Distributed by Littlehampton Book Services, Ltd
Faraday Close, Durrington, Worthing, West Sussex, BN13 3RB
Copyright © Waitrose Ltd, 2017. Waitrose Ltd, Doncaster Road, Bracknell, Berkshire, RG12 8YA

Data management and export by AMA DataSet Ltd, Preston
Printed and bound in Italy by L.E.G.O. S.p.A.

A catalogue record for this book is available from the British Library
ISBN: 978 0 95379 836 0

Maps designed and produced by Cosmographics Ltd, www.cosmographics.co.uk
Mapping contains Ordnance Survey data © Crown copyright and database right 2017
UK digital database © Cosmographics Ltd, 2017. Greater London map and North and South London
maps © Cosmographics Ltd, 2017. West, Central and East London map data © Cosmographics Ltd, 2017
used with kind permission of VisitBritain.

Consultant Editor: Elizabeth Carter
Editor: Rochelle Venables
Content Producer: Ria Martin

The Good Food Guide makes every effort to be as accurate and up to date as possible. All inspections are
anonymous, and Main Entries have been contacted separately for details. As we are an annual Guide,
we have strict guidelines for fact-checking information ahead of going to press, so some restaurants
were removed if they failed to provide the information we required. The editors' decision on inclusion
and scores in *The Good Food Guide* is final, and we will not enter into any discussion on the matter with
individual restaurants.

The publisher cannot be held responsible for any errors or omissions or for changes in the details given
in this Guide. Restaurants may close, change chefs or adjust their opening times and prices during the
Guide's lifetime, and readers should always check with the restaurant at the time of booking.

We would like to extend special thanks to the following people: Iain Barker, Jackie Bates, Ruth
Coombs, Tom Fahey, Alan Grimwade, Joanne Murray, Alan Rainford, Mark Taylor, Steve Trayler,
Andy Turvil, Stuart Walton, Lisa Whitehouse and Blanche Williams. And thanks in particular to all
of our hard-working inspectors.

thegoodfoodguide.co.uk

FSC
www.fsc.org
MIX
Paper from
responsible sources
FSC® C023419

The restaurants included in
The Good Food Guide
are the very best in the UK.

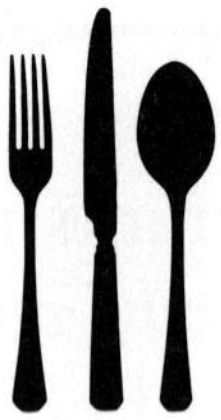

Contents

Introduction

Elizabeth Carter, Consultant Editor

Are we now a country fast on its way to becoming a food-loving nation? The international scorn that was heaped on the UK's culinary efforts just a few decades ago has given way to admiration for a definable, dynamic British cuisine that is moving rapidly towards world-class status. Our homegrown chefs have come of age, not only at the very top but right down through the chain. There is, increasingly, a welcome spread of good-quality restaurants in the middle and lower price bands. Even more striking, there is virtually uniform agreement on the use of the best seasonal produce. The increasing food sophistication of the restaurant-going public helps sustain a higher level of achievement at the cooking end – a happy result for everyone.

While it's impossible not to embrace the exuberance of the UK's restaurant scene, it is currently evolving so fast it can be hard to keep up. Indeed, while I think every edition of *The Good Food Guide* is special, this one is supercharged. The grand old dining-rooms are being seriously challenged – there is a feeling that many are coasting on their long-held reputation of being the best in the country.

There is a very strong sense of the generational passing of the baton - young chefs increasingly want to run their own restaurant as soon as they can, not bothering with the old school 'paying of dues'. And they're not afraid to use the fine-dining moniker – in the modern way, of course: relaxed, engaged and entirely focused on the food. It makes the current restaurant scene a hectic one, but one that is more varied, more accessible, and certainly more exciting.

While chefs such as Gareth Ward (Ynyshir, Wales) and Peter Sanchez-Iglesias (Casamia, Bristol) are overturning tradition and convention at the top end, it's not just about fine-dining. A couple of years ago we reported that high rents were contributing to a geographic shift in London's dining scene, with ambitious young restaurateurs and chefs heading for the residential outer zones to open neighbourhood restaurants. This edition sees a consolidation of that trend with areas such as Deptford (Winemakers, Marcella), Lewisham (Sparrow) and Newington Green (Perilla) now home to chefs who are capturing the city's unique, creative and often eccentric flair.

'There is a very strong sense of the generational passing of the baton – young chefs increasingly want to run their own restaurant as soon as they can, not bothering with the old school 'paying of dues'.

And it's not confined to London – it's happening throughout the country, made possible by the happy coincidence of an increasingly sophisticated and demanding audience of young professionals in almost every corner of the country.

Who's getting it right?

The lower rents outside the capital have attracted some of the UK's most creative and talented young chefs – and they are making it work. We were surprised to be making our way to the centre of Stockport in Greater Manchester, but the endeavour at Samuel Buckley's bravely located, totally quirky, no-frills Where the Light Gets In is completely heartfelt – a work in progress for a young chef who could go far. Ben Crittenden's Stark, with its edgy, no-choice, six-course tasting menu in a tiny converted sandwich bar, sounds very Shoreditch – but this is Broadstairs, Kent. It takes guts to pull this off, but it is done magnificently, with talent and humility. In 2012 Paul Foster impressed us so much we gave him our Up-and-Coming Chef of the Year Award award. His first solo venture, Salt, in Stratford-upon-Avon (crowd-funded, with contributors paying as little as £20 to help kick-start the business), is a textbook lesson in creativity rooted firmly in delightful, delicious cooking.

What's the deal with...

This new breed of chefs is having an impact in other ways. In last year's edition I wondered if the tide was turning against tasting menus in high-scoring restaurants – those nine-or-more courses of artfully rendered food spread over three or four hours with price tags heading north of exorbitant. Well the tide is rushing back in thanks, in part, to young chefs who find the trend fits their cash-strapped first ventures, resulting in less waste and tighter control on costs. But with fewer courses, lower prices and a greater sense of balance, they are making tasting menus exciting, concise and engaging. They have nailed it.

Small plates or sharing plates?

As for that other trend that's been warmly embraced by chefs and restaurateurs across the country - let's be honest, small plates are frequently not designed to be shared. Why the reduction in size if more than one person is supposed to be eating it? If plates are for sharing, there ought to be more, not less, food – after all, a dish featuring a fried egg is best tackled by a solo diner. Moreover, these plates often come out in a random, inhospitable manner. As customers, we have let this weak formula go unchallenged for too long.

'Noise levels are being raised by music played at Glastonbury force.'

Turn it down

Restaurants are getting noisier – that's what our readers, this year in unprecedented numbers, are telling us. Noise levels, already amplified by bare-bones design, are being raised by music played at Glastonbury force. Everyone loves a restaurant that has a buzzing, vibrant atmosphere, but it becomes exhausting and self-defeating when, as one old hand told us: 'I have never heard such loudly amplified music in an eating place. It was so loud that I couldn't hear a word the waitress was saying, and vice versa. We had to gesture and point.' The reporter was not recommending inclusion in the guide.

Talk to us

It is the second decade of the 21st century, and therefore you share, instinctively, all over social media. Please remember to share with us, too, at thegoodfoodguide.co.uk. The real strength of this book is that every single entry represents a random sample of meals eaten by ordinary restaurant customers. We collect, read and count every piece of feedback – and we may well use some of your recommendations in next year's edition.

The Good Food Guide prides itself on the integrity of its expert, anonymous inspections, coupled with continuous feedback from you, the reader. If a restaurant does not have a clear and clean recommendation from our inspectors and readers it will not go in, or stay in, the guide. And we will always act fearlessly on those recommendations, sometimes to the surprise of restaurants that have become famous – but always to the benefit of you, the reader, for whom we produce this guide.

Here are some dishes that I would love to have again, given the chance.

At **Outlaw's Fish Kitchen** we savoured a delicate grey-mullet ceviche layered with orange, fennel and lime – a fresh, simple, yet beautifully put-together dish. From **L'Enclume**, an irresistible, umami-laden braised gem lettuce with English wasabi mayo, fermented mushrooms and a dot of truffle purée. At **James Cochran EC3** a dish of crispy cauliflower – another powerful umami-hit – with base notes of coconut, yoghurt, peanuts and pomegranate. Claude Bosi at **Bibendum** has created a new classic in a clear duck-jelly over a spring-onion soubise, topped with a tiny dice of smoked sturgeon and a generous blob of oscietra caviar.

At **Whatley Manor**, the single oyster with seaweed mignonette was so bright it tingled; it kicked off an exceptional meal from Niall Keating. Bristol's **Casamia** produced an update of sole véronique: perfectly timed fish was embellished with grapes while an intense, eggy sabayon concealed tiny pieces of leek. At the **Sportsman** we devoured a magnificent, full-flavoured and tender roast lamb rack from Ottinge farm, designed as a mini roast dinner and featuring slow-cooked shoulder, vegetables and mint sauce. **108 Garage** in London produced a hunk of char-grilled monkfish balanced by a tart, astringent note of grapefruit custard – an odd idea, and a good one. Finally to **Stark** in Broadstairs, where beautifully cooked pigeon breast was served with a silky dollop of terrific duck-liver mousse, the flavour popping with bitter orange and the crunch of hazelnut.

The Top 50
The UK's best restaurants

1 Restaurant Nathan Outlaw, Cornwall (10)
2 L'Enclume, Cumbria (10)
3 Pollen Street Social, London (9)
4 Restaurant Sat Bains, Nottinghamshire (9)
5 The Fat Duck, Berkshire (9)
6 Restaurant Gordon Ramsay, London (9)
7 Hedone, London (8)
8 Restaurant Andrew Fairlie, Tayside (8)
9 Claude Bosi at Bibendum, London (8) *New*
10 Casamia, Bristol (8)
11 Bohemia, Jersey (8)
12 Ynyshir, Powys (8)
13 Dinner by Heston Blumenthal, London (8)
14 Fraiche, Merseyside (8)
15 Marcus, London (8)
16 Le Champignon Sauvage, Glos (8)
17 Adam Reid at The French, Manchester (8)
18 The Ledbury, London (8)
19 André Garrett at Cliveden, Berkshire (8)
20 Midsummer House, Cambridgeshire (8)
21 Alain Ducasse at the Dorchester, London (8)
22 The Peat Inn, Fife (8)
23 The Kitchin, Edinburgh (7)
24 Sketch, Lecture Room & Library, London (7)

25 The Three Chimneys, Isle of Skye (7) *New*
26 Moor Hall, Lancashire (7) *New*
27 The Greenhouse, London (7)
28 The Ritz, London (7) *New*
29 Castle Terrace, Edinburgh (7)
30 Forest Side, Cumbria (7)
31 Orwells, Oxfordshire (7)
32 Paul Ainsworth at No. 6, Cornwall (7)
33 Restaurant Marianne, London (7)
34 The Waterside Inn, Berkshire (7)
35 Restaurant James Sommerin, Glamorgan (7)
36 Artichoke, Buckinghamshire (7)
37 The Raby Hunt, Durham (7)
38 Whatley Manor, The Dining Room, Wiltshire (7)
39 Restaurant Story, London (7)
40 Simpsons, Birmingham (7)
41 Restaurant Martin Wishart, Edinburgh (7)
42 The Sportsman, Kent (7) *New*
43 Adam's, Birmingham (7)
44 Freemasons at Wiswell, Lancashire (7)
45 Gidleigh Park, Devon (7)
46 Le Gavroche, London (7)
47 Hambleton Hall, Rutland (7)
48 Murano, London (7)
49 The Whitebrook, Gwent (7)
50 The Man Behind the Curtain, Leeds (7) *New*

Editors' Awards

The editors of *The Good Food Guide* are delighted to recognise the following restaurants and chefs for their talent and commitment to excellence.

Chef of the Year
Peter Sanchez-Iglesias
Casamia, Bristol

Chef to Watch
Ben Crittenden
Stark, Broadstairs, Kent

Restaurant of the Year
The Three Chimneys
Isle of Skye, Scotland

Best Pub Restaurant
The Crown
Burchett's Green, Berkshire

Best New Entry
Salt
Stratford-upon-Avon, Warwickshire

Best Front-of-House
Restaurant Sat Bains
Nottinghamshire

How to use
The Good Food Guide

In our opinion, the restaurants included in *The Good Food Guide*
are the very best in the UK; this means that simply getting
an entry is an accomplishment to be proud of, and a
Score 1 or above is a significant achievement.

The Good Food Guide is completely
rewritten every year and compiled
from scratch. Our research list is
based on the huge volume of feedback we
receive from readers, which, together with
anonymous inspections by our experts,
ensures that every entry is assessed afresh.
Please keep the reports coming in: visit
thegoodfoodguide.co.uk for details.

Symbols

We contact restaurants that we're considering
for inclusion ahead of publication to check
key information about opening times and
facilities. They are also invited to participate
in the £5 voucher scheme. The symbols
against each entry are intended for at-a-glance
identification and are based on the information
given to us by each restaurant.

Accommodation is available

£30 It is possible to have three courses,
excluding wine, at the restaurant for
less than £30.

£XX The average price of a three-course
dinner, excluding wine.

£5 The restaurant is participating in our
OFF £5 voucher scheme. See vouchers for
terms and conditions.

 The restaurant has a wine list that
our experts have considered to be
outstanding, either for strong by-the-
glass options, an in-depth focus on a
particular region, or attractive margins
on fine wines.

V We will no longer display the V symbol;
we will list 'v menu' in the details to
indicate that the restaurant has a separate
vegetarian menu.

Scoring

We add and reject many restaurants when we compile each guide. There are always subjective aspects to rating systems, but our inspectors are equipped with extensive scoring guidelines to ensure that restaurant bench-marking around the UK is accurate. As we take into account reader feedback on each restaurant, any given review is based on several meals.

'New chef' in place of a score indicates that the restaurant has had a recent change of chef and we have been unable to score it reliably; we particularly welcome reports on these restaurants.

Readers Recommend

These are direct quotes from our reader feedback and highlight places that have caught the attention of our loyal followers. Reports are particularly welcome on these entries also.

Local Gem

Local Gems highlight a range of brilliant neighbourhood venues, bringing you a wide choice at great value for money. Simple cafés, bistros and pubs, these are the places that sit happily on your doorstep, delivering good, freshly cooked food.

The Good Food Guide scoring system

1 Capable cooking with simple food combinations and clear flavours, but some inconsistencies.

2 Decent cooking, displaying good technical skills and interesting combinations and flavours. Occasional inconsistencies.

3 Good cooking, showing sound technical skills and using quality ingredients.

4 Dedicated, focused approach to cooking; good classical skills and high-quality ingredients.

5 Exact cooking techniques and a degree of ambition; showing balance and depth of flavour in dishes.

6 Exemplary cooking skills, innovative ideas, impeccable ingredients and an element of excitement.

7 High level of ambition and individuality, attention to the smallest detail, accurate and vibrant dishes.

8 A kitchen cooking close to or at the top of its game. Highly individual with impressive artistry. There is little room for disappointment here.

9 Cooking that has reached a pinnacle of achievement, making it a hugely memorable experience for the diner.

10 Just perfect dishes, showing faultless technique at every service; extremely rare, and the highest accolade the Guide can give.

London Explained

London is split into six regions. Restaurants within each region are listed alphabetically. Each main entry and local gem entry has a map reference. Here are the areas covered in each region.

London CENTRAL

Aldwych, Bloomsbury, Covent Garden, Fitzrovia, Holborn,
Hyde Park, Marylebone, Mayfair, Pimlico, Soho, Victoria, Westminster

London NORTH

Archway, Camden, Euston, Finsbury Park, Golders Green, Hampstead,
Islington, Kensal Green, King's Cross, Newington Green, Primrose Hill,
Stoke Newington, Swiss Cottage

London EAST

Bethnal Green, Canary Wharf, City, Clerkenwell, Dalston, Farringdon,
Hackney, Hoxton, Haggerston, Moorgate, Old Street, Shoreditch, Spitalfields,
Tower Hill, Whitechapel

London SOUTH

Balham, Battersea, Bermondsey, Blackheath, Borough, Brixton, Camberwell,
Clapham, Deptford, East Dulwich, Elephant & Castle, Forest Hill, Greenwich,
Herne Hill, Peckham, Putney, South Bank, Southwark, Stockwell, Vauxhall,
Wandsworth, Wimbledon

London WEST

Belgravia, Chelsea, Chiswick, Ealing, Earl's Court, Fulham, Hammersmith,
Kensington, Knightsbridge, Notting Hill, Olympia, Parsons Green,
Shepherd's Bush, South Kensington

London GREATER

Barnes, Croydon, East Sheen, Harrow-on-the-Hill, Kew, Richmond,
South Woodford, Southall, Surbiton, Twickenham, Walthamstow, Wanstead

LONDON

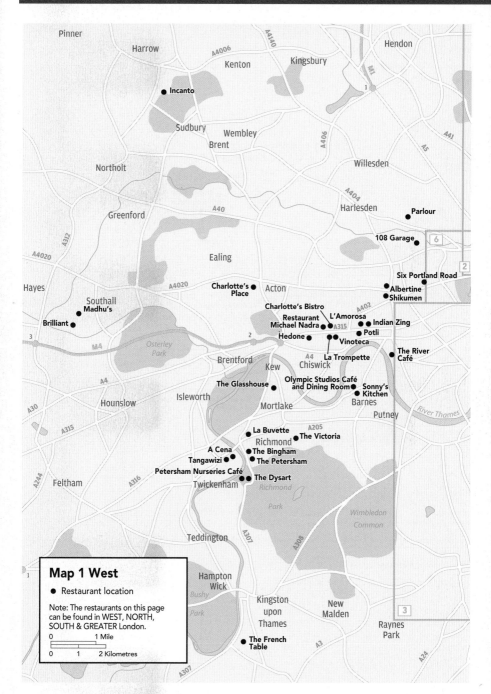

Pinner

Harrow

Kenton

A4006

A4140

Kingsbury

Hendon

M1

1

● Incanto

Sudbury

Wembley

Brent

Northolt

A406

A41

A5

Willesden

A404

Greenford

A40

Harlesden

Parlour
●

A312

108 Garage ●

6

Ealing

2

A4020

Charlotte's ●
Place

Acton

Six Portland Road

● Albertine
● Shikumen

Hayes

A4020

Southall
Madhu's

Brilliant ●

M4

Osterley
Park

3

A4

A30

A315

Charlotte's Bistro

Restaurant   L'Amorosa
Michael Nadra ● ● A315

● ● Indian Zing

Hedone ●   ● Potli
● Vinoteca

A402

A4

La Trompette
●

The River
● Café

Brentford

2

Kew

A4

Chiswick

The Glasshouse ●

Olympic Studios Café
and Dining Room ●

● Sonny's
● Kitchen

Hounslow

Isleworth

Mortlake

Barnes

Putney

River Thames

La Buvette
●

A205

● The Victoria

Richmond

A Cena ●

Tangawizi ● ●

● The Bingham

● The Petersham

Petersham Nurseries Café

● The Dysart

Feltham

A244

A316

Twickenham

Richmond

Park

Wimbledon
Common

Teddington

A307

A308

Map 1 West

● Restaurant location

Note: The restaurants on this page
can be found in WEST, NORTH,
SOUTH & GREATER London.

0   1 Mile

0   1   2 Kilometres

Hampton
Wick

Bushy
Park

Kingston
upon
Thames

New
Malden

3

Raynes
Park

A24

The French
● Table

A3

A307

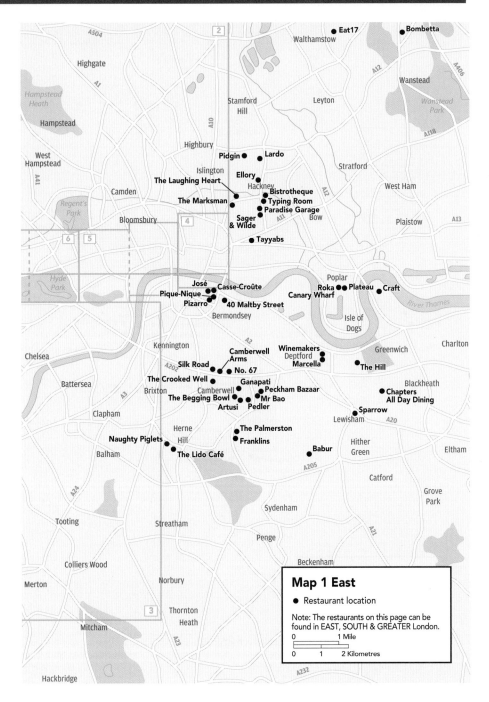

Eat17
Bombetta
Walthamstow

Highgate

A504

A1

Hampstead Heath

Hampstead

West Hampstead

A12

Wanstead

Wanstead Park

A406

A118

Stamford Hill

Leyton

West Ham

A41

Camden

Regent's Park

Highbury

Pidgin
Lardo

Islington

Ellory

The Laughing Heart

Hackney

Bistrotheque

The Marksman

Typing Room

Paradise Garage

Stratford

Bloomsbury

Sager & Wilde

Bow

Plaistow

A13

Tayyabs

Hyde Park

Poplar

José

Casse-Croûte

Roka
Plateau
Craft

Pique-Nique

Canary Wharf

Pizarro

40 Maltby Street

Bermondsey

Isle of Dogs

River Thames

Kennington

Camberwell Arms

Winemakers
Deptford

Greenwich

Charlton

Chelsea

Silk Road

No. 67

Marcella

The Hill

Battersea

A3

Brixton

The Crooked Well

Camberwell

Ganapati

Peckham Bazaar

Blackheath

The Begging Bowl

Mr Bao

Chapters All Day Dining

Clapham

Artusi

Pedler

Sparrow

Lewisham

A20

Herne Hill

The Palmerston

Naughty Piglets

Franklins

Hither Green

Eltham

Balham

The Lido Café

Babur

A205

Catford

Grove Park

A24

Sydenham

Tooting

Streatham

A21

Penge

Colliers Wood

Beckenham

Merton

Norbury

Map 1 East

● Restaurant location

Thornton Heath

Note: The restaurants on this page can be found in EAST, SOUTH & GREATER London.

Mitcham

A23

0   1 Mile

0   1   2 Kilometres

Hackbridge

A232

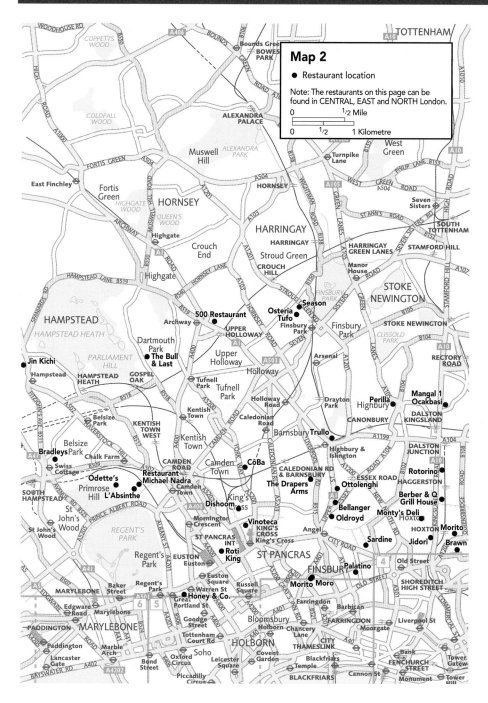

Map 2

● Restaurant location

Note: The restaurants on this page can be found in CENTRAL, EAST and NORTH London.

0   ¹/₂ Mile

0   ¹/₂   1 Kilometre

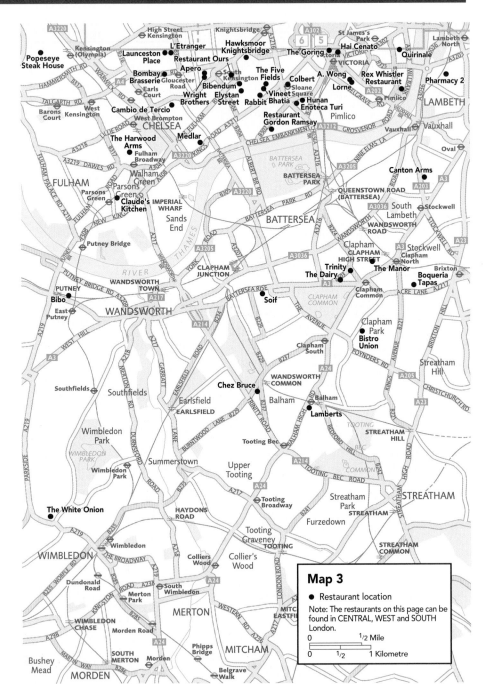

Map 3

● Restaurant location

Note: The restaurants on this page can be found in CENTRAL, WEST and SOUTH London.

0 ——————— 1/2 Mile

0 —— 1/2 —— 1 Kilometre

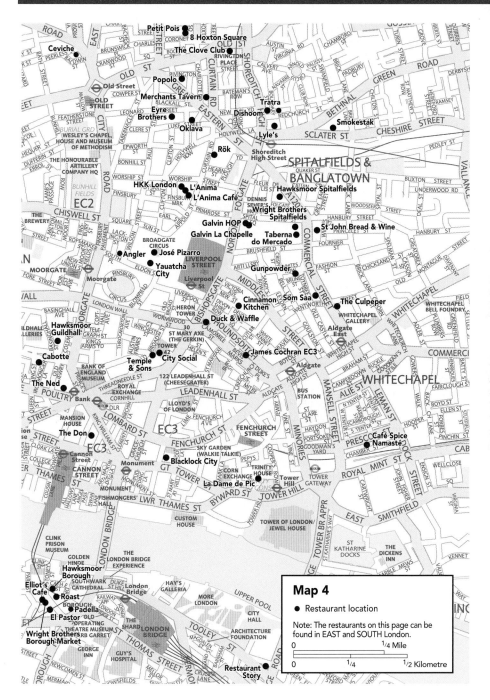

Map 4

● Restaurant location

Note: The restaurants on this page can be found in EAST and SOUTH London.

0   1/4 Mile

0   1/4   1/2 Kilometre

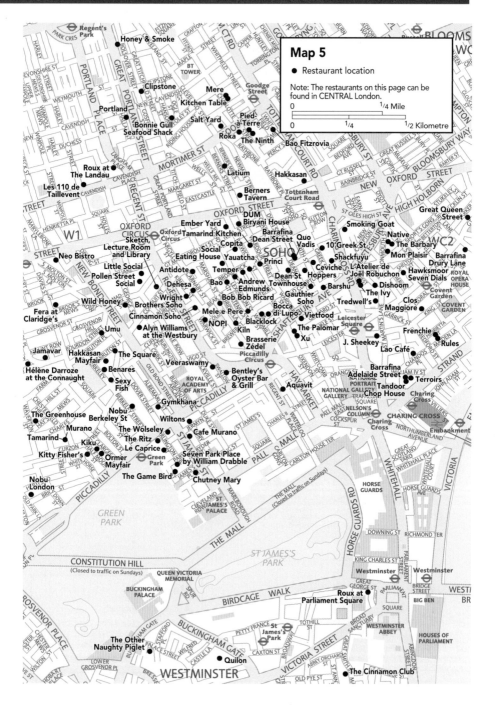

Map 5

● Restaurant location

Note: The restaurants on this page can be found in CENTRAL London.

0 ············· ¹/₄ Mile

0 ············· ¹/₄ ············· ¹/₂ Kilometre

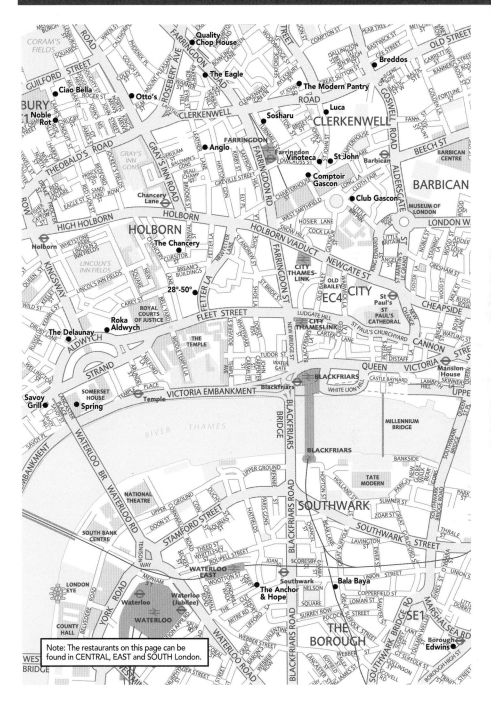

Note: The restaurants on this page can be found in CENTRAL, EAST and SOUTH London.

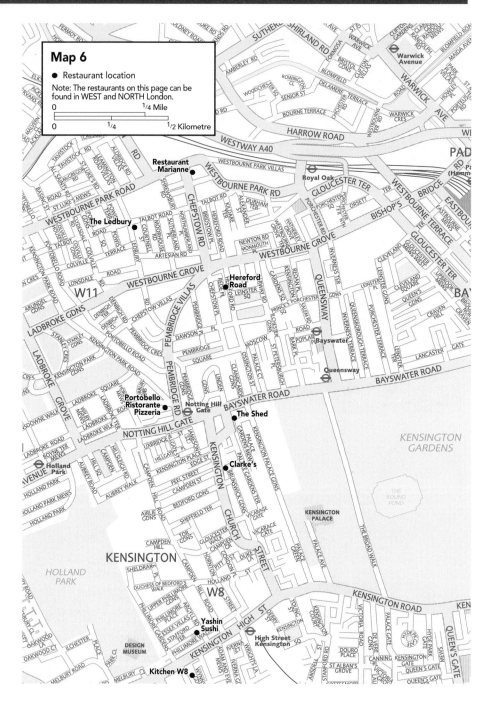

Map 6

- Restaurant location

Note: The restaurants on this page can be found in WEST and NORTH London.

0   1/4 Mile

0   1/4   1/2 Kilometre

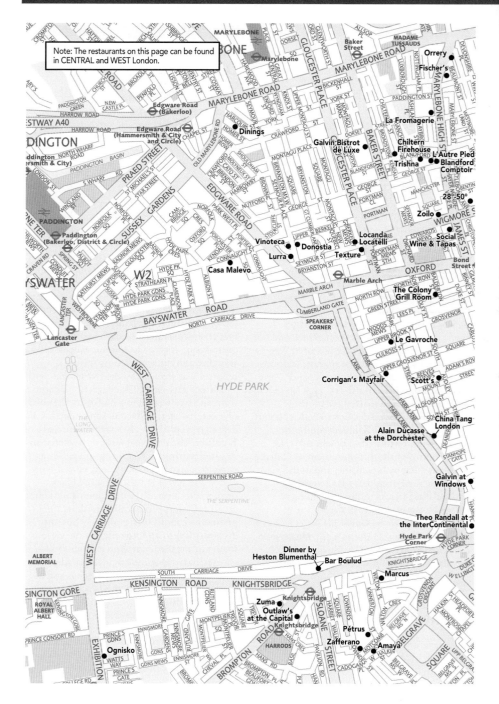

Note: The restaurants on this page can be found in CENTRAL and WEST London.

A. Wong

Cooking score: 5
⊖ Victoria, map 3
Chinese | £40
70-71 Wilton Road, Victoria, SW1V 1DE
Tel no: (020) 7828 8931
awong.co.uk

The narrow frontage in a parade of shops in the humdrum purlieu of Victoria doesn't give much away. If you're wondering where the red lanterns are, note that Andrew Wong takes a forward-looking approach to Chinese food, incorporating much of that country's protean range of regional cooking styles, but subjecting it to a dynamic modernising inspiration that pulls off one sure-fire banger of a dish after another. Historical researches produce a Hong Kong egg waffle with marinated scallop salad credited to the Zhou Dynasty (long before Hong Kong was inhabited, in fact), or street-snack appetisers such as barbecued pork jerky and crispy chicken claw. Excitements come thick and fast among main dishes that take in seared Wagyu beef in mint, chilli and lemongrass, seafood-stuffed braised leaves with cockles and powdered shallot, and stir-fried gai lan greens with dried fish and toasted pine nuts. Creatively conceived desserts include coconut sorbet with poached Xinjiang mulberries, blackberries, yoghurt and mochi rice cake. Explorations of the dim sum menu will make for many a happy lunchtime, and in the evenings, the Forbidden City bar offers cocktails and snacks to the style-hungry. Wines by the glass start at £6.50.
Chef/s: Andrew Wong. **Open:** Tue to Sat L, Mon to Sat D. **Closed:** Sun, 23 Dec to 4 Jan. **Meals:** main courses £8 to £28. Set L £15. Tasting menu £60. **Details:** 64 seats. 10 seats outside. Bar. Music.

Average price

The average price denotes the price of a three-course meal without wine.

★ TOP 50 ★

Alain Ducasse at the Dorchester

Cooking score: 8
⊖ Hyde Park Corner, map 6
Modern French | £100
The Dorchester Hotel, 53 Park Lane, Hyde Park, W1K 1QA
Tel no: (020) 7629 8866
alainducasse-dorchester.com

Contemporary dining in every sense of the term is what to expect in the Dorchester's flagship dining room, consecrated to celestial maître cuisinier Alain Ducasse, represented by Jean-Philippe Blondet. The room itself eschews grand-hotel pomposity in favour of a light, abstractly geometrical design concept. In a room patrolled by staff who are secure in the utter correctness of all aspects of formal service, you're in safe hands, and the modern French cuisine rarely drops below an outstanding level of technique. Negotiating a way through the seven-course taster, a reporter was seduced by the Dorset crab with its sautéed claw and pickled celeriac lasagne to start, and was wafted to paradise by the sauté of lobster with truffled chicken quenelles, a dish that would scarcely have flummoxed Escoffier. The principal meat dish offered an inspired pairing of Welsh venison saddle and a parsnip coated in peanut purée, sauced with coffee and sprinkled with cracked black pepper. Occasionally, a dish doesn't quite fire on all cylinders – the scallop with its gratinated cauliflower, perhaps – but only because it's thrown into relief by the various shades of excellence around it. Four French cheeses arrive in an immaculate parade, each with its separate serving of dressing, and the dessert might be a reinvented vacherin, its meringue positively melting in the mouth, served with coconut ice cream, pomegranate seeds and tropical fruits. A wine list of dazzling stars, starting at £40 and rapidly leaving Planet Earth behind, is overseen by an accomplished sommelier.

Join us at thegoodfoodguide.co.uk

Chef/s: Jean-Philippe Blondet. **Open:** Tue to Fri L, Tue to Sat D. **Closed:** Sun, Mon, 26 to 30 Dec, first week Jan, Easter, 3 weeks Aug. **Meals:** alc £100 (3 courses) to £120 (4 courses). Set L £65 (3 courses). Tasting menu £180 (7 courses). **Details:** 82 seats. V menu. Bar. Wheelchairs. Music. Parking. Children over 10 yrs only.

Alyn Williams at the Westbury

Cooking score: 6

⊖ Oxford Circus, map 5

Modern European | £70

The Westbury Hotel, 37 Conduit Street, Mayfair, W1S 2YF

Tel no: (020) 7183 6426

alynwilliams.com

🛏

Though rarely in the headlines, Alyn Williams is a fine chef with imaginative, skilful cooking, classically French in origin but utterly modern in flavour and presentation. His large airy restaurant just off the Westbury Hotel's main lobby has well-spaced tables and romantic booths with curved button-back banquettes. The staff are young and enthusiastic about the complex cooking they serve. First come light-as-air gougères with Parmesan followed by sourdough bread with black onion seeds and two different butters. Lightly cooked mackerel fillets come with lightly pickled shards of fennel, apple and tiny carrots, the whole bathed with deep seaweed broth and dots of bright green wild garlic oil. The balance of flavour and texture is perfectly managed: lozenges of crisp chicken wings with assertive chilli mayonnaise and vegetable tempura; cod fillet with courgette spaghetti with milky taramasalata sauce and sea vegetables to mix citrus and saltiness, while a rich, gutsy dish of beef cheek is lightened with beetroot, onions and wild garlic purée. An exceptional pre-dessert uses passion fruit sorbet, coffee syrup, white chocolate and saffron, while poached peaches and pannacotta with elderberry sorbet and strawberry ice cream is a magnificent way to end your meal. The wine list could be intimidating but the sommelier can suggest individual labels just right for your food and served in sensible 150ml measures.

Chef/s: Alyn Williams. **Open:** Tue to Sat L and D. **Closed:** Sun, Mon, first 2 weeks Jan, last 2 weeks Aug. **Meals:** set L £30 (3 courses). Set D £65 (3 courses). Tasting menu £80. **Details:** 50 seats. V menu. Bar. Wheelchairs. Music. Parking.

Andrew Edmunds

Cooking score: 2

⊖ Oxford Circus, Piccadilly Circus, map 5

Modern European | £40

46 Lexington Street, Soho, W1F 0LP

Tel no: (020) 7437 5708

andrewedmunds.com

🍾

Andrew Edmunds, tucked away in Soho, has a bistro feel. Cosy and narrow with candles stuck in wine bottles and tightly organised tables, it exudes effortless charm. Some find the basement dining room a touch gloomy, preferring the lighter ground floor with its street views, but all agree that service is friendly with no attempt made at formality. The handwritten daily menu takes in half a dozen dishes per course, delivering robust cooking with a strong emphasis on seasonality. Thus dressed crab with lemon mayonnaise or English asparagus with hot butter could appear on a spring menu, ahead of mackerel fillets with soused carrots, or roast pigeon and beetroot. Portions are substantial, but proceed to ginger pudding with marmalade butterscotch sauce and sighs of satisfaction are guaranteed. It is, however, the predominantly French-led wine list that is the talking point. 'Staggeringly cheap' as one regular puts it, owner Andrew Edmund's passion comes through in a list that offers bargains galore. Bottles from £19.50.

Chef/s: Chris Gillard. **Open:** all week L and D. **Closed:** 25 to 30 Dec. **Meals:** main courses £14 to £35. **Details:** 60 seats. 4 seats outside.

Antidote

Cooking score: 3
⊖ Oxford Circus, map 5
Modern European | £35
12A Newburgh Street, Soho, W1F 7RR
Tel no: (020) 7287 8488
antidotewinebar.com

£5 OFF 🍾

'This is a thoroughly grown-up, laid-back wine bar,' thought one first-time visitor to this small, sunny, L-shaped dining room in a very touristy part of town. All marble counter-tops, wood tables and exposed filament lighting, this 'off-the-main-drag gem' looks out over stylish Newburgh Street. The menu is concise and seasonal, full of things you want to eat. Among 'generous' small plates 'big enough to share', there could be rich, creamy burrata alongside a tangle of salty, bitter, braised cime di rapa, pickled chilli and a delicate grating of lemon zest, and 'stunningly fresh' crab with glossy baked celeriac, a scattering of hazelnuts and a swirl of lovage. At main-course stage, pollack is accompanied by lightly charred cucumber and dressed with dill oil, lemon and salt, a scattering of brown shrimp and creamy whey sauce. Desserts are simple, perhaps a salted-caramel ice cream, while the French-leaning wine list is a thoroughly modern tome full of natural and biodynamic options. Bottles from £25.
Chef/s: John Christie. **Open:** Mon to Sat L and D. **Closed:** Sun, bank hols. **Meals:** main courses £14 to £20. **Details:** 45 seats. 18 seats outside. Bar. Music.

★ NEW ENTRY ★

Aquavit

Cooking score: 3
⊖ Piccadilly Circus, map 5
Nordic | £45
St James's Market, 1 Carlton Street, Mayfair, SW1Y 4QQ
Tel no: (020) 7024 9848
aquavitrestaurants.com

Where there were, until recently, only dingy side streets between Lower Regent Street and Haymarket, the reborn St James's Market now extends its handsome gleaming precinct. Less market than restaurant plaza, it's home to Aquavit, established over 30 years in Midtown Manhattan, now set to seduce the West End with Swedish cheer. Amid light-wood panelling and marble floor tiles, the atmosphere is appropriately light and cool, with glowing abstract tapestry work by Olafur Eliasson evoking forest and coastline. The menu combines some cutting-edge touches in smörgåsbord options such as brilliant matjes herring with tiny potatoes in ash, or blood pudding and lingonberries with diaphanous lardo, while standard starters and mains take a more traditional approach. Monkfish is gently browned and served with pickled fennel in trout roe and chive cream sauce, while a less intuitive cream sauce anoints the long-braised veal cheeks and their gargantuan mound of mash. A side of bacon-and-anchovy-laced Jansson's Temptation makes dauphinois look a little dull, and the early signature dessert is beautifully aromatic burnt cream flavoured with salted liquorice, its surface brûléed and topped with resonant blackcurrant ice cream. Don't miss the wonderful seeded breads, or indeed the aquavit tots, which are full of scented spice and gentle power. Wines start at £6.50 a glass.
Chef/s: Henrik Ritzén. **Open:** all week, all day from 12 (11 Sat and Sun). **Closed:** 24 to 26 Dec, 1 Jan. **Meals:** main courses £24 to £29. Set L £24 (2 courses) to £29. Early D £22 (2 courses) to £25. Sun L £35. **Details:** 114 seats. 20 seats outside. Bar. Wheelchairs. Music.

L'Atelier de Joël Robuchon

Cooking score: 6
⊖ Leicester Square, map 5
Modern French | £90
13-15 West Street, Covent Garden, WC2H 9NE
Tel no: (020) 7010 8600
joelrobuchon.co.uk

With The Ivy almost next door (see entry) and nearby St Martin's Theatre still staging The Mousetrap, this is theatreland incarnate – a perfect location for French superstar Joël

Robuchon's swish London outpost. A discreet black frontage suggests exclusivity and the interior is lavishly tricked out, the whole spread across three floors. L'Atelier is at street level, done out in red and black with Japanese lacquerwork, walls of trailing foliage and stools at the counter. The culinary focus is on appropriately dramatic tasting plates rooted in the traditions of haute cuisine, but super-charged with flashes of innovation: tiger prawns are coated in crunchy rice 'angel hair' perfumed with lime and sumac, for example. Elsewhere, hot foie gras is fashioned with a 'rolled heart' of green apple and hibiscus juice, l'oeuf cocotte given new life with golden chanterelles, 'old' sherry and wild garlic, and suprême of pigeon comes wrapped in cabbage. Desserts could feature a pairing of Earl Grey sorbet with pineapple and citrus confit. 'Découverte' menus offer the chance to sample glasses from a high-rolling wine list. **Chef/s:** Axel Manes and Jeremy Page. **Open:** all week L and D. **Meals:** main courses £25 to £52. Set L and early D £45. Tasting menu £149 (8 courses). **Details:** 88 seats. V menu. Bar. Wheelchairs. Music.

L'Autre Pied

Cooking score: 4
⊖ Bond Street, map 6
Modern European | £50
5-7 Blandford Street, Marylebone, W1U 3DB
Tel no: (020) 7486 9696
lautrepied.co.uk
£5 OFF

Pied à Terre's Marylebone sibling has new muscle in the form of yet another new chef, with Athenian Asimakis Chaniotis now in charge of the kitchen. Although Chaniotis's cooking is formal (the offering encompasses everything from a kindly priced *plat du jour* to caviar signature dish via a set-price carte), the vibe is casual. Pretty green floral columns brighten up what can be quite a dark room. Service, as ever, is relaxed, ultra-efficient and winningly generous with the sourdough. At inspection, the chef's tasting menu delivered hits in the form of a sweet crab and 'just set' vichyssoise layered in an eggshell served in an egg box, and red prawn tartare with morels and Sauternes-pickled mushrooms was beautifully balanced – the delicate, oily cure on the prawns matched wonderfully with sweet pickle in the mushrooms. Tender spring rack of lamb, port, cherry, aubergine compote and pommes soufflés was good, too, and to conclude, mille-feuille, banana and chocolate proved a clever rendition of a classic pairing. The cross-budget wine list opens at £28. **Chef/s:** Asimakis Chaniotis. **Open:** all week L, Mon to Sat D. **Closed:** 23 to 26 Dec, 1 Jan. **Meals:** set L £24 (2 courses) to £29. Set D £40 (2 courses) to £50. Tasting menu £75. **Details:** 48 seats. 9 seats outside. V menu. Music.

★ NEW ENTRY ★

Bao Fitzrovia

Cooking score: 3
⊖ Tottenham Court Road, map 5
Taiwanese | £35
31 Windmill Street, Fitzrovia, W1T 2JN
Tel no: (020) 3011 1632
baolondon.com

Larger and less frenetic than its hugely popular big brother in Soho (see entry), Bao Fitzrovia offers more manageable queues as bookings are taken for the basement dining room. The ground floor is minimalistic in design, dominated by a horseshoe-shaped bar lined with stools, where 'you sit quite close to your neighbour', while wraparound windows let in lots of light. From the xiao chi (Taiwanese snacks) section, 'zingy' pieces of prawn tartare served with shredded raw potato and chilli oil were a big hit at a test meal. The bao (steamed buns) have attracted a legion of followers, and the confit pork loaded with crispy shallots and chilli oil 'did not disappoint'. Equally successful were sticky rice bowls with 'tasty' mapo aubergine teamed with pickled cucumber, and stir-fried squid with Tenderstem broccoli and crispy chicken skin. Rice crêpe filled with peanut ice cream and coriander is the solo dessert. Service is friendly, and for drinks, there's a short list of cocktails and wines (from £25).

Chef/s: Erchen Chang and Shing Tat Chung. **Open:** Mon to Thur L and D. Fri and Sat, all day from 12. **Closed:** Sun. **Meals:** bao £4 to £5. Xiao chi £5 to £9. **Details:** 40 seats. Music.

Bao Soho

Cooking score: 3
⊖ Oxford Circus, map 5
Taiwanese | £35
53 Lexington Street, Soho, W1F 9AS
baolondon.com

'I went for a solo lunch and somehow managed to avoid the usual queues. Staff and service was great – laid-back, swift and efficient,' enthused a reader who found this 'cool, sleek' Soho eatery much to his liking. The drill remains the same, the inevitable queue, then fast-paced service once you've ordered from a short 'dim sum-style' tick-box form. Half a dozen 'delicious bao' are bookended by a selection of excellent xiao chi (snacks) of, say, Taiwanese fried chicken with hot sauce or soft trotter nuggets, and sides such as sweet potato chips with plum pickle ketchup. You may want to order more than one of the light and puffy steamed buns, perhaps 'unctuous' lamb shoulder, confit pork, and crispy soy-milk-marinated fried chicken. For a sweet finish there is just one dessert – a fried bao stuffed with Horlicks ice cream. There is wine (at £22) but oolong tea is probably a better match with the food. In addition to a branch of Bao in Fitzrovia, the Bao team have opened XU, a Taiwanese restaurant and bar (see entries).
Chef/s: Erchen Chang and Shing Tat Chung. **Open:** Mon to Sat L and D. **Closed:** Sun. **Meals:** bao £4 to £5. Xiao chi £3 to £6. **Details:** 24 seats. Music.

Symbols

🛏 Accommodation is available
£30 Three courses for less than £30
£5 OFF £5-off voucher scheme
🍷 Notable wine list

The Barbary

Cooking score: 4
⊖ Covent Garden, map 5
North African | £30
16 Neal's Yard, Covent Garden, WC2H 9DP
thebarbary.co.uk

This follow-up to Soho's Palomar (see entry) arrived not with a whimper but a bang. It's vibey, noisy, hot and heady; whatever the owners learned about working a crowd from their former life in nightclubs, they've introduced here in a more grown-up environment of distressed raw brick and smooth zinc. Yes, you should expect to queue. Perch on stools around the horseshoe bar, behind which chefs and waiters, each one chattier than the next, can't help but convey their enthusiasm for the Barbary's bright North African and Middle Eastern flavours matched by cool wines. Begin with bread, blistered, charred naan e barbari with spicy zhug and harissa for enhanced dipping, ahead of small plates from 'land', 'sea' and 'earth', such as pata negra neck with confit garlic and a lick of sweet date, broccoli with black tahini, or golden kataifi-shrouded prawns. Fudgy pistachio 'hashcake' is a delicious, if unsophisticated, note to finish on. Service is included in the price so the bill's the bill.
Chef/s: Eyal Jagermann. **Open:** Mon to Fri L and D. Sat and Sun, all day from 12. **Closed:** 25 and 26 Dec. **Meals:** main courses £7 to £17. **Details:** 24 seats. V menu. Music. Children over 8 yrs only.

Barrafina Adelaide Street

Cooking score: 4
⊖ Charing Cross, map 5
Spanish | £50
10 Adelaide Street, Covent Garden, WC2N 4HZ
barrafina.co.uk

Like its siblings on Dean Street and Drury Lane (see entries), this branch of Barrafina takes inspiration from Barcelona's Cal Pep – although the style remains very much its own. The format is plain and simple: no bookings, seating at the marble bar, an open kitchen and

a regular menu supplemented by daily specials that are specific to each branch. Everything revolves around the freshest of ingredients, and the output has a palpable directness – premium charcuterie and cheeses, vivacious salad-style assemblages and grilling (plancha or Josper), with the occasional slow-cooked peasant-style dish adding ballast where necessary. Barrafina regulars will know all about the crunchy-yet-gooey croquetas, pan con tomate, chipirones, creamy tortillas and stuffed courgette flowers, but also look to the blackboard for other star turns, especially fish: carabineros (red prawns), cuttlefish with romesco sauce, turbot zarzuela etc. To drink, sherries, cava and Spanish regional wines are all on the money.
Chef/s: Jose Antonio Ceballos Perez. **Open:** all week L and D. **Closed:** 25 and 26 Dec, 1 Jan, bank hols. **Meals:** tapas £3 to £19. **Details:** 29 seats.

Barrafina Dean Street
Cooking score: 5
⊖ Tottenham Court Road, map 5
Spanish | £50
26-27 Dean Street, Soho, W1D 3LL
barrafina.co.uk

Do Sam and Eddie Hart ever put a foot wrong? Modern Spanish tapas served in a light, sleekly designed space has proved a winning formula for their three-strong Barrafina group and it has accrued a strong following. And when the lease on their Frith Street flagship was terminated, they just transported one tiny slice of Spanish life to the ground floor of Quo Vadis (see entry), resulting in marginally more space, more swagger, but with the same no-bookings policy (and no sign of the queue abating). The format remains the same: counter seating with a grandstand view of the chefs cooking, and ingredients given centre-stage prominence. Indeed, quality ingredients get to shine in specials such as 'delicious' piquillo croquetas, deep-fried cod cheeks, whole on-the-bone lemon sole, and arroz de salmonete (red mullet), while a palpable freshness means that traditional dishes such as tortilla (with ham

and spinach, say), grilled sardines, and whole quail with aïoli are reliably superb. Service is impeccable. The short list of Spanish wines is priced by the glass or bottle.
Chef/s: Carlos Manuel Miranda Gomes. **Open:** all week L and D. **Closed:** 25 and 26 Dec, 1 Jan, bank hols. **Meals:** tapas £3 to £19. **Details:** 29 seats. 12 seats outside.

Barrafina Drury Lane
Cooking score: 4
⊖ Covent Garden, map 5
Spanish | £50
43 Drury Lane, Covent Garden, WC2B 5AJ
barrafina.co.uk

Don't expect to make reservations at the Drury Lane branch of Barrafina, where counter and window-ledge seating in a modestly proportioned space means you turn up and try your luck. And when luck's in, you'll be rewarded with vibrant classic Spanish tapas turned out with dispatch and proficiency. Carbs are always a good idea to start, so wolf down a poached duck egg on brioche or a chorizo tortilla, or both, before setting about the fortifying meat options – pork belly in mojo verde, or braised ox tongue – and spanking-fresh seafood, such as soft-shell crab, oysters in vinaigrette, or scallop ceviche. It's all judiciously seasoned and timed, and if you're inclined to assuage guilt over the carbs and fat with some vitamins, look to a side of fennel, pear, radish and dill in mitigation. Finish with cuajada (curdled sheep's cheese), arroz con leche, or palate-coating turrón. Glasses of Spanish wine from £5, or sherry from £6.50, provide perfect lubrication.
Chef/s: Javier Duarte Campos. **Open:** all week L and D. **Closed:** 25 and 26 Dec, 1 Jan, bank hols. **Meals:** tapas £3 to £19. **Details:** 24 seats.

Average price

The average price denotes the price of a three-course meal without wine.

Barshu

Cooking score: 4
⊖ Leicester Square, map 5
Chinese | £35
28 Frith Street, Soho, W1D 5LF
Tel no: (020) 7287 8822
barshurestaurant.co.uk

Held in high regard both inside and outside London's Chinese community, Barshu continues to be popular with everyone who appreciates authentic Szechuan cooking, appealing to a broad mix of Westerners and Chinese. However, this is not a kitchen that plays to the gallery – the massive menu can be off-putting to those not familiar with the cuisine, you need to love garlic and chilli, and while staff are attentive 'they are not particularly friendly'. Recommendations include 'Four Treasures', crisp slices of lotus root, green beans, wood ear mushrooms and bitter melon, served chilled in a fabulous soy-based dressing of finely minced chilli, garlic, ginger and coriander, and delicately sweet steamed scallops with garlic and bean thread noodles. A generous 'tongue-tingling' dry-wok dish of marinated beef with cumin, cooked with peppers, onions, celery, lots of whole garlic cloves and 'a thousand chunks of dried chilli and many Szechuan peppercorns' is a 'delicious dish I'll never forget'. Consider, too, the magnificent platter of crab with chilli and garlic, even the slivered pig's stomach ('in a gorgeous chilli oil sauce'). Saké or beer are the best accompaniments.
Chef/s: Mr Cheng. **Open:** all week, all day from 12. **Closed:** 24 and 25 Dec. **Meals:** main courses £13 to £43. **Details:** 100 seats. Music.

Benares

Cooking score: 5
⊖ Green Park, map 5
Indian | £60
12a Berkeley Square, Mayfair, W1J 6BS
Tel no: (020) 7629 8886
benaresrestaurant.com

A perfect fit for Mayfair, Atul Kochhar's Benares oozes sophistication with its luxurious hand-crafted furniture, leather trim and a flower-strewn pond separating the low-lit dining room from the sleek bar. 'Superb' staff ensure that the place purrs like a vintage Bentley, while the kitchen delights with its elevated renditions of Indian regional cuisine allied to thoughtful European culinary technique and picture-pretty presentation. This is supremely assured cooking noted for its deft touch and dedication to British ingredients. Crispy fried Cornish lemon sole with piquillo dressing makes a fine starter, or you might pick guinea fowl tikka with sweet-and-sour smoked beetroot. To follow, Atlantic hake appears with lemongrass couscous and Tenderstem broccoli pakora, while New Forest venison could be daringly matched with sautéed kale, oyster mushrooms, a biryani and chocolate curry. Occasionally, a more prosaic dish disappoints (whole tandoori chicken with 'curry house' makhani sauce, for example), but desserts such as fennel-and-anise-infused tarte Tatin redress the balance. There are plenty of serious spice-friendly bottles (at a price) on the ambitious wine list.
Chef/s: Atul Kochhar. **Open:** Mon to Sat L, all week D. **Closed:** 24 and 25 Dec, 1 Jan. **Meals:** main courses £26 to £36. Set L and early D £29 (2 courses) to £35. Tasting menu £98 (7 courses). **Details:** 120 seats. V menu. Bar. Wheelchairs. Music. Children over 7 yrs only after 7.30pm.

Join us at thegoodfoodguide.co.uk

Bentley's Oyster Bar & Grill

Cooking score: 4
⊖ Piccadilly Circus, map 5
Seafood | £60
11-15 Swallow Street, Mayfair, W1B 4DG
Tel no: (020) 7734 4756
bentleys.org

Regulars swerve the sedate first-floor restaurant and the heated front terrace, preferring to be in the beating heart of this venerable West End fish restaurant – the compact ground-floor oyster bar where the tables are tight, the atmosphere vibrant and the staff helpful and humorous. Situated on a narrow pedestrianised street straddling Piccadilly and Regent Street, Bentley's has just entered its second century and remains the place to come for spanking-fresh fish and seafood. Proprietor Richard Corrigan has a tremendous respect for good old-fashioned classics, his team serving up oysters, freshly shucked each day, and dishes such as Cornish fish soup, dressed crab (the white and brown meat carefully separated), hot and cold seafood platters, the famous fish pie, fish and chips, turbot and Dover sole. Seafood may be the prominent theme but there's also prime Hereford beef sirloin, Elwy Valley lamb and Ribble Valley chicken, with sides such as skinny chips, buttery mash or spinach. The puddings are good, perhaps a textbook crème brûlée, dark chocolate mousse or bread and butter pudding. The expansive global wine list, arranged by style, has excellent choice by the glass.
Chef/s: Michael Lynch. **Open:** all week L and D. **Closed:** bank hols. **Meals:** main courses £19 to £80. Set L £26 (2 courses) to £29. Sun L £45. **Details:** 130 seats. 60 seats outside. Bar. Music.

Berners Tavern

Cooking score: 5
⊖ Tottenham Court Road, map 5
Modern British | £60
10 Berners Street, Fitzrovia, W1T 3NP
Tel no: (020) 7908 7979
editionhotels.com

Jason Atherton's empire now extends to nine addresses in the capital, and the chef's many fans all agree that this 'gloriously over-the-top', all-day dining room 'bedazzles and charms'. It's a soaring, expansive room, occupying part of the ground floor of the London Edition hotel, and run by 'lovely' staff expressing 'just the right level of attentiveness', with Phil Carmichael at the helm in the kitchen dispatching modern brasserie fare of the highest order. There's something for everyone: prawn cocktail with lobster jelly, avocado and crispy shallot; pimped-up macaroni cheese (an Atherton signature); majestic pork pie (getting the trolley treatment); Josper-grill steak; venison loin with red cabbage, beetroot and bone marrow; or whole Dover sole. Dishes lack pretension, being rather more fun and eager to please, though produce is impeccable and cooked with a fair degree of finesse. If you can squeeze in dessert, the theatrics of baked Alaska (for two), flamed tableside, deserve a table-top drumroll. And it's a 'heaven-sent spot for a tryst' (though your first action at dinner might be to turn your phone-torch on to read the menu). Pricey global wines head swiftly northwards, but the extensive by-the-glass list is rather more forgiving.
Chef/s: Phil Carmichael and Jonathan Wright. **Open:** all week, all day from 7am. **Meals:** main courses £16 to £40. Set L £25 (2 courses) to £30. **Details:** 128 seats. V menu. Bar. Wheelchairs. Music.

Blacklock

Cooking score: 2
θ Piccadilly Circus, map 5
British | £25
24 Great Windmill Street, Soho, W1D 7LG
Tel no: (020) 3441 6996
theblacklock.com
£30

Down in a basement where the business was once of a more sensual nature (well, this is Soho), Blacklock is a thoroughly contemporary kind of steakhouse, with a retro industrial look and a menu that aims to do one thing very well indeed. That thing is cook red meat, and maybe knock up a pretty decent cocktail, too. Go 'skinny' or go 'big' with fabulous steaks, lamb chops, tender pork belly, all sorts, with sides including sweet potatoes roasted in ash for 10 hours, and BBQ baby gem with anchovy dripping. Sunday roasts have built a solid fan base – Cornish lamb leg, say, roasted over English oak. The steak sandwich is available until 6pm. Desserts might be white chocolate cheesecake. Those cocktails arrive on a trolley, and they are good value, with other drink options including Blacklock Brew No. 2 on draught and a few wines by glass, carafe and bottle. There's also a second venue, Blacklock City (see entry).
Chef/s: Modesta Lott. **Open:** all week L, Mon to Sat D. **Closed:** 25 and 26 Dec. **Meals:** main courses £12 to £18. Set L and D £20. **Details:** 65 seats. Bar. Music.

Blandford Comptoir

Cooking score: 3
θ Baker Street, Bond Street, map 6
Modern European | £30
1 Blandford Street, Marylebone, W1U 3DA
Tel no: (020) 7935 4626
blandford-comptoir.co.uk
🍾

Marylebone High Street, with its part village feel, part West End vibe, has plenty of choice from a foodie point of view these days. Just off of the main thoroughfare, Blandford Comptoir strikes an excellent balance

between wine bar and brasserie, its diminutive interior feeling like 'a true Parisian local gem' with seats across a counter in the window, places at a wraparound bar and a selection of small tables in a pretty, mirrored back area. The globetrotting wine list is the absolute star here, as is the advice from the 'young and talented' sommelier (bottles range from £23 to £295, and there's a rare and fine list going up to £1,450). As for food, there's a good selection of small plates, charcuterie, a raw section that takes in oysters, carpaccio, and a lamb cannon. It's the sort of welcome flexibility that suits the brasserie aesthetic really well, one where octopus, pickled fennel and confit lemon makes a flavour-packed start; there's French guinea fowl with celeriac purée, pancetta and cavolo nero to follow, and cheese or pannacotta with fresh strawberries to bring up the rear. A more informal branch – Comptoir Café & Wine – has opened on Weighhouse Street, Mayfair.
Chef/s: Ben Mellor. **Open:** all week, all day from 12. **Meals:** main courses £14 to £24. **Details:** 40 seats. 11 seats outside. Bar. Music.

Bob Bob Ricard

Cooking score: 3
θ Piccadilly Circus, map 5
British/Russian | £45
1 Upper James Street, Soho, W1F 9DF
Tel no: (020) 3145 1000
bobbobricard.com

'It's like The Ivy filtered through the mind of a Russian oligarch,' mused one reader. Perhaps it's the menu's take on comfort food that encouraged the comparison, or the defiance with which contemporary fashion is ignored. That comfort food is both British and Russian in its outlook, and the décor is a shimmering golden display of over-the-top-ness. Every table has its own button to request more Champagne (push and it will come), and the service is decidedly old-school. The cooking is far more sensible and measured. Caviar and vodka shots are a tempting proposition if the budget allows, ditto Champagne, but there are good things to be had with a less indulgent

agenda. Begin with baked oysters Brezhnev (with Parmesan and black truffle, no less), or a fresh-as-a-daisy salmon tartare, before beef Wellington for two, panko-crusted lemon sole, or vegetarian pearl barley risotto. Desserts play the comfort card, too, while the wine list has nothing under 30 quid.
Chef/s: Anna Haugh. **Open:** all week L and D. **Meals:** main courses £18 to £90. **Details:** 130 seats. V menu. Wheelchairs. Music. Children over 12 yrs only.

Bocca di Lupo

Cooking score: 2
Ɵ Piccadilly Circus, map 5
Italian | £50
12 Archer Street, Soho, W1D 7BB
Tel no: (020) 7734 2223
boccadilupo.com

The long, narrow space extends back along bar seating, beneath hovering lights like incandescent soap bubbles, to a cramped but fun rear area, all reliably packed for energetic Italian regional demotic cooking that's mostly high on umami. Certain dishes have stayed the course from the Bocca's early days a decade ago: a vividly colourful salad of truffled radish, celeriac, pomegranate and pecorino, and the carpaccio-sliced sea bream dressed in orange and rosemary. The Tuscan sausages with optional grilled fennel are worth a punt, while high-rolling main dishes take in suckling pig porchetta with roast artichokes, and roast brill with lentils and salsa verde. Among desserts, 'Grandad's balls' are still going strong (deep-fried ricotta dumplings, that is), or try the Piedmontese bonet, a calorific pudding of chocolate, coffee, amaretti, caramel and rum. The Italian wine list opens at £21.50, but there are mature single-vineyard treasures from some of the country's celebrity growers around the nether end.
Chef/s: Jake Simpson. **Open:** all week L and D. **Closed:** 25 Dec, 1 Jan. **Meals:** main courses £8 to £30. **Details:** 75 seats. Wheelchairs.

Bonnie Gull Seafood Shack

Cooking score: 3
Ɵ Oxford Circus, Goodge Street, map 5
Seafood | £40
21A Foley Street, Fitzrovia, W1W 6DS
Tel no: (020) 7436 0921
bonniegull.com

Relive summer beach holidays with spanking-fresh seafood (the kitchen is committed to sustainability, using day boats around the British coast) and a nostalgic setting of blue-and-white linen and tableware, roughly painted boards, marine memorabilia and stripy awnings. A burly croquette stuffed with smooth salt cod, potato and samphire is perked up with brisk kim-chee sauce and radish and rocket salad. Salmon tartare has a luxurious dollop of keta (salmon caviar) and the bright green punctuation of watercress mayonnaise. Fish and chips is a fine piece of haddock attended by thick chips, perfect for dipping into tartare sauce and mushy peas. A plump king scallop arrives in the shell with rich garlic pesto and a scattering of pine kernels, while humble kale leaves are transformed with a light-as-air tempura batter using a special Japanese flour. You can still have simple bowls of cockles or clams with chunks of crusty bread to mop up the juices, and there's always a good selection of oysters. Leave room for puddings such as an irresistible lemon parfait. There's a great wine list of fish-friendly labels as well as cocktails and rare teas. An appealing sibling is at 22 Bateman Street, W1D 3AN.
Chef/s: Christian Edwardson. **Open:** all week L and D. **Meals:** main courses £17 to £23. **Details:** 28 seats. 10 seats outside. Music.

Visit us online

To find out more about The Good Food Guide, please visit thegoodfoodguide.co.uk

Brasserie Zédel

⊖ Piccadilly Circus, map 5
French | £25
20 Sherwood Street, Soho, W1F 7ED
Tel no: (020) 7734 4888
brasseriezedel.com

£30
▼

Images of the Tour Eiffel on the menus should help orient you, as should the ownership of Corbin and King, whose commitment to old-school French brasserie dining remains unwavering. Beautiful 1930s interiors frame a noisily dynamic eating scene that might take you from celeriac rémoulade to boeuf bourguignon to crème brûlée without missing a beat. If you're feeling luxier, you'll likely follow the lobster cocktail and haunch of venison route, finishing perhaps with a coupe of mandarin sorbet libated in Champagne. Vegetarians get a decent look-in, perhaps for fennel and leek gratin, and the French wines, which successfully repel all foreign boarders, start at £22.

Café Murano

Cooking score: 5
⊖ Green Park, map 5
Italian | £35
33 St James's Street, Mayfair, SW1A 1HD
Tel no: (020) 3371 5559
cafemurano.co.uk

Angela Hartnett's winning take on warm-hearted Italian cooking finessed with French technique has found its perfect setting here in swanky St James's where the worlds of fine art and high finance collide with shoppers and Piccadilly tourists. Café Murano doesn't attempt the polish of Murano (see entry), but 'it's a lot more fun'. Sit on smart leather banquettes or high stools at the bar. The menu, divided into classical Italian sections, lets you eat as lightly or as greedily as you wish. Start with cicchetti, small plates of smoked ham or truffle-infused arancini. Elegant antipasti include homemade ricotta with new season's fresh peas and beans lightly dressed with olive oil, while the primi section offers two sizes of rice and pasta dishes, say rabbit risotto or very thin spaghetti perked up with salty anchovies and crisp breadcrumbs, while luxurious squid-ink tagliolini with fresh crab is bathed in a seafood broth that morphs into rich bisque at the bottom of the bowl. The secondi section lists gutsy plates of pork belly with fennel and apricots or a tranche of cod with shrimp and golden raisins. Desserts, dolce, include a classic Amalfi lemon tart and a voluptuously wobbly salted-caramel pannacotta with a rich chocolate sauce. You may need advice on the Italian wine and cocktail list but the staff are exceptionally well informed and helpful.

Chef/s: Sam Williams. **Open:** all week L, Mon to Sat D. **Closed:** 25 and 26 Dec. **Meals:** main courses £18 to £25. Set L and D £18 (2 courses) to £22. **Details:** 86 seats. 4 seats outside. Music.

Le Caprice

Cooking score: 4
⊖ Green Park, map 5
Modern British | £35
Arlington House, Arlington Street, Mayfair, SW1A 1RJ
Tel no: (020) 7629 2239
le-caprice.co.uk

This is what a London restaurant institution looks and feels like. Lurking at the bottom of a side street next to The Ritz, the Caprice is a sleek, well-managed, deeply satisfying venue, where the polished service runs on rails and a menu of modern British food incorporates those Italian and east Asian components that nobody wants to miss out on. Crispy duck salad offers authentically shreddy, sweetly dressed meat in the company of crumbled cashews and pomelo, and even the salmon ceviche is Easterned up with lime, coriander, spring onion and red chilli for a bracing appetiser. Move on to carefully timed cod in an old-school cream sauce, with mussels on the half-shell, or impeccably rendered crackled pork belly with caramelised apple wedges and root hash. Chocoholics will likely forgive a glossy-brown Cru Virunga bar its lack of advertised 'crunch', or go for pannacotta in trifle livery, sharing a tumbler with poached Yorkshire rhubarb, jelly and custard. Glasses start at £8.50 on a brisk international roll call of quality wines. **Chef/s:** Will Halsall. **Open:** all week, all day from 12 (11.30 Sun). **Closed:** 24 to 26 Dec, 1 Jan. **Meals:** main courses £17 to £35. Set L and D £20 (2 courses) to £25. **Details:** 74 seats. 16 seats outside. V menu. Wheelchairs. Music. Parking.

Casa Malevo

Cooking score: 2
⊖ Marble Arch, map 6
Argentinian | £40
23 Connaught Street, Marylebone, W2 2AY
Tel no: (020) 7402 1988
casamalevo.com

'Connaught Street is surprisingly chi-chi these days,' observed one who used to work around here, in the benighted era before Casa Malevo came to enlighten the scene. A chequerboard-floored terrace gives way to a dimly lit clubby room with dark red leather seating and exposed brickwork walls. Argentinian A-grade beef is the calling card, hulking cuts muscling their way off the charcoal grill in the form of butter-soft flank steak with shallots in Malbec sauce, or there are thoroughbred lamb chops glistening with salty fat, dressed in minty, anchovy-rich salsa verde, along with a smear of beetroot purée. Appetise yourself if need be with burnished empanadas (the beef, spring onion, olive and egg version is the best), and perhaps toasted cheese Provoleta, bubbling in its skillet and dressed with roasted red pepper, cherry tomatoes and oregano. A slice of very tired-tasting lemon tart let the side down badly at inspection's end, but cheer is sustained by means of a list of pedigree Argentinian wines, from £24.90.
Chef/s: Jan Suchanek. **Open:** all week L and D. **Meals:** main courses £14 to £30. **Details:** 37 seats. 6 seats outside. Music.

Ceviche

⊖ Tottenham Court Road, map 5
Peruvian | £35
17 Frith Street, Soho, W1D 4RG
Tel no: (020) 7292 2040
cevicheuk.com

It was a big hit from the start and – six years on – this tightly packed homage to Peru remains buzzy, vibrant and energetic. Not surprisingly, it is ceviche that is the real highlight, with the classic don ceviche (fresh sea bass with amarillo chilli tiger's milk, limo chilli, sweet potato and red onion) being a real highlight for one reader, though tender beef heart marinated in pancho chilli and served with choclo corn and rocoto chilli cream, and the quinoa salad have pleased, too. Drink pisco-based cocktails, Peruvian beer or South American wines.

The Chancery

Cooking score: 6
⊖ Chancery Lane, map 5
Modern European | £50
9 Cursitor Street, Holborn, EC4A 1LL
Tel no: (020) 7831 4000
thechancery.co.uk
£5
OFF

Lurking behind the headquarters of Saatchi & Saatchi, the Chancery has grown inexorably in confidence since its opening over a decade ago. The interlinked dining rooms are dazzlingly white with dark seating and minimalist monochrome artwork, and the cooking under Yuma Hashemi is resourcefully inventive in its stylistic reach. Appetisers might be a pork currywurst on Berliner, an oyster with lardo, and a taste of raw beef with kim-chee, productively disorienting the taste-buds as preparation for the concise carte. A more classical French note is sounded by mi cuit foie gras with pear and brioche, or a truffled egg with chanterelles, while main dishes opt for intuitive partnerships of Dover sole with capers, lemon and butter, or 30-day beef fillet with Jerusalem artichoke purée and shallots. The signature dessert is still the multi-textured offering of chocolate in praline, coffee and ganache guises. Presentations are exquisitely clean and precise. A compact wine list, arranged by style, starts at £17.50. **Chef/s:** Yuma Hashemi. **Open:** Mon to Fri L, Mon to Sat D. **Closed:** Sun, 22 Dec to 2 Jan. **Meals:** set L and D £40 (2 courses) to £50. Tasting menu £65. **Details:** 50 seats. 12 seats outside. V menu. Bar. Wheelchairs. Music.

Chiltern Firehouse

Cooking score: 5
⊖ Baker Street, Bond Street, map 6
Modern American | £70
1 Chiltern Street, Marylebone, W1U 7PA
Tel no: (020) 7073 7676
chilternfirehouse.com

When the Victorians built a London fire station in the Gothic Revival style, it's almost as though they intended it to be seamlessly repurposed one day into a chic hotel. The Chiltern has been a magnet for the style set since its launch, and continues to pack them in to its busily designed stylish dining room, where a mix of booth seating, bar-stools and kitchen tables prepares the ground for Nuno Mendes' take on modern American food. Snack on crab-stuffed doughnuts if you will, while perusing the generously proportioned menus. A sense of the world at once comes through in starters that range from house Caesar with crispy chicken skin through Galician octopus with daikon to foie gras terrine with grapefruit and pumpernickel, while mains might offer a satisfying hunk of peat-smoked short rib with charred Hispi, or mimosa-crusted cod with calçots and olives. Most find room for desserts that may be as light as frozen apple pannacotta with shiso granita. A reference list of cutting-edge wine producers keeps the excitement levels high, even if prices will tear a hole in your weekly budget. Start at £22 for a dry white from the south-western Gers.

Chef/s: Nuno Mendes. **Open:** all week L and D. **Meals:** main courses £19 to £44. **Details:** 120 seats. 80 seats outside. Bar. Wheelchairs. Music.

China Tang London

Cooking score: 2
⊖ Hyde Park Corner, map 6
Chinese | £78
The Dorchester Hotel, 53 Park Lane, Hyde Park, W1K 1QA
Tel no: (020) 7629 9988
chinatanglondon.co.uk

Channelling the decadence of 1930s Shanghai, China Tang's dazzling rooms set the scene for something special. The clientele is culled from the international jet set, with polyglot staff in dapper uniforms attending to proceedings. Against a backdrop of sumptuous chinoiserie, carved woodwork, calligraphy and silken drapes, daytime diners enjoy their fill of steamed lobster dumplings, roast pork buns, tofu rolls and other MSG-free dim sum. Dinner, by contrast, focuses on the carte – a pricey run through the familiar regional repertoire taking in everything from 'supreme' fish maw soup to a three-part presentation of Peking duck, via minced pigeon in lettuce leaves, braised fish spiked with Szechuan peppercorns or Cantonese prawns with soy and chilli. Finish with the opulent dessert platter, taking in blood-orange and vanilla pannacotta, poached rhubarb and mascarpone cheesecake, and pistachio macaron. Drinkers pay serious money for serious wines.

Chef/s: Chun Chong Fong. **Open:** all week, all day from 12. **Closed:** 24 and 25 Dec. **Meals:** main courses £18 to £68. Set D £78 (5 courses). **Details:** 120 seats. Bar. Wheelchairs. Music. Children over 5 yrs only after 8pm.

Chutney Mary

Cooking score: 5
⊖ Green Park, map 5
Indian | £70
73 St James's Street, Mayfair, SW1A 1PH
Tel no: (020) 7629 6688
chutneymary.com
£5 OFF

The move from well-heeled Chelsea to even more opulent surroundings in St James's suited Chutney Mary, which has always striven for an aspirational version of the cooking of the Indian Subcontinent. A dining room of dazzling elegance, all towering jardinières and gilded sheen, is the heart of the experience, but for the whole package, have a cocktail in the Pukka Bar before you start. Manav Tuli interprets the regional Indian specialities with creativity and panache, and the likes of whole tandoori lobster in ginger, lime and Kashmiri chilli, or venison samosa in tamarind and date chutney, indicate the elevated nature of it all. Slow-cooked dishes are properly replete with complex layers of seasoning, from the Hyderabadi lamb shank that gets six hours to the undhiyu biryani of Gujarat, with its nine vegetable components, including purple yam and banana. Spelt naan breads offer robust sustenance, and if a bombe surprise of dark chocolate turns up, a long way from home, at the end, who's complaining? The stylistically classified wines are well chosen to stand up to the food.
Chef/s: Manav Tuli. **Open:** Mon to Sat L and D. **Closed:** Sun. **Meals:** main courses £17 to £40. Set L £26 (2 courses) to £30. **Details:** 119 seats. V menu. Bar. Wheelchairs. Music.

Symbols

	Accommodation is available
£30	Three courses for less than £30
£5 OFF	£5-off voucher scheme
	Notable wine list

LOCAL GEM
Ciao Bella

⊖ Holborn, Russell Square, map 5
Italian | £28
86-90 Lamb's Conduit Street, Bloomsbury, WC1N 3LZ
Tel no: (020) 7242 4119
ciaobellarestaurant.co.uk
£30

If the name sounds a bit unreconstructed that's because Ciao Bella has been around since the 1980s (owned by the same team since 1999) and is proudly old-school, right down to the black-and-white showbizzy photos and menu of pasta favourites. Main courses include grilled Dover sole and veal escalope, but it's the pasta that gets most plaudits – spinach and ricotta cannelloni with an aurora sauce, say, or spaghetti con polpette. Prices are fair, and the wine list has good regional Italian options.

The Cinnamon Club

Cooking score: 5
⊖ Westminster, map 5
Indian | £55
30-32 Great Smith Street, Westminster, SW1P 3BU
Tel no: (020) 7222 2555
cinnamonclub.com

Books furnish a room, or so they say, and there's no finer example among London's restaurants than the Cinnamon Club – a civilised sophisticate housed within the baroque splendour of the Old Westminster Library. In many respects, this is the ultimate in 'posh Indian' dining with its high-ceilinged interior, smart contemporary fittings and polished-wood floors – not forgetting those shelves lined with antique tomes. Executive chef Vivek Singh rises to the challenge, matching the swish surroundings with sharply accented food that fuses pinpoint spicing and premium ingredients with homespun tradition and slick European technique. Among the possibilities, you might find fenugreek-scented tandoori cod with curry leaf and lime crumble, roast saddle of Romney Marsh lamb with saffron-tinged rogan josh sauce and pickled root vegetables, or a forward-thinking vegetarian riff involving grilled kohlrabi layered with soya mince, pickled romanesco and achari (pickle) sauce. A couple of token European dishes also feature (courtesy of big-name French chef Eric Chavot), while desserts are in the crossover mode of, say, green cardamom brûlée. Breakfast, business lunches, Sunday feasts, exotic cocktails and a prestigious collection of A-list wines complete a mightily impressive package. **Chef/s:** Vivek Singh. **Open:** all week L and D. **Closed:** 1 May, 29 May, 28 Aug. **Meals:** main courses £17 to £35. Set L £24 (2 courses) to £26. Tasting menu £85 (6 courses). **Details:** 280 seats. Bar.

Cinnamon Soho

Cooking score: 2
⊖ Oxford Circus, map 5
Indian | £25
5 Kingly Street, Soho, W1B 5PF
Tel no: (020) 7437 1664
cinnamonsoho.com
£30

'This is a terrific Indian with moderate pricing, astute spicing and intelligent sourcing,' summed up one visitor to Vivek Singh's all-day diner. Made up of two slim dining spaces at ground and basement levels, it's a 'laid-back environment'. Colourful walls (saffron, cherry pink, grey), simple wooden furniture and easy-going staff help to make this 'a good pit-stop from the shops on Regent Street' and the take on modern Anglo-Indian cooking, offered on a flexible menu of small plates, grills, biryanis and pies, is full of enterprising ideas like rogan josh shepherd's pie. Start, perhaps with assured, spicy crab cakes with curry leaf, then tender pieces of Chettinad-spiced grilled lamb fillets served with a flavoursome masala sauce, and 'make sure you order the fluffy naans'. Finish with Malabar plum cake and cinnamon ice cream. To drink, there are interesting cocktails and a short, spice-friendly wine list (from £21).

Chef/s: Vivek Singh. **Open:** Mon to Sat, all day from 12. Sun 11 to 5. **Meals:** small plates £5 to £20. Set L £12 (2 courses) to £18. Set D £15 (2 courses) to £21. **Details:** 80 seats. 26 seats outside. Wheelchairs. Music.

★ NEW ENTRY ★

Clipstone

Cooking score: 5
⊖ Great Portland Street, map 5
Modern European | £31
5 Clipstone Street, Fitzrovia, W1W 6BB
Tel no: (020) 7637 0871
clipstonerestaurant.co.uk

There's much to like about this stripped-back corner bistro – from the short list of house cocktails, including a superb aged Negroni, to the daily changing menu that brings seasonal, high-quality ingredients together in clever combinations. The approach is dedicated: an umami-rich tartare of ox heart (served with cornichons, anchovy and mustard), and a superlative basil-infused lemon meringue tart ('the pastry chef is probably their best asset') are the standout dishes in a strong list of contenders. As well as the house pickles (orange and yellow carrots, radicchio, red cabbage, mushrooms), young leek tempura with lemon and sorrel mayonnaise is praised, and cuttlefish with clams, Jersey pearls and bacon is subtly worked rather than defiantly robust. Vinophiles will appreciate the carefully curated list that eschews the usual clichés in favour of less fashionable regions and grape varieties: the lip-smacking German Weißburgunder being one such example. House wine is £26.

Chef/s: Stuart Andrew and Merlin Labron-Johnson. **Open:** Mon to Sat L and D. **Closed:** Sun, 23 Dec to 3 Jan, bank hols. **Meals:** main courses £14 to £27. Tasting menu £45. **Details:** 40 seats. 16 seats outside. V menu. Music.

Average price

The average price denotes the price of a three-course meal without wine.

Clos Maggiore

Cooking score: 3
⊖ Covent Garden, map 5
French | £45
33 King Street, Covent Garden, WC2E 8JD
Tel no: (020) 7379 9696
closmaggiore.com

Come summer or winter, there's romance in the air at Clos Maggiore as Covent Garden tourists and celebrating couples clamour for tables in the restaurant's enchanting foliage-garlanded conservatory. The glass roof is opened to the stars on balmy evenings, while twinkling candles and a blazing fire create their own magic in the darker months. Whether you're seated here or in one of the less alluring dining areas, you can expect highly polished French-accented cooking with Mediterranean nuances – perhaps thinly sliced Limousin veal with pickled vegetables, walnut vinaigrette and salsa verde, red mullet with a shellfish faggot, baby artichokes and fennel escabèche or a mighty dish of slow-roast Pyrenean milk-fed lamb 'gremolata' for two. Vegetarians fare particularly well here, while fancy desserts such as the signature caramelised Valrhona chocolate 'sensation' with burnt-honey ice cream and Armagnac jelly are guaranteed to put anyone in the right mood. The wine list is voluminous but accessible, with vintages rolling back the years and quality on every page – plus some superb Coravin selections by the glass.
Chef/s: Marcellin Marc. **Open:** all week L and D. **Closed:** 24 and 25 Dec. **Meals:** main courses £20 to £30. Set L £25 (2 courses) to £30. Set D £28 (2 courses) to £33. Sun L £35. Tasting menu £65 (5 courses). **Details:** 70 seats. V menu. Music. Children at L only.

Visit us online

To find out more about The Good Food Guide, please visit thegoodfoodguide.co.uk

The Colony Grill Room

Cooking score: 3
⊖ Bond Street, map 6
North American | £40
The Beaumont, 8 Balderton Street, Brown Hart Gardens, Mayfair, W1K 6TF
Tel no: (020) 7499 9499
colonygrillroom.com

On the ground floor of the Beaumont Hotel (part of The Wolseley family), the Colony Grill Room has grown-up appeal. Walk past the 'stylish reception and fabulous bar' into the sort of restaurant that 'gets just about everything right' from good food to 'service that instinctively knows how to treat guests'. Here burgundy leather banquettes, parquet flooring, monochrome photos of Hollywood stars, and Art Deco features are nostalgic nods to a more glamorous age. The menu has broad appeal and transatlantic leanings, taking in hot dogs, hamburger, lobster Caesar and New York strip steak. Indeed, a test meal gave the kitchen high-fives all round: for a comforting chicken and sweetcorn chowder, and sea bass 'with lovely crisp skin' served atop caponata made with chunks of aubergine and green olives. To end, choose between bespoke sundaes or a generous slice of apple pie with vanilla ice cream. A well-selected wine list (from £25.50) with some 40 by the glass, rounds things off nicely.
Chef/s: Christian Turner. **Open:** all week, all day from 7am. **Meals:** main courses £12 to £56. **Details:** 100 seats. Bar. Wheelchairs. Music.

Copita

Cooking score: 3
⊖ Oxford Circus, map 5
Spanish | £30
27 d'Arblay Street, Soho, W1F 8EP
Tel no: (020) 7287 7797
copita.co.uk

The counter snakes around the room and fills up fast as diners arrive and bagsy stools for lunch and dinner sittings. A few pavement

tables give access to street life, while the hanging hams, dangling light bulbs and relaxed attitude suit the mood in this part of town. The monthly changing menu deals in high-quality ingredients delivered with simplicity and style. The cured meats and cheeses are hard to ignore – jamon Ibérico of course, and Cañarejal Cremoso cheese with picos. Things are done properly, although that's not to say it's traditional. Sweet potatoes, for example, come with bravas sauce, aïoli and peanuts, squid with celeriac purée and chorizo dressing, and Catalan-style chicken with a sauce of apricots and Pedro Ximénez. To finish, it's hard to get past churros. Every sherry and wine on the list is sold by the glass (bottle prices start at £24), and it's been gathered together with a keen eye on quality.
Chef/s: Khouma Ngedi. **Open:** Mon to Fri L and D. Sat, all day from 1. **Closed:** Sun, 24, 25 and 31 Dec, bank hols. **Meals:** tapas £5 to £10. **Details:** 38 seats. 6 seats outside.

Corrigan's Mayfair
Cooking score: 5
⊖ Marble Arch, map 6
Modern British | £53
28 Upper Grosvenor Street, Mayfair, W1K 7EH
Tel no: (020) 7499 9943
corrigansmayfair.com

To celebrate its 10th anniversary in 2017, Richard Corrigan installed a new watering hole (Dickie's Bar), and appointed Ross Bryans (ex Pollen Street Social – see entry) as chef/patron. With its gentleman's club vibe – hunting theme, low-level illumination, bluish leather and striking light fittings – Corrigan's feels very old-fashioned, but the mood is relaxed, the food much more contemporary than the surroundings. The kitchen's pride in native produce is evident, and raw materials are unsurpassed. 'Fabulous' smoked eel perfectly matched with black pudding hash and apple revealed balanced flavours pointed up by bright accompaniments, while suckling pig three ways (oven-roasted cutlet, confit belly, braised neck) was complemented by kumquat, pumpkin squash, crispy nettle and

granola. It can be difficult choosing between the top-notch cheeses and desserts such as a 'ravishing' pistachio soufflé with chocolate ice cream. Service is 'accomplished and knowledgeable'. The extensive wine list (from £38) is arranged principally by style, but prices, as with the food, are rooted in Mayfair.
Chef/s: Ross Bryans. **Open:** Mon to Fri and Sun L, Mon to Sat D. **Closed:** 25 to 30 Dec. **Meals:** main courses £19 to £44. Set L £28 (2 courses) to £34. Sun L £29. **Details:** 85 seats. Bar. Wheelchairs. Music.

Dean Street Townhouse
Cooking score: 2
⊖ Tottenham Court Road, map 5
Modern British | £40
69-71 Dean Street, Soho, W1D 3SE
Tel no: (020) 7434 1775
deanstreettownhouse.com

From the narrow terrace at the front, via the stool-lined zinc bar, red banquettes, white-clothed tables and art-strewn walls to the smart bedrooms above, this pair of Georgian townhouses lends itself elegantly to the complexity of this whole operation from Soho House. It strikes an instant chord from the moment it opens for breakfast, but it's the classic British brasserie food that forms the nerve centre, and the kitchen lays down an emphatic marker with the likes of twice-baked smoked haddock soufflé, mince and potatoes, ribeye steak with béarnaise, or Dover sole meunière, with a blackberry Bakewell tart to finish. Otherwise, settle in for a high tea of Welsh rarebit, fish fingers or macaroni cheese, or go for the traditional afternoon tea with its tiered array of goodies. It's worth remembering the good-value theatre menu, and booking is essential. The modern, global wine list starts at £23.
Chef/s: Jason Loy. **Open:** all week, all day from 7am (8am Sat and Sun). **Meals:** main courses £15 to £35. Set D £20 (2 courses) to £23. **Details:** 120 seats. 22 seats outside. Bar. Wheelchairs. Music.

Dehesa

Cooking score: 2
⊖ Oxford Circus, map 5
Spanish/Italian | £25
25 Ganton Street, Soho, W1F 9BP
Tel no: (020) 7494 4170
saltyardgroup.co.uk
£30

Although chef/front man Ben Tish has moved on to pastures new, little else has changed at this gregarious Carnaby outpost of the Salt Yard group (see entries). Tables are packed tightly into the small space, while discreet window booths and outdoor seats provide ample opportunities for people-watching. Named after the region that is home to some of Spain's prime acorn-munching porkers, Dehesa naturally features plenty of moreish piggy treats – not only premium-quality jamón but also boldly flavoured plates of, say, grilled Ibérico collar with white onion purée, baby artichokes, pistachio and Pedro Ximénez jus. Following the Salt Yard ethos, the kitchen favours fine-tuned Spanish and Italian 'tapas' in equal measure, from octopus a la plancha with confit ratte potatoes, chorizo ketchup, watercress and migas to twice-baked leek, spinach and Gorgonzola soufflé. Weekend brunch is a bonus for tourists and shoppers alike, while wines plunder the Iberian region to telling effect.
Chef/s: Giancarlo Vatteroni. **Open:** Mon to Fri L and D. Sat and Sun, all day from 10. **Closed:** 25 Dec, 1 Jan. **Meals:** tapas £5 to £10. **Details:** 42 seats. 28 seats outside. Music.

The Delaunay

Cooking score: 3
⊖ Temple, map 5
Modern European | £41
55 Aldwych, Covent Garden, WC2B 4BB
Tel no: (020) 7499 8558
thedelaunay.com

'I love this laid-back, slightly old-fashioned restaurant. It is ideal for Covent Garden Opera House and you can guarantee the timings,' ran the notes of one regular. 'Unfortunately, in the North we lack establishments of this nature, with city centres dominated by chains and rather average outlets,' bemoaned another. Chris Corbin and Jeremy King's café-restaurant in the grand European tradition has many fans, drawn as much by the 'very attentive staff' as by the excellence of the wiener Holstein (try with a side order of kase spätzle – 'cheesy and delicious'). It lends occasion to coffee and cake (pineapple and passion fruit gugelhupf, say), while the all-day menu accommodates all appetites, running from potato rösti with fried eggs for breakfast via wild boar and venison sausages or Hungarian pork goulash, to crustacea. An apple and blackcurrant sorbet, 'very fresh-tasting and full of flavour', makes a fittingly light finish. The European wine list opens at £25.50.
Chef/s: Malachi O'Gallagher. **Open:** all week, all day from 11.30. **Closed:** 25 Dec. **Meals:** main courses £13 to £34. **Details:** 150 seats. V menu. Bar. Wheelchairs.

Dinings

Cooking score: 3
⊖ Marylebone, map 6
Japanese | £50
22 Harcourt Street, Marylebone, W1H 4HH
Tel no: (020) 7723 0666
dinings.co.uk

Austere is an understatement when it comes to describing this modest Japanese restaurant in a tiny Georgian terraced house. To get to the dining room you squeeze through the 'snug at best' ground-floor sushi bar, head down narrow wooden stairs (plenty of grab rails) to a cramped concrete-floored basement with absolutely no décor, limited seating, but plenty of light. You are definitely here for the food, so it's good to know that cooking is vibrant and delicate – and booking essential. The menu combines traditional Japanese cuisine with modern European ideas, and is divided into hot and cold tapas. Nasu miso grilled aubergine with sweet miso, and grilled chilli-garlic black cod are always solid choices, but there's also lobster tempura roll, and nigiri

Japanese Wagyu beef sushi with truffle salsa. While coming across as fresh and quite modern, there's still the feeling of remaining a trusted place for deliciously fresh sushi and sashimi – the classic platters of both (served with miso soup) don't disappoint. Lovely service, too. A glossier, larger Dinings SW3, has opened in Walton House, Walton Street, Chelsea.
Chef/s: Masaki Sugisaki. **Open:** all week L and D. **Meals:** tapas £7 to £29. Sushi and sashimi £4 to £9. **Details:** 28 seats. Music.

Dishoom
Cooking score: 2
⊖ Leicester Square, Covent Garden, map 5
Indian | £30
12 Upper St Martin's Lane, Covent Garden, WC2H 9FB
Tel no: (020) 7420 9320
dishoom.com

Shamil and Kavi Thakrar's lively group of Indian restaurants (four in London, including nearby Kingly Street, one in Edinburgh) proves that while many run-of-the-mill British curry houses are struggling, there is a huge appetite for interesting, authentic cooking served in appealing surroundings. Dishoom recreates the faded glamour of the Irani-run cafés that were once a common sight in Mumbai – think ceiling fans, bentwood chairs, photos of Bollywood stars and a lively bustle (booking is advised, but is only an option for groups of six or more after 5:45). Choice runs from breakfast (Bombay omelette, bun maska and chai) through to lunch and dinner via dishes such as lamb samosas and okra fries, prawn moilee with a bowl of greens, and mango kulfi for dessert. Other Mumbai staples include small plates – maybe chilli cheese toast or keema pau – grills (paneer tikka; seekh kebab) and several biryani options. A big and beautiful drinks menu includes lassis and coolers, Botal soda, various chais (including a Baileys option) and a decent selection of wines and Indian beers.

Chef/s: Naved Nasir. **Open:** all week, all day from 8am (9am Sat and Sun). **Closed:** 25 and 26 Dec, 1 and 2 Jan. **Meals:** main courses £6 to £18. **Details:** 140 seats. 18 seats outside. Bar. Wheelchairs. Music.

Donostia
Cooking score: 3
⊖ Marble Arch, map 6
Spanish | £30
10 Seymour Place, Marylebone, W1H 7ND
Tel no: (020) 3620 1845
donostia.co.uk

The mothership of a chic Basque group of two (see entry for Lurra), small but perfectly formed Donostia goes about its business on a pretty Marylebone street not far from Marble Arch. Regularly rammed with enthusiasts seeking authentic tapas fashioned from top-drawer ingredients – booking is essential – it makes for a thoroughly convivial operation. Come here for platters of Ibérico de bellota chorizo, jamón, salchichón or lomo de presa, pintxos of croquetas made with Ossau-Iraty and Idiazabal sheep's cheese, tempura prawns with ham and mango or mini Galician beef burgers with paprika potatoes, and tapas of crispy fried cod cheeks with aïoli, and pig's cheeks with parsnip purée. Desserts don't stray too far away from tarta de Santiago and torrija. Service is welcoming and helpful – do ask for wine recommendations, there's plenty to lift the spirits among the Spanish regional wines (from £22); good gin and tonic, too.
Chef/s: Joel Donne. **Open:** Tue to Sat L, all week D. **Closed:** 24 Dec to 1 Jan. **Meals:** tapas £10 to £25. **Details:** 40 seats. 10 seats outside. Music.

Symbols

🛏 Accommodation is available
£30 Three courses for less than £30
£5 OFF £5-off voucher scheme
🍾 Notable wine list

DUM Biryani House

θ Tottenham Court Road, map 5
Indian | £27
187b Wardour Street, Soho, W1F 8ZB
Tel no: (020) 3638 0974
dumlondon.com

£30

Descend to a couple of simply decorated dining rooms – bentwood chairs, bare tables, the usual dangling lights, painted concrete floor, splashes of bright colour. The impressive-looking biryanis – lamb, chicken, vegetable – are served thali style with large and small papads, pickles, bhindi pachadi (spiced okra yoghurt) and baingan mirchi salan (baby aubergine in a mild peanut and sesame seed curry). Start with fried yoghurt patties and Andhra tomato chutney, pick a side of, say, Hyderabadi dal tadka, add a couple of paratha and find room, if you can, for Indian milk pudding flavoured with rosewater and cardamom. To drink, there are spiced-up cocktails, beer and a brief selection of wines.

Ember Yard

Cooking score: 4
θ Tottenham Court Road, map 5
Modern European | £30
60 Berwick Street, Soho, W1F 8SU
Tel no: (020) 7439 8057
emberyard.co.uk

The hunger for small plates shows no sign of being sated – and why should it when gems like Ember Yard exist? Chefs at the charcoal grill at the back of this popular, compact Soho spot tame flames with deft hands, letting just the right amount of smokiness and char linger on the softest pieces of octopus (paprika aïoli adds a warmly spiced dimension to this delicious dish) or Jerusalem artichokes, caramelised to sweet nuttiness and served with frills of kale, roast chestnuts and pickled mustard seeds. Pick of the dishes remains the exquisitely delicate Ibérico presa, swirls of whipped jamón butter almost superfluous

such is the memorable flavour of the meat; a plate of chistorra sausage, its punch countered by the gentle syrupy sweetness of colourful peperonata, is a top pick, too. Quince tart with smoked-milk ice cream keeps the charcoal theme running subtly and tastily through a delightful pudding offer. Exceptional, knowledgeable service throughout deserves a mention, as does the terrifc wine list, from £20.

Chef/s: Brett Barnes. **Open:** all week L and D.
Closed: 25 Dec, 1 Jan. **Meals:** tapas £8 to £11. Set L £20. **Details:** 106 seats. 8 seats outside. Bar. Music.

Fera at Claridges

Cooking score: 7
θ Bond Street, map 5
Modern British | £75
49 Brook Street, Mayfair, W1K 4HR
Tel no: (020) 7107 8888
feraatclaridges.co.uk

Simon Rogan may have departed, but the chef's aura still shimmers in this grande dame of London dining rooms. His legacy is bound up not so much in the lofty Art Deco interior, oversized flower arrangements or supremely comfortable sage-green leather seating, more in the inventiveness of the food, and the kitchen's continued dedication to ingredients from hedgerow, woodland and seashore. A whisper-thin wafer topped with a ripple of curd and fairy-garden of petals – served on driftwood, natch – precedes 'snacks'. Believe your waiter's enthusiasm, for they are delicious: confit rabbit in tapioca and onion crumb dipped into tangy lovage purée makes a sublime mouthful, ditto tender curls of squid with sea vegetables on seaweed crackers. The sweetness of plump Gairloch prawns plays beautifully against a scrape of salty-sharp dill and oyster emulsion, and while barbecued white asparagus and crisp-coated sweetbreads look less alluring, the subtle richness of accompanying smoked egg yolk accords the dish delicious depth. Mild monkfish needs something punchier than courgette and mussels to come alive, but the combination of lamb, king oyster mushrooms, nettle purée and crisped belly is masterly. A dome of frozen apple over white chocolate, with hints of fennel, miso and barley, is an invigorating finale. The wine list is brilliantly curated and correspondingly expensive (there's little around the opening £35 mark), but do mine the sommelier's impressive and charmingly imparted knowledge.

Chef/s: Matt Starling. **Open:** all week L and D. **Meals:** main courses £28 to £38. Set L £46. Tasting menu £85 to £110. **Details:** 94 seats. V menu. Bar. Wheelchairs. Children over 5 yrs only.

Fischer's

Cooking score: 2
⊖ Baker Street, Regent's Park, map 6
Austrian | £40
50 Marylebone High Street, Marylebone, W1U 5HN
Tel no: (020) 7466 5501
fischers.co.uk

With its determined air of bygone elegance reinforced by polished wood, brass trim, copious tiling and paintings galore, this brasserie has the look and feel of a 19th-century European café. It's a welcome oasis in a street filled with fairly average European café-culture venues, playing its role as a Viennese café and *konditorei* well, but then the owners are Chris Corbin and Jeremy King of Wolseley fame (see entry). A simple, one-page carte lists the retro comfort food and if the menu changes infrequently, it's because many of the dishes are so popular: wiener schnitzel, käsekrainer (pork and garlic stuffed sausage with Emmental), veal bratwurst, lamb goulash, Sachertorte. The cooking may not be cutting edge, but prices are reasonable for such an affluent area. Breakfast offerings include gröstl (bacon or spinach with paprika-fried potatoes, onions and fried egg). Wines from £25.50.

Chef/s: Maciej Banas. **Open:** all week, all day from 7.30am (8 Sun). **Closed:** 25 Dec. **Meals:** main courses £13 to £26. **Details:** 100 seats. 4 seats outside. V menu. Wheelchairs.

Frenchie

Cooking score: 5
⊖ Leicester Square, Covent Garden, map 5
Modern French | £45
16 Henrietta Steet, Covent Garden, WC2E 8QH
Tel no: (020) 7836 4422
frenchiecoventgarden.com

It's not always easy to find good places to eat in touristy Covent Garden, but this successful Parisian spin-off reboots French cooking with a stylish twist on the classic bistro. Gregory Marchand is a savvy chef who worked at a host of London restaurants before making his name in Paris. Here in London, priority goes to quality British ingredients served in an unshowy, slightly cramped space: a narrow ground-floor room dominated by a long bar (good for dining alone), with an open kitchen-cum-dining room downstairs. It's the very good, modern bistro cooking, however, that's the undoubted star, delivered via concise, seasonal menus. Deftly updated, often surprisingly flavoured dishes have included squid with a winter vegetable pot-au-feu and smoked herring roe, and Ibaiama pork cooked in a salt crust and served with chickpeas, medjool dates and cedrat lemon. Not to be missed are the bacon scones with maple syrup and the smoky bacon ice cream served with a bread-and-butter pudding, and a bittersweet chocolate tart. Service is 'keen and attentive' and gives good advice on the modern wine list (from £28).

Chef/s: Gregory Marchand. **Open:** all week L and D. **Closed:** 24 to 26 and 31 Dec, 1 Jan. **Meals:** main courses £18 to £29. Set L £26 (2 courses) to £29. Tasting menu £45 (4 courses). **Details:** 64 seats. Bar. Music.

Average price ━━━━━╤

The average price denotes the price of a three-course meal without wine.

La Fromagerie

⊖ Baker Street, Bond Street, map 6
Modern European | £25
2-6 Moxon Street, Marylebone, W1U 4EW
Tel no: (020) 7935 0341
lafromagerie.co.uk

£5 £30
OFF

This foodie mecca is so much more than a cheese shop, although nothing can rival the contents of La Fromagerie's temperature-controlled cheese room: French and Italian selections are served in the deli itself or you can sample the wares in the 'café at no. 6'. Plates of charcuterie, terrines and tins of sardines are also on offer here, alongside a short 'kitchen menu' – think broccoli soup with crisp pancetta or seared John Dory with fregola. Baked goods, breakfast and a few European wines complete the picture. There's a branch at 30 Highbury Park, N5 2AA; tel: (020) 7359 7440.

Galvin at Windows

Cooking score: 6
⊖ Hyde Park Corner, Green Park, map 6
French | £79
Hilton Hotel, 22 Park Lane, Mayfair, W1K 1BE
Tel no: (020) 7208 4021
galvinatwindows.com

Putting the 'haute' into haute cuisine, Galvin at Windows on the 28th floor of the London Hilton on Park Lane has been reaching great heights since 2006. The 'reliable and calm restaurant' is so much more than wraparound views. The room itself, large and light, done in a Deco-inspired style, is effortlessly glamorous – just what one wants from a 'special occasion' destination. It's the complete package: as well known for service as it is for its cooking (manager Fred Sirieix is something of a TV personality). It doesn't come cheap, however. The carte, at £79 for three courses, is a steep entry point, though lunch is a steal. Hope for a window table and the likes of Scottish salmon mi cuit, Dorset

crab, Granny Smith and shellfish vinaigrette, then Ibérico pork loin with pipérade, crispy rillettes and sweet potato purée, and apple Tatin with caramel sauce and rosemary ice cream. Wines are as reassuringly classical as the cooking.
Chef/s: Joo Won. **Open:** Mon to Fri and Sun L, Mon to Sat D. **Meals:** main courses £40 to £46. Set L £30 (2 courses) to £35. Alc D £60 (2 courses) to £79. Sun L £55. Tasting menu £115. **Details:** 109 seats. Bar. Wheelchairs. Parking.

Galvin Bistrot de Luxe

Cooking score: 4
⊖ Baker Street, map 6
French | £37
66 Baker Street, Marylebone, W1U 7DJ
Tel no: (020) 7935 4007
galvinrestaurants.com

Baker Street is no match for the Champs-Elysées, but there's a sense of unconfined Gallic largesse about the Galvin brothers' original Bistrot. It's a lively place where mahogany and leather interiors set the tone as smartly garbed waiters work the close-packed tables, delivering elegantly constructed plates of 'satisfying' sure-footed bourgeois food. The signature lasagne of crab with beurre nantaise continues to delight readers ('so light, yet really full of flavour'), but the kitchen wheels out all manner of deftly executed classics and new-wave creations bursting with punchy flavours – from cassoulet or pan-fried calf's liver with spring greens and Alsace bacon to turbot with curried cauliflower, pine nut and raisin dressing. After that, whipped Fourme D'Ambert with caramelised pear and candied walnut has hit the spot, likewise rum baba with crème Chantilly and other true Gallic desserts. 'Superb value' extends to the wine list, which also tips its beret to La Belle France.
Chef/s: Chris Galvin and Max Osborne. **Open:** all week L and D. **Closed:** 25 and 26 Dec, 1 Jan. **Meals:** main courses £15 to £27. Set L £16. Set D £20. Sun L £29. **Details:** 110 seats. V menu. Bar. Wheelchairs.

The Game Bird

Cooking score: 4
⊖ Green Park, map 5
Modern British | £60
The Stafford, 16-18 St James's Place, Mayfair,
SW1A 1NJ
Tel no: (020) 7493 0111
thegamebird.com

🛏

'Beautifully decorated with that mix of antiques, marble, ornate plasterwork, good modern art and formality that only a posh Mayfair hotel can pull off successfully', the Stafford is both relaxed and formal enough to make an evening here a small occasion. Located down a little-known cul-de-sac in the inner recesses of St James's, it's 'a real hidden gem', a grand hotel on a domestic scale. Start with cocktails in the American Bar before heading to the elegant dining area for James Durrant's take on modern British cooking. Familiar strains resound in smoked salmon – they wheel out a trolley laden with different cures – dressed Devon crab, fish and chips, steak and ale suet pudding, Norfolk Black chicken Kiev or the various grills, although there are more contemporary noises in the shape of Orkney scallops served with roasted cauliflower, smoked roe and seaweed butter, and Cornish cod with white onions, Jersey Royals, morels and mint. As the name suggests, seasonal game is a speciality, and this is the place to come if your fancy turns to a traditional Sunday roast. Both Lyle's Golden Syrup sponge with custard and a textbook pistachio soufflé make indulgent finales. Wines start at £33 on the French-leaning list. **Chef/s:** James Durrant. **Open:** all week, all day from 12. **Meals:** main courses £19 to £30. Set L and D £25 (2 courses) to £30. Sun L £30. **Details:** 65 seats. Bar. Wheelchairs. Music.

James Durrant

The Game Bird, Mayfair

What's your favourite game bird?
My favourite would have to be mallard. Wild duck has such a wonderful flavour.

What is your favourite time of year for food?
For me, it would be the end of autumn because that is when the game season opens and the produce really begins to change with the climate. I love to cook hearty comfort food.

Which of your dishes are you most proud of?
A lot of time and work went into perfecting our Norfolk Black Chicken Kiev. As a child I remember the disappointment of being served a chicken Kiev that had burst and lost all its butter, so we have spent a lot of time developing ours to make sure it is packed with filling.

What would you be doing if you weren't a chef?
I stayed on at college to do a one-year art course in preparation for starting a degree in product design and engineering at Liverpool University. I made it around two months into the course before leaving to become a chef.

Gauthier Soho

Cooking score: 6
⊖ Leicester Square, map 5
Modern French | £50
21 Romilly Street, Soho, W1D 5AF
Tel no: (020) 7494 3111
gauthiersoho.co.uk
£5 OFF

The Georgian townhouse near Cambridge Circus offers a refined domestic setting at odds with the Soho norm. If you have to ring a doorbell to get in around these parts, you're likely to be in the market for another kind of experience altogether. The upper dining room is dazzlingly white, with an outsized mirror over the original fireplace and blinds to temper the London glare. Alexis Gauthier offers high-gloss modern French cuisine, underpinned by confident classical technique. Reporters fly into raptures over potent vichyssoise poured over wilted greens and truffle ravioli, or meltingly tender ox cheek with apple and celeriac purée in cider vinegar, as preludes to grandstanding main dishes like Atlantic cod with charred leeks and Jerusalem artichoke in concentrated fish jus. Roast guinea fowl is teamed with a cube of perfect pork belly and slender young carrots, and the concluding note might be chocolate and passion fruit tart with nougatine, or the signature Louis XV, a soul-stirring mousse of 70 per cent dark chocolate. There are Hungarians, Lebanese and Israelis on the magisterial wine list, but the core is a spectacular roll call of French classics, many at peak maturity. A large range by the small glass starts at £9.
Chef/s: Alexis Gauthier. **Open:** Tue to Sat L and D. **Closed:** Sun, Mon, 25 to 30 Dec, bank hols. **Meals:** set L £24 (2 courses) to £30. Set D £50 (3 courses). Tasting menu £75. **Details:** 50 seats. V menu.

Average price

The average price denotes the price of a three-course meal without wine.

★ TOP 50 ★

Le Gavroche

Cooking score: 7
⊖ Marble Arch, map 6
French | £150
43 Upper Brook Street, Mayfair, W1K 7QR
Tel no: (020) 7408 0881
le-gavroche.co.uk

Le Gavroche serves a city vastly different from the one it set out to dazzle some 50 years ago, yet to the delight of its many fans, nothing seems to change – it remains a shrine to classical French cooking. The lavish appeal of the cooking is matched by the equally unchanging, expensively trimmed, green-hued subterranean dining room, which sets out to seduce with its high levels of comfort, old-fashioned gentility (which persists in offering your guests menus without prices), and plentiful staff who are knowledgeable and attentive without being too intrusive – they even manage the dome-removing ceremonies without too much formality. With the emphasis firmly on haute cuisine principles, Michel Roux Jr's cooking takes a journey through luxury ingredients – lobster, foie gras, turbot, langoustine – and heirloom dishes – soufflé suissesse, omelette Rothschild. When the kitchen's sights are focused, it can come up with some very fine cooking, from sweet-roasted Scottish scallops in a Chartreuse velouté with julienne of carrots, and a 'brilliantly succulent' pressed pig's head terrine with braised Hereford snails and parsley purée, to a fat lobe of roasted sweetbread with white asparagus, Ibérico de bellota and toasted hazelnuts, and foamy, well-risen passion fruit soufflé with white chocolate ice cream. For the price, one's hope is always that the cooking is nearly without fault, and generally this is the case, although there were a few lapses at a test dinner. The 'still wonderful value-for-money' set lunch, for example, can deliver a high degree of satisfaction, as one couple discovered at a spring lunch that began with a 'superb and unusual' lightly battered cod's tongue with a

ragoût of petits pois and violet potatoes, smoked bacon and Little Gem, followed by 'a delightful spring-tasting dish' of rump of lamb with parsley, wild mushrooms, broccoli and thyme jus. On the extravagantly great wine list, France is given the full works. Prices are high, but when you look at the pedigree of the Burgundy growers and the Bordeaux châteaux, you can see why.
Chef/s: Rachel Humphrey and Michel Roux Jr. **Open:** Wed to Fri L, Tue to Sat D. **Closed:** Sun, Mon, 2 weeks late Dec, bank hols. **Meals:** main courses £29 to £76. Set L £56. Tasting menu £160. **Details:** 80 seats. V menu. Bar. Wheelchairs.

Great Queen Street

Cooking score: 3
⊖ Covent Garden, map 5
Modern British | £29
32 Great Queen Street, Covent Garden, WC2B 5AA
Tel no: (020) 7242 0622
greatqueenstreetrestaurant.co.uk
£30

Ten years on, this offspring of no-frills, rustic pub-food pioneer the Anchor & Hope (see entry) is considered a veritable theatreland old-timer. Great Queen Street certainly remains unwavering in its commitment to cooking bracing, gutsy, season-led food. The practice of good eating is at the beating heart of this convivial operation, with its moody interior, open kitchen and rough-hewn tables. Expect no facsimile pub grub, but rather a daily changing menu that lists dishes by price, not course, and majors in vigorous flavours brought together with considerable skill. Charred calçot onions with smoky salbitxada and cool goats' curd might start things off, followed by sea trout with monk's beard, dill, potato and cucumber or confit duck leg with chickpeas, pumpkin and chorizo. This is a place to linger – book ahead for Sunday roast – though there is a well-priced set-menu 'Worker's Lunch' that has you handsomely fed and watered within the hour. Indulge with

tarte Tatin for two, or an Alphonso mango and coconut brûlée rice pudding. The judicious Francophile wine list starts at £17.50.
Chef/s: Sam Hutchins. **Open:** all week L, Mon to Sat D. **Closed:** 25 and 26 Dec, bank hols. **Meals:** main courses £16 to £25. Set L £20 (2 courses) to £22. **Details:** 57 seats. 8 seats outside. Bar. Wheelchairs.

★ TOP 50 ★

The Greenhouse

Cooking score: 7
⊖ Green Park, map 5
Modern European | £100
27a Hay's Mews, Mayfair, W1J 5NY
Tel no: (020) 7499 3331
greenhouserestaurant.co.uk
£5 OFF 🍾

As though Mayfair weren't exclusive enough as a restaurant address, the Greenhouse hides itself away in a residential mews, its own little garden extending along the decked entrance approach. Inside, the mood is also green and pleasant, with stylised floral artworks and leaf-coloured seating, a restful backdrop for Arnaud Bignon's contemporary French repertoire. Bignon's food is imaginative and thought-provoking, often rather delicate in conception when compared to the modern British idiom, but resonant in its effects. Lychee, sea beets and ginger are the unexpected accompaniments to an opening offering of sautéed veal sweetbreads, while Scottish langoustines are treated to a bifocal approach, one seared and seasoned with green mango, yoghurt and mint, the other poached and Japanesed with sesame, shiso and pumpkin. Middle and Far Eastern seasonings are enjoyed throughout, as for monkfish in dukkah with banana and lime leaves, or Wagyu Angus beef that comes dressed in yuzu at a hefty supplement. At its least successful, the cooking can feel curiously underpowered – 'the water-bathed turbot with seaweed butter, samphire and spinach purée was not the best we've ever had, and rather sparse on the plate' – but desserts don't lack inventive impetus, when lime pannacotta is sauced with the elements of a mojito cocktail. The wine list (from £35) is one of London's most massive, but a capable sommelier stands ready.

Chef/s: Arnaud Bignon. **Open:** Mon to Fri L, Mon to Sat D. **Closed:** Sun, 25 to 31 Dec. **Meals:** main courses £55 to £75. Set L £35 (2 courses) to £40. Set D £90 (2 courses) to £100. Tasting menu £125. **Details:** 65 seats. V menu. Bar. Wheelchairs.

Gymkhana

Cooking score: 5
↔ Piccadilly Circus, Green Park, map 5
Indian | £65
42 Albermarle Street, Mayfair, W1S 4JH
Tel no: (020) 3011 5900
gymkhanalondon.com

The nabobs of Mayfair are regaled with a re-creation of the days of the Raj at Gymkhana, a period brought into the soft focus of cultural retrospect by means of deeply upholstered leather sofas, stags' heads and antique clocks, under the ornamental turning of ceiling fans. Karam Sethi's Indian cooking is anything but pallidly nostalgic, applying a contemporary sensibility and unusual prime materials to dishes of quartz-like sharpness and definition. Methi keema to begin is made with kid meat, or you might appetise with a duck egg bhurji garnished with lobster and Malabar paratha. A section of kebabs and tikka encompasses peanut and green mango fish with yoghurt-dressed cucumber and carrot pachadi, and the game dishes are quite something – how about muntjac biryani with minted pomegranate raita? Sides such as Rajasthani aubergine add to the allure. Then finish in aromatic style with date and fig rice pudding, or luscious rasmalai with apple preserve. The plethora of set menus is worth anybody's time, and there is a deeply classical Mayfair wine list, from £29, that wouldn't leave even the hautest cuisine feeling naked.

Chef/s: Karam Sethi and Palash Mitra. **Open:** Mon to Sat L and D. **Closed:** Sun, 24 to 26 Dec, 31 Dec to 1 Jan. **Meals:** main courses £15 to £38. Set L £25 (2 courses) to £30. Set D £40 (4 courses). Tasting menu £70 (6 courses). **Details:** 90 seats. V menu. Bar. Music. No children after 7pm.

★ NEW ENTRY ★

Hai Cenato

Cooking score: 3
↔ Victoria, map 3
Italian | £30
Cardinal Place, 2 Sir Simon Milton Square, Victoria, SW1E 5DJ
Tel no: (020) 3816 9320
haicenato.co.uk

Jason Atherton admirably refuses to be typecast. Hard on the heels of Sosharu (Japanese) and Temple & Sons (British), his ninth restaurant in the capital serves New York-style Italian food with a menu that flits from small plates to pasta to pizza to the inevitable ribeye for two. The upper floor blurs the line between bar and restaurant with a boisterous bonhomie and a feeling that this is group-meal territory rather than dinner for two; the tightly organised tables downstairs are much preferred. The cooking is all about no-nonsense robust flavours and there's plenty to entice. Meaty, sweet octopus and Cornish squid served atop braised lentils, bacon, green chilli and salsa verde, and richly flavoured aged beef bolognese with corzetti (flat discs of pasta), tomato, crisp sage leaves, burnt butter and Berkswell cheese are intros to satisfying main courses like charcoal-oven-baked cod served with a dab of anchovy and almond romesco. Pizza is a meal in itself, while baked almond meringue, lemon curd, confit lemon and sour yoghurt sorbet makes a perfect finale. To drink, there are Italian-themed cocktails, and an exciting choice of wines, mostly Italian. Many bottles are under £40, while a few run into three figures.

Chef/s: Frankie Van Loo. **Open:** all week L and D. **Closed:** bank hols. **Meals:** main courses £9 to £30. Set L and early D £15 (2 courses) to £19. **Details:** 60 seats. 38 seats outside. Bar. Wheelchairs. Music.

Hakkasan

Cooking score: 5
⊖ Tottenham Court Road, map 5
Chinese | £65
8 Hanway Place, Fitzrovia, W1T 1HD
Tel no: (020) 7927 7000
hakkasan.com

When this, the original Hakkasan, opened in 2001, it was in a decidedly unfashionable location – but that didn't stop it blazing a trail for a modern style of Chinese dining. Hanway Place has smartened up over the years, but the restaurant remains a surreal place, hidden deep in the bowels of the earth – or so it seems as you head down, down, down stairs to the pair of crepuscular dining rooms – all moody lighting and fretwork screens. An extended list of dim sum is the lunchtime lure, and the kitchen moves from char siu bao and har-gau to more edgy ideas such as black truffle and Dover sole dumplings or gold-leaf lobster with lychee and mustard. The full carte can be revelatory: crispy duck salad with pomelo, pine nut and shallot, wok-fried organic Rhug lamb loin with Pied Bleu mushrooms and salsify, and Atlantic halibut with spicy Szechuan chilli. Sakés and wines (some organic and biodynamic) are fastidiously tailored to the food. It's all staggeringly expensive, so it's worth noting the good deal that is dim sum Sunday.
Chef/s: Goh Wee Boon. **Open:** all week L and D.
Closed: 24 and 25 Dec. **Meals:** main courses £20 to £60. Set L £38. Set D £38 to £128. Sun L £58.
Details: 200 seats. V menu. Bar. Wheelchairs. Music.

Hakkasan Mayfair

Cooking score: 4
⊖ Green Park, Bond Street, map 5
Chinese | £80
17 Bruton Street, Mayfair, W1J 6QB
Tel no: (020) 7907 1888
hakkasan.com

Those branches of Hakkasan in the American cities, the Middle East and India may be more exotically located than staid old Mayfair, but the Bruton Street iteration of the brand, here

since 2010, fires on all cylinders. Eating takes place over two floors, the lower ground offering the cooler space, all wooden screens and lighting levels that are not so much subdued as mercilessly quashed. Aspirational Chinese cooking remains the lure, and the results are dramatic. Adding foie gras to sesame prawn toast for a pre-meal nibble may seem obvious, but the principal dishes are explosive with unexpected levels of intensity. Stir-fried lobster in white peppercorn sauce, chicken smoked in jasmine tea, veal ribs in Zhengjiang vinegar, and exemplary homemade tofu, perhaps in a clay-pot dish with aubergine and Japanese mushrooms in black bean and chilli sauce, are full of commanding tastes and fascinating textures. Fixed-price menus are comprehensive but expensive, but there are stylish dim sum and desserts such as chocolate and olive oil ganache with raspberry sorbet and candied olives. Speciality spirit and liqueur brands are the crown jewels of the drinks list.
Chef/s: Tong Chee Hwee. **Open:** all week, all day from 12. **Meals:** main courses £25 to £60. Set L and early D £38 (3 courses). **Details:** 220 seats. V menu. Bar. Music.

Hawksmoor Seven Dials

Cooking score: 4
⊖ Covent Garden, map 5
British | £50
11 Langley Street, Covent Garden, WC2H 9JG
Tel no: (020) 7420 9390
thehawksmoor.com

The site of the old Watney Combe brewery in Covent Garden is a fitting place for one of the branches of Messrs Beckett and Gott's portfolio of unreconstructed steakhouses. Annual steakathons for the great and good were held on these premises in the Georgian era, and in 1807, the future George IV, who knew a thing or two about eating, got right royally stuffed here. The drill, as throughout the group, is hefty cuts of prime beef, variously garnished and sauced, allowing you to combine, say, a lump of rump with anchovy hollandaise and grilled bone marrow. If you're meating it all the way, a starter portion of potted beef and bacon with Yorkshires is a good way of limbering up, but there are great seafood options, too, including garlic-buttered lobster, or simple crab on toast. The heroic way to finish is with sticky toffee pudding. Inventive cocktails are a good lead-in to a wine list (from £23) that takes no prisoners.

Chef/s: Karol Poniewaz. **Open:** all week L, Mon to Sat D. **Closed:** 24 to 26 Dec, 1 Jan. **Meals:** main courses £12 to £50. Set L and D £25 (2 courses) to £28. Sun L £20. **Details:** 142 seats. Bar. Wheelchairs. Music.

Hélène Darroze at the Connaught

Cooking score: 5
⊖ Bond Street, Green Park, map 5
Modern French | £95
16 Carlos Place, Mayfair, W1K 2AL
Tel no: (020) 3147 7200
the-connaught.co.uk

The old Connaught has scarcely ever felt as glitzy as it has over the past decade, when a vivid green contemporary design was laid gently over the original oak-panelled shell of the principal dining room. This heralded the arrival of Hélène Darroze, who brought an *au courant* French sensibility to proceedings after an Italian intermezzo. It's been nearly a decade now, and while the menu has grown more terse in its descriptions, some dishes remain. The Scottish scallop in its tandoori-spiced carrot purée with bitter citrus and coriander is a delight, the truffled Landais chicken with celeriac and sorrel is probably worth its supplement, and Basque lamb comes in Moroccan array, with Muscat grapes, piquillo peppers and a ras-el-hanout cracker. Other compositions might be more baffling, however. A piece of turbot is under-seasoned except for a vitiating tartness, but then overwhelmed anyway by thick Champagne sabayon. Back on course, a simple dessert of Yorkshire rhubarb with crumbled cashews, rhubarb meringue and ginger is a wholesale

treat. Staff are numerous and omnicompetent, and the wine flights are the best way of finding a way through the enormous opulence of the list.
Chef/s: Hélène Darroze. **Open:** all week L and D. **Meals:** set L £52 (3 courses). Set D £95 (5 courses). Tasting menus £175. **Details:** 65 seats. V menu. Bar. Wheelchairs. Music.

Honey & Co.

Cooking score: 3
⊖ Warren Street, map 2
Middle Eastern | £35
25a Warren Street, Fitzrovia, W1T 5LZ
Tel no: (020) 7388 6175
honeyandco.co.uk

Sarit Packer and Itamar Srulovich's miniscule Middle Eastern eatery has been on a constant roll since opening in 2012 (booking is essential), never failing to deliver lovely, unforgettable flavours. Tables may be a squeeze, but when 'every dish showed off either innovative combinations or exacting technique (and quite often both) but keeping well within the realms of generous, home-style food', nobody is complaining. The emphasis is on quality seasonal ingredients, with a spring menu offering creamy hummus made with fresh broad beans and served with marinated asparagus and soft-boiled egg, and ransom leaf labneh (with minted courgette, currants and pine nut salad). There's a kaleidoscope of flavours in pomegranate molasses-roasted chicken with cracked wheat salad, pomegranate and pistachio or slow-cooked lamb with saffron rice, almonds and golden raisins. For an indulgent finale, feta and honey cheesecake on a kadaif base (shredded filo pastry) won't disappoint. The short list of predominantly European wines opens at £20.
Chef/s: Sarit Packer and Itamar Srulovich. **Open:** Mon to Sat L and D. **Closed:** Sun, 24 to 26 Dec, 31 Dec. **Meals:** main courses £15. Set L and D £29 (2 courses) to £33. **Details:** 26 seats. 6 seats outside. Music.

Honey & Smoke

Cooking score: 4
⊖ **Great Portland Street, Warren Street, map 5**
Middle Eastern | £35
216 Great Portland Street, Fitzrovia,
W1W 5QW
Tel no: (020) 7388 6175
honeyandco.co.uk

'Modern, fuss-free setting, helpful, friendly service, fabulous food and very reasonable prices,' is one appraisal of this warm-hearted purveyor of Middle Eastern food, Sarit Packer and Itamar Srulovich's follow-up to Honey & Co. (see entry). The dining room is 'a bit college-canteeny', filled with plain square tables and 'stacking plastic school-hall chairs' – 'not a place for a date' – but for the greedy, interested diner this is good news. 'Amazing' meze range from msabbaha (very tender and garlicky chickpeas), via burnt celeriac with Urfa chilli butter, sour cream and chives, to 'smoky-flavoured' baba ganoush, and deep-fried cauliflower florets on a smear of full-favoured tahini with a spoonful of tart turmeric-mango relish. The grill delivers Cornish hake kofta with lemons and herbs and 'beautifully seasoned' matbucha sauce or lamb chops in tahini BBQ sauce with charred plums, while desserts include feta and honey cheesecake (with fat blueberries and chunks of deeply roasted almonds) on a finely shredded filo pastry base. Drink classic-with-a-twist cocktails, or wines from a minimal list (from £20).
Chef/s: Sarit Packer and Itamar Srulovich. **Open:** Tue to Sat L and D. **Closed:** Sun, Mon, 24 to 28 Dec, 1 Jan, bank hols. **Meals:** main courses £14 to £35. Set L and D £35. **Details:** 80 seats. Bar. Wheelchairs. Music.

Visit us online

To find out more about
The Good Food Guide, please
visit thegoodfoodguide.co.uk

Hoppers

Cooking score: 3
⊖ **Tottenham Court Road, map 5**
Sri Lankan | £25
49 Frith Street, Soho, W1D 4SG
hopperslondon.com
£30

The Sethi family's Soho hangout is small, fun (once you've got past the inevitable no-reservation queue) and noisy. Certainly not the place for an intimate date (you might be sharing tables), but everyone has a good time. Once you've been squeezed in or placed at the low bar counter, you're in for a treat. Hoppers is all about the flavours of Sri Lanka with a South Indian twist. Dishes impressing reporters include bone-marrow varuval (a mildly spiced curry sauce), devilled shrimps, a rich, buttery, spicy goat roti, an egg hopper (pancake made from fermented lentils and rice) with both pol and seeni sambol and coriander chutney, and a generous short-rib 'buriani'. Portions are small but packed with flavour, and prices are fair. There are no desserts. Spiced-up cocktails, Sri Lankan beer and masala buttermilk are more alluring than the choice of red or white wine. A sibling is due to open in St Christopher's Place in autumn 2017, offering reservations for lunch and dinner.
Chef/s: Karam Sethi. **Open:** Mon to Fri L and D. Sat, all day from 12. **Closed:** Sun, 24 to 26 Dec, 31 Dec to 2 Jan. **Meals:** main courses £10 to £21. **Details:** 36 seats. Music.

The Ivy

Cooking score: 2
⊖ **Leicester Square, map 5**
Modern European | £50
1-5 West Street, Covent Garden, WC2H 9NQ
Tel no: (020) 7836 4751
the-ivy.co.uk

Immovable on its flat-iron corner of Covent Garden, The Ivy has been the haunt of pop idols on furlough, actors on days without matinees, and politicians at the drop of a hat since the desperate days of the Great War.

Embarking on its second century in 2017, the place is in good Art Deco nick, the green banquettes gathered like acolytes around a central mirror-stripped bar, the brasserie menu likewise gathered around a core of old faithfuls as immovable as the venue. They still bang-bang the chicken with peanuts and chilli, and gong bao the tiger prawns with water chestnuts and ginger, quite as if this were Shanghai between the wars, but England's standbys are never far off either, not when haddock, chips and mushy peas, shepherd's pie and Hereford sirloins in bordelaise may be got. A more modern streak finds room for seared foie gras with rhubarb and apple tart, herb-crusted cod with arrabbiata beans, cockles and bacon, and banana and butterscotch Tatin with rum and raisin ice cream. A concise, voguish wine jumble starts at £25, or drink yourself broke with the Sommelier's Picks.

Chef/s: Gary Lee. **Open:** all week, all day from 12. **Closed:** 25 and 26 Dec. **Meals:** main courses £15 to £42. Set L and early D £19 (2 courses). **Details:** 120 seats. Bar. Wheelchairs. Music.

J. Sheekey

Cooking score: 4
⊖ Leicester Square, map 5
Seafood | £55
28-35 St Martin's Court, Covent Garden, WC2N 4AL
Tel no: (020) 7240 2565
j-sheekey.co.uk

'We always promise ourselves that one day we will be brave enough to tackle one of their massive cake stands of assorted shellfish, but so far we have not had the courage to do this – so yet again we had the fish pie,' confided a regular to this long-established theatreland seafooder. Warm and inviting, with small, adjoining dining rooms, Sheekey's may not be the most of-the-moment place but 'everything is efficient – and delicious'. There are contemporary elements (a shrimp and scallop burger with spiced mayonnaise, say) but on the whole the menu is a joyful celebration of classic fish cookery. Standouts

from the many reports received this year have been the dressed crab, buttery potted shrimps, lobster thermidor, Cornish fish stew and skate wing with spiced brown shrimp butter. Service is first class ('good timing as well since this was pre-theatre'), there's Black Angus sirloin for the dissidents and a fish-friendly wine list (from £26) that offers more reds than you may expect.

Chef/s: Andy McLay. **Open:** all week L and D. **Closed:** 25 and 26 Dec, 1 Jan. **Meals:** main courses £18 to £44. **Details:** 75 seats. 40 seats outside. Bar. Wheelchairs. Music.

★ NEW ENTRY ★

Jamavar

Cooking score: 5
⊖ Bond Street, Green Park, map 5
Indian | £50
8 Mount Street, Mayfair, W1K 3NF
Tel no: (020) 7499 1800
jamavarrestaurants.com

This first outpost of the Indian Leela Group has recruited Rohit Ghai from Gymkhana as executive chef (see entry), splashed out on an interior inspired by India's sacred temples (marble floors, mirrors, gold fittings, intricate panelling) and 'served up an absolute corker'. The menu is ambitious and prices 'are what you would expect from a prime Mayfair location', though there is a good-value set menu, all served by 'an effortlessly proficient front-of-house team'. To start there are small plates inspired by Indian street food, perhaps squid with 'lovely spicy undertones' or, from the tandoor, perfectly cooked malai stone bass tikka infused with mace and green cardamom and lifted by an avocado chutney, while Suffolk corn-fed chicken (char-grilled and pulled) with a rich buttery sauce makes a standout main course. Alphonso mango rasmalai on a wheat biscuit base topped with a mixed berry chutney has been described as 'a triumph'. Good cocktails have an Indian bent, and the eclectic wine list (with a dozen bottles in the £23 to £40 range) has whites and reds that are amenable to spices.

Chef/s: Rohit Ghai. **Open:** Mon to Sat L and D. **Closed:** Sun. **Meals:** small plates £8 to £15. Main courses £12 to £30. **Details:** 107 seats. 8 seats outside. Music.

Kiku

Cooking score: 3
⊖ Green Park, map 5
Japanese | £30
17 Half Moon Street, Mayfair, W1J 7BE
Tel no: (020) 7499 4208
kikurestaurant.co.uk

Kiku (the chrysanthemum) took root in Mayfair as long ago as 1978, when Japanese food was very much terra incognita to all but a coterie of business types who had been to Tokyo. Its spare, positively basic look, with simple wood tables along one side and a row of counter seats opposite, helped establish the functional style of Japanese dining out. The extensive menu works very much to the formula, with seafood a prime asset, appearing in everything from the long list of nigiri sushi options to casseroled plaice or mackerel with grated daikon, perfectly crisp tempura and umami-laden dishes such as grilled eel on rice with miso soup. The tofu dishes are texturally correct and dressed in light soy, while delicate meats include the perennial beef teriyaki. Set menus will guide you through the repertoire, concluding with palate-cleansing green tea ice cream. A classy wine list opens at £17.50, although most of the reds are too heavy for the food, which calls out optimally for the separate saké list.
Chef/s: F Shiraishi and Y Hattori. **Open:** Mon to Sat L, all week D. **Closed:** 24 to 27 Dec, 1 Jan.
Meals: main courses £15 to £45. Set L £24 (4 courses) to £34 (5 courses). Set D £59 (8 courses) to £82 (10 courses). **Details:** 99 seats. Wheelchairs.

Visit us online

To find out more about The Good Food Guide, please visit thegoodfoodguide.co.uk

Kiln

Cooking score: 4
⊖ Piccadilly Circus, map 5
Northern Thai | £26
58 Brewer Street, Soho, W1F 9TL
kilnsoho.com

There is nowhere quite like it in London for this style of convention-challenging 'Thai' food. This offshoot of Smoking Goat (see entry) also has a cramped setting and long queues, but fans brave the no-bookings system to experience inventive South-East Asian dishes. Bar seats face an open kitchen where Thai-style dishes are cooked to order on wood-burning grills. The carefully considered dishes change often to reflect seasonality and ingredient availability. A sour turmeric curry champions the fermentation flavours of Burmese and northern Thai cooking, and then unexpectedly marries these with firm-fleshed turbot. A spicy salad of laab also substitutes ocean fish for meat, the whiting a palliative for the pungent aromatic herb we call Vietnamese coriander. Clay pots lend themselves well to slow-cooked glass noodles (vermicelli) baked in a soy dressing, with slices of pork belly and brown crabmeat varying the textures. The wine list is as bold as the robust cooking, and includes 'natural' wines that reflect the offbeat flavours of the dishes.
Chef/s: Nick Molyviatis. **Open:** Mon to Sat L and D. Sun 1 to 8. **Closed:** 25 and 26 Dec. **Meals:** small plates £6 to £9. **Details:** 50 seats. Music.

Kitchen Table

Cooking score: 6
⊖ Goodge Street, map 5
Modern British | £125
70 Charlotte Street, Fitzrovia, W1T 4QG
Tel no: (020) 7637 7770
kitchentablelondon.co.uk

The sheeping and goating at Bubbledogs is done with appealing tongue in cheek. While crowds cram the front room for hot dogs and Champers, a privileged 20 pass through the brown leather curtains in the back corner for counter seats around a small kitchen. A blackboard on the back wall lists the 12 single words that designate tonight's fixed menu. There is no menu card, so listen up to James Knappett's explanations of each dish as soon as everyone's got it. Not the least interest of the cooking is the degree to which many of the little bites are founded on dirt-cheap materials, often the once-scorned outer integuments – radishes on a cracker with potato-skin gel, chicken skin with bacon jam, sourdough toast with whipped butter and beef dripping, Meyer lemon-peel purée with burrata, beetroot marmalade and sour-milk ice cream – and yet the results are hardly ever less than stunning, micro-bombs of intensity, sweetness, sharpness, all in ingenious balance. The show stoppers, such as duck with orange-skin purée and baby turnips, or cured sea trout with green almonds and fennel, are resonantly memorable, and the optional extra two courses, which help to heft the bill north-wards, might include sensational lobster and coral in a bisque containing the brain, scented with lemon verbena, pickled ginger and shiso. Sign up for the wine selection at £70, a tailor-made matching triumph that is all the more impressive for only altering every two dishes.

Chef/s: James Knappett. **Open:** Tue to Sat D only. **Closed:** Sun, Mon, 23 to 27 Dec, 2 weeks Jan. **Meals:** tasting menu £125. **Details:** 20 seats. Bar. Wheelchairs. Music. Children over 12 yrs only.

Kitty Fisher's

Cooking score: 4
⊖ Green Park, map 5
Modern British | £42
10 Shepherd Market, Mayfair, W1J 7QF
Tel no: (020) 3302 1661
kittyfishers.com
£5
OFF

Diminutive and dark, with seating that enforces a certain intimacy and pricing that could rebuff the casually curious, the staff and kitchen have set themselves a high bar for success, but happily they meet it and then some. The short menu, thoroughly English

but not in the least bit old-fashioned, may change on a daily basis, but the attitude and style remain the same: delicate Devon crab acidulated with pickled rhubarb and then brought back to centre with a quirky smoked crème fraîche; meltingly soft leeks forming a bed for crunchy hazelnuts and chicken skin on a pillow of smoked hollandaise; and the house signature, two-person rare-grilled Galician chuleta steak, a carnivorous show stopper. Cocktails and beers are just as popular as the wine list, but those wanting to keep some sort of control on the bill are wise to stick to very drinkable house carafes.

Chef/s: George Barson. **Open:** Mon to Sat L and D. **Closed:** Sun, 25 Dec, Easter, bank hols. **Meals:** main courses £20 to £35. Set L £25 (2 courses) to £35. **Details:** 36 seats. 8 seats outside. Music.

LOCAL GEM

Lao Café

⊖ Charing Cross, map 5
Laotian | £25
60 Chandos Place, Covent Garden, WC2N 4HG
Tel no: (020) 3740 4748
laocafe.co.uk
£30

Anyone used to the now-cosy sweet/sour/salt/fire of London South-East Asian cooking will find this lively if minimal café a walk on the wild side. Brave diners can go all out with deep-fried bugs and herb-fried locusts: the former somewhat reminiscent of spicy walnuts, the latter delivering as much crunch as punch. For the more conservative there are familiar dishes, from papaya salads to char-grilled skewers via steaming hotpots and stir-fried noodles. Though the kitchen is happy to customise the spicing, the entry level is high enough to take no prisoners.

Average price

The average price denotes the price of a three-course meal without wine.

Latium

Cooking score: 2
⊖ Goodge Street, Oxford Circus, map 5
Italian | £35
21 Berners Street, Fitzrovia, W1T 3LP
Tel no: (020) 7323 9123
latiumrestaurant.com

£5
OFF

Following Maurizio Morelli's move to
Margot in Covent Garden, this long-serving
Fitzrovia Italian has reset its culinary compass
and applied some gentle cosmetic
improvements here and there. The dining
room now has a less formal look, with bare
wooden tables, black slate floors and
photographs of Italian city life on peach-
coloured walls creating an easy-going vibe.
Ingredients-led regional cooking is still the
name of the game, with menus following the
traditional four-course format and a special
section devoted to ravioli (a throwback to
Morelli's day). Openers of stewed baby
octopus with chickpea sauce and oregano
could give way to gnocchi with mazzancolle
prawns and artichokes, textbook osso buco
milanese or roast cannon of lamb with
vegetable casserole, broccoli cream and salsa
verde. After that, a dessert of sweet chocolate
ravioli stuffed with ricotta and candied fruits
stays with the programme. The wine list offers
a tempting tour of the Italian regions.
Chef/s: Stefano Motta. **Open:** Mon to Sat L, all week
D. **Closed:** 25 and 26 Dec, 1 Jan. **Meals:** main
courses £16 to £27. Set L and D £18 (2 courses) to
£21. **Details:** 60 seats. Wheelchairs. Music.

Little Social

Cooking score: 5
⊖ Oxford Circus, map 5
Anglo-French | £48
5 Pollen Street, Mayfair, W1S 1NE
Tel no: (020) 7870 3730
littlesocial.co.uk

🍾

Sitting a little skew-whiff to the Pollen Street
Social (see entry), on the same dark back lane
off Regent Street, the Little Social feels like

the younger, rowdier option. A mixture of
booth and banquette seating amid dark wood
makes it feel inviting, as long as a shrilly
amplified compilation of British rock and pop
is on your menu, too. Despite the strong
Parisian cultural signifiers in frames on the
walls, the menu is solidly British, too, even
where it sounds French, taking in crab
mayonnaise and avocado mash on toast, a
creamy soup of roasted celeriac with an egg
and bacon in it, and whole sole meunière. The
mirror-image approach is accorded to cottage
pie, which, served in a cast-iron chafing dish,
arrives in bourguignon guise, with roughly
shredded beef, whole Paris mushrooms and
Alsace bacon under a layer of puréed potato
thin enough to be a gratin topping. The return
ticket home arrives when a nutty apple and
blackberry crumble turns up, silver-served
into a bowl containing a scoop of vanilla ice
cream. Wines by the glass start at £7, and
include a decent Greek Viognier and a lush old
Ribera del Duero.
Chef/s: Cary Docherty. **Open:** Mon to Sat L and D.
Closed: Sun, bank hols. **Meals:** main courses £18 to
£29. Set L £21 (2 courses) to £25. **Details:** 55 seats.
Wheelchairs. Music.

Locanda Locatelli

Cooking score: 4
⊖ Marble Arch, map 6
Italian | £80
8 Seymour Street, Marylebone, W1H 7JZ
Tel no: (020) 7935 8390
locandalocatelli.com

🍾

Discreet, polished, Giorgio Locatelli's Mayfair
flagship has been a home-from-home for fans
of Italian food since 2002 – no wonder it's
now synonymous with a certain brand of
ingredient-led regional Italian cooking. Huge
domed mirrors, pale leather trim and cleverly
designed semi-private spaces provide the
trappings for this chic gastronomic
destination, while the kitchen melds in-the-
blood traditions with a commitment to
provenance. Few would dispute the sheer
magnificence of Locatelli's hand-crafted pasta

(faggotine stuffed with borage, ricotta and walnut sauce, say), the rustic oomph of his snail and nettle risotto or the springtime freshness of his broad bean, rocket and ewes' cheese salad, but that's just the start. Herb-crusted mackerel with stewed onions, slow-cooked suckling pig and garlicky roast squab with lentils are also there for the taking in their appointed season, with Sicilian cannoli, tiramisu or artisan cheeses to follow – served the time-honoured way with honey. The patrician (and pricey) wine list is testament to the sheer diversity of Italian viticulture, with ample temptations by the glass.
Chef/s: Giorgio Locatelli. **Open:** all week L and D. **Closed:** 24 to 26 Dec, 1 Jan. **Meals:** main courses £26 to £33. **Details:** 85 seats. Bar. Wheelchairs.

★ NEW ENTRY ★

Lorne
Cooking score: 4
⊖ Victoria, map 3
Modern British | £38
76 Wilton Road, Victoria, SW1V 1DE
Tel no: (020) 3327 0210
lornerestaurant.co.uk

There's much to like about Lorne. A brilliant addition to an area that's finally finding its feet, food-wise, it's a 'fresh, pretty, modern space', all mirrors, blond wood, marble counter tops and lush green foliage with 'for once, no open kitchen', though there is some counter seating. Ingredients are all and the tone is set immediately with straight-out-of-the-oven sourdough with 'excellent grassy olive oil'. Punchy dishes follow, the short, daily changing menu delivering starters such as 'incredibly tender' cuttlefish 'lightly fried schnitzel style' with violet potatoes and a 'sweet and nutty' bisque romesco balanced by 'lovely acidity' from pickled onions. For mains, lemon sole with baby gem, puntarelle, monk's beard and dashi broth is 'cooked with the lightest of touches and addressed with great respect', while short-rib beef ('so soft and tender') is teamed with pear, cavolo nero and onion vinaigrette. Desserts include rhubarb

with custard, gingerbread and pistachio: 'a lovely combination of sweet and sour'. The wine list (from £22) has some great by-the-glass options.
Chef/s: Peter Hall. **Open:** Tue to Sat L, Mon to Sat D. **Closed:** Sun, 25 Dec to 3 Jan, bank hols. **Meals:** main courses £19 to £22. Set L £22 (2 courses). **Details:** 48 seats. Music.

Lurra
Cooking score: 2
⊖ Marble Arch, map 6
Spanish | £45
9 Seymour Place, Marylebone, W1H 5BA
Tel no: (020) 7724 4545
lurra.co.uk

It has reminded one reporter of her favourite Basque restaurant in Spain, and regulars have a habit of reeling off their favourite plates; there's no doubt this unpretentious tapas bar and Basque grill, a sister to Donostia opposite (see entry), has earned a reputation for running one of the most authentic venues in town. There's plenty to applaud, from the crisp, modern décor with its mix of tables and bar counter seating, to the 14-year aged Rubia Gallega beef (which you can admire in a glass-panelled cabinet as you walk in). Good service is part of the appeal, too. Anchovies and boquerones with mango vinaigrette should not be missed, but highlights this year have been sourdough with bone marrow, wild prawns al ajillo, grilled octopus with piquillo sauce, and the slow-cooked suckling lamb shoulder. Enjoy plates of jamón Ibérico and cheeses, too, and ginger foam is the covetable finale. Drink cocktails or seek advice on the mainly Spanish wine list (from £23).
Chef/s: Charlie Bourn. **Open:** Tue to Sun L, Mon to Sat D. **Closed:** 24 Dec to 2 Jan. **Meals:** main courses £6 to £18. **Details:** 70 seats. 25 seats outside. Music.

Average price

The average price denotes the price of a three-course meal without wine.

LOCAL GEM

Mele e Pere

⊖ Piccadilly Circus, map 5
Italian | £35
46 Brewer Street, Soho, W1F 9TF
Tel no: (020) 7096 2096
meleepere.co.uk

The name translates as 'apples and pears' – quite appropriate, since you need to take the stairs down to Mele e Pere's all-action high-decibel basement. This local hot spot is a classic Soho joint, the kind of venue with a vermouth bar dispensing home-infused concoctions and a menu of assorted seasonal delights – from San Daniele ham with gnocchi fritti or radicchio tart with truffled goats' cheese and guanciale (cured pork jowl) to bigger helpings of wild mushroom risotto or T-bone steak alla fiorentina. Gutsy regional wines, too.

★ NEW ENTRY ★

Mere

Cooking score: 4
⊖ Goodge Street, map 5
International | £55
74 Charlotte Street, Fitzrovia, W1T 4QH
Tel no: (020) 7268 6565
mere-restaurant.com

Monica and David Galetti's new place in restaurant-dense Charlotte Street is so classily discreet you may well walk past its heavy wooden door. But stop, and head down into Mere's cleverly light-filled basement dining room to enjoy fine food and exemplary service in this navy-neutral haven. Butter-tender octopus, charred just so, comes alive with sweet-sharp caper-raisin 'condiment' and gently pokey 'nduja, and there is umami aplenty in fine, mushroom-packed tortellini with Marmite butter, even if that yeast extract only flits like a memory through this surprisingly autumnal dish (served in June). The natural deliciousness of perfectly cooked lobster is smothered under creamy pomme purée, but a main of squab pigeon, breast pink and soft, leg mixed with ras-el-hanout in a crisp pastilla, is praiseworthy. The sweet-

toothed and still-hungry will devour rum-rich banana cream pie; a lighter option could be featherlight yoghurt mousse with elderflower sorbet, which is refreshing, even if some craved more depth of flavour. The beautifully crafted wine list has bottles around the £30 mark, but quickly heads north.
Chef/s: Monica Galetti. **Open:** Mon to Sat L and D. **Closed:** Sun, bank hols. **Meals:** main courses £23 to £38. Set L £35 (3 courses). Tasting menu £70 (6 courses). **Details:** 55 seats. Bar. Wheelchairs. Music.

LOCAL GEM

Mon Plaisir

⊖ Covent Garden, map 5
French | £35
19-21 Monmouth Street, Covent Garden, WC2H 9DD
Tel no: (020) 7836 7243
monplaisir.co.uk

In its infancy when General de Gaulle dropped by during his wartime exile, London's oldest French bistro has delighted generations of Londoners and tourists, all of whom have cosied up amid its posters, flea market bric-à-brac and other curios – note the bar, purloined from a Lyon brothel. Steak tartare recently made a triumphant return to the menu, alongside moules marinière, smoked duck salad with rémoulade, entrecôte béarnaise, noisettes of lamb en croûte and other generous bourgeois platefuls. Cheeses and wines are Gallic to the core.

Please send us your feedback

To register your opinion about any restaurant listed in this guide, or a new restaurant that you wish to bring to our attention, please visit the web address at the bottom of the page. Your feedback informs the content of the book and will be used to compile next year's reviews.

★ TOP 50 ★

Murano

Cooking score: 7
⊖ Green Park, map 5
Italian | £70
20-22 Queen Street, Mayfair, W1J 5PP
Tel no: (020) 7495 1127
muranolondon.com

Neither formal nor stuffy, Angela Hartnett's flagship restaurant caters for a well-heeled rather than hip crowd and, as such, the décor is muted, not attention grabbing. As for the menu – it's complicated. A spin on the classic Italian multi-course offering sees dishes divided into five savoury and one dessert section and diners not only choose which dishes to have, but also how many courses, what size and in what order they are served. While some have found this 'a really fun way of doing things', one reporter noted that 'the young birthday couple next to us really began to fall out after 20 minutes of back-and-forth thinking'. Thankfully, olives, breads, grissini, olive oil and San Daniele ham are placed on the table 'which kept us on track'. Hartnett's cooking has always relied on top ingredients and meticulous craftsmanship. Indeed, a 'beautiful' dish of cured sea bream with kohlrabi, capers, pear and rosemary purée, and the 'wonderful' paper-thin manzo di pozza, served with homemade ricotta, spiced broad beans, spring onion and hazelnut set the tone at an early spring meal. Impressive, too, were button-sized parcels of silky chestnut anolini in a clear, deep-flavoured mushroom consommé topped with a few sprout tops, and monkfish with roasted squash, tempura broccoli and beurre blanc. A 'perfect, barely set, wonderfully wobbly' little pannacotta with oat and macadamia clusters and brown-bread ice cream, or poached Yorkshire rhubarb 'layered up with piped ginger-wine syllabub and some fine crumbs of Cornish fairings' are winning finales. The set lunch continues to offer very good value for the location.

However, while the global wine list may teem with quality, with few bottles under £50, prices are wallet denting.
Chef/s: Angela Hartnett. **Open:** Mon to Sat L and D. **Closed:** Sun, 5 days Christmas. **Meals:** set L £28 (2 courses) to £33. Set D £55 (2 courses) to £90. **Details:** 55 seats. Wheelchairs.

Native

Cooking score: 3
⊖ Covent Garden, map 5
Modern British | £35
3 Neal's Yard, Covent Garden, WC2H 9DP
Tel no: (020) 3638 8214
eatnative.co.uk

A rustic look has been created outside, with overturned packing crates and sprouting foliage framing the glassed entrance of a Covent Garden eatery that could scarcely be more *au courant*. The craze for natural materials – wild garlic, meadowsweet, hay, alexanders, curds and whey – has even crept, like the urban foxes, into the big cities, and is handled with deft panache by Ivan Tisdall-Downes. Fortify yourself with a gin and Prosecco whistle-wetter, before setting about the wild and wonderful to come. Wild boar ragù with buttered salsify, curds and pickled walnuts is one way in, or there might be a kebabed pigeon spiced in ras-el-hanout with beetroot hummus and organic flatbread, illuminated by dukkah and harissa. Fish could be Cornish hake, given the Indian runaround with split pea dhal, cauliflower leaf pakora and pickled seeds, or look to a stonking veggie main such as the clump of sprouting broccoli that comes with a confit egg yolk and Stichelton rye crumb. Desserts kick crème brûlée into touch with the likes of Douglas fir and millet cake in dill oil with a milk crisp. Petit four, anyone? The fudge contains Kentish wood ants. There's a handful of wines, too, from £21.
Chef/s: Ivan Tisdall-Downes. **Open:** Mon to Sat L and D. **Closed:** Sun. **Meals:** set L £25 (2 courses) to £32. Set D £28 (2 courses) to £35. Tasting menu £65. **Details:** 32 seats. Music.

Neo Bistro

Cooking score: 4
⊖ Bond Street, map 5
Modern British | £35
11 Woodstock Street, Mayfair, W1C 2AE
Tel no: (020) 7499 9427
neobistro.co.uk

It's such an unexpected spot to find a restaurant of this quality – 'a quick dash over the road from Debenhams on Oxford Street and you're there'. Alex Harper, formerly head chef at the Harwood Arms, has teamed up with Mark Jarvis of Anglo fame (see entries) to create this honest-to-goodness bistro – all exposed brickwork, dark wood, olive banquette seating and a bare-bones, open-to-view kitchen. The concise menu tempts with earthy, rustic platefuls of seasonal British ingredients, presented with no standing on ceremony. Homemade charcuterie makes the perfect opener, perhaps cured Tamworth pork that's 'tissue-paper-thin and so sweet'. Then 'beautifully flavoured' Cornish crab topped with confit lemon and herring roe with a slick of courgette and basil cream, before principal dishes of, say, Herdwick lamb with turnip and smoked eel. Add some hay-baked new potatoes with 'delicious' mushroom butter on the side, and finish with a deconstructed tart – slices of flaky pastry, very fresh, sweet strawberries, dots of cream and ice cream.
Chef/s: Alex Harper and Mark Jarvis. **Open:** Wed to Sat L, Tue to Sat D. **Closed:** Sun, Mon. **Meals:** main courses £15 to £17. Tasting menu £42

The Ninth

Cooking score: 4
⊖ Goodge Street, Tottenham Court Road, map 5
French-Mediterranean | £50
22 Charlotte Street, Fitzrovia, W1T 2NB
Tel no: (020) 3019 0880
theninthlondon.com

The weathered wood and distressed brick surrounds of Jun Tanaka's informal, double-decker venue make for a laid-back atmosphere with tables and bentwood chairs or bar seating to choose from in the first-floor dining space. French-Mediterranean cooking with strongly earthy appeal, characterised by big savoury seasonings all the way, is the stock-in-trade, and the kitchen makes a good fist of meaty pasta such as osso buco tortellini with hazelnut gremolata, or confit rabbit lasagne with tomato compote. Sea bass arrives shaved into carpaccio slices, dressed in salsa verde and pickled kohlrabi, while salting of meats is a favoured process, resulting perhaps in salt-baked venison with cavolo nero and beetroot. Some feel, with irresistible logic, that if 'all our dishes are made for sharing', there perhaps ought to be more on each plate to go round, but while we ponder that, the tarte Tatin with rosemary ice cream is undoubtedly a dessert built for two. The grab-bag of international wines sticks to the major producers, with small glasses from £7.
Chef/s: Jun Tanaka. **Open:** Mon to Sat L and D. **Closed:** Sun, bank hols. **Meals:** main courses £16 to £27. Set L £19 (2 courses) to £25. **Details:** 84 seats. 8 seats outside. Wheelchairs. Music.

Noble Rot

Cooking score: 4
⊖ Holborn, Russell Square, map 5
British | £35
51 Lamb's Conduit Street, Bloomsbury, WC1N 3NB
Tel no: (020) 7242 8963
noblerot.co.uk

🍾

Halfway between a wine bar and a restaurant, Noble Rot captures the spirit of the times, serving a simple, to-the-point menu and offering a wine list packed with gems at reasonable prices. With close-set tables, dark polished wood and bare floorboards throughout, the look is casual and informal, the welcome warm, the place itself usually busy and noisy. One of the great things about Paul Weaver's cooking is its unabashed simplicity, with the kitchen sending out pork and pistachio terrine or smoked eel with rhubarb and soda bread, and ox cheek with swede mash and turnip tops. Yet ingredients are first class and execution hard to fault, not least when it comes to seafood: the now classic combination of fish (on this occasion Cornish brill) in oxidised Chassagne-Montrachet, for example. It's all designed to comfort and reassure, helped along by a sound grasp of classic technique. Similar contentment is to be found among desserts of warm chocolate mousse or sticky toffee pudding with cream-cheese ice cream. The owners are Mark Andrew and Dan Keeling (co-editors of *Noble Rot* magazine), so it's no surprise that the wine list is a superb collection (from £20) with exemplary choice by the glass.

Chef/s: Paul Weaver. **Open:** Mon to Sat L and D. **Closed:** Sun, Christmas and New Year. **Meals:** main courses £18 to £28. Set L £16 (2 courses) to £20. **Details:** 51 seats. 8 seats outside. Bar. Music.

Nobu Berkeley St

Cooking score: 4
⊖ Green Park, map 5
Japanese | £85
15 Berkeley Street, Mayfair, W1J 8DY
Tel no: (020) 7290 9222
noburestaurants.com

The name that set the benchmark for fashionable modern Japanese restaurants more than two decades ago is now a global phenomenon with a tremendous trickle-down effect. There are chefs who don't even realise that the style they're emulating originated with Nobu Matsuhisa – but here, in his two Mayfair restaurants (Park Lane and Berkeley Street) it's all on show in its original glory. The menu is predictably long and complicated. Regulars may know their way round their shiromi usuzukuri and king crab tempura with ama ponzu, but newcomers should seek out the omikase set menus, which will take them through the house classics, from beautifully presented yellowfin tuna tataki with ponzu via the famous black cod marinated in miso, and beef toban yaki, to chocolate fondant with green-tea ice cream. However, while the cooking is as good as ever, the restaurants have become a victim of their

own success. Once famous as much for A-list customers as its food, they have evolved into something glitzy and loud, calculated to make you spend money, with a custom base of A-list watchers. Service in both restaurants, though polite, can be a little supercilious at times. Nobu Mayfair is at the Metropolitan Hotel, 19 Old Park Lane, W1K 1LB; tel: (020) 7447 4747.
Chef/s: Mark Edwards. **Open:** all week L and D. **Closed:** 25 Dec. **Meals:** main courses £22 to £46. Set L £33 (2 courses) to £40. Tasting menu £110. **Details:** 180 seats. V menu. Bar. Music.

NOPI

Cooking score: 4
⊖ Piccadilly Circus, map 5
Middle Eastern/Mediterranean | £50
21-22 Warwick Street, Soho, W1B 5NE
Tel no: (020) 7494 9584
nopi-restaurant.com

A positive ambience radiates from the moment you step into Yotam Ottolenghi's eatery with its brass ornaments, light-wood furniture and paper-topped tables. The impetus to cater for all comers produces a menu divided into nibbles, sharing dishes, sides and mains, and while the offerings mostly reference the shores of the Mediterranean, there are spiky Asian seasonings here and there, too. Dishes arrive in logical order, rather than the shruggy whenever-they're-ready approach, and are all the more appreciated. Cecina smoked beef with beer-soaked piquillos and crispy garlic heralds some of the exhilarating vegetable specials: a dish of roasted aubergine with dried broad beans and pomegranate, char-grilled sprouting broccoli with tahini and miso, a savoury cheesecake with pickled beetroot, almonds and thyme honey. Main meats might include twice-cooked poussin with lemon myrtle salt in chilli sauce, perhaps paired with exemplary polenta chips in aïoli and Parmesan. Finish with pearl barley malt ice cream in treacly chocolate sauce with biscuit crumbs for scattering over. Exciting cocktails and wines (from £25) that embrace orange and volcanic styles are part of the allure.

Chef/s: Scully Ramael and Yotam Ottolenghi. **Open:** all week L, Mon to Sat D. **Meals:** main courses £20 to £25. Early D £25. Tasting menu £44 to £50. **Details:** 108 seats. Bar. Music.

Les 110 de Taillevent

Cooking score: 4
⊖ Oxford Circus, map 5
French | £45
16 Cavendish Square, Marylebone, W1G 9DD
Tel no: (020) 3141 6016
les-110-taillevent-london.com

🍾

The original concept, exported from Paris more or less intact, is mostly unreconstructed classical French bistro cuisine, accompanied by a choice of no fewer than 110 wines by the glass. To wit, the open-out menu looks a little like an Excel spreadsheet, but is less daunting than it seems. There are four possible wine suggestions with each dish, in small or very small measures, ascending in price from left to right. The food works best as a light-textured lunch, anchored perhaps by turbot in lobster bisque sauce, or poached corn-fed chicken with pommes Anna, Comté and morels. Some dishes stand out better, as in an ingenious opener of baby artichokes (one breaded and fried) in their own purée, offset with puréed anchovies and capers, while others disappear in imperfectly thought-out constructions, such as the warm chocolate mousse with warm 70 per cent chocolate sauce, between which a quenelle of chocolate ice cream disappears like hope. The place looks glossy and sleek enough for an occasion, and staff are admirably well versed.

Chef/s: Raphael Grima. **Open:** Mon to Fri L, Mon to Sat D. **Closed:** Sun. **Meals:** main courses £16 to £37. Set L and D £20 (2 courses) to £25. Tasting menu £48. **Details:** 76 seats. 16 seats outside. Bar. Wheelchairs. Music. Parking.

Ormer Mayfair

Cooking score: 6
⊖ Green Park, map 5
Modern British | £75
Flemings, 7-12 Half Moon Street, Mayfair, W1J 7BH
Tel no: (020) 7499 0000
ormermayfair.com

🛏

Chef Shaun Rankin arrived in London with a reputation for offering some of the best fine dining in the Channel Islands and his first London restaurant, like its Jersey sibling (see entry), takes its name from the prized local abalone. Occupying the basement of Flemings hotel, there's a chic Art Deco mood to the mirrors, panelling, geometric design and leather seating, a smart, polished environment for the high-finance crowd and upmarket visitors to the area. Rankin was an early champion of sustainability, foraging, local sourcing and seasonality, and while he's at home with luxury he has an instinct for pure, clean, modern flavours and the best ingredients, especially seafood. A spectacular starter of red mullet and scallops is presented with a surprising trio of flavours: blood orange, white chocolate and blue cheese – risky but a triumph. Poached oysters are served with nuggets of saffron linguine and caviar, while a tranche of salmon is saved from blandness by calamari, chorizo purée and honey glaze. There are many meat dishes such as secreto, the ultra-lean shoulder of Ibérico pork paired with squid and Asian pear. Puddings include apricot and almond cake with goats' cream cheese and jasmine ice cream. The wine list is aimed at high-rollers but there's plenty for modest tastes, too. Do make sure you enjoy a cocktail beforehand in the luxe Manetta's Bar, one of the best-kept secrets in the capital.

Chef/s: Shaun Rankin and Kerth Gumbs. **Open:** Tue to Sat L, Mon to Sat D. **Closed:** Sun. **Meals:** main courses £29 to £35. Set L £27 (2 courses) to £30. Tasting menu £75 (7 courses). **Details:** 85 seats. V menu. Bar. Wheelchairs. Music.

Join us at thegoodfoodguide.co.uk

Orrery

Cooking score: 4

⊖ Baker Street, Regent's Park, map 6

French | £55

55 Marylebone High Street, Marylebone,
W1U 5RB

Tel no: (020) 7616 8000

orrery-restaurant.co.uk

£5 OFF 🍶

Providing welcome respite from the hum of Marylebone High Street, this urbane offering from the D&D London group makes the most of its first-floor location, with distinctive porthole windows looking out on to the greenery of St Marylebone Church gardens. It's smart and very tasteful without seeming ostentatious – a description that also fits the cooking, which offers a clear-sighted take on French cuisine (albeit classical rather than cutting-edge modern). Bright flavours and neat presentation typify starters such as salmon ballotine with fromage blanc and keta caviar, while mains are mostly from the old-school – tournedos Rossini, lamb rump with carrots, peas and garlicky rosemary jus, herb-crusted sea bass with chive sabayon. Orrery's cheese trolley is replete with Gallic ripeness, and there are sweet pleasures to be had from desserts such as elderflower pannacotta with gariguette strawberries and meringue. The wine list is a roll call of fine vintages, with real depth in France (as you'd expect), and plenty of exceptional bottles from elsewhere; check out the discounted 'love fine wine' deals on Mondays.

Chef/s: Igor Tymchyshyn. **Open:** all week L and D. **Meals:** main courses £20 to £39. Set L £25 (2 courses) to £28. Set D £40. Sun L £30. Tasting menu £67. **Details:** 100 seats. 20 seats outside. Bar. Wheelchairs.

★ NEW ENTRY ★

The Other Naughty Piglet

Cooking score: 4

⊖ Victoria, map 5

Modern European | £30

The Other Palace, 12 Palace Street, Victoria,
SW1E 5JA

Tel no: (020) 7592 0322

theothernaughtypiglet.co.uk

🍶

The second venue from Joe and Margaux Sharratt (see also Naughty Piglets, south London) is housed in Lord Lloyd-Webber's new theatre near Buckingham Palace. Allow time for eating if you're here for a show. Up a sweeping marble staircase, it's a light-filled space adorned with empty bottles, overlooked by a kitchen counter where a young brigade turns out small plates of sublimely creative, flavour-driven dishes, where balance and complexity come together in flashes of potent inspiration. At inspection, it was hard to choose what we loved best, but the XO linguine with confit egg yolk (a cross-fertilisation of Chinese noodles and carbonara), glorious black pudding with strongly vinaigretted cuttlefish and capers, BBQ pork belly with chilli paste and sesame-dressed greens, and the unforgettable pairing of leg and croquetted cheek of spring lamb with anchovy purée and cime di rapa, would have been on the rapidly expanding shortlist. A bowl of rhubarb and custard is just that, served cold with touches of white chocolate crumble; otherwise, go the whole choc hog with brown-butter chocolate crumble and honeycomb. Service could hardly be more knowledgeable or more engaging, and the thrilling wine list is full of biodynamics, oxidation and recherché rarity. Mix and match by the small glass from £5.50.

Chef/s: Joseph Knowlden. **Open:** Tue to Sat L, Mon to Sat D. **Closed:** Sun. **Meals:** small plates £2 to £16. **Details:** 65 seats. Wheelchairs.

Joe and Margaux Sharratt

Naughty Piglets and The Other Naughty Piglet, London

What inspired you to become a chef?

Joe - Watching *Boiling Point*! It inspired me to go and apply for a job with Gordon Ramsay and Marcus Wareing.

What first sparked your interest in wine?

Margaux - Growing up in France, and being raised in a family where spending time around a table was sacred. Food and wine have been part of my life since day one.

What foods could you not live without?

Cheese in general (burrata with olive oil and salt is one of my favourite things to eat - Margaux), but after a long week's work we love ordering a pizza. Add some rocket and a nice bottle of wine - it is heavenly.

What's your favourite dish from your menus?

XO linguine and cured egg yolk, such deliciousness.

...And which is your favourite wine to go with it?

A salty orange wine, a Sicilian Grillo from Nino Barraco.

Otto's

Cooking score: 3
⊖ Chancery Lane, map 5
French | £45
182 Gray's Inn Road, Bloomsbury, WC1X 8EW
Tel no: (020) 7713 0107
ottos-restaurant.com

'You'd think a lunch in early January with just three tables occupied would be a bit flat – not a bit of it,' noted one reader, who chose Otto's for its enthusiastically rendered bourgeois food (scallops with boudin noir, a fine piece of venison and sweet chestnut mousse, to be precise). Run in inimitable fashion by the eponymous Otto Tepassé, this quirkily attired *restaurant de tradition* is idiosyncratically dedicated to preserving the old-school French ways – steak tartare chopped and blended tableside, roast chickens dissected to order and, above all, the mythic pressing of ducks, lobsters and poulardes de Bresse using antique silver contraptions. The latter need ordering in advance, but for sheer audacity and epic spectacle they're unmissable. Alternatively, feast your way through, say, lightly battered calf's brains with sauce gribiche, poached cod fillet with chicken jus and a show-stopping tarte Tatin flambéed with Calvados. Wines are French – and proud of it.

Chef/s: Otto Tepassé. **Open:** Tue to Fri L, Tue to Sat D. **Closed:** Sun, Mon, Christmas and New Year, 2 weeks Aug, bank hols. **Meals:** main courses £20 to £35. Set L £24 (2 courses) to £28. **Details:** 50 seats. No children.

The Palomar

Cooking score: 5
⊖ Piccadilly Circus, map 5
Middle Eastern | £35
34 Rupert Street, Soho, W1D 6DN
Tel no: (020) 7439 8777
thepalomar.co.uk

The melting-pot cuisine of modern Jerusalem – white-hot on its arrival in London in 2014 – still fills this undersized theatreland *boîte* many, many times over. Squeeze in at the zinc-topped kitchen counter or plan ahead and book early to secure a table in the intimate back room. If bread's a sign of a restaurant's intent, the Palomar means business: the Yemeni pot-baked kubaneh is one of its best-loved creations. One's encouraged to mix it up a bit when ordering: something from the raw bar – beef tataki say, with tahini and tomatoes, or cured mackerel 'matbucha' salad with red pepper and quail's egg; something from the grill like the signature 'octo-hummous' (octopus and chickpea msabacha); and maybe a side of truffle-oil-laced mushroom polenta. Noisy, fun and over-friendly – but you will be, too, after an arak and almond cocktail or three. Global wines from £28.

Chef/s: Tomer Amedi. **Open:** all week L and D. **Closed:** 25 and 26 Dec. **Meals:** main courses £13 to £16. **Details:** 46 seats. Wheelchairs. Music. Children in dining room only.

Pied à Terre

Cooking score: 5
⊖ Goodge Street, map 5
Modern French | £80
34 Charlotte Street, Fitzrovia, W1T 2NH
Tel no: (020) 7636 1178
pied-a-terre.co.uk
£5 OFF 🍾

Now regarded as an elder statesman rather than a young turk, this bijou Fitzrovia restaurant promises a vintage blend of poise and pedigree defined by clean lines, velvety chic and contemporary verve – albeit of the low-key variety. Shoehorned into a Victorian townhouse, Pied à Terre's muted dining room purrs with civility and refinement as supremely professional staff go about their business. Meanwhile, chef Andrew McFadden continues to plough his own ultra-sophisticated furrow, with much complexity and arcane culinary technique on show – although everything is driven by fastidious name-checked sourcing. Pembrokeshire crab is paired with avocado, turnips and caviar salt, while Richard Vaughan's suckling pig is teamed up with seasonal companions including parsnips, walnuts and cider; also look for the Lavinton lamb served with

anchovy and a truly revelatory take on ratatouille. To conclude, dazzling desserts such as gariguette strawberries with buttermilk, lemon and vanilla naturally take their cue from the calendar. Pied à Terre's wine offer is indubitably one of the finest in town – two voluminous lists (whites and reds respectively) are stuffed with peerless vintages from top growers worldwide, plus some covetable special 'suggestions'.

Chef/s: Andrew McFadden. **Open:** Mon to Fri L, Mon to Sat D. **Closed:** Sun, last week Dec, first week Jan. **Meals:** set L £30 (2 courses) to £38. Set D £65 (2 courses) to £80. Tasting menu £75 to £145. **Details:** 44 seats. V menu. Bar. Music.

★ TOP 10 ★

Pollen Street Social

Cooking score: 9
⊖ Oxford Circus, map 5
Modern British | £98
8-10 Pollen Street, Mayfair, W1S 1NQ
Tel no: (020) 7290 7606
pollenstreetsocial.com
🍾

You know you're in a place that recognises the desire to eat well in an unstuffy way when a restaurant captures youthfulness without being inconsequential, class without being old-fogeyish, and comfort without being soporific. Jason Atherton's busy flagship restaurant sets the standard on all three counts. Liquid-smooth service curls effortlessly round chattering tables, a superb front-of-house team bringing sublime plate after sublime plate of inventive, joyful food. The eight-course tasting menu opens with afternoon tea – a delightful trio of amuse-bouches, then Parmesan foam and cep powder in a slender cup, on to which is poured satisfyingly savoury mushroom 'tea'. Courses of dazzling deliciousness follow: oyster ice cream is sea-salty refreshing; dots of beluga caviar add glamour to sweet Colchester crab; and a standout piece of John Dory, poached sparingly, is dissolvingly tender, its flavour coaxed out by pieces of crab claw, translucent slivers of green-skinned apple and a deeply flavoursome crab reduction. Lamb, pink of course, yields to the knife, needs nothing more than cauliflower purée, cut with a dash of capers, and baby spinach leaves to bring out supreme flavour. An accompanying hotpot, rich meat under insanely buttery mash and pretty rings of carrot and beetroot, is a meal in itself. An ingenious game of 'guess the ice cream flavour' (five white ices and a sealed envelope) precedes a bowl of fragrant strawberries, a few frozen white berries giving wonderful temperature and textural balance against velvety pannacotta and sharp sorrel granita. The barista behind the forthright espresso that ends the meal (with 'really grand' petits fours) deserves applause. Go for the optional wine flight, or dive into the depths of the full list (and the sommelier's oceanic knowledge) to choose something else from £25.

Chef/s: Jason Atherton and Dale Bainbridge. **Open:** Mon to Sat L and D. **Closed:** Sun, 25 and 26 Dec, 1 Jan, bank hols. **Meals:** main courses £35 to £90. Set L £32 (2 courses) to £37. Tasting menu £98 (8 courses). **Details:** 58 seats. V menu. Bar. Wheelchairs. Music.

Portland

Cooking score: 6

⊖ Great Portland St, Oxford Circus, map 5

Modern British | £50

113 Great Portland Street, Fitzrovia, W1W 6QQ

Tel no: (020) 7436 3261

portlandrestaurant.co.uk

In a place where the bareness of floorboards, tables and light bulbs is standard, it's good to know that the 'cooking here is getting better and better'. Executed with visual flair and great technique, Merlin Labron-Johnson's menus are short, daily changing and give notice that fabulous seasonal ingredients take centre stage. Copious praise continues to pour in from readers, whether singling out a rustic risotto of celeriac, mushroom and truffle or expressing delight at a plate of raw scallop, citrus, radish and caviar. Clever stuff. Other hits have been snacks such as crisp chicken skins topped with delicate liver parfait, candied walnuts and pickled grapes, a cauliflower pannacotta with sea bass tartare and pear, and Cornish cod with oca de Peru (a tuberous root vegetable) and brown-butter sauce. For dessert consider blood orange, pumpkin, frozen cheesecake and Salisbury honey. There's a serious dedication to drink, too, with well-tailored cocktails and a wine list that stays on top of emerging trends (from £25) and offers exemplary choice by the glass.

Chef/s: Merlin Labron-Johnson. **Open:** Mon to Sat L and D. **Closed:** Sun, 23 Dec to 2 Jan. **Meals:** main courses £18 to £30. Tasting menu £45. **Details:** 36 seats. Wheelchairs. Music.

LOCAL GEM

Princi

⊖ Tottenham Court Road, Piccadilly Circus, map 5

Italian | £22

135 Wardour Street, Soho, W1F 0UT

Tel no: (020) 7478 8888

princi.com

A long-time Soho favourite, this self-service Italian bakery (the London offshoot of a Milanese chain) is light, modern and informal, its counter displays of pastries, salads and hot pasta dishes making it just the place to grab a quick bite, whether to eat in or take away. For something more relaxed, head to the adjoining pizzeria for waiter service and exemplary wood-fired pizzas (say burrata with Datterini tomato and basil) or plates of linguine vongole, risotto milanese or slow-cooked beef bollito with salsa verde. It's a great breakfast spot, too, but be prepared to queue – no bookings are taken.

Local Gem

Local Gems are the perfect neighbourhood venues, delivering good, freshly cooked food at great value for money.

Quilon

Cooking score: 4
⊖ St James's Park, Victoria, map 5
Indian | £50
41 Buckingham Gate, Westminster, SW1E 6AF
Tel no: (020) 7821 1899
quilon.co.uk
£5 OFF

Quilon is sufficiently within bolting distance of the Palace of Westminster to feature a division bell, the tolling of which obligates MPs and peers to tear themselves away from the feasting and go to vote. The surroundings in the St James' Court Hotel are a lure in themselves, with contemporary Indian artworks on display in a capacious dining room with gleaming floor space and booth tables. Sriram Aylur draws on south-west coastal culinary traditions, so expect plenty of seafood, ideally opening with Fisherman's Catch, a compendious gathering of peppered shrimp, Goan fish cafreal, a grilled scallop and a crab cake. That could be followed by prawns in rich coconut masala, or halibut and mango curry, but supplementing these are imaginative meat dishes such as delicately stuffed quail legs hot with mustard, and enlivening vegetable mains like coconut, asparagus and snow peas fried in green chillies, curry leaves and mustard seeds. Fusion finishers include chai latte crème brûlée with orange sablé. The wine list we were sent has no prices, but perhaps don't get too optimistic. Think £30 and up.
Chef/s: Sriram Aylur. **Open:** all week L and D. **Closed:** 25 Dec. **Meals:** main courses £22 to £45. Set L £27 (2 courses) to £31. Tasting menu L £36, D £60. **Details:** 82 seats. Bar. Wheelchairs. Music.

Symbols

🛏 Accommodation is available
£30 Three courses for less than £30
£5 OFF £5-off voucher scheme
🍾 Notable wine list

Quirinale

Cooking score: 3
⊖ Westminster, map 3
Italian | £42
North Court, 1 Great Peter Street, Westminster, SW1P 3LL
Tel no: (020) 7222 7080
quirinale.co.uk

'Parliament not sitting, so MPs and their staff were entirely absent but I know it's not normally like that. The place was half empty, but it certainly didn't feel uncomfortable. The tables were spaced far enough apart for nobody to earwig.' So ran the notes of one visitor to this 'grown-up restaurant', where most of the guests are well-dressed regulars looking for highly competent, discreet service, a decent wine list and a menu of familiar dishes. It's not that the kitchen dumbs down. A starter of smoked tuna with crispy fennel, dressed with tangy fresh citrus may be simple, but it's a great example of that genius Italian habit of using the best of ingredients and letting them speak for themselves. A small selection of classic pastas and risottos follow (with a sprinkling of truffle if requested), or move directly to Parmesan-crusted fillet of beef with rösti potatoes or a perfectly cooked fillet of halibut with black olive and pistachio. It's the ideal menu for talking business, and the location, moments from the Palace of Westminster, couldn't be better.
Chef/s: Stefano Savio. **Open:** Mon to Fri L, Mon to Sat D. **Closed:** Sun. **Meals:** main courses £17 to £29. Set L and D £19 (2 courses) to £23. **Details:** 50 seats. Music.

Quo Vadis

Cooking score: 4
⊖ Tottenham Court Road, map 5
Modern British | £50
26-29 Dean Street, Soho, W1D 3LL
Tel no: (020) 7437 9585
quovadissoho.co.uk

Lease issues have compelled the Hart brothers to rearrange their Soho portfolio. Consequently, Quo Vadis has budged up to make room for Barrafina (see entry) on its ground floor and settled into a smaller space in its former bar (with further tables upstairs for QV club members). Small is beautiful for Jeremy Lee. The elegant room, filled with wild flowers and whimsical illustrations, retains its sense of occasion. Here's a world where pristine linen, proper napkins and sparkling glassware still count for something even when the food is as unstuffy as a chicken and bacon suet crust pie or skate knobs, chips and tartare sauce. Seared venison and artichoke salad wrong-footed us somewhat at inspection, the venison served cold (a shade too cold), the artichokes warm, contrary to the waiter's description. Perfectly cooked hake, to follow, with cockle and pea broth was unfashionably rich and buttery – balm for the soul. Pudding was chocolate cake with coffee sauce and a good dollop of whipped cream. The excellent wine list has traditionalist leanings, from £26.

Chef/s: Jeremy Lee. **Open:** Mon to Sat L and D. **Closed:** Sun, 25 and 26 Dec, bank hols. **Meals:** main courses £20 to £28. Set L and D £20 (2 courses) to £23. **Details:** 25 seats. 12 seats outside.

Rex Whistler Restaurant
Cooking score: 3
⊖ Pimlico, map 3
British | £36
Tate Britain, Millbank, Pimlico, SW1P 4RG
Tel no: (020) 7887 8825
tate.org.uk

£5 OFF 📷

Sober, dark parquet and pristine napery in this basement restaurant are brightened up no end by Rex Whistler's vivid wraparound mural, a fantastical hunting scene commissioned by the gallery in the 1920s. However, Garrett Keown's season-led carte is a modern affair. Taking inspiration from exhibits in the rooms above, it treads a neat path, taking in both classic fare, perhaps an impeccable roasted breast of guinea fowl, and more contemporary dishes, albeit grounded in classic technique: tea-smoked celeriac broth with salt-baked celeriac purée, celery and truffle oil packs a

punch for such a delicate dish. On inspection, the Yorkshire mutton – roasted loin, potato hotpot, kidney and minted peas – was a nod to David Hockney's sell-out spring show and showcased superior produce and a deft touch. Caramelised banana tarte Tatin marks an indulgent finish. On Sundays, opt for a plate of meat worthy of Hogarth (his *Roast Beef of Old England* hangs upstairs). Impassioned wine descriptions pepper the outstanding forward-thinking list from head wine buyer Hamish Anderson (claret from a box, anyone?), a generous clutch of which are available by the glass. Expect great cheese, too, from the ever-evolving 'Cheese Please' menu.

Chef/s: Garrett Keown. **Open:** all week L only. **Closed:** 24 to 26 Dec. **Meals:** set L £30 (2 courses) to £36. Sun L £36. **Details:** 80 seats. 30 seats outside. Wheelchairs.

The Ritz
Cooking score: 7
⊖ Green Park, map 5
French | £80
150 Piccadilly, Mayfair, W1J 9BR
Tel no: (020) 7300 2370
theritzlondon.com

🛏

Established by Escoffier in 1904, the dining room at The Ritz is one of the great bastions of classical French cuisine ('I can't think of anywhere else that does it – even Gavroche') where tradition is upheld and service is impeccable. It's a 'true bucket-list restaurant', thought one visitor, wowed by the baroque-style gilded and pillared room with its chandeliers and ceiling frescoes, full-skirted tables and 'be-tailed and be-gloved waiters' who whisk away domes at every course with suitable élan and prepare crêpes suzette at table. In the kitchen, John Williams displays a high degree of technical competence that suffuses everything, with highlights at one meal including an impeccable slab of sweetbread anointed with a textbook Madeira sauce and a generous scattering of black truffle slices – 'all the classicism but not the heaviness'

– and a chestnut velouté, rich, sweet and aromatic, which comes with wild mushrooms and truffle for taste and texture. Venison fillet, tender and flavourful, has a sweet–sour balance of apple and elderberry sauce and a perfectly pan-fried chunk of sea bass is given a touch of modernity with the addition of black quinoa and sea vegetables. The wine list, with six pages alone for Champagnes, is not the place to look for bargains, but the sommelier will happily recommend wines by the glass – starting at around £15.

Chef/s: John Williams. **Open:** all week L and D. **Meals:** main courses £40 to £52. Set L £52 (3 courses). Sun L £59. Tasting menu £95 to £110. **Details:** 90 seats. V menu. Bar. Wheelchairs. Music. Parking.

Roka

Cooking score: 3
⊖ Goodge Street, map 5
Japanese | £60
37 Charlotte Street, Fitzrovia, W1T 1RR
Tel no: (020) 7580 6464
rokarestaurant.com

Roka is world away from the strict etiquette, reverential ritual and formalised theatre of most high-end Japanese restaurants. Instead, this lively performer delivers the goods with a sour, salt and umami intensity against a clean-lined backdrop of knotty, grainy wood and industrial fittings – imagine polished minimalism set to a big-beat soundtrack. There are conventional tables, but it's worth bagging a ringside seat by the robata grill to watch the action as chefs tackle plates of spiced chicken wings with lime, baby back ribs with sansho and cashews or the emblematic black cod marinated in yuzu and miso. There's also a full complement of sparkling-fresh sushi, sashimi and salads, plus some more earthy specialities such as a rice pot packed with Japanese mushrooms and mountain vegetables. While the cooking is impressively on-point, bills are often sumo-sized – especially if you're partial to obscure sakés, sochu cocktails or cosmopolitan wines.

Chef/s: Luca Spiga. **Open:** all week L and D. **Closed:** Christmas. **Meals:** main courses £15 to £72. Tasting menu £66 to £88. **Details:** 88 seats. 24 seats outside. Bar. Music.

★ NEW ENTRY ★

Roka Aldwych

Cooking score: 2
⊖ Temple, map 5
Japanese | £50
71 Aldwych, Aldwych, WC2B 4HN
Tel no: (020) 7294 7636
rokarestaurant.com

There's not much in Aldwych, so this branch of Roka is a welcome addition to the area. It mirrors the branches in Mayfair (North Audley Street) and Canary Wharf with a lively light, bright look, rather than the more cramped Charlotte Street original (see entries). As the open robata grill (with counter seating) indicates, modern Japanese robatayaki cuisine is what Roka is all about, delivering impeccable raw materials and seductive presentation via a well-balanced tasting menu – a good choice if unsure what to order – an à la carte and a popular weekend brunch (though an excellent-value set lunch was drawing the crowds on our visit). Highlights of our 'demonstrably fresh and expertly prepared' meal included Napa cabbage in garlic and hot chilli, beef, ginger and sesame gyoza, pitch-perfect sashimi and a main course of salmon fillet teriyaki with sansho salt. Don't pass on dessert, the rich, velvety pleasure of peanut, vanilla and chocolate sundae is not to be missed.

Chef/s: Cristian Bravaccini. **Open:** all week L, Mon to Sat D. **Meals:** dishes £4 to £70. Set L £33. Tasting menu £66. **Details:** 110 seats. Bar.

Visit us online

To find out more about
The Good Food Guide, please
visit thegoodfoodguide.co.uk

Roux at Parliament Square

Cooking score: 4
Θ Westminster, St James's Park, map 5
Modern European | £59
11 Great George Street, Parliament Square,
Westminster, SW1P 3AD
Tel no: (020) 7334 3737
rouxatparliamentsquare.co.uk

'I've wanted to eat Steve Groves' food ever
since I saw him win *MasterChef: The
Professionals*,' noted one reader who reckoned
'the boy done good' at this outpost of the Roux
empire. Snuggled within the stately
surroundings of the Royal Institution of
Chartered Surveyors, it puts on the style for
Westminster's politicos who like their food
with a side order of old-school civility. Groves
is master of the Roux style, delivering Anglo-
European dishes with an emphatic French bias
and 'flavour combinations that really make
sense' – how about a thick slab of cod with
cucumber, dill, oyster sauce and featherlight
gnocchi? Other good calls range from
mackerel with heritage carrots, citrus and
sesame to Ibérico presa with Cervennes onion
and spelt, while desserts might feature an
'elegantly cheffy' deconstructed cheesecake
with semi-dried kumquats. Service may be
ever so formal, but it's also 'bang-on efficient',
and the wine list is pitched for affluent palates.
Chef/s: Steve Groves. **Open:** Mon to Fri L and D.
Closed: Sat, Sun, Christmas, 31 Dec, bank hols.
Meals: set L £42. Set D £59. Tasting menu £79 (7
courses). **Details:** 53 seats. Bar. Wheelchairs. Music.

Roux at the Landau

Cooking score: 4
Θ Oxford Circus, map 5
Modern European | £52
The Langham, 1c Portland Place, Marylebone,
W1B 1JA
Tel no: (020) 7965 0165
rouxatthelandau.com

🛏

As dining rooms go there can be few more
striking than this oval-shaped former
ballroom. On the ground floor of the

Langham hotel, a vaulted ceiling, wood
panelling and tall bay windows overlooking
All Souls church create 'a timeless elegance' and
there is a 'welcome buzz to the place'. There has
been another change of chef since our last
edition, but Nicolas Pasquier has kept to the
Roux family's take on modern European
cooking with dishes such as 'a beautifully
balanced' white asparagus salad served with
slices of smoked duck, liver and black truffle
and 'meltingly tender' Pyrenean milk-fed
lamb (rack and noisette) teamed with
artichoke barigoule, green harissa and sweet
pepper chutney. Assemblies are well thought
out, not least at dessert stage when a pistachio
soufflé with raspberry sorbet proved 'perfect, I
licked every bit up'. Details are well handled –
from 'excellent' sourdough bread to 'superb'
petits fours. Service is polite, and the set
menus are great value. Anchored in France, the
wine list gathers good labels across the globe.
Prices start at £34.
Chef/s: Nicolas Pasquier. **Open:** Mon to Fri and Sun
L, Mon to Sat D. **Meals:** main courses £20 to £48.
Set L and D £39. Tasting menu £70 (5 courses).
Details: 110 seats. V menu. Bar. Wheelchairs.

Rules

Cooking score: 3
Θ Covent Garden, Leicester Square, map 5
British | £59
35 Maiden Lane, Covent Garden, WC2E 7LB
Tel no: (020) 7836 5314
rules.co.uk

For anyone seeking respite from swipes and
spheres, gels and foams, then Rules may be
just the haven you're craving. Come not for
high fashion, but for the well-executed
cooking of dishes rooted in the classics. Half a
dozen Fines de Claire oysters are sparkling-
fresh and iced to perfection, and the curried
mayonnaise with a Dorset crab salad is pitched
just right so as not to overwhelm the subtle
sweetness of the shellfish. A piece of
impeccably seasoned pan-fried turbot is
everything the so-called king of fish should
be, ditto a superbly tender saddle of rabbit
with black pudding and puréed and whole

peas, but you could happily feast on rose veal with salsify gratin, or leg of Herdwick mutton with artichokes and caper sauce, or satisfying venison suet pudding. A lemon fool delivers beautifully sharp notes, but chocolate lovers may well veer towards a rich chocolate tart with vanilla brûlée centre. Slack service has niggled some diners, although others report it as charming. Wine from £28.

Chef/s: David Stafford. **Open:** all week, all day from 12. **Closed:** 25 and 26 Dec. **Meals:** main courses £19 to £43. **Details:** 96 seats. Bar.

Salt Yard

Cooking score: 2
⊖ Goodge Street, map 5
Spanish/Italian | £30
54 Goodge Street, Fitzrovia, W1T 4NA
Tel no: (020) 7637 0657
saltyard.co.uk
£5 OFF

Salt Yard continues to thrive with its unique take on Spanish tapas and Italian aperitivi. Along with the vivacious atmosphere, ultra-friendly staff and killer cocktails, it's hard to beat settling into a buttery leather high stool and letting one of the team behind the bar talk you through the daily specials and hidden gems on the wine list. Snack on familiar Padrón peppers, boquerones or the fine range of charcuterie and regional cheeses, but tapas are the stars. Octopus is cooked to sweet tenderness and served with firm new potatoes, lemon, chilli and dazzling bursts of saffron, seared hake partnered with vivid green fronds of agretti with a salty tapenade sweetened with tiny sun-dried tomatoes, and wooden platters hold croquetas of haddock with caper aïoli. Don't forget pudding such as the Spanish favourite, doughy churros dipped into warm chocolate sauce. If the ground floor is full, take a seat in the spacious room downstairs or bag a pavement table that catches late afternoon sunshine.

Chef/s: Joe Howley. **Open:** Mon to Fri L and D. Sat and Sun all day from 12. **Closed:** 25 Dec, 1 Jan. **Meals:** tapas £5 to £12. **Details:** 74 seats. 8 seats outside. Bar. Music.

Savoy Grill

new chef/no score
⊖ Charing Cross, map 5
Anglo-French | £58
The Savoy, Strand, Covent Garden, WC2R 0EU
Tel no: (020) 7592 1600
gordonramsay.com

'I remember going here when I was a girl, dining with my parents. I have been back three or four times over the years. It's gorgeous!' The Savoy Grill has many fans. One of London's iconic restaurants, it's been under the guiding hand of Gordon Ramsay and his team for some years. As we went to press, the successor to Kim Woodward had yet to be announced, but the ethos of the place is set to continue. Expect classic British cooking at its very best – proper seafood cocktail, grilled Dover sole, beef Wellington with horseradish cream, as well as a trolleyed lunchtime special of the day. As the first restaurant of Auguste Escoffier in London, diners should also look for some unimpeachable French classics. Expect to be slightly awed by the room – all wood-panelled sobriety and subdued lighting – and remember there's not a hope of finding a bargain, either on the menu or hidden in the wine list.

Open: all week L and D. **Meals:** main courses £23 to £46. Set L and early D £26 (2 courses) to £30. Tasting menu £95. **Details:** 100 seats. V menu. Wheelchairs. Parking.

Scott's

Cooking score: 4
⊖ Green Park, map 6
Seafood | £50
20 Mount Street, Mayfair, W1K 2HE
Tel no: (020) 7495 7309
scotts-restaurant.com

From the doorman's greeting to the art on the walls, Scott's is the epitome of the Mayfair dining experience. Alfresco tables are in high demand on hot days, while inside, its oxblood banquettes, Art Deco accents and wood panelling ooze laid-back luxury. Tables (a little close together) are good for earwigging; the crustacea bar is fun, too. Generally, the kitchen plays by the rules, just the way its well-to-do regulars like it. But there's more to the menu than Dover sole and lobster thermidor: we devoured sautéed monkfish cheeks with snails and bacon served with herby bread for scooping up the silky bordelaise sauce, and thoroughly enjoyed crispy sweetbreads, fried duck egg, asparagus and devilled sauce. If halibut with courgette and cherry tomatoes seemed uninspired, a beautifully cooked golden sea bass was another matter. Puddings are unabashedly comforting: to wit, Bakewell pudding and apple pie. Wines come with big names and big prices. **Chef/s:** David McCarthy. **Open:** all week, all day from 12. **Closed:** 25 and 26 Dec. **Meals:** main courses £19 to £37. **Details:** 120 seats. 20 seats outside. Bar. Wheelchairs. Parking.

Seven Park Place by William Drabble

Cooking score: 6
♨ Green Park, map 5
French | £69
St James's Hotel and Club, 7-8 Park Place, Mayfair, SW1A 1LS
Tel no: (020) 7316 1600
stjameshotelandclub.com

🍷 🍴

Is this the quirkiest of London restaurants, a tiny ornate space tucked into the back of the ground-floor bar of a discreet St James's hotel? A wealth of mirrors, patterned walls, lush buttoned seats and fine table linen may not be everyone's taste but the mayhem of the décor vanishes with the excellence of the cooking. William Drabble cooks unashamedly luxurious food with a light touch, using top-class ingredients and clever combinations, and is a master of transforming humble ingredients into something special: chicken wings partner new season's morels filled with chicken mousseline and glazed with a rich reduction, while slow-cooked rabbit with sage fills a neat ravioli and is served with shellfish poached in butter. A 'boudin' of wood pigeon and foie gras uses thyme crumb to

shape the meat into eye-catching shapes, which are served with baby turnips, wild mushrooms and a rich Madeira sauce. A perfect palate-cleanser is the pre-dessert, a lychee sorbet with mint jelly, and don't miss the zinging passion fruit soufflé, perfectly balanced with a velvety chocolate sauce. The wine list is a scholarly volume with 850 wines from 30 countries – do take advice from top-class sommelier Gonzalo Rodriguez Diaz, who is equally helpful whether you want a simple glass of red or something colossally expensive. **Chef/s:** William Drabble. **Open:** Tue to Sat L and D. **Closed:** Sun, Mon, 21 to 28 Dec. **Meals:** set L £27 (2 courses) to £32. Set D £61 (2 courses) to £69. Menu Gourmand £85. **Details:** 26 seats. Bar. Children over 12 yrs only.

Sexy Fish

Cooking score: 4
♨ Green Park, map 5
Asian | £95
Berkeley Square House, Berkeley Square, Mayfair, W1J 6BR
Tel no: (020) 3764 2000
sexyfish.com

Sexy Fish is a lively place, day or evening – note the 190 or so diners who reliably pack it out, marvelling at (and perhaps subtly trying to outdo) the glamorous décor. Fortunately, there is substance behind the style. The kitchen takes a cross-cultural approach, giving a vigorous spin to Asian flavours and assembling vibrant ideas on the plate. The Mayfair location dictates a fair number of top-end ingredients for top-end prices and you can splash the cash for the opulent likes of caviar, Japanese Wagyu beef and whole lobster, but there's also prawn gyoza with ginger dressing, skewers of maple-glazed belly pork, mixed vegetable tempura with dashi broth, steamed sea bass with mussels, ginger and coriander, and whole baby chicken yakitori. Standout dishes this year have been salt-and-pepper squid, yellowtail sashimi with green mandarin ponzu and myoga, and crispy duck with watermelon, pomegranate and cashew.

Presentation is reliably exquisite, the bar is a popular drinking spot, and the wines match the food.

Chef/s: Bjoern Weissgerber. **Open:** all week, all day from 12. **Closed:** 25 and 26 Dec. **Meals:** main courses £18 to £89. Set L £24 (2 courses) to £36. Tasting menu £82. **Details:** 190 seats. 14 seats outside. V menu. Bar. Wheelchairs.

Shackfuyu

Cooking score: 1
⊖ Tottenham Court Road, map 5
Japanese | £30
14a Old Compton Street, Soho, W1D 4TJ
Tel no: (020) 7734 7492
bonedaddies.com

Hard-edged vibes and a clamorous buzz come with the territory in this Soho eatery, where Ross Shonhan offers a real mash-up of Japanese, Korean and 'Western-influenced' Japanese dishes (called yoshoku in Japan). Lunch brings filled bao (steamed buns), perhaps crispy duck leg with plum sauce, enoki and cucumber pickle; otherwise, expect bold flavours in sharing dishes such as Korean fried chicken wings with a spicy sour sauce, sukiyaki-style Wagyu picanha (rump steak), aubergine miso, sea bass taco with tomatilla salsa, and hot stone rice with sesame, chilli, sweetcorn and beef. There's only one dessert, an unmissable French toast with matcha ice cream. Drink cocktails, craft beer or saké.

Chef/s: Ross Shonhan. **Open:** Tue to Fri L and D. Mon, Sat and Sun, all day from 12. **Closed:** 25 and 26 Dec. **Meals:** main courses £8 to £22. Set L and early D £19 (2 courses) to £22. Tasting menu £30. **Details:** 80 seats. Bar. Music.

Symbols

🛏 Accommodation is available
£30 Three courses for less than £30
£5 OFF £5-off voucher scheme
🍾 Notable wine list

★ TOP 50 ★

Sketch, Lecture Room & Library

Cooking score: 7
⊖ Oxford Circus, map 5
Modern European | £120
9 Conduit Street, Mayfair, W1S 2XG
Tel no: (020) 7659 4500
sketch.london

Be bewitched and bedazzled as you step into the intoxicatingly decadent parallel universe that is Sketch, Lecture Room & Library. Legendary chef Pierre Gagnaire takes top billing, but the day-to-day team, led by Johannes Nuding, who feed the deeply pocketed of Mayfair deserve applause. Flamboyant this place may be, but the ingredients are exemplary and chef skills superb. Choose a theme – Spring, Perfume of the Earth, Duck, for example – and enjoy the medley of small plates that comprises each course. Asparagus sashays through the spring collection, the green in a simple fricassee with toasted pistachio and an emulsified rocket jus, the white in a refreshing cardamom-scented ice cream with raw slivers and an orange reduction. The natural sweetness of turbot, cooked on the bone, is coaxed out by gentle maniguette pepper in the wild turbot line-up; crisp-skinned, flaky-fleshed, it sits well with endive braised in veal jus. Elsewhere, fillets of Goosnargh duck cut like butter and deft textural touches from buckwheat seeds and gingerbread crumb, plus the spicy sweetness of maple syrup and cinnamon, leave your palate dancing. Finish with the signature flight of desserts – pineapple sorbet freshens up nostalgia-laden Battenberg cake, while coriander loukoum with star anise syrup, soya milk and strawberry is a playful cocktail of flavours. The sommelier's impressive knowledge will guide you through the suitably classy wine list.

Chef/s: Pierre Gagnaire and Johannes Nuding. **Open:** Tue to Fri L, Tue to Sat D. **Closed:** Sun, Mon, 2 weeks Dec, 2 weeks Aug. **Meals:** main courses £50 to £65. Tasting menu £120. **Details:** 48 seats. V menu. Bar. Music. Children over 6 yrs only.

Smoking Goat

Cooking score: 3
Θ Tottenham Court Road, map 5
Thai | £30
7 Denmark Street, Soho, WC2H 8LZ
smokinggoatsoho.com

'I love this place,' declared a regular, adding 'the blackboard cocktails are fantastic value and food completely delicious'. If you love smoke, chilli, garlic and fish sauce, slow-cooked meat and hot-as-you-like Thai salads, then Ben Chapman's new-wave Thai restaurant is for you. Sit up front, 'which is a bit like a pub' dominated by a long wooden bar, or head for the little dining room out the back to enjoy the many wonderful things to eat here. Not only the 'gob-smackingly' good fish-sauce chicken wings of gargantuan proportions with their 'glass-crisp skin and confit like interior' that never leave the tiny menu, but also smoked lamb ribs, barbeque beef shortrib – the meat falling off the bone – smoked goat shoulder (for two), and sides of unlimited sticky rice and grilled hispi cabbage with chilli, peanuts and soy. There's a queue at the door most evenings and rapid-fire table turnaround. To drink, there's a concise wine list and a good selection of beers.
Chef/s: Ali Borer. **Open:** Mon to Fri L and D. Sat and Sun, all day from 12. **Closed:** 25 and 26 Dec. **Meals:** main courses £11 to £18. **Details:** 75 seats. Music.

Social Eating House

Cooking score: 6
Θ Oxford Circus, map 5
Modern British | £50
58 Poland Street, Soho, W1F 7NR
Tel no: (020) 7993 3251
socialeatinghouse.com
🍾

The third restaurant in Jason Atherton's proliferating Social group feels right at home in its Soho territory. The worn-in bistro style has a distinctly moody, urban feel, pimped up with leather and industrial fittings (natch). Yet the menu is anything but laid-back; enticing and distinctly top-end modern gastronomic fare is the deal here. Atherton's trademark 'Jars to Share' – maybe ham hock, piccalilli, chicory – are a fun starting point, or a standout starter of lightly smoked, hand-chopped Black Angus tartare (a long-standing SEH dish) might be more your thing. Paul Hood and his head chef Daniel Birk bring highly technical cheffery to play in the sophisticated mains, such as roasted loin of rabbit with confit leg, pancetta, aubergine and miso, morels, wild garlic and purple sprouting broccoli. Elaborate desserts, in keeping with the rest of the menu, are 'a feast for the eyes'. Reverential service sometimes feels at odds with the clubby atmosphere, but it's markedly efficient. The separate imaginative vegetarian menu and a prix fixe lunch are notably good. Head sommelier Jon Kleeman's diverse wine list features plenty of small growers, while leaving ample room for European classics and offering a generous clutch of wines from across the spectrum by the glass. The Blind Pig speakeasy-style bar upstairs is a great spot for a pre-prandial cocktail.
Chef/s: Paul Hood and Daniel Birk. **Open:** Mon to Sat L and D. **Closed:** Sun, bank hols. **Meals:** main courses £18 to £34. Set L £23 (2 courses) to £27. Tasting menu £65. **Details:** 60 seats. V menu. Bar. Music.

Social Wine & Tapas

Cooking score: 5
Θ Bond Street, map 6
Modern British | £29
39 James Street, Marylebone, W1U 1DL
Tel no: (020) 7993 3257
socialwineandtapas.com
🍾 £30

Jason Atherton's intensive restaurant network is in operation everywhere you look in the capital these days, but this cramped, multi-tiered, moodily lit Marylebone venue is the only one to put food and wine on an equal footing. An ambience of deeply endearing charm is matched by the classy output from the kitchen – materials and treatments are varied, ranging from Szechuan-fried chipirones with togarashi (chilli pepper) to mini rose veal burgers with pulled pork and spiced tomato. Recent standouts have included salt-baked beetroot with sairass (fresh, light, sweet sheep's milk ricotta) and honey-glazed fig; a meaty chunk of curried cod 'terrifically partnered with cauliflower, raisin and citrus yoghurt'; and roast suckling pig 'all crisp skin and tender, falling apart meat'. Social Wine & Tapas has so many strengths that few people will leave unhappy. One of those strengths is the wine list chosen by Laure Patry – her formidable wines are all tempting and impressively deep; excellent cocktails, too.

Chef/s: Marcus Rohlen. **Open:** Mon to Sat L and D. **Closed:** Sun, bank hols. **Meals:** tapas £9 to £20. **Details:** 45 seats. Wheelchairs. Music.

Spring

Cooking score: 5
Temple, Waterloo, map 5
Modern European | £65
Somerset House, Lancaster Place, Aldwych, WC2R 1LA
Tel no: (020) 3011 0115
springrestaurant.co.uk

£5
OFF

So enchanting to behold is Somerset House's New Wing under Australian chef Skye Gyngell, it's hard to believe the Inland Revenue ever pushed their pens here. Eau de nil walls, directional floristry, neo-classical columns and 'good soundproofing' (these things matter) have transformed the 'cavernous' space into a grand destination worthy of an 'expensive' treat. As at Petersham Nurseries in arcadian Richmond (see entry) where she found fame, Gyngell's captivating cooking is so seasonal you could set your clock by it: a late winter menu has lamb classically paired with white beans, kale and an assertive lift of harissa, while crab – a favoured ingredient – is treated to white asparagus and saline agretti (vegetables are afforded a high status in Gyngell's kitchen). 'Safe' it may be, but it's 'well judged', too. To wit, a delicately rose-scented custard tart, with buckwheat and poached rhubarb. No less desirable are the set menus including a pre-theatre 'scratch' menu that makes use of 'waste' ingredients. Cocktails, tonics and juices share the 'house' aesthetic, while France and Italy lead the European wine list.

Chef/s: Skye Gyngell. **Open:** Mon to Sat L and D. **Closed:** Sun, 1 week Christmas. **Meals:** main courses £18 to £33. Set L £28 (2 courses) to £32. **Details:** 100 seats. Bar. Wheelchairs.

The Square

Cooking score: 6
Green Park, Bond Street, map 5
Modern European | £105
6-10 Bruton Street, Mayfair, W1J 6PU
Tel no: (020) 7495 7100
squarerestaurant.com

A change of chef alarmed fans of this long-time destination but the Square is in good hands and new owner Marlon Abela, with the Greenhouse and Umu in his portfolio (see entries), is not a man to compromise. Chef Yu Sugimoto trained in Paris, and was most recently head chef of Le Meurice. His cooking marries modern French technique with top-quality British ingredients and an undeniably Japanese elegance and precision that's rare in London. Sweet and succulent Scottish langoustine presented as a sandwich, for example, makes a witty starter, and there are more theatrics with a light-as-air 'soufflé', a bubble of whipped egg white and gelatine holding shards of Devon crab perked up with Espelette pepper, radish and lemongrass. Red mullet is cooked and presented to the table in a roll of fennel stalks, the fillets bathed in a tomato and fennel broth and topped with slivers of lardo. The chef is a whizz at dramatic flavour combinations such as raw Orkney scallop, turned pink by a beetroot marinade and served with curls of seaweed butter, while lightly roasted French pigeon is dressed with a sauce of foie gras, baby artichoke leaves and smoked aubergine purée. Intriguing desserts include coconut ice with sweet and bitter fruits, or clementines with chocolate, gold leaf and the fugitive taste of cloves. The wine list is stupendous, with magnificent vintages and rare bottles. But for those of us who live in the real world, staff will offer wines by the glass and their recommendations are 'a real, and affordable, pleasure'.

Chef/s: Yu Sugimoto and Marco Tozzi. **Open:** Mon to Sat L and D. **Closed:** Sun. **Meals:** set menu £105 (4 courses). Set L £40 (3 courses) to £65. Tasting menu D £125 (7 courses). **Details:** 70 seats.

Tamarind

Cooking score: 4
⊖ Green Park, map 5
Indian | £45
20 Queen Street, Mayfair, W1J 5PR
Tel no: (020) 7629 3561
tamarindrestaurant.com

Make your entrance via the staircase that leads down to this overtly posh subterranean dining room – a lustrous space filled with gold-hued columns, big-statement floral displays and linen-clad tables. Such an inviting, worldly prospect demands fine food, and the kitchen obliges with a cultured take on North Indian cuisine that's as polished as those burnished pillars. Regional specialities are given full-blooded but respectful treatment, from tandoori lamb chops marinated with papaya, fennel and yoghurt to 'dum' biryanis sealed with a pastry lid. But creative reinvention is never far away: broccoli and potato tikki (deep-fried cakes) are served with gooseberry chutney, lobster is given the masala treatment, and halibut keeps company with parsnips, spinach and kasundi mustard sauce. More empathic European detailing also surfaces here and there, from an avocado raita to a mid-course blood-orange sorbet for those sampling the tasting menu. Noteworthy wines are priced for deep pockets.

Chef/s: Peter Joseph. **Open:** all week L and D. **Closed:** 25 and 26 Dec, 1 Jan. **Meals:** main courses £21 to £40. Set L £22 (2 courses) to £25. Sun L £34. Tasting menu £75 (6 courses). **Details:** 85 seats. Music. No children under 5 yrs after 7pm.

Tamarind Kitchen

Cooking score: 3
⊖ Tottenham Court Road, map 5
Indian | £28
167-169 Wardour Street, Soho, W1F 8WR
Tel no: (020) 7287 4243
tamarindkitchen.co.uk
£30

'This is an excellent restaurant – good food, moderate pricing, service that is keen to please and a cool ambience,' noted a visitor to this 'more informal' offshoot of Mayfair's Tamarind (see entry). Bang in the heart of Soho, dining takes place over two floors in 'dark and brooding surroundings', which have been expensively kitted out with velvety seating, low-level lighting and colourful aged-effect walls. The kitchen sticks to familiar ground and dishes such as creamy Malabar tiger prawns in a coconut cream curry and succulent spiced lamb cutlets are delivered with an assured hand, while crispy soft-shell crab with potato and yoghurt salad impressed at inspection. Save room for desserts such as spiced tea brûlée with rose-infused biscotti and ginger jelly. Service is approachable and the moderate pricing is an added bonus. To drink, there are custom-made cocktails and a short wine list from £24.

Chef/s: Peter Joseph. **Open:** Tue to Sun L, all week D. **Meals:** main courses £10 to £15. **Details:** 100 seats.

Tandoor Chop House

Cooking score: 2
⊖ Charing Cross, map 5
Indian | £29
8 Adelaide Street, Covent Garden, WC2N 4HZ
Tel no: (020) 3096 0359
tandoorchophouse.com
£30

Tucked away off the main drag in Covent Garden, this diminutive restaurant brings the high street curry house bang up to date. In a

ramped-up English chophouse setting Marshall amps pump out vintage pop and funk, which bounces off the wood-panelled, breeze-block walls and marble-topped tables. The workhorses here are the three enormous brass tandoor ovens at the front of the open-view kitchen, where chefs take North Indian classics and add their own contemporary twist. Seekh kebab roll with green chutney and pomegranate might lead on to IPA-battered and spiced squid and prawns with chilli chutney. Main courses include four meaty tandoori-cooked lamb chops with a lively spicy coating, and black pepper chicken tikka, perhaps accompanied by tandoor broccoli, black dhal and a bone-marrow naan. Finish with 'coal-roasted' pineapple and honeycomb ice cream or malted kulfi, caramelised banana and salted peanuts. Wines from £21, although most diners opt for cold stubby cans of craft ale.
Open: all week, all day from 11.30 (12 Sat, 1 Sun). **Meals:** main courses £11 to £17. **Details:** Music.

★ NEW ENTRY ★

Temper
Cooking score: 3
⊖ Piccadilly Circus, map 5
International | £40
25 Broadwick Street, Soho, W1F 0DF
Tel no: (020) 3879 3834
temperrestaurant.com

Hipster food hero Neil Rankin gives barbecue the royal treatment at his plush new Soho basement. Wads of cash have been thrown at it, from the glass wine walls and upholstered booths to the vast marble counter encircling the fire pit. Rankin moves London's meat-mania on from Stone Age slabs to something more nuanced: an international hybrid that opens with handmade tacos (soy-cured beef or crab and pork skin maybe) then segues into kebab variants comprising British rare-breed meats, orderable in 100g increments, atop flatbread. Choose tender Cabrito goat or – better – succulent slices of smoky Gloucester Old Spot, and customise with sides and sauces from the global grab-bag ('bewildering at

times, even to our waiter') that includes 'MSG ketchup' (a Parmesan, tomato and anchovy umami bomb) and a textural overload of sweet and popped corn with lamb fat béarnaise. There's a page of mezcals but wine is king: Temper's lengthy list covers anything from 'natural and funky' to 'aromatics and germanics'.
Chef/s: Neil Rankin and George Wood. **Open:** Sun L, Mon D. Tues to Sat, all day from 12. **Meals:** main courses £9 to £10. **Details:** 183 seats. Bar. Wheelchairs. Music.

10 Greek Street
Cooking score: 3
⊖ Tottenham Court Road, map 5
Modern European | £35
10 Greek Street, Soho, W1D 4DH
Tel no: (020) 7734 4677
10greekstreet.com

Small, very tightly packed, with an open kitchen with counter and stools at the back, this unassuming little place has the look of many contemporary eateries these days. But it goes about its business with gusto, proffering earthy, back-to-basics dishes wrought from seasonal British ingredients. Some are simple assemblies, such as a 'very good' small plate of fried duck egg with a couple of nuggets of tender and well-flavoured morcilla topped with a few flakes of Jerusalem artichoke crisps, or a more substantial Gloucester Old Spot with root vegetables, Savoy cabbage and pancetta. Other dishes are more worked, as in beautifully cooked Cornish scallops served with a smooth-textured potato and truffle purée with sea purslane. Chocolate mousse – 'actually a good baked chocolate fondant' with a ball of pistachio ice cream and some honeycomb – hit the mark at a test meal. Otherwise, consider 'charcuterie and cheese and a glass or two of the good-value Languedoc'.
Chef/s: Cameron Emirali and Drake Aldrich. **Open:** Mon to Sat L and D. **Closed:** Sun. **Meals:** main courses £16 to £42. Set D £40. **Details:** 34 seats. 2 seats outside. Music.

Terroirs

Cooking score: 1

⊖ Charing Cross, map 5

Modern European | £30

5 William IV Street, Covent Garden,
WC2N 4DW

Tel no: (020) 7036 0660

terroirswinebar.com

Light and bright with bare brickwork and close-packed tables, the buzz of lively conversation fills the ground floor of this popular wine bar; the cellar restaurant has a 'calmer vibe'. The menu, not overlarge, is set out as small plates, cheese, charcuterie, *plats du jour* and an excellent lunch special – good value when you consider the quality of the ingredients. Isle of Wight tomatoes arrive with fresh cheese, pickled shallots and almonds, salt cod with romesco and a soft-boiled egg, while a more substantial plate of lamb chops arrives with Swiss chard and salsa verde. Of course, wine is no less delightful: modern, well chosen and keenly priced, with excellent choice by the glass or carafe.

Chef/s: Michal Chacinski. **Open:** Mon to Sat L and D. **Closed:** Sun. **Meals:** main courses £18 to £24. **Details:** 100 seats. 6 seats outside. Bar. Music.

Texture

Cooking score: 5

⊖ Marble Arch, map 6

Modern French/Nordic | £75

34 Portman Street, Marylebone, W1H 7BY

Tel no: (020) 7224 0028

texture-restaurant.co.uk

The location, in a red-brick mansion on a corner of Portman Square, is elegant enough, but doesn't quite prepare you for the interior prospect, where bare twigs, miniature lampshades and tables on multiple legs like tipi poles create an ambience of calm Nordic composure. Agnar Sverrisson was in the vanguard of the new Scandinavian cuisine in London when Texture opened a decade ago, and while flavours of his native Iceland are still discernible in the lightly salted cod for main

course and skyr yogurt for afters, they now take their chances amid, respectively, avocado, tomato and chorizo, or strawberries grown in Herefordshire. The level of culinary adventurism remains dynamic, though, and the watchword in the restaurant name is never far away, as in a starter of char-grilled Anjou pigeon with popcorn, sweetcorn and bacon in red wine essence, followed by Cornish turbot and shellfish with shaved and puréed fennel, and then Alphonso mango and passion fruit in a soup with snow peas. Wines by the small glass from £8 open a list that's strong in modern, assertive flavours.

Chef/s: Agnar Sverrisson. **Open:** Wed to Sat L, Tue to Sat D. **Closed:** Sun, Mon. **Meals:** main courses £30 to £44. Set L £29 (2 courses) to £34. Tasting menu £95. **Details:** 50 seats. Bar. Wheelchairs. Music.

Theo Randall at the InterContinental

Cooking score: 6

⊖ Hyde Park Corner, map 6

Italian | £70

InterContinental London Hotel, 1 Hamilton Place, Mayfair, W1J 7QY

Tel no: (020) 7318 8747

theorandall.com

£5 OFF 🛏

Eleven years on, Theo Randall still flies the flag for fine Italian food. His theatre of operations is a windowless dining room in a fine hotel, its muted olive and grey-toned décor and unclothed tables creating a smart but casual look. Success is down to a combination of near-faultless technique and a degree of innovation that eschews novelty in favour of simply putting interesting and complementary flavours together. This may be an old-fashioned way to proceed, but it seems to work, for example in a pyramid of Devon crab served with new season's agretti, bottarga and Daterrini tomatoes. It's the ability to present concentrated flavours without distraction that lifts the cooking to a new realm, be it silky pasta stuffed with slow-cooked veal and pancetta, served with a

chanterelle and porcini sauce, or a dazzling roasted rack of Somerset lamb with roasted globe and Jerusalem artichokes, fennel, baby leeks, carrots, beetroot, turnips and a 'proper' salsa di erbe. Desserts can be as traditional as pannacotta or as straightforward as blood-orange sorbet, but the 'beautiful' Amalfi lemon tart seems to be everyone's dessert of choice. Quality is consistently high on a predominantly Italian wine list, which starts at £38, but soon leaps the £50 barrier.
Chef/s: Theo Randall. **Open:** Mon to Fri L, all week D. **Meals:** main courses £18 to £38. Set L and D £29 (2 courses) to £35. Tasting menu £70. **Details:** 160 seats. Bar. Wheelchairs. Music. Parking.

Tredwells

Cooking score: 2
⊖ Leicester Square, map 5
Modern British | £35
4A Upper St Martin's Lane, Covent Garden, WC2H 9NY
Tel no: (020) 3764 0840
tredwells.com

Multi-level modern British dining in a buzzing venue just off Seven Dials is the lure at Marcus Wareing's Tredwells, where weathered banquettes and bar-stools accommodate a city crowd that may be just on its way to (or from) the theatre. The brasserie-style menus are all about no-nonsense robust flavours, with some eclectic seasonings and modern technique thrown in. A raviolo of confit duck comes strewn in sesame seeds, peanuts, green chilli and pickled cucumber until it doesn't know where it's from, and might lead the charge for sea bass with cocoa beans and parsley root in prawn bisque, or corn-fed chicken with a croquette of its leg, alongside January King cabbage and a smoked egg yolk. To finish, there's a chocolate brownie that bills itself as 'virtuous' and comes with coconut yoghurt, or go the whole villainous hog with gin-and-tonic cheesecake. Wines come at Covent Garden prices, but there are small glasses from £5.

Chef/s: Chantelle Nicholson. **Open:** Mon to Fri L and D. Sat and Sun, all day from 12. **Closed:** 25 and 26 Dec, 1 Jan. **Meals:** main courses £16 to £35. Set L, early and late D £25 (2 courses) to £29. Sun L £28. **Details:** 120 seats. Bar. Wheelchairs. Music.

Trishna

Cooking score: 4
⊖ Baker Street, Bond Street, map 6
Indian | £65
15-17 Blandford Street, Marylebone, W1U 3DG
Tel no: (020) 7935 5624
trishnalondon.com
🍷

The ambience of whitewashed bricks, framed Air India posters of the world's great cities and bare café tables suits the Sethi family's modern Indian eatery in the vibrant heart of Marylebone. Focusing on the cooking of the coastal south-west – Cochin, Kerala and Mangalore – the menu abounds in fresh-tasting seafood with regional spice blends and plenty of coconut. Partridge pepper fry is an appealing mix of rich meat, onion and Keralan spices, served with flatbread, and soft-shell crab is as tenderly chewy as can be, dressed in tomato chutney and green chilli, as well as a little white crabmeat. Main dishes include long-simmered lamb nariyal in a coconut masala with curry leaves, or shellfish pilau, a compendious assembly of black tiger prawns, scallops and lobster with pink peppercorn raita. Finish with apple and blackberry kulfi sprinkled with basil seeds and vermicelli, or the luscious cardamom kheer, boiled rice pudding replete with figs, raisins and pistachios. An impressive wine list is knowledgeable enough to separate even Austria into its regions, and offers intelligent selections for every dish, from £26.
Chef/s: Karam Sethi and Sajeev Nair. **Open:** all week L and D. **Closed:** 24 to 27 Dec, 1 to 3 Jan. **Meals:** main courses £15 to £24. Set L £15 (2 courses) to £35 (4 courses). Set D £28. Sun L £35. Tasting menu £60. **Details:** 80 seats. 6 seats outside. V menu. Music. Children before 7pm only.

28°-50°

Cooking score: 4
⊖ Bond Street, map 6
Modern European | £34
15-17 Marylebone Lane, Marylebone,
W1U 2NE
Tel no: (020) 7486 7922
2850.co.uk
🍷

The self-proclaimed 'wine workshop and kitchen' comes courtesy of Agnar Sverrisson (the chef behind Texture, see entry) – so quality is a watchword. Grab a table on the ground floor, with its striking zinc bar, or head downstairs to the more intimate basement; either way, you can be assured of the kind of food that is now giving modern wine bars a good name. A modest but inviting menu determinedly covers all bases, whether you fancy a plate of oysters, some charcuterie or a seafood platter to share. Alternatively, take the conventional route by ordering sea bream ceviche or beetroot and goats' curd salad followed by braised ox cheek or pan-roasted salmon with soba noodles, dashi and nori. And the wine list? Around 30 are offered by the glass (three sizes), or you can delve into a 'collector's list' of 'fine and rare' vintages garnered from private cellars and established merchants. There's a branch at 17-19 Maddox Street, W1S 2QH, and a further offshoot on Fetter Lane, EC4 (see entry).
Chef/s: Alex Drayton. **Open:** Mon to Sat, all day from 12. **Closed:** Sun, 25 and 26 Dec, bank hols. **Meals:** main courses £16 to £33. Set L and early D £20 (2 courses) to £25. **Details:** 49 seats. 14 seats outside. Bar. Wheelchairs. Music.

Symbols

🛏 Accommodation is available
£30 Three courses for less than £30
£5 OFF £5-off voucher scheme
🍷 Notable wine list

Umu

Cooking score: 6
⊖ Green Park, Bond Street, map 5
Japanese | £145
14-16 Bruton Place, Mayfair, W1J 6LX
Tel no: (020) 7499 8881
umurestaurant.com

A secluded, easily missed Mayfair doorway leads into a small, softly lit dining room of timber, stone and Venetian glass. Dedicated to using the highest-quality wild, line-caught fish, much is made of the *ike jime* – a traditional and humane method of killing fish – now used by the Cornish fishermen who supply most of the catch. Given such obsession about fish, it goes without saying that the dainty morsels of sashimi are exquisite, the sushi excellent and there has been praise for tuna tartare with Exmoor caviar, and crispy skin Dover sole with bonito flakes. Everything makes a full-on visual impact, the cooking is faultless and the service well drilled and friendly. The only downside is the 'eye-watering' prices, especially of you order the kaiseki tasting menu or opt for the Japanese Wagyu beef. But you don't need a wealthy benefactor to eat here, however: set lunches are actually good value for this standard of experience. From the excellent saké list to world-class wines, drinks are expensive, too.
Chef/s: Yoshinori Ishii. **Open:** Mon to Sat L and D. **Closed:** Sun, bank hols. **Meals:** main courses £28 to £95. Set L £35. Kaiseki menu £155 (8 courses). **Details:** 55 seats. Wheelchairs. Music.

★ NEW ENTRY ★

Veeraswamy

Cooking score: 3
⊖ Piccadilly Circus, Oxford Circus, map 5
Indian | £70
Victory House, 99 Regent Street, Mayfair,
W1B 4RS
Tel no: (020) 7734 1401
veeraswamy.com

'I took my mother along, who had last eaten there in 1953,' a reporter confides, giving some indication (with due respect to Mother) of the venerability of Veeraswamy. Indeed, established between the wars, it was the first dedicated Indian restaurant in Britain, and still retains something of a time-worn cachet in its grandiose perch, up a gilded staircase above Regent Street. Personable, smartly attired staff deliver Subcontinental classics rendered with flair and precision. Snack on raj kachori to begin: puri shells filled with colourful vegetable ingredients, bejewelled with pomegranate seeds and laced with fresh coriander chutney. After that, there are crisp crab cakes with chilli, lime and ginger, pink Amritsari lamb chops crusted in pistachios and almonds, in a creamy sauce of cumin, saffron and star anise, or Malabar lobster curry in turmeric, coconut and green mango. Sharply spiced sides take in aloo gobi tossed in curry leaves, coconut and chilli, and meals end with rich wattalapam, a thick coconut palm sugar brûlée, or pineapple and almond halwa tart. A very Regent Street wine list opens with glasses that start at £8 for a Chilean Cabernet Sauvignon rosé.

Chef/s: Uday Salunkhe. **Open:** all week L and D.
Meals: main courses £22 to £44. Set L £30 (2 courses) to £34. Sun L £32. **Details:** 110 seats. V menu. Music.

Vietfood

Cooking score: 2
⊖ Piccadilly Circus, map 5
Vietnamese | £25
34-36 Wardour Street, Soho, W1D 6QT
Tel no: (020) 7494 4555
vietnamfood.co.uk
£30

A shining star on the edge of Chinatown, necessarily small – despite being spread over two floors – and with an unsurprisingly no-frills rustic décor that feels 'polished without tipping too far into engineered', this popular Vietnamese eatery boasts approachable, efficient service. In addition, there's a long menu of modern Vietnamese small plates and classics such as pho and bun (noodles), from which it's near impossible to go wrong. Everyone seems to order the rice-paper

summer rolls with freshwater prawns, char-grilled glazed lemongrass chicken wings, and the 'absolutely fabulous' crispy coconut calamari with sweet chilli herb sauce. Elsewhere, a vibrant salad of grilled chilli sirloin beef with fresh herbs has also been praised, and pandan coconut milk sago with caramel banana is a recommended dessert. Prices are fair. The café-style vibe, with its sense of in-out snacking rather than a long, lingering meal, means queues are inevitable. Drink cocktails or wine (from £17). A sister restaurant, Go Viet, is at 53 Old Brompton Road, SW7 3JS.

Chef/s: Jeff Tan. **Open:** all week, all day from 12.
Meals: Tapas £4 to £9. Main courses £8 to £15.
Details: 90 seats. Wheelchairs. Music.

Vinoteca

Cooking score: 2
⊖ Marble Arch, map 6
Modern European | £32
15 Seymour Place, Marylebone, W1H 5BD
Tel no: (020) 7724 7288
vinoteca.co.uk
🍾

The bottle-green Marylebone outpost of Vinoteca enjoys the same comfortably laid-back but buzzy ambience as its siblings, with a spacious white-walled restaurant and bar on the ground floor, kitted out with bistro furniture and candles, and a private dining room downstairs. Appetising, unpretentious southern European cooking of obvious appeal is the drill, encompassing ham hock and tarragon terrine with cornichons and mustard to start, ahead of roast turbot with artichokes and fennel in vermouth, or pork collar with braised chickpeas, chard and Espelette pepper. If you're just here for bar snacks and plenty of the fruit of the vine, look to sharing platters of Italian cured meats or British cheeses. Sweet tastes are catered for by black cherry frangipane tart with crème fraîche. The great glory of the place is of course its compendious treasure chest of wines, which are grouped by

style, with inspired portfolios of biodynamics, rosés and modern sparklers among the highlights. Bottle prices start at £19.50.
Chef/s: William Lauder. **Open:** Mon to Sat, all day from 12. Sun 12 to 4. **Closed:** bank hols.
Meals: main courses £8 to £18. Set L £13 (2 courses) to £16. **Details:** 55 seats. Bar. Music.

Wild Honey

Cooking score: 4
⊖ Oxford Circus, Bond Street, map 5
Modern European | £50
12 St George Street, Mayfair, W1S 2FB
Tel no: (020) 7758 9160
wildhoneyrestaurant.co.uk

The oak-panelled dining room in the heart of Mayfair opposite St George's church feels like an oasis of sophisticated modern European dining, and is where Anthony Demetre has concentrated his energies since the closure of Soho's Arbutus. The clubby, sumptuous, retro feel, undergirded by abstract art and photographic prints, is relaxing, and nobody need feel hurried if lunch lengthens into the kind of afternoon where you won't get any further work done. Hand-chopped beef tartare with Maldon oyster mayo, or grilled octopus with potato, parsley and aïoli, make bold openers for mains such as Elwy Valley lamb with baby artichokes, sweet dried tomato, anchovy paste and sheep's ricotta, while a gigantic hunk of beef fillet comes with a dinky little tartlet of mushroom hollandaise and gremolata. It all ends on top note with a featherlight sponge filled with boozed-up cream and scattered with sweet nuts and raspberries. Don't miss the canelés that come with coffee. A vast aristocratic wine list opens at £27, or £6 for small glasses.
Chef/s: Anthony Demetre and Greg Csaba. **Open:** Mon to Sat L and D. **Closed:** Sun, bank hols.
Meals: main courses £18 to £29. Set L and D £35 (3 courses). **Details:** 55 seats. Bar.

Wiltons

Cooking score: 4
⊖ Green Park, map 5
British | £67
55 Jermyn Street, Mayfair, SW1Y 6LX
Tel no: (020) 7629 9955
wiltons.co.uk

First established as a shellfish stall by George William Wilton in 1742, becoming a fully fledged restaurant in 1840, Wiltons celebrated its 275th anniversary in 2017. Creature comforts are well catered for in the velvet and wood-lined interior, and there's a lot to like about delightfully old-fashioned thick carpets and proper linen-covered tables. Just like the surroundings, the menu is steeped in tradition, specialising in fish with just a few nods to current fashion; it's all about enjoying food and company. This is the place to come for oysters and top-drawer renditions of classics such as dressed crab, potted shrimps, lobster thermidor and 'cooked to perfection' Dover sole meunière. If fish is out of the question, try beef fillet au poivre or lamb cutlets, or look to the set menu, which delivers a daily roast from the carving trolley. To finish, go for British cheese, a savoury such as Welsh rarebit, or bread-and-butter pudding with vanilla custard. France is accorded its full dignity on a list that's bedevilled by stiff mark-ups.
Chef/s: Daniel Kent. **Open:** Mon to Fri L, Mon to Sat D. **Closed:** Sun, 21 Dec to 2 Jan. **Meals:** main courses £18 to £60. Set L and D £30 (2 courses) to £38. **Details:** 100 seats. Bar. Wheelchairs.

The Wolseley

Cooking score: 2
⊖ Green Park, map 5
Modern European | £37
160 Piccadilly, Mayfair, W1J 9EB
Tel no: (020) 7499 6996
thewolseley.com

As befits a Piccadilly grandee, there's a doorman to let you in at The Wolseley. Once admitted, a soaring room of cast-iron chandeliers and waistcoated waiters greets the eager eye, with gleaming columns and an exquisitely tiled floor the regal backdrop to a tankard of Black Velvet and a plate of chopped liver. You can start and end the day here if you will, and the little treats will keep coming – proper eggs Benedict with lean ham and a doorstop muffin, avocado vinaigrette, beluga and blinis. At the main-service sessions, there are entrées such as smoked haddock Monte Carlo (with poached egg and spinach) or venison loin with parsnip purée in redcurrant jus, and if nothing quite scales the gastronomic heights, you might reflect that it has no such intention. Chocomaniacs will adore the screamingly rich pot au chocolat, while two could make short work of a Kaiserschmarren (shredded pancake served with plum compote). Wines obligingly plump up the bill, by at least £25.50, or £8 a glass.

Chef/s: Maarten Geschwindt. **Open:** all week, all day from 7am (8am Sat and Sun). **Meals:** main courses £14 to £46. **Details:** 165 seats. V menu. Bar. Wheelchairs.

Wright Brothers Soho

Cooking score: 2
⊖ Oxford Circus, map 5
Seafood | £31
13 Kingly Street, Soho, W1B 5PW
Tel no: (020) 7434 3611
thewrightbrothers.co.uk

The Soho outpost of the successful seafood chain is a relaxed place for unhurried all-week eating, with conscientiously treated fish and shellfish dishes in versatile array. There's a raw bar offering lobster and oysters (sign up for shucking classes to help you gain proficiency), a summer courtyard that feels like a precious resource in this district and a well-run main room where obliging staff know the ropes. Bespoke platters may well be the way to go if there's a big hungry crowd of you. Otherwise, look to char-grilled prawns in chilli oil, or monkfish cheeks fried in buttermilk with saffron aïoli and samphire, to get you started, prior to rosemary-roasted gilthead bream with preserved lemon and pickled fennel, or skate wing in crab butter; main courses that give the lie to the idea that fish ought always to

be delicately seasoned. Inspired desserts include spiced plum cake with Greek yoghurt and honey cream, or coconut and lime pannacotta with peanut praline. Wines are roughly grouped by style, from £23.

Chef/s: Jim Abbott. **Open:** all week, all day from 12. **Closed:** 25 and 26 Dec. **Meals:** main courses £16 to £26. Set L £22 (2 courses) to £26. **Details:** 90 seats. 30 seats outside. Bar. Wheelchairs. Music.

★ NEW ENTRY ★

XU

Cooking score: 4
⊖ Piccadilly Circus, map 5
Taiwanese | £30
30 Rupert Street, Soho, W1D 6DL
Tel no: (020) 3319 8147
xulondon.com

The team at Bao (see entry) has come up with another Taiwanese gem, but this time it's not all buns. Inside, 'evocative design' takes in a stylish tea room and private room (with mahjong tables) on the ground floor, with the first-floor dining room a throwback to 1930s Taipei (wood panelling, Art Deco lighting, ceiling fans, green-and-caramel leather booths). The menu features small plates such as bak kwa, the Hokkien name for jerky (aged beef, spicy pork, lamb), and xiao tsai (lotus crisp, chicken feet, lamb sweetbreads), though standouts at inspection were 'numbing' beef tendon soaked in Szechuan chilli vinaigrette and coriander, 'gold coin' (a tiny spring onion disc topped with a rich terrine, red goji berry and Shaoxing wine jelly), and tomato and smoked eel – the flavour heightened by dried soy, daikon and chilli oil. Main courses such as shou pao (marinated chicken with fresh ginger, spring onion and fried chicken skin) are geared for sharing, char siu pork is made from Iberian pigs, and even rice dishes are different (onion lard rice took one reporter 'back to my childhood'). Match the exotic dishes with crafty cocktails (wines from £28).

Chef/s: Erchen Chang. **Open:** Mon to Thur L and D. Fri and Sat, all day from 12. **Closed:** Sun. **Meals:** main courses £12 to £18. **Details:** 68 seats. Bar.

Yauatcha

Cooking score: 4
⊖ Tottenham Court Road, map 5
Chinese | £40
15-17 Broadwick Street, Soho, W1F 0DL
Tel no: (020) 7494 8888
yauatcha.com

A younger offshoot in Broadgate Circle keeps City workers fuelled up (see entry), but Alan Yau's original Yauatcha is top dog when it comes to creative dim sum, esoteric teas and famously good patisserie. As a cleverly conceived sweet-and-savoury hybrid, it operates on two levels: the ground floor is a canteen behind a frosted blue-glass frontage, while downstairs promises a more moody, low-lit trip. Either way, expect superior dim sum delivered with pizazz and artistry: reworked Chinatown standards share the billing with near-legendary venison puffs, scallop and pear skewers, crispy duck rolls and suchlike. Congees and sticky rice add the ballast, or you can progress to bigger plates of octopus salad, lobster vermicelli or jasmine tea-smoked ribs. Alternatively, try the full teahouse experience complete with exquisite macarons and 'petit gâteaux' such as yuzu and ginger crémeux with crumble and rose Chantilly. Smoothies, cocktails and saké are alternatives to the voguish wine list.
Chef/s: Tong Chee Hwee. **Open:** all week, all day from 12. **Meals:** main courses £8 to £39. Set L £30. **Details:** 190 seats. Bar. Music.

Zoilo

Cooking score: 3
⊖ Bond Street, map 6
Argentinian | £45
9 Duke Street, Marylebone, W1U 3EG
Tel no: (020) 7486 9699
zoilo.co.uk

Following a 2016 refurb, the counter facing Zoilo's basement kitchen has been scrapped, although you can still play it casual at the bar on the ground floor. Argentina may be synonymous with slabs of Pampas-reared beef, but deconstructed regional small plates are the order of the day here. The mood is gregarious and sharing is encouraged, so pick your way through all manner of vivid dishes loaded with ripe, bracing flavours: cured sea trout paired with dill mayo, monk's beard ceviche and oat cracker; carrots and quinoa tartare with Amalfi lemons and hazelnut crumble; stone bass with grilled calçots, mussel escabèche and cauliflower. This being 'cocina Argentina', there are also traditional empanadas in new guises and some true-bred beefy cuts for the red-blooded diehards, while the ultra-sweet indulgence of dulce de leche is never far away for dessert. Decent-value wines are culled exclusively from the home country.
Chef/s: Diego Jacquet. **Open:** Mon to Sat L and D. **Closed:** Sun, 1 week Christmas, bank hols (exc Good Friday). **Meals:** sharing plates £6 to £24. **Details:** 39 seats. Wheelchairs. Music.

L'Absinthe
⊖ Chalk Farm, map 2
French | £27
40 Chalcot Road, Primrose Hill, NW1 8LS
Tel no: (020) 7483 4848
labsinthe.co.uk

£30

A local café, serving breakfast, quiches, crêpes and coffee by day, this somewhat scruffy corner site transforms itself in the evening into a classic French bistro, very popular with the locals. The menu is nostalgic 1970s: marinated herrings with potato salad, chicken liver parfait and French onion soup, alongside Toulouse sausage with Puy lentils, duck confit with braised onions and weekly blackboard specials. A generous rump of lamb served with an excellent pommes dauphinoise and a tarte Tatin 'worthy of a much smarter restaurant' delivered cooking that 'is surprisingly good'. Mainly French wines are kindly priced.

Bellanger
Cooking score: 2
⊖ Angel, map 2
French | £35
9 Islington Green, Islington, N1 2XH
Tel no: (020) 7226 2555
bellanger.co.uk

The Corbin and King formula doesn't only succeed at glitzy addresses in the West End. Here, on Islington Green, the all-day drill works to equally alluring effect, in a light-touch Belle Epoque style that extends from front windows that overlook the Green to an intimate, carpeted room at the back, via a long bar with seating. There's an Alsace theme to much of the menu, furnishing tartes flambées and quiches, beery soups and terrines, chicken braised in steely Riesling, and fully loaded choucroute plates that assemble as much pig-related fare as will fit on a heap of pickled cabbage. Elsewhere, proceedings wander happily off-piste for entrecôte in béarnaise, or seared sea bass with Jerusalem artichokes and salsify. A lump of fragrant Munster would

then seem appropriate, perhaps prior to an ice cream coupe with nuts and cream, or you might go light with a single hefty scoop of Gewürztraminer sorbet. The classy wines include a fair bit of Alsace produce, though oddly none of the often wonderful Crémant d'Alsace fizz. Prices open at £22.50.
Chef/s: Brian Scalan. **Open:** all week L and D. **Meals:** main courses £12 to £27. Set L and D £15 to £18. **Details:** 195 seats. 24 seats outside. V menu. Bar. Wheelchairs. Music.

Bradleys
Cooking score: 2
⊖ Swiss Cottage, map 2
French | £36
25 Winchester Road, Swiss Cottage, NW3 3NR
Tel no: (020) 7722 3457
bradleysnw3.co.uk

Simon and Jolanta Bradleys' ever-popular Swiss Cottage restaurant has been punching above its weight since 1992. At a test meal plump scallops with contrastingly crispy chicken wings, peas and shoots made a strong start, followed by flavoursome Gressingham duck breast with crushed turnips and orange. Puddings were more mixed: light yet satisfying crema catalana with vanilla beignets and rhubarb, but a disappointingly lukewarm pear tarte Tatin. However, there's much to enjoy here and a whole host of menus – arguably too many? – including a cracking-value set dinner, Sunday lunch and vegetarian. Unfortunately, disappointing service marred the experience this time round ('the waiter taking the order admitted that he couldn't understand English'), but Bradleys on song is just 'the kind of restaurant you'd love to have on your doorstep': comfortable, airy and informal. The global wine list has attractive drops even at the lower end.
Chef/s: Simon Bradley. **Open:** all week L, Mon to Sat D. **Closed:** bank hols. **Meals:** main courses £18 to £23. Set L £20 (2 courses) to £24. Set D £24. Sun L £27. **Details:** 60 seats. V menu.

The Bull & Last

Cooking score: 3
⊖ Tufnell Park, Kentish Town, map 2
Modern British | £39
168 Highgate Road, Hampstead, NW5 1QS
Tel no: (020) 7267 3641
thebullandlast.co.uk

It feels a bit like a gentrified village pub in the Cotswolds (all farmhouse fittings, stuffed animal heads, big mirrors and pictures of chickens), but the only green expanses you'll see hereabouts are the rolling acres of nearby Hampstead Heath. Otherwise, the Bull & Last plays its part as an elegantly rebooted neighbourhood hostelry where the very decent selection of real ales is overshadowed by some superior pub food. Head upstairs for serious victuals — perhaps pig's cheek with watermelon pickle, basil and sesame followed by lamb rump with pastilla, aubergine, violet artichoke, monk's beard, olives and hazelnuts. If that sounds too fancy for a pub lunch, take a punt on one of the charcuterie and fish boards — or a char-grilled steak with triple-cooked chips — before rounding off with sticky toffee pudding and banana ice cream or a plate of salted-caramel truffles. The owners' terroir-led wine list evolves with the seasons.
Chef/s: Oliver Pudney. **Open:** all week L and D.
Closed: 25 Dec. **Meals:** main courses £16 to £23.
Details: 45 seats. Music.

CôBa

Cooking score: 1
⊖ Caledonian Road, map 2
Vietnamese | £25
244 York Way, Camden, N7 9AG
cobarestaurant.co.uk
£30

'York Way is a long road, so if you're walking from King's Cross, wear comfortable shoes,' advised one reader seeking fulfilment at Damon Bui's Vietnamese joint. Damon credits his mum for the recipes, which means we should probably thank them both for those crab and pork spring rolls, BBQ lamb cutlets and spot-on beef pho. The room is a 'dead cool

urban space' with a cocktail bar dishing out CôBa's Fling, Cô-jito and more. The concise menu starts with small plates — fried butter chicken, say — moving on to 'big bowls' of noodle salads and soup noodles. The wine list is short and sweet (or short and dry, we should say), with a few craft beers in support.
Chef/s: Damon Bui. **Open:** Tue to Fri L, Tue to Sat D.
Closed: Sun, Mon, 2 weeks Dec. **Meals:** main courses £10 to £15. **Details:** 50 seats. Bar.
Wheelchairs. Music.

Dishoom

Cooking score: 2
⊖ King's Cross, map 2
Indian | £30
5 Stable Street, King's Cross, N1C 4AB
Tel no: (020) 7420 9321
dishoom.com

The street name denotes the fact that draught horses were once stabled beneath the railway goods yard and transit shed that is now the King's Cross branch of the Dishoom group. A reimagined Bombay café, of the kind that played host to all walks of life throughout the day, is the concept, and the large menus deal in a mixture of small plates, grills, biryanis and London Ruby Murrays for an enjoyably unstructured approach to Indian feasting. Some quick-fried breadcrumbed squid and perhaps an Iranian-style keema pau, a buttered bun piled with minced lamb and peas, are good places to start, and are well followed by the house take on chicken tikka, made with sweet vinegar rather than yoghurt, or gunpowder potatoes, grilled in their skins, broken up and tumbled about in butter, seeds and herbs. A garlic naan helps fill any gaps, and the must-have dessert is a Malabar Hill version of Eton Mess, scented with rose-petal syrup and preserve. Indian beers and spice-friendly wines add to the bonhomie.
Chef/s: Naved Nasir. **Open:** all week, all day from 8am (9am Sat and Sun). **Closed:** 25 and 26 Dec, 1 and 2 Jan. **Meals:** main courses from £6 to £22.
Details: 250 seats. 20 seats outside. Bar.
Wheelchairs. Music.

The Drapers Arms

Cooking score: 2
⊖ Highbury & Islington, Angel, map 2
British | £30
44 Barnsbury Street, Islington, N1 1ER
Tel no: (020) 7619 0348
thedrapersarms.com

Nestled amid the shady squares and Gothic Revival townhouses of Barnsbury, the Drapers Arms is appropriately attired for this well-heeled postcode, with dapper mint green walls, grand fireplaces, sash windows and chandeliers suspended from lofty ceilings. Signs are this pub is smartening up appearances in the kitchen, too, based on our recent inspection, with confident cooking resting on pillars of seasonality and good sourcing. Our inspection began with ham hock and tomatoes doused in salad cream – arriving in a marvellous jumbled mess – while other trusted classics in attendance include baked St Marcellin, or potted salmon with sourdough crisps and cucumber. Among the mains, expect a whiff of nostalgia in lamb rump with bubble and squeak and mustard sauce, and crisp, clean flavours in mackerel with courgettes, tomatoes and mint. Finish off with rhubarb, orange and ricotta cheesecake. A good range of ales is stocked behind the handsome racing green bar.
Chef/s: Gina Hopkins. **Open:** Mon to Sat L and D. Sun 12.30 to 8. **Meals:** main courses £15 to £30.
Details: 80 seats. Bar.

LOCAL GEM

500 Restaurant

⊖ Archway, map 2
Italian | £27
782 Holloway Road, Archway, N19 3JH
Tel no: (020) 7272 3406
500restaurant.co.uk

£5 OFF £30

Bare tables on a bare floor, lilac walls hung with reproduction classical still-lifes and photographs of Fiats: the scene is set for an Italian café offering sturdily reliable comfort food with a touch of style. Salty beef carpaccio dressed in Parmesan cream and black truffle is an object lesson in umami, and may be followed by crab tagliatelle in a strong bisque sauce. Mains might turn things up a notch for guinea fowl cooked with plums in white wine, accompanied by braised red cabbage and apple, and nobody's complaining when chocolate and pear mousse arrives in a froth of amaretti. House Sardinian varietals are £18.50.

Jin Kichi

Cooking score: 2
⊖ Hampstead, map 2
Japanese | £30
73 Heath Street, Hampstead, NW3 6UG
Tel no: (020) 7794 6158
jinkichi.com

Close-packed tables, lanterns, prints and a counter by the open kitchen might conjure up images of a Tokyo backstreet izakaya, but this is well-to-do Hampstead. Nevertheless, cramped Jin Kichi delivers pinpoint flavours and authenticity from a wide-ranging menu that majors on sushi and yakitori skewers (watch the chefs at work at the robata grill). The former includes a full quota of glistening fresh nigiri and rolls (try the 'inside out' version with grilled eel and egg), while the latter runs from a textbook chicken and spring onion version to more esoteric ideas involving everything from quails' eggs to ox tongue with salt. Also expect assorted appetisers (sliced fishcake with wasabi), grills, noodles and deep-fried dishes (chicken gizzard with ponzu sauce, say). One-plate lunches are a snip (with rice and miso soup included), while Japanese beers, shochu cocktails and saké are alternatives to the rather pricey wine list.
Chef/s: Rei Shimazu. **Open:** Tue to Sun L and D. **Closed:** Mon. **Meals:** main courses £7 to £18. Set L £10 (2 courses) to £19. **Details:** 42 seats. Music.

Average price

The average price denotes the price of a three-course meal without wine.

Our highlights...

Our undercover inspectors reveal their most memorable dishes from another year of extraordinary eating.

Truffled scallops with cured salmon, bergamot gel and artichoke purée at the **Yorke Arms**. It was the kind of starter to remind you that great things can still be done with very familiar ingredients. Its haunting perfumes were a wonderful intro to a great dinner.

At **The Other Naughty Piglet**, a dish of **barbecued pork belly with Korean spices and sesame**, the meat pink and tender, scattered with spring-onion snippings, sauced in mirin, miso and soy, along with raving-hot chilli ketchup paste. A bonfire in the mouth.

But probably best of all, the main meat dish at **OX**. **Mourne Mountain lamb** of such exquisite grassy freshness and tenderness, it made me want to cry. It came with nodules of deep-fried sweetbread, an ocean's surge of sea herbs and miso purée, everything at Force 10. I can still taste it, as they say.

The **chocolate cylinder of banana parfait with bitter orange ice cream and peanut brittle** at the **Springer Spaniel**; similarly, the block of **banana parfait** coated in feathery grated chocolate with lime gel, lime sorbet and stickily honey-roasted peanuts at **Lympstone Manor**.

LOCAL GEM
Mangal 1 Ocakbasi
⊖ Dalston Kingsland, map 2
Turkish | £18
10 Arcola Street, Stoke Newington, E8 2DJ
Tel no: (020) 7275 8981
mangal1.com

£30

Mangal 1 has been serving the community for many a year, and back they come, again and again, for fresh, tender and smoky meat cooked over coals – just like in Turkey. Expect lamb spare ribs, chicken wings, grilled quail, or simply a classic kebab with salad and pide. Stuffed vines leaves, taramasalata, all these are done well. Bring your own booze, and cash. That's not to say it's expensive, it's not, but it is cash only.

Odette's
Cooking score: 4
⊖ Chalk Farm, map 2
Modern British | £43
130 Regent's Park Road, Primrose Hill, NW1 8XL
Tel no: (020) 7586 8569
odettesprimrosehill.com

'The place is buzzy and fun' with an arty atmosphere, emphasised by the cartoons and line drawings that decorate the walls. It's popular with the local intelligentsia – 'you're as likely to sit next to a table of lawyers as musicians and artists' – all here for chef/proprietor Bryn Williams' gutsy, grown-up cooking. Bryn may wear his Welshness on his sleeve, but the menu cherry-picks great ingredients from all over the UK. Kitchen high points are the carefully slow-cooked dishes: beautifully tender glazed pork cheek with scorched onions, a lobster broth giving a big umami finish; Goosnargh duck leg soft enough to eat with a spoon, endive and blood orange cutting through the richness. Smart fish dishes are pretty good, too, say wild brill paired with Jerusalem artichoke and given a classic chicken velouté as a sauce. The shortish wine list is a good eclectic mix, with easy wines by the glass to match the bargain set lunch as well as serious numbers for big occasions.

Chef/s: Bryn Williams and William Gordon. **Open:** Tue to Sun L, Tue to Sat D. **Closed:** Mon, 1 week Christmas. **Meals:** main courses £17 to £28. Set L £17 (2 courses) to £22. Set D £25 (2 courses) to £30. Sun L £30 (3 courses). Tasting menu £49. **Details:** 62 seats. 26 seats outside. Music.

Oldroyd

Cooking score: 3
⊖ Angel, map 2
Modern European | £35
344 Upper Street, Islington, N1 0PD
Tel no: (020) 8617 9010
oldroydlondon.com

£5 OFF

This little high street eatery, and we can't stress the word 'little' strongly enough, means you'll be squeezed in downstairs and up – mind the rickety spiral staircase – but it does encourage a sense of bonhomie. Its popularity is not surprising: the down-to-earth cooking, built around seasonal British produce and offered via a regularly changing shared-plates menu, is exceptional. Creamy whipped cod's roe is simply teamed with radishes and celery salt, asparagus and Welsh Cheddar croquetas get an extra umami hit from truffle mayonnaise, potato gnocchi comes with nettle, broad beans and Berkswell cheese, and a beautifully cooked rose veal osso buco is served with risotto milanese and gremolata – 'the sort of dish I could eat regularly'. As for pudding, it's a hard choice between Amalfi lemon tart with Yorkshire rhubarb and Jersey cream and chocolate mousse with gariguette strawberries and pistachio. Reasonable prices are a plus, and this extends to classic-with-a-twist cocktails and the brief European wine list.

Chef/s: Louis Lingwood. **Open:** all week, all day from 12 (11 Sun). **Closed:** 25 and 26 Dec. **Meals:** main courses £10 to £19. Set L £16 (2 courses) to £19. **Details:** 31 seats. Music.

Osteria Tufo

Cooking score: 2
⊖ Finsbury Park, map 2
Italian | £27
67 Fonthill Road, Finsbury Park, N4 3HZ
Tel no: (020) 7272 2911
osteriatufo.co.uk

£5 OFF **£30**

As resolutely Italian as a Verdi aria, Osteria Tufo is a much-loved establishment on a quiet street corner in N4, where 'the welcome is always warm'. All the same, gondolier-type chintz is mercifully absent in the dining room – all vast windows, chequerboard floors and tightly packed tables – with a menu that covers all corners of the peninsula. Start in the south with a simple antipasti of baked Sicilian aubergine – or dive into the Adriatic with grilled scallops, arriving with a mint, parsley and garlic sauce. Homemade pasta stars elsewhere on the menu – be it incarnated as rigatoni served with gutsy luganica sausage, onions and crumby pecorino romano cheese – or perhaps ravioli stuffed with pumpkin, paired with asparagus, walnuts and Gorgonzola cream. Portions are generous, so it's doubtful if anyone finds room for desserts (tiramisu et al are in attendance), while the all-Italian wine list sees bottles start at £17.

Chef/s: Davide Cimmino. **Open:** Sun L, Tue to Sun D. **Closed:** Mon, 24 Dec to 6 Jan, 20 Aug to 1 Sept. **Meals:** main courses £14 to £19. Sun L £22 (2 courses). **Details:** 30 seats. 20 seats outside. Wheelchairs. Music.

LOCAL GEM

Ottolenghi

⊖ Highbury & Islington, Angel, map 2
Middle Eastern | £35
287 Upper Street, Islington, N1 2TZ
Tel no: (020) 7288 1454
ottolenghi.co.uk

This Upper Street branch of the now four-strong deli-café group is where restaurateur and *Guardian* writer Yotam Ottolenghi first introduced his vibrant Middle Eastern/fusion flavours to an adoring public. Dig into colourful salads from the counter – perhaps heritage tomatoes, burnt lemon and feta yoghurt or seared yellowfin tuna with sesame, soy, honey and ginger – or order hot dishes such as braised beef shin and pickled walnut pastilla from the kitchen. The cake counter is swoon-worthy and the meringues, in particular, are legendary. Wines from £23.

Parlour

Cooking score: 2
⊖ Kensal Green, map 1
Modern British | £35
5 Regent Street, Kensal Green, NW10 5LG
Tel no: (020) 8969 2184
parlourkensal.com

£5
OFF

'The Grey Horse' it says, still visible on the façade, but the old pub was put out to pasture a few years ago and the place was reborn as Parlour, the vision of chef Jesse Dunford Wood. The bones of the old tavern add character to the inside, and these days it's opened up, chilled out and very much of our time – a café, bar, restaurant and all-round hangout. There's a fun retro attitude, so blue cheese custard comes with 'lots of bits to dip', cow pie is 'with or without' (beef we assume), and you might start the day with 'smashed avocado & toasted lazy bread'. Steamed whiting with English asparagus is a serious supper, with 'hot crossed profiteroles' to finish. It's a lot of fun, but they're serious about quality. House wine is £18.50 and the extensive beer range changes weekly.
Chef/s: Jesse Dunford Wood. **Open:** Tue to Sun, all day from 10. **Closed:** Mon, 1 week Christmas, last week Aug. **Meals:** main courses £10 to £24. Set L £15 (2 courses) to £18. Set D £18 (2 courses) to £21. Tasting menu £40. **Details:** 100 seats. 50 seats outside. Bar. Wheelchairs. Music.

★ NEW ENTRY ★

Perilla

Cooking score: 4
⊖ Canonbury, Dalston Kingsland, map 2
Modern European | £30
1-3 Green Lanes, Newington Green, N16 9BS
Tel no: (020) 7359 0779
perilladining.co.uk

Matt Emmerson and chef Ben Marks' modern urban restaurant on the edge of Newington Green reflects the aim to provide great food and drink at kind prices, its endearingly plain countenance – exposed brick, tiled floor, lots of wood, with plenty of light from plate-glass windows – matching the straight-to-the-point cooking perfectly. Based on a zealous enthusiasm for entirely fresh ingredients, the food is a reworking of classic European dishes and flavours. At a June meal we were impressed by raw fish (tuna, sea bream, lemon sole) with sour cherries and gooseberries, by a deconstructed spring pistou soup of peas, fresh basil leaves, potatoes, leafy fronds and pesto, and by a bowl of braised octopus with borlotti beans and grilled hake throat mixed with some rough-torn chunks of bread to mop up juices in the style of a panzanella salad. Flavours are as big as can be, whether a main-course 40-day aged pork chop with pickled elderflower and sea kale, right down to set buttermilk with grilled strawberries and mulberries. As for refreshment, cocktails and gutsy wines from European vineyards suit the food admirably.
Chef/s: Ben Marks. **Open:** Thur to Sat L, Tue to Sat D, Sun 12.30 to 8. **Closed:** Mon. **Meals:** main courses £13 to £20. Tasting menu £38. **Details:** 60 seats.

Restaurant Michael Nadra

Cooking score: 3
⊖ Chalk Farm, map 2
Modern European | £39
42 Gloucester Avenue, Primrose Hill,
NW1 8JD
Tel no: (020) 7722 2800
restaurant-michaelnadra.co.uk
£5 OFF 🍷

Michael Nadra's second London venture,
enticingly billed a 'restaurant, Martini bar and
garden' enjoys a prime spot (in a Grade II-listed
horse tunnel) overlooking the Regent's Canal
in Primrose Hill. It's a large, multi-faceted
space that has ambitions beyond most
neighbourhood joints but falls shy of
'destination' status. As one reporter noted, 'a
little more fun and adventure, both in the food
and from the staff, would help enormously.' In
summary, the restaurant delivers a high
standard of consistent cooking, without
excessively challenging the taste-buds. Expect
nicely done dishes such as suckling pig with
chorizo, choucroute salad and pea shoots, or
Barbary duck breast with Puy lentils, Alsace
bacon and swede fondant. Treacle tart with
clotted cream and raspberry sorbet makes a
lovely finish, and the cheese trolley loaded
with La Fromagerie's finest is well worth
summoning. The wine list, priced 'on the
toppy side', is noteworthy for half-bottles and
a strong showing from Bordeaux and
Burgundy.
Chef/s: Michael Nadra. **Open:** Tue to Sun L and D.
Closed: Mon, 24 to 27 Dec. **Meals:** set L £23 (2
courses) to £28. Set D £ 33 (2 courses) to £39.
Details: 80 seats. 32 seats outside. Bar. Wheelchairs.
Music.

Symbols

🛏 Accommodation is available
£30 Three courses for less than £30
£5 OFF £5-off voucher scheme
🍷 Notable wine list

LOCAL GEM

Roti King

⊖ Euston, map 2
Malaysian | £10
40 Doric Way, Euston, NW1 1LH
Tel no: (020) 7387 2518
rotiking.in
£30

Home-from-home for Malaysians,
Singaporeans and Indonesians now living in
London, Roti King is named after roti canai,
the lightest of paratha served fresh off the
griddle with a bowl of intensely flavoured
curry – mutton being the favourite, rich with
coconut and a heady hit of chilli. There are fish
and chicken options, too, and a cheaper dhal.
Served alongside the famous roti are huge
bowls of laksa, steaming plates of nasi goreng
and an exquisite beef rendang. Easy to ignore
are other dishes from a more recognisable
Chinese list. It is pretty hard to spend more
than £10 per head. Note, the sign on the front
still says 'Euston Chinese', the previous
incumbent, you may have to queue and it's
BYO and cash only.

Season

Cooking score: 2
⊖ Finsbury Park, map 2
Modern British | £25
53 Stroud Green Road, Finsbury Park, N4 3EF
Tel no: (020) 7263 5500
seasonkitchen.co.uk
£5 OFF £30

An evergreen fixture in Finsbury Park from
the height of summer to the depths of winter,
Season's self-proclaimed 'no fuss' philosophy
has won it many fans. The lack of pretension
extends to the battleship-grey dining room,
with its tightly packed tables and smattering
of mismatched pictures, where punters choose
from a succinct menu. Starters show a
preference for simple, precise flavours –
tender wood pigeon breast, for instance, or
deliciously gloopy burrata with chicory, blood
orange and pistachio. A line-up of 58-day
aged steaks form the vanguard of the mains,

with crinkle-cut chips and burnt onion and pomegranate among the signature sides – although vegetarians are catered for with the likes of pumpkin ravioli. Mini rhubarb and custard doughnuts feature among the crowd-pleasing puds – even more popular is the low-mark-up policy on the wine list, where bottles start from £15.50.

Chef/s: Ben Wooles. **Open:** Tue to Sat D. Sun 12 to 8. **Closed:** Mon, 25 to 30 Dec. **Meals:** main courses £10 to £16. **Details:** 35 seats. Music.

Trullo

Cooking score: 3
⊖ Highbury & Islington, map 2
Italian | £35
300-302 St Paul's Road, Islington, N1 2LH
Tel no: (020) 7226 2733
trullorestaurant.com

'Ticks all the right boxes and I only wished there was one in every part of town,' was how one Knightsbridge resident summed up this busy and noisy Islington trattoria. Spread over two floors, there are the usual restaurant trappings – an open kitchen, dark floorboards, wooden chairs, Edison light-bulbs – while the daily changing menu is 'packed with the things you actually want to eat'. There has been praise for crispy artichoke fritti teamed with capers and mint, a plate of 'garlicky, terrific' orecchiette served with purple sprouting broccoli and anchovy and pepped up by a little chilli and Parmesan, and mains of black Hampshire pork chop cooked over burning coal and paired with cannellini beans and salsa verde, and a perfectly timed oven-baked monkfish tail with wilted greens and bottarga. Desserts include the likes of bitter caramel pannacotta. On the wine front, the well-annotated, all-Italian list (from £22) has fashionably esoteric choices alongside some excellent, familiar ones.

Chef/s: Conor J Gadd. **Open:** all week L, Mon to Sat D. **Closed:** 24 Dec to 3 Jan. **Meals:** main courses £13 to £25. **Details:** 93 seats. Music.

Vinoteca

Cooking score: 1
⊖ King's Cross, map 2
Modern European | £30
One Pancras Square, King's Cross, N1C 4BU
Tel no: (020) 3793 7210
vinoteca.co.uk

'A lovely place to go with a group of friends to catch up over wine and lovely food,' notes a reporter about this vast, sprawling, outgoing modern wine bar (part of a group of five spread across central London), within sight of King's Cross and St Pancras stations. It comes with all the right credentials: an exciting modern wine list with reasonable prices and good choices by the glass, an ingredients-led menu with a strong Mediterranean bias, and excellent, well-informed service. The charcuterie board is a promising start, as is heritage tomatoes with barrel-aged feta, followed by whole plaice with a tangle of fashionably spiralised courgettes gently infused with chilli.

Chef/s: Kieren Steinborne. **Open:** all week, all day from 7.30am (10am Sat and Sun). **Meals:** main courses £10 to £21. Set L £13 (2 courses) to £16. **Details:** 80 seats. 40 seats outside. Bar. Wheelchairs.

Angler

Cooking score: 6

Moorgate, map 4

Seafood | £64

South Place Hotel, 3 South Place, Moorgate,
EC2M 2AF

Tel no: (020) 3215 1260

anglerrestaurant.com

A seductive silvery room on the top floor of
the South Place Hotel, Angler offers views of
the City through slanted windows, with
daylight and nocturnal illumination reflected
in wall and ceiling mirrors done in patterns of
silvered foliage. It's a relaxing venue for the
serious business of seafood cookery, in which
Gary Foulkes proves himself a consummate
adept. Fish and shellfish dishes form the
principal scaffolding of the tasting menus,
though meat and vegetable dishes are woven
through them, too. Tartare of yellowfin tuna
with Hass avocado, dressed in wasabi and
shiso, gets things off to a Japanese-inspired
start, before the compass needle spins to the
Med for a serving of roast octopus with
taramasalata and potato in bagna cauda. A
pasta interloper might surface in the form of
rabbit agnolotti with smoked bacon and
cabbage, before Cornish turbot breaks the
surface in the company of line-caught squid in
bonito dashi. Dessert flavours are as enticing as
the surroundings, when Earl Grey cream with
dates and burnt honey is succeeded by a Seville
orange soufflé and ice cream flavoured with
toasted brioche. A French-led wine list is full
of classics, with an imaginative glass selection
from £6.95.

Chef/s: Gary Foulkes. **Open:** Mon to Fri L, Mon to
Sat D. **Closed:** Sun, 26 to 30 Dec. **Meals:** main
courses £32 to £35. Set L £40 (3 courses). Tasting
menu £60 (6 courses) to £90. **Details:** 70 seats. 20
seats outside. Bar. Wheelchairs. Music.

Anglo

Cooking score: 6

Farringdon, map 5

Modern British | £39

30 St Cross Street, Farringdon, EC1N 8UH

Tel no: (020) 7430 1503

anglorestaurant.com

For a masterclass in thoughtful, ingredient-led
cooking, look no further than Anglo. The
chefs here boast glossy pedigrees, but the
menus are as unadorned as the décor
(polished-concrete floors, almost-bare walls,
unfussy tables) is sparse. Three or four
elements per exquisitely presented plate are
enough, and the food is delivered by the chef –
a lovely touch – with a short explanation.
Springy sourdough with tangy yeast butter is
wickedly moreish. White asparagus comes
with its lifelong plate-mates of lemon and dill
with confit egg, and is sublime in its
simplicity. Circular fillets of Cornish cod,
wrapped in kombu and draped with monk's
beard, are sweet against saltier, golden-plump
mussels and the peppery nudge of nasturtium
leaves, while a dish of celeriac, burrata and
shavings of Périgord truffle is both fresh and
indulgent. An exemplary Earl Grey ice cream
balances the sweet-tartness of ribbons of apple
rolled into a puck and topped with a caramel
disc, but you could choose a chocolate ganache
with fresh yoghurt, basil and meringue shards.
There's much to drink at around £35.

Chef/s: Mark Jarvis. **Open:** Tue to Sat L, Mon to Sat
D. **Closed:** Sun, 23 Dec to 4 Jan, bank hols.
Meals: main courses £19 to £25 (L only). Tasting
menu L £39, D £45. **Details:** 30 seats. V menu.
Music.

L'Anima

Cooking score: 4
⊖ Liverpool Street, map 4
Italian | £60
1 Snowden Street, City, EC2A 2DQ
Tel no: (020) 7422 7000
lanima.co.uk

City commuters putting off the journey home from Liverpool Street do well to recharge their batteries at L'Anima, where contemporary Italian style offers a soothing backdrop of textured stone and neutral tones, and the kitchen produces elegantly worked renditions of classic southern Italian food. If some have felt there is a little overgilding of the lily sometimes, that's hardly the case in a refreshingly direct opener of tuna crudo with avocado and mango, nor in the seductive seafood ravioli filled with langoustines and prawns in gently spicy lobster broth. Secondi are good at emphasising the primary flavours, whether it be for a piece of nicely timed monkfish in tomato fondue with capers and black olives, or pavé of succulent lamb with Sicilian-style caponata and aubergine sauce. Simple desserts include moist almond tortino with yoghurt ice cream. The Italian-oriented wine list covers the principal regions, finding more good dry whites than is often the case, with some mature clarets on hand for the sticklers. House blends are £26.50.
Chef/s: Antonio Favuzzi. **Open:** Mon to Fri L, Mon to Sat D. **Closed:** Sun, 2 weeks Christmas, Sat (Aug only), bank hols. **Meals:** main courses £17 to £35. **Details:** 170 seats. Bar. Wheelchairs. Music. Parking.

L'Anima Café

Cooking score: 2
⊖ Shoreditch High Street, map 4
Italian | £31
10 Appold Street, Shoreditch, EC2A 2AP
Tel no: (020) 7422 7000
lanimacafe.co.uk
£5 OFF

A glass city monolith is home to L'Anima Café, which occupies a fair chunk of the ground floor, and fizzes with life in its deli,

bar and restaurant. All that glass and a simply slick interior design make for an egalitarian sort of space, but this is the fringes of the City, so it's more smart than casual. Pop in for a pizza cooked in the wood-fired oven – the crudaiola perhaps, with its creamy burrata and Parma ham topping – or stick around for the full three or four courses. Calamari fritti with chilli jam plays to the gallery, while octopus salad has a bit more of that promised soul. Pasta is a good bet, and among main courses veal milanese is a classic option, or go for grilled tuna with celery and fennel salad. The wine list includes a few international interlopers among its Italian greatest hits.
Chef/s: Antonio Favuzzi. **Open:** Mon to Fri, all day from 11.30. **Closed:** Sat, Sun, 25 and 26 Dec, bank hols. **Meals:** main courses £14 to £20. **Details:** 120 seats. Bar. Wheelchairs. Parking.

LOCAL GEM

Berber & Q Grill House
⊖ Haggerston, map 2
Middle Eastern | £25
338 Acton Mews, Haggerston, E8 4EA
berberandq.com
£30

In a Haggerston railway arch serving grilled meats and vegetables, one can expect cramped, communal seating, loud music 'but surprisingly little noise bounce', and no reservations (except for groups of six or more). You can expect, too, meze-style openers of cauliflower shawarma or golden beets with hazelnuts, beetroot tahini and red chilli, and grilled meats such as pork belly with pomegranate BBQ sauce or green chermoula chicken thighs. Drink innovative cocktails or wines from £19. (Lighter Tel Aviv-inspired offerings can be found at Berber & Q's new Shawarma rotisserie and wine bar at 46 Exmouth Market, EC1R 4QE.)

Average price

The average price denotes the price of a three-course meal without wine.

Bistrotheque

Cooking score: 2
⊖ Bethnal Green, map 1
Modern British | £45
23-27 Wadeson Street, Bethnal Green,
E2 9DR
Tel no: (020) 8983 7900
bistrotheque.com

Industrial styling can be bought off the peg
these days, but this is the real deal, a former
warehouse with a monochrome colour
scheme and a genuine sense of scale. It's not
lacking warmth, though, with the staff doing
their bit and an upbeat mood all round. A seat
at the bar gives close-up views of cocktail
action. The menu speaks a contemporary lingo
– labneh with roast onions and salsa verde,
deep-fried ricotta dumplings with burnt
butter – and has feel-good stuff like fish and
chips alongside cod with romesco sauce. Foie
gras and chicken liver parfait is one way to
begin, or you might go for the seared scallops
with sorrel and Jersey Royal crisps, and, when
it comes to main courses, there is balance
between meat, fish and vegetarian options. To
finish, apple sorbet is fired up with local East
London Liquor Company vodka. Wines open
at £25.
Chef/s: Blaine Duffy. **Open:** Sat and Sun L, Mon to
Sat D. **Closed:** 24 to 26 Dec. **Meals:** main courses
£17 to £25. Early and late D £25 (2 courses) to £29.
Details: 116 seats. Bar. Music.

★ NEW ENTRY ★

Blacklock City

Cooking score: 2
⊖ Monument, map 4
British | £25
13 Philpot Lane, City, EC3M 8AA
Tel no: (020) 7998 7676
theblacklock.com
£30

The second iteration of Blacklock (see also
Blacklock, Soho) lurks in a cellar in the heart
of the City, a short stroll from the Monument.
There's a familiar stripped-down look, with
stained-glass partitions and gnarly old

brickwork behind the bar. Booming music
tests the vocal cords in the lively atmosphere,
and the drill, as at Great Windmill Street, is
hefty cuts of thoroughbred meats – sirloins,
lamb T-bones, pork ribs, smoked bacon chops
– at prices you would pay in the butcher's. Mix
and match them by the platter. It's all good.
Pair with sides of kale and Parmesan, or 10-
hour ash-roasted sweet potato sprinkled with
herbs. Beef-dripping chips are a banker, and
there are sauce options including garlicked
bone marrow and fiery chilli hollandaise. Top
and tail, if you've the capacity, with coal-
roasted scallop and black pudding, and a
serving of bread-and-butter pudding and
vanilla ice cream glugged with bourbon.
There's a short but serviceable wine
miscellany, from £25.
Open: Mon to Fri L and D. **Closed:** Sat, Sun.
Meals: main courses £12 to £18. 'All in' set menu
£20. **Details:** 100 seats. Bar. Music.

Brawn

Cooking score: 4
⊖ Shoreditch, map 2
Modern European | £35
49 Columbia Road, Shoreditch, E2 7RG
Tel no: (020) 7729 5692
brawn.co
🍾

'A lovely local restaurant; it's a real joy to eat
there.' For many readers there's no doubt
Brawn defines a good neighbourhood
restaurant, its stripped-back, rough-edged
décor reflecting the aim of chef/proprietor Ed
Wilson to provide great food and drink
without breaking the bank. His kitchen
majors on broad-shouldered seasonal dishes
with Mediterranean overtones and a finger
firmly on the pulse of today's tastes for robust
combinations. Come here for duck gizzards
with endive, mustard and hazelnuts, or crab
and celeriac rémoulade, with main courses
taking in 'a superb light dish' of pork collar
with creamed potatoes and mustard sauce, or
red mullet with mussels, potato and monk's
beard. Dark chocolate with sea salt and olive
oil, or tiramisu are popular desserts. To drink,

there's a short list of cocktails, beer, cider and sherry, but the lengthy wine list is a pedigree showcase of predominantly European wines worth discovering. Bottles start at £22.

Chef/s: Ed Wilson. **Open:** Tue to Sun L, Mon to Sat D. **Closed:** 24 Dec to 3 Jan. **Meals:** main courses £14 to £22. Sun L £28. **Details:** 70 seats. Wheelchairs. Music.

★ NEW ENTRY ★

Breddos

Cooking score: 3
⊖ Barbican, map 5
Mexican | £25
82 Goswell Road, Clerkenwell, EC1V 7DB
Tel no: (020) 3535 8301
breddostacos.com

£30

Beginning life as a Hackney food truck, Breddos is now a temple to tacos with a permanent address in Clerkenwell. The aesthetic inside is Maya meets metropolitan hipster, with vinyl records spinning on the decks and potted cactuses adorning the tables. Attention nonetheless gravitates to the open kitchen where 12cm tortillas are elevated to a minor art form, made with corn ground using a volcanic stone mill and served with magma-hot salsas. Our inspection found potent, playful flavours in a taco of Baja shrimp with wild garlic, spinach and habanero, and there were detours to the other side of the world with kung pao pork belly taco with Szechuan and spring onion. Tostadas are just as intricate and ambitious – a dish of sublime pulpo, black vinegar, potato and bone marrow stood head, shoulders and tentacles above all others on our visit. Dessert offerings are perfunctory – sorbet trio, for instance – while drinks fly the flag for Mexico, from cooling aguas frescas to tequila-based cocktails from £8. A real winner, though service can be slapdash.

Chef/s: Nud Dudhia. **Open:** Mon to Sat L and D. **Closed:** Sun. **Meals:** tacos £3 to £5. Tostadas £7 to £8. **Details:** 40 seats. Music.

★ NEW ENTRY ★

Cabotte

Cooking score: 3
⊖ Bank, map 4
French | £40
48 Gresham Street, City, EC2V 7AY
Tel no: (020) 7600 1616
cabotte.co.uk

No longer is the City a tumbleweeded desert in the evenings – it's come alive with bars and restaurants catering to a smart business crowd. Cabotte is tucked snugly into the Gresham Street action, a combined wine bar and restaurant from Xavier Rousset of Texture fame (see entry), in partnership with Gearoid Devaney. Here, the theme is Burgundy, the name referencing the little wood huts that dot the region's vineyards. That produces an oeuf en meurette made with a duck egg in sterling winey bourguignon, or jambon persillé with cornichons and capers, to start, but doesn't preclude an efficiently rendered stone bass topped with a Maldon oyster and sea veg in a velouté made with Crémant de Bourgogne. If you haven't already had the egg, that bourguignon stew comes roaring back with beef cheeks en cocotte, but by dessert, the kitchen could be caramelising pineapple, dressed in coconut and juniper with lime and yoghurt mousse. The wine list doesn't just stick to Burgundy, and there are some tempting selections by the small glass or half-bottle carafe. The latter start at £13.

Chef/s: Edward Boarland. **Open:** Mon to Fri L and D. **Closed:** Sat, Sun, last 2 weeks Aug, 25 Dec to 1 Jan, bank hols. **Meals:** main courses £16 to £23. **Details:** 46 seats. Bar. Music.

Symbols

Accommodation is available
£30 Three courses for less than £30
£5 OFF £5-off voucher scheme
Notable wine list

Café Spice Namasté

Cooking score: 2
⊖ Tower Hill, map 4
Indian | £40
16 Prescot Street, Tower Hill, E1 8AZ
Tel no: (020) 7488 9242
cafespice.co.uk
£5
OFF

It may be within easy reach of Brick Lane's
tourists' tour of Indian food, but this richly
decorated restaurant inhabits a very different
world – look for the big banners fluttering
outside. For more than two decades, Cyrus
Todiwala OBE has proved his worth as a
doughty ambassador for his native cuisine,
although artisan British ingredients are at the
heart of his culinary endeavours. Cheltenham
beetroot is packed into samosas, Denham
Estate venison is given the tikka treatment and
there are Goosnargh duck sausages from the
tandoor, while Buccleuch beef fillet is cooked
rare with blisteringly hot red chillies. Todiwala
is a Parsee, so his emblematic version of lamb
dhansak is hard to trump, served with onion
kachumber and a meat kebab embedded in
brown rice. His Goan prawn curry and roasted
pulled pork balchao infused with pickling
spices are further highlights, while desserts
include dinky kulfis. Spice-friendly wines are
mostly sourced from small family vineyards.
Chef/s: Cyrus Todiwala. **Open:** Mon to Fri L, Mon to
Sat D. **Closed:** Sun, 25 Dec to 1 Jan, bank hols.
Meals: main courses £16 to £23. Set L and D £40.
Tasting menu £75. **Details:** 140 seats. Wheelchairs.
Music.

LOCAL GEM

Ceviche

⊖ Old Street, map 4
Peruvian | £30
2 Baldwin Street, Old Street, EC1V 9NU
Tel no: (020) 3327 9463
cevicheuk.com

Housed in an historic workers' dining hall,
Ceviche has brought Peruvian rotisserie
cooking, marinated fish and pisco cocktails to
the previously unsuspecting Old Street

district, supplementing its Soho branch (see
entry). Expect chancho cracklings of pork
belly with chilli jam, spit-roasted chicken
quarters, flame-seared fillet steaks and saltado
peppers, or the house take on citrus-cured fish
such as stone bass. All are sizzling with Latin
flair, hearty in portion and unrestrained in
seasoning, and there's every ethnological
excuse to indulge yourself with chocolate at
the end, unless cassava cake in tamarillo sauce
with quince jelly diverts you. Once you're
thoroughly piscoed, the South American
wines start at £20.

Cinnamon Kitchen

Cooking score: 3
⊖ Liverpool Street, map 4
Indian | £40
9 Devonshire Square, City, EC2M 4YL
Tel no: (020) 7626 5000
cinnamon-kitchen.com

Vivek Singh's City joint is the frisky younger
sibling of Cinnamon Club (see entry), and
with its designer industrial décor, open-to-
view kitchen and modern Indian menu, it's
got the measure of this part of the capital. The
suited and booted can have an express lunch if
required, or linger over the tasting menu (with
a 100-quid wine flight for the big spenders).
British ingredients get a good outing, and
spicing is spot-on. The flavours of Kerala
infuse stir-fried shrimps, with a green mango
chutney on the side, while Kentish lamb is
formed into succulent seekh kebabs and
arrives with a paprika raita. Goan-style pork
cheek vindaloo is a winning curry, or go for a
lamb biryani with aged basmati rice.
Vegetarian courses such as aubergine with
tamarind and peanut crumble don't lack
distinction, and desserts highlight the more
fusion elements. Wines start at £21, with
Anise, the cocktail bar, offering some enticing
alternatives.
Chef/s: Vivek Singh and Ramachandran Raju.
Open: Mon to Fri L, Mon to Sat D. **Closed:** Sun, 25
and 26 Dec, 1 and 29 May, 25 Aug. **Meals:** main
courses £14 to £32. Set L £18 (2 courses) to £21. Set

D £21 (2 courses) to £24. Tasting menu £60.
Details: 150 seats. 70 seats outside. Bar.
Wheelchairs. Music.

City Social

Cooking score: 6
⊖ Liverpool Street, map 4
Modern British | £56
Tower 42, 25 Old Broad Street, City,
EC2N 1HQ
Tel no: (020) 7877 7703
citysociallondon.com

🍾

A City slicker if ever there was one, this suave
outpost of Jason Atherton's Social empire
spreads itself across the 24th floor of the old
NatWest tower, with stunning wraparound
views from every angle of the circular venue.
This is a high-volume, high-decibel
destination done out in brown leather and
dark wood, with shiny metallic ceilings and
horseshoe banquettes, plus an Andy Warhol
original on one wall and a rambunctious bar,
too. Executive chef Paul Walsh's food is all
about freshness, intensity and extraordinarily
vivid flavours – from cured Scottish salmon
with watermelon, saké, cucumber carpaccio
and soy to duck breast with confit leg and
heart, carrot reduction and grilled leeks. There
are char-grilled steaks with duck-fat chips and
béarnaise or peppercorn sauce for the City
crowd, and the kitchen does a nifty line in
pastas and risottos (wild garlic with braised
morels and aged Parmesan, say). To finish,
City Social was the first Atherton venue to
offer pillowy, fluffy soufflés, and they're still
wondrous to behold (try the Yorkshire
rhubarb version in season). The wine list is also
an all-round stunner, stuffed with classy
names, curious discoveries and instantly
appealing by-the-glass selections.
Chef/s: Paul Walsh and Julien Imbert. **Open:** Mon
to Fri L, Mon to Sat D. **Closed:** Sun, bank hols.
Meals: main courses £24 to £36. **Details:** 110 seats.
Bar. Wheelchairs. Music.

The Clove Club

Cooking score: 6
⊖ Old Street, Shoreditch High Street, map 4
Modern European | £75
Shoreditch Town Hall, 380 Old Street,
Shoreditch, EC1V 9LT
Tel no: (020) 7729 6496
thecloveclub.com

The Shoreditch Town Hall is a piece of
Victorian municipal grandeur evolved into an
indispensable arts venue, also housing one of
east London's more eye-catching temples to
the new British cuisine. In surroundings of
canteen-like rough-and-readiness, with the
blue-tiled kitchen on view from bare-wood
tables, a tasting menu format of five or nine
courses explores the range of contemporary
technique with invigorating brio. First up
might be hay-smoked trout tartare in Pink Fir
soup with sansho (Japanese pepper), with a
raw scallop to follow, its delicacy underpinned
by clementine and winter truffle. Red mullet
grilled over hazel wood with calçots and curry
leaves might then pave the way for impeccable
Hebridean lamb, pinkly roasted to sweet
tenderness and offset with prunes, mustard
and mint. A first dessert such as Amalfi
lemonade, served with Cambodian pepper ice
cream, then cedes centre stage to a serving of
Yorkshire rhubarb, aromatic with roses,
accompanied by sheep's milk yoghurt. Wine
pairings at standard or ritzier quality levels are
worth considering. Prices on the main list start
at £7 the small glass.
Chef/s: Isaac McHale and Chase Lovecky. **Open:**
Tue to Sat L, Mon to Sat D. **Closed:** Sun.
Meals: Tasting menus £75 to £110. **Details:** 52
seats. V menu. Bar.

Club Gascon

Cooking score: 5

⊖ Barbican, Farringdon, map 5

Modern French | £50

57 West Smithfield, City, EC1A 9DS

Tel no: (020) 7600 6144

clubgascon.com

Aside from a cool new bar area (Le Bar), Club Gascon's interior is largely unchanged after nigh on 20 years – a room emblazoned with faux-marble walls and extravagant floral displays. From day one, Pascal Aussignac set about distilling the culinary essence of Gascony and unravelling its idiomatic flavours for today's palates – he also instigated small plates long before they became de rigueur everywhere. There's artistry in every department here, from the three kinds of bread with two butters (the lobster version is an 'absolute revelation') to the exceedingly dainty petits fours. Recent successes show the breadth of Aussignac's imagination, from a quinoa risotto 'served within a tulip' to seared scallops with tea-smoked beetroot, hibiscus and wasabi (layer upon layer of sweetness, fragrance and heat) or a clever combination of venison loin, scorched salsify and rhubarb with a floral hint of violet. To finish, Aussignac conjures some seriously pretty and highly technical desserts including a tipsy prune, fennel and pollen soufflé presented in a giant egg cup. A 400-bin treasure trove of wines from France's south-west regions awaits those seeking serious vinous thrills, with back-up from 'vins au verre' by the glass.

Chef/s: Pascal Aussignac. **Open:** Tue to Fri L, Tue to Sat D. **Closed:** Sun, Mon, 23 Dec to 2 Jan. **Meals:** main courses £21 to £29. Set L £25 (2 courses) to £45. Set D £45. Tasting menu £80. **Details:** 42 seats. Bar. Music.

Comptoir Gascon

Cooking score: 3

⊖ Farringdon, Barbican, map 5

French | £28

61-63 Charterhouse Street, Clerkenwell, EC1M 6HJ

Tel no: (020) 7608 0851

comptoirgascon.com

£5 OFF £30

An offshoot of nearby Club Gascon, there's a pleasant hum of activity about this comfortable urban bistro, even at quieter times. The cooking may not surprise or intrigue but you're unlikely to be disappointed by the gloriously unapologetically French comfort food from the south-west, whether duck rillettes, mussels en papillote or saucisse de Toulouse. The list of old favourites also includes onglet de veau with béarnaise and moreish French fries cooked in duck fat, an excellent duck confit served with a 'brilliant' potato cake and bitter leaves with a good mustard dressing, and crème brûlée. A deluxe piggy burger in a brioche bun comes highly recommended, and the côte de boeuf for sharing gets the thumbs-up from many, too. When it comes to dessert, the molten chocolate fondant with pistachio ice cream has been described by one fan as 'perfect'. Wine-wise, it's a short list exclusively from the south-west that could offer more by the glass.

Chef/s: Valentin Verdenet. **Open:** Tue to Sat L and D. **Closed:** Sun, Mon, 24 Dec to 2 Jan, bank hols. **Meals:** main courses £7 to £23. **Details:** 35 seats. 6 seats outside. Wheelchairs. Music.

The Culpeper

Cooking score: 2

⊖ Aldgate East, map 4

Modern European | £35

40 Commercial Street, Whitechapel, E1 6LP

Tel no: (020) 7247 5371

theculpeper.com

Up on the roof is an impressively productive greenhouse supplying seasonal ingredients for Culpeper's kitchen – plus a summertime bar and grill for outdoor gatherings. It's just part of the deal at entrepreneur Nico Treguer's multi-purpose City pub and restaurant-with-rooms. Drink local beers, herb-infused cocktails and trendy international wines in the street-level bar, while foodie interest centres on a first-floor dining room done out in a bright, smart urban style. Come here for plates of Scottish langoustines dressed with tarragon mayonnaise, wood pigeon Wellington or Cornish monkfish with shellfish bisque and samphire. Alternatively, share the spoils from a 50-day aged côte de boeuf or a whole turbot with brown butter, new potatoes, almonds and parsley, before rounding off with lemon posset or bitter chocolate pot. A regular timetable of astronomy events, 'edible botanical drawing' and gardening workshops reflects the chosen pursuits of namesake Nicholas Culpeper – 17th-century herbalist and polymath extraordinaire.

Chef/s: Sandy Jarvis and Antonio Santos da Mota. **Open:** Tue to Fri and Sun L, Tue to Sat D. **Closed:** Mon, 25 to 30 Dec. **Meals:** main courses £13 to £18. **Details:** 38 seats. Bar. Music.

Please send us your feedback

To register your opinion about any restaurant listed in this guide, or a new restaurant that you wish to bring to our attention, please visit the web address at the bottom of the page. Your feedback informs the content of the book and will be used to compile next year's reviews.

★ NEW ENTRY ★

La Dame de Pic

Cooking score: 6

⊖ Tower Hill, map 4

French | £80

Four Seasons Hotel London at Ten Trinity Square, Tower Hill, EC3N 4AJ

Tel no: (020) 3297 3799

ladamedepiclondon.co.uk

When Anne-Sophie Pic announced she was opening her first UK restaurant at a Tower Bridge location, some wondered if this showed a lack of understanding of the capital's restaurant scene. Surely Mayfair is a more natural home for France's top female chef? But it's a shrewd move. Pic's spacious ground-floor restaurant is part of a concerted attempt by Four Seasons to turn this modern hotel (in the striking Port of London Authority building overlooking the Thames) into one of the landmarks of London's luxury constellation. Although the set lunch is a bargain, and the unclothed tables reflect current restaurant trends, the tall windows, high ceilings and a discreet white, brown and caramel colour scheme speak of comfort and money. The menu, meanwhile, speaks of current fashionable things in France: Cornish crab, steamed and seasoned with lovage mayonnaise and layered over blackcurrant and elderflower jelly, perhaps, followed by veal sweetbreads baked with Gruyère and Ethiopian coffee alongside white asparagus and wild garlic leaf, with Pic's signature 'the white mille-feuille' as a fitting finale. This is serious cooking, albeit at a price on the carte and tasting menu. The waiting crew – a skilled team – set it apart. The wines, like the food, don't stint on quality or variety.

Chef/s: Anne-Sophie Pic. **Open:** all week L, Mon to Sat D. **Meals:** main courses £32 to £42. Set L £29 (2 courses) to £39. Tasting menu £105 (6 courses). **Details:** 78 seats. V menu.

Dishoom

Cooking score: 2

⊖ Old Street, Liverpool Street, map 4
Indian | £30

7 Boundary Street, Shoreditch, E2 7JE
Tel no: (020) 7420 9324
dishoom.com

The four-strong Dishoom group is a well-regarded London asset (a fifth branch is in Edinburgh), famed as much for not looking like an Indian restaurant as for a casual approach to its cuisine. This Shoreditch branch, with its hard-edged vibes, clamorous buzz and unfailing congeniality, makes the art of retaining customer loyalty appear effortless. Like its siblings, it opens early enough for breakfast – the bacon naan roll is a big hit – and the cooking gives a spin to trademark Indian classics with Anglo-Indian undertones. Spicy lamb chops, aromatic chicken biryani, mattar paneer, masala prawns and the signature house black dhal, arrive in a seemingly haphazard way, but as a distilled vision of good Indian cooking the dishes are interesting and enticing. Mango kulfi would be an appropriately Indian finale, but there's also chocolate pudding served with a scoop of Kashmiri chilli ice cream. Ales and lagers, cocktails and a spice-friendly wine list (from £20) all help keep the place busy.
Chef/s: Naved Nasir. **Open:** all week, all day from 8am (9am Sat and Sun). **Closed:** 25 and 26 Dec, 1 and 2 Jan. **Meals:** main courses £6 to £23. **Details:** 235 seats. Music.

The Don

Cooking score: 3

⊖ Bank, Cannon Street, map 4
Modern European | £42

The Courtyard, 20 St Swithin's Lane, City, EC4N 8AD
Tel no: (020) 7626 2606
thedonrestaurant.co.uk

🍾

The Don was the mark of Sandeman, importers of port dating back to 1798, and whose former offices are tucked away in a courtyard, making an unusually tranquil setting for a City restaurant. However, the main dining room (there is also a bistro) is modern with well-spaced white-clad tables and showcases abstract artwork by John Hoyland. New chef Frederick Forster has revamped the menu and brought things more up to date, impressing at a test meal with a trio of plump, perfectly cooked Orkney scallops with a crushed pea raviolo, avocado purée and a lemon dressing, and Landes pigeon paired with baked beetroot and Madeira cream. Well-timed turbot with English asparagus, gnocchi and an 'excellent' broth infused with cockles made a handsome main course, with Braeburn apple Tatin and vanilla ice cream a satisfying finale. The wine list is a blockbuster, with a lot of good drinking for all budgets and there's a fine collection of port, sherry and Madeira. It's no wonder that this is a favourite spot for business dining in this part of town.
Chef/s: Frederick Forster. **Open:** Mon to Fri L and D. **Closed:** Sat, Sun, last week Dec, bank hols. **Meals:** main courses £18 to £32. Set L and D £27 (2 courses) to £32. **Details:** 90 seats. Bar.

Duck & Waffle

Cooking score: 2

⊖ Liverpool Street, map 4
International | £35

Heron Tower, 40th floor, 110 Bishopsgate, City, EC2N 4AY
Tel no: (020) 3640 7310
duckandwaffle.com

You'll need a head for heights as lifts whisk you up to this vibrant 24-hour venue on the 40th floor in 40 seconds. Needless to say the cityscape views are some of the most spectacular in the capital, and thankfully the décor doesn't try to compete with the eagle's nest view. Impeccable grazing food is what is on offer, the mix-and-match menu of snacks, small plates and sharing dishes a mash-up of American, Mediterranean and British influences. Expect lots of sweet-savoury combinations, not only in the titular duck and waffle (a successful combination of duck confit, fried duck egg and mustard maple syrup), but also bacon-wrapped dates with linguiça sausage, and maple-glazed cornbread with harissa yoghurt. Otherwise, there could be miso-glazed rabbit with roasted cauliflower, suet biscuit and crispy cabbage, and whole sea bass with potato and samphire ragoût. Cocktails are very good; the wine list is short and modern. A recent offshoot is Duck & Waffle Local, to be found in St James's Market, SW1.

Chef/s: Tom Cenci. **Open:** all week 24-hour opening. **Meals:** main courses £10 to £40. **Details:** 120 seats. Bar. Wheelchairs. Music.

The Eagle

Cooking score: 2
Farringdon, map 5
Modern European | £20
159 Farringdon Road, Clerkenwell, EC1R 3AL
Tel no: (020) 7837 1353
theeaglefarringdon.co.uk
£30

Nowadays, this city pub on the stretch of main road between Clerkenwell Road and Rosebery Avenue may seem like any other high street hostelry, with its stripped-back, knocked around the edges look. But when Michael Belben first took over in 1991, he virtually reinvented London's pub scene, and the Eagle was famed for robust British-Mediterranean dishes and a freewheeling, high-decibel space that never bothered to distinguish between drinkers and diners. Imitated many times over, the basic kitchen behind the bar is now an Eagle signature, as is the fight for tables at busy times. Dishes are hearty enough for one-course meals – even red lentil dhal soup with coconut milk and spinach. Elsewhere there's pork belly with pomegranate molasses, white beans and salsa verde or fish tagine with couscous. Steak sandwich is never off the menu, nor are pastéis de nata. The compact wine list comes by the glass or bottle (from £15.30).

Chef/s: Ed Mottershaw. **Open:** all week L, Mon to Sat D. **Closed:** 10 days Christmas, bank hols. **Meals:** main courses £9 to £16. **Details:** 65 seats. 16 seats outside. Music.

8 Hoxton Square

Cooking score: 3
Old Street, map 4
Modern European | £35
8-9 Hoxton Square, Hoxton, N1 6NU
Tel no: (020) 7729 4232
8hoxtonsquare.com

This is the sibling of 10 Greek Street (see entry), and instead of acting like a too-cool-for-school Shoreditch upstart it operates on a more grown-up level. Its restrained modern interior goes bare on napery and big on brick, with low lighting and requisite pendant lamps (there's courtyard dining for warmer months). Like the simple décor, the food is confidently no-frills, with the kitchen's focus on the best of British produce, with some welcome inflections from warmer climes – prawns with fennel, clementine and 'nduja, say. The daily changing blackboard menu of starters and mains also features small plates, which are served all day and suit each-to-their-own or sharing. Dexter onglet with sprouting broccoli, shallots and horseradish, or meticulously cooked Tamworth pork with celeriac, kale and apple might come next, followed by a blood-orange sorbet with Campari. Sunday roasts are a big draw too. Wine from the ever-evolving list of small-scale producers includes over 20 by the small glass or carafe (£2.50 or £9), but do take note of co-proprietor Luke Wilson's 'Little Black Book' of rarer, fine bottles.

Chef/s: Cameron Emirali and Jesus Sanchez Munoz. **Open:** Tue to Fri L, Mon to Fri D. Sat, all day from 10. Sun 10 to 5. **Meals:** main courses £16 to £20. **Details:** 45 seats. 24 seats outside.

Symbols

Accommodation is available
Three courses for less than £30
£5-off voucher scheme
Notable wine list

Ellory

Cooking score: 3

⊖ London Fields, map 1

Modern European | £35

Netil House, 1 Westgate Street, Hackney,
E8 3RL

Tel no: (020) 3095 9455

ellorylondon.com

Hackney's Ellory is a 'neighbourhood restaurant' fit for arty E8. Tucked beneath the cluster of studios at Netil House, it's not much to look at: the concrete floor, marble bar and record player (played so loud our table vibrated) are the norm round here. What distinguishes Ellory is its commitment to seasonal produce and serious European wines. From the short sharing menu, we enjoyed pristine ingredients cooked with a delicate touch, such as white asparagus, mussels and lardo with a dab of wild garlic cream that melted into the light fish broth just so. Turbot with sorrel and potato purée was simple and elegant, too. Individually, some simpler plates risk underwhelming; taken together in the four-course menu, they find harmony. Alphonso mango sorbet with whipped cream and macadamias was a case in point: pleasant but not technically the equal of preceding plates. Knowledgeable waiters can assist with the unannotated wine list.

Chef/s: Sam Kamienko. **Open:** Sat and Sun L, all week D. **Closed:** 24 Dec to 2 Jan. **Meals:** main courses £15 to £25. Set L £26 (2 courses) to £30. Tasting menu £42. **Details:** 48 seats. Bar. Wheelchairs. Music.

Eyre Brothers

Cooking score: 3

⊖ Old Street, map 4

Spanish-Portuguese | £35

68-70 Leonard Street, Shoreditch, EC2A 4QX

Tel no: (020) 7613 5346

eyrebrothers.co.uk

Portuguese food is having a 'moment', or so says the lifestyle press. This might amuse David Eyre, who has been championing the culinary culture of the Iberian Peninsula at Shoreditch's Eyre Brothers since 2001. As one of this trendy postcode's more grown-up spots, Eyre Bros comprises eating counter, colourfully tiled lounge bar and a 'white tablecloth' dining room. Authenticity and full-on flavour are what counts here, and the extensive menu covers everything from tapas, to eggs, grills and 'special order' whole roast beasts and paellas (pre-order only). Open with simple tapas of stewed beans with garlic and olive oil, gambas al ajillo or one of the generous salads such as home-cured salt cod 'ensalada malagueña' with orange and black olives. Mozambique tiger prawns and massive chuletón T-bones for two to three are the signatures to follow. The all-Iberian wine list starts at £19.

Chef/s: David Eyre. **Open:** all week L, Mon to Sat D. **Meals:** main courses £12 to £25. **Details:** 84 seats. Bar. Wheelchairs. Music.

Galvin HOP

Cooking score: 2

⊖ Liverpool Street, map 4

Modern British | £28

35 Spital Square, Spitalfields, E1 6DY

Tel no: (020) 7299 0404

galvinrestaurants.com

£30

A reworking of the Galvin brothers' Café à Vin, and next to their flagship La Chapelle (see entry), Galvin HOP is a self-styled 'pub deluxe' where beer (Pilsner is dispensed from vast copper tanks on top of the bar) has replaced its predecessor's focus on wine. City suits are drawn to the gourmet dogs and burgers (served with chips) and hearty modern pub classics such as Dorset crab on toast, fish pie and braised Denham Estate venison. There's also a grill section, offering the likes of Saddleback pork cutlet or Loch Duart salmon steak, watercress and homemade crisps. Portions are ample, but it is worth finding room for high-on-the-comfort-factor desserts such as treacle tart with clotted cream or a Valrhona choux bun.

The compact wine list kicks off at £20.50 and rarely looks beyond France and Italy. Around 10 wines are served by the glass or carafe. **Chef/s:** Chris Barrett. **Open:** all week, all day from 11.30. **Closed:** 24 to 26 Dec, 1 Jan. **Meals:** main courses £7 to £20. Set L and D £17 (2 courses) to £20. Sun L £17. **Details:** 65 seats. 100 seats outside. Bar. Wheelchairs. Music. Parking.

Galvin La Chapelle

Cooking score: 5
⊖ Liverpool Street, map 4
French | £70
35 Spital Square, Spitalfields, E1 6DY
Tel no: (020) 7299 0400
galvinrestaurants.com

Built as part of a girl's school in 1890, with time served as a parish hall and gymnasium, Galvin La Chapelle is quite a set-up. Amid the spectacular church-like interior with its striking modern mezzanine is a fine-dining restaurant where Jeff Galvin's luxurious, technically astute and high-gloss cuisine fits the setting like a velvet glove. Of course, there is much from the purebred French repertoire, perhaps a ballotine of Landes foie gras with hazelnut, quince and brioche, and pavé of wild turbot with fennel purée, razor clams and sauce genevoise, but there's also crisp Galician octopus with red pepper dressing, smoked duck breast and Redlove apples, while a dish of golden and ruby beetroot takes a different turn with walnuts, goats' cheese fondue and raspberry dressing. Desserts also flit between different worlds, offering a classic apple tarte Tatin with Normandy crème fraîche, and gariguette strawberry pannacotta with sage crumble and strawberry sorbet. The carefully curated wine list is superb. Top names from classic regions in France come first, including a run of Jaboulet's Hermitage La Chapelle back to 1952, but there's a short, interesting global spread, too.

Chef/s: Jeff Galvin and Eric Jolibois. **Open:** all week L and D. **Closed:** 24 to 26 Dec, 1 Jan. **Meals:** main courses £29 to £39. Set L and D £29 (2courses) to £35. Tasting menu £75. **Details:** 110 seats. 30 seats outside. Bar. Wheelchairs. Music.

Gunpowder

Cooking score: 2
⊖ Liverpool Street, Aldgate East, map 4
Indian | £25
11 White's Row, Spitalfields, E1 7NF
Tel no: (020) 7426 0542
gunpowderlondon.com
£30

Gunpowder promises home-style Indian cooking in a modest package. In this case a tiny, densely packed, bare-brick restaurant with an appealing lack of gimmickry and a humility that comes through in the excellent service and the stripped-down menu with its reasonable prices. First-rate aloo chaat and spicy venison and vermicelli doughnut are fresh and sharp. Spices are distinct and the vegetable dishes – porzhi okra fries, bhuna aubergine and crispy kale salad – particularly noteworthy, while Chettinad pulled duck, which is sandwiched in a light oothappam (rather like a rich lentil pizza), and maa's Kashmiri lamb chops have been praised by reporters. Popular, too, are creamy saag with tandoori paneer and organic baby chicken char-grilled in tandoori spices. Finish with Old Monk rum pudding, a boozy version of bread-and-butter pudding. Drink beer or something from the short wine list, which opens at £20. Sister venue Madame D., focusing on Himalayan cooking, can be found at 76 Commercial Street, E1 6LY.

Chef/s: Nirmal Save. **Open:** Mon to Sat L and D. **Closed:** Sun, 25 and 26 Dec. **Meals:** main courses £8 to £16. **Details:** 28 seats. Music.

Hawksmoor Guildhall

Cooking score: 4
⊖ Bank, map 4
British | £45
10-12 Basinghall Street, City, EC2V 5BQ
Tel no: (020) 7397 8120
thehawksmoor.com

In its wood-panelled ambience, the Guildhall outpost of Beckett and Gott's steakhouse group feels a little like a parliamentary dining room. It's only a T-bone's throw from the site of a Georgian establishment called Dolly's, which may have been London's first ever steakhouse, and the tradition is still going strong today in the form of chateaubriands, porterhouses, sirloins, rumps and ribeyes, sold by judiciously calculated weight, with a choice of sauces – béarnaise, peppercorn, anchovy hollandaise, bone-marrow gravy or a blue cheese version made with Stichelton – and optionally garnished with bacon, fried eggs or lobster. What better than to preface all that with some handsome seafood, perhaps roast scallops in white port and garlic, or a satisfying plate of smoked salmon, and then round it off with a hunk of peanut-butter shortbread or passion fruit cheesecake? In other words, come hungry, is what they're saying. A wine list that gets into four figures completes the picture, though the glasses start at £4.50.

Chef/s: Phillip Branch. **Open:** Mon to Fri L and D. **Closed:** Sat, Sun, 24 to 30 Dec, 1 Jan, bank hols. **Meals:** main courses £12 to £40. Set L and early D £25 (2 courses) to £28. **Details:** 160 seats. Bar. Wheelchairs. Music.

Hawksmoor Spitalfields

Cooking score: 3
⊖ Liverpool Street, Aldgate East, map 4
British | £55
157a Commercial Street, City, E1 6BJ
Tel no: (020) 7426 4850
thehawksmoor.co.uk

Will Beckett and Huw Gott's homage to beef has become something of a dining institution since it opened in 2006. Several branches later, there's still a lot to like about this original

venue, especially the cocktails in the basement bar. Above all, it's a beacon of quality, whether you are in for a massive porterhouse or a simple rump steak 'so tender and delicious' – served with a choice of sauces (say béarnaise or peppercorn) and sides of macaroni cheese, roasted field mushrooms, purple sprouting broccoli with anchovy butter and the like. Start with bone marrow with onions, and go on to baked lemon sole or herb-fed chicken grilled with garlic butter if you're not in the mood for beef. Finish with Amalfi lemon and elderflower meringue tart. There's a strong following for Sunday roasts with all the trimmings, and the wine list features plenty of sturdy reds (from £23) but pitched at deep pockets.

Chef/s: Pavlos Costa. **Open:** Mon to Sat L and D. Sun, all day from 12. **Closed:** 25 and 26 Dec, 1 Jan. **Meals:** main courses £12 to £40. Set L and D £25 (2 courses) to £28. Sun L £20. **Details:** 116 seats. Bar. Music.

HKK London

Cooking score: 6
⊖ Liverpool Street, map 4
Chinese | £88
Broadgate West, Worship Street, City, EC2A 2BE
Tel no: (020) 3535 1888
hkklondon.com

🍾

HKK's muted appearance gives little away, but beyond its polite décor lies prodigious culinary talent and the Hakkasan group's most avant-garde kitchen. White china peaches (a symbol of longevity in Chinese culture) hang over a central serving station in the low-key dining space, where your gaze is naturally drawn towards the glass wall, behind which executive head chef Tong Chee Hwee's team turn out top-flight, innovative food. Unlike the sharing ethos at its sibling restaurants, here the focus is on haute tasting menus that explore the diversity of Chinese cuisine. Traditional Eastern cooking methods, modern tools and artistry coalesce in some extraordinary dishes: wild green Wagyu beef

might start things off, followed by a dim sum 'trio', then the show stopper: exquisite Peking duck served three ways, enabling the lacquered skin and smoky, delicate meat to be savoured in heady isolation. Desserts feature a conflation of cultural influences, taking in classic technique and oriental flourishes to create a Jasmine parfait with poached rhubarb and barley ice cream or perhaps a matcha dacquoise. Notably, all food-friendly wines from the forward-thinking global list are available by the glass, with a specialist saké selection, too.
Chef/s: Tong Chee Hwee. **Open:** Mon to Sat L and D. **Closed:** Sun, 25 and 26 Dec, bank hols. **Meals:** main courses L only £15 to £38. Tasting menu £94. **Details:** 72 seats. V menu. Wheelchairs. Music.

★ NEW ENTRY ★

James Cochran EC3

Cooking score: 5
⊖ Aldgate, map 4
Modern British
19 Bevis Marks, City, EC3A 7JA
Tel no: (020) 3302 0310
jcochran.restaurant

£5
OFF

Laid-back, casual and with a hip utilitarian vibe you don't expect in the City, there's little sign, inside or out, to suggest that seriously good food is on offer – this is a venue that has been through a few incarnations in recent years. But ex-Ledbury chef James Cochran (see entry) has stamped his identity firmly above the door and in the kitchen. His small-plates menu (sharing, of course) is mostly high on umami, from sourdough spread with whipped chicken butter, via smoked cod's roe with radish and seaweed, to the powerful umami-hit in a dish of crispy cauliflower with base notes of coconut, yoghurt, peanuts and pomegranate. Then there's the spectacular full-on crunch in pork kromeski, and the coalition of salt, crunch and creaminess of Jamaican jerk buttermilk chicken, given just a touch of heat from Scotch bonnet jam, while a magnificent main dish of Herdwick lamb (haunch and braised neck), is all sweetness and softness, given heft by kim-chee and wild garlic pesto and underscored by yoghurt. Gentle pricing extends to the short and modern wine list, which opens at £28.
Chef/s: James Cochran. **Open:** Mon to Fri L, Mon to Sat D. **Closed:** Sun. **Meals:** main courses £20 to £26. Tasting menu £45. **Details:** 45 seats. V menu. Bar. Music.

Jidori

Cooking score: 2
⊖ Dalston Kingsland, map 2
Japanese | £20
89 Kingsland Road, Hackney, E8 2PB
Tel no: (020) 7686 5634
jidori.co.uk

£30

Chicken yakitori is the name of the game at this 'cracking little place' on Kingsland Road. Two sticks per portion, from birds brought up at Fosse Meadows Farm in Leicestershire, cooked right there in the room over charcoal on the custom-made grill shipped over from Tokyo. It's an enticing proposition, whether you're perched at the counter with a view of the action, or seated at one of the utilitarian tables. Chicken may rule the roost, but there's also mackerel tartare with mandarin and young ginger ponzu, or spinach ohitashi on the small plates menu, ideal for sharing. Among those yakitori skewers, negima is thigh meat with spring onion, hearts and bacon speaks for itself, and you know what the parson's nose is. Dessert remains a one off – ginger ice cream with miso caramel, sweet potato crisps and black sesame, although a cocktail such as the yuzu daiquiri might be just the thing. Drink Japanese beer, saké and/or whiskey.
Chef/s: Shunta Matsubara. **Open:** Wed to Fri L, Mon to Sat D. **Closed:** Sun. **Meals:** small plates £3 to £8. **Details:** 44 seats. Wheelchairs. Music.

José Pizarro

Cooking score: 2

⊖ Liverpool Street, map 4

Spanish | £28

36 Broadgate Circle, City, EC2M 1QS

Tel no: (020) 7256 5333

josepizarro.com

£30

Among Broadgate Circle's multifarious eating and drinking opportunities, José Pizarro is among the more compelling. The third venture in the group, with legs of Ibérico ham hanging above the counter, and a sensibly short menu that focuses on cured meats, tapas favourites such as croquetas and a few modern additions such as mini Ibérico pork burgers with Manchego and aïoli, or hake with fennel purée. The contemporary space suits the casual vibe, with comfy leather stools and a few tables outside in the Circle. The likes of patatas bravas and spicy prawn fritters have broad appeal, and there's sometimes a little twist such as salsa verde with the boquerones. A selection of charcuterie is a good way to go, with a Spanish cheeseboard (with membrillo) a good meat-free alternative. Drink sherry, Spanish wines or Estrella Damm on draught. A fourth sibling, Little José, is opening in Crossrail Place, Canary Wharf.

Chef/s: José Pizarro. **Open:** Mon to Sat, all day from 11.30. **Closed:** Sun, 2 weeks Dec, bank hols. **Meals:** main courses £12 to £17. **Details:** 40 seats. 24 seats outside. Wheelchairs. Music.

Lardo

Cooking score: 2

⊖ London Fields, map 1

Italian | £27

205 Richmond Road, Hackney, E8 3NJ

Tel no: (020) 8985 2683

lardo.co.uk

£5 OFF £30

Close to London Fields, Lardo has all the accoutrements of a modern city eatery – big glass frontage, open-plan kitchen, café ambience perfect for kicking back, but without the big city prices. Indeed, there's the thrum of constant activity in the tightly packed dining room where appreciative diners of all ages tuck into deftly executed Italian cooking. Passion for quality runs through every aspect, from a selection of salumi to antipasti of spinach, goats' cheese rotolo and walnuts, or cotechino with Puy lentils, and mains of barramundi with roast potatoes, Italian greens, garlic and chilli. Pizza, wood-fired in the Neapolitan style, remains a strength, with praise for tomato, black anise pepperoni, mozzarella and rocket, and pasta is also pitch-perfect. Chestnut torte with gelati is a good way to finish. Gluten- and dairy-free menus are a plus. It's all washed down with imaginative cocktails, and a short, modern wine list bursting with organic and natural options.

Chef/s: Matthew Cranston. **Open:** all week, all day from 12. **Closed:** 24 Dec to 2 Jan. **Meals:** main courses £14 to £20. **Details:** 54 seats. 48 seats outside. Bar. Wheelchairs. Music.

★ NEW ENTRY ★

The Laughing Heart

Cooking score: 3

⊖ Bethnal Green, Hoxton, map 1

International | £35

277 Hackney Road, Hackney, E2 8NA

Tel no: (020) 7686 9535

thelaughingheartlondon.com

The Laughing Heart is one of east London's crop of new-wave wine bars. Its focus is on scintillating small plates and edgy wines in a raucous environment. So far, so Hackney. What gives the Laughing Heart the edge, however, is its 2am closing time. (Don't be surprised to find yourself supping with post-shift hospitality types if you keep those hours.) Tom Anglesea's menu takes fine ingredients and liberates them from their usual regional shackles. Hence stuffed olives with Thai spices; Scottish salmon crudo with pungent nam jim; and tender white asparagus with smoked nori, a dish that's delicious to the point of indecorous. At inspection, gnocchi with confit egg yolk and raw shiitake and Belted

Galloway with fresh sardine butter weren't so well judged. Prices soon mount, particularly once you start wine shopping: the whole list (from such cult producers as Le Coste and Gut Oggau) is available to go.

Chef/s: Tom Anglesea. **Open:** Wed to Sat D. Sun, all day from 12. **Closed:** Mon, Tue. **Meals:** small plates £8 to £20. **Details:** 40 seats. Bar. Music.

★ NEW ENTRY ★

Luca

Cooking score: 3
⊖ Farringdon, Barbican, map 5
Italian | £35
88 St John Street, Clerkenwell, EC1M 4EH
Tel no: (020) 3859 3000
luca.restaurant

This offshoot of the Clove Club (see entry) is a much bigger, slicker operation offering 'none of the scruffy, no-frills charm' of its trailblazing parent. Instead, there's designer décor (caramel, coffee cream, brick and polished wood), a popular, crowded, narrow entrance bar (with bar snacks) widening into a dining area and impressive double-height glass-walled extension. Inspiration is Britalian – aka prime British produce with an Italian accent – so expect a traditionally constructed menu that opens with antipasti such as devilled Cornish spider crab bruschetta or tartare of Hereford beef cured in Italian wine, before gliding on through pasta, say rigatoni with pork sausage, tomato, anchovy and mint, to mains of Hebridean lamb chops with rosemary breadcrumbs and crushed vegetables or Cornish pollack alla puttanesca. The fresh-baked poppy-seed-crusted sourdough, the genuinely committed staff and the excellent cocktails are much appreciated. Likewise the modern Italian wine list (from £26), which makes for fascinating exploration.

Chef/s: Isaac McHale and Robert Chambers. **Open:** Mon to Sat L and D, 12 to 5 Sun. **Meals:** main courses £21 to £25. **Details:** 70 seats. Bar. Wheelchairs. Music.

Lyle's

Cooking score: 5
⊖ Shoreditch High Street, map 4
Modern British | £55
56 Shoreditch High Street, Shoreditch, E1 6JJ
Tel no: (020) 3011 5911
lyleslondon.com

In the white-tiled, concrete-floored and oak-tabled environment of his spartan Shoreditch restaurant, James Lowe's seasonal dishes – on simple, round white plates – stand in for works of art. Lowe hails from the minimalist British school (he was head chef at Fergus Henderson's St John Bread and Wine – see entry) but has found his own clear voice. The lunch menu is mainly small plates, designed, not always terribly well, for sharing. Traditional ingredients are reimagined and reinvigorated, such as Jersey rock oysters and salted gooseberries, a vision in silver and gold; mutton breast and mint sauce; and turbot, sea aster and new season's garlic. Dinner, at £55, represents value for a set four courses that might include Saddleback, artichokes and fennel pollen, sea kale and mussels, and baked cream and rhubarb to finish. Neal's Yard cheese is £9 extra: the homemade crackers are worth the supplement alone. The thoughtfully assembled cellar – France figures high – has some real gems by the glass.

Chef/s: James Lowe. **Open:** Mon to Sat L and D. **Closed:** Sun, 2 weeks Christmas, bank hols. **Meals:** small plates £9 to £24 (L only). Set D £55 (4 courses). **Details:** 44 seats. V menu. Wheelchairs. Music.

The Marksman

Cooking score: 3
⊖ Cambridge Heath, Hoxton, map 1
British | £35
254 Hackney Road, Hackney, E2 7SJ
Tel no: (020) 7739 7393
marksmanpublichouse.com

The heart and soul of this old Hackney Road boozer lives on. They have faith here in the great British institution: a pub it remains. The bar is rich with wooden panelling and is usually stocked with London ales and fashionable craft beers, while some designer touches in the dining room acknowledge the fact that this is indeed the 21st century and Hoxton is just down the road. It's a winning combination, made all the more compelling by the food that comes out of the kitchen. Smoked cod's roe and devilled pig's skin is surf and turf for the hipster generation, clams with purslane and dill is perfect simplicity itself, and Aylesbury duck breast with turnips and anchovy is comforting and restorative. A couple of pies for sharing seem entirely in keeping, and desserts such as a brown-butter and honey tart confirm the capabilities of the team in the kitchen. The European-focused wine list is arranged by style.

Chef/s: Tom Harris and Jon Rotheram. **Open:** Fri and Sat L, Mon to Sat D. Sun 12 to 8. **Meals:** main courses £14 to £24. Set L and D £26 (2 courses) to £35. Sun L £26 (2 courses) to £30. Tasting menu £75. **Details:** 70 seats. 20 seats outside. Bar. Wheelchairs. Music.

Merchants Tavern

Cooking score: 4
♆ Old Street, map 4
Modern European | £45
36 Charlotte Road, Shoreditch, EC2A 3PG
Tel no: (020) 7060 5335
merchantstavern.co.uk

Elements of the Victorian building's industrial past may well be exposed as part of the fashionably retro design, but Angela Harnett's Merchants Tavern is far more chic than shabby. It's a big old space, with a bar with occasional live music and DJs adding to the feel-good vibe, and a restaurant headed up by Neil Borthwick. The menu reflects the seasons and gives equal weight to British and European preparations, thus Portland crab might appear in a nicely balanced salad, and cauliflower risotto gets textural relief from toasted hazelnuts. Braised ox cheek arrives with smoky creamed potatoes, with pickled red onion to cut through its richness, while cuttlefish with polenta and fennel is full of Mediterranean promise. Lemon and basil

posset with salted oats makes for a refreshing finale. The lunch menu might include a chicken, leek and mushroom pie. The classy wine list has some interesting options by the glass and carafe.

Chef/s: Neil Borthwick. **Open:** all week L and D. **Closed:** 25 and 26 Dec, 1 Jan. **Meals:** main courses £17 to £25. Tasting menu £50 to £60. **Details:** 108 seats. Bar. Wheelchairs.

The Modern Pantry

Cooking score: 3
♆ Farringdon, map 5
Fusion | £37
47-48 St John's Square, Clerkenwell, EC1V 4JJ
Tel no: (020) 7553 9210
themodernpantry.co.uk
£5
OFF

Anna Hansen's idea of the modern pantry is famously vast and varied. Both here and in the new City branch, she and her team think nothing of pulling out, say, Scottish salmon, Iranian lime, tomatillos and plantains to use together on a single small plate. It works, in the main, because flavour and texture are refereed with a firm hand, and the effect is breezy and brunch-like even after darkness falls. Start with the house special, sugar-cured-prawn omelette with a kick of smoked chilli sambal and scattering of green chilli, spring onion and coriander, or an asparagus and Jerusalem artichoke salad with a dressing combining lime, sumac and truffle. Mains might be a Thai yellow veg curry or expertly cooked onglet with cassava chips, and puddings such as coconut rice pudding, with garam masala brûlée banana and coconut flakes, are a real highlight. Wine matches are always going to be tricky; try fizz or beer.

Chef/s: Robert McLeary. **Open:** all week L and D. **Closed:** 25 and 26 Dec, Aug bank hol. **Meals:** main courses £16 to £21. **Details:** 100 seats. 36 seats outside. Wheelchairs. Music.

Monty's Deli

Cooking score: 2
⊖ Hoxton, map 2
Jewish | £20
227-229 Hoxton Street, Hoxton, N1 5LH
Tel no: (020) 7729 5737
montys-deli.com

£30

Mark Ogus and Owen Barratt have relinquished their Bermondsey railway arch stall for this permanent part-deli, part-diner spot in Hoxton, much to the delight of their devoted fan base. Channelling the New York Jewish deli aesthetic, Monty's is named in tribute to Mark's grandfather who grew up nearby. Its appealing, spacious modern-retro interior comes complete with worn Victorian wall tiles and chequered floor: nab a stool at the bar and watch the meat being carved and the sandwiches filled, or take a booth. Everything on the no-frills menu is hand-crafted and preserves the best of Jewish culinary heritage, but authenticity is secondary to taste here. Try simple pastrami on rye or a stuffed-to-bursting Reuben special with buttery-soft, hand-carved salt beef and peppery pastrami, pickles, cheese and 'kraut. The chewy bagels, baked on cedar planks wrapped in hessian, won't disappoint the cognoscenti. Weekend brunch brings you salt beef hash and challah French toast and come evening there's a traditional Shabbat dinner (not just on Fridays), meatballs, cholent and Kiddush wines.
Chef/s: Mark Ogus and Owen Barratt. **Open:** Tue to Sat L and D. Sun 11 to 5. **Closed:** Mon. **Meals:** sandwiches £8 to £13. **Details:** 65 seats.

Symbols

🛏 Accommodation is available
£30 Three courses for less than £30
£5 OFF £5-off voucher scheme
🍾 Notable wine list

Morito Exmouth Market

Cooking score: 3
⊖ Farringdon, map 2
Spanish/North African | £30
32 Exmouth Market, Clerkenwell, EC1R 4QE
Tel no: (020) 7278 7007
morito.co.uk

Cram yourself in to one of the little tables along the wall or perch up at the bar in the pint-sized Morito, next door to old-stager Moro (see entry). As bookings are not taken in the evenings, order early and order often for nibbles and small plates of vividly seasoned, authentic Spanish tapas. Croquetas of ham and chicken or salt cod should charge up the appetite for the likes of braised squid with peas and flat beans, lamb chops rubbed with cumin and paprika, and vegetable dishes such as minted smashed courgettes, beetroot borani with feta, dill and walnuts, or the self-styled 'fantastic carrots' with spiced labneh. North African spice notes are never far away, and don't miss the concluding elements, when chocolate and olive oil mousse with hazelnuts, or grilled tetilla cheese with membrillo and walnuts are to hand. Drinking is fun, too, from glasses of pomegranated cava to vermouths, sherries and reliable Spanish wines from £20.
Chef/s: Samantha Clark. **Open:** all week L, Mon to Sat D. **Meals:** tapas £3 to £10. **Details:** 36 seats. 6 seats outside. Wheelchairs. Music.

Morito Hackney

Cooking score: 4
⊖ Hoxton, map 2
Spanish/North African | £30
195 Hackney Road, Hackney, E2 8JL
Tel no: (020) 7613 0754
moritohackneyroad.co.uk

It's 20 years since Sam and Samantha Clark opened Moro in Exmouth market, and the flavours of the southern and eastern Med were put centre stage. They've inspired a lot of chefs in that time, and influenced the culinary landscape, with cookbooks and a trio of restaurants spreading the word (see entries,

Moro and Morito). The newest address, in Hackney Road, puts you in 'holiday mood' even on a wet Wednesday, with its horseshoe marble-topped bar, open kitchen and sunny disposition. The chef hails from Crete, which fits rather nicely, and the menu includes opportunities for meze sharing such as gilda (a classic Basque pintxo, with anchovies, tomato and guindilla peppers), and fried aubergines enriched with date molasses and feta. You might want to keep grilled secreto Ibérico pork with flatbread all to yourself, while the fish plates are no less enticing – horse mackerel, say, with tahini yoghurt and crispy chickpeas. Drink cocktails, sherry or Spanish wines from £17.

Chef/s: Marianna Leivaditaki. **Open:** Tue to Sat L, all week D. **Meals:** tapas £4 to £12. **Details:** 72 seats.

Moro

Cooking score: 5
⊖ Farringdon, map 2
Spanish/North African | £40
34-36 Exmouth Market, Clerkenwell, EC1R 4QE
Tel no: (020) 7833 8336
moro.co.uk

Having negotiated its teenage years, Moro is now riding high as a bullish twentysomething with an undiminished appetite for earthy Moorish food – no wonder it gets rammed inside and out as heady aromas fill the air. Whether you're nibbling tapas at the zinc-topped bar or ensconced in the busy dining room, Moro's forceful interpretation of Spanish and North African cuisine yields delights. Char-grilling and wood-roasting set the gold standard, from sea bass with jewelled rice, chickpeas and tahini to pork belly with patatas a lo pobre and churrasco sauce. Readers also love the calf's liver with cumin yoghurt and crispbread, as well as the stuffed squid with fino sherry, chopped egg, pine nuts and braised spinach – although main ingredients 'sometimes play second fiddle to the garnish'. For afters, rosewater and cardamom ice cream or chocolate and apricot tart beckon. The

drinks list ventures far beyond the Iberian Peninsula in search of treasures – 'orange wine from Georgia, anyone?'.

Chef/s: Sam and Samantha Clark. **Open:** all week L, Mon to Sat D. **Meals:** main courses £18 to £24. **Details:** 90 seats. 20 seats outside. Bar. Wheelchairs.

★ NEW ENTRY ★

The Ned

⊖ Bank, map 4
International | £35
27 Poultry, City, EC2R 8AJ
Tel no: (020) 3828 2000
thened.com

'The Ned transports you back to a time where you could wear a cocktail frock and light a cigarette without being scowled at.' So ran our thoughts on first setting eyes on Soho House's multi-million transformation of the former – and rather grandiose – Midland Bank building in the heart of the City. Designed by Edwin 'Ned' Lutyens in 1924, the ground floor, where most of the hotel's nine restaurants are clustered, is all dark wood, marble floors and pillars with no defined dining or drinking areas – they share the same dramatic, high-ceilinged space and walk the perfect line between special occasion and relaxation. From visits made shortly after opening, Millie's Lounge impressed for its exceptionally well-executed British classics – twice-baked smoked haddock soufflé, 'outstanding' fish and chips, 'perfectly done' mince and potatoes, while Zobler's Delicatessen delivered chicken matzo ball soup 'as good as the one at Russ & Daughters in New York', classic pastrami on rye and perfect NY cheesecake – and it does takeaway. Reports please.

Open: 6am to late. **Details:** Bar. Music.

Average price

The average price denotes the price of a three-course meal without wine.

Oklava

Cooking score: 3
⊖ Shoreditch High Street, map 4
Turkish | £30
74 Luke Street, Shoreditch, EC2A 4PY
Tel no: (020) 7729 3032
oklava.co.uk

Taste-buds need a little love, too, once in a while, so take them pronto to this unpretentious corner spot, a step from frenetic Great Eastern Street. Oklava's contemporary menu and café-like atmosphere sing with all that is relaxed and joyful about Turkish-Cypriot cuisine, so share nicely, quibble politely or argue vociferously over who gets to sweep the last nub of grilled haloumi through a honey-lemon jus, or scoop the final morsel of tender chicken shish through the cacik (cucumber, yoghurt and mint dip). Thankfully, crisp cylinders of börek that burst with salty feta, parsley and warm baharat spices are easily divided, as is the pide flatbread packed with octopus, ricotta, thyme and capers, and the perfectly edgy pickled red cabbage that accompanies it. Even those who eschew sweetness may find their heart skipping with the final beat of the meal: künefe, verjus syrup-soaked shredded pastry packed with mozzarella, scattered with pistachios and served hot so that the cheese remains melting, is deliciously memorable. A carefully curated line-up of Turkish wines cost from £16.
Chef/s: Selin Kiazim. **Open:** Tue to Fri and Sun L, Tue to Sat D. **Closed:** Mon, bank hols. **Meals:** small and sharing plates £6 to £16. Set L £18. **Details:** 46 seats. 12 seats outside. Bar. Wheelchairs. Music.

Visit us online

To find out more about
The Good Food Guide, please
visit thegoodfoodguide.co.uk

Palatino

Cooking score: 3
⊖ Old Street, map 2
Italian | £30
71 Central Street, Clerkenwell, EC1V 8AB
Tel no: (020) 3481 5300
palatino.london

Stevie Parle's new venue in the hinterland between Old Street and the Barbican is an Italian joint inspired by the food of Rome. Although it's conceived in the image of today's brutal design functionalism, with extraction pipes tracking across the ceiling above café tables and booth seating, and an open-kitchen counter populated by busy chefs, the menus hark back nostalgically to the food an earlier generation of British visitors to Italy might have encountered. Stracciatella and anchovies on toast with pickled lemon, a pinch of chilli and a dribble of oil is 'completely delicious' in its simplicity. Homemade pastas are the business, with bombolotti in pork ragù, and tonnarelli (spaghetti, to be pedantic) in cacio e pepe sauce rich with pecorino, both showing up well on inspection. For mains, it might be grilled turbot with agretti, lemon and capers, or sweetly moist meatballs of chicken, pancetta and pistachios with polenta, while pistachio and cinnamon ice cream and honeycomb seem a perfect fit with the densely fabulous chocolate mousse cake. With breakfasts of hot ricotta cakes and fennel sausage, and an all-Italian wine list starting at £4 a glass, Palatino has pretty much all bases covered.
Chef/s: Stevie Parle and Richard Blackwell. **Open:** Mon to Fri, all day from 8am. Sat L and D. **Closed:** Sun. **Meals:** main courses £13 to £20. **Details:** 70 seats. Bar. Music.

Paradise Garage

Cooking score: 4
⊖ Bethnal Green, map 1
Modern British | £33
254 Paradise Row, Bethnal Green, E2 9LE
Tel no: (020) 7613 1502
paradise254.com

East London continues to fill up with good eating, and Robin Gill's third venue, (see also the Dairy and the Manor, south London) in a Bethnal Green railway arch that opens up to the street, is another winner. Bare filament lights dangle over a space that gets pretty raucous when the evening session is motoring, but trades in defiantly unrefined modern plates with strong seasonal emphasis, their taste dial turned up to ten. Charred mackerel tricked out with pickled celeriac and a smoked oyster might kick things off, ahead of venison haunch with beetroot, barbecued chicory and watercress, or else go for the unadorned simplicity of roasted leeks dressed in Parmesan and parsley, before monkfish and cockles, artichoke barigoule and monk's beard, finishing with spiced pumpkin tart with salt caramel and speculoos (Belgian biscuit) ice cream. The short but good wine list is arranged by fruit notes, running from lemony Gaillac to brambly McLaren Vale Shiraz. Prices open at £24.
Chef/s: Simon Woodrow. **Open:** Sat and Sun L, Tue to Sat D. **Closed:** Mon, 1 week Christmas. **Meals:** main courses £19 to £22. Set L and D £20 (2 courses) to £25. Tasting menu £45. **Details:** 60 seats. V menu. Bar. Wheelchairs. Music.

★ NEW ENTRY ★

Petit Pois

Cooking score: 2
⊖ Old Street, Hoxton, map 4
French | £30
9 Hoxton Square, Hackney, N1 6NU
Tel no: (020) 7613 3689
petitpoisbistro.com

Imagine an all-day French bistro in happening Hoxton, in a tranquil enclave of the east London hipster action. The apple-green awning shelters a little terrace where you can snaffle a cheeky Gauloise before heading into the bijou dining room, which is all exposed brickwork and wood floors, with paintings of ballerinas the product of somebody's inner Degas. Service takes the nil-pretension approach, allowing the spotlight to shine on dashingly rendered French cuisine bourgeoise. The chicken liver parfait is enriched with duck fat, the pissaladière a puffy little pillow of sweet onions. It's hard to imagine anything more definitive in such circumstances than steak frites, especially when it offers superb, accurately cooked, rosy rump and hand-cut chips crunchy with sea salt in sharply lemony béarnaise. A handsome whole gurnard arrives swathed in protective paper, stuffed literally to the gills with mussels and given a leek cream libation at the table. The initial buzz for Petit Pois devolved on the chocolate mousse, which is served out as a generous great plop from a large bowl before being dredged with cocoa. A little list of exclusively French wines opens at £24.
Chef/s: Chris Smith. **Open:** all week, all day from 11 (10 Sat). **Meals:** small plates £7 to £11 (L only). Main courses £17 to £19. **Details:** 25 seats. 10 seats outside.

Pidgin

Cooking score: 5
⊖ Hackney Central, map 1
Modern British | £45
52 Wilton Way, Hackney, E8 1BG
Tel no: (020) 7254 8311
pidginlondon.com

Pocket-sized and fashionably unadorned Pidgin may be, but while this neighbourhood spot may lack elbow room, the food certainly packs a punch. Don't expect metaphorical manoeuvre either with the no-choice, weekly changing, fixed-price four-course menu. But why change a thing? This kitchen understands balance, seasons deftly, every dish contributing to create a delightfully coherent meal. A hot nugget of crisp pig's cheek with dots of fig segues into a starter of dribbling-sweet Honeymoon melon on whipped tofu with peppery geranium and pea shoots. Cornish mussels, plumpness a given, pair sweetly with Datterini tomatoes, the bite of cashews and focaccia, and savoury barley miso. Enter lamb – rump, loin, merguez – bound into happy coexistence thanks to lamb-fat yoghurt, ribbons of cucumber, bulgur wheat and rhubarb harissa. There's concord to the end: bibingka – coconut rice cake – flirts deliciously with a sliver of dreamily ripe Alphonso mango, a tangle of candied iced fennel and the slinkiest of duck egg ice creams. The short wine list changes weekly but will always offer something around £25. **Chef/s:** Dan Graham. **Open:** Fri to Sun L, Wed to Sun D. **Closed:** Mon, Tue, 2 weeks Christmas. **Meals:** set L and D £45 (4 courses). **Details:** 28 seats. 4 seats outside.

Plateau

Cooking score: 4
⊖ Canary Wharf, map 1
Modern French | £45
4th Floor, Canada Place, Canary Wharf, E14 5ER
Tel no: (020) 7715 7100
plateau-restaurant.co.uk
£5
OFF

Plateau is becoming a well-liked fixture on the Canary Wharf restaurant scene and for those living in east London 'it is nice to find such a quality restaurant without having to go west of the City'. The interior is all fourth-floor cityscape views, with curving sofa seating, pseudo-marble round tables and soft lighting all fitting in well together. There's been a change of chef since our last edition, but Jeremy Trehout, who previously worked for Pierre Koffmann, delivers polished modern French cooking, steering a course between traditional technique and modern ideas. Pink grapefruit-cured salmon with yuzu compressed cucumber and keta caviar is a light but stimulating opener, if you can be prised away from Cornish crab with avocado and Granny Smith apple. Lamb rump with black garlic, squid ink, pea and aubergine and dry-aged Galician chateaubriand (for two) are the meatier alternatives to baked cod with pink peppercorn crust, spinach and salsify. To finish, try a salted-caramel tart with praline ganache and ginger ice cream. The cocktail list is worth getting stuck into, and there's a good selection of wines by the glass. **Chef/s:** Jeremy Trehout. **Open:** Mon to Fri L, Mon to Sat D. **Closed:** Sun, 25 Dec, 1 Jan. **Meals:** main courses £17 to £30. Set L £28 (2 courses) to £30. Set D £35 (2 courses). Tasting menu £65. **Details:** 120 seats. 30 seats outside. Bar. Wheelchairs. Music. Parking.

★ NEW ENTRY ★

Popolo

Cooking score: 4
⊖ Old Street, map 4
Italian | £25
26 Rivington Street, Shoreditch, EC2A 3DU
Tel no: (020) 7729 4299
popoloshoreditch.com
£5 £30
OFF

Enter a new hybrid form, the tapas and pasta bar, courtesy of Jon Lawson. It was the pasta that floored us at the ex-Theo Randall chef's noisy concrete-counter spot (tables – small ones – are available upstairs): agnolotti del plin, a Piedmont speciality, introduced silky egg pasta, worthy of a maestro, to nonna's slow-cooked veal ragù to powerful effect, while taglierini de sepia, black as pitch, was equally assured. Such serious skills justify the prominence of primi even when they throw the rest of the menu off balance. As to tapas, half-Galician Lawson makes octopus and potatoes, dusted with paprika and drizzled with oil, an almost painterly study in red and gold, and Moorish fried olives and chickpeas prove good snacking with a glass from the (underwhelming) Italo-Spanish list. Effusive service – there's no getting away from the banter at the counter – copes when the no-reservations 'system' doesn't. **Chef/s:** Jon Lawson. **Open:** Tue to Sat L and D. **Closed:** Sun, Mon, 24 Dec to 1 Jan. **Meals:** main courses £9 to £17. **Details:** 33 seats. Music.

Quality Chop House

Cooking score: 3
⊖ Farringdon, map 5
Modern British | £35
94 Farringdon Road, Clerkenwell, EC1R 3EA
Tel no: (020) 7278 1452
thequalitychophouse.com

£5
OFF

Famously uncomfortable benches, mahogany booths and bolted-down tables may lend some puritanical asceticism to this self-styled 'progressive working class caterer', but the born-again Quality Chop House punches well above its weight in the food department – although its beautifully restored Victorian antiquity now comes with modern-day City prices. Diners are lured here by the kind of gutsy fare that summons up a few ghosts of yesteryear: cod croquettes, Galloway mince with dripping toast, Cheddar custard tart and so on. But there's fancy fodder for today's moneyed working classes, too, in the shape of smoked cod's roe with cured egg yolk, guinea fowl with lentils and alexanders or turbot with blood orange and monk's beard. To follow, Neal's Yard cheeses are worth a sniff, or you can try malt chocolate with preserved cherries and gingerbread. Co-owner Will Lander is wine guru Jancis Robinson's son, so check out his earthy, wide-ranging list.
Chef/s: Shaun Searley. **Open:** all week L, Mon to Sat D. **Closed:** 1 week Christmas, Easter Mon.
Meals: main courses £15 to £26. Tasting menu £44.
Details: 70 seats. 6 seats outside. Music.

Roka Canary Wharf

Cooking score: 2
⊖ Canary Wharf, map 1
Japanese | £50
4 Park Pavilion, Canary Wharf, E14 5FW
Tel no: (020) 7636 5228
rokarestaurant.com

One of a quartet of cool, energetic big city eateries serving a menu of modern Japanese robatayaki cuisine, this first-floor Canary Wharf branch, like its siblings, has a robata grill centre stage where you can sit and watch the chefs in action. Uniform, too, is the hard-edged look of pale-wood floors and panelling, with unclothed and rather too close together tables, which makes conversation in a packed restaurant difficult – try a table in the front bar, which is slightly shielded from the restaurant and has the advantage of natural light from the big plate-glass windows. Expect superior sushi and sashimi, a splendid rendition of black cod marinated in yuzu miso, and from a long list of recommendations, salmon fillet teriyaki with sansho salt, and Black Angus ribeye with eryngii mushrooms and wasabi ponzu. The various tasting menus and carte are pricey, but the weekend brunch with its unlimited buffet and free-flowing wine is great value. To drink, interesting cocktails, saké, shochu and style-driven wines.
Chef/s: Cristian Bravaccini. **Open:** all week L and D.
Meals: dishes from £9 to £72. Tasting menu £66.
Details: 89 seats. 40 seats outside. Bar. Wheelchairs. Music.

Rotorino

Cooking score: 2
⊖ Haggerston, Dalston Junction, map 2
Italian | £30
434 Kingsland Road, Hackney, E8 4AA
Tel no: (020) 7249 9081
rotorino.com

Leatherette booths, vintage furniture and Anaglypta wallpaper come together at Stevie Parle's Rotorino to create a buzzy Italian bar and restaurant fit for trendy Dalston. All eyes have been on the River Café alumnus's latest Italian opening, Palatino (see entry), this year, and one can't help feeling Rotorino may be feeling somewhat neglected. At inspection, we found primi up to the usual standard, the pasta correctly al dente (with fiery 'nduja sauce on the casarecce twists) and pea gnudi, gentle in texture and flavour, if irregular in shape and size. But a floppy watercress and courgette salad with anchovy, overdressed and over-seasoned, was as if from another kitchen. Simple meat and fish from the stove or wood grill, such as hanger steak or lemon sole, outshine their accompaniments. Finish with caramel gelato if you can. The wine list is thoughtfully assembled with a producer of the month and specials by the glass.

Chef/s: Stevie Parle and Luigi del Giupice. **Open:** Mon to Sat D. Sun, all day from 12. **Closed:** 24 Dec to 3 Jan. **Meals:** main courses £13 to £19. Set D £15 (2 courses) to £19. **Details:** 90 seats. Bar. Wheelchairs. Music.

Rök

Cooking score: 2
⊖ **Shoreditch High Street, map 4**
Scandinavian | £26
26 Curtain Road, Shoreditch, EC2A 3NZ
Tel no: (020) 7377 2152
roklondon.com

£30

A bare-wood floor, tables and bar form the shell for an intensive exercise in Nordic smokehouse cooking, with accompaniments subjected to any other of the preservation techniques currently in vogue – pickling, fermenting and brine-curing. Indeed, proceedings start with a choice of pickled veg, from carrots, cucumber, fennel, chillied-up cabbage or golden beetroot. Lunch might turn on a hefty sandwich of duck confit, wadded with spring onion, more pickled cucumber and gingery lingonberry jam. Main-course meats such as pigeon or kid take centre stage in the evenings, partnered respectively with Jerusalem artichoke and Muscat grapes, or celery relish, burnt leek and capers, helped along by sides that inveigle fermented anchovies into potato gratin, or simmer winter greens in an antioxidant-rich broth of black tea and seaweed. To finish, there's 'lost bread' (pain perdu? geddit?), served with white chocolate ice cream and blood-orange and rhubarb jam. A second branch is now open at 149 Upper Street, Islington, London N1 1RA.

Chef/s: Matt Young. **Open:** Mon to Fri, all day from 12. Sat D. **Closed:** Sun. **Meals:** main courses £12 to £16. **Details:** 40 seats. Bar.

Sager + Wilde

Cooking score: 3
⊖ **Bethnal Green, map 1**
Modern British | £32
250 Paradise Row, Bethnal Green, E2 9LE
Tel no: (020) 7613 0478
sagerandwilde.com

A welcome revolution in wine drinking has seen a burgeoning appetite for laid-back spots where stellar booze is guaranteed. Housed in a railway arch, dark and moody Sager + Wilde nails this with its democratic approach (40 wines under £40 and small mark-ups). Wine and dine is the agenda here (the original bar on Hackney Road offers bar snacks only). Head chef Chris Leach (ex-Kitty Fisher's and Pitt Cue) keeps things concise, with a menu focused on enticing maximum flavour from (largely British) seasonal produce: standout on inspection was an oozy, soft burrata on a sweet carrot purée. Mains, perhaps Welsh Speckled Face lamb shoulder with salsa verde or Cornish hake with white beans and monk's beard, are simpler affairs but execution is exemplary. For a sweet finish, the lemon tart won't disappoint. The frequently changing and innovative Europe-heavy wine list has no notes, so unless you're a budding oenologist, you're best off talking to your waiter.

Chef/s: Chris Leach. **Open:** Sat and Sun L, all week D. **Meals:** main courses £11 to £35. **Details:** 80 seats. 70 seats outside. Bar. Wheelchairs. Music.

St John

Cooking score: 5
⊖ **Farringdon, map 5**
British | £40
26 St John Street, Clerkenwell, EC1M 4AY
Tel no: (020) 7251 0848
stjohngroup.uk.com

It's not clear whether Fergus Henderson and Trevor Gulliver intended to rewrite the rule book when they opened St John in 1994, but few would deny that this one-time Clerkenwell smokehouse has become an icon of the new British gastronomy. Henderson's once-revolutionary concept of 'nose-to-tail' cuisine has since become common currency in restaurants throughout the land, although no one does it better than St John. Admittedly some of the primal gore has been toned down, but the kitchen still glorifies blood-and-guts freshness, thrifty offcuts, wild pickings and delicacies that were once consigned to the dustbin of poorhouse victuals. Menus change daily in the bare-bones, white-walled dining room, although the emblematic roasted bone marrow and parsley salad is a fixture; otherwise, expect an earthy cabaret of uncompromising seasonal flavours, from verdant nettle and ham soup to pigeon with trotters and prunes or juicy snails with sausage and chickpeas. To conclude, gorgeous fresh-baked madeleines compete with desserts from the annals of British cookery. The food's full-frontal vigour is matched by a gutsy Francophile wine list.

Chef/s: Jonathan Woolway. **Open:** Mon to Fri and Sun L, Mon to Sat D. **Closed:** 25 and 26 Dec, bank hols. **Meals:** main courses £14 to £32. **Details:** 80 seats. Bar. Wheelchairs.

St John Bread and Wine

Cooking score: 3
⊖ Liverpool Street, map 4
British | £35
94-96 Commercial Street, Spitalfields, E1 6LZ
Tel no: (020) 7251 0848
stjohngroup.uk.com

Well into their second decade in the business and St John Bread and Wine still looks the easy-going customer it always was – the staff genuinely committed, the décor unpolished, bordering on the basic. It matches the style of its big brother St John (see entry) with a zealous enthusiasm for nose-to-tail seasonal British produce that helped to establish a trend back in the day, and still delights. Small plates are essentially simple: smoked sprats, their delicious richness cut by sharply pickled red cabbage and pungent horseradish; a heap of beautifully dressed kohlrabi and chervil, scattered with tiny brown shrimp; a satisfying, robust slab of blood cake, topped with a duck

egg and a dab of rich, fruity brown sauce; a tender whole quail with aïoli. At main, chicory and olives are ideal accompaniments to the sweetness of a perfectly grilled mackerel, while, for dessert, the signature Eccles cakes and Lancashire cheese is almost too good to share. A classic cocktail might presage a delve through the list of interesting French country wines at kind prices.

Chef/s: Lee Tiernan. **Open:** all week, all day from 8am (8.30 Sat and Sun). **Closed:** 25 and 26 Dec. **Meals:** small plates £6 to £9. Large plates £15 to £19. **Details:** 64 seats. Bar.

★ NEW ENTRY ★

Sardine

Cooking score: 2
⊖ Old Street, map 2
French | £32
15 Micawber Street, Hoxton, N1 7TB
Tel no: (020) 7490 0144
sardine.london

As small and modest as its namesake fish, this southern French bistro from Stevie Parle and protégé Alex Jackson defies expectations of a gallery canteen (it's housed within the Parasol Unit). Summoning the bonne-femme spirit in such neglected classics as lamb shoulder with white beans and tripe with saffron and tomato, Jackson's cooking is blissfully old-fashioned. Presentation is plain – self-consciously so. Crisp-skinned brill with 'Green Goddess' sauce and a gloriously soupy mass of Puy lentils suggests a commendable 'flavour-first' stance that clearly resonates with the well-to-do gallery-goers and certainly suits the wine cellar's Mediterranean leanings. Occasionally, however, simple tips over into sloppy: pleasingly wobbly ham hock and pig's head terrine deserved better than singed sourdough, but on the whole this is 'hugely enjoyable' food. Seating is around the bar, at wooden tables or a zinc-topped communal one. Bouquets of dried lavender and ochre-glazed jugs are pure Provence.

Chef/s: Alex Jackson. **Open:** Tue to Sun L, all week D. **Meals:** main courses £15 to £20. **Details:** 45 seats.

★ NEW ENTRY ★

Smokestak

Cooking score: 4
⊖ Shoreditch High Street, map 4
Modern British | £25
35 Sclater Street, Shoreditch, E1 6LB
Tel no: (020) 3873 1733
smokestak.co.uk
£30

If only this page was scratch and sniff. Intoxicating wood smoke and barbecue vapours reach your olfactory nerves well before you enter Smokestak's dark realm. This former street-food operation from proprietor David Carter is in a league of its own. Resembling a giant blacksmith's forge, with theatrically lit reclaimed-wood seating (no soft landings here) the real deal comes from the monster rotisserie-style smoker: signature beef brisket cooked low-and-slow until seductively toothsome (in bun or unfettered, it's a winner). True barbecue masters, they take the graft and craft of barbecue seriously here, but it's not all meat. The creative short menu plays to a wider crowd, with bites (crispy pigtails are insanely moreish), fish, salads and sides to lighten the load – so after getting your hands dirty with 30-day dry-aged beef rib or smoked girolles on beef-dripping toast, you can resuscitate yourself with crunchy slaw, then get back to business (should you have the wherewithal) with a sticky toffee pudding. As befits the food, cocktails and beers take the fore.
Chef/s: David Carter. **Open:** Mon to Fri L and D. Sat and Sun, all day from 12. **Closed:** 25 and 26 Dec. **Meals:** main courses £8 to £15. **Details:** 75 seats. 38 seats outside. Bar. Wheelchairs. Music.

Symbols

🛏 Accommodation is available
£30 Three courses for less than £30
£5 OFF £5-off voucher scheme
🍾 Notable wine list

Som Saa

Cooking score: 2
⊖ Aldgate East, map 4
Thai | £30
43a Commercial Street, Spitalfields, E1 6BD
Tel no: (020) 7324 7790
somsaa.com

Natural wood in many forms, exposed brickwork, vintage light fittings, Som Saa has the look of a place designed with today's savvy young diner in mind, with the mostly tattooed staff reflecting the demographic. Cocktails and snacks in the front bar hit the point home. The menu isn't overburdened with the staples of Thai cuisine, choosing instead to focus on vibrant flavours, fresh aromatic salads, interesting curries and grills. Yum mu wan is sweet pork and dandelion in a salad with 'ma-uek' fruit and orange chilli dressing, and when it comes to curries, gaeng gari pla is Cornish plaice in an aromatic yellow sauce with daikon and Thai pickles. Ingredients are carefully chosen – it's back to Cornwall for the lamb that's given a turn in the wok with its offal and 'northern spices'. It is no surprise to hear the guys behind it worked with David Thompson at Nahm. The concise wine list gives due consideration to the food.
Chef/s: Andy Oliver and Mark Dobbie. **Open:** Tue to Sat L, Mon to Sat D. **Closed:** Sun. **Meals:** small plates £8 to £18. **Details:** Bar. Music.

Sosharu

Cooking score: 4
⊖ Farringdon, map 5
Japanese | £45
64 Turnmill Street, Clerkenwell, EC1M 5RR
Tel no: (020) 3805 2304
sosharulondon.com
🍾

Jason Atherton's Clerkenwell restaurant is a Japanese eatery in the loosest sense of the word. Here, a western chef (Alex Craciun) presents his interpretation of Japanese dishes in a format far removed from the capital's traditional Japanese restaurants, but there's no sense it is all for the sake of novelty. Salmon

temaki is an absolute must-try – like a crispy seaweed taco with sushi rice, spiced cabbage, tosazu jelly and avocado. Dishes are designed for sharing and sampling, and in his international box of tricks Mr Craciun has 'very good indeed' chicken karaage, miso-glazed aubergine with crispy shallots, Wagyu beef from the hibachi grill and rice pot (chicken yakitori with shishito pepper and slow-cooked egg) mixed in among the sashimi selection, and desserts such as matcha mille crêpe with a matcha sorbet. Service in the spacious, wood-lined space is excellent, exclusive sakés supplement a wine list full of French classics and artisan gems, and classy cocktails in the basement bar fit the bill, too.
Chef/s: Alex Craciun. **Open:** Mon to Sat L and D. **Closed:** Sun, bank hols. **Meals:** main courses £17 to £28. Set L and D £30 (2 courses). **Details:** 74 seats. Bar. Music.

Taberna do Mercado
Cooking score: 4
⊖ Liverpool Street, Aldgate East, map 4
Portuguese | £35
Old Spitalfields Market, 107b Commercial Street, Spitalfields, E1 6BG
Tel no: (020) 7375 0649
tabernamercado.co.uk

With its outdoor terrace looking out on Spitalfields Market, Nuno Mendes' Taberna is consecrated to informal Portuguese eating, with a mix of traditional petiscos (small plates), tinned fish and bifana sandwiches, as well as more speculative vaults into modernity. You can pick up a beef prego with prawn paste and wild garlic on the fly, or else perch at one of the little café tables amid whitewashed brickwork and set about green bean fritters, pig's ear and pink grapefruit, piri-piri chicken and carrots, and homemade smoked lardo smeared on toast. Cured meats are top-drawer gear, from juicy red wine chouriço to two-year-old presunto ham, and the tinning of fish produces red mullet with navel orange, as well as Cornish mussels and seaweed. Finish with creamy pão de ló, an eggy sponge cake made with olive oil. Acerbic

cocktails are all the rage – the Nautilus Martini comprises that brand of gin with dry white port and pickled kohlrabi – and there are some excellent wines from the one wine country in western Europe least in hock to varietalism. Small glasses start at £4.80.
Chef/s: Nuno Mendes. **Open:** all week L and D. **Closed:** 24 to 30 Dec, 1 Jan. **Meals:** small plates £5 to £15. **Details:** 40 seats. 30 seats outside.

Tayyabs
Cooking score: 2
⊖ Whitechapel, Aldgate East, map 1
Pakistani | £20
83-89 Fieldgate Street, Whitechapel, E1 1JU
Tel no: (020) 7247 6400/9543
tayyabs.co.uk
£30

Crowds continue to descend on this huge, long-established Whitechapel address where the cooking – with its heart in the traditions of the Punjab and Lahore – has stayed true to its Pakistani roots. It's open all day (a tip from regulars is to avoid busy times), portions are generous and prices are reasonable. The extensive menu is built around tandoori dishes and karahi bowls of curry, from lamb chops with a chilli-hot marinade to richly flavoured chicken keema. Shish kebabs and tender mutton tikka are packed with flavour, and there has been praise for vegetarian samosas, methi aloo gajar, and tarka dhal. Breads are good, especially the garlic naan, as are desserts, in particular the rasmalai. Look out for the daily specials. Tayyabs is unlicensed so bring your own wine or beer. Alternatively, drink delicately salted or mango lassi.
Chef/s: Wasim Tayyab. **Open:** all week, all day from 12. **Meals:** main courses £6 to £12. **Details:** 350 seats. Wheelchairs. Music.

Visit us online

To find out more about The Good Food Guide, please visit thegoodfoodguide.co.uk

★ NEW ENTRY ★
Temple & Sons
Cooking score: 3
⊖ Liverpool Street, Bank, map 4
British | £36
22 Old Broad Street, City, EC2N 1HQ
Tel no: (020) 7877 7710
templeandsons.co.uk

We've lost count of the many Jason Atherton restaurants in the capital, but there's no doubt that this informal grill restaurant and all-day deli-bar is another winner. The wedged-shaped double-decker adjacent to Tower 42 is the nearest thing to a neighbourhood restaurant in the City and has built up a strong following for its no-nonsense cooking. The confident menu keeps to the mainly British classics of pork, apple and black pudding sausage roll with buttery mash and HP gravy, wood-fired pork chop, collar and crackling, and Cornish fish stew, alongside a daily selection of simply grilled fish and steaks. While the cooking may not be the most adventurous around, it does show attention to detail and uses good ingredients: slow-cooked poussin finished in the wood grill was pronounced the 'best roast chicken ever'. Beer and imaginative cocktails are offered together with a wine list that appeals to serious wine lovers who aren't interested in trophy bottles and high mark-ups.
Chef/s: Keith Hooker. **Open:** Mon to Sat L and D. **Closed:** Sun, bank hols. **Meals:** main courses £10 to £22. **Details:** 90 seats. 15 seats outside. Bar. Wheelchairs. Music.

Tratra
Cooking score: 3
⊖ Shoreditch, Old Street, map 4
Modern French | £39
Boundary Hotel, 2-4 Boundary Street (entrance in Redchurch Street), Shoreditch, E2 7DD
Tel no: (020) 7729 1051
theboundary.co.uk

In best-selling French cookery writer Stéphane Reynaud, Sir Terence Conran has recruited *un grand nom* for the reboot of the theatrical restaurant at his Boundary Hotel. Reynaud is a butcher's grandson, hence the focus placed on terrines and charcuterie. We were dazzled by the charcuterie 'planche', a selection of ventreche, jambon noir de bigorre, chorizo (and more), in turn silky, glossy, firm and spicy. We only wished smaller portions had been available, the better to explore the rest of the contemporary French country menu. Nothing quite hit the charcuterie's heights but we appreciated nonetheless the bright sharpness that preserved lemon brought to herring and potato salad, the generosity of four fat crevettes with anchovy and caper dressing, even perfectly cooked veal sweetbreads and brown butter with pomegranate and ginger – although the dish was heavy-going on a hot summer's day. The all-French wine list is a wonderful weighty tome. Edited highlights are printed weekly.
Chef/s: Stéphane Reynaud and James Warburton. **Open:** all week D. Sun L. **Closed:** Sun and Mon (May to Sep), bank hols. **Meals:** main courses £16 to £27. **Details:** 100 seats. Bar. Wheelchairs.

28°-50°

Cooking score: 4
⊖ Chancery Lane, map 5
Modern European | £34
140 Fetter Lane, City, EC4A 1BT
Tel no: (020) 7242 8877
2850.co.uk

Agnar Sverrisson's flagship city bar and
restaurant continues to thrive, drawing in
drinkers with an enthusiast's list and diners
with crowd-pleasing bistro dishes.
Considered 'delightfully off the beaten track' it
goes about its business in a convivial
basement, voguishly fitted out with lots of
wood and bare brick. Snacks such as mini
chorizo, pork belly with soy and honey glaze,
and the charcuterie plate are a good way to
start, but the menu also wends its way from
crab salad via lamb rump with ratatouille and
pistou, or spatchcock chicken with the 'best
ever' triple-cooked chips, to a burger with
relish and Cheddar cheese. In addition, set
lunch and early dinner menus are very good
value, and the service pleases everyone. The
wine list does justice, from its Coravin glass
selections to a list that pulls together fine
drinking from reputable names and forward-
looking producers worldwide, all handled
with great insight by the sommelier.
Chef/s: Julien Baris. **Open:** Mon to Fri, all day from
12. **Closed:** Sat, Sun, 25 Dec to early Jan.
Meals: main courses £16 to £35. Set L and early D
£20 (2 courses) to £25. **Details:** 68 seats.
Wheelchairs. Music.

Typing Room

Cooking score: 6
⊖ Bethnal Green, map 1
Modern European | £65
Town Hall Hotel, Patriot Square, Bethnal
Green, E2 9NF
Tel no: (020) 7871 0461
typingroom.com

Dip a toe into edgy E2 at Bethnal Green's old
town hall turned arty hotel by way of the 'very
relaxed and welcoming' marble, oak and brass
surrounds of Lee Westcott's coolly luxurious
Typing Room restaurant. Mr Westcott's a
quietly authoritative figure in the open
kitchen, sending out plate after hand-thrown
plate of his aesthetically evolved new British
cuisine. The offering's been pared back to a set
lunch and tasting menu (vegetarian or not) on
which appear such mainstays as IPA
sourdough with Marmite butter, a signature
study in cauliflower with raisins and capers
and a pig's head 'snack' with smoked apple. The
changing seasons might introduce effective
pairings such as brill, calçots, chicken and
black garlic or venison, burnt quince, monk's
beard and smoked brazil nut. Desserts like
sheep's yoghurt, apple and dill are often on the
savoury spectrum. The list of prestigious
wines, sherries and sakés goes well into three
figures.
Chef/s: Lee Westcott. **Open:** Thur to Sat L, Tue to
Sat D. **Closed:** Sun, Mon, 24 Dec to 2 Jan.
Meals: set L £27 (2 courses) to £32. Tasting menu
£65. **Details:** 38 seats. V menu. Bar. Wheelchairs.

Vinoteca

Cooking score: 2
⊖ Farringdon, Barbican, map 5
Modern European | £32
7 St John Street, Farringdon, EC1M 4AA
Tel no: (020) 7253 8786
vinoteca.co.uk

This lively venue is part of a quintet of cool
London pit-stops owned by Brett Woonton,
Charlie Young and Elena Ares – none coming

Please send us your feedback

To register your opinion about any
restaurant listed in this guide, or a new
restaurant that you wish to bring to our
attention, please visit the web address at
the bottom of the page. Your feedback
informs the content of the book and will
be used to compile next year's reviews.

across as your average wine bar. Here, every bottle on the terrific list is available to take away, and there is a cracking selection by the glass – and many unusual names – while a menu of robust modern European cooking aims for satisfaction rather than aesthetic statements. Platters of cured meats or cheeses are great for a group getting stuck into the wine list, or else there's grilled Scottish mackerel with sweet-and-sour gooseberries or hot-smoked salmon with lemon mayonnaise and radish and samphire salad, then guinea fowl suprême with corn purée, green beans and sauce vierge, or the never-off-the-menu bavette steak with fresh horseradish and hand-cut chips. Finish with dark chocolate and pistachio torte with espresso cream.

Chef/s: Klaudiusz Wiatrak. **Open:** Mon to Sat, all day from 12. **Closed:** Sun, bank hols. **Meals:** main courses £12 to £18. Set L £13 (2 courses) to £16. **Details:** 35 seats. 8 seats outside. Music.

Wright Brothers Spitalfields

Cooking score: 3
Liverpool Street, map 4
Seafood | £40
8a Lamb Street, Spitalfields, E1 6EA
Tel no: (020) 7377 8706
thewrightbrothers.co.uk

With their own oyster farm on Cornwall's Helford river, the Wright Brothers (in fact one Wright, one Hancock) must surely give first dibs on their Frenchman's Creek and Duchy native oysters to their five London restaurants. Battersea is the latest member of the gang (see also entries for Soho, Borough Market and Kensington). The Spitalfields outpost is right in the heart of the action in the old market, with a marble oyster bar, exposed bricks, slinky booths and an outdoor terrace that's indoors (sort of, thanks to the market roof). The oysters will vary – Speciale de Claire from Oléron in France, maybe – with the shellfish platters aways a good bet. Beef tataki with ponzu and crispy garlic shows it's not all about seafood, but it is mostly: shellfish risotto, Scottish halibut sashimi, whole salt-baked sea bream or a straight-up whole lobster

all to yourself. Desserts such as lemon curd cheesecake should be no afterthought. Cocktails and a smart wine list are just the job. **Chef/s:** Richard Kirkwood and Andy Roberts. **Open:** all week, all day from 12. **Closed:** 25 to 27 Dec, 1 Jan. **Meals:** main courses £19 to £27. Set L £22 (2 courses) to £26. **Details:** 64 seats. 37 seats outside. Bar. Music.

Yauatcha City

Cooking score: 1
Liverpool Street, map 4
Chinese | £40
Broadgate Circle, City, EC2M 2QS
Tel no: (020) 3817 9888
yauatcha.com

In a setting that is light and contemporary, Yauatcha City sweeps across a large, semi-circular mezzanine overlooking Broadgate Circle – its location and fast-paced service ensuring that weekday lunches are business orientated. The dim sum menu moves quickly from reworked versions of Chinatown staples (pork and prawn shui mai, char siu) to lobster dumpling with tobiko caviar and ginger, and baked venison puffs. Larger plates also set out to impress: kung pao chicken with cashew nut, jasmine tea-smoked ribs, braised sea bass with tofu, and vegetable congee with choi sum and lotus root. Finish with exquisite patisserie and macarons. Cocktails or an extensive tea menu are alternatives to wine. **Chef/s:** Tong Chee Hwee. **Open:** Mon to Sat, all day from 12. **Closed:** Sun. **Meals:** main courses £16 to £32. Small plates £5 to £10. **Details:** 110 seats. Bar. Music.

The Anchor & Hope

Cooking score: 3
⊖ Waterloo, Southwark, map 5
Modern European | £31
36 The Cut, South Bank, SE1 8LP
Tel no: (020) 7928 9898
anchorandhopepub.co.uk

A heavy curtain draws a near-literal veil between drinkers and eaters at the Anchor & Hope. It's a pub and, given the no bookings policy, you might well find yourself waiting at the bar until you get the call. The unreconstructed décor reflects the no-frills, rustic ethos that has defined the place since it hit the ground running in the early noughties. The menu changes twice a day, keeping everyone on their toes, and what arrives on the plate is likely to be full-flavoured and 'pretty damn appealing'. Inky cuttlefish with chickpeas and aïoli, griddled scallops with blood-orange beurre blanc, braised wild rabbit, or Swaledale lamb shoulder cooked over seven hours... this is great stuff, unflinching and deeply satisfying. Sign off with pear and almond tart. The perky but pricey wine list sticks to the European continent.
Chef/s: Jonathan Jones and Alex Crofts. **Open:** Tue to Sun L, Mon to Sat D. **Closed:** 23 Dec to 2 Jan, bank hols. **Meals:** main courses £11 to £25. **Details:** 50 seats. 32 seats outside. Bar.

Artusi

Cooking score: 3
⊖ Peckham Rye, map 1
Italian | £28
161 Bellenden Road, Peckham, SE15 4DH
Tel no: (020) 3302 8200
artusi.co.uk
£30

A narrow frontage in battleship grey announces the original Artusi (there's now a second venue, Marcella, on Deptford High Street – see entry), Jack Beer's south London homage to Italian rustic cooking. Assemble a group of at least eight and you can eat in family style with a sharing menu at a big table right in front of the tiled kitchen. Menus change daily according to market availability, but can be relied on to offer initial bites along the lines of salt cod with grilled polenta and watercress, or a salad of Jerusalem artichoke, apple, pickled carrot and pecorino, perhaps followed by an intermediate bowl of brodo with tortellini, and then mains such as grilled squid with tomatoes, spinach and mint, or veal meatballs with potatoes and turnip tops. To finish, there are wickedly rich cannoli, filled with home-made ricotta, rhubarb and pistachios, or a simple serving of lemon ice cream perfumed with bay leaf. The short Italian wine list opens with a Sicilian white and Puglian Negroamaro for £20.
Chef/s: Jack Beer. **Open:** Tue to Sat L, Mon to Sat D. Sun 12.30 to 8. **Meals:** main courses £12 to £16. Sun L £20 (3 courses). **Details:** 40 seats. Wheelchairs. Music.

Babur

Cooking score: 2
map 1
Indian | £26
119 Brockley Rise, Forest Hill, SE23 1JP
Tel no: (020) 8291 2400
babur.info
£30

The only restaurant in the guide with a life-sized tiger on the balcony, Babur also has some chops in the longevity stakes. It's been going in Forest Hill for more than 30 years, marked out by a warmly offbeat approach, 'exceptional' service and the creation of many a 'great evening'. They'll go off-menu with a bit of warning, but there's plenty on the 'modern Indian' carte to please most readers. Start with quail breast with black sesame seeds, green papaya salad and sweet chilli, then explore your flexitarian side with a generous vegetarian thali, wild mushroom and pea dosa, or a side of chickpeas soaked in Assam tea with spices. To finish, there's saffron custard with the apricot and fig crumble, and stem ginger and honey in the kulfi. Cocktails are inventive (witness the currytini, with lime, curry leaves and a green chilli) and craft beers include south London brews.

Chef/s: Jiwan Lal. **Open:** all week L 12 to 2.30 (4 Sun), D 6 to 11.30. **Meals:** main courses £14 to £18. Sun L £14 (buffet). **Details:** 72 seats. V menu.

★ NEW ENTRY ★

Bala Baya

Cooking score: 2
⊖ Southwark, map 5
Israeli | £32
Arch 25, Old Union Yard Arches, 229 Union Street, Southwark, SE1 0LR
Tel no: (020) 8001 7015
balabaya.co.uk

The beautifully renovated Union Yard railway arches in Southwark are home to the Union Street Theatre and a few dining spots, the eye-catching standout among which is the Tel Aviv-themed Bala Baya. Sit at the S-shaped zinc counter on ground-floor level for informal nibbling and kitchen views, and climb the metal staircase to the mezzanine beneath the brick arch and views into the apartment block opposite. The menu revolves around small plates, with a 'Grab & Go' lunch deal, as well as a fixed-price arrangement for two plates, pitta with dip, salad and gazoz (Turkish fruit syrup topped with sparkling water). That pitta is exemplary, brown and fluffy with chunky warm hummus to write home about, but the star of the show is 'crispy, sticky, chunky' fried chicken with a jammy bitter orange sauce, puréed squash, harissa and kim-chee. Finish with burnt babka, a smear of chocolate and hazelnut spread served with stewed plums, caramelised pecans and whisked custard.

Chef/s: Eran Tibi. **Open:** all week L, Mon to Sat D. **Meals:** small plates £9 to £12. Set L £20. **Details:** 76 seats. Bar. Music.

Average price

The average price denotes the price of a three-course meal without wine.

The Begging Bowl

Cooking score: 2
⊖ Peckham Rye, map 1
Thai | £30
168 Bellenden Road, Peckham, SE15 4BW
Tel no: (020) 7635 2627
thebeggingbowl.co.uk

Local favourite the Begging Bowl has some covered pavement tables for London's steamier days, but the easy-going blond-wood interior is ready and waiting all year round. They don't take bookings (apart from groups of 8 to 10), but you can get 10 per cent off drinks at the pub down the road while waiting for the call to say your table is ready. Sharing, that's the thing, with five plates recommended per couple. Expect Thai-inspired dishes with real zing. How about crispy squid flavoured with red turmeric, Thai garlic and Kaffir lime leaf, with a sour-chilli dip, stir-fried Hispi cabbage with fermented yellow beans, palourde clams with pickled plums and an aromatic broth, braised beef cheek curry, and a salad of charcoal-grilled guinea fowl with crispy kale, pickled garlic and grilled red chilli dressing. Drink Thai-inspired cocktails, beer on tap or by the bottle, and food-friendly wines from £20.

Chef/s: Jane Alty. **Open:** all week L and D. **Closed:** 25 and 26 Dec, 1 Jan. **Meals:** sharing plates £4 to £16. **Details:** 50 seats. 24 seats outside. Wheelchairs. Music.

Bibo

Cooking score: 2
⊖ East Putney, map 3
Italian | £35
146 Upper Richmond Road, Putney, SW15 2SW
Tel no: (020) 8780 0592
biborestaurant.com

Easy to walk past this clever little Italian without noticing, but it's worth seeking out for unpretentious and proper cooking. The bar dominates the front part of the room – where locals drop in for morning coffee or a glass of wine on their way home from work, possibly tucking into a 'nduja crocchette or some excellent salami. Those in search of a proper meal head to the wide space at the back, where the bentwood tables and chairs may be the same, but there's an air of sophistication supplied by a collection of modern art covering the walls. The food may not be challenging 'but I'd rather eat here than anywhere else on this particular strip'. For zucchini fritti and the likes of roast spatchcock baby chicken served with Delica pumpkin and spinach, it's pretty good and the good-value set menu makes it 'an everyday treat'. There's vanilla pannacotta with red plum compote to finish, and the reasonably priced all-Italian wine list opens at £24.

Chef/s: Stefano Arrigoni. **Open:** Tue to Sun L, Tue to Sat D. **Closed:** Mon, 24 to 28 Dec, bank hols. **Meals:** main courses £14 to £20. **Details:** 70 seats. 12 seats outside. Bar.

Bistro Union
Cooking score: 3
⊖ Clapham South, map 3
British | £30
40 Abbeville Road, Clapham, SW4 9NG
Tel no: (020) 7042 6400
bistrounion.co.uk

There's just a hint of 1950s Britain about this dressed-down sibling of Adam Byatt's big-hitting Trinity (see entry) – note the wooden 'cloak pegs' used for hanging your coats, the shelves of homemade pickles and preserves, the nostalgic enamelware crockery and the specials scribbled on rolls of brown paper. However, the food is several notches up from austerity with its daily offer of Cornish mussels cooked in perry, Barnsley chops with green sauce and poached Yorkshire rhubarb with custard. In addition, the kitchen sends out whole roast chickens with bread sauce and 'pigs in blankets' to share, slow-cooked Jacob's Ladder beef with glazed carrots and mash, cod in seaweed butter and the odd continental interloper such as Swaledale veal bolognese with roast onions and gnocchi. A daily brunch menu, kids' deals, a Sunday supper club

(BYOB), world beers and a list of good-value wines complete a highly appealing neighbourhood package.

Chef/s: Adam Byatt and Jeremy Cuevas. **Open:** Mon to Sat, all day from 9.30. Sun 5.30 to 8.30. **Closed:** 24 to 27 Dec. **Meals:** main courses £14 to £30. Sun supper £26. **Details:** 40 seats. 12 seats outside.

Boqueria Tapas
Cooking score: 3
⊖ Clapham North, Brixton, map 3
Spanish | £25
192 Acre Lane, Brixton, SW2 5UL
Tel no: (020) 7733 4408
boqueriatapas.com
£30

A sleek, minimalist finish, closely packed tables and an all-round energetic buzz add to Boqueria's easy-going appeal. The upbeat attitude is maintained by keen staff. A blackboard – and a blooming giant-sized one at that – lists the daily specials, offering support to a menu that deals in full-flavoured tapas. Cured meats and cheeses are top-drawer stuff, including jamón Ibérico puro de bellota and Idiazabal (a mature sheep's cheese from the Basque region). Suckling pig is 'melt in the mouth stuff', served up with apple sauce and a fat-busting lemon sorbet, while seafood options include cod fritters or the more moderno salmon tartare with avocado and raisin toast. Allow a bit of time if you hanker after black rice with squid and mussels or paella as they're cooked from scratch, and save room for a dessert such as Santiago almond cake. The short, exclusively Spanish wine list includes dry and sweet sherries. There's a second branch on Queenstown Road in Battersea, SW8 4LT.

Chef/s: Julian Gil. **Open:** Mon to Fri D. Sat and Sun, all day from 12.30. **Closed:** 25 Dec, 1 Jan. **Meals:** tapas £5 to £26. **Details:** 100 seats. Bar. Music.

Camberwell Arms

Cooking score: 3
map 1
Modern British | £30
65 Camberwell Church Street, Camberwell,
SE5 8TR
Tel no: (020) 7358 4364
thecamberwellarms.co.uk

Michael Davies has been running the kitchen at this high street pub with commendable reliablility since 2014. To the delight of his many regulars, he is now the owner – and the Camberwell Arms has lost none of its allure. An infectiously buzzy place across two floors, with an open kitchen that keeps an eye on the calendar, there's general approval for the sound sourcing of ingredients, for the down-to-earth cooking that has everyone competing for space in the two dining rooms, and the good, cheerful service. Burrata, blood orange, pistachio and mint should set you up nicely for Middle White pork leg with creamed chard and crispy sage, or a hake and acqua pazza (lightly herbed broth). Otherwise, the undisputed show stoppers are the dishes designed for sharing, say a matchless steak, ale and bone-marrow pie. After that, a simple scoop of grapefruit and Campari sorbet should round things off nicely. There are real ales, but cocktails fit the bill, too, while the short, global wine list starts at £18.
Chef/s: Michael Davies. **Open:** Tue to Sun L, Mon to Sat D. **Closed:** 24 to 27 Dec, 1 Jan, bank hols. **Meals:** main courses £10 to £20. **Details:** 90 seats. Bar. Wheelchairs. Music.

The Canton Arms

Cooking score: 1
⊖ Stockwell, map 3
Modern British | £29
177 South Lambeth Road, Stockwell, SW8 1XP
Tel no: (020) 7582 8710
cantonarms.com

£30

Still a popular neighbourhood hostelry, the Canton Arms also stakes its claim on the food front – thanks (in part) to co-owner Trish

Hilferty, a veteran of London's invigorated pub scene. Eat in the traditional bar or the book-lined dining room from a Med-accented daily menu that might run from Cornish mackerel escabèche to flourless chocolate cake with crème fraîche, via poached rabbit with sherry, ham and baby gem or wild sea bass with artichokes and aïoli. Guest ales and bottled world beers supplement a lively list of food-friendly wines. Note: it's first come, first served, but the owners operate a waiting list – so be patient.
Chef/s: Andrew Lambert. **Open:** Tue to Sun L, Mon to Sat D. **Closed:** 24 Dec to 2 Jan, bank hols. **Meals:** main courses £15 to £17. **Details:** 50 seats. 15 seats outside. Bar. Music.

Casse-Croûte

Cooking score: 4
⊖ London Bridge, Borough, map 1
French | £33
109 Bermondsey Street, Bermondsey, SE1 3XB
Tel no: (020) 7407 2140
cassecroute.co.uk

Readers continue to be hesitant in recommending this 'fantastic' but tiny French bistro 'just in case it becomes more popular than it is'. Push open the door and it is as though 'you have walked into a restaurant in the back streets of Paris', its Gallic theme emphasised by a black-and-white tiled floor, close-packed small tables with paper-topped gingham cloths and walls covered in French posters. A daily changing blackboard of brasserie classics offers just three starters, mains and desserts. The cooking – bourgeois with a rustic edge – takes in fish soup or *croustillants de pied de cochon* (pig's trotters), and rabbit with a well-rendered mustard sauce and excellent potato purée, or veal medallions with a parsley risotto. Desserts are out of the same country-cooking mould – mousse au chocolat or a myrtle tart. Service is well drilled and ungreedy pricing extends to the brief wine list.

Chef/s: Sylvain Soulard. **Open:** Mon to Sat, all day from 12. Sun L. **Closed:** 24 to 28 Dec. **Meals:** main courses £18 to £20. **Details:** 25 seats. Bar.

Chapters All Day Dining

Cooking score: 3
map 1
Modern British | £30
43-45 Montpelier Vale, Blackheath, SE3 0TJ
Tel no: (020) 8333 2666
chaptersblackheath.com

Chapters is the kind of neighbourhood brasserie you'd be thankful to have on your doorstep. Sure, it's never going to win prizes for inventiveness, but the all-day menu will take you from laid-back breakfast (eggs Benedict, grilled kippers) to celebratory dinner. The best dishes are cooked in the Josper: from juicy strips of char-grilled chicken in a Caesar salad, to rosy pink Kentish lamb chump chops. However, steaks and chops come unaccompanied so with sides 'at £3.50 a pop, prices are a bit punchy' for an 'affordable' eatery. Our advice, stick with the good-value main courses and you're on to a winner. Expect the likes of confit duck leg, or crispy-skinned fillets of black bream, which come with all the necessary trimmings. The set weekday menu is a steal, too, especially if the vanilla-rich crème brûlée is on offer. Wine mark-ups are reasonable, although there's not much to excite by the glass.
Chef/s: Nick Simmons. **Open:** all week L and D. **Closed:** 2 and 3 Jan. **Meals:** main courses £12 to £17. Set L £13 (2 courses) to £15. Set D £15 (2 courses) to £18. **Details:** 100 seats. 16 seats outside. Bar. Wheelchairs. Music.

Chez Bruce

Cooking score: 6
⊖ Balham, map 3
Modern British | £55
2 Bellevue Road, Wandsworth, SW17 7EG
Tel no: (020) 8672 0114
chezbruce.co.uk

Way beyond the West End bubble, Bruce Poole continues to set the standard for what a neighbourhood restaurant can and should do. Facing Wandsworth Common and done in soothing cream with none of today's hard edges, it's effectively a very successful contemporary bistro. The menu choice is broad and seasonally responsive, Matt Christmas's cooking direct and straightforward, yet harbouring a streak of inventiveness, too. Half a pink-roasted quail comes topped with its fried egg, some watercress and a thick slice of baked field mushroom stuffed with bacon, onions and breadcrumbs, or there could be crisply coated fishcake with potted shrimp butter, Hispi and chives. Improbable depth is conjured out of crisp-skinned Welsh chicken breast with a ballotine of the thigh stuffed with morels on a slew of peas, and from pinkly roasted duck with asparagus and a layered potato cake. Pure indulgence arrives at dessert stage in the form of a salt-caramel eclair with brown butter ice cream and poached pear. An exemplary list of carefully chosen wines opens with small glasses from £5, following up with Coravin measures of finer things, battalions of half-bottles and a roll call of reference producers from around the world.
Chef/s: Matt Christmas. **Open:** all week L and D. **Meals:** set L £35 (3 courses). Set D £55 (3 courses). **Details:** 80 seats. Wheelchairs.

Craft

Cooking score: 3

⊖ North Greenwich, map 1

Modern British | £45

Peninsula Square, Greenwich, SE10 0SQ

Tel no: (020) 8465 5910

craft-london.co.uk

For the time being, Craft – all three storeys of it – is ploughing a lone furrow amid the cranes and rising tower blocks of the Greenwich Peninsula. The piazza it stands on is a conduit for crowds flocking to the O2, but those who venture in are rewarded with a glass-walled top-floor bar and a restaurant space in shimmering aquamarine, where food from small artisanal producers is the improbable antidote to the corporate gigantism of the neighbourhood. What modern menus call 'snacks' are the appetising intro: brine-pickled vegetables with salted yoghurt and beetroot, and wonderful cod's roe alongside a tiny courgette with its battered flower in parsley emulsion. Even chicken liver parfait is given serious class with pickled walnuts, rhubarb relish and wafer-thin sourdough toast, while the pick of the mains at inspection was perfectly timed turbot with elderberry capers and spinach. Big, bold desserts include a rhubarb and custard spin involving a richly custardy trifle with meringue and cake, and blackberry ice cream with a mountain of heavenly mint granita. Wines from £22 take the artisanal approach, too, with small-batch producers including the avant-garde of Crete, Swartland and Sussex.

Chef/s: Ana Cortes Garcia. **Open:** Sat L, Tue to Sat D. **Closed:** Sun, Mon. **Meals:** main courses £18 to £26. Tasting menus £35 to £55. **Details:** 84 seats. Bar. Wheelchairs. Music. Parking.

Symbols

⌖ Accommodation is available

£30 Three courses for less than £30

£5 £5-off voucher scheme

▮ Notable wine list

The Crooked Well

⊖ Oval, map 1

Modern British | £30

16 Grove Lane, Camberwell, SE5 8SY

Tel no: (020) 7252 7798

thecrookedwell.com

£5
OFF

Something of a local hot spot, you'll find this genteel Victorian pub on a pretty residential street parallel to Camberwell Grove. The spacious bar-cum-dining room has plenty of light flooding through large windows, making it a pleasant place to enjoy a drink or casual meal. A laid-back vibe and service that keeps well on track even during busy periods are matched by good-value modern British dishes such as pigeon breast with raisins, pine nuts and celeriac rémoulade, and whole plaice with samphire, capers, brown butter and grilled lemon, as well as various steaks and the likes of rabbit and bacon pie for two. Wines from £17.50.

The Dairy

Cooking score: 6

⊖ Clapham Common, map 3

Modern European | £48

15 The Pavement, Clapham, SW4 0HY

Tel no: (020) 7622 4165

the-dairy.co.uk

With its little café-style frontage on the northern fringe of the Common, Robin Gill's Dairy stands next to Counter Culture, his south London take on the Basque pintxos bar. The big brother itself is a sober-looking, brown, bare-boarded space, with an open-kitchen hatch and neon-lit bar, the drill a series of small plates classified into appetisers and slightly larger veggie, fish and meat offerings. It is cooking stripped to its essentials, some of it from the rooftop garden, all of it impeccably sourced. Brawn gougères are like airy char siu buns, choux puffs laced with meaty umami, while Raf tomatoes on a burnt-buckwheat pancake are as sweet as new love, discreetly sprigged with horseradish. At inspection, sad to say, monkfish was slightly overcooked and dully garnished with slivered white asparagus, but the year-old Swaledale lamb was resonantly memorable, pink shoulder, pink liver and a slice of spiced leg sausage, along with braised grelots and chard. And an uncomplicated and undeconstructed slice of egg custard tart, innocent of nutmeg, needed only its fragrantly sour apple and elderflower sorbet for company. Coffee came with doughnuts on vanilla-speckled lemon cream. Wines by the glass from £6 are not the most exciting choices for the food, but cocktails inspire confidence.

Chef/s: Robin Gill. **Open:** Wed to Sun L, Tue to Sat D. **Closed:** Mon, 24 to 26 Dec, 1 and 2 Jan. **Meals:** small plates £11 to £13. Set L £25 (4 courses). Tasting menu £48. **Details:** 60 seats. 30 seats outside. V menu. Bar. Wheelchairs. Music.

Edwins

Cooking score: 1
 Borough, map 5
Modern European | £30
202-206 Borough High Street (Upstairs),
Borough, SE1 1JX
Tel no: (020) 7403 9913
edwinsborough.co.uk

Just a few steps from Borough tube, the entrance to Edwins is easily missed: a street door beside a pub leads up to the light, first-floor dining room with its unreconstructed décor – floorboards, polished tables, dangling lights – and retro vibe. The menu is structured and priced to allow one to dip in (via a parade of small plates) or take three courses. Lobster ravioli, pork belly and cauliflower purée, and scallops in filo with harissa mayo, have been standout small plates this year, with praise, too, for baby chicken with spring peas and greens, and the chateaubriand (for two) with béarnaise and bordelaise and hand-cut chips. Wines from £24.

Chef/s: Salim Massouf. **Open:** all week L, Mon to Sat D. **Meals:** main courses £13 to £22. Sun L £25 (3 courses). **Details:** 35 seats. Music.

★ NEW ENTRY ★

El Pastor

Cooking score: 2
 London Bridge, map 4
Mexican | £25
7a Stoney Street, Borough, SE1 9AA
tacoselpastor.co.uk
£30

With a shift of their culinary compass point from Spain to Mexico, Sam and Eddie Hart (along with younger brother James) have stepped into the gastronomic enclave of Borough Market with their homage to tacos, mescal and tequila. It's a cool, curvy and casual joint tucked under railway arches where foodies mingle with tourists and commuters while the kitchen lets rip with a barrage of eye-wateringly punchy flavours. Tacos (blue and white Mexican corn tortillas) are made in-house daily, favourites at our test meal being the 24-hour-marinated pork shoulder with caramelised pineapple, guacamole taquero, white onion and coriander, and the prawns with garlic sauce. Other hits included a ceviche-style starter of sea bass with lime, coriander and Serrano chilli, and a plain cheese quesadilla (folded blue native corn tortilla). Mescal and quality tequilas are available in shots, 150ml or 250ml sizes, and Mexican beers, good cocktails and a handful of Spanish and South American wines complete the picture.

Chef/s: Tomek Baranski. **Open:** Mon to Sat L and D. **Closed:** Sun, 25 and 26 Dec, bank hols. **Meals:** main courses £3 to £9. **Details:** Bar. Music.

Visit us online

To find out more about
The Good Food Guide, please
visit thegoodfoodguide.co.uk

Elliot's Café

Cooking score: 2
⊖ London Bridge, map 4
Modern European | £26
12 Stoney Street, Borough, SE1 9AD
Tel no: (020) 7403 7436
elliotscafe.com
£30

This busy, buzzy eatery opposite Borough Market is a quirky place to eat. It has a worn, rustic look within – a wood-burner and brick walls, small wooden tables and hard seats – and while some readers have found Elliot's Café a little low on creature comforts, there's general approval for the sound sourcing of ingredients and down-to-earth cooking. Many squeeze in here just for the cheeseburger and fat chips, but the regularly changing menu runs to the likes of sharing plates of charcuterie, grilled oysters and 'nduja XO, chicken hearts and lardo, or cheese puffs, salads of crab with heritage tomatoes or grilled peaches, Gorgonzola and sorrel, and grilled Cornish day-boat fish alongside very good steaks. Chocolate fondant with salted caramel and hazelnuts with vanilla ice cream is a well reported dessert. The wine list comprises organic and biodynamic wines sourced from small artisan growers.
Chef/s: Matt Goddard. **Open:** Mon to Sat L and D. **Closed:** Sun, bank hols. **Meals:** sharing plates £2 to £10. **Details:** 50 seats. 12 seats outside.

40 Maltby Street

Cooking score: 2
⊖ Bermondsey, map 1
Modern British | £28
40 Maltby Street, Bermondsey, SE1 3PA
Tel no: (020) 7237 9247
40maltbystreet.com
🍷 £30

A few decades ago it might have been wise to keep shtum about what was going on in the railway arches of Bermondsey, now you can upload photos on Instagram with impunity. At 40 Maltby Street, home of wine supplier Gergovie Wines, which specialises in chemical- and pesticide-free bottles from small European producers, a blackboard announces a daily menu that keeps punters coming in for more than just oenophilia. Like the wines, there's consideration for the environment and sustainability in the sourcing of the ingredients that arrive in relatively simple combinations. Among smaller plates, expect raw asparagus with pea shoots and mint, nettle and anchovy tart, and potted shrimps with Jersey Royals and watercress, with hunkier courses including pot-roast pork neck or brill with laverbread and leek gratin. Save room for warm parkin, apple and custard. It's fun, lively and, as you can't book, worth waiting for if you have to.
Chef/s: Steve Williams. **Open:** Fri and Sat L, Wed to Sat D. **Closed:** Sun, Mon, Tue. **Meals:** main courses £7 to £16. **Details:** 40 seats.

Franklins

Cooking score: 2
map 1
Modern British | £30
157 Lordship Lane, East Dulwich, SE22 8HX
Tel no: (020) 8299 9598
franklinsrestaurant.com

This is what is meant by a local restaurant: a convivial, friendly place that has a good regular following. The handsome Victorian building on Lordship Lane works hard, a small pub-bar at the front with a larger restaurant to the rear (where you can see the chefs at work). The daily menu is a roll call of seasonal dishes – their own farm shop is next door – with dishes a mix of home-grown and European flavours. For openers there could be quail, kohlrabi rémoulade and green sauce or a plate of Isle of Wight tomatoes with mozzarella and basil. To follow, ox tongue is served with dauphinois and sweet onions, or there could be shoulder of lamb with chickpeas, leeks and flat mushrooms. To finish, it's hard to ignore Welsh rarebit, so rarely do such savoury dishes appear on menus these days, but for the sweet-toothed there's prune and almond tart. Drinks run from hand-pulled ales via interesting cocktails to global wins (from £18).

Chef/s: Ralf Wittig. **Open:** all week, all day from 12. **Closed:** 25 and 26 Dec. **Meals:** main courses £15 to £24. Set L £14 (2 courses) to £17. **Details:** 70 seats. 12 seats outside. Bar. Wheelchairs. Music.

Ganapati

Cooking score: 3
⊖ Peckham Rye, map 1
Indian | £30
38 Holly Grove, Peckham, SE15 5DF
Tel no: (020) 7277 2928
ganapatirestaurant.com

A bright spark in Peckham, fans of South Indian food have been beating a path to Ganapati's door since 2004. It's a tiny, well-run place, the atmosphere rarely less than lively – booking is advisable – but it's the colourful, attention-grabbing freshness of the food that draws the crowds. What is on offer is a short menu of dishes that taste distinctively different, spicing is well handled and flavours are more complex and interesting than a standard curry house. After poppadoms with homemade pickles and chutneys, try spiced lamb chops marinated in red wine, garlic and black pepper or the well-reported vegetarian street snacks. Kerala goat curry is a must, too, but other choices include fillet of sea bass in a masala of fresh coriander, fennel, ginger and lemon juice. In addition to excellent thalis and good vegetarian choices, there's a classic gulab jamun for dessert. A short, carefully selected wine list opens at £22.

Chef/s: Aboobacker Pallithodi Koya. **Open:** Tue to Fri L. Sat and Sun all day from 12. **Closed:** Mon, 22 to 29 Dec. **Meals:** main courses £12 to £15. **Details:** 38 seats. 14 seats outside. Music.

★ NEW ENTRY ★

Hawksmoor Borough

Cooking score: 4
⊖ London Bridge, map 4
British | £50
16 Winchester Walk, Borough, SE1 9AQ
Tel no: (020) 7234 9940
thehawksmoor.com

Will Beckett and Huw Gott show they still have the Midas touch with the opening of their latest branch of Hawksmoor. A short walk from London Bridge, on the edge of Borough Market and in the grounds of the 12th-century Winchester Palace, Hawksmoor Borough occupies a mid-19th-century former hop warehouse that was also an auction house for fruit specialists in the 1930s. The kitchen makes good use of suppliers from within the market and menus are centred around the best British grass-fed beef (perhaps a bone-in porterhouse steak) or seafood (maybe South Coast monkfish cooked over charcoal) with a choice of anchovy or béarnaise sauce and sides including exemplary beef-dripping fries and cauliflower cheeses. Finish with the likes of Yorkshire rhubarb pannacotta. Set across two floors with a private dining room in the basement, the wood-panelled dining room has a timeless quality with its parquet floor, comfortable leather chairs and frosted-glass partitions. Wines from £23.

Chef/s: Simon Cotterill. **Open:** Mon to Fri L and D. Sat and Sun, all day from 12. **Closed:** 25 and 26 Dec, 1 Jan. **Meals:** main courses £12 to £60. Set L and D £25 (2 courses) to £28. Sun L £20. **Details:** 140 seats. Wheelchairs. Music.

LOCAL GEM

The Hill
🚇 Greenwich, map 1
Mediterranean | £27
89 Royal Hill, Greenwich, SE10 8SE
Tel no: (020) 8691 3626
thehillgreenwich.com

£30

Locals flock to fill up on sunshine-packed Mediterranean and Latin American flavours at this neighbourhood favourite where warm service and good cooking meld happily. Choose a thin-based 'quattro formaggi' pizza, generous paella, classic patatas bravas or whitebait tapas, or go off-piste for a 'rich, homely, delicious' encocado, an Ecuadorean dish of haddock slow-cooked with coconut, peppers and a hefty hit of turmeric and spice. Churros with homemade (and not over-sweet) dulce de leche is an appropriate finale – but choose tiramisu if you must!

José
Cooking score: 3
🚇 London Bridge, Borough, map 1
Spanish | £23
104 Bermondsey Street, Bermondsey, SE1 3UB
Tel no: (020) 7403 4902
josepizarro.com

£30

Just a few seats are up for grabs at José Pizarro's dinky tapas bar in the middle of Bermondsey Street, so you have to ask yourself one question: 'do I feel lucky?' If your luck is in, you'll get to experience something 'as close to the real thing as you'll find in London', that 'thing' being the sort of honest, earthy, convivial joint that is ten a penny in Andalucia. Blackboards reveal all: classic tortilla, pan con tomate, boquerones and jamón Ibérico alongside baby cuttlefish with black pudding, and lamb cutlets with baby potatoes. The quality of the ingredients stands out, including the plump prawns fired up with chilli and garlic. Rosemary cheesecake is a sweet and fragrant dessert. Drinking is as

much part the fun as the eating, with all the Spanish wines and sherries available by the glass. Little José is the latest addition to the family (in Crossrail Place, Canary Wharf).
Chef/s: José Pizarro. **Open:** Mon to Sat, all day from 12. Sun 12 to 5.15. **Closed:** 24 to 26 Dec, 1 Jan.
Meals: tapas £7 to £14. **Details:** 17 seats. Wheelchairs. Music.

Lamberts
Cooking score: 2
🚇 Balham, map 3
Modern British | £29
2 Station Parade, Balham High Road, Balham, SW12 9AZ
Tel no: (020) 8675 2233
lambertsrestaurant.com

£5 OFF   £30

The residents of Balham have always had a soft spot for Joe Lambert's good-natured neighbourhood eatery, applauding his crusading approach to seasonal British food and his support for independent regional producers. Understated contemporary interiors set the scene for daily market menus and a monthly carte – an enterprising line-up divided into 'field', 'sea' and 'farm' (at least in the evening). Proceedings might begin with some Colchester rock oysters, ahead of gnocchi with wild garlic and walnuts or soused mackerel partnered by Jersey Royals, capers, dill and crème fraîche. Elsewhere, Dorset snails make an appearance, while Dingley Dell pork belly sits alongside earthy companions including black pudding, lentils, spring greens and sauce vierge. The bone-in Shorthorn rib (aged for 35 days) is a sharing favourite, and puddings promise slabs of comforting nostalgia – think treacle tart or Eton mess. Cocktails and London-brewed beers are alternatives to the modestly priced wine list.
Chef/s: Joe Lambert. **Open:** Tue to Sun L, Tue to Sat D. **Closed:** Mon, 25 and 26 Dec, 1 Jan. **Meals:** main courses £14 to £20. Set D £17 (2 courses) to £20. Sun L £24. **Details:** 53 seats. 8 seats outside. Bar. Music.

The Lido Cafe

⊖ Brixton, map 1
Modern British | £30
Brockwell Park, Dulwich Road, Herne Hill,
SE24 0PA
Tel no: (020) 7737 8183
thelidocafe.co.uk

It's quite a treat to visit the listed Art Deco lido in Brockwell Park on a fine day, even more so to eat at its pleasant, amenably priced all-day café (even if the sun isn't shining). Honest intent is the deal with breakfast served throughout the day and lunch bringing the likes of dry-aged Longhorn beef burger with twice-cooked chips, and salads such as beetroot and pear with feta cheese, sunflower seeds, mint and a lemon dressing. Desserts like almond and blackberry tart and raspberry pastel de nata also tempt. Drink cocktails or wine from £21.

The Manor

Cooking score: 5
⊖ Clapham Common, Clapham North, map 3
Modern British | £38
148 Clapham Manor Street, Clapham,
SW4 6BX
Tel no: (020) 7720 4662
themanorclapham.co.uk

Housed in double-fronted premises of battleship grey, guarded by a stone goat *couchant*, the Manor is another in Robin Gill's portfolio of contemporary eateries (see also the Dairy and Paradise Garage). The mix of café tables and high bar-stools is typical of the genre, and at the centre here is a dessert station where you can watch various confections being assembled before your eyes. For the rest, a monthly changing menu of sharing plates (one savoury dish from each of the four sections) supplements the seven-course tasting menu, and the grab-bag approach produces Cornish crab with dulse and barbecued melon in miso, a wee dram of mushroom broth with pickled girolles and pieds bleus, as well as Saddleback pork with braised head, perhaps with courgettes, olives and chickpeas. Menu

descriptions certainly raise the stakes, self-defeatingly sometimes, but then those desserts hurl a fistful of flavours in your direction, maybe malt ice cream with parsnip and beer fudge, and all is well. Wines are fragrantly arranged by fruit aromas, from £23.
Chef/s: Dean Parker. **Open:** Wed to Sun L, Tue to Sat D. **Closed:** Mon, 22 to 29 Dec. **Meals:** main courses £6 to £13. Set L and early D £20 (4 courses). Tasting menu £45. **Details:** 50 seats. V menu. Bar. Wheelchairs. Music.

Marcella

Cooking score: 2
map 1
Italian | £28
165a Deptford High Street, Deptford,
SE8 3NU
Tel no: (020) 3903 6561
marcella.london
£30

This Deptford offshoot of highly regarded Artusi in Peckham (see entry) looks and feels sparsely contemporary – long and narrow with close-set white tables and an open, industrious kitchen where just about everything is made in house, from sourdough bread and pasta to ricotta and ice cream. The regularly changing blackboard-menu bristles with down-to-earth ingredients, so expect small plates of homemade fennel and chilli sausage with salsa verde and peperonata, gnocchi with girolles and peas, or pasta al pomodoro. Alternatively, opt for larger plates of tender whole quail with green beans, chilli and roasted onions, grilled cuttlefish with borlotti and prosciutto or a sharing plate of a magnificent whole bream stuffed with clams and fennel, the highlight of a test meal. Finish with fresh poached peaches and crème fraîche. Laid-back, hard-working staff and happy customers fill the place with joy. Reasonable pricing extends to the brief wine list.
Chef/s: Jack Beer. **Open:** Tue to Fri D only. Sat, all day from 12. Sun L. **Closed:** Mon. **Meals:** main courses from £13. **Details:** 42 seats. Bar.

LOCAL GEM

Mr Bao
map 1
Taiwanese | £20
293 Rye Lane, Peckham, SE15 4UA
Tel no: (020) 7635 0325
mrbao.co.uk

£30

It looks like every restaurant you go to these days – bare brick, bare floorboards, low-slung lights, tight-packed tables, basic seating – but tiny Mr Bao scores as a cheerful, friendly place to eat. Service is speedy and the easy eating menu is excellent value. Choose small plates of, say, fried chicken with miso mayo, prawn dumplings, golden kim-chee, and Tenderstem broccoli with ponzu, before bao (steamed buns) stuffed with pork belly, roasted peanut and coriander or beer-marinated prawns with pickled mooli and spiced spring onions. Drink cocktails rather than the basic choice of red or white.

Naughty Piglets
Cooking score: 2
⊖ Brixton, map 1
Modern European | £29
28 Brixton Water Lane, Brixton, SW2 1PE
Tel no: (020) 7274 7796
naughtypiglets.co.uk

🍾 £30

Joe and Margaux Sharratt have moved their main operation to Lord Lloyd-Webber's new theatre near Buckingham Palace (The Other Naughty Piglet, see entry), but their original (and popular) Brixton wine bar and dining room is still overseen by them: 'only regulars might notice the changes'. Chef Joe Sharratt's East-meets-West approach is still evident in the daily changing menu that might include a globe of burrata perched atop slow-cooked onions, dusted with a sesame-rich dukkah, or a mound of crab garnished with pickled cabbage and ground peanuts. The natural wine list is a draw for many, although a selection of

only ten by the glass (starting at £5.50) is brief for a wine bar; the selection by the bottle is far better, with the cheapest starting at £25. **Chef/s:** Joe Sharratt. **Open:** Thur to Sun L, Tue to Sat D. **Closed:** Mon, 2 weeks Dec. **Meals:** small plates £11 to £16. **Details:** 34 seats. Bar. Music.

LOCAL GEM

No. 67
⊖ Peckham Rye, map 1
Modern European | £17
South London Gallery, 67 Peckham Road, Peckham, SE5 8UH
Tel no: (020) 7252 7649
number67.co.uk

£30

Part of the South London Gallery, this all-day café is a popular venue, especially in fine weather when the front terrace (mercifully set back slightly from the busy A202) and pretty back garden come into their own. It has few pretensions beyond providing fresh, wholesome food, whether for breakfast or weekend brunches, or lunches of generous sandwiches (aubergine with roasted tomato and hummus, say) and plates of Welsh rarebit with pickled red cabbage and leaf salad or Spanish frittata with pickled radish and carrot salad. Cakes and coffee fill in the gaps. Wines from £20.

Padella
Cooking score: 2
⊖ London Bridge, map 4
Italian | £20
6 Southwark Street, Borough, SE1 1TQ
padella.co

£30

It's cheap and full to bursting – unwavering local support ensures long queues – and is certainly good news for visitors to Borough Market. Padella is a place with a mission – nourishing its regulars (and irregulars) with plates of freshly made pasta and an all-comers welcome attitude. It's an unassuming space done out, like it's north London sister Trullo (see entry), in sparse contemporary style with counter seating and an extra dining room downstairs. Trademarks including pappardelle of eight-hour Dexter beef shin ragù, tagliarini of Dorset crab with chilli and lemon, and pici cacio and pepe (quite simply, pasta, butter, pepper and Parmesan) share the short menu with home-baked sourdough, antipasti of Wiltshire burrata with olive oil or bruschetta with baked cannellini beans and salsa rossa, and desserts of pear and almond or chocolate tart. Drinkers can expect Italian-influenced cocktails and a short list of wines by the glass or 500ml carafe.

Chef/s: Ray O'Connor. **Open:** all week L, Mon to Sat D. **Meals:** main courses £6 to £13. **Details:** 75 seats. Wheelchairs. Music.

The Palmerston

Cooking score: 1
map 1
Modern British | £35
91 Lordship Lane, East Dulwich, SE22 8EP
Tel no: (020) 8693 1629
thepalmerston.co.uk

🍾

An agreeable East Dulwich pub, the Palmerston seems happy in its own skin. With wood panelling, scuffed floors, mismatched tables and fireplaces, the setting is unpretentious, informal and welcoming – all things that mark out neighbourhood success stories. Starters range from grilled Brixham squid with tempura tentacles and squid-ink-braised white beans to Italian spring white truffle with ratte potatoes, poached Cacklebean egg and chives, to mains such as skrei cod with peas, brown shrimps, tomato, Prosecco and chive butter, and Sunday roasts of pork loin with apple sauce and prune and sage stuffing. Drink classic cocktails or choose from a wine list that's been put together with obvious care and passion.

Chef/s: James Donnelly. **Open:** all week L and D. **Closed:** 25 and 26 Dec, 1 Jan. **Meals:** main courses £17 to £28. Set L £15 (2 courses) to £18. **Details:** 58 seats. 24 seats outside. Music.

Peckham Bazaar

Cooking score: 2
⊖ Peckham Rye, map 1
Eastern Mediterranean | £35
119 Consort Road, Peckham, SE15 3RU
Tel no: (020) 7732 2525
peckhambazaar.com

'Eastern Mediterranean grilled goodness,' they say, and it's hard to disagree with the likes of grey mullet kebab with chermoula and saffron skordalia. A relaxed, casual place, with lots of natural wood and little by the way of designer affectations, Peckham Bazaar is the place to come for pan-Balkan meze, with the charcoal-fuelled grill bringing a glorious smokiness to much of what comes out of the open kitchen. Seasonal British ingredients loom large, so Cornish mackerel is hot off the grill with caramelised onion pide, and English asparagus might figure in a prawn kebab with dukkah. Salt cod croquettes, grilled quail with chickpea and prune tagine, grilled rabbit with roasted artichokes, it's good, rustic stuff that keeps you coming back for more. The menu changes every day, which further encourages regular return. The wine list focuses on Greek producers.

Chef/s: John Gionleka. **Open:** Sat and Sun L, Tue to Sun D. **Closed:** Mon. **Meals:** main courses £8 to £17. **Details:** 33 seats. 22 seats outside. Wheelchairs. Music.

LOCAL GEM

Pedler

⊖ Peckham Rye, map 1
Modern European | £25
58 Peckham Rye, Peckham, SE15 4JR
Tel no: (020) 3030 5015
pedlerpeckhamrye.com

£5 OFF £30

It's a little rough round the edges (bare brick, close-packed tables) but Pedler works – a convivial, friendly place that has a strong local following and where value for money is a big plus. The flexible, cross-cultural menu works hard, allowing one to dip in or take three courses, starting perhaps with grilled aubergine, honeyed buttermilk and smashed nuts, before moving on to frizzle chicken with all spice and cheesy grits and attitude sauce (which gets rave reviews), before finishing with Yorkshire rhubarb trifle. Cocktails fit the bill, and everything comes by the glass on the wide-ranging wine list.

Pharmacy 2

Cooking score: 3
⊖ Lambeth North, Vauxhall, map 3
Modern European | £35
Newport Street Gallery, Newport Street, Vauxhall, SE11 6AJ
Tel no: (020) 3141 9333
pharmacyrestaurant.com

The 1990s revival is in full swing at Damien Hirst's Newport Street Gallery, where the YBA's cult Notting Hill restaurant Pharmacy has been reborn, medicine cabinets, pill bar-stools and all. The installation is as fascinating for those who remember it from the first time round as it is for those who come to it with fresh eyes. In the kitchen, Fabrizio Puscedu interprets co-collaborator Mark Hix's championing of British ingredients with a broad-minded menu that's an all-day affair, taking in classic dishes from across the continents. At brunch (available until 6pm), it's a toss-up between exotic morning market noodles and brik à l'oeuf de canard or comforting smoked salmon and scrambled eggs. Other hits are linguine with crab and chilli, excellent duck curry with apple pakoras, Sunday roasts and proper puddings (perhaps steamed bergamot marmalade sponge). Full marks for so many sub-£30 bottles on the wine list.

Chef/s: Fabrizio Puscedu. **Open:** Mon to Sat, all day from 12. Sun 12 to 6. **Closed:** Mon, 24 to 26 Dec, 31 Dec, 1 Jan. **Meals:** main courses £11 to £50. Sun L £24 (2 courses) to £28. **Details:** 72 seats. V menu. Wheelchairs. Music.

★ NEW ENTRY ★

Pique-Nique

Cooking score: 3
⊖ London Bridge, Bermondsey, map 1
French | £35
Tanner Street Park, Bermondsey, SE1 3LD
Tel no: (020) 7403 9549
pique-nique.co.uk

Within sight of Tanner Street Park's well-used tennis courts, it really does look like a park café, but, despite the croque-monsieur and coffee served at breakfast, that's where the similarity ends. Pique-Nique, like sister restaurant Casse-Croûte (see entry) a couple of minutes away, serves authentic, hearty, brilliantly rendered French bistro food – 'and boy do they feed you well'. The inside is very simple: café-style tables, bentwood chairs, wood floor, filament light bulbs, with a generous marble-topped bar running along two sides where 'you can see rotisserie chickens turning' – the main attraction on the 'menu autour du poulet de Bresse', where the chicken is served as six courses. In addition, a short carte brings vol-au-vent crammed with mushrooms, topped with crayfish and omelette and finished with a rich sauce nantua, grilled quail with petits pois à la française, or entrecôte and pommes paille (straw fries), and soufflé with warm apricot coulis and ice cream. Service is really personable – take their advice and start proceedings with a dry vermouth.

Chef/s: Sylvian Soulard. **Open:** Mon to Sat, all day from 9. Sun 10 to 5. **Closed:** 1 week Dec. **Meals:** main courses £20 to £22. **Details:** 40 seats. Bar. Wheelchairs. Music.

Pizarro

Cooking score: 4

⊖ London Bridge, Borough, map 1

Spanish | £35

194 Bermondsey Street, Southwark, SE1 3TQ

Tel no: (020) 7378 9455

pizarrorestaurant.com

José Pizarro's post-Brindisa career got underway on Bermondsey Street, home to his dinky tapas bar José and restaurant Pizarro, in 2010. (He's since branched out to the City.) Pizarro is the place to find his more robust dishes, based on a happy marriage of seasonal British ingredients and quality Spanish imports. It's a relaxed place to hang out, with dangling hams and blue-and-white tiles ticking the traditional box; and mid-century chairs and raw brick to bring things up to date. Tapas starters are a twist on classics – gazpacho, crab and quail's egg or caramelised chicory with goats' cheese and cranberries. Heartier dishes follow, perhaps quail en escabèche with rainbow chard stew or hake and clams in salsa verde, then torrija (French toast) with orange-peel ice cream to finish. The beverage list explores Spanish drinking culture in full, from gin tónicas to aged sherries, powerful reds and cava.

Chef/s: José Pizarro. **Open:** all week L and D. **Closed:** last week Dec. **Meals:** main courses £15 to £32. **Details:** 80 seats. Bar. Wheelchairs. Music.

★ TOP 50 ★

Restaurant Story

Cooking score: 7

⊖ London Bridge, map 4

Modern British | £120

199 Tooley Street, Bermondsey, SE1 2JX

Tel no: (020) 7183 2117

restaurantstory.co.uk

The surroundings may be incongruous, and the entrance to the modern glass construction may not be immediately obvious, but the restaurant is pretty clear where it is coming from. Tom Sellers' cooking is deliberately complex, full of daring and invention, and seems designed to test just how far an idea will

go, as if aiming to be the ultimate expression of something. Does it all work? On occasion, the cooking does fall into the 'style over substance' trap, possibly trying a little too hard to shoehorn what is an interesting 'life story' concept into a menu, but dividing the eight- and ten-course tasting menus into a foreword and chapters is an interesting, likeable idea. At its best the cooking has displayed some precise technique: in the 'soft, savoury, hot and crisp' confit rabbit sandwich, the hit of the procession of snacks, and in the timing of pollack, delicate and perfectly cooked, accompanied by a lick of cream sauce with a hint of alexanders and salty roe, dabs of sea buckthorn and parsley gel. Dive into a foamy, briny dish of scallops and you'll find clean, clear flavour with the lemony 'hand of Buddha' a perfect match. A bowl of puréed potato with charcoal oil and green asparagus is pure nostalgia – 'comforting, tasty, smooth, simple' – while the famous beef-dripping candle 'made me smile'. And among highly original desserts, a sensational amalgamation of almonds and dill is a fine balance of texture, temperature and flavour. Service is professional yet relaxed. Drinks do their best to keep up with a selection of bottled beers from London's microbreweries, cocktails, and pedigree wines from £25.

Chef/s: Tom Sellers and Luke Headon. **Open:** Tue to Sat L, Mon to Sat D. **Closed:** Sun, 22 Dec to 3 Jan, Aug bank hol. **Meals:** set L £45. Tasting menu L £80, D £120. **Details:** 37 seats. V menu. Wheelchairs. Children over 6 yrs only.

Roast

Cooking score: 2

⊖ London Bridge, map 4

British | £50

Floral Hall, Stoney Street, Borough, SE1 1TL

Tel no: (020) 3006 6111

roast-restaurant.com

Founded in 2005, Roast has almost achieved 'oldie but goodie' status as regards the British food renaissance. The fact that its handsome high-ceilinged dining room occupies a mezzanine in Borough Market's Floral Hall

also guarantees a captive audience of foodies, tourists and commuters, all of whom relish its mighty cooked breakfasts, Sunday roasts and other gleanings. Regional ingredients receive plenty of exposure here, from the Scrubby Oak apple vinegar served with rock oysters to the Sussex Wagyu beef pressed into service for the house burger. Elsewhere, Dorset crab is matched with avocado, cucumber, white radish and apple, while Isle of Wight garlic adds its pungency to a dish of braised ox cheeks and creamed onion sauce. Hereford steaks, heritage salads and puds such as Kentish cherry pie with yoghurt ice cream complete a rousing package. English labels naturally get top billing on the wide-ranging wine list.
Chef/s: Stuart Cauldwell. **Open:** all week L, Mon to Sat D. **Meals:** main courses £17 to £28. Tasting menu £75. **Details:** 120 seats. V menu. Bar. Wheelchairs. Music.

LOCAL GEM

Silk Road
map 1
Chinese | £15
49 Camberwell Church Street, Camberwell, SE5 8TR
Tel no: (020) 7703 4832

£30

The plain, decidedly no-frills dining room may 'look a bit like a takeaway', but there are far too many long, shared tables and benches. The food is from Xinjiang – a large region of north-western China – the cooking known for strong flavours including pepper, chilli, cumin and the use of wheat noodles – made in-house. It's a very simple concept (no desserts), inexpensive and very, very popular – booking is essential. Pork dumplings, lamb skewers, the big chicken plate, cabbage and chilli, pork with black fungus, and cucumber salad all have their fans. Cash only.

Soif
Cooking score: 1
⊖ Clapham South, map 3
Modern European | £32
27 Battersea Rise, Battersea, SW11 1HG
Tel no: (020) 7223 1112
soif.co

Soif (the name means 'thirst') offers an alluring mix of thrilling terroir-led wines and European bistro food in friendly surroundings – all primary colours, chunky furniture and distressed tiles. Blackboards dotted around the place list the day's fare, an assortment of little and large plates ranging from Christian Parra's boudin noir with quail's egg and mousserons to a tranche of Cornish plaice with asparagus, baby leeks and white wine sauce – plus rustic charcuterie, cheeses and specials from the recently added chargrill. Drink by the glass from a revelatory list that favours organic production, oddballs, obscurities, 'orange' trendies and bottles from the new standard-bearers of natural viticulture. Also look out for Soif's hugely popular 'share table' supper clubs showcasing terroir wines and regional cuisine.
Chef/s: Anthony Hodge. **Open:** Tue to Sun L, Mon to Sat D. **Closed:** 25 Dec to 2 Jan. **Meals:** main courses £16 to £20. **Details:** 56 seats. Bar. Music.

Please send us your feedback

To register your opinion about any restaurant listed in this guide, or a new restaurant that you wish to bring to our attention, please visit the web address at the bottom of the page. Your feedback informs the content of the book and will be used to compile next year's reviews.

★ NEW ENTRY ★

Sparrow

Cooking score: 2
⊖ Lewisham, map 1
International | £30

2 Rennell Street, Lewisham, SE13 7HD
Tel no: (020) 8318 6941
sparrowlondon.co.uk

Stepping boldly into the culinary vacuum of Lewisham, Terry Blake and Yohini Nandakumar's first venture is to be found just around the corner from Lewisham train station. The bare-bones dining room is awash with natural light, tables are close-packed, the kitchen open to view, and there is a casual neighbourhood vibe; good-natured staff make a difference. The kitchen offers fresh, seasonal food without airs or graces, sending out an assortment of sharing dishes with influences from all over. Don't be surprised to see picked Devon crab with coconut and Thai spices or massaman beef brisket with scorched rice challenging Euro contenders such as house-cured salmon with lemon and fennel dressing, brown shrimp and kohlrabi salad or grilled lamb chops with tomato and hazelnut salsa. Desserts such as kefir pannacotta with macerated strawberries are well made. All bottles on the brief, kindly priced European list come by the glass; there's also a cocktail of the day.
Chef/s: Terry Blake and Yohini Nandakumar. **Open:** Sat and Sun L, Tue to Sun D. **Closed:** Mon.
Meals: sharing plates £3 to £9. Main courses £12 to £15. **Details:** 30 seats.

Trinity

Cooking score: 6
⊖ Clapham Common, map 3
Modern European | £60

4 The Polygon, Clapham, SW4 0JG
Tel no: (020) 7622 1199
trinityrestaurant.co.uk

🍾

More than a dozen years after Adam Byatt set up shop here, he remains a hands-on presence and a key part in the friendly, welcoming

atmosphere that keeps guests coming back for more. A couple of years ago the restaurant was refurbished, and the resulting open-fronted light, chic and contemporary space, with tables spilling out under an awning in fine weather, seems to have all bases covered. The kitchen continues to turn out classically inspired dishes with gentle modern touches and a fierce adherence to the seasons. Soused Cornish mackerel with white gazpacho, grapes and tarragon or ravioli of scallop and lobster with lobster soup and a fried oyster typify the fresh, lively flavours, followed perhaps by pot-roast chicken with new season's morels, wild garlic and smoked lardo. To finish, maybe raspberry ripple soft serve with whisky jellies and toasted oats – 'a lovely combo'. The substantial wine list is very strong in France with shorter but still interesting shrift elsewhere. Bottles open at £21.
Chef/s: Adam Byatt. **Open:** all week L and D.
Closed: 25 to 31 Dec. **Meals:** main courses £28 to £35. Set L £35 (2 courses) to £39. **Details:** 48 seats. 18 seats outside. Wheelchairs. Children over 5 yrs only at D.

The White Onion

Cooking score: 3
⊖ Wimbledon, map 3
Modern French | £40

67 High Street, Wimbledon Village, Wimbledon, SW19 5EE
Tel no: (020) 8947 8278
thewhiteonion.co.uk

Chef Frederic Duval knows the recipe for a quality neighbourhood restaurant – he cooked with Eric Guignard at the French Table in Surbiton (see entry) for eight years before taking over the kitchen at the White Onion. With a dining room sporting a bright modern look of cream-and-blue walls, contemporary art, plain tables and wood floor, a kitchen rooted in solid technique and menu driven by excellent raw ingredients, it comes across as a bustling, informal eatery. Build on a delicious beginning of homemade bread (various flavours) with a first course of rabbit ballotine teamed with smoked eel, honey-roasted carrots, pickles and crispy Bayonne ham, then skrei cod with lobster risotto, monk's beard and crispy samphire. For dessert, the raspberry and pistachio mille-feuille with lychee sorbet has been an indulgent hit. The set lunch is excellent value, and a trans-global wine list opens with house selections by the glass or carafe.

Chef/s: Frederic Duval. **Open:** Thur to Sun L, Tue to Sat D. **Closed:** Mon, 25 Dec to 3 Jan, 1 to 15 Aug. **Meals:** main courses £13 to £25. Set L £19 (2 courses) to £23. Set D £33 (2 courses) to £40. Sun L £26. **Details:** 69 seats. Wheelchairs. Music.

★ NEW ENTRY ★

Winemakers

Cooking score: 3
⊖ Deptford, map 1
Modern British | £25
209 Deptford High Street, Deptford, SE8 3NT
Tel no: (020) 8305 6852
thewinemakersclub.co.uk

🍷 £30

A bright spark on Deptford High Street, Winemakers is a tiny wine bar-plus-restaurant that's run with an unselfconscious ease. It has the barest of fittings and little decoration, the food listed on the brief, regularly changing menu is as plain and unadulterated as the green and dark-wood dining room. The tone is set immediately with quality seasonal ingredients – seen in small plates of sweet, crunchy, soft-centred crab croquettes, intensely flavoured deep-fried cornes de boeuf peppers with marinated raisins and crème fraîche, and cured wild turbot with lemon and raw peas, and in main courses of Gigha halibut with peas, broad beans, tomatoes and beurre blanc, and roast herb-fed chicken with courgettes, basil and roast potatoes. Desserts might include warm chocolate sponge or homemade fig and honey ice cream – but the headline attraction is the terrific modern wine list that's bursting with organic and natural options and offers decent choice by the glass.

Chef/s: Rory Shannon and Andrew Gray. **Open:** Fri to Sun L, Tue to Sat D. **Closed:** Mon. **Meals:** main courses £16 to £22. **Details:** Bar.

Wright Brothers Borough Market

Cooking score: 2
⊖ London Bridge, map 4
Seafood | £40
11 Stoney Street, Southwark, SE1 9AD
Tel no: (020) 7403 9554
thewrightbrothers.co.uk

This high-decibel bolt-hole on the edge of Borough Market, with its stark, urban look and lively relaxed atmosphere, is the original of Ben Wright and Robin Hancock's burgeoning seafooder group (in Soho, Spitalfields, South Kensington – see entries). Snagging a table gets harder and harder (do book) or you may be lucky enough to bag a counter stool at the long oyster bar, but either way, you can look forward to some incredibly fresh fish. The open-to-view kitchen's foray into the world of fish cookery is straightforward and full flavoured, from fish soup with all the trimmings, breaded cod cheeks with lemon and mayonnaise or dressed Devon crab, to main courses of whole roasted sea bream with salsa verde, or wild bass fillet, which arrives with mussels, clams and samphire. The pick of desserts may well be an intensely dark chocolate and salted-caramel mousse. To drink, there's a good selection of porters, ales, stouts and sherries, excellent house cocktails and wines start at £21.

Chef/s: Rob Malyon. **Open:** all week L and D. **Closed:** 25 to 27 Dec, 1 Jan. **Meals:** main courses £17 to £20. **Details:** 56 seats. 8 seats outside. Music.

Albertine

Cooking score: 1
☻ Shepherd's Bush Market, Shepherd's Bush, map 1
Modern British | £30
1 Wood Lane, Shepherd's Bush, W12 7DP
Tel no: (020) 8743 9593
albertine.london

Rescued from threatened extinction in early 2017 by Allegra McEvedy, whose mother opened the original venue in 1978, Albertine lives to fight another day. It's been spruced up a touch, but the original wooden pew seating remains in the bare-floorboarded little wine bar at street level. Upstairs is a brightly domestic-looking dining room. The pared-down menus offer simple assembly food, as in smoked trout with warm Jersey Royals, horseradish and capers. Dishes that look unpromising turn out to be ambrosial, as with a forthrightly peppered taglierini cacio e pepe, while simple desserts include chocolate pot with salt caramel. It's all such fun that it will throw a trudge around Westfield into welcome relief. And as if that prospect weren't enough there's an exemplary tour of modern winemaking on offer in the form of a keenly priced list of exciting and offbeat flavours. Say hello to Greek Assyrtiko, biodynamic Nahe Spätburgunder, and sweet red Roussillon.
Chef/s: Roberto Freddi. **Open:** Mon to Sat, all day from 11. **Closed:** Sun. **Meals:** main courses £11 to £16. **Details:** 24 seats. Bar.

Amaya

Cooking score: 4
☻ Knightsbridge, map 6
Indian | £70
15 Halkin Arcade, Motcomb Street, Knightsbridge, SW1X 8JT
Tel no: (020) 7823 1166
amaya.biz

The trend for Indian dining at the opulent end of the scale has been one of the significant features of the most recent restaurant generation, and Amaya follows explicitly in the footsteps of pioneering Chutney Mary (see entry). In slinky Belgravia surroundings, upholstered in eye-popping candy colours and with a grandstanding viewable kitchen where flame-grilling and griddling mesmerise the senses, the eating structure is built around small appetiser dishes that precede the majestic arrival of the main business. The former are stimulating bites of spinach and fig tikki, stuffed portobellos, tamarind-glazed duck liver and suchlike, while the principal dishes take a slightly more traditional tack for chicken slow-cooked in almonds and yoghurt, and mushroom and lentil biryani. Jewel-like miniature desserts, including chocolate rasmalai, pistachio kulfi and rose-scented rhubarb brûlée, complete the picture. A classy wine list to suit the mood doesn't scruple to reach for the skies, but comes with a good glass selection from £8.75.
Chef/s: Karunesh Khanna. **Open:** all week L and D. **Meals:** main courses £25 to £43. Tasting menu L £42. **Details:** 98 seats. Wheelchairs. Parking. No children after 8pm.

L'Amorosa

☻ Ravenscourt Park, Stamford Brook, map 1
Italian | £35
278 King Street, Hammersmith, W6 0SP
Tel no: (020) 8563 0300
lamorosa.co.uk

£5 OFF

After more than a decade heading up the kitchen at big-hitting Zafferano (see entry), Andy Needham swapped Knightsbridge glitz for a more down-home neighbourhood vibe in his own lively gaff. Come here for punchily flavoured, generous and keenly priced regional Italian food served without flimflam – perhaps spiky baby artichokes with green beans and Tropea shallot dressing, roast corn-fed chicken with Amalfi lemon and Pantelleria capers or linguine with Brixham crab, courgette and chilli, followed by chocolate and almond tart. Drink from a promising all-Italian wine list.

Apero

Cooking score: 2
⊖ South Kensington, map 3
Mediterranean | £27
The Ampersand Hotel, 2-10 Harrington Road, South Kensington, SW7 3ER
Tel no: (020) 7591 4410
aperorestaurantandbar.com

Down in the bowels of the Ampersand Hotel, Apero's marble-topped bar dispenses inventive cocktails inspired by famous local residents and South Ken's museums, while diners sit at plush leather chairs surrounded by bare-brick walls and dangling Edison light bulbs. Focusing on bright sunny Mediterranean flavours, the kitchen's all-day offer embraces enticing brunch and lunch deals as well as a line-up of sharing plates, all capably fashioned from native and imported ingredients. Grazing options run from Ibérico ham croquetas to textures of cauliflower with raisins and almonds or roast scallop with samphire and saffron potatoes; otherwise, there are more substantial servings of lamb rump with aubergine caponata or pan-fried duck breast with foie gras, cherries and wild rice. The assortment of Anglo-European cheeses is worth exploring, as are unexpected desserts such as cashew meringue with apple financier and coconut ice cream. France and Italy dominate the short wine list.
Chef/s: Mark Woolgar. **Open:** all week L and D.
Meals: main courses £8 to £18. Set L £13 (2 courses) to £16. **Details:** 48 seats. Bar. Wheelchairs. Music.

Bar Boulud

Cooking score: 4
⊖ Knightsbridge, map 6
French/American | £43
Mandarin Oriental Hyde Park, 66 Knightsbridge, Knightsbridge, SW1X 7LA
Tel no: (020) 7201 3899
barboulud.com

A swift refurb in early 2017 produced new red leather seating, beige banquettes, burgundy walls and mirrors. What hasn't changed is the zinc bar, open-view kitchen and the relaxed mood. Charcuterie and burgers on the French-American brasserie menu (now slightly shortened) continue to grab the limelight and the cooking continues to be sound – note a well-timed roasted monkfish tail wrapped with pancetta, teamed with carrot purée and Tenderstem broccoli and given heft by an excellent diable sauce. However, a regional accent has been introduced, on our visit a 'flaky, cheesy' tarte flambé, followed by choucroute garnie, then a delicious traditional apple tarte, all Alsatian specialities. Elsewhere, the cheese selection (from La Fromagerie) has increased to six – there's now a small cheese trolley. Service is very accommodating. A nifty list of cocktails and beers sits alongside a hefty wine list (from £25) packed with famous labels (including an impressive collection of large-format bottles), but prices are high.
Chef/s: Thomas Piat. **Open:** all week, all day from 12. **Meals:** main courses £21 to £34. Set L and D £18 (2 courses) to £21. **Details:** 135 seats. Bar. Wheelchairs. Music.

Bombay Brasserie

Cooking score: 3
⊖ Gloucester Road, map 3
Indian | £48
Courtfield Road, South Kensington, SW7 4QH
Tel no: (020) 7370 4040
bombayb.co.uk

A valiant trooper among London's Indian restaurants, the Bombay Brasserie has been seducing visitors since the 1980s – although some of its flamboyant glitz and glamour has been softened in recent years. That said, high ceilings, ornate chandeliers and a plant-filled, glass-roofed conservatory still suggest a certain swagger – perfect for a menu that mixes Raj-style luxury with street food and the occasional detour into crossover territory. Picks from the appetisers might range from soft-shell crab with raw mango salad to 'chilli milli' kebabs (spiced vegetable patties wrapped around a 'bullet' chilli), while the tandoor delivers everything from mustard-infused monkfish to ginger-spiked lamb chops. Traditionalists might go for chicken tikka makhani; those of a more adventurous bent could favour the Keralan halibut curry or salli boti (lamb with apricots, jaggery, tomato, vinegar and straw potatoes). Crowds pack in for the Sunday buffet, and the wine list is helpfully annotated by style.

Chef/s: Prahlad Hegde. **Open:** Tue to Sun L, all week D. **Closed:** 25 Dec. **Meals:** main courses £18 to £27. Set L £27. Set D £51. Sat and Sun L £35 (buffet). Tasting menus £58 to £64. **Details:** 105 seats. 120 seats outside. V menu. Bar. Wheelchairs. Music.

Cambio de Tercio

Cooking score: 5
◒ Gloucester Road, map 3
Spanish | £45
163 Old Brompton Road, Earl's Court, SW5 0LJ
Tel no: (020) 7244 8970
cambiodetercio.co.uk

🍷

The vision and personality of owner Abel Lusa has driven success at this casual and lively restaurant for more than two decades. From the beginning, Señor Lusa was determined to champion the best Spanish food and recruited chefs from Madrid to keep menus fresh and relevant. Today the chef is Alberto Criado who reinvents classic dishes like ham croquetas, tortilla with black truffle or spicy patatas bravas, and brings creative magic to new dishes like oysters with blood-orange foam or smoked tuna with anchovy mayonnaise, scallops and tiny new vegetables. Roast halibut is served with rainbow chard, salty cockles and wild garlic cream, while a succulent piece of pluma Ibérica comes with roast pineapple and prunes in sherry brandy. There's an ambitious tasting menu, too. Even traditional desserts are brought up to date: rum baba with hibiscus gel and elderflower sorbet, for instance, or the perennial 'flan' cooked for four hours to smooth sweetness. The Spanish wine list is one of the best in the capital with a list of sherries to win over any

doubters. To reflect Spain's current craze for gin and tonic, a new bar has been created adjacent to the restaurant offering scores of different gins and bespoke mixers and garnishes according to the botanicals. It's great theatre and all part of the fun.

Chef/s: Alberto Criado. **Open:** all week L and D. **Meals:** main courses £19 to £32. Tapas £7 to £26. Tasting menu £45. **Details:** 80 seats. 6 seats outside. V menu. Bar. Music.

Charlotte's Bistro

Cooking score: 3
◒ Turnham Green, map 1
Modern European | £30
6 Turnham Green Terrace, Chiswick, W4 1QP
Tel no: (020) 8742 3590
charlottes.co.uk

£5
OFF

Having experimented with different styles and formats, this sibling of Charlotte's Place in Ealing (see entry) has reverted to its original concept and now fills a niche somewhere between a high street brasserie and a fine-dining destination. Spread over two levels, the interiors are much as before (brown leather banquettes, wall-mounted box lighting), although the kitchen has gone back to its original ethos – namely fixed-price menus with seasonal overtones and a liking for bright flavours. Make a start by ordering confit chicken wings with pea mousse, lemon purée and pickled baby gem, then progress to pan-fried skate with lardo, broccoli and almonds, or meaty maple-glazed duck breast with braised fennel and orange purée. For afters, polenta and pistachio cake with peanuts and Greek yoghurt ice cream sounds suitably international. Some 30 gins are highlights at the all-day bar, while the wine list offers decent drinking at fair prices.

Open: all week L and D. **Meals:** set L Mon to Fri £20 (2 courses) to £25, Sat and Sun £25 (2 courses) to £30. Set D £29 (2 courses) to £35. **Details:** 80 seats. V menu. Bar. Music.

Charlotte's Place

Cooking score: 4
⊖ Ealing Broadway, Ealing Common, map 1
Modern European | £33
16 St Matthew's Road, Ealing, W5 3JT
Tel no: (020) 8567 7541
charlottes.co.uk
£5 OFF

Following a makeover in 2016, this two-tiered sibling of Charlotte's Bistro in Chiswick (see entry) looks bright and shiny with every table now promising views of Ealing Common. All that natural light also helps to point up the exposed brick walls, reclaimed oak doors and stripped-wood floors – it's a pretty picture to be sure, and a fitting backdrop to Lee Cadden's artfully constructed food. Menus change monthly to reflect the market and the calendar, so expect the likes of cured mackerel with cod cheeks, vichyssoise and potato salad in summer, ahead of Clwyd Vale lamb neck and hay-smoked breast accompanied by Jersey Royals and broad beans. Elsewhere, goats' milk yoghurt might be paired with beetroot and sesame, while desserts could include vanilla pannacotta with Yorkshire rhubarb and grapefruit. A dozen wines by the glass or carafe head up a well-constructed list. Ealing is also home to Charlotte's W5 at Dickens Yard, Longfield Avenue, W5 2UQ.
Chef/s: Lee Cadden. **Open:** all week L and D.
Meals: set L Mon to Fri £23 (2 courses) to £28, Sat and Sun £28 (2 courses) to £33. Set D £33 (2 courses) to £39. Tasting menu £34 to £42 (8 courses). **Details:** 50 seats. 14 seats outside. Wheelchairs. Music. Parking.

Clarke's

Cooking score: 4
⊖ Notting Hill Gate, map 6
Modern British | £50
124 Kensington Church Street, Notting Hill, W8 4BH
Tel no: (020) 7221 9225
sallyclarke.com

Sally Clarke's stalwart Kensington dining room, established in 1984, continues to receive plaudits for its 'super-attentive' service and 'no fuss' attitude. This approach matches the kitchen where British and Italian ingredients, flushed with seasonal promise, are respectfully united on a menu occasionally redolent of a bourgeois dinner party. But simple things, such as gazpacho or smoked salmon with capers and crème fraîche, become special things with the right accompaniment – herbed breadsticks in the case of the former, rye wafers the latter: Clarke's baking is rightly famous. Generous mains are 'ably cooked and decoratively presented', for example, roasted turbot on the bone with samphire and Prosecco or Lancashire duck and purple figs. Chocolate brownie comes with peanut ice cream pronounced 'so good that the recipe was requested'. Fireworks are few, but that's not to underestimate the pleasure of prime ingredients perfectly matched with a rare Californian or European bottle from the cellar.
Chef/s: Sally Clarke and Michele Lombardi. **Open:** Mon to Sat L and D. **Closed:** Sun, 10 days Christmas, 10 days Aug, bank hols. **Meals:** main courses £25 to £32. Set L £27 (2 courses) to £32. Set D £39 (3 courses). **Details:** 90 seats. V menu. Bar. Wheelchairs.

★ TOP 10 ★

Claude Bosi at Bibendum

Cooking score: 8
⊖ South Kensington, map 3
French | £85
Michelin House, 81 Fulham Road, South
Kensington, SW3 6RD
Tel no: (020) 7581 5817
bibendum.co.uk

The move from Hibiscus to Bibendum seems to have done Claude Bosi the power of good. Although the cooking had yet to settle into any comfortable rhythm of perfection at inspection, this is first division nonetheless. Refurbishment has re-energised the place, reinforcing the long-held reputation as one of London's most beautiful dining rooms. Now lighter in tone – making the famous pair of stained-glass windows really stand out – Bibendum feels genuinely user-friendly with staff reassuringly civil, without any of the hauteur that can come with a place of this standing. And there has been a subtle modulation in the tone and style of M. Bosi's cooking. He no longer strives for high-wire complexity; the goal is now the accessible elegance of classic French cooking, though naturally, with modern adjustments. Even dishes that look more obviously like bids for haute cuisine seduction – the glorious duck jelly layered over a spring onion soubise and topped with tiny diced smoked sturgeon and a garnish of oscietra caviar – ring honest and true, and when featherlight, wheat-free soupe au pistou dumplings are served with a powerful dollop of Genovese basil and pesto and an intense consommé of Obsiblue prawn, the result is an exquisite balance of flavours. Elsewhere, John Dory is brightened by the depth of flavour in a 24-hour slow-baked Vesuvian tomato, creamy streaks of lime and vanilla sweet-and-sour registering a fleeting, teasing impression, while Brittany rabbit – loin and mini cutlets – with a rich, creamy lobster bisque, artichoke barigoule and a side of perfect potato dauphinois (just to show chef can do it), is an authoritative demonstration. It is possible to play it safe (a chocolate soufflé with Indonesian basil ice cream is immaculate but staid). Incidentals, however, from the eggshell appetiser to petits fours, are all sublime. As is the glorious wine, a formidable treasury taking in the great and the good from all corners of the globe.
Chef/s: Claude Bosi. **Open:** Wed to Sun L, Wed to Sat D. **Closed:** Mon, Tue. **Meals:** main courses L only £28 to £39. Set L £30 (2 courses) to £37. Set-price alc D £85 (3 courses). **Details:** 60 seats.

Claude's Kitchen

Cooking score: 4
⊖ Parsons Green, map 3
Modern British | £36
51 Parsons Green Lane, Parsons Green, SW6 4JA
Tel no: (020) 3813 3223
amusebouchelondon.com

Claude Compton's kitchen may be tiny but he has big ambitions at this little bistro above the Amuse Bouche Champagne bar. As expected, the trappings are par for the course in this part of town (stripped floors, upcycled furniture, dangling Edison light bulbs), but the food has real clarity, plenty of creative impact and an eye for pretty detail. We're not in small-plates territory here, so kick off with a daring pairing of BBQ cuttlefish, ink cracker, green gazpacho and green chilli with back notes of vanilla before tackling pork neck with peas (and shoots), white onion and summer truffle or pollack accompanied by wild garlic, brioche, St George's mushrooms, samphire and San Marzano tomatoes. Menus are brief and to the point, with desserts touting the likes of lemon tart with meringues, shortbread and lemon balm. A full list of Champagnes from the bar down below supplements a short line-up of offbeat wines.
Chef/s: Claude Compton. **Open:** Mon to Sat D only. **Closed:** Sun. **Meals:** main courses £17 to £29. **Details:** 40 seats. Bar. Music. No children.

Colbert

Cooking score: 2
⊖ Sloane Square, map 3
French | £38
50-52 Sloane Square, Chelsea, SW1W 8AX
Tel no: (020) 7730 2804
colbertchelsea.com

Chris Corbin and Jeremy King are master impressionists and here on Sloane Square they've created a vision of a grand Parisian café *par excellence*. While The Wolseley and The Delaunay (see entries) look further into central Europe, Colbert is a French thoroughbred, which looks the part from its oxblood banquettes to its pavement tables. The menu is as classic as the interior design, from croque-madame to omelette au choix, but this is Corbin and King, so you can expect a bit of luxury in the form of caviar served up with blinis and crème fraîche. Puy lentil and superfood salad shows some modern ways have been embraced, but you might keep it *classique* with wild mushroom and leek pithiviers, or leg of lamb with ratatouille. Dessert is an equally comforting foray: tarte au citron, rum baba or salted-caramel eclair. French wines start at £25.50.

Chef/s: Stuart Conibear. **Open:** all week, all day from 12. **Closed:** 25 Dec. **Meals:** main courses £10 to £28. **Details:** 118 seats. 24 seats outside. V menu. Bar. Wheelchairs. Music.

★ TOP 50 ★

Dinner by Heston Blumenthal

Cooking score: 8
⊖ Knightsbridge, map 6
British | £70
Mandarin Oriental Hyde Park, 66 Knightsbridge, Knightsbridge, SW1X 7LA
Tel no: (020) 7201 3833
dinnerbyheston.com

This is a tour de force of a restaurant where virtuosic cooking, supreme service and an oozingly glamorous but comfortable dining room meld like the most perfect of partnerships. Famously scouring culinary archives to find curiously named gems to reinvent, the menu (including the fantastic-value set lunch) demands the focus you'd give an academic treatise. But – oh my – it is worth the effort, delivering knockout dish after knockout dish with meticulous attention to flavour and texture. Rich, smooth chicken liver parfait is contained in an exquisitely crafted citrus gel that even *feels* like a mandarin's dimpled skin in the now legendary meat fruit starter (it's served with very moreish toasted herb-oil sourdough). Frumenty, a 14th-century boiled wheat favourite, is elevated for the discerning 21st-century palate into a dish of tender octopus with gently-smoky 'sea broth' and nutty grains, while 18th-century salamagundy sets soft chicken oysters, sweet salsify, nubs of marrow bone and bitter chicory leaves against a powerful horseradish cream. An Ibérico pork chop is as muscular as it is tender next to a little pile of spelt and ham hock covered in a translucent layer of syrupy lardo di colonnata. Finish with the sweet comfort of tipsy cake, a fluffy brioche drenched in Sauternes-rich cream served with spit-roast pineapple, or brown-bread ice cream with its unforgettable panorama of tastes and texture: sweet-salt caramel, almost savoury ice cream, fresh pear and crunchy oat biscuit. The wine list is long, classy and expensive – of course – but comes with a reassuring side of extremely knowledgeable service.

Chef/s: Ashley Palmer-Watts and Jonny Glass. **Open:** all week L and D. **Closed:** 14 to 27 Aug. **Meals:** main courses £28 to £44. Set L £40. **Details:** 149 seats. Wheelchairs. Children over 4 yrs only.

Elystan Street

Cooking score: 6
⊖ South Kensington, Sloane Square, map 3
Modern European | £70
43 Elystan Street, Chelsea, SW3 3NT
Tel no: (020) 7628 5005
elystanstreet.com

In 2016, Philip Howard left The Square after 25 years as chef and co-owner, banished all thoughts of retirement and rebooted his career with a restaurant in Chelsea. The ground-floor corner site (formerly Tom Aikens), with its light, airy interior, bare tables and colourful furniture has been a striking success from the start. Mr Howard's focus these days is on healthy eating, with protein just one component of a dish and a new emphasis on vegetables, seeds, nuts and on-trend fermenting, but he is too fine a chef for gimmicks: skill and taste are evident even in vegetarian dishes such as griddled sprouts with baked root vegetables, cashew hummus, date jam, chestnuts, pomegranate and pine oil. Otherwise, a creamy symphony of veal tartare with white asparagus, capers, quail's eggs and green olives is given a savoury kick from rustic pecorino cheese. Roast partridge is served with blackened pear, celeriac, chanterelles and chestnuts, while a superb tranche of cod comes with lightly curried lentils, sprouting broccoli, coriander and the whole bathed with almond milk. Desserts include pineapple chunks poached in blueberry juice (almost a fruit soup) and homemade ice creams and sorbets with refreshing flavours like passion fruit, sour cream, grape and green apple. Alongside this modern imaginative food is a splendid wine list with many by the glass (175ml) and at friendly prices.
Chef/s: Philip Howard and Toby Burrows. **Open:** all week L and D. **Closed:** 24 to 28 Dec, spring and summer bank hols. **Meals:** main courses £24 to £36. Set L £35 (2 courses) to £50. Sun L £50. **Details:** 64 seats. V menu. Wheelchairs.

Enoteca Turi

Cooking score: 4
⊖ Sloane Square, map 3
Italian | £49
87 Pimlico Road, Chelsea, SW1W 8PH
Tel no: (020) 7730 3663
enotecaturi.com

£5 OFF 🍾

A year since relocating from Putney, Enoteca Turi appears to have settled well into Belgravia. A new chef has been appointed since the last edition of the guide – Francesco Sodano hails from Naples and his cooking is ambitious, sophisticated, modern and confident. At a test meal, four red Sicilian prawns were perfectly cooked and worked well with a couscous salad perked up by fennel confit and blood orange. Then came maize tagliatelle, served with a wonderfully earthy combination of cured pork cheek and cannellini beans, while a well-cooked fillet of monkfish, wrapped in lardo, was lifted by smoked potato and seafood guazzetto (tomato-based sauce). To finish, the 'exquisitely made' seven-layered chocolate sponge with praline, hazelnut and chocolate mousse was 'heavenly, rich and indulgent'. The spacious, smart yet relaxed dining room is decorated with gold paint, dark wood and large mirrors and service is helpful and attentive. The lengthy wine list pulls together famous labels from all the regions of Italy, and includes some 30 bottles in the £22 to £40 range.
Chef/s: Francesco Sodano. **Open:** Mon to Sat L and D. **Closed:** Sun, 25 and 26 Dec, 1 Jan. **Meals:** main courses £18 to £30. Set L £25 (2 courses) to £29. **Details:** 70 seats. 8 seats outside. Music.

Visit us online

To find out more about The Good Food Guide, please visit thegoodfoodguide.co.uk

L'Etranger

Cooking score: 3
⊖ Gloucester Road, South Kensington, map 3
Modern French | £50
36 Gloucester Road, South Kensington,
SW7 4QT
Tel no: (020) 7584 1118
etranger.co.uk

A sleek, corner site, all black-glass tables and cappuccino walls, with a menu as cosmopolitan as its clientele, L'Etranger is a destination for some, local drop-in for others. The kitchen makes much of its Japanese-influenced French cuisine, which was considered innovative, even intriguing, when the restaurant first opened in 2002, but is a little more familiar nowadays. For example, a very moreish crispy squid with saké and chilli dipping sauce is now a well-known starter, as is a main course of caramelised Alaskan black cod with miso, sushi rice and pickled ginger. Duck breast with pear and swede purée arriving in its own smoke may seem 'a little *de trop*', but is in fact perfectly cooked and full of flavour, as is sea bass, given heft by crisp, vinegared pickled fennel. The menu, for what it offers, is remarkably good value, but those searching for a bargain in the huge, fabulous and very grand wine list will need patience and a magnifying glass.
Chef/s: Peter Tonge. **Open:** all week L, Mon to Sat D. **Meals:** main courses £14 to £32. Set L £20 (2 courses) to £25. Set D £30 (3 courses). Tasting menu £65. **Details:** 65 seats. Bar. Music.

The Five Fields

Cooking score: 6
⊖ Sloane Square, map 3
Modern British | £65
8-9 Blacklands Terrace, Chelsea, SW3 2SP
Tel no: (020) 7838 1082
fivefieldsrestaurant.com

'I loved, loved this dinner,' was all one happy diner needed to say after eating at this small, supremely comfortable restaurant. Others praise the spot-on service and the light,

contemporary décor – but go above all for Taylor Bonnyman's inspired cooking. The snappy, seasonally aware eight-course taster covers a lot of ground (and sea). Dishes brim with stimulating flavours and flashes of brilliance: 'fantastic' scallop with coffee and pine nut might just be the pick of the early courses, though the overall winner for one visitor was the tender, pink pigeon with beetroot and tamarind. Brill with rhubarb and oyster is a balancing act brought off with panache, and there's an almost traditional offering with Longhorn short rib with Périgord truffle and oxtail. Otherwise, a jewel-coloured ball of foie gras (lightly wrapped in beetroot) features on the two-or three-course set-price menu, and seek out the pleasure of sea bass with cockles, clementine and couscous, and an impressive blackcurrant and feuilletine cheesecake. There's quality on a fine international wine list; prices start at £27.
Chef/s: Taylor Bonnyman and Marguerite Keogh.
Open: Mon to Fri D. **Closed:** Sat, Sun, 2 weeks Aug.
Meals: set D £55 (2 courses) to £65. Tasting menu £85 (8 courses). **Details:** 40 seats. Bar. Wheelchairs. Music.

The Goring

Cooking score: 5
⊖ Victoria, map 3
Modern British | £60
15 Beeston Place, Belgravia, SW1W 0JW
Tel no: (020) 7396 9000
thegoring.com

Return visitors find themselves impressed anew at how little seems to change at this genteel residence in the heart of Belgravia, the oldest privately owned hotel in the capital. It's very English and very charming, the plush bar all antiqued gold and deep reds, the David Linley-designed dining room perhaps a touch too beige after the warmth of the bar, but run with comfortable hospitality. Shay Cooper's commanding grasp of classic and modern techniques means there is no superfluous fuss or frippery, just beautiful ingredients and an emphasis on full flavours, and regulars appreciate the old-school touches – the daily roast trolley, the simply prepared Dover sole. There's been praise, too, for Hereford beef tartare, for the salt marsh lamb with preserved lemon, grilled leek heart and smoked garlic potato, and for a set lunch of cep risotto with yellow chanterelles, Ibérico ham and smoked butter, and glazed lobster omelette with duck-fat chips and lobster Caeser salad. The pricey wine list opens at £30.

Chef/s: Shay Cooper. **Open:** Mon to Fri and Sun L, all week D. **Meals:** set L £49. Set D £60. **Details:** 70 seats. 30 seats outside. V menu. Bar. Wheelchairs. Parking.

The Harwood Arms

Cooking score: 5
Fulham Broadway, map 3
British | £43
Walham Grove, Fulham, SW6 1QP
Tel no: (020) 7386 1847
harwoodarms.com

'Superb British food and I enjoyed everything here' – the Harwood Arms shows no signs of slowing down. It's part owned by Brett Graham of the Ledbury (see entry), but is essentially a pub, decked out with lots of wood and sensibly spaced tables with the odd sofa to soften things up. Courteous service helps things along and the daily changing menu is filled with surprises. The cooking may appear straightforward, but it's sophisticated stuff. What strikes most is the freshness of the food, and intensity of flavour. Roast Norfolk quail arrives with 'an awesome' black pudding Scotch egg and mushroom ketchup, while Cornish monkfish is given an extra edge by pork belly, lentils, romanesco and almond crumbs ('even the very buttery mash is faultless'). Puddings such as poached rhubarb with whipped buttermilk and stem ginger ice cream are a fitting finale. The extensive wine list (from £26), takes a global stroll, and there is scope for experimentation due to sensible pricing and plenty of choice by the glass.

Chef/s: Sally Abé. **Open:** Tue to Sun L, all week D. **Closed:** 24 to 26 Dec, 1 Jan. **Meals:** set L £23 (2 courses) to £28. Set D £35 (2 courses) to £43. Sun L £44 to £53. **Details:** 58 seats. V menu. Bar. Wheelchairs. Music.

Hawksmoor Knightsbridge

Cooking score: 4
Knightsbridge, South Kensington, map 3
British | £50
3 Yeoman's Row, Knightsbridge, SW3 2AL
Tel no: (020) 7590 9290
thehawksmoor.com

Only the unassuming entrance is visible from the street and you go down to a dark, moody subterranean bar and dining room – all shades of buff and brown – but everyone agrees that this Knightsbridge branch is a lovely addition to the group. Like the other Hawksmoor venues, this is a modern temple to red meat. Choose your cut and weight from a line-up that includes fillet, ribeye and sirloin, with porterhouse, bone-in prime rib and chateaubriand for the big spenders. All the requisite trimmings are on hand (triple-cooked chips, mash with gravy, creamed spinach, baked sweet potato) as well as a choice of sauces. If steak doesn't appeal, consider something like lobster roll with sriracha mayonnaise and yuzu or char-grilled monkfish. To start the ball rolling there are oysters and starters such as Salcombe crab salad, potted beef and bacon (with Yorkshire pudding) or Old Spot belly ribs. If you've room after all this, choose a devilishly rich sticky toffee pudding or passion fruit cheesecake. Service is good, the cocktails are praised; otherwise, an intelligent selection of wines comes at a price – most are significantly over £40.

Chef/s: Flamur Zeka. **Open:** Mon to Sat L and D. Sun, all day from 12. **Closed:** 25 and 26 Dec, 1 Jan. **Meals:** main courses £12 to £40. Set L and D £25 (2 courses) to £28. Sun L £20. **Details:** 130 seats. Bar. Music.

★ TOP 10 ★

Hedone

Cooking score: 8
⊖ Chiswick Park, map 1
Modern European | £95
301-303 Chiswick High Road, Chiswick,
W4 4HH
Tel no: (020) 8747 0377
hedonerestaurant.com

Anyone who feared the lack of a menu (and no knowledge of what you will eat until it arrives at the table) would prove an uneasy fit has long ago eaten their words. Now catapulted into the premier league of London dining, Mikael Jonsson's cooking comes as a dynamic surprise, the appeal lying not in global dishes and in-your-face flavours, but rather in materials that are well sourced and intelligently handled. There are some unusual combinations – a delicate Parmesan custard served with a liquid umami jelly and topped with chia seeds, which just bursts with savoury intensity – but nothing to cause the wrong kind of palpitations. Mr Jonsson's stock-in-trade is modernist cooking of great technical proficiency that never loses sight of the principle that dishes should be allowed to taste of themselves. Typical is crab claws, served warm to tease out their assertive sweetness, enhanced by a briny velvet crab consommé, dots of hazelnut mayonnaise and diced apple, while a thick spear of asparagus (from Pertuis in the south east of France) has perfect bite, the addition of raw shaved asparagus, dabs of perfectly ripe avocado and a pistachio and primrose cream making for harmonious layering. An intermediate course might supply a remarkably good piece of gurnard with cauliflower purée, romanesco and a coconut-infused cauliflower chutney 'that worked surprisingly well', as a precursor to a notable piece of Bourbonnais lamb, pink, tender, full of flavour, accompanied by artichoke barigoule. Distinctiveness in presentation backs up the compositional ingenuity of dishes, right through to an inconceivably rich warm chocolate mousse balanced by yuzu jelly, a crisp biscuit dusted with praline powder and milk ice cream. The fixed-price format means bills are predictable, just as long as you don't get lost in the excellent wine list – 'the wine pairing is superb' – aimed at those prepared to pay for quality.
Chef/s: Mikael Jonsson. **Open:** Fri and Sat L, Tue to Sat D. **Closed:** Sun, Mon. **Meals:** tasting menu £95 to £135. **Details:** 20 seats.

Hereford Road

Cooking score: 3
⊖ Bayswater, map 6
British | £28
3 Hereford Road, Notting Hill, W2 4AB
Tel no: (020) 7727 1144
herefordroad.org

Notting Hill has grown swankier and less bohemian but Hereford Road stays true to its roots, serving imaginative, authentic British food at reasonable prices. It's a genuine neighbourhood restaurant with a loyal, enthusiastic clientele. Tom Pemberton's cooking is 'simplicity as an art form' and pays precise attention to detail with the right ingredients 'and not an air mile in sight'. Smoked trout with new potato is a menu regular, leek vinaigrette with anchovy is topped with the white and yolk of a freshly boiled egg, and there's a burly lamb shank with carrots or devilled kidneys with mash to mop up the juices. Homely puddings include almond and orange tart, while jam made from zinging summer berries livens up cold rice pudding, perfect for a warm day. The good-value wine list offers many by the glass and half-litre as well as bottles. On-trend organic wines are featured but not overwhelmingly.
Chef/s: Tom Pemberton. **Open:** all week L and D. **Closed:** 23 Dec to 4 Jan. **Meals:** main courses £12 to £17. Set L £14 (2 courses) to £16. **Details:** 66 seats. 6 seats outside. Wheelchairs. Parking.

Hunan

Cooking score: 3
⊖ Sloane Square, map 3
Chinese | £67
51 Pimlico Road, Chelsea, SW1W 8NE
Tel no: (020) 7730 5712
hunanlondon.com

Longevity is revered in Chinese tradition, and Hunan has been ageing gracefully since 1982. The ground-floor dining room is a snug space with a small bar, white walls cheered up by a few Chinese prints, pale-wood floor and furnishings and close-set tables. Mr Peng offers no menu; instead, your order is taken based on your preferences and tolerance level to spiciness. The result is a series of 'consistently executed' small plates: perhaps pickled cucumber and salted peanuts to start, minced chicken soup served in a bamboo pot, 'nicely salty and garlicky' tempura of French beans, sea bream paired with yellow miso, and stir-fried beef ribeye packed with chilli. Elsewhere, Shanghai tofu arrives with cloud ear, and chicken wrapped with beancurd skin is teamed with winter melon and pineapple. Red-bean pancake with almond jelly and matcha ice cream is 'a delightful end'. Care and skill has been lavished on the wine list (from £25), which features some fine Pinot Noir.
Chef/s: Mr Peng. **Open:** Mon to Sat L and D.
Closed: Sun, 2 weeks Christmas, bank hols.
Meals: set L £43. Set D £67. **Details:** 48 seats. V menu.

Indian Zing

Cooking score: 2
⊖ Ravenscourt Park, map 1
Indian | £27
236 King Street, Hammersmith, W6 0RF
Tel no: (020) 8748 5959
indian-zing.co.uk
£5 OFF £30

If you're going to have the word 'zing' in the name of your Indian restaurant it is wise to ensure that what comes out of the kitchen has pungent aromas and zesty spicing, and chef/ patron Manoj Vasaikar duly delivers. The place is done out with Indian artworks on neutral walls, with linen cloths and high-backed faux leather chairs, and there's a covered terrace out back. The menu ranges around the Sub-continent, with the south catching the eye – mussels caldine to start, say, in a herby coconut broth, or a main-course lobster balchao. Shahi chicken korma will bring comfort to many, and duck chettinad and venison kofta curry will pique the interest of the more adventurous. For dessert, fresh figs get a go in the tandoori oven, served with apple, muesli crumble and vanilla ice cream. Efforts have been made to match the wines with the food.
Chef/s: Manoj Vasaikar. **Open:** all week L and D.
Meals: main courses £9 to £22. Set L £14 (2 courses) to £17. Sun L £13 (2 courses) to £17. **Details:** 51 seats. 32 seats outside. Wheelchairs. Music.

Kitchen W8

Cooking score: 6
⊖ High Street Kensington, map 6
Modern European | £48
11-13 Abingdon Road, Kensington, W8 6AH
Tel no: (020) 7937 0120
kitchenw8.com

This is a place that does what it sets out to do: provide a neighbourhood restaurant of a certain calibre for the well-heeled of Kensington. It is comfortable, white-clothed; a relaxed space with top-drawer service that you'd happily linger in long after finishing the (excellent) coffee. The menu pleases without challenging. Ravioli, packed generously with lobster and scallops, are a silkily delicate starter, and while a plate of smoked eel and grilled mackerel needed more welly, faultlessly poached chicken puts things back on track. The dish sings spring with perfectly cooked and seasoned asparagus, morels, grelots, a lick of wild garlic and scattering of pine nuts; lamb, fresh young peas and nettle pesto follows suit. Finish with an oh-so-pretty pudding – some may find them a little soft-textured, but poached apricots and honey ice cream, or raspberries with a light verbena yoghurt and raspberry ripple ice, still hit a sweet spot. The 375ml carafes (from £14) are a welcome sip or two from a wine list that accommodates, thoughtfully, all pocket-depths.

Chef/s: Mark Kempson. **Open:** all week L and D. **Closed:** 24 to 26 Dec, bank hols. **Meals:** main courses £21 to £29. Set L £22 (2 courses) to £25. Set D £25 (2 courses) to £28. Sun L £35. **Details:** 75 seats.

Launceston Place

Cooking score: 5
⊖ Gloucester Road, map 3
Modern European | £50
1a Launceston Place, South Kensington, W8 5RL
Tel no: (020) 7937 6912
launcestonplace-restaurant.co.uk

£5
OFF

An elegant Georgian townhouse that well-heeled locals use for celebrations and occasions, the atmosphere tends to be busy and jolly on any given night, though at the same time comfortable and intimate enough for a classy dinner for two. Ben Murphy's cooking is full of whimsy, delivering beautifully presented, clever combinations of flavours and textures: a miniature clothes peg holds together a wafer of daikon, protecting a mouthful of soft salad with crisp chicken skin – a sort of 21st-century European summer roll; octopus tentacles, sweet and tender as anything, are given a wake-up kick with the addition of tiny chorizo dice, and crunch with deep-fried chicken wing; 'nuts and bolts' is an innovative take on the classic combination of apricots and almonds, which involves sorbets, ice creams and fruit. There's an eight-course tasting menu for those who want the full experience, but enough of the dishes migrate to the main menu to make à la carte just as interesting. Wines start at £25 and climb steeply thereafter.

Chef/s: Ben Murphy. **Open:** Wed to Sun L, Tue to Sun D. **Closed:** Mon. **Meals:** main courses £13 to £30. Set L £20 (2 courses) to £30. Set D £30. Tasting menu £79. **Details:** 60 seats. V menu. Bar. Wheelchairs.

The Ledbury

Cooking score: 8
⊖ Notting Hill Gate, Westbourne Park, map 6
Modern British | £120
127 Ledbury Road, Notting Hill, W11 2AQ
Tel no: (020) 7792 9090
theledbury.com

Brett Graham's theatre of operations is just a stroll from Notting Hill's multicultural epicentre, but is a world away when it comes to style and attitude. The dining room is undistinguished – linen-clad tables, hand-thrown crockery, heavy black drapes, copper light shades – and there's no bar. Success is down to a combination of the relaxed expertise of the front-of-house staff and the attention to detail from a kitchen that regularly displays flashes of culinary genius. From various meals taken this year, nibbles such as a seaweed cracker with smoked mussel mousse and a choux pastry puff with deer and a honey jelly have had readers 'purring with pleasure', but that's just the beginning. Sensational combinations, extraordinarily vivid tastes and contrasting textures abound, from clay-baked white beetroot with English caviar and smoked and dried eel to a dazzlingly precise dish of lobster tail overlaid with thin slices of shiitake mimicking the shell, plus an asparagus spear and tiny dollops of macadamia sauce ('satisfyingly sweet, salt and savoury'). Or perhaps a 'simply stunning' dish of dashi stock-infused hen-of-the-woods wrapped in wafer-thin aged pork lardo, given heft by a smoky BBQ flavour and served with potato emulsion and rosemary oil, to a 'triumph' of a dish of pigeon (tender breast, powerful confit leg, heart and wing) with the addition of cherries, endive, beetroot and onion making 'every mouthful a slightly different but equally enjoyable experience'. Occasionally a dish underwhelms or the flavours become unbalanced, but desserts invariably hit the heights – brown sugar tart with stem ginger ice cream, for example. The wine list saunters across the viticultural globe, picking out inspired choices from heavyweight Bordeaux and German Rieslings to choice Australian picks.

Chef/s: Brett Graham. **Open:** Wed to Sun L, all week D. **Closed:** 25 and 26 Dec, Aug bank hol. **Meals:** set L and D £120 (4 courses). Tasting menu £145 (8 courses). **Details:** 58 seats. V menu. Wheelchairs. Children over 12 yrs only.

★ TOP 50 ★

Marcus

Cooking score: 8
⊖ Hyde Park Corner, Knightsbridge, map 6
Modern European | £85
The Berkeley, Wilton Place, Belgravia,
SW1X 7RL
Tel no: (020) 7235 1200
marcusrestaurant.com

Hidden away inside the Berkeley Hotel, Marcus makes a virtue out of discretion, going about its business with cool aplomb. The refined and clubby dining room looks the part, with well-spaced tables, polished wood, rich leather and silvery-grey tones giving a lesson in studied, gently lit elegance. For some years now, Mark Froydenlund has marshalled the whole culinary set-up but, in early 2017, Marcus Wareing appointed Mark and Shauna Froydenlund as joint chef/patrons, and regulars reckon that they have raised the bar of late. Menus allow you to chart paths of varying lengths, from three standard courses to five or eight tasting dishes. Combinations may be classic enough in themselves, as when Portland crab appears with cucumber, potato, caviar and finger lime, or organic milk-fed lamb is teamed with crispy breast, pea and mint, but the presentations are spare and elegant and the flavours ring true. But Mr Froydenlund is not afraid to be innovative. Confit cod is a masterclass in balancing tastes, wild garlic, Hampshire asparagus and sliver of guanciale (Italian-cured pork cheek) all playing their parts to perfection, offset by the crisp sweetness of tiny pickled turnips, and a nub of puréed boudin noir as an appropriately earthy partner. Delicate, briny clams, rock

samphire and pickled egg (served as a cream in silverskin onions topped with crunchy paprika and garlic-infused breadcrumbs) give a fine piece of Cornish brill a satisfying sweet-tart dimension. In a winning finale, bergamot, meringue and iced tea arrives as a riff on lemon tart combined with the flavours of Earl Grey tea. Professionalism and ease define the service, including the wine advice on a list that plunders France and beyond for big-hitting treasures.

Chef/s: Mark and Shauna Froydenlund. **Open:** Mon to Sat L and D. **Closed:** Sun. **Meals:** set L £55. Set D £85. Tasting menu £120 (8 courses). **Details:** 75 seats. V menu. Bar. Wheelchairs. Children over 12 yrs only at D.

Medlar

Cooking score: 5
⊖ Sloane Square, Fulham Broadway, map 3
Modern French | £49
438 King's Road, Chelsea, SW10 0LJ
Tel no: (020) 7349 1900
medlarrestaurant.co.uk

Since opening in 2011, Joe Mercer Nairne's long, narrow and unobtrusive restaurant has become a huge asset in this sedate part of Chelsea, especially in warm weather when front windows fold back and tables occupy a sunny terrace. His most popular starter, crab ravioli with samphire, brown shrimps, leeks and a light bisque, is so popular it cannot be taken off the menu, while skilful cooking sees nuggets of smoked eel balance a rich foie gras terrine served with beetroot salad and pumpkin seeds, and a salad of calf's brain with aïoli and new potato is refreshed with bitter nasturtium and dandelion leaves. Equally complex is slow-cooked rabbit with creamy white polenta, a crisp slice of ham and sage leaves, though their version of steak and chips is simplicity itself: thick juicy slices with snails, triple-cooked chips and a generous portion of béarnaise. Don't miss puddings like Prosecco and rhubarb jelly with blood-orange sorbet and pistachios, or the superb pineapple financier (in the shape of a small gold bar, hence the name) revved up with coconut ice cream, passion fruit curd and lime. Canny locals favour lunch when the menu is almost exactly the same as the evening à la carte but significantly cheaper. The wide-ranging wine list will please extravagant diners wanting to push the boat out but there are plenty of modest offerings and a decent range by the glass and carafe.

Chef/s: Joe Mercer Nairne. **Open:** all week L and D. **Closed:** 25 and 26 Dec. **Meals:** set L £30 (2 courses) to £35. Set D £41 (2 courses) to £49. Sun L £35. **Details:** 86 seats. 8 seats outside. Wheelchairs.

Ognisko

Cooking score: 3
⊖ **South Kensington, map 6**
Polish | £30
55 Exhibition Road, South Kensington, SW7 2PG
Tel no: (020) 7589 0101
ogniskorestaurant.co.uk

£5
OFF

Found on the ground floor of a stately terraced building opposite the Imperial College Business School, the restaurant of the Polish Hearth Club offers an 'intimate and yet relaxing ambience' with its chandeliers and white-clad tables. Its popularity stems from the reasonable prices and the fact that this is the place to sample vodka – 'even coffee (Polish coffee) is laced with Krupnik vodka'. The menu holds no great surprises, offering a full slate of Polish classics such as beef goulash soup as well as blinis, pierogi or potato pancakes, which all come in small or large portions. Main courses include pork schnitzel (with sautéed potatoes and a fried egg), and kulebiak (salmon in pastry with spinach, buckwheat groats and mushrooms). This is real old-school comfort food so finish with a modest dessert, perhaps spiced caramelised plums with vanilla ice cream. The well-thought out, well-priced wine list is a good match for the food.

Chef/s: Jaroslaw Mlynarczyk. **Open:** all week L and D. **Closed:** 24 to 26 Dec, 1 Jan. **Meals:** main courses £17 to £20. Set L and early D £19 (2 courses) to £22. **Details:** 85 seats. 50 seats outside. Bar. Music.

★ NEW ENTRY ★

108 Garage

Cooking score: 6
⊖ **Westbourne Park, map 1**
Modern British | £40
108 Golborne Road, Notting Hill, W10 5PS
Tel no: (020) 8969 3769
108garage.com

This tiny bare-brick restaurant may have a stark, spare look, but it has a complex taste. Chris Denney's cooking is bold, ultra-modern yet rustic. One minute you're nibbling on some wonderfully crusty sourdough spread with creamy chicken parfait or an intensely flavoured taramasalata, the next you're dipping into a fabulous concoction of raw and al dente Wye Valley asparagus served with an astringent asparagus juice enriched with egg yolk and matcha green-tea powder. Less daring, more elemental, is salt-baked beetroot with sheep's yoghurt, a dollop of caviar supplying a salty tang – nothing fussy about it, just deep, intense flavours. Indeed, every detail makes sense, from the hits of umami in a dish of veal sweetbreads with grilled white asparagus, miso and yeast, via the sweet-salt-sour of crispy pig's head with nasturtium, kohlrabi and piccalilli, to the hunk of char-grilled monkfish balanced by the tart, astringent note of grapefruit custard – an odd idea and a good one. Desserts are on the money, too – especially a simple buttermilk, rhubarb and marjoram confection that has an understated hum of sweetness. Service is casual and pleasant, cocktails fit the bill and the short European wine list starts at a reasonable £18.

Chef/s: Chris Denney. **Open:** Tue to Sat L and D. **Closed:** Sun, Mon. **Meals:** main courses £12 to £25. Set L £25 (3 courses) to £35. Set D £45 (5 courses). **Details:** 38 seats. 4 seats outside. Bar. Wheelchairs. Music.

Outlaw's at the Capital

Cooking score: 6
⊖ Knightsbridge, map 6
Seafood | £62
Capital Hotel, 22-24 Basil Street,
Knightsbridge, SW3 1AT
Tel no: (020) 7591 1202
capitalhotel.co.uk

Situated on a side street between Harrods and Harvey Nichols, the Capital Hotel has an air of understated exclusivity and is 'one of the more intimate of the small luxury London hotels'. In the dining room it is hard to complain about the level of comfort or quality of the décor – soft neutral colours, gentle lighting – or the courteous, efficient and professional service, while Tom Brown's beguiling modern cooking is all about precision, comfort and indulgence. Supremely fresh and sustainable seafood is a hallmark of all Nathan Outlaw restaurants, but in this Knightsbridge outpost there is a meat option for those who fancy getting their teeth into duck with chicory, pistachio and pink grapefruit. The stars of the show, though, are undoubtedly the fish dishes. Some real treats this year have been a lobster risotto with 'a hint of orange, which cut the richness', a superb piece of brill, served with a crisp-fried oyster, smoked hollandaise and asparagus – 'a triumph in every way' – and a beautifully cooked fillet of John Dory in a dark fish-stock reduction. Desserts are impressively rendered, especially a very well-made custard tart with gooseberry and ginger-beer sorbet. The well-curated wine list gives fair shakes around the world, has good choice by the glass and, by Knightsbridge standards, is good value.

Chef/s: Nathan Outlaw and Tom Brown. **Open:** Mon to Sat L and D. **Closed:** Sun. **Meals:** set L £29 (2 courses) to £33. Set D £49 (2 courses) to £62. Tasting menu £85. **Details:** 34 seats. Bar. Music. Parking.

Philip Howard

Elystan Street, Chelsea

After 25 years at The Square, how did it feel starting over in a new kitchen?
Exciting of course - such a blast to get a fresh team together to open a new restaurant.

For those who have loved dining with you at The Square, what can they expect at Elystan Street?
Elystan Street does have a very different feel in general, with emphasis on giving guests a great time with an all round pared back and simpler experience. The food itself is simpler and has moved away from the heavy-hitting style of **The Square**. Happily it has the same soul given that it is born from the same mind!

How do you start developing a new recipe for a dish?
I lock myself away for a few hours, think of the season and think of what I'd like to eat. Simple.

Which dish on the menu is your favourite?
A current favourite is the ajo blanco. It has all the finesse of **The Square**, delivered simply - as we like to do at **Elystan Street**.

Pétrus

Cooking score: 6
⊖ Knightsbridge, map 6
Modern French | £75
1 Kinnerton Street, Knightsbridge, SW1X 8EA
Tel no: (020) 7592 1609
gordonramsay.com

If you've shopped until you've dropped in Knightsbridge, Pétrus is undoubtedly the place to refuel. The smart gleam of the place, emphasised in double-clothed tables, sparkling stemware and impeccably professional yet affable service, is built around a central glass fortification, within which wines that positively demand genuflection slumber in air-conditioned luxury. Lahiru Jayasekara interprets the Gordon Ramsay house style with finely tuned precision, turning out dishes that are essentially founded on classical French principles, but always inflected with elements of the contemporary unexpected. Everything feels as opulent as can be, from the butter-poached lobster with truffled cannelloni, girolles and wood sorrel to fallow deer loin in soubise and a juniper-scented jus, offset by the earthier note of salt-baked beetroot. A genteel gasp of surprise might greet the appearance of Brussels sprouts with Brixham turbot, and another at its garnish of crispy cockscomb. If a gold-leafed chocolate yummy feels a little *de trop*, have a caramelised apple – a rosy-red Braeburn at that. The Pétrus starts at £4,900 for the 2001 and gets dearer. For small glasses of other stuff, start at £6.
Chef/s: Lahiru Jayasekara. **Open:** all week L and D.
Meals: set L £38. Set D £75. Tasting menu £95.
Details: 54 seats. V menu. Bar. Wheelchairs. Music.

Symbols

⬤

🛏 Accommodation is available
£30 Three courses for less than £30
£5 OFF £5-off voucher scheme
🍾 Notable wine list

Popeseye Steak House

Cooking score: 1
⊖ Olympia, map 3
British | £35
108 Blythe Road, Olympia, W14 0HD
Tel no: (020) 7610 4578
popeseye.com

There's nothing avant-garde about Ian Hutchinson's wee chain of steak restaurants (branches can also be found in Putney and Archway). The décor eschews contemporary fashion for a more traditional appearance with dressed tables and big pieces of bovine-inspired art on the walls. The meat comes from Aberdeen Angus cattle reared in Scotland and hung for 28 days, with the menu offering rump (the eponymous popeseye), sirloin, fillet, T-bone and ribeye, all served with chips. Choose your sauce (or sauces), and have a salad on the side if you must. The meat is first-rate, really spot-on. The wine list focuses on beefy reds.
Chef/s: Ian Hutchinson. **Open:** Mon to Sat D only.
Closed: Sun, bank hols. **Meals:** steaks £12 to £70.
Details: 34 seats. Wheelchairs. Music.

Portobello Ristorante Pizzeria

Cooking score: 2
⊖ Notting Hill Gate, map 6
Italian | £33
7 Ladbroke Road, Notting Hill, W11 3PA
Tel no: (020) 7221 1373
portobellolondon.co.uk
£5 OFF

A godsend for Notting Hill, this compact neighbourhood Italian combines a comfortable, laid-back demeanour with cheerful and competent service, forthright cooking and excellent value for money. The canopied and heated front terrace is an all-weather draw, too – 'and they supply lovely blankets just in case'. The à la carte demonstrates chef Andrea Ippolito's appreciation of unreconstructed Italian cuisine, from the unsophisticated pleasures of a wood-fired Neapolitan pizza al metro – 'I

wish I had more friends to take and enjoy one' – to high-quality pasta such as spaghetti vongole, or a rustic dish of octopus in a rich tomato sauce with black olives and chilli on homemade toasted bread, a fine char-grilled veal chop with roasted sweet peppers, and a robust cod alla puttanesca. Desserts show the kitchen's classic side, too, in a well-made tiramisu. The all-Italian wine list has a good selection of organics and starts at £22.
Chef/s: Andrea Ippolito. **Open:** all week, all day from 12. **Closed:** 25 Dec, Easter. **Meals:** main courses £9 to £26. Set L £15 (2 courses). **Details:** 66 seats. 28 seats outside. Music.

Potli

Cooking score: 2
⊖ Ravenscourt Park, Stamford Brook, map 1
Indian | £30
319-321 King Street, Hammersmith, W6 9NH
Tel no: (020) 8741 4328
potli.co.uk
£5
OFF

If you're looking for that elusive 'Indian bazaar experience' down Hammersmith way, this popular neighbourhood eatery might be just the ticket. With its turmeric-yellow walls, paprika-red loo doors, Bollywood posters, metal advertising signs and shelves of provisions, Potli has the 'market kitchen' vibe down to a T, while the illustrated menu maps out a culinary tour of the Subcontinent with stopovers in all the significant culinary provinces. Sharing is the way to go, so check out Mumbai's Chowpatty Beach for pani puris, samosas and suchlike, hit Kolkata's street kiosks or head over to the market of Old Lucknow for its meaty kebabs, tikkas and tandooris. Other niftily spiced hot tips range from Goan pork vindaloo to Odisha-style king prawns and Keralan fish curry, but don't miss the deep-fried chicken 65. The details are spot-on, too, from homemade pickles and chutneys to assorted Punjabi-style breads. Spiced Martinis and spice-friendly wines satisfy the drinkers.

Chef/s: Babul Dey. **Open:** Mon to Sat L and D. Sun, all day from 12. **Closed:** 25 Dec to 1 Jan. **Meals:** main courses £6 to £15. Set L Mon to Fri £11 (2 courses), Sat and Sun £15. **Details:** 80 seats. 16 seats outside. Bar. Wheelchairs. Music.

Rabbit

Cooking score: 1
⊖ Sloane Square, map 3
Modern British | £28
172 King's Road, Chelsea, SW3 4UP
Tel no: (020) 3750 0172
rabbit-restaurant.com
£30

Having scored a hit with the Shed in Notting Hill (see entry), Richard and Oliver Gladwin followed on with this similarly themed eatery on the King's Road. Done out in their distinctive faux-rustic 'country-meets-city' idiom, Rabbit is a mishmash of rough-cut timbers, old tractor seats and 'real trees' from the family farm in Sussex. The brothers are keen on 'food for free', so expect wild pickings in among other seasonal ingredients – perhaps a brown crab 'bomb' with dulse and dill, lamb 'chips' with harissa, lemon and parsley or ox liver with grilled brassicas, kale and figs. Wines include some from the family's Nutbourne vineyard.
Chef/s: Oliver Gladwin and Roland Racz. **Open:** Tues to Sun L, Mon to Sat D. **Closed:** Christmas and New Year, bank hols. **Meals:** small plates £8 to £15. **Details:** 45 seats. Bar. Wheelchairs. Music.

★ TOP 10 ★

Restaurant Gordon Ramsay

Cooking score: 9
⊖ Sloane Square, map 3
French | £110
68 Royal Hospital Road, Chelsea, SW3 4HP
Tel no: (020) 7352 4441
gordonramsayrestaurants.com

Gordon Ramsay's flagship restaurant is a sure-fire gastronomic experience, rock-like in the consistent excellence of the ingredients and the reliably assured technique in the kitchen. The whole operation runs on ultra-smooth castors, thanks to meticulous staff and to the attention of Jean-Claude Breton, who tours the tables discreetly, attending to every need. This contributes to the sense of a quality restaurant firing on all cylinders. Nibble a gougère or two, glance at the menus, sink into the wine list and all is right with the world, an impression reinforced when the excellent breads and amuse-bouches arrive. Matt Abé seems to have settled into the role vacated by Clare Smyth. He has had time to do some thinking, tasting and tweaking and the result is a real treat. The sweet hit of Cornish brown crab is set off by the crunch of young almonds and gilded by elderflower, while fillets of Dover sole are given vigour thanks to fennel, a tangled heap of sea vegetables, mussels and a lovage broth. Rich, sautéed foie gras is balanced by cherries and almond, with chamomile giving an extra flavour dimension. Elsewhere, lavender, fennel, honey and apricot have proved a wonderful match for perfectly roasted pigeon on a Menu Prestige that also included braised confit and roasted Herdwick lamb with a summer vegetable navarin. Desserts, too, have displayed plenty of top-end technique and execution, as in a grown-up caramel milk chocolate (malt mousse, treacle granola, praline and hazelnut milk) and a delightfully sweet riff on strawberries and cream – with lemon verbena-flavoured meringue, buttermilk and Sarawak pepper ice cream. Wines are a star turn. The list shimmers with class and convinces in all regions, from imperious French vintages to a well-chosen bunch by the glass.

Chef/s: Matt Abé. **Open:** Mon to Fri L and D. **Closed:** Sat, Sun, 23 to 27 Dec. **Meals:** set L £65. Set D £110. Tasting menu £145 to £175. **Details:** 42 seats. V menu. Wheelchairs.

★ TOP 50 ★

Restaurant Marianne
Cooking score: 7
⊖ Royal Oak, map 6
Modern European | £85
104a Chepstow Road, Notting Hill, W2 5QS
Tel no: (020) 3675 7750
mariannerestaurant.com

The unassuming frontage on the corner of a Notting Hill mews says little about the vaulting ambition of Marianne Lumb's pocket-sized neighbourhood restaurant. A mere 14 covers per session is what it accommodates, but the restricted dimensions allow for a culinary performance that takes flight from the off. The menu formatting is a five-course taster at lunch, six at dinner, in both vegetarian and omni versions, with a de luxe option for the latter adorned with Alba truffles, Wagyu beef, Scottish langoustines and lardo di Colonnata, as well as a daringly traditional three-course carte at lunch. Marianne's cooking is full of graceful ingenuity, precision detailing and surprises, braising Highland Wagyu brisket in tamarind with rainbow chard, or serving saddle of Forest of Dean muntjac with a gyoza dumpling of the haunch meat and cavolo nero, for mains that linger in the memory. A couple signing up for the lunch taster in October began with Italian tomato consommé garnished with Chinese rose radish, basil and chilli, before confit and carpaccio of heritage beetroots with barrel-aged feta and horseradish, and an unexpected intermediate serving of game-season grouse, and then main-course alternatives of turbot with girolles in cream, and saddle of Rhug salt marsh lamb with spelt, runner beans and potato cannelloni. There is a contemporary French sensibility to many of the dishes, extending to the subtle use of Asian seasonings, and very evident in dessert techniques such as a soufflé of cocoa nibs with raspberries and crème de framboise ganache, or poached rhubarb with pink praline in Champagne sabayon. The introduction of the

Coravin system has allowed the serving of fine wines by the glass. Quality is superb throughout the list; it all starts at £39.
Chef/s: Marianne Lumb. **Open:** Fri to Sun L, Tue to Sun D. **Closed:** Mon, 21 Dec to 4 Jan, Aug bank hol weekend. **Meals:** set L £35. Tasting menu L £65 (5 courses) to £125, D £85 (6 courses) to £145. **Details:** 14 seats. V menu. Music. Children over 12 yrs only.

Restaurant Michael Nadra

Cooking score: 3
⊖ Turnham Green, map 1
Modern European | £39
6-8 Elliott Road, Chiswick, W4 1PE
Tel no: (020) 8742 0766
restaurant-michaelnadra.co.uk
£5 OFF 🍾

While Michael Nadra's north London offshoot feeds the residents of Primrose Hill (see entry), his original place continues to do the business for Chiswick's foodies. Done out in neutral tones with leather banquettes and slate flooring, the low-lit, low-ceilinged dining room has a chic, understated vibe that suits Nadra's accomplished cooking and fondness for sophisticated cosmopolitan flavours. Seafood is always a good call, perhaps salmon ceviche with chilli-pickled cucumber, sweetcorn purée and crisp quinoa followed by grilled 'market fish' accompanied by raw fennel salad, skinny pommes paille and rouille. Other dishes such as belly of suckling pig with chorizo and choucroute or beef fillet and braised cheek with wild mushrooms, spinach and truffled mash remain firmly grounded in European cuisine, while desserts have a familiar ring – chocolate fondant with salted-caramel ice cream, for example. The food is impressively supported by an admirable 200-bin wine list organised by grape variety: a reserve cellar tempts those with fat wallets, but there are also great-value options by the glass and half-bottle.

Chef/s: Michael Nadra. **Open:** all week L, Mon to Sat D. **Closed:** 24 to 26 Dec, 1 Jan. **Meals:** set L £23 (2 courses) to £28. Set D £33 (2 courses) to £39. Tasting menu L £50, D £60 (6 courses). **Details:** 50 seats. Wheelchairs. Music.

Restaurant Ours

Cooking score: 2
⊖ South Kensington, map 3
Modern European | £60
264 Brompton Road, Kensington, SW3 2AS
Tel no: (020) 7100 2200
restaurant-ours.com

Lights don't hide under bushels at Restaurant Ours. From the catwalk 'tunnel' through to the glam dining space and mezzanine bar, glistening with twinkling fairy-light-adorned trees, this is where you'll find affluent millennials and Generation Z in their Instagram-friendly element. Head chef Jarad McCarroll puts every effort into pushing contemporary buttons with haute casual dining: whatever you choose from the seven-section menu of starters, small plates from sea or land, sides, large plates and robata grill dishes, expect hefty prices, particularly for the not-so-'large' dishes, but meticulous technique yields some satisfying flavours. Unapologetically (on occasion, overwhelmingly) rich ingredients abound: witness foie gras and pecorino on chips, or sweet, soft lobster tagliatelle and scallop, crème fraîche and caviar. Wrap things up with salted-caramel doughnuts. Dinner has a nightclub vibe but daytime dining is a more sedate affair. Top-drawer Burgundy and Bordeaux loom large on the Europe-centric list, wines by the glass start at £9.
Chef/s: Jarad McCarroll. **Open:** Sat L, Tue to Sat D. **Closed:** Sun, Mon. **Meals:** main courses £19 to £39. Set L £25 (2 courses) to £28. **Details:** 120 seats. Music. Children before 9pm only.

The River Café

Cooking score: 5
⊖ Hammersmith, map 1
Italian | £85
Thames Wharf, Rainville Road, Hammersmith,
W6 9HA
Tel no: (020) 7386 4200
rivercafe.co.uk

If ever a restaurant was built for summertime revels by the river, this is it. The famous oversized clock, the red log-burning oven, the gleaming bar and the breezy blue-and-white colour schemes all linger in the memory, but nothing can trump the views – especially when the sun is beating down on tables arrayed across the capacious terrace. Since day one, the River Café has been all about seasonal ingredients and the rustic traditions of Italian regional cuisine, with fresh salads and silky handmade pastas complementing the output of aforesaid oven. The cooking's underlying simplicity sometimes seems at odds with the sky-high prices, but no one grumbles after sampling a juicy thick-cut veal chop accompanied by salsa verde, slow-cooked peas and rocket, or char-grilled monkfish with anchovy and rosemary sauce, agretti and broad beans. You might start with a salad of Devon crab, baby artichokes and parsley, while dessert is normally a toss-up between the legendary chocolate nemesis and one of the homemade gelati. The Italian regional wine list is a glory to behold, which is fine if you're on an unlimited budget.
Chef/s: Ruth Rogers. **Open:** all week L, Mon to Sat D. **Closed:** 25 Dec, 1 Jan. **Meals:** main courses £35 to £45. **Details:** 120 seats. 80 seats outside. Bar. Wheelchairs. Parking.

The Shed

Cooking score: 3
⊖ Notting Hill Gate, map 6
Modern British | £30
122 Palace Gardens Terrace, Notting Hill,
W8 4RT
Tel no: (020) 7229 4024
theshed-restaurant.com

There's something of the air of an Art Brut installation here, with odds and ends sourced from wherever they happened to crop up. Some of the table tops rest on barrels that once shipped orange juice from Brazil. A Colman's Mustard sign hangs next to a cartwheel, and an eight-foot tractor hood dangles from the ceiling. It would hardly be Notting Hill without one. The same sense of *omnium gatherum* pervades the modern British menus, too, where carrot hummus with dukkah and caraway crispbread, or a salad of raw Brussels, Braeburn apple, candied walnuts and mature Cheddar, might precede something as abruptly grand as pheasant saltimbocca in white pepper sauce, or cuttlefish with black butter beans in sweet chilli. The resourcefulness of it all wins converts, all the way to reinterpretations of supermarket freezer-cabinet standbys such as Viennetta, or a texturally impeccable match of honeycomb and mascarpone with tarragon sugar. Inventive cocktails of the day lead off a short but good wine slate, from £22 for house French.
Chef/s: Oliver Gladwin and Dominik Moldenhauer. **Open:** Tue to Sat L, Mon to Sat D. **Closed:** Sun, 25 Dec to 1 Jan, bank hols. **Meals:** small plates £8 to £15. Set L £28 (3 courses). Set D £38 (3 courses). **Details:** 60 seats. Bar. Wheelchairs. Music.

Shikumen

Cooking score: 3
⊖ Shepherd's Bush Market, map 1
Chinese | £35
Dorsett Hotel, 58 Shepherd's Bush Green,
Shepherd's Bush, W12 8QE
Tel no: (020) 8749 9978
shikumen.co.uk

Ensconced within the chic Dorsett Hotel,
Shikumen offers upscale Chinese dining,
overlaid with fusion touches of Western
influence, in a glamorous setting of carved
wooden screens and traditional lanterns. The
dim sum are hand-crafted little parcels of
come-and-get-me, including pillowy char siu
buns, umami-laden congee of pork and
century egg, xiao long bao filled with crab
soup, and perfectly glutinous little egg tarts.
Otherwise, the main menu deals in Cantonese
and Shanghainese dishes rendered with brio
and sizzle, from chilli-laced kung po chicken
to braised beef fillet in jasmine tea, with sides
of stir-fried pak choi, asparagus, mushrooms
and lotus root, and speciality accompaniments
such as XO-sauced prawn, scallop and tobiko
in fried rice. Go west, young diner, if you must
for desserts like passion fruit cheesecake, but
you could be negotiating a black sesame ball in
ginger tea, or bracing your olfactory
sensibilities for Musang King puff made with
heavenly stinking durian. Wines from £21.90
supplement an inspired cocktail menu.
Open: all week, all day from 12. **Closed:** 25 Dec.
Meals: main courses £6 to £39. Set L and D £30 to
£50 (3 courses). **Details:** 140 seats. Bar.
Wheelchairs. Music.

Six Portland Road

Cooking score: 2
⊖ Holland Park, map 1
Modern European | £45
6 Portland Road, Holland Park, W11 4LA
Tel no: (020) 7229 3130
sixportlandroad.com

In premises that were once a wine bar of long
standing, a neighbourhood restaurant from
the Terroirs stable (see entry) has been
conjured in leafy Holland Park, just off the
Avenue. European bistro cooking that
combines Italian and French traditions is the
name of the game, and while there are obvious
forays into today's ingredient trends – expect
sea purslane, monk's beard and kale to crop up
here and there – the bedrock is ancestral
European heritage. Look to smoked herring
with potato salad, or rabbit, pork and
pistachio terrine to start, leading on with brill,
bottarga and Pink Firs, or tenderly rich calf's
liver with soft polenta and radicchio in
balsamic. Puddings may be French bistro to
their fingertips, when chocolate mousse comes
with griottines, almonds and crème fraîche,
but the frangipane tart is topped with
Yorkshire rhubarb. A heterogenous list of
great interest finds wines from Irouléguy and
the Jura amid the more well-trodden
pathways. A Rosso Piceno opens the bill
at £22.50.
Chef/s: Pascal Wiedemann. **Open:** Tue to Sun L, Tue
to Sat D. **Closed:** 10 days Christmas, Mon, 2 weeks
Aug. **Meals:** main courses £17 to £32. Set L £15 (2
courses) to £18. **Details:** 36 seats.

La Trompette

Cooking score: 5
⊖ Turnham Green, map 1
Modern European | £50
3-7 Devonshire Road, Chiswick, W4 2EU
Tel no: (020) 8747 1836
latrompette.co.uk

'I was expecting an elegant, grown-up, supremely comfortable experience here – and I was not disappointed,' noted a first-time visitor to Bruce Poole and Nigel Platts-Martin's long-established neighbourhood restaurant. La Trompette sets out a smart stall from the off: heritage grey awnings are suspended over full-length windows that allow passersby to peek into the two rooms inside, where olive-green leather banquettes, walnut chairs, white tablecloths, tasteful modern art, a determinedly neutral palette and honeyed lighting 'combine in the epitome of good taste'. Rob Weston mines a vein of modern Euro-accented dishes with lots of Mediterranean overtones, from a 'well-executed' char-grilled squid with black Ibérico tomatoes, chickpeas and sardine vinaigrette to 'gorgeous ruby red chunks' of roast Berkshire sika deer served with Tropea onion, watercress, 'cheesy, creamy' pommes dauphine and a sharp horseradish cream. As a finale, rhubarb crumble soufflé with rhubarb ripple ice cream is 'quite one of the loveliest soufflés'. Perfectly judged service is 'a masterclass in front-of-house behaviour'. The restaurant's list of wines shines as brightly as ever, its geographical reach astonishing, its prices reasonable.

Chef/s: Rob Weston. **Open:** all week L and D. **Closed:** 25 and 26 Dec, 1 Jan. **Meals:** set L £28 (2 courses) to £33. Set D £45 (2 courses) to £55. Sun L £38. **Details:** 88 seats. 12 seats outside. Wheelchairs.

★ NEW ENTRY ★

Vineet Bhatia London

Cooking score: 6
⊖ Sloane Square, map 3
Indian | £105
10 Lincoln Street, Chelsea, SW3 2TS
Tel no: (020) 7225 1881
vineetbhatia.london
£5 OFF

VBL, the reboot of Vineet Bhatia's Rasoi, is tucked away in a handsome Georgian townhouse on a smart little street not far from Sloane Square. Ring the doorbell to enter and, once inside, the two small rooms are fashionably turned out in pastel shades with leather seating and white linen. Considered a pacesetter among Indian chefs, Mr Bhatia has bravely gone with an evening-only no-choice 'Experience' taster (there's also a vegetarian version). Some might consider this a little against the capital's culinary flow towards more relaxed, approachable dining, but what you get here is 'Bhatia fireworks': a roll call of beguiling, refined Indian dishes underpinned by the chef's Mumbai roots and travels. Open with a trio of small plates that give street food the Bhatia spin: perhaps spice-marinated slow-roasted lamb leg meat and dosa-style rice and lentil pancake with a chutney of coconut and mustard seeds. Menu descriptions are brief. A more substantial 'duck korma' delivers pink duck breast with upam (creamy semolina and polenta porridge with nutty wild mushrooms) and a superb korma sauce. Desserts, like 'chocolate cure' play their part, alongside an array of petits fours. Wines are a serious bunch with some starry names, but the flight of wines matching dishes is recommended.

Chef/s: Vineet Bhatia and Manmeet Bali. **Open:** Tue to Sun D only. **Closed:** Mon, 25 and 26 Dec, 1 and 2 Jan. **Meals:** tasting menu £105. **Details:** 32 seats. V menu.

Vinoteca

Cooking score: 2
⊖ Turnham Green, map 1
Modern European | £30
18 Devonshire Road, Chiswick, W4 2HD
Tel no: (020) 3701 8822
vinoteca.co.uk

Bibulous easy-going Vinoteca now has branches dotted across the capital, with this Chiswick outlet setting the scene for some adventurous sipping. The whole group has a well-deserved reputation for its cosmopolitan brasserie food, and this venue is no exception. Northumbrian stone-baked bread, British cheeses, continental charcuterie and other wine bar staples keep the drinkers satisfied, but it pays to explore the seasonal menu for more enterprising ideas coupled with top-notch wine recommendations by the glass. How about grilled mackerel with fennel, blood orange and rocket paired with a Clare Valley Riesling 2015 (Australia) followed by Berkshire pork with spiny artichokes, farro, black olives and anchovy complemented by a Tetramythos Cabernet Sauvignon 2007, from Greece? To conclude, the bay leaf pannacotta is perfect with a sip or two of Ice Cider 2010 from Leduc-Piedimonte, Quebec. The full wine list is a 250-bin cracker with brilliant global coverage and helpful taste notes, as well as top-drawer by-the-glass selections.
Chef/s: James Robson. **Open:** all week L, Mon to Sat D. **Closed:** 25, 26 and 31 Dec, 1 Jan.
Meals: main courses £13 to £17. Set L £13 (2 courses) to £16. Sun L £20 (2 courses) to £25.
Details: 48 seats. Bar. Wheelchairs. Music.

Symbols

🛏 Accommodation is available
£30 Three courses for less than £30
£5 OFF £5-off voucher scheme
🍷 Notable wine list

Wright Brothers

Cooking score: 2
⊖ South Kensington, map 3
Seafood | £34
56 Old Brompton Road, South Kensington, SW7 3DY
Tel no: (020) 7581 0131
thewrightbrothers.co.uk

With their own oyster beds in Cornwall and unrivalled access to superior bivalves from elsewhere, Wright Brothers have staked their claim as a prime purveyor of *Ostrea edulis* and other marine species. This branch of their flourishing mini-chain is less sprawling than some of its siblings, but it follows the ethos to the letter. Parisian bistro trappings set the tone, and the menu offers a cornucopia of shellfish, fruits de mer and pickings from the Cornish day boats. Around six varieties of oyster (with suitable dressings) get top billing, but you can also sample various 'small' and 'large' plates – perhaps salt cod croquettes with aïoli, fish pie or baked sea bream with fennel, cucumber, yoghurt and mint dressing. Meat eaters aren't ignored, while puddings might include pannacotta with spiced plums. Don't miss the mid-afternoon 'happy hour' (oysters at £1 a pop) or the handsome Mermaid cocktail bar downstairs.
Chef/s: Gareth Clelland. **Open:** all week, all day from 12. **Closed:** 25 to 27 Dec, 1 Jan. **Meals:** main courses £13 to £22. Set L £18 (2 courses) to £20.
Details: 60 seats. Bar. Music.

Yashin Sushi

Cooking score: 4
⊖ High Street Kensington, map 6
Japanese | £50
1a Argyll Road, Kensington, W8 7DB
Tel no: (020) 7938 1536
yashinsushi.com

Yashin offers cutting-edge Japanese food over two floors in elegant premises just off Kensington High Street. Choose from ground-floor counter seating or the more relaxed ambience upstairs, where dark leather banquettes and wall sconces are the drill, for menus of creatively imagined sushi and sashimi. A bite of 'umami tuna', served with Gorgonzola, Parmesan, nori and wasabi, should sufficiently awaken the tastebuds for preparations such as grouper sashimi with summer truffle doused in yuzu, or hot bites like calamari with sansho pepper, and char-grilled sea bass in sour miso. The core of the operation is fixed-price multi-course sushi tasters, including one of the signature rolls, perhaps deep-fried soft-shell blue crab with sweet soy, or stewed beef in egg yolk sauce. The tippest of the top include prime Wagyu sirloin in sushi or carpaccio servings. Saké and yuzu cocktails from £10 and sweet potato shochu make the drinking far more interesting than just sticking to grape wines.

Chef/s: Ryuichi Furukawa. **Open:** all week L and D. **Meals:** sashimi £9 to £28. Tapas £4 to £22. Omakase £30 (8 pieces). **Details:** 37 seats. Music.

Zafferano

Cooking score: 4
⊖ Knightsbridge, map 6
Italian | £45
15 Lowndes Street, Belgravia, SW1X 9EY
Tel no: (020) 7235 5800
zafferanorestaurant.com

Inside this elegant Italian eatery the mood is one of contrasts, with gaily striped upholstery offsetting the stark brick walls, but service is a model of consistent refinement. The cooking has evolved towards a gently modernised version of the traditional Italian format, and Daniele Camera cooks with exuberance and an eye to smart presentation. Deliquescent burrata with puntarelle and anchovy dressing is a palate-priming introduction to one of the primi, perhaps simple pappardelle with wild mushrooms, or the fragrant signature saffron risotto. Mains do creative things with fish, adorning red mullet with spring ratatouille, broccoli cream and balsamic, or teaming roast guinea fowl with chestnut purée and salsify, while desserts keep things simple but pretty, with fruitily garnished passion fruit semifreddo, or densely rich cheesecake and sour cherry ice cream. The proudly Italian-oriented wine list makes room for a shorter roll call of foreigners towards the end. Prices open at £9 a small glass.

Chef/s: Daniele Camera. **Open:** all week, all day from 12. **Closed:** 25 Dec. **Meals:** main courses £27 to £32. **Details:** 170 seats. 20 seats outside. Bar. Wheelchairs. Music.

Zuma

Cooking score: 5
⊖ Knightsbridge, map 6
Japanese | £80
5 Raphael Street, Knightsbridge, SW7 1DL
Tel no: (020) 7584 1010
zumarestaurant.com

This perennially popular upscale emporium is styled after Japan's izakayas (taverns), but Zuma is anything but low-key. Since it opened in 2002, proprietor Rainer Becker has taken the hit formula worldwide. The huge space, furnished with plush upholstery, stone, dark wood and moody recessed lighting, has myriad areas: the main dining room is a sociable space, but the bar, sushi counter and grill is where you can get close to the action. This is cooking of the highest order and the ingredients are impeccable, with the menu's 12 savoury sections (willing waiters will help you navigate) taking in snacks, salads, signature dishes, robata skewers, tempura and sushi – all small and designed for sharing. Soft, silky, warm aubergine salad bursts with umami flavours and chicken skewers from the grill are tender, sweet and sticky. Light-as-air tempura and faultless sushi are exemplary, too. Round off with an ethereal chawan mushi (light egg custard) and brace yourself with a potent saké for the almost inevitably chopstick-trembling moment when the bill arrives.

Chef/s: Rainer Becker and Michael Calenzo. **Open:** all week L and D. **Meals:** sharing plates £5 to £79. Tasting menu £71. **Details:** 150 seats. Bar. Wheelchairs. Music.

A Cena

Cooking score: 2
⊖ Richmond, map 1
Italian | £35
418 Richmond Road, Twickenham, TW1 2EB
Tel no: (020) 8288 0108
acena.co.uk
£5
OFF

A slice of Bella Italia in the shadow of Richmond Bridge, A Cena has been feeding and watering Twickenham locals for more than a decade and shows no signs of flagging. Inside, it's stylish but understated in the suburban mode, with a candlelit bar, smart monochrome décor, mirrors and polished wood, while the kitchen delivers on its promise of capably crafted food with a noticeable regional slant. Classics such as risotto milanese or calf's liver alla veneziana are cooked just so, but also look for more elaborate preparations – perhaps grilled octopus with chilli, lightly pickled cucumber and sour cream, rigatoni with Savoy cabbage, fontina and anchovy or bruschetta-stuffed breast of guinea fowl with red wine, dried porcini and cavolo nero. Desserts range from affogato to a Sicilian orange and almond 'torta' with mascarpone and chocolate. Sunday lunch is 'a delightful and relaxed experience', and Italian regional wines are well-priced.
Chef/s: Nicola Parsons. **Open:** Tue to Sun L, Mon to Sat D. **Closed:** 5 days Christmas, 2 weeks Aug, bank hols. **Meals:** main courses £16 to £24. Sun L £21 (2 courses) to £25. **Details:** 48 seats. Bar. Wheelchairs. Music.

Albert's Table

Cooking score: 3
Modern British | £27
49c Southend, Croydon, CR0 1BF
Tel no: (020) 8680 2010
albertstable.co.uk
£5   £30
OFF

It's fair to say one doesn't go to Croydon for the pretty views, so it will be no surprise to hear that Albert's Table is in an uninspiring road. This makes it all the more of an oasis, and

once inside, the dressed-up tables set the mood for what follows. And what follows is some well-judged modern British tucker. The Britishness extends to a passion for seeking out high-quality ingredients, presented via two menus called Market and Destination. Among opening salvos, poached skate wing finds its way into ravioli, matched with grain-mustard and dill butter sauce, and wild garlic and Kentish new potatoes arrive in a seasonal soup. Glazed shoulder of Colne Valley hogget is as full-flavoured as you'd hope, while pork belly also gets the glazed treatment and is served with a crispy croquette and some ace veggies. Desserts such as treacle sponge are not a high point. Wines start at £22.
Chef/s: Joby Wells. **Open:** Tue to Sun L, Tue to Sat D. **Closed:** Mon. **Meals:** main courses £15 to £26. Set L and D £21 (2 courses) to £27. Sun L £28. **Details:** 60 seats. V menu. Wheelchairs. Music.

The Bingham

Cooking score: 4
⊖ Richmond, map 1
Modern British | £38
61-63 Petersham Road, Richmond, TW10 6UT
Tel no: (020) 8940 0902
thebingham.co.uk
£5
OFF

Part of the draw of this Georgian-era boutique hotel is the setting, particularly in the summer months, when views of the Thames across well-kept gardens are at their most serene. The chandeliered restaurant and beautifully bright bar make the most of those views. Andrew Cole remains at the stoves, his elegantly presented dishes served by attentive staff. Cured trout with white asparagus and lovage pesto has been singled out, but other classy fish dishes include stone bass with baby artichoke and sand carrots. Seasonal ideas also shine through in the meat department, from pork belly with white pudding, samphire, chicory and pineapple to lamb rump with mint miso, Jersey Royals, spring onion and broad beans. Dessert choices typically include dark chocolate ganache with blood orange and granola or rhubarb with frozen vanilla yoghurt and Graham cracker. Set lunches and dinners are good value, too. Partner with wines from an encyclopaedic global list that opens at £26.

Chef/s: Andrew Cole. **Open:** Mon to Sat L and D. Sun 12.30 to 7. **Meals:** main courses £15 to £23. Set L and D Mon to Fri £17 (2 courses) to £20. Tasting menu £50. **Details:** 40 seats. 14 seats outside. Bar. Wheelchairs. Music. Parking.

LOCAL GEM

Bombetta
⊖ Snaresbrook, map 1
Italian | £29
Units 1-5 Station Approach, Wanstead, E11 1QE
Tel no: (020) 3871 0890
bombettalondon.com
£5 OFF £30

Easy to find, being just 50 steps from the Central Line entrance, this Italian grill is 'a delightfully chaotic little place'. Like many a modern London eatery, the concrete floor and ceiling and reclaimed-wood tables make you feel 'a bit like you're eating in a garage'. A slightly ramshackle open kitchen takes up a good half of the room, sending out nibbles of 'brilliant' pig's head bruschetta, and small plates of panzerottini with cured capocollo and fontina cheese, and a generous bowlful of Umbrian lentils and Italian fennel sausage stew – perfect with a glass of wine from the mainly Italian list. On our visit, we found the small plates to be a better bet than the titular bombette (char-grilled parcels of meat and cheese). Don't forget to peek into the fabulous Chefs' Deli next door, where speciality cheeses and meat are sold both wholesale and to the public.

Local Gem 🍴

Local Gems are the perfect neighbourhood venues, delivering good, freshly cooked food at great value for money.

Brilliant
Cooking score: 4
⊖ Hounslow West, map 1
Indian | £25
72-76 Western Road, Southall, UB2 5DZ
Tel no: (020) 8574 1928
brilliantrestaurant.com
£5 OFF £30

The Anand family started Brilliant in the mid-1970s, after an enforced departure from east Africa. From just three dozen covers in those days to the present 265-seat behemoth, it's been quite the journey, and the operation now encompasses a large banqueting suite, a cookery school and its own range of chutneys and pickles. The core activity remains popular Punjabi cooking, now in the capable hands of Dipna Anand, served in an ambience of saffron-hued seating and fish motifs. Marinades and seasonings are diamond-bright, from the tandoori lamb chops in nutmeg, garlic and cardamom, and la-jawab prawns in green chilli, herbs and lime juice, to the timeless appeal of main dishes like chicken karahi with red and green peppers, lamb kofta in masala, or delicately spiced, diced paneer with spinach. Don't forget to include a clay-baked naan, and finish with subtly scented rasmalai with almonds and pistachios. Drink Indian beer, salted or sweet lassi, or house wines at a mere £11.

Chef/s: Dipna Anand. **Open:** Tue to Fri L, Tue to Sun D. **Closed:** Mon, 25 Dec, bank hols. **Meals:** main courses £5 to £14. **Details:** 265 seats. V menu. Wheelchairs. Music. Parking.

La Buvette
Cooking score: 3
⊖ Richmond, map 1
French | £30
6 Church Walk, Richmond, TW9 1SN
Tel no: (020) 8940 6264
labuvette.co.uk
£5 OFF

Once an annexe to St Mary Magdalene church in the pedestrianised centre of Richmond, the Buvette manages to turn an urban setting into something that feels altogether more villagey. The sheltered walled terrace and courtyard help in this regard, and candlelit tables of an evening are a sure fire way into diners' hearts. Buck Carter's menus deal in comforting French and Mediterranean brasserie food that everyone understands. Provençal fish soup with rouille and all the trimmings, Dorset crab with avocado purée and red pepper salsa, and mains such as venison Parmentier or smoked haddock mornay mark a welcome return for the strong French accents of post-war British cooking. A reporter who fed on a nutty salad, steak-frites and a wodge of Brie de Meaux could scarcely have been happier, and if you're in the market for a sweet treat, look to dark chocolate ganache with blood-orange jelly and curd and caramelised oats. The short French wine list opens with Languedoc blends at £18.

Chef/s: Buck Carter. **Open:** all week L and D. **Closed:** 25 and 26 Dec, Good Fri, Easter Sun. **Meals:** main courses £14 to £19. Set L and D £19. **Details:** 44 seats. 34 seats outside.

The Dysart

Cooking score: 5
⊖ Richmond, map 1
Modern British | £43
135 Petersham Road, Richmond, TW10 7AA
Tel no: (020) 8940 8005
thedysartpetersham.co.uk
£5
OFF

The Edwardian Arts and Crafts building overlooking Richmond Park feels pleasantly removed from London's hurly-burly, an impression reinforced by a sojourn on the south-facing terrace, gazing out over the wild flowers. There may be troubles ahead, but while there's music from somebody installed at the Bechstein grand, or a guitarist camped out on the lawn, nothing feels wrong. Kenneth Culhane offers a resourceful menu of modern British food, vividly painted in three dimensions with a huge variety of ingredients. Charred mackerel with kombu-braised daikon in Champagne and ginger is something of a signature, or there could be

salt-baked beetroot in cocoa nibs, prior to wild halibut with lemon celeriac and a Thai top note of green chilli and lime leaves. Herefordshire's Huntsham Court Farm provides pedigree Longhorn beef and Middle White pork, and the textural repertoire of desserts offers plenty of satisfaction, perhaps for wild lime crème brûlée with peanut and almond biscotti. Classic cocktails head up a versatile, confidently chosen wine list, with glasses from £5.25.

Chef/s: Kenneth Culhane. **Open:** Wed to Sun L, Wed to Sat D. **Closed:** Mon, Tue. **Meals:** main courses £21 to £34. Set L and D £25 (2 courses) to £30. Sun L £34. Tasting menu £70. **Details:** 50 seats. 25 seats outside. V menu. Wheelchairs. Music. Parking.

Eat17

Cooking score: 2
⊖ Walthamstow Central, map 1
British | £26
28-30 Orford Road, Walthamstow, E17 9NJ
Tel no: (020) 8521 5279
eat17.co.uk
£30

Eat17, the Walthamstow brand behind cult condiment 'Bacon Jam' and a series of souped up SPAR stores (now in Whitstable and Bishop's Stortford), opened this, their first restaurant and adjoining shop, on newly pedestrianised Orford Road in 2007. It's a British bistro with a global outlook that translates to weekend brunches (fried chicken waffles, with bacon, egg and hot sauce, hails from the 'Elvis' school of American cooking), traditional roasts and a kindly priced carte of both 'basics' (fish and chips, burgers etc) and seasonally adjusted plates. One could eat well on snacks alone – hot wings and blue cheese sauce or char siu bites, say – but pan-fried scallops with grilled courgettes and chilli or lamb rump with peas, broad beans and mint promise a more sophisticated experience. The whitewashed brick space, done up with Danish chairs and a copper bar, rises to the occasion. Wine from £19.95.

Chef/s: Chris O'Connor. **Open:** all week L and D. **Closed:** 25 to 30 Dec. **Meals:** main courses £13 to £22. Set L and D £16 (2 courses) to £18. Sun L £15. **Details:** 70 seats. Bar. Wheelchairs. Music.

The French Table

Cooking score: 3
map 1
French | £45
85 Maple Road, Surbiton, KT6 4AW
Tel no: (020) 8399 2365
thefrenchtable.co.uk

The dark blue frontage and striped awning stand out amid a smart parade of shops, announcing the Guignards' bubbly French bistro. Clean and minimal inside with pale grey walls and slate floor, it's managed by charming front-of-house staff who won't rush you. Eric Guignard thinks outside the box of French culinary tradition, offering crab ceviche to start, productively adorned with kim-chee, passion fruit and an emulsion sauce of brown crabmeat, and then perhaps an enterprising duo of Wagyu beef bavette steak and ox cheek cromesquis in cep sauce, or raclette-crusted cod with Swiss chard pastilla in dill beurre blanc. There may be a feeling at times that the overthinking of dishes can undermine them, as when the foie gras ballotine is overwhelmed by its clove-infused coating, or broccoli gains nothing from being heavily battered in gram flour. Desserts are back on song, though, when a mousse of Valrhona Manjari arrives with raspberry sorbet and a cocoa-nib tuile. Wines are more than just French, with prices opening at £18.95 for southern blends.
Chef/s: Eric Guignard. **Open:** Tue to Sat L and D. **Closed:** Sun, Mon, 25 Dec to 3 Jan, last 2 weeks Aug. **Meals:** set L £20 (2 courses) to £25. Set D £37 (2 courses) to £45. Tasting menu £52. **Details:** 70 seats. V menu. Wheelchairs. Music.

The Glasshouse

Cooking score: 5
⊖ Kew Gardens, map 1
Modern European | £55
14 Station Parade, Kew, TW9 3PZ
Tel no: (020) 8940 6777
glasshouserestaurant.co.uk
£5 OFF ♦

A *restaurant du quartier* that has serenely dominated its quartier since the turn of the millennium, the Glasshouse is within ambling distance of Kew Gardens. Textured white walls offset by a candy-coloured abstract offer a relaxed setting for the Poole and Platts-Martin formula of updated European bistro cooking of eye-catching flair, capably handled here by Berwyn Davies. There's an understated robustness to many dishes, perhaps starting with breast and braised leg of duck with pak choi and grapefruit in teriyaki dressing spiked with wasabi, prior to a main dish of brill and Cornish mussels with parsnip, celeriac purée and an upstanding sauce of verjus and blood orange. Otherwise, it might be corn-fed chicken with saffron cavatelli and three-cornered garlic, garnished with pecans and baby carrots, concluding with passion fruit meringue, caramelised mango and coconut ice cream, or classic tarte Tatin with ginger ice. The wine list has always been a labour of love, with a generous showing of by-the-glass and half-bottle offerings, leading into an exalted line-up that scarcely misses a beat, either in the European regions or across the United States and southern hemisphere. Prices open at £21.
Chef/s: Berwyn Davies. **Open:** all week L and D. **Closed:** 24 to 26 Dec, 1 Jan. **Meals:** set L £28 (2 courses) to £33. Set D £45 (2 courses) to £55. Sun L £38. Tasting menu £70. **Details:** 60 seats. Wheelchairs. Children at L only.

Grand Trunk Road

Cooking score: 3

⊖ South Woodford, map 1

Indian | £30

219 High Road, South Woodford, E18 2PB

Tel no: (020) 8505 1965

gtrrestaurant.co.uk

£5 OFF

One of the movers and shakers of London's Indian gastronomy, Rajesh Suri opened in late 2016 with a fresh conceptual approach to south Asian cooking in an unassuming parade of shops in South Woodford. Inspired by the 16th-century trading route that stretched from Kabul to Kolkata, the menus traverse a broad range of styles. Amritsari battered tilapia in pepper, turmeric and carom seeds with mint chutney, or a Rawalpindi chicken kebab with spinach, cream cheese and coriander, furnish simple appetisers for robustly seasoned, flavour-soaked mains. Lucknow ki nihari (slow-cooked lamb shank in a richly aromatic broth based on an 18th-century recipe) or whole poussin cooked in freshly ground roast spices with paprika and fragrant herbs, elegantly carved at the table, are show-stopping dishes, perhaps accompanied by okra in pickling spices or new potatoes in cumin seeds and leaf coriander. Naan variations include versions stuffed with smoked Applewood cheese or dressed in truffled mushroom oil, while desserts include delightful almond rice pudding with raspberry sauce, and Bengali jamun dumplings in a syrup spiked with cardamom, pistachios and Southern Comfort. Spicy cocktails are the perfect way to start (and finish if you will), and there is an upmarket wine list from £21.50.

Chef/s: Dayashankar Sharma. **Open:** Tue to Sun L, Tue to Sat D. **Closed:** Mon, 25 and 26 Dec, 1 Jan. **Meals:** main courses £15 to £36. Set L £20 (2 courses) to £23. Tasting menu £54. **Details:** 50 seats. V menu. Music. Children over 12 yrs only at D.

Incanto

Cooking score: 3

⊖ Harrow-on-the-Hill, map 1

Italian | £35

41 High Street, Harrow-on-the-Hill, HA1 3HT

Tel no: (020) 8426 6767

incanto.co.uk

£5 OFF

Occupying a former Victorian Post Office, this neighbourhood Italian in villagey Harrow-on-the-Hill receives the stamp of approval from enthusiastic locals. Behind the simple café-deli they flock into the spacious wooden-floored dining room and rear mezzanine to sample high-quality pizzas, homemade pasta and well-constructed main courses featuring prime ingredients. After a freshly fried truffle-scented arancini appetiser, a meal might continue with perfectly springy gnocchi in a rich tarragon and cheese sauce, set off by toasted hazelnuts. Insalata branzino, with meaty strips of cold sea bass, crunchy fennel and orange segments, needed an extra citrus kick, but a main of roast cod with scallops, spinach, samphire and a beurre blanc displayed beautifully balanced flavours. Side dishes costing extra can make for a sizeable bill, and desserts (tiramisu et al) occasionally gild the lily, but Incanto scores highly for its convivial buzz and amenable service. Wine from an Italian-led list starts at £22.

Chef/s: Jerom Patrick. **Open:** Wed to Sun L, Wed to Sat D. **Closed:** Mon, Tue, 25 and 26 Dec, 1 April. **Meals:** main courses £13 to £26. Set L £19 (2 courses) to £21. Set D £21 (2 courses) to £24. **Details:** 65 seats. 12 seats outside. Wheelchairs. Music.

Symbols

⌐	Accommodation is available
£30	Three courses for less than £30
£5 OFF	£5-off voucher scheme
🍾	Notable wine list

Madhu's

Cooking score: 3
map 1
Indian | £25
39 South Road, Southall, UB1 1SW
Tel no: (020) 8574 1897
madhus.co.uk

£30

Over two bright, modern floors on South Road, Madhu's has been part of the community hereabouts for more than 35 years. That's down to the Anand family, several generations of whom have developed the restaurant since 1980. Expect Punjabi cooking via East Africa, which is faithful to tradition and distinctive when it comes to the accuracy of the cooking (and the spicing for that matter). Aloo tikki are 'positively addictive' with their accompanying sweet-and-sour tamarind sauce, tandoori chicken arrives on the bone, full of flavour, and masala fried tilapia is an East African mash-up. Familiar curries stand alongside machuzi kuku and baingan ka bharta. Wines open at £25.
Open: Mon and Wed to Fri L, Mon and Wed to Sun D. **Closed:** Tue. **Meals:** main courses £6 to £13. Set L £15 (2 courses) to £20. Set D £20 (2 courses) to £25. **Details:** 88 seats. V menu. Wheelchairs. Music.

LOCAL GEM

Olympic Studios Café and Dining Room

Hammersmith, map 1
Modern British | £30
Olympic Studios, 117-123 Church Road, Barnes, SW13 9HL
Tel no: (020) 8912 5170
olympicstudios.co.uk

Casual but chic, this café-cum-restaurant, with a plush private cinema attached, is a magnet to local mums for morning coffee or a light lunch, smartening up as the day progresses into evening, and is the haunt of well-dressed families come the weekend. The menu is perfectly attuned to this clientele: offerings range from cheeseburgers and steaks to goats' cheese and beetroot salad and grilled

fish – all long on flavour, size and presentation – served by a competent, young, go-get crew. It's the ideal local for such a well-heeled cosmopolitan neighbourhood.

Petersham Nurseries Café

Cooking score: 3
Richmond, map 1
Modern European | £39
Church Lane, off Petersham Road, Richmond, TW10 7AG
Tel no: (020) 8940 5230
petershamnurseries.com

The Boglione family, owners of Petersham Nurseries, lit out in 2017 for the West End, with Covent Garden retail and catering developments in the offing, but the Richmond nerve centre remains in full force. The Café thrives amid the abundance of a plant nursery and kitchen gardens, the dining area bedded in among trellised foliage in the glasshouse. Plates strewn with edible flowers, herbs and saladings should come as no surprise, but they do come as a delight, with pea shoots and petals garlanding a dish of mussels and saffron gnocchi, while asparagus, radishes and flowers make Portland crab and bottarga into a thing of seasonal beauty. Mains keep things on the lighter side for hake in Vermentino wine, roast chicken on Castelluccio lentils in green sauce, or a veggie offering of roasted courgettes with rainbow chard and spiced chickpeas dressed in minted yoghurt. Top-notch chocolate mousse with raspberries and pistachios is a pleasing conclusion. The tasting-noted, all-Italian wine list has plenty to entice, from £24.
Chef/s: Damian Clisby and Joe Fox. **Open:** Tue to Sun L only. **Closed:** Mon, 24 to 28 Dec. **Meals:** main courses £19 to £30. **Details:** 120 seats. 120 seats outside. Wheelchairs.

Average price

The average price denotes the price of a three-course meal without wine.

On trend...

Out in the field, our inspectors tell us what they've seen trending this year.

Japanese influences: 'Yuzu seems to be popping up a lot.' The versatile citrus fruit has been spotted in desserts in a posset, curd, mousse and jelly, and in savoury dressings, marinades and sauces.

Herbs and edible flowers: 'They make eating a real visual experience as well as a gustatory one.' **Petersham Nurseries** is the place to be if you like to look at, buy and eat flowers.

Tacos: In Clerkenwell, **Breddos** is described as a 'temple to tacos', while others have added them into menus with pairings such as soy-cured beef or crab and pork skin at **Temper** in Soho.

Smoking: 'Food, not cigarettes!' With a lot of restaurants now smoking in-house, we can be treated to more unusual smoked morsels such as meringues (**1887 at the Torridon**) and smoked chocolate ganache (**James Street South**).

Meadowsweet: 'Seems to be everywhere.' A herb in the rose family, often used medicinally and sometimes found in mead (honey wine), the small white flowers give an almond-like flavour.

Soft drinks: Lots of exciting alternatives to branded drinks, such as homemade sodas and cold-brewed coffee.

The Petersham

Cooking score: 3
⊖ Richmond, map 1
Modern British | £45
Nightingale Lane, Richmond, TW10 6UZ
Tel no: (020) 8939 1084
petershamhotel.co.uk

Location is everything at this striking Italian-Gothic country house with ravishing views across water meadows to that famous bend in the Thames – a prospect that probably hasn't changed much since JMW Turner painted it in the 19th century. The dining room makes the most of that view, but the food also merits serious attention, with the kitchen delivering convincing renditions of mainstream modern British dishes. Scallops with plantain, black pudding and parsnip purée could give way to whole Dover sole with heritage potatoes and brown-butter sauce or Creedy Carver duck breast with a tarte fine of caramelised endive, aged prunes and choi sum. One reporter reckoned his 'very well-done and presented' meal was surpassed by a 'really memorable' hot cherry soufflé, and others have praised the Sunday lunch of traditional roast beef, the good-value set meals, and noted that the wine list (from £26) 'is affordable – in part'.
Chef/s: Adebola Adeshina. **Open:** all week L and D. **Closed:** 25 and 26 Dec. **Meals:** main courses £16 to £38. Set L and D £23 (2 courses) to £27. Sun L £40. **Details:** 70 seats. Bar. Wheelchairs. Parking.

Sonny's Kitchen

Cooking score: 2
map 1
Modern European | £34
94 Church Road, Barnes, SW13 0DQ
Tel no: (020) 8748 0393
sonnyskitchen.co.uk

Well established on the Barnes dining scene, Sonny's Kitchen delivers the sort of modern European cooking that has universal appeal. 'It is a typical neighborhood restaurant,' noted one family group, happy to find themselves in good company with quite a few multigenerational families and older groups of friends. That meal produced a burrata salad, simply served with a blood-orange dressing, and sautéed tiger prawns on a bed of smooth jet-black ink hummus with a 'zingy citrus drizzle'. Precisely cooked pollack followed, topped with a hazelnut pesto and served with Hispi cabbage and a smudge of cauliflower purée, its counterpart a 'full of flavour' crab linguine. Pesto linguine from the kids' menu 'was as good as homemade pesto can be', followed by a 'yummy' scoop of banana ice cream 'which at a set price of £7.50 was very good value'. For the adults, a shared blood-orange and cardamom cheesecake proved to be 'fabulous'. Wines from £17.25.

Chef/s: Andrew Chelley. **Open:** all week L and D. **Closed:** bank hols. **Meals:** main courses £15 to £30. Set L and D £20 (2 courses) to £23. Sun L £27. **Details:** 85 seats. Music.

Tangawizi

Cooking score: 2
⊖ Richmond, map 1
Indian | £30
406 Richmond Road, Twickenham, TW1 2EB
Tel no: (020) 8891 3737
tangawizi.co.uk

A neighbourhood Indian restaurant with a soupçon of glam, Tangawizi has been doing its thing near the southern end of Richmond Bridge since 2003. If only a chicken jalfrezi will do, rest assured they have all the old faves, but there's so much more besides. Start with 'herby fish', perhaps tilapia coated in a light mint and coriander batter, or jhinge coco – king prawns marinated in coconut, ginger and garlic, and duly grilled. Vegetarians fare very well indeed, with stellar onion patties ('posh version of the onion bhaji'), and curries such as bhindi koti masala. If you like a creamy curry, try masala liptey chicken, while lamb figures large in the likes of gilafi kebab cooked in the tandoor, or chilli kadai. The naans get good notices, and, to finish, the chocolate samosa is a winner. Cocktails include a Maharaja Mojito, wines start at £15.95, and Cobra and Kingfisher are by the bottle.

Chef/s: Surat Singh Rana. **Open:** all week D only. **Closed:** 25 and 26 Dec, 1 Jan. **Meals:** main courses £7 to £16. Set D £25 (2 courses) to £28. **Details:** 60 seats. Music.

The Victoria

Cooking score: 4
⊖ Richmond, map 1
Modern British | £35
10 West Temple Sheen, East Sheen, SW14 7RT
Tel no: (020) 8876 4238
victoriasheen.co.uk
£5 OFF 🛏

The Victoria has been an independent pub since the days of the monarch whose name it bears, an invaluable local resource in suburban East Sheen, not far from Richmond Park. A walled garden – soon to be expanded, we hear – makes outdoor eating a particular pleasure, while inside is divided between a proper bar and a light-flooded conservatory dining room. At the core of the catering operation are some pub stalwarts, rendered with impressive brio: salmon fishcakes in white wine velouté, steak burgers with triple-cooked chips, saffron risotto, confit duck leg and cassoulet. Prime materials are obviously top-drawer, and underpin some more modern thinking, too – perhaps white quinoa salad with grilled chicken, feta and red pepper to start, with frozen Greek yoghurt, peppered mango, raspberries and chocolate flakes bringing up the rear. British and Irish cheeses with membrillo are a classy alternative to the sweet stuff, and a resourceful wine list opens at £18.50, or £5 a glass.

Chef/s: Paul Merrett. **Open:** all week L and D. **Meals:** main courses £10 to £29. **Details:** 80 seats. 50 seats outside. Bar. Music. Parking.

ENGLAND

Bedfordshire, Berkshire, Buckinghamshire,
Cambridgeshire, Cheshire, Cornwall,
Cumbria, Derbyshire, Devon, Dorset,
Durham, Essex, Gloucestershire & Bristol,
Greater Manchester,
Hampshire (inc. Isle of Wight),
Herefordshire, Hertfordshire, Kent,
Lancashire, Leicestershire and Rutland,
Lincolnshire, Merseyside, Norfolk,
Northamptonshire, Northumberland,
Nottinghamshire, Oxfordshire, Shropshire,
Somerset, Staffordshire, Suffolk, Surrey,
Sussex – East, Sussex – West, Tyne & Wear,
Warwickshire, West Midlands, Wiltshire,
Worcestershire, Yorkshire

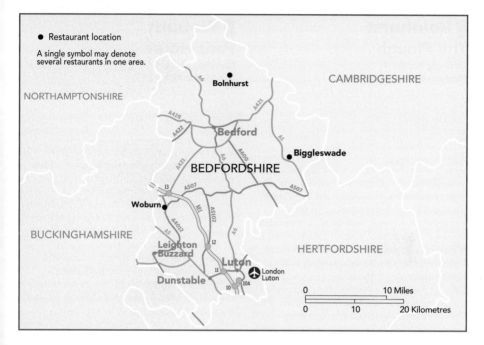

▮ Biggleswade
The Croft Kitchen
Cooking score: 5
Modern British | £45
28 Palace Street, Biggleswade, SG18 8DP
Tel no: (01767) 601502
thecroftbiggleswade.com

£5
OFF

At Kieron and Michael Singh's pair of old cottages the setting is charmingly simple: wood-effect floors, white walls and a central brick fireplace. Crisp white linen adds a sense of occasion, and staff get things off to a smooth start – but none of this prepares you for the clout of the cooking. The thrust of the menu is modern British, but Michael Singh takes that in the broadest sense, travelling via India (red lentil and curry-leaf dhal with sweet potato masala and aubergine pakora) and Asia (blowtorched Scottish salmon with crab, a salt cod won ton, water chestnuts, miso and kimchee) to the more familiar options of pork and black pudding terrine with beetroot, burnt

apple purée and smoked honey dressing or butter-poached free-range chicken breast with en croûte of leg, roasted heritage carrots, quinoa and tarragon jus. Whatever you choose you'll get real precision, refinement and an emphasis on quality ingredients. Round it off with rhubarb, custard, lemon and bergamot. Mostly European wines start at £18.50.
Chef/s: Michael Singh. **Open:** Sat L, Thur to Sat D. **Closed:** Sun to Wed, 26 Dec, 1 week Aug. **Meals:** set L £31. Set D £45. Tasting menu £60. **Details:** 24 seats. Music.

Please send us your feedback

To register your opinion about any restaurant listed in this guide, or a new restaurant that you wish to bring to our attention, please visit the web address at the bottom of the page. Your feedback informs the content of the book and will be used to compile next year's reviews.

▌Bolnhurst
The Plough
Cooking score: 4
Modern British | £36
Kimbolton Road, Bolnhurst, MK44 2EX
Tel no: (01234) 376274
bolnhurst.com

The Plough wears its six centuries of age on its sleeve, with tiny windows dotting the large cream-washed exterior, the inside a mix of stone columns, low ceilings and huge black beams. A conservatory extension offers a second dining room, and there's a restaurant terrace out back, too, next to a deep pond. In this setting of pastoral venerability, Martin Lee offers modern British cooking with clarity and style, without stinting on the pub ethos. A lemon sole at inspection was perfectly timed, served in bubbling brown butter with a verdant wild garlic sauce, as was crisp-skinned whole chicken breast that came with shredded leeks and mashed celeriac in a light but punchy truffle cream. Starters might be goats' cheese brûlée and pickled golden beetroot, topped with smashed hazelnuts, or a traditional seafood risotto aromatised with fennel, dill and chilli. Josper-grilled steaks keep traditionalists happy, and while a pineapple tart with coconut ice cream was a soggy disaster in April, black cherry yoghurt posset should inspire greater confidence, as will the Neal's Yard cheeses. Wines are an enterprising, wide-ranging selection, with standard glasses from £5.

Chef/s: Martin Lee. **Open:** Tue to Sun L, Tue to Sat D. **Closed:** Mon, first 2 weeks Jan. **Meals:** main courses £17 to £30. Set L and D £20 (2 courses) to £25. Sun L £23 (2 courses) to £29. **Details:** 80 seats. 30 seats outside. Bar. Wheelchairs. Parking.

▌Woburn
Paris House
Cooking score: 6
Modern British | £43
London Road, Woburn Park, Woburn, MK17 9QP
Tel no: (01525) 290692
parishouse.co.uk

Paris House may look like a mock-Tudor villa but was originally constructed for the Paris Exposition in 1878 and shipped back, piece by piece, by the Duke of Bedford to a 'gorgeous' setting in Woburn Park. Abandon humdrum expectations of a country-house experience though; all the (comfortable) accoutrements of a modern restaurant are here – undressed, polished tables, wood floors, Tiffany blue velvet chairs, heritage grey walls, simple tableware – while Phil Fanning's cooking is at the very forefront of modern British cuisine, his various tasting menus heady with Asian influences. Summer reporters hugely enjoyed a lunch that took in leche de tigre, a ceviche of hamachi fish in a deep-green tiger's milk broth accented with lime and 'a smack of chilli', as a prelude to a light, frothy confection of morels and alliums that had 'great depth of flavour'. Next, 'very tender pieces' of lamb loin with peas (puréed and whole), rolls of avocado and dots of guacamole was 'a perfect picture of summer eating'. By contrast, that classic combination of pork and eel, served with red pepper and artichoke, was 'hearty and satisfying, but nevertheless done with a delicate and deft hand'. Star of the pair of desserts proved to be an artfully conceived chocolate fondant with chocolate soil, toasted hazelnut and goats' milk ice cream. A conscientiously compiled wine list opens at £28.

Chef/s: Phil Fanning. **Open:** Thur to Sun L, Thur to Sat D. **Closed:** Mon, Tue, Wed, 24 Dec to 3 Jan. **Meals:** tasting menu L £43 (6 courses) to £91, D £91 (8 courses) to £109 (10 courses). Sun L £63 (5 courses). **Details:** 32 seats. V menu. Bar. Music. Parking.

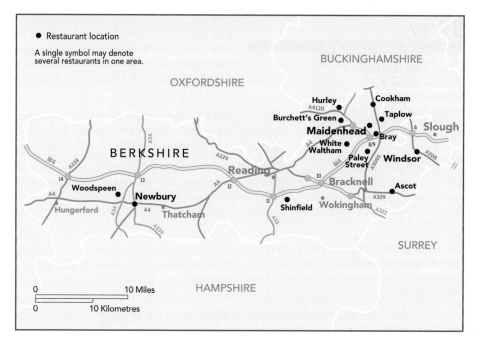

Map legend:
- Restaurant location

A single symbol may denote several restaurants in one area.

OXFORDSHIRE

BUCKINGHAMSHIRE

Hurley
A4130
Burchett's Green
Cookham
Taplow
Maidenhead
Bray
White Waltham
Slough
6
BERKSHIRE
A34
A329
M4
A338
Reading
Paley Street
Windsor
A308
14
13
Woodspeen
Newbury
12
11
Bracknell
A329
Ascot
Hungerford
A34
Thatcham
A339
Shinfield
Wokingham
A322
SURREY

0   10 Miles
0   10 Kilometres

HAMPSHIRE

Ascot

★ NEW ENTRY ★

Restaurant Coworth Park
Cooking score: 6
French | £70
Blacknest Road, Ascot, SL5 7SE
Tel no: (01344) 876600
dorchestercollection.com

Deep in polo country, Coworth Park has struggled somewhat to get its kitchen team together. But with Adam Smith as head chef and Lucy Jones on pastry (and it's quite some pastry), the prospects of eating well in Coworth's smart modern dining room have had a tangible boost. The tasting menu might start with precise canapés and 'wonderful' rosemary-scented bread, followed by an Exmoor caviar and crab tart brimming elegantly with the former. Proceed to a giant morel with cauliflower accompaniments, and a fish course of sea bass and eel with a warm,

foaming sea urchin sauce, and Smith's talent sings loud and clear. Dessert might be a technically impressive assembly of chocolate and malt with a stack of praline cream, biscuit and caramel. Residual niggles include staff who aren't nearly as smooth as the formally dressed tables and a wine list whose lower reaches require swift attention; both are fixable using some of the focus and precision already on show in the kitchen.
Chef/s: Adam Smith. **Open:** Fri to Sun L, Wed to Sat D. **Closed:** Mon, Tue. **Meals:** set L £30 (2 courses) to £35. Set D £45 (3 courses) to £70. Tasting menu £95. **Details:** 60 seats. V menu. Bar. Wheelchairs. Music. Parking.

Symbols

🛏 Accommodation is available
£30 Three courses for less than £30
£5 OFF £5-off voucher scheme
🍾 Notable wine list

■ Bray

The Fat Duck

Cooking score: 9
Modern British | £265
1 High Street, Bray, SL6 2AQ
Tel no: (01628) 580333
thefatduck.co.uk

If there has been a single impulse uniting the divergent strands of culinary modernism, it has been the effort to turn food back into a true experience. In this, as in every other aspect of his work, Heston Blumenthal has been one of the great pioneers, one whose ceaseless explorations and researches have led international sybarites to descend on Bray in their throngs. His primary theme is the recovery of formative taste in those years when our palates were young and new, to which end the present framing of the £265 set menu is that of a family seaside trip, from the thrilled anticipation of the night before to the final tucking up after a slap-up dinner. The various stages of the 24-hour odyssey are realised with astonishing technical panache: the opening macaron of beetroot and horseradish cream; breakfast from variety packs of cereals, all crisped grains and vivid savoury jellies; a Waldorf salad in the guise of a Zoom ice-lolly; the now-famous Sound of the Sea dish of cured seafood eaten to the headphoned accompaniment of susurrating surf. At the climax of it all, the three-course dinner offers alternative choices at each stage, perhaps a superlative crumbed parcel of hay-smoked veal sweetbread with braised Little Gem, then either turbot with a caviar-laden buttery sourdough crouton, or a take on coq au vin with morels, bacon and garlic in red wine, as well as a boned and crisped chicken foot with red wine mayo dip. For the *pièce de résistance*, a magnetised white pillow levitates to spin gently in midair, loaded with frozen milk and meringue bites, as a prelude to a dessert array as white as freshly laundered linen − lychee yoghurt ice cream, vanilla sponge filled with tonka pannacotta, bergamot curd in Earl Grey and lavender mousse. The whole performance is fronted by staff styled as 'storytellers', who stick to the script with impressive tenacity in the manner of museum actors. A significant risk of the childhood concept, especially extended over several hours, is that we recollect that part of being young was yearning to grow up, and it's hard to imagine why, once you had undergone this journey, you would want to repeat it. And yet the magic and its incredible cleverness endure. The wine flights are probably the best way of getting through an extraordinary list of vinous jewels, which reaches from Turkish Chardonnay to mature Uruguayan Tannat, at mark-ups to induce a fit of the giggles.
Chef/s: Heston Blumenthal and Jonny Lake. **Open:** Tue to Sat L and D. **Closed:** Sun, Mon, 2 weeks Christmas. **Meals:** tasting menu L and D £265. **Details:** 42 seats. V menu. Wheelchairs.

The Hind's Head

Cooking score: 4
British | £48
High Street, Bray, SL6 2AB
Tel no: (01628) 626151
hindsheadbray.com

The Hind's Head was given a thoroughgoing makeover in the spring of 2017. It's now divided between a first-floor bar styled the Royal Lounge, designed to look like Hollywood's idea of a hunting lodge, with blunderbuss chandeliers, light fittings fashioned from meat mincers and a 3-D cockatrice on the mantelshelf, and the ground floor, now the dedicated dining area. The menu structure takes a little digestion. 'Mary' is a three-course lunch affair of house specialities, while 'Elizabeth' is the dinner and weekend lunch six-courser. In between comes 'Aleyn', a four-stage parade of premium dishes that change roughly every other month. Basically, it's not claiming to be pub food any more. Ham hock, pork loin and leek terrine with pistachios and piccalilli was unspectacularly satisfactory at a June visit. Much better was the following scallop Waldorf incorporating monk's beard and

raisins among the classic ingredients, while juicily pink duck breast came with noodle-like shreds of celeriac, whole and puréed asparagus, braised endive and a meaty cracker. A surprisingly prosaic white chocolate and lemon cheesecake plated with crumbs and a scoop of biscuity ice cream wasn't a patch on the simpler treacle tart that comes in a generous slab with milk ice. Whatever you do, though, don't miss the Scotch egg. Small glasses of wine from £5.50 head up a list that's weighted towards French classics.
Chef/s: János Veres. **Open:** all week L, Mon to Sat D. **Closed:** 25 Dec. **Meals:** set L Mon to Fri £20 (2 courses) to £25. All week set L £48 (4 courses). Set D £48 (4 courses) to £58. **Details:** 90 seats. Bar. Music. Parking.

★ TOP 50 ★

The Waterside Inn
Cooking score: 7
French | £160
Ferry Road, Bray, SL6 2AT
Tel no: (01628) 620691
waterside-inn.co.uk

Before a certain Heston Blumenthal exploded on to the scene, Bray's reputation for culinary excellence resided entirely with the Waterside Inn – a steadfast defender of civilised dining in a 'restless and sensation-hungry world'. Founded in 1972, this serene performer still has the power to captivate, not least with its picture-book location – a willow-shrouded riverbank redolent of children's stories, with birdsong in the air and boats swaying in their moorings. A high-romantic English idyll you might think, yet everything about the Waterside is suffused with Gallic esprit de corps – not surprising since it has Roux family blood coursing through its veins. Legions of staff (all with specific roles) go about their business with punctilious efficiency, while Alain Roux's kitchen majors in dignified cooking with a patriarchal sense of occasion. The house style is typified by gamey 'masterpieces' such as a pheasant velouté or roast loin of venison en croûte, an

'absolute picture' with broccoli, wild mushrooms, a 'fabulous' Hermitage sauce and blackcurrant vinegar. Masterly seafood cookery also provokes a rapturous response, from flaked Devon crab with ginger-scented cucumber jelly to a dazzlingly precise salad of native lobster with a modish beetroot gel, rocket and crème fraîche – the 'epitome of classical cuisine with apposite modern touches'. By contrast, desserts such as a confection involving creamy yoghurt, raspberries and lime marshmallow seem to create less of an impact. Penny-pinching isn't an option here, so don't flinch at the mark-ups on the aristocratic Francophile wine list.
Chef/s: Alain Roux. **Open:** Wed to Sun L and D. **Closed:** Mon, Tue, 26 Dec to 1 Feb. **Meals:** main courses £54 to £67. Set L Mon to Fri £52 (2 courses) to £64. Sun L £82. Tasting menu £168 (6 courses). **Details:** 70 seats. Bar. Parking. Children over 9 yrs only.

LOCAL GEM

The Crown at Bray
British | £36
High Street, Bray, SL6 2AH
Tel no: (01628) 621936
thecrownatbray.com

Heston Blumenthal's village pub – all winter fires, wonky beams, chatty ambience – perfectly fits its Local Gem status. It's an old pub of obvious charm, much devoted to dining but with well-kept ales and a beer garden, too. The kitchen turns out well-executed dishes, from herring roe on toast with seaweed butter or excellent potted rabbit, via lamb belly with confit potatoes, and a deeply flavoured macaroni cheese with pickled mushrooms, charred spring onion and radish, to good old fish and chips.

Visit us online

To find out more about The Good Food Guide, please visit thegoodfoodguide.co.uk

■ Burchett's Green

★ BEST PUB RESTAURANT ★

The Crown

Cooking score: 6
French | £35
Burchett's Green, SL6 6QZ
Tel no: (01628) 824079
thecrownburchettsgreen.com

It may have real ales, a wood-burner and undressed tables, but the cooking at this 19th-century brick-built village pub is more sophisticated than the country-casual interior suggests. This is down to Simon Bonwick, one of an increasingly rare breed – a wildly talented chef/landlord who respects the traditions of French gastronomy, cooks without compromise and runs his kitchen single-handed. The food is founded on a bedrock of fine ingredients and straddles both traditional and contemporary – Salcombe crabmeat, a generous mound of beautiful white crabmeat, all vibrant and clean flavours, with apple, passion fruit and cashew defining its meaty freshness, for example, or rillettes of sanglier (wild boar) with beer pickles. Equally well considered have been a magnificent pie stuffed with braised haunch of Highland deer and served with rowan sauce, and a generous plate of pink, tender salt marsh lamb rump with garlic and thyme cooking juices. Moreish sourdough rolls are 'the kind to fill your handbag with', potato purée is 'impressive', cheeses are from La Fromagerie and desserts like hot treacle sponge are hailed by one diner as 'too good to miss'. Simon's children lend a hand out front (and in the kitchen), although his eldest son (and co-owner) Dean is charged with running the show and managing the endlessly rewarding 'haggle board' wine list.

Chef/s: Simon Bonwick. **Open:** Thur to Sun L, Wed to Sat D. **Closed:** Mon, Tue, 2 weeks Christmas, 2 weeks Aug. **Meals:** main courses £19 to £26. **Details:** 20 seats. Bar. Wheelchairs. Music. Parking. No children.

■ Cookham

The White Oak

Cooking score: 3
Modern British | £31
The Pound, Cookham, SL6 9QE
Tel no: (01628) 523043
thewhiteoak.co.uk
£5 OFF

Leafy Cookham provides the well-heeled backdrop to this good-looking pub/restaurant, which comes with a drinkers' bar, a smart dining room and a hidden garden for summertime alfresco revelry. Whether you want to quench your thirst or fill up on some capably crafted food, the White Oak can deliver. The kitchen deals in approachable brasserie-style cooking with a dash of metropolitan pizazz and an open-minded approach to ingredients: crispy Cornish squid lines up alongside sweet-pickled carrots, air-dried ham, chorizo mayonnaise and shallots, while Jimmy Butler's pork fillet and treacle-cured belly are combined in true Brit style with caramelised onions, black pudding and Jerusalem artichoke purée. Steaks and line-caught pollack come with triple-cooked chips. And how about a 'toffee crisp' with toasted marshmallow and Nutella, or brioche doughnuts with custard, caramel sauce and hazelnuts for dessert? Set lunches offer decent value and there's a short list of no-nonsense wines at fair prices.

Chef/s: Graham Kirk. **Open:** all week L, Mon to Sat D. **Meals:** main courses £14 to £28. Set L £13 (2 courses) to £16. Set D £16 (2 courses) to £19. Sun L £17. **Details:** 75 seats. 25 seats outside. Bar. Wheelchairs. Music. Parking.

▌Hurley

★ NEW ENTRY ★

Hurley House

Cooking score: 4
Modern British | £45
Henley Road, Hurley, SL6 5LH
Tel no: (01628) 568500
hurleyhouse.co.uk

£5 OFF 🛏

Hurley House has risen, phoenix-like, on the site of what was the old Red Lion pub, refitted for the present day with black slate tiles, rather clubby green leather banquettes and dark wood walls hung with occasional pictures of vegetables. Staff kitted out in lumberjack shirts run the place with smooth efficiency, and there's a large decked terrace for when Berkshire turns balmy. Michael Chapman was at the Royal Oak, Paley Street (see entry), and brings a robust, ingredient-led, unfussy style of cooking with him that emphasises seasonal produce. A first course of 'gorgeously fatty' smoked eel with charcoal-roast kohlrabi, lardo strips, shredded celery and dots of caramel sauce is a resounding success, and is succeeded by thick slices of beef fillet with a plethora of buttery mushrooms piled on creamed spinach, dressed in a glossy bone-marrow sauce, or a whole crisply roasted chicken breast, with pressed thigh, calçot onions, blanched kale, cauliflower purée and a lick of syrupy chicken jus, 'a masterclass in leaving well alone'. Dessert might be chocolate ganache and peanut mousse with bright white hazelnut ice cream. Wines start at £20 for southern French house selections on a list that makes no bones about reaching for the stars.
Chef/s: Michael Chapman. **Open:** all week L, Mon to Sat D. **Meals:** main courses £19 to £35. Set L £24 (2 courses) to £29. **Details:** 48 seats. 60 seats outside. Bar. Wheelchairs. Music. Parking.

▌Maidenhead

Boulters Riverside Brasserie

Cooking score: 2
Modern British | £35
Boulters Lock Island, Maidenhead, SL6 8PE
Tel no: (01628) 621291
boultersrestaurant.co.uk

£5 OFF

Majestically enthroned on its island in the Thames, Boulters enjoys the riparian view through gallery windows that allow you to wave to the occupants of passing boats. Inside, a contented buzz fills the air, as locals pack the place for up-to-the-minute brasserie food full of popular strokes. A chorizo Scotch egg with tarragon mayo, mini-fishcakes in lime and chilli dressing, or Spanish charcuterie prime the appetite for robust main dishes like John Dory with roasted garlic gnocchi, samphire and baby gem in sauce vierge, or breast of Gressingham duck dressed in orange and pistachios with a lyonnaise onion tart. Sides of truffled sweetcorn or red cabbage slaw help things along, while main-course salads provide plenty of variety and freshness. Exotically seasoned finishers are a strong suit, perhaps chocolate and yoghurt mousse with baked spiced pineapple, masala chai ice cream and a spicy tuile. Sicilian house wines are £18.40, or £4.90 a standard glass.
Chef/s: Daniel Woodhouse. **Open:** all week L, Mon to Sat D. **Meals:** main courses £13 to £24. Set L £16 (2 courses) to £20. Sun L £16. **Details:** 130 seats. 40 seats outside. Bar. Wheelchairs. Music. Parking.

▌Newbury

The Vineyard

Cooking score: 4
Modern French | £69
Stockcross, Newbury, RG20 8JU
Tel no: (01635) 528770
the-vineyard.co.uk

£5 OFF 🍷 🛏

Named in honour of owner Sir Peter Michael's California winery, the Vineyard comes tricked out like some über-glitzy West Coast hacienda-with-rooms – although not many ranch houses can boast a 500-piece art collection or a wine cellar holding literally thousands of bottles. This place is all about grandiose aspirations and unabashed opulence, right down to the split-level restaurant – a glamorous backdrop for chef Robby Jenks' highly worked and elaborately detailed creations. Contemporary French themes are embroidered with influences from the Orient, as in Loch Duart salmon with cucumber, English wasabi and dill or slow-cooked chicken with liver parfait and broccoli, blasted with pungent, lip-tingling kim-chee. Other dishes such as saddle of venison with red cabbage, blackberry and chervil root sit much closer to home, while desserts are fancy conceits along the lines of rhubarb parfait with rice pudding and maple syrup. However, the food ultimately plays second fiddle to the contents of the stupendous glassed-in wine 'cave' – some 3,000 bins drawn from the Vineyard's capacious cellar, with an unrivalled selection of Californian treasures and a 'short' list offering no fewer than 100 by the glass.

Chef/s: Robby Jenks. **Open:** all week L and D. **Meals:** set L £24 (2 courses) to £29. Set D £69 (3 courses). Tasting menus £89 (7 courses) to £99. Sun L £39 (3 courses). **Details:** 90 seats. V menu. Bar. Wheelchairs. Music. Parking.

▌Paley Street
The Royal Oak
Cooking score: 4
Modern British | £40
Littlefield Green, Paley Street, SL6 3JN
Tel no: (01628) 620541
theroyaloakpaleystreet.com

Nick Parkinson's handsome 17th-century pub stands on a country road linking a cluster of affluent hamlets and villages. Run with personal charm and good humour, it's an upbeat place that knows how to win friends. People love the way it strikes the right note between traditional and contemporary, and applaud the cooking, whether a herb-crusted halibut on truffled leeks with brown shrimps

and a cream sauce that 'was the most delicious fish dish I have ever eaten', or the 'well worth the 10-minute wait' plum and frangipane tart served with almond ice cream. A well-reported winter lunch took in roast breast and legs of quail with braised chicory, toasted hazelnut and pear salad, then a richly braised shin of veal with a bone-marrow crust, sweetbreads, crisp bacon lardons and broccoli and almonds, with a 'perfect' pannacotta with young pink rhubarb and a sprinkling of coarse white 'Aero' chocolate to finish. Wine is taken seriously, too: reasonable prices (from £19.50), reliable producers, plenty for the French purists, but with some good southern-hemisphere selections.

Chef/s: James Bennett. **Open:** all week L, Mon to Sat D. **Meals:** main courses £19 to £31. Set L £25 (2 courses) to £30. **Details:** 80 seats. Bar. Music. Parking.

▌Shefford Woodlands
READERS RECOMMEND
The Pheasant Inn
Modern British
Ermin Street, Shefford Woodlands, RG17 7AA
Tel no: (01488) 648284
thepheasant-inn.co.uk
'This is a wonderful, welcoming pub. Warm, friendly and efficient service and totally delicious food. We had the côte de boeuf, which was perfectly cooked. Can't recommend it more highly.'

▌Shinfield
L'Ortolan
Cooking score: 5
Modern French | £65
Church Lane, Shinfield, RG2 9BY
Tel no: (0118) 9888500
lortolan.com
£5 OFF

Where once this former rectory stood at the forefront of modern British cooking – from the tenures of Nico Ladenis and John Burton-Race in the 1980s to Alan Murchison in the noughties – it now trades in a more intricately worked modern French style with a seasonal à la carte as the mainstay and a 10-course taster for the splurgers. Tom Clarke continues to head the kitchen, his highly detailed, technically sound cooking deals in canapés and pre-desserts and promises the likes of goose liver terrine with blood orange and honey ahead of loin and belly of pork with dauphinois potatoes, onion and garlic or pan-fried stone bass with seared squid, curry and cauliflower. Fancy desserts bring salted-chocolate parfait with cumin and yoghurt sorbet or a lovely confection of rhubarb (simply poached, with a Champagne sorbet, and in a buttermilk mousse). The cooking is certainly ambitious and refined, and the pedigree wine list matches the culinary aspirations, exploring France in depth but also finding inspiration in shorter choices across the globe.

Chef/s: Tom Clarke. **Open:** Tue to Sat L and D. **Closed:** Sun, Mon, 25 Dec to first week Jan. **Meals:** set L £28 (2 courses) to £32. Set D £58 (2 courses) to £65. Tasting menu £75 (7 courses) to £105 (10 courses). **Details:** 58 seats. V menu. Children over 3 yrs only.

▌Taplow

★ TOP 50 ★

André Garrett at Cliveden
Cooking score: 8
Modern French | £75
Cliveden House, Taplow, SL6 0JF
Tel no: (01628) 607100
clivedenhouse.co.uk

🍷 🛏

'Our story is one of powerful personalities, debaucherous parties and scandalous affairs,' say the owners of Cliveden – but this Berkshire blue-blood has also played host to some serious chefs over the years – a tradition admirably sustained by current incumbent André Garrett. The setting for his invigorating modern French cuisine is a dining room replete with crystal chandeliers, portraits and rich fabrics, all topped off by glorious views of the grounds. The kitchen rightly takes its cue from impeccably sourced ingredients which are gently coaxed and transformed into precise, harmonious and exquisitely balanced dishes, marrying the best of French technique with elements of the modern British style. A plate of English rose veal tartare is gilded with shimeji mushrooms, quail's egg yolk, caviar and a pretty garland of nasturtium flowers, while Wagyu beef from the Earl Stonham estate is given new vigour thanks to carrot and mushroom persillade, bone marrow and truffle mash. Fish is also handled with the utmost dexterity, as in roast fillet of turbot with Pink Fir potatoes, seaweed, celery and borage velouté, while desserts are miracles of technique and artistry – try the fragrant bergamot tart with Earl Grey ice cream and meringue. Service from staff and sommeliers is simply immaculate, and the monumental 'book of wines' offers great treasures galore alongside bottles highlighting viniculture's global diversity. Whether your taste is for a German Spätburgunder or a sparkler from Sussex, it helps to have a healthy bank balance.

Chef/s: André Garrett. **Open:** all week L and D. **Meals:** main courses £28 to £45. Set L £28 (2 courses) to £33. Set D £55 (Mon to Thur). Sun L £60. Tasting menu £98 (8 courses). **Details:** 78 seats. V menu. Bar. Wheelchairs. Music. Parking. No children after 8pm.

The Astor Grill
Cooking score: 3
British/American | £40
Cliveden House, Taplow, SL6 0JF
Tel no: (01628) 668561
clivedenhouse.co.uk

🛏

The brasserie-grill offspring of André Garrett at Cliveden (see entry) shows another side of this famous stately pile's heritage. Sited in the old stables, with the old stalls still in place and plenty of original features, it makes a pleasant pit-stop if you are visiting Cliveden and want a more casual experience. The atmosphere is relaxed enough to cater for those just wanting a drink and half a lobster and chips –

recommended if the weather is fine and there's the chance to sit in the pretty courtyard garden. The menu is peppered with ideas that attempt to please all palates: sautéed wild mushrooms on toast with a poached egg and gremolata, Maryland crab cakes with avocado and tomato and a veal cutlet with béarnaise relish sit happily beside sea bass ceviche with fennel, melon and coriander, or baked fillet of cod with mussel chowder, potato and chilli and lime. Wines from £29.

Chef/s: André Garrett. **Open:** all week L and D. **Meals:** main courses £16 to £32. **Details:** 40 seats. 30 seats outside. Bar. Wheelchairs. Music. Parking.

■ White Waltham
The Beehive
Cooking score: 5
British | £38
Waltham Road, White Waltham, SL6 3SH
Tel no: (01628) 822877
thebeehivewhitewaltham.com

£5
OFF

There's no doubt that chef/proprietor Dominic Chapman's large, handsome brick-built pub on the edge of the village is a showpiece Berkshire hostelry. Inside is fresh and light, a welcoming haven – warm, enveloping, civilised – where the atmosphere is relaxed enough to cater for those who just want to have a drink at the bar. But the food here is bang on the money. What's on offer is a menu of exemplary dishes with a strong seasonal accent. Evergreens such as traditional Sunday roasts are way above the norm and pub diehards can always feast on fish and chips, but potted crab with rosemary and sea salt toast, and peppered haunch of venison with creamed spinach and sauce poivrade are more typical of Dominic's flexible approach to British and classical themes. To finish, a molten chocolate fondant with almond biscuit, toffee sauce and pistachio ice cream succeeds decadently at every step. To drink, local beers compete with the well-annotated, well-travelled wine list (bottles from £18.50).

Chef/s: Dominic Chapman. **Open:** all week L, Mon to Sat D. **Closed:** 25 and 26 Dec. **Meals:** main courses £15 to £28. Set L and D £16 (2 courses) to £20. **Details:** 75 seats. 40 seats outside. Bar. Wheelchairs. Music. Parking.

■ Windsor
★ NEW ENTRY ★
The Oxford Blue
Cooking score: 5
Modern British | £50
10 Crimp Hill, Windsor, SL4 2QY
Tel no: (01753) 861954
oxfordbluepub.co.uk

If you're after serious cooking in a 'polished' but pub-referencing setting, this place could tick your boxes. There is a correspondingly serious price tag – a ploughman's, albeit one plated at table from a trolley bearing a home-smoked leg of ham and hunk of Mrs Kirkham's cheese, costs £15 – but what do you expect with a chef of Steven Ellis's impeccable pedigree at the stove? There's theatre aplenty (despite some 'rather controlled, formulaic' service). Bread arrives in a paper bag that's opened, steaming, in front of you, meat main courses come with a choice of Laguiole knives, and hazelnut brittle petits fours with a hammer. The menu is rich with 'razor sharp' technique: a circle of wafer-thin apple slices is topped with 'irresistibly gelatinous' pig's trotter, panéed black pudding, a quail's egg yolk, and tiny poached crab apple that, with a sauce gribiche, cuts the fat nicely; and a plate of steak and chips is a triumph of 'artistic, technical flourish' even if the 'very good, decently aged' sirloin didn't quite meet one diner's £32 expectations. Top-notch pâtisserie work in a dessert of malt and chocolate mousses, biscuit and wafers of praline and tempered chocolate certainly wows, however. Wine from £19.

Chef/s: Steven Ellis. **Open:** Wed to Sun L and D. **Closed:** Mon, Tue. **Meals:** main courses £19 to £32. Set L £25 (2 courses) to £30. **Details:** 44 seats. 16 seats outside. Bar. Wheelchairs. Music. Parking.

■ Woodspeen
The Woodspeen
Cooking score: 6
Modern British | £46
Lambourn Road, Woodspeen, RG20 8BN
Tel no: (01635) 265070
thewoodspeen.com

£5
OFF

'Attractive modernised and extended former country pub in a minimalist, or at least chintz-free style', a description that marks out the Woodspeen as one of a new breed of country restaurants. It helps that it has a chef with experience at the fancy end of the culinary spectrum, one who has put the place on the culinary map. That is not to say John Campbell is cooking haute cuisine, not a bit of it, for this place is all about classy renditions of food everyone wants to eat, be it crab ravioli with artichoke, lemon and a shellfish bisque or ribeye steak with mushroom gratin and chips. Indeed the menu strikes many alluring modern British chords, whether scallops teamed with pork cheeks, cauliflower and quince, with hazelnut and balsamic dressing, a sharing dish of lobster fish and chips, or hare loin with winter vegetables and truffle pearl barley, parsley root and lemon purée. For dessert, try Manchester tart with banana pannacotta, raspberry and honeycomb. A magisterial list of wines inspires confidence, with quality and value (from £19) in impressive balance throughout.
Chef/s: John Campbell. **Open:** Tue to Sun L, Tue to Sat D. **Closed:** Mon, 26 Dec. **Meals:** main courses £18 to £34. Set L £24 (2 courses) to £29. **Details:** 66 seats. 36 seats outside. Bar. Wheelchairs. Music. Parking.

Fermentation

Beloved by the ancients since time began and now beloved of chefs, too, fermentation is a pet project in every kitchen worth its curing salt. The probiotic benefits are not to be sniffed at, of course, but we're in it for the flavour. Here's where to find it.

At **The Manor** in Clapham, head chef Dean Parker is a leading light in fermentation – he holds masterclasses featuring **kombucha, sourdough** and **salami** and knows the difference between all kinds of **homemade miso**. On the menu, **kefir** might be mixed with crème fraîche to make a dressing with cod cheeks and pickled cucumber.

The story goes that every Korean home maintains their own jar of spicy preserved cabbage, and now that seems to be true of restaurants, too. At the **Ox Club** in Leeds, try the duck served with **Brussels sprout kim-chee**.

Made with an ever-giving 'mother', **sourdough** is a crowd-pleasing and familiar ferment. We love the crackling crust and deep rye heft of the loaf served at **Where the Light Gets In** in Stockport.

Salami is salami because of lactic fermentation. At **Lime Wood** in Hampshire, the little smokehouse has homemade versions, while the house salami at the **Reliance** in Leeds is varied with chilli, fennel or hazelnut.

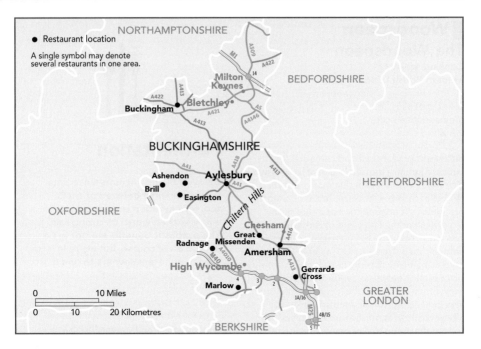

▮ Amersham

Artichoke

Cooking score: 7
Modern British | £48
9 Market Square, Amersham, HP7 0DF
Tel no: (01494) 726611
artichokerestaurant.co.uk
🖢

'I cannot believe how good this place is,' was one reader's reaction after visiting the Artichoke – a restaurant that fits its genteel market-town location like a kid glove. A mood of quiet confidence, goodwill and enthusiasm prevails out front. However, there's no 'self-conscious flashiness' when it comes to delivering the goods – just consider a modernist assemblage of pickled and roasted Jerusalem artichokes arranged in a considered jumble with toasted hazelnuts, chervil and 'ambrosial' truffle gel. But there's respect for the classic ways too: a crab thermidor is presented sans carapace alongside a squid-ink rice cracker like some contorted oyster shell complete with two tiny white 'pearls' (actually steamed scallop bonbons). Elsewhere, nothing says seasonality better than a saddle of venison smoked over Douglas Fir with chervil root, orange curd, pickled red onion and Brussels sprouts or a tranche of briny-fresh plaice on the bone pointed up with oyster leaf, lightly cooked alexanders and a good old foam. To conclude, the signature pear galette gets glowing reviews, likewise the Cambridge burnt cream with new season's rhubarb and rhubarb sorbet. Details such as the unmissable home-baked breads and clever pre-desserts also create good vibrations, as does the intelligently chosen wine list – an imaginative blend of reputable names and exciting newcomers, all impressively managed by sommelier Matteo Scaccabarozzi.

Chef/s: Laurie Gear and Ben Jenkins. **Open:** Tue to Sat L and D. **Closed:** Sun, Mon, 2 weeks Christmas/Jan, 1 week Easter, 2 weeks Aug. **Meals:** main courses £25 to £26. Set L £24 (2 courses) to £28. Set

D £42 (2 courses) to £48. Tasting menu L £38 (5 courses), D £68 (7 courses). **Details:** 48 seats. 2 seats outside. V menu. Music.

LOCAL GEM

Gilbey's
Modern British | £35
1 Market Square, Amersham, HP7 0DF
Tel no: (01494) 727242
gilbeygroup.com

Bang on the market square, a 17th-century former grammar school has been home to Gilbey's since 1989, during which time it has won over more than one generation of locals. The modern British output has moved with the times – seared scallops with a smoked oyster to start, say, followed by ale-braised ox cheeks or stone bass with cauliflower a couple of ways and sea vegetables. Finish with rhubarb and custard crème brûlée, or lemon tart. Wine is a passion, too; bottles start at £18.75.

◼ Ashendon
The Hundred
Cooking score: 4
British | £29
Lower End, Ashendon, HP18 0HE
Tel no: (01296) 651296
thehundred.co.uk
£5 OFF 🛏 £30

Squirrelled away in a little hilltop village, The Hundred was completely renovated in 2013, yet still functions as a country pub – complete with local ales. Nevertheless, its carefully distressed ochre, brick and white walls, its polished flooring and above all the cooking of Matthew Gill (ex-St John, see entry) speak of higher ambitions. Gill's creations feature robust, punchy flavours, most evident in a starter of salted pollack salad teamed with olive-oil-soaked bread, which outshone a homogenous, if sea-fresh, red mullet soup at inspection. Likewise, a main course of tender mutton rump and swede might be perked up with a pickled walnut, and a luscious, fatty

oblong of brisket is paired with broccoli made piquant with anchovy sauce. New potatoes, charged extra, contribute to a sizeable bill, and desserts such as a very sweet rhubarb queen of puddings don't always thrill, but execution is consistently high. The well-thought-out wine list starts at £21.50.
Chef/s: Matthew Gill. **Open:** Tue to Sun L, Tue to Sat D. **Closed:** Mon, 1 week Jan. **Meals:** main courses £14 to £20. **Details:** 38 seats. 20 seats outside. Bar. Music. Parking.

◼ Aylesbury
Hartwell House
Cooking score: 2
Modern British | £62
Oxford Road, Lower Hartwell, Aylesbury, HP17 8NR
Tel no: (01296) 747444
hartwell-house.com
🛏

Once a safe haven for exiled French monarch Louis XVIII, Hartwell House now parades its aristocratic Englishness as part of the National Trust's portfolio. Amid 94 acres of rolling parkland, this Jacobean mansion oozes 'imposing tranquillity' with the smell of wood smoke wafting through the great Gothic hall and well-appointed tables in the 'beautiful, well-lit' Sloane dining room. Chef Daniel Richardson is an old hand at delivering country-house richness, but leavens his efforts with some deft contemporary touches. One 'delightful seasonal lunch' yielded festive cheer in the shape of venison carpaccio with figs followed by pheasant breast with chestnut gnocchi, spiced red cabbage and curly kale, but dinner also brings its share of pretty inducements. Seared scallops are matched with pear ketchup, pickled cauliflower and brawn croquette, while dessert might bring raspberry, lychee and rose tart with Turkish delight. An extravagant French-led wine list promises treasures aplenty, but at a price.
Chef/s: Daniel Richardson. **Open:** all week L and D. **Meals:** set L £26 (2 courses) to £34. Set D £51 (2 courses) to £62. Sun L £38 (3 courses). **Details:** 60 seats. Bar. Wheelchairs. Parking.

Our highlights...

Our undercover inspectors reveal their most memorable dishes from another year of extraordinary eating.

Not an extraordinarily unusual combination of flavours, but a beautiful version of it: **Isle of Skye scallops** with liquid-nitrogen-frozen blood orange, fennel and wakami at newcomer **108 Garage**.

Pan-fried red mullet, fennel salad and Provençal fish sauce at **Ben's Cornish Kitchen**. Perfectly cooked, spankingly fresh Cornish fish with a Gallic twist, eaten a stone's throw from the sea. What's not to like?

Mutton, cauliflower and chard at **Wilsons**. Exceptional and respectful cooking of humble, seasonal ingredients that punched well above its modest menu description.

Baked egg custard tart with rhubarb and nutmeg ice cream at **Castle Bow**. An unimprovable rendition of a classic with tartness from the rhubarb and gentle spice from the nutmeg. Stunning.

Arctic bird's nest at **Aquavit**. The signature dessert from the original. A white chocolate egg of goat's cheese parfait and sea buckthorn yolk, served with a honey-tuile nest, flowers, berries and flecks of gold leaf. A perfect balance of textures and flavours and very pretty.

▉ Beaconsfield
READERS RECOMMEND
No. 5
Modern British
London End, Beaconsfield, HP9 2HN
Tel no: (01494) 355500
no5londonend.co.uk
'Cod main was superb, perfectly cooked with crispy skin and tender, meaty flesh. Gnocchi, mussels and bacon went fantastically well with this dish. I had a side of truffle fries, which again were excellent, crisp and nicely truffled. Dessert was salted–caramel brioche doughnuts. A welcome addition, and a true shining light in the area.'

▉ Brill
The Pointer
Cooking score: 4
Modern British | £40
27 Church Street, Brill, HP18 9RT
Tel no: (01844) 238339
thepointerbrill.co.uk
£5 OFF 🚗

A Pointer dog looks down from the pub sign of this stylishly revamped village local, with a butcher's shop installed next door, and four smart bedrooms (across the road) coming on line in 2017. The Howdens, a farming family of this parish, have created a compelling mix, the pub itself done out with a rustic finish that could grace the pages of any style magazine, and an impressive culinary output that is full of integrity. The farm is the source of much of what follows. Beef tongue is not a cut that gets much of an outing these days, but here it is in a salad with crispy sweetbreads and celeriac slaw, while another starter sees Devon crab with textures of beetroot, Granny Smith apple and the zing of New Delhi spices. Venison pie is a classy version, wild Cornish pollack gets the slow-poached treatment, and a risotto of wild mushrooms is the real deal. Blood-orange posset is a touch of exoticism blown in on the wind. The wine list includes organic, biodynamic and vegan options.

Chef/s: Sebastian Bielecki. **Open:** Tue to Sun L, Tue to Sat D. **Closed:** Mon. **Meals:** main courses £21 to £30. Set L £18 (2 courses) to £23. **Details:** 60 seats. 40 seats outside. Bar. Music. Parking.

◼ Buckingham
Nelson Street
Cooking score: 4
Modern British | £40
53-54 Nelson Street, Buckingham, MK18 1BT
Tel no: (01280) 815556
nelsonstreetrestaurant.co.uk
£5
OFF

Jettison your first impressions. Nelson Street looks every inch the congenial old wine bar it partially is – empty bottles lined up by the windows; polished wooden flooring; modern art on the walls; tealights on the tables – but the food refuses to follow suit. Chef/owner Louis Myhill has transformed his repertoire, producing small-plate meals of playful delights: available in prix fixe and tasting menu formats. Add-ons abound, from amuse-bouches of mackerel marinated in Pimm's (marvellous) and spring roll on shredded lettuce (mundane), to a palate-cleansing drink of apple and mint with lime-infused vinegar. At inspection, highlights included beef tartare matched with a deep-fried oyster and oyster emulsion; crisply fried trout fillet atop a smoky bacon-based dashi broth; and pigeon breast teamed with hazelnut mousse and tart stewed raspberries – but flavour combinations, textural variation and classy presentation are all manifested at this reborn star. Wines from a beefed-up list start at £23.
Chef/s: Louis Myhill. **Open:** Tue to Sat D only. **Closed:** Sun, Mon. **Meals:** small plates £39 (3 courses). Tasting menu £65. **Details:** 45 seats. Wheelchairs. Music.

◼ Easington
The Mole & Chicken
Cooking score: 2
Modern British | £32
Easington Terrace, Easington, HP18 9EY
Tel no: (01844) 208387
themoleandchicken.co.uk
£5
OFF

With sweeping views stretching across miles of Buckinghamshire and Oxfordshire countryside, it's not surprising that this ivy-clad pub-with-rooms makes the most of its gorgeous alfresco terrace – although the tastefully decorated interior has attributes aplenty in the shape of designer fabrics, leather seating and country-chic touches throughout a warren of beamed rooms. Food-wise, devilled kidneys, dry-aged steaks and beer-battered fish are the only pub concessions on a menu that shows a fair degree of ambition. To start, you might plump for hot-smoked eel with Aura potatoes and a crispy poached egg, or goats' curd with beetroot, chicory and caramelised walnuts, while mains cover everything from braised rabbit with fresh pappardelle and wild mushrooms to pan-fried hake with samphire, tomato and mussels. As a finale, go for something indulgent such as warm chocolate fondant with honeycomb ice cream. The concise wine list includes a decent selection by the glass.
Chef/s: Steve Bush. **Open:** all week L and D. **Closed:** 25 Dec. **Meals:** main courses £13 to £26. Set L and D £18 (2 courses) to £24. **Details:** 62 seats. 60 seats outside. Bar. Wheelchairs. Music. Parking.

▮ Gerrards Cross
The Three Oaks

Cooking score: 4
Modern British | £30
Austenwood Common, Gerrards Cross,
SL9 8NL
Tel no: (01753) 899016
thethreeoaksgx.co.uk
£5
OFF

Out of the same arboreally themed stable as
the White Oak, Cookham (see entry), this
solid-looking brick-and-timber hostelry
makes the most of its setting, with a delightful
fenced-in garden for summer meals. Inside,
beams and a brick fireplace blend with shiny
wood floors, pastel colours and tasteful tartan
fabrics – a congenial setting for purposeful
food that's more country restaurant than local
boozer. The kitchen's clear-sighted,
thoughtful approach pays dividends all round,
from starters of cured Cornish mackerel with
red cabbage essence, grape-mustard yoghurt
and sourdough 'sippets' to desserts such as
tonka bean rice pudding with pineapple and
maple compote. In between, the kitchen
applies a respectful but creative approach to
top-drawer ingredients: venison is given
darkly autumnal treatment with curried
parsnips, shallot and Stilton dressing, pickled
walnuts and dark chocolate, while grilled
whole plaice appears alongside St Austell
mussels, mushroom and tarragon emulsion. A
well-chosen Corney & Barrow wine list
rounds things off.
Chef/s: Mikey Seferynski. **Open:** all week L, Mon to
Sat D. **Closed:** 25 Dec. **Meals:** main courses £13 to
£26. Set L 12 (2 courses) to £15. Set D £15 (2
courses) to £19. Sun L £17. **Details:** 70 seats. 30
seats outside. Bar. Wheelchairs. Music. Parking.

Visit us online

To find out more about
The Good Food Guide, please
visit thegoodfoodguide.co.uk

▮ Great Missenden
La Petite Auberge

Cooking score: 2
French | £38
107 High Street, Great Missenden, HP16 0BB
Tel no: (01494) 865370
lapetiteauberge.co.uk
£5
OFF

The county's Francophiles have had Hubert
and Danielle Martel's restaurant in which to
sate their appetite since 1989. They haven't
changed the idiom over the years, which
pleases its many fans, and they continue with
steadfast integrity to offer up a classic French
repertoire. A relaxed professionalism within
helps set the mood for an opening salvo of, say,
a salad of smoked duck breast with proper
French dressing, or gratin of crab and tiger
prawns in a brandy sauce. The soupe de
poisson, though, is a classic many find hard to
ignore. Fresh fish such as fillet of sea bass is
handled well, served simply with fresh herbs
and olive oil, while venison medallions might
come with red cabbage, and calves' liver with a
lime sauce. Desserts deliver on the promise:
tarte au citron and crème brûlée included. The
wine list bristles with Gallic pride.
Chef/s: Hubert Martel. **Open:** Tue to Sat D only.
Closed: Sun, Mon, 2 weeks Christmas, 2 weeks
Easter. **Meals:** main courses £18 to £23. **Details:** 28
seats. Wheelchairs.

▮ Marlow
The Coach

Cooking score: 5
Modern British | £30
3 West Street, Marlow, SL7 2LS
thecoachmarlow.co.uk

This Tudor-style building is owned by Tom
Kerridge and stands much closer to the town
centre than the Hand & Flowers (see entry),
but the Coach is not an extension of the most
famous pub in the country. For a start, you
can't book. It was always the intention to offer
a flexible, relaxed and accessible pub where
everybody is welcome. The design here is

super slick – 'like a high-end hotel bar crossed with a pub' – but although unfamiliar, in terms of modern pub design it is 'totally convincing'. Of course, it's food-focused, with dishes served tapas-style (mussels marinière, for example, will arrive shelled and in a ramekin), so expect to order four or five dishes per person, including, perhaps, salt cod Scotch egg with red pepper sauce and chorizo, a meaty mini burger and a flavour-packed chicken Kiev with delicious cauliflower cheese. The chips with béarnaise sauce continue to be praised, and there's a beef suet sticky toffee pudding with vanilla ice cream to finish. Drink real ales, cocktails or something from the modest wine list.

Chef/s: Nick Beardshaw. **Open:** all week L and D. **Meals:** main courses £6 to £16. **Details:** 45 seats. Bar.

The Hand & Flowers
Cooking score: 5
Modern British | £65
126 West Street, Marlow, SL7 2BP
Tel no: (01628) 482277
thehandandflowers.co.uk

Tom Kerridge's roadside spot is the stuff of bucket-list legend – and it's easy to see why, regardless of the owner's fame. The Hand & Flowers occupies that sought-after ground between fine dining and pub, the informal surroundings of bare tables, cosy nooks (for some, read 'cramped') and exposed brickwork being a backdrop for carefully crafted, tasty food. Ethereally crisp pastry containing haggis, pungent goats' cheese and the finest slivers of swede is a lesson in how to turn ordinary ingredients into an elegant starter. Tenderly pink Cotswold venison starred on a busy main-course plate that included black pudding purée, salt-baked celeriac, ragoût pie and 'cow puff'. A triumphant blackberry soufflé was faultlessly light, hazelnut crumble giving texture and pear sauce a perfect sweet counterpoint to sharp berry; it was a better bet than carrot cake and yoghurt sorbet from the set menu. Some things never change:

whitebait with spot-on Marie Rose sauce; chips that are still worth stealing; and yes, the Essex lamb bun with its sweetbreads and salsa verde keeps its place for good reason. It's worth saving up to eat à la carte rather than economise with the no-choice set, but given that you could wait months before sitting at a prime-time table, there's time for financial planning. The wine list is everything you'd expect, and service deserves a big clap.

Chef/s: Tom Kerridge. **Open:** all week L, Mon to Sat D. **Meals:** main courses £30 to £42. Set L £25 (2 courses) to £30. **Details:** 52 seats. Bar. Parking.

Sindhu
Cooking score: 5
Indian | £40
Compleat Angler, Bisham Road, Marlow, SL7 1RG
Tel no: (01628) 405405
sindhurestaurant.co.uk

The setting is not exactly what one might expect for an Indian restaurant, but a riverside location, overlooking the Thames Weir through mullioned windows with fish motifs, might become in imagination the bank of the Indus, and the splotches of colour in the décor, helped along by striking modern artworks, underscore the theme. Atul Kochhar's menus are founded, as at Mayfair's Benares (see entry), on research into regional cooking, overlaid with touches of European influence. An appetiser pasty is filled with chicken tikka masala and served with chilli pickle and berry chutney, while crisp-fried soft-shell crab with calamari and passion fruit is a red alert to the taste-buds. Mains inveigle some classics such as hefty slow-cooked lamb shank with browned onions and yoghurt amid the more spectacular likes of a fish platter that combines grey mullet, sea trout, scallop and prawn in green mango sauce. Sides of beetroot tossed with red onion and curry leaves, and desserts including rose bhapa doi (steamed curd) and mango kulfi, complete the deal. The vegetarian tasting menu offers one textural and taste seduction after another. Spicy cocktails supplement the well-chosen wines, which start at £24.

Chef/s: Prabhu Ganapati. **Open:** all week L and D. **Closed:** 25 Dec. **Meals:** main courses £19 to £26. Set L £19 (2 courses) to £22. Sun L £25. Tasting menu £65. **Details:** 56 seats. V menu. Wheelchairs. Music. Parking.

The Vanilla Pod

Cooking score: 4
Modern European | £45
31 West Street, Marlow, SL7 2LS
Tel no: (01628) 898101
thevanillapod.co.uk

£5
OFF

What reporters seem to enjoy about the Vanilla Pod is that, although it moves gently with the times, it is still recognisably as it has always been. 'We had not been here for several years but were very pleased to return to this narrow-fronted old building. We greatly enjoyed our lunch because of the combination of very pleasing ambience, style and service with the food.' With this edition, Michael Macdonald celebrates 16 years of serious nurturing, his Anglo-French menus ranging from smoked duck with truffles and a smoked vinaigrette or cep risotto, to potage of plaice with grain-mustard or fillet of lamb with herbs, boulangère potatoes and saffron shallots. Flavour combinations are well considered, while among desserts of rum and raisin cake, or a deconstructed key lime pie, the apple tarte Tatin is highly rated. The wine list is an appealing collection of classical French regions with added attractions from Italy, Spain and the New World.

Chef/s: Michael Macdonald. **Open:** Tue to Sat L and D. **Closed:** Sun, Mon, 24 Dec to 7 Jan, 21 to 24 Apr, 29 May to 5 Jun, 28 Aug to 5 Sept. **Meals:** set L £16 (2 courses) to £20. Set D £20 (2 courses) to £25. Tasting menu £60 (7 courses). **Details:** 38 seats. 12 seats outside. V menu. Bar.

▌Radnage
★ NEW ENTRY ★

The Mash Inn

Cooking score: 5
Modern British | £45
Horseshoe Road, Radnage, HP14 4EB
Tel no: (01494) 482440
themashinn.com

The foraged, fermented and flame-licked food of chef Jon Parry is drawing national interest to Nick Mash's remote Chilterns inn. Parry (ex-Clapham's Trinity, see entry) produces an acutely seasonal carte where garden radish with hay mayonnaise might precede juicy rib of beef, cooked on a locally made wood-grill that's the focus of the open kitchen. But it's the nine-course tasting menu where Parry excels, perhaps starting with 'melt-in-the-mouth' beef crackers, beefed up with salty mushroom powder. In May, a taste of wild garlic – soup, tempura flowers, shredded on toast – might follow, before the likes of asparagus with curds, and a pan-Asian-style dish of cod with sweet peanut-butter-style sunflower seeds, given an umami blast with flaked, dried fish maw. Lamb, pink and perfect, teamed with smoked mash, lovage and sublime gravy triumphed at inspection. True, some ingredients (gorse flowers) seem more for show than flavour, but others (sweet woodruff pannacotta) are a revelation. Glorious countryside (viewed from French windows), a woody little bar (local ales and house-made infusions) and knowledgeable service complete the happy, bucolic picture. Wine from £19.

Chef/s: Jon Parry. **Open:** Wed to Sun L, Wed to Sat D. **Closed:** Mon, Tue. **Meals:** main courses £19 to £30. Set L £19. Tasting menu £55. **Details:** 32 seats. Bar. Wheelchairs. Music. Parking. Children over 15 years only.

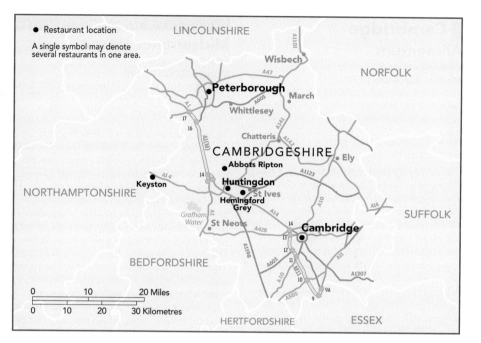

- ● Restaurant location

A single symbol may denote
several restaurants in one area.

LINCOLNSHIRE

NORFOLK

Wisbech

Peterborough

March

Whittlesey

Chatteris

CAMBRIDGESHIRE

Ely

Abbots Ripton

Keyston

Huntingdon

St Ives

Hemingford
Grey

NORTHAMPTONSHIRE

Grafham
Water

St Neots

Cambridge

SUFFOLK

BEDFORDSHIRE

HERTFORDSHIRE

ESSEX

| 0 | 10 | 20 Miles |
| 0 | 10 | 20 | 30 Kilometres |

▮ Abbots Ripton
The Abbot's Elm
Cooking score: 4
Modern European | £35
Abbots Ripton, PE28 2PA
Tel no: (01487) 773773
theabbotselm.co.uk
£5 OFF ▮ ⍾

Following the retirement of Julia Abbey, the
former head chef and restaurant manager of
the Castle Terrace in Edinburgh (see entry)
have been appointed to assume the day-to-day
running of this sizeable and popular pub-
restaurant-with-rooms just outside
Huntingdon. In the kitchen, Roberta Hall has
lost no time in putting her stamp on the menu,
which is now smaller and more bistro in style.
At a test meal, a soft-poached egg, which came
with buttered oyster mushrooms stacked up
on black pudding toast and slathered in bacon
jam, was not only 'a flavour bomb', but also
showed strong technique, while a fillet of hake
'cooked flawlessly' was set on fennel purée,

served with a long-braised but crisp fennel
quarter, with a few olives, almonds and a rich
bisque sauce flavoured with brown crabmeat.
To finish, a white chocolate and ginger
cheesecake had been steamed on top of
poached rhubarb in a Kilner jar and topped
with ginger biscuit crumb. To drink, some 30
or so wines by the glass, carafe or bottle are
complemented by a small selection of fine
wines.
Chef/s: Roberta Hall. **Open:** Tue to Sun L, Tue to Sat
D. **Closed:** Mon, first 3 weeks Jan. **Meals:** main
courses £9 to £26. Sun L £25. **Details:** 80 seats. 50
seats outside. Bar. Wheelchairs. Music. Parking.

Symbols

🛏 Accommodation is available
£30 Three courses for less than £30
£5 OFF £5-off voucher scheme
⍾ Notable wine list

Cambridge

Alimentum

Cooking score: 6
Modern European | £70
152-154 Hills Road, Cambridge, CB2 8PB
Tel no: (01223) 413000
restaurantalimentum.co.uk

£5 OFF

Alimentum is the very model of a contemporary British restaurant. The parquet floor and unclad tables, together with a cherry-red panelled wall, make it look a little like somewhere you might go dancing, but it's all grist to the modern European mill of Mark Poynton's kitchen. On view behind a window, his talented brigade turns out provocatively composed dishes of unusual ingredients, often subjected to the slow cooking that concentrates their character. That applies as much to a simple chicken breast in a welter of alliums and gin as to the gently treated sea bream that is teamed with cauliflower, goats' cheese and PX sherry. Prior to these striking principal dishes, equally considered starters take in Indian-spiced scallop with apple, cumin dhal and coriander yoghurt, or Dingley Dell pork brawn with hazelnuts, smoked bacon and pineapple jam, and desserts include a signature reinterpretation of Battenberg cake of apricot and Amaretto, as well as an almost traditional tarte Tatin made with Braeburns. The wine list has no tasting descriptions, but does boast an impressive roll call of quality producers, French ones leading the pack. Prices open at £27 for Roussillon dry Muscat or Corbières.

Chef/s: Mark Poynton. **Open:** all week L and D.
Closed: 24 to 30 Dec, bank hols. **Meals:** set L £28 (2 courses) to £35. Set D £55 (2 courses) to £70. Tasting menu £80. **Details:** 40 seats. Bar. Wheelchairs. Music.

Average price

The average price denotes the price of a three-course meal without wine.

★ TOP 50 ★

Midsummer House

Cooking score: 8
Modern British | £120
Midsummer Common, Cambridge, CB4 1HA
Tel no: (01223) 369299
midsummerhouse.co.uk

There's a romance about Cambridge that never fails to enchant. Drop the seductive food at Daniel Clifford's legendary common-side restaurant into the mix, and you have a gloriously heady potion. Lively amuse-bouches could include an elfin brik pastry cone of smoked eel, horseradish and puffed rice, or a Bloody Mary and celery espuma with just the right kick to jolt a dozy palate before the five-course tasting lunch (eight at dinner). The chefs in this oh-so-talented kitchen pour such creativity and an unquestionable love of ingredients into every plate that you can overlook moments of slack seasoning, notably in a pumpkin velouté, which needed more lift than Ibérico ham and Parmesan could give. A mouthful of lemon sole and plump prawn sat tastily with agretti and seaweed hollandaise, while there's fulsome praise, too, for 'seriously delicious' red mullet, octopus, fennel and orange, and basil-infused rack of lamb with moreish smoked shoulder and 'quite wonderful, almost old-fashioned' gravy. The sweetness of a white chocolate bombe is punctured by blisteringly refreshing aerated pear and a blueberry purée, while a dark chocolate parfait with passion fruit and yoghurt sorbet nails a perfect sweet-sour balance. Cheese is a generously portioned temptation, and the 'very classy' wine list is everything you'd expect from a restaurant of this standing – though they could get a few more wines around the £30 mark to make it a little more accessible. For some, service is over familiar, though others defend the friendliness and the relaxed atmosphere it fosters.

Chef/s: Daniel Clifford. **Open:** Wed to Sat L, Tue to Sat D. **Closed:** Sun, Mon, 2 weeks Christmas.
Meals: tasting menu £57 (5 courses, L only) to £120 (8 courses). **Details:** 53 seats. V menu. Bar. Wheelchairs. Children over 12 yrs only.

The Dumpling Tree
Chinese | £17
8 Homerton Street, Cambridge, CB2 8NX
Tel no: (01223) 247715
thedumplingtree.com

£30

On the ground floor of a residential block, the Dumpling Tree specialises in dishes from China's south-western Yunnan province. Dumplings don't grow on trees of course; you can see them for yourself being made behind a glass screen upfront. A mixed platter entitled 'Dirty Dozen' is the way to go, including versions with pork and Chinese greens, prawns, beef and dried mushrooms, and coriandered lamb. 'Cross the Bridge' is a signature bowl of homemade rice noodles in chicken broth with meat, vegetables and herbs, and there are fortifying dishes of rice, potatoes and bacon served in copper pots. Dessert dumplings include crispy sunbursts filled with glutinous sweet bean paste. Wines from £18.50.

Fitzbillies
Modern British | £20
51-52 Trumpington Street, Cambridge, CB2 1RG
Tel no: (01223) 352500
fitzbillies.com

£30

Set behind an Art Nouveau façade, Fitzbillies is synonymous with Chelsea buns (a sticky favourite since 1921), but there's plenty more for students, tourists and locals to cheer about. Brunch brings shakshuka, pancakes and porridge, while lunch offers everything from crispy pork belly buns to warm confit duck salad or soup with soda bread. However, afternoon tea is the real treat, with a host of cakes, pastries and scones stealing the limelight. Licensed, but no bookings. There's a little sister at 36 Bridge Street.

Pint Shop
British | £25
10 Peas Hill, Cambridge, CB2 3PN
Tel no: (01223) 352293
pintshop.co.uk

£30

With this one in a Grade II-listed building in Cambridge, and another in Oxford, the Pint Shop concept is built around an ever-changing array of cask and keg ales (not to mention an amazing list of gins), and a menu that specialises in meat cooked over charcoal. Neutral colours, an abundance of wood, *de rigueur* enamel light shades, it's a fun, fashionable place with a menu that aims to please: baby back ribs, pork belly cooked slowly overnight, whole plaice cooked on the coals and dry-aged steaks with straw fries. Wines from £20.

■ Hemingford Grey

The Cock
Modern British | £30
47 High Street, Hemingford Grey, PE28 9BJ
Tel no: (01480) 463609
cambscuisine.com

At the sign of the cockerel, a cream-fronted country inn stands on its village corner by the Ouse, offering real ales to locals, modern British pub food to the dining crowd and warm hospitality to everyone. A kitchen that makes its own pork sausages means business, and the variations – including Marmite and cheese, or tomato, garlic and chilli – extend to mash and sauce options. Fish dishes are chalked on the board when daily deliveries arrive. Bookend these treats with lamb, apricot and rosemary scrumpet and pickled radishes, and a caramel eclair with stout ice cream, and you're sorted. Wines are interestingly drawn from Languedoc-Roussillon, opening at £21.

Empire strikes back

It's the dream of most chefs to have their own restaurant, but sometimes just one isn't enough. An increasing number of restaurateurs are expanding their empires.

In the years since chef Jason Atherton left Gordon Ramsay's company, he has launched his own restaurants in London, New York, Shanghai, Sydney and the Philippines. Atherton has nine in London alone, from his flagship Mayfair restaurant **Pollen Street Social** to the **Berners Tavern** in Fitzrovia. Not a chef wanting to be pigeonholed, it's hard to second guess what Atherton's next move will be. His most recent London openings have been the Japanese restaurant **Sosharu** and the Italian eatery **Hai Cenato**.

Atherton isn't the only Gordon Ramsay-trained chef to have grown one restaurant into an empire since going solo. Since launching her first restaurant, **Murano**, in Mayfair in 2008, Angela Hartnett has opened **Café Murano** and the **Merchants Tavern** in London, as well as **Hartnett Holder & Co.** at the Hampshire hotel, Lime Wood.

And it's not just top London chefs who are finding it hard to stop at one restaurant. In Bristol, Peter Sanchez-Iglesias has followed the success of **Casamia** by launching the **Pi Shop** pizzeria and Spanish bar **Paco Tapas** next door.

◾ Huntingdon

LOCAL GEM
The Old Bridge Hotel
Modern British | £32
1 High Street, Huntingdon, PE29 3TQ
Tel no: (01480) 424300
huntsbridge.com

The Old Bridge is an absolute stunner – towering over the river alongside it, covered in ivy and spread out over a new, stepped terrace that leads into the tastefully restored old hotel. The dining room is part open to the terrace and is refreshingly modern and smart. Monthly menus deliver the likes of venison terrine with apple and date chutney, and stuffed chicken with spinach risotto and crisp cavolo nero, while the wine list (from £19.50) is fairly priced, with a few treats that reflect the brilliant wine shop that is also on site.

◾ Keyston
The Pheasant
Cooking score: 2
Modern British | £30
Loop Road, Keyston, PE28 0RE
Tel no: (01832) 710241
thepheasant-keyston.co.uk

A low-slung pristinely thatched pub in an affluent Cambridgeshire village, this amenable destination is dedicated to the pursuit of gastronomic and oenophile pleasures with its assured cooking and top-class wine list. Rustic beams and open fires shore up the Pheasant's pub credentials (along with ploughman's and other 'traditional classics'), but the kitchen is also tuned to current trends. Ideas and ingredients are garnered from near and far, giving a thoroughly cosmopolitan feel: pan-fried red mullet is served with Moroccan couscous and chermoula dressing, while char-grilled Cornish lamb lines up alongside braised red cabbage and salsa verde. Elsewhere, homemade black pudding appears with mash and curly kale, Jimmy Butler's free-range bangers get a outing, and there are Aberdeenshire steaks for the unreformed. To conclude, Neal's Yard cheeses vie with desserts such as dark chocolate parfait. Former owner John Hoskins MW continues to curate the brilliant 100-bin wine list, which offers superior drinking by the glass or carafe, plus monthly bargains and fashionable thrills at every turn.

Chef/s: Simon Cadge. **Open:** Tue to Sun L, Tue to Sat D. **Closed:** Mon, 2 to 14 Jan. **Meals:** main courses £11 to £23. Set L and D £15 (2 courses) to £20. Sun L £20 (2 courses) to £25. **Details:** 80 seats. 20 seats outside. Bar. Parking.

▌Peterborough

★ NEW ENTRY ★

Prévost

Cooking score: 3
Modern British | £33
20 Priestgate, Peterborough, PE1 1JA
Tel no: (01733) 313623
prevostpeterborough.co.uk
£5
OFF

Most chefs would adopt the tag-line 'flavours without boundaries' without a second thought, but Lee Clarke embraces the notion deeply at his classy city-centre restaurant, using 16 coloured dots to capture the essence of dishes on his three-, five-, or nine-course monthly changing set menus. Cornish mackerel with watercress and smoked herring roe has a blue dot for marine flavours, pale green for brine/salty, and dark green for grassy. Dots against a dessert of lemon thyme, kumquats and oats tell diners to expect citrusy, sour and fresh/fruity tastes – and so on… 'Outstanding' venison, the tenderly pink slices served with Puy lentils and candied and golden beetroot, lift an otherwise 'perfectly nice' dish, while the sweet gooeyness of Italian meringue on a 'kind of deconstructed gooseberry fool' had one diner wanting more, in particular the gooseberry jam. Optional

flights of wine accompany the menus, but there are bottles from £20 and an appealing line-up of cocktails and mocktails.

Chef/s: Lee Clarke. **Open:** Wed to Sat L, Tue to Sat D. **Closed:** Sun, Mon, first 2 weeks Jan, last 2 weeks Aug. **Meals:** set L and D £33 (3 courses) to £50 (5 courses). Tasting menu £75. **Details:** 36 seats. V menu. Bar. Wheelchairs. Music. Children at L only.

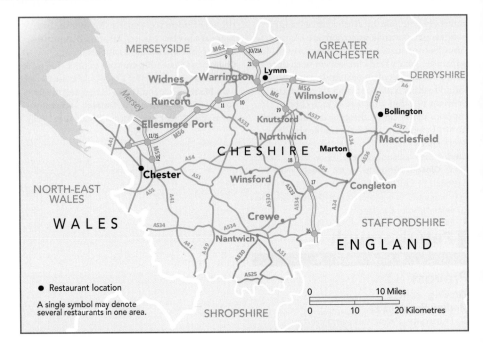

▮ Alderley Edge

Yara

Lebanese/Syrian
29 London Road, Alderley Edge, SK9 7JT
Tel no: (01625) 584040
yara2eat.co.uk

'We ordered everything for sharing: muhammara – a dip, sweetish from the red peppers and crushed walnuts, the latter giving it a bit of texture; tabbouleh with lots of parsley, lots of lemon, more finely chopped walnuts, a tiny amount of bulgur wheat, some tomato and onion – a knockout version; kebab, a main-course affair, one skewer each of chicken, lamb kofta and lamb shish. We had that with really delicious mujadara – rice and lentils, topped with crispy onion. Chicken and kofta were lovely.'

▮ Bollington

The Lord Clyde

Cooking score: 2
Modern British | £35
36 Clarke Lane, Kerridge, Bollington,
SK10 5AH
Tel no: (01625) 562123
thelordclyde.co.uk
£5 OFF

With fine Cheshire countryside in every direction, a small bar that's popular with drinkers and all the signs of a pub that's gone posh, the Lord Clyde has the same appeal as it did during chef Ernst Van Zyl's tenure. But following his departure, the culinary ambitions are less lofty and and dishes not so exhaustively detailed. The new simplicity is shown to good advantage in a starter of heritage tomatoes with goats' cheese – a bit heavy on the onions, but fundamentally good stuff – or chicken liver parfait with good brioche. Mains might be baked locally caught trout with well-dressed quinoa and strands of samphire, or a Sunday roast of rib of beef with a top-hat Yorkshire pudding that would make Aunt Bessie blush. Puddings include a rustic improvement on sticky toffee pudding with a layer of chunky sweet-tart dates under tender sponge. Obliging service and decent wine also repay the journey.

Chef/s: Thomas Clarke. **Open:** Tue to Sun L, Tue to Sat D. **Closed:** Mon. **Meals:** main courses £12 to £23. Set L and D £17 (2 courses) to £20. Tasting menu £45 (5 courses). **Details:** 40 seats. 12 seats outside. Music. Parking.

LOCAL GEM

The Lime Tree

British | £27

18-20 High Street, Bollington, SK10 5PH
Tel no: (01625) 578182
limetreebollington.co.uk

£30

Younger sibling to Didsbury's long-running namesake, Patrick Hannity's Bollington outfit occupies a sizeable chunk of the high street. And there's an 18-acre smallholding in the family, too, so supply lines are entirely traceable. Mrs Kirkham's Lancashire cheese soufflé gets the double-baked treatment, tempura squid and prawns come with sweet chilli and aïoli dipping sauces, while among main courses the feel-good flavours continue with crispy duck leg, the house burger and pan-fried monkfish in a chickpea and chorizo stew. Wines start at £18.

◼ Chester

Joseph Benjamin

Cooking score: 3
Modern European | £27
134-140 Northgate Street, Chester, CH1 2HT
Tel no: (01244) 344295
josephbenjamin.co.uk

£30

Right by the city gate, and closely related to the Porta tapas bar next door (see entry), Joseph Benjamin is a relaxed but suave little restaurant run by brothers Joe (in the kitchen) and Ben (front-of-house). Simple wood furniture and pale walls sensibly play second fiddle to the riot of colour on the plate – from slow-roast pork belly with black bean and chorizo stew to char-grilled swordfish steak with Café de Paris butter, roast cherry tomatoes and matchstick fries. A starter of marinated sardines with blood orange and watercress paves the way for a gutsy, unpretentious but also skilful style of cooking, while an inventive spirit shines through in a dessert of rhubarb crumble with cream-cheese ice cream and poached rhubarb. Besides a few dozen well-chosen wines (lots of accessible, familiar options but also plenty of interest) there's a decent selection of beers and ciders, with an emphasis on small craft producers.

Chef/s: Joe Wright. **Open:** Tue to Sun L, Thur to Sat D. **Closed:** Mon. **Meals:** main courses £11 to £19. **Details:** 38 seats.

★ NEW ENTRY ★

Porta

Cooking score: 2
Spanish | £22
140 Northgate Street, Chester, CH1 2HT
portatapas.co.uk

£30

'Clever use of a small space, all a bit dark and rustico,' thought a visitor to this little tapas bar tucked away at the back of an alley, right next door to big brother Joseph Benjamin (see entry). A small, open-to-view kitchen is at the heart of the place – a lower floor and mezzanine offering informal eating perched on bar-stools at high tables; you can eat outside on picnic-style tables, too. Padrón peppers, patatas bravas, 'creamy' croquetas, cured meats or king prawns a la plancha are typical menu staples, but daily specials could include a 'delicious take on escabèche' with mackerel, or slow-roast ox cheek with pickled walnuts. Desserts such as pistachio and polenta cake and orange curd hit the spot, and all in all 'this is a slick operation with lovely service'. A short wine list (from £18) is just the job.

Chef/s: Joe Wright and José Catala. **Open:** all week D only. **Meals:** tapas £4 to £10. **Details:** Music.

Simon Radley at the Chester Grosvenor

Cooking score: 6
Modern European | £75
Eastgate, Chester, CH1 1LT
Tel no: (01244) 324024
chestergrosvenor.com

Chester's pride and joy, the imperious half-timbered Grosvenor is an asset known for its Arkle Bar and for Simon Radley's formal restaurant. Eating here is a full on 'cosseting experience' as diners relax in the gilded but rather dated hotel dining room (perhaps ready for a revamp?) with a battalion of waiters poised to glide into action. Mr Radley responds with a menu of confident, inventive and playful dishes designed to impress and spring a few surprises: a starter labelled 'cauliflowers' is actually dominated by a tasty fritter of pig's trotter and brawn, with the vegetable consigned to a supporting role as 'flavours of piccalilli', although there's nothing askew about 'tongue and cheek' (veal pastrami and grilled fillet with cracked mustard, hot radish and cipollini onion broth) or Herdwick mutton accompanied by spearmint peas, girolles and ewes' curd – an 'absolute belter' of a dish. To finish, the preserved Catalan tomato stuffed with fruit candy, iced nectar and goats' curd is a marvel of sweet and savoury contrasts, though the cheese trolley – with some British examples among the mainly French selection – is worth exploring. The bread trolley, too, deserves special mention, with its nine different loaves all made in-house. The vast wine list encourages big spending, with page upon page of desirable vintages aimed at free-spirited oenophiles and conservative connoisseurs alike.
Chef/s: Simon Radley and Raymond Booker. **Open:** Tue to Sat D only 6.30 to 9. **Closed:** Sun, Mon, 25 Dec, Jan. **Meals:** set D £75. Tasting menu £99 (8 courses). **Details:** 32 seats. Bar. Wheelchairs. Parking. Children over 12 yrs only.

Sticky Walnut

Cooking score: 4
Modern European | £30
11 Charles Street, Chester, CH2 3AZ
Tel no: (01244) 400400
stickywalnut.com

Sticky Walnut, Burnt Truffle and Hispi are a trio of north west bistros created by chef/proprietor Gary Usher – the last two crowd-funded due to Sticky Walnut's raging success. Mr Usher is certainly on to something. This two-floor restaurant is simply done out, like a good bistro should be, with chunky wooden tables and just a few contemporary affectations. Stay downstairs for the buzz if you can. Walnuts feature with roasted beetroots in a first course, or go for the seldom seen crispy calf's brain ('three cheers for having that on the menu'). It's relatively simple stuff, just what you'd hope for in what is essentially a neighbourhood restaurant: roast hake with herby butter and flaked ham hock, Goosnargh duck boosted by rhubarb and juniper, a whopping chateaubriand to share, and feel-good desserts such as steamed syrup sponge. A canny range of bottled beers supports the sensibly concise wine list.
Chef/s: Luke Richardson. **Open:** all week L and D. **Closed:** 25 and 26 Dec. **Meals:** main courses £15 to £22. Set L £16 (2 courses). Set D £18 (3 courses, Mon to Thur). Sun L £18 (2 courses) to £22.
Details: 55 seats. Music.

Lymm
The Church Green

Cooking score: 2
Modern British | £28
Higher Lane, Lymm, WA13 0AP
Tel no: (01925) 752068
aidenbyrne.co.uk

Aiden and Sarah Byrne have established a winning formula at the big white-fronted pub. With covered outdoor seating to one side, and expansive spaces within, it seems to have all bases covered. Home-grown ingredients form the core of Aiden's modern pub menus, which feature all the poshed-up expected light bites – a soft-centred pork and mustard Scotch egg with celeriac and apple rémoulade, mussels marinière, truffled mushroom arancini – as well as main dishes that are finely judged and satisfying. Roasted cod with purple potatoes and artichokes in hollandaise, or braised beef cheek with giant couscous, glazed carrots and dukkah, are backed up by traditional steaks with beef-dripping chips and sauce options. Sharing platters of seafood, meats and cheeses will keep you occupied a fair while, and to finish, there's apple crumble parfait with blackberries, or pineapple upside-down cake with rum caramel and clotted cream. Wines by the glass from a good selection start at £4.75 for a standard measure, and there are inspiring fruity cocktails, too.

Chef/s: Aiden Byrne. **Open:** all week L, Mon to Sat D. **Closed:** 25 Dec. **Meals:** main courses £18 to £40. Set L and D £24 (2 courses) to £30 (3 courses). **Details:** 86 seats. 94 seats outside. Bar. Wheelchairs. Music. Parking. Children before 8pm only.

▌ Marton
La Popote
Cooking score: 1
French | £40
Church Farm, Manchester Road (A34), Marton, SK11 9HF
Tel no: (01260) 224785
la-popote.co.uk
£5
OFF

There's something of the feel of a French auberge to the Janssens' well-supported country restaurant near Macclesfield, where covered tables in the garden, part of the new Orangery extension, supplement a light-filled, brick-walled main room. Daily specials are the backbone of the kitchen's French bistro output, perhaps the ever-popular Scottish scallops in Champagne beurre blanc, with Herefordshire tournedos and snail gratin, or Dover sole meunière and dauphinois, to follow. A classical rendition of Paris–Brest might close proceedings, unless you fancy looking northwards for cranachan made with caramelised pinhead oatmeal and whisky cream. Wines on a carefully annotated list start at £19.25.

Chef/s: Victor Janssen and Chris Rooney. **Open:** Wed to Sun L, Wed to Sat D. **Closed:** Mon, Tue, 26 Dec to 5 Jan, 1 week summer. **Meals:** main courses £15 to £29. Set L £18 (2 courses) to £23. **Details:** 57 seats. 24 seats outside. Bar. Wheelchairs. Music. Parking. No small children at D.

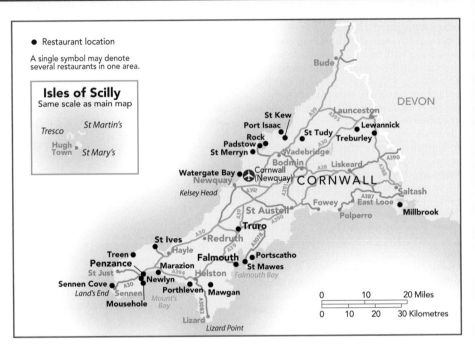

- ● Restaurant location

A single symbol may denote
several restaurants in one area.

Isles of Scilly
Same scale as main map

Tresco   St Martin's

Hugh
Town   St Mary's

Bude

DEVON

St Kew
Port Isaac
Rock   St Tudy   Lewannick
Padstow   Treburley
St Merryn
Wadebridge
Watergate Bay   Bodmin   Liskeard
Newquay   Cornwall   Launceston
Kelsey Head   (Newquay)   CORNWALL
Saltash
Fowey   East Looe
Polperro   Millbrook
St Austell
Truro
St Ives   Redruth
Hayle
Treen   Falmouth   Portscatho
Penzance   Marazion   St Mawes
St Just   Helston   Falmouth Bay
Sennen Cove   Newlyn
Land's End   Porthleven   Mawgan
Mousehole   Sennen   Mount's
Bay
Lizard
Lizard Point

0   10   20 Miles
0   10   20   30 Kilometres

▌Falmouth
Oliver's
Cooking score: 3
Modern British | £32
33 High Street, Falmouth, TR11 2AD
Tel no: (01326) 218138
oliversfalmouth.com

Ken and Wendy Symons' place on the high
street of the surfers' and spa-goers' paradise of
Falmouth looks like an oddball tea room,
with its clumping furniture, naked
floorboards and mesmerising mobiles of fish
idling about the walls. The orientation
naturally is the regional produce of a bountiful
county, with fish and shellfish figuring
prominently, as well as locally reared meats
and game, in a culinary idiom that is *au fait*
with the latest techniques. Bread comes with
whipped flavoured butters to spark the
appetite, which might also be usefully
whetted with tit-bits such as a micro-serving
of octopus and chorizo stew. A gurnard
fishcake with guacamole and rocket salad

might then lead into the main menu,
constructed around fortifying main dishes
like hake baked in a herb and garlic coat with
slow-cooked tomato, spinach and buttery
mash, or venison from the Tregothnan Estate,
served with bubble and squeak and heritage
carrots in port sauce. Finish with a saffron-
poached pear and vanilla sherbet. The little
wine list opens with Piedmontese varietals
at £17.25.
Chef/s: Ken Symons. **Open:** Tue to Sat L and D.
Closed: Sun, Mon, 11 Dec to 8 Jan, bank hols.
Meals: main courses £16 to £26. Set L £16 (2
courses) to £23. Tasting menu £40. **Details:** 28 seats.
Music. Children over 12 yrs only at D.

Symbols

🛏 Accommodation is available
£30 Three courses for less than £30
£5 OFF £5-off voucher scheme
🍷 Notable wine list

Star and Garter

Cooking score: 2
British | £26
52 High Street, Falmouth, TR11 2AF
Tel no: (01326) 316663
starandgarterfalmouth.co.uk

£5 OFF 🍴 £30

Set in a Georgian building opposite Falmouth's old town hall, this sprucely updated pub is full of locals, real ales and wood floors – and is a pretty decent dining destination to boot. The two personas rub along very well indeed, with a bar at the front and the rear dining area offering fabulous views across the estuary to the pastel-painted houses of Flushing quay opposite. The menu reflects an open-minded approach too, accommodating locally caught fish as well as cuts of meat cooked over charcoal. An opener of char-grilled squid with radish and squid-ink aïoli sets the tone for a meal that might move on to smoke-roasted featherblade of beef with cannellini beans, watercress and hazelnuts or brill served with fennel in tomato, mussels, clams and seaweed breadcrumbs. To finish, look no further than Russet apple tart with vanilla ice cream. Wines from £18.
Chef/s: Andi Richardson. **Open:** all week L and D. **Closed:** Tue and Wed (Jan and Feb). **Meals:** main courses £13 to £18. Set L £18 (3 courses).
Details: 60 seats. 60 seats outside. Bar. Music.

LOCAL GEM

Rick Stein's Fish

Seafood | £29
Discovery Quay, Falmouth, TR11 3XA
Tel no: (01326) 330050
rickstein.com

£30

Rick Stein's shoal of fish restaurants extends from Porthleven to Barnes in London, and, like the rest, the cheery Falmouth address deals in you-know-who's signature seafood with a host of global flavours. The sharing board is an ideal opener (Thai fishcakes, piri-piri sardines and more) before an Indonesian curry rich

Tom Adams 🍴

Coombeshead Farm, Lewannick, Cornwall

Tell us about how Coombeshead Farm came to life.
April (Bloomfield) and I met when she came in to eat lunch at **Pitt Cue** in London. I then went to **The Breslin**, and we just kept in touch. I had been keeping pigs at a friend's farm in Cornwall and April would often come to visit when she was in the UK. It was at the farm that the conversations began about starting something together.

Do you prefer the countryside or the city?
A mix is nice, but I grew up in the countryside and I think that is ultimately where my heart lies.

Your menus naturally showcase seasonality; what is your favourite time of year for food?
I've always loved spring as everything is showing so much potential, but autumn always feels beautifully abundant.

Name one ingredient you couldn't cook without?
Dairy. We love brilliant dairy and go to great lengths to ensure we get the right dairy products here. We don't cook with butter very much, except for in our pastries, but it features heavily in our bread course in the evening. I'm not sure we could handle life without butter.

with sea bass, cod and prawns, classic fish and chips or char-grilled tuna with salsa verde. The takeaway counter does steady business, but it's a lovely, contemporary spot to stick around in. The wine list has good options by the glass and carafe.

▮ Lewannick

★ NEW ENTRY ★

Coombeshead Farm

Cooking score: 5
British | £50
Lewannick, PL15 7QQ
Tel no: (01566) 782009
coombesheadfarm.co.uk

🛏

You may feel you're getting back to nature if you find yourself eating sorrel grown on a roof in Shoreditch, but for the full contemporary rustic moderne experience, you need to go wild in the country. Coombeshead is a restored 18th-century farmstead in east Cornwall (download the admirably clear directions from the website), set in 66 acres of meadow and woodland, with sheep springing about the hillsides and Mangalitza pigs snoozing in their sties. The drill is a single sitting for 7.30 dinner, with one big table for 12 just off the quietly industrious kitchen. Tom Adams is partnered out there by Lottie Mew and the near-legendary April Bloomfield, who pops back from New York when she can. Foraged materials and what were once waste bits – potato skin, lard, turnip tops, weeds, whey – back up the in-house curing of pork and excellent organically reared meats from hereabouts. Breads include fantastic sourdough with whipped Guernsey butter, prior to starter dishes served hors d'oeuvres style: in June, they included pickled artichokes and sunflower seeds, shaved asparagus in fermented-milk kefir and garlic, whole radishes on the stalks with crumbled hazelnut, and baby turnips. A bread-based sour meat broth formed a transition to the meat course itself: Dexter beef fillet roasted at low temperature, dressed in Cassis, served

with grains in bread syrup and chard. Dessert was diced rhubarb in nettled cows'-milk curd and wild chamomile. Nibbles in the lounge might include fabulous cured Mangalitza ham with its lardo, and salted hogweed. With gargantuan breakfasts that include cheesy spinach buns and irresistible pork rillettes, even a one-night stay is a memorable experience. Take someone with you and be prepared to make friends. The great wine cellar is a true enthusiast's project, although the only glass options are southern French blends, and Tom's brother's full-throttle Corbières, Les Clos Perdus, at £7.

Chef/s: Tom Adams. **Open:** Thur to Sun D only. **Closed:** Mon, Tue, Wed, Jan. **Meals:** set D £65 (3 courses). **Details:** 12 seats. Bar. Music. Parking. Children over 12 yrs only.

▮ Marazion

Ben's Cornish Kitchen

Cooking score: 5
Modern British | £35
West End, Marazion, TR17 0EL
Tel no: (01736) 719200
benscornishkitchen.com

£5
OFF

Ben Prior opened his compact restaurant on Marazion's main street in 2009, and his understated bistro – stone walls, wood floors – continues to reel in diners with perfectly pitched contemporary cooking. St Michael's Mount can be glimpsed from window tables, which adds to the sense of place for a kitchen that looks to the sea for much of its inspiration. Cooking in step with the seasons, Mr Prior clearly lets great produce do the talking – 'there really wasn't one bum note in the entire meal' was the verdict of one couple. Fish cooking is spot-on – note an accurately timed red mullet with fennel salad and Provençal fish sauce – while confit pork cheek with vegetable slaw, peanuts and sticky Asian sauce 'shows a kitchen not afraid to look beyond the locality for ideas'. A boldly flavoured lamb shoulder, accompanied by pea, lettuce, pancetta fricassee and salsa verde, and pollack with crushed potato, asparagus and herb hollandaise were 'memorable and deceptively simple' main courses. Finish with a 'top-drawer' lemon tart and yoghurt sorbet. Wines from £21.

Chef/s: Ben Prior. **Open:** Tue to Sat L and D. **Closed:** Sun, Mon. **Meals:** set L £18 (2 courses) to £23. Set D £28 (2 courses) to £35. **Details:** 36 seats. Wheelchairs. Music.

◼ Mawgan
New Yard

Cooking score: 3
Modern British | £35
Trelowarren Estate, Mawgan, TR12 6AF
Tel no: (01326) 221595
newyardrestaurant.co.uk

Famously tricky to find, the New Yard restaurant is squirrelled away in a cobbled stableyard on Sir Ferrers Vyvyan's 1,000-year-old Trelowarren Estate, some six miles from Helston. Occupying an old coach house, the venue makes quite an impression with arched floor-to-ceiling windows, a hearth at one end and an open kitchen at the other. Produce from the estate, fish from the Cornish day boats and pickings from local growers provide the building blocks for a succinct menu of unaffected seasonal dishes with plenty of zest: cured brill with tarragon and orange dressing; Morvah chicken with smoked potato sauce, truffle and wild leaves; cod fillet and pork belly with sprouting broccoli, gremolata and aïoli. Also, don't miss the home-baked treacle sourdough, the deep-fried chocolate fondant with torched marshmallow ice cream or the board of artisan Cornish cheeses served with pear and celery jam. Intriguing European names dominate the short, sharp wine list.

Chef/s: Jeffrey Robinson. **Open:** all week L, Mon to Sat D. **Closed:** 3 weeks Jan. **Meals:** main courses £15 to £22. Set L £15 (2 courses) to £19. **Details:** 40 seats. 20 seats outside. Bar. Wheelchairs. Music. Parking.

◼ Millbrook
The View

Cooking score: 3
Modern British | £35
Treninnow Cliff, Millbrook, PL10 1JY
Tel no: (01752) 822345
theview-restaurant.co.uk

£5 OFF

If you're going to call your restaurant The View there's a promise that must be delivered upon to avoid disappointment. And it delivers – from its perch up on the cliffs at Whitsand Bay you can see right up the coast to the Lizard. It's a low-slung property with a terrace out front and decent-sized windows so no one misses out. Seafood out of Looe has a strong showing on the concise, gently contemporary menu. Grilled mackerel with chorizo and parsley is a straight-up first course, while wood pigeon with poached grapes and crispy ham is a land-loving alternative. Roast hake with pancetta and herb butter is another example of classical simplicity, while pan-fried gurnard arrives in the earthy company of portobello mushrooms. A single vegetarian main course might be roast Spanish onion with gnocchi and Cornish Camembert, with rump of lamb with spiced red cabbage for the meat-minded, and iced poppy seed parfait to finish. The wine list has helpfully pithy descriptions.

Chef/s: Matt Corner. **Open:** Wed to Sun L and D. **Closed:** Mon, Tue, seasonal opening winter. **Meals:** main courses £19 to £24. Set L £15 (2 courses) to £19. **Details:** 45 seats. 30 seats outside. Music. Parking.

■ Mousehole
The Old Coastguard

Cooking score: 3
Modern British | £25
The Parade, Mousehole, TR19 6PR
Tel no: (01736) 731222
oldcoastguardhotel.co.uk

'I'm quite a regular here and this was the best I've had here since the Inkens took over' is praise indeed for this long-established hotel, run since 2012 by the owners of the Gurnard's Head in nearby Treen and the Felin Fach Griffin in mid Wales (see entries). The hotel occupies a commanding spot. Lunch in the enclosed subtropical gardens overlooking Mount's Bay can be memorable, particularly if you catch a glimpse of dolphins and seals in the sea below. Inside, the brightly coloured dining room with its chunky farmhouse tables and log fireplace is a draw all year round. The kitchen focuses on local and regional produce – Newlyn dressed crab, for example, teamed with elderflower-pickled cucumber and coriander ketchup. Elsewhere, an ingenious smoked haddock and celeriac farro ('a risotto in all but name') with wild garlic, a runny cured egg yolk adding richness, could precede a robust, rustic dish of perfectly cooked hake on a bed of rich and tender cuttlefish mingled with pinto beans, with sea beet and a 'nduja mayonnaise, and dessert of 'fruity, sticky' prune cake with candied pecans and a delicate Earl Grey ice cream. Wines start at £18.
Chef/s: Matthew Smith. **Open:** all week L and D. **Closed:** second week Jan. **Meals:** main courses £13 to £22. Set L £18 (2 courses) to £21. Set D £20 (2 courses) to £25. Sun L £25 (3 courses). **Details:** 80 seats. 40 seats outside. Bar. Wheelchairs. Music. Parking.

Average price

The average price denotes the price of a three-course meal without wine.

2 Fore Street

Cooking score: 3
Modern British | £32
2 Fore Street, Mousehole, TR19 6PF
Tel no: (01736) 731164
2forestreet.co.uk

'Simple but highly enjoyable' seems to be the general consensus on Joe Wardell's busy little harbourside restaurant which, 10 years on, continues to offer excellent food, value for money, a thriving atmosphere and a sheltered back garden for fine-weather dining. Dishes are as carefully cooked as ever, with most of the work being done by exemplary raw material. Spanking-fresh, locally landed fish and shellfish has been given an emphatic thumbs-up – notably river Exe mussels with white wine, shallot and garlic, superbly cooked gurnard fillets, and brill with prawns, kale, Parmentier potatoes and crème fraîche beurre blanc. The quality of the spiced, braised duck leg and organic shepherd's pie has delighted meat eaters, and everyone loves the Newlyn crab and crayfish mac and cheese. To finish, there may be brown sugar and toasted almond pavlova with poached pear. Wines are a global, affordable selection starting at £17.
Chef/s: Joe Wardell. **Open:** all week L and D. **Closed:** 4 Jan to 10 Feb. **Meals:** main courses £15 to £22. Sun L £15 (2 courses) to £18. **Details:** 36 seats. 26 seats outside. Music.

■ Newlyn
The Tolcarne Inn

Cooking score: 2
Seafood | £32
Newlyn, TR18 5PR
Tel no: (01736) 363074
tolcarneinn.co.uk

Although well and truly on the foodies' map, locals still gather in the bar of this whitewashed inn with their pints of Betty Stogs. Dating from 1717, the Tolcarne may have more than three centuries of maritime history attached to it but it has entered an exciting phase with local chef Ben Tunnicliffe at the tiller. Separated from the waves only by the seawall, this unpretentious harbourside pub is also adjacent to Newlyn fish market, ensuring that the daily catch from day boats goes straight on the menu. That might mean seared scallops, broad beans, mint and vermouth or cracked crab claws, lemon aïoli and cucumber chutney to start. Mains could feature fillet of turbot, baby carrots, romanesco and clams or, if you're in the mood for meat, breast of Cornish chicken, with peas, smoked bacon, lettuce, silverskin onions and mint. Lemon and polenta cake, lemon curd, orange and vanilla mascarpone makes for a zesty finale. Wines from £18.50.

Chef/s: Ben Tunnicliffe and Jake Staebler. **Open:** all week L and D. **Closed:** 25 and 26 Dec. **Meals:** main courses £16 to £20. **Details:** 40 seats. 20 seats outside. Parking.

▮ Padstow

★ TOP 50 ★

Paul Ainsworth at No. 6

Cooking score: 7
Modern British | £57
6 Middle Street, Padstow, PL28 8AP
Tel no: (01841) 532093
paul-ainsworth.co.uk

Understated and smart are how the various dining rooms in this small Georgian town house appear, a mix of slate grey, wood tables and bold wallpaper. It has undergone extensive refurbishment since the last edition of the guide, creating a moody, dark leather-clad bar upstairs and extending the main dining area into the former courtyard. Paul Ainsworth's highly innovative food is presented with a light touch and he enjoys layering dishes with contrasts of textures and carefully worked nuances of flavour – say raw scallops 'as translucent as pearls' with kimchi-style cabbage and the umami hit of an anchovy-laden relish. Perfectly cooked sea bream with crisp skin is enhanced by an accompanying pot of crab topped with oyster leaf and enriched by a bouillabaisse sauce (also

served separately). If there is the odd tiny niggle – a starter of 'superb' ragù of short rib beef would have been better served with normal pasta, not an al dente turnip version – it is brushed lightly away by the pleasure of the homemade sourdough bread served with smoked cod's roe sprinkled with pork crackling, and whipped and caramelised butters. And just as Mr Ainsworth uses his judgement and experience to choose the best local and regional produce, he balances his menu so that energies are preserved for the likes of chocolate with pistachio, olive oil sponge and Caramac. Fast, professional service is delivered by a young team, and knowledgeable dabbling around the globe satisfies most palates and budgets on a wine list that opens at £27.

Chef/s: Paul Ainsworth. **Open:** Tue to Sat L and D. **Closed:** Sun, Mon, 25 and 26 Dec. **Meals:** main courses £30 to £40. Set L £19 (2 courses) to £26. **Details:** 48 seats. V menu. Bar. Music. Children over 4 yrs only.

The Seafood Restaurant

Cooking score: 5
Seafood | £68
Riverside, Padstow, PL28 8BY
Tel no: (01841) 532700
rickstein.com

Rick Stein and Padstow go together like, well, fish and chips – no wonder this Cornish seaside resort has been dubbed 'Padstein'. It all began in 1975, with the launch of this now flagship restaurant overlooking the local quayside. Of course, these days Stein is a global TV star with other things to occupy his time, but his galley master Stephane Delourme ensures that everything is shipshape in the kitchen. Menus depend largely on the catch from the Padstow boats, generously seasoned with creative samplings from Stein's gastro-travelogues: crisp mackerel with green mango and pawpaw salad, Goan cod curry and the gloriously messy Singapore chilli crab are favourites from an ever-evolving, boldly flavoured line-up. You can also indulge in the classics by ordering a mini 'fruits de mer' ahead of hake and chips or char-grilled Dover sole with sea salt and lime. A no-bookings seafood bar satisfies those who crave their Stein fix without the incumbent expense of eating in the restaurant, while the big-hitting wine list features hand-picked selections from the man himself.

Chef/s: Stephane Delourme. **Open:** all week L and D. **Closed:** 25 and 26 Dec. **Meals:** main courses £29 to £58. Set L £40. **Details:** 120 seats. V menu. Bar. Wheelchairs. Music. Children over 3 yrs only.

LOCAL GEM

Rick Stein's Café
Seafood | £24
10 Middle Street, Padstow, PL28 8AP
Tel no: (01841) 532700
rickstein.com

Middle Street is the throbbing hinterland of downtown Padstow, about 30 seconds' walk from the harbourfront, and here's where the budget option of the Stein empire is to be found, behind a roughcast white frontage. It's a proper café, open from midday to mid-evening, with a veggie menu, one for kids, and cocktails for the grown-ups, amid the expected fish specialities. Among the last, grilled sardines spritzed with lime, gurnard Madras curry with basmati, and lemongrass plaice with coriander salsa jump out, and the sunken chocolate cake to finish is something of a favourite. Wines start at £4.70 a glass.

▮ Penzance
The Shore
Cooking score: 3
Seafood | £32
13-14 Alverton Street, Penzance, TR18 2QP
Tel no: (01736) 362444
theshorerestaurant.uk

Bruce Rennie works alone in the kitchen of his restaurant in the centre of Penzance, with arrivals staggered so as not to overload the man at the stove. Mr Rennie cut his teeth with

Martin Wishart and Rick Stein to name but two, and since 2015 he's been turning out some impressive plates of seafood from the waters hereabouts. The dining room is a simply stylish spot with neutral tones and naked wood, with the kitchen drawing on ethically sourced fish from Newlyn's day boats. So get going with trusty mackerel, with pickled oyster and alexanders, or monkfish liver in a fiery vindaloo sauce (complete with a poppadom). It's creative stuff, but not overly fussy – hake, say, with parsley risotto and oyster mushrooms, or sole with Swiss chard and shrimps. To finish, Valrhona Manjari chocolate délice is a classy little number, with passion fruit sorbet and spikes of honeycomb. The fish-friendly wine list kicks off at £18.

Chef/s: Bruce Rennie. **Open:** Fri and Sat L, Tue to Sat D. **Closed:** Sun, Mon. **Meals:** main courses £18 to £20. Set L £19 (2 courses) to £23. **Details:** 26 seats. Music.

▮ Port Isaac
Outlaw's Fish Kitchen
Cooking score: 5
Seafood | £40
1 Middle Street, Port Isaac, PL29 3RH
Tel no: (01208) 881183
outlaws.co.uk

£5
OFF

This unassuming, easy-going harbourside outpost of the Outlaw empire (headquarters is up the steep hill, Restaurant Nathan Outlaw – see entry) is the oldest building in this classic Cornish fishing village. The modest dining room is cheerful and welcoming, with beams, cramped tables, a kitchen in the corner and a 'tiny loo, almost like going into a cupboard'. Simplicity and honest freshness are the hallmarks here and while the raw materials may be local, the kitchen takes a world view of fish cookery. It translates into the kind of cooking our reporters praise fulsomely, though the small sharing plates provoke a dilemma – who's getting the last bite? Particularly enjoyed this year have been raw brill ('with the sweetness of the very fresh') mixed with tart apple and cucumber dressing, a delicate grey mullet ceviche layered with orange, fennel and lime ('a simple, yet beautifully put-together dish'), crisp battered ling with chilli jam, and 'superb' monkfish on the bone with a tangled salad of mangetout, beansprout and peanut. Cheeses are local – Cornish Crumbly, Davidstow Crackler, Helford Blue – and desserts have included a warm, oozy chocolate pudding embedded with fresh raspberries. Service is from young, efficient, happy staff, and the brief, fish-friendly wine list starts at £24.

Chef/s: Tim Barnes. **Open:** Tue to Sat L and D. **Closed:** Sun, Mon, 1 week Christmas, Jan. **Meals:** small plates £7 to £20. **Details:** 24 seats. Wheelchairs. Music.

★ NUMBER ONE RESTAURANT ★

Restaurant Nathan Outlaw

Cooking score: 10
Seafood | £125
6 New Road, Port Isaac, PL29 3SB
Tel no: (01208) 880896
nathan-outlaw.com

It may seem a little odd that Britain's best restaurant is the most modest. Nathan Outlaw shuns all pretension and his restaurant is decorated with restrained good taste, the kind that mixes wood, glass, tactile and visual, the kind that grows on you. An air of individuality and modesty extends to the first-floor dining room with its bare wooden tables and stunning sea views, where Cornish seafood remains paramount, there is no choice and meals are treated as a totality rather than a succession of unrelated courses. This is because Mr Outlaw's food is characterised by absolute freshness of ingredients and by a clear sense of purpose – he follows no fads, copies no recipes, joins no schools. In an opening salvo, cured monkfish is layered with fennel and lemon and dabbed with yoghurt; its counterpart is a simple mound of fresh crabmeat – all at once briny and sweet – topped with a disc of kohlrabi sprinkled with powdered seaweed. Or consider the artistry of nuggets of lobster with thinly sliced young courgette, onion and 'fabulous' smoked mushrooms, each playing off the other in the most exquisite smoky BBQ-style sauce with its base notes of ginger and chilli, while the signature gurnard (at other times red mullet) with its wonderful Porthilly sauce 'never ceases to amaze'. Then meaty turbot, served with St Enodoc asparagus, a sprinkle of bacon and a wonderful tartare hollandaise, gives way to creamy Cornish Jack cheese, celery and walnut tart. Equally deft is the wonderful seasonal confection of strawberries and elderflower – fresh fruit, jelly, shortbread and cream, served with a rhubarb granita – as a prelude to the main dessert of banana, chocolate peanut and lime. Service, led by Stephanie Little, is 'perfect and just happens in the most discreet and attentive way'. As for wine, Damon Little's modern wine list has depth and personality – do take his advice or sign up for the wine flight, a tailor-made matching triumph.

Chef/s: Nathan Outlaw and Christopher Simpson. **Open:** Fri and Sat L, Wed to Sat D. **Closed:** Sun, Mon, Tue, Jan. **Meals:** tasting menu £125 (8 courses). **Details:** 30 seats. Music. Children over 10 yrs only.

LOCAL GEM

Fresh from the Sea

Seafood | £20
18 New Road, Port Isaac, PL29 3SB
Tel no: (01208) 880849
freshfromthesea.co.uk

£30

Callum and Tracey Greenhalgh are a culinary partnership: he takes his boat (the *Mary D*) out daily for lobster, crab and seasonal fish (all sustainably caught), which she prepares and serves for lunch in their tiny café not far from the main car park. Eat in or take-away, the famed crab sandwiches are just part of the deal. Expect dressed crab, smoked salmon, a lobster salad ('great with a glass of crisp white wine'), Porthilly oysters, and homemade apple cake with Cornish clotted cream. House white is £15.

Porthleven

Kota

Cooking score: 4
Fusion/Modern European | £35
Harbour Head, Porthleven, TR13 9JA
Tel no: (01326) 562407
kotarestaurant.co.uk

Grazing on tempura oysters or teriyaki skate wing with charred broccoli in a 300-year-old Cornish corn mill might sound like a curious proposition, but that's the score at Kota – a cute harbourside restaurant-with-rooms run by Kiwi chef Jude Kereama and his wife. With Maori, Chinese and Malaysian blood in his veins, Jude has an instinctive feel for spicy flavours and eclectic East/West mash-ups, although his main ingredients are gleaned from closer to home. Fish from the local boats, Cornish meat and game all figure prominently, and Jude leavens his racy fusion riffs with some modern European influences – as in spiced beef tartare with oyster emulsion, bone-marrow beignet, radishes and avocado, or a three-part chicken dish with roast Jerusalem artichokes, mushrooms and truffled tagliatelle. Big-name Kiwi wines naturally feature on the well-spread global wine list. The owners also run the more casual Kota Kai Bar & Kitchen on Porthleven Harbour Head.
Chef/s: Jude Kereama. **Open:** Tue to Sat D only. **Closed:** Sun, Mon, 25 and 26 Dec, Jan. **Meals:** main courses £14 to £25. Set D £20 (2 courses) to £25. Tasting menu £50. **Details:** 35 seats. Bar. Wheelchairs. Music.

Portscatho

Driftwood

Cooking score: 5
Modern European | £65
Rosevine, Portscatho, TR2 5EW
Tel no: (01872) 580644
driftwoodhotel.co.uk

When it comes to box-ticking seaside attributes, this privately run boutique hotel seems to have it all: a desirable coastal location; fabulous ocean views; acres of gardens; a gorgeous suntrap terrace; plus a private beach and cove reached via a secret wooded path. Driftwood also boasts a bright and breezy restaurant done out in white, blue and sunny yellow shades, with plate-glass windows making the most of the panoramic vistas. Chef Chris Eden matches the setting with an inventory of finely judged, prettily plated dishes inspired by Cornish produce – especially seafood from the local boats. Exotic ingredients and wild pickings also add their own subtle nuances, as in an ingenious starter of cuttlefish, shiitake mushrooms, wild rice, crystallised ginger, samphire and bonito or line-caught pollack with heritage carrots, rainbow chard, almond and seaweed dukkah. Meat dishes bring richer, earthier combos (venison with beetroot, Hispi cabbage, green peppercorns and smoked chocolate), while desserts aim to lighten the mood (try the signature chocolate bar with salted peanut, honeycomb and milk sorbet). Wines are gleaned from top producers worldwide.
Chef/s: Chris Eden. **Open:** all week D only. **Closed:** 11 Dec to 2 Feb. **Meals:** set D £45 (2 courses) to £65. Tasting menu £80 (6 courses) to £95 (8 courses). **Details:** 36 seats. V menu. Bar. Wheelchairs. Music. Parking. Children over 7 yrs only at D.

Rock
The Mariners
Cooking score: 2
British | £30
Rock, PL27 6LD
Tel no: (01208) 863679
themarinersrock.com
£5 OFF

Like everywhere on the front line at Rock, this old pub has been opened up to maximise Camel Estuary views and the summer season overspill, with terraces on the ground and first floor, while big windows let plenty of light into an interior that's all clean modern lines and lots of pale wood. As befits a pub run by Nathan Outlaw (in conjunction with Sharps Brewery), food remains top of the agenda and everything has an instantly recognisable thumbprint. Fresh-from-the-boats seafood gets a good airing, perhaps pickled Porthilly oysters with gherkins, cucumber and jalapeño or breaded ling with apple and cider chutney, gem lettuce, anchovy and tarragon mayonnaise. However, you'll also find ham hock scrumpet served with pease pudding and pickled walnut, and char-grilled half-chicken with satay dressing, peanut salad and coconut rice. Wonderful steamed treacle and lemon sponge with custard stands out among desserts. There's a good choice of bottled or draught ales and a thoroughly accessible wine list opens at £15.
Chef/s: Zack Hawke. **Open:** all week L and D. **Closed:** 25 Dec. **Meals:** main courses £14 to £28. Sun L £26. **Details:** 80 seats. 40 seats outside. Bar. Music.

St Ives
Alba
Cooking score: 2
Modern British | £35
Old Lifeboat House, Wharf Road, St Ives, TR26 1LF
Tel no: (01736) 797222
alba-stives.co.uk
£5 OFF

Part of the enduring appeal of this long-standing restaurant housed in a former lifeboat house is its location overlooking the harbour. So after cocktails in the smart ground-floor bar, climb the stairs to the upper deck, where window seats looking out over the water are highly prized. Light and airy, with white walls dotted with local paintings, it's a relaxed, informal place serving confidently cooked, familiar dishes built around ingredients that are sourced locally. Indeed, locally landed fish and seafood make a strong showing in dishes such as bourride packed with gurnard and mussels with a glossy, garlicky aïoli, or fillet of 'tiptop' brill served with smoked haddock, peas, prosciutto, mint and ratte potatoes. Not in the mood for fish? Then there's Cornish beef fillet with celeriac purée, spinach, baby shallot, smoked Cheddar mash and bordelaise sauce. For dessert, there could be chocolate délice with espresso ice cream, chocolate soil, cocoa nibs and chocolate syrup. The wide-ranging wine list starts at £15.50.
Chef/s: Grant Nethercott. **Open:** all week L and D. **Closed:** 25 and 26 Dec. **Meals:** main courses £18 to £26. Set L and D £22 (2 courses) to £26. **Details:** 26 seats. Bar. Wheelchairs. Music.

The Black Rock

Cooking score: 2
Modern British | £29
Market Place, St Ives, TR26 1RZ
Tel no: (01736) 791911
theblackrockstives.co.uk

£30

Tucked behind the harbour, close to the
Barbara Hepworth Museum, the Black Rock
was, for years, a hardware store run by chef/
proprietor David Symons' family. Art has
played a part in the life of St Ives for many
years, and this is reflected in this laid-back,
contemporary restaurant via a display of
pottery and works by contemporary St Ives
artists. From the hard-working open kitchen
come intelligent, ingredient-driven, please-
all dishes, from a traditional starter of crab
Breton (white crabmeat, mushrooms in port,
béchamel sauce and breadcrumbs) to a classic
Cornish dessert of saffron bread-and-butter
pudding and clotted cream. In between, a
harmonious main course of pan-roasted sea
trout fillet, fricassee of green lentils, fresh peas
and smoked bacon with 'today's potatoes and
vegetables' showcases the premium regional
ingredients. The wine list includes plenty
under £20, with prices from £15.95, and a
selection of Cornish beers and ciders.
Chef/s: David Symons. **Open:** Mon to Sat D only.
Closed: Sun, Nov to Feb. **Meals:** main courses £14
to £23. Set D £18 (2 courses) to £21. **Details:** 40
seats. Bar. Music.

Porthgwidden Beach Café

Cooking score: 1
Seafood | £30
Porthgwidden Beach, The Island, St Ives,
TR26 1PL
Tel no: (01736) 796791
porthgwiddencafe.co.uk

Pitched on one of St Ives' top beaches, with
bracing sea views and fiery sunsets
guaranteed, this little sibling of the
Porthminster Beach Café (see entry) is a sure-
fire crowd-puller. It's easy to see the family
likeness, too, from the whitewashed walls,
funky furniture and big windows to the
preponderance of zingy-fresh Cornish
seafood on the menu. The kitchen favours a
freestyle global approach, serving everything
from moules marinière and crab linguine to
seafood paella or crispy fried squid with miso
dressing and Thai salad. Burgers, steaks and
goats' cheese tart cater to other tastes, while
paninis are added at lunchtime. Choose from
modest, easy-drinking wines.
Chef/s: Robert Michaels. **Open:** all week L and D.
Closed: first 2 weeks Dec, 25 Dec. **Meals:** main
courses £13 to £18. **Details:** 32 seats. 40 seats
outside. Music. Parking.

Porthmeor Beach Café

Cooking score: 1
International | £25
Porthmeor, St Ives, TR26 1JZ
Tel no: (01736) 793366
porthmeorcafe.co.uk

£30

'A special place,' confided a fan of this versatile
beachside café, adding 'more so when a visit
coincides with the amazing sunsets for which
St Ives is famed'. Found in front of Tate St Ives,
the cheery conservatory-style interior has vast
windows looking out over the (genuinely)
white sand, an open kitchen ('these chefs must
have the best views in the UK') and a much-
in-demand terrace for when the weather co-
operates. The flexible all-day menu works
hard. Cornish crab sandwiches or chorizo
burgers vie for attention with tapas of salt-
and-pepper squid or crispy pork belly, with
the evening menu supplying Moroccan-
marinated chicken breast or Thai red prawn
curry. Wines from £17.50. Sister beach cafés at
nearby Porthminster and Porthgwidden (see
entries).
Chef/s: Cam Jennings. **Open:** all week, all day from
9am. **Closed:** 25 and 26 Dec. **Meals:** main courses
£12 to £18. Tapas £3 to £10. **Details:** 31 seats. 90
seats outside. Bar. Wheelchairs. Music.

Porthminster Beach Café

Cooking score: 3
Seafood | £40
Porthminster Beach, St Ives, TR26 2EB
Tel no: (01736) 795352
porthminstercafe.co.uk

The Blue Flag Porthminster beach is a golden beauty and since 1991 it has had the café it deserves – 'when the sun is shining, there is no better place to be'. The white-painted Art Deco building is right on the beach, with a take-away on the sand ('awesome fish and chips', but watch out for the gulls), and the café/restaurant up above with large windows giving uninterrupted sea views. A table on the terrace is the golden ticket in the summer. Australian Michael Smith has been here since 2002 – who'd want to leave? – and his menu focuses on local seafood with plenty of global flavours in the mix: a touch of ponzu enlivens a mackerel pâté, monkfish curry has 'distinctive' spicing, and slow-poached tamarillo appears with vanilla pannacotta. The crab linguine and fish and chips are ever-present classics, with meat options running to pink Cornish duck breast with an accompanying croquette. Wines start at £16.95, or choose a Cornish beer.
Chef/s: Michael Smith and Lee Wilson. **Open:** all week L and D. **Closed:** 25 Dec. **Meals:** main courses £16 to £32. **Details:** 48 seats. 60 seats outside. V menu. Music. Children before 7pm only.

LOCAL GEM

Blas Burgerworks

Burgers | £16
The Warren, St Ives, TR26 2EA
Tel no: (01736) 797272
blasburgerworks.co.uk

£30

Upmarket burger joints are a common sight these days, but this diminutive backstreet restaurant and takeaway really blazed a trail when it opened over a decade ago. It remains a pleasing prospect: burgers made with 28-day-aged Cornish beef sharing the bill with eight different vegetarian and vegan burgers. A meal might take in blue corn tortillas, guacamole and chilli relish, a beef or bean burger with Cornish Gouda, romesco, char-grilled leeks, leaves and aïoli, and deep-fried apple pie with salted caramel and clotted cream. A short drinks menu includes house wines and Cornish beers and ciders.

▋St Kew

St Kew Inn

Cooking score: 2
Modern British | £28
Churchtown, St Kew, PL30 3HB
Tel no: (01208) 841259
stkewinn.co.uk

£30

The beautiful tree-lined garden overlooking St Kew village church receives regular commendations from readers, but there are plenty of attractions inside this tidy 15th-century hostelry, too. A full contingent of heavy beams and worn flagstones awaits, along with a wood-burning range in the bar, while the kitchen uses locally sourced ingredients for a well-spread line-up of enticing visitor-friendly dishes. Warm goats' cheese with fennel and pomegranate salad followed by a plate of Cumberland sausages with Cheddar and leek mash did the business for one reader, but the all-purpose menu embraces everything from braised squid with chorizo and lemon mayonnaise to beer-battered fish and chips, grilled rump steak or beetroot and spinach tagine with couscous and roasted chickpeas. To finish, the 'melt-in-the-mouth' rhubarb crème brûlée with buttery shortbread biscuits also gets a round of applause. Well-kept St Austell beers, good coffee and a creditable wine list complete a winning Cornish package.
Chef/s: Martin Perkins. **Open:** all week L and D. **Closed:** 25 and 26 Dec. **Meals:** main courses £13 to £19. Sun L £23. **Details:** 70 seats. 80 seats outside. Bar. Parking.

St Mawes
Hotel Tresanton

Cooking score: 3
Modern European | £42
27 Lower Castle Road, St Mawes, TR2 5DR
Tel no: (01326) 270055
tresanton.com

£5 OFF

Olga Polizzi's hotel on the Roseland Heritage Coast looks out to sea amid semi-tropical vegetation, towards the beacon of St Anthony's lighthouse, and is the perfect place for recharging the batteries. Taking tea (or something stronger) on the terrace to the sound of lapping waves is what Cornwall is all about, while Paul Wadham keeps things admirably straightforward in the culinary department, incorporating light-touch Mediterranean influences in his treatment of impeccable regional produce. Seafood is a leading suit, with lobster, fennel and saffron risotto, or spaghetti with clams in garlic and chilli, sure-fire bets on that front, but there are also pedigree local meats such as Terras Farm duck, served with roast celeriac, red onion and carrots, or beef fillet and gnocchi, with confit tomato, an oyster mushroom and shallots. Finish lightly with vanilla pannacotta and strawberry compote, or more robustly with Tunisian orange cake and yoghurt sorbet. Zesty cocktails are a good way to start, and wines open at £24.
Chef/s: Paul Wadham. **Open:** all week L and D. **Closed:** 2 weeks Jan. **Meals:** main courses £18 to £42. Set L £25 (2 courses) to £29. **Details:** 70 seats. 90 seats outside. Bar. Wheelchairs. Parking. Children over 6 yrs only in restaurant.

Visit us online

To find out more about
The Good Food Guide, please
visit thegoodfoodguide.co.uk

St Merryn
The Cornish Arms

Cooking score: 1
British | £27
Churchtown, St Merryn, PL28 8ND
Tel no: (01841) 520288
rickstein.com

£30

Rick Stein's revitalised Cornish Arms looks the rustic part with beams, stone walls and log fires, and conforms to everyone's idea of a classic country pub. No bookings are taken so it's best to 'get there as early as possible' or avoid busy times altogether, for service and food have been known to suffer. When on form, the kitchen delivers a menu of uncomplicated, crowd-pleasing dishes such as ploughman's, battered cod or steak and chips, and steak and ale pie, but lamb karahi and wild mushroom risotto aim beyond simple pub grub. It fits the bill, too, for children and canines. Wines from £16.95.
Chef/s: Alex Clark. **Open:** all week L and D. **Closed:** 25 Dec. **Meals:** main courses £11 to £18. **Details:** 140 seats. 130 seats outside. Bar. Wheelchairs. Music. Parking.

Rafferty's

Cooking score: 2
Modern British | £30
St Merryn, PL28 8NF
Tel no: (01841) 521561
raffertyscafewinebar.co.uk

Ed and Nicola Rafferty's café, wine bar and restaurant is at the heart of St Merryn, a village of a couple of thousand souls, not far from good beaches. It's a relaxed and unpretentious place, with beers on tap, a concise wine list that includes fizz and white wine from Cornwall's Camel Valley, and a nifty cocktail bar in the courtyard. The menu mixes British and broader European ideas, with plenty of regional ingredients, and includes a range of 'tapas' to share if you so wish. Those tapas might be fish tostada with a salsa and pickled onions, or crispy Cornish mackerel with tarragon oil and horseradish cream. Beefier appetites might go for steaks (an open sirloin sandwich, say, or 28-day aged ribeye), and other main courses extend to Padstow crab tagliatelle or a vivid green summery vegetarian risotto. Finish with chocolate con churros. Despite the wine bar label, options by the glass are limited.

Chef/s: Alex Scott. **Open:** Sun L, Wed to Sun D. **Closed:** Mon, Tue. **Meals:** main courses £14 to £29. **Details:** 36 seats. 20 seats outside. Bar. Wheelchairs. Music.

▮ St Tudy
St Tudy Inn
Cooking score: 2
Modern British | £32
St Tudy, PL30 3NN
Tel no: (01208) 850656
sttudyinn.com

£5 OFF ▭

In the charming village of St Tudy, opposite a red telephone box, this smart pub-with-rooms is a brilliant local asset, emanating a sense of bonhomie as soon as you set foot in the slate-floored bar with its wood-burner and gaggle of congenial locals. Push your way through to the trio of deceptively spacious interconnecting dining areas, where an understated nautical theme and chef/proprietor Emily Scott's succinctly seasonal menus are to be found. Her dishes are simple and unshowy, reveal a commitment to local and regional suppliers, and offer flavours as big-hearted as the portions. Cauliflower turns up in a pakora with mint, cucumber, coriander and yoghurt and might precede a rustic fish stew of bream, gurnard, clams, prawns, tomato broth and saffron aïoli. If seafood isn't your thing, there's chicken breast, bacon, shallots, sherry, tarragon and Puy lentils. Among desserts, chocolate mousse, hazelnuts and vanilla ice cream catches the eye. Wines, with a generous by-the-glass selection, start at £18.

Chef/s: Emily Scott. **Open:** all week L and D. **Closed:** 25 and 26 Dec. **Meals:** main courses £13 to £24. Set L £18 (2 courses) to £23. Set D £21 (2 courses) to £25. Sun L £13. Tasting menu £50. **Details:** 80 seats. 40 seats outside. Bar. Wheelchairs. Music. Parking.

▮ Sennen Cove
Ben Tunnicliffe Sennen Cove
Cooking score: 1
Modern British | £30
Sennen Cove, TR19 7BT
Tel no: (01736) 871191
benatsennen.com

A custom-built 'surf den' (complete with its own kitchen, pizza oven and resident DJ) is the hot new summertime attraction at Ben Tunnicliffe's timber-framed diner – an all-comers' eatery with surfing and biking memorabilia on the walls and terrific views from wraparound windows overlooking Sennen beach. Food-wise, touristy favourites such as burgers and beer-battered haddock with skin-on chips sit alongside seared scallops with saffron and pickled vegetable dressing, goats' cheese fritters and Indonesian seafood curry, with treacle tart or a squidgy chocolate brownie for afters. There's an intriguing wine list, too. Ben Tunnicliffe also runs the Tolcarne Inn, Newlyn (see entry).

Chef/s: Ben Tunnicliffe. **Open:** all week L, Mon to Sat D. **Closed:** Mon and Tue (winter). **Meals:** main courses £13 to £18. **Details:** 80 seats. 80 seats outside. Bar. Wheelchairs. Music. Parking.

▮ Treburley
The Springer Spaniel
Cooking score: 4
Modern British | £30
Treburley, PL15 9NS
Tel no: (01579) 370424
thespringerspaniel.co.uk

The Spaniel is a big cream-coloured beast on the A388, not far from Launceston. A pleasing mix of rough-and-ready pub and more upmarket dining room is the winning formula, and the versatile menus offer plenty of inspired choice from the modern British

stable. A simple serving of dressed white crab incorporating pearls of salmon roe with watermelon and cucumber makes a light opener, and might be followed by Cajun-spiced lamb rump with a croquette of shredded meat, sweet potato purée and tzatziki, or perhaps fried sea bream with red pepper ketchup and fennel salad. Elements are subtly combined in these dishes, with nothing aiming to knock your socks off, at least until the desserts arrive with a kerpow. Banana parfait encased in chocolate with bitter-orange ice cream and gel, peanut brittle, honeycomb and caramelised banana was a sheer delight at inspection, and good reports are had of the egg custard tart, which might come with roasted peach and matching ice cream. A short wine list, from £5.50 a standard glass, keeps things motoring.
Chef/s: Alistair Fraser. **Open:** Mon to Sat L and D. Sun 12 to 6. **Closed:** 25 Dec, 1 Jan. **Meals:** main courses £12 to £25. Sun L £18 (2 courses) to £22. Tasting menu £45. **Details:** 69 seats. 36 seats outside. Bar. Wheelchairs. Music. Parking.

▌Treen
The Gurnard's Head
Cooking score: 2
Modern British | £33
Treen, TR26 3DE
Tel no: (01736) 796928
gurnardshead.co.uk
£5 OFF 🛏

'Eat, drink, sleep' is the three-pronged motto of this windswept ochre-painted inn high up on the cliffs overlooking a brooding rocky promontory also called Gurnard's Head. The pub's name is emblazoned on the roof for good measure, while all is cosily weatherproof within – from the real ales in the bar to the open fires, comfy sofas and scrubbed-wood tables in the dining room. Given the location, locally caught seafood is a mainstay of the menu: the ugly namesake fish might be partnered by sea buckthorn, carrot, kale, honey and chilli, while cod comes with beetroot, fennel and yoghurt. Other combos could include duck breast, smoky onions and

rhubarb BBQ sauce, and there's curried white chocolate with cumin granola and mango to finish – if you're not in the mood for sticky toffee pudding. Decent-value wines are on offer by the glass or carafe. Related to the Felin Fach Griffin and the Old Coastguard, Mousehole (see entries).
Chef/s: Max Wilson. **Open:** all week L and D. **Closed:** 24 and 25 Dec. **Meals:** main courses £15 to £19. Set L £18 (2 courses) to £21. Set D £21 (2 courses) to £27. Sun L £18 (2 courses) to £23. **Details:** 70 seats. 30 seats outside. Music. Parking.

▌Truro
Tabb's
Cooking score: 5
Modern British | £33
85 Kenwyn Street, Truro, TR1 3BZ
Tel no: (01872) 262110
tabbs.co.uk

Nigel Tabb bestrides the Truro dining scene like a friendly colossus. In an ambience of lilac walls and linened tables, he has created a well-supported local venue that does the old-fashioned things supremely well. There are monthly Sunday roasts, for one thing, of the likes of duck or côte de boeuf, and he supplements a three-stage prix fixe with a carte, rather than setting off along the multi-course tasting route. The cooking has overtones of the modern British style, but with intelligible classical underpinnings, offering pork rillettes with salad, brioche and piccalilli to start, followed perhaps by grilled wing of ray in Chinese guise with sesame broth and chilli oil, or seared loin and braised shin of venison with mushrooms and celeriac in horseradish cream. Alluring desserts embrace nougat glacé with cardamom ice cream and raspberry sauce, or a hot chocolate fondant with black treacle ice cream that's worth the wait. Half a dozen house wines at £17.50 lead an efficiently annotated list.
Chef/s: Nigel Tabb. **Open:** Tue to Sun L, Tue to Sat D. **Closed:** Mon, 25 and 26 Dec, 1 Jan. **Meals:** main courses £16 to £21. Set L and D £20 (2 courses) to £25. **Details:** 28 seats. Bar. Music.

■ Watergate Bay
Fifteen Cornwall
Cooking score: 3
Italian | £50
On the beach, Watergate Bay, TR8 4AA
Tel no: (01637) 861000
fifteencornwall.co.uk

'Welcoming, friendly, cheerful, light and bright and comfortable, overlooking wonderful beach, complete with surfers, dogs and walkers' – our readers are enthusiastic about this modern eatery. Indeed, Jamie Oliver's zingy, confident take on beachside dining has drawn the crowds since opening in 2006. Adam Banks has returned to head the kitchen (he was previously senior sous) after five years cooking in Australia and his seasonal menus are bursting with good ideas. If you can tear yourself away from antipasti of arancini, burrata with hazelnuts or artichoke caponata, there is taglierini with duck and asparagus or gilthead bream with agretti and squid-ink aïoli to start. Main courses bring wood-fired lamb with cannellini beans and salsa verde, or plaice with cockles, fregola and fennel. Lemon and polenta cake with lemon curd and clotted cream makes a great finish. Tasting and sharing menus, and half-portions for kids at lunch, complete the package. Wines from £22.50.

Chef/s: Adam Banks. **Open:** all week L and D.
Closed: 2 weeks Jan. **Meals:** main courses £21 to £27. Set L £26 (2 courses) to £32. Tasting menu £65.
Details: 120 seats. Bar. Wheelchairs. Parking. Children over 12 yrs only after 6.45pm.

LOCAL GEM
The Beach Hut
International | £25
Watergate Bay Hotel, Watergate Bay, TR8 4AA
Tel no: (01637) 860877
watergatebay.co.uk

🛏 £30

This smart but laid-back beachside hangout (all driftwood and glass) is run by neighbouring Watergate Bay Hotel and is so close to the sea that, when the tide is in, it feels like you're floating on the waves. The kitchen delivers dishes with global flavour and broad appeal, along the lines of BBQ-spiced squid with black garlic aïoli, Thai-spiced baked fish of the day with Asian salad, beef chilli, and salted-caramel rice pudding. Breakfast is served, too, as well as tea, cakes and 'extreme' hot chocolate. Wines from £19.

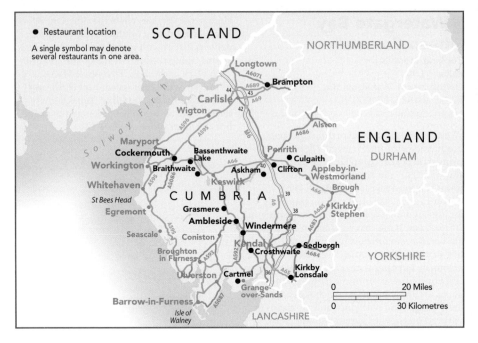

Map legend:
● Restaurant location
A single symbol may denote several restaurants in one area.

SCOTLAND

NORTHUMBERLAND

Longtown

Brampton

Carlisle
Wigton

ENGLAND
DURHAM

Alston

Maryport
Cockermouth
Workington
Braithwaite
Whitehaven
St Bees Head
Egremont

Bassenthwaite Lake
Askham
Keswick

Penrith
Culgaith
Clifton
Appleby-in-Westmorland
Brough

CUMBRIA

Grasmere
Ambleside
Windermere

Kirkby Stephen

Seascale
Coniston
Broughton in Furness
Ulverston
Cartmel

Kendal
Crosthwaite
Sedbergh

YORKSHIRE

Kirkby Lonsdale

Grange-over-Sands

Barrow-in-Furness

0   20 Miles
0   30 Kilometres

Isle of Walney

LANCASHIRE

■ Ambleside
The Drunken Duck Inn
Cooking score: 3
Modern British | £38
Barngates, Ambleside, LA22 0NG
Tel no: (015394) 36347
drunkenduckinn.co.uk

'We love the whole relaxed coal-fired and
dogs-everywhere ambience' ran the notes of
one couple who found this delightful pub
above Ambleside 'busy on a midweek in
October, so goodness knows what it's like in
the summer – we only ever go to the Lakes out
of busy times'. Sometimes pubs hit that
'something for everyone' note pitch-perfectly.
Drop in for a simple lunch of salt beef
sandwich and chips ('the best ever') and jam
roly-poly with custard, or linger over a dinner
of twice-baked cheese soufflé with creamy
Lancashire cheese or confit artichoke and
artichoke dumpling with stout reduction
(brewed on site), then 'really tender' breast and

leg of guinea fowl with creamy wild garlic
potato terrine, a smattering of peas and more
wild garlic. End with rhubarb cobbler and
popcorn ice cream, or strawberries with
yoghurt sorbet and meadowsweet that is
'refreshing and light'. The wine list (from
£21.50) has been chosen with care and with
plenty by the glass.
Chef/s: Jonny Watson. **Open:** all week L and D.
Closed: 25 Dec. **Meals:** main courses £22.
Details: 60 seats. 32 seats outside. Bar. Parking.

Lake Road Kitchen
Cooking score: 6
Modern European | £60
Lake Road, Ambleside, LA22 0AD
Tel no: (015394) 22012
lakeroadkitchen.co.uk

The oscillation of the culinary compass needle
that supplanted the long heyday of
Mediterranean food with the more
challenging ambience of cooler northern
climes is celebrated with single-minded
devotion here. Not just northern English

produce such as Lakeland milk-fed veal, but seafood from the Scottish islands, migrating Norwegian cod, and even king crab from the Arctic fringes, are the stock-in-trade of a kitchen focused on five- and eight-course tasting menus of extraordinary versatility. Reports cite a perfectly timed giant scallop in fennel shavings, dressed in bee pollen and sunflower seeds, the now-famous whole roast cauliflower basted in goat butter, steamed monkfish in chicken dripping, and wild rose-petal granita as dishes to conjure with, but there are more traditionally rooted offerings, too, as when roast squab comes in a Scandinavian livery of lingonberries, girolles and yarrow. A blackberry tart in its own coulis is adorned in lemony oxalis leaves. If some are left a little cold by the style, others praise 'accomplished, innovative cooking with carefully considered flavour combinations'. A short wine list, from £26, just about keeps up.

Chef/s: James Cross. **Open:** Wed to Sun D only. **Closed:** Mon, Tue. **Meals:** tasting menu £60 (5 courses) to £85. **Details:** 21 seats. V menu. Music. Children over 12 yrs only.

Old Stamp House
Cooking score: 5
Modern British | £40
Church Street, Ambleside, LA22 0BU
Tel no: (015394) 32775
oldstamphouse.com

Ryan Blackburn's unassuming restaurant is tucked away down the stone steps of what used to be the local post office in William Wordsworth's day. The simple décor – minimal with dark grey walls and bare tables, a flagstone floor – is the backdrop for intelligent, sophisticated dishes that are 'very, very good indeed'. Pig's trotter baked in 'fluffy, golden' brioche served on top of soubise spinach, with a lobster cracker and lobster sauce points the way, with 'rich, meaty flavours' and top-notch ingredients. On the whole, this is proudly British cooking with fine ingredients such as skrei cod, Herdwick lamb and Cartmel Valley roe deer making seasonal appearances – the latter appearing at a

test meal as a tartare dressed with a lightly smoked beetroot oil with capers and elf caps 'providing acidity and earthiness'. A 'lovely piece' of cod sitting on samphire and potted shrimps, with charred cauliflower and a 'wonderful sweet and savoury' spiced mead velouté really hit the spot, too. Desserts such as a dark chocolate and Unsworth's Yard stout cake, layered with cream and cherry, topped with little blobs of caramelised chocolate, with a slick of cherry sauce on the side, has also won praise. The comprehensive wine list opens at £21.

Chef/s: Ryan Blackburn. **Open:** Wed to Sat L, Tue to Sat D. **Closed:** Sun, Mon, 24 to 26 Dec, first 2 weeks Jan. **Meals:** main courses £19 to £27. Set L £20 (2 courses) to £25. Tasting Menu £65. **Details:** 20 seats. Bar.

▌Askham
Askham Hall
Cooking score: 5
Modern European | £50
Askham, CA10 2PF
Tel no: (01931) 712350
askhamhall.co.uk

Home to the Earls of Lonsdale these past eight centuries, Askham stands in modest seclusion behind hills a few miles from Ullswater. Racier goings-on than the place can ever have known before include parties in the old barn and Indian head massages in the spa, but the core of the operation is surely Richard Swale's elegant modern European cooking, offered in the form of five fixed-price dinner menus a week. Presentations are attractive, and reflect the diligent products of gardening, meat-ageing, charcuterie-curing, as well as astute buying. Roasted Scottish langoustines might appear in spring array with fresh peas and day lily, dressed in the fat of home-reared smoked ham, to be followed by a bavette of Shorthorn beef with Hispi, smoked shallots and triple-cooked chips, or Lowther Estate venison with pommes Anna in mibuna greens, rose hips and bitter chocolate. Autumn visitors might finish with buttermilk pannacotta, served with apple and sorrel sorbet and poached blackberries. The French-oriented wine list opens at £25.50 for Gloucestershire's Three Choirs.

Chef/s: Richard Swale. **Open:** Tue to Sat D only. **Closed:** Sun, Mon, 24 to 26 Dec, 1 Jan to 10 Feb. **Meals:** set D £50 (3 courses). Tasting menu £65 (5 courses). **Details:** 30 seats. V menu. Bar. Wheelchairs. Music. Parking.

■ Bassenthwaite Lake
The Pheasant
Cooking score: 3
British | £30
Bassenthwaite Lake, CA13 9YE
Tel no: (017687) 76234
the-pheasant.co.uk

Matthew Wylie's ancient inn is an agreeable blend of country boozer and upper-crust inn. It's a hugely enjoyable place, something of an all-rounder, with the bar the 500-year-old heart of the place (very busy with locals, not just tourists), and supported by various lounges, the Fell restaurant for special occasions and the down-to-earth Bistro, where everyone feels at home. Here, an upbeat take on pub classics includes ham hock terrine with burnt-apple purée and beetroot and orange chutney or Stornoway black pudding Scotch egg served with a Bloody Mary ketchup. Mains bring the likes of fish and chips, steaks and shepherd's pie, but there's also a rich casserole of venison, crisp confit of Gressingham duck, and hake with pea purée, new potatoes and spring onion, caper and lemon butter sauce. Finish with damson crème brûlée with almond sponge and damson gel. Wines from £18.95.

Chef/s: Jonathan Bell. **Open:** all week L and D. **Closed:** 25 Dec. **Meals:** main courses £14 to £22. Set L and early D £18 (2 courses) to £21. **Details:** 40 seats. 30 seats outside. Bar. Wheelchairs. Parking.

■ Braithwaite
The Cottage in the Wood
Cooking score: 4
Modern British | £55
Magic Hill, Whinlatter Forest, Braithwaite, CA12 5TW
Tel no: (01768) 778409
thecottageinthewood.co.uk

£5 OFF 🛏

The location on a densely forested mountainside may foster a sense of other worldliness, but in practice this Georgian house (now a restaurant-with-rooms) is only a couple of miles from the A66 north of Keswick. The views of Skiddaw from the dining room form a dramatic backdrop for the ambitious cooking of Richard Collingwood, whose style is all about coaxing clean, deep flavours and intriguing textural contrasts from tersely described ingredients. A May dinner, for example, turned up crab with brown crab ice cream, avocado and grapefruit, prior to a serving of 'a beautifully prepared small roll of Herdwick hogget' with purple spouting broccoli and merguez sausage. There's been praise for the six-course 'Taste Cumbria' menu where highlights have included seaweed broth with braised dulse and smoked eel, and veal sweetbreads with wild garlic and morels. Clever desserts put on a thoroughly modern show, too – a dish simply labelled 'gariguette strawberry, sweet cicely' proving to be 'an astonishing line-up of individual and intensely flavoured strawberry-based items'. Wines from £20.

Chef/s: Richard Collingwood. **Open:** Thur to Sat L, Tue to Sat D. **Closed:** Sun, Mon, 25 and 26 Dec, 2 to 24 Jan. **Meals:** set L £20 (3 courses) to £30. Set D £50 (3 courses). Tasting menu £70. **Details:** 36 seats. Bar. Wheelchairs. Parking. Children over 10 yrs only.

▌Brampton
Farlam Hall
Cooking score: 3
Modern British | £48
Hallbankgate, Brampton, CA8 2NG
Tel no: (016977) 46234
farlamhall.co.uk

£5 OFF

One couple, who have been visiting Farlam Hall for more than 20 years, love the 'quiet, settled air' that suffuses this lovingly maintained Lakeland retreat. The Quinion family has been in residence since the mid-1970s, fostering a mood of civilised decorum enlivened by oodles of gracious hospitality. The scene is set for 'an evening full of pleasure', beginning with drinks and canapés in the antique-filled lounges – the warm-up for dinner at 8 in the ornate restaurant. As always, the ever-dependable menu runs to four courses in the 'country house' idiom, perhaps opening with celeriac and apple soup or wild mushroom and spring onion risotto. Mains such as roast loin of Cumbrian lamb or pan-fried monkfish with tomato compote and pesto arrive with a sharing plate of various vegetables, before guests are offered a decent choice of English cheeses and desserts such as salted-caramel mousse. An extensive wine list does its job.

Chef/s: Barry Quinion. **Open:** all week D only. **Closed:** 25 to 30 Dec, 7 to 26 Jan. **Meals:** set D £48 (4 courses). **Details:** 45 seats. V menu. Parking. Children over 5 yrs only.

Please send us your feedback

To register your opinion about any restaurant listed in this guide, or a new restaurant that you wish to bring to our attention, please visit the web address at the bottom of the page. Your feedback informs the content of the book and will be used to compile next year's reviews.

▌Cartmel
★ TOP 10 ★
L'Enclume
Cooking score: 10
Modern British | £145
Cavendish Street, Cartmel, LA11 6PZ
Tel no: (015395) 36362
lenclume.co.uk

A north-west restaurant to be reckoned with and a serious contender on the international food scene, L'Enclume packs a major punch, sure of its stature and pedigree. Simple it is not. What Simon Rogan is good at is cooking, plain and simple – the actual transformation of ingredients from their raw state into deep, deliberate tastes. His inspiration is Cumbria, the fiercely seasonal ingredients impeccable (fruits and vegetables come from his own farm) and there is no choice. The results can be brilliant – '19 courses, a mind-blowing experience' (7 at lunch). It takes considerable nerve and brio to serve raw, diced aged veal in coal oil (with slivers of radish, sorrel and caper jam), or an umami-laden braised gem lettuce with English wasabi mayo, fermented mushrooms and a dot of truffle purée, highlights of one meal. Elsewhere, in an interplay of sweet and tart, diced confit beetroot is layered with beetroot mousse and a runny quail's egg, the whole infused with pine, while rich, sensuous butter-poached turbot is delivered with bay shrimp and kale shoots. These are knockout dishes, no question, and that extends to a pre-dessert of Malling Centenary strawberries in a lovely sweet verbena-infused strawberry juice with coal-infused custard and delicate strawberry jelly. And as a finale, dense nuggets of rhubarb in its own juice, topped by a sweet cicely and buttermilk-aerated mousse dotted with slivers of yoghurt and caramel crisp, is beautifully realised. So too the details such as the breads, and pork and eel with ham fat served as tasty spiky morsels. Service is impeccable, though latterly grown in number, prompting one regular to note 'the second time they remembered we'd been before (which impressed us) – that degree of intimacy and personalisation seems to have gone'. The wine list is magisterial, with top names from classic regions in France and around the globe, but there are plenty of surprises, too, from £35, and good choice by the glass.

Chef/s: Simon Rogan and Marcus Noack. **Open:** Tue to Sun L and D. **Closed:** Mon, 2 to 16 Jan. **Meals:** set L £55 (7 courses). Tasting menu £145. **Details:** 54 seats. V menu. Children at L only.

Rogan & Company

Cooking score: 5
Modern British | £35
Devonshire Square, Cartmel, LA11 6QD
Tel no: (015395) 35917
roganandcompany.co.uk

£5 OFF 🛏

With its prime position in the heart of Cartmel, Simon Rogan's easy-going second restaurant takes pride in the best of British, the short menu a glorious roll call of diligently sourced local and regional ingredients (including fruit and vegetables from L'Enclume's farm), handled with precision. Ancient ceiling beams testify to the building's age, although décor is clean, simple and contemporary and, keeping up standards, impeccable service is knowledgeable, helpful and friendly. Homemade bread comes highly recommended, as does a nibble of creamy smoked roe, while beautifully cooked starters of 'tender, tasty' octopus with sweet heirloom tomatoes, pickled walnut and Ticklemore cheese, or heritage potato in a silky smoked eel cream sprinkled with bacon dashi present 'perfect flavours working in harmony'. Main courses run from lamb flank with onion, nasturtium and kale to sea bass with pine nut, intensely sweet pickled Datterini tomatoes and olive. To finish, chocolate cream with pickled cherries and cocoa nibs is 'elegantly presented and extremely moreish'. To drink, there are inventive cocktails and a brief, global wine list with good choice by the glass.

Chef/s: Peter Smit. **Open:** Mon and Wed to Sun L, Mon and Wed to Sat D. **Closed:** Tue, first week Jan, Wed (Nov to Apr). **Meals:** main courses £18 to £27. Set L £20 (2 courses) to £26. **Details:** 45 seats. Wheelchairs. Music.

■ Clifton
George & Dragon

Cooking score: 3
Modern British | £30
Clifton, CA10 2ER
Tel no: (01768) 865381
georgeanddragonclifton.co.uk

£5 OFF 🛏

Locals and Lakeland tourists alike can thank Charles Lowther for turning this 18th-century pub into a smart, forward-thinking hostelry with a restaurant and bedrooms attached. Cleverly tricked out with slate, oak and other natural materials, the interior is spot-on for cooking that puts great store by regional sourcing. Rare-breed meats and wild pickings supplement a barrow-load of seasonal ingredients from Cumbrian producers and there are plenty of good things to be had, from poached duck egg with warm heritage potato salad, cured yolk and winter truffle to roast pheasant breast with Southern-fried leg, alliums and a splash of Eden Brewery ale. Home-reared Shorthorn beef is aged at sister establishment Askham Hall (see entry), while Herdwick hogget receives an earthy hit from braised barley, parsley root and glazed mushrooms. The well-annotated wine list includes bottles from the owner's private cellar.

Chef/s: Gareth Webster. **Open:** all week L and D. **Closed:** 26 Dec. **Meals:** main courses £14 to £22. Set L and D £15 (2 courses) to £20. **Details:** 104 seats. 60 seats outside. Bar. Music. Parking.

■ Cockermouth
Quince & Medlar
Cooking score: 2
Vegetarian | £28
11-13 Castlegate, Cockermouth, CA13 9EU
Tel no: (01900) 823579
quinceandmedlar.co.uk
£30

Rapidly approaching its third decade, Colin and Louisa Le Voi's Quince & Medlar has become firmly established as a vegetarian restaurant that treats those who eschew meat as grown-ups, offering them a global style of cooking that might even tempt meat-eating companions. Expect starters such as potted chickpea and balsamic red onion pâté with oaty biscuits and cheese shortbread, while among main courses there may be ricotta rotolo – rolled pasta filled with ricotta, sliced and baked with green salsa, pine kernels and chunky tomato relish – or sticky rice fries and star anise and saffron roast fennel with crushed juniper, olives and garlic and a smoky red pepper sauce. There are vegan options for many of the dishes. In more familiar territory, desserts take in chocolate hazelnut torte or coconut and pomegranate pannacotta. Service is affable and chatty. Wines, a succinct global collection, start at £17.40 and stay firmly below £30.
Chef/s: Colin Le Voi. **Open:** Tue to Sat D only. **Closed:** Sun, Mon, 25 and 26 Dec. **Meals:** main courses £16. **Details:** 26 seats. V menu. Music. Children over 5 yrs only.

■ Crosthwaite
The Punch Bowl Inn
Cooking score: 2
Modern British | £33
Lyth Valley, Crosthwaite, LA8 8HR
Tel no: (015395) 68237
the-punchbowl.co.uk
£5 OFF

The Punch Bowl Inn has been a feature of the Lythe Valley for many years, evolving into the well-bred hostelry of today, offering contemporary accommodation, a smart, formal restaurant and more relaxed bar areas. Food remains top of the agenda and everything has an instantly recognizable thumbprint. The kitchen goes about its work with dexterity, whether it is serving 'a very good example' of twice-baked cheese soufflé with wilted spinach or a 'well-flavoured' Goosnargh chicken and ham hock terrine with pickled vegetables. For mains, smoked haddock proves to be 'a silky, delicate piece of fish', accompanied by champ mash, a poached egg and mustard sauce. Applause, too, for good bread rolls and excellent dripping-cooked chips, and visitors have been impressed by a 'lovely' banana soufflé with toffee and lime sauce and a 'sublime' chocolate and salted-caramel mousse. An international wine list starts at £22.50.
Chef/s: Arthur Bridgeman Quinn. **Open:** all week L and D. **Meals:** main courses £13 to £22. Sun L £15. **Details:** 85 seats. 44 seats outside. V menu. Bar. Wheelchairs. Music. Parking.

■ Culgaith

LOCAL GEM
Mrs Miller's
British | £28
Hazel Dene Garden Centre, Culgaith, CA10 1QF
Tel no: (01768) 882520
mrsmillersculgaith.co.uk
£5 OFF £30

Somewhat hidden behind the clusters of outbuildings and enclosures at the back of the garden centre, Mrs Miller's is a tea-room and café that takes a relaxed approach. Lounge on leather sofas before the fire, trifling with a novel from the dresser. Local farm produce goes into the homely menus, resulting in well-seasoned, rillette-textured potted pork with apple and pistachio, and apricot chutney on the side, and then perhaps a fillet of crisped sea bass on mussel risotto, or chicken breast on an underlay of cabbage with fat bacon and onion. Fully loaded desserts include lemon tart with meringue shards, or Baileys crème brûlée.

▮ Grasmere
★ TOP 50 ★

Forest Side

Cooking score: 7
Modern British | £60
Keswick Road, Grasmere, LA22 9RN
Tel no: (015394) 35250
theforestside.com

£5 OFF ▬

Just down the road from Dove Cottage, where the Wordsworths once resided and Thomas De Quincey regularly stupefied himself with laudanum, Forest Side is the model of a modern Lakeland country house. The winding drive leads to a Victorian Gothic stone mansion, within which a contemporary boutique outfit on the grander scale has been conjured. The dining room is an expansive bare-boarded space with enough acreage between tables to keep noise levels on a rein, and staff who are effortlessly knowledgeable and charming with it. Kevin Tickle's period in the Rogan sanctum shines forth from every last foraged leaf and berry; if you still need convincing what aromatic strangeness and fascination can be derived from these once forgotten ingredients, step this way. From the moment a single new potato arrives in a ruff of alfalfa, the surprises keep on coming. A serving of beetroot spheres on Ragstone purée, garnished with an airy sourdough wafer fancifully styled a 'crumpet', might open the multi-course tasting menu, before a corpulent scallop muscles in, its guanciale-topped toasty brown surface echoed by charred onion petals, green leek and a sprinkling of smoky oats. Lemon sole has unsuspected depths of flavour, emphasised by a crowd of weeny Morecambe Bay shrimps in mace butter and sticks of salsify, while the Goosnargh duck is pinkly rendered, earthily matched by celeriac in various textures and intense damson jelly. Crunchy desserts are the rage, so scorched pear comes with a malted cracker, as well as a glass of staggeringly beautiful ginger beer, while a rhubarb composition is garnished with bright green

cubes of biscuit made with minty marigold leaves. Olives, butters and petits fours are sensational, too, and there's plenty of interest on the inspired wine list.
Chef/s: Kevin Tickle. **Open:** Wed to Sun L, all week D. **Meals:** set L £35 (3 courses). Set D £60 (3 courses). Tasting menu £70 (6 courses) to £85.
Details: 50 seats. V menu. Bar. Wheelchairs. Music. Parking. Children over 8 yrs only.

The Jumble Room

Cooking score: 1
International | £35
Langdale Road, Grasmere, LA22 9SU
Tel no: (015394) 35188
thejumbleroom.co.uk

▬

Andy and Chrissy Hill's loveable Jumble is the ultimate in personal hospitality. The idiosyncratic menu and unusual fit-out (featuring plenty of animal portraits) would give any chain-restaurant operator the horrors, which is probably why it's lasted more than 20 years. Start with Morecambe shrimp and pork dumplings or Whitby crab crostini with coriander, basil and chilli. A 'thriller from Manila' main course of seafood and chicken noodles with peanuts is courtesy of Filipino chef James O'Campo, while gingerbread is made to a 150-year-old recipe from Chrissy's family in Grasmere. 'Affordable' wines are from an enthusiastically annotated list.
Chef/s: Chrissy Hill and James O'Campo. **Open:** Mon and Wed to Sun D only. **Closed:** Tue, 10 to 26 Dec, weekends in Jan. **Meals:** main courses £15 to £25. **Details:** 50 seats. 8 seats outside. Music.

Symbols

🥄

▬ Accommodation is available
£30 Three courses for less than £30
£5 OFF £5-off voucher scheme
🍷 Notable wine list

■ Kirkby Lonsdale
Carter at the Sun Inn
Cooking score: 2
British | £34
6 Market Street, Kirkby Lonsdale, LA6 2AU
Tel no: (015242) 71965
sun-inn.info

Jenny and Iain Black may be the new custodians of this historic inn in the centre of Kirkby Lonsdale, but Sam Carter continues to head the kitchen, keeping true food values and a passion for sourcing the finest regional produce at the heart of the operation. Expect to find a traditional beamed bar with real ales and a short bar menu offering the likes of beer-battered fish and chips, and sirloin steak, with a smart, comfortable restaurant at the back. Here, the cooking bristles with up-to-the-minute ideas as well as classical variations, with dishes as diverse as poached hake with mushroom duxelles, brown-butter cauliflower and dill, and rosemary and garlic hogget with Crapaudine beetroot, pickled beetroot, Tenderstem broccoli and creamed potato. Standards remain high for desserts such as rhubarb brûlée or chocolate marquise. Sunday roasts have impressed, too. A compact, fairly priced wine list opens at £18.50.
Chef/s: Sam Carter. **Open:** Tue to Sun L, all week D. **Closed:** 25 Dec. **Meals:** main courses £22. Set D £28 (2 courses) to £34. Sun L £15 (1 course) to £20. **Details:** 59 seats. V menu. Bar. Wheelchairs. Music.

READERS RECOMMEND
The Crossing Point Café
International
7 Market Square, Kirkby Lonsdale, LA6 2AN
Tel no: (015242) 98050
crossingpointcafe.co.uk
'The food here is always inventive and above and beyond what you would expect in a café. They have a range of specials that often involve foraged herbs and bits and pieces from the local landscape.'

■ Sedbergh
Three Hares
Cooking score: 2
Modern European | £28
57 Main Street, Sedbergh, LA10 5AB
Tel no: (015396) 21058
threeharescafe.co.uk
£5 OFF £30

On the narrow little high street of Sedbergh, a Dales town that goes very dark and quiet after nightfall, the black-façaded Three Hares looks a beacon of cheer. Tea room by day, it opens on a few evenings a week for candlelit dinners focused on a menu of local materials, with meats the stars of the show. Hare itself might appear as loin and confit leg on truffled risotto, while good gamey venison loin partnered with black pudding is gently underpinned with swabs of peppery cauliflower purée. Otherwise, start with a Scotch quail's egg and beetroot, or grilled mackerel with a scallop and horseradishy onions, and don't miss the desserts, which will tease you back to schooldays with peanut-butter crunch mousse, with condensed milk ice cream, if you're up for something a little richer than blackberry sorbet and apple. The printed wine list offers some very nice gear by the glass, but no information about vintages.
Chef/s: Nina Matsunaga. **Open:** all week L, Thur to Sat D (Wed to Sun in summer). **Closed:** Mon (winter). **Meals:** main courses £13 to £30. **Details:** 25 seats. 4 seats outside. Music.

■ Windermere
Holbeck Ghyll
Cooking score: 6
Modern British | £68
Holbeck Lane, Windermere, LA23 1LU
Tel no: (015394) 32375
holbeckghyll.com

The new season brings another new chef to the stoves at Holbeck Ghyll in the youthful but extravagantly skilled shape of Jake Jones. While the old place still snoozes contentedly on its hillock above Windermere, with photographic sunsets or rain pelting out of white mist over the water equally captivating, the culinary action is hotting up. Jones brings a new sense of adventure to the menus, with dishes that exude originality, built on the all-important foraged ingredients as well as dazzling prime materials. A dish called 'The Hillside' looks like a particularly rewarding late breakfast bowl, with toasted hay, spring onion bulbs and clumps of enoki weaving their way up a Lakeland fell of sheep's cheese. Duck liver parfait is very light and loose, but convincingly rich, with aromatic notes of pine and verjus, while the main course of suckling lamb is a glorious trio of tender leg, crackled neck and a spicy-crumbed sweetbread ball in a nest of hay. Morels squishy with garlicky stock up the ante. For fish, it could be Gigha halibut in a welter of little shrimps, tiny raw mushrooms, seaweed and a smoky butter sauce. A pre-dessert of crème patissière and hazelnut granola then heralds the arrival of an apple and date creation, with nitro-blasted pie pastry, grainily puréed medjool dates and a screaming green sorbet of wood sorrel the highlights. The wine list is an authoritative document, as confident with Mosel Riesling and Friuli Cabernet Franc as with the crown jewels, with glass prices from £7.25.

Chef/s: Jake Jones. **Open:** all week L and D. **Meals:** set L £35 (2 courses). Set D £68. Tasting menu £70 to £90. **Details:** 28 seats. Bar. Wheelchairs. Music. Parking. Children over 12 yrs only.

lodge, with its heart in the gracious rooms of the original building. Development never seems to flag, and in November 2016 an adjunct to the main dining rooms, Gilpin Spice, was launched, offering dishes inspired by the old Silk Road trading routes. Hrishikesh Desai is a gifted practitioner of the modern British arts, too, as is apparent from menus in the now self-named restaurant, where Indian spices make discreet inroads into many dishes, and multi-layered complexity is guaranteed. Scallop ceviche is dressed in sherry vinegar, orange, ginger and chilli, and accompanied by cumined carrot purée and toasted hazelnuts, before Herdwick arrives in dual guise, the roast fillet and neck braised in Hyderabadi masala, alongside Jersey Royals, asparagus and peas in a gentle yoghurt dressing. Dessert might be almond tart garnished with gariguette strawberries, black pepper meringue, balsamic jelly and basil sorbet. With so many assertive aromatic notes, wines need to step up to the plate, and do so majestically, with a sophisticated and classy collection, from £32.

Chef/s: Hrishikesh Desai. **Open:** all week L and D. **Meals:** set L £35. Set D £65 (4 courses). Sun L £35. Tasting menu £85 (7 courses). **Details:** 58 seats. 26 seats outside. V menu. Children over 7 yrs only.

Hrish at Gilpin Hotel & Lake House

Cooking score: 5
Modern British | £65
Crook Road, Windermere, LA23 3NE
Tel no: (015394) 88818
thegilpin.co.uk

🍷 🛏️

Built as a country retreat in 1901, Gilpin hides among the winding roads around Windermere, its hotel operation expanded into the Lake House that was once a fishing

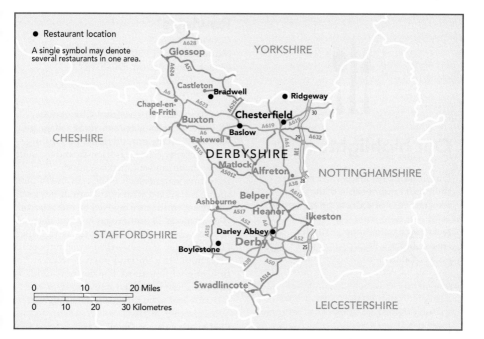

Baslow
Fischer's Baslow Hall
Cooking score: 6
Modern European | £78
Calver Road, Baslow, DE45 1RR
Tel no: (01246) 583259
fischers-baslowhall.co.uk

A seriously bookmarked gastro-destination for nigh on three decades, this grandiose mansion is something of an architectural *trompe l'oeil* — built in 1907 for a vicar with a penchant for mullioned windows, gabled wings and all things archaic. Inside, Baslow Hall signals its civilised pedigree with lofty ceilings, gilt mirrors and extravagant floral displays echoing the kitchen's high ambitions. Ingredients from the hotel's garden, Peak District farms and further afield are liberally scattered throughout the menus, and the result is a repertoire of intricately worked Anglo-European food — from goose liver with rhubarb, pistachio, chocolate and brioche to

roast loin of Cumbrian veal with crispy egg yolk, artichokes, grilled leeks and black truffle dressing. Head chef Rupert Rowley also injects some Asian zing into proceedings (five-spice monkfish with vegetable tempura and squid ink or slow-cooked Derbyshire pork jowl glazed in miso with brown shrimp, coconut and sweet-and-sour sauce, for example), while desserts are deliberately complex constructions such as salted-caramel tart with espresso jelly and mascarpone ice cream. The weighty wine list pleases oenophiles and everyday drinkers alike.

Chef/s: Rupert Rowley. **Open:** all week L and D. **Closed:** 25 and 26 Dec. **Meals:** set L £23 (2 courses) to £30. Set D £63 (2 courses) to £78. Sun L £38 (2 courses) to £45. Tasting menu £65 to £150. **Details:** 60 seats. V menu. Bar. Parking. Children over 8 yrs only (exc Sun L).

Our highlights...

Our undercover inspectors reveal their most memorable dishes from another year of extraordinary eating.

Not French onion soup at **Ynyshir.** So clever - a dashi stock poured over slow cooked onion, with delicate cubes of tofu. So full of umami flavours, served in winsome handmade bowls. It was a very high starting point - you would think it would all go down from there... but it didn't.

From the **Harwood Arms, roast Norfolk quail** with a black pudding Scotch egg and mushroom ketchup. A seemingly straightforward dish that turns out to be quite sophisticated, and the black pudding Scotch egg was packed full of all the right flavours.

Pan-fried sea bass with black quinoa at **The Ritz**: it was very classical, perfectly done and the right size, full of flavour and texture - the ultimate grand comfort food.

Pineapple 'financier', the richness balanced by the flavours of passionfruit curd, lime and coconut ice cream. At **Medlar** in Chelsea.

The **tarte Tatin** at **L'Absinthe**. It was a fairly pedestrian, very grand-mère French dinner and then this slightly scruffy Tatin turned up - never mind the presentation, the flavour was fantastic.

Rowley's

Cooking score: 1
Modern British | £30
Church Lane, Baslow, DE45 1RY
Tel no: (01246) 583880
rowleysrestaurant.co.uk

It's a short, scenic drive from Chatsworth House to Rowley's, a pretty stone village pub with a bar on the ground floor and a dining room upstairs. Service is friendly and the staff know the menu well, making good recommendations such as the crab and salmon spring roll served with sweetcorn, lime confit and sweet chilli sauce enjoyed by one reporter. A 'ginormous' 24-hour sugar-pit beef short rib in Xérès glaze ('sweet and tender') with grilled Hispi cabbage and salt-baked sweet potatoes gives notice that the cooking is hearty, so finishing with steamed 'Rowley poly' with custard might be 'several steps too far – I virtually had to be rolled out of the place'. Wines from £18.50.
Chef/s: Adam Harper. **Open:** all week L, Mon to Sat D. **Closed:** 25 Dec. **Meals:** main courses £15 to £24. Set L £17 (2 courses) to £21. Set D £25 (2 courses) to £31. Sun L £25. **Details:** 80 seats. Bar. Wheelchairs. Music. Parking.

■ Boylestone
The Lighthouse Restaurant

Cooking score: 4
Modern British | £50
New Road, Boylestone, DE6 5AA
Tel no: (01335) 330658
the-lighthouse-restaurant.co.uk
£5 OFF

It's quite tricky to find the Lighthouse as it is in the car park behind the Rose & Crown on the road to Church Broughton – 'we had to u-turn more than once to finally spot it'. However, it clearly doesn't cause much bother, because every table was full when we visited. An attractive brick barn decorated in neutral tones with fat church candles lining the oak beams, it's open for dinner only, working to a tasting menu format of nine courses in the contemporary gastronomic style. Highlights on our visit were sweet langoustine with bacon dashi, lardo, turnip dumpling, kombu and yuzu, a 'beautiful-looking dish' of hand-dived scallop with charred onion, squid cracker, charcoal ash, lemon and crispy onions, and a delicate truffle-stuffed quail with crispy skin, hollandaise, asparagus, truffle gravy and nasturtium. A brace of desserts could bring a bowl of English strawberries with vanilla mousse, toasted rice and meringue, and then a sublime chocolate tree trunk with sour lime mousse, cocoa sorbet and smoked sea salt. A well-annotated and wide-ranging wine list opens at £18.

Chef/s: Jonathan Hardy. **Open:** Wed to Sat D only. **Closed:** Sun, Mon, Tue, first 2 weeks Jan, 2 weeks Jul. **Meals:** tasting menu £50. **Details:** 40 seats. Bar. Wheelchairs. Music. Parking.

■ Bradwell
The Samuel Fox Country Inn

Cooking score: 4
British | £32
Stretfield Road, Bradwell, S33 9JT
Tel no: (01433) 621562
samuelfox.co.uk

£5 OFF 🛏

In the verdant Hope Valley in the heart of Dales country, James Duckett's village inn is named after the inventor of the modern umbrella, who was born in Bradwell. The main dining area feels distinctly more like stepping into somebody's living room than a pub restaurant, and is run with homely hospitality to match. With four evening sessions a week, plus Sunday lunch, Duckett runs a tight ship, and the culinary focus shows in cured sea trout with pickled fennel in orange and saffron sauce, or an ingenious way of serving summer asparagus alongside a boiled egg parcelled in brik pastry and deep-fried. For main, there could be gorgeously squidgy gnocchi with pickled beetroot, charred lettuce and Colston Bassett Stilton, or slow-roast pork belly with crisped cannelloni, spring cabbage and butternut squash, topped

with crackling and sauced with cider. Desserts are on the hefty side, which is as well to know before you set about sticky toffee pudding with stout ice cream. A varied wine list opens at £4.80 a glass.

Chef/s: James Duckett. **Open:** Sun L, Wed to Sat D. **Closed:** Mon, Tue, 2 to 23 Jan. **Meals:** main courses £14 to £28. Tasting menu £49 (7 courses). **Details:** 36 seats. 15 seats outside. V menu. Bar. Wheelchairs. Music. Parking.

■ Chesterfield

LOCAL GEM
Calabria
Italian | £30
30 Glumangate, Chesterfield, S40 1TX
Tel no: (01246) 559944
calabriacucina.co.uk

Calabria is the sun-kissed toe of Italy, Chesterfield is a market town 24 miles north of Derby, and thanks to Vittorio Risorto, the good folk of the latter can get a taste of the former. It's a relaxed place, open for breakfast, lunches including ciabatta sandwiches (salumi with salsa, say) and pasta such as fricelli with mushrooms and Gorgonzola, and an evening menu that might take you from spicy Calabrese bruschetta, via Derbyshire pork chop with sage and onion involtino, to tiramisu. There's a fixed-price evening menu as well, and regional Italian wines.

■ Darley Abbey
Darleys

Cooking score: 3
Modern British | £40
Darley Abbey Mill, Haslams Lane, Darley Abbey, DE22 1DZ
Tel no: (01332) 364987
darleys.com

Housed in a beautiful old mill set on a weir, with most tables offering views of the water, Darleys is considered a special night out by its fiercely loyal customer base, no doubt helped by an unforgettable, heavily draped, pelmeted and cut-glass interior that 'feels smart'.

Jonathan Hobson's confident way with classic preparations deals adroitly with seared scallops, matching them well with braised red lentils, roast ham hock, toasted breadcrumbs and lemon; the skrei cod with curried mussel cream is recommended, too. Among main courses, correctly timed loin of Scottish venison with sweet potato purée, roast Derbyshire parsnips and espresso sauce, and Gressingham duck with Savoy cabbage, salt-baked turnip, pearl barley and treacle sauce have been praised. That same occasion produced a show-stopping caramel banana soufflé with vanilla ice cream. Service is, however, more willing than skilled: 'none were able to answer basic questions or offer advice'. Wines from £18.95.

Chef/s: Jonathan Hobson. **Open:** all week L, Mon to Sat D. **Closed:** 25 Dec for 2 weeks. **Meals:** main courses £23 to £26. Set L £20 (2 courses) to £25. Sun L £30. Tasting menu £50 (7 courses). **Details:** 60 seats. V menu. Bar. Music. Parking.

appear with ricotta dumpling and wild garlic, while a crisp-skinned sea bass is teamed with crabmeat, avocado, a swish of lemongrass butter sauce, diced watermelon and Jersey Royals filled with a chive cream topped with caviar – 'all of it beautifully balanced'. Roasted breast of Norfolk squab, with butternut squash, pea shoots, redcurrant and molasses dressing is well executed, while at dessert stage, the fusion of aromatics, mango, pepper and basil with candied chilli and coconut milk parfait is 'rather thrilling'. The exceptional wine list, arranged by style, features fine vintages and broad-minded global coverage. A page of recommendations neatly summarises the range.

Chef/s: Tessa Bramley and Nathan Smith. **Open:** Tue to Fri L, Tue to Sat D. **Closed:** Sun, Mon, 26 Dec to 5 Jan, 1 week Easter, last week Jul, first week Aug, bank hols. **Meals:** set L £40 (3 courses). Set D £60 (4 courses). Tasting menu £70. **Details:** 48 seats. 20 seats outside. Bar. Wheelchairs. Parking. Children over 10 yrs only.

▮ Ridgeway
The Old Vicarage
Cooking score: 6
Modern British | £70
Ridgeway Moor, Ridgeway, S12 3XW
Tel no: (0114) 2475814
theoldvicarage.co.uk
🍾★

In pastoral surroundings overlooking the Moss Valley conservation area, this comfortable, stone-built early Victorian church house is surprisingly handy for the M1 and the centre of Sheffield. The décor, 'much as you'd expect in an old vicarage', has a comfortable drawing room and a dining room with dark, carved-wood antique chairs at linen-dressed tables with cut crystal and lovely old silverware. For the past 30 years, chef/proprietor Tessa Bramley has devoted plenty of attention to making sure everything runs smoothly. Her cooking, with long-time collaborator Nathan Smith, is led by local and own-grown produce, which is used to create a simple yet sophisticated repertoire of dishes. Thus, new season's asparagus and girolles

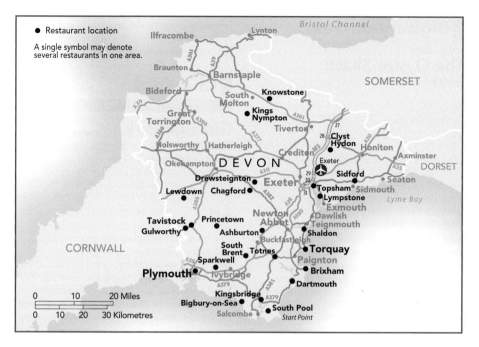

- Restaurant location

A single symbol may denote several restaurants in one area.

Ashburton

★ NEW ENTRY ★

The Old Library

Cooking score: 3
Modern European | £35
North Street, Ashburton, TQ13 7QH
Tel no: (01364) 652896
theoldlibraryrestaurant.co.uk

£5
OFF

Look round the back of the library building to the town car park to find the entrance to Joe Suttie and Amy Mitchell's dynamic all-day venue, which evolved from a pop-up but has now put down deeper roots. Very basic furnishings, photographic prints on the stark white walls and a kitchen that's part of the room create a kick-back atmosphere, and the frequently changing menus, which are provisioned by Devon food heroes, are full of the kinds of enticements that clued-up diners want to see. A little plate of Ibérico sobrasada, spreadable Spanish sausage in paprika-scarlet, comes with rye toast and local honey, puréed beetroot and a pair of cubic pig's cheek croquettes. Next up might be sea bass, roasted in olive oil and dressed with slicks of peperonata, charred fennel, pickled caperberries and asparagus, or perhaps braised lamb shoulder dressed in dukkah with sweet potato purée, apricots and yoghurt. Bright ideas keep rolling through to desserts, which might take in cardamom egg custard tart in a fetching shade of green, served with Amaretto prunes and crème fraîche. A small handful of so-so wines is supplemented by decent ales and ciders to take up the slack.

Chef/s: Amy Mitchell and Joe Suttie. **Open:** Mon and Wed to Sun L, Mon and Wed to Sat D. **Closed:** Tue, 23 Dec to 13 Jan. **Meals:** main courses £17 to £20. Sun L £15 (2 courses) to £20. **Details:** 30 seats. Wheelchairs. Music. Parking.

▐ Bigbury-on-Sea

LOCAL GEM
The Oyster Shack
Seafood | £30
Stakes Hill, Bigbury-on-Sea, TQ7 4BE
Tel no: (01548) 810876
oystershack.co.uk

£5
OFF

This lively seafooder's winning formula takes in plenty of (heated) outdoor seating, a suitably relaxed atmosphere, welcoming and attentive service, and a global approach to cooking locally caught fish and shellfish. There's no doubting the freshness of the raw materials: crispy smelt aïoli, mussels with garlic and white wine and seafood curry have been outstanding. Praise, too, for a good-value lunch of grilled fillet of hake with warm couscous salad, mint, yoghurt and crispy straw potatoes, and lemon posset with lemon drizzle and pistachio gems. Wines from £14.

▐ Brixham

LOCAL GEM
Poopdeck
Seafood | £28
14 The Quay, Brixham, TQ5 8AW
Tel no: (01803) 858681
poopdeckrestaurant.com

£30

The Brixham quayside, where much of the south west's seafood is landed, could scarcely be a more fitting location for an unreconstructed fish restaurant of the old school, perched on the first floor above a shop selling tourist mementoes. Hefty plates of efficiently cooked marine produce include scallop and bacon skewers with balsamic-dressed salad, cider-sauced lemon sole with mussels and leeks, and grilled brill on ratatouille with new potatoes, plus the all-important platters, which are liberally loaded with the good things of the sea. There are a couple of meat dishes, too, while puddings, such as cream-lashed chocolate torte, are the last word in indulgence.

▐ Chagford

★ TOP 50 ★

Gidleigh Park
Cooking score: 7
Modern European | £125
Chagford, TQ13 8HH
Tel no: (01647) 432367
gidleigh.co.uk

The long approach through a seemingly endless network of narrow lanes makes the sight of the mock-Tudor mansion very welcome. A lively stream gushes past the front, woodland presses in, and while 'awe-inspiring' may be overdoing it, this is certainly a magnificent location. Inside it feels properly enveloping with panelled rooms and comfortable sofas. The two dining rooms benefit from well-spaced tables and seem to mandate a sense of occasion, which is amply supplied by rather formal service and by Michael Wignall's intricate and complex dishes. Meals are elaborated further with appetisers and pre-desserts, and modern partnerships abound: in a neat arrangement of cassoulet of shellfish, for example, a triumph of lobster, razor clam, squid, cuttlefish gnocchi and poached quail's egg (and 'all gone in a moment') or, in a mixture of sweet, salt and smoke, cubes of torched eel are given surprising intensity by aerated white chocolate in a starter that's dressed with dabs of jellied consommé and Granny Smith apple dotted with oscietra caviar. This all gives notice that dishes are labour intensive with many tiny elements and intricate combinations. 'Perfectly lightly cooked' turbot is teamed with a nugget of lobster, white asparagus and sea vegetables, flavours intensified by blobs of sardine dressing, while duck appears with St Enodoc asparagus, Douglas fir and parsley cream, Hereford snails and artichokes. With so many bells and whistles, however, dishes can miss the main target – the 'wow' comes from admiring technical achievement rather than from any direct hit on the plate. Nonetheless, this remains a seriously good restaurant, delivering an experience beyond the sum of its parts. As for wine, the list is broad in its scope and authority, stuffed with VIP producers, including plenty of French classics, and with an extensive selection of halves. Bottle entry level is £35.

Chef/s: Michael Wignall. **Open:** all week L and D. **Closed:** 10 days Jan. **Meals:** set L £60 to £75 (7 courses). Set D £125. Tasting menu £145 (10 courses). **Details:** 45 seats. V menu. Bar. Wheelchairs. Parking. Children over 8 yrs only.

■ Clyst Hydon
The Five Bells Inn
Cooking score: 1
Modern British | £35
Main Street, Clyst Hydon, EX15 2NT
Tel no: (01884) 277288
fivebells.uk.com

A thatched inn in a neat country garden, the Five Bells has character on the inside, too, with regulation beams and slate floors. You'll find local ales from Otter Brewery and Butcombe on the pumps, there's a games room and a kitchen that turns out some impressive modern British food. Pub staples such as Scotch egg are done well (a duck egg version with piccalilli), and regional ingredients such as Fowey mussels get a good outing (in Ventons cider sauce, say). Dartmoor Dexter beef makes a fine cottage pie, while grilled plaice might come with romanesco, almonds and sorrel. Expect classic roasts on Sundays.

Chef/s: Ian Webber. **Open:** all week L and D. **Closed:** 25 and 26 Dec. **Meals:** main courses £13 to £20. Set L and early D £16 (2 courses) to £20. **Details:** 74 seats. 80 seats outside. Wheelchairs. Music. Parking.

■ Dartmouth
The Seahorse
Cooking score: 5
Seafood | £45
5 South Embankment, Dartmouth, TQ6 9BH
Tel no: (01803) 835147
seahorserestaurant.co.uk
£5 OFF

A few doors along from the Dartmouth branch of Rockfish (see entry), moored on the south quayside, is the flagship of the Tonks/ Prowse flotilla. Heave open the heavy wood door to enter a high-ceilinged space, walled with wine shelves on one side, with peeps into the kitchen from one end of the banquette on the other. The place runs on well-oiled rails, with unintrusive, flawlessly capable service, and the menu of unreconstructed Italian-based fish cookery is as simple as you like – bowls of mussels, shellfish pasta, rich fish stews and whole charcoal-grilled beasts – with quality ringing out at every mouthful. An inspection lunch of octopus and potato salad in oregano vinaigrette, fire-roasted sea bass on thick peperonata with a side of multitudinous zucchini fritti, and a brace of roast figs in Moscato grappa syrup with amaretto ice cream produced nothing but unalloyed satisfaction. There are one or two meat dishes too, and a list of Italian-led wines of obvious pedigree, from £19.

Chef/s: Jake Bridgewood. **Open:** Tue to Sat L and D. **Closed:** Sun, Mon, 25 and 26 Dec, 1 Jan. **Meals:** main courses £19 to £36. Set L and early D £20 (2 courses). **Details:** 40 seats. 6 seats outside. Bar. Music.

LOCAL GEM

Rockfish

Seafood | £25

8 South Embankment, Dartmouth, TQ6 9BH

Tel no: (01803) 832800

therockfish.co.uk

£30

Overlooking the Dart, this seafood specialist was the first in a chain of six for Mitch Tonks and Mat Prowse. Here they set out the Rockfish stall – sustainable fish, simply cooked, but with a few flourishes (there are three versions of tartare sauce) to keep things interesting. Try devilled Torbay sprats with aïoli, Rockfish fritto misto, Dover sole a la plancha or, if seafood's not your game, a decent haloumi or chicken burger. Puddings are mainly based on the house soft whip ice cream, and there's a neat craft beer list.

■ Drewsteignton
The Old Inn

Cooking score: 4

Modern European | £52

Drewsteignton, EX6 6QR

Tel no: (01647) 281276

old-inn.co.uk

If you take the name at face value and come here expecting a paragon of rustic antiquity, you may be disappointed: this rather plain-looking 17th-century staging post has moved resolutely with the times and now does duty as a warm-hearted, professionally run restaurant-with-rooms – albeit one with a blazing fire in the old stone hearth. Chef/proprietor Duncan Walker cooks with assurance, technical know-how and a feel for proper flavour, eschewing modish foams and smears in favour of thoughtful, coherent assemblages – perhaps grilled fillet of sole with braised endive and citrus juices or sautéed calves' sweetbreads with boudin noir and Savoy cabbage. His smart, gimmick-free dinner menu also nods to current trends (spiced pork belly with scallops and lemongrass, say), although desserts such as tarte Tatin or passion fruit parfait with chocolate and warm fruits show his fondness for well-tried classic themes and French-inspired artistry. Meanwhile, the pin-sharp 40-bin wine list promises some surprisingly fine drinking.

Chef/s: Duncan Walker. **Open:** Fri and Sat L, Wed to Sat D. **Closed:** Sun, Mon, Tue, 3 weeks Jan. **Meals:** set L £32. Set D £46 (2 courses) to £52. **Details:** 16 seats. Bar. Children over 12 yrs only.

■ Gulworthy
The Horn of Plenty

Cooking score: 3

Modern British | £50

Gulworthy, PL19 8JD

Tel no: (01822) 832528

thehornofplenty.co.uk

One of Devon's most inspiringly sited country hotels, the Horn sits on an eminence panoramically overlooking the Tamar Valley, with Cornwall in one sector and Devon in the other. The glassed extension that is the dining room capitalises on that ravishing prospect, and there's an air of genteel tranquillity. Ashley Wright's cooking is fresh, seasonal and colourful, offering Brixham crab with bitter pink grapefruit and avocado purée to kick off a summer lunch, with cured sea trout in dill emulsion to follow. In the evenings, things step up a gear for locally farmed veal with salt-baked swede and shallots, or pan-roasted hake with lobster agnolotti and carrots. South-western produce is the headliner throughout, all the way to cheesecake flavoured with elderflower from the garden, alongside rhubarb sorbet, or immaculate, densely textured lemon posset with Cornish strawberry compote. Themed menus such as a Celebration of Seafood add depth to the operation. Wines start at £5.50 a standard glass.

Chef/s: Ashley Wright. **Open:** all week L and D. **Meals:** set L £20 (2 courses) to £25. Set D £50. Tasting menu £65. **Details:** 50 seats. 20 seats outside. V menu. Bar. Wheelchairs. Music. Parking.

▌Kings Nympton

LOCAL GEM

The Grove Inn

British | £22
Kings Nympton, EX37 9ST
Tel no: (01769) 580406
thegroveinn.co.uk

Hovering on a curve in the road in a slip of a Devon village, the Grove Inn is a great local resource, a place for the exchange of news and the drinking of decent ale. It also furnishes some dependable pub food, along the lines of poppadom-crumbed chicken tikka Scotch egg with lemon mayonnaise for dipping, pan-roasted hake in salsa verde on rapeseed-oiled mash, and the house speciality, a sticky toffee pudding to get stuck into, served with butterscotch sauce and local marmalade ice cream. As well as the beers, there's a serviceable wine list, with standard glasses from £4.

▌Kingsbridge

LOCAL GEM

Beachhouse

Seafood | £30
South Milton Sands, Kingsbridge, TQ7 3JY
Tel no: (01548) 561144
beachhousedevon.com

Why don't more British beaches have eateries like Tamara Costin's 'totally unpretentious' restaurant? And it's not just a source of fish finger sandwiches and bumper breakfasts. The quality of the fish and seafood is second to none, and in providing what visitors to South Milton Sands need, the kitchen has not overlooked the genuine requirement for, say, whole Start Bay crab with mayo and salad, Italian seafood stew with crusty bread, or plaice with caper lemon butter – or a glass of crisp white to go alongside.

▌Knowstone
The Masons Arms

Cooking score: 4
Modern British | £48
Knowstone, EX36 4RY
Tel no: (01398) 341231
masonsarmsdevon.co.uk

Snuggled in an Exmoor backwater, this medieval thatched inn earns full marks for its rural setting. It also promises a beamed bar with real ales, a rocking chair by the fire and a vaulted dining room done out in playful style with bright wooden furniture and knick-knacks. Chef/landlord Mark Dodson once worked alongside Michel Roux, and he treats West Country produce with finesse as well as a broad-minded sensibility: sea bass is paired with white bean ragoût and carrot ketchup, while breast of duck keeps company with pearl barley risotto and plum jam. Meanwhile, the spirit of haute cuisine reappears in an escalope of foie gras sharpened with citrus fruits and a dish of beef fillet with fondant potato, ox cheek, confit onion and red wine jus. 'A touch more sophistication' would be welcome, although desserts such as apricot soufflé with butterscotch ice cream are textbook. Well-chosen wines by the glass.
Chef/s: Mark Dodson. **Open:** Tue to Sat L and D.
Closed: Sun, Mon, first week Jan, Feb half-term, last week Aug. **Meals:** main courses £21 to £25. Set L £21 (2 courses) to £25. Tasting menu £75.
Details: 28 seats. 16 seats outside. Bar. Music. Parking. Children over 5 yrs only at D.

▌Lewdown
Lewtrenchard Manor

Cooking score: 5
Modern British | £50
Lewdown, EX20 4PN
Tel no: (01566) 783222
lewtrenchard.co.uk

Making an appearance in the Domesday Book, Lewtrenchard Manor was given a thorough-going Victorian refit by a certain

Sabine Baring-Gould (of 'Onward, Christian Soldiers' fame), who acquired the mullioned windows, heavy oak panelling and even the front porch from the remnants of other buildings nearby. Nowadays, however, the house is better known as an idyllic retreat, with two antique dining rooms providing the atmospheric backdrop to chef Matthew Peryer's contemporary cooking. Produce from West Country suppliers and Lewtrenchard's kitchen garden are used to creative effect: ceviche of monkfish and Devon crab gets its zing from pickled ginger and Thai purée, while roast fillet of sea bass is given a Mediterranean flavour with crispy salsify, truffle gnocchi and girolles. Devon lamb is a star turn, perhaps served as a duo with spinach, white bean purée and wild garlic, while dessert could be spiced poached pears with toasted crémeux, honeycomb and burnt-honey ice cream. The wine list is a well-rounded global selection with a dozen by the glass.

Chef/s: Matthew Peryer. **Open:** all week L and D. **Meals:** set L £21 (2 courses) to £26. Set D £50. Sun L £28. Tasting menu £69 (7 courses). **Details:** 40 seats. 15 seats outside. V menu. Bar. Wheelchairs. Parking. Children over 8 yrs only at D.

▌Lympstone

★ NEW ENTRY ★

Lympstone Manor

Cooking score: 6
Modern European | £115
Courtlands Lane, Lympstone, EX8 3NZ
Tel no: (01395) 202040
lympstonemanor.co.uk

🍷 🛏

It's been a while since Michael Caines has had a kitchen to call his own. The man is never idle of course, but his departure from Gidleigh Park in 2015 marked a pause. Now he returns, and in some style, in a freshly renovated Georgian manor house that enjoys a panoramic vista over east Devon's rolling sward, with the Exe estuary in the foreground. Elegant, light-toned chic distinguishes the interiors, which centre on a trio of dining rooms hung with original paintings by contemporary artists. The interregnum has given Caines new energy, seen to resonant effect at an early inspection. A warm salad of Cornish lobster, mango and new potato is jointly dressed with curried mayonnaise and a vivid cardamom vinaigrette for a virtuoso opener, which was followed by Powderham lamb from just across the river, with minted pea purée and new broad beans in tapenade jus. Fish might be braised turbot with Exe cockles and mussels in tomato and basil. The vogue for light desserts is celebrated in pistachio soufflé with matching ice cream, and triumphantly in chocolate-coated banana parfait with candied peanuts, salt caramel gel and lime sorbet. A resourceful wine list is overseen by a thoroughly well-versed sommelier, and opens with a great glass selection from £6.

Chef/s: Michael Caines. **Open:** all week L and D. **Meals:** set L £45 (2 courses) to £55. Set D £115 (3 courses). Tasting menu £140 (9 courses). **Details:** 60 seats. Bar. Wheelchairs. Music. Parking. Children over 8 yrs only.

▌Plymouth

The Greedy Goose

Cooking score: 4
Modern British | £32
Prysten House, Finewell Street, Plymouth, PL1 2AE
Tel no: (01752) 252001
thegreedygoose.co.uk

£5
OFF

The location, in what is reputedly Plymouth's oldest building, dating from the early days of the reign of Henry VII, has a lustre all its own, enhanced by the indoor well and a pretty courtyard for either looking out on or sitting in, depending. Ben Palmer's monthly changing modern British repertoire draws them in for the likes of chicken liver parfait with pickled prunes, or an all-inclusive starter of duck egg with an oyster, artichoke, smoked ham and white truffle. Mains are sturdily constructed plates of various cuts – pork belly

and cheek with black pudding, for example, or breast and rolled leg of Creedy Carver duck with wet polenta – while hake appears in Indian livery with sag aloo, a bhaji and yoghurt. As is the way these days, it can all be bundled up into a tasting menu, and desserts mine the best sort of populism with rhubarb and custard or shortbread-crumbed blueberry cheesecake. A fair few wines on the list come in three glass sizes, with standard measures starting at £4.50.
Chef/s: Ben Palmer. **Open:** Tue to Sun L, Tue to Sat D. **Closed:** Mon, 25 to 30 Dec. **Meals:** main courses £14 to £32. Set L and early D £11 (2 courses) to £13. Tasting menu £55. **Details:** 75 seats. 40 seats outside. Bar. Wheelchairs. Music. No children under 4 yrs (exc Sun)

Rock Salt
Cooking score: 2
Modern British | £26
31 Stonehouse Street, Plymouth, PL1 3PE
Tel no: (01752) 225522
rocksaltcafe.co.uk

Rock Salt is the Plymouth-born Jenkins family's labour of love, a vibrant transformation of an old corner boozer in the Stonehouse district into an all-day eatery for the times. Since opening in 2011, the place has been made new, with an airy wood-and-white ambience and lilac tub chairs under the skylight in the extension. David Jenkins cooks modern British bistro food with plenty of Asian influences, seen in sticky pulled pork with papaya, bhaji and peanuts, to mains such as stone bass in Thai mussel chowder with samphire and crab salad. There are big, assertive flavours going on all over the place, extending to vegetarian dishes like chestnut and pumpkin gnocchi with pine nuts and goats' cheese in sage butter, and the hefty burgers that are dressed in tomato and chorizo chutney. Finish by floating off on a blackberry cloud, with poached pear, pear sorbet, meringue and pistachios. Breakfasts, brunches

and a Sunset menu for early birds indicate the determination to keep everyone happy, and wines from £15.95 play their part, too.
Chef/s: David Jenkins. **Open:** all week L and D. **Closed:** 25 and 26 Dec. **Meals:** main courses £11 to £23. Set L £16 (2 courses) to £20. Set D £17 (2 courses) to £20. Sun L £15. Tasting menu £50 (7 courses). **Details:** 80 seats. V menu. Bar. Music.

LOCAL GEM
Lemon Tree Café & Bistro
Modern European | £15
2 Haye Road South, Elburton, Plymouth, PL9 8HJ
Tel no: (01752) 481117
lemontreecafe.co.uk

The Lemon Tree manages to be a vital hub of the villagey suburb of Elburton, despite only being open from 9am to 3 in the afternoon. They will book you in for a meze party in the evening if you're a group of 10 or more. Hot paninis, thick-cut sandwiches, omelettes made with free-range eggs, croque monsieur, it's simple stuff, with smoked haddock chowder and Sicilian meatballs about as racy as it gets. Drink house red, white or Prosecco, and bring cash.

Princetown
Prince Hall Hotel
Cooking score: 3
British | £40
Princetown, PL20 6SA
Tel no: (01822) 890403
princehall.co.uk

There isn't really even a village hereabouts, just a tree-shaded driveway on a turning off the B3357, more or less halfway across Dartmoor, with sheep and cattle ambling along the road. Buried among trees, the Prince Hall is a country house with a lived-in feel, one that welcomes dogs with a dish of snack-treats at reception. Large monochrome prints of ponies, bulls and wild boar glare out from the dining room walls, where nostalgic British cooking from the era before Continental experimentalism started changing everything is the stock-in-trade. A fillet of grilled mackerel comes with sweetly pickled enoki and thick horseradish hollandaise, prior to a serving of sliced Devon beef fillet in garlic and thyme butter on a heap of seasonal veg. Properly tempting desserts include a nifty take on baked raspberry cheesecake, served with a big scoop of piercing mango sorbet. Hearty breakfasts of Dartmoor fare are worth the stay. The serviceable wine list opens with standard glasses at £5.25.

Chef/s: Reece Thompson. **Open:** all week L and D. **Meals:** main courses £15 to £27. Sun L £15. **Details:** 30 seats. V menu. Bar. Parking.

Shaldon

★ NEW ENTRY ★

Ode & Co.
Cooking score: 1
Italian | £20
Coast View Holiday Park, Shaldon, TQ14 0BG
Tel no: (01626) 818450
odetruefood.com
£30

Shaldon's ODE (see entry) has propagated into a café, an outside catering business and now this box-fresh eco-haven sitting in a refined holiday park above the sea on the southern flank of the Teign estuary. Terrace tables allow for the blowing away of cobwebs, or there are window-ledge stools indoors for when it's sheeting down. From the open kitchen counter, pizzas are the main business, 10-inchers made with strong unbleached flour, their bases wafer-thin, blistered in the wood oven. Canonical versions of pepperoni and margherita are offered, but we got stuck into the firecracker chicken, with slivered red chilli, mushrooms and flat parsley. Start with Dorset air-dried ham with mustard-seeded gherkins, citrus-doused olives and rocket, and if the Montezuma chocolate délice is offered, don't swerve it. A short list of wines, beers and juices supplements the decanters of tap water.

Open: Wed to Sun L, Wed to Sat D. **Closed:** Mon, Tue. **Meals:** small plates £4 to £5. Pizzas £8 to £10. **Details:** 70 seats. 30 seats outside.

ODE Dining
Cooking score: 6
Modern British | £55
21 Fore Street, Shaldon, TQ14 0DE
Tel no: (01626) 873977
odetruefood.com
£5 OFF

With two cafés, a travelling pizza van and even a microbrewery on the go, Tim and Clare Bouget are merrily spreading their eco-friendly message across Devon – although their original ODE restaurant still commands most attention. Despite extremely limited opening times and no-choice tasting menus as the only option, this bijou terracotta-tiled dining room is a must-visit, notable for its strictly observed green credentials and crusading approach to organic, local and sustainably sourced ingredients. Creative seasonal cooking is Tim's forte, and he piles on diverse flavours with the sort of brio you'd expect from a well-travelled gastronaut – serving wild garlic tempura with black garlic aïoli, sweet potato blini and goats' curd, for example. Elsewhere, seared loin of fallow deer is given a burnt-onion crust alongside a sugar-cured haunch croquette, roasted carrot and coffee, while caramelised squid is invigorated with Passito sweet wine, salsa verde, almond crumb and Devon flowers. Expect virtuoso desserts such as lemon posset with candied lemon, homemade yoghurt, gin granita and honeycomb. Wines are gleaned from hands-on organic and biodynamic producers.

Chef/s: Tim Bouget. **Open:** Fri and Sat D only. **Closed:** Sun to Thur. **Meals:** tasting menu £55 (7 courses). **Details:** 24 seats. V menu. Music.

Sidford
The Salty Monk
Cooking score: 2
Modern British | £35
Church Street, Sidford, EX10 9QP
Tel no: (01395) 513174
saltymonk.co.uk
£5 OFF 🛏

The site of a monastic salt storehouse back in the 16th century, the Witheridges' restaurant-with-rooms is located in a tranquil spot not far from the coast at Sidmouth. There has lately been some consolidation of the originally twin-track restaurant approach, and a unified new menu offers greater concentration of Andy Witheridge's resources. Classical underpinnings are on show in a starter of scallops, squid and prawns airlifted into a buttery puff pastry basket with julienned vegetables, napped in saffron cream, while main courses feature artful presentations of duck breast, which comes with a herb-crumbled duck confit tartlet, smoked onion purée and champ, or of sea bass, lightly sautéed and served on red wine risotto with a dressing of coriander yoghurt. To finish, there might be baked vanilla cheesecake, served warm with honey-roast figs and vanilla ice cream. A carefully compiled wine list, many organic and biodynamic, is grouped by style and opens at £19.50.
Chef/s: Andy Witheridge. **Open:** Tue to Sat D only. **Closed:** Mon, Jan. **Meals:** main courses £17 to £30. Tasting menu £65. **Details:** 35 seats. 20 seats outside. V menu. Bar. Wheelchairs. Music. Parking.

Average price

The average price denotes the price of a three-course meal without wine.

South Brent
Glazebrook House
Cooking score: 4
Modern British | £43
Wrangaton Road, South Brent, TQ10 9JE
Tel no: (01364) 73322
glazebrookhouse.com
£5 OFF 🛏

Hidden among densely wooded country lanes on the southern fringe of Dartmoor, Glazebrook is something to see inside. Eye-catching elements of the interior design include the ostrich skeleton that greets arrivals in the lobby and the photo mural of a bare-knuckle pugilist of yore who stands guard in the tasting room. There's been a bit of a revolving door in the kitchen in recent years, and the place would benefit from some culinary stability, but Josh Ackland is rising to the challenge. The five-course taster at inspection produced good goats' cheese parfait garnished with spring carrots, followed by a confit duck egg yolk with shredded ham croquette and asparagus. Croquettes and deep-fried items of one sort or another rather over-featured, though never perhaps more satisfyingly as in the deep-fried crumbed oyster that garnished a snowy-white cut of plaice. Creedy Carver duck breast was pink and flavourful, with adequately rendered fat, on a slew of creamy peas, while the chocolate and orange délice with orange ice cream was a refreshing finisher. Accompanying wines on the flight are a touch hit-and-miss for matching, but it's a good list, and there are expertly crafted cocktails in the well-stocked bar.
Chef/s: Joshua Ackland. **Open:** all week L and D. **Closed:** 10 days mid Jan. **Meals:** main courses £16 to £34. Set L £15 (2 courses) to £20. Tasting menu £45 (5 courses) to £64. **Details:** 45 seats. 24 seats outside. Bar. Wheelchairs. Music. Parking.

▌South Pool
The Millbrook Inn
Cooking score: 2
French | £35
South Pool, TQ7 2RW
Tel no: (01548) 531581
millbrookinnsouthpool.co.uk

£5 OFF 🛏

Easily accessible by boat from Salcombe (there's a pontoon for mooring), or by road if you prefer, the picture-book village of South Pool is southern Devon at its most winsome. And in the whitewashed Millbrook Inn it has a country pub in the best modern style. Jean-Philippe Bidart has gone native, in that he brings his French culinary sensibilities to bear on champion regional produce served with flair and imagination. Mackerel ceviche with pickled fennel and cucumber in basil oil may sound modern British enough, but then the menu also offers a terrine of morteau sausage, chicken and guinea fowl with pain de campagne and crab apple jelly, as well as mains like sturdy bouillabaisse with rouille, Gruyère and croûtons, or pan-roasted tenderloin and slow-cooked belly of local pork on a casserole of Puy lentils. 'Don't be put off by the gizzards!' pleads the Sunday lunch menu. As if. Nor are we put off by the chocolate mousse with honeycomb, pecan crumble and raspberry sorbet. Cheeses are an ecumenical mix of French and West Country. Wines come from all over, starting at £21.
Chef/s: Jean-Philippe Bidart. **Open:** all week L and D. **Meals:** main courses £14 to £35. Set L £12 (2 courses) to £15. Set D £25 (3 courses). Sun L £15. **Details:** 45 seats. 45 seats outside. Bar. Wheelchairs.

▌Sparkwell
The Treby Arms
Cooking score: 5
Modern British | £50
6 Newtons Lane, Sparkwell, PL7 5DD
Tel no: (01752) 837363
thetrebyarms.co.uk

When is a village pub not just a village pub? Perhaps when bar nibbles include curried duck hearts, cockles or crispy pig's head and local sourdough arrives with Marmite and cep butter. Or when alongside its dog and walker-friendly 'lively' public bar and garden tables you find a 60-seater fine-dining restaurant. Although Anton Piotrowski has moved on, his replacement, Luke Fearon, continues to combine earthy Dartmoor tradition with an elegant and innovative approach to good food at all levels. Tasting menus, à la carte and set lunches emphasise seasonality and local producers. Starters might include the 'signature' Little Warmer – a comfort blanket of tender braised oxtail with white bean velouté and puffed wild grains. Mains naturally feature prime local cuts but vegetarian dishes stand out, too; wild garlic and barley with textures of fungi, roasted shallot and confit egg yolk surpasses visual and taste expectations. Concluding options include the artfully deconstructed billionaire's shortbread or the more grown-up Devon Blue mille-feuille with sherry vinegar and brown-butter gel – perfectly bridging the gap between sweet and savoury. The wine list, organised by style, features some of the West Country's local vineyards.
Chef/s: Luke Fearon. **Open:** Wed to Sun L and D. **Closed:** Mon, Tue, 25 and 26 Dec, 1 Jan. **Meals:** main courses £15 to £35. Set L £20 (2 courses) to £25 (Wed to Sat). Tasting menu £70. **Details:** 60 seats. 20 seats outside. Bar. Wheelchairs. Music. Parking.

■ Tavistock
The Cornish Arms

Cooking score: 3
British | £26
15-16 West Street, Tavistock, PL19 8AN
Tel no: (01822) 612145
thecornisharmstavistock.co.uk

£5 OFF £30

A pair who have become regulars, despite not living nearby, appreciate being recognised on their every return to the Cornish, which is to be found on the edge of Tavistock, on the western fringe of Dartmoor. The capacious dining areas indicate that this is a pub that takes its food seriously, and John Hooker cooks popular pub dishes that are several cuts above the norm. Seared king prawns on parsley risotto finished with aged Parmesan shows an attention to detail that may take you by surprise, while main could be a whole roast poussin in autumn-truffled array, served with sauté potatoes and buttered spinach, or perhaps a whole baked lemon sole with chips in seaweed béarnaise. Desserts are the whole deal, too, to judge by buttermilk pannacotta with poached mandarin, lime curd and honey cake. Lunchers might feast on sub rolls crammed with pulled pork. Chilean house blends are £15.95.
Chef/s: John Hooker and Will Norrie. **Open:** all week L and D. **Meals:** main courses £11 to £24. **Details:** 75 seats. 75 seats outside. V menu. Bar. Wheelchairs. Music. Parking.

■ Topsham
Salutation Inn

Cooking score: 4
Modern European | £40
68 Fore Street, Topsham, EX3 0HL
Tel no: (01392) 873060
salutationtopsham.co.uk

With a modern, glazed courtyard café, comfortable lounges and a dining room hung with interesting artwork, this early Georgian inn has shaken off its pub shackles and re-invented itself as a restaurant-with-rooms. The all-day café is a popular local spot, and in the evening-only dining room there is a loyal following for Tom Williams-Hawkes' four-, six- and eight-course tasting menus. The quality of the food is undeniably good – native West Country ingredients including local fish, pork, lamb and cheeses define proceedings, and everything, from the bread to the ice creams and petits fours, is homemade. Typical dishes might run to smoked haddock with lightly curried parsnip and poached quail's egg, herb-crumbed pollack with local mussels, leeks and a mussel broth, or pork tenderloin with cabbage and black pudding, then crunchy hazelnut, milk chocolate mousse and milk sorbet. Everything on the short, reasonably priced and global wine list is available by the glass or bottle.
Chef/s: Tom Williams-Hawkes. **Open:** Mon to Sat D only. **Closed:** Sun, 26 Dec, 1 Jan, first 2 weeks Feb. **Meals:** set D £40 (4 courses). Tasting menu £60 (6 courses) to £80 (8 courses). **Details:** 29 seats. Bar. Wheelchairs. Music. Parking.

■ Torquay
The Elephant

Cooking score: 5
Modern British | £40
3-4 Beacon Terrace, Torquay, TQ1 2BH
Tel no: (01803) 200044
elephantrestaurant.co.uk

£5 OFF

Simon Hulstone's place in bright terraced premises to one side of the harbour combines a sense of refinement with a personable front-of-house approach. His kitchen is plentifully supplied by nearly 100 acres of farmland near Brixham, and much of the seafood comes from those environs, too. Streamlining the operation on to one ground-floor level from its previous two seems to have given the old beast new energy, and dishes are well conceived. Gravadlax is given a new spin in the form of a single strip fillet of sea trout bathed in smoked vodka and crusted with pedigree Tellicherry black pepper, accompanied by garlic mayonnaise and pickled cucumber, while tender-as-anything Exmoor venison sliced into thick coins arrives with celeriac variations and a sharp underlay of sauerkraut and apple in truffly jus. Hake may be the pick of the fish, richly served in seaweed and smoked eel butter, and dessert ideas include Tatin spiked with Kikkoman soy, accompanied by an ice cream of Somerset brandy. Wines start at £19.50.

Chef/s: Simon Hulstone. **Open:** Tue to Sat L and D. **Closed:** Sun, Mon, 2 weeks Jan. **Meals:** main courses £16 to £25. Set L £17 (2 courses) to £20. Tasting menu £65. **Details:** 70 seats. Bar. Wheelchairs. Music.

The Orange Tree

Cooking score: 2
Modern European | £33
14-16 Parkhill Road, Torquay, TQ1 2AL
Tel no: (01803) 213936
orangetreerestaurant.co.uk

You'll find Sharon and Bernd Wolf's charming white-fronted eatery hidden away on a quiet back street not far from Torquay's harbour – the kind of setting that might suggest a certain local exclusivity. However, there's nothing too starched or stuffy here (apart from the stiff white linen on the smartly dressed tables). Bernd's exact cooking relies on tiptop supplies of Devon seafood and locally reared meats for a Euro-themed repertoire that might run from Brixham scallops with baby spinach and crab bisque or herb-crusted cod loin accompanied by brown shrimps and pea velouté to roast rump of lamb dressed with wild garlic, piquillo pepper and feta arancini. South Devon steaks are a fixture and free-range Creedy Carver duck makes a regular appearance, while desserts embrace espresso crème brûlée as well as sticky toffee pudding. House wines include selections from the esteemed Villa Wolf estate in Germany – no relation to the restaurant's owners.

Chef/s: Bernd Wolf. **Open:** Tue to Sat D only. **Closed:** Sun, Mon, 26 and 27 Dec, first week Jan, last 2 weeks Oct. **Meals:** main courses £15 to £27. Tasting menu £48 (7 courses). **Details:** 42 seats. Music.

■ Totnes
Rumour

Cooking score: 1
Modern British | £32
30 High Street, Totnes, TQ9 5RY
Tel no: (01803) 864682
rumourtotnes.com

'All round they've got it nailed,' noted one regular, who regards this wine bar and restaurant as a 'treat every time'. You can pop in for a drink or linger over food – the cooking is eclectic and engaging, cherry-picking ideas from far and wide. Among the 'innovative, beautifully presented' offerings might be home-smoked venison carpaccio with red cabbage and onion marmalade; cod loin with cauliflower purée, cauliflower pickles and curried scraps; and a smoked chocolate brownie with chai cream, malt ice cream and coffee soil. As for service, 'it's nice to be recognised and feel special on every visit'. Wines start at £16.95.

Chef/s: Lee Hegarty. **Open:** Mon to Sat L, all week D. **Closed:** 25 and 26 Dec, 1 Jan. **Meals:** main courses £15 to £22. **Details:** 65 seats. Bar. Wheelchairs. Music.

■ Tytherleigh

READERS RECOMMEND
The Tytherleigh Arms

Modern British
Tytherleigh, EX13 7BE
Tel no: (01460) 220214
tytherleigharms.com
'The menu offers wonderful, seasonal dishes using the best of local produce with all food prepared to order. The head chef and his team produce, in our opinion, the best variety of dishes and mouthwatering puddings my wife and I have come across. The dishes we have eaten include fish pie, hake risotto, sea bass risotto, breast of mallard and traditional fish and chips.'

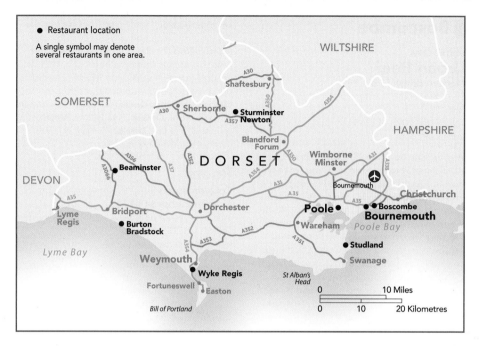

- Restaurant location

A single symbol may denote
several restaurants in one area.

◼ Beaminster
Brassica
Cooking score: 4
Modern British | £30
4 The Square, Beaminster, DT8 3AS
Tel no: (01308) 538100
brassicarestaurant.co.uk

'Excellent food in a very well-run restaurant,'
enthused a first-time visitor to Louise
Chidgey and Cass Titcombe's popular
restaurant. Considered a local asset, there is
much to praise, from the 'wonderfully light,
respectful modernisation' of a listed building
in the town square to the charming service.
Cass's cooking is simple, smart and high
quality, but with just enough tasteful quirky
detail to never be dull – one reader raved
about a 'superb' bruschetta of green tomatoes
and chilli, citing it as an example of 'how to
make simple things delightful'. Wild
mushrooms, hogget and game are seasonal
favourites on short, daily changing menus. At
a spring dinner 'delicious' early-season English

asparagus, and 'generous, beautifully cooked'
turbot fillet with crevettes, haricot beans and
wild garlic were outright winners, but the
kitchen also rolls out excellent braised ox
cheek and orecchiette gratin. Finish with a
slice of loquat frangipane tart or bread-and-
butter pudding. Wines are an affordable, well-
researched tour of European vineyards (from
£20) with good recommendations by the
glass.

Chef/s: Cass Titcombe. **Open:** Wed to Sun L, Wed
to Sat D. **Closed:** Mon, Tue, 25 to 27 Dec.
Meals: main courses £14 to £23. Set L £15 (2
courses) to £19. Sun L £19 (2 courses) to £24.
Details: 40 seats. 6 seats outside. Wheelchairs.
Music.

Symbols

- ⬚ Accommodation is available
- £30 Three courses for less than £30
- £5 OFF £5-off voucher scheme
- ▮ Notable wine list

Boscombe

LOCAL GEM

Urban Reef

Modern British | £30

The Overstrand, Undercliff Drive, Boscombe, BH5 1BN
Tel no: (01202) 443960
urbanreef.com

A stone's throw from Boscombe Pier, Urban Reef shares revamped retro living space with Red or Dead founder Wayne Hemingway's vintage 'beach pods'. It's a bar, café, deli and restaurant, majoring in local produce, with a wood oven for takeaway pizzas. The likes of Dorset rock oysters and New Forest wild mushrooms share a menu with pulled pork and apple-and-cider chutney on sourdough ciabatta. Mains include hand-picked crab linguine with lemon and chilli, and there's local Purbeck ice cream to finish. To drink, it will be a pint of whatever the staff are having.

Bournemouth

The Larderhouse

Cooking score: 2
Modern European | £34

Southbourne Grove, Bournemouth, BH6 3QZ
Tel no: (01202) 424687
thelarderhouse.co.uk

A much-loved neighbourhood restaurant just a few minutes from Southbourne beach, the Larderhouse is considered a 'lucky find' by visitors, and a 'go-to' spot for locals. The zinc bar, air-dried hams and candlelight create a laid-back, unaffected air with a nod to Iberia that extends to the focused menu, where starters of jamón de Teruel with figs, honey and hazelnuts or plump, citrus-cured boquerones might precede perfectly cooked meat and fish from the wood-fired oven that's at the heart of the kitchen. 'Social Suzannes' – as in the spinning serving boards – are a popular sharing option, with a seafood version featuring salmon rillettes, potted shellfish, hake fingers, shell-on prawns and cured fillets. Wood-roasted Sunday lunches

are superb value, while puddings such as the 'divine' pear, malt and almond crumble are mostly from the classic English school. The wine list majors on port, sherry and Madeira, while 'Dorset's best Bloody Mary' is served in the speakeasy-style Library Bar upstairs.
Chef/s: Nick Hewitt. **Open:** Mon to Sat L and D. Sun, all day from 12. **Closed:** 24 to 26 Dec. **Meals:** main courses £15 to £19. **Details:** 45 seats. 50 seats outside. Bar. Wheelchairs. Music.

Roots

Cooking score: 3
Modern European | £36

141 Belle Vue Road, Bournemouth, BH6 3EN
Tel no: (01202) 430005
restaurantroots.co.uk

Blending into an anonymous row of shops, Roots is 'easy to miss from the outside' but the innovative flavour combinations within belie the unassuming exterior. Uncluttered décor – simple wooden tables, bare brick and white walls – provides the backdrop for a seven-course tasting menu whose hits at a test meal included risi e bisi, a light, fresh combination of crispy wild rice, tiny coconut cubes, pea mousse and mint sorbet in a beguiling mix of textures and temperatures. Hake in kohlrabi foam with truffle shavings is well seasoned, sweet and pungent with super-crispy skin, while elderflower parfait with tart raspberries and sweet, hay-infused cream makes a 'stellar' dessert. This is skilful cooking prepared with passion and meticulous attention to detail, served with flair and enthusiasm. Wines start at £19, with ample choice by the glass. Or, for £19.50, a wine tasting with your meal. The 2013 Rheingau Riesling from Schloss Schönborn is exceptional.
Chef/s: Jan Bretschneider. **Open:** Fri to Sun L, Wed to Sat D. **Closed:** Mon, Tue. **Meals:** set L £17 (2 courses) to £22. Sun L £20 (2 courses). Tasting menu £36 to £53. **Details:** 18 seats. V menu. Music.

West Beach
Seafood | £33
Pier Approach, Bournemouth, BH2 5AA
Tel no: (01202) 587785
west-beach.co.uk

Beside the seaside but far from tacky or twee, West Beach is an ozone-laced tonic in beachside Bournemouth. Andy Price has run it for nearly 20 years, and the contemporary iteration is home to new art and solid seafood cookery. From the shell, try moules marinière, hot shellfish in tarragon and butter emulsion, or spiced crusted scallops with Jerusalem artichoke purée and crisp capers. Fish might be halibut with squid-ink and Parmesan gnocchi and a mussel sauce; there's good Dorset beef, too, if you must.

▌Burton Bradstock

Hive Beach Café
Seafood | £30
Beach Road, Burton Bradstock, DT6 4RF
Tel no: (01308) 897070
hivebeachcafe.co.uk

That's the Jurassic Coast right there on the doorstep of this beachside café, but local and sustainable seafood is of just as much interest to visitors as the blissful sea view. Tuck into a West Bay lobster, grilled with garlic butter, or a Weymouth crab sandwich, or Cornish mussels steamed in white wine, and imagine a world where most beaches have such a place. It's open through the year, but check the website just in case. Mostly white wines open at £15.50. A sister joint can be found at West Bay (the Watch House Café), and a third, The Club House, in West Bexington.

▌Poole

Guildhall Tavern
French | £35
15 Market Street, Poole, BH15 1NB
Tel no: (01202) 671717
guildhalltavern.co.uk

£5
OFF

A listed corner property only a couple of minutes from the quay from whence comes much of the fish that appears on the menu, the Guildhall Tavern bills itself as a French seafood restaurant. This means you can expect mussels marinière, skate wing à la provençale and whole sea bass flambéed in Pernod, and if that isn't French enough for you, finish with crêpes suzette. Dorset rack of lamb and beef bourguignon are among meaty options, and the wine list stays true to the motherland. Terrace tables add to the holiday mood.

▌Studland

Pig on the Beach
Modern British | £32
Manor House, Manor Road, Studland, BH19 3AU
Tel no: (01929) 450288
thepighotel.com

A 'delightful, charismatic' country house hotel close to the sands of Studland Bay, this little piggie grows its own fruit and veg and what isn't home-grown won't have come from very far away. The handsome, verdant greenhouse dining room is the setting for the fruits of land and sea – Portland crab tart, with some home-grown red watercress, local cuttlefish in an inky risotto, or Purbeck pigeon matched with new-season rhubarb and a smoky red wine sauce. The smart wine list includes English sparklers.

▋Sturminster Newton
Plumber Manor
Cooking score: 2
Anglo-French | £38
Sturminster Newton, DT10 2AF
Tel no: (01258) 472507
plumbermanor.com

£5 OFF 🛏

A genuine and personable family atmosphere is one reason why the Prideaux-Brunes' long-serving hotel-restaurant has such a loyal following. 'Very English, very charming,' summed up one visitor. In a stunning setting with delightful gardens, Plumber Manor isn't a grand place, rather decorated in a homely manner with open fires, well-worn furniture and portraits of ancestors lining the walls – the house has been in the family since the 17th century. Brian Prideaux-Brune runs things to a tried-and-true formula that doesn't strive after modishness for its own sake, but puts its trust in the value of established practice. His Anglo-French country style covers much familiar territory, some dishes going back a few years – chicken liver parfait, beef Wellington – but meals might also take in a 'tasty' trio of shellfish (crab, crevette, brown shrimp) and 'very fresh, beautifully cooked' brill in a creamy orange sauce with lashings of vegetables on the plate and on the side. Desserts are wheeled in on a magnificent trolley laden with roulades, fresh fruit salads, crème brûlée, mille-feuille and white and dark chocolate mousse cake. Wines from £18.50.

Chef/s: Brian Prideaux-Brune. **Open:** Sun L, all week D. **Closed:** 24 Jan to 1 Mar. **Meals:** set D £30 (2 courses) to £38. Sun L £30. **Details:** 65 seats. Bar. Wheelchairs. Parking.

▋Wyke Regis
LOCAL GEM
Crab House Café
Seafood | £30
Ferryman's Way, Portland Road, Wyke Regis, DT4 9YU
Tel no: (01305) 788867
crabhousecafe.co.uk

It's an enticing proposition and nirvana for anyone who hankers after fresh seafood: a wooden hut overlooking Chesil Beach, with oyster beds on the water's edge, glorious views all round, outside bench tables ready to bag and a menu that sticks to local fish and shellfish. They even grow their own veg. Expect seared scallops with crispy chorizo and squash purée, a whole crab on a wooden board (hammer provided), whole lemon sole with lemon and thyme butter, and those Portland oysters. Wines open at £20.30.

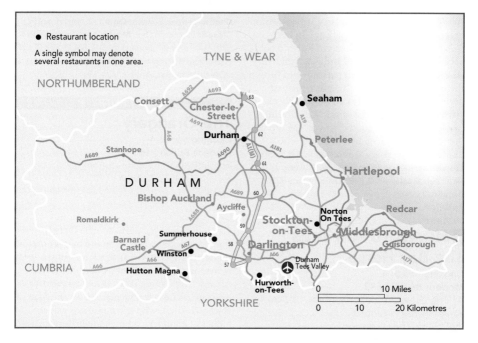

Map legend:

● Restaurant location

A single symbol may denote several restaurants in one area.

NORTHUMBERLAND

TYNE & WEAR

Consett
Chester-le-Street
Seaham
Durham
Peterlee
Stanhope
Hartlepool
DURHAM
Bishop Auckland
Aycliffe
Norton On Tees
Redcar
Romaldkirk
Stockton-on-Tees
Middlesbrough
Summerhouse
Darlington
Guisborough
Barnard Castle
Winston
Durham Tees Valley
CUMBRIA
Hutton Magna
Hurworth-on-Tees
YORKSHIRE

0   10 Miles
0   10   20 Kilometres

▇ Durham
The Garden House Inn
Cooking score: 1
International | £30
Framwellgate Peth, Durham, DH1 4NQ
Tel no: (0191) 3863395
gardenhouseinn.com

Away from Durham's famous cathedral and castle, just north of the train station, this roadside pub still feels like a village local with its dapper interior – bare floorboards, log fire, tall white candles – and range of regional real ales. While drinkers can still sup at the bar, the Garden House's main business is food. The kitchen does a decent job of delivering everything from scallops with curry sauce and brown shrimp bhaji or ham and pease pudding terrine with egg on toast, to burgers, cod and chips or rack of lamb with shoulder shepherd's pie and spring vegetables. Sticky toffee pudding makes a traditional finale. Wines from £17.

Chef/s: Ruari MacKay. **Open:** all week L, Mon to Sat D. **Closed:** 25 and 26 Dec. **Meals:** main courses £10 to £17. **Details:** 104 seats. Wheelchairs. Music.

Restaurant DH1
Cooking score: 3
Modern British | £45
The Avenue, Durham, DH1 4DX
Tel no: (0191) 3846655
restaurantdh1.co.uk
£5 OFF

Stephen and Helen Hardy's personally run restaurant is wedged in on the ground floor of Farnley Tower – a guesthouse occupying a rather grandiose Victorian Gothic residence. The colour purple predominates in the dining room, although all eyes are on the of-the-moment food emanating from Stephen's kitchen – especially his multi-course 'market' menus. Snacks and freshly baked breads provide the opening salvos, while a pair of desserts could yield 'variations on rhubarb' with vanilla and gingerbread or the Rocky

Road (dark chocolate mousse with pistachio, cherry sorbet and marshmallow). In between, there might be a neat pairing of hot and cold beetroot with smoked eel and pear, hake in classic brown butter with parsnips and brown shrimps or an emphatically rustic plate of slow-cooked pork belly and braised cheek with brassicas and cider sauce. Wine flights work well with the food – or you can dip into the reasonably priced list.

Chef/s: Stephen Hardy. **Open:** Tue to Sat D only. **Closed:** Sun, Mon, 25 and 26 Dec, 1 week Jan, 1 week Jul. **Meals:** set D £45. Tasting menu £60. **Details:** 22 seats. V menu. Bar. Wheelchairs. Music. Parking.

▮ Hurworth-on-Tees
The Bay Horse

Cooking score: 4
Modern British | £33
45 The Green, Hurworth-on-Tees, DL2 2AA
Tel no: (01325) 720663
thebayhorsehurworth.com

Drinkers are more than welcome at this upgraded village pub, but one whiff of the bread with sweet white onion is enough to change the thirstiest local's plans to dinner. Hurworth is a lovely village and the Bay Horse is the pub to match, though dishes shout 'restaurant' loud and clear. East Coast fishcake, steaming and crisp, comes with a silky cloud of smoked salmon parfait and fashionably pickled vegetables. Readers have been impressed by 'attentive' staff, and have noted a tendency towards 'creative but rather impractical presentation'. This is very much in evidence in a dark, vibrant plate of succulent herb-stuffed chicken ballotine, dotted and streaked to the edge with sweet potato purée, nuggets of the same and earthy cubes of crisped chorizo. The kitchen's sense of occasion takes account of tradition, though; come Sunday, the Yorkshires are as big as two fists. Pudding might be sticky toffee pudding with a sesame-seed sprinkle, and there's good cheese. Wines from £18.

Chef/s: Marcus Bennett. **Open:** all week L and D. **Closed:** 25 and 26 Dec. **Meals:** main courses £19 to £29. Set L £15 (2 courses) to £19. Set D £23 (2 courses) to £27. Sun L £18. **Details:** 41 seats. 40 seats outside. Bar. Wheelchairs. Music. Parking.

The Orangery

Cooking score: 4
Modern British | £55
Rockliffe Hall, Hurworth-on-Tees, DL2 2DU
Tel no: (01325) 729999
rockliffehall.com

Gorgeous in its proportions, the Orangery is the most majestic part of an old hall whose modern extensions include a fabulous spa, golf course and hotel bedrooms. With views over mature landscaping and a sunny terrace, it's a peaceful if conservative place to eat the food of Richard Allen, whose last posting was at St Helier's Grand Jersey hotel. He brings a little of the sea with him in a tasting menu that kicks off with mussels with white bean cassoulet and a saffron sauce, or an à la carte starter (expect four courses, with frills) of Staithes crab with a bouillabaisse-style dressing and impossibly crisp courgette flower. We'd like to see more of the playfulness evident in a *trompe l'oeil* stick of boozy duck parfait surrounded by nutty garnishes and Ibérico ham, and more oomph in a harissa doughnut served with a classy lamb dish of neat, saucy mince, tongue and best end with a few enlivening sorrel leaves. Pudding might turn 72 per cent chocolate into a milky mousse served with cherry variations, or pair rhubarb with chai spices. Service is reserved but well meaning, and wine is reassuringly expensive.

Chef/s: Richard Allen. **Open:** Tue to Sat D only. **Closed:** Sun, Mon. **Meals:** alc £55 (4 courses). Tasting menu £65 to £95. **Details:** 50 seats. V menu. Bar. Wheelchairs. Music. Parking.

■ Hutton Magna
The Oak Tree Inn
Cooking score: 2
Modern British | £39
Hutton Magna, DL11 7HH
Tel no: (01833) 627371
theoaktreehutton.co.uk

The cottagey interior – beams, open fire, rough stone walls, panelling – makes for a snug, welcoming ambience. It's still very much the village local, and the restaurant to the rear is the rustic setting for Alastair Ross's self-assured and comforting take on modern cooking. He works with the seasons, his compact dinner menus offering four choices per course – starters might include home-cured salmon with crab mayonnaise, pink grapefruit and radish or roast wood pigeon with pearl barley, leeks, sweetcorn and quail's egg. To follow, best end of lamb is teamed with merguez sausage and mash, confit red onions and cabbage, while fillet of silver hake is served with steamed Shetland mussels, new potatoes, fennel and curry. Finish up classically with sticky gingerbread pudding or hot chocolate fondant with chocolate mousse and salted caramel ice cream. Wines are a well-chosen and reasonably priced global collection starting at £18.
Chef/s: Alastair Ross. **Open:** Tue to Sun D only.
Closed: Mon, 24 to 27 Dec, 31 Dec to 2 Jan.
Meals: main courses £22 to £25. **Details:** 20 seats.
Bar. Music. Parking.

■ Norton On Tees
Café Lilli
Cooking score: 2
International | £28
83 High Street, Norton On Tees, TS20 1AE
Tel no: (01642) 554422
lillicafe.co.uk
£30

You can't fake hospitality – and Café Lilli boss Roberto Pittalis and his team have absolutely no need to. An easy-going jumble of a room on Norton's main drag, Café Lilli earns and repays local loyalty with warm service and come-back-soon pricing. The menu, supplemented by big specials blackboards, is pure Continental café with a Northern edge; antipasto comes with Yorkshire Blue cheese, the fish of the day is from Hartlepool and there's as much black treacle ginger sponge as there is hazelnut praline affogato. Everyone gets the warm, cakey bread with a crisp crust, to eat perhaps with roasted tomato and Cheddar soup, which captures the essence of both. Market fish might be sea bream with rich, wobbly baked tomato polenta, gorgeously succulent and buttery sea spinach and a tomato and red pepper relish. There's always pasta, perhaps lobster ravioli with king prawns and samphire, and always Italian wine in flexible measures.
Chef/s: P Wigwam and DJ Poland. **Open:** Tue to Sat, all day from 11. **Closed:** Mon, 25 Dec, 1 Jan.
Meals: main courses £15 to £25. Set D £17 (2 courses) to £22. Sun L £20 (2 courses) to £24.
Details: 70 seats. Bar. Music. Parking.

■ Seaham
★ NEW ENTRY ★
Byron's
Cooking score: 3
Modern British | £45
Seaham Hall, Lord Byron's Walk, Seaham, SR7 7AG
Tel no: (0191) 5161400
seaham-hall.co.uk
£5 OFF

The wild romance of Seaham Hall lies mostly in its past. Today, the house where Byron embarked on his ill-fated marriage is a spa hotel with a mildly blingy dining room named in his honour. If service and wine aren't quite poetry in motion, there are some nice ideas on the plate. Good soda bread is served before, perhaps, a delicate dish of Whitby crab, radish and new-season peas, or scallops with pork belly and vivid piccalilli. Mains might be dry-aged beef with multiple onions and grilled tongue – fatty in the best way – or John Dory with anchovy cream and chunky almonds, and dried and marinated anchovies poised to swim out of an unapologetically crisp wedge of broccoli. Puddings are from the modern school of splodge, but even without much structure the flavours of, say, buttermilk sorbet with blackcurrants, rocket and tarragon are likeably balanced.

Chef/s: Damian Broom. **Open:** Sun L, all week D. **Meals:** main courses £19 to £30. **Details:** 40 seats. Bar. Wheelchairs. Music. Parking.

▌Summerhouse
★ TOP 50 ★
The Raby Hunt
Cooking score: 7
Modern British | £85
Summerhouse, DL2 3UD
Tel no: (01325) 374237
rabyhuntrestaurant.co.uk
£5 OFF 🍾 🛏

Gone are the days when the hunt used to convene outside this remote Georgian inn. The Raby Hunt now plies its trade as an elegant restaurant-with-rooms displaying all the signs of thoughtful transformation. Self-taught James Close is working minor miracles here, cooking at the sharp end of contemporary gastronomy and delivering some astonishingly fine food: one reader likened his 10-course tasting menu (the only option available) to an artfully balanced Japanese kaiseki banquet reimagined in northern England – 'a journey where each dish builds on its predecessor'. Above all, it's about local ingredients subjected to fearsome and resourceful technical wizardry – all in the name of limpid natural flavour. Only the 'freshest and finest' find their way on to the plate, be it a single Lindisfarne oyster (cooked at 62 degrees for ultimate texture) or slivers of ruby-red raw beef dressed with nasturtium and basil. Also consider a disarmingly effective dish of sea bream, the flesh just 'done', the skin just crisp, with swirls of cod's roe cream, a dusting of dried cod's roe powder and some wilted spinach leaves – nothing more. Somewhere along the line, you'll be offered a salad-like collation of seasonal vegetables, and the journey towards sweetness proceeds via an assemblage of warm chocolate mousse with dried black olive and sheep's yoghurt ice cream. Service shows 'skill, knowledge and attention to detail', while the 'masterful' wine list champions terroir, organic and biodynamic names alongside the big-ticket classics.

Chef/s: James Close. **Open:** Sat L, Wed to Sat D. **Closed:** Sun, Mon, Tue, 2 weeks Christmas and New Year. **Meals:** set L and D £85 (10 courses). **Details:** 28 seats. 4 seats outside. Bar. Wheelchairs. Parking.

▌Winston
The Bridgewater Arms
Cooking score: 1
International | £38
Front Street, Winston, DL2 3RN
Tel no: (01325) 730302
thebridgewaterarms.com

Menus and cutlery rather than textbooks and pencils are now the order of the day at this conversion of a 19th-century Church of England school. Landlord Paul Grundy oversees the bar and the kitchen, where ambitious restaurant-style food is given a creditable workout. Starters such as a warm salad of duck breast, pancetta and mango could precede rack of lamb with a leek and potato cake, lobster thermidor or grilled halibut on crab, spring onion and pea risotto, while desserts span everything from tiramisu to a brandy-snap basket filled with honeyed rhubarb and rhubarb ice cream. Fifty wines offer value across the range.

Chef/s: Paul Grundy and Tobias Biggs. **Open:** Tue to Sat L and D. **Closed:** Sun, Mon, 25 and 26 Dec, 1 Jan. **Meals:** main courses £15 to £38. **Details:** 50 seats. 12 seats outside. Wheelchairs. Music. Parking.

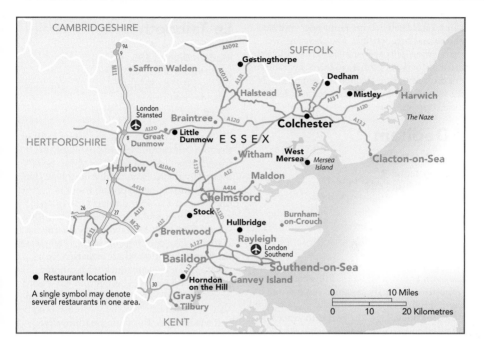

CAMBRIDGESHIRE

SUFFOLK

Saffron Walden

Gestingthorpe

Dedham

Halstead

Mistley

Harwich

London
Stansted

Braintree

The Naze

Colchester

HERTFORDSHIRE

Great
Dunmow

Little
Dunmow

ESSEX

Witham

West
Mersea

Mersea
Island

Clacton-on-Sea

Harlow

Maldon

Chelmsford

Stock

Burnham-
on-Crouch

Brentwood

Hullbridge

Rayleigh

London
Southend

Basildon

Southend-on-Sea

• Restaurant location

A single symbol may denote
several restaurants in one area.

Horndon
on the Hill

Canvey Island

Grays

Tilbury

KENT

0   10 Miles

0   10   20 Kilometres

▊ Colchester
Church Street Tavern

Cooking score: 2
Modern British | £29
3 Church Street, Colchester, CO1 1NF
Tel no: (01206) 564325
churchstreettavern.co.uk

🍶 £30

'Coffee, craft beers, cocktails, snacks, pre-theatre deals, Sunday roasts'… this conversion of a Victorian savings bank is certainly geared up for every eventuality. Opened by Piers Baker from the Sun Inn, Dedham (see entry), the Church Street Tavern is also a tasty proposition if you're looking for some serious food hereabouts. Burgers, omelettes and ramen bowls feed the lunchtime crowds in the bar, while the upstairs restaurant deals in Mersea rock oysters, rare-breed steaks (from East Anglian farms) and more ambitious dishes. On-trend ingredients and big flavours come together in good-looking plates of smoked Lincolnshire eel with apple, ginger,

daikon, soy and lime; anchovy and piquillo pepper tart; or salt cod with cannellini beans, chorizo, salsify and chimichurri sauce. After that, locally made ice creams vie with the likes of chilled rhubarb fondant or steamed syrup sponge. Piers Baker's wine list is notable for its catholic choice by the glass or carafe, plus its covetable 'desert island' bin ends.
Chef/s: Ewan Naylon. **Open:** Wed to Sun L, Wed to Sat D. **Closed:** Mon, Tue, 25 and 26 Dec, first week Jan. **Meals:** main courses £13 to £25. Sun L £21 (2 courses) to £25. **Details:** 85 seats. 15 seats outside. Bar. Wheelchairs. Music.

READERS RECOMMEND
Grain
International
11a North Hill, Colchester, CO1 1DZ
Tel no: (01206) 570005
grain-colchester.co.uk
'The concept is small plates under four headings: Garden, Water, Land and Sweet. From Garden I've had confit parsnip, black cabbage, cranberry and gingerbread. Under

Land, I have eaten a one-hour egg, chorizo, potato and breadcrumb. The chefs are two young men who were trained at the Colchester Institute, went elsewhere to learn the trade and got crowdfunding to open the restaurant. It is the best restaurant in Colchester and deserves local support.'

▍Dedham
The Sun Inn
Cooking score: 3
Modern British | £28
High Street, Dedham, CO7 6DF
Tel no: (01206) 323351
thesuninndedham.com
£5 OFF 🍷 🛏 £30

There are plenty of reasons to linger in pretty Dedham and Piers Baker's 15th-century inn opposite the equally ancient church is one of them. Highly enjoyable, hugely popular and a boon for the village, the Sun is an agreeable blend of rusticity (beams, floorboards, panelling, open fires) and affluent vibes. The easy-going style of the place is much appreciated, too, successfully bridging the divide between country boozer and upper-crust-inn-with-rooms. You can settle in for drinks in the front bar or head for the spacious, timbered dining room for seasonal, produce-driven modern cooking. The starting point is high-quality (often local) raw materials, with pasta and risotto dishes or the likes of poached salt cod with puttanesca sauce, spinach and soft polenta displaying a fondness for things Italian – though the menu also deals in pheasant breast with a leg and ham hock pithiviers and beer-mustard cream. A robust choice of wines has a French and Italian bias and offers both adventure and accessible prices – there's an impressive number under £30; a few elite bottles, too.
Chef/s: Jack Levine. **Open:** all week L and D. **Meals:** main courses £13 to £19. **Details:** 85 seats. 80 seats outside. Bar. Music. Parking.

Le Talbooth
Cooking score: 4
Modern British | £55
Gun Hill, Dedham, CO7 6HP
Tel no: (01206) 323150
milsomhotels.com
£5 OFF 🛏

The magnificent house on the Stour, built in the 16th century and originally where the Ipswich road tolls were collected, has been owned by the Milsom family since 1952. The beamed and timbered dining room is understated, classic and smart with linen-covered tables, and is 'a wonderful place for a special occasion'. Andrew Hirst's careful, craftsmanlike cooking continues, celebrating the best of tradition where it matters, in a terrine of Devonshire duck with candied pistachio, caramelised orange and salt-baked beetroot, for example, or a fillet of Dedham Vale dry-aged beef Rossini with rösti potatoes and Madeira jus. But there are innovative flourishes, too, in a dish of cumin-scented scallops with carrot, pomegranate and crispy chicken tuile or a main-course tenderloin and belly of pork with steamed pork bun, romanesco, Madeira jus and salami. Desserts have included a beautifully risen vanilla custard soufflé with Yorkshire rhubarb and ginger. Service comes in for praise, and the wide-ranging wine list winkles out some interesting wines at all price levels.
Chef/s: Andrew Hirst. **Open:** all week L, Mon to Sat D. **Meals:** main courses £23 to £34. Set L £27 (2 courses) to £34. Sun L £40. **Details:** 80 seats. 60 seats outside. Bar. Wheelchairs. Music. Parking.

Visit us online

To find out more about The Good Food Guide, please visit thegoodfoodguide.co.uk

Gestingthorpe
The Pheasant
Cooking score: 1
Modern British | £25
Church Street, Gestingthorpe, CO9 3AU
Tel no: (01787) 465010
thepheasant.net

From the obscure vegetables grown in the Pheasant's one-acre garden to the coffee beans roasted on a local farm, it seems 'the only way is Essex' at this lovingly run hostelry-with-rooms overlooking the Stour Valley. Green-fingered chef/landlord James Donoghue is a master of all trades, tending the crops, smoking fish and much more besides. You can taste the results in a menu of homespun treats ranging from grilled goats' cheese salad with sweet chilli dressing to char-grilled Cajun chicken or slow-roast pork belly with mash. Just add pies, steaks, beer-battered fish and puds such as rhubarb crumble. Ales and cider are from the region, and an Essex merchant supplies the wine.
Chef/s: James Donoghue. **Open:** Fri to Sun L, Tue to Sun D. **Closed:** Mon. **Meals:** main courses £13 to £20. **Details:** 40 seats. 20 seats outside. Bar. Music. Parking.

Horndon on the Hill
The Bell Inn
Cooking score: 3
Modern European | £33
High Road, Horndon on the Hill, SS17 8LD
Tel no: (01375) 642463
bell-inn.co.uk

Dating from the time of the seventh Henry in the mid-15th century, the Bell looks a treat on a bright day, its cream frontage awash with vivid hanging baskets. Underneath the ancient rafters, the sensitively modernised interiors play host to enterprising modern European cooking founded on assertive flavours presented with refreshing simplicity. First up might be densely textured potted rabbit laced with tarragon and apple, served with toasted brioche, or scallops packaged in maple pancetta with sautéed chard and broccoli purée. Fish and shellfish combinations such as lemon sole in cockle and crayfish brown butter, or sea bass in prawn bisque, appear among sturdy meat mains like herbed pork fillet with chorizo mayonnaise and oyster mushroom in chicken velouté. Finish with Neal's Yard cheeses and grape and apple chutney, or dark chocolate and vanilla cheesecake with pistachios and hazelnut cream. Traditional bar food is also offered, and there is more dining up the road in an adjunct venue, the Ostlers. House Australian is £16.95.
Chef/s: Stephen Treadwell. **Open:** all week L and D. **Closed:** 25 and 26 Dec. **Meals:** main courses £12 to £30. **Details:** 80 seats. 36 seats outside. Bar. Wheelchairs. Parking.

Hullbridge
The Anchor Riverside
Cooking score: 4
Modern British | £30
Ferry Road, Hullbridge, SS5 6ND
Tel no: (01702) 230777
theanchorhullbridge.co.uk

A glance at the menu of this riverside pub suggests it isn't your everyday boozer: kohlrabi and apple crab 'taco' anyone? It's still a pub – a big one at that – but it is the cooking of Daniel Watkins and his team that catches the eye. Head to the expansive, glossy conservatory dining room with its glorious view over the river Crouch and tuck into some impressive mod-Brit food. Lunchtime adds classy versions of ham, egg and chips (duck egg, naturally) and other old favourites to the repertoire; on Sundays it's all about roasts. Asian flavours pepper the menu, from crab and shrimp samosa to char siu smoked pork belly, and there's skill in the execution. Main-course roasted goose, flavoured with beer and honey, gets a lift from hazelnut dukkah, while the sirloin steak arrives on the bone with Marmite butter and hand-cut chips. Finish with a supercharged warm ginger sponge. The globally inspired wine list has good options by the glass.

Chef/s: Daniel Watkins. **Open:** Mon to Sat L and D. Sun, all day from 12. **Closed:** 25 Dec. **Meals:** main courses £14 to £25. Set L and D, Mon to Fri £18 (2 courses) to £20. **Details:** 110 seats. 120 seats outside. V menu. Bar. Wheelchairs. Music. Parking.

▌ Little Dunmow
The Flitch of Bacon
Cooking score: 3
Modern British | £50
The Street, Little Dunmow, CM6 3HT
Tel no: (01371) 821660
flitchofbacon.co.uk

Be warned: this is a restaurant, it is not a pub. Don't expect a meal of pub staples or to leave with a barely-dented wallet, because the Flitch offers the sort of food that Daniel Clifford does best, albeit a relaxed notch down from Midsummer House (see entry). Properly pretty plates are brought from gleaming kitchen (it's open and there are two perches at the pass if you want to get up close) to shiny dining room, by glossy waiters who will ply you with flirty little amuse-bouches and pre-desserts. Fiercely seasonal produce is allowed to show its best side, so a starter of asparagus retains minerally bite, sitting well against tangy Cornish Yarg under a shard of toasted sourdough; ditto firm, nutty Jersey Royals, sweet against rich mackerel and smoky eel. Braver seasoning would have lifted a main of Herdwick lamb, tenderly pink though it is, even if finely-layered potatoes cooked in lamb fat defy resistance. Share a tarte Tatin for a less overwhelming finale than a dessert of dark chocolate with flavours of peanut, lemon and salted caramel. Wine from £17.

Chef/s: Daniel Clifford. **Open:** Thur to Sun L, Wed to Sat D. **Closed:** Mon, Tue. **Meals:** set L £20 (2 courses) to £25. Set D £55 (3 courses). **Details:** 38 seats. Bar. Wheelchairs. Music. Parking.

▌ Margaretting Tye
The White Hart Inn
International
Swan Lane, Margaretting Tye, CM4 9JX
Tel no: (01277) 840478
thewhitehart.uk.com

'So glad we moved to Essex, if only because this lovely countryside pub is now on our doorstep. The pies are amazing, the salt marsh lamb is just incredible, and don't get me started on the real ales. I'm impressed by their gluten-free menu, too. A big thumbs up!'

▌ Mistley
The Mistley Thorn
Cooking score: 2
Modern British | £26
High Street, Mistley, CO11 1HE
Tel no: (01206) 392821
mistleythorn.co.uk

The whitewashed Thorn is a coaching inn from the earliest Georgian era, the original site a headquarters for Witchfinder General Matthew Hopkins. His tireless campaign to spread fear and misery throughout the land is somewhat redeemed by the present incarnation as a sympathetically restored village inn. The beamed interiors are done in grey-boarded walls with terracotta-tiled floors for a modern rustic look, and the kitchen turns out a seafood-led menu that suits the coastal location. Smoked haddock chowder with roast peppers followed by linguine with clams in white wine and garlic could be one route through, and there are Mersea oysters in various guises to gulp down while you ponder. Meat eaters are remembered, too, perhaps with Creedy Carver duck breast, celeriac cake and cavolo nero in marmalade sauce, and comfort puddings such as ginger sponge with cinnamon custard, or the executive chef's

Mom's cheesecake recipe, should send everyone away happy. Wines in all sizes open at £3.25 for a small measure.

Chef/s: Karl Burnside. **Open:** all week L and D. **Closed:** 25 Dec. **Meals:** main courses £10 to £24. Set L £14 (2 courses) to £17. Set D £14 (2 courses) to £18. Sun L £18. **Details:** 90 seats. 14 seats outside. Bar. Music. Parking.

▌Stock
The Oak Room at the Hoop
Cooking score: 1
Modern British | £35
The Hoop, 21 High Street, Stock, CM4 9BD
Tel no: (01277) 841137
thehoop.co.uk

The Hoop's annual beer festival is a boozy reminder that this 450-year-old clapboard pub is still, at heart, a proper old-fashioned drinking den. However, head upstairs to the Oak Room restaurant and you'll discover that it's no slouch in the food stakes either. Expect notable attention to detail and a touch of elegance across the menu, from a salt beef terrine with mustard mayo and toasted sourdough to saddle of venison with beetroot, girolles and ceps. Traditionalists might prefer prawn cocktail followed by steak with 'fat' chips, while puds are of the treacle tart/fruit crumble variety. To drink, look for wines from the nearby New Hall vineyard.

Chef/s: Phil Utz. **Open:** Tue to Fri and Sun L, Tue to Sat D. **Closed:** Mon. **Meals:** main courses £13 to £29. Sun L £25. **Details:** 40 seats. Bar.

▌West Mersea

LOCAL GEM
West Mersea Oyster Bar
Seafood | £20
Coast Road, West Mersea, CO5 8LT
Tel no: (01206) 381600
westmerseaoysterbar.co.uk

£30

A decade on, oysterman Michael Dawson's weatherboarded seafood shack overlooking the Blackwater estuary remains perennially popular. Join the queue of locals and out-of-towners to order impeccably fresh local fish and shellfish to take away (the fish and chips are glorious) or reserve a table to eat in. The dining space is utilitarian, but the all-seafood menu delivers stellar stuff. A plate of renowned Colchester oysters (when in season), or top-grade Mersea Island rocks, come ice-cold and platters-to-share are heaving with crustaceans, molluscs and smoked fish.

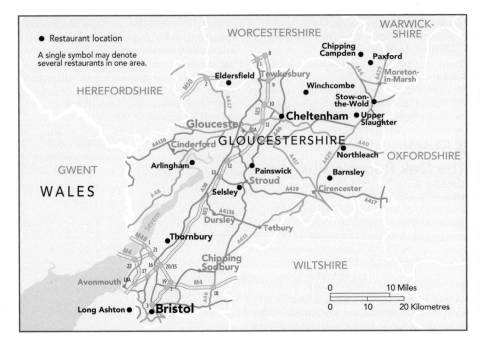

Arlingham
The Old Passage

Cooking score: 2
Seafood | £40
Passage Road, Arlingham, GL2 7JR
Tel no: (01452) 740547
theoldpassage.com

£5 OFF ⏻

'It is a pleasure to go here. I call it "the restaurant at the end of the universe" because it's so tucked away,' noted one fan of Sally Pearce's charming restaurant-with-rooms, adding 'it's a place that particularly lends itself to daytime and summer dining as the views over the river are so lovely'. There has been a change of chef since our last edition, but the menu continues to offer a 'fine selection' of 'extremely fresh' fish and seafood, from Porthilly rock oysters and scallops with pork belly fritter, cauliflower purée and lentils, via 'beautifully cooked' lobster and 'excellent' chips, to pan-roasted brill with calf's tongue, baby onions, butternut squash purée, broccoli

and kale. Not in the mood for fish? Then there's roast duck breast with dauphinois potatoes, baby vegetables and chicory in a pomegranate and red wine jus. There's an impressive cheese tasting plate, too, and a dainty 'gone in three mouthfuls' tarte Tatin among desserts. Wines start at £19.20 for a crisp English white from nearby Newent.
Chef/s: Jon Lane. **Open:** Tue to Sun L, Tue to Sat D. **Closed:** Mon, 25 and 26 Dec, Tue and Wed D (Jan and Feb). **Meals:** main courses £20 to £70. Set L £19 (2 courses) to £25. Tasting menu £68 (6 courses). **Details:** 50 seats. 26 seats outside. Wheelchairs. Music. Parking. Children at L only.

Symbols

⏻ Accommodation is available
£30 Three courses for less than £30
£5 OFF £5-off voucher scheme
🍷 Notable wine list

▌Barnsley
The Potager
Cooking score: 3
Modern European | £37
Barnsley House, Barnsley, GL7 5EE
Tel no: (01285) 740000
barnsleyhouse.com

Barnsley House is quite the looker, its gardens – created by the late garden designer Rosemary Verey – truly romantic. The potager (the exquisite kitchen garden) lends its name and inspiration to the restaurant – all grace and greenery, its tables bedecked with foliage and plentiful windows inviting the outside in. After crusty rolls with a garden herb dip, the menu follows a broadly European tack, with typical options including pork cheeks with celeriac rémoulade and salad leaves, and then venison haunch with a haggis croquette, fondant potato, red cabbage and chestnuts. While garden leaves are a big feature, the desserts also deserve attention: maybe a simple but seductive chocolate fondant with mango sorbet. The bar channels retro cool via 1970s colours and artwork, while the wine list includes an impressive selection by the glass, with the main list divided into categories such as 'old school and serious' and 'curveball reds'.
Chef/s: Francesco Volgo. **Open:** all week L and D. **Meals:** main courses £11 to £30. Set L £24 (2 courses) to £28. **Details:** 40 seats. 24 seats outside. Bar. Parking. Children over 12 yrs only at L, over 14 yrs only at D.

The Village Pub
Cooking score: 2
Modern British | £30
Barnsley, GL7 5EF
Tel no: (01285) 740421
thevillagepub.co.uk

Rambling and rustic on the inside and obviously well looked after, this golden-stoned village hostelry just up the road from

Barnsley House (see entry) is the kind of rural picture townies dream about. The restaurant reinforces the image with its blazing winter fire, summer-terrace tables and strongly rooted policy of sourcing ingredients as locally as possible. The kitchen's gutsy pub classics are strong on flavour. Almost everyone loves to start with nibbles such as black pudding Scotch eggs or onion bhaji. After that it's on to twice-baked Cheddar cheese soufflé or a bowl of restorative leek and potato soup, before mains such as beer-battered haddock and chips, lamb chump with parsley mash and green beans, or a burger with bacon jam, Cheddar and hand-cut chips. Puddings are an honour roll of sticky toffee, apple and pecan crumble and spotted dick and custard. Pedigree British cheeses are another lure. Drink Cotswold craft ales or workaday wines (starting at £20).
Chef/s: Francesco Volgo. **Open:** Mon to Sat L and D. Sun all day from 12. **Meals:** main courses £13 to £21. **Details:** 60 seats. 50 seats outside. Wheelchairs. Parking.

▌Bristol
Adelina Yard
Cooking score: 4
Modern European | £38
3 Queen Quay, Welsh Back, Bristol, BS1 4SL
Tel no: (0117) 9112112
adelinayard.com

Husband-and-wife team Jamie Randall and Olivia Barry have settled into their new roles as proprietors of Adelina Yard, one of a number of recent additions to Bristol's burgeoning food scene – although neither are about to neglect their cooking duties. With time spent in the kitchens of a number of prestigious London addresses, they certainly know what's what when it comes to feeding and watering Bristol's residents. The compact, L-shaped room has a partial open-to-view kitchen delivering cooking that mixes modern British ideas with Scandi influences – say fermented kale with cavatelli (pasta shells), slow-cooked egg and goats'cheese or Brixham crab paired with dill, apple and wood sorrel.

Reporters have praised 'cooked to perfection' fillet of brill served with leeks, 'succulent' Fowey mussels and monk's beard, and enjoyed forced Yorkshire rhubarb with stem ginger and house clotted cream, as well as stout ice cream served with chocolate and popcorn. The concise wine list starts at £20.

Chef/s: Jamie Randall and Olivia Barry. **Open:** Tue to Sat L and D. **Closed:** Sun, Mon, 24 Dec to 9 Jan. **Meals:** main courses £18 to £24. Set L £15 (2 courses) to £17. Tasting menus £42 to £62. **Details:** 30 seats. 10 seats outside. V menu. Wheelchairs. Music.

Bell's Diner

Cooking score: 4
Mediterranean | £35
1-3 York Road, Montpelier, Bristol, BS6 5QB
Tel no: (0117) 9240357
bellsdiner.com

Now into its 41st year, this former grocer's shop in the Bohemian quarter of Montpelier continues to perform well despite a significant change in the kitchen. Sam Sohn-Rethel has left to concentrate on Bellita (see entry); his replacement, Jack Richardson, previously worked at Ballymaloe House in Cork. Mr Richardson's family runs an organic farm in the Cotswolds so using seasonal, local produce comes as second nature to him, and it shows on his small-plates menu. An early July meal produced a parade of 'memorable dishes', including 'spot-on' breaded lamb sweetbreads with a 'punchy' herb and caper mayonnaise, 'super-fresh' clams with lots of shredded smoked ham hock and a deep-flavoured broth, and wild sea trout with crunchy green beans and cherry tomatoes and garlic forming 'a lovely sauce'. A faultless baked vanilla cheesecake with boozy English cherries made for a fine finale. The resourceful wine list (starting at £20 for vibrant Greek house blends) takes in lesser-known regions, including Armenia, Turkey and the Azores, with several by the glass or smaller 'taste' measures.

Chef/s: Jack Richardson. **Open:** Fri to Sun L, Mon to Sat D. **Meals:** small plates £3 to £14. **Details:** 50 seats. Bar. Music. Children before 8pm only.

Bellita

Cooking score: 2
Mediterranean | £25
34 Cotham Hill, Bristol, BS6 6LA
Tel no: (0117) 923 8755
bellita.co.uk
£30

Bellita is a lively, welcoming place with stools at the counter for those who prefer to drink, chat to staff and nibble snacks of potato and Parmesan fritters or boquerones. The kitchen follows a Mediterranean and North African path – small dishes are very much the thing here. Dig into fennel, blood-orange and chicory salad with hazelnuts and mint, and charcoal-grilled Cornish mussels with burnt lemon and extra-virgin olive oil, although you may want to keep to yourself the seductively rich pork cheeks cooked in Pedro Ximénez with cauliflower purée, wild mushrooms and sage. To finish, maybe chocolate, walnut and ricotta tart. As well as cocktails and homemade cordials, a concise but racy wine list is sourced exclusively from female winemakers (from £20), with plenty by the glass and carafe.

Chef/s: Sam Sohn-Rethel and Danny Garland. **Open:** Wed to Sat L, Mon to Sat D. **Closed:** Sun, 25 and 26 Dec. **Meals:** small plates £4 to £15. **Details:** 42 seats. Bar. Wheelchairs. Music.

Birch

Cooking score: 4
Modern British | £26
47 Raleigh Road, Bristol, BS3 1QS
Tel no: (0117) 9028326
birchbristol.co
£30

Little has changed since Birch wowed local residents when it opened in 2014, though one visitor thought the 'decidedly DIY' corner shop conversion 'could do with a bit of money spent on it now the restaurant is so well

established,' before quickly adding 'but this can be forgiven as the food is so good.' Sam Leach still makes everything, from the sourdough bread to the ice cream, and he and partner Beccy Massey grow many of the restaurant's vegetables on their smallholding. The result is a daily changing selection of 'utterly delicious' small plates, plus a couple of mains, showcasing real precision and flair. Simple descriptions, say pickled mackerel oatcake or Jerusalem artichoke, crab and spring onion, belie an astounding complexity of flavour and impressive mastery of complex technical skills, while to finish there could be jam sponge with whortleberry yoghurt ice cream or a local Cheddar and homemade biscuits and plum butter. To drink there is an impressive range of locally sourced beers, ciders and spirits, as well as wines from £20.
Chef/s: Sam Leach. **Open:** Sat L, Wed to Sat D. **Closed:** Sun, Mon, Tue, 2 weeks Christmas, 3 weeks Aug. **Meals:** main courses £12 to £17. **Details:** 24 seats. 6 seats outside. Music.

★ NEW ENTRY ★

Box-E
Cooking score: 4
Modern British | £29
Unit 10, Cargo 1, Wapping Wharf, Bristol, BS1 6WP
boxebristol.com
£5 OFF £30

Bristol foodies warn that this idiosyncratic first venture is currently one of the hardest to book restaurants in the city. Part of Cargo, a development of converted shipping containers on Bristol's rejuvenated harbourside, Box-E is a functional two-container space, allowing room for 14 diners, with four more at the plywood bar next to the open kitchen. Here Elliott Lidstone (ex L'Ortolan, see entry) cooks solo – his wife Tess runs front-of-house – and is making a big impact with his short, seasonal menus. Bursting with imaginative ideas, strong, direct flavours are evident from the outset, in starters such as precisely grilled ox tongue with Jersey Royals, Dijon mustard emulsion

and capers, shallots and salsa verde adding extra punch, and main courses of spot-on roast quail ('seriously succulent') on a bed of herby cannellini beans with more salsa verde and wilted radicchio draped over the top of the bird. Other clever pairings include hake with black lentils and caramelised fennel butter, and a 'light, fluffy' chocolate mousse with passion fruit coulis, pomegranate seeds and grated coconut. As for wine, the list opens at £22, with much of the modern European list priced between £40 and £60.
Chef/s: Elliott Lidstone. **Open:** Wed to Sat L, Tue to Sat D. **Closed:** Sun, Mon. **Meals:** main courses £14 to £22. Tasting menu £45. **Details:** 18 seats. Wheelchairs. Music.

Bravas
Cooking score: 2
Spanish | £15
7 Cotham Hill, Bristol, BS6 6LD
Tel no: (0117) 3296887
bravas.co.uk
£30

It's wise to book for peak times, but if you are struck by a spontaneous urge, note they keep 16 stools unreserved at the front. The pared-back interior and the food displays on the counter, not to mention the smells drifting out of the open kitchen, add to the authentic Spanish vibe. The owners started out with a supper club and the place was born of a love of Spain and its food – jamón croqueta and plump boquerones in vinegar take you right there, as does chorizo cooked in cider, or a cheeseboard with Manchego, Rey Silo and Cabrales (with membrillo). Ibérico pork gets a grilling a la plancha, Hereford skirt steak is fired up with mojo verde, and wild red prawns are simply grilled with a sprinkling of salt. Finish with honey pannacotta and forced rhubarb. The wine list traverses Spain and there are sherries and a G&T list, too.
Chef/s: Mark Chapman. **Open:** Mon to Sat, all day from 11.30. **Closed:** Sun, 24 to 26 Dec. **Meals:** tapas £3 to £7. **Details:** 35 seats. Music.

Bulrush

Cooking score: 5
Modern British | £37
21 Cotham Road South, Bristol, BS6 5TZ
Tel no: (0117) 3290990
bulrushrestaurant.co.uk

£5
OFF

There has been a restaurant on this site for 40 years, which somewhat predates its current youthful custodians, George Livesey and Katherine Craughwell. This may be their first venture but Mr Livesey comes via a number of noteworthy London establishments including St John and Roux at Parliament Square (see entries). Set across two floors, the unassuming décor doesn't quite prepare you for the cutting-edge techniques, global influences and the foraged materials that take the fiercely seasonal dishes to a level way beyond what might be expected from a modest neighbourhood bistro. Blowtorched sole with white gazpacho, almond purée and pickled grapes is one of the starters that regularly turn heads, but the kitchen is equally adept in other departments. Note beautifully cooked Suffolk lamb with wild garlic, pearl barley and turnip tops. Desserts bring the likes of muscovado and miso sponge with hay ice cream and raisin purée. A fixed-price lunch also demonstrates real skill, opening with braised hare with beetroot and rhubarb and going on to confit pork with heritage carrots, roasted onions and arrowgrass. Wines from £20.
Chef/s: George Livesey. **Open:** Thur to Sat L, Tue to Sat D. **Closed:** Sun, Mon, 2 weeks Jan, 1 week May, 2 weeks Aug. **Meals:** main courses £15 to £22. Set L £20 (3 courses). Tasting menu £48. **Details:** 48 seats. V menu. Bar. Music.

Symbols

🛏 Accommodation is available
£30 Three courses for less than £30
£5 £5-off voucher scheme
OFF
🍷 Notable wine list

★ CHEF OF THE YEAR ★
★ TOP 10 ★

Casamia

Cooking score: 8
Modern British | £98
The General, Lower Guinea Street, Bristol, BS1 6SY
Tel no: (0117) 9592884
casamiarestaurant.co.uk

Nearly two years on and Casamia has acclimatised well to its new surroundings – the ground floor of the General, overlooking Bathurst Basin. Inside it is all very informal in an expensively unadorned, monochrome way – tables are clothless, the staff well briefed and relaxed, and chefs interact with the customers without missing a beat; nothing jars here. Enthusiasm for the food is universal: 'once again stunning dish followed stunning dish' is a typical reader's comment. Peter Sanchez-Iglesias's seasonally inspired tasting menus are inventive yet simple, exciting yet carefully controlled for flavour and texture, seen in a procession of dishes of such clarity and cohesion that even bread deserves its status as a separate course. Beetroot risotto surprises with its earthy sweetness offset by a subtle acidity from pickled fennel and beetroot, the whole complemented by yoghurt sorbet and a scattering of pistachios. A trio of brown trout comes as a strip of crisp skin, as roast belly layered with a trout mousse, roe, dashi jelly and lime zest, and as a smoky-flavoured confit loin (topped with a glowing charcoal that's removed at table) served in a crab and ginger dashi broth. And the flavours evoked are strikingly vivid, as in an updating of sole véronique, where a perfectly timed nugget of fish is embellished with grapes and an intense eggy sabayon hiding tiny pieces of leek, or in a lamb two-parter: first a broth, then tender pink loin surrounded by dabs of black garlic, purées of lentil and cherry tomatoes, a micro-heap of nasturtium leaves and a Jersey Royal in lamb fat. It's a theme followed through in desserts – passion fruit (granita, jelly, seeds) topped by a tarragon-flavoured custard and dabs of meringue, served ahead of variations

Join us at thegoodfoodguide.co.uk

of rhubarb, a delicate run through ice and jelly, ginger, rose and cream cheese, both winners at inspection. Care and attention to detail are second to none, and there is nothing complacent about this smooth-running operation; the wine service in particular is highly knowledgeable. This is just as well as the list turns up interesting bottles from around the world.

Chef/s: Peter Sanchez-Iglesias. **Open:** Fri and Sat L, Wed to Sat D. **Closed:** Sun, Mon, Tue. **Meals:** tasting menu £98. **Details:** 35 seats. V menu. Bar. Music.

Flour & Ash

Cooking score: 1
Italian | £20
203b Cheltenham Road, Bristol, BS6 5QX
Tel no: (0117) 9083228
flourandash.co.uk

£30

With the branch in Westbury-on-Trym now closed, focus is firmly on the original venue, a small, family-friendly place by the railway arches at the top of Cheltenham Road. Quirky and great value, the pared-down menu puts the focus on pizza and homemade ice cream, with just a few starters (say mussels in vermouth, cream, dill and tarragon sauce) and sides (polenta chips with truffle oil and Parmesan). Pizzas mix the unusual (ox cheek and red wine ragù) with the more familiar margherita or ventricina (spicy salami). Dark chocolate ice cream is an indulgent finish, beers are mostly local, and wines start at £16.50.

Chef/s: Brendan Baker. **Open:** all week, all day from 12. **Closed:** 24 to 26 Dec, 31 Dec, 1 Jan. **Meals:** main courses £9 to £14. **Details:** 41 seats. Music.

Visit us online

To find out more about The Good Food Guide, please visit thegoodfoodguide.co.uk

---

Greens

Cooking score: 3
Modern European | £29
25 Zetland Road, Bristol, BS6 7AH
Tel no: (0117) 9246437
greensbristol.co.uk

£30

Just off Bristol's Gloucester Road, 'everyday fine dining' is what this Redland neighbourhood restaurant offers, in a 'very relaxed setting'. Service is informal but efficient and the tightly-packed tables and dark mushroom walls create a pleasantly intimate ambience. Menus follow the seasons and while the kitchen plays it safe with comfortingly familiar dishes, the level of cooking is competent and precise. A winter visit opened with a soup of silky butternut squash, studded with chestnuts and spiced with dukkah, and 'impressive' lamb fritters with mint gribiche. 'Meltingly tender' haunch of venison with game sausage, greens, 'intensely flavourful' pumpkin purée and a glossy game sauce followed, with chocolate mousse with milk crumb and a sticky toffee pudding bringing up the rear. The two-course set lunch is considered 'an absolute steal', while wines, many of which are offered by the glass or 500ml carafe, start at £18 for an eminently quaffable bottle of Chilean Merlot.

Chef/s: Martin Laurentowicz. **Open:** Tue to Sat L, Mon to Sat D. Sun, all day from 12. **Closed:** 24 to 30 Dec. **Meals:** main courses £14 to £21. Set L £12 (2 courses) to £16. Set D £18 (2 courses) to £23. Sun L £15. **Details:** 40 seats. 8 seats outside. V menu. Bar. Wheelchairs. Music.

Lido

Cooking score: 3
Mediterranean | £35
Oakfield Place, Bristol, BS8 2BJ
Tel no: (0117) 9339530
lidobristol.com

'I absolutely love this place and took my partner for our anniversary,' noted one regular to this beautifully restored Victorian open-air swimming pool in the heart of Clifton.

Housed in the plate-glass-clad viewing gallery, the restaurant and bar is all about classy cooking in a unique setting. Freddy Bird may rarely be found behind the pass these days, but the influence of his time at Moro is still very much in evidence on the menu. The wood-fired oven is put to good use in a variety of dishes: from roast scallops with sweet herb and garlic butter to leg of lamb with Asturian verdina beans and salsa verde. Puddings include a wide selection of homemade ices with exotic flavours like bay and black pepper or lemon and star anise. A bottle of house wine, from the predominantly Iberian and Italian list, is good value at £18.50.

Chef/s: Freddy Bird. **Open:** all week L and D. **Closed:** 25 and 26 Dec, 1 Jan. **Meals:** main courses £17 to £35. Set L and D £16 (2 courses) to £20. Tasting menu £50. **Details:** 150 seats. 36 seats outside. Bar. Wheelchairs. Music.

Mesa

Cooking score: 2
Modern European | £25
2B North View, Bristol, BS6 7QB
Tel no: (0117) 9706276
mesabar.co.uk

£30

'A great local restaurant,' noted a visitor to Olly Gallery and Julian Faiello's new-look tapas bar, formerly Manna. Mesa is all about tapas 'and it has been packed since it opened'. Caramel-coloured leather banquettes, copper-topped tables and enamel lamps give a sharp, urban feel and the refit has increased covers – 'it feels a lot bigger than it did'. Spain is the major point of reference for the kitchen, but dishes from the Middle East and North Africa make appearances. Highlights of a test meal included Syrian lentils with cumin yoghurt sauce; an Indian-style slow-cooked cauliflower with coriander and spice; hake fillet in salsa verde with white asparagus, and harissa fried lamb shoulder teamed with spiced chickpeas, yoghurt and chilli sauce. Desserts range from Belgian chocolate pot with olive oil chocolate crumble to tarta de

Santiago with whipped cream. A short but carefully curated list of Spanish and Italian wines starts at £17.

Chef/s: Olly Gallery. **Open:** Mon to Sat D only. **Closed:** Sun. **Meals:** tapas £4 to £8. **Details:** 40 seats. Bar. Wheelchairs. Music.

No Man's Grace

Cooking score: 2
Modern European | £32
6 Chandos Road, Bristol, BS6 6PE
Tel no: (0117) 9744077
nomansgrace.com

On the site of a bistro once run by the flamboyant TV chef Keith Floyd (RIP), this corner building in the Bristol suburb of Redland is now the culinary home of chef/proprietor John Watson. Mr Watson previously worked at Casamia (see entry), but his precise techniques and thoughtful presentation owe more to his culinary hero Thomas Keller. There has been a significant change to the menu since the last edition of the guide, with Watson swapping the small-plate format for a more traditional (though concise) à la carte. The cooking remains as confident as before, with the same intuitive flavour combinations on display in dishes such as hand-dived scallop teamed with caramelised cauliflower and grapes, and in a delightful main course of brill with salsify cooked in a seaweed, samphire, gnocchi and crab bisque. For dessert, a light prune and Armagnac soufflé with Lady Grey ice cream is a standout finale. Wines from £18.

Chef/s: John Watson. **Open:** Fri to Sun L, Wed to Sat D. **Closed:** Mon, Tue, last 2 weeks Aug. **Meals:** main courses £15 to £24. **Details:** 34 seats. 24 seats outside. Bar. Music.

Average price

The average price denotes the price of a three-course meal without wine.

The Ox

Cooking score: 3
British | £35
The Basement, 43 Corn Street, Bristol,
BS1 1HT
Tel no: (0117) 9221001
theoxbristol.com

£5 OFF

According to aficionados, descending the spiral marble staircase to the cocooned basement that used to be a bank vault is like walking into a Stateside 'Prohibition-era speakeasy'. There's an almost sepulchral glow to this tremendous dining and drinking venue, with oak paneling, a parquet floor, frosted grape-cluster lamps, vintage mirrors and rich colours. Steak is king here, a temple to the delights of mighty 30oz bone-in ribs or T-bones to share, or ribeye, sirloin and fillet, and served with whatever you fancy paying extra for (triple-cooked chips, mac 'n' cheese, béarnaise sauce et al). It's busy, loud and fun. Start with soft shell crab with calypso mayo or ox heart with baba ganoush and pomegranate molasses, and finish with ginger parkin with clotted cream and rhubarb or a plate of British and Irish cheeses if you want to continue exploring the global wine list. There's a second branch on Whiteladies Road, BS8 2QX; tel: (0117) 973 0005.
Chef/s: Luke Angus. **Open:** Mon to Fri and Sun L, Mon to Sat D. **Closed:** 24 to 27 Dec. **Meals:** main courses £10 to £30. Set L £15 (2 courses) to £18. Early D £15. **Details:** 80 seats. Music.

Please send us your feedback

To register your opinion about any restaurant listed in this guide, or a new restaurant that you wish to bring to our attention, please visit the web address at the bottom of the page. Your feedback informs the content of the book and will be used to compile next year's reviews.

★ NEW ENTRY ★

Paco Tapas

Cooking score: 1
Spanish | £35
3a The General, Lower Guinea Street, Bristol,
BS1 6SY
Tel no: (0117) 9257021
pacotapas.co.uk

£5 OFF

From the team behind Casamia (see entry), this Andalusian-inspired tapas bar sits on the water's edge in Bristol's old General Hospital. The buzz, look and food style is authentic, with legs of jamón hanging from the ceiling over the counter, and an open kitchen where diners perched on high stools can chat to chefs as they cook most dishes over charcoal. Creamy jamón croquetas and wobbly, perfectly seasoned tortillas are a must, although prices soon rise once you hit the meat and fish sections and dishes such as stuffed quail, sobrasada and dates, octopus a la gallega and carabineros prawns from the Canary Islands. Wines start at £27 but there are more than a dozen sherries by the glass including three served from the barrel.
Chef/s: Dave Hazell. **Open:** Fri to Sun L, Wed to Sat D. **Closed:** Mon, Tue, 25 and 26 Dec. **Meals:** tapas £2 to £22. **Details:** 25 seats. 20 seats outside. Wheelchairs. Music.

★ NEW ENTRY ★

Pasta Loco

Cooking score: 3
Italian | £30
37A Cotham Hill, Bristol, BS6 6JY
Tel no: (0117) 9733000
pastaloco.co.uk

£5 OFF

Bristol-born cousins of Italian (and Indian) heritage, Dominic Borel and Ben Harvey have gone into business together in a compact former balti house. With black-topped pine tables and brown-paper-covered lampshades, there's a homespun feel to this warm-hearted neighbourhood joint, which is one of Bristol's hottest new openings of the past year – weekend tables need to be booked about six weeks in advance. Dominic is a big presence, some say the 'best front-of-house in Bristol', while Ben delivers an open-minded take on contemporary, seasonal Italian food. He makes pasta daily, and although it's authentically Italian, is not afraid to throw in the odd curveball, say ravioli of curried goat – as a nod to the cousins' multicultural Bristol background – alongside orzo 'risotto' with peas, mint and feta or a robust pappardelle with wild boar ragù, stuffed breast and a fillet cooked sous-vide. Start with burratina with charred endive, orange and hazelnut and finish with chocolate délice and salt caramel with espresso and grappa pannacotta. A vibrant Italian-leaning wine list starts at £17.

Chef/s: Ben Harvey. **Open:** Tue to Sat L, Mon to Sat D. **Closed:** Sun, 23 Dec to 3 Jan. **Meals:** main courses £10 to £16. Set L £13 (2 courses) to £25. Set D £20 (2 courses) to £30. **Details:** 33 seats. Music.

Prego

Cooking score: 3
Italian | £30
7 North View, Bristol, BS6 7PT
Tel no: (0117) 9730496
pregobar.co.uk

Andrew Griffin may have left to open his own place, but owners Julian Faiello and Olly Gallery are still cooking and with their Italian roots and tiptop ingredients driving the menus 'you can't really see the join'. Indeed, one regular praises this 'proper neighbourhood bistro' for its consistency 'which is why I go back as often as I can'. For starters, a cricket-ball-sized arancini packed with a rich filling of ox cheek and mozzarella with a very garlicky wild garlic and tomato sauce underneath, may be followed by chicken cacciatore in slow-roasted San Marzano tomato ragù with olives, anchovy, Chianti and garlic. Fish always shows up strongly, as in an accurately cooked and very fresh lemon sole on a bed of saffron chickpeas, rainbow chard and salsa rossa, or an excellent fritto misto. A 'huge slice' of amaretti and vanilla cheesecake

with really boozy brandy-poached prunes is a winning dessert. An approachable, all-Italian wine list starts at £16.75.

Chef/s: Julian Faiello, Olly Gallery and Ricky Stephenson. **Open:** Tue to Sun L, Mon to Sat D (Mon, pizza only). **Meals:** main courses £13 to £19. **Details:** 52 seats. 16 seats outside. Wheelchairs. Music.

The Pump House

Cooking score: 3
Modern British | £33
Merchants Road, Bristol, BS8 4PZ
Tel no: (0117) 9272229
the-pumphouse.com
£5 OFF

'We took our kids along, who ate side dishes and bits from the bar menu while we chose from the à la carte, and I came away thinking it was a great place.' Indeed, you'll find cooking with aplomb at this fortress-like Victorian former pumping station overlooking Bristol's floating harbour. From the moreish snacks served at the bar (parsnip wedges with curried mayonnaise) to the tasting menu available at weekends in the mezzanine restaurant, the 'really inventive, exciting menu' is 'full of things you want to order'. Toby Gritten is a keen forager, makes excellent use of local ingredients and changes his dishes with the shifting seasons. In spring, a rabbit and foie gras terrine with forced rhubarb and gingerbread could be followed by a 'gargantuan' portion of 'intensely flavoured' shoulder and crispy breast of Mendip hogget with boulangère potatoes and charred sprouting broccoli. A tasting plate of chocolate and blood orange turns out to be a perfectly executed fondant with a bitter homemade chocolate ice cream, gravel, ganache and orange toffee. The short wine list, starting at £20, jostles for attention with real ales and an enticing rotation of 'gins of the month'.

Chef/s: Toby Gritten. **Open:** all week L, Mon to Sat D. **Closed:** 25 Dec. **Meals:** main courses £16 to £22. Tasting menu £45. **Details:** 80 seats. 100 seats outside. Wheelchairs. Music. Parking.

Peter Sanchez-Iglesias

In 2016, Peter and his family relocated their Casamia restaurant from the leafy Bristol suburb of Westbury-on-Trym to the city's redeveloped General Hospital overlooking the harbourside.

Six months later, the family opened Pi Shop, a pizzeria with a wood-fired oven next to their flagship restaurant. After that, they opened their Spanish tapas bar Paco Tapas to complete their trio of adjacent restaurants.

While Casamia's £98 tasting menu is aimed at the top end of the market, Pi Shop has become a popular family restaurant and Paco Tapas a place for people to enjoy a drink and nibble – often before heading to one of the other two restaurants.

Sanchez-Iglesias says: 'I've seen a lot of new customers coming to Casamia off the back of having a good experience at Paco Tapas and Pi Shop; it all adds to people's understanding about what we are doing. Pi Shop and Paco Tapas feel like an extension of Casamia. It means that rather than having three restaurants dotted all over the place, I don't have to travel back and forth to keep an eye on things.'

Although there are no plans to open more restaurants, Sanchez-Iglesias certainly doesn't rule it out.

The Spiny Lobster

Cooking score: 3
Seafood | £30
128-130 Whiteladies Road, Bristol, BS8 2RS
Tel no: (0117) 9737384
thespinylobster.co.uk
£5 OFF

Mitch Tonks may no longer be at the helm, but physically little has changed at the Spiny Lobster since it left the Rockfish chain at the start of 2017. The décor remains 'reminiscent of an opulent ocean liner's dining room, with an abundance of maritime memorabilia', while the freshest of fish, delivered daily from Devon and Cornwall, continues to be simply but expertly prepared. Starters could be four enormous Atlantic prawns, grilled over charcoal, and adorned with only a glug of olive oil and a sprinkle of sea salt, or wonderfully sweet scallops, roasted in their shells and served in a pool of garlic butter. To follow, a whole gilthead bream, baked al cartoccio with garlic and rosemary and unwrapped on the plate, is accompanied by a side of salsify baked in Parmesan cream. Puddings, if an underwhelming fruitilli (a Tonks recipe of doughnuts with pine nuts and raisins) with chocolate sauce is anything to go by, are not a strong suit. The wine list understandably concentrates on whites, with plenty of good–value bottles from £20.
Chef/s: Neil Roach and Charlie Hearn. **Open:** Tue to Sat L and D. **Closed:** Sun, Mon, 25 to 30 Dec, 1 to 4 Jan. **Meals:** main courses £14 to £30. Set L and D £15 (2 courses) to £18. **Details:** 45 seats. Music.

★ NEW ENTRY ★

Tare

Cooking score: 3
Modern European | £35
Unit 14, Museum Street, Wapping Wharf, Bristol, BS1 6ZA
Tel no: (0117) 9294328
tarerestaurant.co.uk

Part of the Wapping Wharf Cargo shipping-container park that has made Bristol's harbourside a new gastronomic destination,

Tare is the first venture for Matt Hampshire (previously head chef at riverstation across the water). Comprising two shipping containers, the tiny 18-cover space is bright and cheery with splashes of orange lifting the grey walls and unclothed tables – a contemporary setting that suits the ambitious, seasonal dishes emerging from the galley kitchen, often delivered by the chefs themselves. The size of the kitchen and minimal storage space dictates a set five-course menu, a summer meal kicking off in style with a plump and deep-flavoured Ibérico pork cheek croqueta, watermelon pickle and mustard mayonnaise. Pink, juicy Creedy Carver duck breast and ball of confit duck leg wrapped in cabbage followed, with baby turnip dauphinoise, cherry purée and five-spice, while a top-drawer zesty lemon tart with basil-flavoured meringue and strawberries was a fitting conclusion. A concise and intelligent wine list starts at £21.

Chef/s: Matt Hampshire and Joe Wilkin. **Open:** Sat L, Tue to Sat D. **Closed:** Sun, Mon. **Meals:** set L and D £35 (5 courses). **Details:** 18 seats. V menu.

Wallfish Bistro

Cooking score: 4
Seafood | £35
112 Princess Victoria Street, Clifton, Bristol, BS8 4DB
Tel no: (0117) 9735435
wallfishbistro.co.uk

'What a place! I loved everything. The menu was really enticing and the food delivered,' enthused one first-time visitor to this understated Clifton village bistro, adding, 'I'd go here again and again. Ask for a table on the ground floor, with its upside-down metal colander lights, stripped wood tables and comfy banquettes.' Chef/patron Seldon Curry's simple treatment of excellent local produce delivers 'walloping flavours'. Clearly the focus is on fish and seafood, but there's plenty for meat eaters in the mains section – try the sirloin steak with onions, lovage and garlic and a bowl of 'really moreish, wondrously crunchy chips'. To start,

Herefordshire snails (the eponymous wallfish) are served with bone marrow and mushrooms in a rich garlic sauce, or there could be 'beautifully executed' crab with Jerusalem artichoke and a poached bantam's egg. Three 'glistening fillets' of West Bay mackerel arrive with sea beet in a pool of pungent grain mustard reduction, while puddings include chocolate mousse with salt caramel, crème fraîche and peanut. The well-chosen wine list starts at £15, or try a locally brewed beer or Bristolian gin aperitif.

Chef/s: Seldon Curry. **Open:** Wed to Sun L and D. **Closed:** Mon, Tue. **Meals:** main courses £15 to £22. Set L and D £13 (2 courses) to £16 (Wed to Fri). **Details:** 38 seats.

Wilks

Cooking score: 6
Modern French | £53
1-3 Chandos Road, Bristol, BS6 6PG
Tel no: (0117) 9737999
wilksrestaurant.co.uk
£5
OFF

Tucked away in the residential Redland district of Bristol, James Wilkins' place is an elegantly understated venue, with grey walls showcasing the work of local artists and photographers, and a service approach that is a model of calm civility. Dishes are ingeniously composed to bring out the best in prime materials, much of which is thoroughbred West Country produce, in a cooking style that owes more than a little to modern French thinking. Squab pigeon breast royale with a parfait of the liver and its own jus offset with a note of sweet vinegar is a delicately poised starter, and could be the prelude to red mullet fillets in their Mediterranean gear of black olives, avocado and lemon with romanesco and bouillabaisse sauce, or perhaps haunch and saddle of local roe deer with morels on toast, white asparagus and a jus scented with juniper and thyme. A sphere of cocoa meringue is a technical marvel, coming with poached pear, chocolate Chantilly and hazelnut ice cream.

Look to the sommelier's selections of wines of the week, but the list has decent drinking all through, from £24.

Chef/s: James Wilkins. **Open:** Thur to Sun L, Wed to Sun D. **Closed:** Mon, Tue, 3 weeks Christmas, 3 weeks Aug. **Meals:** main courses £24 to £30. Set L £24 (2 courses) to £29. Tasting menu £58 to £78. **Details:** 28 seats. V menu. Wheelchairs. Children over 6 yrs only at D.

Wilsons

Cooking score: 5
Modern British | £32
22a Chandos Road, Bristol, BS6 6PF
Tel no: (0117) 9734157
wilsonsrestaurant.co.uk

'It just gets better each time,' declared a regular to this low-key converted shop, considered something of a hot spot since it opened in 2016. Prior to opening his first solo venture, Jan Ostle earned his culinary stripes at the likes of L'Enclume and the Clove Club (see entries) and the pedigree shines through. In a simple, no-frills, whitewashed room with black floorboards and an open kitchen at the far end, Mr Ostle keeps frippery to a minimum. The blackboard-only menu is in step with the seasons as an early spring meal showed: a 'frothy' wild garlic soup topped with a perfectly timed slow-cooked egg, then a piece of hake, accurately cooked sous-vide, teamed with chestnut mushrooms, leek and hazelnuts, both dishes revealing a resourceful range of techniques and textures. As for dessert, a flawless crème brûlée was, according to one reader, among 'the best tastes I have experienced this year'. Wines from £18.

Chef/s: Jan Ostle. **Open:** Wed to Sat L, Tue to Sat D. **Closed:** Sun, Mon. **Meals:** main courses £16 to £18. **Details:** 28 seats. Wheelchairs. Music.

Average price

The average price denotes the price of a three-course meal without wine.

Hart's Bakery

British | £8
Arch 35, Lower Approach Road, Bristol, BS1 6QS
Tel no: (0117) 9924488
hartsbakery.co.uk

£30

Hart's Bakery is to be found in a converted railway arch beneath Bristol's Temple Meads railway station, its hidden-from-view location only adding to its reputation as the city's busiest foodie hub. Baker Laura Hart has created something quite special and as her artisan bakery café has only a handful of trestle tables, queues are inevitable. Open from breakfast through to mid-afternoon, those in the know drop by for worth-a-detour Cheddar cheese toasties, straight-from-the-oven pork and black pudding sausage rolls, pea, mint, ricotta and Parmesan tarts, or roast heritage carrots with whipped ricotta, walnuts, leaves and malted wheat sourdough, all accompanied by excellent Bristol-roasted coffee.

Pi Shop

Italian | £18
The General, Lower Guinea Street, Bristol, BS1 6FU
Tel no: (0117) 9256872
thepishop.co.uk

£5 OFF £30

'Definitely a pizza place for grown-ups, despite a kids' menu and a tin of crayons being offered when I visited with my two toddlers,' thought one mum, impressed as much by the 'stonking cocktail list' as by the 'premier league' pizzas. The stark white space is dominated by the huge, copper-clad oven that delivers five classic and four regularly changing pizzas: the anchovy, olive and basil 'JR' is named in memory of Jonray Sanchez-Iglesias, whose brother Peter owns Pi Shop (as well as the neighbouring Casamia and Paco Tapas, see entries). Don't expect starters, and there's just ice cream for dessert.

LOCAL GEM
Sky Kong Kong
Korean | £15
Unit 2, Haymarket Walk, Bristol, BS1 3LN
Tel no: (0117) 2399528
skykongkong.co.uk

£30

It's not the greatest location, just off the Bear Pit roundabout, next to the bus station, but this tiny, organic Korean café is worth seeking out. Wizzy Chung does all the cooking herself, makes her own soy sauce, miso and chilli paste, and uses allotment vegetables and herbs. The good-value menu changes daily, perhaps with tuna tartare with watermelon preceding grilled sea bass or beef on a fiery kim-chee base, with rice and a tray of sides including anchovies, wild mushrooms and spinach. The lunchtime bento boxes have a loyal following and booking is essential in the evening. Unlicensed, so BYO.

LOCAL GEM
Spoke & Stringer
Spanish | £30
The Boathouse, Unit 1, Lime Kiln Road, Bristol, BS1 5AD
Tel no: (0117) 9259371
spokeandstringer.com

£5
OFF

With Brunel's iconic SS *Great Britain* directly opposite, Spoke & Stringer occupies a great harbourside location. Owned by the adjacent clothes and bike shop, this Spanish-style bar has a bit of a split personality: a prime brunch spot by day, busy tapas joint after dark. Pintxos are one way to go, but cooked-to-order tapas dishes such as charred octopus with peperonata and mojo verde or lamb cutlets with baba ganoush, pomegranate, preserved lemon and mint are tempting, too. Wines from £19.

READERS RECOMMEND
The Cauldron
International
98 Mina Road, Bristol, BS2 9XW
Tel no: (0117) 9141321
thecauldron.restaurant
'Even for a city well-known for its independent streak and quirky restaurants, the Cauldron is a genuine one-off. Everything is cooked over wood in cast-iron cauldrons and a wood-fired oven, and produce is so local that some suppliers deliver on foot or bicycle from nearby plots. The cider-braised pork belly with apple, parsnip, carrot and pickled red cabbage is worth the detour in itself.'

■ Cheltenham
★ TOP 50 ★
Le Champignon Sauvage
Cooking score: 8
Modern French | £67
24-26 Suffolk Road, Cheltenham, GL50 2AQ
Tel no: (01242) 573449
lechampignonsauvage.co.uk

David and Helen Everitt-Matthias celebrated their 30th anniversary at the Champignon in 2017. It is thus one of those restaurants that reaches back into the previous generation of culinary history, but is still at the forefront of modern development. A reader summarises the appeal: 'there are some restaurants that earn their spurs with scientific cheffery, and can be very interesting, too. Then there are other places that succeed by serving plates of food that you really, really want to eat. This is firmly in the latter category.' The grey-walled, elegantly accoutred room still looks simple enough, its artworks evoking town and country, but it's what's on the plate that matters. David's cooking combines skilfully assured technique and imagination with the confidence to leave well alone once the components of a dish are in striking harmony, as witness an autumn dish of perfectly timed wood pigeon with black pudding and puréed squash in a chocolate-laced reduction, 'one of the finest main courses I have ever eaten'. Profound impact is conjured from obvious, as well as less familiar, components, so that a starter cannelloni filled with roast kid is matched by variant textures of beetroot, while a modern classic pairing of scallops and maple-glazed chicken wings, leaking umami from every pore, gains even greater resonance from baby parsnips fragranced with woodruff. Fish dishes rise to the aromatic challenge, too, when miso-glazed cod arrives in geranium and coconut broth, while the favoured dessert has been bergamot parfait with orange jelly and liquorice cream. Lunches remain an outstanding bargain, and the wine list ranges authoritatively across the French regions and beyond, from £24.

Chef/s: David Everitt-Matthias. **Open:** Tue to Sat L and D. **Closed:** Sun, Mon, 2 weeks Christmas, 3 weeks Jun. **Meals:** set L £27 (2 courses) to £34. Set D £53 (2 courses) to £67. **Details:** 38 seats.

★ NEW ENTRY ★

Koj

Cooking score: 2
Japanese | £30
3 Regent Street, Cheltenham, GL50 1HE
Tel no: (01242) 580455
kojcheltenham.co.uk

MasterChef 2013 finalist Andrew Kojima's casual restaurant and cocktail bar started life as a pop-up, which may explain the 'slightly DIY vibe', and offers a different take on Japanese food. There's no sushi on the fairly short menu, instead you can mix and match from a list of small dishes, steamed buns (say slow-cooked lamb belly) and sides, which come out as they're ready and are designed to share. After 'a quick lesson in how (and how much) to order', dive in and try a 'standout' beef shoga yaki salad, a 'really excellent' white miso soup, and crispy shiitake mushrooms with a yuzu dipping sauce. The Anglo-Japanese micro-puddings include several flavours of mochi ice cream and a yuzu posset 'zinging with citrus'. A wide range of sakés and Japanese beers are

the focus of the drinks list, bespoke cocktails come from the first-floor Kampai cocktail bar; wine is just one red (£18), one white (£30). **Chef/s:** Andrew Kojima. **Open:** Sat L, Wed to Sat D. **Closed:** Sun, Mon, Tue. **Meals:** small plates £4 to £9. **Details:** 25 seats. Bar.

Lumière

Cooking score: 5
Modern British | £65
Clarence Parade, Cheltenham, GL50 3PA
Tel no: (01242) 222200
lumiere.cc

£5
OFF

Understatement is the key to Jon and Helen Howe's discreet venue in the Regency district of town. Behind the black door with its small awning, a room done in soothing shades of aubergine and cream is adorned with contemporary artworks and glass pieces to make an elegant setting for Jon Howe's carefully considered modern British compositions. From the moment the appetisers arrive – including perhaps kombu and sumac breadsticks for dunking in taramasalata – it's clear that concentrated thought has gone into everything. Fish dishes are replete with the kinds of bright, upstanding flavours that properly enhance the main item, such as crab in black cannelloni, pickled fennel and blood-orange butter to partner red mullet on samphire, while thoroughbred meats include West Country beef with onion and wheat beer purée, trompettes and Périgord truffle, or succulent mallard with its sweet-natured companions of pear and medjool dates. The eight-course tasting menus remain the obvious way to take in the whole experience, culminating as they do with desserts such as Valrhona Guanaja and vanilla cheesecake with brown-bread ice cream. Creative cocktails and speciality gins lead off a wine list that opens at £18.

Chef/s: Jon Howe. **Open:** Fri and Sat L, Wed to Sat D. **Closed:** Sun, Mon, Tue, 2 weeks winter, 2 weeks summer. **Meals:** set L £35 (3 courses). Set D £65 (3 courses) to £60. Tasting menu £65. **Details:** 24 seats. V menu. Bar. Music. Children over 8 yrs only.

Purslane

Cooking score: 6
Seafood | £39
16 Rodney Road, Cheltenham, GL50 1JJ
Tel no: (01242) 321639
purslane-restaurant.co.uk

There's an appealing intimacy to the Fulfords' neighbourhood restaurant on a central but quiet side street. The small, pleasant dining room is done in muted tones with a large Roman-numeralled clock on the wall, and the service tone is appreciated for its unshowy civility. Gareth Fulford hails from a family of butchers, so it isn't entirely surprising that he grew up thinking of fish and seafood as a rare treat, but here they are intended to be anything but a rarity. Start with an oyster or two in Cabernet Sauvignon vinegar, before setting about Oban scallops with orzo, sweetcorn and (of course) sea purslane, dressed to striking effect in parsley pesto, or there's fabulous crab salad, the brown meat encased in a crisp-shelled bonbon, the sweetness of the white enhanced by puréed and shaved carrot. For main, it could be megrim sole with garganelli pasta and romanesco in Périgord truffle butter, or hake with crispy polenta, clams and pancetta in a featherlight seafood sauce. Aged Highgrove beef is on hand, too, and the finishing reward could be muscovado rice pudding with poached pear, honeycomb and brazils. A short international wine list opens at £20.
Chef/s: Gareth Fulford. **Open:** Tue to Sat L and D. **Closed:** Sun, Mon, 24 to 27 Dec, 2 weeks Jan, 2 weeks Aug. **Meals:** main courses £18 to £20. Set L £14 (2 courses) to £17. Set D £39 (3 courses). Tasting menu £60. **Details:** 34 seats. 4 seats outside. Music.

Symbols

🛏 Accommodation is available
£30 Three courses for less than £30
£5 OFF £5-off voucher scheme
🍷 Notable wine list

▮ Chipping Campden
The Chef's Dozen

Cooking score: 3
Modern British | £45
Island House, High Street, Chipping Campden, GL55 6AL
Tel no: (01386) 840598
thechefsdozen.co.uk

A table under the shade of a weeping willow tree is the summertime must-have at this intimate neighbourhood restaurant, or you can chill out in the first-floor dining room amid period features and smart modern furniture. The restaurant's name gives a clue to what's on offer – a dozen similarly sized dishes from which diners generally choose four. Readers have enjoyed many inspired creations, from an amuse-bouche of apple, cucumber and lovage soup to a 'heavenly' raspberry and orange-curd soufflé with elderflower ice cream – all 'perfectly timed'. In between, local boy Richard Craven looks to his home turf for inspiration – think heritage tomato with Wigmore cheese, granola and nasturtium or beetroot (heritage, again) with ox tongue, wild horseradish and crispy barley. For mains, fish could be gurnard with parsnips, mussels and curry, meat a hay-smoked lamb with sweetbreads and sheep's cheese. The mood is relaxed, service is 'excellent' and there are some pleasing wines to set things off.
Chef/s: Richard Craven. **Open:** Sat L, Tue to Sat D. **Closed:** Sun, Mon. **Meals:** Set L and D £45 (4 courses). Tasting menu £65. **Details:** 26 seats. 20 seats outside. Music.

▮ Eldersfield
The Butchers Arms

Cooking score: 5
Modern British | £45
Lime Street, Eldersfield, GL19 4NX
Tel no: (01452) 840381
thebutchersarms.net

Praise comes thick and fast for this 16th-century red-brick rural pub with 'serious wizardry going on in the kitchen' and a 'really

laid-back and relaxed' atmosphere. Push open the ancient, warped wooden front door to enter the cosy low-ceilinged rooms with mismatched wooden furniture and hop-wreathed beams. There might be a few locals propping up the small bar, but most people are here to eat chef/patron James Winter's intensely flavourful food. At a test meal, crispy pig's cheeks proved to be a croquette of succulent, slow-cooked meat 'with a perfect crunch outside', shot through with subtle Chinese spicing and served with fried quails' eggs and a silky romesco sauce with great depth of flavour. A main of honey-roast duck breast ('topped with a layer of perfectly crispy fat') and served with lentils, bacon and rocket and a Parmesan beignet was also 'flawlessly cooked', while roast hake arrived with a round of pork belly and 'a golden roasted slice from a cake of compressed layers of potato slices'. Portions are generous but do find room for 'textbook' pistachio macarons with Amalfi lemon curd and a 'delicious' passion fruit sorbet. The short, carefully chosen wine list starts at £23.50.
Chef/s: James Winter. **Open:** Fri to Sun L, Tue to Sat D. **Closed:** Mon, 2 weeks Christmas, 2 weeks Aug. **Meals:** main courses £23 to £30. **Details:** 30 seats. Bar. Parking. No children under 10 yrs.

◼ Long Ashton
The Bird in Hand
Cooking score: 2
British | £34
17 Weston Road, Long Ashton, BS41 9LA
Tel no: (01275) 395222
bird-in-hand.co.uk

£5
OFF

Run by the team behind Bristol harbourside's Pump House (see entry), this affable village boozer is a short drive from the city centre and takes its food seriously, right down to walls covered with pages ripped from old Mrs Beeton cookbooks. Locals still congregate in the chummy bar, where you might try the Scotch eggs that made one reader 'weep with pleasure', but those in the know grab one of the scrubbed wooden tables in the teal-coloured dining room. Shelves of homemade pickles and chutneys are signs of an industrious kitchen and many of the ingredients on the short carte are wild or foraged. Strongly seasonal dishes are simple and honest: Cornish scallops with Jersualem artichokes and apples might be followed by whole St Ives Bay lemon sole with cockles and seaweed butter sauce. Puddings could feature tonka bean pannacotta with poached pear and almonds. To drink, local ales compete with a good-value wine list from £16.50.
Chef/s: Sylvester Platek. **Open:** all week L, Mon to Sat D. **Meals:** main courses £16 to £20. **Details:** 46 seats. 25 seats outside. Bar. Music. Children before 9pm only.

◼ Northleach
The Wheatsheaf Inn
Cooking score: 3
Modern British | £35
West End, Northleach, GL54 3EZ
Tel no: (01451) 860244
cotswoldswheatsheaf.com

🛏

This handsome, wisteria-clad 17th-century coaching inn on the edge of Northleach's pretty market square is everything you might expect from a well-groomed country hostelry. Now reinvented as a smart boutique dining-pub-with-rooms with a tranquil landscaped garden and draught ales for local drinkers, there's an unpretentious confidence about the place and a menu that's as appealing as the fire-warmed bar is cosy. Starters such as wood pigeon and foie gras terrine with pickled pears or soft polenta with nettles, peas, goats' curd and lemon, and mains like new season's rump of lamb with roasted spring carrots and salsa verde or organic chicken, mushroom and tarragon pie with mashed potato and kale make the most of the region's rich larder. Comforting desserts include blackberry crème brûlée or raspberry and vanilla custard tart. The carefully chosen and wide-ranging wine list, arranged by country, opens at £19.

Chef/s: Devon Boyce. **Open:** all week L and D.
Meals: main courses £13 to £18. Set L £13 (2
courses) to £15. **Details:** 70 seats. 40 seats outside.
Bar. Music. Parking.

Painswick
The Painswick
Cooking score: 4
Modern British | £40
Kemps Lane, Painswick, GL6 6YB
Tel no: (01452) 813688
thepainswick.co.uk

What was once known as Prospect House was
built on wool money in the Georgian era, but
conjured into its present magnificence by the
great Arts and Crafts architect Detmar Blow
in 1902. It's been carefully nurtured by its
present owners into a modern-day country
hotel, a place where afternoon tea on the
terrace is a must, the parquet-floored dining
room makes an equally relaxing setting, and
the menus of modernised British cooking,
courtesy of Michael Bedford, offer plenty to
entice. A smoked salmon soufflé provided a
memorable opener for one reporter, or there
could be a tartlet topped with truffled
butternut and pumpkin, adorned with
saladings. Mixing meat and fish produces a
main course of stone bass with beef shin ravioli
and buttered greens, while duck leg gets the
classic French daube treatment with red wine,
bacon, mushrooms and button onions, or
skate wing comes in Chinese livery with soy
and ginger and a serving of prawn toast.
Chef/s: Michael Bedford. **Open:** all week L and D.
Meals: main courses £14 to £28. **Details:** 40 seats.
24 seats outside. V menu. Bar. Music. Parking.

Paxford
★ NEW ENTRY ★
The Churchill Arms
Cooking score: 2
British | £34
Paxford, GL55 6XH
Tel no: (01386) 593159
churchillarms.co

With its atmospheric flagstoned bar, the
inglenook filled with logs and a wood-burner,
and a scrubbed-up, easy going dining area
leading out to the beer garden, Nick Deverell-
Smith's revitalised inn is the perfect village
hostelry. It can be thought of as a gentrified
pub in three parts: where drinkers are
welcome, where the menu offers pub classics
(such as fish and chips) as well as a familiar run
through the modern brasserie catalogue, and
where there are two comfortable bedrooms
upstairs. Drinkers and diners generate a lively
buzz and reports have praised a host of things
from 'the amazing' smoked haddock soufflé
with chive velouté to beautifully timed whole
Cornish bream, calf's liver with confit bacon,
cider onions and buttery mash, and roast wild
partridge 'perfectly cooked and full of flavour',
accompanied by polenta and roast cauliflower.
To finish, the glazed lemon tart is highly rated.
To drink there are real ales or a global wine
selection.
Chef/s: Nick Deverell-Smith. **Open:** Tue to Sun L,
Tue to Sat D. **Closed:** Mon. **Meals:** main courses
£15 to £26. Set L £15 (2 courses) to £20.
Details: Bar.

◼ Selsley
The Bell Inn
Cooking score: 1
British | £25
Bell Lane, Selsley, GL5 5JY
Tel no: (01453) 753801
thebellinnselsley.com

£5 OFF £30

With views across the pretty Woodchester Valley, this 'lovely old stone building' has been classily refurbished and extended, providing all the warmth, welcome and rusticity you could wish for, along with a touch of boutique class. The kitchen aims for a mix of traditional and modern cooking, baking bread daily, offering lunchtime sandwiches or beef burger and triple-cooked chips on the 'pub classics' menu, while a typical evening meal might include pressed ham and leek terrine with chicken liver parfait and crostini, and confit Barbary duck leg with Puy lentils and wild mushrooms. For dessert, maybe bitter chocolate fondant with tonka bean ice cream. Wine prices start at £16.
Chef/s: Mark Payne and Jack Dowdswell. **Open:** all week L, Mon to Sat D. **Closed:** first week Jan. **Meals:** main courses £11 to £17. **Details:** 55 seats. 30 seats outside. Bar. Wheelchairs. Music. Parking.

◼ Stow-on-the-Wold

LOCAL GEM
The Old Butchers
Modern European | £35
7 Park Street, Stow-on-the-Wold, GL54 1AQ
Tel no: (01451) 831700
theoldbutchers.com

The old butcher himself would be heartened to see the charcuterie on offer in his one-time shop. Peter and Louise Robinson offer top-quality Spanish meats cut to order, while the menu is full of well-judged combinations and bold flavours: lamb's sweetbreads with wild garlic mayonnaise, crab and quail Scotch egg, ox cheek bourguignon with grilled ox tongue, or Cornish mussels spiced up with 'ndjua.

Even the burger is a cut above – Ruby Red rump cooked over charcoal. The concise wine list opens at £18.75.

◼ Thornbury
Ronnies
Cooking score: 3
Modern European | £39
11 St Mary Street, Thornbury, BS35 2AB
Tel no: (01454) 411137
ronnies-restaurant.co.uk

Hidden away in an increasingly deserted shopping precinct, chef/proprietor Ron Faulkner's well-appointed restaurant is certainly low-key, despite its enduring popularity. Now in its tenth year, this 17th-century former schoolhouse has a loyal local following, but works well as a special destination with bare stone walls, warm lighting and neutral colours creating a relaxed look. The modern European dishes are informed by Faulkner's classical background (he trained under the legendary Anton Mosimann) and he delivers 'exemplary plates of seasonal combinations'. An early summer meal started with a well-balanced crab cannelloni, burnt pineapple adding sweetness and acidity along with sweet pepper and crunch from radish. It was followed by a precisely cooked fillet of turbot topped with a hazelnut crust and served with shallots and calçot onions. To finish, a caramelised white chocolate cheesecake was teamed with intense Cheddar Valley strawberries. A good-value international wine list (bottles from £19) offers a dozen by the glass.
Chef/s: Ronnie Faulkner. **Open:** Tue to Sun L, Tue to Sat D. **Closed:** Mon, 25 and 26 Dec, 2 weeks Jan, bank hols. **Meals:** main courses £15 to £25. Set L £15 (2 courses) to £20. Sun L £21 (2 courses) to £25. **Details:** 58 seats. Wheelchairs. Music.

Average price

The average price denotes the price of a three-course meal without wine.

Liam Finnegan
Castle Bow, Taunton, Somerset

Your menu showcases seasonality; what is your favourite time of year for food?
I love all times of year and enjoy watching the changes in food across the seasons. Spring for freshness, summer for light dishes and intense flavours, autumn for its abundance and finally winter for its comforting, heartier food.

Name one ingredient you couldn't cook without.
Love - pure and simple.

Who are your greatest influences?
My family, friends and team inspire me daily and have done all through my career. We don't follow food trends or watch what's going on, we just like to cook food that we love to eat.

When you get home at the end of a long day, what do you like to eat?
High fat, high sugar, washed down with a good red.

Do you have a guilty junk-food pleasure?
Stinky cheese and crusty bread.

LOCAL GEM
Romy's Kitchen
Indian | £25
2 Castle Street, Thornbury, BS35 1HB
Tel no: (01454) 416728
romyskitchen.co.uk

£5 OFF £30

Now with an MBE to her name, Kolkata-born Romy Gill started out hosting dinner parties before opening her own restaurant in a rather quaint Grade II-listed building. What she offers is a world away from the high street curry house, so expect a short menu featuring the likes of tamarind-infused Parsee chicken, Keralan goat curry and anardana gosht (lamb cooked with pomegranate seeds). Sides include chilli-spiked pickled onions, and there's locally made chai ice cream to finish. Wines suit the spicy flavours to a T.

▮ Upper Slaughter
Lords of the Manor
Cooking score: 5
Modern British | £73
Upper Slaughter, GL54 2JD
Tel no: (01451) 820243
lordsofthemanor.com

The creeper-covered Cotswold stone house began life as a rectory in the Georgian era, and found itself serving as a billet for the US army during the last war, before becoming a country hotel in the 1970s. It looks the business outside and in, through to a low-ceilinged, cocoon-like panelled dining room, where new chef Charles Smith now rules the roost. Smith's CV is of the blessed, incorporating stints at New York's Per Se and Mayfair's Westbury (see entry), and his menus here avoid over-complexity in favour of a direct, ingredient-led approach. Choose from tasters of five or seven courses for dinner, with a three-course prix fixe at weekend lunches. Standout dishes have been Wye asparagus part-wrapped in brik pastry and deep-fried, served with a mousseline of duck egg and caviar, a confidently focused main course of butter-roasted turbot with braised fennel, preserved lemon purée and foaming vermouth cream, and another of Belted Galloway beef in classic bordelaise with Alsace bacon, puréed Jerusalems and a side of irresistible truffled mash. Textbook just-set crème brûlée is unmoulded and partnered with a harvest of strawberries and their sorbet and some honeycomb for a bravura finale. The wine list here has long been a masterpiece. Bereft of notes but teeming with quality, it has fine sections of rosés, German Rieslings, Italians, and English wines, at markups that shouldn't offend. Prices start at £28.

Chef/s: Charles Smith. **Open:** Sat and Sun L, all week D. **Meals:** set L £30 (2 courses) to £38. Set D £73. Tasting menu £90. **Details:** 50 seats. V menu. Bar. Parking.

◼ Winchcombe
5 North Street
Cooking score: 6
Modern European | £54
5 North Street, Winchcombe, GL54 5LH
Tel no: (01242) 604566
restaurant5northstreet.co.uk

Despite the grandeur of its reputation, there's still a warmly comfortable air to Gus and Kate Ashenford's Cotswold restaurant. Walls in red or left in bare brick, memorabilia from the Waterside Inn (see entry, Bray), where they met, and a general air of friendly efficiency add up to a winning formula. The cooking maintains a taproot in French classical gastronomy, but the labour-intensive, mightily effective dishes then light out into more modern territory. A quail opener that offered the breast and bacon-stuffed leg topped with its fried egg comes with a cornucopia of other ingredients, including asparagus and cep slivers, to resemble a mini-main course, while cured sea trout comes with a goats' cheese cake, pickled radish, dill-scented beetroot and tomato chutney. The mains themselves are likewise richly busy but well-judged plates: pink Longhorn beef with braised cheek and confit tongue, Jerusalem

artichoke purée and roasted carrots, or poussin with redcurrants, bacon jam and puréed watercress. To finish, there might be a banana study combining caramelised fruit with gooey cake and superb sorbet, interspersed with shards of hazelnut meringue and slashed with toffee sauce. More wines by the glass would help. What there are start at £6.

Chef/s: Marcus Ashenford. **Open:** Wed to Sun L, Tue to Sat D. **Closed:** Mon, 1 week Jan, 2 weeks Aug. **Meals:** main courses £18 to £26. Set L £27 (2 courses) to £32. Set D £45 (2 courses) to £54. Sun L £36. Tasting menu £74. **Details:** 26 seats. V menu. Music.

Wesley House
Cooking score: 2
Modern European | £39
High Street, Winchcombe, GL54 5LJ
Tel no: (01242) 602366
wesleyhouse.co.uk
£5 OFF 🛏

This ancient restaurant-with-rooms hops from a ramshackle, half-timbered exterior into a rather old-fashioned, cluttered lounge. But head to the long, thin dining room (all exposed stone or cream walls, black beams, white-clad tables, fresh flowers, evening candles) and you will find cooking that is comfortingly familiar but in the modern manner. So expect pressed ham hock terrine with piccalilli purée, say, or sole goujons with tartare sauce, followed by crisp pork belly with champ, roast apple, creamed Savoy cabbage and red wine, or confit duck leg with spiced red cabbage, green beans and ginger and honey-soy dressing. In addition, there are various steaks (from ribeye to T-bone), fish from Cornwall, a good selection of regional artisan cheeses and the likes of warm plum frangipane with griottine cherries, clotted cream and chocolate crisp to finish. A short wine list opens at £19.

Chef/s: Cedrik Rullier. **Open:** Tue to Sun L, Tue to Sat D. **Closed:** Mon. **Meals:** main courses £16 to £38. Set L £15 (2 courses) to £20. Set D £20 (2 courses) to £25. Sun L £22. **Details:** 60 seats. Bar. Music.

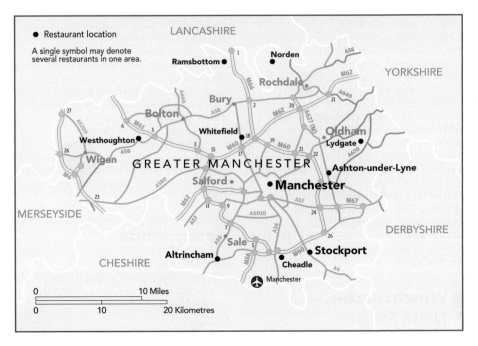

▌Altrincham

★ NEW ENTRY ★

Porta

Cooking score: 2
Spanish | £22
50 Greenwood Street, Altrincham, WA14 1RZ
Tel no: (0161) 4656225
portatapas.co.uk
£30

An import from across the county border in
Chester, this low-key tapas bar fits
comfortably into Altrincham's burgeoning
community of food businesses. Standards are
high and the small plates come at pace, with
the semi-open kitchen knocking out solid
classics and a handful of intensely flavoured
house specials. Crisp, charred purple
sprouting broccoli with punchy romesco is a
standout veg dish, while presa Ibérica with
grassy mojo verde is cooked boldly pink – a
challenge for some, a delight for others. Ox
cheek is slow-roasted until melting, then
crisped in slices and matched cleverly with
caperberries and an intense, fragrant oil
heavily loaded with anise. Puddings are
limited and plain, but the chocolate mousse
with honeycomb is worth a look. Service in
the small dark-wood-dominated ground-
floor dining room (there's an upstairs and a
few pavement tables, too) is breezy and
relaxed, and the Iberian wine list includes
enough sherry to keep purists going. No
reservations.
Chef/s: Joe Wright. **Open:** Tue to Fri L and D. Sat
and Sun, all day from 12. **Meals:** tapas £4 to £10.
Details: 55 seats. Wheelchairs. Music.

Sugo

Cooking score: 3
Italian | £30
22 Shaw's Road, Altrincham, WA14 1QU
Tel no: (0161) 9297706
sugopastakitchen.co.uk

This titchy pasta joint's menu may be written
mainly in Italian, but one correspondent notes
that they 'absolutely know the meaning' of one

British word – hospitality. Sugo's liveliness, informality and communal tables 'may not suit for a romantic dinner for two', but dishes such as bruschetta with lemon ricotta, grilled chicory and salsa verde continue to make readers swoon. They find sophistication and complexity (and occasionally a heavy hand with the chilli) in pasta with pancetta and creamy, long-cooked cannellini beans or 'perfectly seasoned', herby ragùs combining wild boar and beef shin with 'nduja, or Tuscan fennel sausage with white wine and grilled fennel. If you think the main menu is brief (though no barrier to finding something that appeals), try the dessert or wine lists, both small but agreeably formed; homemade chocolate tart, with a slightly bitter edge, is the standout pud.

Chef/s: Alex De Martiis. **Open:** Tue to Thur D. Fri and Sat, all day from 12. **Closed:** Sun, Mon, first 2 weeks Jan, 2 weeks Aug. **Meals:** main courses £11 to £23. **Details:** 25 seats. Wheelchairs. Music. No children Fri and Sat D.

▌Ashton-under-Lyne

LOCAL GEM
Lily's Vegetarian Indian Cuisine
Indian vegetarian | £10
75-83 Oldham Road, Ashton-under-Lyne, OL6 7DF
Tel no: (0161) 3394774

£30

At some point in the life of this guide, Lily's will move to new premises, so do check before planning to combine a meal here with a trip to IKEA – currently a five-minute walk away. The bright, basic café is tacked on to an Indian supermarket and has a reputation for fast, authentic Indian vegetarian cooking. Expect outstanding bhel puri, crisp vegetable samosas, and chilli paneer, then mains of chana masala (spicy chickpeas), aloo gobi (potatoes and cauliflower) and jaipuri (mixed vegetable paneer with cashew nuts in a sweet-and-sour sauce). Finish with carrot halwa. Unlicensed.

▌Cheadle

LOCAL GEM
Aamchi Mumbai
Indian | £25
2A Gatley Road, Cheadle, SK8 1PY
Tel no: (0161) 4283848
aamchimumbai.co.uk

£5 OFF   £30

The street food of Mumbai provides the inspiration and the mainly vegetarian classics get meals off to a racing start. Bhel puri, idli sambar (rice dumplings with lentil soup and chutney) and masala dosa (crisp pancake filled with lightly spiced potato) are all 'good stuff'. Moving on, curries are well made. Lamb bhuna has been pronounced 'as good as ever', as has a 'tasty' chicken saagwala with well-rounded spicing and an excellent spinach sauce. There are the usual breads and rice. House wines are £14.95, but beer or lassi is a better bet.

▌Lydgate
The White Hart
Cooking score: 4
Modern British | £33
51 Stockport Road, Lydgate, OL4 4JJ
Tel no: (01457) 872566
thewhitehart.co.uk

£5 OFF

Overlooking Oldham's urban sprawl, the White Hart is a dyed-in-the-wool northern hostelry classily re-garbed for our times. Local drinkers congregate in the bar, but this venue is primarily in the hospitality business, hosting events of all kinds as well as offering an eclectic range of food. Best bet is in the warm, rustic Brasserie – a cosy home from home spread over two of the inn's original rooms, with an all-purpose menu of snazzy cosmopolitan dishes. Whether you're after tandoori roast cod with parsnip and apple or Norfolk quail with smoked garlic sausage and choucroute onions, the kitchen can oblige. Also expect steaks, fish specials, roasts and local classics such as crispy haddock and chips,

plus desserts ranging from rice pudding to tarte Tatin. Alternatively, trade up to the Dining Room for more elaborate cooking and highly worked tasting menus. An extensive international wine list suits the food.
Chef/s: Michael Shaw. **Open:** all week L and D. **Closed:** 26 Dec, 1 Jan. **Meals:** main courses £14 to £29. Set L £18 (2 courses) to £20. Sun L £27. **Details:** 100 seats. 50 seats outside. Bar. Wheelchairs. Music. Parking.

▌Manchester

★ TOP 50 ★

Adam Reid at The French

Cooking score: 8
Modern British | £65
The Midland, 16 Peter Street, Manchester, M60 2DS
Tel no: (0161) 2354780
the-french.co.uk
£5 OFF

Having re-established The French as a serious destination, Simon Rogan has departed the Midland hotel, leaving former lieutenant Adam Reid in charge. Nothing about the new-look restaurant is second best. In shades of blue-grey, with an open counter where chefs interact with customers, the refit will please anyone who felt exposed in the vast expanses below spherical chandeliers (still here, but less dominant). A Mancunian soundtrack and end-of-week lunches with a six-course option boost the bid for accessibility, and service, always 'kind and professional', is also more relaxed. And readers' take on the food? 'It's not as intricate and, frankly, that's an improvement'. Highlights of a tasting menu in early summer might include asparagus fried with a light, crisp coating and warm truffled Tunworth mousse to dip, or a rather wintry but otherwise winning bomb of slow-cooked trotter with a popping crackling carapace. Beef tartare is still here, but lightly dressed in mushroom catsup with tiny vegetable dice and just a breath of charcoal: a delicate raw take on a summer stew. Fish cookery (as in sea trout,

served with pickled elderflower hollandaise) is everything you'd hope, dark ale bread deserves its status as a separate course, and Cumbrian lamb makes a show of the fat as well as the lean, served with sticky ramson jus, peas and lettuce. A fragile sugar 'clementine' filled with white chocolate mousse and passion fruit sorbet is, unapologetically, a real (and skill-packed) dessert. With wine as good as ever and an easy-going atmosphere in which to drink it, this is close to being the complete package.
Chef/s: Adam Reid. **Open:** Fri and Sat L, Tue to Sat D. **Closed:** Sun, Mon, 1 week Dec, 2 weeks Aug. **Meals:** main courses £10 to £14 (L only). Set L and D £65 (6 courses) to £85. **Details:** 52 seats. V menu. Wheelchairs. Music. Children over 8 yrs only.

Australasia

Cooking score: 2
Pan-Asian | £45
1 The Avenue, Spinningfields, Manchester, M3 3AP
Tel no: (0161) 8310288
australasia.uk.com

Enter the glass pyramid and descend to another hemisphere... this is Australasia, a subterranean pan-Asian restaurant and bar. It's a futuristic entrance to be sure, and no less fun once you're below ground in the airy and rather smart, neutrally decorated contemporary space. The menu focuses on the flavours of Australia, Indonesia and Japan, and sharing is probably the best way to go to really get a taste of the place. Tuck into beetroot with goats' cheese bonbons, black cod roasted in a hoba leaf, or hand-dived scallops with pork and apple, and keep an eye on the robata grill for the likes of Cambodian beef skewers. Bigger plates run to roast and confit lamb with basil jus, or barramundi and clams with carrot and ginger purée, with flavours packing a punch. There's sushi and sashimi, too, and East-meets-West desserts such as lychee and ginger pannacotta. Drink pan-Asian cocktails, saké or wines starting at £23.
Chef/s: Maros Sorovka. **Open:** all week, all day from 12. **Meals:** main courses £14 to £29. **Details:** 147 seats. Bar. Wheelchairs. Music.

El Gato Negro

Cooking score: 2
Spanish | £30
52 King Street, Manchester, M2 4LY
Tel no: (0161) 6948585
elgatonegrotapas.com

Slinky city-centre premises present a reflective front to the bustle of the street, but behind the disguise, there's a ground-floor bar, with a restaurant space above it, and an open-air rooftop bar with a closable cover in the unthinkable event of a Manchester downpour. The deal is Spanish tapas, and Simon Shaw gleaned much of his technique on forays into Catalonia and the Basque country. Original Spanish materials such as acorn-fed jamón Ibérico de bellota, and Manchego with bittersweet green figs, are out of the top drawer, and the traditional small plates are brought off with confidence and flair. Look to char-grilled lamb skewers with spiced chickpea purée and harissa, or octopus with capers, shallots and allioli, for evidence of that, but there are contemporary flourishes, too – sugar-cured mackerel with salt-baked celeriac and pink grapefruit salad. Spiced aubergine with onion confit on lavosh helps up the nutrient intake, and you can sugar up at the end with tangerine cheesecake and milk chocolate crémeux. A range of tonic waters is an asset of a drinks list that features cool cocktails and quality Spanish wines from £18.
Chef/s: Simon Shaw. **Open:** Tue to Thur L, Mon to Thur D. Fri to Sun, all day from 12. **Meals:** tapas £4 to £15. **Details:** 40 seats. Bar.

Greens

Cooking score: 2
Vegetarian | £26
43 Lapwing Lane, West Didsbury, Manchester, M20 2NT
Tel no: (0161) 4344259
greensdidsbury.co.uk
£30

For long one of the UK's best-known vegetarian venues, Greens maintains good standards from year to year (the restaurant turns 28 in 2018). In his search for modern vegetarian ideas, Simon Rimmer takes a global view, his menu offering a take on Chinese duck and pancakes (slices of deep-fried oyster mushrooms with plum sauce and a spring onion, cucumber and pickled ginger salad) or a spiced, fried tofu katsu curry with jasmine rice, and a spring onion and carrot sesame salad. Elsewhere, a plate of bangers and mash consists of Lancashire cheese, sage and onion sausages teamed with mustard mash, roasted beets, beer gravy and onion marmalade, and the kitchen even puts a spin on vegetarian clichés such as the nut roast – a satisfying combination of pecan, cashew and almond. Finish with a citrusy orange and lemon posset or sticky toffee pudding with salted-caramel sauce and Chantilly cream. Wines from £17.
Chef/s: Simon Rimmer. **Open:** Tue to Sat L, Mon to Sat D. Sun, all day from 12.30. **Meals:** main courses £13 to £14. Sun L £17 (3 courses). **Details:** 74 seats. 8 seats outside. V menu. Music.

Hawksmoor

Cooking score: 4
British | £45
184-186 Deansgate, Manchester, M3 3WB
Tel no: (0161) 8366980
thehawksmoor.com

Mancunians can't move for blow-ins from the London restaurant scene at the moment, and Hawksmoor is one of 'a comparatively rare breed of restaurants that just exudes professionalism'. The fact that 'everything is as it should be' is down to a cracking front-of-house team and a kitchen that knows how to deliver beefy savour to the sexily dark bar and lighter but equally buzzy restaurant. Start with beetroot and hazelnut salad with horseradish crème fraîche dressing, or Flintstone-channelling bone marrow and onions, but don't forget that you're 'here for the steak'. Sold by weight or as a Manc lunch special of rump and chips, it's all beautifully charred and a compliment to conscientious beef farmers everywhere. Ladle on hollandaise laced with Stichelton or anchovy, sop with a

butter lettuce salad, and finish with passion fruit cheesecake or one of the house tributes to classic confectionery. Wines from the Coravin or red-led main list do it all justice.
Chef/s: Szymon Szymczak. **Open:** Mon to Sat L and D. Sun, all day from 12. **Closed:** 25 and 26 Dec, 1 Jan. **Meals:** main courses £12 to £35. Set L and D £25 (2 courses) to £28. Sun L £20. **Details:** 137 seats. Bar. Wheelchairs. Music.

★ NEW ENTRY ★

Hispi
Cooking score: 3
Modern British | £32
1C School Lane, Manchester, M20 6RD
Tel no: (0161) 4453996
hispi.net

Rarely bettered in the north west, chef/owner Gary Usher's talent is for giving the people what they want – and who doesn't want an easy-going neighbourhood bistro with deeply satisfying, switched-on cooking? The team has 'got it right straight from the start' with a simple bare-brick fit-out, positive, open service and 'exactly the right take on seasonality'. To start, that might mean purple carrots with horseradish-spiked yoghurt and melting nuggets of smoked garlic, or ox tongue with sauce gribiche and lettuce hearts, grilled so they're both melting and crisp. The signature dish is braised featherblade with truffle and Parmesan chips and a changing roster of vegetable garnishes; at inspection, as well as during one reader's visit, it was 'absolutely delicious, but not piping hot'. Bread and puddings really earn their keep; dessert might be a huge cloud of whipped fromage blanc paired with forced rhubarb, meringue and pistachio. In line with the food, wines are well chosen and well priced.
Chef/s: Gary Usher and Richard Sharples. **Open:** all week L and D. **Meals:** main courses £15 to £24. Set L and early D £16 (2 courses) to £19. **Details:** 85 seats.

Indian Tiffin Room
Cooking score: 3
Indian | £23
2 Isabella Banks Street, Manchester, M15 4RL
Tel no: (0161) 2281000
indiantiffinroom.com
£30

The Indian Tiffin Room folk have had fun with their follow-up to the much loved – but tiny – Cheadle original. They've really gone for it visually: stacked shipping containers, sculptural neon lights and murals bring colour to this spacious glass-sided box. From the lively menu of street snacks, South Indian tiffin, thalis and more, there's always room for the ITR's benchmark bhel puri, goat keema pav and masala dosa. Readers speak highly also of a clever beetroot shami kebab, lamb dalcha with lentils and 'a good kick of chilli' (both dishes from the broader dinner menu) and steamed rice and lentil idly – 'lovely soft dumplings'– with sambar and a chutney trio. For afters, go traditional with rose-scented gulab jamun. Unlike the Cheadle branch (Chapel Street, Cheadle, Cheshire, SK8 1BR; tel: 0161 4912020) the Manchester ITR has the advantage of a full bar doing lassis, beers and spice-loaded cocktails.
Chef/s: Selvan Arul. **Open:** Mon to Fri L and D. Sat and Sun, all day from 1. **Closed:** 25 Dec, 1 Jan. **Meals:** main courses £8 to £15. **Details:** 100 seats. V menu. Bar. Wheelchairs. Music. Parking.

The Lime Tree
Cooking score: 3
Modern British | £32
8 Lapwing Lane, West Didsbury, Manchester, M20 2WS
Tel no: (0161) 4451217
thelimetree.co.uk

'Always reliable modern British food,' was the verdict of one regular to this well-liked bistro. Now in its fourth decade, the Lime Tree glides along, keeping pace with changing fashion and maintaining links with local produce, including that from its own farm. The result is a roster of imaginative seasonal dishes that might see English asparagus teamed with roast red peppers and Cheshire goats' cheese, or a well-reported smoked salmon mousse served with a dollop of horseradish cream and a little pea shoot salad. Local game shows up well in main courses, say haunch of Macclesfield forest venison (with wild mushrooms, celeriac purée, roast garlic mash and game jus), as does Goosnargh chicken breast, served Spanish style (stuffed with chorizo, paprika, onions and garlic, with a butternut squash risotto). Desserts might bring salted-chocolate caramel tart with vanilla ice cream. Good-value early-evening meal deals, weekend brunch, and Sunday roasts are also part of the excellent package. The wine list makes good reading and good drinking.

Chef/s: Jason Parker and David Hey. **Open:** Tue to Sat L and D. Sun 12 to 6. **Closed:** Mon, 25 and 26 Dec, 1 and 2 Jan, bank hols. **Meals:** main courses £13 to £19. Set D £15 (2 courses) to £18. Sun L £19 (2 courses) to £22. **Details:** 70 seats. 30 seats outside. Bar. Wheelchairs. Music.

Lunya

Cooking score: 1
Spanish | £20
Barton Arcade, Deansgate, Manchester,
M3 2BB
Tel no: (0161) 4133317
lunya.co.uk
£5 OFF £30

Peter and Elaine Kinsella's Spanish delicatessen in Barton Arcade is rammed with good things, and diners heading upstairs to the restaurant don't miss out. You can happily build lunch or dinner from the deli, perhaps good jamón, cold-smoked Cantabrian tuna loin with bacalao mousse, escalivada with romesco and a comprehensive selection of vinegar and oil to go with the house sourdough. Among the tapas classics, there are some Catalonian curiosities including a version of cannelloni with turkey, chicken livers and squid, the alt-paella fideuà, and

zarzuela, the saffron-spiked fish stew. The Spanish wine list represents a comprehensive regional tour.

Chef/s: Erica Bell. **Open:** all week, all day from 12. **Closed:** 25 Dec, 1 Jan. **Meals:** tapas £5 to £19. **Details:** 138 seats. 20 seats outside. V menu. Bar. Wheelchairs. Music.

Manchester House

Cooking score: 5
Modern British | £60
Tower 12, 18-22 Bridge Street, Manchester,
M3 3BZ
Tel no: (0161) 8352557
manchesterhouse.uk.com

Manchester House is in a period of reassuring stability. If you loved it before, with its laid-back service and Manc design detail, you will love it again. Multi-course menus are still the real focus of chef Aiden Byrne's efforts; diners are nudged towards the 10- or 14-course tasting menus by a brief and rather unbalanced à la carte. Nevertheless, a combination of greatest hits and new ingredients (we pronounce txogitxu 'Basque beef') makes it a 'good place for dinner'. Starters might be squab with crisped gingerbread and foie-filled 'cherry', or spot-on halibut with resonant mushroom broth. Tasting mains could be pork belly with apple, lemon thyme and lovage, and there are some neat details – feathery crackers with the cheese, and an effective back note of liquorice in a chocolate and hazelnut dessert – to come. Bedenimed staff are 'a credit' to the enterprise, and the view from the bar on the 12th floor's not bad either.

Chef/s: Aiden Byrne. **Open:** Tue to Sat L and D. **Closed:** Sun, Mon. **Meals:** main courses £35 to £58. Set L £23 (2 courses) to £28. Set D £50 (3 courses) to £60. Tasting menu £95. **Details:** 76 seats. Bar. Wheelchairs. Music.

The Rabbit in the Moon

Cooking score: 4
East Asian | £75
Urbis Building, Cathedral Gardens, Todd
Street, Manchester, M4 3BG
Tel no: (0161) 8048560
therabbitinthemoon.com

The duplex restaurant space at the top of Urbis
is a curiosity. Awkward, with limited views, it
demands imagination. That's the promise of
Michael O'Hare and his protégé Luke
Cockerill, who have installed all the graffiti,
Beastie Boys and clever cocktails a restaurant
could need. Almost everything is black, from
the umami-dusted snack rocks to the heavy
curtains (a nod to O'Hare's true original, in
Leeds) and even the loo roll. A £75 tasting
menu is an unlikely vehicle for doing things
differently. This one sacrifices balance and
variety for a surfeit of salt, savour and fat in
small-bite dishes from XO veal sweetbreads to
salmon skin inari pockets carrying the breath
of the fryer. But just as ennui sets in,
something fabulous is delivered: a pink-
sprinkled oyster with dehydrated ginger, or a
frozen half plum with a tiny ball of yuzu
cream, encased in cocoa butter like a trompe
l'oeil stone. As a wise rabbit might say from
space: patience, earthlings. You'll get what you
came for. It just might take a while.
Chef/s: Luke Cockerill. **Open:** all week D only.
Meals: tasting menu £75 (17 courses). **Details:** 30
seats. Bar. Music.

Refuge

Cooking score: 2
International | £50
Oxford Street, Manchester, M60 7HA
Tel no: (0161) 2335151
refugemcr.co.uk

After several tumbleweed years, Manchester's
landmark hotel (once The Palace, now
refurbed and reborn as The Principal) had

been running with a serious personality
deficit. In a move of bold genius, DJs-come-
hospitality stars Luke Cowdrey and Justin
Crawford (of Volta in West Didsbury) were
brought in to look after the food, drink and –
whisper it – vibes. The change is wholesale
and heartening, with the glorious tiled
interior revived, protected and channelled
into a series of easy-going, welcoming spaces.
At its best, there's nowt wrong with the Volta
approach – bold flavours, small plates – and
it's been brought lock, stock and char-grilled
flatbread to the Refuge dining room. Winners
here include tuna tartare with whipped
avocado and a whisper of passion fruit, smoky,
cumin-scattered mutabal, and a painterly
radicchio and orange salad with pomegranate,
orange blossom and a big whack of salt. Both
well-meaning, positive floor staff and an
apparently harried kitchen team drop the ball
occasionally, but when they nail the right flow
of dishes and the way to treat an apple tart, this
really will be a refuge.
Chef/s: Alex Worrall. **Open:** Mon to Fri L and D, Sat
and Sun, all day from 12. **Meals:** small plates £4 to
£12. Sharing plates £26 to £60. **Details:** 167 seats.
Bar. Wheelchairs. Music.

TNQ

Cooking score: 2
Modern British | £31
108 High Street, Manchester, M4 1HQ
Tel no: (0161) 8327115
tnq.co.uk

£5
OFF

A constant in a whirl of inconstancy, TNQ has
more than earned the status that seems to come
with its handsome corner spot opposite the
old Smithfield market. Owner Jobe Ferguson
opened it in 2004 and has since launched
trendier places, but it's still the go-to
recommendation for readers advising those
who want to go out to eat and 'be certain of
having a nice time'. The menu is studded with
local stars, such as the smoked Goosnargh
duck breast served with pickled vegetables and
truffle game chips, or the powerful Shorrocks
Lancashire Bomb put to a variety of good uses

including a wild garlic and cheese soufflé. Mains might be halibut with caramelised fennel, crab gnocchi, chive buerre blanc and preserved lemon or, at lunch, pies such as shepherd's with pickled red cabbage. Sticky toffee pudding is, of course, a perennial favourite. Wines are chosen partly for their medals, but start at £18.

Chef/s: Anthony Fielden. **Open:** Mon to Sat, all day from 12. Sun 12 to 7. **Closed:** 25 and 26 Dec, 1 Jan. **Meals:** main courses £13 to £24. Set L £15 (2 courses) to £19. Set D £30 (3 courses). Sun L £15. **Details:** 68 seats. 60 seats outside. Wheelchairs. Music.

★ NEW ENTRY ★

Umezushi
Cooking score: 4
Japanese | £35
4, Mirabel Street, Manchester, M3 1PJ
Tel no: (0871) 8118877
umezushi.co.uk

Umezushi has found its niche not just under the railway arches but as Manchester's premier purveyor of sushi and sashimi – and the grilling's not bad, either. Necessarily small, unsurprisingly wood-lined, Umezushi boasts approachable, efficient service, and a menu from which it's near impossible to go wrong. Crisp vegetable pickles, each distinctively preserved in sour-sweet variations, might precede hosomaki stuffed with spring onion and fatty tuna, or nigiri draped with sea bream; it's all cut beautifully, with the rice seasoned just so. A hand roll filled with hot, rich, smoky eel has good flavour despite an element of squish, while slippery, shape-shifting steamed chawan mushi, topped with okra, edamame and chunks of crab, gives savoury custard a good name. From the specials board, it's worth looking the charred salmon head in the eye. Decent value extends to the drinks list, and though the temptation is to drop in for sushi and a beer at the kitchen bar, the wise move is to book.

Chef/s: Omar Rodriguez Marrero. **Open:** Tue to Sun all day from 12. **Closed:** Mon, 23 to 30 Dec, 1 week summer. **Meals:** sushi £3 to £9. Sushi platters £18 to £56. Donmono £7 to £40. Set L £15. Tasting menu £54. **Details:** 18 seats. Wheelchairs. Music.

Wing's
Cooking score: 3
Chinese | £45
Heron House, 1 Lincoln Square, Manchester, M2 5LN
Tel no: (0161) 8349000
wingsrestaurant.co.uk

Navigating a reliable course through Manchester's myriad Chinese restaurants is never easy, but readers make a strong case for this 'old favourite' close to the city centre. You can expect the warmest of welcomes from the proprietor and his brigade of 'efficient servers', while the interior promises privacy with lots of booths, screens and discreet partitions. The menu is a 200-dish monster with variety in every department: Cantonese staples such as stir-fried beef in black bean sauce are reliably on point, but it pays to explore the more esoteric corners of the menu, too. Among the highlights worth discovering are Singapore black pepper lobster, a claypot of stewed brisket, and braised bamboo fungus with tofu. On Sundays, big family parties arrive en masse, lured in by the prospect of spot-on dim sum: scallop dumplings with crab roe, steamed pork buns, spring onion pancakes, shredded duck and beancurd rolls etc. Wines from £25.

Chef/s: Mr Chi Wing Lam. **Open:** all week, all day from 12 (4 Sat, 1 Sun). **Meals:** main courses £15 to £45. Set L and D £35 to £55. **Details:** 85 seats. V menu. Bar. Wheelchairs. Music.

Yuzu

Cooking score: 3
Japanese | £20
39 Faulkner Street, Manchester, M1 4EE
Tel no: (0161) 2364159
yuzumanchester.co.uk

£30

Perched on the edge of Chinatown, Yuzu sports a no-frills interior and only a small number of seats. It doesn't look all that from the outside, either, but it's worth making a reservation; diners come again and again for essentially deeply traditional and 'absolutely lovely' Japanese food – and the cost is fair, if not cheap. With no sushi on the menu, the headline act is an enticing variety of sashimi served over sushi rice in a donburi bowl, backed up by spot-on tempura, noodle dishes (try the kishimen – a flat, broad wheat-flour noodle with prawns and vegetable tempura), and daily blackboard specials. You might start with excellent grilled chicken yakitori or gyoza (freshly made prawn dumplings). Lunchtime specials 'are still a good deal' and there's a cosy atmosphere and excellent service. In the absence of a wine list, to accompany the food there's beer or a good selection of saké.
Chef/s: David Leong. **Open:** Tue to Sat L and D. **Closed:** Sun, Mon, 2 weeks Christmas. **Meals:** main courses £8 to £17. Set L £9 (2 courses). **Details:** 28 seats. Music.

LOCAL GEM

Albert Square Chop House

British | £29
The Memorial Hall, Albert Square, Manchester, M2 5PF
Tel no: (0161) 8341866
albertsquarechophouse.com

£30

It may promise 'a gastronomic voyage round the British Isles', but there's no doubting where this chop house's real allegiances lie. Cheese and onion pie, corned beef hash, Barnsley chops and honey-roast bacon with pease pudding all sing of the north-west – and old Lancashire in particular. Meaty grills also make their sizzling presence known, while puddings such as baked custard tart, Eccles cakes and fruit flapjack crumble are as nostalgic as a brass band. Don't pass on the tantalising wine list.

LOCAL GEM

The Pasta Factory

Italian | £24
77 Shudehill Street, Manchester, M4 4AN
Tel no: (0161) 2229250
pastafactory.co.uk

£5 OFF   £30

Shudehill's 19th-century bank building is arguably in its most rewarding phase, as an unpretentious café specialising in fresh handmade pasta. There are usually three kinds of ravioli filling, perhaps prosciutto served with Piedmontese Toma, or goats' cheese with sage and pumpkin sauce, or mushrooms, garlic, parsley and cashews with black truffle and porcini sauce. For less fuss, bucatini arrabbiata or aglio e olio are easy wins. Kindly service means you might linger longer than intended, perhaps with wine from £16.

LOCAL GEM

Teacup Kitchen

Modern British | £18
55 Thomas Street, Manchester, M4 1NA
Tel no: (0161) 8323233
teacupandcakes.com

£30

Doing a roaring trade in easy comfort and quality brews, Teacup Kitchen has belonged to the Northern Quarter since DJ and producer Mr Scruff opened up in 2005. Not surprisingly, breakfasts (French toast with salted caramel, almonds and raspberries, perhaps) are served all day and lunches have moved with the times; right now it's all spiced cauliflower salad and asparagus and haloumi flatbreads. Teacup is also justifiably known for its eye-popping display of robust baking in all the colours of the rainbow – including, of course, rainbow cake.

Volta

Modern European | £25
167 Burton Road, West Didsbury, Manchester,
M20 2LN
Tel no: (0161) 4488887
voltafoodanddrink.co.uk

£30

The after-hours lifeblood of pulsating Burton Road, Volta earned its reputation with robust small plates and the kind of quality vibes that can only come from the leadership of two DJs turned hospitality pioneers. Their new set-up in Manchester (Refuge, see entry) has taken some attention from the original, but here in West Didsbury signature dishes like smoked feta with beetroot, hazelnut and dill, crisp shredded lamb shawarma, char-grilled hanger steak or sweet potato fries have mostly kept their shine. Desserts are simple, but no worse for that.

▌Norden

Nutters

Cooking score: 2
Modern British | £35
Edenfield Road, Norden, OL12 7TT
Tel no: (01706) 650167
nuttersrestaurant.co.uk

Established by much-missed restaurateur Rodney Nutter and his wife Jean, Nutters is run with gusto by son Andrew, who recently opened a pub, The Bird, in nearby Birtle. In terms of both its local reputation and its home above Rochdale, in a manor house surrounded by lawns, Nutters is in an enviable position. Its culinary niche might be some distance from the cutting edge, but there's an insistence on local produce, as well as treating guests warmly and well, which serves it admirably. At dinner, a generous list of specials (plus separate veggie menu) means there's no end of choice. The default serving size is large, and dishes such as sticky short-rib fritters with cucumber spaghetti, wasabi and black sesame, or lemon and herb scallops with confit

chicken drumstick and black pudding, can be heavier than anticipated. The mini 'sweetshop' dessert plate is a crowd-pleaser, and there's a roaring trade in Lancashire cheese. Wines can be pretty serious, but start at accessible.
Chef/s: Andrew Nutter. **Open:** Tue to Sun, L and D. **Closed:** Mon, 25 to 27 Dec, 1 and 2 Jan, bank hols. **Meals:** main courses £18 to £27. Set L £17 (2 courses) to £20. Sun L £25. Tasting menu £44. **Details:** 146 seats. V menu. Bar. Wheelchairs. Music. Parking.

▌Ramsbottom

Baratxuri

Cooking score: 2
Spanish | £25
1 Smithy Street, Ramsbottom, BL0 9AT
Tel no: (01706) 559090
levanterfinefoods.co.uk

£30

The fact that Ramsbottom can support more than one quality Spanish outfit (and that, as we went to press, this one, the much-admired sibling of Levanter, was knocking through into the shop next door) is testament to the skilled hospitality of owners Joe and Fiona Botham. Their pursuit of and belief in great ingredients, no matter how obscure (witness smoky cod throat pil-pil) brings a compelling set of flavours to the Lancashire hills. Even with the new dining room, this tastefully tiled pintxos bar with benefits shouldn't feel less than cosy. Tables can expect to share small dishes of seared Sanlúcar prawns with black squid-ink bomba rice or Goosnargh egg yolks whipped and served with wild mushrooms, truffles and crisp slices of sourdough. From the new wood-fired oven, dishes cooked whole and cut at the table include milk-fed lamb with green salad, olive oil and Jerez vinegar. An all-Spain wine list is great value, topping out at £45 for an aged cava.
Chef/s: Rachel Stockley. **Open:** Wed D. Thur to Sat, all day from 12. Sun 12 to 7. **Closed:** Mon, Tue, first week Jan. **Meals:** pintxos from £2. Sharing platter £35. **Details:** 24 seats. Music. Children before 7.30pm only.

Levanter

Cooking score: 2
Spanish | £35
10 Square Street, Ramsbottom, BL0 9BE
Tel no: (01706) 551530
levanterfinefoods.co.uk

Big tapas flavours and zero pretension are Levanter's stock-in-trade. They might have the finest handmade spicy morcilla, unpasteurised goats' milk cheese or Galician beef rib for miles, but they'd no sooner show off about it than charge through the nose for it. It's a package that suits foodie Ramsbottom, which has embraced dishes like grilled figs with hazelnut butter, chicken wings cooked with sobrasada and onions, or chickpeas grilled with cumin and breadcrumbs until crisp and sizzling. As well as making chickpeas irresistible, the kitchen also opens the doors on tinned and preserved fish, serving a big sharing board with two glasses of manzanilla thrown in, or fresh Cantabrian anchovies with garlic and parsley. That Galician dairy beef is a treat grilled crustily as a kilo steak with salted peppers and tomatoes, and could aptly be followed by baked cheesecake. Wines are Spanish and inviting, though there's room on the list for more sherry.
Chef/s: Sam McGlynn. **Open:** Wed D. Thur to Sat, all day from 12. Sun 12 to 7.30. **Closed:** Mon, Tue, first week Jan. **Meals:** tapas £4 to £9. **Details:** 24 seats. Music.

■ Salford

READERS RECOMMEND

Vero Moderno

Italian
4 Vimto Gardens, Chapel Street, Salford, M3 5JF
Tel no: (0161) 6371160
veromoderno.co.uk

'This is not your standard anglicised Italian gaff. Here they've taken some classics and stayed true to their essence but have given them an up-to-date spin: there was an absolute delight of an aubergine starter – slices breaded and fried – served with a tomato sauce, with basil hitting high notes and mozzarella melting over it all; there was a generous portion of gnocchi, perfectly light and dressed with nuggets of sausage and wild broccoli; there was pizza marinara – an object lesson in the craft of pizza cooking – with perfectly crisp, thin dough and everything you could want in a tomato sauce.'

■ Stockport

Easy Fish Company

Cooking score: 1
Seafood | £30
117 Heaton Moor Road, Stockport, SK4 4HY
Tel no: (0161) 4420823
theeasyfishco.com

If there's one thing better than a good fishmonger, it's a good fishmonger that does the cooking for you. The Easy Fish Co. is just that – alongside the fresh catch, there's a full-service restaurant which romps far beyond beer-battered haddock to grilled sardines on toast with chorizo and caper sauce, tempura soft-shell crab with mango chilli salsa, and lots of white wine under £30. At their best, dishes are 'fresh, light and full of flavour,' though there are misses as well as hits – keep it simple with one of the platters, or ask staff for their favourites. Food can take its time coming out of the kitchen – 'you get to the finger-tapping stage,' said one reporter.
Chef/s: Steve Kanaris. **Open:** Tue to Sat, all day from 12. **Closed:** Sun, Mon. **Meals:** main courses £13 to £22. **Details:** 35 seats. Wheelchairs. Music.

★ NEW ENTRY ★

Where the Light Gets In

Cooking score: 5
Modern European | £75
7 Rostron Brow, Stockport, SK1 1JY
Tel no: (0161) 4775744
wtlgi.co
£5
OFF

Where the light gets in is also where the customers get in – through a door, up some stairs, off an alley, near a barbers', opposite a

church in Stockport. As diners arrive in the vague area of Samuel Buckley's comfortably idiosyncratic restaurant, a member of staff stands in the window and waves them in. Diners sit amid bare brick between a comfy lounge area, complete with wood-burning stove, and an island kitchen that completely exposes the bearded brigade and their art. No one say 'hipster'; Buckley worked at L'Enclume and Juniper, and his endeavour here is heartfelt. Dinner is roughly eight courses; no menu, total seasonality and some fabulous moments of deft cooking anchored by a generous loaf of rye sourdough for the table to share. Hits include a tiny cup of powerful duck broth, Faroe Islands plaice served all-white with salt-baked kohlrabi and two pale, almost vanilla-sweet sauces, and a thick muddle of herbs to go with with wild garlic and a slab of Suffolk pork. It's a set-up that can, of its nature, brook no compromise; disabled access is non-existent and the menu changes for no man, even if he is a vegetarian. With no wine list, drinks (and drink prices) are unfathomable unless you take the pairing. It's to be hoped that, in time, fixes will be found, but WTLGI is already worth finding.
Chef/s: Samuel Buckley. **Open:** Wed to Sat D only. **Closed:** Sun, Mon, Tue. **Meals:** tasting menu £75. **Details:** 30 seats. Music. No children.

◼ Westhoughton
Provenance
Cooking score: 1
Modern British | £28
46-48 Market Street, Westhoughton, BL5 3AZ
Tel no: (01942) 812398
provenancerestaurant.co.uk
£5 OFF £30

Above a deli of the same name (or a Food Hall as they call it), Provenance Restaurant does indeed make use of what's stocked downstairs, with just about all the ingredients available to purchase, and all the butchery done on the premises. The dining room is light, bright and contemporary. A sizeable menu covers a lot of bases, from lunchtime sandwiches, through 'favourites' such as fish and chips and steaks

with classic sauces, but there's also turbot with a herby crumb, and lobster thermidor. A fashionable curried scallops opener precedes a white chocolate sphere finisher, which reveals a host of exotic flavours. Wine from £17.
Chef/s: Lewis Gallagher. **Open:** Mon to Sun L, Tue to Sat D. **Closed:** 26 Dec, 1 Jan. **Meals:** main courses £9 to £34. Sun L £19 (3 courses). Tasting menu £45. **Details:** 46 seats. Bar. Music.

◼ Whitefield
★ NEW ENTRY ★
One88
Cooking score: 2
Modern British | £30
188 Bury New Road, Whitefield, M45 6QF
Tel no: (0161) 2800524
one88whitefield.co.uk

Long associated with big-city cooking but without a place to call his own, well-regarded chef David Gale has settled in the suburbs. Some of Manchester's most exciting food stories are beginning out of town, but Gale is no hip, faux-humble show-off: his aim in his Whitefield brasserie is, simply, to please. Warm service and pleasantly neutral décor make One88 easy to like, and locals emphatically do. There's a distinctively north Manchester character in dishes such as chilli cheese toast topped with almost moussey Lancashire cheese and pink pickled onions, or salt beef brisket with steamed baby vegetables, crushed beetroot and horseradish mash. Veal escalope with fried duck egg, anchovy, capers and artichoke dressing is rich, sharp and robust, though there's also courgette spaghetti with crushed hazelnuts for the healthy crowd. Puddings such as a raspberry custard tart need work, though there's nothing wrong with the sherbety sorbet served alongside. Wines from £16.
Chef/s: David Gale. **Open:** all week, all day from 10. **Meals:** main courses £11 to £20. **Details:** 74 seats.

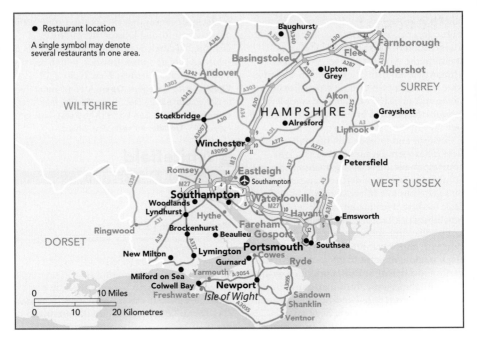

▌Alresford
Pulpo Negro

Cooking score: 4
Spanish | £30
28 Broad Street, Alresford, SO24 9AQ
Tel no: (01962) 732262
pulponegro.co.uk
£5
OFF

'A real find outside London, and better than a lot I've eaten at in Spain,' enthused one fan of Andres Alemany's 'pukka tapas bar'. The L-shaped room has bench seating around most of the edges, mixed chairs and plain wooden tables with a Mediterranean-style tiled bar at one end, behind which is the kitchen. Brilliant charcuterie sets the tone, there's exemplary Catalan tomato bread to nibble while you explore the menu, and gambas al ajillo, tortilla sobrasada, pintxos morunos (tender, well-marinated pieces of pork fillet) and courgette fritters sprinkled with Manchego and served on a smoky tomato and paprika sauce deliver big, pugnacious flavours. Here is a kitchen that

clearly tastes its food. The highlight for one reporter was gypsy potatoes with ceps and egg yolk – 'a bowl of utter, delicious comfort' – while whiskey tart, 'not so much a tart, more like a trifle', demanded you 'dig deep to reap the rewards'. No wonder that for one diner, distance is no object: 'This place is a 40-minute drive from home, but we would head back there in a heartbeat.' Expect pitch-perfect service and a savvy all-Spanish wine list with good choice by the glass.

Chef/s: Andres Alemany. **Open:** Tue to Sat L and D. **Closed:** Sun, Mon, 25 and 26 Dec, 1 Jan, bank hols. **Meals:** tapas £3 to £13. **Details:** 44 seats. 12 seats outside. Bar. Wheelchairs. Music. Children over 5 yrs only.

Symbols

🛏	Accommodation is available
£30	Three courses for less than £30
£5 OFF	£5-off voucher scheme
🍷	Notable wine list

◼ Baughurst
The Wellington Arms

Cooking score: 4
Modern British | £37
Baughurst Road, Baughurst, RG26 5LP
Tel no: (0118) 9820110
thewellingtonarms.com

'The first thing you notice about this pub is how immaculate it is. The gardens are beautifully laid out, the whole place seems to shine.' Reporters are in agreement that Simon Page and Jason King have done Baughurst proud during their 13-year residence at this handsome pub-with-rooms. And while there's no doubt that the Wellington Arms plays the part of a busy local perfectly, these days it is better known for its food. Jason King's kitchen is an enterprising place noted for industriousness and dedication to local produce, with the emphasis firmly on provenance and home production, including the rearing of hens, pigs and sheep, and the growing of vegetables. The cooking confirms 'how much standards have improved in this country' by blending the traditional and the contemporary on a menu that moves confidently from a rich game terrine or twice-baked Cheddar soufflé to roast rack of home-reared lamb with caponata, basil and pine nuts. A fortifying finish sees stem ginger and golden syrup sponge served with 'proper' custard. To drink, there are regional ales alongside a well-chosen wine list.

Chef/s: Jason King. **Open:** all week L, Mon to Sat D. **Meals:** main courses £12 to £25. Set L £17 (2 courses) to £20. **Details:** 40 seats. 25 seats outside. Wheelchairs. Music. Parking.

◼ Beaulieu
The Terrace Restaurant

Cooking score: 5
Modern British | £70
Montagu Arms Hotel, Palace Lane, Beaulieu, SO42 7ZL
Tel no: (01590) 612324
montaguarmshotel.co.uk

The Montagu Arms enjoys a commanding presence in this picturesque New Forest village. On the corner of the high street, oft-visited by the local ponies, guests will find the hotel's fine-dining restaurant helmed by Roux Scholar Matthew Tomkinson. (For teas or more casual bites, try the hotel's Monty's Inn.) Inside all is cosseting and comfortable, with panelled walls, double-clothed tables and garden views let down only by 'granny's front room' carpet. From high prices follow high expectations. At its finest, Tomkinson's cooking is elegant and technically accomplished, the ingredients in harmony, the seasoning on point. Veal sweetbreads grenobloise, black garlic purée, confit lemon, a 'pressing' of rabbit, prune and black pudding with parfait liver and celeriac rémoulade, and chocolate crémeux with delicate walnut ice cream and coffee macaroon exemplify the style perfectly. However, some dishes on the newly introduced set lunch are less convincing – 'as if from a different kitchen'. The 300-bin wine list leans towards minimal-intervention, small-producer wines.

Chef/s: Matthew Tomkinson. **Open:** Wed to Sun L, Tue to Sun D. **Closed:** Mon. **Meals:** set L £25 (2 courses) to £30. Set D £55 (2 courses) to £70. Sun L £38. Tasting menu £90. **Details:** 60 seats. 40 seats outside. Bar. Wheelchairs. Parking. Children at L only.

Brockenhurst

LOCAL GEM
The Pig
Modern British | £38
Beaulieu Road, Brockenhurst, SO42 7QL
Tel no: (01590) 622354
thepighotel.com

Take one grey-stone Georgian mansion, turn it into a laid-back boutique hotel, transform the glasshouse into a horticulturally themed dining room and allow self-sufficient foodie enterprise to do the rest. What isn't home-grown is resolutely local, and the result is a menu that positively blooms with dewy freshness. How about a crispy gull's egg with alexanders, Hampshire salami and Lymington crab, a 'three corner' garlic risotto or BBQ Wiltshire beef rump with herb salad and shaved fennel? Wines are suitably offbeat.

Emsworth
36 on the Quay
Cooking score: 4
Modern European | £58
47 South Street, Emsworth, PO10 7EG
Tel no: (01243) 375592
36onthequay.co.uk
£5 OFF

On a corner plot overlooking Emsworth Quay – part of Chichester harbour – Ramon and Karen Farthing's restaurant-with-rooms has been delighting regulars for some 20 years. While muted cream tones and heavily dressed tables might not be to everyone's taste these days, excellent home-baked sourdough brings things bang up to date, and although duck pastrami, duck liver parfait, plum chutney, pumpernickel and duck sandwich from the succinct à la carte may sound somewhat over the top, the reality is 'a very attractive plate of rich pickings'. Or perhaps opt for an 'exemplary' loin of veal and crisp pieces of kidney – 'both with exceptional flavour' – served with a mound of cauliflower and Tunworth cheese and earthy turnip tops. Bar

the odd conceptual stumble, this is food with flair. Finish with just-set vanilla and yoghurt pannacotta, honeycomb crisps, warm rhubarb doughnut and 'fragrant' hibiscus and rhubarb tea. 'Very pleasant, not over-formal' service gets the nod, too. Wines open at £21.50.
Chef/s: Gary Pearce. Open: Tue to Sat L and D. Closed: Sun, Mon, 25 and 26 Dec, 2 weeks Jan, 1 week May, 1 week Oct. Meals: set L £24 (2 courses) to £29. Set D £48 (2 courses) to £58. Tasting menu L £30, D £65. Details: 50 seats. Bar. Wheelchairs.

Grayshott

LOCAL GEM
Applegarth
International | £28
Applegarth Farm, Headley Road, Grayshott, GU26 6JL
Tel no: (01428) 712777
applegarthfarm.co.uk
£30

The main engine of this rural enterprise in the midst of the Hampshire countryside is a well-stocked farm shop, through which you walk to the pretty all-day restaurant (so much more than a café) with its covered terrace overlooking a well-tended garden (and central fire pit for special events). At lunch choose sandwiches (maybe Sussex Charmer cheese, tomato, red pepper jam and watercress) or antipasti boards or, from the main menu, baked local asparagus in a mustard and Cheddar cheese sauce, maple-glazed short ribs with charred spring cabbage and parsley mash, and a boozy chocolate and Kahlúa trifle with passion fruit sauce. It's deservedly popular, especially at weekends, and it's wise to book.

Local Gem

Local Gems are the perfect neighbourhood venues, delivering good, freshly cooked food at great value for money.

Isle of Wight
The Little Gloster
Cooking score: 4
Modern European | £35
31 Marsh Road, Gurnard, Isle of Wight,
PO31 8JQ
Tel no: (01983) 298776
thelittlegloster.com
£5 OFF

From sprouted rye bread and Danish Gamle Ole cheese to an array of infused aquavits, this beguiling family-run restaurant-with-rooms brings some welcome Scandi style to the Isle of Wight. Inside, billowing drapes, nautical trimmings, stripped wood and wraparound windows add a feeling of light and air, while the kitchen is busy from breakfast onwards. Fixed-price dinners are worth considering, sharing feasts are perfect for big parties, and the full menu points up its Nordic allegiances with the likes of home-cured gravadlax and frikadeller (Danish meatballs). Other possibilities might range from precisely fashioned Bembridge crab cakes with rhubarb and ginger pickle to char-grilled local steaks, burgers and specials such as fillet of day-boat cod with cauliflower purée and tempura cavolo nero tops, while boozy ice creams and sorbets are alternatives to calorific desserts including clementine and pistachio pavlova with crème Chantilly. Ample cocktails and local beers supplement a well-spread wine list.
Chef/s: Ben Cooke and Jay Santiago. **Open:** Tue to Sun L and D. **Closed:** Mon, Sun to Wed (Oct to May), 24 to 27 Dec, 1 Jan to 8 Feb. **Meals:** main courses £10 to £25. Set D Wed and Thur only £16 (2 courses) to £20. Tasting menu £45 to £90. **Details:** 85 seats. 55 seats outside. Wheelchairs. Music. Parking.

Thompson's
Cooking score: 5
Modern British | £50
11 Town Lane, Newport, Isle of Wight,
PO30 1JU
Tel no: (01983) 526118
robertthompson.co.uk
£5 OFF

He starred at the George in Yarmouth, matched the hushed elegance of the Hambrough, but now Robert Thompson is turning heads in his own right – in a gently refurbished listed building overlooking Newport town centre. The building's original beams, timbers and exposed brickwork have been retained, but an open kitchen and the glow of copper lamps make it all feel very modern. Mr Thompson is a keen supporter of the island's producers and their wares, from whipped Green Barn goats' cheese with Jerusalem artichokes, burnt onion and black truffle to exemplary seafood (hake with King cabbage, pickled walnuts and pommes dauphine on the side), but he delivers fresh, elaborate and finely judged cooking across the board. Just consider the contrasts and textures involved in a dish of Chart Farm fallow deer crusted with juniper berries and pepper and served with roasted apple, sweet-and-sour blackberries and glazed venison faggot or the dark chocolate brownie with salted-caramel and caramelised banana ice cream that is a stunning reworking of the chef's Valrhona Manjari chocolate délice. The evolving wine list showcases some noteworthy independent growers.
Chef/s: Robert Thompson. **Open:** Tue to Sat L and D. **Closed:** Sun, Mon, 2 weeks Feb/Mar, 2 weeks Nov, 25 Dec. **Meals:** main courses £17 to £29. Set L £24 (2 courses) to £29. Tasting menu L £49 (5 courses), D £65 (6 courses). **Details:** 50 seats. Bar. Wheelchairs. Music.

The Hut

Modern British | £30
Colwell Bay, Colwell Chine Road, Isle of Wight,
PO40 9NP
Tel no: (01983) 898637
thehutcolwell.co.uk

Right on the beach, next to a row of colourful beach huts, the Hut has expansive windows if the weather isn't playing ball, and a decked terrace if it is. A bright and breezy sort of place, the menu takes in feel-good global stuff such as Indonesian fish curry, cheeseburger in a brioche bun, and grilled lobster with garlic butter and fries. You might kick off with fish tacos, move on to crab gnocchi or ribeye steak, and finish with Eton Mess. Drink cocktails on the deck – 'blissful'.

▌Lymington
The Elderflower

Cooking score: 4
Modern British | £40
4-5 Quay Street, Lymington, SO41 3AS
Tel no: (01590) 676908
elderflowerrestaurant.co.uk

🛏

Physically, much has improved at Andrew du Bourg's restaurant-with-rooms since it opened in 2014. The long, low-ceilinged room has had a proper lick of paint and a new, soft carpet put in. Tables – once bare – are now double-clothed and a lounge area has been established at one end of the room, creating 'a smart but modern restaurant'. A restaurant manager has been recruited, who may insist on 'donning a white glove to place food and cutlery', but is very easy to talk to and 'doesn't go in for airs and graces'. The general impression is of a kitchen given over to restless experimentation, which leads to not a few grumps. A 'piece of nicely cooked cod' with crab velouté, a tulip filled with white crabmeat and tapioca 'spilling out on to a blob of pink peppercorn sour cream', has been a recent success, but general niggles caused one

reporter to think he may have been better trying 'les petites assiettes', a choice of 16 small, simple dishes, along the lines of beetroot, apple and walnut salad, crispy cod cheeks and confit mallard leg with caramelised chicory, chickpeas and roast garlic. Wines from £18.
Chef/s: Andrew du Bourg. **Open:** Tue to Sun L, Tue to Sat D. **Closed:** Mon, 26 Dec, 1 Jan. **Meals:** main courses £21 to £26. Tasting menu £60 (7 courses). **Details:** 36 seats. Music. Children over 12 yrs only at D Fri and Sat.

▌Lyndhurst
Hartnett Holder & Co.

Cooking score: 3
Italian | £55
Lime Wood Hotel, Beaulieu Road, Lyndhurst,
SO43 7FZ
Tel no: (02380) 287167
hhandco.com

🛏

'Oh the joys of the New Forest on a sunny spring day!' mused one reader who navigated her way past cyclists, camera-toting sightseers and the odd pony to reach this smartly chilled-out addition to the Lime Wood Hotel. 'Fun dining rather than fine dining' is the mantra, with Luke Holder manning the stoves and Angela Hartnett adding her own distinctive contribution to the big-hearted, ingredients-led Italian food. A dish of Parmesan gnocchi with morels, wild garlic and crispy onions is 'delicious in its simplicity', while melting lamb shank (no steak knife needed) arrives alongside a herby mélange of sausage and beans. Readers have also lapped up the buttery richness of a porcine 'cheek and jowl' duo with celeriac and (more) morels, as well as a 'wonderfully frou-frou' pink rhubarb and rice pudding trifle served in a glass sundae bowl. A leather-bound A4 wine list yields potable pleasures galore.
Chef/s: Luke Holder and Angela Hartnett. **Open:** all week, all day from 12. **Meals:** main courses £18 to £53. Set L £20 (2 courses) to £25. Sun L £38. **Details:** 62 seats. 40 seats outside. Bar. Wheelchairs. Music. Parking.

New dish on the block

With the world at their fingertips, chefs' references and techniques are evolving at breakneck pace. Our favourite restaurants are the ones where staff are glad to explain each dish - but a bit of advance knowledge never hurts.

Everyone likes cheese on toast, and at **Dishoom** they like it with Cheddar, spring onions, green chilli and a fried egg. On the menu, you're looking for **Kejriwal**, and you can also find a version at **One88** in Whitefield, Bury, topped with pink pickled onions.

Inspired by chef Stephen Toman's adventures with buttered beef at Noma, **lard-aged beef**, preserved for up to three weeks under a pristine white carapace of lard, is protected as it gathers age and flavour. At **Ox** in Belfast, it's served with spelt, girolles, wild asparagus and **lovage** - which, in case you need to ask, tastes like celery.

Has Anne-Sophie Pic found the new yuzu? At **La Dame de Pic** in London, she uses **mikan**, a Japanese citrus with a foot in both satsuma and mandarin camps, to bring brightness to a crab dish.

Looking for a change from paella? Think **fideuà**, made with short lengths of noodles instead of rice in the familiar wide pan at Liverpool's **Lunya**.

Milford on Sea
La Perle
Cooking score: 2
British | £35
60 High Street, Milford on Sea, SO41 0QD
Tel no: (01590) 643557
laperle.co.uk

Sam Hughes' restaurant in the heart of the old village is a pearl indeed; properly rooted in its environment, even a quick glance at the menu gives a clue to the local topography – New Forest venison, South Coast fish, Lymington lobster and Isle of Wight garlic (not all on the same plate, though). There's a retro homeliness to the décor, and plenty of classical refinement in the kitchen's output (which might be partly due to the chef's time with Raymond Blanc). A warm salad pitches up with smoked sausage, lardons and lyonnaise potatoes, and the fish soup has local produce in abundance. Keyhaven lamb, its shoulder served up as tender confit, comes with mint and caper sauce, while it's a rich lobster sauce that brings a lustre to roasted hake. A Rosary goats' cheese and local honey parfait is a creative way to sign off, with its accompanying mead ice cream, dehydrated black olives and lemon syrup. Home-infused spirits join a lively drinks list, with wines from £20.
Chef/s: Sam Hughes. **Open:** Tue to Sat L and D. **Closed:** Sun, Mon. **Meals:** set L £17 (2 courses) to £35. Set D £30 (2 courses) to £37. Tasting menu £55 (5 courses). **Details:** 28 seats.

★ NEW ENTRY ★

Verveine
Cooking score: 4
Seafood | £50
98 High Street, Milford on Sea, SO41 0QE
Tel no: (01590) 642176
verveine.co.uk
£5
OFF

Verveine is 'an intimate, modern place with an open kitchen, eccentrically at the rear of a wet fish shop'. Décor is contemporary coastal in muted shades of grey, throwing the spotlight right where it belongs – on to 'colourful, outlandish' dishes. A starter of sweet, tender baby squid, for example, contrasts with sharp redcurrants, crunchy kohlrabi and burnt aubergine, while smoked bass in 'its natural surroundings' comes served on a rock with pickled seaweed and plants foraged from the seashore. The main event is a daily choice of fresh fish or shellfish with one of four imaginative garnishes: scallops with Chinese cabbage, salt-baked pineapple and a citrusy ponzu sauce hit all the right notes at inspection. Finish with a deconstructed banoffee pie. Dishes arrive in all manner of outlandish crockery – some billowing dry ice – and there's a vanilla and olive oil jelly baby reclining in the petits fours. The reasonably priced, fish-friendly wine list is big on Burgundy and large on the Loire.

Chef/s: David Wykes. **Open:** Tue to Sat L and D. **Closed:** Sun, Mon, 24 Dec to 12 Jan, bank hols. **Meals:** main courses £19 to £28. Set L £17 (2 courses) to £29. Set D £34 (2 courses) to £50. Tasting menu £48 (4 courses) to £90. **Details:** 28 seats. V menu. Wheelchairs. Music. Children over 8 yrs only.

■ New Milton
Chewton Glen, The Dining Room
Cooking score: 4
Modern British | £60
Chewton Glen Hotel, Christchurch Road, New Milton, BH25 6QS
Tel no: (01425) 275341
chewtonglen.com

With its long approach, croquet facilities, swings in the trees, spa treatments and so forth, this lavishly modernised country house is quite the tonic for an urban escapee. Drinks are taken in the bar before moving through to one of several dining areas, although most reports centre on meals taken in the conservatory. The carte is a surprisingly long document in the old grand-hotel style. Prefaced with a section of oysters and caviar, mains are supplemented by four grilled dishes

(sole to sirloin), a roast-of-the-day trolley, and seven side dishes. At a summer dinner, dressed Devonshire crab with pickled daikon and celeriac and apple remoulade proved to be 'a very generous timbale', loin of Quantock lamb came with an underlay of crunchy-fresh peas interspersed with bacon and shreds of lettuce, and a shoulder meat 'bonbon' on a slick of strongly minted pea purée, while passion fruit cheesecake arrived with 'a sublime scoop' of lychee ice cream. The wine list opens at £30.

Chef/s: Simon Addison. **Open:** all week L and D. **Meals:** main courses £21 to £42. Set L £27. Tasting menu £70. Sun L £40. **Details:** 180 seats. 40 seats outside. Bar. Wheelchairs. Music. Parking.

■ Petersfield
Annie Jones
Cooking score: 3
Modern European | £40
10a Lavant Street, Petersfield, GU32 3EW
Tel no: (01730) 262728
anniejones.co.uk
£5
OFF

This cheerily stylish restaurant offers more than you'd expect, both in terms of size and food offerings, with an outside terrace and lively tapas bar extending choice. In the restaurant, panelled walls, high-backed chairs and wood floors create a homely feel. Here, the cooking references rustic European traditions yet feels elegant and assured: think poached duck egg with truffle butter, potato foam and jamón Ibérico; pan-roasted fillet of beef with heritage carrots and braised shallots; and vanilla pannacotta with blackberry and apple crumble, lemon foam and an orange beignet. Little extras such as sourdough bread or a bowl of fat olives (a spectrum of purples and greens) impressed, too, while the wine list is divided between Old World and New World, with a good showing from classic favourites.

Chef/s: Andrew Parker. **Open:** Thur to Sun L, Wed to Sat D. **Closed:** Mon, Tue, first week Jan. **Meals:** set L £28 (2 courses) to £35. Set D £30 (2 courses) to £40. Sun L £17. **Details:** 34 seats. Bar. Music.

JSW
Cooking score: 6
Modern British | £55
20 Dragon Street, Petersfield, GU31 4JJ
Tel no: (01730) 262030
jswrestaurant.com

If you're wondering whose initials those are, the answer is Jake Saul Watkins, chef and owner of this intimate little restaurant. Occupying what was a 17th-century coaching inn, JSW reflects that low-key approach with heavy old beams and a glass-covered well alongside some classy contemporary touches. There's also something refreshingly uncluttered about Jake's cooking, although terse descriptions conceal a great deal of labour-intensive detailing behind the scenes. Scallops are a favourite starter, perhaps served with lightly spiced mussels and borage or accompanied by 'cauliflower cheese' purée, truffle oil and pretty nasturtiums. Britain's seasonal larder is also well represented by up-to-date plates of fallow deer with shallot tart, hay-baked parsnip and coffee sauce or textures of lamb with salt-baked turnip and a 'wondrous' shepherd's pie. Tasting menus are the default setting for special occasions, complete with forward-thinking desserts such as baked English custard with rhubarb, ginger-beer jelly and gingerbread (a British classic disassembled). Easy mark-ups are a feature of the connoisseur's wine list, with lesser-known terroir names alongside the important big hitters, and a splendid choice of half-bottles.
Chef/s: Jake Saul Watkins. **Open:** Thur to Sat L, Wed to Sat D. **Closed:** Sun, Mon, Tue, 2 weeks from 25 Dec, 2 weeks spring, 2 weeks summer. **Meals:** set L £35 (2 courses) to £45. Set D £45 (2 courses) to £55. Tasting menu £65 (6 courses) to £90

(8 courses). **Details:** 50 seats. 28 seats outside. V menu. Wheelchairs. Parking. Children over 6 yrs only.

▌Portsmouth
Abarbistro
Cooking score: 2
International | £28
58 White Hart Road, Portsmouth, PO1 2JA
Tel no: (023) 9281 1585
abarbistro.co.uk

On the cobbles, a short stroll from Gunwharf Quays and the Isle of Wight ferry, this capably run 'bar bistro' is perfectly pitched for the Portsmouth scene, dishing up everything from burgers and steaks to popular Sunday roasts. Once a hotel and watering hole, it now puts on a bright contemporary face (scrubbed tables, conservatory, waterside terrace etc), while the kitchen tackles a mixed bag of eclectic brasserie food with satisfying results. Pick through the menu and you might find chicken satay, oriental duck and pomegranate salad or a Seychelles-style curry of monkfish and red snapper alongside ham hock terrine with homemade piccalilli, lentil shepherd's pie or herb-crusted cannon of lamb with fondant potato and shallot purée. Desserts also cover a lot of ground, from apple and blackberry crumble tart to cardamom-infused rice pudding with mango sorbet. Real ales, cocktails and a clutch of good-value wines keep the drinkers happy.
Chef/s: Mark Andrew. **Open:** all week, all day from 12. **Closed:** 25 and 26 Dec. **Meals:** main courses £11 to £22. Set L and D £18 (2 courses) to £23. **Details:** 100 seats. 80 seats outside. Bar. Wheelchairs. Music.

▋Southampton

The Dancing Man
British | £25
1 Bugle Street, Southampton, SO14 2AR
Tel no: (023) 8083 6666
dancingmanbrewery.co.uk

£30

The former wool house, built by Cistercian monks in 1338 and the only surviving free-standing medieval warehouse in Southampton, is now home to the Dancing Man Brewery and its light-filled, atmospheric first-floor dining room, where you'll find a simple menu of modern British brasserie staples. Start, perhaps, with smoked haddock, hake, bacon and Applewood Cheddar fishcakes with homemade tartare sauce, ahead of chicken, ham and leek pie, or 'cooked to perfection' lamb shank, and totally irresistible desserts, say a rich chocolate stout mousse with Baileys cream. Drink from a list of the on-site micro-brewery's award-winning beers.

▋Southsea
Restaurant 27
Cooking score: 4
Modern European | £50
27a South Parade, Southsea, PO5 2JF
Tel no: (023) 9287 6272
restaurant27.com

'Overall plush but minimal in style, dark chocolate brown and beige décor, contrasting dark red drapes, a nice bar area. It reminded me of the interior of more upmarket Japanese restaurants in its styling.' So ran the notes of one visitor, reporting on the complete refurbishment and restructuring of Kevin Bingham's innovative modern restaurant. Local and regional produce form the backbone of two tasting menus ('they are willing to do a bit of mixing and matching'), but inspiration for dishes comes from wider-spread European roots. Meals start with 'enticing little extras': whipped onion on a little toast, blue cheese choux bun, a pre-

starter of rich onion velouté. Start, perhaps, with a simple dish of smoked mackerel with cucumber and caviar, and go on to umami duck with smoked maize and a rich duck reduction or a 'beautiful thick-cut piece' of Romsey trout, roasted with a crisp skin, served with wild asparagus and a simple hollandaise sauce. Presentation is praised, especially a dessert that's a take on afternoon tea: a light scone-shaped croissant with rhubarb jam and cream plus a quenelle of chocolate mousse and a little bowl of blossom scent with liquid nitrogen to mimic tea. Service is charming. Wines start at £19.50.
Chef/s: Kevin Bingham. **Open:** Sun L, Wed to Sat D. **Closed:** Mon, Tue, 25 and 26 Dec, 1 Jan. **Meals:** set L £32 (3 courses). Set D £45 (3 courses). Tasting menu £46. **Details:** 34 seats. V menu. Bar. Music.

▋Stockbridge
The Greyhound on the Test
Cooking score: 2
Modern British | £38
31 High Street, Stockbridge, SO20 6EY
Tel no: (01264) 810833
thegreyhoundonthetest.co.uk

Traditional country pursuits are big hereabouts, and the Greyhound's name references not only the dogs that once ran with the local hunt, but also the river revered by devotees of fly fishing. The Test actually meanders past the garden, while the inn's spacious, airy interior has been dressed up with scrubbed tables, polished floors, prints and other country-chic accessories. The kitchen nods to its pubby roots with grills, Sunday roasts and fish and chips on Fridays, but the rest of menu is cosmopolitan brasserie fare with a confident global slant – perhaps soy-cured halibut with cucumber, apple, crab and wasabi or curried guinea fowl breast with poached egg, raisins, curry velouté and Bombay potato terrine. Things on toast, oysters, sharing boards and desserts such as dark chocolate mousse with caramelised banana complete a satisfying line-up. There are real ales on tap, plus a substantial wine list with a dozen by the glass.

Chef/s: Chris Heather. **Open:** all week L and D. **Closed:** 25 and 26 Dec. **Meals:** main courses £14 to £30. Set L £15 (2 courses) to £20. Sun L £24 (2 courses) to £30. **Details:** 62 seats. 30 seats outside. Bar. Music. Parking.

LOCAL GEM
Woodfire
Mediterranean | £20
High Street, Stockbridge, SO20 6EX
Tel no: (01264) 810248
woodfirestockbridge.co.uk

£5 OFF   £30

A one-time pumping station for the river Test, and later still a petrol station, it's all about the naked flame at this high street address these days – damn fine pizzas cooked in the wood oven and served up to an appreciative local crowd. It's bright and informal, with good-quality ingredients making the difference; a pizza topped with porcini mushrooms, cherry tomatoes and buffalo mozzarella, a melting panini filled with prosciutto, aubergine and provola cheese, hearty salads, sharing platters and a few pasta options. A short wine list opens at £18.50.

▉ Upton Grey
The Hoddington Arms
Cooking score: 2
British | £30
Bidden Road, Upton Grey, RG25 2RL
Tel no: (01256) 862371
hoddingtonarms.co.uk

£5 OFF

Affectionately known as 'The Hodd', this ever-so-welcoming village pub has virtues galore – thanks, in part, to its 'accommodating hosts'. Locals, travellers and even hungry dog walkers drop by for 'excellent' and 'reasonably priced' lunches, although the kitchen saves its best for the evening sessions. The old guard might go for pub-grub classics such as crispy

cod goujons followed by ham, egg and chips, while those with more adventurous palates could be swayed by ballotine of home-cured Loch Duart salmon with beetroot and horseradish dressing, ahead of a 'perfect spring main' of roast skate scattered with shrimps and served with 'lovely' crushed heritage potatoes, or slow-braised beef with salt-baked carrot and beef-dripping mash. After that, the Amalfi lemon posset with blood-orange sorbet, jelly and crunchy meringue is a sound bet. Local ales and a short list of international wines keep the drinkers happy – especially in summer, when the pub's outdoor pizza oven and cabana BBQ are in full swing.

Chef/s: Chris Barnes and Tom Wilson. **Open:** all week L, Mon to Sat D. **Closed:** 1 Jan. **Meals:** main courses £13 to £25. Set L £22 (2 courses) to £27. Sun L £28. Tasting menu £35 (6 courses). **Details:** 60 seats. 60 seats outside. Bar. Wheelchairs. Music. Parking.

▉ Winchester
The Black Rat
Cooking score: 3
Modern British | £40
88 Chesil Street, Winchester, SO23 0HX
Tel no: (01962) 844465
theblackrat.co.uk

The chunky wooden tables, bare-brick walls and shelves of ephemera at this quirky restaurant give little hint of the serious intent in the kitchen. But take a look at the menu and the signs are there: from the idiosyncratic, good-quality ingredients – anyone for bacon granola, perhaps served with guinea fowl, black garlic gnocchi, nettle purée and spring greens, or a dish of wild boar teamed with black pudding, crispy ears, celery, walnut, pear and hogweed? At a test meal celeriac 'velouté' had a decidedly rustic texture, and veal loin, though beautifully presented, was curiously tasteless, 'presumably the result of time spent in a water bath'. However, some dishes show real skill and the best are those that keep things simple – a game terrine or a tender ballotine of chicken, say – while vanilla pannacotta, and caramelised banana cake with popcorn are the pick of desserts. For 'experimentation without a hefty price tag', the weekend lunch menu is worth trying.

Chef/s: John Marsden-Jones. **Open:** Sat and Sun L, all week D. **Closed:** 2 weeks Christmas, Easter and Sep. **Meals:** main courses £19 to £25. **Details:** 40 seats. 16 seats outside. Bar. Music.

The Chesil Rectory

Cooking score: 4
Modern British | £34
1 Chesil Street, Winchester, SO23 0HU
Tel no: (01962) 851555
chesilrectory.co.uk

Spread over two wonky floors, and chock-full of hunting prints and taxidermy, this centuries-old restaurant often ranks highly in surveys of the UK's most romantic venues. Though it would be easy for this historic gem to rely on its film-star looks alone, it maintains a loyal following with its fine French-inflected dishes and well-considered wine list. There's a sound grasp of the nuances of flavour and texture in a warm salad of cauliflower, which combines florets roasted to nutty perfection, with crunchy shavings of the raw veg, finished off with lightly-pickled local mushrooms and toasted almonds. Likewise, a main of Middle White pork loin is offset by a shard of crispy crackling and butter-drenched kale. The wine list includes wallet-friendly selections by the glass and bottle, including the local Hattingley Valley Classic Cuvée, a worthy rival to many a Champagne. Friendly service completes the hat-trick.

Chef/s: Damian Brown. **Open:** all week L and D. **Closed:** 25 and 26 Dec, 1 Jan. **Meals:** main courses £14 to £20. Set L and D £18 (2 courses) to £22. Sun L £23 (2 courses) to £28. **Details:** 75 seats. Bar. Music. Children at L only.

◼ Woodlands Hotel TerraVina

Cooking score: 3
Modern European | £45
174 Woodlands Road, Woodlands, SO40 7GL
Tel no: (023) 8029 3784
hotelterravina.co.uk

£5 OFF ▮ 🍴

Master sommelier Gerard Basset and his wife Nina opened their eco-hotel in a handsome porticoed building on the eastern fringe of the New Forest a decade ago. The intention was to let the great outdoors come indoors to a degree, and the natural colours and generous use of light woods make a restful backdrop for Gavin Barnes' French-inflected contemporary cooking. An autumnal opener might be rich wild mushroom velouté with chestnut and apple ravioli, or there may be terrine of confit duck with pear and black garlic mayonnaise. Local materials come into their own in a main course of chalkstream trout with pickled alexanders, and there is no undue bashfulness about offering fine ribeye with good chips, leeks and sugar snaps. Fifteen minutes will fly by while you wait for a passion fruit soufflé to rise, the better to drop a scoop of mango sorbet into it. With Basset at the helm, you'd expect a doozy of a wine list, and TerraVina obliges. There is discernment and imagination written all through it, and mark-ups don't feel as though they are tugging at their moorings. Explore with confidence, from £18.75.

Chef/s: Gavin Barnes. **Open:** all week L and D. **Meals:** main courses £20 to £29. Set L £22 (2 courses) to £27. Sun L £25 (2 courses) to £33. Tasting menu £65. **Details:** 56 seats. 26 seats outside. V menu. Bar. Wheelchairs. Parking.

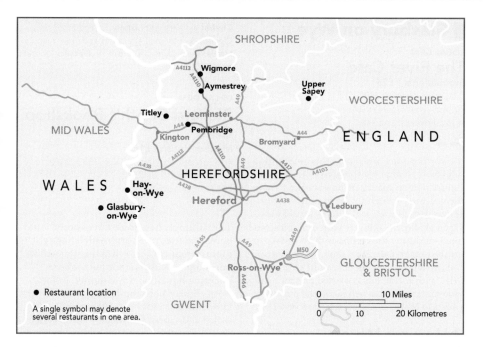

Map showing restaurant locations across Herefordshire, including SHROPSHIRE, Wigmore, Aymestrey, Upper Sapey, WORCESTERSHIRE, Titley, Leominster, MID WALES, Kington, Pembridge, Bromyard, ENGLAND, HEREFORDSHIRE, WALES, Hay-on-Wye, Hereford, Ledbury, Glasbury-on-Wye, Ross-on-Wye, M50, GLOUCESTERSHIRE & BRISTOL, GWENT.

- Restaurant location

A single symbol may denote several restaurants in one area.

0   10 Miles
0   10   20 Kilometres

Aymestrey

★ NEW ENTRY ★

The Riverside

Cooking score: 3
British | £30
Aymestrey, HR6 9ST
Tel no: (01568) 708440
riversideaymestrey.co.uk

£5 OFF 🛏

On the Mortimer Trail and fronting the river Lugg, the Riverside has been a popular refreshment stop for walkers and fishermen for centuries. However, now that the kitchen has upped its game, there's a steady stream of diners 'arriving hungry and leaving well satisfied'. Local produce abounds – herbs and vegetables from the kitchen garden, pork from local farms, trout from the river outside – prepared and presented beautifully on locally made pottery. Starters of local pressed chicken leg on a crunchy sunflower-seed base is sweetened with onion confit or mussels cooked with local angelica and local cider might be followed with hay-baked Shropshire guinea fowl breast with a gentle, sweet malted barley broth and carrots or wild-caught gurnard with wild herbs and hazelnut. Generous (though not gigantic) portions may make puddings redundant, but those who can manage are rewarded with excellent slow-baked bread-and-butter or excellent raspberry sorbet alongside seriously chocolatey délice. Wines from £17.

Chef/s: Andrew Link. **Open:** all week L, Mon to Sat D. **Meals:** main courses £14 to £26. Set D £25 (3 courses). Sun L £18 (2 courses) to £21. **Details:** 60 seats. 30 seats outside. Bar. Music. Parking.

Visit us online

To find out more about The Good Food Guide, please visit thegoodfoodguide.co.uk

▌Glasbury-on-Wye

LOCAL GEM
The River Café
International | £25
Glasbury-on-Wye, HR3 5NP
Tel no: (01497) 847007
wyevalleycanoes.co.uk

It's worth paying homage to this unassuming café-bar-restaurant at the Wye Valley Canoe Centre. The riverside setting is second to none, the welcome as friendly for passing walkers and tourists as it is for the many loyal locals. Open all day, breakfast is a top deal, but come lunch or dinner the emphasis shifts to take in mushroom and tarragon soup, say, very good cod and chips or excellent roast hake, and pork belly with soft polenta, roasted beetroot and vine tomatoes. Bakewell tart is the pick of puds and there's a modest selection of wines.

▌Hay-on-Wye
St John's Place
Cooking score: 1
Modern British | £32
Lion Street, Hay-on-Wye, HR3 5AA
Tel no: (07855) 783799
stjohnsplacehay.tumblr.com

Described as a 'very basic environment, limited menu . . .but original combinations by someone who can cook imaginatively,' this pint-sized, weekend-only restaurant shoehorned into the meeting room of an ancient chapel has locals competing for space. Julia Robson's cooking is down-to-earth, her short, weekly changing menus putting an abundance of seasonal ingredients through their paces. An April dinner, for example, delivered duck egg with asparagus, potato and lovage, then hogget shoulder with monk's beard, radishes and wild garlic, and beignets with fennel sugar and lemon curd to finish. There's an equally short wine list with biodynamic house wine at £18.

Chef/s: Julia Robson. Open: Fri and Sat D only. Closed: Sun to Thur, Christmas and New Year. Meals: main courses £15 to £19. Details: 25 seats. Music. Cash only.

LOCAL GEM
Richard Booth's Bookshop Café
Modern British | £18
44 Lion Street, Hay-on-Wye, HR3 5AA
Tel no: (01497) 820322
boothbooks.co.uk

The strikingly handsome three-storey bookshop features an armchaired library room and cinema, as well as the stone-tiled café hung with author portraits, where lingering lunches and two dinner sessions a week (Friday and Saturday) are offered. Dinner might well be smoked salmon with rocket and capers, followed by Asian-styled pork belly with braised red cabbage, while the all-day menu keeps you carbed up with pulled brisket sandwiches, rhubarb slaw and chips, or black bean burgers with tzatziki, then lemon polenta cake with raspberry jam and cream, while you turn the pages of an improving volume. Come festival time, the joint is jumping.

▌Pembridge
LOCAL GEM
The Cider Barn
Modern British | £30
Dunkertons Cider Mill, Pembridge, HR6 9ED
Tel no: (01544) 388161
the-cider-barn.co.uk

Housed in a Grade II-listed, 400-year-old barn attached to Dunkerton's pioneering organic cider mill, this café/restaurant is a terrific destination in its own right. Local produce is the theme, but there's nothing folksy or homespun about the results – think smoked duck with poached pear, gingerbread and parsnip purée followed by Hereford beef fillet and braised cheek with Jerusalem artichoke, sautéed Hispi cabbage, confit garlic and shallot jam. For afters, don't miss the doughnuts with fennel sugar and lemon curd. Wines from £17.95.

■ Titley
The Stagg Inn

Cooking score: 4
Modern British | £36
Titley, HR5 3RL
Tel no: (01544) 230221
thestagg.co.uk

£5 OFF 🍷 🚗

Steve and Nicola Reynolds will be celebrating 20 years at the Stagg in 2018, and it says a great deal about their devotion to duty that they've managed to maintain this one-time drovers' inn as a proper country boozer while investing it with serious gastronomic clout. There are real ales and ciders on tap and no piped music to disturb the hum of conversation. Meanwhile, Steve's kitchen delivers fine-tuned food with plenty of flair and an eye on the regional larder: locally reared beef is a headline act (especially on Sundays), but the seasonal repertoire takes in everything from Hereford snails with watercress and garlic croûtons to a festive dish of venison loin and slow-cooked haunch with salt-baked celeriac, fig and chestnuts. With snacks in the bar, artisan cheeses from the 'three counties' and puds including apple and ginger cake with elderflower ice cream, this is a rousing package. Nicola's knowledgeably chosen wine list is peppered with reputable growers and eclectic grape varieties, all at pain-free prices.
Chef/s: Steve Reynolds. **Open:** Wed to Sun L and D.
Closed: Mon, Tue, 25 and 26 Dec, 1 week Jan/Feb, 1 week Jun/Jul, first 2 weeks Nov. **Meals:** main courses £14 to £25. Sun L £23. **Details:** 70 seats. 20 seats outside. V menu. Bar. Parking.

Nose-to-tail eating

Nose-to-tail eating used to be all about things that had… well, a nose and a tail. That definition is being stretched, but there's still plenty of unusual protein on the nation's menus.

You can't move for pig's cheek, but be prepared to fossick with chopsticks and there's some serious texture and flavour in the chargrilled **salmon head** at **Umezushi** in Manchester. Don't worry about looking it in the eye – it'll be obscured by a scattering of greenery.

Secreto pork, the little-known treat cut from behind the shoulder by Spanish butchers, is the chewy, smoky element in the Chinese bacon butty, made with a steamed bao bun, at Michael O'Hare's **Rabbit in the Moon**.

Formerly considered to be good only for milk in the UK, **dairy beef** is having a moment, mainly if it's Spanish and comes as a huge, well-aged and charred steak known as **txuleta**. Try it at **Paco Tapas** in Bristol or **Chiltern Firehouse** in London.

If you like your offal in one resonant hit, try **Smoking Goat**'s offal Mondays. You might encounter **salted deep-fried ox heart**, Northern-style **chicken offal laab**, **lambs' liver jungle curry** or **stewed beef tongue soup**.

█ Upper Sapey

★ NEW ENTRY ★

The Baiting House
Cooking score: 1
Modern British | £30
Upper Sapey, WR6 6XT
Tel no: (01886) 853201
baitinghouse.co.uk

A proper local for modern times, there's a decent, well-stocked bar with county beers and ciders on tap, and a decent, if short, selection of wines. But unlike many community pubs, the food here is worth a try. Though decent sandwiches, fish and chips and homemade soup are the favourite choices for weekday lunches, the kitchen steps up in the evening, with pork belly with chorizo, and smoked mackerel and salmon pâté. Make sure you book for Sunday lunch, where beetroot and goats' cheese salad and a roast or two, followed by sticky toffee pudding, are the order of the day.
Chef/s: Charles Bradley. **Open:** Tue to Sun L, Tue to Sat D. **Closed:** Mon. **Meals:** main courses £12 to £17. **Details:** 40 seats. 50 seats outside. Bar.

█ Wigmore
The Oak
Cooking score: 3
British | £30
Ford Street, Wigmore, HR6 9UJ
Tel no: (01568) 770424
theoakwigmore.com

A converted house and barn on a crossroads at the heart of a peaceful slip of a village, the Oak has an appealing mixture of old stone walls and clean-lined modern design inside. Rory Bunting is a Wigmore boy who went out into the world of aspirational gastronomy and came back again to deliver the glad tidings, and the reputation of the place is spreading. Artfully conceived dishes that deliver plenty of punch include starter soufflés such as leek

and Snowdonia Bomber with cumined cauliflower purée, or oxtail terrine with pickled St George mushrooms, and mains that bring on a welter of good things in careful balance. Sautéed haunch and confit belly of lamb with artichoke purée and black garlic and mint jus is founded on fine local materials, or there may be gurnard and calamari with anise-spiked shallot purée and wilted pak choi, sauced in Pernod. Dessert seductions take in chocolate and stout fondant with matching ice cream, or summery strawberry and elderflower custard with vanilla shortbread. The cooking deserves a wider range of wines than the tiny list that starts at £18.
Chef/s: Rory Bunting. **Open:** Wed to Sun L, Wed to Sat D. **Closed:** Mon, Tue. **Meals:** main courses £15 to £30. Sun L £15 (1 course) to £22 (3 courses). **Details:** 50 seats. 20 seats outside. Bar. Wheelchairs. Music. Parking.

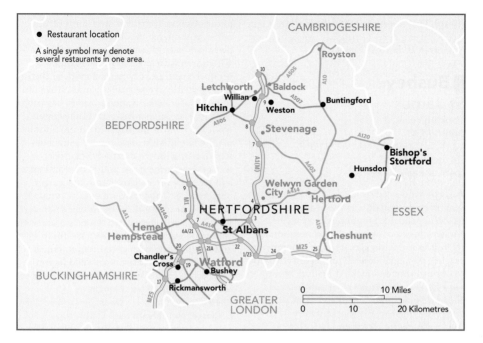

- ● Restaurant location

A single symbol may denote
several restaurants in one area.

CAMBRIDGESHIRE

Royston

Letchworth   Baldock
    Willian   Buntingford
Hitchin   Weston

BEDFORDSHIRE   Stevenage

                                Bishop's
                                Stortford
                        Hunsdon

                Welwyn Garden
                City
HERTFORDSHIRE   Hertford   ESSEX

Hemel   St Albans
Hempstead

                        Cheshunt

Chandler's   Watford
Cross   Bushey
BUCKINGHAMSHIRE
        Rickmansworth

GREATER
LONDON

0   10 Miles
0   10   20 Kilometres

▊ Bishop's Stortford
Water Lane
Cooking score: 1
Modern British | £29
31 Water Lane, Bishop's Stortford, CM23 2JZ
Tel no: (01279) 211888
waterlane.co
£30

The one-time home of the Hawkes brewery is
a self-declared bar and restaurant, part of the
family-run Anglian Country Inns group that
includes The Fox in Willian (see entry) and the
Brancaster Brewery among its portfolio. An
atmospheric vaulted cellar bar and capacious
ground-floor restaurant show the bones of the
18th-century building. The menu plays to the
gallery, serving piled-high burgers (jerk
chicken, say, or salt beef and Swiss cheese),
sharing boards, and steaks with a host of extras
if desired. Kick off with coronation prawn
cocktail, and finish with double chocolate
brownie with popcorn ice cream. House wine
is £17.50.

Chef/s: Adam O'Sullivan. **Open:** Wed to Sat, all day
from 12. Sun 10 to 4. **Meals:** main courses £12 to
£18. Sun L £19 (2 courses) to £24. **Details:** 80 seats.
Bar. Wheelchairs. Music.

▊ Buntingford

LOCAL GEM
Pearce's Farmshop & Café
International | £25
Hamels Mead, Buntingford, SG9 9ND
Tel no: (01920) 821246
pearcesfarmshop.com
£30

If you fancy a bowl of Sri Lankan chicken
curry (or something similarly exotic) while
driving along the A10, this enterprising café/
farm shop might fit the bill. Done out in
breezy style with green-painted beams and
floor-to-ceiling windows (great rural views
guaranteed), it offers breakfast, brunch,
afternoon tea and everything in between.
Specials such as said curry are top picks, but
also expect sandwiches, burgers, beetroot

risotto, Thai noodle broth, fishcakes and so on – plus cakes galore. Drink East Anglian beers or Corney & Barrow wines.

▮ Bushey
St James
Cooking score: 1
British | £45
30 High Street, Bushey, WD23 3HL
Tel no: (020) 8950 2480
stjamesrestaurant.co.uk

A deep-windowed frontage looks into a smart vermilion-walled dining room at Alfonso La Cava's dependable neighbourhood venue. Modern bistro cooking with contemporary references is the stock-in-trade, in a range that extends from grilled scallops in pancetta with roast butternut and pickled shallots, through roast lamb rump with a rosemary-blasted shepherd's pie, puréed peas and mint jelly, to satisfying finishers like the signature Toblerone cheesecake with black cherry compote. A separate vegetarian menu offers beetroot textures with horseradish cream, followed perhaps by spiced roast cauliflower with gnocchi and winter pesto. The simple wine list covers many of the classic appellations, with house selections in all three colours at £16.95.
Chef/s: Matt Cook. **Open:** all week L, Mon to Sat D. **Closed:** 25 and 26 Dec, bank hols. **Meals:** main courses £7 to £24. Set L £17 (2 courses) to £22. Set D £19 (2 courses) to £24. Sun L £26. **Details:** 100 seats. V menu. Bar. Wheelchairs. Music.

▮ Chandler's Cross
Colette's
Cooking score: 5
Modern British | £65
The Grove, Chandler's Cross, WD3 4TG
Tel no: (01923) 296010
thegrove.co.uk

🛏

Not much of a stretch from central London, the Georgian Grove is the former residence of the Earls of Clarendon, now a deep-piled,

luxurious hotel retreat with all the golf and facials you can handle. The kitchens are patrolled by an enormous brigade of chefs, who not only help Russell Bateman to produce some glossily refined modern British food, but also oversee the organic cultivation of much of it in the walled gardens. Colette's, with its wide strip mirrors and lime-green colour scheme, is the flagship dining option, a place where roast scallops arrive bathed in hazelnut and brown-butter hollandaise, or foie gras is simmered in ginger beer and spices and served with poached apple and ginger beer caramel. Top-drawer prime materials at main might see Norfolk Black chicken sauced with Tunworth cheese in a thyme jus scattered with pine nuts, or turbot given the full bells-and-whistles job with caviar cream. Finish aromatically with saffron baba and lemon verbena ice cream. What the wine list lacks in scope, it makes up for in quality.
Chef/s: Russell Bateman. **Open:** Sun L, Tue to Sun D. **Closed:** Mon. **Meals:** set D £65 (3 courses). Sun L £55. Tasting menu £85. **Details:** 45 seats. V menu. Bar. Wheelchairs. Music. Parking. Children at Sun L only.

▮ Hitchin
Hermitage Rd
Cooking score: 2
Modern British | £28
20-21 Hermitage Road, Hitchin, SG5 1BT
Tel no: (01462) 433603
hermitagerd.co.uk
£30

With generous internal proportions and a bar that invites hours of dawdling, Hermitage Road has become a fine place to eat and drink. Indeed, the place has come a long way since its days as a town-centre nightclub. At its heart is a sound kitchen offering up a vision of contemporary dining with sharing boards and plates of well-crafted dishes that combine good sense with present-day cooking techniques. Steaks dominate, served with classic sauces and sides such as sweet potato fries or iceberg, blue cheese and bacon, but the menu's broad remit takes in everything from a pork belly steamed bun with kimchi mayo, and Brancaster mussels with white wine and parsley cream, via cauliflower cheese to sea bass with pumpkin, orange, spinach and red pepper risotto. Desserts tread a steady path from sticky toffee and pecan pudding to blood-orange and lemongrass posset. Decent wines from £17.50.

Chef/s: Kumour Uddin. **Open:** Mon to Fri L and D. Sat and Sun, all day. **Meals:** main courses £13 to £18. **Details:** 150 seats. Bar. Wheelchairs. Music.

■ Hunsdon

LOCAL GEM
The Fox & Hounds
Modern British | £35
2 High Street, Hunsdon, SG12 8NH
Tel no: (01279) 843999
foxandhounds-hunsdon.co.uk

James and Bianca Rix's village pub ticks all the right boxes with its crackling winter fires, beams and summer beer garden, especially as it manages to combine its dual role as local hostelry and upmarket eatery with agility. The feel is relaxed and the menus keep things simple but maintain interest with dishes such as roast mallard with treviso and blood orange or venison haunch with duck-fat potato cake and red cabbage, while from the Josper oven come char-grilled squid with romesco salsa or skate wing with sprouting broccoli and capers. Wines from £17.50.

■ Rickmansworth

LOCAL GEM
Café in the Park
International | £15
The Aquadrome, Frogmoor Lane, Rickmansworth, WD3 1NB
Tel no: (01923) 711131
thecafeinthepark.com

£5 OFF £30 ⬇

'Wow, loved this place and trying to find an excuse to get there again soon – so wish I had one like this near me,' enthused one visitor to this café at the Aquadrome in Rickmansworth

park. And no wonder. With its reasonable prices, simple food and informal atmosphere, everything about the place feels right. The menu is a wonderful mix of Mediterranean and Middle Eastern flavours anchored by great British staples, from breakfasts of shakshuka (eggs baked in tomato sauce) to a good old sausage sarnie, from lunches of falafel with harissa and yoghurt, and squash and barley risotto, to burgers made with 21-day Aberdeen Angus beef. Wines from £18.

■ St Albans

Lussmanns
Cooking score: 1
Modern European | £28
Waxhouse Gate, off High Street, St Albans, AL3 4EW
Tel no: (01727) 851941
lussmanns.com

£5 OFF £30 ⬇

'Lussmanns is always a pleasure,' declared a fan of Andrei Lussmann's relaxed, all-day brasserie, a brilliant local asset and the original of a group of five Herts-based venues. The menu is rooted in great British ingredients (among them organic beef and lamb, woodland-reared pork and sustainable fish) and is a please-all affair of cheeseburgers, 'excellent' fishcakes, steak frites, with a few ambitious plates thrown in. These range from wild rabbit with Monmouthshire spiced chorizo linguine, to hake with Chichester clams, confit of fennel, sea purslane and new potatoes. Desserts hit the comfort zone with sticky date pudding or lemon posset with almond bastoncini and toasted pistachios. Staff are 'friendly and helpful'. Wines from £16.95.

Chef/s: Bogdan Cozma. **Open:** all week, all day from 12. **Closed:** 25 and 26 Dec. **Meals:** main courses £13 to £25. Set L and early D £13 (2 courses) to £16. **Details:** 105 seats. Wheelchairs. Music.

Thompson St Albans

Cooking score: 5
Modern British | £55
2-8 Hatfield Road, St Albans, AL1 3RP
Tel no: (01727) 730777
thompsonstalbans.co.uk

There's a suburban feel to the outside of Phil Thompson's place, with its weatherboarded frontage and backyard summer tables, but inside, the dining room goes for a racier look in crimson and grey, with smartly dressed tables and colourful artworks. Backing up his weekly changing tasting menus with a seasonally developing carte, Thompson brings a lightly applied modern sensibility to dishes founded on thoroughbred prime materials. Applewood-smoked sea trout and potato dauphine laced with crab make a convincing pairing in a starter that also finds room for beetroot, compressed radicchio and smoked roe, and may be the prelude to honey-glazed duck with Chinese-style crispy duck tongue, tarragon-braised carrots and clementine. Fish is boldly treated, perhaps butter-roasted John Dory in ink-black tagliatelle, wild mushrooms and salsify, sauced with verjus, the tartness of which is neutralised by something sweet to follow, such as apple crumble and custard soufflé with condensed milk ice cream and caramel. A stylistically grouped wine collection opens with Chilean varietals at £22.
Chef/s: Phil Thompson. **Open:** Wed to Sun L, Tue to Sat D. **Closed:** Mon, 2 to 10 Jan. **Meals:** main courses £25 to £35. Set L £19 (2 courses) to £21. Set D £21 (2 courses) to £25. Sun L £30. Tasting menu £60. **Details:** 90 seats. 18 seats outside. V menu. Bar. Wheelchairs. Music.

LOCAL GEM

The Foragers

Modern British | £24
The Verulam Arms, 41 Lower Dagnall Street, St Albans, AL3 4QE
Tel no: (01727) 836004
the-foragers.com

£30

'Still dishing up decent stuff,' notes a regular to this likeable pub that's a five-minute walk from the cathedral, and where wild foods enliven the likes of local game, birch-smoked lamb shank, roasted hake and even cocktails. Starters of spätzle (noodles) made with nettle, three-cornered leek and hogweed, scattered with salty Scottish sea lettuce and kohlrabi, and mains of slow-roasted pork belly with scrumpy and apple sauce and alexander seed mash, greens and gravy define the cooking perfectly. Drink real ales or wines from £18.

■ Weston

LOCAL GEM

The Cricketers

Modern British | £21
Damask Green Road, Weston, SG4 7DA
Tel no: (01462) 790273
thecricketersweston.co.uk

£30

Cricket bats play their part both decoratively around the bar and practically as you'll discover as you order food, while references to the game pepper the menu. A proper pub, run by the regional Anglian Country Inns group, it's a genuine all-rounder with real ales, pub classics such as fish and chips and a wood-fired pizza oven turning out the Inswinger, topped with goats' cheese and caramelised onions. The likes of coq au vin and veggie quiche are done well. Wines open at £17.50.

■ **Willian**
The Fox
Cooking score: 2
Modern British | £29
Willian, SG6 2AE
Tel no: (01462) 480233
foxatwillian.co.uk

The family-run Anglian Country Inns has turned the Fox, a Georgian village hostelry lurking between Willian's church and its pond, into the image of a contemporary country pub. Inside are a suite of guest rooms, a light-toned bar area and a breezy dining room adorned with vulpine paintings and a blackboard menu of daily specials. Local sourcing is a *sine qua non* of such set-ups, and Sherwin Jacobs gets creative with a pork duo that comprises pancetta-wrapped tenderloin and pig's cheek cannelloni with cavolo nero and cider-braised heritage carrots, or perhaps baked plaice that comes with roast portobellos, cauliflower and chard, in a beurre noisette incorporating almonds and Lilliput capers. Before that, you could appetise with a bowl of curried mussel and saffron chowder with a smoked trout potato cake and slaw, and then round things off with the house take on lemon meringue pie, served with ginger shortbread, raspberries and yoghurt ice cream. A concise but wide-ranging wine selection starts at £17.50.
Chef/s: Sherwin Jacobs. **Open:** all week L and D.
Meals: main courses £14 to £22. **Details:** 100 seats.
80 seats outside. Bar. Wheelchairs. Music. Parking.

Our highlights...

Our undercover inspectors reveal their most memorable dishes from another year of extraordinary eating.

From **Murano**, the wonderful **chestnut anolini in mushroom consommé** – little pasta parcels with a silky, mousse-like chestnut filling in a glistening and deep-flavoured broth with a few sprout leaves wilted in.

At **Ormer Mayfair - secreto of Ibérico pork with calamari, chorizo chutney, Asian pear**. I loved this dish – its fantastic flavours and textures made me desperate to buy a wood-burning oven for home-use.

Beef fudge at **Ynyshir** – using Wagyu beef dripping as the dairy element. A weird sensation but very, very good. And original.

Feta and honey cheesecake from **Honey & Smoke**: This has to be the best cheesecake I've ever eaten. The crisp and buttery kadaif pastry base was topped with thick and soft feta cheesecake and finished with honey syrup, darkly toasted almonds and plump blueberries – I could eat it for breakfast, lunch and dinner!

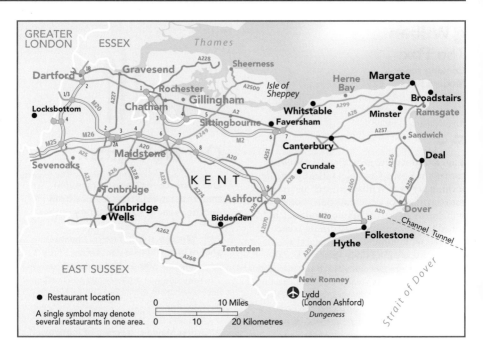

▋Biddenden
The West House

Cooking score: 5
Modern European | £45
28 High Street, Biddenden, TN27 8AH
Tel no: (01580) 291341
thewesthouserestaurant.co.uk

Half-hidden in a row of weavers' cottages
smack in the middle of pretty Biddenden,
Graham Garrett's warm-hearted little
restaurant exudes a hospitable vibe, while his
kitchen is known for its ability to conjure
unexpected delights from locally sourced
ingredients. As for the menu, plain-speaking
dish descriptions conceal a great deal of
technical know-how and culinary nous:
poached egg with Ibérico ham dressing,
brown butter sabayon and crispy kale is a
witty modern take on a popular pub dish;
charred monkfish cheeks are served Indian-
style with tandoori cauliflower and mussel
masala; grilled lamb rump receives classic
accompaniments including shepherd's pie
croquette, sprouting broccoli and caper sauce.
This is clever, high-end cooking with an
underlying instinct for true tastes and
flavours. And with light-hearted desserts such
as a Paris–Brest involving dulce de leche,
banana mousse and frozen banana, there's also
a hint of mischief about Garrett's approach to
all things gastronomic. The gently priced
global wine list is a classy compendium, with
lots of minimum-intervention 'natural'
vintages, English labels, offbeat numbers and
a generous selection by the glass or carafe.
Chef/s: Graham Garrett and Tony Parkin. **Open:** Tue
to Fri and Sun L, Tue to Sat D. **Closed:** Mon, 24 to 27
Dec, 1 Jan. **Meals:** set L £25. Set D £38 (2 courses)
to £45. Tasting menu £60 (6 courses). **Details:** 35
seats. V menu. Music. Parking.

Average price 🍴

The average price denotes the price
of a three-course meal without wine.

▉ Broadstairs

Albariño

Cooking score: 2
Spanish | £22
29 Albion Street, Broadstairs, CT10 1LX
Tel no: (01843) 600991
albarinorestaurant.co.uk
£5 OFF £30

Bringing sunny Spain to this quaint corner of
south-east Kent, Steven and Stephanie Dray's
diminutive tapas spot on a narrow
thoroughfare exudes good cheer. Its yellow
walls, colourful tiles, bar and bistro seating set
an informal tone as Steven goes about his
business, proffering generous plates of tapas,
punctuated with stellar local ingredients.
Along with a board of chalked-up daily
specials, the menu kicks off with snacks –
chickpea and fennel chips are justly popular –
cheese and cured meat boards, and takes in the
gamut of typical Spanish tapas (Padrón
peppers, patatas bravas and tortilla). Seafood is
either given a lick of heat on the plancha (try
gambas and octopus) or roasted to perfection,
and there are creative vegetarian offerings,
too. Meat dishes are rather more workmanlike, but satisfying nonetheless. Needless to
say, Albariño – Spain's signature thirst
quencher – is the choice tipple here, although
plenty of sherries are also available. If your
constitution can withstand it, proceed to the
belt-loosener puddings.
Chef/s: Steven Dray. **Open:** Sat L, Mon to Sat D.
Closed: Sun, 25 and 26 Dec, 1 Jan. **Meals:** tapas £5
to £13. **Details:** 26 seats. Bar. Wheelchairs.

Symbols

🛏 Accommodation is available
£30 Three courses for less than £30
£5 OFF £5-off voucher scheme
🍷 Notable wine list

★ CHEF TO WATCH ★
★ NEW ENTRY ★

Stark

Cooking score: 5
Modern European | £45
1 Oscar Road, Broadstairs, CT10 1QJ
Tel no: (01843) 579786
starkfood.co.uk

Ben and Sophie Crittenden's simple 12-seater
restaurant with a galley kitchen tucked in the
corner gives a sense that something special is in
store. Ben (ex West House, Biddenden, see
entry) has had a good grounding in
technically sharp cooking, but with his
mastery of different textures and, sometimes,
ingenious simplicity, the cooking here is a
little bit more. What's on offer is a six-course,
no-choice tasting menu that gets right to the
point – no small talk and the flavours come at
you out of nowhere. Cured mackerel, for
example, is offset by a smear of sweet-tart
rhubarb, pickled cucumber and the
caramelised sweetness of onion, tender pigeon
breast matched by a silky dollop of duck liver
mousse, the flavour popping with bitter
orange and the crunch of hazelnut, while
perfectly timed hake comes in a bowl with a
few spoonfuls of 'lovely' broth with
asparagus, pungent wild garlic and potato. A
pre-dessert of pistachio sponge with lemon
and shavings of fennel – 'an unexpectedly
daring combination' – heralds sweet treats
such as chocolate crémeux, its sweetness offset
by the malty tones of barley and toasted milk.
To sum up, there is serious dedication to food
and drink here – our meal was really well
balanced, the dynamics modulated from one
dish to the next – with interesting wine
pairings. Otherwise, there's a very brief,
reasonably priced list with bottles from £17.
Chef/s: Ben Crittenden. **Open:** Tue to Sat D.
Closed: Sun, Mon, 25 and 26 Dec. **Meals:** tasting
menu £45 (6 courses). **Details:** 12 seats. Music.

Wyatt & Jones

Cooking score: 2
Modern British | £32
23-27 Harbour Street, Broadstairs, CT10 1EU
Tel no: (01843) 865126
wyattandjones.co.uk
£5 OFF

It's been doing Broadstairs proud for nigh on five years, and this hard-grafting local asset perched beneath the York Gate arch keeps on spreading the gospel. Made up of three stepped fishermen's cottages, the view of Viking Bay from the lower dining room cheers the senses, and the menu of creative, seasonal dishes eschews pretension in favour of big, hearty flavours. Pig's head terrine with wild rocket and smoked apple purée is a fine way to start, and main dishes do their bit, too, perhaps with a sturdy Sussex beef loin with braised ox cheek and bone-marrow butter mash, or else Aylesbury duck leg with bubble and squeak topped with an egg (that's if you can resist the mussels in garlic cream with chips). Warm crab tart has been well reported, and everyone has a good word for the sticky toffee pudding. On the drinks front there's a 'vast array of gins', house cocktails, Kentish beers and ciders and a mainly European selection of wines from £19.
Chef/s: Craig Edgell. Open: Wed to Sun L, Wed to Sat D. Closed: Mon, Tue, 25 and 26 Dec. Meals: main courses £12 to £22. Details: 60 seats. Bar. Wheelchairs. Music.

◼ Canterbury
The Goods Shed

Cooking score: 2
Modern British | £32
Station Road West, Canterbury, CT2 8AN
Tel no: (01227) 459153
thegoodsshed.co.uk

For 15 years the Goods Shed has enjoyed loyal support among the residents of Canterbury, the cavernous Victorian railway shed an oddly fascinating setting for such an unusual venture: a six-day-a-week farmers' market with bakery, food, wine and beer stalls, as well

as a restaurant on the upper tier serving food that's fiercely seasonal and locally sourced (much from the market). With high-arched windows, plain-wood tables, cheerful service and 'a happy buzz', it's the kind of neighbourhood restaurant that can give a neighbourhood a good name, feeding the faithful with the likes of tender octopus with a silky bean purée and herb relish, then guinea fowl with potato rösti, Hispi cabbage, cider and lardons or a fine piece of hake with new potatoes, clams and asparagus. Finish with artisan British cheeses, that's if you can resist the orange and almond cake with crème fraîche. Wines are a European selection with a few by the jug or glass.
Chef/s: Rafael Lopez. Open: Tue to Sun L, Tue to Sat D. Closed: Mon, 25 to 27 Dec, 1 Jan. Meals: main courses £15 to £24. Details: 60 seats. Parking.

◼ Crundale
The Compasses Inn

Cooking score: 4
Modern British | £30
Sole Street, Crundale, CT4 7ES
Tel no: (01227) 700300
thecompassescrundale.co.uk
£5 OFF

Such has been this modest 14th-century country pub's success since Robert and Donna Taylor took over in 2013 it is now advisable to book – especially at weekends. A bucolic location, hop-strewn beams and open fires reinforce the image of an ever-so-English pub – there's even a proper bar with Shepherd Neame ales – but the main interest is in cooking that shines with seasonal goodness and remarkable depth of flavour. Robert's menus are all about vivid modern British combinations, from Marmite-glazed pigeon with celeriac purée and hazelnut granola to 40-day aged Kentish beef with ox cheek, given heft by smoked chips, balsamic-glazed onions, English-mustard clotted cream and mushroom ketchup. He's dedicated to sourcing the best seasonal ingredients, handles fish cookery with aplomb – try roasted cod loin with cockle, potato and sweetcorn chowder – and, while puddings may be fairly traditional in range, they are very good: perhaps almond tart with glazed prunes and cinnamon ice cream. Wines from £16.50.

Chef/s: Robert Taylor. **Open:** Tue to Sun L, Tue to Sat D. **Closed:** Mon, bank hols. **Meals:** main courses £15 to £22. Set L £15 (2 courses) to £18. **Details:** 60 seats. Bar. Music. Parking.

Deal

★ NEW ENTRY ★

Frog and Scot

Cooking score: 3
French | £32
86 High Street, Deal, CT14 6EG
Tel no: (01304) 379444
frogandscot.co.uk
£5
OFF

Tightly packed tables and wooden chairs set a no-frills and informal tone at this popular, bustling high-street venue. With prices that keep locals returning, Frog and Scot is a big hit, especially as everyone is put at ease by a mood that's as personable as can be. Blackboard-scrawled menus are constantly updated to reflect availability and seasonality, with seafood well to the fore: perhaps beautifully cooked seared scallops on a rich, truffley cauliflower purée with a nugget of excellent black pudding, a bowl of plump mussels with saffron, spices and cream, or baked fillet of very fresh hake with an intense crab bisque and a heap of finely sliced cabbage. Intelligent flavour combinations and confident cooking were the themes running through a winter lunch that included roast breast and confit leg of Aylesbury duck with spiced roasting juices, and a dessert of a 'really well-made' warm chocolate mousse with a blood-orange ice cream. The mainly French wine list starts at £19.

Chef/s: David Gadd. **Open:** Wed to Sun L, Wed to Sat D. **Closed:** Mon, Tue. **Meals:** main courses £15 to £25. Set L £14 (2 courses) to £17. Tasting menu £60. **Details:** 52 seats. 8 seats outside. Bar. Music.

Victuals & Co.

Cooking score: 2
Modern British | £37
2-3 St George's Passage, Deal, CT14 6TA
Tel no: (01304) 374389
victualsandco.com
£5
OFF

Locals show loyalty to Andy and Suzy Kirkwood's restaurant for good reason – it's worth knowing about if you're in the area. It's a comfortable, atmospheric and sociable place characterised by a tiny bar and various dining rooms with pale painted floorboards, marble-topped tables, brightly patterned upholstered chairs and art-covered walls. The kitchen hitchhikes round the globe for ideas, picking up everything from crispy pork belly with Asian dressing, baby gem lettuce, chilli dip and pickled carrot to a Thai green curry. Elsewhere, a starter of crab bisque – 'deep flavour and creamy' – with a couple of mini brown crab toasts might be followed by hake with roast tomato, thyme and olive sauce, rösti and greens. If it's meat you're after, 28-day aged pedigree Sussex beef with salsa verde and fries is one option, while apricot French toast with wild fennel ice cream is a satisfying dessert. On Sunday evenings the kitchen likes to use up remaining stocks of food with a good-natured 'raid the larder' menu. Wines from £19.50.

Chef/s: Suzy Kirkwood, Ayesha Harris and Callum Grundon. **Open:** Sat and Sun L, Wed to Sun D. **Closed:** Mon, Tue, Jan, 1 week Jun, 1 week Oct. **Meals:** main courses £18 to £26. Set L £21 (2 courses) to £25. **Details:** 40 seats. 10 seats outside. Bar. Music. Children over 9 yrs only at D.

Visit us online

To find out more about
The Good Food Guide, please
visit thegoodfoodguide.co.uk

Faversham
Read's

Cooking score: 6
Modern British | £60
Macknade Manor, Canterbury Road,
Faversham, ME13 8XE
Tel no: (01795) 535344
reads.com

David and Rona Pitchford's Georgian manor house continues to delight visitors. It glides along as a polished restaurant-with-rooms, where staff do their level best from greeting to farewell to make all feel welcome, and the kitchen's output is dependent on seasonal and local supplies – as well as produce from its own kitchen garden. The cooking is thoroughgoing British modernism, carefully considered, classy but unfussy, delivering much gratification in the form of a pressing of pickled herring with Charlotte potatoes, apple and a light horseradish dressing, and loin of Kentish lamb with hotpot potato, carrot purée and cabbage with vegetable brunoise. Hot black cherry soufflé with vanilla ice cream is a handsome, generous end-note, though the selection of British cheese makes a fine alternative. Read's also springs surprises on the wine front: the authoritative list has pedigree growers and vinous treasures in abundance. The budget-conscious need not worry, however; prices start at £25 and the Best Buys list provides excellent, wide-ranging choice for under £30.
Chef/s: David Pitchford. **Open:** Tue to Sat L and D. **Closed:** Sun, Mon, 25 to 27 Dec, 2 weeks Jan, 2 weeks Sept. **Meals:** set L £28. Set D £50 (2 courses) to £60. Tasting menu £65. **Details:** 55 seats. 20 seats outside. Bar. Wheelchairs. Parking.

Local Gem

Local Gems are the perfect neighbourhood venues, delivering good, freshly cooked food at great value for money.

Folkestone
Rocksalt

Cooking score: 2
Seafood | £35
4-5 Fishmarket Road, Folkestone, CT19 6AA
Tel no: (01303) 212070
rocksaltfolkestone.co.uk

'There's not too many good dining options in the immediate area. This will be our first port of call next time we're passing through.' So noted a first-time visitor to Mark Sergeant's harbourside restaurant. On warm days much is made of the sea-facing location when glass sliding doors open on to a terrace, creating a Continental vibe; inside there's a neutral contemporary finish. Menus make the most of local ingredients and seasonal produce, with the focus firmly on fish – say creamed smoked coley 'thermidor' with a poached egg, followed by baked cod with heritage tomatoes, wild garlic and spring leeks. But there's also fried pig's jowl with caramelised cream onions and nasturtium pesto, and spiced lamb neck fillet with curried cauliflower and sweetbread bhaji, as well as steaks. Elsewhere, good sourdough bread comes with excellent 'very smoky' taramasalata, cheeses are from Kent and Sussex, and Kentish gypsy tart is the pick of desserts. Wines from £17.
Open: all week L, Mon to Sat D. **Meals:** main courses £13 to £28. Set L Mon to Fri £22 to £25. **Details:** 84 seats. 44 seats outside. Bar.

Hythe

LOCAL GEM
La Salamandre

French | £15
30 High Street, Hythe, CT21 5AT
Tel no: (01303) 239853

Everyone agrees that Alain Ronez's little French café-patisserie is 'a fantastic addition to Hythe High Street'. Light lunches of French onion soup, croque monsieur, tartiflette and the lightest of quiche lorraine (served with a beautifully dressed salad) have all been praised, as has the sunny service, welcoming vibe and tempting cakes to eat in or take-away. Almond croissants and pains aux raisins sell out quickly to in-the-know locals, who also pop in for breakfasts of omelettes or scrambled egg and smoked salmon. Unlicensed. Cash only.

Locksbottom
Chapter One
Cooking score: 6
Modern European | £40
Farnborough Common, Locksbottom,
BR6 8NF
Tel no: (01689) 854848
chapteronerestaurant.co.uk

Uptown food at downtown prices has always been the big selling point at Chapter One – Andrew McLeish's unerringly consistent restaurant deep in Kent's commuter belt. Behind its handsome mock-Tudor façade, the dining room gives off a cosmopolitan vibe – although it still feels like a genuine neighbourhood eatery with a brigade of 'delightful' staff happily attending to every detail. McLeish's cooking is impressively skilful and technically clever without ever seeming abstruse – note roast asparagus with confit duck egg yolk, hazelnut dressing and celeriac rémoulade or a compression of pig's head with smoked pork jowl, pickled cockles and anchovy mayonnaise. Other dishes such as treacle-cured salmon accompanied by charred spring onions, coriander, ginger and lemongrass purée show that McLeish is wise to the ways of the world, while traditionalists will be delighted by his squab Wellington and Josper-grilled steaks. To finish, try something elaborate such as chocolate fondant with milk ice cream and ginger jelly. A 'wonderful' manager is eager to guide diners through the wine list, which ranges from Kentish locals and French aristocrats to serious New World contenders – all at fair mark-ups. In short, there's 'absolutely nothing to criticise'.

Chef/s: Andrew McLeish and Dean Ferguson.
Open: all week L and D. **Closed:** 2 to 4 Jan.
Meals: set L £30. Set D £40. Sun L £25. Tasting menu £55 (6 courses). **Details:** 100 seats. 16 seats outside. V menu. Bar. Wheelchairs. Music. Parking.

Margate

LOCAL GEM
GB Pizza Co.
Italian | £17
14a Marine Drive, Margate, CT9 1DH
Tel no: (01843) 297700
greatbritishpizza.com
£5 OFF £30

A real sense of loyalty and affection radiates from reports we receive about this 'gem on the seafront' especially now it's become a rather smart cookie thanks to a light pastel and neon makeover. A go-to family-friendly place for locals, GB Pizza lives up to its name by using local and Kentish produce as toppings for 'consistently good' thin-crust pizzas baked in the wood-fired oven. Choose between British chorizo and chilli, Chandler & Dunn ham and mushroom, or a Margat-rita, washed down with Kentish beer or cider, or a glass of Prosecco. Wines from £16.

LOCAL GEM
Greedy Cow
British | £15
3 Market Place, Old Town, Margate, CT9 1ER
Tel no: (01843) 447557
thegreedycow.com
£5 OFF £30

Tucked inside the Old Town, just off the splendid seafront, the Greedy Cow is a rough-and-ready daytime spot for sandwiches and more substantial lunch plates, with a few tables outside and the rest in a cheery upper room reached via a steep, narrow-treaded staircase. Glazed buns with fully loaded burgers, or BBQ-sauce-laden pulled pork, served with red cabbage and apple coleslaw and pickled gherkins, and – for those with ample carb capacity – majestic homemade cakes such as banana and white chocolate loaf and moist, almondy Bakewell are the integral components of a happy Margate day. The takeaway service is a welcome local resource.

Hantverk & Found
Seafood | £28
18 King Street, Margate, CT9 1DA
Tel no: (01843) 280454
hantverk-found.co.uk

£5 OFF £30

This tiny seafooder in a back street of Margate's old town has earned itself a solid local reputation. It's a spare (cramped) operation built around a few tables (avoid the basement overspill if you can) noted for an easy-going flexibility. The kitchen's lively global repertoire is scribbled on a pair of blackboards, perhaps buttery potted shrimp with lovely toasted rye bread or a Puy lentil, beetroot, pomegranate and feta salad dressed with cobnut oil. Mussels with bacon, leeks, cider and cream has been a hit, with lemon and blood-orange posset a splendid dessert. There's an affordable modern wine list, too.

Roost
British | £25
19 Cliff Terrace, Margate, CT9 1RU
Tel no: (01843) 229708
roostmargate.com

£5 OFF £30

'The kind of food you want to eat on a day by the sea' sums up this friendly breakfast-lunch-dinner spot overlooking the North Sea. Under new ownership, its expanded menu (children are well looked after, too) offers the likes of seaweed salt-and-pepper squid or whitebait with tartare sauce, which you might follow with classic rotisserie chicken (various dimensions, various sides), the 'Roost Dog' – chorizo and crayfish with sweet potato fries –

or a tempura soft-shell crab burger. Finish with 'legendary' salted-caramel tart. A bottle of Merlot or Sauvignon Blanc costs £20.

▌Minster
The Corner House
Cooking score: 1
British | £29
42 Station Road, Minster, CT12 4BZ
Tel no: (01843) 823000
cornerhouserestaurants.co.uk

🛏 £30

'Homemade' is a strong thread running through this popular and warmly run local restaurant. The kitchen clearly makes the most of its village setting and responds to the best of what's available: one evening, a rather magnificent whole honeycomb was paraded, to serve at the table with ice cream. Elsewhere, there's rabbit, ham and black pudding with homemade pear chutney, 'really excellent, perfectly pink' duck with a dauphinois and carrots 'three ways' adding sweet, sharp and crunch, or 'really top-notch' fillet of bream with warm tartare sauce and triple-cooked chips. There's chocolate and ale cake with malt cream to finish. Keen pricing extends to the wine list, which opens at £16.50.
Chef/s: Pedrag Kostic. **Open:** Wed to Sun L, Tue to Sat D. **Closed:** Mon. **Meals:** main courses £17 to £20. Set L £13 (2 courses) to £17. Sun L £18 (2 courses) to £22. **Details:** 48 seats. 16 seats outside. Bar. Wheelchairs. Parking.

▌Tenterden
The Swan
Modern British
Chapel Down Winery, Small Hythe Road, Tenterden, TN30 7NF
Tel no: (01580) 761616
swanchapeldown.co.uk
'We visited the restaurant before our visit to the on-site winery. The ingredients were local and very fresh – the asparagus with local goats' cheese was fantastic, and the rhubarb

dessert was also enjoyed. Wines were competitively priced and obviously from the winery.'

▉ Tunbridge Wells
Thackeray's
Cooking score: 5
Modern European | £55
85 London Road, Tunbridge Wells, TN1 1EA
Tel no: (01892) 511921
thackerays-restaurant.co.uk
£5 OFF

Facing the grassy common amid a cluster of grand villas, the former home of the author of *Vanity Fair* is Tunbridge's oldest house, dating from the time of the Restoration. Inside is absolutely not about contemporary clean lines, but is all skew-whiff angles, lopsided staircases and low dipping ceilings. It makes a charming setting for some forward-looking modern European cooking, now in the hands of returning chef Patrick Hill. His dishes are intricately composed, with strong counter-pointing flavours and visual panache. First up might be poached lobster with violet potato salad and pickled leeks in lovage-scented vichyssoise dressing, or pot-roast quail with pesto and green tapenade, tarragon cream cheese and tomato jelly, before main courses embrace the likes of roast monkfish tail and cheek ceviche with smoked onions, cumined carrot cream and curry oil. Pork comes in as many ways as you can handle: roast loin, confit belly, pork and chorizo raviolo and a shoulder spring roll, along with spiced Puy lentils, charred sweetcorn and Hispi. If you're hankering for something simple by dessert stage, look to raspberry soufflé with matching sorbet and white chocolate crème anglaise. An extensive classic wine list opens at £21.
Chef/s: Patrick Hill. **Open:** Tue to Sun L, Tue to Sat D. **Closed:** Mon. **Meals:** set L £18 (2 courses) to £20. Set D £55 (3 courses). Tasting menu £78. **Details:** 70 seats. 40 seats outside. V menu. Bar. Wheelchairs. Music.

Vittle and Swig
Modern British
26-28 Camden Road, Tunbridge Wells, TN1 2PT
Tel no: (01892) 544522
vittleandswig.co.uk
'They have totally transformed the space into a modern and relaxed environment. My favourite dishes include venison carpaccio, beef shin and the chateaubriand with Café de Paris butter. Presentation is immaculate and the use of local ingredients and flavours is stunning.'

▉ Whitstable
★ NEW ENTRY ★
Harbour Street Tapas
Cooking score: 4
Spanish | £26
48 Harbour Street, Whitstable, CT5 1AQ
Tel no: (01227) 273373
harbourstreettapas.com
£5 OFF £30

Small, utilitarian and full of light from large windows on two sides, the biggest draw of this self-confident and upbeat tapas bar is the owners' aim to provide great food and drink without breaking the bank. Chef Tim Wilson and front man Lee Murray have a zealous enthusiasm for entirely fresh ingredients, and their menu of Spanish-inspired small sharing plates, cheese and charcuterie is really pulling in the crowds – despite the no-bookings policy (groups can book the upstairs dining room). Simplicity is the watchword and dishes gain impact thereby, with special praise for broad bean hummus on toasted sourdough and a robust beetroot salad with pistachio sauce. Fish is bracingly fresh, whether a 'standout dish' of cod, chickpea and chorizo, or a chunk of hake with a slick of rich, buttery Seville orange sauce, but tender slices of venison with a sweet-sour Pedro Ximénez red cabbage show meat cookery is top-drawer,

too. Sherries and a modest selection of Spanish wines (all by the glass, from £4) complete a sociable offer.
Chef/s: Tim Wilson. **Open:** Wed to Sat L, Tue to Sat D. Sun 12.30 to 5. **Closed:** Mon. **Meals:** tapas £8 to £12. **Details:** 48 seats. Bar.

JoJo's

Cooking score: 4
Tapas | £30
2 Herne Bay Road, Whitstable, CT5 2LQ
Tel no: (01227) 274591
jojosrestaurant.co.uk

Following a refit, JoJo's front half is now a cocktail and tapas bar with counter seating, a few tables and no reservations taken. Past the bar is the dining room, light and airy with wood floor, bare-wood tables, an open kitchen and views of the North Sea, although you will need to book ahead to sample the food here. The style remains personal, unpretentious, informal: tailor-made for socialising over plates of charcuterie, tzatziki with flatbread, and calamari deep-fried in beer batter with garlic mayo. Sourcing remains as impeccable as ever, and while sharing plates of mutton and feta koftas, fish goujons and lamb cannon (thinly sliced and seared with mint jelly) are old favourites never off the menu, specials can bring the freshest grilled local dab fillet with a beautifully dressed green salad, char-grilled chilli squid, and char-grilled courgettes baked with white wine, cream and mozzarella. Finish with the likes of salted-caramel tartlet. A brief wine list opens at £18.
Chef/s: Nikki Billington, Sam Clowes, Buddy Rowden and Florin Sirghi. **Open:** Thur to Sun L, Wed to Sat D. **Closed:** Mon, Tue. **Meals:** tapas £5 to £13. **Details:** 70 seats. 20 seats outside. Bar. Wheelchairs. Music.

Visit us online

To find out more about The Good Food Guide, please visit thegoodfoodguide.co.uk

---

★ NEW ENTRY ★

Samphire

Cooking score: 2
International | £34
4 High Street, Whitstable, CT5 1BQ
Tel no: (01227) 770075
samphirewhitstable.co.uk
£5
OFF

Enjoy a delicious fill of Kentish produce at this established, comfortable, locally popular Whitstable bistro, where 'the food is on the up again' according to local spies. It's a place where the day-boat catch of the day could become a dish of gurnard with purple sprouting broccoli, or pan-fried bream with new potato and chorizo hash, or where the meat offer could tempt with local lamb and rosehip harissa. Come for conventional bistro fare by all means – kedgeree, fishcakes or gnocchi with wild mushrooms are all praised – but look out for some more unusual options, too, such as dosa-spiced potato cake with fermented chilli or an elegantly presented miso and chilli mackerel, the fish skin scorched crisp and the whole served with gently pickled carrot and fennel and a seaweed and sesame cracker. A chocolate ganache on a crumb base with blood-orange sorbet is an 'absolute delight', and there's love, too, for a pistachio cake with cardamom ice cream. Wine from £18.95.
Chef/s: Greig Hughes. **Open:** all week L and D. **Closed:** 25 and 26 Dec. **Meals:** main courses £14 to £20. **Details:** 40 seats. Music.

★ TOP 50 ★

The Sportsman

Cooking score: 7
Modern British | £40
Faversham Road, Seasalter, Whitstable, CT5 4BP
Tel no: (01227) 273370
thesportsmanseasalter.co.uk

The Sportsman could hardly be lower key if it tried. Stephen Harris is confident enough to do things his way rather than follow restaurant fashion. A recent refit has improved facilities and brightened things up, providing space enough for all to enjoy the generously proportioned tables of reclaimed wood, while service is smooth and friendly, and never overbearing – the idea is to relax, to enjoy food, drink and hospitality. The repertoire includes an eight-course tasting menu (to be ordered when booking, although a truncated version is available on the day) and a blackboard à la carte of long-standing favourites, the latter suiting the ingredient-focused ethos but matching the pub setting by being simpler in concept and execution. Indeed, dazzling freshness and supremely good raw materials (from a finely honed network of local suppliers) are the kitchen's hallmarks, shown with breathtaking execution on our tasting menu, whether crab with sweet and creamy hollandaise spooned over the top, or the renowned slip sole grilled with seaweed butter. Then there was a full-throttle thrill in slurping down three different types of oyster – natural with a nugget of homemade chorizo, creamily poached and topped with caviar, or buried under a stunning apple granita – and undeniable pleasure in licking the remains of the glossy vin jaune sauce that accompanied a chunk of brill topped with an intensely flavoured smoked pork rasher. A real treat was the mini roast dinner – a magnificent, full-flavoured and tender roast lamb rack – served with slow-cooked shoulder, a selection of vegetables and mint sauce. Equally impressive, a mini mushroom and celeriac tart with a runny egg yoke hidden under celeriac foam; the bread – sourdough, focaccia and soda bread – with home-churned butter and Seasalter salt; and a light, intense Bramley apple soufflé with salted-caramel ice cream that brought up the rear. The short, reasonably priced wine list opens at £17.95.

Chef/s: Stephen Harris and Dan Flavell. **Open:** Tue to Sun L, Tue to Sat D. **Closed:** Mon, 25 and 26 Dec. **Meals:** main courses £20 to £25. Daily tasting menu £50 (5 courses), full tasting menu £65 (8 courses). **Details:** 50 seats. Wheelchairs. Music. Parking. No children at D.

Wheelers Oyster Bar

Cooking score: 4
Seafood | £36
8 High Street, Whitstable, CT5 1BQ
Tel no: (01227) 273311
wheelersoysterbar.com

It still feels like a well-kept secret, even though the striking pink-and-blue building on the high street has been adopted as one of this famous seaside town's more iconic images. A beacon for lovers of stunning seafood, Wheelers remains a tiny place with a big reputation: the front oyster bar seating just four at counter-stools, while the small, quirky back parlour (thankfully unchanged since expansion added a further room) can squeeze sixteen at four tables. A bring-your-own affair – there's The Offy over the road – the kitchen delivers impeccable renditions of smoked haddock baked with Gruyère rarebit on a smoked haddock and mustard chowder, then roasted stone bass, teamed with coriander mash, sweet pepper piperade and prawn and mussel broth and finished with local shellfish, brown shrimps and samphire or, everyone's favourite, lobster lasagne with a leek and wild crab ragoût. Homemade bread has been praised, and chocolate, date and pecan sponge with toffee sauce and caramel ice cream has stood out among straightforward comfort desserts.

Chef/s: Mark Stubbs. **Open:** Thur to Tue, 4 sittings all day from 1. **Closed:** Wed, 2 weeks Jan. **Meals:** main courses £20 to £22. **Details:** 16 seats. Wheelchairs.

Please send us your feedback

To register your opinion about any restaurant listed in this guide, or a new restaurant that you wish to bring to our attention, please visit the web address at the bottom of the page. Your feedback informs the content of the book and will be used to compile next year's reviews.

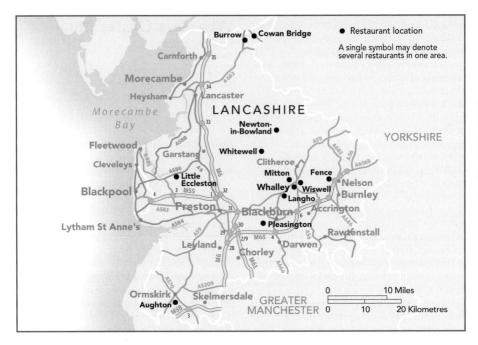

▌Aughton

★ TOP 50 ★

★ NEW ENTRY ★

Moor Hall
Cooking score: 7
Modern British | £65
Prescot Road, Aughton, L39 6RT
Tel no: (01695) 572511
moorhall.com

Not long after opening, readers feel that Mark Birchall's Lancashire restaurant-with-rooms 'will be a great success'. We agree; there's not much to quibble with at this Grade II-listed hall, with its substantial glass-walled restaurant extension providing cool contrast with the open fires and ornate panelling of the old house. Birchall's 'wonderful skill' did his former boss Simon Rogan a great deal of credit at L'Enclume (see entry). Here, there's a greater sense of luxury; the style is less ascetic, less vegetal, more obviously complex, though

he still has the confidence to send out a single curl of rich, funky pancetta as the opening snack in set dinners of five or eight courses. Dishes issue from a vast and well-staffed open kitchen at quite a pace; blink, but don't miss a snack of tender oyster in a milky pool of crème fraîche, offset by fine-grained dill snow. Birchall has brought his beef tartare with him and turned it into an umami-rich assembly of shallot, mustard and barbecued celeriac with definite shades of char-grilled burger. He's equally adept at pairing scallop with charred cauliflower and barley bound in an intense chicken jus, or adding just-bitter, crystal-clear turnip broth to furls of asparagus filled with white and brown crab. Wine is big on genuinely offbeat grapes and interesting producers, and like all the team, wine staff wear their knowledge lightly. Continued development will include a dairy, brewhouse and diffusion-line restaurant in a converted barn, but Moor Hall really is already a destination.

Chef/s: Mark Birchall. **Open:** Wed to Sun L and D. **Closed:** Mon, Tue, middle 2 weeks Jan, first 2 weeks Aug. **Meals:** Set L £35 (3 courses) to £45. Tasting menu £65 to £95. **Details:** 50 seats. V menu. Bar. Wheelchairs. Music. Parking.

Burrow
The Highwayman
Cooking score: 2
British | £29
Main Road, Burrow, LA6 2RJ
Tel no: (01524) 273338
highwaymaninn.co.uk
£30

Nigel Haworth and Craig Bancroft have definitely hit on the formula for a successful modern country inn with the Highwayman, part of their Ribble Valley Inns group, by blending a traditional yet classy country look – stone floors, open fires, decent real ale – with thoroughly modern cooking (and a few old favourites). Lancashire hotpot, twice-baked Lancashire cheese soufflé with beetroot relish and cream sauce, fish and chips, and Cumbrian lamb cutlets with fondant potato, braised red cabbage and mint jelly sit next to chorizo and crispy chilli squid salad, seafood platters, breaded sage and onion chicken lollipops, and a black pea and chilli burger with Shorrocks chilli Lancashire cheese. Among desserts, dark chocolate slice with vanilla ice cream and hot salted-caramel sauce has been praised. The terrace comes into its own when the sun shines. Gentle pricing extends to the well-chosen, well-annotated wine list, which opens at £17.
Chef/s: Kristian Fisher. **Open:** Mon to Sat, all day from 12. Sun 12 to 8. **Meals:** main courses £10 to £25. **Details:** 110 seats. 50 seats outside. Bar. Wheelchairs. Music. Parking.

Cowan Bridge
Hipping Hall
Cooking score: 5
Modern British | £55
Cowan Bridge, LA6 2JJ
Tel no: (01524) 271187
hippinghall.com
£5 OFF

A pristine oasis in 12 acres of grounds twixt Lancashire, Yorkshire and Cumbria, this former gentleman's residence wears its history lightly, teasing visitors with lush lawns, oil paintings and plush sofas, before playing its trump card – a medieval hall complete with a minstrels' gallery. This is the dining room, but don't expect banquets served to the sound of madrigals and lutes; instead, chef Oli Martin cooks in the present tense, gilding his dishes with foraged pickings and playing with contemporary themes. Dish descriptions are terse ('monkfish, cabbage, pear', 'beef, turnip, hay'), but there's no arguing with the technique or the commitment to harmonious seasonal pairings. A dish of mackerel is invigorated with lovage and mustard, pigeon keeps company with salt-baked celeriac and juicy elderberries, while halibut is matched with kohlrabi and shrimps. To finish, an alliance of chocolate, beetroot and hibiscus taps into the culinary zeitgeist, likewise a combo of quince, lemon balm and barley. Each dish comes with a suggested wine from the hotel's enterprising list – a dedicated and knowledgeably annotated compendium showcasing the fruits of organic and biodynamic viticulture.
Chef/s: Oli Martin. **Open:** Sat and Sun L, all week D. **Meals:** set L £30 (4 courses). Set D £55. Tasting menu £65 (6 courses) to £75 (9 courses). **Details:** 32 seats. Bar. Music. Parking. Children over 8 yrs only.

▌Fence
White Swan

Cooking score: 6
British | £32
300 Wheatley Lane Road, Fence, BB12 9QA
Tel no: (01282) 611773
whiteswanatfence.co.uk

It may have a reputation for food, but Gareth Ostick and Tom Parker strive to maintain the pubbiness of this down-to-earth village local – it's still a good spot for a pint of Timothy Taylor's. In the kitchen Tom has forged dependable links with the local food network and takes trouble over quality raw materials – note locally shot game, local raw-cream butter – and distinguishes himself with enthusiasm and honest effort (note the bar laden with Kilner jars filled with flavoured gins and brandies). He may be an inventive cook, but never loses touch of what works well together, so expect tried-and-tested combinations, say stuffed jacket skin and Lancashire cheese with pickles and herring roe, or pork belly with lentils, ras-el-hanout and chorizo, followed by 48-hour-cooked lamb with winter cabbage, shallot and potato or wild sea bass with warm tartare and confit lemon. To finish, maybe Valrhona chocolate soufflé, peanut-butter ice cream sandwich and hot caramel. Selections from the short wine list open at £17.

Chef/s: Tom Parker. **Open:** Tue to Sun L, Tue to Sat D. **Closed:** Mon. **Meals:** main courses £15 to £25. Set L and D £20 (2 courses) to £25. Tasting menu £40 (5 courses). **Details:** 40 seats. 20 seats outside. Wheelchairs. Music. Parking.

Please send us your feedback

To register your opinion about any restaurant listed in this guide, or a new restaurant that you wish to bring to our attention, please visit the web address at the bottom of the page. Your feedback informs the content of the book and will be used to compile next year's reviews.

▌Langho
Northcote

Cooking score: 6
Modern British | £60
Northcote Road, Langho, BB6 8BE
Tel no: (01254) 240555

£5 OFF 🍷 🚗

Reporters remain firm in their copious enthusiasm for one of Lancashire's finest, a brick-built country manor in the beguiling Ribble Valley, north of Blackburn. In the dining room, an opulent modernist space, Nigel Haworth and Lisa Allen devise dishes of remarkable intensity, employing the latest techniques to memorable effect. The five-course summer taster delivered rose veal tartare with burnt leek and garden sorrel, an onion in its skin with whipped Wilja potato and onion ash, sea trout with wild mushrooms and foraged herb tea, milk-fed spring lamb with buttermilk, whey, peas and mint, and a final dazzling take on strawberries and cream to one pair of delighted punters. People appreciate the reference points – treacle-glazed salmon with lime and ginger foam and pickled ginger is awash with Japanese piquancy, while Southport shrimp porridge with tomato sauce is a counterblast to the snail original chez Blumenthal – and the lightness of touch, even humour, that characterises it all. A deconstructed Lancashire hotpot somehow acquires a deep-fried oyster, while for afters, there might be an apple-shaped cheesecake coated in white chocolate, served with cider sorbet. The wine list is a masterpiece of studious research, with flights of vintages of the classics and some modern biodynamics. Prices open at £28.

Chef/s: Nigel Haworth and Lisa Allen. **Open:** all week L and D. **Meals:** main courses £25 to £60. Set L £24 (2 courses) to £34. Set D £40 (2 courses) to £75. Sun L £42. Tasting menu £90. **Details:** 50 seats. 40 seats outside. V menu. Bar. Wheelchairs. Music. Parking.

Little Eccleston
The Cartford Inn

Cooking score: 2
Modern British | £27
Cartford Lane, Little Eccleston, PR3 0YP
Tel no: (01995) 670166
thecartfordinn.co.uk

Patrick and Julie Beaume's remodelled 17th-century coaching inn is extremely good at winning converts with its delightful rural location (on the banks of the river Wyre) and agreeable blend of rusticity, quirkiness and creature comforts – as one fan noted, 'whenever we visit something new appears... it is an interesting building lined with eclectic art, old wood and art glass'. A meal here can be as hearteningly simple as an in-house deli meat platter or a large bowl of mussels, but British classics like oxtail, beef and ale suet pudding have their say and there's praise for nibbles of 'light and unctuous' arancini, and shrimps with saffron aïoli, as well as venison cobbler in a rich gravy, and a 'light but rich' dish of braised, roasted and confit rabbit with tagliatelle, mustard and tarragon sauce and wild mushrooms. A Lancashire cheese plate is hard to resist, but then so is peanut-butter parfait. Good-value wines from £16.
Chef/s: Patrick Beaume. **Open:** Tue to Sat L, Mon to Sat D. Sun, all day from 12. **Closed:** 25 Dec. **Meals:** main courses £12 to £23. **Details:** 90 seats. 20 seats outside. Wheelchairs. Music. Parking. No children in restaurant.

Mitton
The Three Fishes

Cooking score: 2
British | £27
Mitton Road, Mitton, BB7 9PQ
Tel no: (01254) 826888
thethreefishes.com

The first of the Ribble Valley Inns group, the Three Fishes set the bar when it opened in 2004. It now has four pub siblings, each firmly focused on a local and regional ethos, which is co-owner Nigel Haworth's *raison d'être* after all (see entry for Northcote). The white-painted inn still holds on to its pub spirit – local cask ales and all – but the finish is smart and contemporary. The kitchen turns out plenty of regional flavours such as Haworth's renowned Lancashire hotpot, or the county's famous cheese in a twice-baked soufflé, but there's also crispy chilli squid with lime, chilli and caramel dressing reflecting a more expansive modern British style. The Scotch egg is a posh venison number, wild Cumbrian rabbit might find its way into a lattice pie, and do keep an eye on the specials. Finish with a proper rice pudding. The informative wine list kicks off at £16.95.
Chef/s: Ian Moss. **Open:** all week, all day from 12. **Meals:** main courses £10 to £25. **Details:** 120 seats. 40 seats outside. Bar. Wheelchairs. Parking.

Newton-in-Bowland
Parkers Arms

Cooking score: 2
Modern British | £30
Hallgate Hill, Newton-in-Bowland, BB7 3DY
Tel no: (01200) 446236
parkersarms.co.uk

'A little bit shabby but nevertheless welcoming, with a nice open log fire to take the chill off what was a bright but cool day,' noted one visitor to Kathy Smith and Stosie Madi's thriving traditional inn at the heart of the Forest of Bowland, between Clitheroe and Slaidburn. While fish and chips or gammon and egg are on offer along with other pub favourites, there are surprises on the menu, too. Crab gratin Caribbean-style or charcoal-grilled cuttlefish with new season's potatoes and wild garlic mayo as a prelude to one of Stosie Madi's famed pies (with curried Skipton goat, perhaps) or an 'excellent thick slab' of roast hake and roasted Wye Valley asparagus with crushed Jersey Royals in lemon butter sauce – 'classic but good'. Desserts might range from a simple lemon posset to a Lebanese-style almond and semolina cake with orange blossom and pomegranate yoghurt. The wine list, supplied by the excellent Byrne's at Clitheroe, is reasonably priced (from £19.50). **Chef/s:** Stosie Madi. **Open:** Wed to Fri L and D. Sat, all day from 12. Sun 12 to 6. **Closed:** Mon, Tue. **Meals:** main courses £15 to £28. Set L and D £20 (3 courses). **Details:** 70 seats. 100 seats outside. Parking.

◼ Pleasington

LOCAL GEM
The Clog & Billycock
British | £27
Billinge End Road, Pleasington, BB2 6QB
Tel no: (01254) 201163
theclogandbillycock.com

£30

Part of Nigel Haworth's Ribble Valley Inns group, refurbishment in 2017 saw the addition of a gin bar to bring even more refinement (and fun) to this classy pub. The cooking, as with the rest of the gang, relies on tight local supply lines to bring a regional flavour, so Lancashire black pudding with spiced onion jam and a free-range egg sits alongside classic fish and chips, and a modern take on chicken in a basket (crumbed buttermilk Goosnargh chicken). First-class steaks, daytime sandwiches, local ales: the Clog & Billycock is a class act.

◼ Whalley
Food by Breda Murphy
Cooking score: 3
Modern British | £34
41 Station Road, Whalley, BB7 9RH
Tel no: (01254) 823446
foodbybredamurphy.com

There have been big changes at this suburban house beside Whalley rail station, with a recent transformation doubling the size of the restaurant. The popular little deli remains in situ, but regular evening openings now join the usual breakfast, lunch and afternoon tea repertoire. Menus celebrate British ingredients, especially local produce – perhaps

Bowland beef (char-grilled with a sweet onion glaze, pickled carrots and crispy smoked potato), and Farnsworth's pork and apple sausages 'from up the road' (with creamy potatoes, leek and marjoram fondue and cider jus). Big impact flavours came through in a starter of salt-baked beetroot with smoked feta, dill croûtes and fennel granola, and in a main course of plump fillet of red mullet, served with wilted baby spinach, 'excellent' fennel bonbons and caper vermouth sauce, while whiskey and date sponge with honey ice cream and parsnip crisps inspired one reporter to declare 'forget sticky toffee pudding – this is much better'. A well-crafted wine list, organised by style, offers some good-value drinking, starting at £19.50. **Chef/s:** Gareth Bevan. **Open:** Tue to Sun L, Fri and Sat D. **Closed:** Mon. **Meals:** main courses £14 to £28. Sun L £25. **Details:** 100 seats. 14 seats outside. Bar. Wheelchairs. Music. Parking.

◼ Whitewell
The Inn at Whitewell
Cooking score: 2
Modern British | £34
Forest of Bowland, Whitewell, BB7 3AT
Tel no: (01200) 448222
innatwhitewell.com

Surrounded by the sylvan expanses of Bowland Forest, with a river running close by, 'The Whitewell' hardly looks like an inn at all. This hugely extended medieval pile is now a splendid country retreat with more than its share of mighty log fires, flagstones and antiques spread across myriad spaces, as well as an impressive art collection. Food-wise, eat in the bar from a menu of pub classics with add-ons, or graduate to the formal restaurant (evenings only) for more ambitious fare along the lines of seared scallops with pea purée or char-grilled beef fillet with shallots and tarragon butter. Lancashire produce gets a decent look-in, from roast Goosnargh chicken to rack of Burholme lamb with lemon and mint jelly, while puddings are promoted as 'wholesome and sometimes nursery-like'. The owners are also vintners with their own wine shop and a comprehensive list tailored to all palates and pockets.

Chef/s: Jamie Cadman. **Open:** all week L and D. **Meals:** main courses £16 to £26. **Details:** 180 seats. 20 seats outside. Bar. Wheelchairs. Parking.

■ Wiswell

★ TOP 50 ★

Freemasons at Wiswell

Cooking score: 7
Modern British | £45
8 Vicarage Fold, Wiswell, BB7 9DF
Tel no: (01254) 822218
freemasonswiswell.co.uk
£5 OFF ▲

A frequent challenge these days is how to transform an old village inn into somewhere competing in the top echelons of British dining, while still retaining the welcoming ethos of the local hostelry. The Freemasons, once a trio of workers' cottages, manages this trick with unflappable aplomb. The flagstone floors are strewn with old rugs; the period pictures and venerable furniture look as old as time, though there is talk this year of a chef's table and even a roof garden to come. Set in the lush Ribble Valley, the inn has become a nerve centre of vanguard northern cooking under Steven Smith, with fine prime materials and heritage techniques refracted through a prism of thoroughgoing innovation. The fillings of brioche pies change with the seasons, oxtail one moment, rabbit and langoustines the next, while roast hake in its fondue of Procter's Kick Ass Cheddar is a sure-fire way of starting as you mean to go on. A winter visitor enjoyed the pairing of scallops and black pudding that preceded halibut amid a welter of Lancashire shrimps, but the kitchen is confident with East-West confabulations too, offering a whole roast squab with yakitori-dressed liver and hen-of-the-woods in XO sauce. A little sweet-savoury hoisin enhances the blood-orange and rhubarb sauce that anoints a dessert of honey-roasted winter roots, while Amalfi lemon meringue pie gets

not just the deconstruction treatment, but a head-turning dry-ice display, too. Alongside these pyrotechnics, an equally dazzling wine list, categorised by style, offers broad-minded range of choice, from £4.95 a standard glass.

Chef/s: Steven Smith and Matthew Smith. **Open:** Wed to Sat L and D. Sun 12 to 6. **Closed:** Mon, Tue, 2 weeks Jan. **Meals:** main courses £24 to £38. Set L and D £20 (2 courses) to £25. Sun L £30. Tasting menu £70. **Details:** 70 seats. 20 seats outside. V menu. Bar. Wheelchairs. Music. Parking.

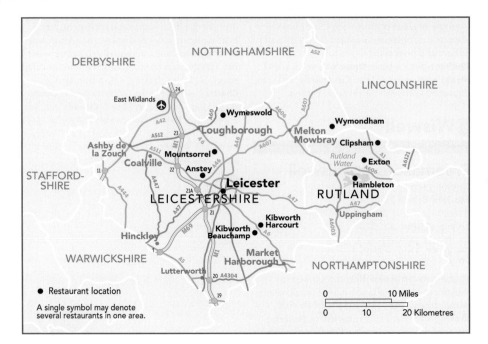

Map showing restaurant locations in Leicestershire and Rutland, with surrounding counties: Derbyshire, Nottinghamshire, Lincolnshire, Staffordshire, Warwickshire, Northamptonshire. Locations include East Midlands, Wymeswold, Wymondham, Loughborough, Melton Mowbray, Clipsham, Ashby de la Zouch, Mountsorrel, Coalville, Anstey, Rutland Water, Exton, Leicester, Hambleton, RUTLAND, Uppingham, Kibworth Harcourt, Kibworth Beauchamp, Hinckley, Market Harborough, Lutterworth.

● Restaurant location

A single symbol may denote several restaurants in one area.

0   10 Miles
0   10   20 Kilometres

▌Anstey

LOCAL GEM

Sapori
Italian | £35
40 Stadon Road, Anstey, LE7 7AY
Tel no: (0116) 2368900
sapori-restaurant.co.uk

Popular for its scratch cooking and consistent standards, this family-run outfit just outside Leicester has local feeling on its side. An airy dining room in shades of blue is the backdrop for neatly finished dishes that delight more than they surprise. Signature dishes include confit cod with caponata and a main course of pork tenderloin with pancetta, chestnuts, butternut squash purée and black truffle sauce. Pudding might be hazelnut crème brûlée with mango sorbet – homemade, of course. Vini bianchi e rossi from £16.

▌Clipsham

The Olive Branch
Cooking score: 2
Modern British | £35
Main Street, Clipsham, LE15 7SH
Tel no: (01780) 410355
theolivebranchpub.com

Hugely popular locally, Sean Hope and Ben Jones' hostelry suits many different occasions from an alfresco lunch ('in the lovely little courtyard area') to a special-occasion dinner. Inside it's all country-pub charm – 'hints of gingham, a row of wellies' – alongside a deli and wine shop selling a small selection of local items and its own range of chutneys, pesto and dressings. And the kitchen is bang on the money when it comes to food, offering an admirable mix of pub classics (fish and chips, steaks) alongside clever ideas for more inquisitive palates. Beetroot and apple salad with nasturtium, as well as roast breast of pigeon and confit leg pastilla with Israeli couscous and pomegranate, could precede perfectly cooked fillet of sea trout served with a colourful array of heritage tomatoes, a smattering of ricotta and light gnocchi, with elderflower and Champagne parfait with gooseberry compote to finish. It's all backed up by 'really pleasant' service. Drinks do their best to keep up with well-kept craft ales and well-chosen wines from £19.50.

Chef/s: Sean Hope. **Open:** all week L and D. **Meals:** main courses £15 to £25. Set L £18 (2 courses) to £22. Set D £33. Sun L £28. **Details:** 50 seats. 30 seats outside. V menu. Bar. Wheelchairs. Music. Parking.

■ Exton
Fox & Hounds

Cooking score: 2
Modern European | £35
19 The Green, Exton, LE15 8AP
Tel no: (01572) 812403
afoxinexton.co.uk

Facing the village green in the heart of an England that hasn't much moved on since the Armistice, the Fox & Hounds is a delightful 17th-century coaching inn that has been sensitively modernised with boutique rooms and outdoor tables among the attractions. The main dining area, meanwhile, looks built to withstand the worst the Rutland winter can do, with ceiling beams and solid stone walls to encase you. Local farmers supply thoroughbred meats, while fish is from the Lowestoft day boats, and the kitchen turns out global dishes that describe an arc from beef tataki in orange, ginger and chilli with lotus root crisps, to mains like cod cheeks and chorizo in smoked bacon cream, or roast rump and braised belly of lamb with a faggot of its offals, accompanied by onion purée and charred romanesco in sherry jus. Finish with a plate of chocolate variations, including mousse, torte and Valrhona soil, with poached cherries. Wines start at £19.

Chef/s: David Graham. **Open:** all week L and D. **Meals:** main courses £13 to £25. Set L and D £15 (2 courses) to £18. Sun L £20. Tasting menu £45. **Details:** 32 seats. 35 seats outside. Bar. Wheelchairs. Music. Parking.

■ Hambleton
★ TOP 50 ★
Hambleton Hall

Cooking score: 7
Modern British | £69
Ketton Road, Hambleton, LE15 8TH
Tel no: (01572) 756991
hambletonhall.com

'This admirable hotel remains a very good place to stay and dine for a night,' commented one couple, fans of the aristocratic Victorian edifice of Hambleton Hall, which presides, like a petit château, over landscaped terraces, sculpted topiary and colourful flowerbeds, while the interior exudes polish and civilised comfort – testament to the diligence of hands-on custodians Tim and Stefa Hart. Chef Aaron Patterson has also put in the shifts, but his appetite for classically detailed seasonal food is as keen as ever. Delicate painterly images of feathers and leaves decorate the beautiful menus, which herald cohesive calendar-friendly ideas overlaid with pertinent grace notes: in January, a starter of salt-baked celeriac, hickory and apple strikes just the right balance of texture and flavour, while 'impeccable' mains rely on rich, potent accompaniments – dark chocolate with fallow deer, liquorice with loin and shoulder of rabbit, pipérade and rosemary sauce with Lavinton Farm lamb. Fish can be slow-cooked octopus with miso broth or turbot with chervil root, clams and sea vegetables, before desserts such as a pear and blackberry terrine with caramel ice cream have diners reaching for the superlatives yet again. The whole masterly show is fleshed out with dainty amuse-bouches, brilliant breads and 'chocolates etcetera', while able young staff 'know how to look after their tables'. Tim

Hart's authoritative hand-picked wine list favours 'the little guy', so expect quirky oddballs among the lordly Old World vintages; popular 'wines of the moment' offer the best value.

Chef/s: Aaron Patterson. **Open:** all week L and D. **Meals:** set L £29 (2 courses) to £38. Set D £69. Sun L £58. Tasting menu £92 (6 courses). **Details:** 60 seats. V menu. Bar. Parking. Children over 5 yrs only.

▉ Kibworth Beauchamp
The Lighthouse
Cooking score: 3
Seafood | £29
9 Station Street, Kibworth Beauchamp, LE8 0LN
Tel no: (0116) 2796260
lighthousekibworth.co.uk
£5 OFF £30

Not every seafood restaurant needs to be overlooking the sparkling briny, and Sarah and Lino Poli's place in landlubbing Leicestershire is a case in point. With marine-themed pictures hung about, and a nautical blue-and-white frontage, the place looks as refreshing as a sea breeze, and the extensive and varied menus will put an edge on your appetite too. Many find it hard to tear themselves away from the excellent fish and chips with tartare sauce and mushy peas, but the kitchen also strikes out for the Mediterranean for tiger prawns wrapped in pancetta with bean stew, and further still to east Asia, whence come mussels in Thai coconut broth, or gilthead bream in Chinese-style vegetable broth with crispy prawn won tons. If you're more meat than fish, look to ox cheeks braised in red wine. Things end on a high with espresso-laced affogato or chocolate torte with mandarin sorbet. Wines arranged by style start at £16.50.

Chef/s: Lino Poli and Tom Wilde. **Open:** Tue to Sat D only. **Closed:** Sun, Mon, 25 and 26 Dec, 1 Jan, bank hols. **Meals:** main courses £7 to £22. Set D £15 (2 courses) to £18. **Details:** 60 seats. Music.

▉ Kibworth Harcourt

LOCAL GEM
Boboli
Italian | £29
88 Main Street, Kibworth Harcourt, LE8 0NQ
Tel no: (0116) 2793303
bobolirestaurant.co.uk
£5 OFF £30

Boboli's warm-hearted Italian vibe makes this all-day place one that people return to time and again. Start a typical meal with antipasti – speck, bruschetta, or octopus and potato salad maybe – before ordering the inevitable lasagne 'as Lino's (the chef's) Mamma makes it' or homemade beetroot ravioli with goats' cheese. Pan-fried calf's liver with polenta, and osso buco alla milanese – braised shin of veal with saffron risotto – continue the classic Italian line-up that, *naturalmente*, includes pizzas. What else would you finish with but tiramisu? The all-Italian wine list opens at £16.50.

▉ Leicester

LOCAL GEM
Delilah
Modern European | £20
4 St Martins, Leicester, LE1 5DB
Tel no: (0116) 2963554
delilahfinefoods.co.uk
£30

An appealing all-day eatery and delicatessen housed in a former Victorian bank, Delilah is a place to combine a bite to eat with delicious food shopping. Grab a table on the airy mezzanine for a lunch of bresaola and Stichelton salad, or morcilla, pancetta and butter-bean stew. If you're in the mood to share, the Connoisseur's Experience platter combines the finest of deli ingredients – Ibérico ham, duck rillettes crostini, black truffle Gouda or baked Picodon goats' cheese, for example. A vast array of cakes and pastries will fully satisfy sweet cravings. Wine from £14.

▉ Mountsorrel
John's House
Cooking score: 6
British | £47
Stonehurst Farm, 139-141 Loughborough
Road, Mountsorrel, LE12 7AR
Tel no: (01509) 415569
johnshouse.co.uk
£5
OFF

Farmhouse restaurants are quite the thing these days, a movement in which John Duffin has been at the forefront, returning to his roots on the family holding near Loughborough to run an idiosyncratic operation that has charm written all over it. Many of the ingredients are naturally home-grown, supplemented by pedigree regional supplies, and the level of inventive energy is breathtaking. With appetisers of an oxtail and pine dumpling done in the deep-fryer on the end of a twig, and a squid bun with smoked eel, crispy chicken skin and elderflower, an assault on the senses is prepared. From the starters, beef carpaccio and ox tongue are dressed with coal oil and given a herbaceous lift with lovage, or there might be a raviolo of ratte potato with a cured egg yolk, truffle and Comté. Farm-bred meats are incomparable, whether Old Spot piglet belly and loin with aubergine and peanut purée, passion fruit and an Indian-spiced sauce, or beautifully tender lamb with its sweetbreads, hen-of-the-woods, puréed alliums and goats' curd, while fish might be poached halibut with crab, winter brassicas and English wasabi. Desserts, too, combine intricacy and aromatic grace, as when pine ice cream and white chocolate mousse are accompanied by raspberries and intense lemon sauce. An intelligently composed wine list opens with Argentinian Malbec at £28.

Chef/s: John Duffin. **Open:** Tue to Sat L and D.
Closed: Sun, Mon, 1 week Dec, 2 weeks Aug.
Meals: set L £24 (2 courses) to £28. Set D £42 (2 courses) to £47. Tasting menu £70 (8 courses).
Details: 30 seats. V menu. Bar. Music. Parking.

The Good Food Guide Scoring System

Score 1: Capable cooking with simple food combinations and clear flavours.

Score 2: Decent cooking, displaying good technical skills and interesting combinations and flavours.

Score 3: Good cooking, showing sound technical skills and using quality ingredients.

Score 4: Dedicated, focused approach to cooking; good classical skills and high-quality ingredients.

Score 5: Exact cooking techniques and a degree of ambition; showing balance and depth of flavour in dishes.

Score 6: Exemplary cooking skills, innovative ideas, impeccable ingredients and an element of excitement.

Score 7: High level of ambition and individuality, attention to the smallest detail, accurate and vibrant dishes.

Score 8: A kitchen cooking close to or at the top of its game. Highly individual with impressive artistry.

Score 9: Cooking that has reached a pinnacle of achievement, making it a hugely memorable experience.

Score 10: Just perfect dishes, showing faultless technique at every service; extremely rare and the highest accolade the Guide can give.

▌Wymeswold
The Hammer & Pincers

Cooking score: 2
Modern European | £39
5 East Road, Wymeswold, LE12 6ST
Tel no: (01509) 880735
hammerandpincers.co.uk

£5
OFF

Originally the village blacksmith's, the appropriately named Hammer & Pincers is full of surprises – note the ever-changing display of contemporary artwork from the Galerie Gartenhaus in Germany. Once you've eyed up the exhibits, focus your attention on the smart-looking beamed dining room, where chef/proprietor Daniel Jimminson offers a menu of ambitious modern food with an Anglo-European complexion. Regional produce has a big say here, from twice-baked Beauville cheese soufflé with chicory salad and rhubarb chutney to dry-aged Welland Valley beef with Pedro Ximénez sherry, braised short rib, wild garlic potatoes and charred grelot onion, although fish comes up from Cornwall – perhaps monkfish with asparagus, peas, morels and Champagne velouté. Leicestershire's gamekeepers, butchers and artisan growers also dictate the daily specials, and it's no surprise to see celebrated local heroes gracing the cheeseboard. Austrian-born Sandra Jimminson oversees a wine list featuring bottles from her homeland and a decent by-the-glass Coravin selection.

Chef/s: Daniel Jimminson. **Open:** Tue to Sun L, Tue to Sat D. **Closed:** Mon, 24 and 25 Dec. **Meals:** main courses £17 to £27. Set L and D £23 (2 courses) to £27. Tasting menu £40 (7 courses) to £50 (10 courses). **Details:** 46 seats. 30 seats outside. Bar. Music. Parking.

▌Wymondham
The Berkeley Arms

Cooking score: 3
Modern British | £30
59 Main Street, Wymondham, LE14 2AG
Tel no: (01572) 787587
theberkeleyarms.co.uk

Louise and Neil Hitchen's village hostelry elicits delighted reactions from many readers. That's thanks in part to a careful balance of pubby approachability, genuine civility and warmth – 'I instantly thought this was somewhere I'd like to return to' – and Neil's simple but alluring cooking. Everybody seems to find everything 'delicious', and reporters have applauded local game, from a starter of mallard duck breast ('beautifully cooked, rare, thin slices') with orange, hazelnut and beetroot salad, to a main course braised shoulder of 'absolutely delicious' venison with mash, caramelised walnuts, poached pear and 'a very rich gravy'. Elsewhere, there could be a generous portion of pork fillet, belly and black pudding with fondant potato and apple cider sauce. Desserts have been a particular highlight for many, and a delicate buttermilk pudding with red-wine-poached fruits (fig, blackberries and quince) garners as much praise as the homemade petits fours plate. The wine list keeps it short, with bottles from £18.50.

Chef/s: Neil Hitchen. **Open:** Tue to Sun L, Tue to Sat D. **Closed:** Mon, first 2 weeks Jan, 2 weeks summer. **Meals:** main courses £13 to £25. Set L £15 (2 courses) to £20. Set D £19 (2 courses) to £23. Sun L £20 (2 courses) to £24. **Details:** 48 seats. 24 seats outside. Bar. Wheelchairs. Parking.

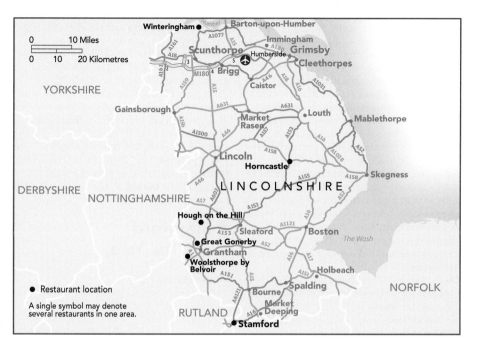

Great Gonerby
Harry's Place
Cooking score: 4
Modern French | £65
17 High Street, Great Gonerby, NG31 8JS
Tel no: (01476) 561780
£5
OFF

As of September 2018 Harry and Caroline
Hallam will have been running Harry's Place
on their own for 30 years. Hats off, raise a
glass, book a table. The dining room in their
rather handsome old house seats just 10, and it's
very much like being a guest in their family
home (which is indeed the case). Caroline
looks after matters front-of-house while
Harry cooks a classically inspired menu
offering a couple of choices at each course.
Local celeriac might appear in a soup as one
opener, or go for Orkney king scallops with a
spiced marinade. Among main courses,
Lincolnshire salt marsh teal comes with a
classic red wine sauce, and fillet of turbot is
served with samphire and a lightly creamy
sauce. Among desserts, a cherry brandy-
fuelled jelly comes with yoghurt and a touch
of black pepper. The wine list starts at £28.
Chef/s: Harry Hallam. **Open:** Tue to Sat L and D.
Closed: Sun, Mon, 25 and 26 Dec, 2 weeks Aug,
bank hols. **Meals:** main courses £40. **Details:** 10
seats. Parking. Children over 5 yrs only.

Horncastle
Magpies
Cooking score: 5
Modern British | £49
73 East Street, Horncastle, LN9 6AA
Tel no: (01507) 527004
magpiesresturant.co.uk

Old-fashioned charm is a much underrated
virtue in the era of modern brutalism, and the
Gilberts' restaurant with three rooms, set in a
terrace of converted cottages, emphasises the
point. Low ceilings and a gentle cream décor
are enhanced by a log-burner in winter, and
there's a patio for aperitifs on warmer

evenings. Despite the atmosphere of traditionalism, Andrew Gilbert has absorbed much from the modern British repertoire, for broadly based menus that might take in ballotine of partridge with chestnut and apple stuffing, pressed foie gras and Black Muscat jelly, as a prelude to steamed halibut with gravadlax and potato terrine on lemongrass beurre blanc, or goose breast in gin and juniper with baby leeks, duck leg confit and a haggis bonbon. Desserts are artfully conceived, defying anybody to resist them, by means of orange and hazelnut Grand Marnier trifle with orange marmalade sorbet, or classic glazed lemon tart with lemonade and a syrup of limoncello and lime. A conscientiously compiled wine list from £19.30 does each of its regions proud, and is well provisioned with half-bottles.

Chef/s: Andrew Gilbert. **Open:** Wed to Fri and Sun L, Wed to Sun D. **Closed:** Mon, Tue, 26 to 30 Dec, first week Jan. **Meals:** set L £22 (2 courses) to £27. Set D £43 (2 courses) to £49. Sun L £22 to £27. **Details:** 34 seats. Bar. Wheelchairs. Music.

◼ Hough on the Hill
The Brownlow Arms
Cooking score: 2
British | £40
Grantham Road, Hough on the Hill, NG32 2AZ
Tel no: (01400) 250234
thebrownlowarms.com

The Brownlow stands in a picture-pretty village north of Grantham, a stone-built country inn from the Stuart era that has been tastefully modernised. An outdoor terrace looks out over greensward, while the dining room has the look of an upmarket restaurant with smartly clothed tables set with quality accoutrements. Ruaraidh Bealby's food steps up to the plate with carefully composed dishes that mix traditional pub appeal – prawn and crayfish cocktail in Marie Rose with apple and cucumber, or a game version of shepherd's pie with braised peas and lettuce – with ideas that are straight out of the modernist repertoire. Main course might be pan-roast duck breast

with a foie gras fritter and pak choi in orange and griottine jus, or stone bass, prawn and scallop with peas and broad beans in linguine dressed with chilli oil. Seasonal awareness produces a cold-weather winter berry compote with matching parfait, mulled wine sorbet and pistachio mascarpone, but there's sticky toffee pud, too. House Chilean varietals from Echeverria are £19.95.

Chef/s: Ruaraidh Bealby. **Open:** Wed to Sun L, Tue to Sat D. **Closed:** Mon, 25 and 26 Dec, bank hols. **Meals:** main courses £15 to £29. Sun L £25 (2 courses) to £28. **Details:** 80 seats. 30 seats outside. Bar. Music. Parking. Children before 8pm only.

◼ Stamford
No. 3 The Yard
Cooking score: 1
Modern British | £30
3 Ironmonger Street, Stamford, PE9 1PL
Tel no: (01780) 756080
no3theyard.co.uk
£5
OFF

It's a gift of a location just off the high street, and on a sunny day 'sitting in the courtyard with a glass of rosé, it's very pleasant'. The restaurant itself comes with a modern conservatory although the main dining area is upstairs – 'a much darker affair'. There's a main menu with some appealing dishes, starters of home-cured salmon with celeriac rémoulade and beetroot gel, say, and mains of crispy duck leg with white-wine-poached pear and caramelised pecan. The courtyard menu has slightly lighter, less formal options along the lines of pork and chorizo flatbread burger with sweet potato fries or fish goujons with pea purée and tartare sauce. Finish with raspberry and white chocolate brûlée. Drink cocktails or wine (from £17.50).

Chef/s: Sam Carson. **Open:** Tue to Sun L, Tue to Sat D. **Closed:** Mon, 26 Dec, 1 Jan. **Meals:** main courses £14 to £23. **Details:** 64 seats. 20 seats outside. Bar. Wheelchairs. Music.

▌Winteringham
Winteringham Fields

Cooking score: 6
Modern European | £45
1 Silver Street, Winteringham, DN15 9ND
Tel no: (01724) 733096
winteringhamfields.co.uk

In the quiet village of Winteringham, six miles west of the Humber Bridge, Colin McGurran continues to build on his reputation for original and intricate dishes that embrace the twin tropes of seasonal and local supported by a smallholding from which he sources much of the restaurant's produce. One reader found the richly furnished public rooms 'oppressive' but the updated dining room with slate walls, contemporary lighting and modern textiles is more restful. At dinner the no-choice 'surprise' menu of seven or nine courses with matching wines is a showcase for a full-stretch extravaganza of Mr McGurran's highly crafted dishes. The cheaper lunch menu was much enjoyed by one reporter, who made a 150-mile round trip to eat here, praising everything from an 'amazing' appetiser of tomato gazpacho with mustard ice cream to a 'superb' pork belly with pea and mint purée. We largely concur, sampling cod cheeks with featherweight tempura pork belly followed by Herdwick lamb and pickled turnip, finishing on a definitive chocolate soufflé with a banana and passion fruit sorbet. Wines begin at a manageable £24 for Blue Ridge Chardonnay and rise to dizzying heights.
Chef/s: Colin McGurran. **Open:** Tue to Sat L and D. **Closed:** Sun, Mon, 2 weeks Dec, 2 weeks Aug. **Meals:** set L £45 (3 courses). Tasting menu L £60, D £75 to £85. **Details:** 60 seats. V menu. Bar. Wheelchairs. Music. Parking.

▌Woolsthorpe by Belvoir
Chequers Inn

Cooking score: 1
Modern British | £30
Main Street, Woolsthorpe by Belvoir, NG32 1LU
Tel no: (01476) 870701
chequersinn.net

This 17th-century country pub still possesses much of its old character with real fires, beams and cosy corners as touchstones to its past as a farmhouse. Its culinary outlook is more contemporary, with the kitchen's output neatly slipping between past and present. While the likes of sausage, mash and onion gravy and fish and chips shows willingness to play the comfort card, there's much more besides. Scallops, for example, with curried cauliflower purée and a cauliflower pakora, or a main course that matches two generous char-grilled pork cutlets with black pudding pommes Anna, confit apple and Calvados cream. Finish with white chocolate blondie (sponge) with sweet-and-sour raspberries and raspberry sorbet. Liquid refreshment comes in the form of local ales, cocktails and a well-spread wine list.
Chef/s: Keith Martin. **Open:** all week L and D. **Closed:** 26 Dec, 1 Jan. **Meals:** main courses £12 to £25. Sun L £16 (2 courses). **Details:** 120 seats. 80 seats outside. Bar. Wheelchairs. Music. Parking.

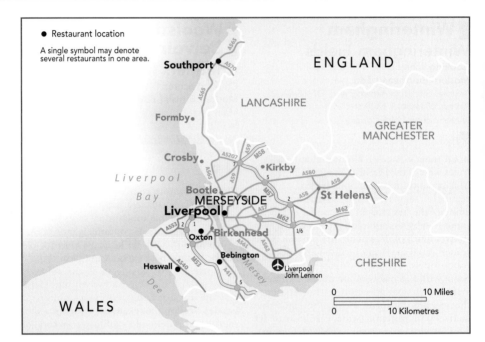

▌Bebington

LOCAL GEM

Claremont Farm Café
British | £22
Old Clatterbridge Road, Bebington,
CH63 4JB
Tel no: (0151) 3341133
claremontfarm.co.uk

£30

This cheerfully run farm shop/café is
everything you might hope for – down-to-
earth, welcoming, with plenty of enterprise,
skill and industry at work. Seasonal raw
materials (much of it farm grown or reared)
shine brightly on menus that start with
generous breakfasts, go on to lunches of Welsh
rarebit toasted sandwich or slow-braised
shoulder of Claremont lamb served with
potato and onion hotpot, kale salsa and
roasted carrot, with daily specials scrawled on
a blackboard wall and homemade cakes filling
in the gaps. Children have their own menu.

▌Heswall

Burnt Truffle
Cooking score: 3
Modern European | £34
104-106 Telegraph Road, Heswall, CH60 0AQ
Tel no: (0151) 3421111
burnttruffle.net

Part of a growing crowdfunded empire
known jokingly as 'the elite bistros of the
world', Burnt Truffle really is a cut above on
the Wirral. A refurbishment means there's
more space downstairs for locals to get stuck in
to Gary Usher's great-value early-evening
menu. It's £18 for a glass of wine and three
courses of honest, thoughtfully conceived
food, but best to think of it as £21 and add the
excellent sourdough with truffle and walnut
butter. Later, from the full carte, try
cauliflower soup with rocket pesto or pickled
herring with taramasalata and roasted
beetroot, followed by whole roasted quail
with hazelnut and pomegranate salad and
cauliflower cheese, an exotic proposition with

its feet on the ground. Desserts are dominated by trifles, mousses and custards (such as tonka bean with fromage blanc, dark chocolate and hazelnuts). Wirral beers appear alongside a simple wine list with plenty under £35.

Chef/s: Gary Usher. **Open:** Tue to Sat L and D. Sun 12 to 8. **Closed:** Mon, 25 and 26 Dec. **Meals:** main courses £14 to £24. Set L £15 (2 courses) to £18. Early D £18 (Tue to Fri). Sun L £18 (2 courses) to £22. **Details:** 53 seats. 21 seats outside. Wheelchairs. Music. Parking.

▉ Liverpool
The Art School
Cooking score: 5
Modern European | £69
1 Sugnall Street, Liverpool, L7 7DX
Tel no: (0151) 2308600
theartschoolrestaurant.co.uk
£5 OFF

As Liverpool's gastronomic scene aims for the stars, its resurgence in recent years is in no small part the work of Paul Askew. Housed in what was once a children's home, in the hinterland between the city's two cathedrals, the Art School is a hotbed of creative energies, as befits the HQ of a chef/patron who is also joint chairman of the Royal Academy of Culinary Arts' northern region. In an understated minimalist space beneath a wide skylight, various menu formulas are offered, from vegan through fish to omnivore diets, and the level of invention never lets up. With a welcoming glass of Charles Heidsieck inside you, you might set forth on the Excellence format with Cornish red mullet, accompanied by brown shrimp risotto in squid ink with chanterelles, prior to dry-aged Cumbrian rose veal sirloin, appearing alongside a cabbage parcel, salsify and puréed white beans, or perhaps roast hake with smoked pork lardons, charred onions and Puy lentils, sauced with cider. A dessert plate for sharing will prove hard to pass up, unless you're determined to hog the dark chocolate torte with praline, caramel popcorn and griottines all to yourself. Wines are a distinguished selection arranged between Old and New Worlds, from £26.

Chef/s: Paul Askew. **Open:** Tue to Sat L and D. **Closed:** Sun, Mon, 25 and 26 Dec, 1 week Jan, 1 week Aug. **Meals:** set L £24 (2 courses) to £30. Set D £69 (3 courses). Tasting menu £89. **Details:** 48 seats. V menu. Bar. Wheelchairs. Music. Children at L and early D only.

Delifonseca Dockside
Cooking score: 1
International | £28
Brunswick Quay, Liverpool, L3 4BN
Tel no: (0151) 2550808
delifonseca.co.uk
£5 OFF £30

Turn right for the well-stocked deli or left for the restaurant – 'it is clearly very popular with lots of folk coming and going all the time'. The menu of the day is chalked on a huge board offering soups and main dishes, or there's a printed menu that covers breakfast dishes (say eggs florentine), sandwiches, salads, sharing platters of charcuterie, and the likes of 'very very tasty' rare-roasted Welsh Black beef with rocket, a light drizzle of basil oil and shavings of Parmesan. Desserts include crème brûlée or a comforting crumble. The varied drinks list takes a world tour with wine starting at £16.50.

Chef/s: Marc Lara. **Open:** Mon to Sat, all day from 12. Sun 12 to 5. **Closed:** 25 and 26 Dec, 1 Jan. **Meals:** main courses £11 to £21. Sun L £12. **Details:** 66 seats. 24 seats outside. Wheelchairs. Music. Parking.

Fonseca's
Cooking score: 1
Modern European | £30
12 Stanley Street, Liverpool, L1 6AF
Tel no: (0151) 2550808
delifonseca.co.uk
£5 OFF

'Quite a cool set-up' was the first impression of one visitor to Candice Fonseca's city-centre bar-cum-dining room. The interior blends retro and modern elements and feels relaxed and informal but 'special, too'. The kitchen pleases all comers with its blackboard menu of

mainly modern European dishes with a hint of invention, with dishes ranging from the pleasing familiarity of Cumberland sausage with pulled pork mash in rich honey-mustard gravy to spiced Herdwick mutton and apricot tagine with pomegranate couscous. Duck egg custard tart with vanilla ice cream and poached rhubarb is 'lovely stuff'. Drink cocktails or something from the wide-ranging, well-annotated wine list.
Chef/s: Alban Parnell. **Open:** Sat L, Tue to Sat D. **Closed:** Sun, Mon, 26 to 30 Dec. **Meals:** main courses £12 to £25. **Details:** 60 seats. Bar. Music.

The London Carriage Works

Cooking score: 2
Modern British | £44
Hope Street Hotel, 40 Hope Street, Liverpool, L1 9DA
Tel no: (0151) 7052222
thelondoncarriageworks.co.uk

This busy city restaurant is situated in an impressive palazzo-style building in the heart of old Liverpool, sharing the location with the Hope Street Hotel whose guests it serves. Understated in style, the open-plan interior offers informal eating in the bar area and a more formal restaurant space – a popular pre-theatre dining spot with the Everyman and the Philharmonic Hall nearby. Two generous slices of char-grilled tuna 'cooked perfectly rare' with gently pickled carrot, swede and baby corn or rare pigeon breast with carrot, courgette and focaccia crumb are well-constructed openers and might preface pan-fried salmon with endive, crushed potato and a slick of beurre blanc or crispy pork belly and pork cheek with caramelised apple purée. Comforting desserts include rum-soaked prune cake with spiced caramel and clotted cream or a green apple pannacotta crumble with caramelised apples. An extensive wine list suits all pockets, from £18.95.

Chef/s: David Critchley. **Open:** all week L and D. **Meals:** main courses £10 to £35. Set L and D £22 (2 courses) to £28. **Details:** 60 seats. Bar. Wheelchairs. Music. Parking.

Lunya

Cooking score: 2
Spanish | £26
18-20 College Lane, Liverpool One, Liverpool, L1 3DS
Tel no: (0151) 7069770
lunya.co.uk

£30

In the heart of Liverpool, with Liverpool One just round the corner, Peter and Elaine Kinsella's converted 300-year-old warehouse is the perfect Spanish retreat. Cheery vibes and energetic staff give an infectiously convivial buzz and there's also plenty of action in the kitchen, which delivers some cracking tapas and genuine Catalan/Spanish flavours. Most dishes are superb according to reporters, who have singled out cauliflower and Manchego frituras served with a romesco sauce, chorizo in white wine with fennel seeds, albondigas, pollo al moro (slow-cooked chicken in preserved lemon and Moroccan spiced broth) and lamb chops with aubergine purée. Even desserts such as crema catalana and churros and chocolate are high on tradition. The service is relaxed, and if you can't get enough of the speciality cheeses and Ibérico charcuterie, you can always stop off at the deli on the way out. The equally patriotic wine list features encyclopaedic coverage of native grape varieties and vineyards. Rarities abound and prices are reasonable (from £18.75). Lunya has also expanded to Manchester (see entry).

Chef/s: Dave Upson. **Open:** all week, all day from 12. **Closed:** 25 Dec, 1 Jan. **Meals:** tapas £5 to £19. Set L £10 (2 courses) to £14. Set D £13 (2 courses) to £20. **Details:** 142 seats. 30 seats outside. V menu. Bar. Wheelchairs. Music.

Cooking over fire

Whether cooking over fire can be deemed a trend is perhaps a question worth asking. After all, people have been doing it for thousands of years.

However, it is growing in popularity all over the country as high profile restaurants like **Temper**, **Kiln** and **Kitty Fisher's** all pay homage to our apparently insatiable love of a good barbecue.

Honey & Smoke, the Middle Eastern grill restaurant from Sarit Packer and Itamar Srulovich, is wowing critics as vegetables, meat and even fruit get the hot grill treatment.

Outside London, there's a more back-to-basics approach. Stuart Tattersall at the **Gunton Arms** in north Norfolk employs a bit of theatre, cooking venison from the Gunton Estate on a vast inglenook fire.

And in his tiny **Pea Porridge** restaurant in Bury St Edmunds, Justin Sharp's cast-iron charcoal oven, Bertha, smoulders pretty much around the clock.

These days, the fire 'thing' is about letting great ingredients sing for themselves with minimum fuss; it's about applauding an ingredient for its inherent flavour, not for a technique that's been applied. Ultimately, it's about returning to a very natural way of cooking.

★ **NEW ENTRY** ★

Maray

Cooking score: 1
International | £23
91 Bold Street, Liverpool, L1 4HF
Tel no: (0151) 7095820
maray.co.uk
£30

Inspired by the falafel eateries of the Marais district in Paris, the folk behind this small contemporary café offer food that leans towards the Middle East and have developed quite a following for their interesting range of small plates. F.H.T (falafel, hummus, tabbouleh) is considered something of a signature dish, but there's also burrata mozzarella with pea velouté, honeycomb and lovage, and hot-smoked lamb shawarma with watermelon and saffron yoghurt. Puddings offer an 'inspired, deeply chocolatey' Fernet-Branca chocolate tart with cream and mint. Cocktails are a speciality but the wine list, though short, is well chosen, with prices starting at £18.50.
Chef/s: Sam Grainger and Liv Alarcon. **Open:** all week, all day from 12. **Closed:** 25 and 26 Dec, 1 Jan. **Meals:** main courses £6 to £9. **Details:** 43 seats. V menu. Bar. Wheelchairs. Music. Parking.

Salt House Tapas

Cooking score: 3
Spanish | £20
1 Hanover Street, Liverpool, L1 3DW
Tel no: (0151) 7060092
salthousetapas.co.uk
£5 OFF £30

Whether you eat inside — at table or perched on a bar seat — or in the heated outside space, this lively tapas bar has 'a great vibe and staff are very professional and friendly'. Found in the heart of Liverpool city centre, the bare-wood industrial look fits the laid-back style of inspired small plates. You might choose a zingy fattoush salad, 'succulent' chicken thighs with shallots, peas and salsa verde or salt-baked beetroot with slow-roast grapes, mustard and hazelnut dressing and Idiazabal (sheep's) cheese, you'll find 'great flavour combinations that have been put together very skilfully'. Elsewhere, sea bass with courgette, 'nduja and burnt lemon, a single, plump seared king scallop in its shell with wakame (kelp) butter, crusty sourdough served with a PX vinegar-olive oil mix, and the 'nice little choice of sherries' have been praised. There's a gin bar, too, cocktails and a mainly Spanish wine list (from £16.95).

Chef/s: Martin Renshaw. **Open:** all week, all day from 12. **Closed:** 25 Dec. **Meals:** tapas £5 to £9. Set L £13. **Details:** 80 seats. 30 seats outside. V menu. Bar. Wheelchairs. Music.

60 Hope Street
Cooking score: 2
Modern British | £48
60 Hope Street, Liverpool, L1 9BZ
Tel no: (0151) 7076060
60hopestreet.com

Those who weren't aware that Liverpool had a Georgian quarter should set a course for Hope Street, a long thoroughfare that extends an ecumenical bridge between the Anglican and Metropolitan Catholic cathedrals. Somewhere in between, at number 60, the Manning brothers' elegant restaurant extends over three floors, a lower-ground lounge and a private first-floor room sandwiching an elegantly appointed restaurant. Classic modern British dishes are the drill, from seared king scallops with confit roe under a sausage-meat and lemon crumb, to roast chicken breast with smoked parsnip purée and toasted farro, or sea bream with braised leeks in verjus sauce, for main. A deep-fried jam sandwich with Carnation milk ice cream is the kind of treat Liverpool once thrived on, while today's trendsetters look to the more sophisticated likes of coffee, mascarpone and walnut tart. The ambitious wine list (from £19.95) is full of helpful descriptions, and when you've run dry, check out the after-dinner cocktails.

Chef/s: Neil Devereux. **Open:** Mon to Sat L and D. Sun 12 to 8. **Closed:** 26 Dec. **Meals:** main courses £14 to £33. Set L and D £25 (2 courses) to £30. Sun L £30 (3 courses). **Details:** 200 seats. 20 seats outside. Bar. Music.

Spire
Cooking score: 5
Modern British | £36
1 Church Road, Liverpool, L15 9EA
Tel no: (0151) 7345040
spirerestaurant.co.uk

It may be a stone's throw from Penny Lane and the day-tripping Beatles trail, but don't expect 'a four of fish' (or anything more risqué) at the Locke brothers' classy Liverpool eatery. 'Outstanding food at very fair prices' brings in diners from far and wide, most of whom are 'thoroughly delighted' by the kitchen's efforts and the stylish split-level space with its spiral staircase, bare tables and brick walls lined with contemporary artworks. There's culinary artistry on the plate, too, as the kitchen fashions fine-looking dishes such as pan-fried halibut with baby potatoes and broad beans in a lemon and dill chowder or herb-crusted rump of salt marsh lamb with aubergine purée, caramelised red onion, baby red pepper and feta. 'Obvious skills and outstanding presentation' are evident across the board, from jazzy starters of seared duck with smoked duck pâté, duck fritters and pineapple purée to desserts such as chocolate and mint fondant with choc-chip ice cream. Readers applaud the attentive 'but not obtrusive' service, while the wine list offers interesting drinking at manageable prices.

Chef/s: Matt Locke. **Open:** Tue to Fri L, Mon to Sat D. **Closed:** Sun, 25 and 26 Dec, first week Jan. **Meals:** main courses £16 to £23. Set L £15 (2 courses) to £18. Set D £17 (2 courses) to £20. **Details:** 70 seats. Music.

Etsu
Japanese | £25
25 The Strand (off Brunswick Street),
Liverpool, L2 0XJ
Tel no: (0151) 2367530
etsu-restaurant.co.uk

£5 OFF £30

Located across the road from the famous
'Three Graces' (the Liver, Cunard and Port of
Liverpool buildings), David Abe's Japanese
restaurant is a spacious, relaxing place – all
light wood and dark-tiled floor. Lunchtime
brings bento boxes, donburi rice bowls, mild
and creamy Japanese curries, and soup
noodles, but the repertoire runs to niku gyoza
(handmade pork and vegetable dumplings),
yakitori skewers, various tempura and
tonkatsu, and the full-range of sushi, sashimi
and maki rolls. Saké and shochu supplement a
brief wine list.

▌ Oxton

★ TOP 50 ★

Fraiche
Cooking score: 8
Modern French | £88
11 Rose Mount, Oxton, CH43 5SG
Tel no: (0151) 6522914
restaurantfraiche.com

Squirrelled away in an upmarket corner of
suburbia, Fraiche unfolds layer by layer. Its
understated frontage – closed blinds, sober
paintwork and a rather forbidding door – hint
at exclusivity. The interior is darkly clubby,
with room for just four well-spaced tables,
with two more squeezed into a rear
conservatory, the lights violet and purple, the
walls a screen for video projections chosen to
suit the time of year: autumnal leaves and
gardens for a November visit. While you may
struggle to make out the colours of your meal
amid the purple glow, there's no denying that
maximum atmosphere has been coaxed from
this unassuming little building. Flavours are

big-booted and bold on Marc Wilkinson's no-
choice menu, a carrot amuse-bouche
delivering a concentrated, fresh blast of
vegetable sweetness via carrot sorbet wrapped
in marinated carrot, while Nordic salmon is
paired with the sweet tang of pineapple and
bergamot cream, then finished with crunchy
almond. The quality of ingredients shines out
in every course, from fat, melt-in-the-mouth
scallops with truffle and artichoke three ways
– crisped, puréed and pickled – to a pearly
roast sea bass with a squid-ink crisp, charred
sweetcorn and a sauce that tingles with
gingery, lemony vigour. After that, rich,
caramelised, slightly salty Pink Fir potatoes in
a pot that billows wood smoke, and then it's on
to roast Dexter beef with a rich jus, charred
onion, carrot, cabbage and a fine lattice of
crisped potato. At this point you are asked to
choose 'sugar' or 'salt'. The latter leads to sheep's
cream mousse with walnut crisp and orange,
and then a platter of crunchy homemade
biscuits and pungent cheeses, each served with
its own accompaniment, from white wine
jelly to honey, scooped from its honeycomb at
the table. Then on to a trolley laden with petits
fours – you get to pick five – as a finale to a
meal of unexpected twists and turns and
endless invention.
Chef/s: Marc Wilkinson. **Open:** Sun L, Wed to Sat D.
Closed: Mon, Tue, 25 and 26 Dec, 2 weeks Sept.
Meals: tasting menu £88. Sun L £48. **Details:** 12
seats. 4 seats outside. Bar. Music. Children over 10
yrs only at D.

▌ Southport

Bistro 21
Cooking score: 4
Modern European | £29
21 Stanley Street, Southport, PR9 0BS
Tel no: (01704) 501414
bistro21.co.uk

£30

A block back from the hurly-burly of Lord
Street, Bistro 21 is a clean-lined contemporary
space, all white tiles and mirrors. Run by a
small team of friendly staff, it's made a
successful pitch to be Southport's destination

town-centre venue, with a menu of modern European cooking built around a core of signature dishes. Start with smoked haddock and pea risotto topped with a poached egg and Parmesan, or panko-crumbed black pudding fritters with Stilton and chilli. Explosive, finely tuned flavours distinguish main dishes too, when herb-crusted cod comes with spinach cream, pesto crumbs and mash, while the Moroccan lamb shoulder with raisined couscous and red pepper purée is a sweet and tender delight. A novel approach to tasting menus allows you to choose a set number of courses from what otherwise looks like a carte, and meals end with black cherry frangipane tart and vanilla ice cream, or salt-caramel chocolate pot. The short wine list opens with house South Africans at £14.95.

Chef/s: Michael Glayzer. **Open:** Tue to Sat L and D. **Closed:** Sun, Mon. **Meals:** main courses £16 to £25. Set L £12 (2 courses). Set D £16 (2 courses). Tasting menu £20. **Details:** 28 seats. V menu. Bar. Wheelchairs. Music.

Bistrot Vérité
Cooking score: 3
French | £31
7 Liverpool Road, Southport, PR8 4AR
Tel no: (01704) 564199
bistrotverite.co.uk

Marc Vérité's *restaurant du quartier* is a valued local resource, sitting neatly behind its potted shrubs in the smart shopping district of Birkdale village. Remaining true to his roots in a gently modernised French bistro tradition, the chef/patron conscientiously puts in the hours here to ensure a level of inspired consistency. Certain stalwarts such as ribeye steaks in béarnaise or peppercorn sauces, and the grilled fish dishes that come with a welter of local shrimps in rich bisque sauce, crop up reliably on the otherwise frequently changing menus, which find room for the likes of Moroccan-spiced king prawns with Caesar salad, garlic-roasted lamb rump with provençale accompaniments, and a blackboard listing of alluring finishers such as chocolate pavé with peanut brittle, salt caramel and

raspberries. Michaela Vérité leads the front-of-house with efficient bonhomie. The wine card doesn't trouble itself with vintage details, but leads off with house Duboeuf at £17.95.

Chef/s: Marc Vérité. **Open:** Wed to Sat L, Tue to Sat D. **Closed:** Sun, Mon, 25 and 26 Dec, 1 Jan, 1 week Feb, 1 week Aug. **Meals:** main courses £13 to £29. Set L £17 (2 courses). **Details:** 45 seats. 16 seats outside. Music.

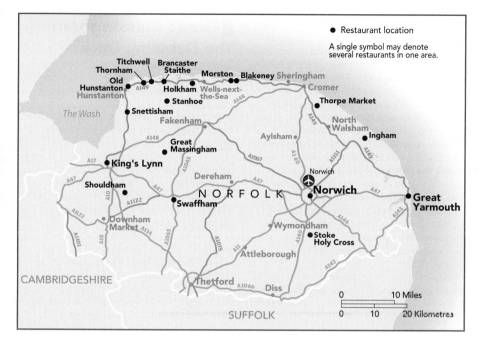

▉ Blakeney
The Moorings

Cooking score: 2

Modern British | £30

High Street, Blakeney, NR25 7NA

Tel no: (01263) 740054

blakeney-moorings.co.uk

By day a relaxed coffee-and-cake or soup, salad and sandwich pit-stop, by night channelling 'proper restaurant' with charm, this friendly neighbourhood spot, a stone's throw from the quay at Blakeney, is worth checking out. The menu leans towards seafood (of course), so start with fish soup with rouille and croûtons, a crab risotto or a platter of smoked fish from local supplier, Simon Letzer. Want more fish? A panaché of monkfish, scallops and mussels in saffron jus could fit the bill, or for something meatier choose rack of lamb with roast celeriac and squash, or pan-fried loin of local venison with braised red cabbage. Co-owner and chef Angela Long is well known in these parts for

her pastry skills, so don't miss her summer pudding, or plum and almond tart with raspberry sorbet. There's enough to choose from on a wine list with several bottles around the £17 mark.

Chef/s: Richard and Angela Long. **Open:** Tue to Sun L, Tue to Sat D. **Closed:** Mon (Dec and Jan). Tue to Thur (Feb, Mar and Nov). **Meals:** main courses £15 to £23. Sun L £19 (3 courses). **Details:** 50 seats. Music.

▉ Brancaster Staithe
The White Horse

Cooking score: 2

Modern British | £30

Brancaster Staithe, PE31 8BY

Tel no: (01485) 210262

whitehorsebrancaster.co.uk

🛏

This roadside pub is firmly anchored on coastal north Norfolk's lively food scene, and rightly so. Fran Hartshorne plunders the local area to create an appealing menu that blends posh pub staples with more sophisticated fare. In the bar, think Red Poll steak, fish pie to share, a pan of mussels raked from the marshes behind the pub, or in summer, lobster from the courtyard barbecue. The dining room with its (mesmerising) view is the place to enjoy classy starters such as queen scallops with celeriac, oats, apple and pancetta, or soy-and-ginger-cured trout with yuzu and yoghurt. You could follow these with tender Red Poll beef cheeks, or stone bass with spelt, Marsh Pig chorizo, squid and black garlic. A sharing assiette of desserts solves any decision-making angst and might include lemon tart, baked Alaska, blackberry parfait or coffee pannacotta with a hazelnut crémeux. Those with a less sweet tooth will devour the devoutly Norfolk cheeseboard. Wine from £17.50.

Chef/s: Fran Hartshorne. **Open:** all week L and D. **Meals:** main courses £14 to £22. **Details:** 100 seats. 100 seats outside. Bar. Wheelchairs. Music. Parking.

LOCAL GEM
The Jolly Sailors
British | £23
Brancaster Staithe, PE31 8BJ
Tel no: (01485) 210314
jollysailorsbrancaster.co.uk
£30

An endearing coastal bolt-hole with good intentions and a big heart, Anglian Country Inns' lively, rustic village hostelry deals in locally brewed ales and gutsy food. The menu delivers pub classics along the lines of steak and Brancaster Ale pie, fish or scampi and chips and ploughman's platters, as well as stone-baked pizzas, specials from its own smokehouse (rack of ribs with BBQ sauce, say) and local mussels. It fits the bill for walkers, children and canines – the beer garden is a bonus – and the service team clearly enjoy what they do. Wines from £17.50.

▌Great Massingham
The Dabbling Duck
Cooking score: 2
British | £26
11 Abbey Road, Great Massingham, PE32 2HN
Tel no: (01485) 520827
thedabblingduck.co.uk
🛏 £30

Saved from extinction by a couple of local farmers a few years back, this pub-with-rooms is thriving under the stewardship of Mark and Sally Dobby. It's right in the heart of the village, locals gather in the bar, and children have their own tasteful wooden play area in the garden, where you'll also find the wood-fired oven from which pizzas are served on Friday and Saturday nights. In the kitchen they know how to do the simple things well (the burger is made with Red Poll beef), but also delve into contemporary territory, pairing duck liver pâté with pickled rhubarb and a malt loaf with liquorice butter, and stone bass with cockle popcorn and pollen beurre blanc. Ingredients are carefully chosen, game features in season and the 'malt teaser' is a creative dessert with an array of malty treats and a Tia Maria crisp. Drink cask ales or wines from £16.50.

Chef/s: Dale Smith. **Open:** all week, all day from 12. **Meals:** main courses £12 to £23. **Details:** 100 seats. 30 seats outside. Bar. Wheelchairs. Music. Parking.

▌Great Yarmouth
Seafood Restaurant
Cooking score: 1
Seafood | £35
85 North Quay, Great Yarmouth, NR30 1JF
Tel no: (01493) 856009
theseafood.co.uk

Christoper and Miriam Kikis have been serving up fresh fish in this one-time pub a short walk from the quay since 1979, and not much has changed in almost 40 years. The charming old-school service and traditional décor remain steadfastly immune to fashion.

Among first courses, the likes of spicy seafood soup and calamari are joined by frogs' legs and a Greek-style salad, while main courses mostly come with sauces (lemon sole with blue cheese, for example). Local lobsters come fresh from the tank, and fillet steak arrives on its own or as part of a surf and turf with prawns, crawfish or half of one of those lobsters. House wines start at £16.75.

Chef/s: Christopher Kikis. **Open:** Mon to Fri L, Mon to Sat D. **Closed:** Sun, 2 weeks Christmas, 2 weeks May, bank hols. **Meals:** main courses £14 to £37. **Details:** 40 seats. Children over 7 yrs only.

▊ Holkham
The Victoria
Cooking score: 2
British | £38
Park Road, Holkham, NR23 1RG
Tel no: (01328) 711008
holkham.co.uk

Refurbished by Lord and Lady Leicester, owners of the Holkham Estate, this substantial Victorian inn sports the tell-tale signs of post-millennial country gentrification: duck-egg blue panelling, stuffed fauna (encased seabirds), bare wooden furniture and flooring. It also boasts splendid views to the sea marshes. Food has firm links to the locality: fresh, fleshy oysters; duck livers in creamy grain-mustard sauce; and Holkham venison (tender medallions served with venison suet pudding). Crab, a Norfolk staple, might appear as a special of 'thermidor' with meaty tempura lobster, rissole-like beignet and salty 'thermidor broth'. Execution occasionally faltered at inspection, but to finish, chocolate torte was a spoon-bendingly dense joy. Prompt service and plentiful wine by the glass (from £19 a bottle) are further pluses.

Chef/s: Michael Chamberlain. **Open:** all week L and D. **Meals:** main courses £13 to £30. **Details:** 86 seats. 76 seats outside. Parking.

Scoring - Explained

Local Gems, scores 1 and 2
Scoring a 1 or a 2 in The Good Food Guide, or being awarded Local Gem status, is a huge achievement. We list the very best restaurants in the UK; for the reader, this means that these restaurants are well worth visiting if you're in the area – and you're extremely lucky if they are on your doorstep.

Scores 3 to 6
Further up the scale, scores 3 to 6 range from up-and-coming restaurants to places to watch; there will be real talent in the kitchen. These are the places that are well worth seeking out.

Scores 7 to 9
A score of 7 and above means entering the big league, with high expectations of the chef. In other words, these are destination restaurants, the places you'll long to talk about – if you're lucky enough to get a booking.

Score 10
This score is extremely rare, with chefs expected to achieve faultless technique at every service. In total, only eight restaurants have achieved 10 out of 10 for cooking since the scoring system was introduced in 1998.

See page 12 for an in-depth breakdown of The Good Food Guide's scoring system.

▌Ingham
The Ingham Swan
Cooking score: 3
Modern European | £38
Sea Palling Road, Ingham, NR12 9AB
Tel no: (01692) 581099
theinghamswan.co.uk

£5 OFF 🍽

A centuries-old watering hole turned foodie destination, this trusty village inn is also a terrific stopover for bird-watchers or those cruising the nearby Broads. Built in medieval times as an adjunct to Ingham Priory, the Swan now provides sustenance of a different kind – thanks to chef/proprietor Daniel Smith and his Norfolk farm. Expect pretty restaurant-style dishes with modern accents and lots of ingredients on the plate – from garlicky lobster tails with Brancaster mussels, samphire, spiral potato and shellfish consommé to pork belly and tenderloin with a pulled pork cake, dauphinois potatoes, salt-baked swede, sprouting broccoli, braised red onion and red wine jus. Occasionally, things get too cluttered, but there's a return to form with desserts such as a contemporary take on peach Melba (as seen on *Great British Menu* 2016). Dishes are offered with apt suggestions from a classy, cosmopolitan wine list; otherwise, ales from local heroes Woodforde's are on tap.

Chef/s: Daniel Smith and Alex Clare. **Open:** all week L and D. **Closed:** 25 and 26 Dec. **Meals:** main courses £17 to £27. Set L £18 (2 courses) to £23. Set D £24 (2 courses) to £28. Sun L £28. Tasting menu £50 (6 courses). **Details:** 50 seats. 20 seats outside. V menu. Bar. Music. Parking.

▌King's Lynn
Market Bistro
Cooking score: 2
Modern British | £28
11 Saturday Market Place, King's Lynn, PE30 5DQ
Tel no: (01553) 771483
marketbistro.co.uk

£5 OFF £30

Richard and Lucy Golding have banged the drum for under-loved King's Lynn for several years, offering 'seasonal British food' (for which, read 'Norfolk where possible' because this place promotes the county's bounties) to an increasingly hungry audience. Sourdough bread is moreishly warm and fresh, perfect for trapping every drop of a beetroot gazpacho that pools, crimson and silky, around a tian of crabmeat, decorated with dill, mini spheres of cucumber and heritage tomatoes. Home-smoked salmon is a winner too, its sweet butter-softness balanced by a cracking sesame tuile and candied beetroot. Tender salt marsh lamb could follow: again, the flavour balance is deft, tomatoes, broad beans and capers providing edge as well as colour. To finish, choose a delicate galette with sweet-sharp rhubarb sorbet, crème pâtissière, rhubarb gel and a scattering of pistachio, over the 'cream tea' pudding where the gentle flavour of the strawberries, clotted cream ice cream and a fragrant Earl Grey macaron is overwhelmed by a hefty scone. Wine, including bottles from Norfolk's award-winning Winbirri Vineyard, from £17.

Chef/s: Richard Golding. **Open:** Wed to Sat L, Tue to Sat D. **Closed:** Sun, Mon. **Meals:** main courses £14 to £24. Set L £17 (2 courses) to £23. **Details:** 45 seats. Wheelchairs. Music.

Marriott's Warehouse

Modern British | £25
South Quay, King's Lynn, PE30 5DT
Tel no: (01553) 818500
marriottswarehouse.co.uk

£5 OFF £30

A new charcoal oven is the latest addition to the culinary armoury at Marriott's – a 16th-century warehouse conversion down by King's Lynn waterfront. In a buzzy setting of beams and local artwork, the kitchen sends out breakfasts, lunchtime sandwiches, burgers and other crowd-pleasers, while the globetrotting evening menu moves up a notch for the likes of pigeon pie with bramble gravy, five-spiced duck kebabs, pork belly with chorizo mash or grilled skate with chilli and caper butter. All wines come by the glass.

◼ Morston
Morston Hall

Cooking score: 6
Modern British | £75
The Street, Morston, NR25 7AA
Tel no: (01263) 741041
morstonhall.com

🍾 🛏

Buoyed by tributes such as 'faultless in every respect', things are going swimmingly at Morston Hall. Pitched somewhere between a full-dress country house hotel and a come-as-you-please hideaway by the coast, Galton and Tracy Blackiston's sturdy Jacobean mansion sets about its business in a 'caring, thoughtful and extremely comfortable manner'. Assemble at 7.15 for dinner at 8 – a triumphant seven-course tasting menu offering a procession of technically astute dishes crafted from top-drawer seasonal ingredients (many of them local). Introductory items might include a juicy caramelised scallop with gentle cauliflower purée and a 'sublime' peanut sauce, while centrepieces could be brilliantly timed North Sea plaice with sea-fresh Brancaster mussels bathed in their own sauce or a piece of

Holkham venison partnered by salt-baked beetroot, polenta, cavolo nero and white pepper jus. To finish, readers have drooled over the rich, warming Morston chocolate bar with milk ice cream ('small on the plate, but great on taste') and marvelled at the trolley of 'knowledgeably presented' cheeses. Well-drilled staff really know their stuff, while wine matches offer pure class by the glass from a prestigious list loaded with classy labels.
Chef/s: Galton Blackiston and Greg Anderson.
Open: Sun L, all week D. **Closed:** 24 to 26 Dec, Jan.
Meals: set D £75 (7 courses). Sun L £47. **Details:** 40 seats. V menu. Bar. Wheelchairs. Parking.

◼ Norwich
Benedicts

Cooking score: 5
Modern British | £36
9 St Benedict's Street, Norwich, NR2 4PE
Tel no: (01603) 926080
restaurantbenedicts.com

Richard Bainbridge's shop conversion in the city centre looks satisfyingly stripped back, with wood surfaces surrounding you in walls, floor and tabletops. It's a modern bistro for the times, with an approach to British cooking that modernises some decidedly unmodern-sounding offerings, from mash and gravy to rhubarb and custard. The former, which may be the opening gambit on the six- or eight-course taster, is light as air but full of concentrated buttery, meaty flavour. 'We all stand for Jerusalem' is the conceptual-art title of a dish that teams that puréed vegetable with parsley sponge, local lamb and a generous waft of truffle, while a serving of cod is shoehorned into a crunchy lettuce leaf, taco-fashion, and served with Brancaster mussels in blood orange and a spicy dash of XO sauce. These are dishes you may well have seen on the *Great British Menu*, now faithfully recreated before your very eyes. A reporter begged to differ with our doubts last year about Nanny Bush's trifle with its milk jam, but rum baba or chocolate praline tart offer solid reinforcements. A concise wine list opens at £21.

Chef/s: Richard Bainbridge. **Open:** Tue to Sat L and D. **Closed:** Sun, Mon, 24 Dec to 10 Jan, 8 to 23 Aug. **Meals:** set L £16 (2 courses) to £20. Set D £29 (2 courses) to £36. Tasting menu £48 to £59. **Details:** 32 seats. V menu. Music.

Roger Hickman's

Cooking score: 5
Modern British | £50
79 Upper St Giles Street, Norwich, NR2 1AB
Tel no: (01603) 633522
rogerhickmansrestaurant.com
£5 OFF

This discreet address has long been a go-to destination for Norwich foodies, and current incumbent Roger Hickman knows how to keep customers satisfied. Devoted regulars and first-timers rub shoulders in the dining room, which exudes personable civility amid a setting of modern artworks and neatly laid tables. Hickman's spirited cooking is all about clear seasonal contrasts, be it a plate of cured and smoked mackerel with gooseberry, horseradish and dill or roasted John Dory accompanied by artichoke, pickled shallots and caramelised onion. He can summon up muscular, meaty flavours, too – think loin of venison with braised red cabbage, fig, kale and celeriac or a dish of duck embellished with duck egg, turnip, broad beans, grains and truffle. The cheese selection is well worth exploring, while desserts embrace traditional themes (forced rhubarb with ginger, blood orange and custard) as well as exotic crossovers (lime parfait with creamy rice pudding, coconut, mango gel and pineapple). The thoughtfully chosen wine list features some classy growers and a dozen by-the-glass selections.
Chef/s: Roger Hickman. **Open:** Tue to Sat L and D. **Closed:** Sun, Mon, first week Jan. **Meals:** set L £20 (2 courses) to £25. Set D £38 (2 courses) to £47. Tasting menu £63 (7 courses). **Details:** 45 seats. Music.

Shiki

Cooking score: 3
Japanese | £26
6 Tombland, Norwich, NR3 1HE
Tel no: (01603) 619262
shikirestaurant.co.uk
£30

Occupying a three-storey house on Tombland, this Japanese eatery is the real deal with its little sushi bar out front, rows of bench seating, low tables and obliging staff. Chef/manager Shunsuki Tomii is moving the dinner menu towards izakaya-style 'otsumami', a succession of sharing plates brought out when they're ready – perhaps oshitashi (blanched greens with sesame and seaweed broth), tori kara (deep-fried chicken thighs with sweet plum vinegar) and seafood tempura or shogayaki (pan-fried pork slices with ginger sauce). After that, diners are encouraged to round off in traditional style with 'shime' – the Japanese holy trinity of rice, miso soup and pickles. The result is a telling blend of innovation and authenticity buoyed by top-drawer ingredients. Meanwhile, bargain-priced lunchtime deals bring in crowds of students and tourists hungry for the excellent bento boxes, donburi rice bowls, katsu curries, noodles and 'on the board' sushi deals. Drink green tea, saké, beer or wine.
Chef/s: Shunsuki Tomii. **Open:** Mon to Sat L and D. **Closed:** Sun, 2 weeks Jan, 1 week Aug, 1 week Sept. **Meals:** small plates £5 to £12. **Details:** 60 seats. 30 seats outside. Wheelchairs. Music.

Local Gem

Local Gems are the perfect neighbourhood venues, delivering good, freshly cooked food at great value for money.

▌Old Hunstanton

The Neptune

Cooking score: 5
Modern European | £60
85 Old Hunstanton Road, Old Hunstanton,
PE36 6HZ
Tel no: (01485) 532122
theneptune.co.uk
£5 OFF 🚗

Don't choose this gem of a roadside restaurant
to be wowed by flash techniques or
challenging combinations; do come for the
deft touch of a talented chef who takes first-
rate ingredients and coaxes them into full
song. Norfolk asparagus on vivid pea purée is a
generous reminder of spring, peppery pea
shoots and gently giving textures balanced by
kernels of salted-caramel popcorn and crisply
fried sprout leaves. Tender quail – a healthy
portion – sits tastily on pomegranate-studded
couscous with a swirl of mint yoghurt. Fish is
cooked faultlessly. Subtle hake flakes and
shines against the nutty flavour of morels,
young broad beans, spinach, monk's beard and
the butteriest creamed potato, while meatier
turbot comfortably accommodates punchy
aubergine, artichoke, leek and wild garlic. A
honey parfait with gariguette strawberries and
mint ice cream doesn't quite hit the same high,
but it's hard to resist the sugar-cinnamon
churros and hot chocolate sauce dip that come
with coffee. The Old World-leaning wine list
opens at a not-insignificant £25 but there is
plenty by the glass and half-bottle, too.
Chef/s: Kevin Mangeolles. **Open:** Sun L, Tue to Sun
D. **Closed:** Mon, 26 Dec, 3 weeks Jan, 1 week Nov.
Meals: set D £45 (2 courses) to £60. Sun L £30 (2
courses) to £38. Tasting menu £75. **Details:** 22 seats.
Bar. Music. Parking. Children over 10 yrs only.

▌Shouldham

LOCAL GEM

King's Arms

Modern British | £27
28 The Green, Shouldham, PE33 0BY
Tel no: (01366) 347410
kingsarmsshouldham.co.uk
£30

Saved by the village in 2013, this community
pub overlooking the village green has all the
rustic accoutrements you'd expect, given its
17th-century vintage (worn bricks, log fires,
low ceilings), plus a great selection of local
craft ales. And in an area poorly served for
eating out, beer-battered cod and homemade
pies shows the kitchen is willing to do the
populist thing (and do it well), alongside the
likes of pork belly and dauphinois, and sea bass
with Tenderstem broccoli, salsa rossa and
herbed potato cake. Wines from £16.50.

▌Snettisham

LOCAL GEM

The Rose & Crown

Modern British | £28
Old Church Road, Snettisham, PE31 7LX
Tel no: (01485) 541382
roseandcrownsnettisham.co.uk
🚗 £30

With its views of the local cricket pitch, roses
climbing the walls and crooked beams galore,
this revitalised medieval inn is everyone's idea
of a quaint village hostelry – although smart
contemporary touches, boutique bedrooms
and big helpings of modern food tell a
different tale. Typical picks from the menu
might range from wild mushroom and pearl
barley risotto to Thai-style sea bass 'en
papillote' with glass noodles, supported by a
fistful of pub staples. East Anglian beers and
wines from Adnams satisfy the drinkers.

Stanhoe
The Duck Inn
Cooking score: 3
Modern British | £30
Burnham Road, Stanhoe, PE31 8QD
Tel no: (01485) 518330
duckinn.co.uk
£5 OFF

Readers' enthusiasm for this welcoming pub-with-rooms close to the north Norfolk coast continues, with both locals and visitors drawn by chef/proprietor Ben Handley's resourceful modern British cooking. He offers a compact, bang-up-to-date menu with the food driven by well-sourced local and regional produce. Reporters have praised a starter of cod cheeks with vanilla velouté, chorizo, mussels and leeks, and a main course of 'as it should be' pan-roast sirloin of aged Norfolk beef with miso, onions and mushrooms with skinny fries. Classic techniques and flavour combinations are evident, too, in the likes of poach-roast breast of free-range Norfolk chicken with rosemary-baked potatoes, salt-baked celeriac and jus noisette. And for pudding, it's a hard choice between sticky toffee apple pudding, toffee sauce and vanilla ice cream or hazelnut praline parfait with a cherry and hazelnut financier. Wines from £14 with around 20 by the glass and carafe. **Chef/s:** Ben Handley. **Open:** Mon to Sat L and D. Sun 12 to 8. **Closed:** 25 Dec. **Meals:** main courses £10 to £25. Sun L £14. **Details:** 90 seats. 50 seats outside. Bar. Wheelchairs. Music. Parking.

Stoke Holy Cross
Stoke Mill
Cooking score: 4
Modern British | £40
Mill Road, Stoke Holy Cross, NR14 8PA
Tel no: (01508) 493337
stokemill.co.uk

Norfolk has more than its share of wind- and water-powered mills, but this fine weatherboarded construction on the outskirts of Norwich also stakes its claim as part of the county's foodie heritage. Formerly home to Jeremiah Colman's mustard-grinding empire, it's a now a tranquil contemporary restaurant dealing in seasonally accented modern cuisine. Light, airy, open-plan interiors provide a suitably relaxed backdrop for cooking that shows an impressively sure touch and a feel for regional produce – perhaps local asparagus with truffle oil, wild garlic, risotto and Parmesan or 12-hour beef cheek pointed up with mustard (of course), onions, spinach and carrots. Starters might range from Cromer crab salad with crispy squid or duck liver parfait with plum chutney, while desserts could herald the likes of glazed crème brûlée with elderflowers or a signature chocolate orange egg with chocolate-orange soil. The well-considered, fairly priced wine list includes bottles from Norfolk's talked-about Winbirri Vineyard. **Chef/s:** Andrew Rudd. **Open:** Wed to Sun L, Wed to Sat D. **Closed:** Mon, Tue. **Meals:** main courses £16 to £27. Set L £19 (2 courses) to £22. Sun L £28. Tasting menu £45. **Details:** 65 seats. Bar. Music. Parking.

The Wildebeest
Cooking score: 2
Modern British | £34
82-86 Norwich Road, Stoke Holy Cross, NR14 8QJ
Tel no: (01508) 492497
thewildebeest.co.uk

Daniel Smith spent 10 years cooking at the original Wildebeest Arms before decamping to the Ingham Swan (see entry), but now he's back as chef/proprietor overseeing this re-branded eatery on the outskirts of Norwich. Gone are the lurid mustard-yellow walls and African masks, although the open-plan look is much as before, and the food still arrives via an open kitchen. Produce from the owners' Norfolk farm is combined with prime regional ingredients for a frequently changing menu of seasonal dishes loaded with a veritable shopping list of components: how about lamb 'pencil' fillets with rosemary mash, goats' curd, shiitake mushrooms, braised peas, crispy Parma ham and local mizuna salad? To start, Cromer crab is a perennial favourite (with watermelon, garlicky crayfish, burnt lemon purée and coriander, perhaps), while dessert could be strawberry pannacotta with textures of strawberry, meringue and aerated white chocolate. The knowledgeably annotated wine list includes some cracking New World names.

Chef/s: Daniel Smith. **Open:** all week L and D. **Closed:** 25 and 26 Dec. **Meals:** main courses £17 to £27. Set L £18 (2 courses) to £23. Set D £24 (2 courses) to £28. Sun L £28. Tasting menu £45 (7 courses). **Details:** 65 seats. 24 seats outside. Wheelchairs. Music. Parking.

∎ Swaffham

Strattons Hotel

Cooking score: 2
Modern British | £30
4 Ash Close, Swaffham, PE37 7NH
Tel no: (01760) 723845
strattonshotel.com

Set in an East Anglian microclimate that is one of the driest regions of Britain, Strattons is a handsome red-brick listed building turned boutique eco-hotel. An on-site café-deli is only half of the catering arm, which also extends to an attractive semi-basement restaurant hung with amply proportioned local landscape paintings. Jules Hetherton is determined to put the Norfolk Brecks on the map with seasonal menus that look far and wide for culinary inspiration. A pasty of slow-cooked venison with pickled pink turnips, beetroot crisps and raisin purée, or the signature smoked haddock soufflé with horseradish cream, might be the preamble to sea bass in salsa verde with fennel and celery, or spiced quail with its own samosa, served with a nutmeg-poached pear, curried lentils and coriander oil. A lengthy roll call of populist desserts might include prune frangipane tart with Cognac ice cream, or pear and hazelnut sponge with custard. An extensive cocktail list and well-chosen wines, from £20.50, complete the deal.

Chef/s: Jules Hetherton. **Open:** Sun L, all week D. **Closed:** 1 week Christmas. **Meals:** main courses £14 to £18. **Details:** 40 seats. 14 seats outside. Bar. Music. Parking.

∎ Thornham

LOCAL GEM

Shuck's

International | £30
Drove Orchards, Thornham Road, Thornham, PE36 6LS
Tel no: (01485) 525889
shucksattheyurt.co.uk

It may look 'an unpromising tent from the outside' but a quirkier, cosier, more comfortable place to eat you'd be hard-pressed to find. Phil Milner's compact all-day menu in this family-friendly, fairy-lit yurt offers dishes packed with local flavour: a generous bowl of plump Brancaster mussels in a fragrant thyme-and-apple-infused cream; lightly tempura-battered cod cheeks perfectly paired with punchy local black pudding; and Red Poll burgers with Norfolk Dapple cheese. Phil's curries have a loyal following, and his sticky toffee pudding will soothe any lingering cravings sweetly. The wine list is straight-forward and good value (from £16.50).

∎ Thorpe Market

The Gunton Arms

Cooking score: 3
British | £35
Cromer Road, Thorpe Market, NR11 8TZ
Tel no: (01263) 832010
theguntonarms.co.uk

A panelled bar with bare floorboards and high stools is in keeping with the rural setting, but it's in the faintly *Twin Peaks*-sounding Elk Room that the serious business of the Gunton is transacted. Flaring antlers preside over a log-burning fire, and the roasting of meats on the open flames has a thrillingly Paleolithic air. Cuts of mature Angus beef, ribs and steaks, Blythburgh pork chops, even juicy pork and leek sausages, heading for their predestined partners of mash and onion gravy, emerge properly seared and appetising, and goose-fat roasties are not to be sneezed at either. Standbys of the pub food ethos supplement these heroic offerings, and meals are bookended by whole dressed crabs or smoked salmon and soda bread, and buttermilk pudding with rhubarb, or white chocolate and strawberry cheesecake. It's worth saving room for it all, and there are plenty of wines by the glass (from £5) to ease its passage, with bottles from £20.

Chef/s: Stuart Tattersall. **Open:** all week L and D. **Closed:** 25 Dec. **Meals:** main courses £12 to £25. **Details:** 90 seats. 100 seats outside. Bar. Wheelchairs. Music. Parking.

▉ Titchwell
Titchwell Manor
Cooking score: 4
Modern European | £35
Titchwell, PE31 8BB
Tel no: (01485) 210221
titchwellmanor.com

'We liked it here,' was all one satisfied diner needed to say. It's not surprising: this family-run hotel rejects the coastal cliché of washed-out neutrals in favour of funky colour, youthful style and food that attracts a loyal following. Come for a straightforward lunch – a cauldron of cockles is exactly what it claims to be, and a fish pie brims deliciously with seafood under crisp-topped Emmental mash, a tangle of softened leeks and brown shrimps on the side. Dive into the Norfolk-championing Conversation menu to explore this kitchen's more adventurous palate, and – admittedly – some dishes that divide opinion. Perfectly cooked lemon sole, and delicate red mullet with bouillabaisse, red pepper, fennel and monk's beard compensate for a starter of crab with a set cream and 'plain odd' frozen avocado that cried out for texture and acidic bite. Tart rhubarb and deliciously bitter chocolate sorbet challenge the shards of super-

sweet meringue and soothing cream in a superbly balanced final act, however. A £19.50 Portuguese rosé opens the wine offer.

Chef/s: Eric Snaith. **Open:** all week L and D. **Meals:** main courses £13 to £29. **Details:** 70 seats. 20 seats outside. V menu. Bar. Wheelchairs. Music. Parking.

▉ Wells-next-the-Sea
READERS RECOMMEND
Wells Crab House
Seafood
38 Freeman Street, Wells-next-the-Sea, NR23 1BA
Tel no: (01328) 710456
wellscrabhouse.co.uk

'To start, a simple bowl of shell-on prawns in a sweet chilli sauce – yes, it's messy to eat, but it's absolutely lovely. I find it hard to resist game, even in a specialist seafood place, and here a couple of pigeon breasts are carefully cooked, so they're still soft and juicy. We both ordered local dressed crab as the main course. It's as light, delicate and summery as you like, the balance between white and brown meat just perfect. Everything was absolutely spot-on. And, to think, we were eating this probably a matter of yards from where the crabs were landed.'

Readers recommend

A 'readers recommend' review is a genuine quote from a report sent in by one of our readers. We intend to follow up these suggestions throughout the year to come.

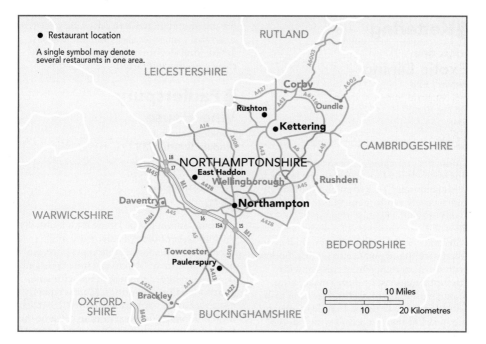

▮ East Haddon

The Red Lion

Cooking score: 4
Modern British | £30
Main Street, East Haddon, NN6 8BU
Tel no: (01604) 770223
redlioneasthaddon.co.uk

£5 OFF 🛏

You'd be hard pushed to find much else in the way of diversion in East Haddon, but fortunately the Red Lion is well equipped to handle the ambassadorial role single-handed. It's an invaluable local resource, an authentic village inn with a slate-floored bar extending into a dining area (and a cookery school on the opposite side of the gravelled car park). The menu offers an extensive tour of modern classic British dishes, but any trace of the formulaic is banished by the evident determination to exceed expectations with every dish. The Scotch egg is an object lesson, a savoury mix of Cumberland sausage and black pudding on a puddle of violently yellow piccalilli mayonnaise, or there may be potted mackerel with celeriac coleslaw and sourdough croûtons. At inspection, the grilled sea bream was terrific, its crisp salted skin and delicate flesh a perfect contrast, the accompaniments of intense homemade pesto and char-roasted sweet potato cleverly judged, or you might look to turkey escalope stuffed with apricot and sage and wrapped in pancetta. Irresistible desserts take in gin and lime cheesecake, or a wonderful lemon version of Bakewell with berries and whipped cream. The short wine list, from £4.50 a glass, just about does.
Chef/s: Chloe Haycock. **Open:** all week L, Mon to Fri D. **Closed:** 25 Dec. **Meals:** main courses £11 to £18. **Details:** 104 seats. 50 seats outside. Wheelchairs. Music. Parking.

Average price

The average price denotes the price of a three-course meal without wine.

▮ Kettering

Exotic Dining

Indian | £28
3-5 Newland Street, Kettering, NN16 8JH
Tel no: (01536) 411176
dineexotic.co.uk

Ignore the unprepossessing surroundings of this town-centre Indian-fusion restaurant and venture upstairs. Tucked among the lengthy and bizarrely exotic menu (choose kangaroo, camel or reindeer steaks if you wish) are the likes of gently spiced sea bass with sweet-sour tamarind sauce, or a fine southern Indian dosa filled with spiced potato and sambar. Follow with methi murgh, tender chicken with fragrant fenugreek, or jhinga malai, king prawn with mustard seed and coconut milk. Service is keen. To drink, a chilled Cobra hits the spot, but there's a decent wine list, too.

▮ Northampton

Bread and Pullet

Modern British | £30
176 Wellingborough Road, Northampton, NN1 4DZ
Tel no: (01604) 638520
breadandpullet.co.uk

Small modern British tapas plates may be everywhere now, but they are still relatively uncommon in Northampton, where the restaurant stretch of Wellingborough Road now plays host to Adam Church's turbo-charged caff. Chunky wood tables and breadboards on the wall set the tone for stimulating bites such as browned lemony cod and buttered samphire, creamed cabbage with braised ham hock, jerked lamb chops with citrus mayo, and grilled Tenderstem with crumbled smoked hazelnuts. Spicy bottled relishes and locally produced cakes and ice creams take up the slack. Afternoon teas are a feature on certain red-letter days. Be prepared to scream your order above the music levels. Drink local ales or flavoured ciders, though there are a few wines, too.

▮ Paulerspury

Vine House

Cooking score: 3
Modern British | £33
100 High Street, Paulerspury, NN12 7NA
Tel no: (01327) 811267
vinehousehotel.com

The long-running Vine House is undoubtedly the highlight of sleepy Paulerspury, and benefits from the formidable experience and professionalism of Marcus and Julie Springett. In a low-ceilinged room adorned with semi-abstract landscape paintings, Marcus's quietly assured country cooking has garnered a strong local following. Simplicity can so often be the boldest statement, as is the case with a plate of cured beetroot, creamy goats' cheese, onions caramelised in balsamic vinegar and pickled apple, the whole thing given a gentle chilli back note. Main might be turbot fillet dressed in smoked bacon mayonnaise with new season's asparagus, or lamb saddle in its spring greenery of crushed peas and a salsa verde doubly fragrant with basil and mint. Dessert might look like something nutritious from the breakfast buffet, when a bowl of plum fool arrives topped with thick crème fraîche and a scattering of puffed toasted oats. The short wine list starts at £17.50 for Chilean varietals.
Chef/s: Marcus Springett. **Open:** Mon to Sat D only. **Closed:** Sun, 1 week Christmas. **Meals:** set D £33. **Details:** 33 seats. Bar. Music. Parking. Children over 8 yrs only.

∎ Rushton
Rushton Hall, Tresham Restaurant

Cooking score: 3
Modern British | £55
Desborough Road, Rushton, NN14 1RR
Tel no: (01536) 713001
rushtonhall.com

£5
OFF

Rushton is a country estate on the colossal scale, a palatial edifice that was once home to generations of the Tresham family, whose illustrious scions beadily watch you at your aperitifs from their numerous portraits in the Great Hall. The dining room, too, is a vast expanse, patrolled by staff operating at all levels of formality and supplied with enthusiastic renditions of the modern British idiom by Adrian Coulthard. On the plate, the dishes may be more straightforward than they sound: a starter serving of cured mackerel with egg yolk, deep-fried onion threads and borage flowers is a nice spring thing. Main courses lead on to pedigree meats such as Jacob's Ladder of 28-day Aberdeenshire beef with root veg and horseradish mayonnaise, or perhaps cod with celeriac purée and sea herbs in butter sauce. Dessert might offer a busy-looking plate of Valrhona textures, with mousse, aerated chunks and minty white chocolate ice cream among its seductions, while a lemon study comprises meringue, shortbread and sorbet. A decent wine list keeps prices reasonable in the circumstances, with glasses from £7.
Chef/s: Adrian Coulthard. **Open:** Sun L, all week D. **Meals:** set D £55. Sun L £30. **Details:** 40 seats. Bar. Wheelchairs. Music. Parking. Children over 12 yrs only at D.

Our highlights...

Our undercover inspectors reveal their most memorable dishes from another year of extraordinary eating.

The **XO linguine with salt-cured egg yolk** at **The Other Naughty Piglet** was a shatteringly beautiful thing. As the yolk burst, it created the egginess that mimicked a carbonara sauce along with the diced Parma ham, but the seasonings of dried seafood and soy turned the thin pasta back into Chinese noodles. Joyous ingenuity matched to exquisite flavour-drenching.

The principal meat dish at **Kitchen Table**, was **pink-roasted junipered duck breast** with baby turnips and a screamingly intense orange purée made from the rind only. A simple but effective amplification of a classic idea.

The glossy, chewy **dark chocolate and coffee ganache** with passion fruit ice cream and coffee sauce at **Eipic** was sensational. But my absolute favourite: **barbecued scorched pear on a malted cracker** with ginger Anglaise and a tumbler of homemade ginger beer at **Forest Side** – a haunting riff on two basic flavours, but pursuing both to the last syllable of intensity.

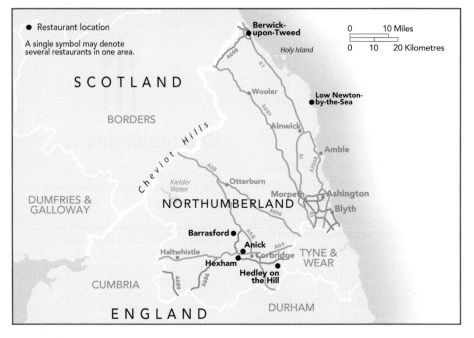

- Restaurant location

A single symbol may denote several restaurants in one area.

0   10 Miles
0   10   20 Kilometres

SCOTLAND

BORDERS

Cheviot Hills

DUMFRIES & GALLOWAY

Kielder Water

NORTHUMBERLAND

CUMBRIA

ENGLAND

Berwick-upon-Tweed

Holy Island

Wooler

Low Newton-by-the-Sea

Alnwick

Amble

Otterburn

Morpeth

Ashington

Blyth

Barrasford

Anick

Haltwhistle

Corbridge

Hexham

Hedley on the Hill

TYNE & WEAR

DURHAM

▊Anick

LOCAL GEM

The Rat Inn

British | £27

Anick, NE46 4LN

Tel no: (01434) 602814

theratinn.com

£5 OFF   £30

This splendid old drovers' inn, with lovely views over the Tyne Valley, all beams, roaring fire, rustic furniture and real ales within, is the textbook setting for some modern pub food. It reels in long-distance diners with a daily blackboard menu of locally sourced, seasonally inspired dishes: grilled sardines with caponata and rocket, ground rib burger 'in our own bun' with tomato salsa, Swiss cheese and chips, or roast Northumberland rib of beef (for two) with a simple peppercorn sauce. Wines from £15.95.

▊Barrasford

The Barrasford Arms

Cooking score: 2

Modern British | £25

Barrasford, NE48 4AA

Tel no: (01434) 681237

barrasfordarms.co.uk

£5 OFF   £30

Set in the rolling wilds of the North Tyne Valley, the stone-built Victorian pub with expansive gardens is a local magnet for salmon-fishers, hikers, quoiters and dartists, among others, anybody with an appetite for traditional country hospitality and heartily satisfying, well-crafted pub cooking. A pair of smartly turned-out dining rooms, supplemented by outdoor seating, are the setting for Tony Binks' locally supplied menus, which run the rule over duck and pistachio terrine with clementine-kumquat marmalade and toasted fruit bread, followed by seared salmon and broccoli in hollandaise, or marinated lamb rump with dauphinois and fine beans in red wine. The lunch menu might deliver a classic pheasant pie with bacon, cabbage and shallots, served with creamy mash, and if Northumberland Nettle is on, don't miss the cheese course. Sweeter things include rhubarb and white chocolate trifle with amaretti. Hand-pumped ales and a kindly priced wine list from £14.95 add to the conviviality.

Chef/s: Tony Binks. **Open:** Tue to Sun L, Tue to Sat D. **Closed:** Mon, 25 and 26 Dec, bank hols. **Meals:** main courses £12 to £19. Set L £15 (2 courses) to £19. Sun L £17 (2 courses) to £20. **Details:** 60 seats. 10 seats outside. Bar. Wheelchairs. Music. Parking.

■ Berwick-upon-Tweed

LOCAL GEM
Audela
Modern British | £30
41-47 Bridge Street, Berwick-upon-Tweed, TD15 1ES
Tel no: (01289) 308827
audela.co.uk

£5
OFF

'A delight on our doorstep' and 'an oasis of good cooking': local readers are certainly enamoured of Audela – an easy-going neighbourhood eatery that 'oozes calmness and relaxed sophistication'. Chef/owner Craig Pearson's twice-baked Northumberland cheese and leek soufflé remains a favourite pick from the menu, but other ideas also show undoubted skill and creativity: a 'refreshing' tian of local crab, roast pigeon with plums and spring cabbage, and desserts such as 'perfect' rice pudding scented with orange have all pleased. Wines from £15.95.

■ Hedley on the Hill
The Feathers Inn
Cooking score: 3
British | £29
Main Street, Hedley on the Hill, NE43 7SW
Tel no: (01661) 843607
thefeathers.net

£5 £30
OFF

The food at the Feathers is as firmly rooted in the landscape as the foundations of the rock-solid old inn itself. Chef/landlord Rhian Cradock has been running the place for a decade and in that time has kept it very much as a community hub, but it's his cooking that's really put the place on the map. Local farms are central to the supply line, all waste is recycled and they even sell their own produce at Jesmond Food Market. British ideas mix with French classicism and some Mediterranean sunshine in a repertoire that is first and foremost about the ingredients themselves. The potted North Sea brown shrimps are simply perfect, or how about whisky-cured local grouse with pickled roots and crab apple jelly? Among main courses, North Sea mackerel is powered up with chilli, garlic and anchovies, fish and chips is a fine version and hare Wellington is a smart reworking of a classic. Finish with burnt Northumbrian cream. Regional ales man the pumps; wines start at £16.

Chef/s: Rhian Cradock. **Open:** Thur to Sun L, Wed to Sat D. **Closed:** Mon, Tue, first 2 weeks Jan. **Meals:** main courses £11 to £15. **Details:** 35 seats. 14 seats outside. Parking.

▌Hexham
Bouchon Bistrot
Cooking score: 4
French | £29
4-6 Gilesgate, Hexham, NE46 3NJ
Tel no: (01434) 609943
bouchonbistrot.co.uk
£5 OFF £30

Gregory Bureau's neighbourhood French bistro is *très sympathique*. It has the air of an English country pub that has been blown across the Channel in high winds, with French posters, an open fire, deep pink carpet and exposed stonework the setting for a menu of classically based cuisine bourgeoise, more than capably rendered by Nicolas Kleist. Summer reporters hugely enjoyed a visit that took in langoustine soup with aïoli croûtons, well-dressed landaise salad with duck breast, a sole véronique to do Escoffier proud, and perfectly pink lamb noisettes with Provençal tomato in thyme jus. One or two more contemporary notes are struck, for seared scallops with pea purée and piquillos perhaps, but essentially there's little reason to veer off the beaten track, all the way to properly caramelised crème brûlée, profiteroles or a rum-drenched baba served with pineapple carpaccio and coconut. A handful of *vins étrangers* inveigle themselves among a predominantly French list, which opens at £16.50 for house Duboeuf.
Chef/s: Nicolas Kleist. **Open:** Mon to Sat L and D. **Closed:** Sun, 24 to 26 Dec, bank hols. **Meals:** main courses £13 to £22. Set L £15 (2 courses) to £16. Set D £16 (2 courses) to £17. **Details:** 130 seats. Wheelchairs. Music.

▌Low Newton-by-the-Sea
LOCAL GEM
The Ship Inn
British | £25
Newton Square, Low Newton-by-the-Sea, NE66 3EL
Tel no: (01665) 576262
shipinnewton.co.uk
£30

A whitewashed pub set in a square of fishermen's cottages just 50 yards from the North Sea, this Northumberland stalwart continues to cheer visitors by providing good beer – from its own microbrewery next door – and unfussy food, alongside beams, wood floors and rough stone walls. The menu cleverly mixes the familiar (lunchtime sandwiches, ploughman's, steaks) with locally caught crab, mackerel, or hake fillet with beetroot, chilli and cucumber salsa. To finish, there could be comforting apple crumble and cream or local cheeses. Wines from £16.75.

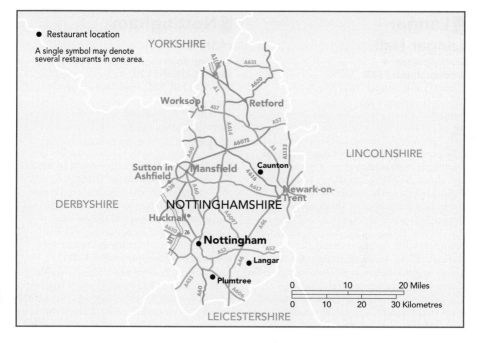

- Restaurant location

A single symbol may denote several restaurants in one area.

YORKSHIRE

Worksop · Retford

Sutton in Ashfield · Mansfield · Caunton

Newark-on-Trent

DERBYSHIRE

NOTTINGHAMSHIRE

LINCOLNSHIRE

Hucknall

· **Nottingham**

· Langar

· Plumtree

LEICESTERSHIRE

0   10   20 Miles

0   10   20   30 Kilometres

◼ Caunton

Caunton Beck

Cooking score: 2
Modern European | £25
Main Street, Caunton, NG23 6AB
Tel no: (01636) 636793
wigandmitre.com

£5 OFF   £30

'It's just a lovely country pub by a beck full of ducks,' writes Valerie Hope of Caunton's finest, and let there be no 'just' about it. It will look like an oasis of civilisation after a gruelling interlude on the A1, and although the place has been around since the Tudor era, it can't ever have looked as vibrantly fresh as it does now, with its pink carpet and russet walls. The kitchen works to a formula of modern, internationally inspired pub food, interleaving the likes of roast pigeon with Persian-spiced bulgur wheat and cavolo nero, and butternut and chestnut risotto with Colston Bassett Stilton, among the more obvious stalwarts such as battered prawn cocktail, beef bourguignon with mustard mash, and the kinds of puddings that induce purrs of delight. Under that last head, read chocolate brownie and coffee pannacotta, treacle tart, and a crème brûlée zested up with orange and cinnamon. House vins de pays de l'Hérault at £14.95 lead the charge on a creditably versatile list.

Chef/s: Valerie Hope and Ben Hughes. **Open:** all week, all day from 12. **Closed:** 25 Dec. **Meals:** main courses £12 to £16. Set L and D £15 (2 courses) to £18. **Details:** 100 seats. 40 seats outside. Bar. Wheelchairs. Parking.

Please send us your feedback

To register your opinion about any restaurant listed in this guide, or a new restaurant that you wish to bring to our attention, please visit the web address at the bottom of the page. Your feedback informs the content of the book and will be used to compile next year's reviews.

Langar
Langar Hall
Cooking score: 4
Modern British | £43
Church Lane, Langar, NG13 9HG
Tel no: (01949) 860559
langarhall.com

The present-day Georgian house at Langar rises with a soft orange glow at the end of its tree-lined driveway, and there's an agreeable feeling of relaxed hospitality to the place, an impression reinforced by the portrait of its late owner, Imogen Skirving, that hangs just outside the dining room. A handsome room complete with a foliaged chandelier and statuary of half-clad human figures in the Greek manner makes an elevated backdrop for finely wrought contemporary cooking. Croquettes of braised pig cheek are adorned with weeny pickled vegetables – radish, carrot and cauliflower – and dressed with dots of smooth piccalilli, as a delicate prelude to sautéed turbot with miso-glazed octopus and salt-baked kohlrabi in black garlic sauce, a main course exuding umami from its every pore, or perhaps a carb-heavy Indian number that combines Goan beef curry with a terrine of Bombay potato, Peshwari naan, raita and basmati. Ingenious desserts take in cheesecake mousse in a mango gel tube with black pepper and sheep's yoghurt sorbet, or glorious bitter chocolate tart with sharp raspberry sorbet. An efficient wine list starts with southern French varietals at £19.95.
Chef/s: Gary Booth and Ross Jeffery. **Open:** all week L, Mon to Sat D. **Meals:** set L £20 (2 courses) to £27. Set D Mon £25 (2 courses) to £30, Tue to Thur £38 (2 courses) to £43, Fri and Sat £55. Sun L £40. **Details:** 60 seats. 20 seats outside. Bar. Wheelchairs. Parking.

Nottingham
Hart's
Cooking score: 3
Modern British | £38
Standard Hill, Park Row, Nottingham, NG1 6GN
Tel no: (0115) 9881900
hartsnottingham.co.uk

Tim Hart's modern brasserie (with rooms in the adjoining hotel) doesn't attempt to shake the foundations of the city, but it is a crowd puller, with a strong business contingent during the week. Versatile menus mix influences in true modern style. The best dishes see British ingredients treated with minimal fuss, so expect twice-baked Lincolnshire Poacher and haddock soufflé with a rocket and caper salad, and 'a large piece of well-cooked' sea trout atop asparagus and radish with dukkah dressing. There's chocolate mousse, served with shards of praline, some fruit compote and hazelnut cream to finish. A special shout-out goes to the sourdough, from Hambleton Bakery: in 'a nice touch', baked goods are on display and for sale by the front door. Service can be 'overly formal, of the type where your wine is stashed in a bucket an anxiety-inducing distance away from you'. However, there is quality across the board on the international wine list. Arranged by style, it comes with eloquent tasting notes and fair prices.
Chef/s: Daniel Burridge. **Open:** all week L and D. **Closed:** 1 Jan. **Meals:** main courses £17 to £27. Set L £19 (2 courses) to £24. Set D £22 (2 courses) to £28. Sun L £25. **Details:** 80 seats. Bar. Wheelchairs. Parking.

The Larder on Goosegate

Cooking score: 2
Modern British | £30
16-22 Goosegate, Hockley, Nottingham,
NG1 1FF
Tel no: (0115) 9500111
thelarderongoosegate.co.uk

£5
OFF

Occupying a stately Victorian structure in Hockley – Nottingham's hipster precinct – the Larder on Goosegate was once the original headquarters for Jesse Boot of Boots the Chemist. Inside, deferential nods to the businessman abound – from original signing to apothecary bottles now employed as vases – all arranged around a handsome dining room with high ceilings and tall windows. The kitchen today serves up doses of modern British cooking – with uncluttered flavours in starters like ham hock terrine with pickled vegetables, or perhaps grilled mackerel with beetroot and horseradish. Mains show some flair in the kitchen – think tender lamb rump accompanied by spiced aubergine, broccoli and goats' curd – while a fragrant dish of sea trout, shrimps, broad beans and sea vegetables impressed on inspection. Puddings pull no punches – chocolate brownie with vanilla ice cream, for instance, or elderflower parfait with Southwell strawberries. House wines start at £17.50, with a stellar array of beers from Nottingham and (say it quietly) Derby available by the bottle. Service can be a bit sluggish.
Chef/s: David Sneddon. **Open:** Fri and Sat L, Tue to Sat D. **Closed:** Sun, Mon. **Meals:** main courses £13 to £22. Set L and D £15 (2 courses) to £18. **Details:** 65 seats. Music.

Symbols

🍴   Accommodation is available
£30   Three courses for less than £30
£5 OFF   £5-off voucher scheme
🍷   Notable wine list

★ TOP 10 ★
★ BEST FRONT-OF-HOUSE ★

Restaurant Sat Bains

Cooking score: 9
Modern British | £95
Lenton Lane, Nottingham, NG7 2SA
Tel no: (0115) 9866566
restaurantsatbains.com

🍷 🛏

Just outside Nottingham, in a leafy lane off the thunder of the A52, a repurposed Victorian farmhouse in red brick offers one of the country's most singular dining experiences. Since taking over in 2005, Sat and Amanda Bains have turned the place into a coveted destination. Above all else, they understand that dining here is, for many, a once-in-a-lifetime experience and it is their duty to make that experience unique – in a relaxed and fun way. And they succeed. The warm service is spot-on, making every diner 'feel like the most special person in the room'. In addition, refurbishment of guest rooms continues and the dining room has been remodelled, too, with unclothed deer-hide tables furnished with artisan wooden accoutrements. There's also a bench in the kitchen where, with chefs bustling, you're positioned in the eye of the culinary storm. The glasshouses and garden plots that surround the place pour forth strawberries, nasturtiums, herbs and much else besides into a kitchen where creativity is permanently on maximum impulse drive. Choose seven or ten courses of a tasting menu printed on filmy plastic and wrapped around the table lamp, with coloured dots indicating the relative levels of each of the five taste categories pertaining to each dish. Thus briefed, you can relax into the enjoyment of terrific, high-powered contemporary cooking, opening perhaps with a little cornet of horseradish ice cream. Textural elements are explored with great diligence, as when a pair of scallops – one raw, one not – are veiled with sheets of elderflower jelly and dotted with dried tomato and strawberry. The vogue for breakfast theming produces a bowl of chicken muesli, in which frozen liver parfait and dried skin combine with cranberries and green beans for something that transcends its unprepossessing appearance. Wood-fired Nicola potatoes arrive delicately pulverised with cream cheese on kombu jelly, topped with Siberian baerii caviar, and are followed by a take on beef tartare that's like 'the angel-twin of a Big Mac', slicked with mushroom ketchup and smoked mayo for an umami-soaked effect. For the main meat, there could be lamb in two servings, first a tender ragù on kohlrabi 'tagliatelle' in nutmeg emulsion, then a slightly overwrought serving of pressed Asian-spiced shoulder with lemon purée amid a tumult of other ingredients. The pick of desserts is a cylinder of chocolate mousse topped with cumin-dusted yoghurt pannacotta, and the conclusion, a glass box of Thai spices that flavour a kulfi-like cube of ice cream and candyfloss, ends things with a flourish. The same approach to flavour analysis informs a stupendous wine list that seeks out the best in modern viniculture. Everything is there as an emblematic representative of its style, from young, enterprising growers in both hemispheres. Bottles open at £33.

Chef/s: Sat Bains and John Freeman. **Open:** Wed to Sat L and D. **Closed:** Sun, Mon, Tue, 1 week Dec, 2 weeks Jan, 1 week Apr, 2 weeks Aug. **Meals:** tasting menu £95 (7 courses) to £110 (10 courses). **Details:** 48 seats. V menu. Bar. Wheelchairs. Music. Parking. Children over 8 yrs only.

LOCAL GEM

Delilah

Modern European | £20
12 Victoria Street, Nottingham, NG1 2EX
Tel no: (0115) 9484461
delilahfinefoods.co.uk

£30

Housed in a former bank, this long-running deli-cum-café has lost none of its vim and remains an understandably popular venue that pulls in the crowds with high-quality food. Take your pick from a fashionably modern medley – charcuterie and cheese platters, daily brunch dishes, to an array of grazing plates. You might find blood-orange balsamic and honey-glazed chorizo, salads of oak roast salmon or panzanella, and flatbread pizza, say heritage tomatoes, basil, buffalo mozzarella and black olive tapenade. The eminently affordable wine list (from £15) is a model of small, mostly European producers.

■ Plumtree
Perkins Bar & Bistro

Cooking score: 2
Modern British | £35
Station House, Station Road, Plumtree, NG12 5NA
Tel no: (0115) 9373695
perkinsbarbistro.co.uk

Noted for its attractive surroundings, nostalgia for the Victorian railway station it once was is part of the charm of this well-maintained red-brick building and conservatory overlooking the single track – still used occasionally as a test line. It has been run by the Perkins family since 1982 and their good-value bistro repertoire covers everything from old favourites such as plaice goujons with minted pea purée and tartare sauce, and calf's liver with Provençal herbs, creamed potato, char-grilled bacon, fried onions and grain-mustard cream sauce, to Moroccan spiced rump of lamb with apricot and almond quinoa, onion seed bhaji and a carrot and cumin purée. Three-course lunches are a snip for dishes like pearl barley and confit duck risotto, fillet of cod with pommes Anna, celeriac purée, braised fennel and salsa verde, then lemon posset with raspberry and whisky ice cream. Sunday lunches have also been commended. Wines from £16.50.

Chef/s: Sarah Newham. **Open:** all week L, Mon to Sat D. **Meals:** main courses £12 to £22. Set L £14 (2 courses) to £17. Set D £17 (2 courses) to £19. Sun L £17. **Details:** 74 seats. 24 seats outside. Bar. Wheelchairs. Music. Parking.

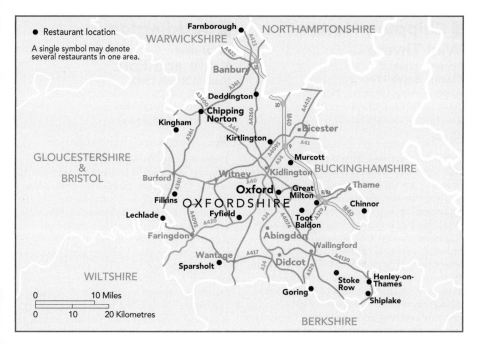

- Restaurant location

A single symbol may denote
several restaurants in one area.

Farnborough
NORTHAMPTONSHIRE
WARWICKSHIRE
Banbury
Deddington
Chipping Norton
Kingham
Kirtlington
Bicester
Murcott
GLOUCESTERSHIRE & BRISTOL
Burford
Witney
Kidlington
BUCKINGHAMSHIRE
Oxford
Great Milton
Thame
Filkins
OXFORDSHIRE
Chinnor
Lechlade
Fyfield
Toot Baldon
Faringdon
Abingdon
Wallingford
Wantage
Sparsholt
Didcot
WILTSHIRE
Stoke Row
Henley-on-Thames
Goring
Shiplake
BERKSHIRE

0   10 Miles
0   10   20 Kilometres

◼ Chinnor
The Sir Charles Napier

Cooking score: 6
Modern British | £47
Sprigg's Alley, Chinnor, OX39 4BX
Tel no: (01494) 483011
sircharlesnapier.co.uk

For more than 40 years, Julie Griffiths has run
'the Napier' by her own quirky rules, filling
the place with animal sculptures, surreal curios
and vintage furniture of the 'well-worn'
variety. After a spell in the doldrums, this
lovably eccentric Chiltern charmer is on song
once again – and better than ever, thanks to
the arrival of chef Gerd Greaves from the
Oxford Kitchen (see entry). Regulars may
recognise one or two old favourites on the
unconditionally seasonal menu (the twice-
baked smoked haddock and Cheddar soufflé,
for example), but Greaves brings his own 'free-
thinking' style to proceedings: consider two
'toasty' scallops on a circle of soubise-style

onion purée with a crispy boned chicken wing
and petals of charred shallot or an 'absolutely
precise' ballotine of quail partnered by a
caraway-scented sauce, creamed leeks and
artichoke purée. Big flavours, superb
technique and exact butchery are the
hallmarks of meat dishes including an assiette
of suckling pig with salt-baked celeriac, pear
and sorrel, while desserts make their own
impact – as in a dense chocolate and peanut
terrine brilliantly offset by a pink grapefruit
sorbet. 'Common-sense service' is appreciated,
although things can get shambolic during
extended Sunday lunches – no doubt fuelled
by a wine list that's 'absolutely chock-full of
bargains'. Growers and vintages are top-
drawer, and classy drinking is a given.
Chef/s: Gerd Greaves. **Open:** Tue to Sun L, Tue to
Sat D. **Closed:** Mon (exc bank hols), 3 days
Christmas, first week Jan. **Meals:** main courses £23
to £30. Set L Tue to Fri £20 (2 courses). Set D Tue to
Thur £20 (2 courses). Tasting menu £65. **Details:** 70
seats. 70 seats outside. V menu. Bar. Parking.
Children over 6 yrs only at D.

▮ Chipping Norton

Wild Thyme

Cooking score: 2
Modern British | £40
10 New Street, Chipping Norton, OX7 5LJ
Tel no: (01608) 645060
wildthymerestaurant.co.uk

£5 OFF

Scuffed, sanded and distressed in true shabby-chic style, with painted chairs, a big old stone fireplace and 'smart-minimal' table settings, this neighbourly restaurant-with-rooms suits affluent Chipping Norton in a dressed-down casual kind of way (watch out for regular art and music events). Chef/co-owner Nick Pullen bakes bread in-house and puts great store by locally sourced ingredients. To begin, there might be home-cured carpaccio-style venison with an assortment of nicely cooked asparagus, sun-blush tomatoes, capers, mozzarella pieces, herbs and a little hat of crisp straw potatoes, or a well-balanced and enjoyable plate of panko-crusted scallops baked with cauliflower purée. After that, a dish of lamb loin, kidney and potato terrine with a generous mélange of braised fennel, courgettes, roast tomato and asparagus has outshone a rather bulky assemblage involving Todenham Manor pork, mash, sauerkraut and carrots. Finish off with a set of rhubarb desserts. The wine list is a modest selection, starting at £18.50, and promises some good picks at fair prices.

Chef/s: Nicholas Pullen. **Open:** Thur to Sat L, Tue to Sat D. **Closed:** Sun, Mon, 1 week summer, 1 week winter. **Meals:** set L and midweek D £20 (2 courses) to £25. Set D £33 (2 courses) to £40. **Details:** 35 seats. Wheelchairs.

Local Gem

Local Gems are the perfect neighbourhood venues, delivering good, freshly cooked food at great value for money.

▮ Deddington

LOCAL GEM
Knife and Fork

Modern British | £45
Clifton Road, Deddington, OX15 0TP
Tel no: (01869) 336954
knifeandforkeatery.co.uk

Tanya and John Young's unique restaurant 'pops up' weekly (Fridays and Saturdays only) in their Oxfordshire farmhouse-cum-B&B. As such, it's only loosely a 'restaurant', but the cooking – 100 per cent gluten-free (Tanya is herself a coeliac) – is certainly restaurant standard. The tasteful dining room comes with two communal tables (seating 16 in total), which makes for a fun, sociable evening. A five-course surprise menu could deliver cauliflower soup with Red Leicester and bacon, a simple but well-done assembly of roasted vegetables and hazelnuts dressed with yoghurt and olive oil, and a beautifully cooked chicken suprême with gooey dauphinois. To conclude, cheese with superb gluten-free crackers then chocolate torte. Unlicensed, so BYOB. Book well in advance.

▮ Farnborough

LOCAL GEM
The Kitchen

British | £30
Main Street, Farnborough, OX17 1DZ
Tel no: (01295) 690615
thekitchenfarnborough.co.uk

£5 OFF

The former Inn at Farnborough has been reinvented as the Kitchen, offering inspired country food with the accent on seasonal freshness. Modern nibbles of ox cheek croquettes or flowerpot bread with whipped butter start things off, and the menu is littered with fashionable ideas ranging from warm smoked mackerel with apple, kale and pumpkin salad to spinach gnocchi with duck egg, wild mushrooms, sage and hazelnut.

Char-grilled steaks and burgers naturally come with beef-dripping chips, 'laid-back' Sunday lunch has been praised and 'nothing is too much trouble' for the staff. Wines from £17.50.

Filkins
The Five Alls
Cooking score: 3
Modern British | £32
Filkins, GL7 3JQ
Tel no: (01367) 860875
thefiveallsfilkins.co.uk
£5 OFF

Flagstone floors, mismatched antique furniture, ancient beams, local ales, cider and a delightful garden out back signal that the Five Alls is a comfortable country inn with all the necessary attributes, although most people come here for the food served in the traditional bar and dining room. The long menu covers a lot of ground (too much, according to some readers), moving from restaurant-style interpretations of the pub classics to eclectic superfood salads, Thai-style mussels, Double Gloucester cheese soufflé or chump of lamb with imam bayaldi, couscous and garlic cream. However, reports have detailed some unqualified successes from starters of 'wonderful' devilled kidneys and 'excellent' pasta nero with seafood, to mains of a fricassee of rabbit, and confit duck leg with Asian salad. While there have been some question marks over the service, others have praised the 'willing approach'. The carefully chosen international wine list receives a proper thumbs-up.
Chef/s: Sebastian Snow. Open: all week L, Mon to Sat D. Closed: 25 Dec. Meals: main courses £13 to £23. Set L and D £18 (2 courses) to £24. Sun L £26. Details: 100 seats. 50 seats outside. Bar. Wheelchairs. Music. Parking.

Fyfield
The White Hart
Cooking score: 3
Modern British | £33
Main Road, Fyfield, OX13 5LW
Tel no: (01865) 390585
whitehart-fyfield.com
£5 OFF

The Dissolution did for the Fyfield Chantry, as was, and it became a village inn, but renovations in the 1960s exposed the Tudor arch-braced roof to admiring view, and the original Great Hall and minstrels' gallery are once more a grand place to dine. Mark Chandler cooks in the modern idiom, as to both format – sharing boards of meze, fish and antipasti are popular – and style. The kitchen garden supplies the materials for dishes such as salt-baked and pickled beetroot with goats' cheese cream and blackberries, or sharply etched parsnip and apple soup boosted with scrumpy. Substantial mains take in rump of lamb with a black olive and feta tart and char-grilled vegetables, or crisp-skinned stone bass on crushed new potatoes with clams, pickled Little Gem and wild garlic oil. Finish with lime and ginger cheesecake, garnished with an avalanche of tropical fruit, mango purée and coconut sorbet. Wines are grouped by style with good notes, opening at £18.
Chef/s: Mark Chandler. Open: Tue to Sun L, Tue to Sat D. Closed: Mon. Meals: main courses £12 to £25. Set L £17 (2 courses) to £20. Sun L £26 (2 courses) to £29. Details: 60 seats. 40 seats outside. Bar. Music. Parking.

▌Goring
The Miller of Mansfield
Cooking score: 4
British | £40
High Street, Goring, RG8 9AW
Tel no: (01491) 872829
millerofmansfield.com
£5 OFF 🛏

The Galers have put down roots in their redbrick Georgian village inn on the Oxon-Berks border, where boutique guestrooms and a well-stocked beamed bar are the comforting adjuncts to a culinary operation with its finger on the modern regional English pulse. Nick's nine-course tasting menu is the summit of the kitchen's output, but if you're in for a more traditional pub approach, there's still plenty to entice. Start with a ham hock and trotter croquette with piccalilli and turmeric mayo, or even a bowl of tomato soup with maple bacon and a quail's egg, as intros to satisfying main dishes like locally farmed chicken with hay-smoked cabbage and a lemony chicken jus. Fish might be spiced monkfish tail with buttered Cornish potatoes and creamed sweetcorn, sauced in Pernod. To finish, get stuck into some eggy bread, which comes decked out in pistachios, along with yuzu curd and pomegranate sorbet. The wine list runs through the styles, from elegant and zesty to hearty and robust, starting at £19.
Chef/s: Nick Galer. **Open:** all week L and D. **Closed:** 27 and 28 Dec. **Meals:** main courses £15 to £26. Set L £18 (2 courses) to £22. Sun L £26 (2 courses) to £31. Tasting menu £60. **Details:** 56 seats. 40 seats outside. Bar. Wheelchairs. Music.

▌Great Milton
Le Manoir aux Quat'Saisons
Cooking score: 7
Modern French | £150
Church Road, Great Milton, OX44 7PD
Tel no: (01844) 278881
belmond.com
🛏

Le Manoir generates such love and affection that it seems almost churlish to find fault with Raymond Blanc's consummate country-house experience. From the moment you're greeted (by name) as you step from your car, this aristocrat proves its pedigree as a five-star getaway – rooms 'elegantly furnished with Gallic taste', terraces for flutes of Champagne, magical gardens to stroll around. Meanwhile, the kitchen is attuned to its French master's voice, delivering food that can satisfy and seduce. Flavours of the season are paramount: staples such as the jellied terrine of garden beetroot with horseradish sorbet still draw top reviews, likewise disparate dishes ranging from a 'perfect' assiette of lamb with white asparagus, broad beans and rosemary jus to fillet of brill with oyster, cucumber, wasabi, seaweed and samphire. Similarly, desserts such as the gariguette strawberry 'delight' with Kirsch sabayon and marshmallow are all about well-honed craftsmanship rather than showboating. Those with critical palates may find the cooking frustratingly erratic for the prices, detecting technical shortcomings here and there, but dining at Le Manoir remains a special-occasion treat – lubricated by a French-led wine list tailored to celebrations.
Chef/s: Raymond Blanc and Gary Jones. **Open:** all week L and D. **Meals:** main courses £50 to £58. Set L £85 (5 courses) to £130. Set D £41 (5 courses) to £162. **Details:** 80 seats. V menu. Bar. Wheelchairs. Music. Parking.

▌Henley-on-Thames
Shaun Dickens at the Boathouse
Cooking score: 5
Modern British | £45
Station Road, Henley-on-Thames, RG9 1AZ
Tel no: (01491) 577937
shaundickens.co.uk

The Boathouse's Thames-side setting is an obvious trump card, and, whether chilling on the decked terrace or gazing through the dining room's glass frontage, there are wonderful just-messing-about-on-the-river views. However, the big draw here is Shaun Dickens' cooking – his intricate, light, modern dishes delivered with 'bags of flair and surprise'. Welsh lamb, for example, arrives as a trio (pink loin, melting belly and tender kidney) with wild garlic, charred shallot, monk's beard and lemon gel providing balance and a showboating lamb jus adding the final gloss. Likewise starters 'are the real deal', the ordinarily sounding 'broccoli' proving to be perfectly timed florets teamed with preserved lemon, roast garlic and almond, while desserts such as 'blood orange' – with polenta cake, dehydrated milk (wafer) and cream cheese (roll) – add a final flourish. The dining room looks the part: as light, clean-lined and contemporary as the food, service is 'spot-on' and wines are a real strength, with bags of interest (from £21) and an admirable selection by the glass.
Chef/s: Shaun Dickens and James Walshaw. **Open:** Wed to Sun L and D. **Closed:** Mon, Tue. **Meals:** main courses £20 to £26. Set L £26 (2 courses) to £30. Tasting menu £52. **Details:** 50 seats. 30 seats outside. V menu. Bar. Wheelchairs. Music.

▌Kingham
The Kingham Plough
Cooking score: 4
Modern British | £42
The Green, Kingham, OX7 6YD
Tel no: (01608) 658327
thekinghamplough.co.uk

The Plough encapsulates many people's idea of what a country pub should be like. The Cotswold-stone building overlooks a small village green; its bar, all stone and plaster walls, beams and open fires, creates a homely atmosphere that's continued in the pair of dining rooms, one papered in a bold sage, the other dark red, with polished-wood tables and rugs on the floor. The kitchen treats food seriously yet without pretension. What Emily Watkins is good at is familiar combinations of quality ingredients, mostly sourced from a network of well-chosen suppliers. Starters such as duck liver parfait with carrot marmalade and dandelion and carrot salad come with homemade carrot brioche, for example. Main courses are given extra shine by pedigree components, as in a dish of slow-cooked collar of Tamworth pork with 'hungry gap' (greens) and almond pesto and buttered swede. To conclude, there might be a forced rhubarb Alaska. This is unaffected cooking where incidentals charm too: good bread, homemade ice creams, fantastic regional specimens on the mighty cheeseboard, all backed up by local ales, ciders and a wine list that offers good drinking from £24.
Chef/s: Emily Watkins and Thomas Waller. **Open:** all week L, Mon to Sat D. **Closed:** 25 Dec. **Meals:** main courses £16 to £24. Set L and D £16 (2 courses) to £20. **Details:** 55 seats. 24 seats outside. Bar. Wheelchairs. Music. Parking.

The Wild Rabbit

Cooking score: 4
Modern European | £52
Church Street, Kingham, OX7 6YA
Tel no: (01608) 658389
thewildrabbit.co.uk

£5 OFF 🛏

The Wild Rabbit poses many questions. Is it a pub, a restaurant, a brasserie? As to identity, its pitch is as a modern British inn in a quiet village. Expectations are high – partly on account of its owner's Daylesford fame and evident commitment to high quality, partly on account of the prices – so the food has a lot to live up to. At its best the food can be a sheer delight, perhaps Cornish lemon sole with green asparagus, morels, barbecue calçots and smoked-eel butter or tender veal rump with fricassee of braised veal, confit onion and truffle curd. But the cooking doesn't always flatter the amazing produce available and seasoning can be awry, as in a first course of roasted and marinated mackerel with forced rhubarb, turnip and horseradish and an 'underwhelming' frozen dill buttermilk. Puddings, however, seem to be on a roll, judging by recent reports of 'perfect' Cox's apple served with a couple of crisp, richly caramelised shards of puff pastry and creamy custard ice cream. Impeccable service from smartly clad, attentive, polite and accommodating staff also plays a part in achieving a relaxed, professional atmosphere. The sommelier gives good advice on the short, international wine list.
Chef/s: Tim Allen. **Open:** all week L and D.
Meals: main courses £20 to £32. **Details:** 40 seats. Bar. Wheelchairs. Music. Parking.

Symbols

🛏 Accommodation is available
£30 Three courses for less than £30
£5 OFF £5-off voucher scheme
🍾 Notable wine list

▌Kirtlington

LOCAL GEM
The Oxford Arms

Modern British | £30
Troy Lane, Kirtlington, OX5 3HA
Tel no: (01869) 350208
oxford-arms.co.uk

It's the entire package that appeals at this 19th-century village pub, a welcoming, fire-warmed hostelry with bags of rustic personality where the atmosphere is relaxed enough to cater for those who just want a pint of Hook Norton at the bar. Chef/landlord Bryn Jones is also bang on the money when it comes to food, his no-nonsense menu offering appealing ideas, taking in 28-day aged ribeye steak or handmade venison burger with triple-cooked chips, as well as black miso salmon with ginger and garlic pak choi. Desserts hit the comfort zone and wines start at £17.

▌Lechlade
The Plough

Cooking score: 3
British | £29
Lechlade, GL7 3HG
Tel no: (01367) 253543
theploughinnkelmscott.com

🛏 £30

Seventeenth-century stone inns like the Plough are a reasonably common sight in this corner of the Cotswolds but, even so, it's difficult not to be impressed by its picture-pretty setting. A short walk from the summer retreat of the Victorian writer and designer (and co-founder of the Arts and Crafts Movement) William Morris – now a popular tourist attraction in its own right – the Plough stands on the border where Oxfordshire becomes Gloucestershire and is run by the same team behind the Five Alls at Filkins (see entry). Rug-strewn flagstone floors, exposed stone walls and a drinkers' bar – local ales, sandwiches, burgers – tells one side of the story, but a carte of simple, modern cooking and bedrooms complete the package. Kiln-smoked local trout with fennel, cucumber, watercress, blood orange and pomegranate might be followed by steak and ale pie with creamed potato and roasted carrots, while caramelised chilled rice pudding with apricot jam and cinnamon shortbread is a great way to finish. Wines from £18.

Chef/s: Matthew Read. **Open:** Tue to Sun L and D. **Closed:** Mon. **Meals:** main courses £12 to £19. **Details:** 40 seats. 40 seats outside. Bar. Parking.

◼ Murcott
The Nut Tree Inn

Cooking score: 5
Modern British | £46
Main Street, Murcott, OX5 2RE
Tel no: (01865) 331253
nuttreeinn.co.uk

£5
OFF

With a name like the Nut Tree Inn, you might expect rusticity – and this entrancing 15th-century hostelry doesn't disappoint. From the heavily thatched roof, thick stone walls and nearby village pond to the growing patch and porkers rooting around in the open air, it's a purposeful vision of pastoral bliss – but with the bonus of seasonally attuned contemporary food. Inside, the place fulfils its pub duties with real ales, low beams and wood-burning stoves, but siblings Michael and Mary North have other things on their mind: home-baked breads and home-cured salmon lay down a marker for pitch-perfect flavoursome plates of, say, scorched diver-caught scallops with potato mousse, cauliflower 'couscous' and curry oil or ballotine of Cotswold White chicken with smoked potato purée and morel sauce. There's no shame in offering BLTs or beer-battered cod in the bar, although proceedings move up a notch for dessert – perhaps Valrhona chocolate ganache with coffee foam and cardamom ice cream. Organic and biodynamic labels feature heavily on the forward-thinking wine list.

Chef/s: Michael and Mary North. **Open:** Tue to Sun L, Tue to Sat D. **Closed:** Mon, 26 Dec to 16 Jan. **Meals:** main courses £18 to £35. Tasting menu £65 (8 courses). **Details:** 70 seats. 36 seats outside. V menu. Bar. Music. Parking.

◼ Oxford

★ NEW ENTRY ★

Arbequina

Cooking score: 3
Spanish | £26
74 Cowley Road, Oxford, OX4 1JB
Tel no: (01865) 792777
arbequina.co.uk

£30

High stools at the stainless-steel counter make for real conviviality at this neighbourhood tapas bar created by the team behind Oli's Thai (see entry). If you don't want to be so close to the kitchen action, perch on a school-salvage seat at the more conventional tables – but wherever you sit, enjoy a wedge of tortilla with just the right gooey interior and thin-cut potatoes, a plate of blistered Padrón peppers or some grilled spring onions that stand in for calçots on a generous bowl of chunky romesco sauce. Less familiar dishes include beetroot borani – beets smothered in dill, walnuts, gherkins and sheep's cheese – and a standout cocido montañés, a rich meat broth that brims with beans, sausage, morcilla, carrot and crunchy croûtons. A custard tart is an appropriate finale to a relaxed, taste-packed meal that won't break the bank. The compact all-Spanish wine list plugs sherry in proper measures, though there are bottles from £18.

Chef/s: Ben Whyles and Norberto Pena Nunez. **Open:** Thur to Sat L, Mon to Sat D. **Closed:** Sun. **Meals:** tapas £4 to £8

Branca

Cooking score: 1
Modern European | £25
110-111 Walton Street, Oxford, OX2 6AJ
Tel no: (01865) 556111
branca.co.uk
£5 OFF £30

The address may be in the smart Jericho district, but Branca takes an all-comers attitude to feeding Oxford's hungry, and sunning them on the garden terrace when appropriate. 'They make you feel welcome,' explains a reader, 'and the bustle makes you feel young.' Hallelujah. Stone-baked pizzas, risottos, pasta dishes such as rigatoni with a plethora of mushrooms, and one reporter's 'delicious Good Friday hake with a blob of crab butter', are the kind of thing to expect. Showpiece meat dishes include harissa-spiced lamb leg steak with braised white beans, and variously sauced sirloin and rump steaks. Sunday roasts are another valuable resource. Wines from £18.50.

Chef/s: Jamie King. **Open:** Mon to Fri, all day from 12. Sat and Sun, all day from 10. **Meals:** main courses £11 to £20. Set L and D £15 (2 courses). **Details:** 100 seats. 60 seats outside. Bar. Wheelchairs. Music.

Cherwell Boathouse

Cooking score: 2
Modern British | £35
50 Bardwell Road, Oxford, OX2 6ST
Tel no: (01865) 552746
cherwellboathouse.co.uk
£5 OFF

With more than 80 punts for hire, a glorious wine cellar and the prospect of carousing on a gorgeous decked terrace by the river, this enchanting Oxford institution is wholeheartedly devoted to earthly pleasures and serious relaxation. Dating from 1904, the Cherwell Boathouse is also a fine shout for capably handled Anglo-European food, offering all manner of seasonal treats from shellfish fregola or pear, shallot and goats' cheese tarte Tatin to fillet of sea trout with crab croquette, green beans and crab bisque foam, or roast venison loin with braised red cabbage and bitter chocolate jus. Ribeye steaks and slow-cooked pork belly strike a more traditional note, while comfortingly calorific desserts might include banoffee pie, chocolate cheesecake or apple, pear and raisin streusel tart with crème anglaise. Meanwhile, the all-embracing wine list is a rare treat with pages of pedigree global selections, mouthwatering possibilities from the French aristocrats and heaps of new-wave New World stuff – all at realistic prices.

Chef/s: Nick Welford. **Open:** all week L and D. **Closed:** 25 to 30 Dec. **Meals:** main courses £17 to £24. Set L and D £23 (2 courses) to £28. **Details:** 65 seats. 45 seats outside. Bar. Wheelchairs. Music. Parking.

Gee's

Cooking score: 2
Mediterranean | £40
61a Banbury Road, Oxford, OX2 6PE
Tel no: (01865) 553540
gees-restaurant.co.uk

Glasshouse sounds so much more evocative than conservatory, but however one refers to this Victorian gem, it's a 'beautiful place to eat', surrounded by olive trees that reflect the Mediterranean aspirations of the menu. It's been here since the 1980s, so it really isn't out of place to call it an Oxford institution. British seasonal produce gets a decent showing in European-inspired dishes that bring Italy and Spain to mind in particular. Salt cod croquettes with saffron aïoli is a classic done well, while a salad of beetroot, ricotta and hazelnuts has surely been appropriated as a modern British classic by now. Fettuccine with wild boar ragù is a posh spag bol, char-grilled whole sea bass has roasted fennel and capers for company, and baked aubergine parmigiana is a vegetarian option full of flavour. Desserts are on message, although you might find a good old crumble, too. Drink cocktails, bottled beers or wines from £22.

Chef/s: Russell Healey. Open: all week, all day from 12 (9.30am Sat and Sun). Meals: main courses £15 to £24. Set L £14 (2 courses) to £17. Details: 80 seats. 40 seats outside. Bar. Wheelchairs. Music.

The Magdalen Arms
Cooking score: 3
Modern British | £25
243 Iffley Road, Oxford, OX4 1SJ
Tel no: (01865) 243159
magdalenarms.co.uk
£30

The bare-naked tables and floor, russet and purple walls and post-ironic candles on the tables make this big pub worth the trip up the Iffley Road, where the academic quarters feel a world away. And there's a rough-and-ready back terrace for when the sun comes out. What's on the menu is robust, brawny helpings of modern pub food, with the emphasis on punchy flavours and assertive seasonings. Porcini soufflé with Parmesan cream offers a big socking hit of umami to get you going, before main plates such as lamb shoulder with gratin potatoes and pickled red cabbage, or stuffed mackerel with salsa verde and pickled cucumber, make their appearance. 'This is my go-to in Oxford,' confides a reporter. 'The produce is very high-spec and, while simple, the cooking is incredibly reliable.' Finish with a chocolate and coffee pot, or a wodge of pear frangipane tart with vanilla ice cream. Lacing the Prosecco with the juice of local medlars makes a good aperitif, and the wines start at £19 for Languedoc house blends.
Chef/s: Tony Abarno. Open: Tue to Sun L, all week D. Closed: 24 to 26 Dec, 1 Jan. Meals: main courses £10 to £35. Details: 150 seats. 150 seats outside. Bar. Wheelchairs. Music.

Average price ⚄

The average price denotes the price of a three-course meal without wine.

Oli's Thai
Cooking score: 3
Thai | £25
38 Magdalen Road, Oxford, OX4 1RB
Tel no: (01865) 790223
olisthai.com
£30

It seats little more than a couple of dozen people at a time, and, given its popularity, securing a table feels like a prize in itself. This diminutive restaurant opened back in 2013 and word spread fast. The unpretentious interior, the keen staff, the upbeat vibe, it doesn't count for much if the cooking isn't up to snuff, but here the tastes and aromas of Thai cooking hit home. Crispy chickpea salad is a simple enough proposition, as is sweetcorn fritters with slaw and sweet chilli, but the distinct spicing and zingy flavours hit home. Aubergine curry, chicken green curry, deep-fried sea bass... the menu suits sharing, so everyone gets a go. Confit duck panang is a signature dish worthy of the name. Dessert is a choice of custard tart or macarons. The wines on the short list suit the food, or drink Thailand's Chang lager.
Chef/s: Ladd Thurston and Anthony Fossacuzza. Open: Tue to Sat L, Wed to Sat D. Closed: Sun, Mon, 2 weeks Dec. Meals: main courses £11 to £15. Details: 27 seats. 4 seats outside. Wheelchairs. Music. Children over 7 yrs only at D.

The Oxford Kitchen
Cooking score: 3
Modern British | £40
215 Banbury Road, Oxford, OX2 7HQ
Tel no: (01865) 511149
theoxfordkitchen.co.uk

It may be a little out of the centre of the city, but Summertown's indubitably contemporary Oxford Kitchen is no suburban wallflower. Today's favoured natural colours abound, pop art prints hang on the exposed brick walls and the cooking of John Footman is bang on when it comes to meeting modern expectations. A tasting menu gives the opportunity for a full workout if you so desire. Chicken wing pressé

gets things off to a winning start (from the fixed-price carte), with its earthy accompaniments of celeriac and morels, and the runny yolk of a hen's egg. Presentation is eye-catching, techniques are modern, but it's the flavours that linger in the mind – loin of venison, say, with chocolate and juniper sauce, or roasted monkfish tail with quinoa and turkey jus. There's a jazzed up burger, too, and desserts like black cherry soufflé with a perky ground cocoa 'gelato'. Dessert cocktails and an interesting cheese selection prolong the fun.
Chef/s: John Footman. **Open:** Tue to Fri L and D. Sat, all day from 9am. Sun 9 to 4. **Closed:** Mon, 2 weeks Jan. **Meals:** main courses £20 to £27. Set L £20 (2 courses) to £25. Set D £35 (2 courses) to £40. Tasting menu £55. **Details:** 80 seats. 8 seats outside. V menu. Wheelchairs. Music.

LOCAL GEM
Turl Street Kitchen
Modern British | £21
16-17 Turl Street, Oxford, OX1 3DH
Tel no: (01865) 264171
turlstreetkitchen.co.uk

🛏 £30

A charity foundation in a handsome Georgian town house, 'all paper tablecloths and tap water and volubly if breathlessly run', flies the green flag with pride – eco-friendly principles define just about everything, from waste disposal to the ethically sourced food. The kitchen delivers tasty, generous dishes along the lines of organic broccoli and potato soup, grilled Barnsley chop with shaved fennel and green salsa, good English cheeses and custard tart with English strawberries – all at reasonable prices.

Local Gem 🍴

Local Gems are the perfect neighbourhood venues, delivering good, freshly cooked food at great value for money.

▮ Shiplake
★ TOP 50 ★
Orwells
Cooking score: 7
Modern British | £52
Shiplake Row, Shiplake, RG9 4DP
Tel no: (01189) 403673
orwellsatshiplake.co.uk

🍷

On the edge of Binfield Heath, five miles outside Henley, Ryan Simpson and Liam Trotman's rural destination continues to make serious waves. A whitewashed Georgian pub from the outside, it cleverly transforms within to a stylish country restaurant, albeit one retaining its original beamed structure. The level of ingenuity being generated by a kitchen on turbo-drive, fuelled by its own gardens and beehives, is prodigious, the opening statement of intent a nibble that adds a telling dollop of oscietra caviar to a piece of crisply battered chicken in a cheeky homage to KFC. The fast-food witticisms continue with scallop and mushy peas in tartare with shoestring fries in scrunched newspaper, sprayed with vinegar mist, before the main-menu dishes start arriving. Foie gras is pointed up with assertive flavours every which way – rhubarb, liquorice, pistachios and fungi – before sensational plaice seasoned with snippets of bacon in a deep brown verjus, or perhaps tender Wiltshire lamb with crosnes, sprout tops, broccoli and squash for a thoroughly classical production. A cleansing pre-dessert of sorrel sorbet with sweet beet and ginger, might then herald a rhubarb and custard stack incorporating mousse and biscuit layers, while the populist touch returns in 'Bounty Pebble', a shiny chocolate stone containing coconut ice cream, dressed with aerated chocolate and honeycomb. The signature dessert at the moment is a soufflé-light honey sponge spiced with ras-el-hanout. The almost slapstick playfulness of a lot of the food may not be everyone's idea of fun, but the elevated technique on show throughout is breathtaking. And the picture is completed by

a superlative wine list at better-than-fair mark-ups that tracks down outstanding growers all over, opening with an excellent selection in all sizes, from £5.50 the standard measure.
Chef/s: Ryan Simpson and Liam Trotman. **Open:** Wed to Sun L, Wed to Sat D. **Closed:** Mon, Tue, first 2 weeks Jan, 1 week Apr, 2 weeks end Aug/Sept. **Meals:** main courses £22 to £35. Set L £25 (2 courses) to £30. Set D £30 (2 courses) to £35. Tasting menu £95. **Details:** 40 seats. 20 seats outside. Bar. Wheelchairs. Music. Parking.

▮ Sparsholt
The Star Inn
Cooking score: 2
Modern British | £32
Watery Lane, Sparsholt, OX12 9PL
Tel no: (01235) 751873
thestarsparsholt.co.uk
£5 OFF 🛏

A pretty prospect, sitting comfortably beneath the ancient Ridgeway path, the 300-year-old Star Inn is niftily endowed with smart wooden furniture, blue tartan blinds, dried hops draped across a black-beamed ceiling and black flagstone floors in the airy conservatory dining room. The kitchen's offer is pitched 'a step above the norm', portions are never measly and the set-lunch menu is an 'absolute bargain'. At a test meal, a creamy Roquefort mousse arrived as 'a generous quenelle' served alongside a salad of apple matchsticks, shredded celery, pickled red onion and truffle (though minus advertised caramelised walnuts), while lamb shoulder was 'a huge chunk of meat' and came with 'a sizeable wodge of champ' and a 'big dollop' of redcurrant chutney. Desserts tend towards the likes of ginger and rhubarb trifle or sticky toffee soufflé. Service is 'friendly and effective', beers are well kept and wines offer excellent value by the glass or carafe.
Chef/s: Matt Williams. **Open:** Mon to Sat L and D. Sun 12 to 8. **Meals:** main courses £14 to £22. Set L £19 (2 courses) to £22. **Details:** 60 seats. 50 seats outside. Bar. Parking.

Desi Delights

There's no contest – the UK is easily Europe's best place for Indian restaurants. What's more, the variety and quality of the food has soared.

Most local curry houses are run by those of Bangladeshi heritage, so it's worth examining their menus for genuine Bengali dishes; keep an eye out for ingredients such as shatkora, mustard seeds and freshwater fish.

However, the cooking style that dominates northern India and Pakistan is Punjabi cuisine. Bread is the dominant staple here, chargrilled tandoori food is popular, and curries tend to be rich and meaty. Butter chicken is a Punjabi classic, as is the lentil-based dhal makhani.

With the trend for street food, you're increasingly likely to find beach snacks such as bhel puri, which originated in Mumbai. Also from western India, the sweet, veg-based food of Gujarat is served in many north-west London establishments, and Goan dishes are gaining appeal – look for pork vindaloo.

Especially distinctive from the curry-house norm, though, is southern Indian cuisine. Vegetarian cooking predominates here, and dishes such idli sambar and masala dosa are especially enticing.

▊ Stoke Row

The Crooked Billet
Modern British | £35
Newlands Lane, Stoke Row, RG9 5PU
Tel no: (01491) 681048
thecrookedbillet.co.uk

Paul Clerehugh's 17th-century pub is extremely good at winning friends with its delightful rural location (down a single-lane farm track) and agreeable air of rusticity. The easy-going style of the place is much appreciated, too. You can eat at mismatched tables in the country-cosy dining room and expect earthy British heritage cooking with a feel for seasonality – say onion tart baked with local Nettlebed cheese and tomato compote, Old Spot pork belly with baked quince, mustard mash and thyme gravy, and strawberry and almond Bakewell with custard sauce. The drinks list accommodates cocktails as well as wide-ranging cosmopolitan wines, from £22.

▊ Toot Baldon

The Mole Inn
Cooking score: 2
International | £32
Toot Baldon, OX44 9NG
Tel no: (01865) 340001
themoleinn.com

The 300-year-old village inn is a true country hostelry, brimming with atmosphere and abundant in what can only be described as character – from a mishmash of open fires, bare brick and scuffed stone, distressed beams and panelled walls, bare floorboards and floor tiles. Culinary eclecticism may also be expected, and menus (plus lunchtime sandwiches and fish and chips, and full-on Sunday lunch) show British tradition with some global gatherings. Shredded duck and pork belly with chilli, bean shoots, lime, coriander and rocket salad, and cod fillet with linguine, samphire, fish cream sauce with brown Devon crab, tomatoes and soft herbs, show decent

ingredients and flavour combinations that work. Or you could try matching a 28-day aged steak with a bottle of the Mole Inn's 'real underground ale'. Desserts include sticky date pudding with toffee sauce and vanilla ice cream. There is a lovely garden for summer eating, service is helpful and friendly, and the wine list opens at £19.

Chef/s: Gary Witchalls. **Open:** all week L and D. **Closed:** 25 Dec. **Meals:** main courses £16 to £19. Set L and D £18 (2 courses) to £24. **Details:** 67 seats. 50 seats outside. Bar. Wheelchairs. Music. Parking.

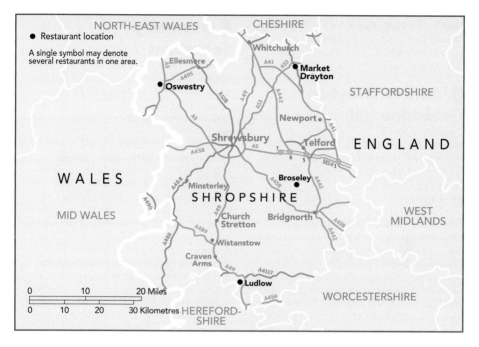

■ Broseley

The King & Thai
Thai | £45
The Forester Arms, Avenue Road, Broseley,
TF12 5DL
Tel no: (01952) 882004
thekingandthai.co.uk

£5
OFF

A feeling of quality and substance pervades
this former pub where Suree Coates has been
cooking for over a decade. She has the measure
of her customers – the cooking is very
Western-friendly and dishes are succinctly and
accurately described. There is plenty of variety
in all departments, from lok chin tod
(skewered pork balls with sweet chilli dipping
sauce) or tom yam goon (tiger prawns in a hot-
and-sour soup) to duck red curry or stir-fried
chicken and vegetable noodles. Wines
from £18.

■ Ludlow

The Green Café
Cooking score: 1
Modern British | £19
Mill on the Green, Ludlow, SY8 1EG
Tel no: (01584) 879872
thegreencafe.co.uk

£30

With Ludlow's ancient castle looming in the
background, the river Teme bubbling along
nearby and the expanses of Millennium Green
ready to be enjoyed, this converted watermill
provides daytime sustenance for locals and
tourists. The affix 'green' also extends to the
lunch menu, which is peppered with eco-
friendly ingredients: there's always a soup
(organic chicken, white bean and pancetta
minestrone) ahead of pasta, salads, omelettes
and puds along the lines of warm ginger cake
with apple sauce. To drink, Shropshire-
brewed beers and local ciders line up alongside
10 French regional wines.

Chef/s: Clive Davis. **Open:** Tue to Sun L only.
Closed: Mon, 2 Jan to 1 Feb. **Meals:** main courses
£7 to £11. **Details:** 30 seats. 25 seats outside.
Wheelchairs.

■ Market Drayton
Goldstone Hall

Cooking score: 3
Modern British | £48
Goldstone Road, Market Drayton, TF9 2NA
Tel no: (01630) 661202
goldstonehall.com

£5 OFF 🍷 🛏

It boasts one of the largest and most
productive restaurant kitchen gardens in the
UK, but the lovely walled garden at this
handsome country pile is just one of the
attractions – throw in an oak-panelled dining
room and Victorian conservatory and you're in
true Agatha Christie territory. The building is
Georgian, although there has been a dwelling
on this site since the Middle Ages. It's a family-
run affair with all the attendant care and
attention to detail, not least in the kitchen,
where Christopher Weatherstone takes a
broadly modern British approach with home-
grown and local ingredients – maybe cured
salmon with oyster emulsion and fennel,
ahead of loin and braised neck of lamb with
swede and black cabbage. The combination of
garden and kitchen turns out some great meat-
free options, too – crispy polenta with
textures of onion and sage, for instance. The
substantial global wine list includes a good
selection of vegetarian and biodynamic
options, plus plenty of half-bottles.
Chef/s: Chris Weatherstone. **Open:** all week L and
D. **Closed:** 26 Dec. **Meals:** set L £27 (2 courses) to
£32. Set D £48. Sun L £36. **Details:** 60 seats. 25
seats outside. Bar. Wheelchairs. Music. Parking.

■ Oswestry
Sebastians

Cooking score: 3
French | £45
45 Willow Street, Oswestry, SY11 1AQ
Tel no: (01691) 655444
sebastians-hotel.co.uk

🛏

With its ancient beams, heavy wood
panelling, blazing fires and barewood floors,
Sebastians looks every inch the redoubtable
English coaching inn, although this 17th-
century watering hole now plies its trade as a
civilised restaurant-with-rooms serving food
with a broad-minded French accent. Mark
Sebastian Fisher's concise monthly menus
tread a line between bourgeois classic and
nouvelle eclectic, with amuse-bouches, mid-
course sorbets and post-prandial chocolate
truffles all called into play. A starter of duck,
pistachio and pear terrine could share the
billing with warm fillet of mackerel,
guacamole and grapefruit salad, while mains
take in everything from fillet and belly of
pork with black pudding, ratatouille and cider
sauce to a selection of fish in tomato, saffron
and sweet pepper sauce with braised fennel. To
finish, soak up the boozy delights of honey
sponge pudding with whisky caramel and
mead ice cream. There are some useful half-
bottles on the French-led wine list.
Chef/s: Mark Sebastian Fisher. **Open:** Wed to Sat D
only. **Closed:** Sun, Mon, Tue, 24 and 25 Dec, 1 Jan.
Meals: set D £45 (5 courses). **Details:** 32 seats. 15
seats outside. Wheelchairs. Music. Parking. Children
over 12 yrs only.

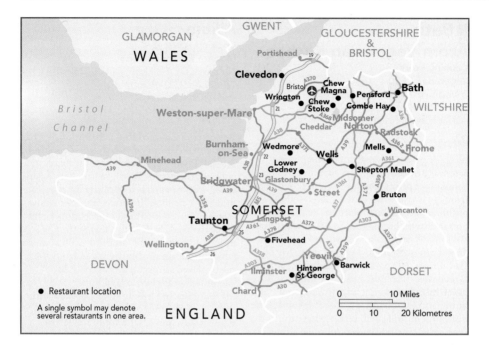

▪ Barwick
Little Barwick House
Cooking score: 5
Modern British | £50
Rexes Hollow Lane, Barwick, BA22 9TD
Tel no: (01935) 423902
littlebarwick.co.uk

🍷 🛏

'Little Barwick House is a story of enthusiastic enterprise,' declares a devotee of Tim and Emma Ford's hideaway – a Georgian dower house in three acres of grounds; others are simply amazed that the couple have maintained such high standards during their 17-year residency. Like the building, Tim Ford's painstaking food 'doesn't defer to fashion' ('an assurance that the menu didn't feature froths and foams was decisive in securing our booking,' admitted one happy soul). Instead, he fashions dishes of unwavering consistency from top-drawer ingredients: hand-dived West Bay scallops arrive with pea purée and crispy pancetta, while Gressingham duck breast sits well with wild mushroom risotto and new season's asparagus. There's also familiarity in the shape of Cornish turbot with Champagne sauce or local lamb enriched with aubergine and garlic confit, before dessert brings banana tarte Tatin with star anise ice cream. The authoritative wine list caters to 'every conceivable taste', with strong global coverage, some tasty off-piste excursions and around 30 tiptop selections by the glass.

Chef/s: Tim Ford. **Open:** Wed to Sat L, Mon to Sat D. **Closed:** Sun, first 3 weeks Jan. **Meals:** set L £28 (2 courses) to £31. Set D £44 (2 courses) to £50. **Details:** 40 seats. 12 seats outside. Bar. Parking. Children over 5 yrs only.

Symbols

🥄

🛏 Accommodation is available
£30 Three courses for less than £30
£5 OFF £5-off voucher scheme
🍷 Notable wine list

Bath
Acorn Vegetarian Kitchen
Cooking score: 3
Vegetarian | £30
2 North Parade Passage, Bath, BA1 1NX
Tel no: (01225) 446059
acornvegetariankitchen.co.uk
£5
OFF

Its golden Bath-stone frontage may come across as just another pretty face, but this place is full of surprises. Dating from 1622 – the frontage was added a century later – the building was the birthplace of the British postal system, but nowadays offers vegetarian cooking of singular ambition and creativity. The credit goes to Steven Yates, formerly of Bath Priory (see entry) and the late Sienna in Dorchester, who now heads the kitchen. At lunch he offers snappy sides (cashew nut butter and sourdough, polenta chips and garlic mayonnaise) and small plates (pine nut risotto with slow-cooked Brussels sprouts) alongside a kindly priced set lunch. At dinner, oven-roasted Jerusalem artichokes with a toasted sunflower-seed butter and a touch of pink grapefruit is a typical opener, while walnut agnolotti in a rich mushroom stew with salsify, kale and haricot beans is typical of his kaleidoscopic but eminently sensible use of ingredients. To finish, try rhubarb with almond Amaretto cream, fennel sorbet and almond buckwheat crumb. The wide-ranging wine list is mostly vegan, and full of interest.
Chef/s: Steven Yates. **Open:** all week L, Mon to Fri D. **Closed:** 25 and 26 Dec. **Meals:** set L £18 (2 courses) to £23. Set D £27 (2 courses) to £33. Sun L £19. **Details:** 34 seats. V menu. Music.

Symbols

- Accommodation is available
- £30 Three courses for less than £30
- £5 OFF £5-off voucher scheme
- Notable wine list

Allium
Cooking score: 4
Modern European | £35
Abbey Hotel, 1-3 North Parade, Bath, BA1 1LF
Tel no: (01225) 461603
abbeyhotelbath.co.uk

Reporters are agreed that a change of chef has not dented Allium's 'seriously good' cooking. Rupert Taylor continues the tradition of cooking the best of British with a pan-Asian twist – his menu has something for everyone, offering a canny split between snacks, sharing plates and brasserie classics like haddock and triple-cooked chips with 'a lovely fresh pea purée and homemade tartare', as well as more adventurous dishes. Start with an 'enjoyable' miso-glazed salmon with compressed cucumber, gooseberries and yuzu mayonnaise, and follow with a 'packed with flavour' roast rump of lamb with baby gem, white onion purée, salsa verde and Jersey Royals. Puddings are a highlight if poached rhubarb with jasmine, pistachio cake, green-tea crumble and rhubarb sorbet is anything to go by. The funky, theatrical décor, adorned with a 'fascinating range' of modern art from the owners' private collection, helps you forget you're in a hotel dining room. The efficient service is 'really friendly and welcoming'. Wine, from an eclectic, regularly changing list, starts at £24.
Chef/s: Rupert Taylor. **Open:** all week L and D. **Meals:** main courses £15 to £25. Set L and D £20 (2 courses) to £25. Sun L £28. **Details:** 62 seats. 40 seats outside. Bar. Wheelchairs. Music.

The Bath Priory
Cooking score: 5
Modern European | £80
Weston Road, Bath, BA1 2XT
Tel no: (01225) 331922
thebathpriory.co.uk

Formerly of The Ritz (see entry), Michael Nizzero brings a similar sense of opulence to the Priory with his delicate, flawlessly presented food. A meal here feels like an occasion. In fine weather, arrive early to wander round the stunning gardens or, at the very least, bag a table by the window as, by comparison, the dining rooms are 'tastefully beige' in marked contrast to some of the hotel's antique-stuffed public spaces. An amuse-bouche of Little Gem gazpacho poured (at the table) over cubes of torched mackerel and tiny balls of apple and yoghurt proved to be an 'extraordinarily delicious' introduction. An intense chicken consommé (again poured at table) beautifully complemented the wild mushroom cappelletti and cauliflower couscous, while lamb loin arrived perched on a fragrant basil cream ('so vibrant and fresh') accompanied by a tube of mandolined courgette stuffed with lightly spiced fregola. Occasionally, the balance of flavours belies the kitchen's ambition, though not in the case of salted-caramel fondant with banana sorbet, butterscotch 'and lime shaved at the table for extra drama', a dish declared 'exemplary'. A friendly sommelier will navigate you through the encyclopaedic wine list, which starts at £28 and 'ends at a second mortgage'.

Chef/s: Michael Nizzero. **Open:** all week L and D. **Meals:** set L £30 (3 courses). Set D £85 (3 courses). Sun L £35. **Details:** 50 seats. Parking. Children over 12 yrs only.

★ NEW ENTRY ★

Chez Dominique

Cooking score: 2
Modern French | £28
15 Argyle Street, Bath, BA2 4BQ
Tel no: (01225) 463482
chezdominique.co.uk
£5 OFF £30

Chris Tabbitt used to work as sous-chef at Bibendum (see entry) and his French-inspired menu has all the hallmarks of a chef who once cooked dishes created by Simon Hopkinson. His first solo venture is a cosy contemporary French bistro close to Pulteney Bridge, alcoves and fireplaces acting as a reminder of the building's Georgian heritage, but with bare floorboards and unadorned tables, duck egg

blue walls and clusters of bare filament bulbs dangling from the ceiling adding a modern touch. An early-summer test meal delivered a 'super-fresh' Dorset crab mayonnaise with broad beans, baby gem and dill, followed by precisely cooked rump of lamb teamed with a well-balanced caponata, roast tomatoes and a robust jus. A perfectly molten chocolate fondant was paired with a toffee-like salted-caramel ice cream and chopped hazelnuts. The prix fixe menu is excellent value and geared towards diners heading to the nearby Bath Theatre Royal. The French-heavy wine list starts at £19 and offers 10 by glass.

Chef/s: Chris Tabbitt. **Open:** all week L, Mon to Sat D. **Closed:** 25 and 26 Dec. **Meals:** main courses £14 to £21. Set L and D £14 (2 courses) to £17. **Details:** 40 seats. Music.

The Circus

Cooking score: 2
Modern European | £32
34 Brock Street, Bath, BA1 2LN
Tel no: (01225) 466020
thecircusrestaurant.co.uk
£5 OFF

In a quiet street located between Bath's famed Circus and Royal Crescent, Alison Golden's popular restaurant continues to attract many loyal locals as well as visitors. With its greens and greys, white cornicing and original fireplaces, the narrow Georgian room is relaxed, although one solo diner, put in one of the two tiny window alcoves, found it to be 'possibly the most uncomfortable seating I have ever had the misfortune to be offered'. The food here is inspired by Elizabeth David and Jane Grigson and the concise menus are in step with the seasons. Start with red mullet fillets marinated in blood orange and lemon juice served with smoky aubergine purée, olive tapenade and prosciutto, before moving on to rabbit, chicken and crayfish 'cooked in good stock' with calasparra rice, piquillo peppers, chorizo, white wine and saffron. To finish, there's dark chocolate and star anise truffle, white chocolate and stem ginger mousse with miso caramel. Wines from £17.70.

Chef/s: Alison Golden, Máté Andrasko and Tom Bally. **Open:** Mon to Sat L and D. **Closed:** Sun, 3 weeks Dec. **Meals:** main courses £17 to £20. **Details:** 50 seats. 8 seats outside. Music. Children over 7 yrs only.

Corkage

Cooking score: 2
Modern European | £20
132a Walcot Street, Bath, BA1 5BG
Tel no: (01225) 422577
corkagebath.com

The original idea was a short-lived pop-up within a wine shop but now Marty Grant and Richard Knighting's 'convivial and bustling neighbourhood wine bar' is here to stay. Tables are hard to secure – booking essential – with diners squeezed into every corner of the intimate space, happy to sit cheek by jowl beneath a sail-like ceiling and wait for the tersely written blackboard menu to be explained in detail. Among the small plates might be cumin roast cauliflower, followed by slow-cooked pork belly with giant couscous and beetroot or bream with broad beans and pickled lemon dressing. Pear and frangipane tart is one way to end a meal. With 50 wines served by the glass and an interesting selection of bottles from £19.50, it's 'brilliant from a wine perspective', although the absence of a printed wine list ('and price tags not visible when ordering') means your final bill might surprise you.

Chef/s: Richard Knighting. **Open:** Thur to Sat L, Wed to Sat D. **Closed:** Sun, Mon, Tue. **Meals:** main courses £8 to £14. **Details:** 38 seats. Wheelchairs. Music. Children before 8.30pm only.

Average price

The average price denotes the price of a three-course meal without wine.

The Dower House

Cooking score: 3
Modern European | £72
Royal Crescent Hotel, 16 Royal Crescent, Bath, BA1 2LS
Tel no: (01225) 823333
royalcrescent.co.uk

Having celebrated its 250th anniversary in 2017, Bath's Royal Crescent Hotel still cuts it as an iconic social and cultural destination. Fans of Georgian architecture and spa treatments should have a field day here, but food lovers are also well served by the elegant Dower House restaurant. Overlooking a sheltered secret garden, this relaxed venue offers sophisticated contemporary cooking against a soothing backdrop of soft fabrics, muted tones and silk wallpaper. The evening's menu is a fixed-price six-course affair that might begin with a sherry-spiked cep espuma, and conclude with an elegantly modern pairing of poached peach and lavender pannacotta with honeycomb and Champagne. In between, sharp execution is the hallmark of, say, Cornish mackerel ceviche with horseradish sorbet or Anjou squab accompanied by beetroot chutney, hay-baked potato, beetroot variations and rainbow chard. Prices are true to the patrician setting – a theme that extends to a heavy-duty international wine list.

Chef/s: David Campbell. **Open:** all week D only. **Meals:** set D £72 (6 courses). **Details:** 45 seats. 100 seats outside. V menu. Bar. Wheelchairs. Music.

Menu Gordon Jones

Cooking score: 5
Modern British | £55
2 Wellsway, Bath, BA2 3AQ
Tel no: (01225) 480871
menugordonjones.co.uk

The location on a traffic-choked corner isn't exactly auspicious, but when Gordon Jones opened his restaurant in 2012, it quickly became a gastronomic destination. The dining room is basic and small, a mix of bare tables, IKEA-style blinds and an antler chandelier, with the chef's personal playlist of rock music in the background. Diners still seem to love the no-menu 'surprise' concept, 'although we did struggle to catch the dish descriptions from the quick-talking, low-volume staff or perhaps the music – Kings of Leon, Smiths, Bowie – was a little too loud'. But the cooking is confident, thoughtful, light of touch and perfectly in step with the seasons – a late May menu saw 'wild sea trout and Alphonso mango both on the menu' – and an element of surprise amplifies the open kitchen's fearlessly experimental cooking. A paper bag filled with homemade bread accompanied by test tubes of dipping oils, and snacks such as Dorset snails, might lead on to sweet-and-sour pepper soup with chorizo and Parmesan, then smoked haddock arrives with crispy pheasant egg and leeks or suckling spring lamb tart with cauliflower cream and Puy lentils. And that Alphonso mango appeared with saffron and pistachio kulfi, English raspberries and chocolate crémeux in a 'memorable dessert'. Wines from £26.

Chef/s: Gordon Jones. **Open:** Tue to Sat L and D. **Closed:** Sun, Mon. **Meals:** set L £50 (5 courses). Set D £55 (6 courses). **Details:** 22 seats. V menu. Wheelchairs. Music. Children over 12 yrs only.

The Olive Tree

Cooking score: 4
Modern British | £55
The Queensberry Hotel, 4-7 Russel Street, Bath, BA1 2QF
Tel no: (01225) 447928
olivetreebath.co.uk

£5 OFF

Comfort and seemingly effortless chic is what the Queensberry is all about, as well as location – the elegant Georgian townhouse hotel is just two minutes' walk from the Royal Crescent. Reporters find its restaurant hard to fault for service and food, and note that it has a sense of occasion without being too formal or stuffy: 'so much fun, from the amuse-bouche to the petits fours, and great wine parings to boot'. Spread over three lower-ground-floor rooms, the Olive Tree delivers well-practised

six- or seven-course tasting menus of modern British dishes, offering concentrated flavours teased from top-quality raw materials. Excellent langoustine with basil gnocchi in an intense bisque, and a melt-in-the-mouth duck liver torchon with rhubarb, Champagne and gingerbread have been singled out, along with English rose veal with cauliflower cheese, grelot onions and hazelnut. Carefully wrought desserts include a 70 per cent Valrhona chocolate confection with custard, yoghurt and passion fruit. It all comes with a good-value wine list that's obviously a labour of love, full of fascinating selections from around the globe.

Chef/s: Chris Cleghorn. **Open:** Fri to Sun L, Tue to Sun D. **Closed:** Mon, 1 week in: Jan; Jul/Aug, Nov. **Meals:** main courses £24 to £26. Set L £26 (2 courses) to £34. Tasting menu £68 (6 courses) to £80. **Details:** 60 seats. V menu. Bar. Music.

LOCAL GEM

King William

Modern British | £30
36 Thomas Street, Bath, BA1 5NN
Tel no: (01225) 428096
kingwilliampub.com

£5 OFF

Despite outward appearances, this is one city pub where food definitely takes precedence over pints of beer – although drinkers are warmly welcomed. When it comes to the seasonal, robust modern British cooking, visitors relish everything they are offered, from confit of Gressingham duck with fig and port purée, via hake with squid-ink linguine, black pudding, black garlic and Kalamata olive tapenade, or roasted beef rump with baked beef suet pudding, to rhubarb, orange and gingerbread trifle. A thoughtfully assembled choice of wines opens at £18.

Yak Yeti Yak
Nepalese | £25
12 Pierrepont Street, Bath, BA1 1LA
Tel no: (01225) 442299
yakyetiyak.co.uk

£30

Occupying the basement of three converted Georgian townhouses close to Bath railway station, this cheerful, multi-roomed restaurant serves inexpensive and proper Nepalese home cooking. Whether you sit on traditional floor cushions or eat at cramped tables, the kitchen delivers flavours that are subtle and light, and vegetarians are well catered for. 'Delicious' deep-fried, crispy spiced salmon pieces followed by lamb bhutuwa with fried rice delighted one reporter, or there could be fragrant steamed pork momo dumplings or chicken stir-fried with green chillies, peppers, tomato and spring onion. Wines from £15.90.

■ Bruton
Roth Bar & Grill
Cooking score: 3
Modern British | £28
Durslade Farm, Dropping Lane, Bruton, BA10 0NL
Tel no: (01749) 814700
rothbarandgrill.co.uk

£30

On a 1,000-acre working farm that supplies the restaurant with meat from rare-breed animals reared in the surrounding fields, this bucolic barn conversion is a unique combination of great food and fine art. It's part of the Hauser & Wirth gallery, the neon-chandeliered cocktail bar, café and restaurant strewn with interesting artwork, all of which sets the scene for enjoyably no-frills cooking that relies on top-drawer produce. As well as steaks from the salt room, burgers, charcuterie and salads, main courses might take in grilled Dorset sea bass, watercress, baby gem and radish, or crispy pheasant breast with wild

garlic, wet polenta and chilli. Forced rhubarb and Mallorcan almond tart with clotted cream is one way to finish, although there is a board of excellent local cheeses from Westcombe Dairy and Montgomery. Local artisan ales and ciders complement a lively wine list (from £24).
Chef/s: Steve Horrell. Open: Tue to Sun L, Fri and Sat D. Closed: Mon, 25 and 26 Dec, first week Jan. Meals: main courses £12 to £28. Set L and D £20 (2 courses) to £25. Sun L £18. Details: 100 seats. 80 seats outside. V menu. Bar. Wheelchairs. Music.

■ Chew Magna
The Pony & Trap
Cooking score: 5
Modern British | £40
Knowle Hill, Chew Magna, BS40 8TQ
Tel no: (01275) 332627
theponyandtrap.co.uk

Out in the rural interstice of Bristol and Bath, the Eggletons' whitewashed country pub looks very much the unvarnished part, with tables on the back lawn, and a jolly, tile-floored interior with clothless tables under a low ceiling. Josh Eggleton is a man on a mission to bring the finest of West Country and south-western produce to the fore, presented in a cooking style that mixes stalwart tradition – steamed mussels in local cider, pork chop and black pudding with spiced apple – with excursions into showboating modernism. Among the latter have been scallop ceviche with seaweed, elderflower and blackcurrant oil, and a timbale of shredded lobster with sheep's curd and toasted sourdough, while best end and breast of lamb with red pepper purée and a polenta chip offers unimpeachable local meat. Cleanse the palate with a gin ice lolly, before nutmegged rice pudding and strawberry sorbet closes the deal. Wines arranged by style open at £4.75 for a standard glass.
Chef/s: Josh Eggleton. Open: all week L and D. Closed: 25 Dec. Meals: main courses £18 to £27. Sun L £35 (3 courses). Details: 64 seats. 25 seats outside. Music. Parking.

Chew Stoke

LOCAL GEM
Salt & Malt
British | £22
Chew Valley Lake, Walley Lane, Chew Stoke,
BS40 8TF
Tel no: (01275) 333345
saltmalt.com

£30

On the northern edge of the Mendip Hills
Area of Outstanding Natural Beauty, Salt &
Malt sits by the Chew Valley Lake. Open for
breakfast, lunch and dinner, it's a café, tea
room and take-away, where breakfast can set
you up for the day, fish and chips is done
properly (it's the speciality of the house) and
stone bass might arrive in a rich turbot sauce.
It's a family affair, and a proper foodie family at
that – the Eggletons of Pony & Trap fame (see
entry). Wines start at £18.

Clevedon

LOCAL GEM
Murrays
Italian | £24
87-93 Hill Road, Clevedon, BS21 7PN
Tel no: (01275) 341555
murraysofclevedon.co.uk

£30

Reuben Murray picked up a civic award for
the renovation work involved in extending his
neighbourhood eatery, which now embraces
an Italian-themed restaurant, wine bar and
deli. A pizza and sandwich menu suits
shoppers and locals on the go, while the full
line-up covers a lot of ground from home-
cured bresaola with capers and artichokes to
chicken Caesar salad, penne with 'nduja or
poached hake fillet in a light cream broth with
shrimps, spinach and fennel. Promising Italian
regional wines, too.

Combe Hay
The Wheatsheaf
Cooking score: 3
Modern British | £36
Combe Hay, BA2 7EG
Tel no: (01225) 833504
wheatsheafcombehay.com

Beer has been brewed in this idyllic spot
outside Bath since the 1500s, with some of the
original parts of the building dating from that
time, and it's been a pub since the 18th century.
The white-painted inn has character inside
and out, with today's rustic-chic incarnation
done out in heritage colours. A Taste of the
West Country menu reveals a passion for
regional produce, and a seven-course tasting
menu gives the kitchen team full rein to
express themselves. Seared foie gras with
poached hen's egg and toasted muffin shows
recognition of classic ways, while crispy chilli
beef with minty yoghurt has more
contemporary leanings. Brill is roasted whole,
chateaubriand is for two to share, and Exmoor
partridge Kiev might appear under the West
Country banner. There is fish and chips, too,
and desserts extend to dark chocolate délice
with peanut-butter ice cream. The wine list
sticks to European territories, and is
particularly big on Bordeaux.
Chef/s: Eddy Rains. **Open:** Tue to Sun L, Tue to Sat
D. **Closed:** Mon, 1 week Jan. **Meals:** main courses
£20 to £25. Set L and D £24 (2 courses) to £29. Sun L
£21 (2 courses) to £27. Tasting menu £60.
Details: 55 seats. 80 seats outside. V menu. Bar.
Music. Parking.

▌Fivehead
The Langford

Cooking score: 6
Modern British | £39
Langford Fivehead, Lower Swell, Fivehead,
TA3 6PH
Tel no: (01460) 282020
langfordfivehead.co.uk

With its flagstoned halls, intricate plasterwork ceilings, cracked beams and ancient graffiti scrawled on to stone lintels, this fine-looking early-Tudor manor house positively oozes antiquity – although current owners Olly and Rebecca Jackson are keen to promote the Langford as a contemporary retreat *par excellence*. The building itself is surrounded by seven acres of parkland, with orchards and a productive kitchen garden yielding a constant supply of seasonal ingredients for Olly's high-spec modern cooking. Readers have been bowled over by the 'fabulous' food ('mouth-watering' fillet of hake, 'show-stopping' rolled cannon of sirloin), but weekly fixed-price menus also suggest restraint, intelligence and a refreshing lack of showboating. Home-smoked duck breast is a star attraction (perhaps served with walnuts and pickled peaches or with a leg croquette and medlar jelly), while mains could take in anything from slow-cooked belly and pancetta-wrapped loin of pork with red cabbage, celeriac and beetroot to pan-fried cod with romanesco, leeks and salsify. After that, the Langford's orchard contributes to 'beautifully presented' desserts such as iced apple parfait with apple and cinnamon sorbet. France is a major player on the well-spread wine list.
Chef/s: Olly Jackson. **Open:** Wed to Fri L, Tue to Sat D. **Closed:** Sun, Mon, 25 and 26 Dec, first 2 weeks Jan, 23 Jul to 7 Aug. **Meals:** set L £28 (2 courses) to £33. Set D £39. **Details:** 20 seats. Wheelchairs. Music. Parking. Children over 8 yrs only.

▌Hinton St George
The Lord Poulett Arms

Cooking score: 2
Modern British | £30
High Street, Hinton St George, TA17 8SE
Tel no: (01460) 73149
lordpoulettarms.com

A pub since 1680, it's not difficult to imagine 17th-century folk wandering up the street and into this thatched inn. Original features coexist with appropriately rustic furniture, but rest assured it's a stylish place, with a kitchen that turns out some bright modern food. Goats' curd is a fashionable ingredient to start with, but here it's turned into a pannacotta and served with piccalilli and toast, or cockles and tomatoes might come together in a risotto with samphire salad. Main courses include fish and chips and Somerset hot dog, although this kitchen can also turn out skrei cod with truffle emulsion and chestnut gnocchi, and river Exe mussels with English chorizo and local cider. The cheese platter is English through and through, while, among desserts, banana sundae with salted-caramel popcorn appeals to the inner child. The wine list is cleverly put together to aid decision making.
Chef/s: Philip Verden. **Open:** all week L and D. **Closed:** 25 and 26 Dec, 1 Jan. **Meals:** main courses £14 to £20. Set L and early D £16 (2 courses, Mon to Sat) to £20. Sun L £19 (2 courses) to £23. **Details:** 60 seats. 65 seats outside. Bar. Music. Parking.

▌Lower Godney

LOCAL GEM
The Sheppey

International | £28
Lower Godney, BA5 1RZ
Tel no: (01458) 831594
thesheppey.co.uk

'We're half barn, half London club,' say the owners of the Sheppey – an oddball watering hole in the heart of the Somerset Levels famed for its live music sessions, home-brewed God Beer and 'really good' food. Steaks and burgers come from the BBQ, but also look for trendy items ranging from fried chicken with bulgur pilaf and mushroom ketchup to 'perfectly cooked' sea bream with fennel and samphire. Just add bags of 'character and confidence', modest prices and staff who 'really enjoy their jobs'.

▊ Mells
Talbot Inn

Cooking score: 3
Modern British | £35
Selwood Street, Mells, BA11 3PN
Tel no: (01373) 812254
talbotinn.com

Horse-drawn carriages may no longer trundle through the archway that fronts this stone-built 15th-century inn, but the Talbot plays the heritage card with its massive oak doors, roaring fires and even a banqueting-style grill room where meat and fish are cooked over a magnificent open fire and served at long communal tables (weekends only). There's also something wholly traditional about the bar and the quaint dining areas, whether you're supping a pint of Talbot Ale or tackling some generously portioned food. Ploughman's and pub staples share the billing with more modern combos such as lightly cured monkfish with pickled mussels, cauliflower and puffed wild rice or rump steak with smoked beetroot, bone marrow, horseradish butter and chips. To finish, West Country cheeses compete with sturdy puddings such as egg custard tart or sticky rum sponge with grilled pineapple and coconut ice cream. Wines are also a cut above.
Chef/s: Pravin Nayar. **Open:** all week L and D.
Meals: main courses £13 to £22. **Details:** 80 seats.
30 seats outside. Bar. Music. Parking.

▊ Pensford

LOCAL GEM
The Pig

Modern British | £35
Hunstrete House, Pensford, BS39 4NS
Tel no: (01761) 490490
thepighotel.com

Set amid beautiful gardens and dedicated to sourcing the finest locally grown ingredients (from its own huge kitchen garden where possible), you'd be hard-pressed to find a nicer place to have lunch on a summer's day. The hotel may be Georgian, but the restaurant channels a potting-shed vibe, which suits the vivid modern British combinations on the menu, say a just-picked-that-morning dish of Victoria rhubarb served with goats' curd, orange and walnuts, and Wiltshire wild boar chop with chorizo and char-grilled Jersey Royals. Wines from £20.

▊ Shepton Mallet

LOCAL GEM
Blostin's

Anglo-French | £35
29 Waterloo Road, Shepton Mallet, BA4 5HH
Tel no: (01749) 343648
blostins.co.uk

£5 OFF

Now well into their fourth decade as custodians of this affable neighbourhood bolt-hole, Nick and Lynne Reed certainly know how to keep their customers satisfied. Eschewing fashionable trends in favour of dependable cooking founded on sound principles (and sound regional ingredients), their fixed-priced dinner menus might offer the likes of salmon fishcakes with apple and beetroot salad, chicken breast with mushrooms and Marsala, and sticky toffee pudding with butterscotch sauce. Seasonal specialities add variety, and fair pricing extends to the 40-bin wine list.

▌Taunton

Augustus

Cooking score: 5
Modern British | £30
3 The Courtyard, St James Street, Taunton,
TA1 1JR
Tel no: (01823) 324354
augustustaunton.co.uk

A glassed extension projecting into the little courtyard announces the presence of Augustus, while whitewashed walls, a bare floor and blackboard create a modern bistro ambience within. Richard Guest's town-centre venue offers easily comprehensible, big-hearted plates of European-influenced flavour, with a little Asian element, perhaps Thai-style avocado and peanut salad, folded in for good measure. Otherwise, expect calamari fritters with herbed mayonnaise, or seared foie gras with Jerusalem artichoke and toasted hazelnuts, to open proceedings, before robust mains such as whole lemon sole with creamed Hispi and clams, or venison pie with faggots, greens and mash, make their appearances. It's the kind of menu on which you'll confidently assume a ribeye steak and fries may be got, and will find it happily partnered with baked chorizo and peppers. Desserts offer populist indulgences like salt caramel and chocolate Paris-Brest, or treacle tart with ginger ice cream. An equitably spread wine list does the job, with bottles from £17.

Chef/s: Richard Guest. **Open:** Tue to Sat L and D.
Closed: Sun, Mon, 23 Dec to 6 Jan. **Meals:** main courses £13 to £25. **Details:** 40 seats.

Brazz

Cooking score: 1
British | £29
Castle Bow, Taunton, TA1 1NF
Tel no: (01823) 252000
brazz.co.uk

The Chapman family has run the Castle Hotel since 1950, but they keep things current with this recently refurbished brasserie. Modern in style but sticking to the classics when it comes to the food, Brazz is the cheerful all-day sibling of the Castle Bow restaurant next door (see entry). The broad menu is fairly priced and is acutely aware of seasonality and provenance. Lunchtime sandwiches, fish and chips, steaks and salads appeal, but look to the carte for fishcake with slow-cooked leeks, lemon butter and chive sauce, which could be followed by roast Somerset lamb rump and braised shoulder, served with courgette, tomato, and dauphinois potatoes. Finish with chocolate mousse with raspberry sorbet or the excellent board of local cheeses. Wine from £16.95.

Chef/s: Liam Finnegan. **Open:** all week L and D.
Closed: 25 Dec. **Meals:** main courses £10 to £20.
Set L and early D £12 (2 courses). **Details:** 52 seats.
12 seats outside. Bar. Music. Parking.

Castle Bow

Cooking score: 6
Modern British | £38
Castle Green, Taunton, TA1 1NF
Tel no: (01823) 328328
castlebow.com

With its imposing stone battlements, arched windows and ancient rose garden, Taunton's Castle Hotel (once a Norman fortress) looks like antiquity personified, yet its kitchen has been in the vanguard of reinvented British cuisine since Gary Rhodes' tenure back in the 1980s. The elegant flagship dining room is done out in vintage style with mirrored walls and Art Deco lampshades, but Liam Finnegan's cooking is modern: seasonal, simple and confident, backed up by pin-sharp service. An amuse-bouche of pea and shallot soup and three exceptional homemade, 'still-warm' breads opened a 'superlatively good meal' for one reporter. Brixham crab tortellini – three delicate, silky parcels of handmade pasta generously filled with very fresh white crabmeat – topped with a frothy, creamy bisque 'with bursts of orange and a salty grassiness from sea herbs' reveals a chef who has tailored his food to the needs of his customers rather than aiming to show off how clever he is. Next up, Stream Farm Dexter beef is a sensation, soft and tender with 'such a depth of flavour' and teamed with watercress purée, roasted courgettes and garlic, and an 'utterly delicious' crisp, breadcrumbed potato dauphine. A 'wobbly' slice of egg custard tart 'with the thinnest, crispest pastry', a few pieces of poached forced rhubarb and an intense nutmeg ice cream ensured a triumphant finale. Since taking over the hotel in the 1950s, the Chapman family has accrued a magnificent wine cellar filled with fine vintages and bargains by the glass.

Chef/s: Liam Finnegan. **Open:** Wed to Sat D only. **Closed:** Sun, Mon Tue, Jan. **Meals:** main courses £19 to £21. Tasting menu £60 (6 courses). **Details:** 36 seats. Bar. Music. Parking. Children over 5yrs only.

The Willow Tree

Cooking score: 4
Modern British | £33
3 Tower Lane, Taunton, TA1 4AR
Tel no: (01823) 352835
thewillowtreerestaurant.com

You would be unlikely to stumble across this small, secluded old house beside a canal by accident, even though it's in the centre of Taunton; those who know where it is consider it worth the journey. Dinner is the main business (booking is essential) and proceedings in the beamed dining room are overseen by the attentive Rita Rambellas, while behind the scenes Darren Sherlock takes care of the food – both work on the principle that customers' enjoyment is their only goal. Darren keeps an eye on the seasons and appealing options might include Cornish scallops with lightly curried creamed leeks, Jerusalem artichoke purée and basil oil, homely roast cod with Puy lentils cooked with root vegetables and smoked bacon, and slow-cooked belly of pork with crackling, purple sprouting broccoli, greens and polenta cooked with sage and garlic. Desserts meet with

reporters' approval too, especially bread-and-butter pudding. Wines are fairly priced, starting at £19.95.

Chef/s: Darren Sherlock. **Open:** Tue, Wed, Fri and Sat D only. **Closed:** Sun, Mon, Thur, Jan, Aug. **Meals:** set D £28 (Tue and Wed), £33 (Fri and Sat). **Details:** 25 seats. Music.

Wedmore
The Swan

Cooking score: 2
Modern British | £28
Cheddar Road, Wedmore, BS28 4EQ
Tel no: (01934) 710337
theswanwedmore.com

It's hard to miss the Swan as you pass through Wedmore. From the outside the well-maintained Georgian coaching inn exudes a sense of tradition, but grown-up chic is what you get the moment you walk through the doors. While it has been spruced up with some style, the Swan has not lost its attraction as a pub – the bar with its bare boards, scrubbed and polished tables and leather chairs has become a fixture on the local scene over the years – and visitors describe it as 'relaxing', 'unpretentious' with 'friendly service'. The food is stylish, too, the menu mixing pub classics (steaks, burgers, chicken and smoked ham hock pie), alongside contemporary ideas such as Cornish crab on toast with grilled fennel, rocket, lemon and capers, ahead of pork belly stuffed with nettles and served with Pink Fir potatoes, beetroot, spring greens and apple sauce, then buttermilk pannacotta with honey-roasted rhubarb and pumpkin-seed praline. Wines from £18.

Chef/s: Tom Blake. **Open:** all week L and D. **Meals:** main courses £13 to £24. **Details:** 65 seats. 52 seats outside. Bar. Music. Parking.

▌Wells
Goodfellows

Cooking score: 4
Seafood | £36
5 Sadler Street, Wells, BA5 2RR
Tel no: (01749) 673866
goodfellowswells.co.uk
£5
OFF

'We went out of our way to visit this restaurant, and were very glad we did' – so say readers who pitched up at Adam Fellows' egalitarian eatery. Goodfellows is a two-pronged operation, with a daytime café out front ('spring vegetable quiche and a lovely salad followed by superb chocolate cake'), and a formal dining area surrounding the open-plan kitchen with more intimate tables upstairs. Fresh fish arrives each day from Brixham, and Mr Fellows uses the haul for dishes that are self-assured, big on flavour but 'not overly fussy' – perhaps scallops with black pudding, apple and a boozy juniper reduction or a classy plate of turbot aligned with celeriac purée, Savoy cabbage, roast chervil root and truffle jus. Although seafood is the main attraction, every item is 'extra special', from confit duck terrine with Puy lentil salad and hazelnut vinaigrette or saffron polenta with Cerney goats' cheese to caramelised passion fruit tart with exotic fruity accompaniments. Wines are a well-priced European bunch.
Chef/s: Adam Fellows. **Open:** all week L, Wed to Sat D. **Closed:** 25 and 26 Dec. **Meals:** main courses £13 to £24. Set L £22 (2 courses) to £26. Tasting menu £50 (5 courses). **Details:** 50 seats. 15 seats outside. Music.

▌Wrington
The Ethicurean

Cooking score: 4
Modern British | £35
Barley Wood Walled Garden, Long Lane, Wrington, BS40 5SA
Tel no: (01934) 863713
theethicurean.com

Taking 'sense of place' and sustainability to a passionate level, this beautifully rustic restaurant draws both inspiration and ingredients from the 'quite bewitching setting' of a Victorian walled garden. Produce that isn't used immediately is preserved, so ingredients in their pickled or fermented guise feature frequently on the twice-daily changing menu. Light lunches might include parsnip, carrot and anise soup, a Cheddar and cider Welsh rarebit, or monkfish with fermented chilli aïoli. The evening Full Feast is five 'extremely tasty' courses that could offer shiitake, parsnip and cauliflower (crisp ribbons of parsnip on sharp/savoury mushroom ketchup with toasted cauliflower), a perhaps too-dainty portion of hake, mussels and sea vegetables, or a standout duck dish with sharp pickled and sweet puréed carrot, and the flowering heads of an overwintered brassica. The accompanying duck reduction had one enthusiast 'in raptures' such was its depth of flavour. Finish with hearty apple cake, clotted cream ice cream and honeycomb; similarly 'sumptuous' cakes will tempt around coffee or afternoon tea time – you have been warned! There is plenty to excite on the drinks front, with cider made on site, beer brewed locally, lively cocktails, kombucha and wine from £22.
Chef/s: Simon Pedro Miller and Iain and Matthew Pennington. **Open:** Tue to Sun L, Tue to Sat D. **Closed:** Mon. **Meals:** main courses £16 to £23. **Details:** 60 seats. 40 seats outside. Bar. Wheelchairs. Music. Parking.

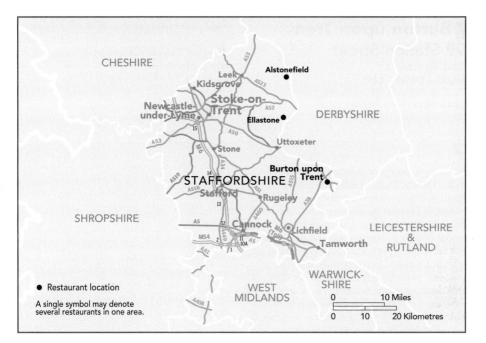

◼ Alstonefield
The George
Cooking score: 2
Modern British | £36
Alstonefield, DE6 2FX
Tel no: (01335) 310205
thegeorgeatalstonefield.com

A lovely stone-built Georgian country inn opposite the green in a Peak District village near Ashbourne, the George has been in the same family ownership for three generations. With views over Dovedale, and a thoroughly welcoming interior of lime-plastered walls, rustic furniture and candles, it fits the bill for a rural watering hole to perfection, and the menu of up-to-date pub cooking is where people most want to see the modernising touch show its hand. It does so with a starter of mackerel smoked in-house, fired up with horseradish, and served with a mixture of salt-baked and pickled heritage beets, or with bruschetta topped with wood pigeon, woodland mushrooms and bitter leaves,

dressed with blackberry jam. A 'proper pie' for main is an easy sell, crammed with red wine-braised steak and local blue cheese, while fried cod in shellfish cream with sea veg awaits fish lovers. Rhubarb and vanilla pannacotta with honeycomb is one of the lighter ways to finish, or get stuck into treacle tart with apple compote and orange mascarpone sorbet. A short wine list opens at £18.
Chef/s: Kelvin Guest. **Open:** all week L and D.
Closed: 25 Dec. **Meals:** main courses £16 to £30.
Details: 40 seats. 40 seats outside. Bar. Wheelchairs. Parking.

Please send us your feedback

To register your opinion about any restaurant listed in this guide, or a new restaurant that you wish to bring to our attention, please visit the web address at the bottom of the page. Your feedback informs the content of the book and will be used to compile next year's reviews.

▌Burton upon Trent
99 Station Street
Cooking score: 1
Modern British | £29
99 Station Street, Burton upon Trent,
DE14 1BT
Tel no: (01283) 516859
99stationstreet.com
£30

Behind a neatly grey-painted shopfront close
to the station, Daniel Pilkington delivers a
modern British repertoire that is rooted in the
seasons. Judicious combinations of ingredients
show classical leanings, and there are
interesting ideas, too. Pigeon and port make a
flavour-packed pie among first courses, or go
for cured salmon, 'pressure marinated' with
beetroot, lime, coriander and sea salt. The
char-grill turns out Bromley Hurst steaks –
ribeye, say – while chicken breast is roasted
with butter and thyme and arrives with confit
leg and hazelnut risotto. Finish with bread-
and-butter pudding. The wine list has good
options under £20 a bottle.
Chef/s: Daniel Pilkington. **Open:** Thur to Sun L,
Wed to Sat D. **Closed:** Mon, Tue. **Meals:** main
courses £13 to £22. Set L £14 (2 courses) to £15. Set
D £26 (3 courses). Sun L £18. **Details:** 40 seats. Bar.
Wheelchairs. Music.

move on to classy versions of shepherd's pie or
fish and chips, or consider hay-baked shoulder
of hogget. The carefully compiled wine list is
arranged by style.

▌Ellastone

LOCAL GEM
The Duncombe Arms
Modern British | £30
Main Road, Ellastone, DE6 2GZ
Tel no: (01335) 324275
duncombearms.co.uk

Original features, heritage colours,
comfortable corners, local ales and a terrace
with a countryside view, the Duncombe Arms
has the look of a country pub of our times.
Similarly, the culinary output includes
traditional and contemporary flavours in feel-
good combinations. Get going with potted
kippers with a zesty orange and fennel salad,
or crispy pig's head with pickled mushrooms,

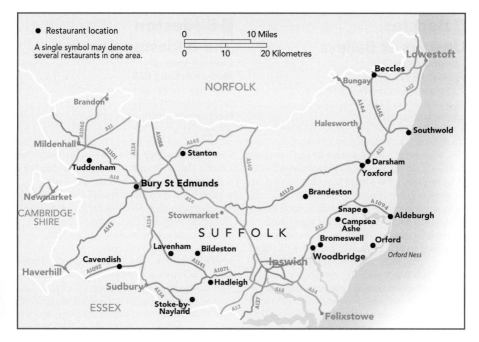

Restaurant location

A single symbol may denote several restaurants in one area.

0 — 10 Miles
0 — 10 — 20 Kilometres

NORFOLK

Lowestoft
Beccles
Bungay
Brandon
Halesworth
Southwold
Mildenhall
Darsham
Tuddenham
Yoxford
Stanton
Newmarket
Bury St Edmunds
Brandeston
CAMBRIDGE-SHIRE
Stowmarket
Snape
Aldeburgh
Campsea Ashe
SUFFOLK
Bromeswell
Orford
Lavenham
Bildeston
Woodbridge
Orford Ness
Cavendish
Haverhill
Ipswich
Sudbury
Hadleigh
ESSEX
Stoke-by-Nayland
Felixstowe

▌Aldeburgh

Regatta

Cooking score: 1
Modern British | £30
171-173 High Street, Aldeburgh, IP15 5AN
Tel no: (01728) 452011
regattaaldeburgh.com

Chef/proprietor Robert Mabey has run his welcoming restaurant for 27 years, suggesting a rare level of reliability and consistency. Local seafood is a big player on the menu: fish soup has real depth of flavour, while spot-on timing is a feature of dishes such as tiger prawn tempura, scallops with crispy bacon and new potatoes or sea bream with Mediterranean vegetables. The kitchen also pleases with the likes of pork, chicken and pistachio terrine, while raspberry soufflé and chocolate tart with vanilla Chantilly cream have been praised. Wines from £15.

Chef/s: Robert Mabey. **Open:** Tue to Sat L and D.
Closed: Sun, Mon, 24 to 26 and 31 Dec, 1 Jan.
Meals: main courses £12 to £27. **Details:** 90 seats.

LOCAL GEM

The Aldeburgh Market

Seafood | £21
170-172 High Street, Aldeburgh, IP15 5AQ
Tel no: (01728) 452520
thealdeburghmarket.co.uk

£5 OFF   £30

Aldeburgh Market is a daytime restaurant, shop and all-round foodie haven where you can stock up on deli produce made on the premises or pick out some fresh fish for your dinner (Carl, the 'fish-counter maestro', will talk you through the day's catch). Open for breakfast and closing in the late afternoon (it varies in summer in particular), grab a seat in the diminutive dining room or a pavement table and tuck into potted shrimps, South Indian fish curry or beer-battered fish and chips. Veggies fare well, too. Finish with blueberry and honey cheesecake. A short wine list opens at £15.95.

▌Beccles
Upstairs at Baileys

Cooking score: 2
Spanish | £32
2 Hungate, Beccles, NR34 9TL
Tel no: (01502) 710609
upstairsatbaileys.co.uk
£5 OFF

Yes, you are in a quiet market town in deepest Suffolk, but head upstairs from Baileys, itself a delightful deli, for a meal that channels Spain to its sunny core. Friday or Saturday evenings offer the real deal – lunch is far simpler – when an array of tapas precedes a menu of Spanish favourites. Break into just-made croquetas to find béchamel packed with diced Ibérico ham; scallops with robustly flavoured homemade black pudding are silky-shiny; or play the Russian roulette proposed by pan-fried Padrón peppers. Follow with roast lamb with Mediterranean vegetables, paella made in the traditional way with prawn-head stock and a bite to the bomba rice, or more Ibérico pork, this time shoulder with a black garlic sauce. The pastry leaves in a pretty mille-feuille are an exquisitely crisp foil to the generous amount of berries, crema catalana and Chantilly cream that they contain. Owner Xavier Esteve will happily advise on wines from his all-Spanish list, which opens with an £18 Albariño.

Chef/s: Xavier Esteve and Maria Elliston. **Open:** Tue to Sat L, Fri and Sat D. **Closed:** Sun, Mon. **Meals:** main courses £16 to £22. Set L £10 (2 courses) to £15. Set D £27 (2 courses) to £32. **Details:** 38 seats. Music.

▌Bildeston
The Bildeston Crown

Cooking score: 5
Modern British | £35
104 High Street, Bildeston, IP7 7EB
Tel no: (01449) 740510
thebildestoncrown.com
£5 OFF

Chris and Hayley Lee's return to the Bildeston Crown after a sojourn in Newmarket has been a cause for celebration hereabouts, with readers heralding a new-found vitality in every department. Decked out in farmhouse-chic style, with log fires, distressed wood, antiques and artworks, this thoughtfully restored 15th-century inn is now a 'stylish operation with no fuss' – but heaps of culinary kudos. Whether you are nibbling on curried vegetable croquettes, slurping Colchester oysters or partaking of the pub's new-wave take on chicken Kiev, there's much to enjoy. Classily rendered classics such as char-grilled Red Poll rump steak with braised shin and chips share the limelight with more ambitious dishes including rabbit and duck liver Wellington with confit leg, carrot and tarragon, although one reader singles out the superlative fish – perhaps grilled red mullet with ratatouille, artichoke and basil. 'Young, interested staff' lift the mood, and the well-spread wine list features an excellent by-the-glass selection.

Chef/s: Chris Lee. **Open:** all week L and D. **Meals:** main courses £14 to £22. Set L £15 (2 courses) to £20. **Details:** 80 seats. 30 seats outside. Bar. Wheelchairs. Music. Parking.

Brandeston

LOCAL GEM
The Queen
Modern British | £28
The Street, Brandeston, IP13 7AD
Tel no: (01728) 685307
thequeenatbrandeston.co.uk

£5 OFF 🚗 £30

Alexander Aitchison, the chef at this unpretentious family-run village pub ('it's done up but not too done-up – nothing pretentious') clearly knows a thing or two about cooking meat – Longhorn beef brisket from nearby Kenton Hall flakes deliciously after slow, tender cooking, and sits sweetly next to silky-smooth carrot purée and the satisfying flavours of roast onion, cavolo nero and plenty of gravy! Enjoy the same careful touch with meltingly good pork belly, its fattiness cut sharply with tart rhubarb and mustardy pak choi. Puddings could benefit from simplification, but the celebration of East Anglian cheeses is worth a mention.

Bromeswell
The Unruly Pig
Cooking score: 4
Modern British | £29
Orford Road, Bromeswell, IP12 2PU
Tel no: (01394) 460310
theunrulypig.co.uk

£5 OFF £30

This carefully curated roadside pub is the result of immense research and investment – which has paid off in spades. It is comfortable and contemporary, the welcome as warm to wet dogs and their owners as it is to finer diners coming for Dave Wall's accomplished cooking. A charcoal grill helps with some of the magic – try a starter of bone marrow with caramelised onion, or a main of seared duck breast with shallot purée and potato terrine – but this is no one-trick-pony of a kitchen. Smoked mackerel and oyster velouté is refined, sea-salty and sweet with celery and apple, while butter-roasted poussin with

salsify, leeks and truffle emulsion is a masterclass in succulence and flavour. Come back another day for a burger, albeit one served in a brioche bun with Roquefort mayonnaise and hand-cut chips. The treacle tart is exemplary, blood orange and crème fraîche sorbet keeping it mercifully distant from the sickly spectrum. The owner's love of wine is poured into a list that sashays seductively through some fantastic vintages, but also offers day-to-day glugs and a £15 'wine of the month'.
Chef/s: Dave Wall. **Open:** Mon to Sat L and D. Sun 12 to 8. **Meals:** main courses £14 to £18. Set L and D £15 (2 courses) to £18. **Details:** 90 seats. 40 seats outside. V menu. Bar. Wheelchairs. Music. Parking.

Bury St Edmunds
Maison Bleue
Cooking score: 5
Modern French | £45
30-31 Churchgate Street, Bury St Edmunds, IP33 1RG
Tel no: (01284) 760623
maisonbleue.co.uk

Come to this 'effortlessy elegant' town-centre spot for white-clothed tables and service that is as gracious and relaxed as the food is delicious. Whisper-fine ravioli are packed with sweet brown shrimps and turbot, the flavour lifted by peppery notes of radish and baby red chard, while exuberant colour from pickled brassica florets, pink petals, citrus segments and golden beetroot ignites a dish of plump tempura langoustine and delicate crabmeat. Staying fishy, the taste and texture of impeccably cooked halibut is balanced beautifully by slivers of dried beef, but Pascal Canevet's touch is equally assured with meat – an exquisite Aberdeen Angus fillet is served with truffle velouté, or saddle of rabbit with snails and parsley sauce. There's flirty, summery deliciousness in a dessert of marinated strawberries, pistachio-studded meringue, morsels of cheesecake and fresh yoghurt ice cream, although chocolate lovers will adore a tartlet with memorable salted-caramel sauce. The wine list sweeps through

France's finest vineyards, nodding politely to other countries *en passant*. There's enough around the £20 mark, and plenty by the glass or 50cl carafe.
Chef/s: Pascal Canevet. **Open:** Tue to Sat L and D. **Closed:** Sun, Mon, 2 weeks Sept, 23 Dec to 15 Jan. **Meals:** main courses £22 to £29. Set L £20 (2 courses) to £25. Set D £37 (3 courses). **Details:** 60 seats. Music.

1921 Angel Hill
Cooking score: 4
Modern British | £36
19-21 Angel Hill, Bury St Edmunds, IP33 1UZ
Tel no: (01284) 704870
nineteen-twentyone.co.uk

Whet your appetite for Zack Deakins' 'exquisitely flavoured' food with a flight of imaginative canapés – try a morsel of vodka-cured cod or lightly curried frog's leg – as you read his beautifully crafted menu. Dishes celebrate local ingredients (think Denham Estate lamb or venison, locally shot partridge, Mersea crab) without being restrictively slavish. A watercress velouté delivers its velvety promise deliciously, a vivid green pool dotted with shades of crimson beetroot and the plump gold of a confit egg yolk. It's almost too pretty to eat – ditto salt cod squid-ink tortellini and chorizo with bright curls of carrot and segments of sweetcorn. Zack's eye may be artistic but there's never a compromise on taste here: note a delicately spiced hake with nuggets of confit parsnip and Parmentier potatoes or an irresistibly creamy and perfectly seasoned wild garlic risotto with white asparagus and blewit mushrooms that sings of spring. White chocolate cheesecake with confit blood orange and thyme is – is the word still allowed? – deconstructed, but nonetheless delicious. Many applaud the reasonably priced wine list (from £19.95), and give full marks for the 'informed, brisk, but not hurried' service in this comfortable, elegant spot.

Chef/s: Zack Deakins. **Open:** Mon to Sat L and D. **Closed:** Sun, 24 Dec to 5 Jan. **Meals:** main courses £16 to £25. Set L £18 (2 courses) to £21. Tasting menu £70. **Details:** 50 seats. Bar. Wheelchairs. Music.

Pea Porridge
Cooking score: 4
Modern British | £35
28-29 Cannon Street, Bury St Edmunds, IP33 1JR
Tel no: (01284) 700200
peaporridge.co.uk

Striding confidently into its eighth year, Justin Sharp's restaurant shows no signs of slowing down – 'lives up to expectations every time, never falters in my opinion' is one fan's heartfelt comment. The old ovens of the former bakery are on display along with beams and exposed brickwork and a lot of effort has gone into creating a mood that is warm and unpretentious. Exceptionally good food is the deal here, and it is 'worth travelling a long way...the sweetbreads and also the special of ox cheek were gloriously successful'. The daily changing menus are an appealing mix of broadly based European dishes and intelligent and confident craftsmanship. There's a foundation of solid simplicity in wood-fired dishes such as starters of mackerel with Yorkshire rhubarb and salmoriglio (a sauce of olive oil, lemon, garlic and oregano), and mains of veal T-bone with curly kale, chanterelle mushrooms, garlic and gremolata, while desserts might include a classic tarte Tatin with Calvados ice cream. Lovers of organic and boutique producers are in for a treat on a confidently chosen, mainly European wine list noted for good value (from £19).

Chef/s: Justin Sharp. **Open:** Thur to Sat L, Tue to Sat D. **Closed:** Sun, Mon, 2 weeks Christmas, 2 weeks summer. **Meals:** main courses £14 to £24. Set L and D £15 (2 courses) to £19. **Details:** 46 seats. Music. Babies at L only.

Ben's

Modern British | £31

43-45 Churchgate Street, Bury St Edmunds,
IP33 1RG
Tel no: (01284) 762119
bensrestaurant.co.uk

'Ben's is a fantastic restaurant, which offers something different,' runs one appraisal of this jolly, warm-hearted neighbourhood eatery 'in a town predominantly filled with chain restaurants'. The cooking is all about simple satisfaction, from Gressingham duck, black pudding and potato terrine with piccalilli, via braised lamb, pea and mint shortcrust pie with creamy mash and a redcurrant reduction, to the 'best Sunday roast ever'. Finish with rhubarb and vanilla meringue tart or a plate of Suffolk Farmhouse cheeses. Wines from £18.

The Angel

Modern British

3 Angel Hill, Bury St Edmunds, IP33 1LT
Tel no: (01284) 714007
theangel.co.uk

'Food at the Angel has really perked up recently. My red pepper gazpacho and sorrel sorbet was just stunning, and the plaice was beautiful with charred cherry tomatoes and monk's beard. Pimm's jelly with basil granita, meringue and strawberries had my friend in raptures!'

◼ Campsea Ashe

The Dog and Duck

British | £30

Station Road, Campsea Ashe, IP13 0PT
Tel no: (01728) 746211
dogandducksuffolk.co.uk

Once nothing to bark or quack about, this family-run roadside pub has been transformed into a tasty spot on the edge of attractive Woodbridge. Drop in for good pub staples or enjoy the on-trend likes of salt-baked and pickled heritage beetroots with quinoa and pumpkin salad, followed by nicely pink lamb rump, harissa yoghurt and falafel, or scallops with a seaweed and nut gremolata. Loosen the waistband to indulge in the millionaire's shortbread tart. Wine from £16.50.

◼ Cavendish

The George

Cooking score: 1
International | £27

The Green, Cavendish, CO10 8BA
Tel no: (01787) 280248
thecavendishgeorge.co.uk
🛏 £30

There may be handpumps dispensing Suffolk ales in the bar but this 16th-century beamed hostelry now makes its living as a country restaurant-with-rooms rather than a village pub. While readers have good things to say about the devilled kidneys and the oxtail casserole, the kitchen ventures well beyond Britain's borders in search of culinary inspiration. On a typical day, you might find beetroot risotto, sea bass with udon noodles and confit duck with Jerusalem artichoke purée alongside steaks, burgers, fish specials and lunchtime sandwiches. Finish with dark chocolate cheesecake with Baileys cream or Yorkshire rhubarb 'many ways'. Easy-drinking wines from £16.95.

Chef/s: Lewis Bennet. **Open:** all week L, Mon to Sat D. **Closed:** 24 to 26 Dec, 30 to 31 Dec. **Meals:** main courses £12 to £20. Set L and D £15 (2 courses) to £18. **Details:** 50 seats. 30 seats outside. Bar. Music.

▌Darsham
Darsham Nurseries

Cooking score: 3
International | £25
Main Road (A12), Darsham, IP17 3PW
Tel no: (01728) 667022
darshamnurseries.co.uk
£30

This ludicrously lovely café on the side of the A12 is a pit-stop for many a weary driver heading for Suffolk's honeypot coastal spots. There are plants to buy, a delightful shop to browse and sensationally tasty, confident food to choose from a perfectly formed small plate menu. Shy vegetables are nudged into the limelight, cauliflower charred just enough to tease out its reticent flavour and supported – not overwhelmed – by a lemony, herby yoghurt, saffron butter and pine nuts; Jerusalem artichokes are sweet against nutty Puy lentils and tahini; and kale is given a sweet-sour-umami lift from a miso and apple dressing. Tender morsels of lightly crisped cod cheek stay in their natural sea-salty firmament thanks to strands of monk's beard, and the deep creaminess of a blood-orange and juniper posset is cut deftly by citrus segments. A compact wine list offers just what's necessary, while homemade seasonal cordials will keep drivers hydrated.
Chef/s: Lola DeMille. **Open:** all week L, Thur to Sat D. **Closed:** 25 and 26 Dec, 1 and 2 Jan. **Meals:** main courses £9 to £15. **Details:** 30 seats. 20 seats outside. Wheelchairs. Music. Parking.

▌Hadleigh
The Hadleigh Ram

Cooking score: 2
Modern British | £30
5 Market Place, Hadleigh, IP7 5DL
Tel no: (01473) 822880
thehadleighram.co.uk

'Bottomless brunch', steak nights, vegan menus, a gin list, private dining facilities – this venerable watering hole has certainly upped its game since the current team took

over in 2013. Inside, it feels more like a smartly updated bar/restaurant with pretty fabrics and contemporary colour schemes brightening the mood – although heavy exposed beams are reminders of the Ram's longevity. On the food front, sharing boards and 'market' specials flesh out a menu that is pitched well above the pub norm – think chicken consommé with marinated chicken 'oysters', herb gnocchi and poached enoki mushrooms or rump and confit belly of Lavenham lamb with goats' curd dauphinois, char-grilled baby gem, grelot onion and Madeira jus. Also look for Shetland mussels and local game in season, burgers (beef with chorizo and jalapeño rarebit, say) and smart desserts such as Morello cherry crème brûlée with sour cherry sorbet. 'Classic' and 'contemporary' wines from around £20.
Chef/s: Oliver Macmillan. **Open:** all week L, Mon to Sat D. **Meals:** main courses £12 to £24. **Details:** 50 seats. 25 seats outside. V menu. Bar. Wheelchairs. Music.

▌Lavenham
The Great House

Cooking score: 5
Modern French | £48
Market Place, Lavenham, CO10 9QZ
Tel no: (01787) 247431
greathouse.co.uk

A family with interests in the weaving business built and extended the Great House in the 14th and 15th centuries. It owes its present pristine white façade to a Georgian makeover, and its 30-year-plus career as a modern country restaurant-with-rooms to the unwavering commitment of Régis Crépy, who continues to oversee the intricately constructed menus of contemporary French food that have brought the place to prominence. Time has not stood still, not when skate wing with mussel mayonnaise comes with quinoa, or king scallops with smoked cauliflower purée and powdered dried roe, but there is a strong classical foundation to dishes, too. Main courses are multi-layered but coherent assemblages, perhaps Scottish beef fillet with Puy lentils in sherry vinegar and an emulsion sauce of foie gras, or the Anjou pigeon that comes with braised red cabbage and griottes in a reduction of port sharpened with raspberry vinegar. An enthusiastic reporter advised not overlooking the 'fantastic cheese selection', if you can resist the lure of Suffolk honey parfait with apple and Calvados mousse and almond tuiles. Glasses from £5.50 lead the charge on an authoritative wine list, which has its heart in the French regions, but is cosmopolitan enough to include Brazil and Macedonia.

Chef/s: Régis Crépy. **Open:** Wed to Sun L, Tue to Sat D. **Closed:** Mon, Jan, 2 weeks summer. **Meals:** main courses £20 to £30. Set L £20 (2 courses) to £25. Set D £32 (2 courses) to £37. Sun L £37. **Details:** 50 seats. 20 seats outside. Music.

Orford
The Crown & Castle

Cooking score: 3
British/Italian | £37
Market Hill, Orford, IP12 2LJ
Tel no: (01394) 450205
crownandcastle.co.uk

The red-brick inn by the river estuary has a 12th-century turreted castle for next-door neighbour, but has quite enough cachet of its own. With tables on a broad terrace outside, as well as a simply refurbished interior that maintains a comfortingly domestic feel, the place has plenty going for it. Ruth Watson keeps a firm hand on the tiller, overseeing the transition to head chef of Rob Walpole during his predecessor's maternity leave, and the Anglo-Italian brasserie cooking is as attractive as ever. Fish is a big deal, as was attested by spring visitors who enjoyed fritto misto with aïoli to start, and then expertly timed crisp-skinned cod with octopus and cauliflower fritter in a sharply piquant dressing. Otherwise, there may be locally bagged roast pheasant, served with creamed cavolo nero and porcini and Parmesan orzo. Finish with a combination of ices – perhaps blood-orange

and blackberry sorbets and hazelnut ice cream – or classic lemon tart dolloped with crème fraîche. A well-compiled, chatty wine list opens at £20.

Chef/s: Ruth Watson and Rob Walpole. **Open:** all week L and D. **Meals:** main courses £16 to £25. **Details:** 50 seats. 30 seats outside. V menu. Children over 8 yrs only at D.

Snape
The Plough & Sail

Cooking score: 1
Modern British | £25
Snape, IP17 1SR
Tel no: (01728) 688413
theploughandsailsnape.com

'A very well-run, attractive pub' warmed by log fires in the winter and with a very sheltered courtyard for the summer months, the Plough & Sail is a valuable local resource and a popular refuelling point for visitors to Snape Maltings. Restorative food comes in the shape of filling staples (beer-battered fish and chips with crushed, minted peas) and more upbeat dishes, perhaps spiced king prawn and vegetable bhaji with mango and chilli compote, or lamb rump, served two ways, with braised fennel, pumpkin fritter, fine beans and jus. Sandwiches and Sunday roasts play their part, while puddings might feature vanilla crème brûlée. Wines start at £15.50.

Chef/s: Oliver Burnside. **Open:** all week L and D. **Meals:** main courses £12 to £17. **Details:** 100 seats. 50 seats outside. Bar. Wheelchairs. Music. Parking.

Please send us your feedback

To register your opinion about any restaurant listed in this guide, or a new restaurant that you wish to bring to our attention, please visit the web address at the bottom of the page. Your feedback informs the content of the book and will be used to compile next year's reviews.

▐ Southwold

Solebay Fish Co.

Seafood | £20

Shed 22e, Blackshore, Southwold, IP18 6ND
Tel no: (01502) 724241
solebayfishco.co.uk

£30

A trip to this stretch of coast isn't complete
without a dip into this welcoming quayside
eatery. Book ahead – people throng here on
summer weekends – and look forward to
garlicky-grilled lobster with chunky chips,
pan-fried sea bass or Dover sole (and chips), or
a dozen Colchester oysters. Sharing platters
(make your own combo if you like) fit the
laid-back vibe; crab, home-smoked mackerel,
crevettes and all manner of other shellfish
crowding generously on to the dish. A bottle
of Pinot Grigio opens the short wine list
at £18.

▐ Stanton

The Leaping Hare

Cooking score: 3
Modern British | £39
Wyken Hall, Stanton, IP31 2DW
Tel no: (01359) 250287
wykenvineyards.co.uk

£5
OFF

As slices of English countryside go, the Wyken
Estate is nigh on perfect. Livestocked fields,
woodland walks, a vineyard, weekly farmers'
market and stunning garden wrap around a
beautiful Elizabethan manor house – and the
elegant converted barn is a rather lovely place
to eat in. The appealing menu will never shock
or startle, but the food rings with a confident
sense of place. Start with carpaccio of estate
venison with a pear and walnut salad, or
sublimely simple asparagus with rocket,
poached egg, a drizzle of olive oil and
Parmesan. Lamb or hogget is the meat to
choose, perhaps a rack of Wyken lamb, turnip
dauphinois and carrots from nearby Elveden,
although a clattering pile of river Deben

mussels with Aspall cyder and bacon cream is
just as tempting. Finish with a pear tart and
chocolate sorbet. To drink? Bottles from the
estate vineyard, some award-winning, are
priced from £22.

Chef/s: Simon Woodrow. **Open:** all week L, Fri and
Sat D. **Closed:** 25 Dec to 6 Jan. **Meals:** main courses
£15 to £22. Set L £16 (2 courses) to £19. Set D £28.
Details: 45 seats. Wheelchairs. Parking.

▐ Stoke-by-Nayland

The Angel Inn

Cooking score: 2
Modern British | £28
Polstead Street, Stoke-by-Nayland, CO6 4SA
Tel no: (01206) 263245
angelinnsuffolk.co.uk

£5   £30
OFF

Like many of its neighbours in this photogenic
Suffolk village, the Angel was originally half-
timbered, although its façade was bricked over
in later years. Improvements continue apace
now that this well-endowed pub-with-rooms
is part of the locally based Suffolk Country
Inns group – not least in the kitchen, where
chef Mark Allen's team work to an accessible
menu for all seasons. Local ingredients pop up
here and there, with some neat twists applied
to the classics – think sausages and sweet
potato mash with sprout tops and veal gravy,
chorizo-crusted cod with spicy homemade
baked beans or ribeye steaks with pink
peppercorn butter. Retro fans might fancy the
prawn cocktail but there's also southern-fried
soft-shell crab, while desserts could feature
white chocolate bavarois with hazelnut
praline. Lunchtime sandwiches, fish and chip
suppers on Friday and keenly priced wines by
the glass or carafe complete a well-rounded
package for visitors to Constable country.
Chef/s: Mark Allen. **Open:** all week L and D.
Meals: main courses £12 to £28. Set L £15 (2
courses) to £17. Sun L £20. **Details:** 60 seats. 24
seats outside. Bar. Music. Parking.

Our highlights...

Our undercover inspectors reveal their most memorable dishes from another year of extraordinary eating.

White asparagus at Anglo. The combination of asparagus, duck egg, lemon and dill is just perfect. Nature clearly means them to be together forever – so let them!

The fish at Neptune (hake with morels, spinach, young broad beans, or turbot with artichoke, aubergine and wild garlic) was cooked as if by the king of the sea himself.

Roast jowl and trotter sauce at Tuddenham Mill, because you could taste the care that had gone into making it, and for its unabashed old-school vibe.

Chicken broth with spring vegetables at Sketch, which was deeply flavoursome, simple and fresh – a real feel-good bowl of great food.

Kunefe at Oklava. Hands down the best dessert. Hot, crisp and sweet with a layer of sharpness, it was rich and utterly, utterly moreish. But maybe also **Pidgin's bibingka, mango, candied fennel, crumble and duck egg ice cream**, a deliciously genius agglomeration of flavours and textures – daring, thoughtful, not too sweet.

■ Tuddenham
Tuddenham Mill

Cooking score: 6
Modern British | £42
High Street, Tuddenham, IP28 6SQ
Tel no: (01638) 713552
tuddenhammill.co.uk

£5 OFF 🛏

Roasted jowl with trotter sauce? Fanny Cradock or Mrs Beeton maybe – but 30-something Lee Bye and his young brigade? Deeply connected with his own East Anglian heritage, Bye treads a sometimes playful line between old-school flavours and utterly contemporary, refined cooking. The jowl is cooked for 14 patient hours until fat and flesh transform into a syrupy, salty sweetness that collapses almost indecently in the mouth; a glossy, savoury trotter sauce, the bite of spelt and a tangle of on-trend agretti make it a memorable dish. Humble Fenland produce is celebrated as determinedly as the silkiest foie gras or classiest turbot – Vichy carrots in particular, finished with thyme and wild honey, are much more than a support act. Dishes rarely miss a flavour or textural beat, delicate sea trout ceviche as pretty as the subtle taste is balanced thanks to salty herring roe, fresh cucumber and peppery nasturtium. Finish with a picture-perfect mille-feuille, its sweet lemon cream balanced by fresh goats' milk ice, plump poached blueberries, sour sorrel and the flaky crunch of pastry. The three-course set lunch is a steal, and there's plenty to drink by the glass with bottles from £19.95.

Chef/s: Lee Bye. **Open:** all week L and D.
Meals: main courses £20 to £45. Set L £18 (2 courses) to £23. Early D £20. Set D £32 (2 courses) to £41. Sun L £28. Tasting menu £55. **Details:** 50 seats. 40 seats outside. V menu. Bar. Wheelchairs. Music. Parking.

■ Woodbridge
The Riverside

Cooking score: 1
Modern British | £27
Quay Street, Woodbridge, IP12 1BH
Tel no: (01394) 382174
theriverside.co.uk

£5 OFF £30

Handily placed for Woodbridge station and the marina, this long-running enterprise is part of a renowned theatre/cinema complex and holidaymakers' haunt (note the ice cream kiosk outside). Pre-matinee tapas lunches and special 'dinner and film' deals pull in the crowds, but the regular menu also has plenty of red-carpet appeal. Sound regional ingredients play their part, although flavours are global – from locally made merguez sausages with mustard mash or Dingley Dell pork T-bone with chorizo and crispy Parma ham to Goan seafood curry or pan-fried cod with black pudding, greens and smoked salmon sauce. Creditable wines by the glass or carafe.
Chef/s: Dan Jones. **Open:** all week L and D.
Closed: 25 and 26 Dec. **Meals:** main courses £10 to £22. **Details:** 45 seats. 34 seats outside. Bar. Wheelchairs. Music.

LOCAL GEM
The Table

International | £25
3 Quay Street, Woodbridge, IP12 1BX
Tel no: (01394) 382428
thetablewoodbridge.co.uk

£5 OFF £30

'It may be simple brasserie stuff, but in a lovely, unpretentious town-centre spot with sunny courtyard and bags of atmosphere,' summed up one fan of owner/chef Vernon Blackmore's warren-like eatery. Noted for his curries (try the coconut chicken), Vernon also delivers a 'lovely spread' of cakes and bakes during the morning, light lunches, then evening candles and the likes of soy-braised

beef croquette with chilli jam, and local cod fillet with thyme risotto and red wine jus. Wines from £17.

■ Yoxford
Main's

Cooking score: 1
Modern British | £30
High Street, Yoxford, IP17 3EU
Tel no: (01728) 668882
mainsrestaurant.co.uk

Jason Vincent and Nancy Main's 'lovely business' in a former draper's shop is obviously a treasured local – on a busy Thursday evening 'Nancy knew everyone apart from us'. Good wholesome seasonal ingredients find favour and Jason's dedication to the local cause shows itself in the straightforward cooking of dishes such as pheasant and bacon terrine with quince jelly, Brancaster mussels with smoked haddock, white wine, cream and dill, pot-roast free-range chicken, and saffron rice pudding with anise-poached rhubarb. Wines from £16.
Chef/s: Jason Vincent. **Open:** Thur to Sat D.
Closed: Sun to Wed. **Meals:** main courses £12 to £26. **Details:** 35 seats.

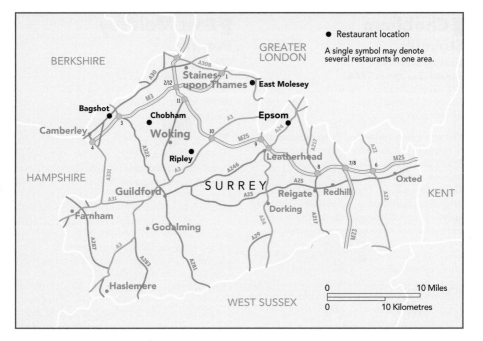

A single symbol may denote several restaurants in one area.

▮ Bagshot
Matt Worswick at the Latymer

Cooking score: 6
Modern European | £65
Pennyhill Park Hotel, London Road, Bagshot, GU19 5EU
Tel no: (01276) 486156
pennyhillpark.co.uk

£5 OFF 🛏

A long drive leads through 125 acres of parkland to this ivy-clad country house, now a hotel/spa/country club complex. The interior is distinguished by a sense of comfort and style, although the contrast between Pennyhill Park's corporate playground and the intimacy of the Latymer couldn't be more striking. Matt Worswick's cooking unites faultless technique with clear and original flavour combinations. The format remains unchanged – tasting menus at lunch and dinner – and the result is a measured procession of precise, carefully crafted flavours. That might mean tender braised octopus with sesame and miso, poached lobster with spiced crab and a shellfish bisque, and fillet of Sussex beef with roast sweetbread, mushroom duxelles and red wine sauce, concluding with a parade of desserts: a mini strawberry cornet; passion fruit cream with mango gel and coconut ice cream; and chocolate délice with milk crumble and yoghurt sorbet. The set-menu format means that bills are predictable, just as long as you don't get lost in the global wine list – aimed at those prepared to pay for quality; house selections start at £34.

Chef/s: Matt Worswick. **Open:** Fri and Sat L, Wed to Sun D. **Closed:** Mon, Tue, first 2 weeks Jan. **Meals:** tasting menu L £35 (5 courses) to £49. Tasting menu D £55 (5 courses) to £100. **Details:** 50 seats. V menu. Bar. Wheelchairs. Parking. Children over 12 yrs only.

▌Chobham
Stovell's

Cooking score: 6
Modern European | £45
125 Windsor Road, Chobham, GU24 8QS
Tel no: (01276) 858000
stovells.com

The renovated Tudor farmhouse on the edge of the village may have mind-your-head beams and gnarled timbers, mullioned windows and a log-burner in the bar, but the dining room looks comfortably modern with beige seating and crisp white linen. Fernando Stovell is an ambitious chef, noted for skill, technique and not a little panache. After a period of change in the kitchen he is full of ideas and plans – regulars 'can't wait for him to move up another gear'. From a parade of extras, like between-course 'little awakenings' and bread, a course in its own right, featuring a giant tapioca crisp and spreads from pork dripping to guacamole, it is obvious that contemporary ideas are the driving force. Flavours are paramount in an innovative main course of 'stunning' South Coast cod confit in a 'fathoms-deep' tasting bouillabaisse with morels and ramsons. Mr Stovell's Mexican heritage occasionally comes through in dishes such as a signature sea bass with guajillo and ancho chillies, char-grilled over citrus wood with pico de gallo pescado a la talla (designed to share), while showy desserts might deliver a Valrhona chocolate bombe with salted caramel and raspberry sorbet. Service is slick. The steller wine list has plenty by the glass; bottles start at £22.
Chef/s: Fernando Stovell. **Open:** Tue to Sat L and D. **Closed:** Sun, Mon, first 2 weeks Jan. **Meals:** set L £18 (2 courses) to £23. Set D £37 (2 courses) to £45. **Details:** 60 seats. 25 seats outside. V menu. Bar. Music. Parking.

▌East Molesey
Petriti's

Cooking score: 3
Modern European | £27
98 Walton Road, East Molesey, KT8 0DL
Tel no: (020) 8979 5577
petritisrestaurant.co.uk
£30

Handily placed across the river from Hampton Court Palace, Tom and Nargisa Petriti's restaurant is a boon to the neighbourhood and a venue fuelled by high aspirations. A recent paint job has given the dining room a darker, cosier feel, although the overall impression is still one of low-key sophistication in the suburbs. Tom is a diligent procurer of ingredients, buying locally and from London's markets for other supplies. The result is an amazing-value set menu that rolls with the seasons, offering prettily arranged plates such as beetroot risotto with smoked Applewood cheese or guinea fowl with purple sprouting broccoli, quince and truffled tortellini. Otherwise, fish is always worth a punt, from red mullet with radish, fennel and grapefruit to sea bream with 'surf and turf' vegetables, seaweed butter and herring caviar. To conclude, try passion fruit soufflé with elderflower custard. Fifteen wines by the glass head up a well-assembled list.
Chef/s: Tom Petriti. **Open:** Tue to Sun L, Tue to Sat D. **Closed:** Mon, first 2 weeks Jan. **Meals:** set L and D £21 (2 courses) to £27. Tasting menu £49 (6 courses). **Details:** 70 seats. V menu. Wheelchairs. Music. Parking. Children over 6 yrs only

Epsom

Dastaan

Cooking score: 4
Indian | £25
447 Kingston Road, Epsom, KT19 0DB
Tel no: (020) 8786 8999
dastaan.co.uk
£5 OFF £30

Its location may not fill you with confidence, 'being set in a rather nondescript parade of takeaways and shops off the main dual carriageway', but Dastaan is well worth seeking out. Rustic, unpretentious, relaxed and brimful of atmosphere, it's been put together on a shoestring. Colours are vivid, with chocolate-brown or turmeric-yellow walls and hot-pink or yellow bench-style banquettes, it's all permeated by the heady aroma of spices – and it's anything but your regular curry house. Owner Sanjay Gour (previously head chef of the Tamarind collection and then of Gymkhana, see entries) and head chef Nand Kishor (Trishna and Gymkhana) deliver 'the real deal', from the pani puri – crisp little spheres containing a 'kicking' chickpea salad, with a hole in the top through which to pour the accompanying jaljeera (a cooling yet spicy liquid) that ate in one 'explosive' mouthful, to Malabar prawns, a Keralan-inspired aromatic, coconut-laced dish 'of intelligent subtlety' or perhaps a spicy and tangy pork vindaloo. Naans are light and buttery, rice fragrant and service cheery and informed. The wine list is short, with four by the glass.
Chef/s: Nand Kishor. **Open:** Sat and Sun L, Tue to Sun D. **Closed:** Mon. **Meals:** main courses £8 to £12. **Details:** 50 seats. Wheelchairs. Music.

Our highlights...

Our undercover inspectors reveal their most memorable dishes from another year of extraordinary eating.

At **Dastaan**, little **pani puri**: crisp spheres containing a 'kicking' chickpea salad with a hole in the top to pour in the accompanying jal-jeera (a cooling yet spicy liquid), then eaten in one 'explosive mouthful'. These were like fireworks and so much fun; street food informality but execution by a top chef's hand. So memorable.

Welsh lamb at **Shaun Dickens at the Boathouse**. A trio of perfectly pink loin, melting belly and tender kidney, balanced with wild garlic, charred shallot, monk's beard and lemon gel, with a showboating lamb jus adding the final gloss. With tiny broad-bean flowers to decorate, it's a marriage made in heaven with presentation to thrill.

Pain perdu, honeycomb and vanilla ice cream at **The Ninth**. An absolutely stunning rendition of the classic, almost melt-in-the-mouth, with a soufflé-esque softness, a lovely milky flavour and a perfectly browned outer. Topped with a fresh, light honeycomb to lift things and a quenelle of good vanilla ice cream to accompany, too. Cracking dessert.

Ripley
The Anchor

Cooking score: 3
Modern British | £35
High Street, Ripley, GU23 6AE
Tel no: (01483) 211866
ripleyanchor.co.uk

On Ripley village's charming high street, the vintage brick-and-timber-fronted Anchor stands out from the crowd. It may trace its roots back to the 16th century but the interior cleverly blends the old and the new – pastel tones with exposed brick, lead-light windows, beams and smart wood furniture. With cosy snugs, a small bar, dining areas and a trump-card alfresco courtyard, it is run with positive enthusiasm. There are local ales for drinkers, while diners are drawn by the heavy commitment to local seasonal produce and dishes that have a light, modern touch. The menu reflects British and broader European styles, so roasted, crispy-skinned pink duck breast comes with sarladaise potatoes, shallot and balsamic, and lemon sole with spring onion gnocchi, caper and raisin purée and a verjus reduction. Accurate, careful cooking continues to the end, where Earl Grey pannacotta with blood orange and caraway praline will be waiting. There are lunch and early-evening deals, while the wine list (from £22) offers a dozen by the glass and carafe.
Chef/s: Michael Wall-Palmer. **Open:** Tue to Sat L and D. Sun 12 to 8. **Closed:** Mon, 25 Dec.
Meals: main courses £12 to £26. Set L and early D £18 (2 courses) to £22. Sun L £32. **Details:** 45 seats. 20 seats outside. Bar. Wheelchairs. Music. Parking.

★ NEW ENTRY ★

The Clock House

Cooking score: 5
Modern British | £55
High Street, Ripley, GU23 6AQ
Tel no: (01483) 224777
theclockhouserestaurant.co.uk

Serina Drake is now the sole owner of the restaurant formerly known as Drake's, the new name picking up on the landmark clock fronting this handsome Georgian building. While her former sous-chef, Fred Clapperton, has taken over the kitchen, little else has changed. The rear walled garden (for summer drinks) remains a hidden gem and inside, stripped-back wall timbers and tall street-side windows sit comfortably alongside warm pastel shades and contemporary seating. On the food front, Mr Clapperton's refined, modern approach takes a sophisticated if simpler route than previously, delivering intricate dishes full of colour, texture and flavour via a series of fixed-price offerings – from à la carte to tasting menus. Brill is given an exotic spin with spiced pumpkin, fat mussels, coconut, ginger and lemongrass, while beef (12-hour slow-roasted short rib) is served with sweetbreads, brassicas and trumpet chanterelles. Blackberry, hibiscus, apples and shortbread make an accomplished light finale. In addition, canapés, petits fours and breads hit the spot, the set lunch is considered a very good deal and service is 'very good'. The wine list is dominated by classic French regions but has a global outlook.
Chef/s: Fred Clapperton. **Open:** Wed to Sat L and D. **Closed:** Sun, Mon, Tue, 25 Dec, 1 Jan, 1 week Easter, 2 weeks Aug. **Meals:** set L £26 (2 courses) to £30. Set D £45 (2 courses) to £55. Tasting menu £70. **Details:** 40 seats. V menu. Bar. Music.

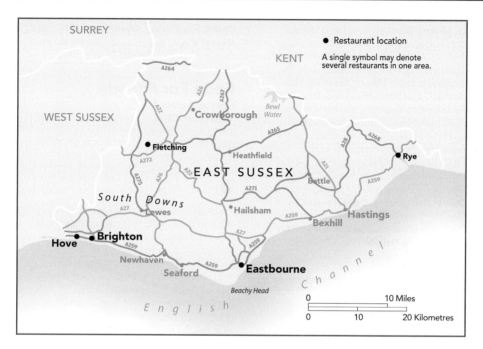

SURREY

KENT

● Restaurant location

A single symbol may denote several restaurants in one area.

A264

WEST SUSSEX

A26 A267

A22

Crowborough

Bewl Water

A265

A28 A268

Fletching

A272

Heathfield

Rye

A275 A26

EAST SUSSEX

A21

A271

Battle

A259

South Downs

A27

Lewes

Hailsham

A259

Bexhill

Hastings

Hove

Brighton

A259

A27

A259

Newhaven

Seaford

Eastbourne

Beachy Head

C h a n n e l

E n g l i s h

0   10 Miles

0   10   20 Kilometres

◾ Brighton
Bincho Yakitori
Cooking score: 2
Japanese | £20
63 Preston Street, Brighton, BN1 2HE
Tel no: (01273) 779021
binchoyakitori.com
£30

Preston Street is rammed full of restaurants, but its reputation has long been for quantity, not quality, so when David Biney rocked up in 2015 to realise his passion for Japanese izakayas, things started to look up. After three years working in Japan, David has nailed the casual izakaya vibe: basic décor, a few seats on the counter by the charcoal grill, an energetic soundtrack and full-flavoured dishes to share. From the grill come yakitori skewers of chicken thigh and deliciously tender pork belly, or try the more outré chicken hearts, or quail's egg with bacon. Lamb chops, fiery Korean chicken wings... it's all good stuff, and the veggie courses are no less punchy (tofu

with kimchi, say). Keep an eye on the daily specials, too. Drink saké, Japanese beer or wines from £17.50.
Chef/s: Tomo Ishii. **Open:** Tue to Sun D only.
Closed: Mon, 24 Dec to 6 Jan. **Meals:** dishes £4 to £16. **Details:** 32 seats.

The Chilli Pickle
Cooking score: 2
Indian | £28
17 Jubilee Street, Brighton, BN1 1GE
Tel no: (01273) 900383
thechillipickle.com
£30

With its playschool colours, stencilled walls and shelves of provisions visible behind an imposing glass frontage, Chilli Pickle isn't your average curry house – still, you'd expect nothing less from Brighton. Alun Sperring earned his stripes at London's Cinnamon Club (see entry) and his invigorating take on Indian regional cuisine is noted for its freshness, zest and complexity. Readers also applaud his

'excellent presentation and very good garnishing', typical flourishes from a chef who cares about the little details. Sussex ingredients make a significant contribution (try the locally landed red bream sizzled in the tandoor), but the menu ranges far and wide from Goan prawn puri vindaloo to Nepalese chicken dal bhat (a home-style 'village' curry) and Hyderabadi biryanis perfumed with rosewater. Sunday brunch is a family buffet, while lunch includes great-value railway trays and all-inclusive 'king thalis'. World beers and aromatic wines match the food perfectly.
Chef/s: Alun Sperring. **Open:** all week L and D. **Closed:** 25 and 26 Dec. **Meals:** main courses £14 to £19. Set D £25 (2 courses) to £28. Sun L £25 (2 courses) to £28. **Details:** 115 seats. 18 seats outside. Wheelchairs. Music.

★ NEW ENTRY ★

Cin Cin
Cooking score: 2
Italian | £30
13-16 Vine Street, Brighton, BN1 4AG
Tel no: (01273) 698813
cincin.co.uk
£5
OFF

The guys behind Cin Cin started off by fuelling up festival-goers and corporate do's with proper Italian grub from the back of their old Fiat van (or rather the side of it). They've now laid some foundations in Brighton's North Laine, and have 20 seats at their 'Bar & Kitchen', where you get to sit on a surprisingly comfy stool at the counter within close proximity to the open kitchen. It's a chilled-out, feel-good place, where relatively simple things are done well and many of the dishes are ideal for sharing. Antipasti such as creamy burrata drizzled with balsamic or a salumi board for two will get you in the mood. The seasons are duly followed, with May presenting asparagus, cooked just so, with confit egg yolk and Parmesan a couple of ways, or rabbit crocchette with 'addictive' wild garlic pesto. Pasta is handmade, fazzoletti, say, with black bream and capers, while the aperitifs and wines are Italian all the way.

Chef/s: Jamie Halsall. **Open:** Tue to Sat L and D. **Closed:** Sun, Mon, 25 and 26 Dec. **Meals:** main courses £9 to £12. **Details:** 20 seats. Music.

Food For Friends
Cooking score: 1
Vegetarian | £26
17-18 Prince Albert Street, The Lanes, Brighton, BN1 1HF
Tel no: (01273) 202310
foodforfriends.com
£30

Food for Friends is a smart-casual sort of place with an urban vibe that has, over the years, morphed from a laid-back old-school wholefood restaurant into a well-regarded local asset, famed for its contemporary vegetarian cooking. Dishes are substantial but refined, with influences from the Mediterranean, Middle East and Asia. Five-spice crispy tofu with sesame and tamari-marinated aubergine and a cardamom, tomato and lemongrass relish, might be followed by ginger-beer-battered haloumi with triple-cooked chips, pickled quails' eggs, wakami, samphire and crushed lemon peas. Wines from £17.95.
Chef/s: Tomas Kowalski. **Open:** all week L and D. **Closed:** 24 and 25 Dec. **Meals:** main courses £13 to £15. Set L £18 (2 courses) to £24. Set D £24 (3 courses). Sun L £18. **Details:** 75 seats. 25 seats outside. V menu. Wheelchairs. Music.

The Gingerman
Cooking score: 3
Modern British | £37
21a Norfolk Square, Brighton, BN1 2PD
Tel no: (01273) 326688
gingermanrestaurants.com

Ben McKellar is approaching the end of his second decade at his discreet restaurant near the seafront – the flagship of his Brighton-based Gingerman group. It is very much a local – the sort we all wish we had nearby. Good-quality materials such as local gurnard and Trenchmore Farm beef establish a firm foundation, and the kitchen does exactly what it sets out to do, producing imaginatively conceived and skilfully prepared dishes. Monkfish, for example, is teamed with Parma ham, red pepper and chorizo arancini, fennel purée, spiced tomato chutney and asparagus, and a main-course chicken is served with its crispy leg, a boudin blanc and veal sweetbread, as well as smoked garlic purée, broad beans, lettuce, girolles and parsley oil. Soufflés, say passion fruit (with banana sorbet and coconut and peanut crunch) are a big hit. The set lunch is very good value and well-paced service adds to the appeal. Wines are a worldy bunch, starting in Spain at £18.

Chef/s: Ben McKellar and Mark Charker. **Open:** Tue to Sun L and D. **Closed:** Mon, 2 weeks from 1 Jan. **Meals:** set L £17 (2 courses) to £20. Set D £32 (2 courses) to £37. Sun L £25. **Details:** 32 seats. Music.

★ NEW ENTRY ★

Isaac At

Cooking score: 3
Modern British | £35
2 Gloucester Street, Brighton, BN1 4EW
Tel no: (07765) 934740
isaac-at.com

This young, passionate team are truly dedicated to the concept of local and seasonal ingredients, with food miles duly counted (honey, Hove, 2 miles), and wines exclusively from Sussex. The small dining room and open-plan kitchen has a design motif that is stylish contemporary simplicity itself, and they're not afraid to use the 'fine dining' moniker (but this is the modern way, so relaxed, engaged and focused on the food). The necessity to pay a down payment to secure a table raises an eyebrow, but it is a small venue and they're obviously affected by no-shows. What you get, though, is some very good cooking with great attention to detail. Things get going with first-rate bread – 'out-blooming-standing'. Among an array of creative courses, a generous amount of perfectly cooked brill is matched with Jerusalem artichoke purée and kohlrabi, and 'pink and tender' lamb rump with their version of babaganoush. The core ingredients

get to shine. A dessert of alexanders bud ice cream with cherry tomatoes (dehydrated and then rehydrated with rhubarb syrup) makes for an impressive finish. English wines start at £21.

Chef/s: Isaac Bartlett-Copeland. **Open:** Sat L, Tue to Sat D. **Closed:** Sun, Mon, 23 Dec to 7 Jan, 1 week Easter, 1 to 21 Aug. **Meals:** set L and D £35 (4 courses). Tasting menu £47. **Details:** 20 seats. V menu. Music. Children over 12 yrs only.

★ NEW ENTRY ★

Pike & Pine

Cooking score: 4
Modern European | £55
1d St James's Street, Brighton
Tel no: (01273) 686668
pikeandpine.co.uk

The restaurant scene here has finally started to match the vibrancy and energy of the city. This recent arrival is full of beans – coffee and trendy plates in the daytime café, Redroaster, morphing into an evening restaurant, Pike & Pine, where Matt Gillan serves up contemporary tasting menus. The botanical theme, with hanging fake plants and marble tables, is a bit different from the usual modern schtick ('more like a boutique than a restaurant'), while the soundtrack provides a repetitive beat. Some counter seats provide a good view of the open kitchen. Highlights thus far include a plate of beetroot tartare, watercress purée and a perfectly runny crispy egg yolk – 'so much more than the sum of its parts' – and stone bass with a plump morel, rich jus and Hispi cabbage that has no right to taste this good. Among dessert courses, fennel ice cream is a perfect foil to honey pannacotta, with crunchy honeycomb and silky yoghurt. Drink cool cocktails or wines from the exceedingly reasonable opening price of £17.50.

Chef/s: Matt Gillan. **Open:** Wed to Sun D only. **Closed:** Mon, Tue. **Meals:** tasting menu £55 (6 courses) to £65 (8 courses). **Details:** V menu. Music.

Plateau

Cooking score: 1
Modern European | £40
1 Bartholowmews, Brighton, BN1 1HG
Tel no: (01273) 733085
plateaubrighton.co.uk

It's the French meaning of the word 'plateau' that holds sway at this restaurant and wine bar, with sharing plates such as a fishy one with tandoori mackerel, crispy buttermilk gurnard and sea trout with an Asian salad. There are solo main courses if sharing's not for you. A European flavour and some Asian influences inflect an output where crab is the centrepiece of a pretty dish with watermelon and cucumber (lightly pickled and vibrant sauce), and Roscoff onions arrive in a wonderfully rustic dish with goats' curd and hazelnuts. Onglet steak with frites, capsicum risotto, it's simple stuff done well, with a wine list that focuses on the natural, organic and biodynamic.
Chef/s: Dan Cropper. **Open:** all week L and D. **Meals:** main courses £10 to £12. Set L £16 (2 courses) to £20. **Details:** Bar.

The Restaurant at Drakes

Cooking score: 4
Modern European | £45
43-44 Marine Parade, Brighton, BN2 1PE
Tel no: (01273) 696934
therestaurantatdrakes.co.uk

£5 OFF 🛏

A boutique hotel on the seafront, in a town hardly deficient in such attractions, Drakes is the kind of place where, reclining in your bathtub, you may well wave to the crowds below heading towards the pier. Drakes, meanwhile, is to be found in the nether reaches, in a basement room that, with its dazzling white background and rolled grey banquettes, does it best not to feel submerged at all. Andy Vitez maintains a confident touch on the tiller, offering modern European dishes of direct appeal, building up to a five-course taster that includes cheese at no supplement.

Expect gutsy seafood chowder with Sussex pancetta, garnished with herb-crusted razor clams, before marinated wild boar steak and matching ragoût, with sweet-natured accompaniments of candied red cabbage and quince purée, or perhaps poached Arctic char with violet potatoes, salmon roe and crackled sea trout skin. A light dessert of pineapple soufflé chilled out with lime and tequila ice cream should set you up nicely for Brighton's nocturnal fleshpots. Wines by the glass from £6 head up a compendious list.
Chef/s: Andy Vitez. **Open:** all week L and D. **Meals:** main courses £12 to £16. Set L £20 (2 courses) to £25. Set D £34 (2 courses) to £45. Tasting menu £60 to £95. **Details:** 40 seats. Bar. Parking.

Riddle & Finns

Cooking score: 1
Seafood | £35
139 King's Road Arches, Brighton, BN1 2FN
Tel no: (01273) 821218
riddleandfinns.co.uk

Doubling as a Champagne and oyster bar, this seafood specialist makes much of its prime position underneath the arches on Brighton's beachfront. Big platters of fruits de mer are the headliners here, but the lengthy menu covers all bases from whole Dover sole to Keralan seafood curry. In between, take a punt on sautéed squid with chorizo and chilli, bouillabaisse or fillet of Shoreham cod with pearl barley risotto, butternut squash purée, cavolo nero and hazelnuts. Meat eaters and vegetarians are accommodated, and there's useful back-up from a cosmopolitan drinks list. There's also a bijou no-bookings outlet at 12B Meeting House Lane.
Chef/s: Luke Webb. **Open:** all week, all day from 12. **Meals:** main courses £15 to £42. Set L and early D £15 (2 courses). **Details:** 48 seats. 50 seats outside.

Average price

The average price denotes the price of a three-course meal without wine.

The Salt Room

Cooking score: 3
Modern British | £40
106 King's Road, Brighton, BN1 2FN
Tel no: (01273) 929488
saltroom-restaurant.co.uk

Nabbing such a prime spot opposite the skeletal remains of the West Pier and the i360 tower was a canny move by the owner of the city's Coal Shed restaurant (see entry). Attached to the side of the Hilton Metropole, the Salt Room is busy much of the time, but keen service keeps pace. It's a big space (bigger still when the sea-facing terrace comes into play), with an interior design of urban and retro inclination. Keep an eye on the blackboard for specials, quite possibly cooked on the Josper charcoal grill – monkfish, say, for two to share, with wild garlic and monk's beard, or a whopping bone-in sirloin. Get going with cuttlefish in a 'richly satisfying' red wine sauce, or keep it simple with coal-roasted king prawns. Gurnard with 'super-tender' octopus competes with a full-monty 'surf board' among main courses (oysters, crab, langoustines et al). There's attention to detail right through to a modern take on rhubarb and custard. Drink cool cocktails and well-chosen wines starting at £18.50.
Chef/s: Dave Mothersill. **Open:** all week L and D. **Closed:** 25 to 27 Dec. **Meals:** main courses £14 to £28. Set L and early D £15 (2 courses) to £18. **Details:** 98 seats. 45 seats outside. Bar. Wheelchairs. Music.

Semolina

Cooking score: 1
Modern European | £27
15 Baker Street, Brighton, BN1 4JN
Tel no: (01273) 697259
semolinabrighton.co.uk
£5 OFF £30

Some way away from the tourist hubbub, Semolina is sought out by savvy locals for its sensible prices, engaging service and 'darn good cooking'. Expect a relaxed bistro vibe, but plenty of professionalism too, with chef/

proprietor Orson Whitfield in the kitchen turning out a broadly modern European repertoire based on a good amount of regional produce. Kick off with hot-smoked salmon, followed by cod with Jerusalem artichokes or slow-cooked Jacob's Ladder with truffle polenta. Brighton gin looms large in a fun list of cocktails, local Ridgeview fizz is 'just divine' and the concise wine list opens at £17.
Chef/s: Orson Whitfield. **Open:** Wed to Sat L, Tue to Sat D. **Closed:** Sun, Mon, 1 week Christmas, 2 weeks Jan, 2 weeks Aug. **Meals:** main courses £11 to £18. Set L £12 (2 courses) to £15. **Details:** 28 seats. Music.

The Set

Cooking score: 2
Modern British | £35
Artist Residence, 33 Regency Square, Brighton, BN1 2GG
Tel no: (01273) 324302
thesetrestaurant.com
£5 OFF

The boho Artist Residence hotel's food and drink output is in the creative hands of Semone Bonner and Dan Kenny, with The Set Café delivering the likes of crab mac 'n' cheese and the Cocktail Shack doling out inspiring libations. The Set Restaurant itself seats only 20, has offbeat recycled décor and a tiny open kitchen, offering the choice of three rather reasonably priced set menus, one of which is vegetarian. Tomatoes take centre stage in an opening salvo, brined, dried and jammed, with fiery kim-chee and soothing goats' curd, followed by trout from a chalk stream in Hampshire, with compressed watermelon and crab in various guises. Modern techniques and ideas don't overshadow the fabulous ingredients, so pork belly is as tender as it gets, with equally tender octopus, and peaches and pickled chicory providing the sweet and sharp. Among sweet courses, chocolate, popcorn and peanuts are 'best friends forever'. Paired drinks are £27 per flight.
Chef/s: Dan Kenny and Semone Bonner. **Open:** all week L and D. **Meals:** set L and D £29 to £35. **Details:** 20 seats. V menu. Bar. Music. No children.

Silo

Cooking score: 3
Modern British | £30
39 Upper Gardner Street, Brighton, BN1 4AN
Tel no: (01273) 674259
silobrighton.com

£5 OFF

In the only British constituency ever to elect a Green MP, Silo fits the bill. Its furniture and supporting structure are all made from recycled materials, and the place incorporates its own flour mill, processes its own almond milk, churns its own butter, and so forth. A Victorian warehouse in the North Laine, haunt of alternative retailers and eateries, provides the setting, and Douglas McMaster's kitchen offers a menu (printed on recycled brown paper) of advanced natural cooking. Expect to start with a serving of shiitake mushrooms and celeriac in whey, before the favoured fish, gurnard, turns up cured and partnered with potato and sea buckthorn. Alternatively, a whole leek – fermented and charred – is served as a veggie show stopper, in curd sauce with dumplings. The three menu formats are designed along vegetable, fish and meat lines. The last might deliver pork loin with carrots and mizuna, while a dessert of rhubarb and cacao parfait looks the best sweet bet. There are wines from £27, as well as distinctly groovy cocktails.
Chef/s: Douglas McMaster and James McIlveen.
Open: all week L, Tue to Sat D. **Closed:** 25 and 26 Dec. **Meals:** main courses £14 to £18. Set L £20 (3 courses). Set D £28 (3 courses). **Details:** 50 seats. V menu. Bar. Wheelchairs. Music.

64 Degrees

Cooking score: 4
Modern European | £30
53 Meeting House Lane, Brighton, BN1 1HB
Tel no: (01273) 770115
64degrees.co.uk

It's just a wee stroll from the seafront into the Lanes to Scotsman Michael Bremner's 64 Degrees, a restaurant named after the temperature that secures his perfect egg yolk.

Sit cheek by jowl with your neighbours at one of the few chunky wooden tables or grab a stool at the open kitchen counter and watch the chefs at work. A spirited, boisterous place, it's wise to book. Small plates arrive to be shared, savoured and devoured, with modern cooking techniques used to measured effect, and the sterling ingredients get room to shine. Squid arrives as tender as you like, with crispy tentacles, fermented fennel and a perky black bean sauce, a cauliflower course is a veggie star turn, and meat lovers can get hands-on with gloriously tender glazed lamb to wrap in Savoy cabbage leaves, a fiery gochujang sauce for company. A 'stonking' chocolate, coffee and hazelnut dessert plays with temperature and texture to winning affect. The compact wine list is arranged by style.
Chef/s: Michael Bremner and Samuel Lambert.
Open: all week L and D. **Closed:** 25 and 26 Dec, 1 Jan. **Meals:** small plates £12 to £29. **Details:** 22 seats. Music. No children after 9pm.

Terre à Terre

Cooking score: 3
Vegetarian | £33
71 East Street, Brighton, BN1 1HQ
Tel no: (01273) 729051
terreaterre.co.uk

£5 OFF

Meat-free on East Street for nearly a quarter of a century, Terre à Terre continues to flex its vegetarian muscles. If at times the 'humorous' menu seems like an impenetrable text, the knowledgeable staff can always help with contextualisation. The simple, unpretentious dining room extends out back and they can really pack them in while managing to keep everything going along nicely. Asian flavours pepper the 'inventive, unique' menu, but the world is truly their (veggie) oyster, so you might start with KFC, a zingy Korean-inspired cauliflower number, or go for a 'mince pie' made with hot Twineham Grange cheese. Main-course 'ding dong dengaku' is a vegan and gluten-free option inspired by Japanese cuisine, with deftly handled hits of sweet, sour and umami, with haloumi playing the protein role in a 'filling' take on fish and chips. Among desserts, churros lack the hoped for lightness. The wine list is entirely organic and vegetarian.

Chef/s: Judith Lang. **Open:** all week, all day from 12 (11am Sat and Sun). **Closed:** 24 to 26 Dec. **Meals:** main courses £15 to £16. Set L £25 (2 courses) to £33. Set D £33 (3 courses). **Details:** 100 seats. 15 seats outside. V menu. Wheelchairs. Music.

LOCAL GEM

The Coal Shed

Modern British | £40

8 Boyces Street, Brighton, BN1 1AN
Tel no: (01273) 322998
coalshed-restaurant.co.uk

£5
OFF

Younger brother to the Salt Room (see entry), this Josper-fuelled eatery has become a local hit with its confident offer of well-hung Scottish beef and luxury seafood. Dry-aged steaks and juicy lobsters are the big money-spinners, but there's much more besides – perhaps crab and saffron ravioli followed by roast lamb loin and faggot with pearl barley, boulangère potatoes and baby carrots. Still hungry? Try doughnuts with espresso mousse and Amaretto. Beefy reds stand out on the wine list – BYO on Mondays (£5 corkage).

LOCAL GEM

Curry Leaf Cafe

Indian | £26

60 Ship Street, Brighton, BN1 1AE
Tel no: (01273) 207070
curryleafcafe.com

£30

Everything about this cheerfully decorated eatery encourages a relaxed approach to Indian food. Pop in for a lunchtime masala dosa and flavours of the South Indian streets (especially the light and crisp vegetable samosas), or go the whole hog at dinner with a starter of Hyderabadi lamb chops, before a main course such as an aromatic fish curry or Goan pork vindaloo. Vegetarians fare very well indeed,

and to finish, there is mango ice cream. Drink spicy cocktails, craft beers or spice-friendly wines from £18.

▌Eastbourne

The Mirabelle

Cooking score: 4
Modern European | £44
The Grand Hotel, King Edward's Parade, Eastbourne, BN21 4EQ
Tel no: (01323) 412345
grandeastbourne.com

£5
OFF

Living it large on Eastbourne's seafront since 1875, 'The White Palace', as it is known with justifiable hubris, is a landmark and a touchstone for old-school formality and grandeur. Its main restaurant, the Mirabelle, is that way inclined, too, staunchly formal and grown up, with an engaging service team who dress exceedingly smartly and expect you to do the same. The fixed-price carte has moved gently with the times, with Gerald Röser's signature pike mousseline soufflé joined by the likes of a new-fangled burrata salad with pickled rhubarb and pomegranate molasses among opening salvos. If a fillet of lamb with mini shepherd's pie might be said to lack a little finesse, the general consensus is that the Mirabelle remains the town's fine-dining high-water mark. Finish with a rich dark chocolate parfait served up with a coffee and mascarpone macaron. The wine list gives good account of the region, and not just the fizz.

Chef/s: Gerald Röser. **Open:** Tue to Sat L and D. **Closed:** Sun, Mon, first 2 weeks Jan. **Meals:** set L £22 (2 courses) to £26. Set D £38 (2 courses) to £44. Tasting menu £64. **Details:** 50 seats. Bar. Wheelchairs. Music. Parking.

Local Gem

Local Gems are the perfect neighbourhood venues, delivering good, freshly cooked food at great value for money.

▮ Fletching

LOCAL GEM
The Griffin Inn
Modern British | £32
Fletching, TN22 3SS
Tel no: (01825) 722890
thegriffininn.co.uk

£5 OFF 🛏

'Still a lovely pub, atmospheric bars, pleasant traditional dining room, great terrace and an amazing garden,' the Griffin has all the character you'd hope for alongside regional ales and a killer countryside view from the garden. The menu sweeps through the south east before heading off to foreign shores, so Rye Bay scallops with black pudding hash sits alongside Asian-inspired tuna. South Downs lamb and Sussex beef fly the local flag, and a risotto primavera might be the vegetarian option. The summer weekend BBQs are great fun. The wine list is a well-constructed, serious work.

▮ Hove

★ NEW ENTRY ★
etch.
Cooking score: 5
Modern European | £40
216 Church Road, Hove, BN3 2DJ
Tel no: (01273) 227485
etchfood.co.uk

£5 OFF

Whether you watched Steven Edwards win *MasterChef: The Professionals* a few years back, or just got wind of it via the social media buzz, etch. (lower-case, full stop) certainly hit the local dining scene with a vengeance in 2017. It's a class act with an open kitchen and dashing contemporary design, and evident passion is shown for the fruits of the land and sea hereabouts. The menu evolves weekly with multi-course tasting menus of four, six or eight courses. Expect to get going with a brace of snacks including the signature mushroom doughnut, before the 'gloriously glazed'

Marmite brioche with seaweed butter. Pea and mint pack quite a punch in Mr Edwards' hands, a light, frothy and flavour-packed bowl setting the tone, followed by locally caught grey mullet with scallop roe cream and a couple of ways with lettuce, then yielding pork belly with a 'potentially addictive' crackling powder. There's confidence and intelligence in the matching of flavours, not least in a chocolate and rapeseed course that combines sweet, sour and salty notes. The concise wine list makes a big thing of regional English sparkling wine, quite rightly.
Chef/s: Steven Edwards. **Open:** Sat L, Wed to Sat D. **Closed:** Sun, Mon, Tue, last 2 weeks Dec. **Meals:** tasting menu £40 (4 courses) to £60. **Details:** 38 seats. Music. Children over 8 yrs only.

The Ginger Pig
Cooking score: 3
Modern British | £35
3 Hove Street, Hove, BN3 2TR
Tel no: (01273) 736123
gingermanrestaurants.com

🛏

Just a stroll from the pleasurable inducements of Hove Lawns and the seafront, this one-time hotel now does duty as a pub with serious foodie credentials. Launched in the noughties as part of the Brighton-based Gingerman group, it caters to drinkers as well as diners – although there's little doubt who fares best here (check out the private dining room). Lively modern cooking with a seasonal accent takes in roast pigeon breast with beetroot purée, pickled quince, port and radicchio, and roast cod loin with olive oil mash, sauce vierge and ham-fried carrots. Other ideas such as pickled mussels with whipped cod's roe, fennel salad and potato crisps or a cheese burger with smoked chilli mustard, pickles and dripping chips are bang on-trend, while puddings might offer cranberry and walnut tart with treacle custard. To drink, real ales or cocktails from an impressive list compete with a sharp list of global wines.

Chef/s: Robin Koehorst. **Open:** all week L and D. **Meals:** main courses £13 to £23. Set L and early D Mon to Fri £15 (2 courses) to £18. **Details:** 100 seats. 10 seats outside. Bar. Wheelchairs. Music.

The Little Fish Market

Cooking score: 5
Seafood | £55
10 Upper Market Street, Hove, BN3 1AS
Tel no: (01273) 722213
thelittlefishmarket.co.uk

£5
OFF

Hove may be united in municipal alliance with neighbouring Brighton, but it maintains its own distinct character, and here in the hinterland between Church Road and the seafront, Duncan Ray's fish restaurant is a beguiling proposition. The emphasis on the bounty of the sea is apt enough in a coastal venue, but the polish accorded to it lifts the place far above the norm. The fixed menu might bring you a Carlingford oyster in Jersey cream scented with elderflower, prior to Loch Duart salmon with crab, fennel and potato salad, and then a pair of principals, cod in beurre noisette with brown shrimps, and brill with chicken and morels in sherry. Sometimes a meat dish is inveigled in, but generally given a waft of sea breeze, too – say pork belly with cockles – and proceedings conclude with the likes of wild strawberry mille-feuille or passion fruit nougat glacé. Breads such as olive fougasse come with home-churned cultured butter. The short wine list, from £23, is all about bright modern flavours.
Chef/s: Duncan Ray. **Open:** Sat L, Tue to Sat D. **Closed:** Sun, Mon, 1 week Easter, 2 weeks Sept, 1 week Dec. **Meals:** set L £20 (2 courses) to £25. Tasting menu £55. **Details:** 20 seats. V menu. Music. Children over 12 yrs only.

▌ Rye
Landgate Bistro

Cooking score: 2
British | £30
5-6 Landgate, Rye, TN31 7LH
Tel no: (01797) 222829
landgatebistro.co.uk

While there's a certain cottagey charm, with low ceilings and some bare brick, at Martin Peacock and Nilla Westin's tiny restaurant by Rye's 14th-century Landgate, a face-lift has overlaid it all with a gentle contemporary feel – it feels classic but modern. Mr Peacock works hard at the stove, respects seasonal ingredients and knows his home patch when it comes to supplies – from locally caught fish via marsh lamb to new-season wild garlic. The result is a menu that might involve tender local squid braised in red wine with aïoli and go on to lemon sole fillets in white wine and tarragon with crispy kale and crushed Pink Fir potatoes or breast and confit leg of Gressingham duck served with Puy lentils, potato gnocchi and wild spinach. There's an excellent selection of British cheeses if puddings such as apple tartlet served with Valrhona white chocolate ice cream don't appeal. Wines from £19.20.
Chef/s: Martin Peacock. **Open:** Sat and Sun L, Wed to Sat D. **Closed:** Mon, Tue, 24 to 26 and 31 Dec. **Meals:** main courses £15 to £20. Set L £16 (2 courses) to £20. Set D Wed and Thur £19 (2 courses) to £23. Sun L £16 (2 courses) to £20. **Details:** 32 seats. Bar. Music.

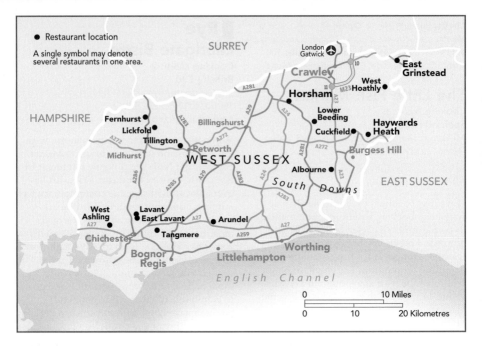

▮ Albourne
The Ginger Fox

Cooking score: 3
Modern British | £35
Muddleswood Road, Albourne, BN6 9EA
Tel no: (01273) 857888
gingermanrestaurants.com

This neatly thatched, whitewashed country inn stands in a pretty garden, has views over the South Downs and is owned by the Brighton-based Gingerman group. It's relaxed and unstuffy, with real ales and a welcoming attitude towards children, but the main interest is in the cooking – its approach echoing the group's mix of rustic informality and upmarket, often gutsy British dishes. There's a feel for combining diverse flavours with a commitment to local produce, one where black pudding Scotch egg with apple purée and celeriac rémoulade, or even Welsh rarebit with Sussex ale, may be served alongside mallard breast and confit leg with braised cabbage, salsify, swede purée and

mushroom jus, or Redlands Farm beef fillet with creamed spinach, onion fondant, Brighton Blue cheese croquette and duck-fat chips. Brioche pain perdu (caramelised pear, walnut crumble, muscovado ice cream and pear chutney) is a handsome, generous endnote. Wines from £18.

Chef/s: Ben McKellar and Mark Bradley. **Open:** all week L and D. **Closed:** 25 Dec. **Meals:** main courses £14 to £24. Set L £16 (2 courses). **Details:** 62 seats. 88 seats outside. Bar. Music. Parking.

Please send us your feedback

To register your opinion about any restaurant listed in this guide, or a new restaurant that you wish to bring to our attention, please visit the web address at the bottom of the page. Your feedback informs the content of the book and will be used to compile next year's reviews.

▌Arundel
The Parsons Table
Cooking score: 3
British | £32
2 & 8 Castle Mews, Tarrant Street, Arundel,
BN18 9DG
Tel no: (01903) 883477
theparsonstable.co.uk
£5
OFF

At the end of a short mews not far from the
castle (though nowhere in Arundel is that far
from the castle to be fair), this seriously
accomplished venue offers up classically
inspired contemporary cooking. Lee and Liz
Parsons have experience at the top end of
cheffing and management respectively, and
their well-designed restaurant, unpretentious
but in vogue, is noted for attention to detail
and high standards. The weekly changing
menu is bolstered by daily specials, and much
is made of the fact ingredients are sourced
locally. Pulled ham hock croquettes with
homemade piccalilli is a feel-good opener, or
go for an equally satisfying seafood chowder.
Among main courses, Barbary duck breast
arrives perfectly pink with a cherry port sauce,
while the catch of the day is 'locally sourced
fish simply prepared'. Finish off with spiced
poached pear with almond streusel and honey
and ginger ice cream. The concise wine list
starts at £17.50.
Chef/s: Lee Parsons. **Open:** Tue to Sat L and D.
Closed: Sun, Mon, 24 to 27 Dec, 1 week Feb, 1
week end Aug. **Meals:** main courses £15 to £20.
Tasting menu £60. **Details:** 34 seats. Music.

The Town House
Cooking score: 3
Modern British | £30
65 High Street, Arundel, BN18 9AJ
Tel no: (01903) 883847
thetownhouse.co.uk
£5
OFF

The Georgian market town of Arundel,
sheltering beneath its magnificently preserved
castle, is the setting for a Regency house that

has its own claim on architectural
exquisiteness. Look upwards in the dining
room, and above you is an imported 16th-
century Florentine ceiling of gilded carved
walnut, a breathtaking feature. Lee Williams'
cooking has evolved over the past decade to
incorporate more modernist touches among
the classics of French fine dining. Home-
smoked Barbary duck dressed in honey and
mustard with pickled wild mushrooms could
be the curtain-raiser for roast monkfish in
fennel and mussel butter sauce, or perhaps
fillet of Sussex venison with roasted salsify,
buttered Savoy and confit potato in chestnut
jus. Simple dessert temptations run to
griottine frangipane tart with clotted cream,
and chocolate marquise with honeycomb in
white chocolate sauce. The lunch menu is
something of a bargain. House Grenache
Blanc and Merlot are £19.50 on a reliable core
list that's supplemented by a glitzier slate of
Bordeaux and Burgundy.
Chef/s: Lee Williams. **Open:** Tue to Sat L and D.
Closed: Sun, Mon, 25 to 27 Dec, 1 to 3 Jan, 2 weeks
Easter, 2 weeks Oct. **Meals:** set L £18 (2 courses) to
£22. Set D £26 (2 courses) to £30. **Details:** 24 seats.
Music.

▌Cuckfield
Ockenden Manor
Cooking score: 5
Modern French | £65
Ockenden Lane, Cuckfield, RH17 5LD
Tel no: (01444) 416111
hshotels.co.uk
🛏

Part of the privately owned Historic Sussex
Hotels group, there's no disputing the lineage
of Ockenden Manor – built in the middle of
the 16th century and extended over the years,
it has a prime position in eight acres with 'just
beautiful' views from the restaurant. When the
French doors are open on to the terrace, it's
pretty special. Stephen Crane cooks in a
refined modern French style that suits the
formality of the space, with regional
ingredients bringing a sense of place, and a
creative, contemporary touch. Home-smoked

mackerel stars in an opening course (after copious canapés) with beetroot in various guises and horseradish cream, while English asparagus soup with home-smoked salmon and cream cheese soldiers is a spring and summer treat. Newhaven turbot with pearl barley, chorizo and fennel salad, and Goodwood Estate lamb with a Middle Eastern spin put those local ingredients centre stage, with desserts such as red cherry soufflé ensuring it all comes to a close in fine style. The impressive wine list opens at £29.
Chef/s: Stephen Crane. **Open:** all week L and D. **Meals:** set L £23 (2 courses) to £30. Set D £65. Sun L £40. Tasting menu £90. **Details:** 75 seats. V menu. Bar. Wheelchairs. Parking.

■ East Grinstead
Gravetye Manor
Cooking score: 5
Modern British | £70
Vowels Lane, East Grinstead, RH19 4LJ
Tel no: (01342) 810567
gravetyemanor.co.uk

An uxorious Sussex merchant had Gravetye built for his good lady towards the end of the first Elizabeth's reign, but it was as the home of Victorian master gardener William Robinson that the place began to come into its own. The long approach through parkland to the stone manor itself creates a gathering sense of anticipation, rewarded by the prospect of a panelled dining room with dramatic marble fireplace. George Blogg has a productive kitchen garden and peach house to keep the kitchen supplied all year, and works it into broadly based menus of carefully composed British dishes. Miso-glazed Orkney scallops with baby radish and a seaweed sesame cracker, or duck liver with roasted hen-of-the-woods, watercress and wild garlic seeds, might be the opening gambits, before seared sea trout and squid with a fishcake, fennel, monk's beard and saffron aïoli makes its multifarious impression. Meats are treated inventively but intuitively, perhaps saddle and shoulder of hogget with potato-wrapped

haggis, sprouting broccoli and mint jellies. Close the deal with lemon and ginger posset, seasoned with blood orange and sumac and served with gin-and-tonic sorbet. A wine list of formidable regional reach and stupendous quality makes a particular feature of English sparklers, and there's a good glass selection from £11. NB: Gravetye will be closed from January to April 2018 for redevelopment of its restaurant operations.
Chef/s: George Blogg. **Open:** all week L and D. **Closed:** 2 Jan to 30 Apr (for refurbishment). **Meals:** set L £30 (2 courses) to £40. Set D £40. Sun L £50. Tasting menu £85. **Details:** 50 seats. 20 seats outside. Bar. Wheelchairs. Music. Parking. Children over 7 yrs only.

■ East Lavant
The Royal Oak Inn
Cooking score: 1
Modern British | £35
Pook Lane, East Lavant, PO18 0AX
Tel no: (01243) 527434
royaloakeastlavant.co.uk

A village pub on the southern edge of the South Downs, not a million miles from the sea, the Royal Oak has old beams, a real fire and rather smart rooms if you're looking to stop over. The kitchen turns out classy versions of pub staples such as fish and chips and properly aged steaks, but there's also the likes of duo of local pork (seared tenderloin, confit belly) with pear purée and a rich cider jus, and a specials board to keep an eye on. Friendly staff, regional ales and a well-annotated wine list only add to its appeal.
Chef/s: Fran Joyce. **Open:** all week L and D. **Meals:** main courses £16 to £30. **Details:** 55 seats. 35 seats outside. Bar. Wheelchairs. Music. Parking.

Visit us online

To find out more about
The Good Food Guide, please
visit thegoodfoodguide.co.uk

Fernhurst
The Duke of Cumberland Arms

Cooking score: 4
Modern British | £35
Henley Hill, Fernhurst, GU27 3HQ
Tel no: (01428) 652280
dukeofcumberland.com

With its rustic beamed bar, real ales on draught, a roaring fire in winter and tiered gardens overlooking the South Downs National Park, this spruce 16th-century hostelry is the very image of a quintessential Sussex country pub. But venture into the smart modern extension and you'll realise that the Duke of Cumberland is also a serious destination restaurant. Simon Goodman's kitchen proves its mettle with a monthly repertoire of ambitious (but manageable) dishes inspired by regional and home-grown produce: wild pigeon breast with celeriac purée, black pudding and wild mushrooms; pea, prawn and crayfish risotto; blackened South Coast monkfish with pomme purée and tomato sauce. Other carefully judged ideas such as Chinese five-spice pork wraps suggest a free-roaming sensibility, while desserts could usher in anything from treacle sponge to a wildly extravagant chocolate sphere with 'snowball foam', strawberry powder, nutmeg ice cream and other embellishments. The food is backed by a well-chosen wine list.
Chef/s: Simon Goodman. **Open:** all week L, Tue to Sat D. **Closed:** 25 and 26 Dec. **Meals:** main courses £15 to £30. **Details:** 75 seats. 132 seats outside. Bar. Wheelchairs. Music. Parking.

Haywards Heath
Jeremy's

Cooking score: 4
Modern European | £36
Borde Hill Garden, Balcombe Road, Haywards Heath, RH16 1XP
Tel no: (01444) 441102
jeremysrestaurant.co.uk
£5
OFF

Gorgeously located amid the resplendence of Borde Hill Garden, the celebrated Edwardian parkland created around an old Tudor house, Jeremy Ashpool's venue is a particular hit in summer. Its own Victorian walled garden supplies the kitchen with much of its fresh produce, and it all ends up on the finely crafted contemporary menus that include a five-course taster on the first Tuesday of the month. There has always been an appealing lightness and delicacy to Ashpool's cooking, which more than ever suits the mood of the times, encompassing brill ceviche with oyster emulsion sauce, avocado, lime and coriander to begin, following on with Ryeland lamb on rösti, with butternut, leeks and kale, or a pairing of John Dory and squid with pak choi, noodles, mango and sea lettuce. Dessert might be as fanciful as grapefruit mousse with labneh and pomegranate, or as stalwart as sticky toffee pudding and vanilla ice cream. A far-reaching wine list arranged by style starts at £19.50.
Chef/s: Jeremy Ashpool. **Open:** Tue to Sun L, Tue to Sat D. **Closed:** Mon, first 2 weeks Jan. **Meals:** main courses £15 to £26. Set L £22 (2 courses) to £28. **Details:** 55 seats. 45 seats outside. Bar. Wheelchairs. Music. Parking.

▮ Horsham
Restaurant Tristan
Cooking score: 6
Modern British | £45
3 Stans Way, East Street, Horsham, RH12 1HU
Tel no: (01403) 255688
restauranttristan.co.uk

'I can't quite believe Tristan Mason's restaurant has been here for 10 years,' mused one fan, perplexed by the passage of time, and grateful the town has been blessed with such a place for a decade. The 16th-century bones of the building give character to the first-floor restaurant, open to the rafters with an understated contemporary finish; there's also a rather smart café/bar on the ground floor. Tristan's four-course fixed-price carte is supported by a couple of highfalutin tasting menus, a slightly smaller – and cheaper – lunch and midweek dinner option, plus veggie and pescatarian menus which are 'a cut above'. Expect precise and innovative cooking, where first-class ingredients are turned into rather inspiring and pretty-looking plates such as a crab opener, with Jerusalem artichokes and mushrooms, or an inspiring combination of pork belly, smoked eel and the yolk of a duck egg. Dish descriptions are simple ('lamb/kid/goat'), the resulting flavours and technical dexterity anything but, all the way to a dark chocolate délice dessert. Wines start at £28.
Chef/s: Tristan Mason. **Open:** Tue to Sat L and D. **Closed:** Sun, Mon, 25 and 26 Dec. **Meals:** set L £25 (3 courses) to £30. Set D £45. Tasting Menu £65 (6 courses) to £80. **Details:** 34 seats. V menu. Bar. Wheelchairs. Music. Children over 10 yrs only.

Readers recommend ◢━━━

A 'readers recommend' review is a genuine quote from a report sent in by one of our readers. We intend to follow up these suggestions throughout the year to come.

▮ Hurstpierpoint
READERS RECOMMEND
The Fig Tree
Modern British
120 High Street, Hurstpierpoint, BN6 9PX
Tel no: (01273) 832183
figtreerestaurant.co.uk
'Excellent food: pigeon breast with duck liver and sea trout ballotine with smoked fillet for starters, followed by quail and duck and a pistachio and chocolate dessert. Beautifully cooked, beautifully presented, high quality.'

▮ Lavant
The Earl of March
Cooking score: 2
Modern British | £30
Lavant Road, Lavant, PO18 0BQ
Tel no: (01243) 533993
theearlofmarch.com
£5
OFF

This Sussex stalwart – now in its eleventh year – is quite a local asset, with Giles Thompson's pub playing the roles of casual drinkers' den and full-on restaurant with great style. People love the way the menu strikes the right note between traditional and contemporary. They applaud the cooking, 'a mix of pub classics with more ambitious dishes, often using locally sourced game or seafood', and coupled with the beautiful location and the friendly service, it is no wonder booking ahead is recommended – especially in fine weather when the 'sizeable outdoor seating' comes into its own. A winter meal yielded 'excellent' devilled whitebait with tartare sauce, pan-fried pigeon and salted ox tongue served with parsnip purée and honey mead jelly, and local venison teamed with salsify, winter greens and forest mushrooms. Sticky toffee pudding for dessert 'meant a happy ending, helped by the moreish whiskey-and-honey ice cream from the nearby Caroline's Dairy'. The wine list covers most bases with bottles from £21.50.

Chef/s: Adam Hawden. **Open:** all week L and D. **Closed:** 25 Dec. **Meals:** main courses £23 to £25. Set L and D £22 (2 courses) to £25. **Details:** 70 seats. 60 seats outside. Bar. Wheelchairs. Music. Parking.

Lickfold
The Lickfold Inn
Cooking score: 6
Modern British | £48
Highstead Lane, Lickfold, GU28 9EY
Tel no: (01789) 532535
thelickfoldinn.co.uk

Built in 1460 and now boasting the tidiest of 'restored Tudor' makeovers – all fancy brickwork and blackened timbers – the Lickfold Inn still does duty as a Sussex watering hole, complete with real ales and a blazing fire in the hearth. But one glance at the bar menu will alert you to the fact that there's something else going on here – tempura cauliflower or pine chicken wings, anyone? It all makes sense when you discover that Tom Sellers from London's Restaurant Story (see entry) has adopted the place as his out-of-town bolt-hole, installing Graham Squire to run a gleaming state-of-the-art kitchen that also serves the rustic-chic dining room upstairs. Here the menu takes flight, mixing new British and Nordic themes across a creative, full-strength repertoire that's described with fashionable brevity and delivered with dazzling panache: 'artichoke, brown butter and fig'; 'lamb rump, burnt gem and monk's beard'; 'black bream, Cornish mussels and cauliflower'. To finish, try the Yorkshire rhubarb 'mess' or the baked cheesecake made with Dirty Vicar cheese (from Surrey). A concise, thoughtfully chosen wine list provides the happiest of endings to this story.
Chef/s: Graham Squire. **Open:** Wed to Sun L, Wed to Sat D. **Closed:** Mon, Tue, 25 Dec, 2 to 16 Jan. **Meals:** main courses £26 to £30. Set L £20 (2 courses) to £26. Sun L £35. Tasting menu £45 (5 courses) to £70 (7 courses). **Details:** 38 seats. Bar. Music. Parking.

Lower Beeding
The Crabtree
Cooking score: 2
Modern British | £28
Brighton Road, Lower Beeding, RH13 6PT
Tel no: (01403) 892666
crabtreesussex.co.uk
£30

Dating from the 16th century, this foursquare old coaching inn on the road betwixt Horsham and Shoreham has a lovely garden out back to get you away from those mechanised carriages that whizz along the A281 out front. The natural charm of the old inn remains, with local ales at the pumps and some 'pub classics' on the menu. The kitchen does a good version of fish and chips, but there's much more going on to attract the dining crowd: seared scallops with roast chorizo and cauliflower purée is a modern classic to be sure, while devilled chicken livers on toast with pickled rhubarb is a fabulous partnership. European influence runs deep in slow-cooked pork belly with three-bean and pancetta cassoulet, and in a fishy number of hake with lemon and garlic risotto. Likewise, desserts flit between English classics and European flavours. Wines start at £18.50.
Chef/s: Nolan Bott. **Open:** all week L, Mon to Sat D. **Closed:** 25 Dec. **Meals:** main courses £15 to £22. Set L £16. **Details:** 70 seats. 150 seats outside. Bar. Wheelchairs. Music. Parking.

The Pass
Cooking score: 4
Modern British | £80
South Lodge Hotel, Brighton Road, Lower Beeding, RH13 6PS
Tel no: (01403) 891711
exclusive.co.uk

Sweeping views to the South Downs from the lawn showcase the Sussex countryside, and of South Lodge's two restaurants, the Camellia catches those views through French doors, while the Pass has you in the kitchen instead.

Perched on posh stools or high banquettes, watch the team work first-hand, or via TV monitors, and meet them as they bring your food to the table – a country view is not required. 'It's fun', 'it's a gimmick', it is certainly fashionable. Every course on Ian Swainson's no-choice tasting menus (eight or ten at dinner) has a title, even if the title is 'Untitled 2'; this is modern, creative, experimental stuff. 'Walk the line' is a luxe snail course, 'Seeing Red' a crimson tide of roasted duck, beetroot, red cabbage and duck liver, 'lobster thermidor' a modern interpretation of classic flavours, and desserts are no less striking: 'Solar Eclipse', say, with its brilliant yellows of lemon posset and curd and evocative white truffle ice cream. A wine flight takes away the worry of trying to match wine and food.

Chef/s: Ian Swainson. **Open:** Fri to Sun L, Wed to Sun D. **Closed:** Mon, Tue, 25 Dec, 2 weeks Jan. **Meals:** tasting menu L £40 (6 courses) to £50. Tasting menu D £80 (8 courses) to £90. **Details:** 28 seats. V menu. Children over 12 yrs only.

◼ Tangmere
Cassons
Cooking score: 3
Modern British | £39
Arundel Road, Tangmere, PO18 0DU
Tel no: (01243) 773294
cassonsrestaurant.co.uk

£5
OFF

On the South Coast artery road, outside of Chichester and close to Goodwood, Cassons occupies a couple of 18th-century cottages built long before the motorcar claimed the land out front. Once inside, it's peaceful enough, with Cass (Mr Casson) the host and New Zealander Viv (Mrs Casson) leading the line in the kitchen. The menu is modern, but sensibly so, with classical combinations and a good amount of regional produce. Seafood looms large – Selsey crab, say, given an Asian flavour with daikon, a tangy salad and ginger mayonnaise, and do check the menu for the 'fish of the day'. Suckling pig gets the trio treatment (loin, belly and confit leg), with potato mille-feuille and cider reduction, game

is a seasonal treat to look out for (fillet of roe deer perhaps) and Sunday lunch includes classic roasts. Desserts such as tarte Tatin with ginger cake and crème brûlée mousse confirm the technical proficiency on show. Wines start at £21.

Chef/s: Vivian Casson. **Open:** Sun L, Tue to Sat D. **Closed:** Mon, Christmas to New Year. **Meals:** main courses £23 to £26. Sun L £23 (2 courses) to £28. **Details:** 38 seats. 14 seats outside. Bar. Music. Parking.

◼ Tillington
The Horse Guards Inn
Cooking score: 2
British | £30
Upperton Road, Tillington, GU28 9AF
Tel no: (01798) 342332
thehorseguardsinn.co.uk

With jumbled vintage décor, real fires, evening candles and a glorious garden with clucking hens, this honest-to-goodness country hostelry feels just right, so comfortable and easy is the atmosphere. The welcome is as friendly for passing trade as it is for the many loyal locals, prompting one first-time visitor to declare that 'the owners should be very proud of themselves'. The kitchen makes much of local and regional produce but isn't immune to the charms of Toulouse sausage, chorizo or a well-made aïoli. Highlights include South Downs venison haunch with Sussex pudding, button onions, beetroot and red wine sauce, and cod fillet with new potatoes, aïoli, almonds, lemon and wild garlic. Crowd-pleasing lunches have taken in twice-cooked pork belly with duck egg, chips and mustard, while desserts range from flourless blood-orange cake with orange and mint salad and crème fraîche to good old sticky toffee pudding with muscovado sauce and vanilla ice cream. Drink real ales or wines from £17.60.

Chef/s: Mark Robinson. **Open:** all week L and D. **Closed:** 25 and 26 Dec. **Meals:** main courses £11 to £22. **Details:** 50 seats. 40 seats outside. Bar. Music.

West Ashling
The Richmond Arms
Cooking score: 4
Modern British | £32
Mill Road, West Ashling, PO18 8EA
Tel no: (01243) 572046
therichmondarms.co.uk
£5 OFF

That van parked on the forecourt does a roaring trade in wood-fired pizzas in the evenings, and gives some indication of the innovative approach taken at the Richmond, a white-fronted village pub not far from Chichester. Rotisserie Sunday roasts, retooled bar snacks, such as crispy chorizo rolls or gremolata-crumbed haloumi fries with tartare sauce, and a wittily conceived principal menu of demotic modern cooking are served forth at chunky tables in the bar or in slightly softer-focused formality in the restaurant. An undrawn Anglesey snipe is roasted and served with toast to pique the taste-buds, prior to the arrival of roast cod with green chorizo and saffron potatoes, or charcoal-roasted Ibérico pork with charred broccoli, sweet potato and quince aïoli. Traditionalists need look no further than a Funtington bavette with chips in dripping and some greens to salve the conscience, the better to enjoy an Alaska made with chocolate and Harvey's porter, or dulce de leche brûlée with caramelised banana ice cream. A collection of sharp, astringent and lusciously syrupy wines, as occasion demands, starts at £18.95.
Chef/s: William Jack and Theo Tzanis. **Open:** Wed to Sun L, Wed to Sat D. **Closed:** Mon, Tue, 18 Dec to 11 Jan, 1 week Jul, 1 week Oct. **Meals:** main courses £16 to £27. **Details:** 98 seats. 30 seats outside. Bar. Wheelchairs. Music. Parking.

West Hoathly
The Cat Inn
Cooking score: 2
Modern British | £29
North Lane, West Hoathly, RH19 4PP
Tel no: (01342) 810369
catinn.co.uk
£5 OFF £30

Local ales, real fires, oak beams, a pretty terrace – this rustic 16th-century village hostelry seems to have it all. It's a welcoming place much loved by locals and visitors – and it's a nice place to stay. The kitchen casts its net wide, offering prime seasonal ingredients in a lively, hubble-bubble mix of European and classic British flavours with a few twists from further afield (perhaps cauliflower and turmeric couscous with sag aloo purée, spiced falafel, curry oil and pickled sultanas). You can't go wrong with locally smoked ham, egg and chips or a prime-aged Sussex beef burger, but there's also haunch of Sussex roe deer, and salmon with chorizo, cannellini beans, roasted red pepper, leek and cavolo nero. To finish, fine local cheeses are a feature, while blackberry parfait with lemon curd, hazelnut financier, spiced blackberries and sorrel is a comforter with a difference. The well-annotated wine list starts at £18.50.
Chef/s: Alex Jacquemin. **Open:** all week L and D. **Closed:** 25 Dec. **Meals:** main courses £14 to £26. **Details:** 85 seats. 45 seats outside. Wheelchairs. Parking. Children over 7 yrs only.

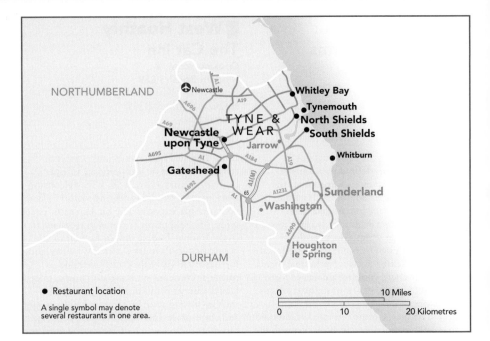

● Restaurant location

A single symbol may denote several restaurants in one area.

0   10 Miles
0   10   20 Kilometres

▌Gateshead
Eslington Villa
Cooking score: 2
Modern British | £30
8 Station Road, Low Fell, Gateshead, NE9 6DR
Tel no: (0191) 4876017
eslingtonvilla.co.uk

As Gateshead and its big Geordie sister thrum relentlessly not far away, there's something to be said for the serenity of a large Victorian house with a couple of acres of landscaping. Eslington regulars know exactly what they're going to get, and the package now includes a refurbished bar, lounge and conservatory dining room. The greenery makes it a pleasant spot for lunch, which cleaves to classics such as Yorkshire beetroot with goats' cheese and honey or fishcake with spinach, parsley sauce and a poached egg. At dinner, local nods include the homemade pease puddng with a pressing of ham hock and a main course of North Sea hake with celeriac, samphire and

spiced prawns. Nevertheless, technique and inspiration are fundamentally French – until it comes to puddings, when sticky toffee pudding, chocolate brownie with muscovado cream or apple and cinnamon cake with mascarpone ice cream make generously proportioned appearances. There's a relatively basic international wine line-up, with the lion's share under £35.

Chef/s: Jamie Walsh. **Open:** all week L and D. **Closed:** 25 and 26 Dec, 1 Jan. **Meals:** set L and early D £17 (2 courses) to £20. Set D £25 (2 courses) to £29. Sun L £21. **Details:** 90 seats. 20 seats outside. Bar. Wheelchairs. Music. Parking.

Symbols

🛏 Accommodation is available
£30 Three courses for less than £30
£5 OFF £5-off voucher scheme
🍾 Notable wine list

◾ Newcastle upon Tyne

Artisan

Cooking score: 3
Modern British | £30
16 Stoddart Street, Newcastle upon Tyne,
NE2 1AN
Tel no: (0191) 2605411
artisannewcastle.com
£5 OFF

The Biscuit Factory is the UK's largest
independent gallery, the very heart of the
city's cultural quarter, and the artisan
restaurant therein rises to the challenge of its
location with its visually impressive and
creative food. A groovy glass wall gives a
glimpse into the gallery. Take the à la carte or
tasting route (pre-booking is required for the
latter). Andrew Wilkinson's contemporary
cooking is impressive, but it isn't wacky, so
combinations make sense and everything
hangs together nicely. Citrus-cured salmon
and dressed crab gets a flourish from an oyster
emulsion, and hand-rolled gnocchi is a veggie
main course enriched by goats' curd and
truffle. A tasting of Northumbrian lamb
confirms the passion for regional ingredients,
and you might find Lindisfarne oysters if
you're lucky. Desserts such as dark chocolate
crémeux, blood-orange and pistachio ice
cream maintain the artistry to the end. There's
an early-evening menu if you're off to do
something cultural. Wines start at £18.95.
Chef/s: Andrew Wilkinson. **Open:** Wed to Sun L,
Wed to Sat D. **Closed:** Mon, Tue, 24 to 26 Dec, 1
Jan. **Meals:** main courses £14 to £25. Set L £15 (2
courses) to £20. Set D £20 (2 courses) to £24. Sun L
£25. Tasting menu £40. **Details:** 70 seats. 15 seats
outside. Bar. Wheelchairs. Music. Parking.

Visit us online

To find out more about
The Good Food Guide, please
visit thegoodfoodguide.co.uk

Blackfriars Restaurant

Cooking score: 1
British | £37
Friars Street, Newcastle upon Tyne, NE1 4XN
Tel no: (0191) 2615945
blackfriarsrestaurant.co.uk
£5 OFF

First-time visitors to Blackfriars get a
genuinely pleasant shock when they turn off
the main drag in central Newcastle and
stumble upon a medieval quarter complete
with 13th-century Dominican friary. Once
the monks' refectory, the restaurant's
authenticity is evident from the thick stone
walls, wood panels and kitchen viewed
through the old fireplace. The food is far less
archaic, with locally sourced ingredients to the
fore in modern dishes such as broad bean and
wild garlic risotto or herb-crusted black cod
with heritage potatoes, beetroot and
hollandaise, although spiced apple crumble
with vanilla custard is a more old-fashioned
dessert. Wines from £23.
Chef/s: Christopher Wardale. **Open:** all week L,
Mon to Sat D. **Closed:** 25 and 25 Dec, bank hols.
Meals: main courses £12 to £26. Set L £15 (2
courses) to £18. Set D £18 (2 courses) to £21. Sun L
£21 (3 courses). **Details:** 72 seats. 30 seats outside.
Music.

The Broad Chare

Cooking score: 4
Modern British | £29
25 Broad Chare, Newcastle upon Tyne,
NE1 3DQ
Tel no: (0191) 2112144
thebroadchare.co.uk
£30

'A well-run operation, as one might expect
from a Terry Laybourne establishment,'
declares a fan of this popular dining pub,
struck as much by the friendly service as by the
classy but accessible cooking. Begin amid the
warm glow of the snug, traditional bar – all
wood floors, craft beers and bar snacks – then
move to the more refined dining room
upstairs for your meal. The surroundings fit

the casual ethos very well. Small plates such as potted shrimps or game terrine really hit the spot, and a main course of butter-roast cod with asparagus and sea aster is right on the money. At the meaty end of the spectrum, the dry-aged ribeye with watercress and steak butter ticks all the right boxes. For dessert, try the ginger syrup sponge and custard, or look to the selection of English cheeses. Besides great beers, there's an appealing selection of wines from £17.50.

Chef/s: Dan Warren. **Open:** all week L, Mon to Sat D. **Closed:** 25 and 26 Dec, 1 Jan. **Meals:** main courses £10 to £20. **Details:** 74 seats. Bar. Music.

Cook House

Cooking score: 2
Modern British | £16
20 Ouse Street, Newcastle upon Tyne, NE1 2PF
cookhouse.org

£5 OFF £30

What do you need to set up in the restaurant trade? In Anna Hedworth's case, a pair of shipping containers sufficed. Herein, she runs the whole show, as you can see from the dining space that looks into her little kitchen domain. Wood-burners keep things toasty on chilly northern days, and the bill of fare, mainly light lunchtime dishes, is chalked up on a board. There's no licence, so bring your own wine, and no chip-and-pin machine, so factor in a trip to the cashpoint, too. Thus readied, prepare for roast pork belly and mint salad dressed in pickled red onion and sesame, cold rare beef with egg and new potatoes, or a dollop of smoked mackerel pâté with pickled fennel and toast. A plate of local cheeses with spiced apple chutney, or a hunk of dark chocolate and almond cake, will fill any remaining gaps. If you forgot the wine, Anna's homemade still lemonade has plenty of tang.

Chef/s: Anna Hedworth. **Open:** Mon to Sat 9.30 to 3.30. **Closed:** Sun. **Meals:** main courses £5 to £8. **Details:** 20 seats. 8 seats outside. Music. Cash only.

House of Tides

Cooking score: 5
Modern British | £70
28-30 The Close, Newcastle upon Tyne, NE1 3RF
Tel no: (0191) 2303720
houseoftides.co.uk

Found on the old quayside close to the Tyne Bridge, mullioned windows, exposed stone walls and rusting steel girders in the downstairs bar are reminders of the 16th century heritage of this former merchant's house. Head upstairs to the first-floor dining room and there is something Alice-in-Wonderlandish about the sloping polished boards and gnarled pillars. There is no doubt this is 'a slick operation' with an army of front-of-house staff, but 'it remains unstuffy, buzzy and not at all uptight' and the cooking seems to be 'gaining momentum'. The descriptions on Kenny Atkinson's tasting menu are terse 'to give an element of surprise' – crab teamed with apple and dill; lamb with hen of the woods and lovage, for example, preceded by top-notch amuse-bouches, including squid ink cracker with smoked cod's roe, and 'memorably good' fermented rye bread with cultured butter. Dessert proved to be the hit at a May meal. Gariguette strawberries and curry leaf proved to be a fascinating and surprising flavour match, with dark chocolate, hazelnut and gold leaf pushing all the right buttons when it comes to richness and luxury. Wines from £25 with a dozen served by the glass.

Chef/s: Kenny Atkinson. **Open:** Fri and Sat L, Wed to Sat D. **Closed:** Sun, Mon, 24 Dec to 8 Jan. **Meals:** Tasting menu L £55. Tasting menu D £70. **Details:** 70 seats. V menu. Bar. Wheelchairs. Music. Parking. Children over 8 yrs only.

Average price

The average price denotes the price of a three-course meal without wine.

Jesmond Dene House

Cooking score: 2
Modern British | £40
Jesmond Dene Road, Newcastle upon Tyne,
NE2 2EY
Tel no: (0191) 2123000
jesmonddenehouse.co.uk

This gothic stone Arts and Crafts mansion, a short drive from the city centre in one of Newcastle's more upmarket suburbs, is now a modern country house hotel. Whether you choose to dine in the conservatory overlooking the lovely gardens, or in the more sombre dining room, the kitchen sources top-drawer regional ingredients to produce contemporary dishes of a generally high standard. Slow-cooked ox tongue with goats' curd, pickled cucumber and oyster might lead on to a main course of wild turbot with Jersey Royals, capers and brown butter, while caramelised banana, aerated fudge and banana ice cream displays a strong skills set in the pastry department. The ambitious à la carte prices are geared more towards celebration meals and expense accounts but the early-evening set menu offers better value for the more casual diner. The global wine list opens at £25 but there are 18 served by the glass.
Chef/s: Michael Penaluna. **Open:** Mon to Sat L and D. Sun, 12 to 7. **Meals:** main courses £16 to £28. Set L £20 (2 courses) to £22. Early D £21 (2 courses) to £25. Sun L £22 (2 courses) to £26. Tasting menu £55. **Details:** 70 seats. 28 seats outside. Bar. Wheelchairs. Music. Parking.

★ NEW ENTRY ★

The Patricia

Cooking score: 3
Modern European | £35
139 Jesmond Road, Newcastle upon Tyne,
NE2 1JY
Tel no: (0191) 2814443
the-patricia.com

'There may be prettier spots in Jesmond,' noted a visitor to Nick Grieves' first venture on the busy coast road out of Newcastle upon Tyne, 'but it's been a hot spot since it opened its doors in December 2016.' Named after Mr Grieves' grandmother, Patricia is an unassuming, candlelit space, and the deep aubergine walls dotted with old French posters and dark floorboards give a warm French bistro feel, even if the ingredient-driven cooking is modern British in style. Although Grieves is self-taught, he has spent time at the River Café and Fera and was clearly paying attention when it comes to treating prime raw materials with respect and integrity. At a test meal, a simple dish of spanking-fresh picked Cornish spider crab mixed with sliced violet artichokes clearly relied on the best quality and freshest ingredients. At main course, massive flavours were evident in a dish of tender slow-cooked lamb that was teamed with Jersey Royals, broad beans, peas and a punchy, mint-heavy salsa verde, while at dessert stage, a rich but fluffy chocolate mousse was lifted by hazelnuts, miso caramel and preserved cherries. An interesting and carefully curated wine list opens at £19.50.
Chef/s: Nick Grieves. **Open:** Wed to Sat L, Tue to Sat D. **Closed:** Sun, Mon, 2 weeks Jan, 1 week Aug, 1 week Nov. **Meals:** main courses £16 to £27. **Details:** 30 seats. Bar. Wheelchairs. Music.

Peace & Loaf

Cooking score: 4
Modern British | £38
217 Jesmond Road, Newcastle upon Tyne,
NE2 1LA
Tel no: (0191) 2815222
peaceandloaf.co.uk
£5 OFF

A surprisingly off-centre location, in a row of shops beside a busy main road, seems to work for Peace & Loaf. Set across three floors, the contemporary décor may be quirky but the informal service is perfectly pitched with a refreshingly relaxed 'anything goes' approach. A *MasterChef: The Professionals* 2010 finalist, Dave Coulson's cooking has high aspirations – his dishes regularly hit the spot with seasonal flavours aplenty, whether you choose from the good-value set menus, the carte or 10-course taster. A starter of octopus bolognese with wild garlic, Parmesan and squash packs an immediate punch, and might be followed by full-flavoured mains such as 40°C halibut with chicken pie, creamed potato and mushroom or sirloin of beef with beetroot, short rib, mash, bone marrow and tarragon. Artfully presented desserts include rhubarb, blood orange and black olive. Starting at £19.95, the well-chosen wine list offers plenty of good drinking under £30, with plenty by the glass.

Chef/s: David Coulson. **Open:** all week L, Mon to Sat D. **Closed:** 25 and 26 Dec, 1 and 2 Jan. **Meals:** main courses £17 to £26. Set L £18 (2 courses) to £22. Set D £22 (2 courses) to £26. Sun L £26. Tasting menu £75. **Details:** 54 seats. Wheelchairs. Music.

21

Cooking score: 3
Modern British | £35
Trinity Gardens, Quayside, Newcastle upon Tyne, NE1 2HH
Tel no: (0191) 2220755
21newcastle.co.uk

Rebooted in 2015 with a suave new look and a truncated name, Terry Laybourne's Tyneside flagship (formerly Café 21) remains one of the hot tickets on Newcastle's waterfront. The interior now has a warmer, richer tone thanks to polished floorboards and leather banquettes, while the kitchen continues to deliver cosmopolitan brasserie food with bags of flavour. Fixed-price deals offer particularly 'good value', although the whole repertoire is a user-friendly mix of updated regional classics and more eclectic ideas. To start, try a warm salad of Craster kippers with ratte potatoes and endive or grilled Spanish black pudding and white bean casserole, before tackling fishcakes with buttered spinach and parsley cream or Asian-style pork belly with fragrant rice. To finish, 21's tarte Tatin has been well received, or you might fancy rose pannacotta

with strawberries and 'iced gems'. The smart wine list opens with 15 house selections by the glass or carafe.

Chef/s: Chris Dobson. **Open:** all week L and D. **Closed:** 25 and 26 Dec, 1 Jan. **Meals:** main courses £16 to £32. Set L £19 (2 courses) to £23. Early D £21 (2 courses) to £25. Sun L £21 (2 courses) to £25. **Details:** 120 seats. V menu. Bar. Wheelchairs. Music.

LOCAL GEM
Bistro Forty Six
Modern British | £28
46 Brentwood Avenue, Newcastle upon Tyne, NE2 3DH
Tel no: (0191) 2818081
bistrofortysix.co.uk

£5 OFF   £30

In an appealing row of shops and bars close to the West Jesmond Metro station, this intimate, simply decorated bistro has found its groove since chef Max Gott took over in 2016. Reporters note food is clearly improved, the modern British menu making sure seasonal and local produce feature prominently: Northumbrian wood pigeon with smoked belly pork and radish and pomegranate, for example, then two 'nicely cooked' fillets of sea bass with mussels in a rich bisque with potatoes, kale and asparagus. Puddings include bitter chocolate tart ('very good pastry') and berry compote. A short wine list starts at £16.95.

LOCAL GEM
Caffè Vivo
Italian | £32
29 Broad Chare, Newcastle upon Tyne, NE1 3DQ
Tel no: (0191) 2321331
caffevivo.co.uk

Tacked on to Newcastle's Live Theatre, next to the law courts on the Quayside, Terry Laybourne's lively all-day enoteca has a deli look from the outside, with hams, salamis and bunches of chillies hanging in the window. It's a slick operation, delivering straightforward Italian cooking at fair prices – the flexible menus built around antipasti, salads, pasta and lunchtime sandwiches. In the evening, expect dishes such as char-grilled lamb chops with rosemary roast potatoes and salmoriglio, or a fish stew of mussels, cockles, calamari, prawns, sea bass, scallops and langoustines, with Prosecco jelly, fresh cream and raspberries to finish. Wines from £16.50.

LOCAL GEM

Cal's Own

Italian | £25
1-2 Holly Avenue, Newcastle upon Tyne, NE2 2AR
Tel no: (0191) 2815522
calsown.co.uk

£30

Calvin Kitchin started out as a joiner but he learnt how to make pizza by watching YouTube videos and now has accreditation from the Naples-based Associazione Vera Pizza Napoletana. Located in the heart of West Jesmond, his neighbourhood pizzeria specialises in Neapolitan pizzas cooked in the wood-fired oven. Try the signature marinara pizza topped with San Marzano tomato sauce, garlic, oregano, basil, sea salt and extra-virgin olive oil, perhaps with an extra topping of spicy smoked salami from Calabria.

READERS RECOMMEND

Starks Kitchen

Modern British
205-207 Chillingham Road, Newcastle upon Tyne, NE6 5LJ
Tel no: (0191) 2658436
starkskitchen.co.uk
'This is a fantastic café and restaurant. It's fine-dining food but in a local café setting. The couple who are front-of-house are friendly and welcoming and always go the extra mile. The two chefs provide an exciting, ever-changing menu using top-quality local ingredients.'

Tyneside Bar Café

International
Tyneside Cinema, Pilgrim Street, Newcastle upon Tyne, NE1 6QG
Tel no: (0191) 2275522
tynesidecinema.co.uk
'The food is always clever and delicious, and I know that they are passionate about using special, local suppliers. Recent dishes include ricotta gnocchi with walnut pesto, smoked mackerel with greens and beetroot, and market fishcake.'

■ North Shields

Irvins

Cooking score: 2
Modern British | £25
Union Road, The Fish Quay, North Shields, NE30 1HJ
Tel no: (0191) 2963238
irvinsnewcastle.co.uk
£5 OFF £30

Occupying the entire ground floor of a former trawlermens' stores on North Shields' historic Fish Quay, Irvins is an impressive building with sweeping stone arches, floor-to-ceiling windows, slate and parquet floors and a well-stocked deli section next to the bar. From the white-tiled open kitchen food is served all day, starting with breakfast and going on to an attractively priced set lunch and then dinner. Local and regional sourcing is at the heart of the seasonal menu, with plenty of seafood from the North Sea landed at the fish market across the road. A generous bowl of 'seriously fresh and huge' mussels with garlic, cream and wine might lead on to a dish of 'delicious' spiced monkfish with turmeric rice or, for meat fans, dry-aged rump steak with a fried duck egg and chips. Desserts play the comfort card, perhaps chocolate torte or stem ginger cake with vanilla ice cream. A short wine list of around 20 bottles starts at £18.50 and most are available by the glass.

Chef/s: Graeme Cuthell. **Open:** Wed to Sun, all day from 10 (9 Sat and Sun). **Closed:** Mon, Tue. **Meals:** main courses £12 to £21. Set L and D £16 (2 courses) to £26. Sun L £25. **Details:** 72 seats. 8 seats outside. Bar. Wheelchairs. Music.

The Staith House
Cooking score: 2
Modern British | £30
57 Low Lights, Fish Quay, North Shields, NE30 1JA
Tel no: (0191) 2708441
thestaithhouse.co.uk

From the outside, John Calton's quayside pub 'doesn't look that much', but inside 'it's lovely, light and airy with blues and greens on the distressed walls, nautical artefacts, maps on the ceiling and pictures of the Fish Quay in its heyday'. It also feels like a pub, with stools at the bar, real ales 'in excellent nick' and staff who are friendly and helpful – 'nothing is too much trouble for them'. And, in an area dominated by fish and chip cafés and takeaways, you don't expect to find such confident, well-executed cooking either. Pub classics like fish and chips with mushy peas remain a big seller, but the kitchen displays plenty of ambition in dishes such as 'perfectly cooked' king scallops with a creamy Jerusalem artichoke purée, wild leeks, wild garlic and locally foraged seaweed butter, in North Sea halibut with thinly sliced raw cauliflower, home-smoked bacon, hazelnuts and watercress, and in Goosnargh guinea fowl with a samosa of the leg, curried lentils, coriander, cucumber and lime. Desserts might include treacle tart with pineapple, fresh mint, rum, coconut and lime sorbet. Wines from £18.50.
Chef/s: John Calton and James Laffan. **Open:** all week L, Mon to Sat D. **Closed:** 25 and 26 Dec. **Meals:** main courses £13 to £26. **Details:** 45 seats. 40 seats outside. Wheelchairs. Music. Parking. Children before 7.30pm only.

■ South Shields
LOCAL GEM
Colmans
Seafood | £15
182-186 Ocean Road, South Shields, NE33 2JQ
Tel no: (0191) 4561202
colmansfishandchips.com

£30

This venerable fish and chip venue (established in 1926) has passed through five generations of the same family and is considered by many readers as one of the few outstanding 'chippies' of its kind left in the UK, unpretentious and no-nonsense. High-quality fish from local boats and properly fried chips is what they do, and they do it well, whether hake, cod, haddock, sole, plaice, lobster or handmade fishcakes – all served by friendly, smiling staff. The short wine list starts at £14.95.

■ Tynemouth
★ NEW ENTRY ★
Riley's Fish Shack
Cooking score: 1
Seafood | £18
King Edward's Bay, Tynemouth, NE30 4BY
Tel no: (0191) 2571371
rileysfishshack.com

£30

A tucked-away, glass-fronted shipping container on a sheltered beach facing the North Sea, Riley's Fish Shack is a genuine find, and although it has appeared on TV as one of the UK's 'hidden restaurants', the secret is well and truly out now. High-quality North Sea seafood stars on the daily changing menu (there are flat-iron or onglet steak wraps, too), and while a no-bookings policy means queues for the few tables are inevitable, everything is served in cardboard boxes so you can always take your food on to the beach itself. Choose from oysters, salt cod fishcakes, chilli fish empanada, Craster kipper wraps, wood-baked cod and haricot beans, salted hake pan-fried with caper butter, or smoky monkfish kebab marinated in lemon, rosemary and white wine and served with fried potatoes and salad. Wines (poured into plastic tumblers) from £16.50.

Chef/s: Adam Riley. **Open:** Mon and Wed to Sun L, Wed to Sat D. **Closed:** Tue. **Meals:** main courses £6 to £14. **Details:** 12 seats. 16 seats outside.

▌Whitburn

LOCAL GEM
Latimer's
Seafood | £25
Shell Hill, Bents Road, Whitburn, SR6 7NT
Tel no: (0191) 5292200
latimers.com

£30

Robert Latimer was once a creel fisherman in the Scottish islands, but has now pitched camp in a coastal seafood shack at the mouth of the Wear. It's a retail outlet, too, with the day's wares chalked up outside, but the smart move is to set up on the decked terrace beneath the striped awning and tuck in. Expect smoked fish chowder, day-boat fish cooked en papillote with lemon and chives, or impressive seafood platters of lobster, crab, smoked salmon, mussels and much more besides. How about an oyster and Champagne breakfast to blow away the cobwebs? The place is now licensed, with £14 house wines.

▌Whitley Bay

LOCAL GEM
The Roxburgh
British | £30
4 Roxburgh House, Park Avenue, Whitley Bay, NE26 1DQ
Tel no: (0191) 2531661

If the Roxburgh sounds like a posh restaurant, it ain't. If it makes an underwhelming first impression, don't worry. Enter clutching your chosen tipple (it's BYOB), and you'll likely be won over by the rustic simplicity of the space, the great tunes being played and the nose-to-tail cooking of Gary Dall. The short menu is chalked up on a blackboard: char-grilled ox tongue doner kebab as a starter, followed by pig three ways (belly, head and cured), or a risotto with onions, and to finish, what else but Stoners Delight (a creamy chocolate number).

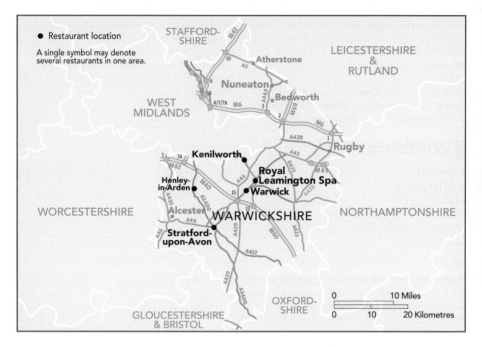

- **Restaurant location**

A single symbol may denote several restaurants in one area.

STAFFORD-SHIRE

LEICESTERSHIRE & RUTLAND

Atherstone

Nuneaton

WEST MIDLANDS

Bedworth

Kenilworth

Rugby

Royal Leamington Spa

Henley-in-Arden

Warwick

WORCESTERSHIRE

Alcester

WARWICKSHIRE

NORTHAMPTONSHIRE

Stratford-upon-Avon

OXFORD-SHIRE

GLOUCESTERSHIRE & BRISTOL

0   10 Miles
0   10   20 Kilometres

◼ Henley-in-Arden
Cheal's of Henley

Cooking score: 5
British | £50
64 High Street, Henley-in-Arden, B95 5BX
Tel no: (01564) 793856
chealsofhenley.co.uk

In a prime position on the high street, Matt Cheal's restaurant occupies a 17th-century cottage with beamed ceilings and a venerable air. Smart linens and quality glassware banish all thought of the rustic – this is a venue for serious contemporary cooking with ingenious presentations and juxtapositions, offered via a series of fixed-price menus that ascend in complexity to the six-course taster. Cheal was at Simpsons in Birmingham (see entry) before lighting out here on his first solo venture, and while one or two dishes can feel as though they are still finding their feet, there is plenty to enthuse. A pairing of dressed Cornish crab and citrus-cured sea trout comes in a productive motley of avocado mousse, blood

orange, borage and trout roe with a wild rice crisp to start. Duck breast roasted in five-spice with blackberries in red wine sauce was a hit for one pair of reporters, or there may be a sea-scented combination of skate and mussels with samphire and marine herbs in saffron cream. Desserts lack nothing in opulence, when a chocolate and praline bombe arrives with a high-octane malted sauce, and the Continental cheeses with membrillo are in admirably fine fettle. A knowledgeably composed wine list full of trending producers opens with half-litre carafes from £13.
Chef/s: Matt Cheal. **Open:** Wed to Sun L, Wed to Sat D. **Closed:** Mon, Tue, 25 and 26 Dec, 21 Aug to 5 Sept. **Meals:** set L £23 (2 courses) to £30. Set D £30 (2 courses) to £40. Sun L £40. Tasting menu £75. **Details:** 40 seats. Bar. Wheelchairs. Music.

Average price

The average price denotes the price of a three-course meal without wine.

▌Kenilworth
The Cross at Kenilworth
Cooking score: 6
Modern British | £48
16 New Street, Kenilworth, CV8 2EZ
Tel no: (01926) 853840
thecrosskenilworth.co.uk
£5 OFF

The Cross wears its glossy reputation with appealing modesty. Start a meal in this informal, relaxed place with creamy yet fresh wild garlic soup, chunks of potato giving bite, and cod flakes a delicious depth of flavour, or a delicate plate of jewel-coloured baby beetroot. The latter is a masterclass in balancing tastes, sweet beet, tart apple, tangy honey-vinegar dressing and gently salty goats' cheese all playing their parts to perfection. Pigeon, pink and butter-soft to cut, is a standout main, a puck of homemade black pudding an appropriately earthy partner. The flavour of beautifully cooked monkfish is somewhat lost against a powerful bordelaise sauce, however, though the onion risotto and fleshy sea beet leaves do give the dish a satisfying sweet-bitter dimension. For a dramatic finale, the chocolate sphere deserves applause, melting theatrically when a passion fruit sauce is poured over to reveal a sharp coconut sorbet and mango compote. A sublimely feather-light toffee soufflé is just as show-stopping, leaving diners questioning the role of the accompanying citrus yoghurt ice cream. There's plenty to drink from £24, and an exciting choice of gins will keep non-drivers' thirst quenched.
Chef/s: Adam Bennett. **Open:** all week L, Mon to Sat D. **Closed:** 25 and 26 Dec, 1 Jan. **Meals:** main courses £25 to £34. Set L £25 (2 courses) to £30. Tasting menu £65. **Details:** 83 seats. 24 seats outside. V menu. Bar. Wheelchairs. Music. Parking.

▌Leamington Spa
Restaurant 23
Cooking score: 4
Modern British | £55
34 Hamilton Terrace, Leamington Spa, CV32 4LY
Tel no: (01926) 422422
restaurant23.co.uk

The pristine Victorian building may seem very grand, but it houses a modern operation, offering a lounge bar and fair-weather patio, as well as the soft-hued ground-floor dining room. Chef Curtis Stewart endeavours to maintain the excitement of his predecessor, Peter Knibb, with much complexity and arcane culinary technique on show. However, a test meal found the cooking in need of sharper focus, ranging from superb via quietly competent to oddly off-kilter. Highlights were ponzu-marinated sashimi tuna, with tartare, fermented kohlrabi and kohlrabi crisp, passion fruit, miso and bonito jelly, and an impressive, umami-laden homemade pasta with a rich mushroom ragù, balsamic caviar, shaved Parmesan and English truffle. A pre-dessert of lemon meringue pie – tartness cut by the creaminess of Italian meringue, a sliver of charred fresh lemon adding an extra dimension – was pronounced 'one of the best desserts I've had this year'. Service is thoroughly professional. The wine list focuses on Europe with a brief look at the New World.
Chef/s: Curtis Stewart. **Open:** Tue to Sat L and D. **Closed:** Sun, Mon, 25 and 26 Dec, 1 to 16 Jan, 14 to 29 Aug. **Meals:** main courses £22 to £35. Set L £20 (2 courses) to £25. Tasting menu £55 (6 courses) to £70. **Details:** 60 seats. Bar. Wheelchairs. Music.

▌Stratford-upon-Avon
No. 9 Church St

Cooking score: 2
Modern British | £35
9 Church Street, Stratford-upon-Avon,
CV37 6HB
Tel no: (01789) 415522
no9churchst.com

'A shining oasis in the desert of Stratford-upon-Avon,' is the considered opinion of one who has eaten in the first-floor dining room of this quirky little restaurant in the centre of town many times. The setting is relaxed, comfortable and welcoming, with chef/proprietor Wayne Thomson's modern British cooking based on soundly sourced ingredients, perhaps smoked roe deer loin with pickled mushrooms and truffle purée, and Black Pig Co. rare-breed pork loin with maple-glazed carrots, Savoy cabbage, mash and apples and walnuts. Lunches and pre-theatre dinners (the RSC is just a seven-minute walk away) are also popular, with praise for a rustic-style pâté, a rare steak bavette with caramelised onion relish and good chips, and warm chocolate and pecan brownie with peanut-butter ice cream. Small touches like 'proper napkins, tasty butters and petits fours' can't be faulted. Wines (from £16.50) are a reasonably priced global selection.
Chef/s: Wayne Thomson. **Open:** Tue to Sat L and D. **Closed:** Sun, Mon, 25 and 26 Dec, 1 to 5 Jan. **Meals:** main courses £14 to £25. Set L and early D £15 (2 courses) to £20. Tasting menu £43 (5 courses) to £60 (9 courses). **Details:** 40 seats. Bar. Music.

Please send us your feedback

To register your opinion about any restaurant listed in this guide, or a new restaurant that you wish to bring to our attention, please visit the web address at the bottom of the page. Your feedback informs the content of the book and will be used to compile next year's reviews.

Salt

Cooking score: 5
Modern British | £37
8 Church Street, Stratford-upon-Avon,
CV37 6HB
Tel no: (01789) 263566
salt-restaurant.co.uk

'I very much hope that Stratford embraces him,' enthuses a visitor to Paul Foster's understated little restaurant. It's been firing on all cylinders since opening in March 2017, with Mr Foster building on the promise he showed in 2012 when he won our Up-and-Coming Chef award – as a first solo venture it is certainly worth a culinary detour. Located about 'five minutes from the tourist-tastic centre of town,' Salt is simply and inexpensively decorated with plain pine tables and chairs, whitewashed walls, a beamed ceiling and an open-to-view kitchen delivering 'serious, exciting cooking from a seriously talented chef'. A cured mackerel fillet is deemed 'sweet and delicate' by one diner, similar praise being poured on two fat, glossy, golden oyster mushrooms, seasoned with a scattering of salted egg yolk shavings and served over a slice of fatty bacon. Continue the fish theme if you will (a large, roasted, meaty fillet of sea bass perhaps, with gem lettuce, dressed seaweed and gentleman's relish), but pinkly perfect lamb rump with slow-cooked neck, curried cauliflower, and herb sauce (with some charred cauliflower and broccoli) makes a superb main. Creative combinations abound at dessert stage where a whipped lime curd is teamed with fennel and yoghurt meringue and yoghurt parfait. Wines from £18.
Chef/s: Paul Foster. **Open:** Wed to Sun L, Wed to Sat D. **Closed:** Mon, Tue, 2 weeks Dec, 1 week spring, 2 weeks Aug. **Meals:** set L £15 (2 courses) to £20. Set D £32 (2 courses) to £37. Sun L £23. **Details:** 35 seats. 10 seats outside. V menu. Music.

▌Warwick

Tailors

Cooking score: 3
Modern British | £40
22 Market Place, Warwick, CV34 4SL
Tel no: (01926) 410590
tailorsrestaurant.co.uk

A mini Singer sewing machine, displayed alongside a host of awards, reminds diners of the origins of this appealing town-centre restaurant, and the root of its name. Run enthusiastically by Mark Fry and Dan Cavell, it's a place to enjoy a fantastic-value lunch – including a tasting-menu option – or linger over a more extensive evening offer. There's a deft balance to flavours throughout the meal: nettle and fennel soup punches above its silky weight with deliciously seasoned freshness, and superb homemade sourdough bread means none is wasted, while the richness achieved from slow-cooking the meat elevates a venison ragù into something more than a run-of-the-mill pasta dish. On-song fish cooking means pollack flakes as it should and sits tastily next to butternut squash purée, little gnocchi and an edgy balsamic jus. Be warned: the chips that come with a butter-soft fillet steak are moreish. A simple almond cake with rhubarb and Chantilly cream rounds things off well. There's wine from £18.95.
Chef/s: Dan Cavell. **Open:** Tue to Sat L and D.
Closed: Sun, Mon, 1 week Christmas. **Meals:** set L £17 (2 courses) to £21. Set D £30 (2 courses) to £40. Tasting menu £60. **Details:** 28 seats. V menu. Music.

READERS RECOMMEND

Micatto

Italian
62 Market Place, Warwick, CV34 4SD
Tel no: (01926) 403053
micatto.com
'A kitchen operating on full throttle with excellent regional food to include, in our case, small squid in piquant tomato sauce; outstandingly flavoured lamb; potatoes from Calabria; and a fine chicken breast.'

A taste of crowdfunding

With banks increasingly reluctant to lend money to start-up businesses, crowdfunding has become the only viable option for many restaurateurs.

Whether it's a reward system where people are given incentives such as free meals in return for investing their money, or an equity-based arrangement where investors effectively buy a share of the business, raising money this way has almost become the norm.

In recent years, there have been countless success stories of new restaurants that have only been able to open because of crowdfunding, including Nordic-influenced Harrogate restaurant **Norse** and the influential **Clove Club** in London.

Without crowdfunding, Paul Foster's first solo project, **Salt** in Stratford-upon-Avon, probably wouldn't have opened as soon as it did. The former chef from **Restaurant Sat Bains** and **Tuddenham Mill** raised £100,000, hitting the final total just a few hours before the campaign closed.

After the success of his **Sticky Walnut** restaurant in Chester, chef/owner Gary Usher has since launched three different Kickstarter campaigns, all reaching their targets and bringing his restaurants, **Burnt Truffle**, **Hispi** and most recently, **Wreckfish,** to life.

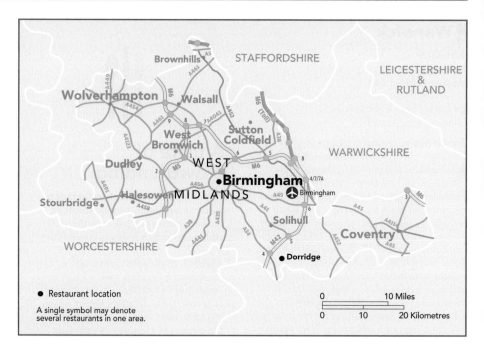

Birmingham

Adam's

Cooking score: 7
Modern British | £65
New Oxford House, 16 Waterloo Street,
Birmingham, B2 5UG
Tel no: (0121) 6433745
adamsrestaurant.co.uk
£5
OFF

The transformation from a temporary pop-up
in a sandwich shop to the present occupation
of New Oxford House, a gracious and
attractive venue in the city centre, is a
characteristically modern success story. Adam
Stokes' cooking now sees the light of day in
elegant surroundings, from the checkerboard-
floored bar with counter seating to a simply
accoutred dining room with unclothed tables,
as well as a ringside chef's table for the curious.
And it's elegant cooking too, but in a style that
makes a virtue of its lack of pretentiousness.

Eight-course tasting menus (or three if you
prefer) are the core of the operation, and what
impresses readers is the potency that dishes
achieve through remarkably simple means. A
winter lunch that included veal sweetbreads
with chorizo, Jerusalem artichoke and
hazelnut, and scallop with cauliflower,
almonds and smoked salmon as a precursor to
majestically intense venison with shiitake,
chervil root and apple, and 'one of the best
lamb dishes ever' with baby turnip, miso and
wild rice, offered one soaring triumph after
another. That meal ended with the *de rigueur*
pre-dessert, followed by chocolate with salted
caramel, peanut and sesame seed, and a
'fabulous refreshing dish of a variation of
apple, lemon walnut and ginger sponge'.
Service is consistently praised as impeccable,
with particular plaudits for the sommelier,
who oversees a strong, varied list that finds
some tempting mavericks as well as inspired
French and Italian classics. Wines by the glass
start at £7.

Chef/s: Adam Stokes. **Open:** Tue to Sat L and D. **Closed:** Sun, Mon, 3 weeks Dec to Jan, 2 weeks summer. **Meals:** set L £35 (3 courses). Set D £60 (3 courses). Tasting menu £85. **Details:** 50 seats. V menu. Bar. Wheelchairs. Music.

Carters of Moseley
Cooking score: 6
Modern British | £65
2c Wake Green Road, Moseley, Birmingham, B13 9EZ
Tel no: (0121) 4498885
cartersofmoseley.co.uk

Wedged in among a parade of shops not far from the centre of Moseley, Carters may look like your average neighbourhood eatery, albeit one capable of serving up the likes of squid with swede dashi and back fat, or pine mushroom porridge with Moliterno al tartufo cheese. The setting may be understated and informal, but ambition runs high in the kitchen. Brad Carter now focuses all his efforts on fiercely creative tasting menus that point to a prodigiously industrious kitchen – note the excellent home-baked bread, home-cured charcuterie and fermented vegetables, as well as the empathy for foraged ingredients and Asian riffs. Seasonal standouts might range from snacks of raw kohlrabi with pine and salad burnet to a sweet assemblage of black rice with Cornish kombu seaweed via monkfish with artichoke, sea kale and bacon fat or wild duck with onion squash. Partner Holly Jackson is a confident, knowledgeable and cheery presence out front, and the wine list offers a concise but considered selection of classy bottles. Also check out the esoteric choice of world beers.
Chef/s: Brad Carter. **Open:** Tue to Sat L and D. **Closed:** Sun, Mon, first 2 weeks Jan, first 2 weeks Aug. **Meals:** set L £45 (4 courses) to £65 (6 courses). Set D £65 (6 courses) to £85 (8 courses). **Details:** 32 seats. V menu. Bar. Wheelchairs. Music. Parking. Children over 8 yrs only.

Edmunds
Cooking score: 3
French | £50
6 Brindleyplace, Birmingham, B1 2JB
Tel no: (0121) 6334944
edmundsrestaurant.co.uk
£5 OFF

A small, intimate restaurant, Edmunds Bistro de Luxe (to give its full title) is both relaxed and formal enough to make a meal here a special occasion. Didier Philipot has a determinedly French approach to food, his classical cooking style built around conscientious sourcing, traditional technique and modern ideas. Caramelised Skye scallops, for example, are sensitively cooked and accompanied by wild mushrooms, parsley cream and tarragon crisp. Elsewhere, black pudding 'boudin noir' is teamed with a sweet/tart combination of caramelised apple, mashed potato and Dijon mustard sauce, and Cornish sea bass might be confidently and skilfully matched with a potato pancake, wilted spinach, cream of saffron and fresh mussels. Desserts are simple, maybe hot toffee soufflé with chocolate ice cream or a chocolate and griottine cherry eclair with pistachio ice cream. On the wine front, France leads the way, followed by Italy, the Iberian Peninsula and the southern hemisphere; bottles from £23.
Chef/s: Didier Philipot. **Open:** Tue to Fri L, Tue to Sat D. **Closed:** Sun, Mon. **Meals:** main courses £16 to £28. Set L and early D £19 (2 courses) to £24. Tasting menu £60. **Details:** 46 seats. Wheelchairs. Music.

Harborne Kitchen

Cooking score: 4
Modern British | £29
175-179 High Street, Birmingham, B17 9QE
Tel no: (0121) 4399150
harbornekitchen.com
£5 OFF £30

The inhabitants of Harborne are looking kindly on Jamie Desogus' gregarious, good-natured restaurant and it's easy to see why. A surprisingly large space, it's divided into a front bar and back dining room – a straight-up blend of pale wood, grey walls and dangly light bulbs, with an open kitchen giving a grandstand view of Mr Desogus and his team toiling away. It strikes just the right note for a neighbourhood venue. No surprise then that the place is usually buzzy. It keeps regulars returning with a menu that plays off the seasons, producing fresh, modern, vibrant dishes with vivid flavours – perhaps seared mackerel with kombu tartare and diced Granny Smith apple or a well-reported duck liver parfait, with Yorkshire rhubarb, buttermilk mousse, spiced loaf and chicken skin. Mains might include miso pollack with cauliflower couscous and a superb ginger and lime dhal or a 35-day aged beef rump served with Roscoff onion, shallot purée and leek, while chocolate cream, peanut mousse, miso and malted milk is proving a firm favourite. Drinks-wise, cocktails are good and everything comes by the glass or bottle on the short, imaginative and kindly priced wine list.
Chef/s: Jamie Desogus. **Open:** Thur to Sat L, Tue to Sat D. **Closed:** Sun, Mon, 25 to 27 Dec, 1 Jan, 1 week Feb, 2 weeks Aug, 1 week Oct. **Meals:** set L £18 (2 courses) to £23. Set D £23 (2 courses) to £29. Sun L £29. Tasting menu £55. **Details:** 50 seats. V menu. Bar. Wheelchairs. Music.

Lasan

Cooking score: 3
Indian | £50
3-4 Dakota Buildings, James Street, St Paul's Square, Birmingham, B3 1SD
Tel no: (0121) 2123664
lasan.co.uk
£5 OFF

Birmingham is known as the UK's curry capital, but for those seeking something more than your average curry house, Lasan puts on a high-class show. The dining room is sleek and cool, the contemporary Indian cuisine 'definitely different to the popular Indian food served elsewhere'. The kitchen makes an impressive use of native British produce, from free-range Wiltshire Downlands lamb (served as cutlets with soft galouti patty, lightly pickled red onion and green chutney) to sirloin of Herefordshire beef (perhaps a 13-hour braised blade with salt beef bartha, wilted kale, south Indian stone moss and anise sauce). Elsewhere, wild halibut might appear with a slow-cooked onion and gourd, crisp Keralan curry leaf and chilli pakora, and a sauce of Nellori coconut milk infused with tamarind. Among the vegetables, look for sweet potato kofta roundels with a tempered Rajasthani yoghurt sauce, braised squat aubergines and home-style lentils. The short, global wine list (from £20) offers plenty of suggestions for matching with particular dishes.
Chef/s: Aktar Islam and Gulsher Khan. **Open:** Mon to Fri L, Mon to Sat D. Sun, all day from 12. **Closed:** 25 Dec, 1 Jan. **Meals:** main courses £17 to £25. Tasting menu £50. **Details:** 66 seats. Bar. Wheelchairs. Music. Children over 10 yrs only.

Opus

Cooking score: 2
Modern British | £35
54 Cornwall Street, Birmingham, B3 2DE
Tel no: (0121) 2002323
opusrestaurant.co.uk

£5 OFF

With the name picked out in giant lettering in the front windows, you can hardly miss the grey-façaded venue in the Snow Hill quarter. Inside is surprisingly formal for a modern urban eatery, with white linens, leafy-green suede banquettes and framed pictures, but the cooking is straight out of the contemporary British city repertoire. Start with something fairly robust in the form of a whole roast quail with blackeye bean cassoulet and honey- and balsamic-glazed radicchio in Madeira jus, or more delicately with goats' cheese mousse if you will, before the main business brings on roast monkfish with tomato, chorizo and wild garlic risotto, or two cuts of Cornish lamb with minted pea purée, saffron potatoes and asparagus. Four-week aged beef from British and Irish farms comes off the char-grill in fillet and sirloin cuts served with triple-cooked chips and a choice of sauces. Keep it light at dessert stage with raspberry and blueberry parfait garnished with fresh berries and granola crumble. A well-written wine list opens at £21.
Chef/s: Ben Ternent. **Open:** Mon to Sat L and D.
Closed: Sun, 24 to 26 Dec, Easter, bank hols.
Meals: Set L and D £25 (2 courses) to £33. Tasting menu £45 (5 courses). **Details:** 85 seats. V menu. Bar. Wheelchairs. Music.

Purnell's

Cooking score: 5
Modern British | £68
55 Cornwall Street, Birmingham, B3 2DH
Tel no: (0121) 2129799
purnellsrestaurant.com

£5 OFF

Glynn Purnell's flagship restaurant is a highly valued destination in Birmingham, the smart-casual dining room, with its linen-free tables,

suits low-key suppers and business lunches, yet is buzzy and impressive enough for a special occasion. Mr Purnell dresses his food with a designer's brio, reinventing some of the old ways for today's inquisitive palates. His hottest signature dishes are fascinating forays down memory lane (taste of cheese and pineapple) or a nod towards Brum's famous balti houses (monkfish masala with Indian red lentils, carrots, coconut and coriander), all underpinned by real skill. Six- or nine-course seasonal tasting menus are the restaurant's USP, with avid supporters praising poached duck egg yolk with cauliflower, black pudding, bacon and birch syrup, as well as slow-cooked neck of Wiltshire Downlands lamb with Jerusalem artichoke, wild garlic and puffed rice, and a masterful blood-orange tartlet with meringue, pink peppercorn honeycomb and lime. The wine list is classically French-led but New World and modern styles are well represented; bottles from £25.
Chef/s: Glynn Purnell. **Open:** Tue to Fri L, Tue to Sat D. **Closed:** Sun, Mon, 2 weeks Christmas, 1 week Easter, 2 weeks Aug. **Meals:** set L £35 to £45 (5 courses). Tasting menu £68 (6 courses) to £88 (9 courses). **Details:** 45 seats. Bar. Wheelchairs. Music. Children over 10 yrs only.

Purnell's Bistro

Cooking score: 2
Modern British | £30
11 Newhall Street, Birmingham, B3 3NY
Tel no: (0121) 2001588
purnellsbistro-gingers.com

'Certainly will go again on next trip to Birmingham' – Glynn Purnell's bar and bistro combo, a short walk from New Street station, continues to delight. Design is slick, with the front-loaded Ginger's Bar offering a serious list of inventive cocktails, table service and please-all bar snacks. But many prefer to push straight through to the pair of dining rooms at the back, where 'service is very good' and the classic bistro menu has been put together by someone who understands life's simple pleasures: 'totally irresistible focaccia', 'outstanding' beetroot and ginger-cured salmon with pickled ginger and beetroot and horseradish cream, and braised pork belly with creamed cabbage and lyonnaise potato terrine. Elsewhere, a 'stunning-looking' celeriac velouté with sour apple and crème fraîche, and ox cheek rendang with coconut rice, have been enjoyed. The prix fixe lunch and early-bird menu are considered excellent value.

Chef/s: Glynn Purnell. **Open:** all week L, Mon to Sat D. **Closed:** 25 to 31 Dec, 1 Jan. **Meals:** main courses £15 to £25. Set L and D £16 (2 courses) to £20. Sun L £20 (2 courses) to £22. **Details:** 70 seats. Bar. Wheelchairs. Music.

★ TOP 50 ★

Simpsons

Cooking score: 7
Modern British | £65
20 Highfield Road, Edgbaston, Birmingham, B15 3DU
Tel no: (0121) 4543434
simpsonsrestaurant.co.uk
£5 OFF

In a city with strong gastronomic credentials, Simpsons continues to set the benchmark for top-end dining in Birmingham – despite new contenders snapping at its heels. Occupying a handsome Georgian townhouse in Edgbaston, this Brum veteran has quietly evolved and matured over the years, with a cookery school and boutique bedrooms cited as further incentives for bookmarking a visit. Simpsons' Greek-inspired landscaped gardens promise serenity, while the conservatory dining room backing on to trim lawns offers a dressed-down setting for Luke Tipping's sublime spin on contemporary British cuisine. Everything is driven by top-drawer ingredients and impressive technique, from a duck egg with Jerusalem artichoke, hazelnut and watercress to belly of suckling pig with carrot purée, smoked carrots, barley, charred onions and Hispi cabbage. Pairings are sometimes surprising, but nothing is ever superfluous and each component fully justifies its inclusion on the plate – be it cauliflower

porridge and almond milk with a serving of smoked eel or a scattering of yeast flakes and lingonberries enhancing a dish of Creedy Carver duck. To finish, you might veer towards the trolley of British cheeses accompanied by rye crackers and pickled onions or give in to sweet temptation with a historically informed dessert of quince, spiced bread and milk ice cream. Divided into colourful categories such as 'steely and mineral' or 'supple and fragrant', the authoritative wine list culls fine vintages from across the globe, with high-rolling Coravin selections for those who want to sample class by the glass.

Chef/s: Luke Tipping. **Open:** Tue to Sun L, Tue to Sat D. **Closed:** Mon, 25 Dec, bank hols. **Meals:** set L £30 (2 courses) to £35. Set D £65. Sun L £35. Tasting menu £85 (8 courses). **Details:** 75 seats. 20 seats outside. V menu. Bar. Wheelchairs. Music. Parking.

Turners at 69

Cooking score: 4
Modern British | £45
69 High Street, Harborne, Birmingham, B17 9NS
Tel no: (0121) 4264440
turnersat69.co.uk

In Harborne, which is about a 10-minute drive from the city centre, Richard Turner's restaurant remains something of a celebratory destination, despite a slight tweak to the name and modifications to the menu. The expensive tasting menu has been ditched in favour of a classy à la carte, bolstered by a keenly priced weekday set lunch. Mr Turner's cooking has a timeless quality – though it's not dated – and matches the compact, smartly mirrored and chandeliered interior with its two rows of white-clothed tables. Here you'll find 'a very good' venison tartare served with heritage beetroot and chestnuts, 'a good balance of flavours and textures' in a dish of salmon with deep-fried oyster, pickled cucumber, wasabi and dill, alongside a rich bouillabaisse with saffron, chilli and samphire, and aged Longhorn beef with béarnaise sauce and chips

cooked in duck fat. Desserts hit the comfort zone with either duck egg crème brûlée and Yorkshire rhubarb or apple tarte Tatin.
Chef/s: Richard Turner. **Open:** all week L, Mon to Sat D. **Meals:** main courses £22 to £25. Set L £19 (2 courses) to £35. Sun L £33 (2 courses) to £39. **Details:** 26 seats. Children over 12 yrs only.

Two Cats Kitchen
Cooking score: 2
North-Eastern European | £48
27 Warstone Lane, Jewellery Quarter, Birmingham, B18 6JQ
Tel no: (0121) 2120070
twocatskitchen.com
£5
OFF

This small, intimate restaurant is not easy to find – invisible from the street, look for it at the end of a passage between two jewellery shops. The lovely old building with its stained-glass windows was once a gold forge – an industrial feel is hinted at in the exposed brickwork and iron beams. Chef/proprietor Niki Astley is a proponent of a thoroughly modern kind of cooking, that of north-eastern Europe, and with modern combinations and techniques on show aims to impress with his seven-course tasting menu. From the homemade sourdough bread and smoked butter, via finely sliced cauliflower topped with a perfectly runny egg and hazelnut crumb, and the contrasting flavours of smoked and dried beetroot with fermented damson, to monkfish tail with liver, served with buttermilk, dill and an eastern European dark bread, and a stunning finale of birch, oak and pine, this is cooking that can hit the heights. The wine list is brief and there's a selection of interesting beers.
Chef/s: Niki Astley. **Open:** Sat L, Tue to Sat D. **Closed:** Sun, Mon, 2 weeks from 24 Dec, 2 weeks July. **Meals:** tasting menu £48 (7 courses). **Details:** 24 seats. Music.

▮ Dorridge
LOCAL GEM
The Forest
Modern British | £29
25 Station Approach, Dorridge, B93 8JA
Tel no: (01564) 772120
forest-hotel.com
£5 OFF ⏻ £30

Pull up at this unassuming station hotel for brasserie-style food delivered by an excellent front-of-house team. Haloumi 'chips' with garlicky, nicely textured chimichurri is a generous 'nibble', and a separate small-plates menu tempts with the likes of Red Leicester soufflé with red grape and smoked date purée. Pan-fried sea trout is accompanied by a sweet-sharp blood orange and braised fennel, while a delicate lemon and green tea roulade is as prettily plated as it is fresh-tasting. Gin-love is evident: come by train and kick off with the Forest aperitif of gin, rose syrup and Prosecco.

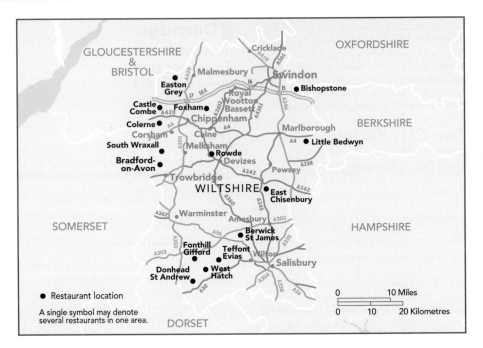

Berwick St James
The Boot Inn
Cooking score: 1
British | £26
High Street, Berwick St James, SP3 4TN
Tel no: (01722) 790243
theboot.pub

£30

With ceramic tankards hanging above the mighty inglenook, Wiltshire-brewed Wadworth ales on handpump and a pretty beer garden outside, this 18th-century roadside inn upholds local tradition and public-house virtues with a vengeance. It also does a good line in (almost) unreformed British victuals, from smoked haddock rarebit (that old Gary Rhodes classic) to roast chicken breast with braised pearl barley and leeks. Elsewhere, corned beef fritters are contemporised with a quail's egg and raw tomato vinaigrette, ribeye steaks come with

polenta chips, and rice pudding gets a kick from blood orange and pistachios. Wine drinkers can pick from a workmanlike list.
Chef/s: Giles Dickinson. **Open:** Tue to Sun L, Tue to Sat D. **Closed:** Mon, 25 Dec, first 2 weeks Feb. **Meals:** main courses £12 to £18. **Details:** 30 seats. 24 seats outside. Music. Parking.

Bishopstone
Helen Browning's Royal Oak
Cooking score: 3
British | £28
Cues Lane, Bishopstone, SN6 8PP
Tel no: (01793) 790481
helenbrowningorganics.co.uk

£5 OFF £30

Standing proud and foursquare in a Wiltshire village not far from Swindon, the Royal Oak is the centrepiece of a thriving organic farm, where smart guest rooms (more added in 2017) and the crisp country air are part of the allure. What isn't grown and reared on site is carefully sourced from ethical suppliers and producers, and transformed into unpretentious, hearty comfort food served in loin-girding portions. Start with smoked mackerel salad with crispy lardons and a poached egg for a good introduction to a menu built around superior pork – roast belly in lentil stew, schnitzel with coleslaw, braised cheeks and horseradish mash – as well as flavourful game, such as pheasant slow-cooked in white wine and tomato with black pudding mash, or perhaps a grilled salmon steak on salsa verde. Puddings push all the right buttons for sticky toffee in rum-laced toffee sauce with banana, or lemon posset with lemon curd and raspberries. The short wine list, from £20.50, does its best to keep up.

Chef/s: Paul Winch. **Open:** all week L and D. **Meals:** main courses £12 to £27. **Details:** 70 seats. 70 seats outside. Bar. Wheelchairs. Parking.

◼ Bradford-on-Avon

LOCAL GEM

Bunch of Grapes
French | £25
14 Silver Street, Bradford-on-Avon, BA15 1JY
Tel no: (01225) 938088
thebunchofgrapes.com

£5 £30
OFF

The longest-serving pub in Bradford-on-Avon has an invitingly venerable feel inside, with a cheery bar on the ground floor, and a bare-boarded dining room upstairs, dominated by a huge, encouraging image of an artichoke. Steve Carss cooks an ambitious Anglo-French menu of modernist inclinations, dressing rabbit rillettes in red pepper chutney, citrus crème fraîche and onion ash, prior to cramming hake and cockles into a chowder with wild mushrooms and sunflower shoots for character, and then shoehorning poached pear into a crêpe that comes with dark chocolate and vanilla ice

cream. Wood-fired roasts pack them in on Sundays. A small list of unusual French wines from £18 is an asset.

◼ Castle Combe

The Bybrook
Cooking score: 6
Modern British | £66
The Manor House Hotel, Castle Combe, SN14 7HR
Tel no: (01249) 782206
manorhouse.co.uk

🛏

Do take a moment to glance around Castle Combe if you've not been before. Medieval English villages rarely look more ravishing than this. The ivy-smothered Manor House will hardly disappoint either, with its hefty stone walls and venerable panelling, the bevies of impeccably trained staff and an expansive dining room that gazes out over the listed Italian gardens. Rob Potter sources from the kitchen plots as well as from surrounding Wiltshire for modern British dishes that don't go off the outré deep end, but do display bundles of impressive technique. Fillet of mackerel with Cornish crab, mooli, avocado and charred cucumber with caper and raisin purée is a beautifully constructed beginner, and might preface loin of Wiltshire lamb and belly, with sweetbread, boudin, potato terrine, caramelised onion, morel mushrooms and lamb jus, or there may be fillet of Gigha halibut with buttered lettuce, sea purslane, cockles and mussels in chive-strewn beurre blanc. The finishing line is reached with a 'superb' chocolate délice, or with a phalanx of fine regional cheeses. Limited-availability wines are the stars of a list that opens at £25.50.

Chef/s: Robert Potter. **Open:** Sun L, all week D. **Meals:** set D £66 (3 courses). Sun L £35. Tasting menu £89. **Details:** 60 seats. V menu. Bar. Music. Parking. Children over 11 yrs only.

▌Colerne

Restaurant Hywel Jones by Lucknam Park

Cooking score: 5
Modern British | £87
Colerne, SN14 8AZ
Tel no: (01225) 742777
lucknampark.co.uk

🍷 ⇌

Reclining in 500 acres of grounds bordered by copses and lawns, this Palladian mansion offers a hospitality package gilded with antiques and stuffed with fine-dining largesse. To celebrate Hywel Jones' tenure as head chef, Lucknam's flagship Park restaurant has been renamed and gently refurbished – although the unabashed opulence of this one-time ballroom remains undiminished. Eating here is a measured full-dress experience, from G&Ts and canapés in the drawing room to dinner amid silk drapes and chandeliers dangling from a hand-painted ceiling. Serious money is involved, but in return you can expect intricate modern cooking underpinned by sound technique. To start, duck liver might be served two ways with chicory, spiced mandarin and sweet wine, while fastidious sourcing yields Brecon lamb, Wiltshire pork and day-boat fish (grilled red mullet with Cornish shellfish, sea vegetables and verjus butter, say). Desserts such as rhubarb soufflé with stem ginger ice cream also know how to sparkle. Vintage old-school classics and 'adventurous niche wines' sit side by side on the masterly list, with ample flights, half-bottles and by-the-glass selections adding to the enjoyment.

Chef/s: Hywel Jones. **Open:** Sun L, all week D. **Meals:** set D £87. Sun L £45. Tasting menu £110 (8 courses). **Details:** 65 seats. V menu. Bar. Wheelchairs. Parking. Children over 5 yrs only.

▌Donhead St Andrew

The Forester

Cooking score: 2
Modern British | £30
Lower Street, Donhead St Andrew, SP7 9EE
Tel no: (01747) 828038
theforesterdonheadstandrew.co.uk

Make sure it's the right saint you're heading for. There is a Donhead St Mary, too. Her confrère lies nearby though, and is home to a thatched country pub buried among tiny lanes not far from Wardour Castle. A beautiful garden awaits in summer, and the oak-beamed and panelled interior feels properly cocooning in the chillier seasons, with cask-conditioned ales and a carefully thought-out short wine list on hand to crank up the cheer. Andrew Kilburn's cooking has plenty to say for itself too, incorporating Eastern modes for a tempura prawn starter that comes with Thai-spiced green papaya salad, and coming over all Italian for linguine with venison ragù and Parmesan. Locally reared meats are the stars of the show, perhaps Style Farm beef featherblade with root veg rösti and Savoy cabbage. Start by snacking on cockle popcorn, and finish with something equally out of the ordinary, like Seville orange tart and fennel sorbet. Those wines open with a Chilean Sauvignon at £19.

Chef/s: Andrew Kilburn. **Open:** Tue to Sun L, Tue to Sat D. **Closed:** Mon. **Meals:** main courses £15 to £28. Set L and D £19 (2 courses) to £23. **Details:** 60 seats. 25 seats outside. V menu. Wheelchairs. Parking.

East Chisenbury
The Red Lion Freehouse
Cooking score: 5
Modern British | £40
East Chisenbury, SN9 6AQ
Tel no: (01980) 671124
redlionfreehouse.com
£5 OFF 🛏

In a pastoral backwater not far from Salisbury Plain, this immaculately thatched, self-styled village 'freehouse' comes complete with a boutique B&B across the road and a serious gastronomic reputation. Guy and Brittany Manning arrived here with gilt-edged culinary CVs and have done sterling work ever since, baking bread, curing charcuterie, growing green stuff and supporting the local foodie network. Strong flavours and uncluttered plates of bold French-accented food are the norm – from a 'paysanne' salad of goose ham with bitter leaves and rye to roast loin of local venison with glazed chicory, chestnut purée and sauce poivrade. Chateaubriand, pissaladière and confit duck fix the culinary compass, although you might find steamed salted cod with rice cake and dashi broth too. After that, the 'tres leches' cake with avocado ice cream, lime curd and cocoa nibs sounds unmissable. The Red Lion has its full pubby quota of beams, open fires and microbrewery ales, but also note the classy artisan wine list (including around 20 by the glass).
Chef/s: Guy Manning. **Open:** all week L and D. **Meals:** main courses £20 to £30. Set L and D £20 (2 courses) to £25. Tasting menu £85. **Details:** 65 seats. 30 seats outside. Bar. Music. Parking.

Easton Grey
★ NEW ENTRY ★
Grey's Brasserie
Cooking score: 3
Modern British | £32
Whatley Manor, Easton Grey, SN16 0RB
Tel no: (01666) 822888
whatleymanor.com
£5 OFF 🛏

It may sound rather grand with its stately Cotswold-stone good looks and pretty gardens, but Whatley Manor doesn't lord it – just the opposite, in fact. The whole place is run with a mix of personable good humour and common courtesy – no furtive tiptoeing or doffing-of-caps pomposity here. The Dining Room is the hotel's gastronomic flagship (see entry), but the hotel's second restaurant is run by the same keen kitchen brigade and puts on a convincing show. Its unpretentious approach is matched by some appealing, soothing food and the menu offers a familiar run through the modern brasserie catalogue, from homemade sausage roll with brown sauce, via omelette Arnold Bennett, to roast chicken with pomme purée or pollack with spring leeks, bacon and a creamy wild garlic sauce. For a simple finish try English custard tart with an intensely flavoured blackcurrant sorbet. The short wine list is equally accessible (from £27), with plenty by the glass.
Chef/s: Niall Keating. **Open:** all week L and D. **Meals:** main courses £15 to £32. Set L £29 (2 courses) to £36. **Details:** 70 seats. 24 seats outside. Bar. Wheelchairs. Music. Parking.

Whatley Manor, The Dining Room

Cooking score: 7
Modern British | £99
Whatley Manor, Easton Grey, SN16 0RB
Tel no: (01666) 822888
whatleymanor.com

£5 OFF ♦ 🛏

Whatley Manor stands at the end of a long drive, a spectacular country house of Cotswold stone with a full complement of modern facilities including spa, boardroom, cinema and two dining rooms (see entry, Grey's Brasserie). Tranquillity reigns, as indeed it must have done pretty much since the house was built in the 18th century. You could be forgiven for thinking that the surroundings would inspire a sleepy version of country-house cooking, but sights have always been trained higher than that. Since our last edition, Niall Keating has taken over the kitchen. He is a chef whose cooking has pursued an interesting trajectory – from Restaurant Sat Bains (see entry) and Benu in San Francisco, to Kong Hans Kaelder in Copenhagen, combining modern juxtapositions with classical technique along the way. Eating takes place at generously spaced tables in a pair of adjoining dining rooms with chefs nipping out of the kitchen to serve diners alongside the pitch-perfect front-of-house team. The opening salvo of the evening tasting menu is terrific – one minute you're nibbling on a crisp, spiced sesame cracker dotted with Exmoor caviar, the next you're slurping up an oyster in a fabulous seaweed mignonette. Every detail makes sense, from the subtle hints of sweet-and-sour in a nugget of mackerel served with preserved raspberries and raspberry foam, to the deftness of an egg white custard with tamari and seaweed, its umami hit contrasting with the salty pop of salmon roe. There are big flavours in a risotto with chorizo that's topped with raw, cubed scallop, in the richness of a spring lamb cutlet with dill pickle and horseradish. Desserts also hit the high notes, whether an aloe vera, grape and olive oil palate cleanser, or the superb matcha with chocolate and lime. The connoisseurs' wine list strides through each of the headline regions with inspiring confidence, offering plenty of classics and new discoveries, starting at £40.
Chef/s: Niall Keating. **Open:** Wed to Sun D only. **Closed:** Mon, Tue. **Meals:** tasting menu £99 (12 courses). **Details:** 44 seats. 24 seats outside. V menu. Bar. Wheelchairs. Music. Parking. Children over 12 yrs only.

▪ Fonthill Gifford
Beckford Arms

Cooking score: 3
Modern British | £30
Hindon Lane, Fonthill Gifford, SP3 6PX
Tel no: (01747) 870385
beckfordarms.com

🛏

An 18th-century inn on the edge of the 9,000-acre Fonthill Estate, the Beckford Arms cuts a dash with its creeper-covered façade, 'oh so tasteful' interior and lush garden. Real fires keep it toasty in winter, and when the French doors open on to the terrace in the summer, it's 'a little piece of heaven'. The menu plays it safe with a house burger and fish and chips, but they're done well, and starters such as devilled chicken hearts and livers, and goats' curd gnocchi with local beets and caramelised walnuts really show the cut of the kitchen's jib. Main-course slow-roast pork belly, Puy lentils and celeriac purée is full of earthy satisfaction, and oven-baked cod with chimichurri, pickled radish and a salad of braised fennel and celery shows contemporary sensibilities. Fennel marshmallow is a creative accompaniment to a lemon dessert of custard and sorbet, with almond biscotti providing le crunch. Arranged by style, the wine list kicks off at £18.
Chef/s: Nigel Everett. **Open:** all week L and D. **Closed:** 25 Dec. **Meals:** main courses £12 to £22. **Details:** 54 seats. 34 seats outside. Bar. Music. Parking.

▌Foxham
The Foxham Inn
Cooking score: 1
Modern British | £30
Foxham, SN15 4NQ
Tel no: (01249) 740665
thefoxhaminn.co.uk
£5 OFF 🛏

Some five hundred years of history are etched into parts of this family-run brick-built pub-with-rooms – although you wouldn't guess it from the ambitious food served in the high-raftered, open-plan extension. Local ingredients are given creditable up-to-date treatment, as in slow-cooked lamb belly with celeriac, kale and red wine sauce, rabbit and kidney pie with artichoke purée or pancetta-wrapped saddle of rabbit stuffed with truffle mousse. Steaks and pub classics also get a workout, while lemon polenta cake or sticky toffee pudding jazzed up with Horlicks ice cream are typical desserts. Real ales and easy-drinking wines satisfy drinkers.
Chef/s: Neil Cooper. **Open:** Tue to Sun L, Tue to Sat D. **Closed:** Mon, first 2 weeks Jan. **Meals:** main courses £14 to £23. **Details:** 60 seats. 24 seats outside. Wheelchairs. Music. Parking.

▌Lacock

READERS RECOMMEND
Sign of the Angel
Modern British
6 Church Street, Lacock, SN15 2LB
Tel no: (01249) 730230
signoftheangel.co.uk
'A wonderful 15th-century pub in a beautiful setting. I ordered lamb rump and dumpling, spinach and rosemary crumb, creamed potato, baby carrots and smoked garlic sauce. The lamb was pink, tender and juicy, and the accompanying roast carrots and potato purée were tasty and well cooked. The dumpling was boldly flavoured – a bit like a faggot – and there were wilted baby spinach leaves to mop up the gravy.'

Niall Keating 🍴
Whatley Manor, The Dining Room, Easton Grey, Wiltshire

What can diners expect when they eat with you at The Dining Room?
We talk of dining experiences: a sequence of dishes inspired by different cuisines, designed to make our guests stop a moment, ponder over the flavours, and make them want to talk about the dishes. When our guests have questions about a dish, there will always be a chef on hand in the restaurant to give a thorough explanation - the additional information seems to be very much wanted by our guests and it appears to add to the whole experience.

How did you go about compiling your menu - what were your influences?
The current menu is an expression of the different styles of cuisine I have enjoyed working with, combined with my own creative ideas and my many trips to the food markets of Korea, San Francisco and Copenhagen. Working with some of the UK's finest suppliers is also a source of inspiration. My kitchen team also have 'project nights' where I encourage them to dip into their creative reserves to present new ideas - without question, this inspires me too.

▌Little Bedwyn
The Harrow at Little Bedwyn

Cooking score: 6
Modern British | £50
High Street, Little Bedwyn, SN8 3JP
Tel no: (01672) 870871
theharrowatlittlebedwyn.com
£5 OFF

Roger and Sue Jones ditched the suffix 'inn' many moons ago, so don't come to the Harrow expecting a ploughman's or farming paraphernalia. Instead, this handsome Wiltshire retreat is a country restaurant of inestimable class with an astonishing wine cellar to boot. Muted modern colours and leather chairs create a soothing tone in the two dining rooms, where diners are treated to cooking of real dexterity and assurance. Proceedings open with an amuse-bouche – perhaps an Arbroath smokie milkshake in a dinky glass bottle. After that, expect a procession of dishes defined by fastidiously sourced ingredients, sumptuous flavours and contrasting textures – from 'succulent' seared yellowfin tuna with Asian spices and minted couscous to Pembroke lobster salad with fennel and citrus dressing. Elsewhere, Périgord truffles are lavished on plates of Highland beef and Northumberland roe deer, while desserts such as a fresh berry soufflé are similarly impressive. Brilliant wine pairings are plucked from a staggering wine list stuffed with remarkably fine drinking – look to Germany, Alsace and South Africa for the biggest thrills. Otherwise, take the plunge by ordering from the premium Coravin selection by the glass.
Chef/s: Roger Jones and John Brown. **Open:** Wed to Sat L and D. **Closed:** Sun, Mon Tue, Christmas and New Year. **Meals:** set L £40 (5 courses). Set D £50 (6 courses). Tasting menu £75 (8 courses). **Details:** 34 seats. 24 seats outside. V menu. Wheelchairs. Music.

▌Rowde
The George & Dragon

Cooking score: 3
Modern British | £32
High Street, Rowde, SN10 2PN
Tel no: (01380) 723053
thegeorgeanddragonrowde.co.uk
£5 OFF

Not the most picturesque inn in the county perhaps, but full of character and period charm nonetheless, the George & Dragon dates from the 16th century and has been specialising in seafood for quite a while now. Check out the blackboards to see what's been shipped up from St Mawes in Cornwall that very day. Scallops, perhaps, pan-fried and plated up with crispy black pudding and a belly pork salad, or roast monkfish wrapped in Parma ham with wild mushrooms and a grainy mustard sauce. The sharing seafood platter is full of good things, and, if you crave meat, devilled kidneys on toast or char-grilled ribeye steak are no afterthoughts. Finish in true British fashion with raspberry posset with lemon shortbread or apple and berry crumble. Drink draught ales or something from the concise global wine list (starting at £19).
Chef/s: Tom Bryant. **Open:** all week L, Mon to Sat D. **Closed:** 25 Dec. **Meals:** main courses £14 to £26. Set L and D £17 (2 courses) to £20. Sun L £20. **Details:** 36 seats. 38 seats outside. Bar. Music. Parking.

▌South Wraxall
The Longs Arms

Cooking score: 3
Modern British | £32
South Wraxall, BA15 2SB
Tel no: (01225) 864450
thelongsarms.com

From the outside it might look like a regulation roadside boozer, but the stone-built Longs Arms is a hostelry with hidden talents. It not only doubles as a local watering hole and village shop, with Wadworth ales on

handpump and essential provisions for sale over the bar, but also boasts an unpretentious restaurant. Chef/landlord Rob Allcock learned his craft in some high-end West Country kitchens, and it shows: just consider a gutsy plate of Wiltshire kid loin and kidney with elderberry jelly, pistachios and Wye Valley asparagus. Yes, the menu spells out the provenance of its main ingredients, be it mackerel from Cornwall (sweet-cured and served with garlic mayo, orange and Thai basil) or Goosnargh chicken breast (from Lancashire) with home-smoked bacon, Jersey Royals, hen-of-the-woods mushrooms and wild garlic. There's some pub grub too, plus desserts including Seville orange marmalade parfait with honeycomb and mint. The wine list comprises two dozen good-value wines.
Chef/s: Rob Allcock. **Open:** Wed to Sun L, Wed to Sat D. **Closed:** Mon, Tue, 3 weeks Jan, 1 week Sept. **Meals:** main courses £11 to £32. **Details:** 38 seats. 30 seats outside. Wheelchairs. Music. Parking.

▌Teffont Evias
Howard's House Hotel
Cooking score: 3
Modern British | £47
Teffont Evias, SP3 5RJ
Tel no: (01722) 716392
howardshousehotel.co.uk
£5 OFF 🛏

A late Jacobean dower house in the Cranborne Chase AONB, the stone-built Howard's still contains plenty of original amenities, from wine cellars to fireplaces. There's a real sense of its locality, too, in Nick Wentworth's menus, which start from the kitchen garden and build upwards, with the option of cookery lessons based on those foraged ingredients that are now everywhere. Combinations make enlightening statements about the prime materials, as when pickled beetroot from the garden and horseradish mayonnaise lend sharpness to home-smoked halibut, while a pairing of sheep's curd and poached pear with black pepper biscuit and sherry vinegar caramel is an inspired assemblage. Main courses are more classically based, perhaps

roast breast of guinea fowl with onion rösti, wild mushrooms and roasted shallots in red wine jus, or lemon sole fillets with pak choi in crab bisque. Plenty of fruit makes its way into desserts like apple and cherry crumble, rum-roasted pineapple, or passion fruit soufflé with mango and passion fruit sorbet. Ardèche blends at £19 lead off an engagingly cosmopolitan wine list.
Chef/s: Nick Wentworth. **Open:** all week L and D. **Closed:** 24 to 27 Dec. **Meals:** alc £37 (2 courses) to £47. Tasting menu £65. **Details:** 30 seats. 30 seats outside. Bar. Wheelchairs. Music. Parking.

▌West Hatch
LOCAL GEM
Pythouse Kitchen Garden
British | £20
West Hatch, SP3 6PA
Tel no: (01747) 870444
pythousekitchengarden.co.uk
£30

The walled kitchen garden is the heart of Pythouse Kitchen Garden, with a charming boho-rustic café that is also open on Friday and Saturday evenings. Consider glamping, an event or even getting married... it is a lovely spot. During the day you might tuck into a seasonal board, an organic burger or simply coffee and a cake, while the supper menu runs to confit pheasant with vegetable rösti, and seared hake with braised Puy lentils and roasted fennel. The seasonal vegetables are fab, Sunday roasts are the business and the setting is wonderfully tranquil.

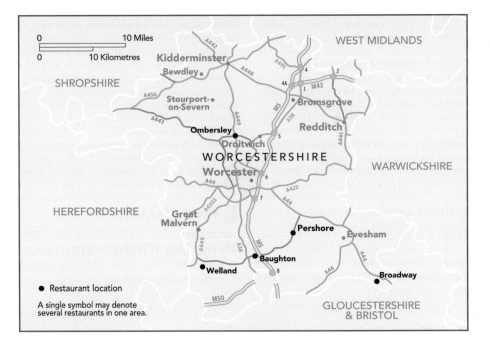

▮ Baughton

LOCAL GEM

The Jockey Inn
Modern British | £28
Pershore Road, Baughton, WR8 9DQ
Tel no: (01684) 592153
thejockeyinn.co.uk

£30

It was a regional winner in last year's Local
Restaurant Awards, and reporters are in no
doubt that Rebekah Seddon-Wickens'
rejuvenated village inn continues to charm. It's
a proper local with real ales and fish and chips,
beamed ceilings and real fires. In the mood for
more fancy stuff? Then head to the restaurant
for dishes such as braised pork bonbons with
Bramley apple, onion and sage crackling, and
fillet of turbot with saffron-infused haricots
blancs and Chardonnay and saffron reduction.
Finish with caramel pannacotta with warm
ginger cake. Wines from £14.95.

▮ Broadway

Russells of Broadway
Cooking score: 3
Modern British | £40
20 High Street, Broadway, WR12 7DT
Tel no: (01386) 853555
russellsofbroadway.co.uk

£5 OFF

A film-set vision of English pastoral,
Broadway is well served by Neil Clarke's
boutique restaurant-with-rooms. Quirky
artworks and bare stone walls add some
character to the otherwise 'rather bland'
interior, while the kitchen sets about
delivering simple yet refined bistro-style
food. There's nothing confused about hand-
dived scallops with braised pork belly and
turnip purée, although a starter of smoked
pigeon breast with seared foie gras, brioche
and fig chutney struck one reader as an odd
presentation with an identity crisis.
Elsewhere, local ingredients are well
represented, while dry-aged fillet of beef

forms part of a creditable 'meat and three veg' combo. The food doesn't always live up to expectations, but desserts such as a 'superb' dark chocolate crémeux with caramelised banana and burnt-milk ice cream show what the kitchen is capable of achieving. Staff are chirpy, even if they're not au fait with the passionately curated wine list.

Chef/s: Neil Clarke. **Open:** all week L, Mon to Sat D. **Closed:** Mon bank hols. **Meals:** main courses £15 to £32. Set L and D £20 (2 courses) to £24. Sun L £25 (2 courses) to £29. **Details:** 60 seats. 25 seats outside. Bar. Wheelchairs. Music. Parking.

▌Ombersley
The Venture In

Cooking score: 4
Modern European | £43
Main Road, Ombersley, WR9 0EW
Tel no: (01905) 620552
theventurein.co.uk

You're not absolutely guaranteed an encounter with the resident ghost at Toby Fletcher's place, a 15th-century timbered house on the high street of a Severn village, but there's plenty of historical atmosphere to absorb anyway. Crooked beams and upright hospitality make an attractive combination to back up the contemporary Anglo-French bistro cooking, which might kick off with a heterogeneous selection of seafood hors d'oeuvres, or then again, seared scallops in a pairing with confit pork belly, seasoned with Chinese five-spice. Smoking of main ingredients is done in-house, and produces wonderful Gressingham duck breast and leg, with duck hash and a casserole of bacon, apple and peppercorns in cider jus. Fish might be sea bass with prawn and tarragon risotto and a shellfish emulsion, while the dessert indulgences take in Valrhona and nut brownie with chocolate sauce, or orange marmalade sponge with Grand Marnier anglaise and chocolate and orange ice cream. A spread of house wines at £18 and £19 heads up a usefully annotated international list.

Chef/s: Toby Fletcher. **Open:** Tue to Sun L, Tue to Sat D. **Closed:** Mon, 1 week Christmas, 1 week Mar, 1 week Jun, 2 weeks Aug. **Meals:** set L £29 (2 courses) to £33. Set D £43. Sun L £33. **Details:** 32 seats. Bar. Music. Parking. Children over 10 yrs only.

▌Pershore
Belle House

Cooking score: 2
Modern British | £37
5 Bridge Street, Pershore, WR10 1AJ
Tel no: (01386) 555055
belle-house.co.uk

A big picture of Evesham asparagus catches the eye in this spacious, airy restaurant, while high ceilings and arched front windows are reminders that Belle House was once Pershore's fire station. However, there's nothing to set alarm bells ringing these days: the mood is sedate and rather grown-up, service is personable – you're left to pour your own wine (hooray) – and the cooking is sound. Old-school brasserie classics such as crab fettuccine, twice-baked cheese soufflé with Waldorf salad and lemon meringue pie dominate the concise fixed-price menus, although there's also room for the odd off-piste foray – duck breast and liver kebab with chicory tart, charred broccoli and plum sauce, say. Recent reports suggest that the whole outfit is starting to feel 'just a little tired and old-fashioned' but applaud the 'excellent value'. Wines by the glass come courtesy of a Verre de Vin system, and there's a fascinating deli/traiteur next door.

Chef/s: Steve Waites. **Open:** Wed to Sat L and D. **Closed:** Sun, Mon, Tue, 25 to 30 Dec, first 2 weeks Jan. **Meals:** set L £18 (2 courses) to £27. Set D £29 (2 courses) to £37. Tasting menu £45 (6 courses). **Details:** 70 seats. Bar. Wheelchairs. Music.

▋Welland
The Inn at Welland
Cooking score: 4
Modern European | £30
Hook Bank, Drake Street, Welland, WR13 6LN
Tel no: (01684) 592317
theinnatwelland.co.uk
£5
OFF

'Always a pleasurable experience,' noted one fan of this smart country inn. With the Malvern Hills on panoramic display outside and decorated with taste within, this sought-after Worcestershire destination is noted for top-notch food. The kitchen casts its net wide, offering a lively mix of Mediterranean and classic British flavours. Venison carpaccio is partnered with baby leaves, quails' eggs and fresh horseradish for a contemporary classic opener, or you might head towards chunky woodland pork terrine with roast garlic purée and a crisp hen's egg. Game shows up well in main courses, too, as does spring lamb, which comes as a herb-crusted rack with petit ratatouille, potato dauphinois and a red wine and basil jus, while hake hauled in from Cornwall appears with herb and garlic potatoes, Provençal vegetables, lemon and dill and a beurre blanc. Real ales are 'the icing on the cake', but don't ignore the affordably priced wine list with plenty of decent drinking from £15.95.
Chef/s: Alex Boghian. **Open:** Tue to Sun L, Tue to Sat D. **Closed:** Mon, 25 and 26 Dec, 31 Dec, 1 Jan. **Meals:** main courses £13 to £25. Sun L £26. **Details:** 80 seats. 40 seats outside. Wheelchairs. Music. Parking.

▋Worcester
READERS RECOMMEND
Saffrons Bistro
International
15 New Street, Worcester, WR1 2DP
Tel no: (01905) 610505
saffronsbistro.co.uk
'I would like to commend this bistro. There is nothing grandiose about the cooking but ample choice of wholesome food – cod for my wife and a 10 oz steak for me. The owners do all the front-of-house work efficiently and cheerfully. The plain wood floor and straightforward seating suit the building in a narrow Worcester Street. Service and atmosphere are excellent.'

Readers recommend

A 'readers recommend' review is a genuine quote from a report sent in by one of our readers. We intend to follow up these suggestions throughout the year to come.

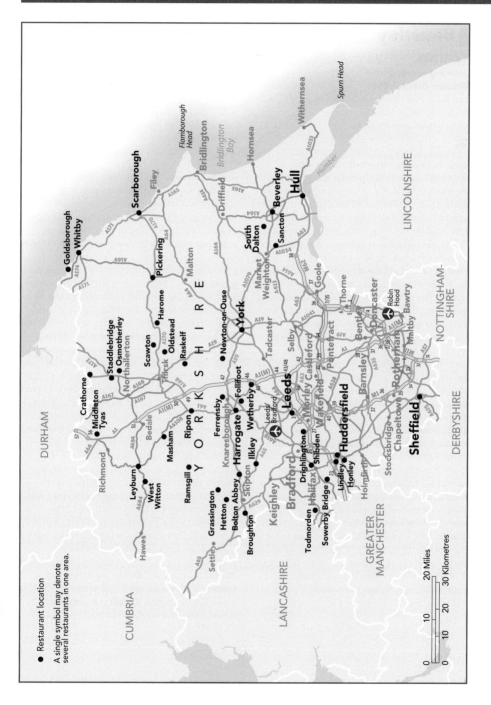

▊ Beverley
Whites
Cooking score: 5
Modern British | £50
12a North Bar Without, Beverley, HU17 7AB
Tel no: (01482) 866121
whitesrestaurant.co.uk

John Robinson's detached corner site
overlooking Beverley's town walls is about as
pared back as can be. A varnished wood floor,
small unclothed tables, plain shelf units and an
open kitchen hatch is about the sum of it,
although the rooftop terrace is an asset on
balmy days. What this means is that the focus is
entirely on what comes out of that little
kitchen, and one January reporter was left in
no doubt about that: 'a cool and unfettered
masterclass of top-notch cooking'. Robinson
tasks himself with tasting menus of four or
nine courses, an ambitious aim in the limited
circumstances, but the results are regularly
stunning. An early course of smoked eel
mousse with chicken skin vinaigrette, pickled
radish and caviar sets the modernist tone, and
could be followed by quail cooked gently
sous-vide for 10 hours and partnered with
pickled cucumber, apple and miso. Pork belly
has had an even more sedate 54 hours, and the
balsamic vinegar it's dressed in a hundred
years, but the rhubarb dessert is all stinging-
sharp freshness, with jam, jelly and roasted
elements underpinned by chocolate and
walnut délice and orange and thyme cream.
Wines are reasonably priced, from £18.50,
with a few upmarket selections interspersed.
Chef/s: John Robinson. **Open:** Sat L, Tue to Sat D.
Closed: Sun, Mon, 2 weeks Christmas, 1 week Aug.
Meals: set L £23 (4 courses). Set D Tue to Thur £25
(4 courses). Tasting menu £50 (9 courses).
Details: 20 seats. Wheelchairs. Music.

▊ Bolton Abbey
The Burlington
new chef/no score
Modern British | £70
The Devonshire Arms, Bolton Abbey,
BD23 6AJ
Tel no: (01756) 710441
burlingtonrestaurant.co.uk

It may be called the Devonshire Arms, but the
building in which the Burlington is set is
essentially a country house, though not an
imposing or even grand one. The grounds are
beautifully tended, the interiors are as
expected – dark, polished panelling and
tables, oddment antiques and quirky
paintings, patterned deep-pile carpets, even a
grand piano. The dining room itself is formal
– although the all-glass wine cellar built here
is a standout feature. However, Paul Evans,
who arrived after the publication of last year's
guide, has now departed. The good news is
that Paul Leonard, who spent two years as
head chef at the Isle of Eriska in Oban, Argyll
(and previously at Restaurant Andrew Fairlie
– see entry) will head the kitchen. New menus
are unavailable as we go to press, but a meal
taken while Mr Evans was cooking produced
'a superb meal here – great setting, pricing and
service'. We are certain standards will be
maintained. The great tome of a wine list
remains the same – packed full of treats at
superb prices and reflecting a huge base of
suppliers, great cellar management and years
of investment. Do take the advice of the
sommelier – he has mastered the art of
combining his own, natural personality with a
flair for the occasion. He knows his list
backwards.
Chef/s: Paul Leonard. **Open:** Tue to Sun D only.
Closed: Mon. **Meals:** set D £70 (5 courses). Tasting
menu £80 (8 courses). **Details:** 66 seats. Bar.
Wheelchairs. Parking. Children over 7 yrs only.

The Devonshire Brasserie

Cooking score: 3
Modern British | £35
The Devonshire Arms, Bolton Abbey,
BD23 6AJ
Tel no: (01756) 710710
devonshirebrasserie.co.uk

The Brasserie in the Devonshire Arms has the bright, airy, expansive feel of a community centre, with contemporary landscape paintings and a tumult of clashing colours in the chairs and cushions, although the Dales views (from the terrace) are something else. Regionally based dishes are the stock-in-trade, perhaps starting with pressed Dales ham hock with pickled veg and mustard gel, and sharing platters of charcuterie or seafood for working up an appetite. At main, Nidderdale lamb gets an outing with couscous, feta and Mediterranean accompaniments in a scented jus of mint and cumin, while the more populist offerings include beer-battered Whitby haddock or 55-day aged steak cuts, both with triple-cooked chips. Vegetarians look to sweet potato and chickpea curry on cardamom rice, and the enticing finishers include custard tart with nutmeg ice cream, or lemon posset with strawberry sorbet. A good selection of wines by the glass heads up a value-conscious list.
Chef/s: Sean Pleasants. **Open:** all week L and D.
Meals: main courses £15 to £32. **Details:** 70 seats.
40 seats outside. Wheelchairs. Music. Parking.

▌Broughton

LOCAL GEM
The Bull

British | £22
Broughton, BD23 3AE
Tel no: (01756) 792065
thebullatbroughton.com
£30

Part of Nigel Haworth's Ribble Valley Inns Group, the Bull has been knocking about since 1709 and is looking in fine fettle these days. The charm of the original building remains and the food – as at its Lancashire compadres – includes a local flavour in a broadly appealing repertoire. The twice-baked cheese soufflé is made with Yorkshire Blue, ploughman's and sandwiches are good versions, fish and chips and burgers are done right, and 21-day aged steaks hit the spot. Drink regional beer or wines from £16.95.

▌Crathorne
Crathorne Arms

Cooking score: 2
British | £35
Crathorne Village, Crathorne, TS15 0BA
Tel no: (01642) 961402
thecrathornearms.co.uk

'Good to see him back and on form,' cheered a fan of owner Eugene McCoy, happily recalling Mr McCoy's time at the 'totally eccentric and much revered' Cleveland Tontine. True to form, antiques and bric-a-brac furnish a series of rooms in this whitewashed village pub and the menu follows the old Tontine French-bistro-meets-modern-British style – 'it's all very comforting' and adds up to a welcoming local offering food you really want to eat. Starters range from classic prawn cocktail to seared chicken livers with crispy bacon, brioche croûtons and port wine reduction, while 'sublime, tasty' main courses include steaks with a choice of sauces, as well as pancetta-wrapped wild rabbit with a nut-crusted leg and pommes Anna, and whole char-grilled sea bass with sauce skordalia (potato and garlic). For dessert, look no further than banana split with toffee popcorn ice cream and candied peanuts. A short but wide-ranging wine list starts at £18.65.
Chef/s: David Henry. **Open:** Tue to Sun L, Tue to Sat D. **Closed:** Mon, 25 and 26 Dec, 1 to 5 Jan.
Meals: main courses £12 to £24. Set L and D £19 (2 courses) to £22. Sun L £15. **Details:** 65 seats. 20 seats outside. Bar. Wheelchairs. Music. Parking.

▌Drighlington
Prashad

Cooking score: 2
Indian Vegetarian | £26
137 Whitehall Road, Drighlington, BD11 1AT
Tel no: (0113) 2852037
prashad.co.uk
£5 £30
OFF

Prashad evolved from a deli 24 years ago, becoming a Bradford institution along the way. Surroundings are comfortable – a long restaurant on different levels – and it is a 'slick operation' with the kitchen dealing in mainly Gujarati vegetarian food but making a few excursions elsewhere in the Subcontinent. Sharing a tasting platter is one way to experience a range of starters, perhaps pattra (griddled vegetable parcels), kopra pethis (garlic-infused coconut dough ball) or hara bara kebab (mashed pea and cauliflower, crisp and richly spiced). Masala dosa filled with spiced potato and onion lentil broth and served with fresh coconut chutney is a complete meal, bhindi (okra) served with fenugreek and tomato is a lighter option. There is plenty of heat but a jug of cooling lassi might do the trick, or there are 'zero chilli' options. A palate cleansing fruit and spice sorbet is a fitting end or there's date and ginger ice cream. The wine list (£15.95) has been chosen to complement the spicy food.
Chef/s: Minal Patel. **Open:** Sat and Sun L, Tue to Sun D. **Closed:** Mon, 25 Dec. **Meals:** main courses £12 to £20. Tasting menu £46. **Details:** 80 seats. V menu. Bar. Wheelchairs. Music. Parking.

▌Ferrensby
The General Tarleton

Cooking score: 4
Modern British | £30
Boroughbridge Road, Ferrensby, HG5 0PZ
Tel no: (01423) 340284
generaltarleton.co.uk
🛏

A local asset for the past 21 years, John and Claire Topham's really quite skilful balancing act delivers a brilliant restaurant-with-rooms in pub clothing. The GT is a captivating destination thanks to an interior that blends the pubby virtues of exposed stone, brick, beams and open fires with a comfortable country-house feel. And the menu of creatively retooled pub classics and modern British ideas is another big hit, noted for 'overall quality and value for money'. 'Little moneybags' is an old favourite and 'still a treat for the seafood lover', while ewes' cheese, English mustard and leek soufflé, slow-braised sticky pig's cheeks and Yorkshire fish pie is food that comforts rather than challenges. Sunday lunch brings a well-reported roast saddle of pork with black pudding, apple sauce and good gravy, there's a wonderful all Yorkshire cheeseboard, a perfect dark chocolate fondant and a well-considered list of wines that packs value, with prices from £22.
Chef/s: John Topham and Marc Williams. **Open:** all week L and D. **Meals:** main courses £14 to £27. Set L and D £15 (2 courses) to £19. **Details:** 120 seats. 60 seats outside. Bar. Music. Parking.

▌Follifoot

★ NEW ENTRY ★

Horto

Cooking score: 5
Modern British | £54
Rudding Park Hotel, Follifoot, HG3 1JH
Tel no: (01423) 871350
ruddingpark.co.uk

£5 OFF 🛏

This elegant and contemporary restaurant grew from a summer pop-up to a permanent posting earlier this year with the opening of the Rudding Park Hotel's stunning new spa – and it's hit the ground running. The cool white space, with splashes of vivid colour from original artwork, makes a fitting setting for chef Murray Wilson's (formerly of Norse and the Yorke Arms – see entries) mature and confident dishes, often marked by contrasting textures as well as original combinations. Inspired by head gardener Adrian Reeve's kitchen garden, Wilson places fruit and vegetables at the heart of the menu. His 'kitchen garden salad' is a winning collation of leaves and herbs served with bacon and millet and a dinky bread roll with an intense herb butter alongside. Whitby crabmeat comes with garden-fermented kombucha, and later in the seven-course menu, a tiny cornet of sorbet is bursting with sorrel and tarragon. Other standout dishes include a pot of smoked eel, millet grains and buttermilk and a dish of whipped mozzarella cheese, with a caramelised tomato slice and an intensely flavoured 'tomato water'. The quality wine list starts at £35 a bottle and all are available by the glass from £9.
Chef/s: Murray Wilson. **Open:** all week D only.
Closed: 25 Dec. **Meals:** alc £54 (3 courses). Tasting menu £64. **Details:** 36 seats. 36 seats outside. V menu. Bar. Wheelchairs. Music. Parking.

▌Goldsborough

The Fox & Hounds

Cooking score: 5
Modern European | £36
Goldsborough, YO21 3RX
Tel no: (01947) 893372

'Hidden gem' is the only phrase for this pub-turned-restaurant, found down a country lane in a hamlet of no more than a couple of farms and a glimpse of the sea. It operates without a website and with limited evening opening, but Jason Davies' cooking is straightforward, exact and invariably superb. In the cosy dining rooms with just a handful of tables you might start with salmon carpaccio or crab linguine with chilli, lemon and fennel; on another day it might be crab risotto – brown crabs are caught all along this coast. Follow with wild sea trout or turbot served with heritage potatoes, Datterini tomatoes and a piquant anchovy and rosemary sauce. But it's not all fish. You may find char-grilled lamb cutlets, roast suckling pig or superb steak. Finish with a couple of perfectly ripe cheeses, chocolate torte or something fruity like white peaches in Amaretto and crème fraîche or an apricot and almond tart. Sue Davies knows her wine and curates a quality list starting at £20.
Chef/s: Jason Davies. **Open:** Wed to Sat D only.
Closed: Sun, Mon, Tue, Christmas, bank hols.
Meals: main courses £18 to £30. **Details:** 18 seats.

▌Grassington

Grassington House

Cooking score: 3
Modern British | £35
5 The Square, Grassington, BD23 5AQ
Tel no: (01756) 752406
grassingtonhousehotel.co.uk

£5 OFF 🛏

Sitting proud to one side of the town square in a charming and dynamic Dales village, the Ruddens' operation is all things to all people – a handy local watering hole with good wines and beers, a hotel with its own entrance and, squeezed between the two, a restaurant that extends from an interior room with ornately carved fireplace into a glassed extension with halogen lights. Modern bistro fare is John Rudden's stock-in-trade, and there are some neat touches. A scorched mackerel fillet comes with beetroot crackers, horseradish crème fraîche and a quenelle of pickled mackerel tartare, ahead of fine homemade pasta such as cauliflower cream ravioli in sauce soubise topped with onion rings, hake fillet on fabulous crushed Jersey Royals in beurre blanc, or breast and leg of Goosnargh duck with parsnip three ways – fondant, crisps and cumined purée. Something served as Eton mess in early May was entirely bereft of its whipped cream, a weird lapse indeed, but egg custard tart and sticky toffee pudding are much more the real thing. Wines are from £19.95.

Chef/s: John Rudden and Andrew Collop. **Open:** all week L and D. **Closed:** 25 Dec. **Meals:** main courses £14 to £26. Set L and D £16 (2 courses) to £18. **Details:** 44 seats. 36 seats outside. Bar. Wheelchairs. Music. Parking.

∎ Harome
The Pheasant Hotel

Cooking score: 4
Modern British | £50
Mill Street, Harome, YO62 5JG
Tel no: (01439) 771241
thepheasanthotel.com

🍷 🍴

'I would return here like a shot,' enthused one reader who was bowled over by the Pheasant – a clever conversion of Harome smithy and surrounding barns, with a glass-roofed conservatory and snug bar vying for attention alongside the smartly attired dining room. Menus from legendary restaurants are on display, although chef/co-owner Peter Neville is very much his own man. There are wonderfully simple dishes such as de-shelled mussels in a light but punchy wild garlic cream with sautéed leeks, but there are more complex ideas, too – perhaps plaice véronique tweaked with raisin verjus, black radish, Kaffir lime and gnocchi. Mr Neville also shows his

muscular side with a stonking dish of roast squab pigeon, carved into pieces and arranged on a 'deep, glossy, almost black' sauce dotted with morels and broad beans – 'superb on every front'. To finish, a sweet-savoury asparagus and white chocolate pannacotta with strawberry sorbet shows the influence of Neville's mentor, Claude Bosi. It's also worth spending time with the revamped wine list – a thoughtful compendium noted for its serious choice, affable prices and inviting house selections.

Chef/s: Peter Neville. **Open:** all week L and D. **Meals:** main courses £20 to £32. Set L £25 (2 courses) to £33. Sun L £29 (2 courses) to £34. Tasting menu £65. **Details:** 60 seats. 75 seats outside. Bar. Wheelchairs. Music. Parking.

The Star Inn

Cooking score: 6
Modern British | £45
High Street, Harome, YO62 5JE
Tel no: (01439) 770397
thestaratharome.co.uk

🍷 🍴

They might have called it the Star with its millennial future in mind, for the beautiful 14th-century thatched inn with magnificent cruck-framed (timber-arched) roof is the prime player in the district. Picture-crammed walls, ancient settles and stone-flagged floors in the bar maintain the rural roots, while in the high-class dining room, Andrew Pern's cooking is given the elegant setting it deserves. Working at the forefront of modern technique with thoroughbred Yorkshire produce, he isn't afraid of technical innovation: celeriac is fashioned into a shell for braised wild rabbit alongside a clay pot of mushroom purée and pickled roots into which a 'forager's broth' is poured. Yellowfin tartare dotted with wasabi mayo rests on red cabbage purée with a raw egg yolk crown, and the signature crisp-fried black pudding and apple caramel is still a winner. Saddle of roe deer, char-grilled and pink, with coffee-scented carrot, molasses bread and sweet potato purée is a majestic meat dish, while Bakewell pudding arrives as a pastry cylinder of frangipane with an ooze of cherry jam in the middle, offset by sheep's milk ice cream and pistachio custard. In addition to this wizardry, an authoritatively compiled wine list has temptations in every direction, from £22.50.

Chef/s: Andrew Pern and Stephen Smith. **Open:** Tue to Sat L, Mon to Sat D. Sun 12 to 6. **Meals:** main courses £21 to £34. Set L and D £20 (2 courses) to £25. Sun L £19. Tasting menu L £55, D £85. **Details:** 100 seats. 60 seats outside. V menu. Bar. Wheelchairs. Music. Parking.

■ Harrogate
Norse

Cooking score: 3
Scandinavian | £35
28a Swan Road, Harrogate, HG1 2SA
Tel no: (01423) 313400
norserestaurant.co.uk

£5
OFF

Since its first appearance in the guide two years ago, Norse has made quite a name for itself as a standout destination. This edition marks a huge step forward in its development as a restaurant, with the team having moved from Baltzersens on Oxford Street into permanent premises in Swan Road; the new location is certainly allowing Norse to firm up its own identity. Tasting menus have been ditched in favour of a dozen seasonally rotating small plates. An excellent bowl of Whitby crab, with cucumber jelly, horseradish and pea sorbet evidence Simon Jewitt's ability to utilise what is abundant, fresh and local, and simpler plates such as Ken's salad ('a beautifully fresh-tasting medley of vegetables and leaf, elegantly configured'), and thinly sliced hasselback potatoes with Cheddar, broccoli and lovage cream ('entirely delicious') exhibit a confidence and understanding of true Nordic process. It has one of the best selections in the region of gins, craft beer and wines by the glass. Bottles start at £22.

Chef/s: Simon Jewitt. **Open:** Wed to Sat L, Tue to Sat D. **Closed:** Sun, Mon, 25 and 26 Dec, 1 Jan. **Meals:** main courses £12 to £19. Set L £15 (2 courses) to £18. Set D £18 (2 courses) to £22. **Details:** 36 seats. 10 seats outside. V menu. Music.

Orchid

Cooking score: 2
Pan-Asian | £30
Studley Hotel, 28 Swan Road, Harrogate, HG1 2SE
Tel no: (01423) 560425
orchidrestaurant.co.uk

Within the solidly traditional Studley Hotel, Orchid is a contemporary space where Kenneth Poon has been overseeing a pan-Asian menu since 2005. Classic dishes from the countries of the Pacific Rim loom large on the menu – mostly China, Hong Kong, Thailand and Malaysia. Japan gets a mention, too, with beef tataki among first courses, or go for bang-bang chicken (Szechuan), or Thailand's famous som tum salad. Kurma kambing lamb is a Malaysian curry, none too fiery, with 'weeping tiger' a good option for heat lovers. Sea bass appears a number of ways such as crispy fried with a sweet-and-sour Thai sauce, and noodles such as pad thai are a good bet. To finish, it has to be chilled mango pudding, and note Sunday lunch is a buffet. The helpfully annotated wine list has options by the glass, with bottles opening at £19.90.

Chef/s: Kenneth Poon. **Open:** Mon to Fri and Sun L, all week D. **Closed:** 25 and 26 Dec. **Meals:** main courses £9 to £22. Set L £13 (2 courses) to £15. **Details:** 60 seats. 16 seats outside. Bar. Music. Parking.

★ NEW ENTRY ★

Restaurant 92

Cooking score: 4
Modern European | £45
92-94 Station Parade, Harrogate, HG1 1HQ
Tel no: (01423) 503027
restaurant92.co.uk

At 23, Michael Carr has already done three years at Claridge's under the aegis of Gordon Ramsay and 18 months with Alyn Williams at the Westbury (see entry), so to learn that he has been cooking since he was 14 years old comes as no surprise. Ambitious is scarcely the word, an impression reinforced by the level of investment undertaken at these premises in a converted stone-built residential terrace opposite Waitrose. Amid handsomely minimalist décor in sophisticated grey with deep windows, the cooking is all about surprise through familiarity. A DIY approach to French onion soup involves tugging on a little tag of thyme on a whole onion to reveal a tangle of caramelised shreds and pommes dauphine, into which you pour your broth. Another starter turns ham, egg and chips into a piece of cured five-spiced duck with tiny vinegar-powdered fries, a truffle-oiled yolk and a blob of densely jammy ketchup. There's clearly as much energy applied to the conceptions of dishes as to their execution, but it pays off tellingly. Mains encompass barbecue-glazed pork belly done in lager with puffed crackling and a whole turnip, while fish could be curried monkfish with crispy octopus and chorizo jam. For such ingenuity, prices are very restrained, and the populist impulse extends to sticky toffee pudding and caramel sauce with burnt-butter ice cream. Lucky Harrogate. A compact wine list is keenly priced, too, from £17.50.
Chef/s: Michael Robert Carr. **Open:** Wed to Sun L, Wed to Sat D. **Closed:** Mon, Tue, first 2 weeks Jan. **Meals:** main courses £18 to £27. Set L £18 (2 courses). Sun L £30. Tasting menu £68. **Details:** 60 seats. 12 seats outside. V menu. Bar. Music. Children over 12 yrs only at D.

Sasso

Cooking score: 3
Italian | £35
8-10 Princes Square, Harrogate, HG1 1LX
Tel no: (01423) 508838
sassorestaurant.co.uk
£5
OFF

Sasso is the name of the town in Emilia-Romagna, not far from Bologna, from whence chef/patron Stefano Lancellotti hails, and here in genteel Harrogate, he evokes a convincingly vivid impression of it. There is a feel-good atmosphere to the place, and a sense of exemplary value in the pre-theatre menu deal that one of our regular reporters treasures. The main menu is traditionally structured, with pasta dishes particularly strong – the bolognese ragù with traditional lasagne is an object lesson – but antipasti such as gingery crab cakes in lemon and garlic sauce should not be missed either. At main, there may be calf's liver in a pancetta and sage coating in smoky red wine sauce, on a bed of spinach, sultanas and pine nuts, as well as mushroom-crusted sea bass in saffron cream. Finish with generous helpings of affogato and Amaretto, or the lemon tart that comes splashed with blueberry sauce and partnered with limoncello sorbet. An Italian-led wine list opens at £15.75.
Chef/s: Stefano Lancellotti. **Open:** Mon to Sat L and D. **Closed:** Sun, 25 and 26 Dec, 1 Jan. **Meals:** main courses £15 to £24. Set L £10 (2 courses) to £14. Set D £20 (2 courses) to £24. **Details:** 104 seats. 24 seats outside. Music.

LOCAL GEM

Stuzzi

Italian | £25
46b Kings Road, Harrogate, HG1 5JW
Tel no: (01423) 705852
£30

Italian products line the shelves at this spirited venue, which has a heated covered terrace out front. It kicks off with breakfast, shimmies into lunchtime sharing plates, sandwiches and wood-fired focaccia pizzette, before the evening arrives and more of those sharing plates. The menu changes every day, so you might get Negroni-cured salmon with squid-ink pane carasau (Sardinian flatbread), arancini filled with rich beef ragù, orecchiette pasta with roasted red pepper and chilli sauce, and beef cheeks slow braised in Montepulciano. Whatever you choose, it's simple, honest and good. The wine list is Italian all the way.

▌Hetton
The Angel Inn
Cooking score: 3
Modern British | £40
Hetton, BD23 6LT
Tel no: (01756) 730263
angelhetton.co.uk

🍶 🛏

Signposted off the B6265 in the heart of the Dales, the Angel is one of our longest-serving entries, a country pub with serious dining since the era when such places were rare as hen's teeth. The filo moneybag of seafood in lobster sauce, on the menu since the 1980s, has been preserved for the nation, but there is plenty of inventive energy in the cooking to keep things up to date. Roast cod with smoked bacon and peas in vivid orange crayfish sauce was hugely enjoyable at inspection, and although the risotto that came with roast pigeon needed better timing, the bird and its liver were excellent, accompanied by white carrots and spinach in good red wine jus. Finish with crisply torched banana crème brûlée and shortbreads. The wine list here has long been a treasure and repays exploration for its constantly updated gleanings, with small glasses starting at £4.
Open: all week L and D. **Meals:** main courses £16 to £27. **Details:** 100 seats. 40 seats outside. Bar.

▌Honley
Mustard & Punch
Cooking score: 2
British | £30
6 Westgate, Honley, HD9 6AA
Tel no: (01484) 662066
mustardandpunch.co.uk

An old-school bistro opposite the Honley car park, Mustard & Punch has all the trappings of bare floors and tables, antique Champagne posters and a bustly, babbly atmosphere you hope to find. It's been doing its community, not to mention nearby Holmfirth, proud for well over 20 years, and the happy crowds on a weekday evening tell their own story. Staff motor between ground floor and basement with impressive agility, delivering plates of unpretentiously presented, big-hearted flavour. Pigeon breast with game liver parfait, plum jam and thyme toasts to begin is an unmitigated delight, or there could be king prawns with crab and sweetcorn arancini. For main, pink sea trout is beautifully timed and comes in a textbook hollandaise with tomato salsa, but the Barbary duck breast desperately needs more lubrication than a dab of vinaigrette. Finish with well-made, intensely zesty desserts like lemon tart and raspberry sorbet, or passion fruit parfait. Wines start at £5.50 a glass. A second venue just across the street, Punch Bar and Tapas, does exactly what it says on the tin.
Chef/s: Richard Dunn. **Open:** Tue to Sat D only.
Closed: Sun, Mon, first week Jan. **Meals:** set D £23 (2 courses) to £26. **Details:** 52 seats. Bar. Wheelchairs. Music.

Huddersfield

Epicure Bar & Kitchen

Cooking score: 2
Modern British | £25
37-39 Queensgate, Huddersfield, HD1 2RD
Tel no: (07980) 373699
epicurebarandkitchen.co.uk
£5 OFF £30

'It's an unglamorous spot,' noted a visitor to this modest, stone terraced house on a busy dual carriageway, adding 'but that's missing the point'. A café at heart – you can still 'score a faultless flat white' with your breakfast eggs Benedict, while lunchtime brings baguettes and burgers – but the kitchen ups the ante with daily changing specials. Expect the likes of black pudding and smoked bacon Scotch egg, 'the yolk only just set' and the accompanying spicy red cabbage cutting the richness, or confit duck leg with a pulled duck and orange croquette, and an 'After Hours' menu that features 'a standout' dish of aged rump carpaccio with tiny pillows of deep-fried Manchego, or pressed ox tongue on chorizo mash, in addition to bubble and squeak – 'a clever, featherlight riff on the classic'. The wine list is short – four whites, four reds – but 'intelligently selected', starting at 16.50.
Chef/s: Lewis Myzak. **Open:** all week L, Fri and Sat D. **Meals:** main courses £9 to £12. **Details:** 50 seats. Music.

Hull

1884 Dock Street Kitchen

Cooking score: 2
Modern British | £45
Humber Dock Street, Hull, HU1 1TB
Tel no: (01482) 222260
1884dockstreetkitchen.co.uk
🍾

With black panelling, padded banquettes, chandeliers and glass cabinets housing a bountiful wine and Champagne collection,

this spacious former shipping office invites indulgence. 'Unpretentious, relaxing but most importantly serving excellent food,' noted one reader, enthusiastically describing the chestnut and venison suet pudding as 'most enjoyable'. Elsewhere the à la carte offers Lindisfarne oysters or North Sea plaice with salsify and lemon purée. A midweek set menu featured a refined beetroot cured salmon and a melting braised lamb shoulder with broad beans though suffering a little from an over-sweet apricot sauce. The substantial wine list opens at £18, rising to three figures, with many available by the glass and carafe, and there is a substantial gin list. The black-and-gold theme continues at the cheerful 1884 Wine and Tapas Bar across the Marina with a short menu of familiar Spanish tapas. Good service throughout.
Chef/s: Laura Waller. **Open:** Tue to Sun L, Mon to Sat D. **Closed:** first week Jan. **Meals:** main courses £19 to £30. Set L and D £20 (2 courses) to £25. **Details:** 92 seats. 20 seats outside. Bar. Wheelchairs. Music.

Ilkley

The Box Tree

Cooking score: 6
Anglo-French | £65
35-37 Church Street, Ilkley, LS29 9DR
Tel no: (01943) 608484
theboxtree.co.uk
🍾

Famously flamboyant and unorthodox in its original incarnation (under owners Malcolm Reid and Colin Long), the Box Tree sports a more sober demeanour these days. There have been changes of personnel in the kitchen of late, but chef/patron Simon Gueller's team continue to deliver 'top-quality classical cooking' with all the panache you would expect from a much-decorated Yorkshire veteran. Refinement and technical virtuosity are a given here, from exquisitely presented plates of grilled mackerel fillet and tartare with caviar, cucumber, radishes and pungent horseradish ice cream to mignon of veal osso buco with crispy sweetbreads, morels and

Madeira. Ingredients are paramount, too, whether it's hand-dived scallops, Yorkshire venison or locally reared beef – perhaps served in earthy fashion with roasted shallot purée and beer-pickled onions. Seasonal soufflés (black cherry, for example) are the showstoppers when it comes to dessert, or you could keep it local with Yorkshire rhubarb and custard. All the little details are 'spot-on', as are the personable ever-attentive staff. Peerless vintages from the greatest terroirs and a clutch of new-wave contenders lend weight to the distinguished wine list. **Chef/s:** Simon Gueller. **Open:** Fri to Sun L, Wed to Sat D. **Closed:** Mon, Tue, 26 to 30 Dec, first week Jan. **Meals:** set L £38. Set D £65. Sun L £38. Tasting menu £80 (6 courses). **Details:** 50 seats. Bar. Music. Children over 5 yrs only at L, over 10 yrs only at D.

Leeds
Brasserie Forty 4
Cooking score: 2
Modern British | £30
44 The Calls, Leeds, LS2 7EW
Tel no: (0113) 2343232
brasserie44.com

On the banks of the river Aire in the Calls complex, this long-running venue may be starting to look its age but it continues to satisfy its loyal regulars with an unpretentious range of classic brasserie dishes. The converted 18th-century corn mill has an industrial look that suits its history and waterside location. The service is good and the cooking is hard to fault, with the kitchen sticking to tried-and-tested favourites. A test meal opened with crispy king prawns teamed with a fresh, fiery and fragrant sweet chilli, ginger and coriander dip. It was followed by thick slices of pink, perfectly cooked lamb rump served with Puy lentils, pickled shallots and a rich mint and lamb sauce. The old-school desserts are of the rib-sticking variety – think chocolate fondue, crumble and cheesecake – although a well-made blueberry and almond tart with lemon curd ice cream 'was lighter than expected'. A broad wine list starts at £19.95.

Chef/s: David Robson. **Open:** Tue to Sat L and D. **Closed:** Sun, Mon, 25 and 26 Dec, bank hols. **Meals:** main courses £14 to £27. **Details:** 85 seats. 18 seats outside. Bar. Music. Children over 2 yrs only.

Crafthouse
Cooking score: 2
Modern European | £40
Level 5, Trinity Leeds, 70 Boar Lane, Leeds, LS1 6HW
Tel no: (0113) 8970444
crafthouse-restaurant.com

It might sit above a shopping centre, but the D&D group's Crafthouse is ready to serve a more corporate crowd. Sleek marble detailing, heavy chairs and the lesser-spotted napkin ring send Josper-fired smoke signals to the city's lunching professionals. But partial rooftop views, low lighting and lots of glass give the main dining room a bit of night-time glamour for those who seek it. To start, try the truffle cheese pillows with yuzu gel, cucumber and pickled apple, or charcoal salmon with daikon, burnt butter and dandelion, followed by Atlantic halibut with cauliflower, curry and a chicken oyster; all the modern flourishes are present and correct. Desserts such as lemon drizzle cake with honey, chamomile and matcha or glazed Valrhona mousse with maple, caramel and pecans are done very well indeed. Wines feature a pair blended by D&D sommeliers as well as a handful of 'limited' specials.

Chef/s: Lee Murdoch. **Open:** Tue to Sat L, Mon to Sat D. Sun, all day from 12. **Closed:** 25 Dec. **Meals:** main courses £13 to £24. Set L and early D £19 (2 courses) to £24. Tasting menu £65. **Details:** 144 seats.

Visit us online

To find out more about The Good Food Guide, please visit thegoodfoodguide.co.uk

The Man Behind the Curtain

Cooking score: 7
Modern British | £75
68-78 Vicar Lane, Leeds, LS1 7JH
Tel no: (0113) 2432376
themanbehindthecurtain.co.uk

There is no doubt that Michael O'Hare's cooking demonstrates a flair that leaves others bewildered on the starting line, though as a restaurant, The Man Behind the Curtain is still in a formative stage. By the time you read this, Mr O'Hare will have moved out of the edgy, left-field gallery-cum-metropolitan-loft bar he created at the top of Flannels to an expensively styled, marble-clad space on the ground floor, where the 10- to 14-course taster experience is expected to be largely the same. First there are the little taste bombs, like a vivid red slider of veal sweetbreads, pickled shiitake mushrooms, basil and mint in a fluffy sriracha rice bun that 'delivers a freight-train-load of flavour'. Fleeting, teasing contrasts appear in a mini 'doughnut' of foie gras, white chocolate, passion fruit and dehydrated raspberry. Worthy of note is 'ackee and saltfish', which explores the powerful flavours of the Caribbean, while 'emancipation' is fish and chips 'repackaged by Fendi'. Then comes Iberian pork cooked two ways, enlivened by an explosion of ajo blanco across black slate, puréed and fresh whole anchovies, a slow-cooked runny egg yolk in its (edible) shell, a sauce of fino sherry and pig's trotter pulling it all into focus, smoked-bread cinders adding some heft. Drink Spanish house beers or sommelier picks from the succinct wine list (from £30).
Chef/s: Michael O'Hare. **Open:** Thur to Sat L, Tue to Sat D. **Closed:** Sun, Mon. **Meals:** tasting menu £60 to £90. **Details:** 42 seats. Music.

Ox Club

Cooking score: 3
Modern British | £32
Headrow House, The Headrow, Leeds, LS1 6PU
Tel no: (07470) 359961
oxclub.co.uk
£5 OFF

Leeds' foodie flame is burning bright, with pop-ups, festivals, street traders and markets all contributing to a vibrant range of edible possibilities. Ox Club was born out of this movement – executive chef Ben Davy is a key city player – and fire is at the heart of this compact restaurant tucked into the base of multifariously funky Headrow House. The wood-fired grill is in constant use, with a menu centred around charred offerings such as pork neck with barbecued potato and rhubarb ketchup or duck with Brussels sprout kim-chee, grilled heart, won ton and radish. Starters like sea trout with rhubarb, rose, cultured cream and rye cracker are no less of the moment. It's an agreeable collection of influences, capably plated and served, with industrial edges softened (except in the penitentiary-style toilets) by contemporary design touches. To finish, try blue cheese mousse with pickled grapes, celery granita and oats, and perhaps a pint in the adjoining beer hall.
Chef/s: Ben Iley. **Open:** Sat and Sun L, Tue to Sat D. **Closed:** Mon, 25 and 26 Dec, 1 Jan. **Meals:** main courses £12 to £17. Early D £17 (2 courses) to £20. Sun L £13. **Details:** 39 seats. Bar. Wheelchairs. Music.

The Reliance

Cooking score: 3
Modern British | £25
76-78 North Street, Leeds, LS2 7PN
Tel no: (0113) 2956060
the-reliance.co.uk
£30 ▼

On the edge of the city in the trendy Northern Quarter, this converted Victorian cloth mill is now a relaxed bar and dining room – 'reminds

me of the Anchor & Hope in Waterloo, actually,' (see entry) noted one visiting southerner. Grab a comfortable chair in the downstairs bar and settle down with a pint of one of the five local real ales on draught or wander up to the high-ceilinged dining room – stripped floorboards, candlelit Formica-topped tables, open-plan kitchen – where a board of home-cured charcuterie using Yorkshire rare-breed pork is one way to open your account here. A late winter test meal produced a starter of cool, creamy labneh with smoky charred spring onion, sumac and blood orange, and a robust main course of meltingly tender ox cheek with turnip and wild garlic. Yorkshire rhubarb mille-feuille was a delicate and refined finish. An intelligently curated list includes natural and orange wines, and starts at £15.50.
Chef/s: Tom Hunter. **Open:** all week, all day from 12 (11 Sun). **Closed:** 25 and 26 Dec, bank hols. **Meals:** main courses £12 to £17. **Details:** 120 seats. Bar. Wheelchairs. Music.

Salvo's
Cooking score: 2
Italian | £25
115 Otley Road, Headingley, Leeds, LS6 3PX
Tel no: (0113) 2755017
salvos.co.uk
£30

A strike away from Headingley's famous cricket ground, Leeds landmark Salvo's has been run by the Dammone family since 1976 – they marked their 40th anniversary with a major refurbishment. Everybody agrees that it appears more spacious, lighter, fresher – with grey walls, exposed brick, orange banquettes, industrial-looking leather chairs and huge monochrome photos (floor to ceiling in some cases) of Salvo and wife Nunzia in Italy in the 1950s. A charming trattoria with broad appeal, students and young families home in on the 'fantastic and well-priced' pizzas and pasta dishes – the pappardelle with a rich and meaty British rose veal ragù and aged Parmesan impressed at a test meal. Others splash out on mains such as sea bass, braised peas, artichokes,

asparagus, prosciutto and mint, or Yorkshire lamb rump, cannellini beans, spring cabbage and salsa rossa. Desserts play the populist card, perhaps pannacotta with blood-orange jelly and pistachio or homemade tiramisu. Wines from £17.50.
Chef/s: Gip Dammone and Jonathan Elvin. **Open:** Mon to Fri L and D. Sat and Sun, all day from 12. **Closed:** 25 and 26 Dec, 1 Jan. **Meals:** main courses £8 to £25. Set L £12 (2 courses). Set D £15 (2 courses). Sun L £16. **Details:** 80 seats. 20 seats outside. Bar. Wheelchairs. Music.

The Swine that Dines
Cooking score: 4
Modern British | £23
58 North Street, Leeds, LS2 7PN
Tel no: (07477) 834227
£5 OFF £30

'It's still as close as you can get to being invited for tea at a top chef's house.' If only all dinner invitations were as accomplished as the offer at The Swine that Dines. Stuart and Jo Myers' evening reincarnation of their daytime caff, the Greedy Pig, now offers a tasting menu-come-small plate selection, designed for two to share. Value is hard to deny with dishes including fresh juts of Yorkshire rhubarb with beetroot, labneh and radishes; lentils with shallots, beautifully pungent wild garlic, migas and mustard seeds, while a swede pommes Anna with piccalilli showed real skill and brought an added level of refinement to the cooking. Exceptional sourdough sourced from local micro-bakery, Roops, makes for happy mopping and as an accompaniment to a classy Old Spot pork terrine (with prune ketchup and toasted pistachios). The BYOB policy, coupled with excellent service, ensures that the laid-back, homely vibe of this mini-bistro is preserved for all to enjoy.
Chef/s: Stuart Myers. **Open:** Thur to Sat D only. **Closed:** Sun to Wed, 1 week Christmas, 2 weeks Aug. **Meals:** tasting menu £45 (for 2, sharing). **Details:** 16 seats. Music.

Tharavadu

Cooking score: 2
Indian | £35
7-8 Mill Hill, Leeds, LS1 5DQ
Tel no: (0113) 2440500
tharavadurestaurants.com
£5
OFF

In a side street by the central railway station, Tharavadu is the city's first Keralan restaurant and it lives up to its name ('ancestral home') as it has become a favoured spot for fans of South Indian cooking. Spacious with a no-frills look, the restaurant serves a vast selection of authentic and traditional dishes, from starters of kidilan erachi (lamb cooked in spices and sautéed with onions) and masala dosa to stand-out seafood dishes like marari prawn masala (king prawns with ginger, garlic, cinnamon, tomato and curry leaves) and marinated whole sea bass stuffed with shrimps and vegetables. Vegetarian dishes make a good show, too, perhaps a curry of spinach and paneer tempered with garlic, onion and spices. Homemade breads such as paratha and puri are a speciality and desserts include vattayappam fudge cake (steamed rice cake stuffed with toffee, topped with chocolate sauce). Wines from £15.50.

Chef/s: Ajith Nair and Rajesh Nair. **Open:** Mon to Sat L and D. **Closed:** Sun, 24 to 26 Dec. **Meals:** main courses £9 to £18. **Details:** 80 seats. Music.

★ NEW ENTRY ★

Vice & Virtue

Cooking score: 2
Modern European | £45
68 New Briggate, Leeds, LS1 6NU
Tel no: (0113) 3450202
viceandvirtueleeds.co.uk

The name is a tongue-in-cheek reference to the fact that this was once a strip club. Climb the steep stairs and the first stop is the low-lit cocktail bar with a low stage where you might expect a pole dancer to appear rather than a mixologist brandishing a hefty cocktail and wine list. Once you get the call, you are taken up to the dining room with its Art Deco touches and open-view kitchen. Three different tasting menus are offered, each with optional wine flights. At first it all 'seems a bit style-over-substance' until an amuse-bouche of prawn gyoza with curry emulsion makes you realise there is solid technical skill and innovation in the kitchen. Surf and turf of 'perfect' lobster ravioli in a rich bisque with shredded ox cheek topped with a crevette is 'a smart dish' and a modern take on the the classic combo. Guinea fowl teamed with saffron potato, black pudding bonbon and powdered smoke makes an arresting main course, and there is organic apple strudel with apple gel, caramel ice cream and salted-caramel sauce to finish.

Chef/s: Luke Downing. **Open:** Sat L, Wed to Sat D. Sun, 12 to 8. **Closed:** Mon, Tue. **Meals:** tasting menu £35 (5 courses) to £55 (10 courses). **Details:** Bar. Music.

LOCAL GEM

Friends of Ham

Modern European | £25
4-8 New Station Street, Leeds, LS1 5DL
Tel no: (0113) 2420275
friendsofham.com
£30

'A friend of ham is a friend of ours', they say at this charcuteria a few minutes walk from the train station. It's a cool and casual gaff with chunky wooden tables, stools at the counter and some excellent craft beers by tap and bottle (friends of beer as well, it turns out). Choose from a long list of top-quality cured meats and cheeses – Serrano Grand Reserva, Mrs Kirkham's Lancashire, Monte Enebro – or go for a sharing board. They've got boquerones and salads, too, a brunch menu and a wine list opening at £18. A second branch is in Ilkley, while Ham & Friends opened in the Northern Quarter's Grand Arcade in spring 2017.

Zucco

Italian | £28
603 Meanwood Road, Leeds, LS6 4AY
Tel no: (0113) 2249679
zucco.co.uk

£30

A bustling neighbourhood restaurant in one of the leafier corners of Leeds, this wedge-shaped dining room cuts quite a dash with its subway tiles, black-and-white tiled floor and copper-panel ceiling. Styled on an Italian bacaro, small plates are the thing here, perhaps a spinach, Gorgonzola and walnut pizzetta followed by rabbit, pancetta, white wine and potatoes or braised beef pappardelle with grana Padano. Classic cocktails and an all-Italian wine list from £16.80 add to the conviviality and buzz.

▌Leyburn
The Sandpiper Inn

Cooking score: 2
Modern British | £33
Market Place, Leyburn, DL8 5AT
Tel no: (01969) 622206
sandpiperinn.co.uk

The creeper-covered Sandpiper is the sort of traditional stone-built 17th-century inn that pub purists love, while moving with the times just enough to ensure it's not stuck in the past. Real ales on tap, cosy snugs, a couple of charming bedrooms; it's got a lot going for it, not least in the culinary department, where the candlelit dining room is the setting for some gently contemporary grub. Caramelised pork belly and seared scallops is a modern match, here served with butternut squash purée, while the equally on-trend Scotch egg is a game version with beer ketchup. Among main courses, the grilled rib burger keeps to the theme, or go for crispy duck leg with chestnut mushrooms and mash, or grilled sea bass with leek and smoked salmon risotto. Yorkshire

rhubarb Eton mess results in a happy ending. Real ales, 100 malt whiskies and fairly priced wines make for good drinking.
Chef/s: Jonathan Harrison. **Open:** Tue to Sun L and D. **Closed:** Mon, 2 weeks Jan. **Meals:** main courses £14 to £21. **Details:** 40 seats. 26 seats outside. Bar. Music. Parking.

▌Lindley
Eric's

Cooking score: 3
Modern British | £45
73-75 Lidget Street, Lindley, HD3 3JP
Tel no: (01484) 646416
ericsrestaurant.co.uk

Home of a famous brass band and a striking Art Nouveau clock tower, Lindley is also becoming known for Eric Paxman's intimate neighbourhood-style restaurant. It's a likeable antidote to most high street eateries – smart and comfortable with a robust attitude to provenance and seasonality – and reporters certainly approve the welcoming atmosphere and applaud the kitchen's efforts. Mr Paxman draws on classical skills and global influences in ambitious, often complex dishes such as pan-fried scallops with a crisp, 'delicately flavoured' spring roll of crab and lobster and lemongrass velouté, and 'thick slivers' of char-grilled venison steak over a delicate truffle ravioli and rich girolle mushroom ragoût, served with roast field mushrooms, parsley, sweet maple syrup and creamy Gorgonzola cheese, while a sticky date jam melted into venison gravy 'providing contrasting sweetness to the gamey flavour'. Finish in style with lemon tart, lemon curd, pavlova, poached blackberries, blackcurrant and lavender sorbet. A good-value wine list starts at £19.45.
Chef/s: Eric Paxman. **Open:** Tue to Fri and Sun L, Tue to Sat D. **Closed:** Mon. **Meals:** main courses £20 to £29. Set L and D £20 (2 courses) to £25. **Details:** 70 seats. V menu. Bar. Music.

Masham

Samuel's

Cooking score: 4
Modern British | £58
Swinton Park, Masham, HG4 4JH
Tel no: (01765) 680900
swintonestate.com

Should you labour under the lingering apprehension that everything up north is on the grim side, get a load of Swinton. It's a sprawling 20,000-acre estate with a crenellated castle at its heart, home to the various earldoms and baronies of the Cunliffe-Lister family since Victoria's golden jubilee. Maybe change out of your ripped jeans. The dining room, with its carved fireplace, ceiling mouldings and views over the deer park, seems to mandate a sense of occasion, which is amply supplied by Chris McPhee and Mehdi Amiri's seasonal dishes. With game from the estate and produce from the walled garden, it's a local affair, starting perhaps with curds and crisped rice to garnish a truffled-up heap of garden saladings, and going on to loin and haunch of venison with garden beets and shallots. Further afield, the Dales might supply beef for braising with woodland mushrooms and pickled onions, or there may be monkfish tail, served in an earthy bedding of black trompettes, truffled cauliflower gratin, dill pasta and beurre blanc. More dill crops up as a filling for the meringues that come with lemon parfait, olive oil jelly and fennel. Small Coravin measures of wine lead off an enterprising list, with bottles from £25.
Chef/s: Chris McPhee and Mehdi Amiri. **Open:** Sat and Sun L, all week D. **Closed:** 2 days Jan.
Meals: set L £38 (3 courses). Set D £58 (3 courses). Sun L £28. Tasting menu £70. **Details:** 120 seats. Bar. Wheelchairs. Music. Parking. Children over 8 yrs only.

Middleton Tyas

The Coach House

Cooking score: 3
Modern British | £38
Middleton Lodge, Kneeton Lane, Middleton Tyas, DL10 6NJ
Tel no: (01325) 377977
middletonlodge.co.uk

Occupying a converted stable block attached to Middleton Lodge (a lavishly restored 18th-century manor in expansive grounds), the Coach House looks a picture of refined rusticity with its high-raftered ceiling, tiled floors, distressed plaster walls and farmhouse tables. A two-acre smallholding is due to open on the estate in 2018, but – for now – the kitchen supplements its supplies of Yorkshire produce with home-grown herbs and wild pickings. Ideas are culled from the front line of modern British cooking, and the results are bang on-trend: XO crab with puffed pork, heritage carrot salad; sea bream with oyster mayonnaise, compressed cucumber, dill and apple; saddle of venison with blackberry vinegar, cabbage and almond granola. Steaks and chops are shown the char-grill, while desserts keep it fashionable with, say, BBQ pineapple, coconut and gingerbread ice cream. Kids get a decent deal, Sunday lunch is a traditional roast and the wine list does its job.
Chef/s: Gareth Rayner. **Open:** all week L and D.
Meals: main courses £15 to £24. Set L £15 (2 courses) to £20. **Details:** 84 seats. 32 seats outside. Bar. Wheelchairs. Music. Parking.

Newton-on-Ouse

The Dawnay Arms

Cooking score: 3
Modern British | £35
Moor Lane, Newton-on-Ouse, YO30 2BR
Tel no: (01347) 848345
thedawnayatnewton.co.uk

The Dawnay is a real boon for the area and 'a beautiful place for a drink in summer' when the large garden, 'dotted with pub tables, and stretching away to a willow-flanked stream', comes into its own. Inside, it's smart but not engineered, and still feels like a pub, hop-draped, with beams, open fires, menu blackboards, comfy, high-backed chairs, church pews and bare-wood tables that extend into a more modern, well-lit extension. Chef/proprietor Martel Smith's classy but accessible cooking delivers substance as well as style, offering pork belly, long-braised, then roasted to be both crisp and juicy, forming a base for four golden scallop halves and served with black pudding, some apple purée and raw apple matchsticks, and ballotined chicken thigh stuffed with mousse made from the breast and buried in butter-loaded mushrooms flecked with a tarragon cream sauce, and served alongside asparagus and a little pot of tangy leek and Fountains Gold Cheddar risotto. Drink local ales or wine from £18.95.

Chef/s: Martel Smith. **Open:** Tue to Sun L, Tue to Sat D. **Closed:** Mon, 2 and 3 Jan. **Meals:** main courses £14 to £27. Set L and D £14 (2 courses) to £19. Sun L £20. **Details:** 80 seats. 40 seats outside. Bar. Wheelchairs. Music. Parking.

◼ Oldstead
The Black Swan
Cooking score: 6
Modern British | £95
Oldstead, YO61 4BL
Tel no: (01347) 868387
blackswanoldstead.co.uk

Tommy Banks is a man on a mission. He has transformed his family's Dales pub into an immaculate restaurant-with-rooms – or rather a hybrid, comprising a well-tended pubby bar and a stylish upstairs dining room with a dash of Nordic minimalism, all underpinned by the family's two-acre smallholding. From the moment you're presented with the tasting menu, written on cream parchment with a wax seal, you know this is going to be different. With potted beetroot plants on each table and a signature dish involving slow-cooked crapaudine

beetroot in beef fat, there's no doubting Banks' favourite vegetable, but the symbiotic 'foraging and farming' approach yields all manner of creations – from a sensational steamed bun filled with confit chicken balanced by a suitably sour lovage emulsion to a dessert of 'cleansing' sheep's milk ice cream with white chocolate and pine gel. Sometimes the zealous pursuit of self-sufficiency and cutting-edge technique comes at the expense of honest-to-goodness enjoyment, but there's no doubting that Banks' efforts are to be admired. 'Obsessively enthusiastic' staff are clearly tuned into the restaurant's ethos, while esoteric home-infused cocktails support a diagrammatic wine list that marries age and oak with freshness and aromatic qualities. Excellence is the hallmark, with 100ml Coravin selections adding to the pleasure.

Chef/s: Tommy Banks and Will Lockwood. **Open:** Sat L, all week D. **Meals:** Sat L £60. Tasting menu £95 (12 courses). **Details:** 50 seats. V menu. Bar. Music. Parking. Children over 10 yrs only.

◼ Osmotherley
Golden Lion
Cooking score: 2
Anglo-European | £30
6 West End, Osmotherley, DL6 3AA
Tel no: (01609) 883526
goldenlionosmotherley.co.uk

Beams and mirrors, pews and pots of flowers; the welcoming and candlelit Golden Lion has all you can ask of a village inn, including a fire that never goes out and a crowd-pleasing menu of steak and kidney pie, calf's liver and onions or its own chicken Kiev. Chicken paillard from the blackboard specials menu comes with a well-dressed salad, spaghetti vongole with mussels is 'nicely dressed with olive oil and lemon', and the halibut with saffron risotto is excellent. Portions are generous, the chips are good, kids are well catered for and afters come from the sticky toffee and treacle sponge and custard school of puddings. Staff look the business in white aprons, but the service is relaxed, efficient and charming. Wine comes from a standard list or there's a choice of four real ales including the estimable Timothy Taylor's Landlord. It's advisable to book for evenings and weekends at this convivial inn that knows what it's doing.

Chef/s: Christopher and Judith Wright. **Open:** Wed to Sun L, all week D. **Closed:** 25 Dec. **Meals:** main courses £11 to £23. **Details:** 67 seats. 16 seats outside. Wheelchairs. Music.

▋ Pickering
The White Swan Inn

Cooking score: 1
British | £36
Market Place, Pickering, YO18 7AA
Tel no: (01751) 472288
white-swan.co.uk

A grand old hotel with family credentials and a wealth of stone-floored nooks, the White Swan lives and breathes antiquity. Not surprisingly, its please-all menu is exactly what you might expect in such historic market-town surroundings – a line-up running all the way from lunchtime sandwiches to rare-breed steaks and chops from the Bertha grill, via a few more fancy ideas such as grilled hake with sautéed heritage potatoes, shrimp and hazelnut butter. Sadly, execution isn't always what it should be and service can be lackadaisical, although the revamped 60-bin wine list deserves full praise.

Chef/s: Darren Clemmitt. **Open:** all week L and D. **Meals:** main courses £14 to £26. Set L £15 (2 courses) to £20. **Details:** 62 seats. 20 seats outside. Bar. Wheelchairs. Parking.

Visit us online

To find out more about
The Good Food Guide, please
visit thegoodfoodguide.co.uk

▋ Ramsgill
The Yorke Arms

Cooking score: 6
Modern British | £65
Ramsgill, HG3 5RL
Tel no: (01423) 755243
yorke-arms.co.uk

£5 OFF

The former shooting lodge buried deep in the Yorkshire Dales is a long, low building covered in clambering ivy, looking a little as though it's in hiding, with the river Nidd running alongside. Inside, it feels properly enveloping, with low-ceilinged panelled rooms, and an atmosphere of solicitous civility created by impeccable staff. Frances Atkins cooks to what is at bottom a deeply traditional template, which doesn't preclude modernist touches, but does mean that dishes are based on unimpeachable seasonal domestic ingredients that are allowed their say before anything else is done to them. That's eloquently proved by meat dishes such as spring lamb – loin and shoulder – with sheep's curd, broad beans and fronds of nettly mint, or by quail, its legs smokily barbecued, the breast filled with a herbed mousse, with artichoke purée, asparagus and peas. Before either might come seared scallop and cured salmon, dressed with a blob of bergamot gel and shavings of scented truffle, while desserts aim to please with hazelnut crunch, red berries and balsamic syrup, or a duo of chocolate mousse and lemon tart with great clumps of popcorn and salted-milk ice cream. Wines are a very classical bunch, with some half-bottles and an excellent glass selection.

Chef/s: Frances Atkins. **Open:** Tue to Sat L and D. **Closed:** Sun, Mon. **Meals:** main courses £25 to £35. Set L £45. Tasting menu £85 (8 courses). **Details:** 40 seats. 20 seats outside. Bar. Music. Parking.

Raskelf

★ NEW ENTRY ★

Rascills

Cooking score: 3
Modern British | £37
Village Farm, Howker Lane, Raskelf, YO61 3LF
Tel no: (01347) 822031
rascillsrestaurant.vpweb.co.uk

Picture the scene: a converted café bolted on to the side of a 1960s bungalow located down a dirt track, with chickens and sheep penned in beyond the car park, a plastic French door and a mishmash of green seating, mirrors and laminate floors in the pastel-walled dining room – 'it's one of the oddest-looking restaurants I've come across,' observed a well-travelled reader. Rascills is now home to Richard and Lindsey Johns, who made their name at the Artisan in Hessle – although their new set-up clearly has more modest aspirations. Lindsey is a charming hostess, while Richard's cooking is described as 'generous, skilled and interesting, but not overdone'. It's also reliable stuff, from an 'incredibly bright' wild garlic soup with semi-dried ham to honey-glazed Goosnargh duck breast or roasted sea bream partnered by a 'superbly made' pea risotto, pea shoots and a drizzle of herb oil. For afters, plump for the 'dessert plate'. Three dozen 'budget-first' wines suit the set-up.
Chef/s: Richard Johns. **Open:** Wed to Sat D. Sun L (last Sun in month only). **Closed:** Mon, Tue, bank hols. **Meals:** main courses £11 to £14 (L only). Set D £30 (2 courses) to £37. Sun L £26. Tasting menu £50 (5 courses). **Details:** 22 seats. 10 seats outside. Bar. Wheelchairs. Music. Parking.

Symbols

🛏 Accommodation is available
£30 Three courses for less than £30
£5 OFF £5-off voucher scheme
🍷 Notable wine list

Ripon

Lockwoods

Cooking score: 1
Modern British | £27
83 North Street, Ripon, HG4 1DP
Tel no: (01765) 607555
lockwoodsrestaurant.co.uk
£30

A pretty blue frontage with hanging baskets announces the valuable local resource that is Matthew Lockwood's modern bistro. Blackboard menus cover a lot of ground, including on-trend items like black pudding Scotch egg with smoked bacon jam, seafood fritto misto with caper and parsley mayo, and the all-important Asian notes that transform pork belly by braising it in coconut and serving it with egg noodles in a thin Vietnamese-style broth. Ingeniously constructed finishers might include banana cake served with spiced roast pineapple and brown-sugar ice cream. Don't overlook the Wensleydale Blue if it's on. House Spanish blends are £16.95.
Chef/s: Robert Harvey and Richard Sharp. **Open:** Tue to Sun L, Tue to Sat D. **Closed:** Mon, 25 and 26 Dec, 1 and 2 Jan. **Meals:** main courses £13 to £17. Early D £14 (2 courses) to £17. **Details:** 65 seats. V menu. Bar. Wheelchairs.

Sancton

The Star Inn

Cooking score: 4
Modern British | £34
King Street, Sancton, YO43 4QP
Tel no: (01430) 827269
thestaratsancton.co.uk
🍷

Transformed from a 'grubby roadside boozer' into a smartly turned out foodie destination with its own shop, the Star Inn still welcomes travellers, walkers and locals – much as it did back in the 18th century. It may be deep in the touristy Yorkshire Wolds, but that's an asset when it comes to sourcing ingredients for the kitchen's full-flavoured endeavours. To begin,

The Good Food Guide 2018

you might find sticky pig's cheek with homemade black pudding, burnt-apple purée and clapshot, while the carnivorous cavalcade continues with everything from rack of lamb rolled in herbs with pressed shoulder, garlicky potato terrine and spring greens, to prized cuts of 60-day salt-aged beef from Kirkby Malzeard. If fish is your fancy, consider beetroot-cured gravadlax followed by pan-roast cod with creamy crab and fennel risotto, braised fennel and chanterelles. To finish, treacle and liquorice tart says Yorkshire, as does poached rhubarb and gingerbread with Bird's custard 'shards' and parkin ice cream. The fascinating global wine list shows confident buying and a liking for off-piste producers, with helpful notes and fair mark-ups throughout. **Chef/s:** Ben Cox. **Open:** Tue to Sun L and D. **Closed:** Mon, 1 Jan, bank hols. **Meals:** main courses £12 to £29. Set L £17 (2 courses) to £19. **Details:** 80 seats. 32 seats outside. Bar. Wheelchairs. Music. Parking.

■ Scarborough

Lanterna
Cooking score: 3
Italian | £38
33 Queen Street, Scarborough, YO11 1HQ
Tel no: (01723) 363616
lanterna-ristorante.co.uk
£5
OFF

'It can feel like being stuck in Monty Python's 'Four Yorkshiremen' sketch,' quips one reader who wouldn't miss her annual visit to this landmark Scarborough ristorante. Lanterna's determinedly old-fashioned ambience is one of its enduring charms, as senior cricket fans and locals rub shoulders with thespians (famous or otherwise) from the nearby theatre. Chef/proprietor Giorgio Alessio is renowned for his fish cookery and regularly picks up the 'freshest ever' supplies from the town's market – his 'beautifully delicate' tempura-battered ling, Scarborough woof and turbot in white wine sauce have all received rave reviews. You can also eat handsomely by ordering some homemade pasta (tagliolini

with veal and pecorino, say) followed by fillet steak enriched with a sauce of Taleggio cheese, cream and grappa. Not surprisingly, Piedmont-born Giorgio also celebrates the native truffle season with due generosity – and he whisks a mean zabaglione, too. A classy collection of directly imported Italian wines does the food full justice. **Chef/s:** Giorgio Alessio. **Open:** Tue to Sat D only. **Closed:** Sun, Mon, 25 and 26 Dec, 1 Jan, last 2 weeks Oct. **Meals:** main courses £15 to £49. **Details:** 32 seats. Music.

LOCAL GEM
Eat Me Café
Modern British | £18
2 Hanover Road, Scarborough, YO11 1LS
Tel no: (07445) 475328
eatmecafe.com
£5 £30
OFF

This bright, easy-going café opposite the train station and directly behind the Stephen Joseph Theatre gives off a healthy buzz, part of which, no doubt, comes from the approving murmurs of those partaking of its changing array of daily specials and popular staples. Come for breakfast or coffee and cake, otherwise the repertoire spans everything from sandwiches to Welsh rarebit with bacon or Thai green curry. Taking centre stage are various burgers, 'the best I've had in the UK', and there's an evening menu three days a week. Wines from £12. Cash only.

■ Scawton

The Hare Inn
Cooking score: 6
Modern British | £70
Scawton, YO7 2HG
Tel no: (01845) 597769
thehare-inn.com
£5
OFF

'Meltingly tender goujons of Yorkshire pig cooked sous-vide, ingenious mackerel two ways, sea bass with sea vegetables and edible sand' – just some highlights from one reader's superlative lunch at the family-run Hare. '13th-century inn, 21st-century restaurant' proclaims the slogan – and you'd better believe it. With its thick stone walls, cosy corners and scrubbed tables, this ancient hostelry suits its isolated North York Moors location to a T, although the food tells a very different story. Chef/co-proprietor Paul Jackson is defying the odds by shunning touristy pub clichés and going for broke with a choice of two 'slowly changing' multi-course tasting menus bursting with creativity and serious-minded accomplishment. Between the tantalising snacks and the 'fine coffee', you might encounter anything from razor clams, cleverly partnered by crayfish, kohlrabi and sea herbs, to Holme Farm venison with butternut squash, hen-of-the-woods mushrooms and leeks. To finish, an enigmatically titled mini dessert of 'milk – honey' might precede a concoction of rhubarb with buttermilk. Service is 'detailed, considerate and friendly', while spot-on wine pairings are gleaned from a concise well-considered list. New accommodation should be ready in spring 2018.

Chef/s: Paul Jackson. **Open:** Sat L, Wed to Sat D. **Closed:** Sun, Mon, Tue, 2 weeks Jan, 1 week Jul, 1 week Nov. **Meals:** set L £55 (6 courses). Set D £70 (9 courses). **Details:** 22 seats. V menu. Bar. Wheelchairs. Music. Parking. No children.

◼ Sheffield

★ NEW ENTRY ★

Jöro

Cooking score: 4
Modern European | £28
Krynkl, 294 Shalesmoor, Sheffield, S3 8US
Tel no: (0114) 2991539
jororestaurant.co.uk

Housed in a pile of refurbished shipping containers – alongside a gym, hair salon, design studio and gallery – Jöro is super cool. Chunky wooden tables, candles, fresh flowers, low lighting, and 'chill-out clubby music with a bit of Lou Reed and Nick Cave thrown in' set

the scene, while Luke French can be viewed in the open kitchen building up meals via a series of snacks and small plates. He excels at no-holds-barred seasonal cooking; indeed, his dishes can change daily depending on available produce and his menu is ambitious yet deceptively simple, as in a plate of green, white and wild asparagus with just a light dusting of Parmesan and a hit of lovage cream. Poached breast of chicken wrapped in wilted spinach with more wild asparagus and spring onions in a deeply flavoured chicken sauce delighted one reporter, who went on to praise cannon, 'nicely charred' rib and 'sticky, deeply flavoured' ragù of local lamb atop broad beans, mint and cucumber ketchup. Sorbet of coriander and apples with apple caramel and apple crisp – 'the poshest toffee apple ever' – is the 'perfect finish'. An intelligent wine list starts at £22.

Chef/s: Luke French. **Open:** Wed to Sat L and D. **Closed:** Sun, Mon, Tue, 29 Oct to 4 Nov, 24 to 30 Dec. **Meals:** main courses £10 to £20. Set L and D £28 (3 courses). Tasting menu £45. **Details:** 50 seats. Wheelchairs. Music.

Rafters

Cooking score: 4
Modern British | £45
220 Oakbrook Road, Nether Green, Sheffield, S11 7ED
Tel no: (0114) 2304819
raftersrestaurant.co.uk
£5 OFF

There's an appealing contrast at Rafters between the smart table settings and genteel furnishing and the exposed brickwork of the walls, a classic contemporary backdrop for a Sheffield old-stager. These days, Tom Lawson offers an unmistakably progressive menu of modern dishes, with eight-course tasting menus, in both omnivore and vegetarian versions, the core of the operation. The combinations may be classic enough in themselves, as when whipped Stilton appears with pear and walnuts, or torched mackerel is garnished with cucumber and dill, but the presentations are spare and elegant and the flavours ring true. Main items might take in wild sea bass with mussels and leeks, and venison with beetroot and juniper alongside a slab of potato terrine, while Yorkshire's rhubarb season, the envy of England, is celebrated in the exotic company of white chocolate and coconut. Pre-selected wine flights are inspired and apposite, from a list that is arranged by style, opening with glasses from £4.50.

Chef/s: Thomas Lawson. **Open:** Sun L, Wed to Sun D. **Closed:** Mon, Tue, 25 to 27 Dec, 1 to 9 Jan, 27 Aug to 4 Sept. **Meals:** set D £45. Sun L £34. Tasting menu £60. **Details:** 38 seats. V menu. Music.

■ Shibden
Shibden Mill Inn
Cooking score: 2
Modern British | £32
Shibden Mill Fold, Shibden, HX3 7UL
Tel no: (01422) 365840
shibdenmillinn.com
£5 OFF ⊨

'The journey doesn't get any easier,' remarked one reporter who got lost trying to find this whitewashed and wisteria-clad country pub tucked into a sheltered, almost hidden valley. Arrive on a fine summer's day and bag a seat on the charming front terrace – it's a perfect lunch spot. And with low dark beams, exposed stone walls and open fires, this ancient and atmospheric hostelry is always welcoming and cosy inside. The kitchen matches the very traditional looks with pub classics (sausage and mash, fish pie, good Whitby crab sandwiches), but is also bang up to date with a menu that features local produce, including game, with the kitchen garden providing leaves and vegetables in season. Sea bream, squid-ink pasta with brown crab ketchup is 'a delicate, good-looking dish and full of flavour', followed by chocolate fondant with cocoa sorbet, white chocolate tuilles and dark chocolate sauce. Wines start at £19.99.

Chef/s: Darren Parkinson. **Open:** all week L and D. **Closed:** 25 and 26 Dec. **Meals:** main courses £18 to £23. Set L and D £15 (2 courses) to £18. **Details:** 88 seats. 50 seats outside. Bar. Music. Parking.

■ South Dalton
The Pipe & Glass
Cooking score: 5
Modern British | £46
West End, South Dalton, HU17 7PN
Tel no: (01430) 810246
pipeandglass.co.uk
🍷 ⊨

With afternoon tea and savouries, Sunday roasts and a 'little people's menu' on the table, James and Kate Mackenzie's striking Wolds pub goes all out for inclusivity. Cellar work and dutiful innkeeping count for a great deal here, but the Mackenzies have higher aspirations when it comes to the sustenance served in their commodious conservatory-style dining room. James's finely judged food shows refinement above its pubby station, although he invests his cooking with bags of generosity and seasonality. Picking winners is hard: some might favour a salt beef hash cake with a fried quail's egg, Yorkshire rhubarb ketchup and crispy pickled onion rings followed by BBQ rump of lamb and braised breast with broccoli, pickled girolles and mead sauce; others could plump for some home-cured duck bresaola ahead of sausages with bubble and squeak. Yes, there's a lot of meat on the menu. Artisan British cheeses get a commendable airing, while desserts such as 'five reasons to love chocolate' go way beyond mere comfort. The knowledgeably assembled wine list is a drinker's delight with thoughtful food-matching categories, easy mark-ups and a terrific by-the-glass selection.

Chef/s: James Mackenzie. **Open:** Tue to Sun L, Tue to Sat D. **Closed:** Mon (exc bank hols), 2 weeks Jan. **Meals:** main courses £14 to £32. **Details:** 80 seats. 60 seats outside. V menu. Bar. Wheelchairs. Music. Parking.

Sowerby Bridge

Gimbals

Cooking score: 4
International | £30
76 Wharf Street, Sowerby Bridge, HX6 2AF
Tel no: (01422) 839329
gimbals.co.uk
£5
OFF

The Upper Calder Valley is quite a food lovers' destination these days and, more than two decades down the line, Simon and Janet Baker's restaurant remains at the forefront, its eclectic decoration ('mosaic glass mirrors and plenty of gilded ones, baubles and beads on the lamp shades') matched by a highly individual approach to modern cooking. Local and regional ingredients appear in dishes that draw influences from all over: for example, an 'absolutely beautiful' pile of cod cheeks teamed with crispy saffron, turmeric and lime tempura with chimichurri aïoli, or piri-piri lemon chicken breast with chicken, apricot and pistachio ballotine with romesco sauce. Closer to home there could be Yorkshire beef fillet with beef tea and fries and very good English cheeses. Desserts include chocolate and espresso brownie with salted-caramel ice cream, and lemon tart with mango sorbet. It is all 'excellent value for money', including wines from £17.50.
Chef/s: Simon Baker. **Open:** Tue to Sat D only.
Closed: Sun, Mon, 24 to 28 Dec. **Meals:** main courses £13 to £24. Set D £19 (2 courses) to £23. Tasting menu £25. **Details:** 55 seats. V menu. Bar. Music.

Please send us your feedback

To register your opinion about any restaurant listed in this guide, or a new restaurant that you wish to bring to our attention, please visit the web address at the bottom of the page. Your feedback informs the content of the book and will be used to compile next year's reviews.

Staddlebridge

The Cleveland Tontine

Cooking score: 3
Modern British | £35
Staddlebridge, DL6 3JB
Tel no: (01609) 882671
theclevelandtontine.co.uk

The legendary Tontine, run for 35 years by Eugene McCoy (see Crathorne Arms), has changed hands twice since his departure. The new owners spent a year stripping and painting only to sell on last year to Provenance Inns who run nine well-respected eating pubs across north Yorkshire. The zany excess of the McCoy years has been moderated though the public rooms are still striking. Happily the delightful mirrored and candlelit dining room remains largely unchanged. The *menu du jour* has seafood pancake, fish and chips and ribeye steak, while the comprehensive à la carte offers a sophisticated goats' cheese cannelloni with a modish scattering of pickled cauliflower florets and candied pecans. Halibut is accompanied by crayfish tails and caper butter, venison with mushrooms, red cabbage and a creamy mash. At dessert choose from crêpes suzette, chocolate fondant or affogato. A helpful wine list has many by the glass, bottles starting at £16.95.
Chef/s: John Muigana. **Open:** all week L and D.
Meals: main courses £14 to £29. Set L and D £19 (2 courses) to £22. **Details:** 120 seats. 40 seats outside. Bar. Music. Parking.

Todmorden

Blackbird

Cooking score: 2
International | £28
23 Water Street, Todmorden, OL14 5AB
Tel no: (01706) 813038
blackbirdbar.co.uk
£5 £30
OFF

'I really wish I didn't live so far away,' noted one visitor to this understated restaurant right in the middle of town. There's a 'blink-and-you'll-miss-it exterior' opening into two cosy but pleasantly sparse dining areas – exposed brickwork and simple furniture – an atmosphere that is relaxed and homely, with deceptively simple, 'supremely confident' cooking from a kitchen that shows real flair in the sourcing of ingredients and in the deft handling of flavour. The extensive, tapas-style menu runs from Sicilian meatballs to crescent momo (Tibetan-style dumplings), and from haloumi chips to chermoula pork ('good, punchy flavours') and is designed to make you sit up and take notice. Dishes singled out for praise have included oxtail filo bonbons filled with tender, full-flavoured meat braised in Rioja, and melt-in-the-mouth chicken basquaise 'packing a good paprika punch'. Desserts favour simple classics such as crème brûlée ('perfectly done') or caffè affogato, while drinks run from Continental and local beers to an affordable list of well-chosen wines (from £17).

Chef/s: Emmaline Horton. **Open:** all week L and D. **Closed:** 25 and 26 Dec, 1 Jan. **Meals:** tapas £5 to £8. **Details:** 44 seats. Wheelchairs. Music.

The White Rabbit

Cooking score: 4
Modern British | £35
1 White Hart Fold, Todmorden, OL14 7BD
Tel no: (01706) 817828
whiterabbittodmorden.com
£5
OFF

At first glance, you might be mistaken for thinking this quirkily designed little restaurant just outside Todmorden train station is one of the many quaint tea rooms that line the streets of this pretty market town. But as with Alice in Wonderland, the White Rabbit is full of surprises – melting clocks, an old cast-iron range sprayed with green graffiti and plenty of rabbit figurines – but is immediately welcoming. A hanging sign telling diners to 'feed your head' is clearly a statement of intent for a kitchen that conjures vibrant, thoughtful dishes from the very best local ingredients. A precisely cooked starter of seared king scallops with a cauliflower

pancake and Gruyère sauce and cauliflower crisps (a twist on cauliflower cheese), followed by pan-fried venison fillet with an assortment of wild mushrooms and a rich, well-made port jus, and pear délice teamed with pear textures and salted caramel formed the components of an 'excellent lunch'. Wines from £17.50.

Chef/s: David and Robyn Gledhill. **Open:** Wed to Sat L and D. **Closed:** Sun, Mon, Tue, 26 and 27 Dec, last 2 weeks Aug. **Meals:** main courses £17 to £22. Tasting menu £35 (5 courses) to £55. **Details:** 22 seats. V menu. Music.

▉ West Witton
The Wensleydale Heifer

Cooking score: 2
Seafood | £40
Main Street, West Witton, DL8 4LS
Tel no: (01969) 622322
wensleydaleheifer.co.uk
£5
OFF

Given its beefy North Country moniker, it's somewhat surprising to discover that the eccentrically decorated Wensleydale Heifer deals primarily in fresh seafood rather than slabs of red meat – that's all down to chef/ proprietor David Moss. Deep in the Dales, this boutique hotel-cum-restaurant is jam-packed with curios and oddball touches (note the risqué seaside cartoons in the loos), and there's more fun to be had when picking your way through the menus. David's retro prawn cocktail is laced with Jack Daniel's, his cod goujons are dipped in batter revved up with Black Sheep bitter, and he does intriguing things with lobsters (try the version with spicy roquito peppers, garlic, coriander and herb butter). If fish isn't your thing, there are also steaks galore, plus roast chicken, gammon joints and desserts such as rhubarb and custard pannacotta. True to form, the illustrated wine list looks more like a tongue-in-cheek Victorian magazine.

Chef/s: David Moss. **Open:** all week L and D. **Meals:** main courses £17 to £48. Set L and D £21 (2 courses) to £25. Sun L £27. **Details:** 75 seats. 40 seats outside. Bar. Wheelchairs. Music. Parking.

▮ Wetherby

LOCAL GEM

Mango

Indian Vegetarian | £25
12-14 Bank Street, Wetherby, LS22 6NQ
Tel no: (01937) 585755
mangovegetarian.com

£30

This small, family-owned-and-run South Indian vegetarian restaurant is found down a small but centrally located side street, where a light, bright contemporary look and utterly charming service distinguishes it from run-of-the-mill curry houses – as does the 'extremely tasty' freshly cooked food. The menu takes in dishes from Gujarat to the deep south and ranges from the familiar Indian spring rolls, vegetable samosas, onion bhajis and masala dosas to the more unusual dhokra (delicately spiced gram-flour cakes), ravaiya nu shaak (peanut and aubergine curry), and a dessert of rasmalai (milk dumplings in cardamom-infused milk). Licensed.

▮ Whitby

Bridge Cottage Bistro

Cooking score: 3
Modern British | £30
East Row, Sandsend, Whitby, YO21 3SU
Tel no: (01947) 893438
bridgecottagebistro.com

Only a short hop from the tourist throngs of the town, but sitting in an idyllic spot only yards from the beach at Sandsend, overlooking the East Row Beck, Alex Perkins' bistro operation is a stylish place for all-day eating. Brunches and cake-centred afternoon teas fill in the spaces between main services, the menus for which are chalked on to the wall. The cooking is impeccably seasonal, and the aspirational intention signalled from the off with excellent sourdough and whipped goats' butter. Flavour combining shows clear confidence in a starter of cured sea trout with pickled apple, cucumber and skyr, while a spring visit

devolved on rack of local lamb with delightfully light and fresh pea croquettes, asparagus and salsa verde. A top-value fish-themed tasting menu looks a particular steal, and desserts to beat the band take in pistachio cake, or chocolate mousse with a sorbet and caramel of blood orange. What's not to like? Sad to say, friendly but inattentive service, which will surely be addressed before too long. A small but eclectic group of wines opens at £4.50 a glass.
Chef/s: Alexander Perkins. **Open:** Tue to Sun L, Thur to Sat D. **Closed:** Mon. **Meals:** main courses £12 to £26. Tasting menu £30. **Details:** 28 seats. 26 seats outside. Bar. Wheelchairs. Music. Parking.

▮ York

Le Cochon Aveugle

Cooking score: 4
French | £50
37 Walmgate, York, YO1 9TX
Tel no: (01904) 640222
lecochonaveugleyork.com

The spirit of French bistronomy runs through this 'blind pig' – although chef/co-proprietor Josh Overington plays fast and loose with the concept. Spread over two floors on historic Walmgate, this small venue recently underwent some refurbishment, enabling the kitchen to feed its customers in freshened-up surroundings. 'Dining by surprise' is the stated aim, with a 'blind' no-choice menu that changes from day to day and allows Mr Overington to throw down plenty of small-plate challenges. So what can you expect? Perhaps nasturtium ice cream with onion squash velouté, hand-dived scallop with Douglas Fir butter or squab with heritage beets and 'tasty paste relish', ahead of left-field desserts such as a beeswax canelé with morello cherry and warm chamomile milk. The food is matched by exclusively French wines from small indie producers. The owners' Cave du Cochon wine bar is at 19 Walmgate.
Chef/s: Joshua Overington. **Open:** Tue to Sat D only. **Closed:** Sun, Mon, 25 and 26 Dec, 2 weeks Jan, bank hols. **Meals:** set D £50 (6 courses) to £70 (9 courses). **Details:** 30 seats. Bar. Music.

Melton's

Cooking score: 5
British | £38
7 Scarcroft Road, York, YO23 1ND
Tel no: (01904) 634341
meltonsrestaurant.co.uk
£5 OFF

In more than a quarter of a century, Melton's has accumulated many return customers, They value 'the same friendly welcome and smiling service', as well as continuing investment in keeping the small dining room both comfortable and classy. Strangers are welcome, too, and Michael Hjort's cooking is a perennial lure to this lovely corner of York. Dishes take account both of modern technique and the local larder, as in a clever take on beef carpaccio with vivid egg yolk purée and crunchy shallot rings. A main course of just-cooked hake is given a punchy Beaufort cheese crust and set on a lovely tangle of sweet leeks and sour pickled mushrooms, and confidence in the classics is rewarded by a floaty prune and brandy soufflé. Lunch and early dinner represents 'good Yorkshire value for money', and an accomplished wine list includes thoughtfully made (and often modestly priced) matches for popular dishes.
Chef/s: Michael Hjort and Calvin Miller. **Open:** Tue to Sat L and D. **Closed:** Sun, Mon, 2 weeks from 24 Dec. **Meals:** main courses £18 to £24. Set L and early D £26 (2 courses) to £30. Tasting menu £45. **Details:** 40 seats. Music.

★ NEW ENTRY ★

Mr P's Curious Tavern

Cooking score: 3
Modern British | £30
71 Low Petergate, York, YO1 7HY
Tel no: (01904) 521177
mrpscurioustavern.co.uk

As part of his expansion across Yorkshire – see entries for the original Star at Harome, and York's Star Inn the City – Mr P (aka Andrew Pern) brings his clever and comforting dishes to this city-centre venture. 'Curious' here means modish clutter in a pseudo 'olde-worlde' tavern, with Toby jugs, tankards, a stuffed snowy owl and salamis hanging from Grade II-listed beams, conspiring to make an agreeable setting for small-plate dining. Croque M'Lass is a fried-bread sandwich of smoked salmon, Comté and quail's egg. Potted confit duck comes with toasted brioche and truffled honey, and a super-crisp taco filled with lobster, smoked sweet corn, avocado and pine nuts is Mr Pern at his creative best. Reporters have struggled with the small-plate concept – food that comes 'as its cooking and preparation time dictate' – concluding it delivers an erratic meal and is perhaps 'not a sociable way to eat'. However, for the most part, Mr P 'delivers enjoyable dishes with a difference'.
Chef/s: Stuart Snell. **Open:** Mon to Thur and Sun L, Mon to Thur D. Fri and Sat, all day from 11. **Closed:** 25 Dec and 1 Jan. **Meals:** small plates £5 to £18. Tasting menu £35. **Details:** 80 seats. Music.

The Park

Cooking score: 3
Modern British | £60
Marmadukes Town House Hotel, 4-5 St Peter's Grove, York, YO30 6AQ
Tel no: (01904) 540903
marmadukestownhousehotelyork.com
£5 OFF

Occupying a Victorian gentleman's residence just minutes from York's Roman walls, Marmadukes Town House Hotel is home to all manner of boutique delights – not least the Park restaurant, tucked away in a smart glass-roofed extension. Adam Jackson's local reputation precedes him, but he has raised the bar a notch in this latest venture by focusing on an eight-course tasting menu of savvy modern dishes bursting with finely honed flavours and textures. It's a brave (and mischievous) chef who can offer cheesy Lancashire 'bomber' bread with ham hock and pickle ahead of asparagus with summer truffle and egg, but Jackson manages to pull it off – and that's not all. Diners might also be treated to plates of salmon with asparagus, mussels and samphire, or beef with carrots and boulangère potatoes, while desserts such as rhubarb and ginger fool take their cue from Yorkshire's bounty. Dishes come with thoughtful wine suggestions from a wide-ranging list.

Chef/s: Adam Jackson. **Open:** Tue to Sat D only. **Closed:** Sun, Mon, first 2 weeks Jan. **Meals:** set D £60 (8 courses). **Details:** 24 seats. Bar. Wheelchairs. Music. Parking. Children over 12 yrs only.

★ NEW ENTRY ★

The Rattle Owl

Cooking score: 3
Modern British | £34
104 Micklegate, York, YO1 6JX
Tel no: (01904) 658658
rattleowl.co.uk

Just beyond medieval Micklegate Bar, the southern gateway to the city, the admirable Rattle Owl provides casual dining in a 17th-century building of rustic brick, light oak furnishings and Roman remains, discovered during the renovations and now part of the restaurant's wine cellar. A regularly changing menu might offer a lunch of soup, open sandwich or a comforting dish of new potato hash with tomato, olives and capers followed perhaps by liquorice rice pudding and blood oranges. Dinner gears up a little with a refined chicken and black pudding roulade and a prettily presented rhubarb ripple parfait with honey, gin gel and Chantilly cream. Wines, mostly organic, begin at £19 and are also available from their shop, which at the weekend operates as a bakery, part of a commendable small-business residency.

Chef/s: Jamie Hall. **Open:** Wed to Sun L, Tue to Sat D. **Closed:** Mon, 24 to 26 Dec, 1 to 10 Jan. **Meals:** main courses £16 to £19. Set L and D £14 (2 courses) to £18. **Details:** 42 seats. Wheelchairs. Music.

Average price

The average price denotes the price of a three-course meal without wine.

★ NEW ENTRY ★

Skosh

Cooking score: 4
Modern British | £25
98 Micklegate, York, YO1 6JX
Tel no: (01904) 634849
skoshyork.co.uk
£30

The clue is in the name: Skosh comes from the Japanese word *sukoshi*, meaning 'little' or 'small', and this exciting new arrival on York's Micklegate is based on an original menu of snacks and small plates from which diners choose three or four of each. Neil Bentinck's menu changes frequently, but the ceramic 'hen's egg' filled with a fluffy mousse of richly flavoured Dale End Cheddar and a surprise sweet-sour mix of mushroom and Pedro Ximénez in the base, has been a favourite from the start. Plates progress in size and price through the likes of cured sea trout with Thai flavours served in gem lettuce 'cups' and a superb char-grilled octopus with black olive caramel, on to more substantial plates of hake topped with dukkah, a splash of miso and a soothing cauliflower purée or crisp lamb belly with charred Hispi cabbage. A concise wine list starting at £20 completes an accomplished meal at this audacious new arrival.

Chef/s: Neil Bentinck. **Open:** Wed to Sun L, Wed to Sat D. **Closed:** Mon, Tue, 25 and 26 Dec, 1 to 10 Jan, 8 to 16 May, 4 to 19 Sept. **Meals:** small plates £3 to £15. **Details:** 38 seats. Music.

The Star Inn the City

Cooking score: 1
British | £42
Lendal Engine House, Museum Street, York, YO1 7DR
Tel no: (01904) 619208
starinnthecity.co.uk

The external beauty and charm of Andrew Pern's reworked old engine house is undeniable. If a restaurant could typify York purely in its setting and aesthetic, this would surely be it. Breakfast is a delightful experience on a bright morning overlooking

the river Ouse, on a sizeable outdoor terraced area that should be a staple on any trip to York, even just for a drink. A recent refurbishment has made room for a copper tank containing 500 litres of unpasteurised Pilsner Urquell that means – with an extensive wine list (from £22) and gin menu – all are catered for. The menu focuses on showcasing classic flavours from around the region and has a clear focus on seasonal or locally sourced produce such as crab salad with brown crab ketchup, curried granola, apple and coriander, and Beverley duck breast with Tomlinson's rhubarb. Staff are extremely welcoming and family friendly.
Chef/s: Matt Hunter. **Open:** all week L and D.
Meals: main courses £16 to £32. Set L and D £17 (2 courses) to £22. **Details:** 175 seats. 80 seats outside. Bar. Wheelchairs. Music.

Walmgate Ale House

Cooking score: 2
International | £28
25 Walmgate, York, YO1 9TX
Tel no: (01904) 629222
walmgateale.co.uk
£30

Michael Hjort's ale-house-cum-bistro has a long history: the listed building dates from just after the English Civil War and the loft is reputed to be haunted. There's been a reorganisation of the menu since the last edition, with more use made of blackboards. An Anglo-European flavour runs through dishes such as warm beetroot and goats' cheese flatbread, and fillet of stone bass with tapenade crumb and tomato and fennel sauce. Alternatively, you could try a hearty Longhorn rump steak with herb butter, onion rings and chips or a vegetarian main of pea pancakes with cauliflower purée and spiced cauliflower and finish with sticky toffee pudding. The international wine list has broad appeal, with much available by the glass.
Chef/s: Michael Hjort. **Open:** Tue D. Wed to Sun, all day from 12 (9.30 Sat and Sun). **Closed:** Mon, 2 days Christmas and New Year. **Meals:** main courses £13 to £21. Set L and D £16 (2 courses) to £18.
Details: 105 seats. Bar. Wheelchairs. Music.

Mannion & Co.

Modern British | £20
1 Blake Street, York, YO1 8QJ
Tel no: (01904) 631030
mannionandco.co.uk
£30

'Lots of tea rooms in York, many of them good, this one is consistently excellent.' Andrew Burton's daytime bistro-deli-bakery, a stone's throw from York Minster, stands out for many reporters. Sandwiches, deli boards, good bread and proper homemade scones and cakes are crowd-pullers, but there's honest cooking in dishes such as Yorkshire rarebit with bacon, chorizo with thyme and Manchego gnocchi, and boudin noir with crispy pancetta and fried duck egg. No booking means it's first come, first served. Wines from £18. Another branch has opened at 5 Castlegate, Helmsley, YO62 5AB.

SCOTLAND

Borders, Dumfries & Galloway,
Lothians (inc. Edinburgh),
Strathclyde (inc. Glasgow), Central, Fife,
Tayside, Grampian, Highlands & Islands

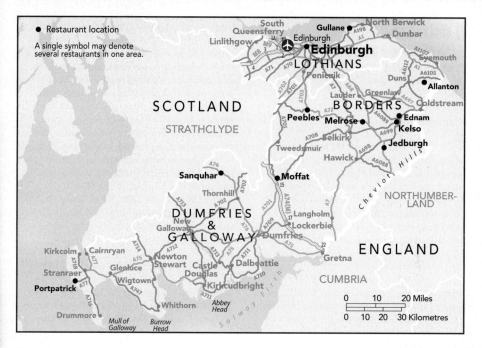

- Restaurant location
- A single symbol may denote several restaurants in one area.

SCOTLAND

STRATHCLYDE

LOTHIANS

BORDERS

DUMFRIES & GALLOWAY

ENGLAND

CUMBRIA

NORTHUMBERLAND

| 0 | 10 | 20 Miles |
| 0 | 10 | 20 | 30 Kilometres |

Allanton

Allanton Inn
Cooking score: 2
Modern British | £25
Allanton, TD11 3JZ
Tel no: (01890) 818260
allantoninn.co.uk
🛏 £30

At the north-eastern end of the Border country, Allanton is an unassuming hamlet of stone-built houses with a two-storey Georgian inn at its heart. It's very much a family affair, under the aegis of William and Katrina Reynolds and sons, and they work assiduously to create the kind of warm-hearted welcome expected in a country pub. With local artworks and fresh flowers to adorn the inside, and sweeping views over Berwickshire from the beer garden, its winning formula is sealed by menus of homely Scottish cooking that balance tradition and modernity. A chunky terrine of local game with honey-baked figs and tomato chutney could be the prelude to sea bass with mussels, tarka dhal, buttered kale and coriander salad, or apricot-stuffed pork belly roulade and haggis dauphinois in mustard sauce. A sharing platter of that terrine with seafood, olives and tomatoes could be the best lunchtime option, and puddings include coconut and lime brûlée with homemade shortbread. Scottish cheeses are top-drawer, while wines open with Chilean Sauvignon and Merlot at £15.50.
Chef/s: Lee Cessfard. **Open:** all week L and D. **Closed:** 25 and 26 Dec. **Meals:** main courses £12 to £24. **Details:** 50 seats. 40 seats outside. Music.

Symbols

🛏 Accommodation is available
£30 Three courses for less than £30
£5 OFF £5-off voucher scheme
🍾 Notable wine list

Ednam
Edenwater House

Cooking score: 4
Modern British | £44
Ednam, TD5 7QL
Tel no: (01573) 224070
edenwaterhouse.co.uk

Jeff and Jacqui Kelly's affectionately run B&B occupies a converted manse in the Tweed Valley borderlands – a haven of repose for travellers, but also worth seeking out for its Lilliputian restaurant. Those who book for dinner can expect an unhurried four-course deal full of bright ideas, all designed to show off Jacqui's skilful way with eclectic mix-and-match flavours. In practice, that might mean seared sea bass on a warm kale salad with sautéed potato 'buttons', sprout 'shells', crispy capers and wasabi mayo or an equally complex assemblage of Gressingham duck breast on carrot rösti with a mélange of Chinese cabbage, snow peas and egg noodles, all dressed with orange honey and star anise jus. Intricacy also characterises desserts such as mango and coconut semifreddo with passion fruit coulis and tropical fruit salsa. Pre-selected wines by the glass are offered with each dish, or you can pick from the ever-changing global list.
Chef/s: Jacqui Kelly. **Open:** Thur to Sat D only. **Closed:** Sun to Wed, Dec to mid Mar. **Meals:** set D £44 (4 courses). **Details:** 16 seats. Bar. Parking. Children over 12 yrs only.

Jedburgh
The Caddy Mann

Cooking score: 3
Modern British | £25
Mounthooly, Jedburgh, TD8 6TJ
Tel no: (01835) 850787
caddymann.com

The rolling landscape of the Borders, criss-crossed by the Tweed on its way to the sea at Berwick, produces a wealth of hearty ingredients. Many find their way into the capable hands of Ross Horrocks. Although initial impressions of the low red buildings on the Jedburgh to Kelso road may be more café than culinary, it's quickly clear that a classical pedigree and personal touch underpin this homely family business. Unctuous Borders lamb slow-cooked for 18 hours is a worthy signature dish but the daily menu may also showcase local deer, hare, lobster and squirrel as well as a laudable vegetarian range. A smoked partridge starter with mulled pears and pressed wild game reflects the surrounding woodlands, while flaky North Sea cod is paired with smoked pancetta, leeks and mushrooms in creamed cider. Come hungry! Flavours are big and portions generous. House wines start at a very reasonable £14.50 a bottle with local brews also available.
Chef/s: Ross Horrocks. **Open:** Tue to Sun L, Fri and Sat D. **Closed:** Mon, 25 and 26 Dec. **Meals:** main courses £13 to £21. **Details:** 50 seats. 20 seats outside. V menu. Wheelchairs. Parking.

Kelso
The Cobbles

Cooking score: 2
Modern British | £27
7 Bowmont Street, Kelso, TD5 7JH
Tel no: (01573) 223548
thecobbleskelso.co.uk

Tucked just off Kelso's main square, this is the kind of pub you'd love as your local – nurturing food, friendly service, unique craft beers from the local Tempest brewery (six on draught plus seasonal and special edition brews) and a lively buzz. Chef Daniel Norcliffe focuses on local suppliers and crowd-pleasing recipes – his classic pub menu is delivered with aplomb, supplemented by daily specials. A satisfyingly chunky chicken and ham hock terrine with pineapple chutney and olive-oil-infused sourdough might be followed by truffled beef shin macaroni that's more comforting than a cuddle. Desserts are unexpectedly elegant with 'banana loaf' offering multiple takes on the fruit through patisserie, ice cream, caramel and parfait and imaginative sorbet choices including avocado and elderflower. A separate steak menu showcases well-matured Hardiesmill Aberdeen Angus with precision cooking of less common cuts such as bavette and bullet. A small wine choice is available but it's the beers that take centre stage.

Chef/s: Daniel Norcliffe. **Open:** Mon to Fri L and D. Sat and Sun, all day from 12. **Closed:** 25 and 26 Dec. **Meals:** main courses £11 to £30. **Details:** 60 seats. 16 seats outside. Bar. Music.

▌Melrose

Burts

Cooking score: 2
Modern British | £38
Burts Hotel, Market Square, Melrose, TD6 9PL
Tel no: (01896) 822285
burtshotel.co.uk

🛏

Tweeds and tartans along with rods and mounted trophies in the restaurant underscore the local 'hunting, shooting, fishing' feel of this traditional market-square hotel. There's a classic treatment of core Scottish ingredients: Teviot smoked salmon, simply served with thinly sliced brown bread, or plump caramelised scallops on melting pork belly with a contrasting kick of fennel and apple, for example. As well as a selection of grills, from which tender lamb cutlets are a standout, you might find braised venison with a turnip and celeriac gratin or a grilled plaice fillet smothered in creamy seafood chowder on salmon tortellini. Warm pear tart with salted-caramel ice cream and almond custard offers nursery-style comfort. The formal restaurant feels primarily aimed at residents, while the relaxed bistro bar offers a more contemporary menu. Wines from £18.50.

Chef/s: Trevor Williams. **Open:** Sat and Sun L, all week D. **Closed:** 6 to 13 Feb. **Meals:** main courses £15 to £26. **Details:** 60 seats. 24 seats outside. Bar. Music. Parking. Children over 8 yrs only.

▌Peebles

Osso

Cooking score: 2
Modern British | £32
Innerleithen Road, Peebles, EH45 8BA
Tel no: (01721) 724477
ossorestaurant.com

Opening its doors at 10 in the morning, Osso sates the local community with its brunches (or breakfast for later risers), soups and sandwiches, and if you're up for something rather more urbane, you can also swing by for celeriac risotto with artichokes and winter truffle. When it comes to the evening, the candles come out and the cheerful café becomes an equally cheerful and rather good wee bistro. Warm cured sea bass with seaweed potato, kohlrabi and some herbs foraged from the beach shows that the kitchen is keeping up with the times. Loch Duart salmon arrives with some clams in a lick of dashi, and glazed short rib of beef is matched with a moreish combination of bone marrow and salt-baked potato. Desserts are an inspiring bunch, too: baked pineapple, say, fired up with coconut, chilli and coriander. A few cocktails and a short wine list complete the picture.

Chef/s: Ally McGrath and Stuart Smith. **Open:** all week 10 to 4.30, Tue to Sat D. **Closed:** 25 Dec, 1 Jan. **Meals:** main courses £16 to £25. Set D £22 (2 courses) to £28. **Details:** 38 seats. 6 seats outside. Wheelchairs. Music.

Please send us your feedback

To register your opinion about any restaurant listed in this guide, or a new restaurant that you wish to bring to our attention, please visit the web address at the bottom of the page. Your feedback informs the content of the book and will be used to compile next year's reviews.

∎ Moffat
The Limetree
Cooking score: 4
Modern British | £29
Hartfell House, Hartfell Crescent, Moffat,
DG10 9AL
Tel no: (01683) 220153
hartfellhouse.co.uk

£5 £30
OFF

Hartfell House is a guesthouse of the old
school, seemingly immune to the vagaries of
fashion, with the handsome Victorian
building providing generously proportioned
spaces done out with comforting formality.
The Limetree occupies the dining room and
offers the same sense of correctness, with
white linen and candles. Head chef Matt
Seddon's cooking is British in a broad sense,
inasmuch as ideas and influences come from
far and wide, and regional ingredients play
their part. A vegetarian risotto of butternut
squash and goats' cheese is a European-
influenced opener, with Chinese-spiced
grilled pork and Asian-flavoured cucumber
salad showing an altogether more exotic side.
Loin of venison with venison sausage and a
truffled mushroom and potato gratin owes
much to French classical cooking, with grilled
fillet of bream looking further south with its
accompanying chorizo, char-grilled red
peppers and aubergine. For dessert, apple
crumble ice cream is a clever foil to date and
ginger pudding. Wines open at £16.

Chef/s: Matt Seddon. **Open:** Tue to Sat D only.
Closed: Sun, Mon, 24 and 25 Dec, 10 days Jan, 10
days Oct. **Meals:** set D £29 (3 courses). **Details:** 24
seats. Wheelchairs. Parking.

∎ Portpatrick
Knockinaam Lodge
Cooking score: 5
Modern British | £68
Portpatrick, DG9 9AD
Tel no: (01776) 810471
knockinaamlodge.com

£5
OFF

An isolated grey-stone hunting lodge
enveloped in its own cove and private bit of
beach will feel like Knockinaam heaven's door
to most, and certainly must have done for
Churchill and Eisenhower when they met
here during the Second World War. Panelled
interiors and winter fires help you get bedded
in, while Tony Pierce is on hand to provide
sustaining modern Scottish dishes that show
regional produce at its best. The set menu
changes daily, and never fails to feel like an
occasion. A late February evening opened
with grilled halibut and fennel in an emulsion
of blood orange, before proceeding via its
intermediate soup course (celeriac and
pancetta slicked with white truffle oil) to a
slow roast of superlative Angus beef fillet with
pied de mouton mushrooms, rösti and shallot
purée in Madeira jus. To conclude, there's a
choice of either British and French cheeses
with walnut and sultana bread, or vanilla
pannacotta with poached William pear,
honeycomb and ginger caramel. A resourceful
list of modern wines draws in a harvest of
stunning quality in all regions, at prices that
are not necessarily forbidding. French
classicists are comprehensively spoiled for
choice, but there are authoritative Italian,
Spanish and American sections, too. It opens
at £23.

Chef/s: Tony Pierce. **Open:** all week L and D.
Meals: set L £40 (4 courses). Set D £68 (5 courses).
Sun L £33 (4 courses). **Details:** 20 seats. Bar. Music.
Parking. Children over 12 yrs only at D.

Scott Smith ≡🍴

Norn, Edinburgh

What do you enjoy most about being a chef?

I enjoy working with the best produce every day and working with a great team. Putting all your time and effort into the food and guest experience and then getting to see the enjoyment it brings is a great feeling; it makes all the long hours worth it.

Name one ingredient you couldn't cook without.

I love using butter. I don't use it to excess, but just a little is a great way to add extra flavour and richness to a dish.

What is the most unusual preparation technique you use?

We do quite a bit of self-seasoning by drying out the trimmings of vegetables. Take asparagus, for example: we blend the dried trimmings with a little salt and then use this flavoured salt to season the prepared vegetables. This achieves a nice little boost to the flavour of the finished product.

And finally...tell us something that will surprise your diners.

We have never bought a single block of butter into the restaurant. All the butter we have used, for the bread and the cooking, has all been made in-house since day one.

▌Sanquhar
Blackaddie House Hotel

Cooking score: 4
Modern British | £63
Blackaddie Road, Sanquhar, DG4 6JJ
Tel no: (01659) 50270
blackaddiehotel.co.uk
🛏

Recently refurbished but still very much of the old school, Blackaddie is an extension of a 16th-century house with loose Burns connections and a river that almost feels like its own. The odds are already stacked in chef/owner Ian McAndrew's favour; all he has to do is add 'memorable' cooking using local produce that tastes of itself. A menu priced to set expectations high might open with mi cuit fish with a seasonal garnish or pork terrine with apple purée, tomato marmalade and pickled mushrooms, followed by duck with seared foie gras, confit carrot and mille-feuille potatoes and an Armagnac and raisin jus, or roast hake with black rice, spinach and sea vegetables. Readers rate the Scottish cheeses with homemade oatcakes, or there's praline mousse with bitter orange, blood-orange jelly and whisky ice cream. The wine list is pure country house hotel, starting at £22.50.
Chef/s: Ian McAndrew. **Open:** all week L (bookings only) and D. **Meals:** set L £30 (2 courses) to £40. Set D £63 (4 courses). Tasting menu £80. **Details:** 20 seats. Bar. Music. Parking.

▌Edinburgh

Aizle

Cooking score: 4
Modern British | £45
107-109 St Leonard's Street, Edinburgh,
EH8 9QY
Tel no: (0131) 6629349
aizle.co.uk

'Heading south from Waverley station, we taught our taxi driver a Scots word he didn't know – aizle, a glowing hot ember or spark.' A short ride or brisk walk from the centre, Aizle has got contemporary dining nailed: relaxed, rustic and retro vibe, passionate and enthusiastic service, and creative, seasonal food that appears on a blackboard as a mysterious list of ingredients. Multiple courses arrive in succession (five of them, and pretty generous sizes), starting with 'outstanding' bread with 'addictive' burnt onion salt and an array of little 'snacks'. A first course proper of Wye Valley asparagus with nori and lomo hails the start of spring before perfectly cooked Loch Awe sea trout with crisp spring cabbage and silky crab. Flavours resonate and balance is achieved, not least in a third course when Gartmorn Farm duck is partnered with chicory kimchi. A ricotta and blood-orange dessert is a refined and fiery finale (thanks to a wee bit of Szechuan pepper). Well-chosen wines start at £26, and homemade soft drinks make drivers feel loved.
Chef/s: Stuart Ralston. **Open:** Wed to Sun D only. **Closed:** Mon, Tue, 25 Dec to mid Jan, 2 weeks Jul. **Meals:** set D £45 (5 courses). **Details:** 35 seats. V menu. Wheelchairs. Music.

Angels with Bagpipes

Cooking score: 4
Modern European | £40
343 High Street, Royal Mile, Edinburgh,
EH1 1PW
Tel no: (0131) 2201111
angelswithbagpipes.co.uk

Situated among the tourists and trinkets of the Royal Mile, this Guide stalwart continues to present pleasing, traditional Scottish dishes

with a contemporary twist, wearing its sophistication lightly. The smart setting, across two floors – the upper floor the more characterful and bustling – is smartly decorated in grey with touches of copper and bronze. Head chef Fraser Smith raids an enviable Scottish larder to good effect, with dishes like an elegant darne of smoked salmon with lemon and horseradish mascarpone setting a confident tone. Rabbit loin and black pudding, pearl barley and crispy kale is both comforting and flavoursome. Lamb loin is served unusually but successfully with feta, pine nuts and a salsa verde. Haggis with neeps and tatties bravely manages to look graceful with a shard of pancetta, a haggis bonbon and a whisky sauce, while an agreeable dessert of whisky parfait with toasted oats, raspberries and marshmallow has echoes of Scottish cranachan. A comprehensive wine list starts with Verdejo at £21.
Chef/s: Fraser Smith. **Open:** all week, all day from 12. **Closed:** 2 weeks Jan. **Meals:** main courses £15 to £32. Set L £18 (2 courses) to £22. Tasting menu £35 (4 courses) to £50. **Details:** 70 seats. 16 seats outside. V menu. Bar. Wheelchairs. Music.

Cafe St Honoré

Cooking score: 4
French | £35
34 North West Thistle Street Lane, Edinburgh,
EH2 1EA
Tel no: (0131) 2262211
cafesthonore.com
£5 OFF

The place could hardly exude a more Parisian air if you stumbled upon it in the back streets of Montmartre, and yet Neil Forbes' homely bistro has taken root in a side-lane of Edinburgh's New Town, where its chequerboard floor, bentwood chairs and overall brown look are quite at home. His cooking, while retaining one or two French gestures – ham hock terrine and brioche, praline parfait – is otherwise Scottish to its fingertips, its founding materials all credited to their growers and producers. Expect to start with Belhaven smoked salmon, cured in-house, with heritage potato and dill salad, before moving on to Scotch pork belly with organic Berwickshire salami and braised lentils, finishing with organic chocolate fondant and Katy Rodger's Fintry crème fraîche. Hearty portions – one reader only just negotiated a way through the generosity of confit duck breast and beetroot tart – are the norm. Scottish gins and single malts back up a French-based wine list, from £19.50. **Chef/s:** Neil Forbes. **Open:** all week L and D. **Closed:** 24 to 26 Dec, 1 Jan. **Meals:** main courses £15 to £25. Set L £16 (2 courses) to £20. Set D £18 (2 courses) to £24. Sun L £20. **Details:** 48 seats. Music.

★ **NEW ENTRY** ★

Cannonball

Cooking score: 2
Modern British | £34
Cannonball House, 356 Castlehill, Edinburgh, EH1 2NE
Tel no: (0131) 2251550
contini.com

This recent expansion of the Italo-Scot Contini family's food orbit owes its name to stray Jacobite ordnance in the outer wall, allegedly from the castle next door. In a building steeped in history, the menu is unsurprisingly rooted in Scots classics, including the eponymous 'cannonballs' – an idiosyncratic presentation of Findlay's haggis with whisky and marmalade. Seasonal starters might include local asparagus with homemade ricotta and a refreshing lemon dressing. A comforting dish of Clash Farm pork belly celebrates everything porcine: pulled, puréed and preserved. Eyemouth lobster and dry-aged Aberdeen Angus from the Tweed Valley reinforce Scotland's surf and turf credentials. Desserts see Eton mess transported to Edinburgh thanks to inclusion of the local gin distillery's elderflower liqueur. Add in a wide whisky range, local craft beers and gins and this is a solid take on Scottish cuisine in an enviable location attractive to Edinburgh's many visitors.

Chef/s: Marcin Medregal and Emma Mills. **Open:** Tue to Sat L and D. **Closed:** Sun, Mon, 25 and 26 Dec, 2 weeks Jan. **Meals:** main courses £14 to £32. Set L £15 (2 courses) to £22. Set D £26 (2 courses) to £34. Tasting menu £45 to £55. **Details:** V menu. Bar. Wheelchairs. Music.

★ **TOP 50** ★

Castle Terrace

Cooking score: 7
Modern French | £70
33-35 Castle Terrace, Edinburgh, EH1 2EL
Tel no: (0131) 2291222
castleterracerestaurant.com

A deep blue outline of Edinburgh castle on the end wall reflects the mighty monument just outside. With crisp white tablecloths, funky wallpaper and a gold ceiling, Castle Terrace offers culinary pampering to a mix of business lunchers, tourists and celebratory eventers. An aperitif trio presages the meal to come – elegantly styled, cleverly delivered and with a tasty twist – while the table d'hôte, à la carte and tasting menus (including vegetarian version) are equally artfully conceived. Bursting with the joys of spring, a seasonal tagliatelle vibrant with peas, beans, wild garlic and summer truffle offers the freshest taste of the garden, while spelt risotto, with crispy ox tongue and pork collar, is a heartier choice. Mains demonstrate both technical assurance and quality ingredients: cod with fennel and orange flakes plumply on to its multi-textured companions, while Gartmorn Farm duck is perfectly balanced against both rich and sharp complements, including rhubarb and ginger. Desserts allow creative free rein with a mango and lime marshmallow a visual masterpiece showcasing multiple technical skills. The cheese trolley navigates esoterically through goat and ewe to blue, hard and delightfully pungent. An extensive wine list will suit the classicists with large budgets as well as those exploring value and idiosyncrasy. Imaginative cocktails and classic pours may attract those of more diverse spirituous preferences.

Chef/s: Dominic Jack. **Open:** Tue to Sat L and D. **Closed:** Sun, Mon, 23 Dec to 15 Jan, 1 week Jul, 1 week Oct. **Meals:** set L £33 (3 courses). Set D £70 (3 courses). Tasting menu £80. **Details:** 75 seats. V menu. Bar. Wheelchairs. Music. Children over 5 yrs only.

Contini

Cooking score: 1
Italian | £35
103 George Street, Edinburgh, EH2 3ES
Tel no: (0131) 2251550
contini.com

Locals show loyalty to Contini for good reason – and it's worth knowing about if you are in the area. Described by one visitor as 'a lovely, family-friendly space – white with splashes of shocking pink and an open central kitchen', it has a busy atmosphere and a menu that is noted for kind prices and smaller portions for children and the elderly. Dishes such as agnolotti (homemade egg pasta filled with spinach, nutmeg and ricotta) can be followed by the likes of fritto misto or slow-cooked oxtail in a rich tomato sauce, Italian cheeses or a range of desserts, say tiramisu or homemade doughnuts. Italian wines from £20.50. Other branches at the Scottish National Gallery and Cannonball Restaurant and Bar overlooking the Castle.
Chef/s: Carina Contini. **Open:** Mon to Sat L and D. **Closed:** Sun, 25 and 26 Dec. **Meals:** main courses £14 to £24. Set L £16 (2 courses) to £20. Set D £22 (2 courses) to £28. **Details:** 120 seats. 30 seats outside. Bar. Wheelchairs. Music.

★ NEW ENTRY ★

Dishoom

Cooking score: 2
Indian | £30
3 St Andrew Square, Edinburgh, EH2 2BD
Tel no: (0131) 2026406
dishoom.com

The Edinburgh outpost of the Dishoom family offers the same high-energy experience as its four London siblings (see entries in Covent Garden, King's Cross, Shoreditch and

Soho). Over three boisterous floors on St Andrew Square, a thoroughly modern kind of Indian experience awaits, inspired by the Irani cafés of old Mumbai, with a charcoal grill on the ground floor, a basement bar – The Permit Room – and a first-floor dining room of considerable acreage. Open from 8am for brekkie, the kitchen turns out Anglo-Indian food all day long, with that charcoal grill providing murgh malai (chicken thighs as tender as they come and properly marinaded), and spicy lamb chops given a proper good go to maximise their flavour. Chicken Ruby is an old-school curry and biryanis are the real thing, while the more trendy end of the spectrum offers lamb raan bun and slaw. A list of cocktails, beers, wines and chai covers most bases.
Chef/s: Naved Nasir. **Open:** all week, all day from 8am (9am Sat and Sun). **Closed:** 25 and 26 Dec, 1 and 2 Jan. **Meals:** main courses £6 to £17. **Details:** 156 seats. Bar. Wheelchairs. Music.

Field

Cooking score: 2
Modern British | £28
41 West Nicolson Street, Edinburgh, EH8 9DB
Tel no: (0131) 6677010
fieldrestaurant.co.uk
£30

It's only a wee room, sitting just 22, so it's wise to plan your visit ahead. An intimate place, Field's culinary output is modern and creative, ambitious but measured, and, for one reader, a dinner of caramelised cauliflower fritter, hake with shellfish velouté and toffee apple parfait was enough to encourage a return visit posthaste. Pre-eminent ingredients bring a local flavour to proceedings, such as the salmon that is cured in G&T and comes with tonic jelly, compressed cucumber and dill mayo, or the pan-roasted partridge given an equally contemporary spin with confit baby turnips, tattie scone and a punchy haggis jus. A pre-theatre and early-evening menu is outstanding value for money. For dessert, that toffee apple parfait arrives with a streusel and apple blossom, or go for the honey tart offset

with almond ice cream. The annotations on the global wine list confirm the owner's passion for environmental and ethical concerns.
Chef/s: Georgia Cass. **Open:** Tue to Sun L and D. **Closed:** Mon, 25 and 25 Dec, 28 Aug to 8 Sept. **Meals:** main courses £12 to £25. Set L £13 (2 courses) to £17. **Details:** 22 seats. Music. Children over 5 yrs only.

Fishers Bistro
Cooking score: 1
Seafood | £30
1 The Shore, Leith, Edinburgh, EH6 6QW
Tel no: (0131) 5545666
fishersrestaurantgroup.co.uk

A much-loved Leith stalwart, Fishers nails its maritime colours to the mast with nautical prints, model boats, a mermaid figurehead and a menu driven by supplies of Scottish seafood. The kitchen offers a rolling line-up of bistro-style dishes, where starters of Anstruther langoustine tails or pan-fried squid with chorizo could give way to Shetland monkfish with peas à la française or Gigha halibut with merguez sausage and Puy lentil cassoulet, while puddings are old faithfuls such as pavlova or crème brûlée. Wines are a good fit for the food. The 'no-frills' Shore Bar next door also promises 'very decent' cooking, as well as live jazz and boozy revels.
Chef/s: Andrew Bird. **Open:** all week, all day from 12 (12.30 Sun). **Closed:** 25 and 26 Dec, 1 Jan. **Meals:** main courses £13 to £40. Set L £15 (2 courses) to £19. **Details:** 40 seats. 12 seats outside. Bar.

★ NEW ENTRY ★

Forage & Chatter
Cooking score: 3
Modern British | £31
1A Alva Street, Edinburgh, EH2 4PH
Tel no: (0131) 2254599
forageandchatter.com

Forage & Chatter epitomises owner Cameron McNeil's passion for local sourcing and relaxed conviviality. In a couthie corner of the West End, interconnecting bar and dining spaces flow through a sylvan backdrop of mossy tones, hewn timber, stone and plants. Light flows through the conservatory with its potting-shed vibe. Both service and food are thoughtful, honest and clearly delight – 'blown away by the quality, clean plates all round'. Moreish dough balls with mushroom-powdered yoghurt and fresh herb pesto demonstrate ambition from the off. Beetroot, fennel and citrus salad unleashes a flavour burst of colours, textures, sharpness and sweet. Perfectly crisped hake flakes cleanly with added umami from a briny seaweed sauce and samphire. Desserts are indulgent but carefully conceived – so a rich chocolate ganache is balanced by the savoury notes of rosemary ice cream and streusel crunch. A kindly priced wine list offers some original takes on popular varietals across major wine regions.
Chef/s: Liam Massie. **Open:** Tue to Sat L and D. **Closed:** Sun, Mon. **Meals:** main courses £15 to £22. Set L £15 (2 courses) to £18. **Details:** 42 seats. Bar. Music.

Galvin Brasserie de Luxe
Cooking score: 3
French | £39
Waldorf Astoria Edinburgh, The Caledonian, Princes Street, Edinburgh, EH1 2AB
Tel no: (0131) 2228988
galvinbrasseriedeluxe.com

🛏️

'I'm a bit of a Galvin fan,' admitted one reporter, 'so it was interesting to see how the Galvin brand has adapted to the Edinburgh market.' Very well indeed, it seems, with the Galvin brothers now a firm fixture on Edinburgh's dining scene. On the ground floor of the famous Caledonian hotel, their Brasserie de Luxe is modelled on a Parisian bistro, right down to the glamorous circular bar, polished staff and assured regional French repertoire. Well-defined flavours and unshowy presentation are a given in classic starters such as escargots à la bourguignonne or the more location-appropriate haggis with crushed swede and carrot. Elsewhere, show-stopping crustacean options and *plats du jour* (coq au vin, maybe) appear alongside the likes of confit duck leg with braised red cabbage and boudin noir, or fish and steaks from the grill. To finish, there's Valrhona chocolate fondant and pistachio ice cream or rhubarb custard soufflé with rhubarb ripple ice cream. The mainly French wine list starts at £24.

Chef/s: Jamie Knox. **Open:** all week L and D. **Meals:** main courses £19 to £33. Set L and D £18 (2 courses) to £21. Sun L £19. **Details:** 120 seats. Wheelchairs. Music.

The Gardener's Cottage

Cooking score: 2
Modern British | £50
1 Royal Terrace Gardens, London Road, Edinburgh, EH7 5DX
Tel no: (0131) 5581221
thegardenerscottage.co

For once, a folksy restaurant name means what it says: this rustic shack among the flowerbeds of Edinburgh's Royal Terrace Gardens really was once home to its resident horticulturist. Nowadays, however, it's a forward-thinking eatery done out with Sunday school chairs, communal tables, paint-splattered floorboards, flowers and antique cutlery – an Anglo-Scandi mash-up that's reflected in a daily menu of reinvented British heritage food tweaked with Nordic ferments, pickles and influences from faraway lands. You can mix and match at lunchtime, although you'll reap richer rewards by homing in on the multi-course dinner menu. Typical on-trend assemblages might run from carrot with buckwheat, 'fresh cheese' and cauliflower or lamb with asparagus, beetroot, walnut, lovage and honey to dessert plates of apple, marjoram and brown butter. Fresh sourdough sets the ball rolling (with a choice of dips and nibbles), while two dozen wines offer decent drinking by the glass or carafe.

Chef/s: Dale Mailley and Edward Murray. **Open:** all week L and D. **Closed:** 25 to 27 Dec, 1 to 3 Jan. **Meals:** main courses £12 to £19 (L only). Set L £30 (5 courses), Set D £50 (7 courses). **Details:** 30 seats. Music.

★ TOP 50 ★

The Kitchin

Cooking score: 7
Modern British | £75
78 Commercial Quay, Leith, Edinburgh, EH6 6LX
Tel no: (0131) 5551755
thekitchin.com

Leith's waterfront makes for an appetising vista on a bracing day, but turn to Tom Kitchin's place in an old whisky warehouse, and you'll quickly feel the lure of the great indoors. The place retains some of the feel of its former purpose, the cave-like interior with its brick pillars enhanced by stone walls and etched glass screens to divide the space. Kitchin's philosophy of establishing tangible connections between nature and plate may be the worldwide norm now, but he has been practising it for longer than most. The menus are a tour of heathland, hillside and coastline, with thoroughbred Scottish produce gleaned and gathered along the way. Hand-harvested Orkney scallops are baked in the shell and strewn with seasonal late-winter vegetables and chestnuts in a positively traditional sauce of white wine, vermouth and herbs. Impressive depth is evoked from shellfish cannelloni adorned with crabmeat, celeriac and orange in a bisque of green crab. Less obvious meat offerings may take in hare royale with gnocchi, carrots and celeriac, while Borders roe deer appears as exceptional peppered loin, its tenderness emphasised by sweet accompaniments of apple and quince, along with root veg mash, resonantly sauced in red wine. Desserts then cleave to a French classicism, to excellent effect, as in apple and caramel mille-feuille with Calvados ice cream and toffee sauce, or the wondrously rich chocolate soufflé with pumpkin ice cream. The wine list, like all the best, is a constant work in progress, with pedigree producers, experimental modern oddballs and mature vintages in bewildering profusion. One or two under the base price of £35, or £13 a small glass, would surely help.

Chef/s: Tom Kitchin. **Open:** Tue to Sat L and D.
Closed: Sun, Mon, 23 Dec to 13 Jan, 4 to 8 Apr, 25
to 29 Jul, 10 to 14 Oct. **Meals:** set L £33. Set D £75.
Tasting menu £85. **Details:** 80 seats. V menu. Bar.
Wheelchairs. Music. Parking. Children over 5 yrs
only.

★ NEW ENTRY ★

Norn

Cooking score: 5
Modern European | £40
50-54 Henderson Street, Edinburgh, EH6 6DE
Tel no: (0131) 6292525
nornrestaurant.com

Norn gives an understated nod to Danish
design, but even with plush carpet feels a little
sparse. A warmer intimacy develops as the
'lovely enthusiastic chefs' personally introduce
and serve their creations. They exude passion
for authenticity and provenance from food to
wine (an eclectic range of natural and
biodynamic bottles start at £27). An emphasis
on foraging, pickling and fermenting is
evidenced through a downstairs window into
a world of neatly labelled science projects.
Menus are highly seasonal, ingredient-led and
change daily. Crab, artichoke and sorrel sees
sweet crustacean paired with earthy tubers
slow-cooked to caramel and spiked with sharp
sorrel and delicate artichoke crisps. 'Pigeon,
salsify, kale' gives a satisfyingly ferrous hit of
rusticity. It's not faultless; a pine, sea
buckthorn and chocolate dessert is a triumph
of ambition over cohesion, but in general this
is thoughtful, confident cooking.
Chef/s: Scott Smith. **Open:** Tue to Sat D only.
Closed: Sun, Mon, 2 weeks Jan, 1 week Oct.
Meals: tasting menu £40 (4 courses) to £65.
Details: 36 seats. Wheelchairs. Music.

Visit us online

To find out more about
The Good Food Guide, please
visit thegoodfoodguide.co.uk

Number One

Cooking score: 6
Modern British | £75
The Balmoral, 1 Princes Street, Edinburgh,
EH2 2EQ
Tel no: (0131) 5576727
roccofortehotels.com

It's hard to make a basement look good, but
they've done well at the Balmoral Hotel,
where the large dining room feels
sophisticated and exclusive with well-spaced
tables, subdued lighting, red-lacquered tiles
on the walls and black-framed pictures from
the Royal College of Art. Head chef Brian
Grigor's food fits the setting well, first-class
materials are generally impeccably handled,
with complex culinary detailing in dishes such
as hand-dived scallops with prune ketchup,
crispy chicken wing and leek oil, and sautéed
foie gras served with poached rhubarb, confit
duck leg and marzipan crumb. By relying on
clever techniques and the artful composition
of dishes, he layers on flavours and textures, in
a dish of organic pork, say, with medjool date,
white turnip and Cox's apple or wild halibut
teamed with roast langoustine, squid farfalle
and cauliflower purée. Desserts? Think
banana and honey mousse with a sugar-blown
pear and a streusel crumb. The wine list
accords France its full dignity, but good
drinking abounds elsewhere and there is
plenty by the glass. Bottles from £30.
Chef/s: Jeff Bland and Brian Grigor. **Open:** all week
D only. **Closed:** 2 weeks Jan. **Meals:** set D £75 (3
courses). Tasting menu £80 (4 courses) to £110.
Details: 65 seats. V menu. Bar. Wheelchairs. Music.

Ondine

Cooking score: 4
Seafood | £55
2 George IV Bridge, Edinburgh, EH1 1AD
Tel no: (0131) 2261888
ondinerestaurant.co.uk

A discreet glass door leads to the first-floor
dining room and what Ondine calls 'a proper
seafood restaurant where people can roll up

their sleeves and truly relax'. Up to a point. The smartly upholstered chairs, monochrome décor and service that inclines towards the formal suggest suits rather than shirtsleeves; then again, if you are splashing out on their 'grand fruits of the sea' – lobster, oysters, crab, cockles, razor clams, mussels, scallops and langoustines – you might actually want to knuckle down in shirtsleeves with a set of lobster crackers. Oysters on ice are shipped in from all corners of the British Isles, while wild sea bass ceviche or brown crab served with dainty crumpets and squid in a lighter-than-light tempura batter and an Asian dipping sauce continue the starters. Generous mains cover the range from fish and chips to lobster thermidor via lemon sole with capers and brown shrimps and sea bass with chanterelles and lentils. Proper seafood indeed, matched with an accessible wine list and Muscadet sur Lie at £29.

Chef/s: Roy Brett. **Open:** Mon to Sat L and D. **Closed:** Sun, 24 to 27 Dec. **Meals:** main courses £16 to £48. Set L and D £19 (2 courses) to £24. **Details:** 86 seats. Wheelchairs. Music.

The Pompadour by Galvin
Cooking score: 6
French | £60
Waldorf Astoria Edinburgh, The Caledonian, Princes Street, Edinburgh, EH1 2AB
Tel no: (0131) 2228975
thepompadourbygalvin.com

One of Edinburgh's more celebrated restaurants is in its best-known hotel, and the Pompadour at the Caledonian has been impressively revitalised by Chris and Jeff Galvin – the brothers behind a mini empire in London and beyond. Luxury is a given in this palatial first-floor dining room – a vision of *belle époque* swagger complete with courtly plasterwork, long drapes and hand-painted Chinese panels. Scottish produce meets French haute cuisine in the kitchen, which interprets the high-end Galvin style with spectacular results. The brothers' signature lasagne of crab with beurre nantais makes the

most of crustacea from North Berwick, while Highland lamb shank is paired with crowdie (cheese) ravioli, pipérade and sauce niçoise. Other ideas, such as a terrine of foie gras served with winter fruits poached in Douglas Fir or a dish of wild halibut and langoustine in shiitake dashi show that the kitchen isn't totally bound by French convention, although Gallic themes return in the shape of tarte Tatin, blood-orange soufflé or Valrhona chocolate crémeux with passion fruit sorbet. The expansive wine list oozes class.

Chef/s: Dan Ashmore. **Open:** Sat L, Wed to Sun D. **Closed:** Mon, Tue, first 2 weeks Jan. **Meals:** main courses £32 to £38. Set L and D £29 (2 courses) to £35. Tasting menu £55 (5 courses) to £75 (7 courses). **Details:** 60 seats. Wheelchairs. Music. Parking.

Purslane
Cooking score: 2
Modern British | £35
33a St Stephen Street, Stockbridge, Edinburgh, EH3 5AH
Tel no: (0131) 2263500
purslanerestaurant.co.uk
£5 OFF

Well suited to Edinburgh's trendy Stockbridge district, chef/proprietor Paul Gunning's bijou basement restaurant is a surprisingly low-key setting for cooking that aims so high. Gunning used to work at Number One at the Balmoral Hotel (see entry), which informs his style, although prices are in line with the informality of a dining room that has close-packed tables and reclaimed wood-clad walls. Quail breast with maple glaze, sweetcorn mousse and cauliflower is a typical starter, while lamb rump with boulangère potatoes, artichokes, olive purée and red wine jus is a well-executed classic, as is fillet of hake with fennel and tomato compote, saffron potatoes, kale and romesco sauce. For dessert, consider chocolate and coffee parfait with smoked-milk ice cream or poached rhubarb, pistachio mousse, caramelised orange and orange sorbet. Wines start at £18 on a list that has plenty by the glass.

Chef/s: Paul Gunning. **Open:** Tue to Sun L and D. **Closed:** Mon, 25 and 26 Dec, 1 Jan. **Meals:** set L £15 (2 courses) to £18. Set D £30 (2 courses) to £35. Tasting menus £45 (5 courses) to £55. **Details:** 24 seats. Music. Children over 6 yrs only.

★ TOP 50 ★

Restaurant Martin Wishart

Cooking score: 7
Modern French | £85
54 The Shore, Leith, Edinburgh, EH6 6RA
Tel no: (0131) 5533557
martin-wishart.co.uk

You could be forgiven for mistaking Martin Wishart's for just another restaurant, but the understated exterior belies serious cooking (and pricing) from the man who has been operating at the top of his game for some 18 years. The flagship of four Wishart restaurants, and where it all started on a shoestring in 1991, has today a deservedly unrivalled reputation north of the border based on Wishart's Scottish take on what he describes as 'traditional and modern French cuisine'. There is an à la carte, but you may well be guided towards one of three six-course tasting menus: classic, fish or vegetarian. Good bread, clever amuse-bouches and a series of superb plates take diners from a ceviche of halibut, mango and passion fruit to a more involved plate of brown shrimps, buttermilk jelly, dill and horseradish or an impeccable rose veal tartare with wild mushrooms and white wine sauce. Along the way you might come by warm langoustine and oysters, marinated Orkney scallop or ravioli of snails. An additional cheese course showcases Scottish and French cheeses, a pre-dessert features pear and a silky salted caramel, finishing with a definitive chocolate mousse with coconut sorbet and fine petits fours. One reader criticised the service but our inspection visit found an easy charm in the front-of-house team while remaining attentive and professional. The sommelier oversees a substantial and quality wine list that starts at £29 and rises vertiginously.

Chef/s: Martin Wishart. **Open:** Tue to Sat L and D. **Closed:** Sun, Mon, 25 and 26 Dec, 3 weeks Jan. **Meals:** main courses £35. Set L £32 (3 courses). Set D £85 (4 courses). Tasting menu £85. **Details:** 50 seats. V menu. Wheelchairs. Music. Children over 7 yrs only.

Rhubarb at Prestonfield

Cooking score: 4
Modern British | £55
Prestonfield House, Priestfield Road,
Edinburgh, EH16 5UT
Tel no: (0131) 2251333
prestonfield.com

Nothing succeeds like excess in James Thomson's outrageously baroque restaurant at the 17th century Prestonfield House in the shadow of Arthur's Seat. From the peacocks on the lawn ('There's your main course,' quipped the taxi driver), to the kilted concierges, from the outrageous antler furniture in the Whisky Room to the gilded antiques and ancestral portraits of the Tapestry Room, Thomson's glorious extravagance extends across the public rooms to two glittering dining rooms lit by chandeliers and more candles than the Vatican. The table d'hôte offers decent value, with prices rising more steeply for the elaborate à la carte, offering the likes of beef carpaccio, asparagus with morels and truffle gnocchi, and reliable mains of lamb, turbot or sirloin steak with all the trimmings. The cheeseboard provides a selection of Scottish or Continental cheeses, while desserts are more pedestrian with chocolate brownie and ice cream and crème brûlée. Wines start at £24.

Chef/s: John McMahon. **Open:** all week L and D. **Meals:** main courses £18 to £40. Set L £20 (2 courses) to £25. Set D £36 (3 courses). **Details:** 120 seats. 40 seats outside. Wheelchairs. Music. Parking. No children after 7pm.

The Scran & Scallie

Cooking score: 2
Modern British | £30
1 Comely Bank Road, Edinburgh, EH4 1DT
Tel no: (0131) 3326281
scranandscallie.com

Sheepskins draped over tartan chairs, Scandi furnishings, Timorous Beasties wallpaper and a menu that touts 'yer starters' and 'oor specials': welcome to Scran & Scallie – an auld Scottish 'pub with dining', as envisioned by chefs Tom Kitchin and Dominic Jack (see entries for The Kitchin and Castle Terrace). 'From nature to plate' is the familiar mantra, and the concept is realised via a fuss-free mash-up of traditional 'scran' (Scottish dishes) and more up-to-date ideas ranging from leek and potato soup (with haggis and a fried egg, of course) to Orkney scallop with cauliflower and cured beef or chicken with roast pumpkin caponata. Pies and steaks play to the pubby theme, while 'yer puddins' might include chocolate fondant with buttermilk ice cream. 'Scallies' (aka children) have their own menu and a special 'corner', allowing grown-ups to explore a wine list pitched well above the Edinburgh pub norm; while you're at it, don't miss the Scottish beer flights.
Chef/s: James Chapman. **Open:** Mon to Fri L and D, Sat and Sun, all day from 12. **Closed:** 25 Dec. **Meals:** main courses £10 to £24. Set L £15 (Mon to Fri). **Details:** 75 seats. Bar. Wheelchairs. Music.

Taisteal

Cooking score: 2
International | £29
1-3 Raeburn Place, Edinburgh, EH4 1HU
Tel no: (0131) 3329977
taisteal.co.uk

Near the Water of Leith in Stockbridge, Taisteal, meaning 'travel' or 'journey' in Gaelic (and formerly Field Grill House), offers menus that meander like the river itself. Dishes juxtapose flavours and origins in a scrapbook of chef Gordon Craig's travels, ranging from the southern Mediterranean through Thailand, Indonesia or India. A starter of Singapore squid with squid-ink risotto sees dark Italianate rice pungent with Kaffir lime and ginger. Rabbit ballotine with silky wild garlic pesto and pillowy gnocchi is firmly rooted in European rusticity but tikka monkfish with lentils and masala sauce heads East again. Desserts offer further fusions as mango cream is matched with a tingling cardamom ice or white chocolate pannacotta with yuzu mousse. It's imaginative, although some combinations work better than others and technical delivery and service can vary. Cocktails and craft beers supplement a wine list less widely travelled than the menu itself.
Chef/s: Gordon Craig. **Open:** Tue to Sun L and D. **Closed:** Mon, 25 and 26 Dec. **Meals:** main courses £13 to £17. Set L and D £10 (2 courses). **Details:** 40 seats. Music.

Timberyard

Cooking score: 4
Modern British | £50
10 Lady Lawson Street, Edinburgh, EH3 9DS
Tel no: (0131) 2211222
timberyard.co

Foraging, butchery, curing, growing your own... this shabby-chic conversion of a Victorian warehouse ticks all the boxes as an urban eatery for our times. Run by five members of the Radford family, Timberyard is divided up into various beamed communal spaces, with warming stoves indoors and fire pits in the courtyard. Expert regional sourcing is a given, and Ben Radford's seasonal menus are loaded with bright modish flavours. Graze on plates of different sizes or trade up to one of the tasting menus; either way, expect lots of northern European nuances from duck egg with truffle, mushroom and smoked butter to turbot with clams, salsify, sea beet and artichoke. Elsewhere, pigeon is colourfully paired with elderberries, beetroot and chard, while a dessert of buttermilk, sea buckthorn and carrot is bang on-trend. Drinks play a major role here, from heady floral cocktails and small-batch beers to enterprising, eclectic wines with a strong 'natural' bias.

Chef/s: Ben Radford. **Open:** Tue to Sat L and D. **Closed:** Sun, Mon, 24 to 26 Dec, first week Jan, 1 week mid Apr, 1 week mid Oct. **Meals:** main courses £15 to £25. Set L £15 (2 courses) to £20. Tasting menu £55 (4 courses) to £75 (8 courses). **Details:** 65 seats. 30 seats outside. V menu. Bar. Wheelchairs. Music. Children over 12 yrs only at D.

21212

Cooking score: 5
Modern British | £70
3 Royal Terrace, Edinburgh, EH7 5AB
Tel no: (0131) 5231030
21212restaurant.co.uk

Given chef Paul Kitching's reputation for eclectic, even eccentric cooking, it might seem unexpected to find him holed up in an extravagantly decorated Victorian townhouse at one end of Edinburgh's longest terrace. For those who don't already know, 21212's moniker refers to the fact that lunchtime menus involve two starters, one soup, two mains, one cheese and two desserts – although dinner quickly moves into 31313 mode. It's all about breaking rules, challenging preconceptions and having fun as Kitching packs his plates with a carnival of components designed to baffle and surprise: the cryptically named '1 C x 7' comprises seven ingredients all beginning with the letter 'C', while 'fish and chops' incorporates creamed horseradish, olive, prawn, spinach and peanuts – you get the idea. The jokes also come thick and fast as the kitchen sends out desserts with names like 'spring forward' (rhubarb and ginger compote, sweetcorn, cashews and trifle). Kitching's flamboyant antics conceal a sound culinary intelligence, impressive technical ability and an astute eye for Instagrammable presentation. A serious list of eclectic wines offers ample opportunities by the glass.
Chef/s: Paul Kitching. **Open:** Tue to Sat L and D. **Closed:** Sun, Mon. **Meals:** set L Tue to Fri £28 (2 courses) to £55 (5 courses), Sat £32 to £55 (5 courses). Set D Tue to Fri £70 to £85 (5 courses), Sat £85 (5 courses). **Details:** 38 seats. Children over 5 yrs only.

Valvona & Crolla Caffè Bar

Cooking score: 3
Italian | £26
19 Elm Row, Edinburgh, EH7 4AA
Tel no: (0131) 5566066
valvonacrolla.co.uk
£5 OFF | £30

Striding confidently into its 22nd year, Mary Contini's deli-restaurant shows no sign of slowing down. For an Edinburgh institution (with a walk-on part in Alexander McCall Smith's *Scotland Street* novels), the modest deli-shop frontage looks nothing from the outside. But push open the door and walk past hams, cheeses, pasta and wine to the large, airy café at the back. Here you can kick-start your day with a full breakfast, delicious pastries and excellent coffee. Those who prefer to wait awhile can tuck into spicy Italian sausage with lentils and mashed potato; fritto misto; pizzas, maybe topped with buffalo mozzarella, roasted red peppers and red onion; or pasta, possibly orecchiette with broccoli, anchovies, garlic and extra-virgin olive oil – the list may be predictable, but it's all done well. Cap it all off with polenta, pistachio and almond cake served with crème fraîche and red berries. There's a compact all-Italian wine list (from £20) or you can buy a bottle from the deli and just pay £10 corkage.
Chef/s: Mary Contini. **Open:** Mon to Sat 8.30 to 5.30. Sun 10 to 4.30. **Closed:** 25 and 26 Dec, 1 and 2 Jan. **Meals:** main courses £13 to £16. Set L £16 (2 courses) to £20. **Details:** 60 seats. Music.

The Wee Restaurant

Cooking score: 3
Modern European | £36
61 Frederick Street, Edinburgh, EH2 1LH
Tel no: (0131) 2257983
theweerestaurant.co.uk
£5 OFF

Behind a plum-coloured exterior set in an imposing stone terrace in the New Town, the Woods' second Wee Restaurant (there's an original in North Queensferry – see entry, Fife) is a simple affair, with unclothed tables and brickwork washed in yellow and white. At the core of operations is a brasserie menu of French-inflected Scottish food, with Highland beef from the char-grill a strong draw. King scallops accompanied by boudin noir and celeriac rémoulade are very much *au courant*, while mains might deliver Perthshire lamb on pea and garlic risotto in red wine jus, or grilled sea bass in spring array with Jersey Royals, asparagus and rocket in hollandaise. Finish with tarte Tatin and Calvados ice cream, or a selection of Ian Mellis cheeses. The *menu du jour* offers exemplary value for dishes such as pork rillettes and cornichons, braised beef shin with mash, and île flottante in crème anglaise. Wines start at £20.75.

Chef/s: Michael Innes. **Open:** Tue to Sun L and D. **Closed:** Mon. **Meals:** main courses £21. Set L and D £16 (2 courses) to £20. **Details:** 38 seats. Music.

LOCAL GEM

Tanjore
Indian | £18
6-8 Clerk Street, Edinburgh, EH8 9HX
Tel no: (0131) 4786518
tanjore.co.uk

£30

Most Indian domestic kitchens are a woman's preserve – and so it is here, with owner Mrs Boon Ganeshram doing most of the work behind the scenes. Named after the historic city of Tanjore, this café-style eatery celebrates the Tamil cooking of the Subcontinent's southern provinces – so expect dosas and idli dumplings galore, alongside regional specialities ranging from spicy chicken fry to Keralan fish moilee, lamb biryani and potent 'karaikudi' fired up with Chettinad spices. Unlicensed, but you can BYOB or drink soothing lassi.

▍Gullane
La Potinière
Cooking score: 5
Modern British | £39
34 Main Street, Gullane, EH31 2AA
Tel no: (01620) 843214
lapotiniere.co.uk

This neat, one-room restaurant (with a hint of the house-proud living room) is run with well-honed proficiency by owners Mary Runciman and Keith Marley. The short, regularly changing menu is well judged, with just two choices at each course at both lunch and dinner. On our visit, starters were a velvety pea and asparagus soup and a delicate blue cheese mousse served with pickled plums and their own-grown salad leaves. A main of salmon, new potatoes, asparagus and mangetout was finished with a subtle orange and Pernod sauce, while the alternative of poached chicken and mustard mash was elevated by a confident assembly of mushroom, bacon and shallots. Don't arrive expecting rare or high-end ingredients, nor especially speedy service, but with excellent breads, intricate desserts and a thorough wine list starting at a very reasonable £19, La Potinière represents adept and effective cooking and honest value.

Chef/s: Mary Runciman and Keith Marley. **Open:** Wed to Sun L, Wed to Sat D. **Closed:** Mon, Tue, Jan, bank hols. **Meals:** set L £22 (2 courses) to £27. Set D £39 (3 courses) to £45. **Details:** 24 seats. Wheelchairs. Parking.

▌Annbank

Browne's

Cooking score: 4
Modern European | £42
Enterkine House Hotel, Annbank, KA6 5AL
Tel no: (01292) 520580
enterkine.com
£5 OFF ⊨

Built for a shipping magnate in the 1930s, and regally approached via a lengthy tree-lined drive through a 300-acre woodland estate, Enterkine House is a model of baronial splendour complete with lovely views over the river Ayr. Much of its reputation is down to the ambitious food served for dinner in the pine-floored restaurant, where chef Paul Moffat is well into his second decade; but his cooking has lost none of its zest or creativity – just consider Scottish langoustines with celery risotto, quail's egg and avocado oil or venison loin with cocoa, stout, gingerbread and red cabbage purée. European themes dominate, but there's also room for an exotic foray or two

– perhaps dashi-poached halibut with pak choi or caramel pannacotta with apple, rum, cinnamon and yuzu. Lunch is an altogether simpler affair. Wine recommendations are worth noting, and the full list is a well-travelled compendium.
Chef/s: Paul Moffat. **Open:** all week L and D.
Closed: 1 Jan. **Meals:** main courses L £9 to £16. Set D £42. **Details:** 40 seats. Wheelchairs. Parking.

▌Ballantrae

Glenapp Castle

Cooking score: 5
Modern British | £45
Ballantrae, KA26 0NZ
Tel no: (01465) 831212
glenappcastle.com
£5 OFF ⊨

Standing proud on a grassy hillock overlooking a lake, Glenapp Castle looks like something out of a Sir Walter Scott novel – all stone turrets, crenellations and castellated walls. Built for the Deputy Lord Lieutenant of

Ayrshire back in 1870, this magnificent grey-stone pile is now a country retreat riding high on baronial pomp – not least in the dramatic red-and-gold dining room with its rich-patterned carpets, floor-to-ceiling drapes and glittering chandeliers. By contrast, the food strikes a more contemporary note, although there's nothing to scare the horses in a daily line-up that might run from Ballantrae lobster bisque with saffron rouille to a soufflé made with blackcurrants from Glenapp's garden. In between, the kitchen melds French themes with Scottish ingredients – think grilled mackerel fillet with caviar, pickled beetroot and raspberry vinaigrette or roast cannon of Girvan lamb with a black pudding crust, pea purée and mint jus. As you might expect, Burgundy and Bordeaux lead the charge when it comes to the grand international wine list.

Chef/s: David Alexander and Tyron Ellul. **Open:** all week L and D. **Meals:** set L £40. Set D £45. Sun L £40. Tasting menu £65 (6 courses). **Details:** 40 seats. Wheelchairs. Parking. Children over 5 yrs only.

Dalry

Braidwoods

Cooking score: 5
Modern British | £48
Drumastle Mill Cottage, Dalry, KA24 4LN
Tel no: (01294) 833544
braidwoods.co.uk

Fashioned from two whitewashed mill cottages out in the Strathclyde sticks (but within striking distance of Glasgow), Nicola and Keith Braidwood's rugged country restaurant has been trundling along quietly for more than two decades – and shows no signs of waning. Nicola runs the modest 24-cover dining room with warmth and unobtrusive civility, while Keith's cooking melds incisive seasonal flavours with spot-on technique from the classic school of gastronomy. Pan-roast quail breast with confit leg and sweetcorn velouté or Arran Blue cheese pannacotta with a salad of roasted baby beetroot could open proceedings, before sturdy mains put the emphasis on big, deep flavours – from roast

Lanarkshire pork fillet and black pudding with Savoy cabbage and caper sauce to grilled North Sea halibut on crushed potatoes and courgettes with Arran mustard butter. It's also worth shelling out a supplement for the prime fillet of Cairnhill Farm beef. To conclude, a quintet of British artisan cheeses competes with desserts such as chilled caramelised rice pudding with poached William pears. The wine list is a well-balanced compendium gleaned from top growers worldwide.

Chef/s: Keith Braidwood. **Open:** Wed to Sun L, Tue to Sat D. **Closed:** Mon, 25 Dec to 31 Jan, first 2 weeks Sept. **Meals:** set L £28 (2 courses) to £32. Set D £48 (3 courses) to £52 (4 courses). Sun L £32. **Details:** 24 seats. Parking. Children over 5 yrs only at L and over 12 yrs only at D.

Glasgow

★ NEW ENTRY ★

Alchemilla

Cooking score: 3
Middle Eastern | £35
1126 Argyle Street, Glasgow, G3 8TD
Tel no: (0141) 3376060
thisisalchemilla.com

Alchemilla takes simple ingredients and lets them sing in a sparse but sociable space. Indeed, expectations of the comforts associated with fine dining could bring disappointment – this is about the food not the fittings. Imaginative flavours, uber-freshness and creativity are the stars at the unashamedly functional tables and stools surrounding the open kitchen. From the small-plate menu deliberately geared to epicurean grazing and sharing, you might be inspired by zesty octopus with blood orange and thyme or grilled ox heart with pomegranate and chilli. Lighter options include a palate-tingling salad of shaved kohlrabi, fennel, mint and tarragon or flavour-packed caramelised cauliflower with nutty tahini and pistachio. Homemade sourdough or granary mops up the juices. Just three desserts for the sweet finish but who can resist salted-chocolate torte or a perfect orange polenta cake? Cheery staff are as likely to be conjuring cocktails as advising on the short and quirky wine list.

Chef/s: Rosie Healey. **Open:** all week, all day from 12. **Meals:** small plates £7 to £13. **Details:** Bar.

Brian Maule at Chardon d'Or

Cooking score: 4
French | £51
176 West Regent Street, Glasgow, G2 4RL
Tel no: (0141) 2483801
brianmaule.com

Brian Maule's well-honed recipe of classical cuisine in formal style remains well attuned to the mix of celebrating families, smart dates, formal business types, cocktail quaffers and genteel lunchers that populate his white-linen tables. The cooking may not surprise or intrigue but with prime ingredients and refined Gallic technique, you're unlikely to be disappointed by what's on the plate. A chicken and sweetbread lasagne is a light but intensely flavoursome pasta morsel reposing on slow-cooked winter squash. Main courses showcase each lead ingredient with typically French focus on the protein. So assiette of pork is an homage to everything porcine; tender fillet, braised cheek and confit shoulder all set off by satisfyingly fat, salty lardons and crackling – just the merest smear of pomme purée and truffled jus to align the elements. The signature tarte Tatin with butterscotch sauce and creamy vanilla ice guarantees *entente cordiale* at the close. An unsurprisingly Old World wine list offers solid if predictable choice.

Chef/s: Brian Maule. **Open:** Tue to Sat L and D. **Closed:** Sun, Mon, 25 and 26 Dec, 1 and 2 Jan, bank hols. **Meals:** main courses £28 to £29. Set L £22 (2 courses) to £25. Tasting menu £60. **Details:** 150 seats. V menu. Bar. Music. No children after 6pm.

Cail Bruich

Cooking score: 6
Modern British | £40
725 Great Western Road, Glasgow, G12 8QX
Tel no: (0141) 3346265
cailbruich.co.uk

£5 OFF

Proof positive that eating out in Glasgow 'has very much improved', Cail Bruich puts on quite a show with its stylish copper lampshades, original art, polished floorboards and tweed-cushioned banquettes. It can feel a tad cramped in the dining room, but there are no complaints when it comes to Chris Charalambous' contemporary food – especially his impressively good-value tasting menus. Snacks of kohlrabi with smoked cheese and onion or crispy haggis with cabbage and spiced dates give way to a roster of plates full of complex nuances and unusual ideas: mackerel with creamy smoked cod's roe, celery, apple and lemon is a top pick, closely followed by stone bass with cauliflower, raisin, mussel and satay sauce. There's Perthshire venison and Goosnargh duck, too, plus some novel desserts such as warm artichoke cake with gorse flowers and vanilla ice cream or toasted-hay parfait with rhubarb and crème fraîche. To drink, cool aperitifs, sakés, malt whiskies and an impressive choice of world beers sit alongside a zesty assortment of keenly priced global wines.

Chef/s: Chris Charalambous. **Open:** Wed to Sat L, Mon to Sat D, Sun 1 to 7. **Closed:** 25 and 26 Dec, first week Jan. **Meals:** set L £20 (2 courses) to £25. Set D £30 (2 courses) to £40. Sun L £25. Tasting menu £45 (6 courses) to £55 (8 courses). **Details:** 42 seats. V menu. Music. Children over 5 yrs only.

Crabshakk

Cooking score: 2
Seafood | £35
1114 Argyle Street, Glasgow, G3 8TD
Tel no: (0141) 3346127
crabshakk.com

Launched in 2009 and still packing 'em in, this seafood specialist is true to its punning slogan. 'Cracking good food' is the order of the day, whether you're tackling a whole brown crab with the implements provided, slurping through a bowl of shellfish chowder or dissecting a whole grilled Scottish lobster. There are oysters on ice, 'wee' fish and chip suppers and plates of smoked fish, too, although it pays to investigate the specials board, which goes out of its way to offer something a bit more sophisticated every session – perhaps pan-fried black bream with romesco sauce, charred green onions, asparagus and salt-baked potatoes. It's fish all the way, apart from a token steak dish and a vegetarian risotto, while puddings and cheese are definitely an afterthought. Enjoy it all in a cramped setting of elbow-to-elbow tables, with an industrial steel staircase and a glass-clad bar dispensing gluggable fish-friendly wines.
Chef/s: David Scott. **Open:** all week, all day from 12. **Meals:** main courses £9 to £27. **Details:** 53 seats. 6 seats outside.

Eusebi Deli

Cooking score: 2
Italian | £21
152 Park Road, Glasgow, G4 9HB
Tel no: (0141) 6489999
eusebideli.com

A short stroll from Kelvingrove Park, Eusebi Deli is open all day, every day – once across the threshold, it's hard to tear yourself away. The family have been importing produce from Italy for over 40 years and whether you want something to eat in the park, to cook at home, or breakfast, lunch or dinner on the premises, it's all quality stuff. They buy well,

they cook well. Antipasti might include their own ricotta with I Ciacca Millefiori honey and toasted pagnotta, or octopus calabrese, while the cured meat selection is second to none. Pasta is made on the premises – beef agnolotti del plin, or squid-ink bavette with Scottish seafood – and pinsa (pizza) add further to its usefulness. Slow-cooked shoulder of mutton with salsa verde is a main course with serious flavours, and, among desserts, check out the ice creams or tiramisu. The wine list is 100 per cent Italian.
Chef/s: Sebastian Wereski. **Open:** all week, all day from 8am (9am Sun). **Closed:** 25 and 26 Dec, 1 to 3 Jan. **Meals:** main courses £10 to £22. Set L £14 (2 courses) to £17. **Details:** 74 seats. 16 seats outside. Wheelchairs. Music.

Gamba

Cooking score: 3
Seafood | £40
225a West George Street, Glasgow, G2 2ND
Tel no: (0141) 5720899
gamba.co.uk
£5 OFF

Briny-fresh sustainably sourced seafood is the lure at Derek Marshall's rock-solid fish restaurant – a sound bet in Glasgow's West End since 1998. Some find the atmosphere in this soft-toned basement-with-windows a touch drab, but there's nothing flat about the food on offer. Derek's exotic fish soup with crab, ginger and prawn dumplings has been a fixture since day one, but the menu generally reflects what the market can provide – perhaps sardines with sun-dried tomato, citrus and crème fraîche, lobster thermidor or Gigha halibut with king prawns, artichoke, bitter orange and leeks. The kitchen also brings on board lots of Asian influences, from Thai mussel stew or sashimi of yellowfin tuna to seared hand-dived scallops with lemon teriyaki dipping sauce. Meat fans are offered fillet of Scotch beef and veggies have barley risotto, while desserts run from hazelnut parfait to frozen chocolate and peanut-butter cake. Well-priced wines suit the food.

Join us at thegoodfoodguide.co.uk

Chef/s: Derek Marshall. **Open:** Mon to Sat L, all week D. **Closed:** 25 and 26 Dec, first week Jan. **Meals:** main courses £19 to £30. Set L and pre-theatre D £20 (2 courses) to £24. **Details:** 62 seats. Bar. Music.

The Gannet
Cooking score: 3
Modern British | £40
1155 Argyle Street, Glasgow, G3 8TB
Tel no: (0141) 2042081
thegannetgla.com
£5
OFF

A gritty urban conversion of a derelict tenement building in Glasgow's increasingly hip Finnieston district, this neighbourhood eatery looks totally on-trend with its rugged stonework, bare light bulbs, wooden planking and shiny metallic ducts snaking across the ceiling. Shades of brown dominate the interior – a modish backdrop for food that comes with lots of modern inflections. Scottish ingredients figure prominently, from Shetland squid served with confit chicken wings, ink and chicken juices or 'excellent' Perthshire partridge with caramelised onion, quail's egg and leaves to slow-cooked Borders lamb or Inverness roe deer accompanied by crisp potato, sweet-and-sour beetroot purée and heritage beets. To finish, salted-caramel fondant is a signature dessert, but readers also like the 'very moreish' Guinness ice cream presented on a café au lait biscuit base. Tapas-style small plates are also popular at lunchtime, while 'Champagne Sunday' deals come with a complimentary glass of bubbly from the serviceable wine list.
Chef/s: Ivan Stein and Peter McKenna. **Open:** Thur to Sat L, Tue to Sat D. Sun 1 to 7.30. **Closed:** Mon, 25 and 26 Dec, 1 and 2 Jan. **Meals:** main courses £16 to £23. Set L and early D £20 (2 courses) to £24. Sun L £30. **Details:** 55 seats. Bar. Wheelchairs. Music. Children before 8pm only.

111 by Nico
Cooking score: 2
Modern European | £22
111 Cleveden Road, Glasgow, G12 0JU
Tel no: (0141) 3340111
111bynico.co.uk
£5 £30
OFF

Taking a leaf out of Jamie Oliver's book, chef/proprietor Nico Simeone has set up an 'academy' to educate disadvantaged youngsters in the ways of the kitchen – not bad for a neighbourhood restaurant in suburban Glasgow. His chosen trainees have a hand in what reaches the tables at 111, and there's plenty of creativity on show – as well as a desire to offer unbeatable value. Nico's fixed-price menus always showcase Scottish ingredients, but inspiration is global: herb-crusted plaice might be teamed up with apple, lemongrass and kohlrabi, while grey mullet receives Mediterranean treatment with butternut squash, cavolo nero, anchovy and olives. Speyside beef shin is worth its supplement (especially when paired with celeriac, ox tongue and pommes Anna), and there are some lively ideas for vegetarians (wild mushrooms with goats' cheese, leeks, broccoli and walnuts, for example). To conclude, enjoy the drama of crème brûlée with coffee and flaming caramel. Well-priced wines, too.
Chef/s: Modou Diagme. **Open:** Thur and Fri L, Tue to Fri D. Sat and Sun, all day from 12. **Closed:** Mon. **Meals:** set L and D £19 (2 courses) to £22. Tasting menu £30 (5 courses). **Details:** 44 seats. Wheelchairs. Music. No children.

Stravaigin
Cooking score: 1
International | £32
28 Gibson Street, Glasgow, G12 8NX
Tel no: (0141) 3342665
stravaigin.co.uk

A beamed room with rough stone walls and a design of meat cleavers is the setting for an appealing modern bistro that begins with prime Scottish ingredients but brings its global imagination to bear. Confidence in combining produces lively assemblages such as pan-roast cod and crispy chicken wing with golden beetroot and Jerusalem artichoke, then roast duck breast with confit leg pastilla accompanied by puffed wild rice, orange and five-spice chicory, and Korean-style ssamjang cashew spice paste. Ingredients keep on coming in desserts, too, perhaps white chocolate mousse with toffee popcorn, yoghurt sorbet and caramelised banana. A slate of Scottish gins shows time hasn't stood still. Wines start at £18.45.

Chef/s: Nathan Kidney. **Open:** all week, all day from 10 (11 Sat and Sun). **Closed:** 25 Dec, 1 Jan. **Meals:** main courses £16 to £27. Set L £14 (2 courses). Set D £16 (2 courses) to £19. **Details:** 120 seats. 10 seats outside. Bar. Wheelchairs. Music.

★ NEW ENTRY ★

Turnip & Enjoy

Cooking score: 2
International | £28
393-395 Great Western Road, Glasgow, G4 9HY
Tel no: (0141) 3346622
turnipandenjoy.co.uk
£30

Its shopfront setting on Great Western Road may feel somewhat understated but the ambition and flavour emanating from Turnip & Enjoy's tiny kitchen provide colour and character aplenty. Favouring hearty ingredients and bold taste combinations, a lightness of touch is nonetheless evident when needed. A starter of blackened mackerel and crab is well matched with fresh orange and fennel – bergamot gel and a fennel pollen muffin accenting the high notes. The generous main of corn-fed chicken with punchy homemade venison haggis arrives on a silky artichoke purée with truffle jus adding further depth. For dessert, chervil root and toffee apple breathe new life into a very untraditional but delicious cheesecake. Wines cover the normal territories and the five-course tasting menu offers an accessible overview of the chef's abilities. Atmosphere and temperature

may prove a little cool at quiet times, although during busier sessions the limited cooking space can impact service and consistency.

Chef/s: Martin Connor. **Open:** Tue to Sun L and D. **Closed:** Mon. **Meals:** main courses Fri and Sat D only £14 to £24. Set L £15 (2 courses) to £19. Early D Fri and Sat and Set D Tue to Thur and Sun £19 (2 courses) to £22. **Details:** 40 seats.

Ubiquitous Chip

Cooking score: 5
Modern British | £40
12 Ashton Lane, Glasgow, G12 8SJ
Tel no: (0141) 3345007
ubiquitouschip.co.uk

'Evergreen' is an appropriate descriptor for this Glasgow institution known simply by locals as 'The Chip'. While the lush foliage festooning the indoor courtyard is a contributory factor, it is their ability to keep food, flavours and atmosphere enduringly fresh and relevant that really earns the epithet. Under the careful stewardship of the Clydesdale family since 1971, they've pulled off the trick of subtly reinventing without losing authenticity or core values. Their confident interpretation of modern Scottish cuisine is proudly seasonal, showcasing trusted local suppliers and available as a brasserie or full restaurant experience. A duck ham and liver parfait starter is creatively paired with dehydrated ginger cake and pickled cherries in an explosive mouth sensation of bitter, sweet, crunch and cream. Plump cod loin luxuriates in its truffle and hazelnut crust on a satisfyingly earthy artichoke, barley and brown-butter bed. Simple-sounding desserts such as peanut-butter parfait with raspberry sorbet offer mini adventures in texture and technique combining into memorable wholes. Wine and whisky enthusiasts can't fail to be tempted by the extensive offerings.

Chef/s: Andrew Mitchell. **Open:** all week L and D. **Closed:** 25 Dec, 1 Jan. **Meals:** main courses £16 to £35. Set L and early D £17 (2 courses) to £22. Sun L £22. **Details:** 115 seats. 20 seats outside. V menu. Bar. Wheelchairs.

LOCAL GEM

The Finnieston
Seafood | £32
1125 Argyle Street, Glasgow, G3 8ND
Tel no: (0141) 2222884
thefinniestonbar.com

£5
OFF

With exposed brick, low ceilings and wood floors, this casual seafood restaurant has held on to the character of the old pub it once was and is 'a great place to stumble across'. According to regulars 'as much effort and emphasis is put into the cocktails and the bustling bar area as the food', which explains the lively buzz and the pressure on tables. Braised octopus with squid-ink emulsion could precede sea trout with langoustine bisque and barley risotto, peas, broad beans and herbs. Most of the brief but wide-ranging wine list comes by the glass, carafe or bottle.

LOCAL GEM

Number 16
Modern British | £30
16 Byres Road, Glasgow, G11 5JY
Tel no: (0141) 3392544
number16.co.uk

£5
OFF

Small is definitely beautiful in this exceptionally wee mid-terrace restaurant, where the cosy atmosphere and concise menu combine with a big personality to compensate for the lack of size. Scottish ingredients are very much in evidence but influences come from far and wide: witness smoked duck with pickled kohlrabi, watercress, baby radish and wasabi mayonnaise; and roast chicken with pomme purée, braised red cabbage, heritage carrots and red wine jus. To finish, maybe a coconut popsicle with Malibu pipette and pineapple. Wine prices and choices are pleasantly accessible.

LOCAL GEM

Ox and Finch
International | £30
920 Sauchiehall Street, Glasgow, G3 7TF
Tel no: (0141) 3398627
oxandfinch.com

Popular as ever, with its bare brickwork, upcycled materials, open kitchen and the small sharing plates concept ticking all the right contemporary boxes, this informal, sociable venue satisfies a local, group-grazing crowd. The kitchen takes a globetrotting approach, offering grilled prawns with saffron dhal, pickled cucumber and tandoori yoghurt, as well as slow-cooked pork belly served alongside smoked polenta, capers and golden raisins. As for dessert, pineapple carpaccio served with coconut ice cream, tarragon and lime is no less creative. Wines from £17.75.

LOCAL GEM

Porter & Rye
British | £40
1131 Argyle Street, Glasgow, G8 8ND
Tel no: (0141) 5721212
porterandrye.com

Gaindykehead Farm in Airdrie supplies the beef that forms the backbone of the menu at Porter & Rye, with the meat dry-aged in the restaurant to maximise the flavour of the steaks – 10oz onglet, say, or 28oz porterhouse for two to share. Toppings include garlic king prawns, sides might be black garlic mash, while starters such as confit Bute sea trout are on the creative side. It all takes place in an effervescent contemporary space, with cocktails and a late-night menu.

Helensburgh

★ NEW ENTRY ★

Sugar Boat

Cooking score: 2
Modern British | £28
30 Colquhoun Square, Helensburgh,
G84 8AQ
Tel no: (01436) 647522
sugarboat.co.uk

£30

Sugar Boat opened in May 2017 on Helensburgh's refurbished Colquhoun Square, just a cormorant's flight from the 1974 Clyde wreck after which it's named. With its all-day bar/bistro approach, the menu is reminiscent of owner Will Smith's previous Arbutus and Wild Honey establishments in London. Diminutive dishes can be combined for small-plate sharing or built into a more structured meal offering relatively uncomplicated but flavour-filled treatments of prime ingredients. Openers might include hearty hand-cut pappardelle with a light mustard and shredded rabbit sauce, perhaps followed by a perfectly grilled 'butcher's cut' steak with beef-dripping boulangère potatoes laced with confit shin. Side dishes such as grilled Little Gem with 'nduja spicy pork are welcome additions to the core offering. Warm cherry clafoutis or a more local fruit-laden Ecclefechan tart ensure a sweet finish. The eclectic and imaginative wine selection grouped (largely) by varietal starts from a very affordable £15.
Chef/s: Scott Smith. **Open:** all week L and D.
Meals: main courses £11 to £17. **Details:** Bar.

Symbols

◖━━━

🛏 Accommodation is available
£30 Three courses for less than £30
£5 OFF £5-off voucher scheme
🍾 Notable wine list

Isle of Colonsay

LOCAL GEM

The Colonsay

Modern British | £28
Scalasaig, Isle of Colonsay, PA61 7YT
Tel no: (01951) 200316
colonsayestate.co.uk

🛏 £30

This white-fronted hotel dates from the mid-18th century and stands proud above the pier and harbour. It offers views across to Jura and Scarba and is a welcome redoubt on such a remote island. In the dining room the obvious choices are Colonsay oysters, fresh fish such as halibut with leek mash and herb cream, garden-grown salad leaves, and honey ice cream (made with local honey), but there's also navarin-style lamb shank and Angus beef burger if you are not in the mood for fish. There are Scottish cheeses, too, and wines from £14.

Isle of Mull
Café Fish

Cooking score: 3
Seafood | £33
The Pier, Main Street, Tobermory, Isle of Mull,
PA75 6NU
Tel no: (01688) 301253
thecafefish.com

£5 OFF

'I'd had a fabulous day of seaborne wildlife, so came here for more,' quipped one visitor following a memorable trip to Café Fish. Perched atop the old CalMac ferry building overlooking Tobermory harbour, this is a fiercely independent set-up delivering 'knock 'em dead stuff' with the emphasis firmly on quality and freshness – you can even watch the catch being landed if you're lucky. The owners have their own boat, hence much of the menu depends on the weather and the haul – check out the daily specials to see what's on. Traditionalists can have their chosen fish simply grilled, while glistening shellfish platters are great for sharing; otherwise, tackle a bowl of moules marinière ahead of haddock mornay or seared Mull scallops with pomegranate, ginger and raspberry glaze. Glengorm steaks, Moroccan-spiced chicken and superfood salads swim against the tide, while creamy puddings might include pavlova or chocolate sundae. Wines from £18.50. **Chef/s:** Liz McGougan. **Open:** all week L and D. **Closed:** 28 Oct to 17 Mar. **Meals:** main courses £12 to £26. **Details:** 38 seats. 62 seats outside. Music. Parking. No children under 5 yrs at D.

Ninth Wave

Cooking score: 4
Modern British | £56
Bruach Mhor, Fionnphort, Isle of Mull, PA66 6BL
Tel no: (01681) 700757
ninthwaverestaurant.co.uk

When it comes to getting away from it all, Carla Lamont's restaurant is truly far away from the hubbub of modern life, on the south-western tip of the Isle of Mull. The former bothy has been sensitively extended and fits seamlessly into the landscape, from whence Carla gets most of the ingredients that feature on the menu. The kitchen garden plays its part, as do local farms and local waters. Carla is Canadian and has a passion for Asian ingredients, growing wasabi and Kaffir lime in the garden, thus Inverlussa mussels and clams arrive in a coconut and ginger broth, with tamarind gel and braised daikon, and local pork loin is served with pork and prawn won tons and a spicy vinaigrette. The combination of local and Asian flavours is beautifully handled. Among sweet courses, green-tea and chocolate torte with green-tea pannacotta, chocolate glaçage and green-tea shortbread reveals the confidence and skill in the kitchen. The wine list has excellent organic and biodynamic options.
Chef/s: Carla Lamont. **Open:** Wed to Sun D only. Seasonal openings apply, please check website. **Closed:** Mon, Tue, winter. **Meals:** set D £48 (3 courses) to £68 (6 courses). **Details:** 18 seats. Wheelchairs. Parking. Children over 12 yrs only.

▌Kilberry
The Kilberry Inn

Cooking score: 3
Modern British | £38
Kilberry Road, Kilberry, PA29 6YD
Tel no: (01880) 770223
kilberryinn.com
£5 OFF 🛏

'Not easy to get to but worth the effort' is the considered opinion of one who braved the miles of single-track road and came away impressed that in such a remote location 'good produce and service are consistently on offer'. The modesty of Clare Johnson and David Wilson's low-slung whitewashed cottage with its red tin roof – think beams, exposed stone, a log fire – is matched by a deliberately simple cooking style that is spare yet elegant, with flavours that ring true. Shellfish, for example, is 'incredibly fresh and of premium quality', with Loch Fyne langoustine simply grilled with saffron and black olive butter, or hand-dived king scallops served with celeriac purée and a saffron vinaigrette, while roast rack of Tayvallich Blackface lamb, teamed with braised lettuce and fondant potatoes, offers unimpeachable local meat. Puddings mix the stalwart tradition of sticky toffee pudding with a more modern olive oil cake, poached pear and blackberry sorbet. Interesting wines reflect David Wilson's personal interest and explorations, opening with an Australian Chardonnay (£22) and a Pays d'Oc Pinot Noir (£23).
Chef/s: Clare Johnson. **Open:** Fri to Sun L, Tue to Sun D. **Closed:** Mon, 1 Jan to mid Mar. **Meals:** main courses £16 to £24. **Details:** 26 seats. 12 seats outside. Music. Parking.

Visit us online

To find out more about
The Good Food Guide, please
visit thegoodfoodguide.co.uk

■ Kilchrenan

READERS RECOMMEND
Kilchrenan Inn
British
Kilchrenan, PA35 1HD
Tel no: (01866) 833130
kilchrenaninn.co.uk
'We ate here on a Friday evening and were both extremely surprised by how busy the restaurant was in December given it is very much off the beaten track. There is a lovely wood-burning stove in the bar. The menu is relatively small but all dishes were delicious. I had their own smoked mackerel to start and then pheasant pie, which had come from the local shoot. My husband had a Scotch egg to start and then oxtail and clapshot.'

■ Kilmarnock

LOCAL GEM
Titchfield's
International | £22
6-10 Titchfield Street, Kilmarnock, KA1 1PH
Tel no: (01563) 530100
titchfields.co.uk

£5 OFF £30

A ray of sunshine in an otherwise rather uninspiring shopping centre, Titchfield's delivers easy bistro charm with menus running from breakfast to dinner. The style is broadly European, with small plates offered alongside hearty dishes such as a burger made with aged short rib beef. Other options include bruschetta of seasonal Scottish foraged mushrooms, Ayrshire lamb, grilled and slow-cooked, with local vegetables and lamb sauce, and a 'clootie' doughnut with cloutie dumpling, toffee sauce and ice cream. All wines are available by the glass.

■ Loch Lomond

Martin Wishart at Loch Lomond
Cooking score: 6
Modern French | £75
Cameron House on Loch Lomond, Loch Lomond, G83 8QZ
Tel no: (01389) 722504
martinwishartlochlomond.co.uk

If Martin Wishart's acclaimed Edinburgh restaurant (see entry) gives off the air of a suave, expensively garbed man about town, his country outpost by the bonnie banks of Loch Lomond has more of a country vibe – without resorting to Brigadoon clichés. Ravishing views are a given here, but there's as much to admire in the light, airy dining room, with its eye-catching designer detailing, lime green chairs and chocolate leather seats with zebra-striped backs. Wishart's deputy Graeme Cheevers cooks with real poise, applying pin-sharp modern French technique to scrupulously sourced seasonal Scottish ingredients – in line with his mentor's culinary ethos. Tasting menus show off the kitchen's full repertoire, opening perhaps with citrus-marinated sea bream, quinoa, avocado and ponzu. After that, lemon sole with Brussels sprouts, parsnip cream and vermouth cappuccino is a textbook pairing, likewise BBQ onglet of Black Angus beef accompanied by celeriac, bone marrow and caramelised onion. Intricate desserts such as chestnut parfait and Cox apple mousse with apple caramel and cinnamon ice cream are also designed to highlight the kitchen's masterly skills. Wines from France and Europe dominate the serious-minded wine list.
Chef/s: Graeme Cheevers. **Open:** Sat and Sun L, Wed to Sun D. **Closed:** Mon, Tue, 25 and 26 Dec, first 2 weeks Jan. **Meals:** set L £32. Set D £75. Tasting menu £80 (6 courses) to £95 (8 courses). **Details:** 42 seats. V menu. Wheelchairs. Music. Parking.

▋Oban
Ee-Usk
Cooking score: 1
Seafood | £28
North Pier, Oban, PA34 5QD
Tel no: (01631) 565666
eeusk.com
£30

Oban is synonymous with fish, and this modern eatery overlooking the harbour not only scores with its supremely fresh seafood but also has cracking views of the Argyll coast to boot. Against a backdrop of glass and steel, visitors can enjoy everything from plates of Loch Creran oysters *au naturel* or whole dressed crab to old-school favourites such as salmon and prawn mornay, battered haddock or sea bass with creamed leeks and savoury mash. 'Grand' seafood platters are spot-on for two to share, while desserts continue the traditional theme with lemon cheesecake or sticky toffee pudding. Wines from £16.50.
Chef/s: David Kariuki. **Open:** all week L and D.
Closed: 25 and 26 Dec, 1 Jan, 3 weeks Jan.
Meals: main courses £13 to £30. Set L and D £15 (2 courses) to £18. **Details:** 100 seats. 20 seats outside. Wheelchairs. Music. Children over 12 yrs only at D.

▋Strachur
Inver
Cooking score: 6
British | £35
Strathlachlan, Strachur, PA27 8BU
Tel no: (01369) 860537
inverrestaurant.co.uk
🛏

Plumb on the shores of Loch Fyne, where ospreys fish the bay and a pair of castles looms in the middle distance, Pamela Brunton and Rob Latimer's restaurant is housed in an 18th-century ferryman's cottage with adjacent boatshed. The supreme tranquillity of the place is enhanced by a dining room that keeps things spare and clean, with unclothed pale-wood tables and loch views to conjure with. Pamela's kitchen works in harmony with what the environs have to offer, offering ingredients that may be surprising and new to city diners. Fried beef tendon or cod's roe tart might kick off the fixed-price menu, as curtain-raisers to fine Isle of Bute lamb with leeks both young and mature, gentled with ewes' milk yoghurt, in a medium of soured barley broth, or there could be mackerel, its bracing freshness underscored by mussels and nettles. The vegetarian option might see yeast and kelp added to a central composition of potatoes and egg yolk, while desserts beguile the senses with bergamot-scented chocolate and chestnut dacquoise, or parsnip ice cream with clementine jelly. A tiny wine list does its resourceful best to step up to the plate, from £17.50.
Chef/s: Pamela Brunton. **Open:** Wed to Sun L and D. **Closed:** Mon, Tue, Wed and Sun D (off-season), 3 Jan to mid Mar. **Meals:** main courses £11 to £26. Set D £45 (4 courses). **Details:** 40 seats. 18 seats outside. V menu. Bar. Music. Parking.

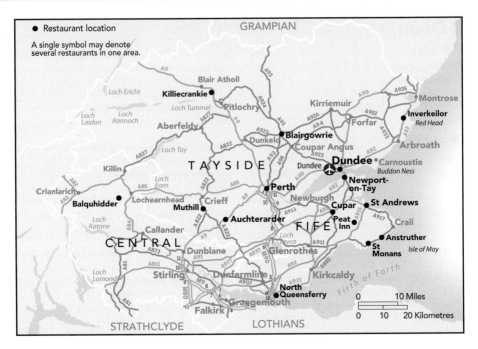

Balquhidder
Monachyle Mhor
Cooking score: 5
Modern British | £65
Balquhidder, FK19 8PQ
Tel no: (01877) 384622
mhor.net

Monachyle is an architecturally fascinating Jacobite safe house that weathered the unsafest of times gone by to become the present-day centrepiece of the Lewises' farmstead. Overlooking a brace of lochs at the end of a long single-track road, it's a beautiful spot for an exercise in near self-sufficiency, with beef, lamb, pork and venison supplied from the estate, hens laying eggs for breakfast and the kitchen garden turning out vegetables, saladings and herbs in plenty. The cooking has plenty of voguish dash too, for dishes such as Scrabster monkfish with braised fennel, parsnip, smoked lardo and Parmesan, or home-reared Tamworth pork with apple, kale,

charred leek and sage. At main, Monachyle's own Blackface lamb turns up in Med-inspired guise with pearl barley, chorizo, confit tomato, black olives and capers, or there could be incomparable Gigha halibut with a harvest home of salsify, swede and cavolo nero, scented with tarragon. Rose petals and rhubarb in Prosecco are the fragrant garnishes for a dessert of coconut and white chocolate mousse, or go for unpasteurised cheeses with homemade oatcakes and chutney. A wine list of great authority and reach opens at £24.
Chef/s: Marysia Paszkowska. **Open:** all week L and D. **Closed:** 8 to 24 Jan. **Meals:** set L £24 (2 courses) to £30. Set D £65. Sun L £34. **Details:** 42 seats. 16 seats outside. V menu. Bar. Wheelchairs. Music. Parking.

Visit us online

To find out more about
The Good Food Guide, please
visit thegoodfoodguide.co.uk

Deliciously Scottish

Unsurprisingly, Scotland's food specialities reflect its geography, climate and culture.

Today we're spoiled for choice with Scottish ingredients. Most of the UK's seafood catch is landed along Caledonia's coastline. Alongside haddock, halibut and herring, two thirds of the world's langoustines and a growing culinary seaweed range come from Scotland.

Prime meats include beef, wild venison, hare, feathered game and succulent borders lamb - not forgetting, of course, that wee haggis beastie. The Vikings popularised 'salting' and 'smoking' - still evident with salmon and dishes such as Shetland reestit mutton.

Crops, too, are important; oats for porridge, obviously, but also the ever popular oatcakes and pinhead oatmeal. The mild summers of the eastern shires are perfect for berries - the native tayberry engendering oat/berry desserts such as cranachan.

The Scots' sweet tooth is not just a stereotype. Hearty bakery goods like clootie dumpling and fruit-laden Selkirk bannock sit alongside the ubiquitous shortbread and tooth-aching treats like tablet or Irn Bru. Wash it all down with a dram? Thirty-eight bottles of whisky are exported every second.

LOCAL GEM

Mhor 84

Modern British | £30
Balquhidder, FK19 8NY
Tel no: (01877) 384646
mhor.net

While this offshoot of Monachyle Mhor (see entry) may seem thrown together with artistic exuberance, the approach is actually very well thought out. The cooking adds touches of luxury to largely familiar dishes (steak with chips) and majors on the quality of the raw materials – drawn invariably from the Lewis family's own farm, bakery and fish shop. Flexibility is key: smart enough for a celebration meal, while families can enjoy a casual lunch. Creamy Loch Creran oysters or aromatic Gressingham duck with hoisin sauce and pancakes precede cod with chorizo and cannellini bean stew, and rhubarb and ginger cheescake. Wines from £19.50.

▌Anstruther
The Cellar

Cooking score: 6
Modern British | £60
24 East Green, Anstruther, KY10 3AA
Tel no: (01333) 310378
thecellaranstruther.co.uk

The ancient stone walls and gnarled beams could tell a tale or two of the venue's previous lives as cooperage and smokehouse, but the focus has been firmly gastronomic in recent generations. Billy Boyter's acquisition of the old Cellar in 2014 kept the place in local hands, and his modern Scottish approach has given the seasonal, regionally bolstered menus renewed impetus. Seafood remains a strong point, from a serving of smoked haddock with a cured egg yolk to local crab with spiced tomato and smoked onion jelly, to a majestic main course of hake and mussels with leeks and sea kale in brown-butter foam. Meatier offerings also make bold statements, as when a winter serving of truffled beef cheek in Anster cheese crops up in second place on the tasting menu, or the main-course option is Black Isle hogget with January King cabbage, kohlrabi and yoghurt. Scottish cheeses with beetroot and orange chutney are hard to resist, unless you're waylaid by a fashionable fruit-and-veg assembly of Jerusalem artichoke ice cream and calamansi with chocolate cream and hazelnuts. An international miscellany of dependable wines opens at £18.
Chef/s: Billy Boyter. **Open:** Thur to Sun L, Wed to Sun D. **Closed:** Mon, Tue, 24 to 26 Dec, 3 weeks Jan, 1 week May, 10 days Sept. **Meals:** set L £35 (5 courses). Set D £60 (7 courses). **Details:** 28 seats. Bar. Music. Children over 12 yrs only.

▌Cupar
Ostlers Close

Cooking score: 4
Modern British | £43
25 Bonnygate, Cupar, KY15 4BU
Tel no: (01334) 655574
ostlersclose.co.uk

For 33 years Jimmy and Amanda Graham have been nourishing and nurturing visitors to their cosy restaurant off Cupar's main street. Their dedicated approach to local Scottish seasonality extends to harvesting their own kitchen garden and foraging wild mushrooms. A regularly changing and personalised menu might feature a home-grown beetroot tarte Tatin with celeriac rémoulade and goats' cheese and honey ice cream. Main courses showcase long-standing, trusted suppliers, so a generous selection of perfectly cooked cuts of turbot, hake, halibut, monkfish and scallop celebrating Scotland's coastline sits delicately with boulangère potatoes, summer vegetables individually matched to fish and a light saffron sauce. A creamy buttermilk pannacotta with Earl Grey syrup is balanced by the more playful tartness of garden rhubarb and sweet cicely. With notification a bespoke vegetarian menu offers uncommon choice. Their thoughtful wine list demonstrates personal insight with better than average non-alcoholic choices recognising its drive-to location for many.
Chef/s: Jimmy Graham. **Open:** Tue to Sat D only. **Closed:** Sun, Mon, 25 and 26 Dec, 2 weeks Jan. **Meals:** main courses £24 to £28. **Details:** 26 seats. V menu. Children over 6 yrs only.

Newport-on-Tay

★ NEW ENTRY ★

The Newport

Cooking score: 4
Modern British | £50
1 High Street, Newport-on-Tay, DD6 8AB
Tel no: (01382) 541449
thenewportrestaurant.co.uk

Chef/patron Jamie Scott won *MasterChef: The Professionals* in 2014 and two years later introduced his imaginative take on local and foraged ingredients to the newly refurbished Newport. Offering panoramic views over the Tay, the glazed frontage of his airy restaurant creates an indoor-outdoor atmosphere 'with sunsets to die for'. The small-plates menu – starting with 'nibbles' and then categorised simply as 'land', 'sea', 'ground' and 'garden' – is designed for sharing and grazing, with diners impressed by 'the use of unusual ingredients'. Crispy cod cheeks or a delicate pig's head and langoustine dumpling are tempting precursors to sweet buttery hake with dulse and alexanders, or tiny local Pittormie artichokes with sheep's milk, peas and barley. Tender mutton loin comes with wild garlic and crisped-up belly, while buttermilk chicken with apple is genuinely finger-licking good. Desserts are no less impressive; a rhubarb soufflé with ground ivy and clove custard is a scene-stealer.
Chef/s: Jamie Scott. **Open:** Wed to Sun L, Tue to Sat D. **Closed:** Mon, 25 and 26 Dec, 1 to 14 Jan. **Meals:** small plates £6 to £14. Sun L £30. Tasting menu £45 (5 courses) to £65. **Details:** 54 seats. 12 seats outside. V menu. Bar. Music. Parking.

North Queensferry

The Wee Restaurant

Cooking score: 3
Modern European | £36
17 Main Street, North Queensferry, KY11 1JG
Tel no: (01383) 616263
theweerestaurant.co.uk
£5 OFF

Although they've branched out with a second Wee Restaurant in Edinburgh (see entry), Craig and Vikki Wood's original neighbourhood eatery is still wowing the crowds. Hidden beneath the Forth Bridge in a stone-clad building with a chequered history (jail, ironmonger's, post office), this place packs a lot of energy and conviviality into a relatively confined space – with the added incentive of assured bistro-style cooking at highly competitive prices. Craig's thoughtfully rendered food is shot through with bourgeois French influences, although he takes his cues from Scottish produce: Aberdeen smoked haddock and saffron soup is embellished with Puy lentils and parsley oil, while roast hake is presented with white bean cassoulet, chorizo, fennel, morcilla and octopus tempura. Meat eaters have braised ox cheek or slabs of seriously aged Black Isle beef with gratin dauphinois and Café de Paris butter, ahead of Gallic-themed desserts such as warm rhubarb frangipane tart. Drink from a list of well-chosen, food-friendly wines.
Chef/s: Craig Wood. **Open:** Tue to Sun L, Tue to Sat D. **Closed:** Mon. **Meals:** set L £16 (2 courses) to £20. Set D £29 (2 courses) to £36. Sun L £23. **Details:** 38 seats. Music.

▌Peat Inn

★ TOP 50 ★

The Peat Inn
Cooking score: 8
Modern British | £50
Peat Inn, KY15 5LH
Tel no: (01334) 840206
thepeatinn.co.uk
£5 OFF 🍷 🛏

The Inn has stood here in one incarnation or another since the mid-18th century, and is of sufficient local note for its surrounding village community, which accreted gradually around it, to be named after it, rather than the habitual reverse. Hospitality has been the name of its game since Georgian coach horses clopped exhaustedly up, and in the Smeddles, it has the best of latter-day custodians, tending the place in finest country-house style. That means an amicable approach in the elegantly reappointed dining room, and an enterprising kitchen headed up by Geoffrey Smeddle, dedicated to shining the spotlight on thoroughbred Scottish produce. An autumn visit began in delicate but seductive style with sea bream tartare, garnished with lobster, textured cauliflower and dill crème fraîche, and led on to roast fillet and confit pork with black pudding, its accompaniments – smoked potato mousseline, young carrots, Savoy cabbage and poached apple – in flawless balance. Pedigree meats have included 60-day dry-aged beef rump, Cairngorm roe deer and Clackmannanshire duck, while fish could be beautifully textured wild turbot with salsify gratin, romanesco and onion velouté. Old-fangled technical skills always inspire confidence, so a perfectly airborne mirabelle plum soufflé with Armagnac-laced custard is a delectation, but so too is a délice of Scottish artisan dark chocolate (yes, Scottish, from 'bean to bar') with pear mousse, chocolate crackling and pear sorbet. A splendidly discerning wine list, arranged regionally, opens with fine wines by the small glass, beginning with Henri Bourgeois Sancerre at £9.50. Bottles go from £26.

Chef/s: Geoffrey Smeddle. **Open:** Tue to Sat L and D. **Closed:** Sun, Mon, 25 and 26 Dec, 1 to 4 Jan. **Meals:** main courses L £16 to £23, D £23 to £30. Set L £22. Set D £50. Tasting menu L £45 (4 courses), D £70 (6 courses). **Details:** 50 seats. V menu. Bar. Wheelchairs. Music. Parking. Children over 7 yrs only at D.

▌St Andrews

The Seafood Ristorante
Cooking score: 3
Seafood | £50
The Scores, Bruce Embankment, St Andrews, KY16 9AB
Tel no: (01334) 479475
theseafoodristorante.com
£5 OFF 🍷

A slight tweak to the name hints at change since our last edition (in ownership and chef). But that's all. Snagging a window table in this modernist glass cube still delivers spectacular views of nesting fulmars, the famous West Sands and the incoming tide beneath you (literally). The open kitchen and informed, well-measured servers continue to offer an informal backdrop to the real stars: fresh local seafood and the incomparable vista. This is all about the simple joy of being by the sea and eating what comes out of it – minimal intervention and maximum flavour. A starter of smoked haddock rarebit adds a maritime twist to the holy trinity of bacon, allium and cheese. Sweetly flavoured St Andrews Bay lobster needs no adornment beyond a guilty drizzle of garlicky butter, while crisp-skinned hake has an imaginative winter pairing of chestnut and pumpkin. Desserts offer greater complexity with a ginger pannacotta, new-season rhubarb and blood orange bringing a compelling play of sprightly tastes and textures. The wine list is a pleasurable browse offering an interesting selection by the glass, and an extensive range of quality classics by the bottle, as well as some interesting alternatives, all brought together by an enthusiastic and knowledgeable sommelier.

Chef/s: David Aspin. **Open:** all week L and D. **Closed:** 25 Dec, 1 Jan, 7 to 14 Jan. **Meals:** main courses £21 to £30. Set L £18 (2 courses). **Details:** 66 seats. 28 seats outside. V menu. Wheelchairs. Music.

▮ St Monans
Craig Millar at 16 West End
Cooking score: 3
Modern British | £45
16 West End, St Monans, KY10 2BX
Tel no: (01333) 730327
16westend.com
£5
OFF

This refurbished harbourfront restaurant provides a surprisingly spacious and elegant enclave among the jumble of winding streets and diminutive fishing cottages of the traditional East Neuk village of St Monans. Expansive picture windows and a summer terrace afford sublime views over the same briny waters that offer primary ingredients and inspiration. Craig Millar's cooking shows constancy, with a regular recipe roster that may include a visually striking squid-ink risotto with scallops and black pudding or prime cod loin with a powerful chorizo, butter-bean and goats' cheese stew. A lighter touch is displayed in a delicate pea mousse – the sweetness well balanced by pickled mushrooms and salty Parmesan crisps. Chocolate crémeux with malt ice cream and salted caramel is a fittingly sweet epilogue. The compact menu with its fishy focus does mean, however, limited choice if you are in the mood for meat (or are vegetarian) and the wine list is unlikely to surprise.
Chef/s: Craig Millar. **Open:** Wed to Sun L and D. **Closed:** Mon, Tue, 24 to 26 Dec, 2 weeks Jan. **Meals:** set L £22 (2 courses) to £28. Set D £45. Sun L £28. Tasting menu £60. **Details:** 40 seats. 20 seats outside. Bar. Wheelchairs. Parking. Children over 12 yrs only at D.

GFG scoring system

Score 1: Capable cooking with simple food combinations and clear flavours.

Score 2: Decent cooking, displaying good technical skills and interesting combinations and flavours.

Score 3: Good cooking, showing sound technical skills and using quality ingredients.

Score 4: Dedicated, focused approach to cooking; good classical skills and high-quality ingredients.

Score 5: Exact cooking techniques and a degree of ambition; showing balance and depth of flavour in dishes.

Score 6: Exemplary cooking skills, innovative ideas, impeccable ingredients and an element of excitement.

Score 7: High level of ambition and individuality, attention to the smallest detail, accurate and vibrant dishes.

Score 8: A kitchen cooking close to or at the top of its game. Highly individual with impressive artistry.

Score 9: Cooking that has reached a pinnacle of achievement, making it a hugely memorable experience.

Score 10: Just perfect dishes, showing faultless technique at every service; extremely rare and the highest accolade.

Auchterarder

★ TOP 10 ★

Restaurant Andrew Fairlie

Cooking score: 8
Modern French | £110
Gleneagles Hotel, Auchterarder, PH3 1NF
Tel no: (01764) 694267
andrewfairlie.co.uk

The gazillions spent on the Gleneagles upgrade have succeeded in making a palatial stopover even more opulent than ever. A staggering 850 acres, not quite all of it golf course, extends around the house, but within it all, as though undaunted by the outside world, too aloof to look upon it through anything as prosaic as windows, Andrew Fairlie's autonomous restaurant sails on serenely. It's definitely a mood-altering space, the low lighting and shimmering artworks creating a sultry ambience for Fairlie's finely wrought contemporary cooking. A French approach to outstanding Scottish produce, including vegetables, herbs and flowers from the kitchen garden, results in dishes that have an obvious classical gloss, perhaps opening with a pairing of caramelised veal sweetbreads and mushroom tart with onion soubise in jus gras. Scallops are marinated before a light roasting, their sweetness offset by the assertiveness of baby fennel and dill. Main courses show principal materials to their best advantage, so that the incomparable Highland roe deer and its little game bonbon are supported by nothing more complicated than a port sauce, but the kitchen also has the confidence to team stone bass and pork belly in a harmonious partnership, deepened with Madeira jus. Technically accomplished desserts might offer a flawless combination of passion fruit soufflé with coconut ice cream and mango coulis. A gargantuan wine list is on the forbidding side of magnificent, starting at £30.
Chef/s: Andrew Fairlie and Stephen McLaughlin. **Open:** Mon to Sat D only. **Closed:** Sun, 25 and 26 Dec, 3 weeks Jan. **Meals:** alc £110 (3 courses).

Tasting menu £155 (8 courses). **Details:** 50 seats. V menu. Wheelchairs. Music. Parking. Children over 12 yrs only.

Blairgowrie

Kinloch House Hotel

Cooking score: 5
Modern British | £53
Dunkeld Road, Blairgowrie, PH10 6SG
Tel no: (01250) 884237
kinlochhouse.com

Family-owned Kinloch House stands in 25 acres of its own woodland and parkland, bashfully swathed in ivy, an early Victorian country house that wears most of its grandeur on the inside. Here, an oak-panelled hall and portrait gallery lead to a light-toned dining room, where pastoral pictures and discreet service create a properly relaxed atmosphere. Steve MacCallum applies an equally light touch to the produce of Scottish hills and waters, from Arbroath lobster with shaved fennel in citrus dressing to local Perthshire lamb, its neck braised, the best end roasted, with potato purée in rosemary sauce. One reporter was roundly convinced by a dinner that took in seared king scallops and pork belly with aubergine purée, honey-roast duck breast with chanterelles, braised lentils and puréed parsnip in prune and apple sauce, and then creamy vanilla pannacotta with blueberries, every dish more creatively and innovatively designed than the menu suggests. Wines by the glass come at £8.50, bottles from £27.
Chef/s: Steve MacCallum. **Open:** all week L and D. **Closed:** 14 to 29 Dec. **Meals:** set L £20 (2 courses) to £26. Set D £53. Sun L £30. **Details:** 36 seats. Children over 7 yrs only at D.

Visit us online

To find out more about The Good Food Guide, please visit thegoodfoodguide.co.uk

Little's

Cooking score: 2
Seafood | £35
4 Wellmeadow, Blairgowrie, PH10 6ND
Tel no: (01250) 875358
littlesrestaurant.co.uk

Willie Little not only cooks at his restaurant but also uses his own fishmongers nearby for a same-day trawler-to-table delivery of the freshest seafood. The setting is informal and homely, conveniently located on the town's green heart of Wellmeadow. Personal touches appear in quirky wine selections (from £21) and seaweed condiments. The daily fish specials that complement the short menu grace an old classroom roller blackboard. Ingredients rather than technical or design flourishes are centre stage here. A crisp smoked haddock croquette bathes in a silken curried cauliflower purée. Lightly battered turbot (oh the indulgence!) is served with a Mediterranean chickpea and tomato broth and peppery local land cress. Desserts ooze comfort: blood-orange posset with rhubarb is a seasonal standout. Weekdays also feature Willie's 'Something Fishy' fixed-price piscatorial selection. An unexpected boutique pizza range offers idiosyncratic combinations such as chorizo, black pudding, scallop and apple as an alternative in this fish-led bistro.
Chef/s: Willie Little. **Open:** Fri and Sat L, Tue to Sat D. **Closed:** Sun, Mon, 25 Dec, 1 Jan, first 2 weeks Nov. **Meals:** main courses £14 to £26. Set L and D £22 (2 courses). **Details:** 38 seats. Wheelchairs. Music.

Symbols

- Accommodation is available
- £30 Three courses for less than £30
- £5 £5-off voucher scheme
- Notable wine list

█ Dundee

★ NEW ENTRY ★

Castlehill

Cooking score: 6
Modern British | £35
22 Exchange Street, Dundee, DD1 3DL
Tel no: (01382) 220008
castlehillrestaurant.co.uk
£5 OFF

Castlehill sits unassumingly on a quiet street just back from Dundee's fast-evolving waterfront, with décor and design that succeed in being stylish without being over-formal. No need for modesty though around chef Graham Campbell's exact and ambitious cooking – described by regulars as 'divine and by far the best fine dining in Dundee'. Graham's unapologetic Scottish focus brings intriguing combinations to his table d'hôte and tasting menus, with dainty but flavour-packed portions at surprisingly accessible prices. Simple recipe descriptors belie their complexity; an amuse-bouche of pea velouté bursting with spring freshness is bejewelled with jellied ham hock, while wild rabbit sees a perfect gem of loin crowning an umami-laden artichoke and pearl barley risotto – piquant with aged balsamic and micro-leaves. Chicken transcends its sometimes dull reputation – plumply brined with oats and chestnut mushrooms. A spruce sorbet with lemon espuma and fennel meringue, or white chocolate with strawberry and meadowsweet play with your sensory expectations for dessert. The wine list offers some kindly price points for a restaurant of this standard and interestingly matched flights.
Chef/s: Graham Campbell. **Open:** Tue to Sat L and D. **Closed:** Sun, Mon, 24 to 26 Dec, 1 and 2 Jan, 1 week Aug. **Meals:** set L £14 (2 courses) to £18. Set D £30 (2 courses) to £35. **Details:** 40 seats. Wheelchairs. Children before 8pm only.

▌Inverkeilor

Gordon's

Cooking score: 5

Modern British | £65

Main Street, Inverkeilor, DD11 5RN

Tel no: (01241) 830364

gordonsrestaurant.co.uk

Despite founder Gordon Watson's sad death in 2016, this close-knit family-run restaurant-with-rooms is 'still a joy to visit' – wife Maria 'deals brilliantly' with front-of-house, while son Garry is an increasingly confident and commanding presence in the kitchen. Occupying a sympathetically restored Victorian house in a tiny village not far from Lunan Bay, Gordon's oozes personal pride and character, and readers confirm that 'standards are as high as ever'. Impressive details such as the home-baked breads and biscuits set the bar high, and the kitchen responds with dishes that are full of vitality and dazzle. The signature twice-baked Mull Cheddar soufflé continues to thrill, but other ideas are designed to show off the kitchen's more creative side – from sea bream ceviche dressed with mango, coconut and pomegranate to turbot with char-grilled sweetcorn, crispy chicken wings and burnt cabbage. Elsewhere, 'amazingly tender' Angus beef fillet and featherblade with onion jam, celeriac purée and Rioja jus wows, while a 'divine' pistachio crème brûlée claims the plaudits for dessert. Well-annotated wines are a spot-on match for the food.

Chef/s: Garry Watson. **Open:** Sun L, Tue to Sun D. **Closed:** Sun (winter only), Mon, Jan. **Meals:** set L £35. Set D £65 (4 courses). **Details:** 24 seats. Parking. Children over 5 yrs L, over 12 yrs D.

Average price ≡🍴

The average price denotes the price of a three-course meal without wine.

▌Killiecrankie

Killiecrankie Hotel

Cooking score: 2

Modern British | £42

Killiecrankie, PH16 5LG

Tel no: (01796) 473220

killiecrankiehotel.co.uk

£5 OFF

Built in 1840 for a local vicar with a liking for dramatic views, this personally run hotel stands in wooded grounds overlooking the Pass of Killiecrankie. Owner Henrietta Fergusson keeps things just so, while chef Mark Easton knows what his customers demand in such surroundings – solid country-house cooking with a few gentle contemporary touches, but nothing too outré. Scottish ingredients have their moment in the formal restaurant, where the dinner menu might open with Arbroath smokie terrine wrapped in smoked salmon, or sautéed wood pigeon and wild mushrooms on olive oil toast. Mains (with helpful wine suggestions) could feature Aberdeen Angus beef, moorland game or fish (perhaps grilled sea trout fillet with saffron potato, fennel and samphire butter sauce), while desserts such as dark chocolate and salted-caramel torte are exactly what you might expect. Pub-style lunches are served in the bar, and the wine list offers ample choice at keen prices.

Chef/s: Mark Easton. **Open:** all week D only. **Closed:** 3 Jan to mid Mar. **Meals:** set D £42 (4 courses). **Details:** 30 seats. Bar. Parking.

▌Muthill

Barley Bree

Cooking score: 3

Anglo-French | £42

6 Willoughby Street, Muthill, PH5 2AB

Tel no: (01764) 681451

barleybree.com

The arched entrance gives notice that the Bouteloups' restaurant-with-rooms was once a coaching inn, and it retains a sympathetic air of the local hostelry inside, with its bare-boarded floor, beamed ceiling, exposed stone walls and old-fashioned furniture. Things come winging up to date with one glance at Fabrice Bouteloup's menus, which take a distantly but recognisably French approach to the modern Scottish idiom. A duo of pig's cheek and black pudding with beetroot purée confirms that, and the expected Asian note comes in a starter of scallops and mussels with soba noodles and pak choi in wasabi broth alight with coriander and chilli. Pedigree meats such as Gartmorn duck – the breast and confit leg with wild mushrooms and artichoke – and fish such as hake, given an Italian spin with orzo pasta and pesto, are the mainstays of the principal courses, and things end on a light note with vanilla pannacotta and a salad of rhubarb and blood orange. Wines, which include a decent Macedonian red from the Vranec grape, start at £18.95.

Chef/s: Fabrice Bouteloup. **Open:** Wed to Sun L and D. **Closed:** Mon, Tue, 24 to 26 Dec, 1 week Jul. **Meals:** main courses £15 to £23. Set L £17 (2 courses) to £23. **Details:** 40 seats. 12 seats outside. V menu. Bar. Music. Parking.

▌Perth

Deans

Cooking score: 3
Modern British | £33
77-79 Kinnoull Street, Perth, PH3 1LU
Tel no: (01738) 643377
letseatperth.co.uk

Deans is a true family affair with Willie in the kitchen and wife Margo and sons out front. Their crimson-and-silver accented domain caters to a mixed crowd of genteel locals, theatre-goers, tourists and city professionals. Willie's cooking is grounded in classical technique and finely honed through the raw heat of culinary competitions where ambition and precision bring success. A starter of local Ochil pheasant ballotine with a goats' cheese glaze, smoked celeriac purée and prune and port sauce is a well-balanced blend of sweet and sharp to bring out the best of the delicate, moist meat. Though the focus is confidently

carnivorous, a baked truckle Cheddar cheesecake on a meltingly short oat base provides an indulgently wobbly mouthful to win admirers beyond those of a vegetarian inclination. Modest portions make desserts inevitable and an iced mango and lychee parfait with winter berry crumble successfully twins the tropics with tasty tradition. Wines from £19.

Chef/s: Willie Deans. **Open:** Tue to Sun L, Tue to Sat D. **Closed:** Mon, 2 weeks Jan, 1 week Nov. **Meals:** main courses £14 to £29. Set L £14 (2 courses) to £19. Set D £18 (2 courses) to £22. **Details:** 70 seats. Bar. Wheelchairs. Music.

The North Port

Cooking score: 3
British | £32
8 North Port, Perth, PH1 5LU
Tel no: (01738) 580867
thenorthport.co.uk

Andrew Moss and Karen Milne took over this long-standing bistro in 2014, after working at The Ubiquitous Chip in Glasgow (see entry). Tucked away behind Perth's Concert Hall, in a wood-panelled Georgian building that might look more like a quaint old tea room, this is a restaurant delivering pin-sharp food worthy of a detour. Glorying in local produce from a supply chain of trusted suppliers, foragers and day boats, everything is made from scratch, from the bread and butter to the rowanberry jam served with Scottish cheeses at the end. In between, a meal might start with West Coast mackerel, beetroot, Knockraich crème fraîche, dill and cucumber, and go on to Black Isle rump, lamb belly with Jerusalem artichoke, kale, hazelnuts and Joker IPA gravy. The seasonal flavours continue with dessert of toasted oat mousse, rhubarb sorbet, oat praline and rhubarb jelly. The well-judged wine list starts at £17.95.

Chef/s: Andrew Moss. **Open:** Tue to Sat L and D. **Closed:** Sun, Mon, 2 weeks Christmas. **Meals:** main courses £13 to £22. Set L £13 (2 courses) to £16. Early D £16 (2 courses) to £19. **Details:** 32 seats. V menu. Music.

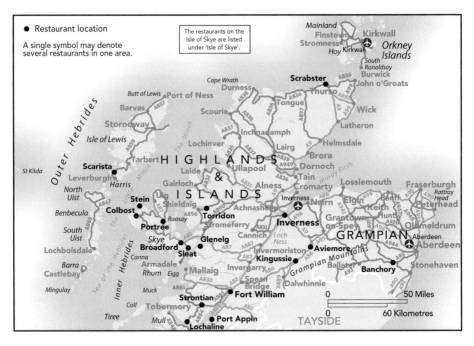

▊ Banchory

The Cowshed

Cooking score: 2
Modern British | £25
Raemoir Road, Banchory, AB31 5QB
Tel no: (01330) 820813
cowshedrestaurant.co.uk
£5 £30
OFF

Forget mucky farmyard buildings, straw bales
and lowing cattle, this Cowshed is an on-
trend mix of sleek chrome and wood trappings
with a snazzy glassed-in wine cellar, outdoor
decking and bright airy conservatory –
although views of the surrounding
countryside help to keep everyone grounded.
The Buchans aim to please, peppering their
menus with robust, comforting staples in new
guises: how about panko-crusted Stornoway
black pudding with spiced apple purée,
fishcakes with 'puffed' capers or grilled lamb's
liver accompanied by crushed oatmeal
potatoes and salted-onion marmalade. There
are haggis-topped burgers, local Deeside pies

and hot chicken schnitzels, too, while an on-
site chippy adds to the populist ethos – don't
miss the 'chip shop' chips. Toasted paninis and
open sandwiches make handy lunchtime
snacks, while puds might run to pineapple
fritters or crème brûlée with local double
cream. Around 20 wines from around £20
complete the offer.
Chef/s: Graham Buchan. Open: all week L, Wed to
Sun D. Closed: 25 to 27 Dec, 1 to 9 Jan.
Meals: main courses £9 to £25. Details: 80 seats. 20
seats outside. Wheelchairs. Music. Parking.

Please send us
your feedback

To register your opinion about any
restaurant listed in this guide, or a new
restaurant that you wish to bring to our
attention, please visit the web address at
the bottom of the page. Your feedback
informs the content of the book and will
be used to compile next year's reviews.

▌Acharacle

READERS RECOMMEND

Mingarry Park

Modern British
Mingarry, Acharacle, PH36 4JX
Tel no: (07791) 115467
mingarryparkhouse.co.uk

'We were very happy with the meal. All the food was locally sourced and freshly prepared. Great portion sizes, very attentive waitresses and beautiful views. We had a pigeon breast starter, cod and chips for main and chocolate mousse for dessert. All was absolutely delicious and packed with flavour.'

▌Aviemore

Mountain Café

Cooking score: 2
International | £20
111 Grampian Road, Aviemore, PH22 1RH
Tel no: (01479) 812473
mountaincafe-aviemore.co.uk
£30

It doesn't get more outdoorsy than Aviemore in the heart of the Cairngorms, and the Mountain Café is a recommended ascent to the upper floor of an outdoor shop where mountaineers, walkers, skiers and anyone else with a hearty appetite and a weakness for their 'show-stopper' cakes are amply refuelled. Portions here are big bordering on excessive. New Zealander Kirsten Gilmour is behind this cultish café that runs from breakfast – granola, pancakes, banana bread or all-day breakfast – until late afternoon. Mains bring steak melt flatbread featuring minute steak, Emmental and red onion jalapeño jam and proper chips or maybe Lebanese chicken salad, piled high with grains, cucumber, mango and pomegranate. If it's too much to contemplate a cake from the lavish display, they'll box one up. Vegetarians and vegans are well catered for and they make good things for kids. You may have to queue on the stairs but service is swift,

efficient and friendly. There's a short wine list, Cairngorm brewery beers and New Zealand cider.

Chef/s: Kirsten Gilmour. **Open:** all week 8.30 to 5 (5.30 Sat and Sun). **Closed:** 25 and 26 Dec, 1 Jan. **Meals:** main courses £9 to £12. **Details:** 50 seats. 12 seats outside. Music. Parking.

▌Fort William

Crannog

Cooking score: 1
Seafood | £35
Town Pier, Fort William, PH33 6DB
Tel no: (01397) 705589
crannog.net
£5 OFF

Head towards the pier on Loch Linnhe and you'll spot a roof that is a colour match for the lobster you may well be acquainted with very soon. Crannog has been here for donkey's years and continues to offer fantastically fresh seafood in a relaxed setting. It's not entirely about the fruits of the sea – you can have a twice-baked cheese soufflé, haunch and saddle of venison or a vegetarian dish if you so desire. The main menu runs to roast Mallaig monkfish with crab potato cake, but keep an eye on the evening blackboard, with oysters, mussels, langoustines, crab and lobster winning the day. Drink Scottish beer or something from the serious wine list.

Chef/s: Stewart MacLachlan. **Open:** all week L and D. **Closed:** 25 and 26 Dec, 1 Jan. **Meals:** main courses £15 to £25. Set L £15 (2 courses) to £19. **Details:** 55 seats. Wheelchairs. Music. Parking.

Lochleven Seafood Café

Cooking score: 2
Seafood | £40
Onich, Fort William, PH33 6SA
Tel no: (01855) 821048
lochlevenseafoodcafe.co.uk

With its prime position overlooking Loch Leven, Alison Grieve's easy-going seafooder is in an especially captivating spot, with large windows looking out over the water to the Pap of Glencoe mountain. The décor is simple and contemporary, and the venue relaxed, unpretentious and full of beans – this is a seriously busy place, a real honeypot for tourists and booking ahead is advisable. Shellfish gets a good outing: oysters from Loch Creran are served with a raspberry dressing, scallops are as fresh as can be, mussels (cooked in cider) come from the loch outside, wonderfully big langoustines (with lemon and mayonnaise) are incredibly firm and sweet, and there's a very good spaghetti alle vongole. There's also whole roasted megrim sole with salsa verde and samphire salad, steak for those who must, and almond frangipane and Calvados ice cream or sticky toffee pudding to finish. The short, European wine list starts at £16.

Chef/s: Scott Fraser. **Open:** all week L and D. **Closed:** 31 Oct to 10 Mar. **Meals:** main courses £8 to £45. **Details:** 35 seats. 15 seats outside. Wheelchairs. Parking.

■ Glenelg
The Glenelg Inn
Cooking score: 2
British | £35
Glenelg, IV40 8JR
Tel no: (01599) 522273
glenelg-inn.com

🛏

'Wonderfully atmospheric whitewashed inn, very dark and cosy and a wonderful position,' noted a visitor to this friendly village hostelry on the banks of the Sound of Sleet, over-looking the Isle of Skye. It's all very informal, eat in the bar or dining room and choose from a short, simple, daily changing menu that showcases locally sourced produce. That could mean home-smoked wood pigeon with shallot purée, charred shallots, pickles and rye, and hand-dived Isle of Skye scallops with roe purée, apple and cider vinegar, but visitors have come away full of praise for fresh langoustine, very good haddock and chips, venison haunch and meltingly tender blade of beef. Do save room for desserts such as lemon posset with thyme and sea salt shortbread or

sticky toffee pudding – 'it's hard to fault the enjoyment of it all'. Booking recommended. Wines from £17.95.

Chef/s: Verity Hurding. **Open:** all week L and D. **Closed:** Mid Nov to 1 Mar. **Meals:** main courses £12 to £21. **Details:** 50 seats. 30 seats outside. Wheelchairs. Music. Parking.

■ Inverness
Chez Roux at Rocpool Reserve
Cooking score: 3
French | £40
Rocpool Reserve Hotel, 14 Culduthel Road, Inverness, IV2 4AG
Tel no: (01463) 240089
rocpool.com

£5 OFF 🛏

This heavily branded Highland fling from French master Albert Roux takes place in a smart, classically styled hotel dining room complete with polished tables, pale leather chairs and cheffy cartoons on the walls. Hushed elegance sums up the mood, service is keen to please and the food is French country cooking with a refined twist – although much depends on the seasonal Scottish larder. Monsieur Roux's legendary twice-baked soufflé is made with Mull Cheddar as well as Gruyère, Campbells Gold ribeye steaks arrive with chipped potatoes and béarnaise sauce, while breast of mallard is served with chestnut boudin, crispy confit, poached pear and game jus. Fancy desserts also have that Roux stamp, from glazed lemon tart to black cherry and white chocolate chiboust with hazelnut crunch and blackberry sorbet. A fixed-price 'RouXpress' menu is served until 6, and the wine list is impressively stocked with classy bottles from the French regions and beyond.

Chef/s: Darin Campbell. **Open:** all week L and D. **Closed:** Mon and Tue (Jan and Feb only). **Meals:** main courses £17 to £26. Set L £25 (2 courses) to £33. Set D £26 (2 courses) to £35. Sun L £33. **Details:** 60 seats. 12 seats outside. Bar. Wheelchairs. Music. Parking.

Rocpool

Cooking score: 2
Modern European | £38
1 Ness Walk, Inverness, IV3 5NE
Tel no: (01463) 717274
rocpoolrestaurant.com
£5 OFF

Confusingly, Inverness has two Rocpools – the other is Chez Roux at Rocpool Reserve (see entry). This one is close by the river Ness and has a modern menu that responds to season and sourcing. Scottish produce features heavily on the à la carte with the likes of Shetland mussels, west coast king scallops, Arbroath smokies, Speyside venison and Strathdon Blue cheese, while the dishes themselves roam the globe. Sea bream with chilli and coriander is served with jasmine rice, while beef cheek is paired with wild mushroom risotto. While there is adventure in many of the dishes, pairings aren't always entirely successful. Individually, a savoury crème brûlée and warm figs with caramelised walnuts were both excellent but didn't sit easily together on the plate. More successful was turbot with Puy lentils, mushrooms and cotechino. Triple-chocolate praline tart tempts at dessert. There are good-value lunch and early-evening deals, and a well-constructed wine list (from £17.95) comes complete with tasting notes plus some special reserves.
Chef/s: Steven Devlin. **Open:** Mon to Sat L and D. **Closed:** Sun, 24 to 26 Dec, 1 to 3 Jan. **Meals:** main courses £13 to £24. Set L £17 (2 courses). Set D £19 (2 courses). **Details:** 55 seats. Wheelchairs. Music.

Please send us your feedback

To register your opinion about any restaurant listed in this guide, or a new restaurant that you wish to bring to our attention, please visit the web address at the bottom of the page. Your feedback informs the content of the book and will be used to compile next year's reviews.

▌Isle of Harris
Scarista House

Cooking score: 2
Modern British | £45
Scarista, Isle of Harris, HS3 3HX
Tel no: (01859) 550238
scaristahouse.com

Tim and Patricia Martin's converted Georgian manse has a great deal going for it – not least its stunning prospect overlooking a gorgeous sandy beach, with views of the rolling Atlantic thrown in for good measure. Given the remote location, it's no surprise that the couple have to rely on their own talents and what is to hand: they bake bread, grow what they can in this unforgiving climate, procure fish from the local boats and buy free-range meat from their farming neighbours. The result is a no-choice dinner menu that promises comforting satisfaction rather than cutting-edge thrills – think Uist crab tart followed by navarin of Lewis lamb with aubergine purée, buttered carrots, courgettes and dauphinois potatoes. After that, you might be offered local raspberries and strawberries with Champagne and elderflower jelly or hot chocolate fondant with ginger ice cream and salt caramel. Wine drinkers have some cracking deals by the glass.
Chef/s: Tim and Patricia Martin. **Open:** all week D only. **Closed:** Dec to Feb. **Meals:** set D £45. **Details:** 22 seats. V menu. Parking. Children over 8 yrs only.

▌Isle of Skye
Birlinn Restaurant

Cooking score: 2
British | £45
Hotel Eilean Iarmain, Isle Ornsay, Sleat, Isle of Skye, IV43 8QR
Tel no: (01471) 833332
eileaniarmain.co.uk
£5 OFF

Birlinn restaurant and its informal sister bar Am Praban are part of the Eilean Iarmain hotel on an idyllic peninsula overlooking the

Sound of Sleat and Knoydart mountains. Whether joining residents for the table d'hôte or enjoying a hearty bar meal of local venison or langoustines fresh from the pier end, the focus is on old-style Highland hospitality complete with tweeds, tartans and simple family comforts. The set-dinner menu offers three choices for each course and might start with local pigeon breast or scallops paired with black pudding. Best end of lamb sees two hearty chops cooked perfectly pink with well-rendered fat simply accompanied by dauphinois potatoes, kale and a shallot balsamic jus. A hot chocolate fondant with candied pistachios presages the possibility of a coffee and a wee dram in the wood-panelled lounge, overseen by an antiquated stuffed eagle.
Chef/s: Martin Nel. **Open:** all week D only. **Meals:** main courses £15 to £25. Set D £35 (2 courses) to £45. **Details:** 15 seats. Bar. Music. Parking.

Creelers of Skye

Cooking score: 2
French | £28
Lower Harrapool, Broadford, Isle of Skye, IV49 9AQ
Tel no: (01471) 822281
skye-seafood-restaurant.co.uk
£5 OFF £30

'Our building is little more than a shack,' admit the owners of this immensely likeable eatery, but don't be fooled: once inside, you'll discover a pleasurable space done out like a low-key art gallery, with local canvases on the walls and a menu that promises the honest delights of Scottish seafood (and more besides), cooked with a conspicuous Gallic touch. On a clear day, you can also gaze across Broadford Bay and watch as the fishermen haul in creels loaded with squat lobsters. The day's line-up depends on the catch, so expect anything from steamed mussels à la landaise to braised monkfish in a light soy and Pernod cream reduction – not forgetting a show-stopping Marseille bouillabaisse (served authentically in two stages). However, the menu is not exclusively fish or exclusively French: chicken cacciatore and tagliatelle milanese also feature, ahead of desserts such as cloutie dumpling with a cranachan 'chaser'. Fairly priced wines, too.
Chef/s: David Wilson. **Open:** Tue to Sat, all day from 12. **Closed:** Sun, Mon, Nov to Feb. **Meals:** main courses £15 to £20. **Details:** 28 seats. 8 seats outside. Wheelchairs. Music. Parking.

★ NEW ENTRY ★

Dulse & Brose

Cooking score: 3
British | £35
9-11 Bosville Terrace, Portree, Isle of Skye, IV51 9DG
Tel no: (01478) 612846
bosvillehotel.co.uk

Located in the Bosville hotel, Dulse & Brose accentuates its identity from the outset with its eponymous seaweed butter and porridge-oat bread presented on a rustic board. Decorated with Hebridean tweeds and placemats mapping the island's key food suppliers and producers, it vaunts its Skye heritage. Ham hock and chicken terrine with Glendale leaves and apples sees a flavoursome and chunky serving set atop locally grown baby kale, nasturtium and chicory with apple in a bittersweet medley. Mains are presented on cast-iron platters, and you'll find hearty dishes such as a pressed ingot of pork belly with Sconser scallops on a celeriac and grain-mustard rémoulade. A crumbly baked cheesecake featuring Blairgowrie strawberries, shortbread and mango sorbet might close this simple but well-presented tour around Scotland's larder. Alongside the narrow but perfectly adequate wine choice, the drinks list features extensive Scottish gins and local beers from the island's craft brewery.
Chef/s: Peter Cullen. **Open:** all week L and D. **Closed:** 25 Dec. **Meals:** main courses £14 to £22. **Details:** 54 seats. Bar. Wheelchairs. Music.

Kinloch Lodge

Cooking score: 5
Modern British | £75
Sleat, Isle of Skye, IV43 8QY
Tel no: (01471) 833214
kinloch-lodge.co.uk

The bright-white former hunting lodge glows out above the Sound of Sleat amid the wilds of Skye, a gloriously remote setting in which to banish one's ephemeral concerns. The Macdonalds have been in charge since the early 1970s, and the refined elegance of the place is conscientiously maintained, to the extent lately of a new look in the dining room, where ash-grey walls throw the Georgian oil portraits into relief, and Marcello Tully's cooking shines as brightly as ever. Tully favours a broadly French approach to his cornucopia of stellar Scottish produce, shown to its best advantage on the seven-course tasting menu. Combinations are carefully considered, as when pigeon breast, black pudding and beetroot all contribute their richness to an early course dressed in citrus jus, while Chinese seasoning gives point to a modern classic pairing of pork cheek and scallop, alongside sweetly pickled fennel. That underlying out-of-the-ordinary note conjures a passion fruit jus for quail with honeyed vegetable mousse, and the enjoyment of fruit elements comes into its own at dessert, with raspberries to sauce the chocolate espuma, and apple crumble parfait and matching sorbet sharpened with blackcurrants. An authoritative wine list comes with exhaustive notes, and is particularly good in the southern hemisphere. Standard glasses start at £7.95.
Chef/s: Marcello Tully. **Open:** all week L and D.
Meals: set and Sun L £36 (2 courses) to £39. Set D £75 (5 courses). Tasting menu £85. **Details:** 45 seats. V menu. Bar. Wheelchairs. Music. Parking. Children at L and early D only.

Our highlights...

Our undercover inspectors reveal their most memorable dishes from another year of extraordinary eating.

Seasonal tagliatelli with peas, beans, wild garlic and summer truffle at **Castle Terrace.** Simple, fresh summer-on-a-plate, with the added luxury of generous shaved fresh truffle.

Orbost Farm beef with new season garlic – celebrated fourfold through confit flank, pressed tongue, short-rib and fillet, accompanied by Jerusalem artichoke and salsify at **Three Chimneys**. Local, very personal, farm-to-fork and nose-to-tail. Love the honesty and depth of flavour from the 'lesser cuts'.

Spruce sorbet with lemon espuma and fennel meringue at **Castlehill,** a pre-dessert that brought unusual flavours and textures and which prompted a genuine intake of breath (in a good way).

Apple crumble, charcoal vanilla ice cream, rye and oats from **Aquavit.** OK, it's just a crumble, but this a superior version of the classic with a healthy kick and the best I've ever tasted! Served in a copper pan, it's a winter warmer. The stewed-apple base with its lovely little clove backnote and bags of oat-and-rye-filled crumble atop (really lovely texture), served with delicious vanilla ice cream.

Loch Bay

Cooking score: 4
Seafood | £40
1-2 Macleod's Terrace, Stein, Isle of Skye,
IV55 8GA
Tel no: (01470) 592235
lochbay-restaurant.co.uk

Michael Smith made his name as chef/director of the nearby Three Chimneys (see entry), before decamping to this converted fisherman's cottage in a conservation village. With help from his French wife, Laurence, he has refined the interiors, adding some modern blue/grey tones and enlivening the space with old mirrors. The food has been given a shake-up too, with a skilfully executed 'fruits de mer' tasting menu now making waves alongside the regular carte. The former might list anything from brown crab 'flory' with Glendale mesclun (salad) to lobster and prawn 'pot-au-feu', while the latter could involve mussel and spinach soup or roast hake 'Rockerfeller' alongside pot-roast pigeon with chanterelles, apple and brambles or beef short rib and tongue with cauliflower and pickles – all sound local stuff. After that, expect reinvented Auld Scottish puds such as a cloutie dumpling soufflé. To drink, local beers and Highland malts vie with some keenly chosen wines.
Chef/s: Michael Smith. **Open:** Wed to Fri and Sun L, Tue to Sat D. **Closed:** Mon, Jan. **Meals:** set L £30. Set D £40. Sun L £40. Tasting menu £60 (6 courses). **Details:** 22 seats. V menu. Music. Parking.

★ NEW ENTRY ★

Scorrybreac

Cooking score: 3
British | £39
7 Bosville Terrace, Isle of Skye, IV51 9DG
Tel no: (01478) 612069
scorrybreac.com
£5
OFF

Scorrybreac ('speckled rock' in Gaelic) is the brainchild of local chef Calum Munro. Working abroad with great produce arriving from his home island of Skye he felt inspired

to return and celebrate its local provenance in situ. His elegantly styled but tiny 20-seater restaurant fulfils this ambition – though its small scale can be challenging for both elbow room and availability – the quality of sourcing and love of ingredients and flavour combinations are evident throughout. A compact menu, perhaps constrained by kitchen space, might open with sweet and crumbly maple oat bread served with caramelised butter. A properly meaty Highland beef tartare is thoughtfully enhanced with rapeseed aïoli and shaved Letterfinlay smoked Cheddar. Perfectly caramelised hake is served with some of the sweetest Portree crabmeat imaginable. To close, the popular Talisker whisky chocolate fondant with espresso ice cream cleverly combines dessert and digestif.
Chef/s: Calum Munro. **Open:** Tue to Sun D only. **Closed:** Mon, 25 and 26 Dec, Jan to Mar. **Meals:** set D £33 (2 courses) to £39. **Details:** 20 seats. Music.

★ RESTAURANT OF THE YEAR ★
★ TOP 50 ★

The Three Chimneys

Cooking score: 7
Modern British | £65
Colbost, Isle of Skye, IV55 8ZT
Tel no: (01470) 511258
threechimneys.co.uk

A sensitive refurbishment of this modestly proportioned former coastal cottage and its luxurious neighbouring bedrooms concluded with a brand-new kitchen in 2017 that pays dividends in enhanced culinary capacity. Head chef Scott Davies focuses on provenance and authenticity. His menus reflect Skye's culinary heritage and ancient Nordic connections and most ingredients come from a 20-mile radius. Truly evangelistic about respecting ingredients, his cooking cherishes native-breed animals such as Soay lamb, wild deer and Iron Age pigs from nose to tail. Orbost Highland beef bathed in the pungent sweetness of new-season garlic is celebrated fourfold through confit flank, pressed tongue, short rib and fillet – each miniature mouth-marvels in their own right, together a bovine masterclass. Local fish and shellfish are equally revered; Dunvegan crab from the loch outside offsets the sweet white flesh with a savoury brown-meat mousse, aromatic pickled fennel and floral bee pollen. Such imaginative recipe design with vibrant flavour combinations and deft executions mean the kitchen has little need of gadgets or technical trickery to impress. Desserts reinforce the ethos of artful simplicity – witness a hedgerow forage elevated to gastronomic glory in pressed apple with bramble, elderberry and hazelnut. Extensive wine choices with expert sommelier support span the price range while indulgent gin and whisky options are perfect for a contemplative moment in the lounge overlooking the loch.

Chef/s: Scott Davies. **Open:** all week L (1 Apr to 11 Nov only) and D all year. **Closed:** 10 Dec to 19 Jan. **Meals:** set L £38. Set D £65. Tasting menu £90. **Details:** 40 seats. V menu. Bar. Wheelchairs. Music. Parking. Children over 8 yrs only at D.

▍Kingussie
The Cross

Cooking score: 4
Modern British | £55
Tweed Mill Brae, Ardbroilach Road, Kingussie, PH21 1LB
Tel no: (01540) 661166
thecross.co.uk

🍷 🛏

With the waters of the Gynack Burn tumbling close by and four acres of riverside gardens teeming with flowers, this converted Victorian tweed mill is a holidaymaker's dream, but The Cross has a great deal more to offer than languorous pastoral contentment. The current team is also capable of delivering some very fine food and hospitality, amid a setting that blends original beams and rough stone walls with contemporary artwork. In the kitchen, seasonal Scottish produce receives accomplished treatment with lots of intricate flourishes: seared John Dory might be paired

with crispy pork belly, young spinach, baby onions and sauce épices, while loin of local venison arrives with creamed cabbage, braised oxtail, pickled beets and celeriac. Beef fillet, lobster and sea bass maintain the luxurious feel, before desserts herald the likes of green apple parfait with cinnamon doughnuts and cider jelly. The long wine list is a dazzler, with French classics and New World contenders offering impressive value across the range. Great whisky flights, too.

Chef/s: David Skiggs. **Open:** all week L and D. **Closed:** Christmas, Jan (exc Hogmanay). **Meals:** set L £30. Set D £55. Sun L £30. Tasting menu £65 (6 courses). **Details:** 26 seats. 12 seats outside. V menu. Bar. Wheelchairs. Parking.

▍Lochaline
The Whitehouse

Cooking score: 5
Modern British | £45
Lochaline, PA80 5XT
Tel no: (01967) 421777
thewhitehouserestaurant.co.uk

If you're arriving by private launch from Mull, head for the snazzy new pontoons at Lochaline. Others will have to make do with the A861 and the little Ardgour ferry. Either way, it's worth the journey to find the foursquare white building next to the village shop that looks out over the tranquil waters of the Sound. Inside is done in a cheeringly domestic fashion, with chunky bare tables and little landscape prints, and the welcome is reliably warm. Mike Burgoyne is doing exciting things with fabulous Highland produce, presented in the form of a land-and-sea menu from which you select two, four or six courses, as temptation dictates. Ardshealach smoked trout with a quail's egg and wild horseradish might open proceedings, before pressed ham hough with pickles and piccalilli offers a different smoky mouthful. Gigha halibut is poached in seawater and matched with wormwood and fennel pollen, before squab pigeon scented with woodruff is teamed with black pudding crumble and black-ale jam. The aromatic note is sustained

to the end, when Mull tea and chocolate cloutie comes with Tobermory whisky toffee and a shot of single malt. Wines open at £19.95.
Chef/s: Mike Burgoyne. **Open:** Tue to Sat L and D. **Closed:** Sun, Mon, Nov to end Mar. **Meals:** set L and D £25 (2 courses). Tasting menu £45 (4 courses) to £65. **Details:** 26 seats. 8 seats outside. V menu. Wheelchairs. Parking.

▌Port Appin
Airds Hotel
Cooking score: 3
Modern British | £56
Port Appin, PA38 4DF
Tel no: (01631) 730236
airds-hotel.com

Having made a 500-mile trip to dine here, one reader came away full of praise for Airds' spot-on blend of 'excellent service and heavenly food'. The fabulous views across Loch Linnhe haven't changed much since this converted ferry inn first appeared in the Guide more than 40 years ago, but the hotel itself has seen lots of changes. Recent refurbishment has given the small, tasteful dining room a more relaxed contemporary vibe, while chef Chris Stanley is shoring up Airds' gastronomic reputation with his highly intricate cooking – a 'subtle combination of tastes and textures'. Scottish ingredients figure prominently, with 'extraordinarily delicious' fish and seasonal game leading the pack – perhaps monkfish with braised oxtail, girolles and smoked gnocchi or loin of venison with Jerusalem artichoke, beetroot and juniper. The cheeseboard earns a special mention, alongside desserts such as lemon parfait with gin sabayon and thyme. Well-chosen wines are arranged by grape variety.
Chef/s: Chris Stanley. **Open:** all week L and D. **Closed:** first 2 weeks Dec. **Meals:** set L £19 (2 courses) to £24. Set D £56. Sun L £22. Tasting menu £76 (7 courses). **Details:** 32 seats. 20 seats outside. V menu. Bar. Wheelchairs. Parking. Children over 9 yrs only at D.

▌Scrabster
The Captain's Galley
Cooking score: 4
Seafood | £54
The Harbour, Scrabster, KW14 7UJ
Tel no: (01847) 894999
captainsgalley.co.uk

The guide's most northerly restaurant sits above Scrabster Harbour: a ferry terminal, fishing port and oil and gas facility. Not the most promising location, but this superb little fish restaurant in a former salmon bothy and ice house is run with bags of personality by Jim and Mary Cowie. Jim, a former fish trader, only buys and cooks what is landed beneath his window, which translates to a dinner of cured herring followed by langoustines dripping in herb and garlic butter, a heady prawn and scallop bisque then saithe (pollack), Cajun blackened with sweetcorn succotash and sweet potato while a piece of flaking hake is beautifully paired with fennel, asparagus, artichokes and roast hazelnuts. A mid-course sorbet surprised with sea buckthorn and grapefruit; a dessert of ginger crème brûlée and lemon posset was a delight. Wines are standard. Beers include a lovely amber ale from the Black Isle. A similar, but cheaper menu is served in next door's informal Seafood Bar.
Chef/s: Jim Cowie. **Open:** Thur to Sun L and D. **Closed:** Mon, Tue, Wed, Jan. **Meals:** main courses £25 to £32. Set L £28 (3 courses). Set D £54 (5 courses). Tasting menu £72. **Details:** 25 seats. 25 seats outside. V menu. Wheelchairs. Music. Parking.

Please send us your feedback

To register your opinion about any restaurant listed in this guide, or a new restaurant that you wish to bring to our attention, please visit the web address at the bottom of the page. Your feedback informs the content of the book and will be used to compile next year's reviews.

▋Strontian
Kilcamb Lodge
Cooking score: 4
Modern British | £35
Strontian, PH36 4HY
Tel no: (01967) 402257
kilcamblodge.co.uk
£5 OFF 🛏

With the lovely Loch Sunart on Scotland's Ardnamurchan Peninsula all but lapping at its door, Kilcamb Lodge is a beautifully situated country house hotel. Lunch and dinner are served in the small Driftwood brasserie or the sunny more formal dining room – the menu is the same for both – and with an emphasis on seafood you might begin with Orkney crab and seaweed cake served with beetroot and salmon crème fraîche with an original kick from a wasabi and apple sorbet. Pickled cauliflower and a tomato and caper salsa provide contrast to tender scallops and a silky cauliflower purée. Chef Gary Phillips may have a tendency to overload on ingredients, as in the cod with a pistachio and mustard crust, a wild mushroom and Parma ham tart, roast celeriac, mussels and samphire, but portions are generous and cooking is exact. Pleasing service from a friendly team. A standard wine list starts at £23.50

Chef/s: Gary Phillips. **Open:** all week L and D.
Closed: 1 to 15 Dec, 2 Jan to 2 Feb. **Meals:** main courses £16 to 21. Set L £28 (3 courses). Set D £39 (3 courses). Tasting menu £69 (7 courses).
Details: 40 seats. 12 seats outside. V menu. Bar. Wheelchairs. Music. Parking. Children over 5 yrs only in restaurant.

▋Torridon
★ NEW ENTRY ★
1887 at the Torridon
new chef/no score
Modern European | £60
The Torridon, Torridon, IV22 2EY
Tel no: (01445) 791242
thetorridon.com
🛏

The Torridon, a turreted gothic mansion on the shores of Loch Torridon, is a luxury hotel of baronial splendour that has developed a dining room worthy of its pampering surroundings. The food is now in the capable hands of Ross Stovold, who comes with experience at Alimentum (see entry) and the Isle of Eriska. He assumed his position just as we were about to go to press, but we are sure that, like his predecessor David Barnett, his menus will continue to reference top Scottish produce and the Torridon's kitchen garden. A spring inspection, for example, taken before Mr Stovold took over, featured a full-flavoured spelt risotto with asparagus, Mimolette cheese and Torridon ham, and a delicate fillet of Scrabster-landed halibut served with peas, morels and broad beans. At dessert, lemon parfait with shards of smoked meringue came with a clever celery sorbet. Wines begin at a reasonable £23 and rise exponentially towards their special collection. If you fancy a dram their Whisky Bar claims a choice of 350.

Chef/s: Ross Stovold. **Open:** all week D only.
Closed: Jan, Mon and Tue (Feb and Mar).
Meals: set D £50 (3 courses) to £75. **Details:** 36 seats. Bar. Wheelchairs. Music. Parking. Children over 10 yrs only.

WALES

Glamorgan, Gwent, Mid-Wales, North-
East Wales, North-West Wales, West Wales

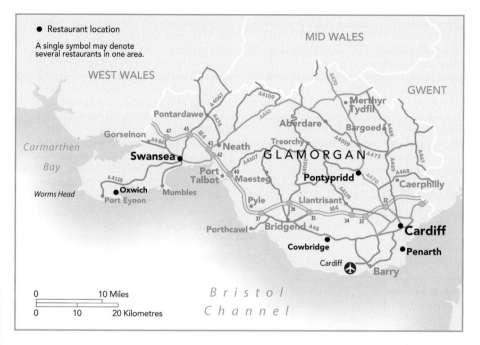

- Restaurant location

A single symbol may denote several restaurants in one area.

MID WALES

WEST WALES

GWENT

Merthyr Tydfil

Pontardawe

Aberdare

Bargoed

Gorseinon

Carmarthen

Neath

Treorchy

GLAMORGAN

Swansea

Bay

Port Talbot

Maesteg

Pontypridd

Caerphilly

Oxwich

Worms Head

Port Eynon

Mumbles

Pyle

Llantrisant

Porthcawl

Bridgend

Cardiff

Cowbridge

Penarth

Cardiff ✈

Barry

0   10 Miles

B r i s t o l

0   10   20 Kilometres

C h a n n e l

▌Cardiff

Arbennig
Cooking score: 3
Modern British | £29
6-10 Romilly Crescent, Cardiff, CF11 9NR
Tel no: (029) 2034 1264
arbennig.co.uk
£30

Meaning 'special' in Welsh, Arbennig occupies a spacious building in one of Cardiff's greener suburbs, just a short walk from the city centre. Set across two floors, service is friendly and welcoming from the off. A test meal produced some assured cooking of well-sourced seasonal ingredients treated with respect and minimal fuss. A well-handled starter of char-grilled Wye Valley asparagus with chilli, garlic and hazelnut was followed by super-fresh and accurately timed plaice fillet teamed with charred octopus, sea parsley butter and purple sprouting broccoli, while a dessert of raspberry sorbet, meringue, vanilla ice cream and fresh raspberries was an interesting take

on Eton mess. Wines from £17.95. If you want something even more informal, the restaurant's new Arbennig Emporium deli/café next door also serves a decent breakfast.
Chef/s: John Cook. **Open:** Thur to Sat L and D. Sun 11.30 to 6. **Closed:** Mon, Tue, Wed. **Meals:** main courses £15 to £25. Set L £15 (2 courses). Sun L £15 (2 courses) to £17. **Details:** 60 seats. 16 seats outside. Bar. Music. Parking.

★ NEW ENTRY ★

Asador 44
Cooking score: 2
Spanish | £40
14-15 Quay Street, Cardiff, CF10 1EA
Tel no: (029) 2002 0039
asador44.co.uk
£5
OFF

From the Bar 44 group (see entry, Cowbridge) comes Asador 44, styled on the asador grill restaurants of northern Spain – right down to the tiles, marble-topped tables and open kitchen with wood-fired grill. Directly opposite the main entrance to the Principality rugby stadium, it's a large venue in a former pub where unfussy cooking includes rare-breed meats displayed in glass-fronted dry-aging units, and whole turbot, Galician beef and Segovian milk-fed lamb are all cooked over wood. An inspection meal opened with slices of seared spiced tuna and avocado simply dressed with fruity olive oil, lemon and micro-coriander. Next up, a fillet of hake smoky from the charcoal grill, accompanied by Albariño clams and a pool of mossy, piquant salsa verde. Tempting as the walk-in cheese room selection was (there are 11 Spanish cheeses) our meal finished with tarta de queso cheesecake and Tempranillo blueberries. Service is 'knowledgeable and faultless'. An almost exclusively Spanish wine list (with plenty by the glass) starts at £21.

Chef/s: Owen Morgan. **Open:** Tue to Sat L and D. **Closed:** Sun, Mon, 25 and 26 Dec, first week Jan. **Meals:** main courses £11 to £20. **Details:** 84 seats. V menu. Bar. Wheelchairs. Music.

Bully's
Cooking score: 2
Modern French | £37
5 Romilly Crescent, Cardiff, CF11 9NP
Tel no: (029) 2022 1905
bullysrestaurant.co.uk

'Bully's is a great little neighbourhood restaurant – the sort of place most of us want around the corner,' said one happy diner. Russell Bullimore has certainly imbued his laid-back restaurant with bags of feel-good personality: an arty, eclectic one-off, it's cheerfully stuffed with mismatched furniture, crockery, bric-à-brac and family memorabilia. In the kitchen, things are equally upbeat, the cooking taking its cue from the gutsy flavours of French cuisine, while respecting the British seasonal larder. The result is cooking of a high order: scallops with hazelnut, celeriac and apple, for example, or Wye Valley asparagus ravioli with Parmesan, wild garlic and pea sauce. For a main course, 'pink, tender, juicy' rump of lamb is served with rosemary and garlic fondant potatoes, braised leeks,

caramelised onions and lamb sauce, while sea bass is teamed with Provençal vegetables, saffron potatoes, cockles and a rich bouillabaisse sauce. Desserts include chocolate tart with orange and Chantilly cream. As befits a neighbourhood bistro, there are excellent prix fixe deals, and a short, well-anotated list of wines from across the viticultural globe.

Chef/s: Christie Matthews. **Open:** Wed to Sun L, Wed to Sat D. **Closed:** Mon, Tue. **Meals:** main courses £15 to £26. Set L £20 (2 courses) to £25. Set D £25 (2 courses) to £30. Sun L £13. **Details:** 40 seats. Music.

Casanova
Cooking score: 1
Italian | £30
13 Quay Street, Cardiff, CF10 1EA
Tel no: (029) 2034 4044
casanovacardiff.com

In the shadows of the Principality (Millennium) Stadium, this unassuming little bistro-style restaurant is now in its 12th year. There's a genuinely warm welcome and the generous set-price menu centres around traditional regional cooking. Dishes include crispy breast of lamb with a chickpea and butternut squash compote and roast lemon purée to start, then southern Italian fish stew with new potatoes, tomatoes, garlic and chilli. Finish with pears poached in white wine, saffron and vanilla. Wines from an all-Italian list start at £17.85.

Chef/s: Antonio Cersosimo. **Open:** Mon to Sat L and D. **Closed:** Sun, 25 and 26 Dec, bank hols. **Meals:** set L £14 (2 courses) to £18. Set D £25 (2 courses) to £30. **Details:** 36 seats. Music.

Symbols

Accommodation is available
Three courses for less than £30
£5-off voucher scheme
Notable wine list

Chapel 1877

Cooking score: 2
Modern European | £35
Churchill Way, Cardiff, CF10 2WF
Tel no: (029) 2022 2020
chapel1877.com
£5 OFF

A smartly converted Methodist chapel built in the French Gothic style, Chapel 1877 comprises a lively ground-floor bar and more sedate mezzanine restaurant with entertaining views of the bustle below. It's a great looker inside and out, with restaurant seating including secluded booths as well as ringside seats, and its location in the heart of the city makes it a good option on a night out. Ryan Mitchell has been promoted to head chef; his kitchen is responsible for afternoon teas, as well as an à la carte and a seven-course tasting menu. Typical of his modern Welsh style are bruschetta of Wye Valley asparagus with a poached Burford Brown egg; roast rump of Welsh lamb with scorched gem lettuce, Parmentier potatoes, fine beans, olives and tomato; and a hot chocolate-orange fondant with chocolate ice cream and candied oranges. The wine list has a wide reach, with most bottles under £30.
Chef/s: Ryan Mitchell. **Open:** all week L, Mon to Sat D. **Closed:** 26 and 27 Dec, 2 and 3 Jan. **Meals:** main courses £12 to £29. Set L £13 (2 courses). Sun L £19 (3 courses). Tasting menu £59 (7 courses). **Details:** 180 seats. 16 seats outside. Bar. Music. Children over 5 yrs only at D.

Mint and Mustard

Cooking score: 2
Indian | £35
134 Whitchurch Road, Cardiff, CF14 3LZ
Tel no: (029) 2062 0333
mintandmustard.com

It has spawned offshoots in Penarth, Taunton and Chepstow, but the original Cardiff branch of Mint and Mustard still defines the house style and continues to deliver the goods. Vibrant colours, polished floors, banquettes and Indian artwork set the mood, while the menu backpacks across the Subcontinent. Dishes from Kashmir, Goa and Hyderabad sit alongside Himalayan venison curry and Coorgi-style wild boar, although the kitchen's main geographical focus is to the south and west – Kerala in particular. That region's seafood specialities hold pole position, from crab porichathu (deep-fried soft-shell crab with masala seasoning) or tiger prawns marinated in chillies and turmeric, to sea bass cooked in a banana leaf with seafood pilau and moilee sauce. Otherwise, make a beeline for the meaty tandooris. Vegetarians have five-spice paneer or baby mango curry, while the signature 'chocomosa' (a sweet take on the savoury samosa) delights everyone. Spice-friendly wines do their job.
Chef/s: Santhosh Kumar Nair. **Open:** all week L and D. **Closed:** 25 and 26 Dec. **Meals:** main courses £9 to £15. Tasting menus £37 to £47. **Details:** 90 seats. Wheelchairs. Music.

Purple Poppadom

Cooking score: 3
Indian | £30
Upper Floor, 185a Cowbridge Road East, Cardiff, CF11 9AJ
Tel no: (029) 2022 0026
purplepoppadom.com
£5 OFF

Chef Anand George made his name at the Mint and Mustard (see entry), but he's now cooking at this vibrant first-floor eatery wedged in among a parade of suburban shops. Purple hues and splashes of yellow brighten up the contemporary dining room, but the décor plays second fiddle to Anand's ambitious food, which marries Indian tradition with European technique and highly elaborate, Instagram-ready presentation. How about a trio of cheese-based specialities 'fresh from the creamery' (including saffron-infused tandoori paneer and warm goats' cheese with peppered beetroot and spinach salad), slow-cooked beef with 'chunks' of tapioca, shallots and chilli relish or tiger prawns cooked with raw mango, fresh ginger and coconut milk? Seekh kebabs, chicken tikka makhani and Kashmiri rogan josh strike a more familiar note, although desserts return to freewheeling mode for tandoori pineapple and rose-petal crème brûlée. The eclectic wine list includes a brace from India.

Chef/s: Anand George. **Open:** Tue to Sat L and D. Sun, all day from 1. **Closed:** Mon, 25 and 26 Dec, 1 Jan. **Meals:** main courses £13 to £19. Set L £11 (2 courses). Sun L £20. Tasting menu £45 (6 courses). **Details:** 68 seats. Music.

◼ Cowbridge

Bar 44

Cooking score: 2
Spanish | £25
44c High Street, Cowbridge, CF71 7AG
Tel no: (0333) 3444049
bar44.co.uk

One of three branches (also in Penarth and Cardiff), this modern first-floor venue is noted locally for its top-notch tapas. Large bay windows overlook the town centre (a separate second-floor lounge provides extra space for events and parties) and the menu offers ample choice. There are familiar options such as charcuterie and cheeses and rousing renditions of hot tapas classics, say lamb meatballs with red wine, cider-poached chorizo, jamón Ibérico croquetas, chipirones with mojo rojo and lime, and prawn and piquillo tortilla. But there are more creative choices, too, along the lines of Rioja-braised ox cheek with celeriac, oyster mushroom and sage, and grilled sea bream with Jerusalem artichoke, pancetta and romesco. Pistachio and olive oil cake with lemon thyme ice cream and apple is one way to finish. Drink cocktails, Spanish beers and ciders, and do check out the wine list that serves as an education in Spanish wines.

Chef/s: Felix Orellana Cadena. **Open:** Tue to Sun, all day from 12. **Closed:** Mon, 25 Dec. **Meals:** tapas £2 to £9. Set L Mon to Fri £11. Sun L £13. **Details:** 55 seats. Music.

Hare & Hounds

Cooking score: 1
British | £30
Maendy Road, Cowbridge, CF71 7LG
Tel no: (01446) 774892
hareandhoundsaberthin.com

A proper pub with a raft of real ales lined up in the ever so traditional bar, the Hare & Hounds continues pretty much as it has done for the last 300 years or so. But if you head into the dining room (two rooms actually), you'll find a more pared-back, rustic style and an open kitchen serving up Welsh octopus with crispy suckling pig. The chef served time at St John and the Anchor & Hope, so passion for home-grown, local and foraged food is a given. Mackerel and mussel cawl, steamed brill with laverbread butter, roast milk-fed Torgelly Farm lamb, sweetbreads and smoked bacon; it's flag-waving stuff. Finish in style with Champagne rhubarb soufflé. Wines open at £13.95.

Chef/s: Tom Watts-Jones. **Open:** Wed to Sun L, Wed to Sat D. **Closed:** Mon, Tue. **Meals:** main courses £11 to £20. Set L £17 (2 courses) to £20. Tasting menu £55. **Details:** 35 seats. 20 seats outside. Bar. Wheelchairs. Music. Parking.

◼ Newport

Vic North Café

International
Market Street, Newport, SA42 0PH
Tel no: (01239) 820777
vicnorth.co.uk

'Very good food... the best ever mackerel fillets and excellent, elegant salads. Another good meal – this time supper – potted ham, Catalan fish stew and lemon cream with fennel biscotti.'

Oxwich

Beach House

Cooking score: 5
Modern British | £45
Oxwich Beach, Oxwich, SA3 1LS
Tel no: (01792) 390965
beachhouseoxwich.co.uk
£5 OFF

Slap bang on the sands overlooking Oxwich Bay, the Beach House offers expansive Gower Peninsula views. Like sister restaurant Coast at Saundersfoot (see entry), the interior of this detached building mirrors the view from the terrace outside, with sand-coloured leather upholstery and sea-blue fabrics set against wood floors and white walls. It's also a bit of a well-kept secret – 'my taxi driver had lived in the area all his life and didn't even know about it'. The chef here is Hywel Griffith, whose CV includes notable stints at Ynyshir and the Freemasons at Wiswell (see entries), and his menu is full of seafood and fish from day boats, and from lobster pots in the bay itself, as well as top-drawer local meat and game. A starter of courgette flower and white crab meat fritter ('light, crisp, crunchy') accompanied by tomato, artichoke, basil and olive, might precede sweet Oxwich Bay lobster served with crisp breadcrumbed nuggets of soft, creamy sweetbread, charred gem lettuce, fondant potato and grapefruit butter sauce. As a finale, a light, fruity bara brith soufflé is partnered by smoky lapsang souchong ice cream. Wines from £22.
Chef/s: Hywel Griffith. **Open:** Wed to Sun L and D. **Closed:** Mon, Tue, 2 weeks Jan. **Meals:** main courses £19 to £28. Set L £24 (3 courses). Tasting menu £50 (5 courses) to £70. **Details:** 49 seats. 40 seats outside. V menu. Bar. Wheelchairs. Music. Parking.

Penarth

Restaurant James Sommerin

Cooking score: 7
Modern British | £50
The Esplanade, Penarth, CF64 3AU
Tel no: (029) 2070 6559
jamessommerinrestaurant.co.uk
£5 OFF

Overlooking Penarth's seafront, James Sommerin's restaurant is the smartly impressive go-to venue for modern British cooking for miles around. With white-clad tables and restful colours – including pale teal banquettes, which reflect the blues and greens of sea and sky outside – 'the beautiful room' has 'modern, uncluttered and stylish' down to a fine art. What better way to start than with impressive canapés, including 'quite the best goats' cheese gougère I have ever tasted' and a fine selection of breads, as a way in to dishes such as butter-poached lobster with a buttery lobster and sweetcorn bisque, broccoli, fennel, carrot and toasted seeds? Scallops could follow, neatly sliced and interspersed with matchstick pieces of apple and topped with a rich caviar sauce, while meat is imaginatively handled if the 'rosy, tender' Welsh lamb that impressed at inspection (and served with small discs of turnip, tender broad beans and a 'dark and deeply savoury' cumin sauce) is anything to go by. A deconstructed lemon tart with plump, fermented blueberries makes a 'fresh, bright and satisfying' palate cleanser, before a perfectly risen raspberry soufflé, a molten raspberry coulis at its heart, cooled by a dollop of rosemary ice cream. Service, led by Louise Sommerin, is pitched perfectly and the wine list is a serious global affair, with plenty of interest at the lower end.
Chef/s: James Sommerin. **Open:** Tue to Sun L and D. **Closed:** Mon. **Meals:** main courses £18 to £28. Tasting menu £60 (6 courses) to £80 (9 courses). **Details:** 50 seats. Bar. Wheelchairs. Music.

▌Pontypridd
Bunch of Grapes

Cooking score: 2
Modern British | £30
Ynysangharad Road, Pontypridd, CF37 4DA
Tel no: (01443) 402934
bunchofgrapes.org.uk
£5
OFF

Once a watering hole for narrowboat workers and bargees on the now-closed canal, this higgledy-piggledy Victorian pub really is tucked away, despite being fairly central in Pontypridd and just a five-minute walk from the train station. It's well worth seeking out for its range of ales, many of them made by the owners' Otley Brewing Company, and great atmosphere. Warmed by a wood-burner, it's a proper community boozer with a buzzy wood-clad bar serving homemade curries and sandwiches, but the kitchen displays greater ambition in the small restaurant and conservatory at the back. Alongside steaks from a local butcher (including a 'spot-on' fillet of beef with morels, silky pommes mousseline and asparagus), there are starters such as a light and seasonal goats' curd gnocchi with peas and lettuce, and lamb with black garlic, brassicas and white wine. Finish with a playful dessert of banana with crunchy, caramelised sugar, peanut ice cream and a light caramel sauce given a citrusy lift from yuzu ('very addictive'). Wine from £16.90.
Chef/s: Thomas Munton. **Open:** all week L, Mon to Sat D. **Meals:** main courses £14 to £25. Sun L £18 (3 courses). **Details:** 70 seats. 24 seats outside. Bar. Music. Parking.

▌Swansea
Café TwoCann

Cooking score: 2
Modern British | £35
Unit 2, J Shed, Kings Road, Swansea, SA1 8PL
Tel no: (01792) 458000
cafetwocann.com
£5
OFF

If it weren't for the close-packed tables and chairs, you might mistake this glass-fronted warehouse conversion for a gift boutique – note the display cabinets and shelves stocked with bespoke jewellery, leather bags, scarves, candles and suchlike. Part of the SA1 waterfront development overlooking Swansea's Sail Bridge, Café TwoCann functions as casual neighbourhood drop-in by day and an upmarket bistro by night. Burgers, sandwiches, jacket potatoes, omelettes and other café staples give way to dishes with a bit more restaurant clout – think Welsh goats' cheese and apple croustade with toasted brioche, Thai-spiced Gower mussels with handmade focaccia or duck breast with beetroot purée, black cherries and red wine jus. Steaks, pasta and daily fish specials bulk out the menu, while dessert might be sticky toffee pudding or lemon posset with meringue, macaroon, chocolate soil and fresh berries. Breakfast, afternoon tea, cocktails and two dozen easy-drinking wines complete the picture.
Chef/s: Matt Griffiths. **Open:** Wed to Mon L, Wed to Sat D. **Closed:** Tue, 25 and 26 Dec. **Meals:** main courses £10 to £24. Set L and D £20 (2 courses) to £25. **Details:** 49 seats. 24 seats outside. Wheelchairs. Music.

Didier & Stephanie

Cooking score: 4
French | £30
56 St Helen's Road, Swansea, SA1 4BE
Tel no: (01792) 655603

A white-fronted townhouse with steps leading up to the front door has been home to a fondly regarded classical French bistro in the

Symbols

▬⬛ Accommodation is available
£30 Three courses for less than £30
£5
OFF £5-off voucher scheme
🍷 Notable wine list

heart of the city since 2000. News reached us early in 2017 that the owners were intending to sell up and move on to pastures new, but for the time being, Didier Suvé's unreconstructed French cooking maintains its solidly loyal customer base. These are dishes of the *cuisine grandmère* generation, interpreted with honesty and aplomb, on menus that might open with warm crab mousse in white wine sauce, or oxtail terrine with horseradish dressing, and move on seamlessly to sea bass in saffron sauce, herb-crusted hake in beurre blanc, or properly preserved duck leg confit with shallots. Favoured sweet finishings that hark back a century and more encompass nougat glacé with red fruit coulis, and pear poached in spiced red wine with ice cream. Wines start at £15.90.

Chef/s: Didier Suvé. **Open:** Tue to Sat L and D. **Closed:** Sun, Mon, 2 weeks Christmas and New Year. **Meals:** main courses £16 to £20. Set L £17 (2 courses) to £20. Set D £23 (2 courses) to £31. **Details:** 25 seats. Music.

Hanson at the Chelsea

Cooking score: 4
Modern European | £38
17 St Mary Street, Swansea, SA1 3LH
Tel no: (01792) 464068
hansonatthechelsea.co.uk

Diners ensconced in Andrew and Michelle Hanson's convivial eatery can enjoy some of the finer things in a cosy yellow-walled dining room that fuses breezy bistro-style simplicity with some rustic touches. Andrew's unfussy but sophisticated food relies heavily on Welsh ingredients, with seafood stealing most of the limelight in dishes such as roast salmon carré with Alsace bacon and wild mushroom risotto or thick-cut cod fillet with slow-cooked leeks and pancetta, truffle oil mash and Penclawdd cockle butter sauce. Otherwise, the kitchen produces finely judged, meaty specialities ranging from a classic take on steak Diane to honey-roast Gressingham duck breast with sweet potato dauphinois, seared cherries, orange, figs and port-infused pink peppercorn jus. To finish,

keep it sociable by ordering a sharing plate of mini desserts or explore the selection of Welsh cheeses. Well-chosen, fairly priced wines also hit the mark.

Chef/s: Andrew Hanson. **Open:** Mon to Sat L and D. **Closed:** Sun, bank hols. **Meals:** main courses £13 to £25. Set L £15 (2 courses) to £19. Tasting menu £40 (7 courses). **Details:** 40 seats. Music.

Slice

Cooking score: 4
Modern British | £42
73-75 Eversley Road, Swansea, SA2 9DE
Tel no: (01792) 290929
sliceswansea.co.uk

Behind a clean white frontage, the café-like ambience of Messrs Harris and Bannister's vibrant venue in the Sketty district embraces chunky chairs and bare floorboards, as a backdrop to some lively modern Welsh cooking. Either choose three courses à la carte, or combine half a dozen of them into a taster format. Sterling prime materials are on display in principal dishes such as wild boar loin, belly and cheek with pickled red cabbage, celeriac fondant and apple, or a double-act of roast brill and langoustine with fashionable cauliflower accompaniments and a rich langoustine beurre blanc. Prior to that, there are carefully considered openers like truffle-scented textures of Jerusalem artichoke with crispy quail's eggs, or barbecued mullet on clam linguine, and the art of sweet temptation is practised ruthlessly for desserts such as pear frangipane tart with a purée of golden raisins and PX sherry, as well as brown-sugar ice cream. A broadly spread wine list opens at £17 for Languedoc varietals in all three colours.

Chef/s: Chris Harris and Adam Bannister. **Open:** Fri to Sun L, Thur to Sun D. **Closed:** Mon, Tue, Wed, 1 week Apr, 1 week Jul, 2 weeks Oct. **Meals:** set L £29 (2 courses) to £32. Set D £42. Tasting menu L £48, D £55. **Details:** 16 seats. V menu. Music.

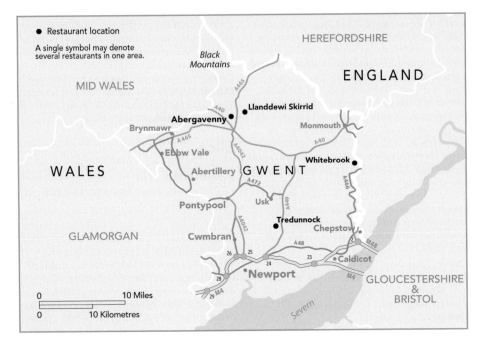

Abergavenny

1861

Cooking score: 4
Modern British | £39
Cross Ash, Abergavenny, NP7 8PB
Tel no: (01873) 821297
18-61.co.uk

£5 OFF

Named in reference to its date of construction, Simon and Kate King's place is a stone-built country restaurant in the hinterland between Abergavenny and Monmouth. A display of jams, jellies and pickles, as well as shelves of cookbooks, creates a welcoming homey atmosphere, and Simon King is an ardent proselytiser for Monmouthshire produce, not to mention that of his father-in-law's vegetable nursery. Various fixed-price menus and a carte are crowned by an impressive seven-course Prestige taster. At inspection, it comprised beetroot and lavender risotto with Parmesan crisps, a colourful overture to a seared scallop with foie gras and elderberries,

spinach-bedded hake in Champagne cream, and then a principal dish of pinkly roasted lamb loin with a cinnamon-spiced lamb and apricot boudin, char-grilled vegetables and crushed butter-beans. Nobody gets away with one dessert these days, so a light, sweet intro of elderflower pannacotta and red gooseberries, followed by a similarly flavoured soufflé with rhubarb sauce and sorbet, are all the more appreciated for being sensitively judged. Wines offer a good spread at reasonable prices, from £18.

Chef/s: Simon King. **Open:** Tue to Sun L, Tue to Sat D. **Closed:** Mon, first 2 weeks Jan. **Meals:** main courses £21 to £25. Set L £24 (2 courses) to £27. Set D £38. Sun L £30. Tasting menu £65. **Details:** 40 seats. V menu. Bar. Music. Parking.

Average price

The average price denotes the price of a three-course meal without wine.

Top of the box

With the cost of setting up a fixed location restaurant spiralling, it's no wonder more start-ups are looking to upcycled shipping containers as a more economical way to launch their business.

It is estimated that there are around 17 million shipping containers around the world, although only a third are being used. Discarded containers tend to remain stacked up in ports, but a number of entrepreneurial restaurateurs are transforming these stainless steel boxes into restaurants across the UK.

From lobster rolls at **Riley's Fish Shack** on the beach at Tynemouth to Elliott Lidstone's contemporary fine dining at his 18-cover **Box-E** restaurant on the quayside at Bristol's new box-park Cargo, shipping container eateries are opening all the time.

In Newcastle-upon-Tyne, Anna Hedworth has gained a national reputation for the seasonal dishes served in her two-container restaurant **Cook House**, and **Craftworks** on Lemon Quay in Truro continues to draw a crowd with its vibrant global street food.

Built to withstand the elements and cheaper to run, shipping containers are especially attractive to start-ups testing the market before taking the bigger step to open a bricks-and-mortar business.

The Hardwick

Cooking score: 3
Modern British | £35
Old Raglan Road, Abergavenny, NP7 9AA
Tel no: (01873) 854220
thehardwick.co.uk

Like the Walnut Tree at nearby Llanddewi Skirrid (see entry), the Hardwick has shed most of its pubby baggage and is now comfortable in its new skin. Pitched as a cosmopolitan restaurant-with-rooms, it promises an appealing blend of low-beamed rusticity and comfy sofas across three rambling spaces, all dedicated to the business of eating. High prices remain a bugbear, but Stephen Terry's kitchen can still deliver an exceptionally spirited menu 'full of different, interesting dishes'. Highlights from recent samplings have included tender pork loin on butter beans with pieces of crispy ham hock, and a 'wonderful creation' involving lamb and mint salsa verde wrapped in a thin strip of pasta. Mr Terry's famous deep-fried black pudding now appears with pickled fennel, apple and mustard sauce, there's beer-battered haddock if you want it, and desserts are mostly reinvented classics such as chocolate mousse or lemon crunch. The classy modern wine list is spot-on for sophisticated palates.
Chef/s: Stephen Terry. **Open:** all week L and D. **Meals:** main courses £8 to £18. **Details:** 100 seats. 25 seats outside. Bar. Wheelchairs. Music. Parking.

▪ Llanddewi Skirrid
The Walnut Tree

Cooking score: 5
Modern British | £60
Llanddewi Skirrid, NP7 8AW
Tel no: (01873) 852797
thewalnuttreeinn.com

'Have been eating in this restaurant for over twenty years: Franco Taruschio's heyday, and now Shaun Hill. In a way the two regimes are similar — classic cuisine, seasonal ingredients and a very good reasonably priced wine list.' It's good to know that, a decade down the line, Shaun Hill continues to take a genuinely unaffected approach to things – it's as if the ghost of Elizabeth David is hovering near the stove. The strength of this rustic country restaurant has always been the superb quality of the ingredients, the simplicity of the cooking and the outstanding sauces. Indeed, one reporter was so blown away by a dish of cèpes (with artichoke, potato, garlic and parsley), he spent the next two days searching the Forest of Dean for the funghi. Enjoyable, too, has been Brillat-Savarin and black truffle omelette, veal kidneys with streaky bacon and Cassis sauce, and Seville orange meringue pie. As for wine, the emphasis is on personal favourites rather than carefully planning out the list, so expect plenty of smaller and artisan producers (mainly European), with some top-end classics thrown in for good measure. Bottles from £26.

Chef/s: Shaun Hill and Roger Brook. **Open:** Tue to Sat L and D. **Closed:** Sun, Mon, 1 week Christmas. **Meals:** main courses £15 to £30. Set L £25 (2 courses) to £30. **Details:** 50 seats. 12 seats outside. Bar. Wheelchairs. Parking.

▌Monmouth

READERS RECOMMEND

#7 Church Street
Modern European
7 Church Street, Monmouth, NP25 3BX
Tel no: (01600) 712600
numbersevenchurchstreet.co.uk
'As we sauntered along a narrow cobbled alleyway in the beautiful town of Monmouth we saw this attractive French-style café. Outside were a few painted tables and chairs, with couples sitting relaxed in the shade. We discovered it was not so much a café as a lovely little restaurant. The food was excellent; compliments to the chefs. My husband ordered the Caesar salad, which was very fresh and crispy. I chose the pork sandwich, oh-so-juicy pork and a touch of sweet apple sauce; it was delicious. We will definitely make more visits and can highly recommend it.'

▌Tredunnock
The Newbridge on Usk
Cooking score: 3
Modern British | £37
Tredunnock, NP15 1LY
Tel no: (01633) 451000
celtic-manor.com
🛏

A handsome black-and-white country inn facing a bridge over the river Usk, the Newbridge is enviably located for getting away from it all, and its terrace for summer dining is a precious resource in the pastoral surroundings. Country walks for the enterprising will help build an appetite for the rustic Welsh cooking on offer, which is presented with a certain contemporary flair and features an array of local-market fish, thoroughbred meats and Welsh cheeses. A hungry pair might share a stacked seafood platter including peppered mackerel, mussels cooked in Taffy cider, potted salmon and more. For mains, pork loin with black pudding and prunes vies for attention with slow-cooked beef cheek and mash on lentils and turnips, and if a trio of cheeses (perhaps Pant-Ysgawn goat, Snowdonia Black Bomber and Perl Las Blue) with pear chutney doesn't tempt, look to baked passion fruit cream with oats and fudge for sweet relief. Welsh wines in all styles from Ancre Hill in the Wye Valley are worth a punt.

Chef/s: Adam Whittle. **Open:** all week L and D. **Meals:** main courses £17 to £34. Set L £16 (2 courses) to £20. Set D £20 (2 courses) to £25. Sun L £25. **Details:** 80 seats. 45 seats outside. Bar. Wheelchairs. Music. Parking.

■ Whitebrook

The Whitebrook

Cooking score: 7
British | £59
Whitebrook, NP25 4TX
Tel no: (01600) 860254
thewhitebrook.co.uk

£5 OFF 🍷 🛏

'We took a walk along the river, then up through the woods to the restaurant. On arrival, we had drinks on the terrace, with a bowl of water for our dogs.' And that's in deep December. Buried in the Wye Valley, only a few miles from the ruins of Tintern Abbey, the Whitebrook enjoys its pastoral location to the utmost, as well it might. The brook babbles by outside, while within it is very fresh, light and stylish. Chris Harrod makes a thoroughgoing effort to bring a sense of the changing seasons to his kitchen, which pursues the foraging route more enthusiastically than most. Just trust to those 'forest findings' that crop up in an opening course to accompany roast Jerusalem artichokes with goats' curd, nuts and seeds. Reporters who came amid the bounty of autumn were thrilled by a tasting menu that began with mugwort-smoked beets and black pudding, and went on to an Orkney scallop with apple, turnip and wood sorrel. Technique is mobilised to telling effect throughout – the mushrooms that come with an egg yolk have been slow-cooked for an hour to bring out their deep earthiness – while the local suckling pig is braised to ultimate tenderness and set alongside sweetly rooty caramelised celeriac and pear. The scent of hedgerows and herbaceous borders continues into desserts such as violet and blueberry cocktail with rose and lemon thyme, or an aerated raspberry mousse with herb sorbet and a little soil (cocoa, not humus). It's a charming and dazzling experience all told, including 'some of the nicest service – super efficient and friendly', and a list of organic, biodynamic and natural wines. Start with a glass of Sylvain Bailly's delicate Sancerre Rosé (£6.25), and proceed from there.

Chef/s: Chris Harrod. **Open:** Wed to Sun L, Tue to Sun D. **Closed:** Mon, first 2 weeks Jan. **Meals:** set L £29 (2 courses) to £35. Set D £59 (3 courses). Sun L £35. Tasting menu £47 (5 courses) to £74. **Details:** 28 seats. V menu. Bar. Wheelchairs. Music. Parking. Children over 12 yrs only at D

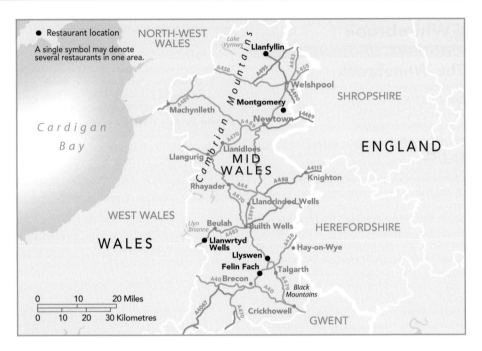

● Restaurant location

A single symbol may denote several restaurants in one area.

NORTH-WEST WALES

Lake Vyrnwy — Llanfyllin

Cambrian Mountains

A458 A495 A483 A458

Welshpool

Machynlleth Montgomery A490 SHROPSHIRE

A489 Newtown A489

Cardigan Bay

A470 Llanidloes MID WALES ENGLAND

Llangurig

A4113 A488 Knighton

Rhayader A44

A470 Llandrindod Wells

WEST WALES A483

Llyn Brianne Beulah Builth Wells HEREFORDSHIRE

WALES ● Llanwrtyd Wells A483 A438

Llyswen ● Hay-on-Wye

Felin Fach ● Talgarth

A40 Brecon A40 Black Mountains

0 10 20 Miles
0 10 20 30 Kilometres

A4067 A470 Crickhowell GWENT

Felin Fach
The Felin Fach Griffin
Cooking score: 4
Modern British | £38
Felin Fach, LD3 0UB
Tel no: (01874) 620111
felinfachgriffin.co.uk

Over the years Charles and Edmund Inkin have worked wonders with this mid 18th-century coaching inn – though be warned, the entrance can look 'unloved'. Once inside, however, it is warm, relaxed, with real fires, plump leather sofas and newspapers to read. As for food, the starting point is good-quality materials, and the kitchen offers an inviting selection of contemporary dishes. Maybe try the board of Trealy Farm charcuterie, or cauliflower and cumin tempura with a goats' cheese fondue, before gnocchi with wild garlic, cottage cheese and chilli seed granola, or Bwlch venison chop with faggot, swede and confit onions. Sunday roasts are well

reported, and there's a good selection of British and Irish cheeses, while dessert brings 'a really effective' passion fruit posset with cucumber and coriander. The wine list is pitched just right, with modest pricing and a huge amount of variety.
Chef/s: Ben Ogden. **Open:** all week L and D.
Closed: 25 Dec, 4 days early Jan. **Meals:** main courses £16 to £21. Set L £19 (2 courses) to £24. Set D £24 (2 courses) to £29. Sun L £27 (3 courses).
Details: 60 seats. 30 seats outside.

Llanfyllin
Seeds
Cooking score: 1
Modern British | £29
5 Penybryn Cottages, High Street, Llanfyllin, SY22 5AP
Tel no: (01691) 648604

Mark and Felicity Seager run an 'atmospheric restaurant with great ambience and are very welcoming'. Cosy, cottagey and

unpretentious, with a wood-burning stove adding to the charms, their long-standing, evening-only venue fits the bill if you are in the area. Readers report success with simple, familiar fare such as linguine and wild mushrooms with sherry cream sauce, and rack of Welsh lamb with Dijon and herb crust. Desserts include white chocolate cheesecake with salted-caramel sauce. Wines from £16.
Chef/s: Mark Seager. **Open:** Wed to Sat L and D. **Closed:** Sun, Mon, Tue. (Wed and Thur winter.). **Meals:** main courses £14 to £20. Set D £25 (2 courses) to £28. **Details:** 20 seats. 6 seats outside.

▌Llanwrtyd Wells
Carlton Riverside
Cooking score: 4
Modern British | £32
Irfon Crescent, Llanwrtyd Wells, LD5 4SP
Tel no: (01591) 610248
carltonriverside.com

£5
OFF

Occupying 'the second oldest building in the smallest town in Britain', this long-serving restaurant-with-rooms makes the most of its setting by the south bank of the river Irfon. Chef Luke Roberts is now the owner, although nothing much has changed, from the shelves lined with cookbooks to the gently reassuring food served in the refined dining room. Polished-wood tables and a big picture window (with river views) provide the backdrop to Luke's concise menus, which come liberally peppered with Welsh ingredients. Carmarthen air-dried ham is served with pea and shallot salad, sea bass is partnered by roast tomato salsa and wilted spinach, while pan-fried venison benefits from a wimberry and port jus. This is classic mainstream stuff, right down to capably crafted desserts such as chocolate fondant with raspberry jelly, apricot purée and honey ice cream. The global wine list includes a generous selection of half-bottles.
Chef/s: Luke Roberts. **Open:** Mon to Sat L and D. **Closed:** Sun, 20 to 30 Dec. **Meals:** main courses £17 to £27. Set L £15. Tasting menu £45. **Details:** 18 seats. Bar. Music. Children over 5 yrs only.

▌Llyswen
Llangoed Hall
Cooking score: 5
Modern British | £75
Llyswen, LD3 0YP
Tel no: (01874) 754525
llangoedhall.co.uk

There are few more picture-perfect places than this beautiful, ancient house in a fabulous setting. The grand fireplace dominates the deep-sofa'd drawing room, where the view of the gardens from old lead-lighted windows would make 'the perfect backdrop for afternoon tea'. The dining room has the full country house hotel accoutrements – full-skirted tables and thick carpet, with white-glove-wearing waiters dancing attendance. The hotel is very proud of its kitchen – expect tasting menus of four or more courses, topped and tailed with delicate canapés and petits fours. There's a strong emphasis on local, even home-grown, organic produce, which is delicately rendered into intricate, clever dishes strewn with flowers and herbs that are almost too pretty to eat: a squid-ink cracker dotted with weeny pink shrimps, a light curry sauce and careful cubes of mango making a deconstructed coronation prawn canapé; a ceviche scallop wrapped around an intense nest of seaweed, beautified with a spoonful of oscietra; a cannon of local lamb served perfectly pink, on a bed of crispy, slow-cooked shoulder, its simple jus lifted with herbs and local asparagus. The wine list, supplied by respected local merchants Tanners, has everything diners need without going over the top.
Chef/s: Nick Brodie. **Open:** all week L and D. **Meals:** tasting menus £74 (4 courses) to £95. Set L £25 (3 courses). Sun L £25. **Details:** 40 seats. V menu. Bar. Wheelchairs. Parking.

▌Montgomery
The Checkers

Cooking score: 6
French | £65
Broad Street, Montgomery, SY15 6PN
Tel no: (01686) 669822
checkerswales.co.uk

The result of working/family partnership between an impressively qualified French chef and two sisters of Shropshire farming stock, the Checkers is a centuries-old Montgomery drinking den recast as a country-style restaurant-with-rooms. Drinks are served in the rustic-chic lounge, while dinner proceeds at a leisurely pace in an elegantly appointed room done out with vintage scrubbed tables, panelling and arty prints. Stéphane Borie's food may be rooted in Gallic haute cuisine, but he is also in tune with the seasonal Welsh larder. Intriguing home-baked breads and canapés open the show, while the evening's menu might run from wild trout with cauliflower and tarragon dressing, via a zingy pink grapefruit and Champagne granita to grilled fillet of Celtic Pride beef accompanied by smoked pomme mousseline, spinach purée and red wine jus. M. Borie's mastery of the repertoire also shows in textbook desserts such as a rhubarb crumble soufflé with stem ginger ice cream. The no-choice tasting menu isn't to everyone's taste, but this is seriously refined cooking backed by a 100-strong wine list that ventures well beyond the French borders.
Chef/s: Stéphane Borie. **Open:** Tue to Sat D only.
Closed: Sun, Mon, 3 weeks Jan, 1 week summer.
Meals: set D £65 (6 courses). **Details:** 30 seats. Bar.
Wheelchairs. Children over 7 yrs only.

GFG scoring system

Score 1: Capable cooking with simple food combinations and clear flavours.

Score 2: Decent cooking, displaying good technical skills and interesting combinations and flavours.

Score 3: Good cooking, showing sound technical skills and using quality ingredients.

Score 4: Dedicated, focused approach to cooking; good classical skills and high-quality ingredients.

Score 5: Exact cooking techniques and a degree of ambition; showing balance and depth of flavour in dishes.

Score 6: Exemplary cooking skills, innovative ideas, impeccable ingredients and an element of excitement.

Score 7: High level of ambition and individuality, attention to the smallest detail, accurate and vibrant dishes.

Score 8: A kitchen cooking close to or at the top of its game. Highly individual with impressive artistry.

Score 9: Cooking that has reached a pinnacle of achievement, making it a hugely memorable experience.

Score 10: Just perfect dishes, showing faultless technique at every service; extremely rare and the highest accolade.

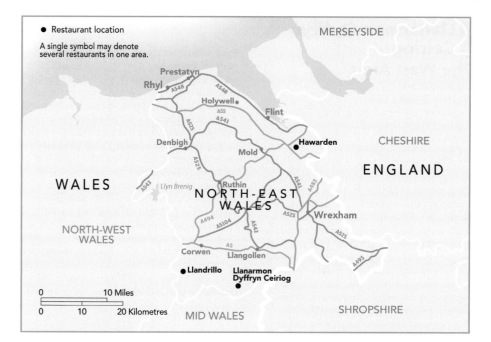

Hawarden

The Glynne Arms

Cooking score: 3

International | £28

3 Glynne Way, Hawarden, CH5 3NS

Tel no: (01244) 569988

theglynnearms.co.uk

£5 OFF £30

As descendants of Victorian prime minister William Gladstone, Charles Gladstone and family are not only heirs to the Hawarden Estate, but also run a farm shop, manage the online shopping hub Pedlars and oversee the Glynne Arms – a 200-year-old coaching inn by the gates of Hawarden Castle. Done out in quirky style, it offers a wide-ranging repertoire with steaks and sausages from the shop getting special billing on the menu, alongside pies, burgers and charcuterie boards. The remainder of the line-up is an eclectic cook's tour taking in the likes of chorizo-stuffed squid with smoked chilli oil, gilthead bream with ramen noodles or a mixed plate of

pork cuts with black pudding, celeriac rösti, black cabbage and sticky lentil jus. Nibbles such as whitebait with harissa aïoli are served at the bar, while puddings might include chocolate fondant with blood orange. To drink, six local ales and Wrexham lager compete with a modest wine list.

Chef/s: Adam Stanley and Chris Moran. **Open:** all week, all day from 12. **Meals:** main courses £12 to £25. Sun L £11. **Details:** 75 seats. 32 seats outside. Bar. Wheelchairs. Music. Parking.

Please send us your feedback

To register your opinion about any restaurant listed in this guide, or a new restaurant that you wish to bring to our attention, please visit the web address at the bottom of the page. Your feedback informs the content of the book and will be used to compile next year's reviews.

Llanarmon Dyffryn Ceiriog
The West Arms

Cooking score: 1
Modern British | £32
Llanarmon Dyffryn Ceiriog, LL20 7LD
Tel no: (01691) 600665
thewestarms.co.uk

£5 OFF

An 'unreconstructed country pub, but definitely not faded,' noted one visitor to this rambling, fire-warmed old charmer in the depths of the North Wales countryside. Its inglenooks, flagstones and gnarly old timbers speak for themselves, and the cooking runs from honest, hearty lunchtime fare to more poised evening creations – maybe fillet of oak-smoked Ceiriog trout with textures of beetroot and horseradish ahead of Welsh mountain lamb fillets with pearl barley, honey-roasted seasonal vegetables and a port wine jus. A substantial wine list complements a good selection of ales.
Chef/s: Grant Williams. **Open:** Mon to Sat L and D. Sun, all day from 12. **Meals:** main courses £15 to £27. Sun L £13. **Details:** 150 seats. 80 seats outside. Bar. Wheelchairs. Music. Parking.

Llandrillo
Tyddyn Llan

Cooking score: 6
British | £65
Llandrillo, LL21 0ST
Tel no: (01490) 440264
tyddynllan.co.uk

It's been a decade and a half since Bryan and Susan Webb upped sticks from London and headed for the tranquillity of North Wales, but the move suited them to a T. At the heart of their opulent country hotel is a civilised dining room pleasantly adorned with greenery in both the colour scheme and table decorations. Bryan's cooking remains in touch with its mingled roots in Anglo-French

classicism, and there are six- and nine-course tasters for exploring the repertoire. Langoustine bisque has all the requisite richness and comes with rocking rouille, while red mullet is briefly grilled and paired with aubergine purée in chilli and garlic oil. At main, there are approving notices for Label Anglais chicken leg with morels in luxurious tarragon cream, as well as confit duck with its faggot and morteau, sauced with cider and apple. Desserts are their best when simplest, perhaps mirabelles poached in brandy with vanilla ice cream, or prune frangipane tart. Wines by the glass from £6.50, or half-litre carafe from £17, lead off a list that capably covers the major producing countries.
Chef/s: Bryan Webb. **Open:** Fri to Sun L, Wed to Sun D. **Closed:** Mon, Tue, 2 weeks Jan. **Meals:** set L £29 (2 courses) to £36. Set D £55 (2 courses) to £65. Sun L £36. Tasting menu £80 (6 courses) to £95. **Details:** 16 seats. Bar. Wheelchairs. Music. Parking.

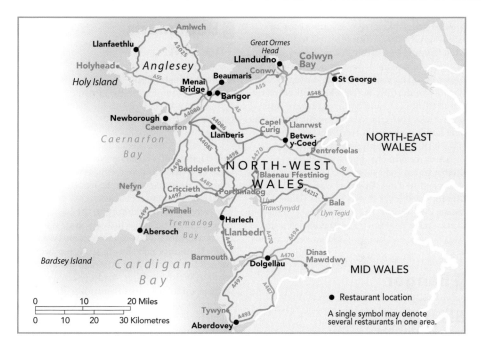

Aberdovey
Seabreeze
Cooking score: 1
British | £30
6 Bodfor Terrace, Aberdovey, LL35 0EA
Tel no: (01654) 767449
seabreeze-aberdovey.co.uk
£5
OFF

'A great atmosphere reflecting the coastal location,' sums up one visitor to this suitably bright and breezy restaurant on the seafront at Aberdovey. Against a backdrop of stonework and exposed wood, the big-hearted cooking focuses on local ingredients first and foremost. 'Perfectly cooked' salt cod fritters have garnered particular praise and might precede slow-roasted pork belly with carrot purée, fondant potato, buttered greens and Marsala sauce. Get your sweet fix from dark chocolate tart and hazelnut ice cream. Service, 'friendly, attentive but not intrusive' for one reporter, deserves plaudits, as does the 'very reasonably priced' wine list, starting at £15.

Chef/s: Henry Benson. **Open:** all week D only. **Closed:** 25 and 26 Dec, 2 to 20 Jan. **Meals:** main courses £13 to £21. **Details:** 40 seats. 8 seats outside. Music.

Abersoch
Porth Tocyn Hotel
Cooking score: 2
Modern British | £47
Bwlch Tocyn, Abersoch, LL53 7BU
Tel no: (01758) 713303
porthtocynhotel.co.uk

The mountain range visible across Cardigan Bay includes Snowdon itself, and this prize view is best enjoyed from the terrace. The gloriously situated white-painted hotel has been in the same family since 1948 and the Fletcher-Brewers have kept it steadfastly away from passing fad and fashion. It's a traditional, family-friendly place, with a kitchen that turns out classically focused dishes with a modern touch or two. A crab bonbon and

pickled vegetables arrive as support for an opening salvo of sardines stuffed with the Med flavours of sun-blush tomatoes and basil butter, while main courses run to roast duck breast with spicy stir-fried veg, or sea bream with a wonderfully herby Montpellier butter. For dessert, plum and apple crumble comes with sticky toffee sauce and vanilla ice cream. The lunch menu is shorter than the evening carte with some lighter options. The informative wine list opens at £19.
Chef/s: Louise Fletcher-Brewer, Darren Henton-Morris and Ian Frost. **Open:** all week L and D. **Closed:** early Nov to 2 weeks before Easter. **Meals:** main courses £12 to £26 (L only). Set D £40 (2 courses) to £47. Sun L £26. **Details:** 50 seats. 50 seats outside. Bar. Parking. Children over 5 yrs only at D.

■ Bangor

LOCAL GEM
Blue Sky Café
International | £20
Ambassador Hall, 236 High Street, Bangor, LL57 1PA
Tel no: (01248) 355444
blueskybangor.co.uk
£5 OFF   £30

There are 'blue skies' over this converted Second World War dance hall – at least on the painted beamed ceiling above this café/live music venue. The eclectic menu covers all bases, from 'cowboy breakfasts' and Belgian waffles to meze platters and merguez lamb patties 'in a basket', but also check out the 'chef specials' – perhaps crispy Asian-style pork belly in a barm or chorizo, lentil and vegetable stew. Kids do well here, while drink ranges from Welsh ales, lagers and ciders to a fistful of wines.

■ Beaumaris
The Loft
Cooking score: 4
Modern British | £50
The Bull, Castle Street, Beaumaris, LL58 8AP
Tel no: (01248) 810329
bullsheadinn.co.uk
£5 OFF   🍴

In 2017, the Bull's Head (as was) celebrated 400 years of feeding and watering travellers through Beaumaris, from those who rattled here in horse-drawn coaches to the era of the four-wheel drive. Standing in the lee of Edward I's castle, it has history on its side. A converted loft is a fashionable amenity, and here a contemporary dining space has been created beneath the low rafters to showcase modern Welsh cooking. Andrew Tabberner stepped up to head chef in autumn 2016, and maintains the monthly changing fixed-price menu format of his predecessor. April proceedings began with a light, fresh crab, spiced tomato, radish and lovage salad with dill emulsion, and turned on a main course of eloquently flavoured rolled Anglesey lamb shoulder with smoked bacon, slender new carrots and wild garlic. Another main, roasted plaice T-bone with mussels and samphire may have been oddly lacklustre, but desserts did the business with chocolate mousse and orange sorbet, and a regionally unimpeachable apple mille-feuille, its luscious layer of caramel seasoned with Halen Môn sea salt. A resourceful wine list leads with four house wines at £23.
Chef/s: Andrew Tabberner. **Open:** Wed to Sat D only. **Closed:** Sun, Mon, Tue, 25 and 26 Dec, 1 Jan. **Meals:** set D £50. **Details:** 40 seats. Bar. Children over 7 yrs only.

Parla Italiano?

It's one of the most popular cuisines in the world with good reason, but navigating the menus in many Italian restaurants can be as stressful as sitting a GCSE language exam.

Whether you are eating in a pizzeria, trattoria or osteria, decoding unfamiliar dishes under the headings of antipasti (appetisers), zuppa (soup), insalata (salad), primi piatti (first course), secondi piatti (main course) and dolce (dessert) can be as demanding as untangling your bowl of spaghetti.

Of course, if you have a Pavarotti-sized appetite, you can order the whole lot, but most people in the UK tend to opt for a more traditional three courses of antipasti or soup followed by secondi piatti and dolce.

And then there's the ingredients themselves. What's the difference between a lardon and lardo? The former is a cube of pork fat, the other is a strip of cured pork back fat. Why go for tardivo over radicchio when they are essentially the same bitter leaf?

A basic knowledge of Italian menu terms can be an advantage when it comes to ordering dessert. Ask your waiter for a 'bacio' at the wrong time and you may end up causing quite a scene. After all, this delicious hazelnut and chocolate ice cream translates as 'kiss' in Italian.

▮ Betws-y-Coed

LOCAL GEM
Bistro Betws-y-Coed
British | £26
Holyhead Road, Betws-y-Coed, LL24 0AY
Tel no: (01690) 710328
bistrobetws-y-coed.co.uk

£5 OFF £30

A traditional stone building, home to a traditional bistro, this local favourite allows Welsh ingredients to shine on its bilingual menu. Wood figures large in the cosy interior. The Conwy river, estuary and lush green valley provide many of the ingredients, although there are some broader influences, too (veal cooked in lentil dhal, say, or risotto of smoked haddock). Rump of Welsh lamb is marinated in honey and balsamic, and fillet of hake is topped with Welsh rarebit, while dessert might bring forth warm orange cake with lemon posset and pink grapefruit sorbet. Wines open at £15.50.

▮ Dolgellau
Mawddach
Cooking score: 2
Modern British | £25
Llanelltyd, Dolgellau, LL40 2TA
Tel no: (01341) 421752
mawddach.com

£30

The tiny community of Llanelltyd near Dolgellau is home to the Dunn brothers' farming enterprise, where one of the barns has been converted into a supremely relaxing restaurant. Leather chairs, a slate floor and the fabulous prospect towards Cader Idris, with sheep peaceably grazing in the foreground, makes for one of North Wales' more enviable locations. Ifan Dunn celebrates the surroundings with lively contemporary cooking designed with regional bragging rights in mind. A plate of Trealy Farm charcuterie with caponata, pickles and olives gives its Italian counterpart a run for its money, or you might start with crab linguine enriched with 'nduja. The Mediterranean influence surfaces again in a treatment of locally reared free-range duck with Parmesan polenta and spiced aubergine, while fish might be cod fillet on a casserole of lentils and tomatoes, dressed in gremolata. An appreciation of today's pudding tastes supplies warm ginger cake with salt-caramel ice cream and ginger nuts, or there are fine Welsh cheeses with grape chutney and sourdough. Italian and Chilean house wines are £16.50. **Chef/s:** Ifan Dunn. **Open:** Thur to Sun L, Thur to Sat D. **Closed:** Mon, Tue, Wed, 2 weeks Apr, 2 weeks Nov. **Meals:** main courses £13 to £17. Sun L £25. **Details:** 50 seats. 40 seats outside. Bar. Wheelchairs. Music. Parking. Children over 5 yrs only at D.

Harlech
Castle Cottage
Cooking score: 2
Modern British | £40
Y Llech, Harlech, LL46 2YL
Tel no: (01766) 780479
castlecottageharlech.co.uk

Harlech Castle, a mighty medieval structure built in the 1280s, is a near neighbour to Glyn and Jacqueline Robert's restaurant-with-rooms. They've run their place, which is made up of two 16th-century cottages, since 1989, the business now comprising seven bedrooms and an atmospheric restaurant with original features and a gently contemporary finish. Glyn is a chef with a passion for the region's ingredients, so you might kick off with a trio of Welsh salmon before Cefn Llan Farm duck a couple of ways (pan-roasted breast and a duck and leek bonbon). Influences come from further afield, too, thus hand-carved Serrano ham comes with roasted figs and cantaloupe melon, and local wild sea bass and king prawns with a white wine and basil cream sauce. A tasting menu kicks off with canapés in the bar. Summer fruits set in Champagne jelly with clotted cream ice cream is a seasonal treat. The wine list gives equal attention to Old and New Worlds.

Chef/s: Glyn Roberts. **Open:** all week D only. **Closed:** 24 to 26 Dec, 3 weeks Nov. **Meals:** set D £40 (3 courses). Tasting menu £45. **Details:** 35 seats. Bar. Music. Parking.

Llanberis
LOCAL GEM
The Peak
Modern British | £28
86 High Street, Llanberis, LL55 4SU
Tel no: (01286) 872777
peakrestaurant.co.uk
£5 OFF **£30**

Whether you are in need of sustenance after attempting Snowdon's peak or just want a cosy evening, this warm, welcoming restaurant is the place to be. There's nothing cluttered or fancy about Angela Dwyer's cooking, which aims to please with local produce and casual bistro favourites such as smoked mackerel pâté and slow-roasted lamb shank with fluffy mash and rosemary and redcurrant jus. Otherwise, coconut-coated prawns with a cucumber and coriander salad and soy dipping sauce, followed by home-cured belly of pork with Taffy cider sauce, are typical choices. Wines from £15.95.

Llandudno
Jaya
Cooking score: 2
Indian | £32
36 Church Walks, Llandudno, LL30 2HN
Tel no: (01492) 818198
jayarestaurant.co.uk

Nothing about Jaya is quite what one expects from a neighbourhood Indian restaurant. It's in a red-brick house that encompasses a stylish bar, as well as a minimally accoutred dining room with glass tables and spindly chandeliers. The culinary orientation is Punjabi North India, with a little influence from the Kenyan Asian tradition, the latter resulting in chilli mogo, a starter of cassava fried in garlic and red chilli, or another of spice-rubbed chips with

fruity chutney, and main-course curries in East African masala spices. The more familiar offerings embrace gingery lamb tikki or fish pakora with chilli jam to start, ahead of turbo-charged karahi prawns with red and green peppers and ajwain, or lightly spiced mattar paneer. Griddled chapatis make fine vehicles for sopping up all the juices, and there's refreshing strawberry falooda to finish. Tasting-menu special events are worth diarising, and Valentine's Day in 2017 was celebrated with a murder-mystery evening. Australian house wines are £16.95.
Chef/s: Steve Bloor. **Open:** Thur to Sat D only. **Closed:** Sun to Wed, 23 Dec to 12 Jan. **Meals:** main courses £11 to £14. **Details:** 20 seats. Bar. Music. Parking. Children over 6 yrs only.

▉ Llanfaethlu
The Black Lion Inn
Cooking score: 1
Modern British | £29
Llanfaethlu, LL65 4NL
Tel no: (01407) 730718
blacklionanglesey.com
🛏 £30

The good times returned to the Black Lion in 2012 when Mari and Leigh Faulkner revamped this listed 18th-century country inn on the A5025 between Valley and Cemaes Bay. The bar keeps the character of the original building and three draught ales confirm its pub status, with the menu focused firmly on regional ingredients. Y Cwt Mwg smoke-house provides the duck, which comes in a salad with caramelised oranges, while many of the vegetables, fruits and herbs are own-grown. Tuck into rare-breed steaks, local lamb (braised shoulder perhaps) or fish of the day with creamy garlic mussels, and finish with chocolate and orange fondant. The concise wine list opens at £17.
Chef/s: Wayne Roberts. **Open:** Thur to Sun L, Wed to Sat D. **Closed:** Mon, Tue, 10 days Jan. **Meals:** main courses £14 to £24. Sun L £15 (1 course) to £25. **Details:** 70 seats. 20 seats outside. Bar. Wheelchairs. Music. Parking.

▉ Menai Bridge
Sosban and the Old Butcher's
Cooking score: 6
Modern British | £65
Trinity House, 1 High Street, Menai Bridge, LL59 5EE
Tel no: (01248) 208131
sosbanandtheoldbutchers.com

The setting could hardly be more ordinary: a double-fronted former butcher's shop at the top end of an Anglesey high street, painted pallid green, next door to a place selling mobility scooters. Abandon humdrum expectations, all who enter here, because Stephen and Bethan Stevens' venue is at the very forefront of modern Welsh cooking. The nine-course menu offers no choice, but is constructed from whatever is available and good on each of the three evenings a week the place opens. Reindeer moss is a wild lichen boosted with anchovy and malt for an opener, to be followed by an unmistakably regional speciality of lamb cheek in laverbread. Next up is crackly chicken skin with leeks and mushroom, before a serving of creamed Jerusalem artichoke with goats' cheese and pancetta. The fulcrum of the whole presentation might be pitch-perfect celeriac risotto adorned with apple and coffee, before the main business brings on Coed y Brenin venison in smoky yoghurt with beetroot and black garlic. Only after that does fish arrive, perhaps cod with a little oxtail and yeast, before the pair of desserts marches in – sliced rhubarb topped with a custard bubble, and then a winning combination of lemon ice encased in wickedly dark chocolate strewn with black olive. A provocatively short wine list does its best to keep up, from £20.
Chef/s: Stephen Owen Stevens. **Open:** Sat L, Thur to Sat D. **Closed:** Sun to Wed, Jan, Christmas and New Year. **Meals:** L menu £40. Tasting menu D £65. **Details:** 16 seats. V menu. Children over 12 yrs only.

LOCAL GEM

Freckled Angel

Modern British | £27
49 High Street, Menai Bridge, LL59 5EF
Tel no: (01248) 209952
freckled-angel-fine-catering.co.uk

£30

A move down the high street (from 35 to 49) has resulted in more seats for eager diners and a bigger kitchen for chef/proprietor Mike Jones. His take on Welsh tapas – British ingredients served as small sharing plates – is a big hit, which isn't surprising given braised lamb knuckle comes with crushed carrot and herb salsa, and baked lemon sole with Menai mussels, and Perl Las is twice-baked in a soufflé and arrives with balsamic-infused grapes. Finish with an orange and Earl Grey pannacotta. Wines open at £16.50.

Newborough
The Marram Grass

Cooking score: 4
British | £35
White Lodge, Penlon, Newborough, LL61 6RS
Tel no: (01248) 440077
themarramgrass.com

£5
OFF

Not the most attractive building, this extended potting shed – a long, low building with a corrugated iron roof and pretty pagoda-covered area outside – blasted into the national spotlight when it opened a few years back. This is very much Liam and Ellis Barrie's home turf and the brothers have siphoned off all their energy and passion into making this former greasy spoon (on a campsite) a special work-in-progress. Fresh local ingredients and simple, accurate cooking bring droves of diners – booking is essential – and Ellis's cooking bears evidence of serious thought, with flair and originality running strongly through the short menu. Anglesey goats' cheese mousse is teamed with smoked beetroot, festive apple salsa and kale pesto, while a main course of pan-roasted cod is

served with a split-leek masala sauce, potato mousse, crisped shallots, garlic and potatoes. To finish, an indulgent chocolate and hazelnut délice with chocolate tuile, macaron, jelly and soil is a must if it's on. The wine list (from £15) is arranged helpfully by style.
Chef/s: Ellis Barrie. **Open:** Thur to Sun L and D. **Closed:** Mon, Tue, Wed. **Meals:** main courses £10 to £20. **Details:** 40 seats. 20 seats outside. Parking.

St George
The Kinmel Arms

Cooking score: 4
Modern British | £35
The Village, St George, LL22 9BP
Tel no: (01745) 832207
thekinmelarms.co.uk

£5
OFF

With its 'pantry' for purchasing edible goodies, plus a tea room and the owner's artworks on display, there's much more to the Kinmel Arms than beer. In a wooded setting not far from Abergele, this is a diamond for holidaymakers as well as locals, who frequent the place for its please-all food – a satisfying freestyle take on contemporary pub/brasserie cooking bolstered by old favourites such as chicken Caesar salad. Given the pub's proximity to the bracing expanses of Colwyn Bay, it's no surprise that seafood gets star billing – perhaps turbot in verdant company with wasabi, romanesco and sea herbs or spiced monkfish dressed up with carrots, lentils, lemongrass and chervil velouté. Meat eaters might prefer herb-crusted loin of veal with white asparagus and wild mushrooms, while puds could feature a version of île flottante with pistachio and mandarin. The Welsh cheeseboard is worth a look, and the wine list reads well.
Chef/s: Chad Hughes. **Open:** Tue to Sat L and D. **Closed:** Sun, Mon, 25 Dec, 1 Jan. **Meals:** main courses £18 to £30. Early D £15 (2 courses) to £19. **Details:** 64 seats. 30 seats outside. Bar. Wheelchairs. Music. Parking.

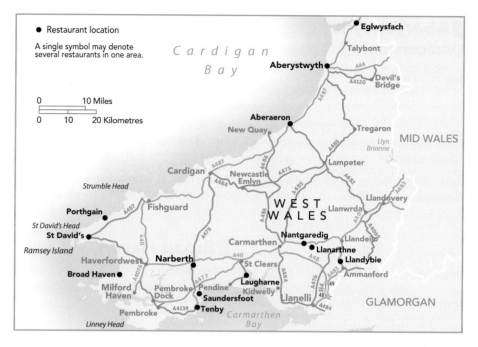

▮ Aberaeron
Harbourmaster

Cooking score: 2
Modern British | £35
Pen Cei, Aberaeron, SA46 0BT
Tel no: (01545) 570755
harbour-master.com

There's no shortage of colour on Aberaeron's
waterfront, but the vivid blue/violet exterior
of this former harbourmaster's office easily
trumps its neighbours – and rightly so. Since
arriving in 2001, Glyn and Menna Heulyn
have transformed the place into a standard-
bearer for Welsh hospitality. Drinks and
bistro-style dishes are served in the warehouse
extension, but the main action takes place in
the original building with its bare-boarded,
maritime-blue dining room. Welsh
ingredients define the daily menu, which
promises big flavours and eclectic ideas
ranging from warm smoked salmon with
burnt apple purée and Brecon Gin-infused
cucumber to breast and samosa of local
pheasant with Savoy cabbage, pancetta and
Madeira sauce. Also expect a nifty take on fish
and chips involving haddock fillet and potato
'scraps', plus old-fashioned desserts such as
apple crumble and custard. Well-chosen
international wines.
Chef/s: Ludo Dieumegard. **Open:** all week L and D.
Closed: 25 Dec. **Meals:** main courses £11 to £22.
Set D £35. Sun L £19 (2 courses) to £25.
Details: 100 seats. 15 seats outside. Bar.
Wheelchairs. Parking.

Please send us
your feedback

To register your opinion about any
restaurant listed in this guide, or a new
restaurant that you wish to bring to our
attention, please visit the web address at
the bottom of the page. Your feedback
informs the content of the book and will
be used to compile next year's reviews.

▌Aberystwyth
Ultracomida
Cooking score: 2
Spanish | £20
31 Pier Street, Aberystwyth, SY23 2LN
Tel no: (01970) 630686
ultracomida.co.uk
£30

'Our first visit last year was so pleasing (and so unusual to find in Aberystwyth) that we returned to this excellent, authentic Spanish deli and tapas bar. As before, we arrived early to get good seats at the large round tables and give ourselves time to sample more from the extensive menu. It is very popular and quickly filled, creating a very happy buzz.' Praise indeed, and there is no shortage of vocal support for this local eatery of the best sort – just a few yards from the seafront. Expect a trademark mix of Spanish flavours grounded in charcuterie and cheeses and offering classics such as albondigas, chipirones (fried baby squid), chorizo al vino, gambas al ajillo and tortilla. Elsewhere, slow-cooked pig's cheek in PX sherry with garlic mash, and slow-cooked rabbit (falling off the bone) with a fine vegetable stew have been endorsed. Drink Spanish beer, cider or sherry or choose from a modestly priced, all-Spanish wine list. Another branch is at 7 High Street, Narberth; tel: (01834) 861491.
Chef/s: Cheryl Price. **Open:** all week L, Mon to Sat D. **Closed:** 25 and 26 Dec, 1 Jan. **Meals:** tapas £4 to £7. **Details:** 32 seats.

Readers recommend

A 'readers recommend' review is a genuine quote from a report sent in by one of our readers. We intend to follow up these suggestions throughout the year to come.

READERS RECOMMEND
Pysgoty
Seafood
The Harbour, South Promenade, Aberystwyth, SY23 1JY
Tel no: (01970) 624611
pysgoty.co.uk
'We only come on holiday to the area to eat here. The first night we had scallops with Ibérico ham, followed by local lobster grilled with herbs. The second night I had crab with a tomato salsa, then roasted turbot with new-season asparagus. They are dedicated to providing their customers with the best, and consistently do just that.'

▌Broad Haven
LOCAL GEM
The Druidstone
Global | £35
Broad Haven, SA62 3NE
Tel no: (01437) 781221
druidstone.co.uk

Twenty acres of grounds and magnificent views over St Brides Bay add to the pleasures of this homely Victorian country hotel on the Pembrokeshire cliffs. The owners have been in residence for more than four decades and are not about to change their successful formula. As always, the menu is loyal to local ingredients and a global outlook, with dishes ranging from beetroot-cured salmon gravadlax with root vegetable rémoulade to pepper-crusted fillet steak on a bed of wok-fried baby vegetables, while cherry cheesecake can feature among desserts. Wines from £16.50.

Eglwysfach

★ TOP 50 ★

Ynyshir

Cooking score: 8
Modern British | £110
Eglwysfach, SY20 8TA
Tel no: (01654) 781209
ynyshir.co.uk

£5 OFF 🍷 🛏️

It may be a destination restaurant, but it doesn't take long to realise that this fine country manor house 'doesn't have too much truck with tradition and convention'. The house itself is charming but informal: the bar could happily grace a brasserie or town house in any busy metropolis, while the tiny dining room is open to the kitchen and 'it's the chefs rather than the waiters who bring each course'. Gareth Ward's menu is a clever and meticulous no-choice affair – a celebration of local produce infused with Japanese flavours and real skill. But most of all, his cooking is about flavour. 'Not French Onion Soup' offers confit alliums with seaweed and tiny cubes of tofu, covered with dashi, a veritable explosion of sweet-savoury umami flavours. Lamb spare ribs, salted and slow-cooked for hours, are finished briefly in a Green Egg barbecue and are tender yet crisp – the very essence of lamb – 'and best eaten with fingers'. Duck liver is melted and re-formed with soya to make the lightest mousse and served with a grating of smoked eel and concentrated birch sap. Fudge hits the ultimate salt-savoury note with the use of Wagyu beef dripping in place of cream, while tiramisu is constructed at the table with rich gels of sugar and coffee, frozen mini-balls of cream and coffee sprinkled over the top. So, allow plenty of time – lunch consists of at least nine courses and takes more than two hours, and dinner will take around four. With this much to eat on such a culinary journey you may think the chef's table, with at least 19 courses, de trop, but halfway through the meal, you'll be wondering why you didn't go the whole hog because you won't want it to

stop. The extensive wine list ranges wide, offering thought-provoking bottles and glasses.
Chef/s: Gareth Ward. **Open:** Tue to Sat L and D. **Closed:** Sun, Mon, new year, 1 week Apr, 2 weeks summer, 1 week Nov. **Meals:** tasting menu L £40 (9 courses). Chef's Table L £110. Tasting menu D £110 (18 courses). Chef's Table D £130. **Details:** 20 seats. V menu. Bar. Music. Parking. Children over 12 years only.

Laugharne

The Cors

Cooking score: 3
Modern British | £35
Newbridge Road, Laugharne, SA33 4SH
Tel no: (01994) 427219
thecors.co.uk

£5 OFF 🛏️

In the lee of the ruined castle, overlooking the Coran estuary, The Cors is a country villa with plenty of rural style. A couple of acres of exceedingly pretty landscaped gardens are not the least of its seductions, and inside the place is decorated in rather racy fashion, its low-lit, crimson-walled dining room enhanced by light through partly stained-glass windows. Nick Priestland offers relatively straightforward modern Welsh bistro cooking, with refined prime materials to the fore. Expect a savoury crème brûlée to start, full of the beguiling richness of smoked haddock, prior to roast rack of salt marsh lamb, crusted in rosemary and garlic and served in caramelised onion gravy, or perhaps wild Pacific salmon with cavolo nero and locally gathered samphire in lemon chive sauce. Finish with classic sticky toffee pudding. The wine list makes a virtue of brevity, opening with Languedoc house blends at £16.95, or £5 a glass.
Chef/s: Nick Priestland. **Open:** Thur to Sat D only. **Closed:** Sun to Wed, 25 and 26 Dec, last 2 weeks Nov. **Meals:** main courses £17 to £30. **Details:** 30 seats. 10 seats outside. Bar. Wheelchairs. Music. Parking. Children over 12 yrs only.

▌Llanarthne
Wright's Food Emporium

Cooking score: 3
Modern British | £22
Golden Grove Arms, Llanarthne, SA32 8JU
Tel no: (01558) 668929
wrightsfood.co.uk
£30

On the back road from Llandeilo to
Carmarthen, Simon and Maryann Wright's
Food Emporium may be out of the way but is
definitely worth the detour. With bright plain
rooms and lots of mismatched tables, it majors
on breakfast and lunches, only opening in the
evenings on Fridays and Saturdays. The
blackboard-scrawled menu is built around
seasonal and local produce, including produce
available from the deli and adjoining wine
room. Like the décor, there is nothing
cluttered or fancy about the food, which aims
to please with its mix of sandwiches (pork
belly cubano or toasted Welsh rarebit with
'nduja), quiches and charcuterie, and more
elaborately worked dishes such as paper-thin
slices of cured beef topped with shavings of
aged Parmesan, linguine tangled with
Cardigan Bay crabmeat, garlic and chilli, and
deep-fried aubergine with honey, cumin and
labneh. There is a ood selection of homemade
cakes, and lubrication comes from a short list
of modern European wines.
Chef/s: Aled Evans, Charlotte Pasetti and Stefan
Emamboccus. **Open:** Wed to Mon, 9am to 7pm.
(Tue and Sun 11am, Fri and Sat til late). **Closed:** 25
and 26 Dec, 1 Jan. **Meals:** main courses £10 to £16.
Details: 80 seats. 20 seats outside. Wheelchairs.
Music. Parking.

▌Llandybie
Valans

Cooking score: 1
International | £25
29 High Street, Llandybie, SA18 3HX
Tel no: (01269) 851288
valans.co.uk
£30

Once a florist's, this cheery family-run outfit
is still a trusty local – although blooms and
bouquets have given way to plates of unfussy,
but carefully rendered bistro food. Welsh
ingredients figure prominently, but the
kitchen meanders far and wide for inspiration
– Thai meatballs and eggs Benedict share the
billing with pork stroganoff and confit of
Gower salt marsh lamb with redcurrant sauce.
Mighty joints of Carmarthenshire beef are
slow-cooked for six hours, fish specials vary
with the market and there's always a decent
choice of desserts, from lemon and blueberry
pavlova to chocolate-chip-cookie cheesecake.
Quaffable everyday wines.
Chef/s: Dave Vale. **Open:** Tue to Sun L, Tue to Sat D.
Closed: Mon, 26 Dec to 3 Jan. **Meals:** main courses
£17 to £22. Set L and D £13 (2 courses) to £18. Sun L
£16 (2 courses) to £19. **Details:** 32 seats.
Wheelchairs. Music.

▌Nantgaredig
Y Polyn

Cooking score: 4
Modern British | £35
Capel Dewi, Nantgaredig, SA32 7LH
Tel no: (01267) 290000
ypolyn.co.uk

The location is as invitingly remote as ever,
but Y Polyn is now reaping the benefits of a
custom-built extension offering additional
space upstairs. Nevertheless, this one-time
tollhouse still makes the most of its scrubbed-
up folksy interiors, matching the laid-back
mood with a feisty assortment of culinary
ideas culled from Europe and beyond. Big,
bold flavours and straight-talking
presentation are the hallmarks of dishes as

Symbols

⬤

🛏 Accommodation is available
£30 Three courses for less than £30
£5 OFF £5-off voucher scheme
🍶 Notable wine list

diverse as warm ham hock with crispy poached egg and parsley sauce or roast rump of lamb with caponata and salsa verde. Venison from Dinefwr Park might appear as a ragù with pappardelle and pangritata, while fish comes all the way from Brixham (perhaps whole sand sole with cockles, baby spinach, red chard, artichoke hearts, caper and anchovy butter). Respect for ingredients also shows in the superb homemade sourdough bread, top-drawer Welsh cheeses and desserts such as Carmarthenshire cream and yoghurt pannacotta. House wines from £18.

Chef/s: Susan Manson, Phil Leach and Alix Alliston. **Open:** Tue to Sun L, Tue to Sat D. **Closed:** Mon. **Meals:** main courses £16 to £20. Set L £14 (2 courses) to £17. Set D £28 (2 courses) to £35. Sun L £24 (2 courses) to £29. **Details:** 100 seats. 20 seats outside. Bar. Wheelchairs. Music. Parking.

▌Narberth
The Grove

Cooking score: 6
Modern British | £59
Molleston, Narberth, SA67 8BX
Tel no: (01834) 860915
thegrove-narberth.co.uk

£5 OFF ▮ ⊨

Bucolic surroundings and an eclectic mix of architecture including Neo Gothic, Arts and Crafts and Jacobean make a striking first impression at The Grove, which is fast becoming one of Wales' premier dining destinations. The kitchen has come on in leaps and bounds under the guidance of executive chef Allister Barsby, who was previously head chef at Gidleigh Park when Michael Caines was in residence (see entry). Mr Barsby's approach is as eclectic as the surroundings: scallops might be paired with smoked eel, parsnip, curry and lime, while Preseli lamb shares a plate with turnips, charred leeks, capers and mint. To finish, try roasted pineapple with caramelised brioche, pineapple sage, pistachio and black pepper ice cream. You can choose from a five-course taster, an eight-course chef's signature or take the à la carte option, while lunch brings a superb-

value three-course menu. The weighty wine list is one for enthusiasts and newbies alike, with helpful notes and a decent range of price points.

Chef/s: Allister Barsby. **Open:** all week L and D. **Meals:** set L £24 (3 courses). Set D £59 (3 courses). Tasting menu £75 (5 courses) to £94 (8 courses, D only). **Details:** 50 seats. V menu. Bar. Wheelchairs. Music. Parking. Children over 11 yrs only after 7pm.

▌Porthgain
The Shed

Cooking score: 1
Seafood | £30
Porthgain, SA62 5BN
Tel no: (01348) 831518
theshedporthgain.co.uk

'An unpretentious can-do atmosphere and friendly, energetic staff – what a brilliant place,' was the view of one visitor to this old stone building beside Porthgain harbour. The Shed started out in 2001 as a tea room for boat trippers, nowadays it's a bistro with seafood as the star. A fish and chip menu draws the crowds, but the kitchen's repertoire extends from 'perfectly cooked' hake and 'delicious' crab cakes to mussels with Welsh cider, leek and tarragon cream, and monkfish tail and tiger prawn curry in Thai coconut sauce. When it comes to dessert, warm walnut tart with whisky butterscotch sauce is a great way to finish. Wines from £15.95.

Chef/s: Caroline Jones and Brian Mullins. **Open:** all week L and D (Apr to Sept). **Closed:** Mon and Tue, Sun D (Oct to Mar). **Meals:** main courses £17 to £21. **Details:** 50 seats. 64 seats outside.

⬛ St David's

LOCAL GEM
Cwtch
Modern British | £33
22 High Street, St David's, SA62 6SD
Tel no: (01437) 720491
cwtchrestaurant.co.uk

£5 OFF

The Welsh word 'cwtch' conjures up snuggly warmth – a perfect description of this family-run eatery known for its neighbourly approach, pared-back rustic interiors and sympathetic cooking. Local and regional ingredients set the scene for skilfully handled dishes ranging from Solva crab and fennel filo parcels to a duo of Welsh lamb with Kalettes, rosemary and redcurrant jus, while desserts could bring lemon posset or toffee apple and oat crumble tart. Affordable well-chosen wines, too.

⬛ Saundersfoot
Coast
new chef/no score
Modern British | £42
Coppet Hall Beach, Saundersfoot, SA69 9AJ
Tel no: (01834) 810800
coastsaundersfoot.co.uk

£5 OFF

Casual, flexible and family-friendly, this coastal outing from the owners of The Grove at Narberth (see entry) occupies a purpose-built cedar-clad complex overlooking Coppet Hall Beach and Carmarthen Bay. Pizazz without frippery seems to be the maxim here, from the clean-lined interiors and suntrap terrace to the skilfully constructed menu – a roster of appealing dishes inspired by Welsh produce (especially seafood from Saundersfoot harbour). However, as we prepared for publication, chef Will Holland announced he will leave Coast in the autumn of 2017 to take up the executive chef role at the Ocean restaurant in the Atlantic Hotel, Jersey (see entry). Previously, vegetarians and 'little people' have had their own menus, fixed-price

'market' deals offered decent value and there are plenty of knowledgeably chosen wines, too.
Open: Wed to Sun L and D (all week L and D Easter and summer hols). **Closed:** Mon, Tue, second week Jan. **Meals:** main courses £16 to £26. Tasting menu £65 (6 courses). **Details:** 54 seats. 40 seats outside. V menu. Bar. Wheelchairs. Music. Parking.

⬛ Tenby
The Salt Cellar
Cooking score: 3
Modern British | £38
The Esplanade, Tenby, SA70 7DU
Tel no: (01834) 844005
thesaltcellartenby.com

£5 OFF

First off, it isn't actually in a cellar, but it does occupy the lower-ground floor of the Atlantic Hotel, on the clifftop overlooking the South Beach: a stand-alone business comprising restaurant, bar and terrace. The dining area is a clean white space with coastal pictures on the gleaming walls and simple, undressed tables. Seafood is a strength, showing up well in an Asian-seasoned crab salad with wasabi, avocado and soy, or citrus-poached salmon with pickled apple and fennel and a boozy jelly of whisky and mead. At main, the rump and shin of 21-day aged Pembrokeshire beef with smoked mash will have plenty of support, or there could be butter-roasted hake with potato terrine and sea herbs in caper and almond butter. Finish with banana malt cake, or dark chocolate tart with espresso mascarpone and hazelnuts. The short wine list explores today's fashionable flavours, from Albariño to Malbec, with prices opening at £16.95.
Chef/s: Duncan Barham and Matt Flowers. **Open:** all week L and D. **Closed:** Mon and Tue (Dec and Jan), 23 to 26 Dec, 2 to 6 Jan. **Meals:** main courses £16 to £24. Set L £15 (2 courses) to £19. Sun L £20 to £25. **Details:** 44 seats. 20 seats outside. V menu. Bar. Wheelchairs. Music.

CHANNEL
ISLANDS

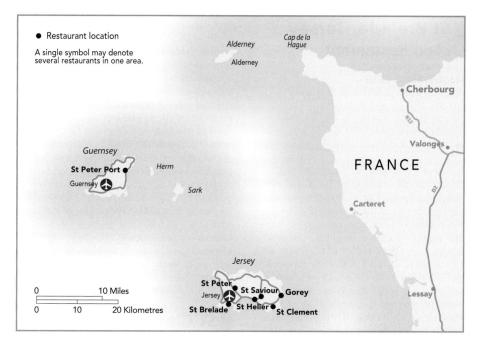

▮ Gorey, Jersey

Sumas

Cooking score: 2
Modern British | £38
Gorey Hill, St Martin, Gorey, Jersey, JE3 6ET
Tel no: (01534) 853291
sumasrestaurant.com
£5
OFF

Sumas sits proud on a steep hill overlooking Gorey harbour, with views of Mont Orgueil castle from the terrace. Inside, coolly whitewashed stone walls and varnished beech-board floors give the place an auberge-like feel. Service maintains a tone of relaxed affinity, while chef Dany Lancaster supplies the modern British brio. A nicely caramelised scallop foursome appears in simple East Asian salad array with daikon, peanuts, watercress and lime, while fine local oysters are poached in their shells and napped with beurre blanc. Seafood is generally accorded its deserved respect, as for a main of roast brill topped with crab raviolo on piles of shredded fennel in

smoked butter, but there are well-conceived meat dishes, too, including venison saddle with salt-baked roots, sprout leaves and chanterelles in bitter chocolate. Fruit-based desserts take in caramelised pineapple with passion fruit parfait, or a tangerine frangipane tart with matching ice cream. Bottles from £19 lead the bistro-style wine list.
Chef/s: Dany Lancaster. **Open:** all week L, Mon to Sat D. **Closed:** late Dec to mid Jan. **Meals:** main courses £17 to £26. Set L and D £20 (2 courses) to £25. **Details:** 35 seats. 20 seats outside. Bar.

Please send us your feedback

To register your opinion about any restaurant listed in this guide, or a new restaurant that you wish to bring to our attention, please visit the web address at the bottom of the page. Your feedback informs the content of the book and will be used to compile next year's reviews.

▌St Brelade, Jersey

Ocean Restaurant
new chef/no score
Modern British | £65
Atlantic Hotel, Le Mont de la Pulente, St
Brelade, Jersey, JE3 8HE
Tel no: (01534) 744101
theatlantichotel.com

🛏

An air of old-school 'posh' pervades the
Atlantic Hotel, a high-profile holiday
playground complete with spectacular sea
views, subtropical palm trees and a Hockney-
esque azure swimming pool – plus a swanky
full-dress restaurant done out in maritime
shades. Long-serving chef Mark Jordan is to
step down in October 2017, to be replaced by
Will Holland, from Coast in Pembrokeshire
(see entry). If Mr Holland's past performance
is anything to go by, it seems likely that the
restaurant will continue to deliver a cuisine
heavily biased towards Jersey seafood, one
where lobster, crab and bivalves are given top-
end treatment, with the likes of prime Jersey
beef representing 'the land'. Wines from top
French growers will continue to loom large on
the heavyweight list.
Chef/s: Will Holland. **Open:** all week L and D.
Closed: 3 Jan to 8 Feb. **Meals:** set L £23 (2 courses)
to £28. Set D £55. Sun L £33. Tasting menu £85 (7
courses). **Details:** 60 seats. V menu. Bar. Music.
Parking.

Oyster Box
Cooking score: 3
Seafood | £34
Route de la Baie, St Brelade, Jersey, JE3 8EF
Tel no: (01534) 850888
oysterbox.co.uk

An expansive room extending from a mosaic-
tiled bar to gallery windows overlooking St
Brelade's Bay, with a broad terrace for outdoor
dining, expresses the Oyster Box's umbilical
link to the sea, and seafood remains very much
its centre of gravity. Local rock oysters in
Champagne butter are a reliable intro to full

first courses such as grilled mackerel with
horseradish and watercress, moules marinière,
or crab on toast with avocado and garlic mayo.
A decent selection of meat mains fills out the
options, though, including suckling pig with
cabbage and shallots in mustard and cider
sauce, if you can resist the lure of roast cod
with peas and Jersey Royals, or poached
smoked haddock on mussel and leek risotto,
topped indispensably with a poached egg. If
the weather approaches tropical, finish with
Jamaican rum pudding in toffee sauce, served
with rum and raisin ice cream, or there are
good British farmhouse cheeses. House wines
are South Africa's Fish Hoek Sauvignon and
Merlot at £19.50.
Chef/s: Tony Dorris. **Open:** Tue to Sun L, all week D.
Closed: 25 and 26 Dec, 1 Jan. All day Mon and Sun
D in winter. **Meals:** main courses £12 to £30.
Details: 90 seats. 60 seats outside. Bar. Wheelchairs.
Music.

▌St Clement, Jersey

LOCAL GEM
Green Island Restaurant
Mediterranean | £40
Green Island, St Clement, Jersey, JE2 6LS
Tel no: (01534) 857787
greenisland.je

Named after a grass-topped rock off shore,
Green Island beach is a corker, and this
restaurant and beach hut is as much a part of
the landscape as the golden sand. Seafood is
the main focus (but not the sole focus), so rock
up and tuck into Royal Bay oysters, local crab
and lobster, skate wing with brown butter,
and monkfish with red lentil and ham hock
dhal. Among meat options, crispy duck leg
might come with Chinese pancakes. Desserts
include crème brûlée; wines open at £17.25.

Visit us online

To find out more about
The Good Food Guide, please
visit thegoodfoodguide.co.uk

St Helier, Jersey

Bohemia

Cooking score: 8
Modern European | £59
The Club Hotel & Spa, Green Street, St Helier,
Jersey, JE2 4UH
Tel no: (01534) 880588
bohemiajersey.com

Enveloped within the Club spa hotel,
Bohemia cuts a rather sober figure, with its
ruby leather seating, dark-wood walls and
double-linened tables, a muted setting for
some of the most exuberant cooking to be had
throughout the Channel Islands. Steve Smith's
generous, adventurous food employs a
fascinating range of technique, and when a
dining room is run by prompt, interested and
engaging staff, the whole experience seems
flawless. There are more menu formats than
there are days in the week, but once you've
lighted on one, what arrives is dynamic and
inexhaustibly creative to the last mouthful.
The Prestige taster at a June visit opened with a
brace of corpulent oysters in foaming oyster
cream with a twist of caviar-dotted cucumber,
and was followed by a waterbathed bantam
egg surrounded by fresh whole peas and sweet
purée with twists of ham. This is a style of
cooking that refuses the easy cliché, so firmer-
than-usual foie gras parfait arrives with cured
duck ham and gésiers, with a film of sea
buckthorn jelly, candied pistachios, kumquat
and ginger biscuits that snap, then melt, in the
mouth. At the summit of the whole
performance were butter-roasted turbot,
garnished with Roscoff onion filled with its
gratinated purée and a meaty sauce spiked
with mustard seeds, and then 60-day sirloin
with morels and asparagus, alongside pressed
ox cheek on toast and coarse tartare dotted
with capers and cured egg yolk. The pick of
the dessert parade was a square of popcorn
mousse coated in white chocolate, with sharp
lime sorbet and salt-caramel parfait
sandwiched in slices of syrupy sponge. A

broad choice of wines by the glass, from
£7.50, opens a list that's deeply upholstered
with classics, and is overseen by an
authoritative sommelier.
Chef/s: Steve Smith. **Open:** Mon to Sat L and D.
Closed: Sun, 24 to 29 Dec. **Meals:** main courses
£22 to £36. Set L £18 (2 courses) to £25. Set D £59
(3 courses). Tasting menu £75. **Details:** 66 seats. V
menu. Bar. Wheelchairs. Music. Parking.

The Green Olive

Cooking score: 3
Mediterranean | £35
1 Anley Street, St Helier, Jersey, JE2 3QE
Tel no: (01534) 728198
greenoliverestaurant.co.uk
£5 OFF

Tucked away in the business district, with a
first-floor dining room overlooking the
esplanade, Paul Le Brocq's place has risen again
from a calamitous fire with a snazzy refurb.
Shades of green frame a wood-toned room,
with a *trompe-l'oeil* wallpaper effect of wood
panels, and ample light flooding in through
blinded windows. Plenty of island produce
makes its way into modern fusion cooking
that retains a strong bistro element, brought
off with appreciable verve and generosity. A
trio of caramelised scallops comes with
cauliflower variations of purée, curry-roasted
and raw, along with Earl Grey raisins, apple
and pine nuts for a zesty opener, while Caesar
salad is brilliantly reconceived as lightly
grilled Little Gems with chicken thighs,
battered anchovies and crisp bacon in garlicky
buttermilk mayonnaise. Pick of the mains is a
vast serving of roast cod in herb crust with
baby leeks and silky mash, with a side of
mussels and chorizo, or there may be duck
roasted in five-spice and honey with pak choi,
celeriac fondant and purée and tamarind jus.
Finish with coconut pannacotta and pineapple
in a Kilner jar. The little wine list opens at
£17.95 for Argentinian house wines.
Chef/s: Paul Le Brocq. **Open:** Tue to Fri L, Tue to Sat
D. **Closed:** Sun, Mon, 23 Dec to 23 Jan. **Meals:** main
courses £15 to £22. **Details:** 45 seats. Music.

Ormer

Cooking score: 5
Modern European | £50
7-11 Don Street, St Helier, Jersey, JE2 4TQ
Tel no: (01534) 725100
ormerjersey.com

Secreted on a narrow street in St Helier's business district, Ormer is Shaun Rankin's smartly impressive go-to venue for modern European cooking. With seating in mustard leather and blue suede, and a frontage opening out into the Jersey sunshine, the place has relaxation down to a fine art. What better than to start with some superb sourdough and golden island butter, as a way in to fusion dishes such as crabmeat bound with apple, pear, coriander and chilli, with wafers of gingerbread and crumbled peanuts? Fish is imaginatively handled, as when turbot is crusted in pine nuts and served with roasted and puréed cauliflower with samphire and sea purslane, while meat might be lamb saddle with goats' cheese agnolotti and a smear of black garlic purée, or pork belly with pressed Asian pear, grilled calamari and a schmooze of chorizo and tomato purée. To finish, there may be buttermilk pannacotta with rhubarb variations and ginger-beer jellies, or a study in cherry that partners soufflé and sorbet with chocolate-coated ice cream to match. A wine list of surpassing quality accompanies, the glass options from £5.50 augmented by Coravin selections, leading on to a stellar core collection of serious producers.
Chef/s: Shaun Rankin. **Open:** Mon to Sat L and D. **Closed:** Sun, 25 to 27 Dec. **Meals:** main courses £28 to £35. Set L £22 (2 courses) to £27. Tasting menu £75. **Details:** 70 seats. 24 seats outside. V menu. Bar. Wheelchairs. Music.

Tassili

Cooking score: 5
Modern European | £45
Grand Jersey Hotel, The Esplanade, St Helier, Jersey, JE2 3QA
Tel no: (01534) 722301
handpickedhotels.co.uk
£5 OFF

A spa hotel of a certain era on the esplanade overlooking St Aubin's Bay, the Grand Jersey is home to the Tassili dining room, a split-level space that partly enjoys those marine views but fades into corporate blandness further in. Nicolas Valmagna makes a resourceful splash with contemporary Anglo-French cooking in a number of tasting formats – Land and Sea, Jèrriais (Jersey produce all the way to a local cheese) and vegetarian – as well as a three-course carte. The production rises and falls through an evening, opening boldly with a generous lobe of seared goose foie gras garnished with duck ham, sweetcorn ice cream and sweet wine jelly, or perhaps fine local crab with passion fruit gel, diced mango and coconut foam. Perfectly poached lobster in an intense bisque with celeriac purée offers the best kind of simplicity, while meat might be lamb loin and sweetbread with a tempura-battered anchovy, wild garlic pesto and Jersey Royals. The grand finale is a set of chocolate and orange variations, incorporating a wiggly strip of blancmange and an ice cream of tonka beans. Italian house wines at £21, and a serviceable selection by the glass from £5, head a stylistically categorised list from big producers.
Chef/s: Nicolas Valmagna. **Open:** Tue to Sat D only. **Closed:** Sun, Mon, 1 to 4 Jan. **Meals:** set D £45 (3 courses). Tasting menu £62 to £75. **Details:** 22 seats. V menu. Bar. Wheelchairs. Music. Parking. Children over 12 yrs only.

St Peter, Jersey
Mark Jordan at the Beach

Cooking score: 3
Modern British | £36
La Plage, La Route de la Haule, St Peter,
Jersey, JE3 7YD
Tel no: (01534) 780180
markjordanatthebeach.com

Mark Jordan may have bowed out as chef in charge of the Atlantic Hotel's Ocean Restaurant in St Brelade (see entry), but he still maintains an interest in this laid-back eatery across the road from the beach at St Peter. Nautical trinkets, wicker chairs and seaside artwork create a backdrop that's tailor-made for the holiday crowd as well as Jersey locals, and the cooking follows suit – although Jordan's pedigree guarantees that even the signature burgers are a cut above. Overall, the menu is a considered run through the mainstream brasserie repertoire, homing in on the likes of crab and sweetcorn risotto, coq au vin and pan-roasted fillet of John Dory with samphire, orange, vanilla butter sauce and Jersey Royals (naturally). Locally landed lobsters are given the luxurious thermidor treatment, while fine-tuned desserts could feature almond pannacotta with dark chocolate ice cream and coffee syrup. The diverse international wine list also has broad appeal.
Chef/s: Mark Jordan and Alex Zotter. **Open:** all week L and D. **Meals:** main courses £15 to £22. Set L £20 (2 courses) to £25. Early set D £28. Sun L £28. **Details:** 50 seats. 30 seats outside. Bar. Music. Parking.

St Peter Port, Guernsey
La Frégate

Cooking score: 4
Modern British | £40
Beauregard Lane, Les Cotils, St Peter Port,
Guernsey, GY1 1UT
Tel no: (01481) 724624
lafregatehotel.com
£5 OFF 🛏

All agree that the location of this extended 18th-century manor house is superb, set high on a hill overlooking the harbour. Long-standing chef Neil Maginnis sails confidently through the tricky waters of modern cuisine, fashioning dishes that dovetail British ingredients with contemporary French technique and Asian influences. He serves hand-dived scallops with warm Thai-spiced crabmeat and coriander butter sauce, and bass fillet with truffled cauliflower purée, sautéed pak choi and soy-honey dressing, but counterbalances any arcane tendencies with some back-to-the-roots blockbusters – fillet of beef with roasted garlic dauphinoise, woodland mushrooms and Madeira jus, for example. To finish, an intense passion forest délice forms a clever alliance with pine raspberry syrup, caramelised mango, dark chocolate soil and sugar lace, although Mr Maginnis is equally at home with a traditional crêpe suzette. Brilliant-value lunches maintain the tempo. A dozen or so wines by the glass (from £7) head the serious, well-annotated wine list.
Chef/s: Neil Maginnis. **Open:** all week L and D. **Meals:** main courses £19 to £25. Set L £20 (2 courses) to £25. Set D £37. Tasting menu £65. **Details:** 70 seats. 20 seats outside. V menu. Bar. Wheelchairs. Music. Parking.

Da Nello

Italian | £45
46 Lower Pollet, St Peter Port, Guernsey,
GY1 1WF
Tel no: (01481) 721552
danello.gg

£5
OFF

With rough granite walls, exposed ships' timbers and a lovely covered courtyard, this converted 15th-century building has bags of character to match its capably executed Italian food. Seafood from the Guernsey boats gets a decent airing (think oysters with shallot and red wine vinaigrette, scallops meunière or fettuccine with crab), while those in the mood for meat should look to the char-grill for beef tagliata, veal paillard or rack of lamb with a boozy port jus. To drink, pick something Italian from the good-value international wine list.

followed by deep-water turbot with a fricassee of woodland mushrooms, sweet potato and tarragon, or perhaps a bold partnership of Lough Erne lamb loin, braised shoulder and lightly curried local crab with butternut squash and aubergine. English and French artisan cheeses are the alternative to dashing desserts such as a raspberry and lemon omelette flambéed in raspberry vodka. The gargantuan wine list has something for all tastes and price points, in an arc from classed-growth Bordeaux to Californian Viognier, with biodynamics and a good glass selection to boot. Bottles start at £28, glasses £7.
Chef/s: Andrew Baird. **Open:** all week L and D.
Meals: set L £25 (2 courses) to £30. Set D £53 (2 courses) to £60. Sun L £45. Tasting menu £80 (7 courses). **Details:** 90 seats. 35 seats outside. V menu. Bar. Music. Parking.

▪ St Saviour, Jersey

Longueville Manor

Cooking score: 5
Modern British | £60
Longueville Road, St Saviour, Jersey, JE2 7WF
Tel no: (01534) 725501
longuevillemanor.com

🍷 🛏

The broad-arched doorway of Longueville leads into a stone manor steeped in history, founded in Norman times and still cock of the walk in the St Helier area. Its career as a country house hotel under the Lewis family began in the early 1980s and hasn't missed a beat, not least as a result of the long incumbency of Andrew Baird in the kitchens. Framed drawings and brocade-backed chairs create a refined feel in the dining room, and the cooking is a suitably Anglo-French amalgam that feels right in the geographical circumstances. A warm salad of goats' cheese and beetroot fondant with Sicilian blood orange and sorbet is a neatly contrasting composition to raise the curtain, and could be

NORTHERN IRELAND

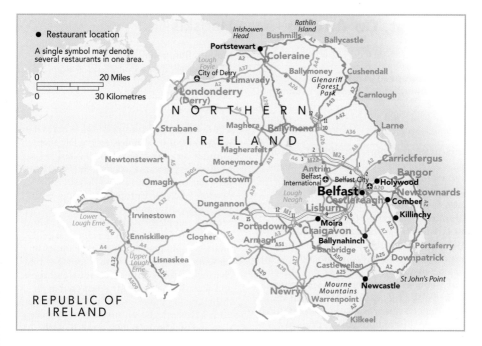

Ballynahinch, Co Down

★ NEW ENTRY ★

The Bull & Ram

Cooking score: 2
Modern British | £28
1 Dromore Street, Ballynahinch, Co Down,
BT24 8AG
Tel no: (02897) 560908
bullandram.com
£30

The Bull & Ram is an architectural gem on a very busy roundabout junction in the centre of a modest Down market town. It was once a butcher's shop, opening just as the Great War did, a time when such premises were white-tiled temples to meat. It retains its hanging rails, chequerboard floor and a fine herring-bone oak ceiling, the room extending to a semi-open kitchen at the back. Modern Irish bistro food is the name of the game, with a solid backbone of quality burgers and fish and

chips to keep the crowds coming. At the more aspirational end, expect good Dundrum crab with pickled carrot and mayonnaise on Melba toast, and fortifying mains such as char-grilled chicken with feta, crushed potatoes, broad beans and peas, and hake topped with sliced chorizo on a bed of buttery champ. Our inspector's gooseberry fool fair lit up the day with delicious cream, tart compote and shards of shattered honeycomb. A little wine list needs its vintages and some producers filling in, starting anyway at £18.

Chef/s: Kelan McMichael. **Open:** Wed to Sat all day from 12. Sun 12 to 8. **Closed:** Mon, Tue.
Meals: main courses £13 to £17. Sun L £25 (3 courses). **Details:** 70 seats.

Symbols

🥄 Accommodation is available
£30 Three courses for less than £30
£5 OFF £5-off voucher scheme
🍷 Notable wine list

▌Belfast, Co Antrim

Eipic

Cooking score: 6
Modern European | £40
28-40 Howard Street, Belfast, Co Antrim,
BT1 6PF
Tel no: (028) 9033 1134
michaeldeane.co.uk

Eipic is the fine-dining section of a tripartite set-up, Deanes, that also features meat and fish venues in expansive premises just along from City Hall. A pair of white double-doors admits you into a tenebrously lit dining room, illuminated by a trio of silver-foil moons along one wall and a giant wine cave. Danni Barry is a formidably talented practitioner of the contemporary gastronomic style, working to a set-menu format of either six courses, or a three-course digest thereof. A spring visit turned up a brik tartelette of seasonal veg, including fat tips of asparagus, with bacon jam on brown-butter hollandaise, prior to a serving of turbot with sea flora and pickled celeriac. Meats might see roasted quail with spiced yoghurt precede wonderful Mourne lamb rump with sweet-and-sour turnips, cime di rapa and grilled cabbage in mustard sauce, and then it's on to a brace of desserts, perhaps strawberries with sheep's yoghurt and elderflower, and then utterly sublime coffee-flavoured chocolate ganache with passion fruit ice cream. Canapés alone are astonishing, as witness a bowl of crab ice cream topped with Parmesan crunch, and the wine pairings, in the capable hands of a French sommelier, are offered in either shot or glass servings so you can pace yourself. Glasses start at £5.95.
Chef/s: Danni Barry. **Open:** Fri L, Wed to Sat D. **Closed:** Sun, Mon, Tue, 20 to 27 Dec, 1 Jan, 12 to 15 Apr, 12 to 27 Jul. **Meals:** tasting menu £40 to £60. **Details:** 30 seats. V menu. Bar. Wheelchairs. Music.

Average price

The average price denotes the price of a three-course meal without wine.

Hadskis

Cooking score: 2
Modern European | £30
33 Donegall Street, Belfast, Co Antrim,
BT1 2NB
Tel no: (028) 9032 5444
hadskis.co.uk

The fashionably unadorned look – bare tables, walls and floor – emphasises the fact that eating is very much the focus at Niall McKenna's place, named after the family that once ran an iron foundry on this site. A mixture of classic European cooking, with pasta, gnocchi and charcuterie front and centre, is supplemented by daily specials and café-style offerings from the charcoal grill. Sharp and pungent flavours are paramount, informing crispy squid with romesco sauce, charred mackerel with horseradish and apple, and accessible, generously composed main dishes such as stone bass, lentils and ham hock with salsa verde, bacon ribs with red cabbage slaw and pickles, or ricotta gnocchi with oyster mushrooms and crispy leeks. One-plate lunches for the kind of price you've probably got rattling round your pocket in loose change include Clonakilty black and white puddings with potato salad and a fried egg. A broad-based wine sheet features many good producers and starts at £18.
Chef/s: Cathal Duncan. **Open:** all week, all day from 12 (11 Sat and Sun). **Closed:** 25 and 26 Dec, 1 Jan, Easter Sun, 12 Jul. **Meals:** main courses £13 to £23. **Details:** 90 seats. 16 seats outside. Bar. Wheelchairs. Music.

Il Pirata

Cooking score: 3
Italian | £20
279-281 Upper Newtownards Road,
Ballyhackamore, Belfast, Co Antrim, BT4 3JF
Tel no: (028) 9067 3421
ilpiratabelfast.com
£5 OFF £30

If you're looking for hang-loose rustic Italian cooking presented with flair this is the place to come, with the emphasis on big rollicking flavours happily banishing all memory of the venue's previous consecration to fried chicken. A huge station clock, dangling filament lights and rough-plank table tops set the mood for meals that may begin with nibbles such as goat meatballs in caper and raisin vinaigrette, or fried duck ravioli with truffled aïoli. Thus primed, you can get stuck into the more familiar likes of pork and fennel sausage pizzetta, butternut squash risotto with sage butter and Parmesan, or larger plates such as a hunky piece of smoked hake with caponata and salsa verde. A separate vegetarian and vegan menu is a welcome consideration, and few will balk at the irresistible-looking dolci, which might include carrot cake, with rosewater mascarpone and pistachio brittle standing in for the usual cream cheese and walnuts. Fruity cocktails and wines from £18 help things along nicely.

Chef/s: Marc Heron. **Open:** all week, all day from 12. **Closed:** 25 and 26 Dec. **Meals:** main courses £9 to £19. Set L £10 (3 courses). **Details:** 80 seats. V menu. Wheelchairs. Music. Parking.

James Street South

Cooking score: 5
Modern European | £35
21 James Street South, Belfast, Co Antrim, BT2 7GA
Tel no: (028) 9043 4310
jamesstreetsouth.co.uk

Tucked away in a little city-centre back street, lurking for the time being amid Belfast's ongoing building development, JSS (as city-dwellers know it) is a breezy whitewashed modern eatery with all the smooth, airy class of a Docklands apartment complex. Staff cope, mostly charmingly, with a formidable press of business, and the format of modern urban cooking, supplemented by four- or five-course tasting menus, is what urban sophisticates want. At inspection, we were impressed by grilled scallops with curry spices, roasted cauliflower and almonds, as well as Guinness-cured salmon in sesame broth with apple and pickled mushrooms, while a majestic hunk of Antrim beef fillet in

chocolate-dark glaze, served with sea greens, pastrami and a side of stonking great chips in their skins, was perfectly on point, but were less convinced by a confit rabbit leg that was only saved from bland insufficiency by its sage coating. At an autumn taster, the star dish was grilled monkfish cheeks with peas and minty pesto, topped with Ibérico chorizo. A stick of smoked chocolate ganache with sour cream and lovely hazelnut ice cream is a grand way to finish. The confidently chosen wine list opens at £19, or £5.25 a glass.

Chef/s: David Gillmore. **Open:** Wed to Sat L, Mon to Sat D. **Closed:** Sun, 24 to 26 Dec, 1 Jan, Easter Mon to Wed, 1 week Jul. **Meals:** main courses £16 to £28. Set L and D £19 (2 courses) to £22. Tasting menu £50 to £80. **Details:** 60 seats. Bar. Wheelchairs. Music.

Mourne Seafood Bar

Cooking score: 3
Seafood | £35
34-36 Bank Street, Belfast, Co Antrim, BT1 1HL
Tel no: (028) 9024 8544
mourneseafood.com

The city cousin of the waterside original on Dundrum Bay, Mourne Seafood Bar uses the same supply lines to ensure local urbanites get the best stuff landed at Annalong and Kilkeel. A no-frills interior, blackboards bringing news of the catch and cheerful staff make for a happy atmosphere. Plain and simple langoustines with homemade mayonnaise is one way to start, or oysters as they come, but this kitchen is just as happy to pickle mackerel and put it in a pâté with scallop ceviche. Check out the whole baked fish of the day. Salt-and-chilli squid, fish and chips, seafood paella with a twist (orzo pasta, not rice) and char-grilled Irish ribeye if you must — the menu has broad appeal. For dessert, pecan pie comes with chocolate sauce and bourbon vanilla ice cream. Drink draught beer (including Guinness) or wines from £16.75.

Chef/s: Steven Hughes. **Open:** all week L and D. **Closed:** 24 to 26 Dec, 1 Jan, 17 Mar, 1 Apr, 12 Jul. **Meals:** main courses £11 to £26. **Details:** 80 seats. Wheelchairs. Music. Children before 9pm only.

The Muddlers Club

Cooking score: 3
Modern European | £45
Warehouse Lane, Belfast, Co Antrim, BT1 2DX
Tel no: (028) 9031 3199
themuddlersclubbelfast.com

Down a narrow lane containing a host of converted warehouses, the Muddlers Club in the city's Cathedral Quarter is an urban hot spot with a thoroughly modern outlook via an open-to-view kitchen, industrial styling, lots of natural wood and a proper buzz. A list of cocktails, its own house beer and an inspiring menu matches the up-to-date mood. Gareth McCaughey and his team deliver hearty flavours with no lack of refinement: scallops with a piquant hit from the accompanying chorizo, say, plus celeriac purée and the sweet hit of golden raisins. Salt-aged beef with fiery horseradish and bone-marrow sauce has the same appeal, with monkfish featuring in a monochrome assembly with squid ink (save for the addition of broccoli and dill). To finish, there's plenty of comfort to be found in a dessert of pear, toffee and cardamom. Just about everything on the concise wine list is available by the glass.
Chef/s: Gareth McCaughey. **Open:** Tue to Sat L and D. **Closed:** Sun, Mon, 24 to 26 Dec, 1 to 10 Jan, 1 week Easter, 10 to 24 Jul. **Meals:** main courses £15 to £20. Set L £15 (2 courses) to £20. Tasting menu £45. **Details:** 50 seats. Bar. Wheelchairs. Music. Children before 9pm only.

OX

Cooking score: 6
Modern European | £25
1 Oxford Street, Belfast, Co Antrim, BT1 3LA
Tel no: (028) 9031 4121
oxbelfast.com
£5 OFF £30

On the Lagan riverside with the graceful steel torsion of the Beacon of Hope sculpture right outside, OX is in the vanguard of Northern Irish gastronomy. The high-ceilinged space with its backboarded banquettes and unclothed, candlelit tables is overlooked by a slinkier mezzanine level, and the whole place buzzes with enthusiastic staff and excited diners. The dinner format is a five-course taster, with extra bits fitted around it. At our spring visit, the performance glided through a stately crescendo, a strategically cleverer approach than starting at fortissimo. Lobster with peas and pickled mussels paved the way for a serving of asparagus with a rich dressing of whipped Coolattin Cheddar cream, but it was the fish – turbot in opulent bisque with dill gnocchi, bergamot and oyster leaves – and then, transcendently, a show-stealing serving of Mourne Mountain lamb with its sweetbreads, roasted cauliflower, sea herbs and a splot of miso purée that was as unabashedly rich and savoury as a spoonful of hoisin. Dessert was great, too, though: a layered bowl of baked ginger and brown-sugar cream, coconut ice cream and lime foam. Wine pairings suit the dishes to perfection, a Lebanese Shiraz-Cabernet blend turning wishfully into cru classé claret with that lamb. Mix and match your own, if you prefer, from £7 a small glass.
Chef/s: Stephen Toman. **Open:** Tue to Sat L and D. **Closed:** Sun, Mon, 2 weeks Dec, 1 week Apr, 2 weeks Jul. **Meals:** set L £20 (2 courses) to £25. Tasting menu £50. **Details:** 40 seats. V menu. Bar. Wheelchairs. Music.

Shu

Cooking score: 4
Modern European | £32
253 Lisburn Road, Belfast, Co Antrim, BT9 7EN
Tel no: (028) 9038 1655
shu-restaurant.com
£5 OFF

The name references a primordial Egyptian god, but there's nothing antiquated about Shu – the hottest ticket on Lisburn Road since the turn of the millennium. A sophisticated buzz energises this Belfast brasserie, and Brian McCann's cooking is exactly what's required in such lively cosmopolitan surrounds – sharply tuned flavours, confident technique, trendy compositions and seriously good value

across the board. Ingredients (and influences) are pulled in from far and wide, so don't be surprised to see smoked eel with salt-baked beetroot sharing the bill with roast curried cauliflower, chickpea, spinach and almond salad or a main course of roast stone bass with chestnut and thyme risotto up there alongside beef bourguignon. Irish ingredients such as Clandeboye pigeon have their moment, steaks are given the 'Himalayan salt' treatment, while desserts offer surprises along the lines of new season's blood-orange trifle with tonka bean custard. Impressive, keenly priced wines, too.
Chef/s: Brian McCann. **Open:** Mon to Sat L and D. **Closed:** Sun, 24 to 26 Dec, 1 Jan, 12 and 13 Jul. **Meals:** main courses £13 to £27. Set L £11 (2 courses) to £14. Set D £19 (2 courses) to £23. **Details:** 80 seats. Bar. Music.

LOCAL GEM

The Ginger Bistro
International | £35
7-8 Hope Street, Belfast, Co Antrim, BT12 5EE
Tel no: (028) 9024 4421
gingerbistro.com

This sociable bistro in the centre of the city is known for popular dishes built around European and Asian flavours. A big bowl of local mussels is served with chorizo and tomato, for example, while a warm salad of smoked duck comes with mango, papaya, rocket and mint. Mainstays such as squid and dips (garlic mayo, sweet chilli, pickled ginger) and sirloin steaks are complemented by the likes of hake with garlic tiger prawns, stir-fried greens, soy and pickled ginger and noodles, and desserts such as poached pears, Champagne jelly, vanilla custard and meringues. Wines from £18.

▌Comber, Co Down
The Old Schoolhouse Inn
Cooking score: 4
Modern British | £32
100 Ballydrain Road, Comber, Co Down, BT23 6EA
Tel no: (028) 9754 1182
theoldschoolhouseinn.com
 £5 OFF ⌖

A restaurant-with-rooms, rather than a traditional inn, this ever-evolving Irish stalwart occupies what was once a primary school – although you wouldn't know it from the recently modernised interiors or the charcoal-toned dining room. Chef/proprietor Will Brown served time in London kitchens such as The Square (see entry), and it shows in his confident contemporary menu – an epigrammatic line-up of clever ideas ranging from snacks of crab doughnuts to desserts such as chocolate délice with artichoke, or treacle tart with blood orange and malt ice cream. Woodland plants, beach gleanings and pickings from the Schoolhouse kitchen garden are used to telling effect in clear-flavoured seasonal dishes ranging from mackerel with smoked eel, apple, celery and walnut to chicken with charred leeks, smoked potato and kale. Quality is the watchword, value is never in doubt (check out the bargain set deals) and fair pricing extends to the short, savvy wine list.
Chef/s: Will Brown. **Open:** Wed to Sun L, Wed to Sat D. **Closed:** Mon, Tue, 2 to 13 Jan. **Meals:** main courses £15 to £30. Set L £14 (2 courses) to £18. Set D £15 (2 courses) to £20. Sun L £25. Tasting menu £45. **Details:** 50 seats. 15 seats outside. V menu. Bar. Wheelchairs. Music. Parking.

Holywood, Co Down

LOCAL GEM

The Bay Tree

Modern British | £20

118 High Street, Holywood, Co Down,
BT18 9HW

Tel no: (028) 9042 1419

baytreeholywood.co.uk

£5 OFF £30

A fixture on the high street for many years,
William Farmer's all-day café is to be found in
the courtyard of a listed building. The star
attraction is the 'amazing' cinnamon scones
(you can buy them to take home), but there's
much more besides. Drop in for breakfast,
pick from the user-friendly lunch menu (a
warm salad of Puy lentils with goats' cheese
and walnuts) or nip in for coffee and cakes.
Friday night dinner could bring crispy pork
belly salad with roasted celeriac, juniper,
mango and lime, and lamb's liver with
pomegranate and lemon sauce, cardamom-
scented rice and sugar snap peas. Wines
from £16.

Killinchy, Co Down

Balloo House

Cooking score: 2

Modern British | £27

1 Comber Road, Killinchy, Co Down,
BT23 6PA

Tel no: (028) 9754 1210

balloohouse.com

£5 OFF £30

Set back from the very occasional traffic along
the A22, stranded between villages, Balloo
House is a valued local resource, a white-
fronted pub-cum-country restaurant that
comprises several interconnecting, stone-tiled
rooms run with personable charm. A plethora
of menus is offered, but don't worry too much
about sticking to one or the other. The drill is
modern pub food cooked with gusto, from a
bowl of battered whitebait on vinaigretted
Asian slaw with garlic mayo and chilli sauce
dips, to crispy pork belly with spring cabbage,

homemade black pudding, toffee apple and
potato boxty, or crisply grilled sea bass on
heritage tomato vinaigrette with potato
terrine. At the end, there may be sustaining
apple crumble with gingerbread ice cream, or
a glass of milk chocolate mousse liberally
garnished with summer's first strawberries
and a couple of little doughnuts. Breads are
lovely, served with tapenade and butter. A
short wine offering has most glasses at £4.95.
Chef/s: Danny Millar and Grainne Donnelly. **Open:**
all week, all day from 12. **Closed:** 25 Dec.
Meals: main courses £11 to £24. Set L and D £14 (2
courses) to £18. Sun L £22. **Details:** 80 seats. 18
seats outside. Bar. Wheelchairs. Music. Parking.

Moira, Co Armagh

Wine & Brine

Cooking score: 3

Modern British | £30

59 Main Street, Moira, Co Armagh, BT67 0LQ

Tel no: (028) 9261 0500

wineandbrine.co.uk

£5 OFF

Since scooping the guide's 'Local Restaurant
of the Year Award' for 2017, Chris and Davina
McGowan have added a new lounge bar to
their admirable town-centre eatery. There's a
great deal going on behind this venue's listed
Georgian frontage, not least a passion for
pickling and preserving (hence the 'brine' of
the title). Chris's homemade black pudding
'sausage rolls' come with the house ketchup,
cured egg yolk is scattered over crab ravioli
with shellfish velouté, while smoking is the
technique of choice for everything from
beetroot to bone marrow. Menus are peppered
with Irish produce, from pressed skate wing
and pork belly with fermented carrot and
dashi to a fruity dish of roast corn-fed
Thornhill Farm duck with spiced pineapple
and kumquat. For afters, keep it local with a
baked Armagh apple and Connemara whiskey
cream. Generous portions are matched by
exceedingly fair prices, and the modest wine is
exactly what's required.

Chef/s: Chris McGowan and Jonny Davison. **Open:** Tue to Sat L and D. Sun 12 to 6. **Closed:** Mon, first 2 weeks Jan, 2 weeks Jul. **Meals:** main courses £17 to £30. Set L £14 (2 courses) to £18. Sun L £25. Tasting menu £48. **Details:** 80 seats. V menu. Bar. Wheelchairs. Music.

▌Newcastle, Co Down

Vanilla

Cooking score: 3

Modern British | £41

67 Main Street, Newcastle, Co Down, BT33 0AE

Tel no: (028) 4372 2268

vanillarestaurant.co.uk

Newcastle looks as though it might have been constructed by a film studio with money to burn, an utterly charming seaside town with the Mourne Mountains looming in startling proximity over it. In the season, it fills up with golfers here for proceedings at the Royal Down, and if they've any sense, they'll make it to Vanilla. This modern bistro is a long low-lit room run with commendable efficiency, trading in fairly labour-intensive contemporary Irish cooking. That's certainly the case with a great raviolo pillow stuffed with salmon, lobster and langoustine, garnished with ribboned carrot and fennel in Parmesan emulsion, scattered with smoked bacon, and with a main course of local duck breast with cabbage in both colours, the red stewed sweetly and tartly, with potato and carrot gratin and a delicately ginger-infused jus. Finish on a lighter note with lemon custard and gingerbread sorbet. A short but serviceable wine list opens at £18.95.

Chef/s: Darren Ireland. **Open:** all week L and D. **Closed:** 25 and 26 Dec, 1 Jan. **Meals:** main courses £18 to £24. Set L and early D £17 (2 courses) to £21. **Details:** 36 seats. 6 seats outside. Bar. Wheelchairs. Music. Parking.

▌Portstewart, Londonderry

Harry's Shack

Cooking score: 4

Seafood | £28

116 Strand Road, Portstewart, Londonderry, BT55 7PG

Tel no: (028) 7083 1783

£30

Harry's is beginning to look like a little empire in the making. There is now a third venue, Harry's of Derry in the Craft Village, to join the siblings at Bridgend on the Donegal border and the present incarnation on the Portstewart strand. Sitting on the exposed north coast, the Shack is subject to every vicissitude the north Atlantic weather systems can throw at it, but on quiescent days, the long shed is an atmospheric bolt-hole for Derek Creagh's admirably robust bistro cooking. Start with a flavour-laden St Tola goats' cheese pannacotta saladed up with beetroot, apple and fennel, or mussels from Mulroy Bay doused in Irish cider, as preambles to sturdy mains like venison neck with red cabbage, roots and mustard mash in peppercorn sauce, or a seafood-stuffed pasta dish that offers squid, cockles and mussels in creamy-sauced spaghetti with pancetta. Finish with the signature chocolate pot that's impregnated with chunks of blondie (not brownie) and topped with salt-caramel ice cream. Harry's is now licensed, so you no longer have to take your own bottle.

Chef/s: Derek Creagh. **Open:** all week summer L and D. Call for winter openings. **Meals:** main courses £12 to £15. **Details:** 65 seats. 30 seats outside.

ATLAS MAPS

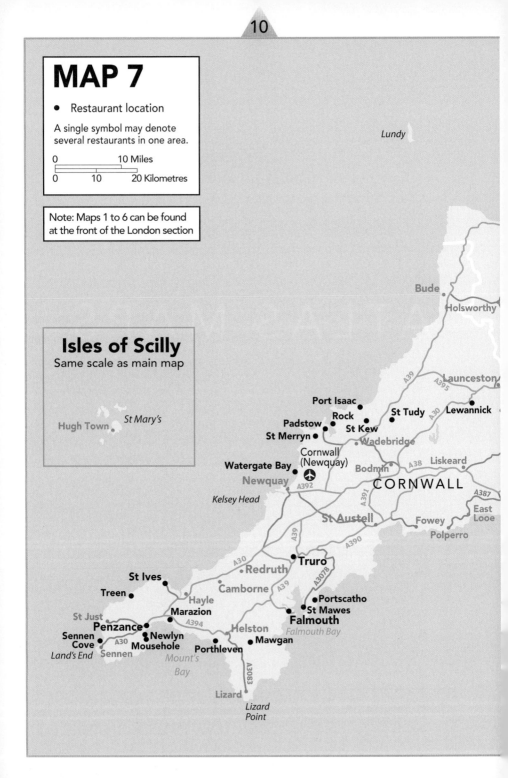

MAP 7

- Restaurant location

A single symbol may denote
several restaurants in one area.

0   10 Miles

0   10   20 Kilometres

Note: Maps 1 to 6 can be found
at the front of the London section

Isles of Scilly
Same scale as main map

Hugh Town   St Mary's

Lundy

Bude

Holsworthy

Launceston

Port Isaac

Rock   St Tudy   Lewannick

Padstow   St Kew

St Merryn

Wadebridge

Cornwall
(Newquay)   Bodmin   Liskeard

Watergate Bay

Newquay

CORNWALL

Kelsey Head

St Austell   Fowey

East
Looe

Polperro

Truro

Redruth

Camborne

St Ives

Treen

Hayle

Portscatho

St Mawes

St Just

Marazion

Falmouth

Penzance

Helston

Falmouth Bay

Sennen
Cove   Newlyn
Mousehole   Porthleven   Mawgan

Land's End   Sennen

Mount's
Bay

Lizard

Lizard
Point

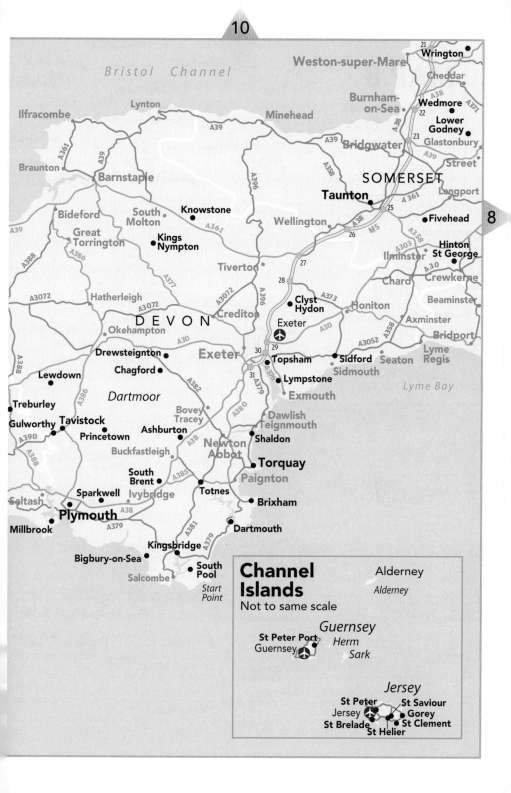

Bristol Channel

Weston-super-Mare

21 Wrington

Cheddar

Burnham-on-Sea

Wedmore A38 A371

Lower Godney

22

23 Glastonbury

Bridgwater A39

Street

Lynton

Minehead

A39

A38

Ilfracombe

Braunton

Barnstaple

A361

A39

A39

Knowstone

Bideford

South Molton

Kings Nympton

A361

A388

Great Torrington

A386

A39

A3072

Hatherleigh

A3072

A3072

DEVON

Okehampton

Drewsteignton

Chagford

Lewdown

A386

Dartmoor

Treburley

Gulworthy

Tavistock

A390

Princetown

A388

Buckfastleigh

Saltash

Sparkwell

Ivybridge

Plymouth

A38

Millbrook

A379

Bigbury-on-Sea

Kingsbridge

A381

A379

Salcombe

South Pool

Start Point

SOMERSET

Taunton

25

A361

Langport

Wellington

26

M5

Fivehead

A358

Ilminster

A303

Hinton St George

Tiverton

27

28

Chard

A30

Crewkerne

Clyst Hydon

A373

Honiton

Beaminster

Crediton

A396

Exeter

30

29

Topsham

Sidford

Seaton

Axminster

A3052

Bridport

Lyme Regis

31

A379

Lympstone

Sidmouth

Exmouth

Lyme Bay

Bovey Tracey

A380

Dawlish

Teignmouth

Newton Abbot

Shaldon

Ashburton

A38

Torquay

Paignton

Totnes

Brixham

Dartmouth

A382

Wellington

A38

Fiveheadd

Crediton

Exeter

Exeter

A30

Seaton

Hatherleigh

Okehampton

A30

A3052

A377

A396

A382

A380

A381

South Brent

A385

8

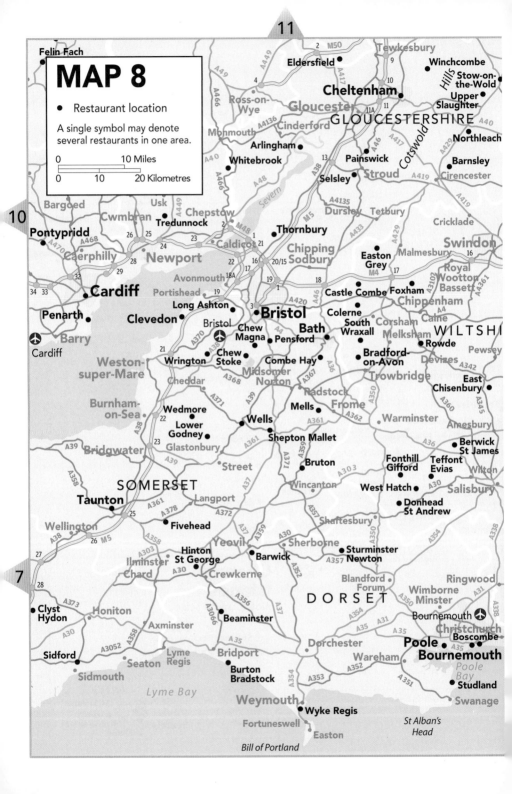

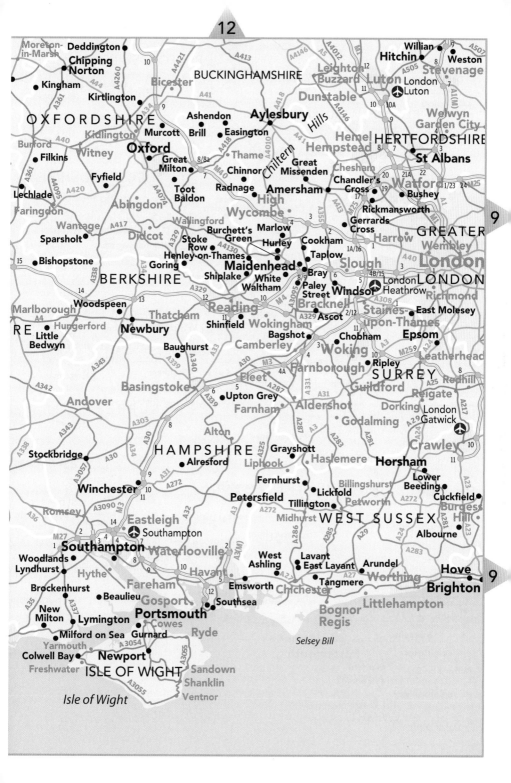

Moreton-in-Marsh
Deddington
Chipping Norton
Kingham
10
Kirtlington
Bicester
BUCKINGHAMSHIRE
A413
A41
A4421
A413
A4146
A5
A4012
A260
A44
A361
A34
Williar
Hitchin
Weston
Leighton
Buzzard
Luton
London
Luton
Stevenage
A505
A1(M)
12
11
10
10A

OXFORDSHIRE
Ashendon
Aylesbury
Hills
A41
A418
A4146

Kidlington
Murcott
Brill
Easington
Thame
Chinnor
Great Missenden
Hemel Hempstead
Chesham
HERTFORDSHIRE
St Albans
Welwyn Garden City
9
8 7
3

Burford
Filkins
Witney
Oxford
Great Milton
8/8a
7
A40
A4010
Chiltern
A41

Fyfield
Radnage
Amersham
Chandler's Cross
Watford
Bushey
20
21A
22
19
1/23
24
A25
17

Lechlade
Abingdon
Toot Baldon
High
Rickmansworth
Gerrards Cross
A4095
A420
A4074
A355

Faringdon
Wantage
Sparsholt
A417
Wallingford
Wycombe
Burchett's Green
Marlow
Cookham
Harrow
GREATER
Wembley
London
LONDON
4
3
2
1
9

Didcot
Stoke Row
Henley-on-Thames
Hurley
Taplow
Slough
A329
A4130
1/16
A40
3

15
Bishopstone
Goring
Shiplake
Maidenhead
White Waltham
Bray
Paley Street
Windsor
London Heathrow
Richmond
4B/15
8/9
6
5
1

BERKSHIRE
A329
Reading
Bracknell
Staines-upon-Thames
East Molesey
13
12
10
2/12

Marlborough
Woodspeen
Thatcham
Shinfield
Wokingham
Ascot
11
14
A4
RE
Little Bedwyn
Hungerford
Newbury
Baughurst
Camberley
Bagshot
Chobham
Woking
Epsom
Leatherhead
A343
A339
A340
A33
A30
M3
3
4
10
M25
A24

A342
Basingstoke
Fleet
Farnborough
Ripley
SURREY
Redhill
4A
6
5
A287
A331
A31
A25
8

Andover
Upton Grey
Aldershot
Guildford
Dorking
Reigate
London Gatwick
A303
A339
Farnham
Godalming
A29
A217

Alton
Grayshott
Crawley
10
8
A30
A31
A281
A283

Stockbridge
HAMPSHIRE
Alresford
Liphook
Haslemere
Horsham
11
A325
A338
A3057
A30
A34
A31
A272

Winchester
Fernhurst
Lickfold
Billingshurst
Lower Beeding
9
10
11
A31
A272
A3
Petersfield
Tillington
Petworth
A272
Cuckfield
Burgess Hill

Romsey
Eastleigh
Southampton
Midhurst
WEST SUSSEX
Albourne
A3090
M3
A32
A3
A286
A285
A29
A24
A281

M27
Southampton
Waterlooville
West Ashling
Lavant
East Lavant
Arundel
Hove
A283
A27
9
2
3
4
7
14
1
8
9
10
2

Woodlands
Lyndhurst
Hythe
Havant
Emsworth
Chichester
Tangmere
Worthing
Brighton
5
12

Brockenhurst
Beaulieu
Fareham
Gosport
Southsea
Littlehampton
A35
A337

New Milton
Lymington
Portsmouth
Cowes
Ryde
Bognor Regis
Selsey Bill

Milford on Sea
Gurnard
A3054
Yarmouth
Colwell Bay
Newport
A3055
Sandown
Freshwater
ISLE OF WIGHT
Shanklin
Ventnor

Isle of Wight

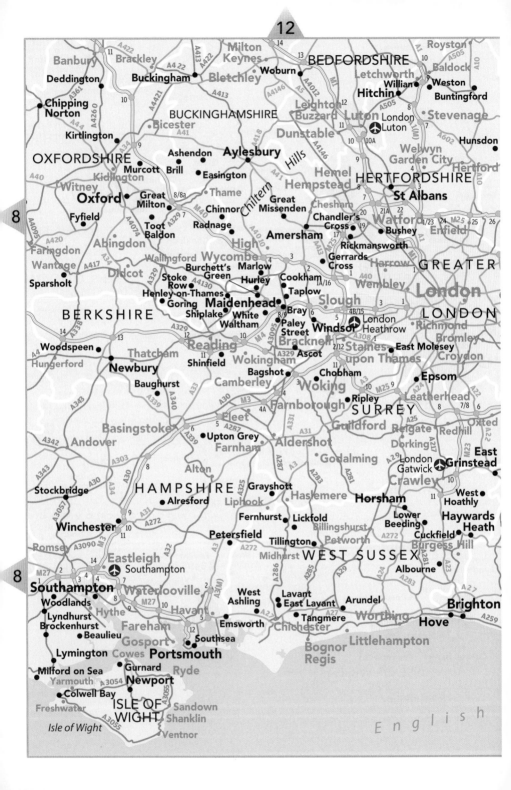

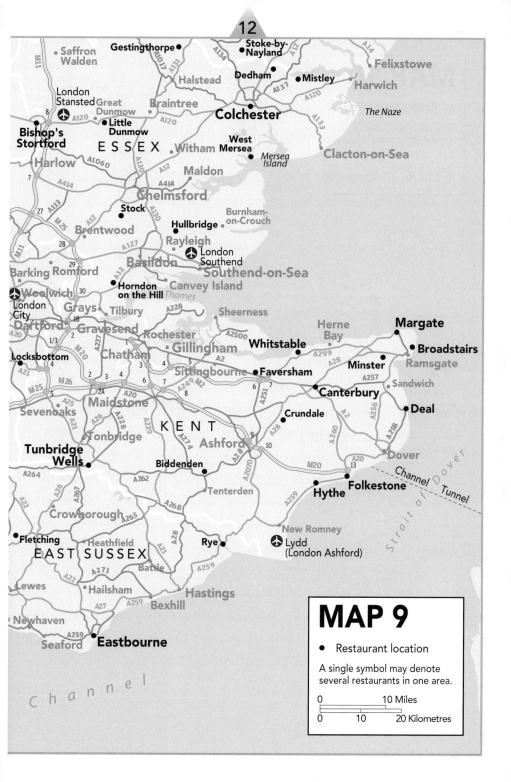

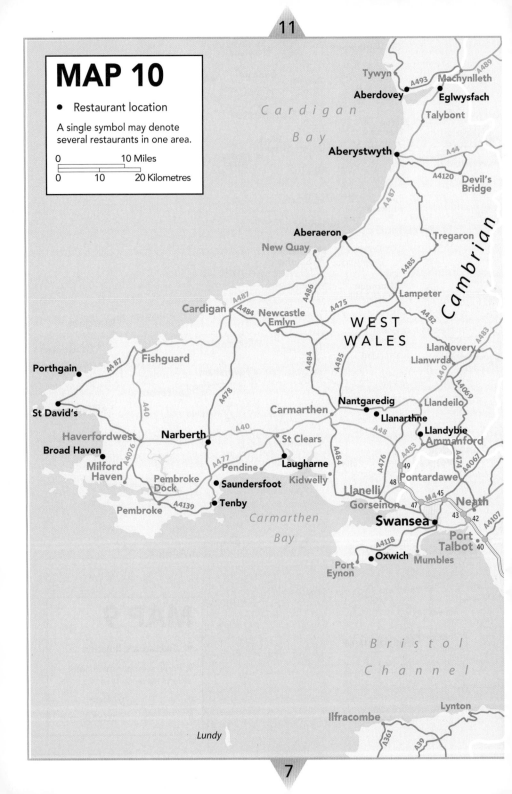

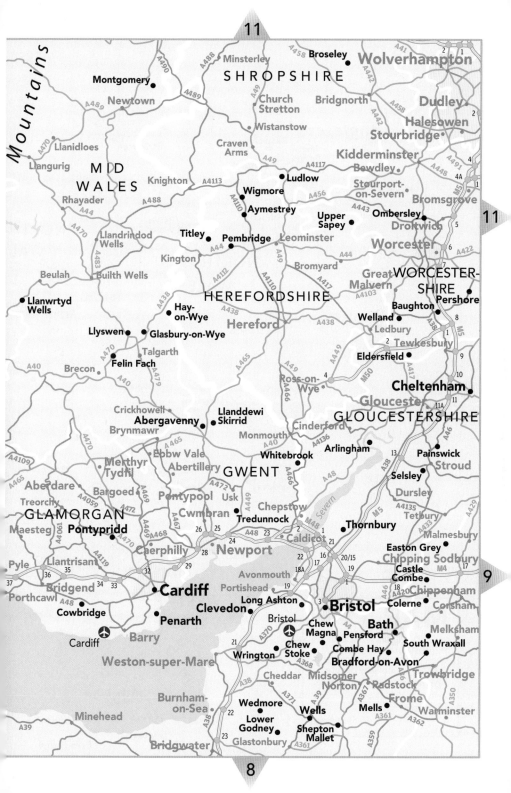

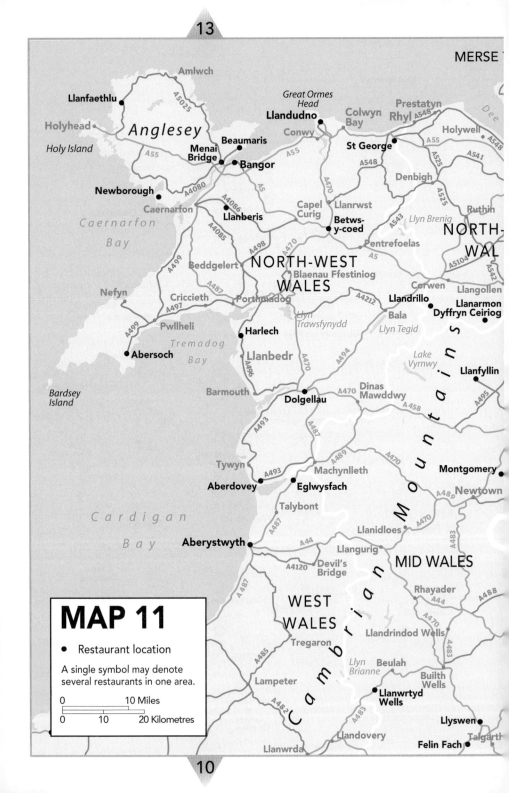

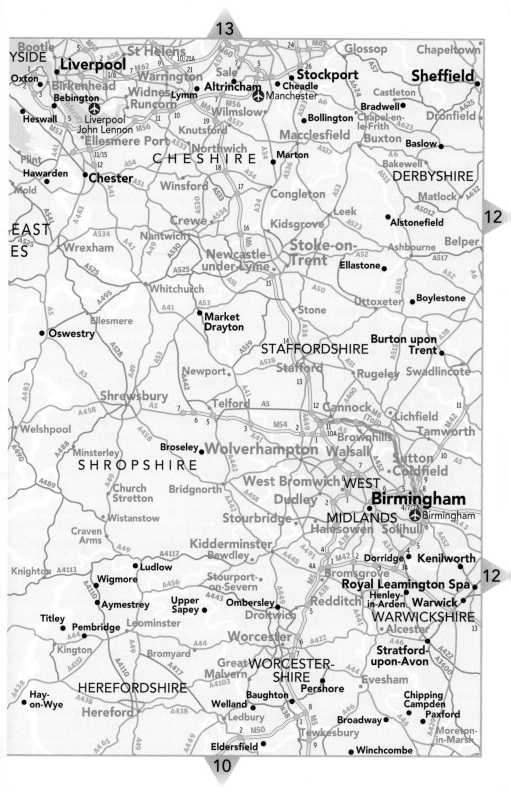

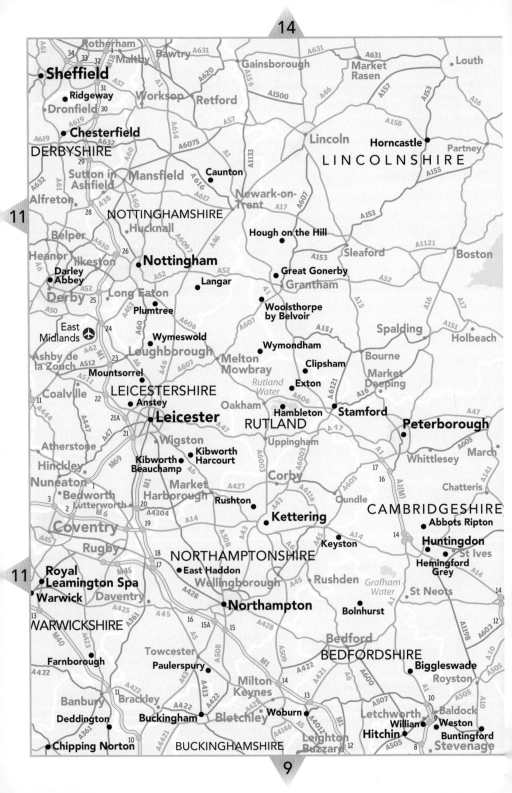

Rotherham
Maltby
Bawtry A631
A631
A631
Louth
Sheffield
Gainsborough
Market
Rasen
Ridgeway
Worksop
Retford
A1500
Dronfield
Chesterfield
Lincoln
Horncastle
Partney
DERBYSHIRE
L I N C O L N S H I R E
Sutton in
Ashfield
Mansfield
Caunton
Alfreton
Newark-on-Trent
NOTTINGHAMSHIRE
Belper
Hucknall
Hough on the Hill
Heanor
Ilkeston
Nottingham
Sleaford
Boston
Darley
Abbey
Great Gonerby
Derby
Long Eaton
Langar
Grantham
Plumtree
Woolsthorpe
by Belvoir
East
Midlands
Wymeswold
Spalding
Holbeach
Loughborough
Wymondham
Ashby de
la Zouch
Mountsorrel
Melton
Mowbray
Clipsham
Bourne
Market
Deeping
Coalville
LEICESTERSHIRE
Rutland
Water
Exton
Anstey
Oakham
Hambleton
Stamford
Leicester
RUTLAND
Peterborough
Wigston
Uppingham
Atherstone
Kibworth
Harcourt
Whittlesey
March
Hinckley
Kibworth
Beauchamp
Corby
Chatteris
Nuneaton
Bedworth
Market
Harborough
Oundle
CAMBRIDGESHIRE
Lutterworth
Rushton
Kettering
Abbots Ripton
Coventry
Keyston
Huntingdon
St Ives
Rugby
NORTHAMPTONSHIRE
Hemingford
Grey
Royal
Leamington Spa
East Haddon
Wellingborough
Rushden
Grafham
Water
St Neots
Warwick
Daventry
Northampton
Bolnhurst
WARWICKSHIRE
Bedford
BEDFORDSHIRE
Farnborough
Towcester
Paulerspury
Biggleswade
Royston
Milton
Keynes
Banbury
Brackley
Letchworth
Baldock
Deddington
Buckingham
Bletchley
Woburn
Willian
Weston
Hitchin
Buntingford
Chipping Norton
BUCKINGHAMSHIRE
Leighton
Buzzard
Stevenage

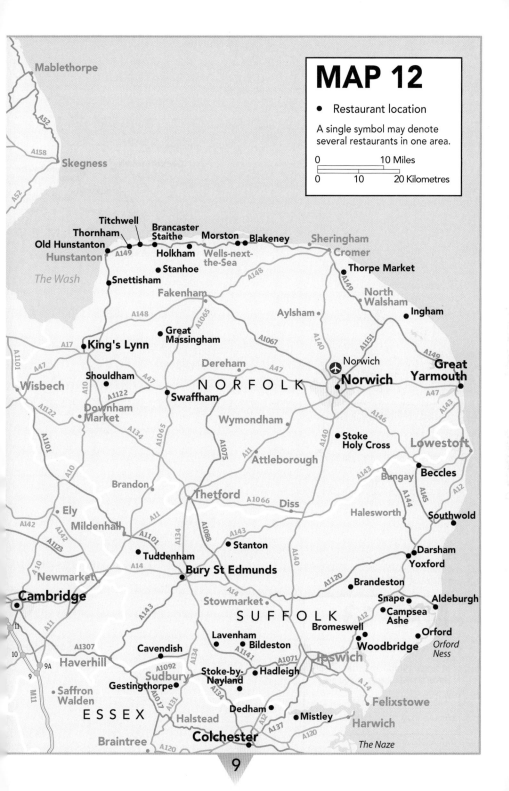

MAP 12

● Restaurant location

A single symbol may denote
several restaurants in one area.

0   10 Miles
0   10   20 Kilometres

Mablethorpe

A52

A158

Skegness

A52

The Wash

Titchwell
Thornham   Brancaster
Staithe   Morston   Blakeney   Sheringham
Old Hunstanton   Cromer
Hunstanton   A149   Holkham   Wells-next-
Stanhoe   the-Sea   Thorpe Market
Snettisham   A148
Fakenham   North
Walsham
A148   Aylsham●   Ingham
A1065
Great
King's Lynn   Massingham   A1067
A17
Dereham   Norwich   Great
Shouldham   A47   A47   Yarmouth
Wisbech   A10   Norwich
A1122   Swaffham   A47
A1122   Downham
Market   N O R F O L K
A134   A1065   Stoke
A101   Wymondham   Holy Cross   Lowestoft
A1075
Attleborough
A140
Brandon   Bungay   Beccles
Thetford   A1066   A145
Ely   Diss   Halesworth   Southwold
A142   Mildenhall   A143
A112   A1101   A134   A1088   Stanton
A10   Tuddenham   A14   Darsham
Newmarket   Bury St Edmunds   Yoxford
A14   A1120   Brandeston
Cambridge   Stowmarket ●   Snape ● Aldeburgh
A143   S U F F O L K   Campsea
Lavenham   Bromeswell   Ashe
A1307   Cavendish   Bildeston   Woodbridge   Orford
A1092   A1141   Orford
Haverhill   A1071   Ipswich   Ness
9A   Stoke-by-
Sudbury   Nayland   Hadleigh   A14
Saffron   Gestingthorpe●   A134
Walden   Dedham ●   Mistley   Felixstowe
E S S E X   Halstead   Harwich
Braintree   A120   Colchester   The Naze

9

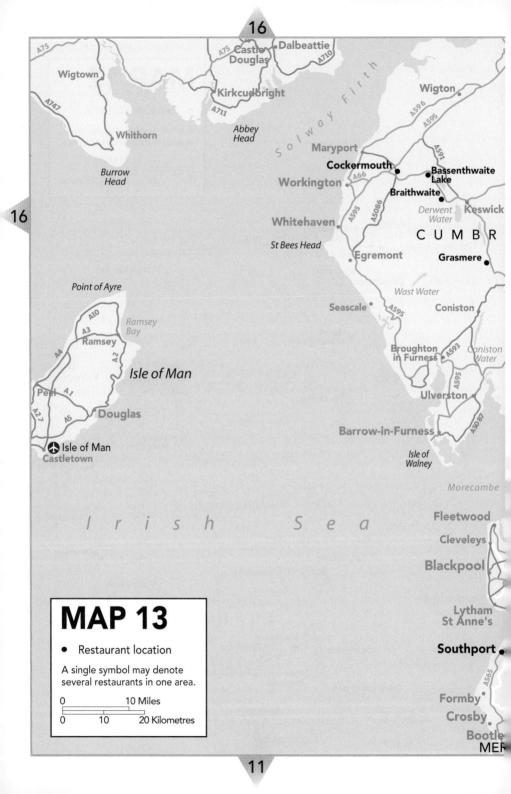

MAP 13

- Restaurant location

A single symbol may denote
several restaurants in one area.

```
0            10 Miles
0     10        20 Kilometres
```

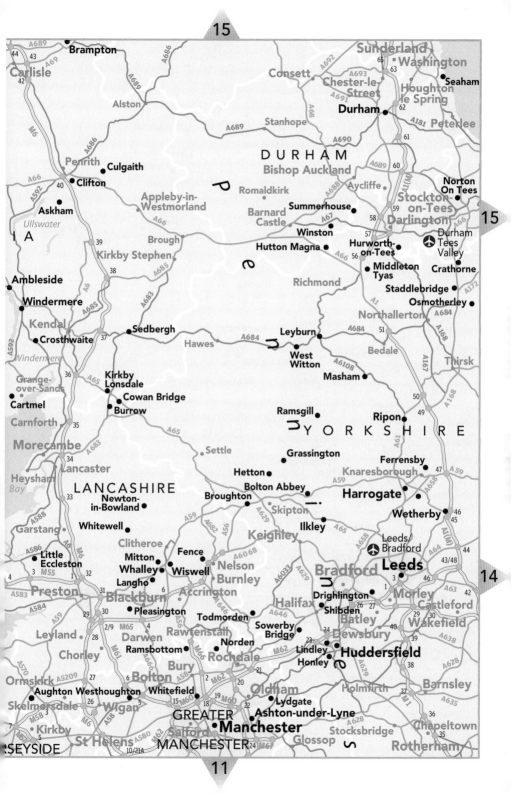

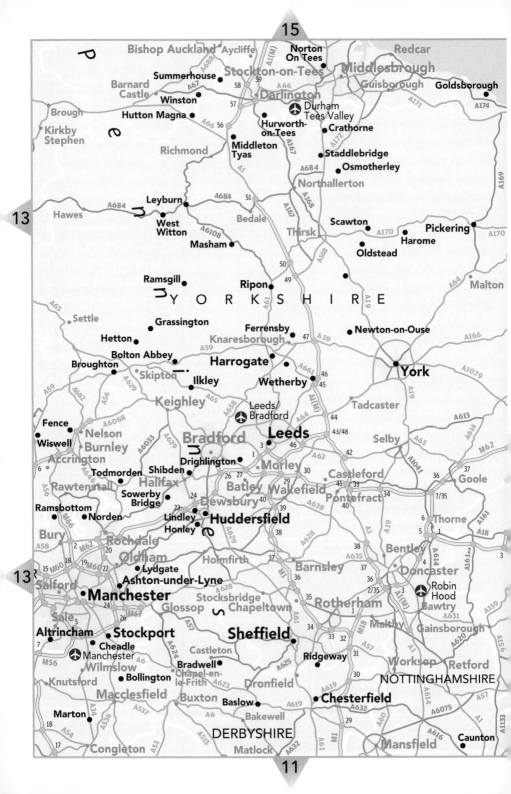

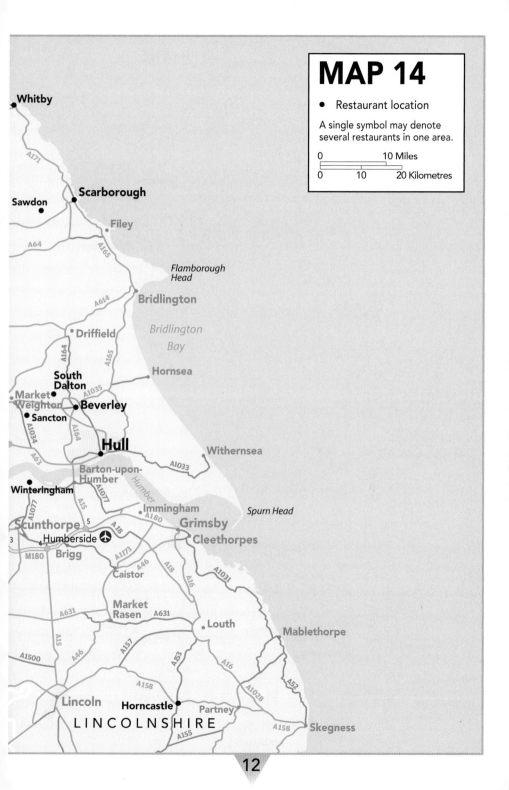

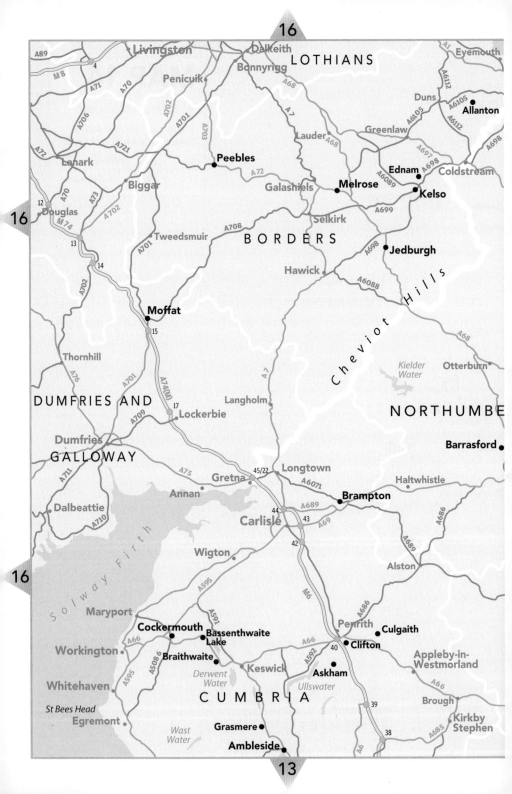

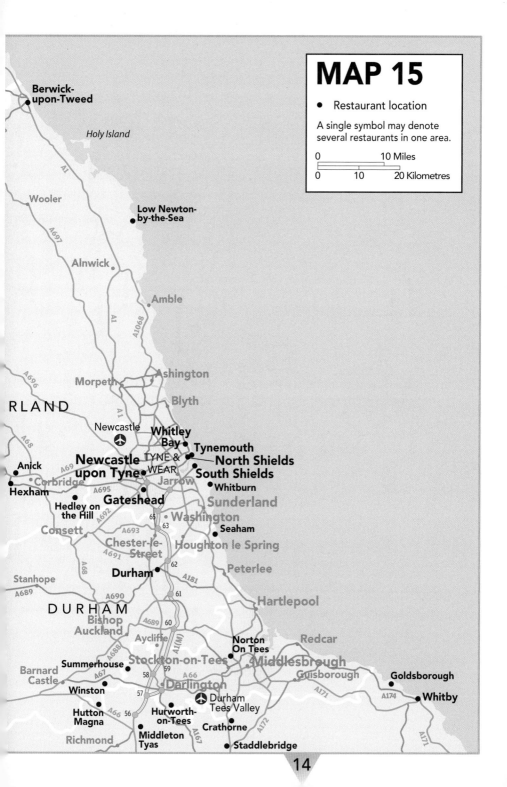

MAP 15

● Restaurant location

A single symbol may denote
several restaurants in one area.

0   10 Miles
0   10   20 Kilometres

Berwick-
upon-Tweed

Holy Island

Wooler

Low Newton-
by-the-Sea

Alnwick

Amble

Ashington

Morpeth

Blyth

RLAND

Newcastle

Whitley
Bay

Tynemouth

Anick

Newcastle
upon Tyne

TYNE &
WEAR

North Shields

South Shields

Corbridge

Jarrow

Hexham

Gateshead

Whitburn

Hedley on
the Hill

65

Sunderland

Washington

Consett

63

Chester-le-
Street

Seaham

Houghton le Spring

Stanhope

62

Durham

Peterlee

A689

61

Hartlepool

DURHAM

Bishop
Auckland

60

Aycliffe

Norton
On Tees

Redcar

Summerhouse

Stockton-on-Tees

Middlesbrough

Barnard
Castle

58

59

Guisborough

Goldsborough

Winston

57

Darlington

Durham
Tees Valley

Whitby

Hutton
Magna

56

Hurworth-
on-Tees

Crathorne

Richmond

Middleton
Tyas

Staddlebridge

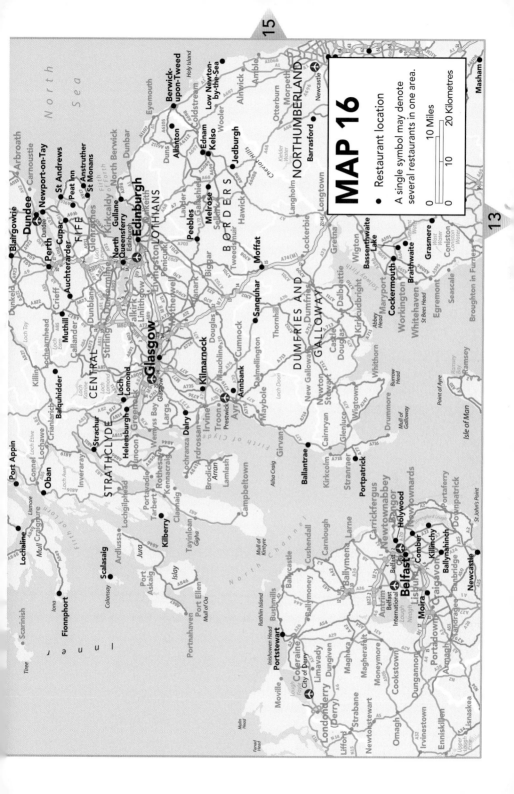

Note: The INDEX BY TOWN does not include London entries.

Join us at thegoodfoodguide.co.uk

Join us at thegoodfoodguide.co.uk

Join us at thegoodfoodguide.co.uk

Join us at thegoodfoodguide.co.uk

Join us at thegoodfoodguide.co.uk

Thank you

This book couldn't have happened without a cast of thousands.
This is just a sample of the many contributors to whom thanks are due.

Anthony Abrahams
Alasdair Adam
Judith Adam
William Adams
Robert Afia
John Aird
Zain Ali
Ali Alibhai
Doreen Allen
Joseph Allen
Tessa Allingham
Tom Alves
Simon Amey
Carol Andrews
Sebastian Anstey
Irene Archer
Graham Armstrong
Hilary Armstrong
Charmian Asher
Michael Ashwood
Viv Astling
Margaret Atherton
Paul Atkins
Clifford
    Attewell-Hughes
Frank Attwood
James Baird
Iain Barker
Joshua Barnes
Penny Barr
Mark Barrett
Alger Barrington
Phil Barron
John Bartholomew
Jackie Bates

Tracy Batt
Tim Battle
Edward Bayfield
Sydney Bayley
Elizabeth Beattie
David Bell
John Bence
Frank Benfield
Jill Bennett
Toby Berryman
W J Best
Marc Billings
David Bingle
Chris Birch
Tim Bishop
Mark Bixter
Stephanie Bliss
Andy Boase
Lexi Mai Bolt
Neil Booth
Melissa Bosher
Andrew Bowers
Iain Bowles
Anthony Bradbury
Ruth Brice
Celia Brigstocke
L C Briscoe
Anthony Brooke
Jasper Browell
Michael Brown
Angie Bryant
Tim Buchanan
Malcolm Budd
Alison Burgess
Jonathan Burt

Tim Caley
Ian Campbell
Margaret Campbell
David Carter
Robert Cassen
Matt Chalwin
Gill Chapman
Katharine Chater
Sue Chesterman
Richard Christopher
John Chute
Margaret Clancy
Tim Clare
James Clark
Gabrielle Clarke
Colin Clarkson
William Clegg
Mark Clifton
David Coleman
Sara Coles
Sarah Coles
Duncan Collins
Laurene Collot
Solene Collot
Adam Conteh
Mark Cooke
Derek Cooknell
Ruth Coombs
Dawn Corbett
Helen Corcoran
Russell Corn
Aidan Cox
Martin Cox
TJ Cox
Karl Craig-West

James Crosby
Charlotte Croser
Sam Croucher
Robert Curley
Eddie Dallas
Amber Dalton
Phillip Darnton
Sharon Davidson
Alun Davies
Jenny Davis
Lydia Dean
Nicholas Dee
Andrea D'Ercole
Amandine
    Desquartiers
Leana Dickie
Guy Dimond
Barbara Dittrich
Martin Dodd
Clifford Dolley
Michael Doupe
Hamish Dow
Rachel Drake
Stephen Drew
Yvonne Dumsday
John Dunford
Alan Dunn
Francis Durham
Lindsay Easton
Jayne Edwards
Julian Edwards
Mark Edwards
Osian Edwards
Steven Edwards
Josh Eglin

Gary Elflett
Keith Elmitt
Anne Marie Evans
Margaret Evans
Gordon Fenn
Clare Fielding
Neville Filar
Sebastian Finch
Paul Fisher
Justin Fleming
Adam Fligiel
Christine Flint
Sean Foley
Alison Fountain
David Fowler
Laura Fox
Rachel Fox
Silvana Franco
Alice Frewin
Stephanie Gallagher
Simon Gamage
Anthony Gannon
Becky Gardner
Miles Gasston
Stephen Gerrard
David Gibbon
Elspeth Gibbon
Philip Godfrey
Lynne Gollop
Jonathan Goodall
Martin Goode
Pauline Goodson
Philippa Gordon
Michael Graham
Lesley Granger
David Grant
Florence Grant
Karla Graves
Marcus Gray
Karen Green
Peter Green
Tessa Green
Tony Green
Thomas Greenall
John Gregory
Brian Griffiths
John Griffiths
Alan Grimwade
Ian Gunning

Vivien Haigh
Jake Hall
Terry Halloran
Brian Harley
Sophie Harper
Phil Harriss
John Hartley
Tom Harvey
Nicholas Harvey-Hills
Ged Hawkswell
Ray Haydock
Natalie Hayes
Alan Heason
Anne Heason
Becker Helen
Jane Henley-King
Michael Hesketh
Michael Hession
Karen Higgins
John Holland
David Holt
Aaron Hopkins
Genevieve Horsted
Richard Howells
Caroline Hubbert
Dennis Huckerby
Sally Humphries
Toby Hunter
Caroline Hurt
Joyce Hutchinson
Peter Iles
Will Ingarfill
C Ireland
Jennifer Isaac
Annabel Jackson
Linda Jackson
Robert Jamieson
Alison Jarvis
Ian Jarvis
Martin Jeeves
Angela Jefferson
Elizabeth Jeffery
Simon Jenkins
Carla Jones
Ian Jones
Oxana Jones
Simon Jones
Todd Kane
Brendan Keane

Akram Khadr
Mina Kim
Allen King
Mike King
Keith Kingham
Ray Kirby
Mark Kirkbride
Rick Kirkbride
Bart Kistemaker
Adrian Knight
Margaret Knight
Piers Krause
Gautam Krishna
Ian Laidlaw-Dickson
Michael Lane
Robin Lane
David Le Fevre
Samantha Leach
Alan Leaman
Alice Lee
Andrew Lees
Imogen Lees
Alfred Lennon
Carol Leslie
David Lewis
Irene Lewis
Matthew Lewis
Daniel Leyden
Robert Lightbody
Ann Lincoln
Tracie Linehan
Robert Llewellin
Chanin Lloyd
Malcolm Lloyd
David Locke
Steve Locklin
Jenny Loveless
Jeremy Lucas
Ryta Lyndley
Gerard M
David Mabey
Peter
  Mackenzie-Williams
Lili Mackintosh
Hugh Mackintosh CBE
Lucy Macleod
Caroline Maddison
Jan Maish
Fiona Malcomson

James Malcomson
Adrian Markley
Charles Markus
Lydia Marshall
Stjohn Marston
Basil Martin
Graham Martin
Ian Martin
John Martin
Lily Martin
Linda Martin
Nigel Martin
Valerie Martin
Simon Mather
Raffaele Mattei
Jonathan Maxfield
David McBrien
Ashley Mcdermott
Dale McGleenon
Stuart McIntosh
Thomas McKenzie
Carina McLellan
Ian McMillan
Nick McNally
Judith Merriman
Anna Merton
Hilary Metcalf
Robert Michael
Scott Middleton
Zhivko Mihaylov
Birgit Miller
Andy Mitchell
Alison Mitton
John Moder
Joanna Moffatt
Mike Moffatt
Adam Moliver
Stephen
  Montgomery
Colin Morison
James Morley
Niall Morrison
Amabel Mortimer
Andrew Morton
John Moss
John Moy
Martin Muers
John Mullard
Emily Munday

James Murphy
Andrew Murray
Joanne Murray
Lisa Napier-Raikes
Brett Newman
Jeffrey Ng
Laura Nickoll
Lesley Nsh
Viv O'Connell
Donna Ogden
Kevin O'Mahoney
Hannah Osborne
Richard Osborne
Deborah Owen
Desmond Palmer
Ulick Palmer
Philip Papworth
Gary Paterson
John Patterson
Henry Pavlovich
Avril Peters
Brian Pettifer
Evelyn Phillips
Valentine Mark
  Phillips
David Pickup
David Porter
Sherry Porter
Charlie Portman
  Olive
Julie Pressey
Nic Preston
Robert Preston
Michael Price
Nigel Price
Sandra Price
Manju Prince
Hamish Pringle
Hugh Proudman
Barbara Pryor
Patricia
  Pulford-Lustig
Ben Purser
Matt Putt
Alan Rainford
Belinda Raitt
Christine Ramsay
Ronald Rankine
Deborah Raven

Liz Rawlins
Peter Raynor
Paul Reed
Thomas Riby
Gareth Richards
Tom Richards
Marjorie Richardson
Richard Rigby
Cassandra Rigg
Florence Riley
Martin Riley
Sarah Riley
Zach Riley
Steve Rimington
James Robbins
Amanda Roberts
Elin Robinson
Anne Rogers
Wendy Rogers
Colin Roth
Clare Rowe
Stephen Ruffle
Willie Runte
Emma Russell
Jeremy Russell
Anthony Saber
Jane Sackville West
Mark Sadler
Keith Salway
Paul Samson
J.A.T. Saul
Isabel Saunders
Peter Savage
Derek Sayer
Rebekah Schiff
Richard Schofield
Theo Schofield
Danielle Sebire
Bryony Sees
David Sefton
Geoffrey Senior
Jennifer Sharp
Frank Shaw
Robert Shaw
Asif Sheikh
Monica Shelley
Angela Shelton
Gilbert Short
Dan Shute

Alan Sillitoe
Richard Sim
Tony Simister
Steve
  Simmons-Huzzard
Godfrey Small
Sandra Smieszek
Oliver Smith
Mary Somers
Hayley Soper
John Southern
John Speller
Kathy St Quintin
Geoff Stanley
Emily Stanton
William Steele
Amy Stephenson
Anna Stevens
Hugo Stevenson
Allen Stidwill
Robert Stobo
John Stott
Emma Sturgess
Derek Sumpter
Thomas Sundblad
Pete Surefour
Michael Sutcliffe
Peter Tallentire
Daniel Tapper
Cyril Taylor
Jean Taylor
Mark Taylor
Willie Tham
Tina Thompson
Bettina Thomson
Bob Thurlow
Anthony Timoney
Deirdre Timoney
Carole Tomlinson
Ward Tomlinson
Joy Towler
Steve Trayler
Ian Treder
John Turner
Kate Turner
Jill Turton
Andrew Turvil
Andrew Tye
Claire Tyler

Jessica Valenghi
Jonathan Varey
Andrew Varghese
Susan Vaughan
Becky Volker
Nick Wagner
Alison Wakelin
David Wakeling
Sarah Wales
Charlotte Walker
Garry Walker
Jane Walker
Richard Wall
Lee Walsh
Thomas Walsh
Stuart Walton
Jo Warwick
Donna Weeks
Iola Wellings
Keith Wells
Stacey Whatling
Jenny White
Lisa Whitehouse
Richard Whitley
Karen
  Whittingham-Brown
Emma Wilcox
Rosie Wild
Eileen Wilde
Kenneth Wilkins
Eileen Wilkinson
Blanche Williams
Kathleen Williams
Lottie Williams
Mike Williams
Anne Williamson
Ian Wilson
Jane Wilson
Ralph Wilson
John Winepress
Matthew Winnie
David Wood
Kathy Woolley
Andrew Worby
Amanda Wragg
Jackie Wyatt
Sarah Wyndham
Anne Yelland
Harry Yeo

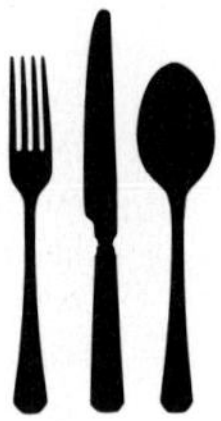

Longest serving

The Good Food Guide was founded in 1951. The following restaurants have appeared consistently since their first entry in the guide.

The Connaught, London, 65 years
Gravetye Manor, West Sussex, 61 years
Porth Tocyn Hotel, Gwynedd, 61 years
Le Gavroche, London, 48 years
Ubiquitous Chip, Glasgow, 46 years
Plumber Manor, Dorset, 45 years
The Druidstone, Pembrokeshire, 45 years
The Waterside Inn, Berkshire, 45 years
Airds Hotel, Argyll & Bute, 42 years
Farlam Hall, Cumbria, 41 years
Hambleton Hall, Rutland, 39 years
The Seafood Restaurant, Padstow, Cornwall, 37 years
The Sir Charles Napier, Oxfordshire, 37 years
Le Caprice, London, 36 years
Little Barwick House, Somerset, 36 years
Paris House, Bedfordshire, 35 years
Ostlers Close, Fife, 35 years
The Angel Inn, Hetton, 34 years
Brilliant, London, 33 years
Clarke's, London, 33 years
Le Manoir aux Quat'Saisons, Oxfordshire, 33 years
Blostin's, Somerset, 32 years

Read's, Kent, 32 years
The Castle at Taunton, Somerset, 32 years
The Three Chimneys, Isle of Skye, 32 years
Tyddyn Llan, Llandrillo, 32 years
Wilton's, London, 32 years
Launceston Place, London, 32 years
Northcote, Lancashire, 31 years
The Lime Tree, Manchester, 31 years
The Old Vicarage, Ridgeway, 30 years
Cherwell Boathouse, Oxford, 30 years
Le Champignon Sauvage, Glos, 29 years
Quince & Medlar, Cumbria, 29 years
Harry's Place, Lincolnshire, 28 years
Bibendum, London, 28 years
The Great House, Suffolk, 28 years
Ynyshir, Powys, 28 years
Crannog, Fort William, 28 years
La Petite Auberge, Buckinghamshire, 28 years
The Chester Grosvenor, Cheshire, 28 years
Eslington Villa, Tyne & Wear, 27 years
Melton's, York, 27 years
Horn of Plenty, Devon, 27 years
Castle Cottage, Gwynedd, 26 years
Kilcamb Lodge, Highlands, 25 years

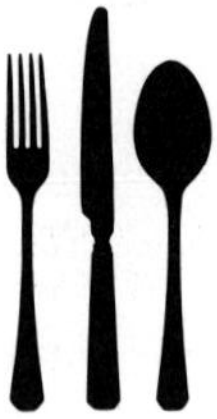

History of the guide

The Good Food Guide was first compiled by Raymond Postgate in 1951. Appalled by the British post-war dining experience, Postgate formed The Good Food Club, recruiting an army of volunteers to inspect restaurants anonymously and report back. His aim was simple: 'to raise the standard of cooking in Britain' and 'to do ourselves all a bit of good by making our holidays, travels and evenings-out in due course more enjoyable'. Following the success of The Good Food Club, the volunteers' reports were compiled and *The Good Food Guide* was published.

Although much has changed since the very first edition of *The Good Food Guide*, including the addition of expert restaurant inspectors, the ethos of the original book remains. *The Good Food Guide* is about empowering diners, helping them to find the very best places to eat and encouraging restaurants to offer the best possible food, service and experience.

Tell us your thoughts

The Good Food Guide receives reports from members of the public throughout the year, and it's your list of recommendations that creates the longlist for possible inclusion. Every piece of feedback we receive is read by our editorial team and will go on to inform our reviews of restaurants featuring in the guide.

Write to us using our website: thegoodfoodguide.co.uk